W9-DEU-531

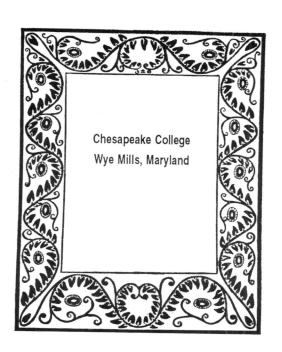
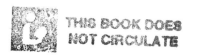

Encyclopedia of
Capital Punishment in the United States

Encyclopedia of Capital Punishment in the United States

by

LOUIS J. PALMER, JR.

McFarland & Company, Inc., Publishers

Jefferson, North Carolina, and London

Library of Congress Cataloguing-in-Publication Data

Palmer, Louis J., 1956–
Encyclopedia of capital punishment in the United States /
by Louis J. Palmer, Jr.
p.   cm.
Includes index.
ISBN 0-7864-0944-4 (illustrated case binding : 50# alkaline paper) ∞
1. Capital punishment — United States — Encyclopedias.   I. Title.
HV8694.P35   2001   364.66'0973'03 — dc21   00-58396

British Library cataloguing data are available

Cover image © 2001 IndexStock.

Manufactured in the United States of America

*McFarland & Company, Inc., Publishers
Box 611, Jefferson, North Carolina 28640
www.mcfarlandpub.com*

To my mother, Maggie,
for her guidance, devotion and grace

Contents

Preface

The legal history of capital punishment in the United States dates back to the founding of the nation. The American colonists brought capital punishment with them from Europe and, except for a brief period between 1972 and 1976, the punishment has always been a living instrument in Anglo-American jurisprudence. The primary purpose of this encyclopedia is to provide a comprehensive A to Z source of information on the legal, social and political history and present status of capital punishment in the nation. The breadth of coverage provided by the entries in this encyclopedia are especially critical at this juncture of capital punishment's history. Tremendous pressure is being brought both domestically and internationally to remove capital punishment from every penal code in the United States. The outcome of the struggle between opponents and proponents of the death penalty will be resolved in large part by the understanding or lack of understanding of the punishment by the majority of the nation's citizenry. This encyclopedia should serve not only as a tool for academic researchers, but for laypersons on both sides of the debate.

Every effort has been made to present the material in this encyclopedia in a manner that makes it readily understandable to a lay audience. Obviously, the lowest common denominator of some issues simply does not shed its legal trappings, nor its terminology. Cross references have been provided that should enable nonspecialist researchers to gain access to all of the material.

While it is not practical to summarize the entire encyclopedia in this preface, some discussion of its highlights is in order. First, the encyclopedia has an entry for virtually every capital punishment opinion issued by the United States Supreme Court, from its inception through 1999. (The Supreme Court case entries do not include memorandum opinions. Also, the Supreme Court, during its early years,

would periodically issue opinions that did not state what punishment a defendant received; consequently some cases that appeared to be capital punishment cases were not included in the encyclopedia simply because of the lack of certainty on the punishment.) The Supreme Court case entries summarize the important legal issue(s) presented by a case. The cases actually provide a synopsis of the history of capital punishment, because they shaped the manner in which capital punishment was allowed to operate in the nation.

A second important type of entry in the encyclopedia is that of each jurisdiction which has (or does not have) capital punishment. The capital punishment jurisdiction entries summarize the relevant death penalty laws of each jurisdiction, as well as provide information on the judicial structure of each jurisdiction.

Several special types of entries have been included in the encyclopedia. Almost 200 entries set out the status of capital punishment in the nations of the world. Numerous entries are included which summarize famous and not so famous capital prosecutions. Entries have been included for many of the organizations that are for or against capital punishment. Special entries discuss the impact of capital punishment on African Americans, Asian Americans, Hispanic Americans, Native Americans, women, and foreign nationals. Entries have been included which look at the history of each current method of execution in the nation. Additionally, a special entry has been provided which examines capital punishment by the military. A wealth of diverse statistical data accompany many of the entries.

Louis J. Palmer, Jr.
Pocatalico, West Virginia
Summer 2000

1

THE ENCYCLOPEDIA

A

Abandonment Defense The abandonment defense is generally used in criminal prosecutions involving two or more co-defendants. It is usually asserted by a defendant alleging that he or she was part of a conspiracy or plan to commit the crime charged, but that prior to completion of the crime he or she abandoned all involvement in the matter. In capital murder prosecutions the abandonment defense may be asserted at the guilt phase for the purpose of establishing innocence, or at the penalty phase as a mitigating circumstance. The abandonment defense is an affirmative defense that must be proven by the defendant. *See also* **Affirmative Defenses**

Abduction *see* **Kidnapping**

Abettor *see* **Aider and Abettor**

Abscond *see* **Escape**

Absentia *see* **Tried in Absentia**

Abu-Jamal, Mumia Mumia Abu-Jamal was sentenced to death for the 1981 murder of a police officer by the State of Pennsylvania on May 25, 1983. An aborted scheduled execution of Mumia in 1999 caused protests in cities throughout the United States and in nations around the world. Supporters of Mumia, who include international heads of states, legislative bodies, celebrities and organizations, believe that he is innocent of murder and should receive a new trial.

Mumia was born in Philadelphia, Pennsylvania, on April 23, 1954. In 1981 he worked as a radio journalist in Philadelphia, and moonlighted as a taxi cab driver. On the evening of December 9, 1981, Mumia was moonlighting as a cab driver when he came upon a police officer scuffling in the street with a motorist. The motorist was Mumia's brother.

The evidence introduced at Mumia's trial established that he approached the police officer struggling with his brother. Testimony revealed Mumia had a gun and that it was used to shoot the officer initially in the back. The police officer managed to fire a shot that struck Mumia in the abdomen. Further testimony during the trial indicated that Mumia approached the fallen officer and fired point blank into his face killing him.

Subsequent to Mumia being sentenced to death, his prosecution aroused national and international attention. Evidence surfaced indicating that someone else at the scene of the murder actually shot the police officer and fled. The police were unable to match the bullets that struck the officer with bullets from Mumia's gun. A key prosecution witness allegedly recanted testimony and stated that a police officer told the witness to lie and say that Mumia shot the victim. Mumia has always maintained his innocence.

While on death row Mumia wrote two books that received international acclaim: *Live from Death Row* and *Death Blossoms*. The support and recognition Mumia has gained while on death row includes: an honorary law degree from the New School of Law in San Francisco, California; being made an honorary vice president of the National Lawyer's Guild; being named an honorary citizen of the Central District of Copenhagen, Denmark and Palermo, Italy; recipient of the Solhvervfonden Foundation Award; and the establishment of the Committee to Save Mumia Abu-Jamal which included Whoopi Goldberg, Harry Belafonte, Edward Asner, Ossie Davis, Mike Farrell and Julian Bond.

Access to Counsel *see* **Right to Counsel**

Accessory After the Fact *see* **Law of Parties**

Accessory Before the Fact *see* **Law of Parties**

Accomplice *see* **Accomplice Liability**

Accomplice Liability   For all practical purposes, accomplice liability is nothing more than a legal phrase that describes conduct of a principal in the second degree and accessory before the fact, without distinguishing presence or absence at the crime scene. As a general matter, a person is liable as an accomplice if he or she provided assistance or encouragement, or failed to perform a legal duty with the intent thereby to facilitate or promote the commission of a crime.

A defendant can be an accomplice to murder even though his or her participation in the killing, when compared to that of the principal, is relatively passive. To hold a defendant liable as an accomplice for a homicide committed by another, the prosecutor need only show that the defendant intended to promote or facilitate a crime, and there is no need to show that the defendant specifically intended to promote or facilitate a murder. A murder prosecution under the accomplice liability theory does not require the defendant participate in the actual murder.

Where an accomplice purposely aids in the commission of murder, he or she is said to have the same intent as the principal. However, in determining whether murder is the appropriate charge against an accomplice to a homicide, it is necessary to look at his or her state of mind and not that only of the principal. Moreover under the accomplice liability theory it is not necessary that the defendant be shown to have the intent to commit murder after deliberation and premeditation; it is enough to establish the defendant had the intent purposely to promote the commission of murder.

Imposition of the death penalty on a capital felon found guilty as an accomplice is constitutionally permissible, so long as the guilt phase jury finds the accomplice killed, attempted to kill, or intended that a killing occurred.

Accusation   Accusation is a legal term used to refer to the three principal types of criminal charging instruments: complaint, information, and indictment. An accusation conveys nothing more than that a person has been charged with a crime. An accusation is not evidence of guilt. *See also* **Complaint; Grand Jury; Prosecution by Information**

Accusatory Body   In Anglo-American jurisprudence the phrase "accusatory body" is used to refer to a grand jury. The phrase can be, but rarely is, associated with a prosecutor who charges a person with a crime in an information or a citizen who brings a criminal charge against a person through a complaint. An accusatory body does nothing more than charge a person with committing a crime. An accusatory body is distinguished from the petit jury, which has the responsibility of determining a defendant's innocence or guilt. *See also* **Complaint; Grand Jury; Prosecution by Information**

Acquittal   Acquittal is a legal pronouncement that a prosecutor failed to establish beyond a reasonable doubt that a defendant committed a charged crime. An acquittal may be rendered by a petit jury or a trial judge. Once an acquittal has been rendered, constitutional double jeopardy principles prohibit reprosecution of a defendant for the crime to which the acquittal attached. *See also* **Double Jeopardy Clause**

Actual Innocence Claim   The actual innocence claim is a legal theory that is used by a capital felon who has exhausted direct appeals and initial collateral or habeas corpus attacks on the judgment rendered against him or her. The actual innocence claim permits a court to hear the merits of a successive, abusive, or defaulted claim for relief, if failure to do so would result in a miscarriage of justice. The miscarriage of justice exception applies where a capital felon alleges he or she is "actually innocent" of the capital crime for which he or she was convicted or the death penalty which was imposed.

In order for a capital felon to establish actual innocence of the crime for which he or she was convicted, it must be shown that, in light of new evidence, it is more likely than not that no reasonable jury would have found the defendant guilty beyond a reasonable doubt. To show actual innocence of the punishment imposed a capital felon must show by clear and convincing evidence that, but for a constitutional error, no reasonable jury would have found him or her eligible for the death penalty.

Between the period 1973 and 1999, there were 82 people released from death row because of evidence of their innocence. Researchers have estimated that since 1900 there have been 23 persons executed who were innocent.

Death Row Inmates Released After Proving Their Innocence 1973–1999

Name	Year Convicted	Year Released	State
David Keaton	1971*	1973	FL
Samuel A. Poole	1973	1974	NC
Wilbert Lee	1963*	1975	FL
Freddie Pitts	1963*	1975	FL
James Creamer	1973	1975	GA
Thomas Gladish	1974	1976	NM
Richard Greer	1974	1976	NM
Ronald Keine	1974	1976	NM
Clarence Smith	1974	1976	NM
Delbert Tibbs	1974	1977	FL
Earl Charles	1975	1978	GA
Jonathan Treadway	1975	1978	AZ
Bary Beeman	1976	1979	OH
Jerry Banks	1975	1980	GA
Larry Hicks	1978	1980	IN
Charles R. Giddens	1978	1981	OK
Michael Linder	1979	1981	SC
Jonny Ross	1975	1981	LA
Annibal Jaramillo	1981	1982	FL
Lawyer Johnson	1971	1982	MA†
Anthony Brown	1983	1986	FL

Name	Year Convicted	Year Released	State
Neil Ferber	1982	1986	PA
Clifford H. Bowen	1981	1986	OK
Joseph G. Brown	1974	1987	FL
Perry Cobb	1979	1987	IL
Darby W. Tillis	1979	1987	IL
Henry Drake	1977	1987	GA
John H. Knapp	1974	1987	AZ
Vernon McManus	1977	1987	TX
Anthony R. Peek	1978	1987	FL
Juan Ramos	1983	1987	FL
Robert Wallace	1980	1987	GA
Richard N. Jones	1983	1987	OK
Jerry Bigelow	1980	1988	CA
Willie Brown	1983	1988	FL
Larry Troy	1983	1988	FL
William Jent	1980	1988	FL
Earnest Miller	1980	1988	FL
Randall D. Adams	1977	1989	TX
Jesse K. Brown	1983	1989	SC
Robert Cox	1988	1989	FL
Timothy Hennis	1986	1989	NC
James Richardson	1968*	1989	FL
Clarence Brandley	1981	1990	TX
Patrick Croy	1979	1990	CA
John C. Skelton	1983	1990	TX
Dale Johnston	1984	1990	OH
Gary Nelson	1980	1991	GA
Bradley P. Scott	1988	1991	FL
Charles Smith	1983	1991	IN
Jay C. Smith	1986	1992	PA
Kirk Bloodsworth	1984	1993	MD
Federico Macias	1984	1993	TX
Walter McMillian	1988	1993	AL
Gregory Wilhoit	1987	1993	OK
James Robison	1977	1993	AZ
Muneer Deeb	1985	1993	TX
Andrew Golden	1991	1994	FL
Joseph Burrows	1989	1994	IL
Adolph Munson	1985	1995	OK
Robert C. Cruz	1981	1995	AZ
Rolando Cruz	1985	1995	IL
Al Hernandez	1985	1995	IL
Sabrina Butler	1990	1995	MS
Vern Jimerson	1985	1996	IL
Dennis Williams	1979	1996	IL
Roberto Miranda	1982	1996	NV
Gary Gauger	1993	1996	IL
Troy L. Jones	1982	1996	CA
Carl Lawson	1990	1996	IL
Ricardo Guerra	1982	1997	TX
Benjamin Harris	1985	1997	WA
Robert Hayes	1991	1997	FL
Randall Padgett	1992	1997	AL
Robert Miller	1988	1998	OK
Curtis Kyles	1984	1998	LA
Shareef Cousin	1996	1999	LA
Anthony Porter	1983	1999	IL
Steven Smith	1985	1999	IL
Ron Williamson	1988	1999	OK
Ronald Jones	1989	1999	IL
Clarence Dexter	1991	1999	MO

Source: Death Penalty Information Center, *Innocence* (1999).
*Death sentence invalidated by the decision in *Furman v. Georgia,* 408 U.S. 238 (1972).   †State no longer has death penalty.

Actus Reus Actus reus literally means conduct of a person. The phrase is used to refer to the element of an offense that involves prohibited conduct. The actus reus is one of two elements that make up criminal offenses. The second element is called mens rea or mental state. No crime may legally exist without an actus reus, while some regulatory crimes, called strict liability offenses, may exist without a mens rea. Examples of the actus reus element of a capital offense would be: causing death, causing death while committing another crime, causing the death of a police officer, and causing death by using a bomb. In each of the examples, the mental state of the defendant is not relevant to actus reus. The mental state is relevant for the second element, i.e., the mens rea. *See also* **Mens Rea**

Adams v. Texas *Court:* United States Supreme Court; *Case Citation:* Adams v. Texas, 448 U.S. 38 (1980); *Argued:* March 24, 1980; *Decided:* June 25, 1980; *Opinion of the Court:* Justice White; *Concurring Statement:* Justice Brennan; *Concurring Statement:* Chief Justice Burger; *Concurring Statement:* Justice Marshall; *Dissenting Opinion:* Justice Rehnquist; *Appellate Defense Counsel:* Melvyn Carson Bruder argued; J. Stephen Cooper and George A. Preston on brief; *Appellate Prosecution Counsel:* Douglas M. Becker argued; Mark White, John W. Fainter, Jr., Ted L. Hartley and W. Barton Boling on brief; *Amicus Curiae Brief Supporting Prosecutor:* None; *Amicus Curiae Brief Supporting Defendant:* 1.

Issue Presented: Whether the decision in *Witherspoon v. Illinois* was violated by a statute used by Texas to exclude members of the venire from jury service because they were unable to take an oath that the automatic penalty of death would not affect their deliberations on any issue of fact?

Case Holding: The ruling in *Witherspoon v. Illinois* was violated by a statute used by Texas to exclude members of the venire from jury service because they were unable to take an oath that the automatic penalty of death would not affect their deliberations on any issue of fact.

Factual and procedural background of case: The defendant, Adams, was charged with capital murder by the State of Texas. During jury selection the trial court excluded potential jurors if the jurors stated that they would be "affected" by the fact that the death penalty would be automatically imposed if they answered three statutory penalty phase questions in the affirmative. The exclusion was based upon a state statute that required removal of potential jurors who were unwilling or unable to take an oath that the automatic penalty of death would not affect their deliberations on any issue of fact. The three penalty phase questions concerned (1) whether the defendant's conduct causing the death at issue was deliberate, (2) whether the defendant's conduct in the future would constitute a continuing threat to society, and (3) whether his conduct in killing the victim was unreasonable in response to the victim's provocation, if any.

The jury that was selected convicted the defendant of capital murder and sentenced him to death. On appeal, the Texas Court of Criminal Appeals rejected the defendant's contention that the prospective jurors had been excluded in violation of the United States Supreme Court's decision in *Witherspoon v. Illinois*, which held that a state may not constitutionally execute a death sentence imposed by a jury culled of all those who revealed during voir dire examination that they had conscientious scruples against or were otherwise opposed to capital punishment. The United States Supreme Court granted certiorari to consider the issue.

Opinion of the Court by Justice White: Justice White found that the statute used to exclude potential jurors violated the Court's ruling in *Witherspoon*. The opinion provided the following basis for its judgment:

> Based on our own examination of the record, we have concluded that [the statute] was applied in this case to exclude prospective jurors on grounds impermissible under *Witherspoon* and related cases. As employed here, the touchstone of the inquiry under [the statute] was not whether putative jurors could and would follow their instructions and answer the posited questions in the affirmative if they honestly believed the evidence warranted it beyond reasonable doubt. Rather, the touchstone was whether the fact that the imposition of the death penalty would follow automatically from affirmative answers to the questions would have any effect at all on the jurors' performance of their duties. Such a test could, and did, exclude jurors who stated that they would be "affected" by the possibility of the death penalty, but who apparently meant only that the potentially lethal consequences of their decision would invest their deliberations with greater seriousness and gravity or would involve them emotionally. Others were excluded only because they were unable positively to state whether or not their deliberations would in any way be "affected." But neither nervousness, emotional involvement, nor inability to deny or confirm any effect whatsoever is equivalent to an unwillingness or an inability on the part of the jurors to follow the court's instructions and obey their oaths, regardless of their feelings about the death penalty. The grounds for excluding these jurors were consequently insufficient under the Sixth and Fourteenth Amendments. Nor in our view would the Constitution permit the exclusion of jurors from the penalty phase of a Texas murder trial if they aver that they will honestly find the facts and answer the questions in the affirmative if they are convinced beyond reasonable doubt, but not otherwise, yet who frankly concede that the prospects of the death penalty may affect what their honest judgment of the facts will be or what they may deem to be a reasonable doubt. Such assessments and judgments by jurors are inherent in the jury system, and to exclude all jurors who would be in the slightest way affected by the prospect of the death penalty or by their views about such a penalty would be to deprive the defendant of the impartial jury to which he or she is entitled under the law
>
> We repeat that the State may bar from jury service those whose beliefs about capital punishment would lead them to ignore the law or violate their oaths. But in the present case Texas has applied [the statute] to exclude jurors whose only fault was to take their responsibilities with special seriousness or to acknowledge honestly that they might or might not be affected. It does not appear in the record before us that these individuals were so irrevocably opposed to capital punishment as to frustrate the State's legitimate efforts to administer its constitutionally valid death penalty scheme. Accordingly, the Constitution disentitles the State to execute a sentence of death imposed by a jury from which such prospective jurors have been excluded.

The judgment of the Texas Court of Criminal Appeals is con-

sequently reversed to the extent that it sustains the imposition of the death penalty.

Concurring statement by Justice Brennan: Justice Brennan issued a concurring statement indicating: "Although I join the Court's opinion, I continue to believe that the death penalty is, in all circumstances, contrary to the Eighth Amendment's prohibition against imposition of cruel and unusual punishments."

Concurring statement by Chief Justice Burger: The Chief Justice issued a statement stating that he concurred in the Court's judgment.

Concurring statement by Justice Marshall: In his concurring statement, Justice Marshall stated that he "continue[d] to believe that the death penalty is, under all circumstances, cruel and unusual punishment prohibited by the Eighth and Fourteenth Amendments."

Dissenting opinion by Justice Rehnquist: Justice Rehnquist dissented from the Court's decision. He argued that Texas' exclusion statute did not violate *Witherspoon*. Justice Rehnquist stated that he saw "no reason why Texas should not be entitled to require each juror to swear that he or she will answer [the three penalty phase] questions without regard to their possible cumulative consequences." It was said that the procedure employed by the Texas statute presented no greater risk to defendants than any capital punishment procedure approved by the Court. *See also* **Witherspoon v. Illinois**

Adamson v. California

Court: United States Supreme Court; *Case Citation:* Adamson v. California, 332 U.S. 46 (1947); *Argued:* January 15–16, 1947; *Decided:* June 23, 1947; *Opinion of the Court:* Justice Reed; *Concurring Opinion:* Justice Frankfurter; *Dissenting Opinion:* Justice Black, in which Douglas, J., joined; *Dissenting Opinion:* Justice Murphy, in which Rutledge, J., joined; *Appellate Defense Counsel:* Morris Lavine argued and briefed; *Appellate Prosecution Counsel:* Walter L. Bowers argued and briefed; *Amicus Curiae Brief Supporting Prosecutor:* None; *Amicus Curiae Brief Supporting Defendant:* None.

Issue Presented: Whether the Constitution prohibited the prosecutor from commenting upon the defendant's failure to explain or deny evidence against him?

Case Holding: The Constitution did not prohibit the prosecutor from commenting upon the defendant's failure to explain or deny evidence against him.

Factual and procedural background of case: The defendant, Adamson, was convicted of capital murder and sentenced to death by the State of California. The California Supreme Court affirmed the judgment. In doing so, the appellate court rejected the defendant's contention that the Fifth Amendment prohibited the prosecutor from commenting on his failure to explain or deny the evidence against him (the defendant did not take the stand). The United States Supreme Court granted certiorari to consider the issue.

Opinion of the Court by Justice Reed: Justice Reed held that under the laws of California it was permissible for the prosecutor and trial judge to comment on a defendant's failure to explain or deny evidence. It was said that the issue was a state matter insofar as the Fifth Amendment provided only a federal right, not a right imposed upon the states. Justice Reed wrote: "It is settled law that the clause of the Fifth Amendment, protecting a person against being compelled to be a witness against himself, is not made effective by the Fourteenth Amendment as a protection against state action[.]" The judgment of the California Supreme Court was affirmed.

Concurring opinion by Justice Frankfurter: Justice Frankfurter concurred in the Court's decision. He wrote separately to indicate that "[l]ess than 10 years ago, Mr. Justice Cardozo announced as settled constitutional law that while the Fifth Amendment, which is not directed to the States, but solely to the federal government, provides that no person shall be compelled in any criminal case to be a witness against himself, the process of law assured by the Fourteenth Amendment does not require such immunity from self-crimination[.]"

Dissenting opinion by Justice Black, in which Douglas, J., joined: Justice Black dissented from the Court's decision. He argued that the Fifth Amendment was applicable against states through the Fourteenth Amendment. Justice Black wrote:

> In my judgment ... the language of the first section of the Fourteenth Amendment, taken as a whole, was thought by those responsible for its submission to the people, and by those who opposed its submission, sufficiently explicit to guarantee that thereafter no state could deprive its citizens of the privileges and protections of the Bill of Rights....
>
> I would follow what I believe was the original purpose of the Fourteenth Amendment — to extend to all the people of the nation the complete protection of the Bill of Rights.... I would therefore hold in this case that the full protection of the Fifth Amendment's proscription against compelled testimony must be afforded by California. This I would do because of reliance upon the original purpose of the Fourteenth Amendment.

Dissenting opinion by Justice Murphy, in which Rutledge, J., joined: Justice Murphy dissented from the Court's decision. He believed that the Fifth Amendment was applicable against the states. Justice Murphy wrote as follows:

> Moreover, it is my belief that this guarantee against self-incrimination has been violated in this case. Under California law, the judge or prosecutor may comment on the failure of the defendant in a criminal trial to explain or deny any evidence or facts introduced against him. As interpreted and applied in this case, such a provision compels a defendant to be a witness against himself in one of two ways:
>
> If he does not take the stand, his silence is used as the basis for drawing unfavorable inferences against him as to matters which he might reasonably be expected to explain. Thus he is compelled, through his silence, to testify against himself. And silence can be as effective in this situation as oral statements.
>
> If he does take the stand, thereby opening himself to cross-examination, so as to overcome the effects of the provision in question, he is necessarily compelled to testify against himself. In that case, his testimony on cross-examination is the result of the coercive pressure of the provision rather than his own volition. Much can be said pro and con as to the desirability of allowing comment on the failure of the accused to testify. But policy arguments are to no avail in the face of a clear constitutional command. This guarantee of freedom from self-incrimination

is grounded on a deep respect for those who might prefer to remain silent before their accusers.... Accordingly, I would reverse the judgment below.

Case note: The position taken by the dissenting opinions would eventually become the position adopted by the Court.

Adjournment *see* Time Between Guilt Phase and Penalty Phase

Admissible Evidence *see* Rules of Evidence

Adversarial Criminal Justice System
The Anglo-American criminal justice system is adversarial. It places the government, represented by a prosecutor, against the defendant. The system requires that a neutral judge preside over the contest. The defendant is constitutionally guaranteed the right to have assistance of counsel and a jury to decide the facts of the case.

In an effort to balance the weight and resources of the government against an individual defendant, the system requires that the defendant's innocence be presumed. The effect of the presumption of innocence is that of placing the burden upon the government to prove a defendant is guilty of a charged crime. Thus, a defendant does not have to prove his or her innocence. Additionally, elaborate rules of evidence and procedure are used in the criminal justice system to ensure fair treatment to the defendant and the government. Although the Federal Constitution does not require appellate review of a criminal conviction, all jurisdictions in the criminal justice system provide for an initial right to appeal a conviction. *See also* **Burden of Proof at Guilt Phase; Burden of Proof at Penalty Phase; Rules of Criminal Procedure; Rules of Evidence**

Adverse or Hostile Witness *see* Examination of Witness

Advisory Jury *see* Binding/Nonbinding Jury Sentencing Determination

Affirm *see* Appellate Review of Conviction and Death Sentence

Affirmative Defenses
The Anglo-American criminal justice system is unique in affording defendants a presumption of innocence and requiring prosecutors prove guilt beyond a reasonable doubt. In spite of placing the burden of proof of guilt on prosecutors, defendants are generally required to prove any affirmative defense that is offered. Examples of affirmative defenses include: insanity, alibi, self-defense, intoxication and defense of another. In most instances a defendant must prove an affirmative defense by a preponderance of the evidence. Failure to prove an affirmative defense does not mean that a defendant is guilty of a crime. The prosecutor must always prove a defendant's guilt beyond a reasonable doubt regardless

of the outcome on an affirmative defense. *See also* **Burden of Proof at Guilt Phase**

Afghanistan   The death penalty is carried out in the nation of Afghanistan. It was reported that in 1998, Afghanistan executed 10 prisoners. The legal system of the nation is based on Shari'a (Islamic) law. Afghanistan does not have a constitution.

The nation officially changed its name in 1997, to that of the Islamic Emirate of Afghanistan. Tremendous political instability existed in the country throughout the 1990s, due to internal religious and ethnic fighting. The nation is ruled by Mullah Omar and a six-member ruling council. Afghanistan's former president, Burhanuddin Rabbani, is in exile. Afghanistan does not have a constitution, operative legislative laws, nor an independent judiciary. With no functioning nationwide judicial system, local authorities rely on some interpretation of Shari'a law and traditional tribal codes of justice.

Afghanistan utilizes four methods of execution: stoning, firing squad, throat slitting, and hanging. Adhering strictly to Shari'a law, Afghanistan allows the relative of a murder victim to carry out the death sentence. Executions are held in public. In February of 2000, several thousand people gathered in an Afghanistan sports stadium to watch a ten year old boy execute the murderer of his father. The defendant, Mohammed Hashim, was shot four times with a rifle by the youth. *See also* **International Capital Punishment Nations**

African Americans and Capital Punishment

African Americans have historically condemned capital punishment on a single ground: Blacks made up a disproportionate number death penalty victims. This argument was the primary basis of all death penalty statutes being struck down through the United States Supreme Court decision in *Furman v. Georgia*, 408 U.S. 238 (1972).

Historical data supported the pre–*Furman* racial attack on capital punishment by blacks. For example, between the period 1930–1972, blacks made up 53.5 percent of all persons executed in the United States. However, during this same time period the total black population never surpassed 15 percent of the nation's total population. The decision in *Furman* recognized the enormous racial disparity and declared that it was

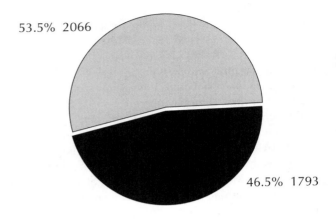

AFRICAN–AMERICANS EXECUTED 1930–1972

53.5% 2066

46.5% 1793

■ AFRICAN–AMERICANS

■ ALL OTHERS

Source: Bureau of Justice Statistics, Capital Punishment (1977).

not by chance that blacks made up the majority of the people executed in the nation.

Under post–*Furman* capital punishment jurisprudence many blacks are still arguing that the death penalty is imposed in a racially discriminatory manner. However, post–*Furman* statistical data does not provide the irrefutable supporting evidence of racial discrimination that characterized pre–*Furman* death penalty data. For example, blacks represented only 35.1 percent of all those executed between the period 1976–1999. While it is arguable that the percentage of blacks executed during the latter period was high, relative to their total population in the nation, this figure would not, standing alone, support changing the death penalty system a second time.

While the statistical data of executions during the post–*Furman* era lacks moral persuasion for changing the death penalty system, blacks have made a compelling case for change through evidence of persons actually sentenced to death, but not executed. Blacks contend that a definite pattern has developed indicating undue racial discrimination in persons actually sentenced to death. A snap shot of the death row

Erica Yvonne Sheppard was convicted of capital murder by the State of Texas. She initially declined all appeals and, in 1999, was scheduled to be the first Africa-American female executed since the reinstatement of capital punishment in 1976. However, through the intervention of family members and the Rev. Jesse L. Jackson, Sheppard changed her mind and agreed to have her case go through the appeal process. (Texas Department of Criminal Justice)

Left to right: *Charles Sanders, Grady B. Cole, and J. C. Levine were executed on January 8, 1943, by the State of Arizona. The three men were convicted of robbing and killing a taxi driver. (Arizona Department of Corrections)*

AFRICAN–AMERICANS EXECUTED 1976–1999

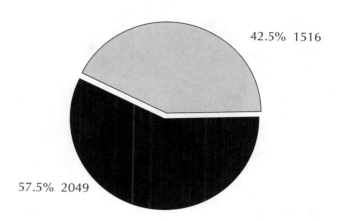

35.1% 210

64.9% 388

■ AFRICAN–AMERICANS
■ ALL OTHERS

AFRICAN–AMERICANS ON DEATH ROW APRIL 1999

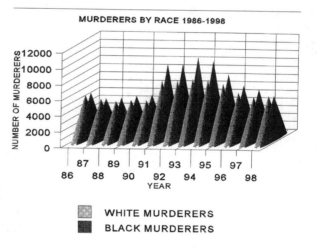

42.5% 1516

57.5% 2049

■ AFRICAN–AMERICANS
■ ALL OTHERS

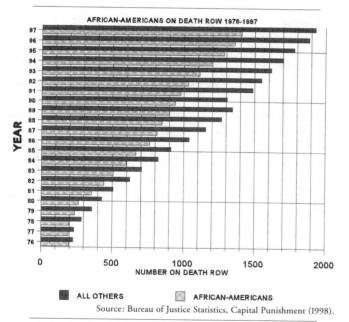

Source: Bureau of Justice Statistics, Capital Punishment (1998).

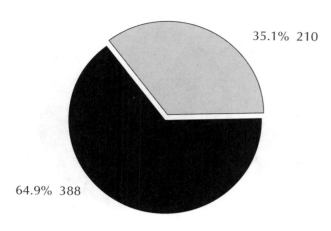

population in April of 1999 revealed that blacks made up 42.5 percent of the nation's death row population.

Opponents of the death penalty race theory contend that blacks and their supporters have focused upon the wrong set of numbers, in determining whether post–*Furman* capital punishment is racially dispensed. It has been postured that the correct numbers to look at involve the race of actual murderers. For example, between the period 1986–1998, the number of known black and white murderers totaled 172,218. Out of that total, blacks comprised 54.2 percent of the known black and white murderers. Although known black murderers outnumbered known white murderers during this period, more white murderers received death sentences than black murderers. Thus, it is argued that post–*Furman* capital punishment is not racially dispensed.

Age and Capital Punishment *see* **Juveniles**

Age of Felon Mitigator In a majority of capital punishment jurisdictions the age of felon mitigator is a statutory mitigating circumstance. A few jurisdictions specifically require that a capital felon must be under 18 at the time of the murder in order to invoke the statutory age mitigating circumstance.

The chronological youth of a capital felon at the time of the offense may be considered by the jury at the penalty phase as a mitigating factor against imposition of the death penalty. Courts have held that, while chronological age may be relevant, chronological age is not dispositive of this mitigator. That is, a capital felon may be chronologically well along in years, but mentally and emotionally he or she may be an adolescent. Therefore, a capital felon may utilize age as a mitigator where he or she is chronologically old, but mentally and emotionally he or she is child-like.

JURISDICTIONS USING AGE OF FELON MITIGATOR

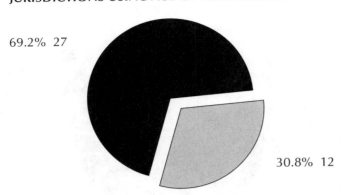

69.2% 27

30.8% 12

■ AGE OF FELON MITIGATOR JURISDICTIONS

■ ALL OTHER JURISDICTIONS

JURISDICTIONS USING AGE OF FELON AGGRAVATOR

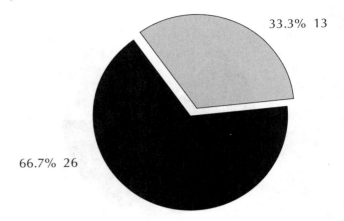

33.3% 13

66.7% 26

■ AGE OF VICTIM AGGRAVATOR JURISDICTIONS

■ ALL OTHER JURISDICTIONS

Age and Gender of Murderers 1994

Age of Murderer	Total Murderers	Male	Female
Under 1	–	–	–
1 to 4	–	–	–
5 to 8	1	1	–
9 to 12	38	30	8
13 to 16	1,536	1,435	101
17 to 19	3,366	3,222	144
20 to 24	3,897	3,600	297
25 to 29	2,293	1,985	308
30 to 34	1,679	1,434	245
35 to 39	1,225	1,006	219
40 to 44	827	702	125
45 to 49	555	478	77
50 to 54	302	257	45
55 to 59	176	158	18
60 to 64	129	109	20
65 to 69	93	82	11
70 to 74	65	60	5
75 & over	70	65	5

Source: U.S. Department of Justice, Federal Bureau of Investigation, *Uniform Crime Reports* 16, Table 2.6 (1995).

A majority of capital punishment jurisdictions that utilize age as a statutory mitigating circumstance do not specify any specific age. However, as a practical matter juries are more likely than not to give significance to age when it concerns a capital felon who committed a murder when he or she was under 18 or a senior citizen. This point was alluded to in *State v. Ramseur*, 524 A.2d 188 (N.J. 1987) where the New Jersey supreme court suggested that age should be a mitigating circumstance only when the capital felon is relatively young or relatively old. *See also* **Mitigating Circumstances**

Age of Victim Aggravator   A large minority of capital punishment jurisdictions provide that the age of a victim of murder is a statutory aggravating circumstance that permits the imposition of the death penalty. There is no unity among capital jurisdictions regarding the age of a victim which constitutes a statutory aggravator.

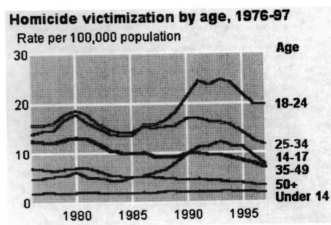

Source: Bureau of Justice Statistics, Homicide Trends in the United States (1998).

Age and Gender of Murder Victim 1994

Age of Victim	Total Victims	Male	Female
Under 1	257	150	107
1 to 4	470	263	207
5 to 8	103	46	57
9 to 12	120	60	60
13 to 16	944	770	174
17 to 19	2,307	2,052	255
20 to 24	4,088	3,514	574
25 to 29	3,231	2,626	605
30 to 34	2,917	2,209	708
35 to 39	2,249	1,687	562
40 to 44	1,565	1,236	329
45 to 49	1,007	773	234
50 to 54	680	520	160
55 to 59	444	331	113
60 to 64	342	252	90
65 to 69	284	182	102
70 to 74	244	145	99
75 & over	70	65	5

Source: U.S. Department of Justice, Federal Bureau of Investigation, *Uniform Crime Reports* 16, Table 2.5 (1995).

Research has shown that the murder of teenagers and young adults increased dramatically in the late 1980s while rates for older age groups declined. The murder rate for 14–17 year olds increased almost 150 percent from 1985 to 1993. While 18–24 year olds experienced the highest homicide. Murder rates for children under age 14 have remained stable and low. *See also* **Aggravating Circumstances**

Aggravated Battery Aggravator   Aggravated battery has been made a statutory aggravating circumstance when murder results therefrom. Two capital punishment jurisdictions, Georgia and Virginia, have made aggravated battery a statutory aggravating circumstance. The crime of aggravated battery is not the same as the crime of battery. Aggravated battery occurs when there is serious injury to a victim. The crime of battery can be a mere touching of a victim.

A "fine" legal distinction is made between aggravated battery and murder, insofar as the victim of aggravated battery is also the victim of murder. The aggravated battery component of capital murder requires the victim not die immediately, but suffer severe injuries before eventual death. *See also* **Aggravating Circumstances**

Aggravating Circumstances   The United States Supreme Court has ruled that the death penalty cannot be imposed arbitrarily upon all defendants who commit murder. The imposition of the death penalty must be reserved for a small class of murderers out of the sum total of murderers. To comply with this constitutional mandate, capital punishment jurisdictions have statutorily created certain factors that permit imposition of the death penalty. Two approaches have developed in meeting the narrowing requirement.

A minority of capital punishment jurisdictions utilize death-eligible special circumstances to trigger a capital prosecution and special statutory issues to impose the sentence of death. The majority of capital punishment jurisdictions uti-

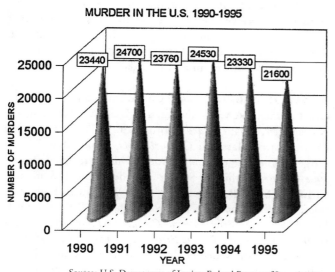

MURDER IN THE U.S. 1990-1995

Source: U.S. Department of Justice, Federal Bureau of Investigation, *Uniform Crime Reports* 106, Table 7 (1996).

lize a procedure that involves narrowing death penalty prosecution through the use of death-eligible special circumstances, and narrowing the actual imposition of the death penalty through the use of aggravating circumstances. There are two types of aggravating circumstances: non-statutory aggravators and statutory aggravators.

Both procedures perform a function that is not constitutionally required. The Federal Constitution only requires narrowing the class of defendants for death penalty treatment once. The narrowing may occur at the guilt phase or penalty phase. However, under both schemes used by capital punishment jurisdictions, the constitutional narrowing occurs twice: at the guilt phase and at the penalty phase.

Statutory Aggravating Circumstances: The phrase, "statutory aggravating circumstances" refers to unique factors created by legislators which, if found to exist by the penalty phase factfinder, will constitutionally permit the death penalty to be imposed upon capital offenders. In the case of *Zant v. Stephens*, 462 U.S. 862 (1983) the United States Supreme Court held that no capital felon may validly be sentenced to death unless at least one statutory aggravating circumstance was proven against him or her. The statutory aggravating circumstance requirements have replaced the pre-*Furman v. Georgia*, 408 U.S. 238 (1972) arbitrariness in imposing the death penalty, and are the sole criteria that permits the death penalty to be imposed.

In the case of *Tuilaepa v. California*, 114 S.Ct. 2630 (1994) the United States Supreme Court established two conditions that must be satisfied in order for a statutory aggravating circumstance to be constitutionally valid. First, the statutory aggravating circumstance must not be a factor that could be applied to every defendant convicted of murder. For example, the mere fact that a victim died could not be a constitutionally valid statutory aggravating circumstance that allows imposition of the death penalty. The reason being, in every murder the victim dies. A statutory aggravating circumstance must be some factor that would have application to only a subclass of murders.

The second requirement announced in *Tuilaepa*, is that a statutory aggravating circumstance cannot be set out in a manner that makes it vague, i.e., it must have a common sense meaning that a jury would understand. If the bare language of a statutory aggravating circumstance does not provide the factfinder with sufficient direction as to its meaning, use of the aggravator may still survive constitutional scrutiny if the jurisdiction's appellate court has construed the aggravator so as to adequately channel the factfinder's discretion.

Non-Statutory Aggravating Circumstances: Non-statutory aggravating circumstances are any case-specific factors of a murder which make the murder especially egregious. Non-statutory aggravators are not set out in statutes. The death penalty cannot be imposed solely upon the proven existence of a non-statutory aggravator. Non-statutory aggravators serve only to support imposing the death penalty, upon proof of the existence of a statutory aggravator. Courts have reasoned that consideration of non-statutory aggravators do not unduly prejudice capital felons, because the factfinder can only consider such evidence if it first finds at least one statutory aggravating circumstance against a defendant.

Prosecutors do not have a carte blanche right to introduce any and all non-statutory aggravating evidence. Trial courts must preclude irrelevant or highly prejudicial non-statutory aggravating evidence. Generally, courts will limit non-statutory aggravating evidence to a capital defendant's prior criminal record, evidence that would be admissible at the guilt phase, and evidence to rebut matters raised in mitigation by the defendant.

Courts have held that prosecutors may use evidence of any type of uncharged crime against a capital felon at the penalty phase, as a non-statutory aggravator. Hearsay evidence of crimes that did not result in prosecution or conviction is admissible at the penalty phase so long as such evidence is both relevant and reliable. Prosecutors may inform the penalty phase jury that a capital felon has planned other offenses, when there is evidence to corroborate the allegation.

Distinguishing Statutory Aggravators from Death-Eligible Special Circumstances: Death-eligible special circumstances and statutory aggravating circumstances are both factors which are created by legislators. The purpose of death-eligible special circumstances and statutory aggravating circumstances are the same. Both seek to narrow the class of murders and murderers that are subject to death penalty treatment. The function of death-eligible special circumstances and statutory aggravating circumstances are different. The function of a death-eligible special circumstance is that of merely triggering death penalty consideration for those whose conduct fall within their sphere of proscriptions. The function of a statutory aggravating circumstance, on the other hand, is that of causing the death penalty to be imposed.

Death-eligible special circumstances are elements of capital offenses and, as such, are constitutionally required to be proven beyond a reasonable doubt at the guilt phase. If a death-eligible special circumstance is not so proven at the guilt phase, then a defendant could not be subject to capital sentencing. Statutory aggravating circumstances are not elements of capital offenses. They are not constitutionally required to be proven beyond a reasonable doubt, and the proof of their existence is made at the penalty phase.

Many death-eligible special circumstances are also duplicated as statutory aggravating circumstances. Most jurisdictions utilize only a few death-eligible special circumstances that are the same as some of their statutory aggravating circumstances. However, four capital punishment jurisdictions, California, Louisiana, New York, and Virginia, duplicate all of their death-eligible special circumstances as statutory aggravating circumstances. Notwithstanding such duplication, each of the four jurisdictions require proof of both types of "circumstances" at the guilt phase and penalty phase.

Distinguishing Statutory Aggravators from Special Statutory Issues: Four capital punishment jurisdictions, Oregon,

Texas, Utah, and Washington, do not utilize statutory aggravating circumstances. These jurisdictions allow death-eligible special circumstances to fulfill the constitutional narrowing at the guilt phase. In *Jurek v. Texas*, 428 U.S. 262 (1976) the United States Supreme Court indicated that the constitution permitted the narrowing process to occur at the guilt phase and did not require more. Notwithstanding the pronouncement in *Jurek*, the four jurisdictions utilize, at the penalty phase, special statutory issues that must be addressed by the factfinder in deciding whether to impose the death penalty. *Jurek* upheld the constitutionality of using special statutory issues, instead of statutory aggravating circumstances, at the penalty phase.

Although special statutory issues and statutory aggravating circumstances serve the same purpose, i.e., they both are used to determine whether to impose the death penalty, they differ in one respect. Special statutory issues are constant for all capital felons, in that special statutory issues are a series of questions that are asked in all capital prosecutions. However, statutory aggravating circumstances vary with the particular facts of each capital homicide. *See also* **Death-Eligible Offenses**

Aider and Abettor

An aider and abettor is a person who participates in a crime, but who is not considered a principal, i.e., the person who actually committed the crime. Statutes generally permit an aider and abettor to be prosecuted and punished as though he or she actually committed an offense. An exception to this general rule has been constitutionally carved out for capital murder.

Under the Federal Constitution an aider and abettor to capital murder may be prosecuted and found guilty for the crime. However, the Constitution has been interpreted to require specific conduct by the aider and abettor be shown before a death sentence may be imposed upon him or her.

A death sentence may not be imposed upon an aider or abettor who neither took life, attempted to take life, nor intended to take life. An aider and abettor convicted of capital murder may receive a sentence of death if his or her participation in the crime is major and his or her mental state was one of reckless indifference to the value of human life. *See also* **Tison v. Arizona; Enmund v. Florida**

Ake v. Oklahoma

Court: United States Supreme Court; *Case Citation:* Ake v. Oklahoma, 470 U.S. 68 (1985); *Argued:* November 7, 1984; *Decided:* February 26, 1985; *Opinion of the Court:* Justice Marshall; *Concurring Opinion:* Chief Justice Burger; *Dissenting Opinion:* Justice Rehnquist; *Appellate Defense Counsel:* Arthur B. Spitzer argued; Elizabeth Symonds, Charles S. Sims, Burt Neuborne, and William B. Rogers on brief; *Appellate Prosecution Counsel:* Michael C. Turpen argued; David W. Lee on brief; *Amicus Curiae Brief Supporting Prosecutor:* None; *Amicus Curiae Brief Supporting Defendant:* 5.

Issue Presented: Whether the Constitution requires that an indigent defendant have State appointed access to psychiatric assistance to prepare a defense based on his or her mental condition, when his or her sanity at the time of the offense is seriously in question?

Case Holding: When an indigent defendant has made a preliminary showing that his or her sanity at the time of the offense is likely to be a significant factor at trial, the Constitution requires the State provide the defendant with court appointed expert psychiatric assistance on this issue

Factual and procedural background of case: The record of the case indicated that the defendant, Glen Burton Ake, was arrested and charged in 1979, by the state of Oklahoma, with murdering a couple and wounding their two children. The trial court initially determined that the defendant was incompetent to stand trial and therefore had the defendant committed to a state mental hospital. Six weeks after the defendant's commitment, the State's chief forensic psychiatrist informed the trial court that the defendant had become competent to stand trial.

The defendant was indigent and had court appointed counsel. To enable defense counsel to prepare and present a defense adequately, defense counsel indicated that a psychiatrist would have to examine the defendant with respect to his mental condition at the time of the offense. Defense counsel argued that the federal Constitution required the trial court to either arrange to have a psychiatrist perform the examination, or to provide funds to allow the defense to arrange for one. The trial court rejected defense counsel's argument that the federal Constitution required that an indigent defendant receive the assistance of a psychiatrist when that assistance is necessary to the defense.

The defendant was tried for two counts of murder in the first degree and for two counts of shooting with intent to kill. At the guilt phase of trial, his sole defense was insanity. The jury rejected the defendant's insanity defense and returned a verdict of guilty on all counts. The defendant was subsequently sentenced to death on each of the two murder counts, and to 500 years imprisonment on each of the two counts of shooting with intent to kill.

On appeal to the Oklahoma Court of Criminal Appeals, the defendant argued that, as an indigent defendant, he should have been provided the services of a court appointed psychiatrist. The appellate court rejected this argument, observing: "We have held numerous times that, the unique nature of capital cases notwithstanding, the State does not have the responsibility of providing such services to indigents charged with capital crimes." The United States Supreme Court granted certiorari to consider the issue.

Opinion of the Court by Justice Marshall: Justice Marshall made a fundamental legal observation at the outset of the Court's opinion. It was said that: "This Court has long recognized that when a State brings its judicial power to bear on an indigent defendant in a criminal proceeding, it must take steps to assure that the defendant has a fair opportunity to present his defense. This elementary principle, grounded in significant part on the Fourteenth Amendment's due process guarantee of fundamental fairness, derives from the belief that

justice cannot be equal where, simply as a result of his poverty, a defendant is denied the opportunity to participate meaningfully in a judicial proceeding in which his liberty is at stake."

The opinion proceeded to focus upon the conditions under which the participation of a psychiatrist was significant enough to the preparation of a defense, so as to require a State to provide an indigent defendant with access to competent psychiatric assistance in preparing his or her defense. Justice Marshall outlined a three pronged test to address the issue. The first prong of the test seeks a determination as to the private interest that will be affected by the action of the State. Under the second prong an analysis is required to determine the governmental interest that will be affected if the safeguard is to be provided. The third prong seeks to determine the probable value of the additional or substitute procedural safeguards that are sought, and the risk of an erroneous deprivation of the affected interest if those safeguards are not provided.

In applying this test abstractly to the issue of appointment of psychiatric assistance, Justice Marshall reached the following conclusions. First, it was said that the private interest in the accuracy of a criminal proceeding is, in and of itself, compelling. That is, a defendant's interest in the outcome of the State's effort to overcome the presumption of innocence is self-evident and is given great weight in the analysis.

Next, in looking at the interest of the State, the opinion refuted Oklahoma's suggestion that providing such assistance would result in a staggering economic burden to the State. Justice Marshall noted that many States, including the federal government, make psychiatric assistance available to indigent defendants. It was concluded that the State's interest in denying the assistance of a psychiatrist is not substantial, in view of the compelling interest of both the State and the defendant in an accurate disposition of a case.

In turning to the final issue of the probable value of the psychiatric assistance sought, and the risk of error in the proceeding if such assistance is not offered, Justice Marshall made the following determinations. It was said that when the State has made the defendant's mental condition relevant to his or her criminal culpability and to the punishment he or she might suffer, the assistance of a psychiatrist is crucial to the defendant's ability to present a meaningful defense. While acknowledging that psychiatry is not an exact science, Justice Marshall added that "[b]y organizing a defendant's mental history, examination results and behavior, and other information, interpreting it in light of their expertise, and then laying out their investigative and analytic process to the jury, the psychiatrists for each party enable the jury to make its most accurate determination of the truth on the issue before them." With that observation in view, the opinion found that there was an extremely high risk of an inaccurate resolution of a case, when necessary psychiatric assistance is denied to a defendant.

The ultimate conclusion from Justice Marshall's abstract analysis of the application of the three pronged test was "that when a defendant demonstrates to the trial judge that his sanity at the time of the offense is to be a significant factor at trial, the State must, at a minimum, assure the defendant access to a competent psychiatrist who will conduct an appropriate examination and assist in evaluation, preparation, and presentation of the defense."

In turning to the facts of the case presented to the Court, the opinion found that the defendant established that he was indigent and that his sanity was a major issue at the trial, therefore it was constitutional error to deny him free access to psychiatric assistance. The judgment of the Oklahoma Court of Criminal Appeals was reversed and a new trial ordered.

Concurring opinion by Chief Justice Burger: Chief Justice Burger wrote a brief concurring opinion wherein he pointed out that he believed the Court's holding should be narrowly interpreted as applying to capital prosecutions, and not to non-capital cases.

Dissenting opinion by Justice Rehnquist: Justice Rehnquist dissented on two primary grounds. First, he argued that the facts of the case did not warrant the creation of a rule of law that required appointment of a psychiatrist for an indigent defendant merely upon " a preliminary showing that his sanity at the time of the offense is likely to be a significant factor at trial[.]" Justice Rehnquist argued that a higher standard should be erected that would entitle a defendant to appointment of psychiatric assistance. He did not believe that the facts of the case reached the level necessary to require appointment of psychiatric assistance.

Next, it was reasoned by Justice Rehnquist that even if the rule announced by the Court was necessary, "the constitutional rule announced by the Court is far too broad." Justice Rehnquist indicated that the majority opinion should have expressly limited "the rule to capital cases, and make clear that the entitlement is to an independent psychiatric evaluation, not to a defense consultant."

Akins v. Texas *Court:* United States Supreme Court; *Case Citation:* Akins v. Texas, 325 U.S. 398 (1945); *Argued:* April 30, May 1, 1945; *Decided:* June 4, 1945; *Opinion of the Court:* Justice Reed; *Concurring Statement:* Justice Rutledge; *Dissenting Opinion:* Justice Murphy; *Dissenting Statement:* Chief Justice Stone and Black, J.; *Appellate Defense Counsel:* A. S. Baskett argued; W. J. Durham on brief; *Appellate Prosecution Counsel:* Benjamin T. Woodall argued and briefed; *Amicus Curiae Brief Supporting Prosecutor:* None; *Amicus Curiae Brief Supporting Defendant:* None.

Issue Presented: Whether defendant established racial discrimination in grand jury selection due to the jury commissioners' refusal to select more than one black to serve on a grand jury?

Case Holding: The defendant did not establish racial discrimination in grand jury selection due to the jury commissioners' refusal to select more than one black to serve on a grand jury, because the Constitution does not guarantee racial proportionality on a grand jury.

Factual and procedural background of case: The defendant, Akins, was convicted of capital murder and sentenced to death by the State of Texas. The Texas Court of Criminal Appeals affirmed the judgment. In doing so, the appellate court rejected the defendant's contention that his prosecution violated the Federal constitution, because the grand jury commissioners would not permit more than one black person to sit on a grand jury. The United States Supreme Court granted certiorari to consider the issue.

Opinion of the Court by Justice Reed: Justice Reed held that "[t]he Fourteenth Amendment forbids any discrimination against a race in the selection of a grand jury." However, the opinion indicated that limitations were imposed upon the right of participation on a grand jury. Justice Reed wrote: "Fairness in selection has never been held to require proportional representation of races upon a jury. Purposeful discrimination is not sustained by a showing that on a single grand jury the number of members of one race is less than that race's proportion of the eligible individuals. The number of our races and nationalities stands in the way of evolution of such a conception of due process or equal protection. Defendants under our criminal statutes are not entitled to demand representatives of their racial inheritance upon juries before whom they are tried. But such defendants are entitled to require that those who are trusted with jury selection shall not pursue a course of conduct which results in discrimination in the selection of jurors on racial grounds."

Justice Reed reasoned further that: "The mere fact of inequality in the number selected does not in itself show discrimination. A purpose to discriminate must be present which may be proven by systematic exclusion of eligible jurymen of the proscribed race or by unequal application of the law to such an extent as to show intentional discrimination." The opinion concluded that the record in the case failed to establish "that the commissioners deliberately and intentionally limited the number of [blacks] on the grand jury list." The judgment of the Texas Court of Criminal Appeals was affirmed.

Concurring statement by Justice Rutledge: Justice Rutledge issued a statement indicating he concurred in the Court's decision.

Dissenting opinion by Justice Murphy: Justice Murphy dissented from the Court's decision. He believed the Constitution encompassed the defendant's claim and that the defendant's rights were violated. Justice Murphy wrote:

It follows that the State of Texas, in insisting upon one [black] representative on the grand jury panel, has respected no right belonging to [the defendant]. On the contrary, to the extent that this insistence amounts to a definite limitation of [black] grand jurors, a clear constitutional right has been directly invaded. The equal protection clause guarantees [the defendant] not only the right to have [blacks] considered as prospective veniremen but also the right to have them considered without numerical or proportional limitation. If a jury is to be fairly chosen from a cross section of the community it must be done without limiting the number of persons of a particular color, racial background or faith — all of which are irrelevant factors in setting qualifications for jury service. This may in a particular instance result in the selection of one, six, twelve or even no [blacks] on a jury panel. The important point, however, is that the selections must in no way be limited or restricted by such irrelevant factors....

Our affirmance of this judgment thus tarnishes the fact that we of this nation are one people undivided in ability or freedom by differences in race, color or creed.

Dissenting statement by Chief Justice Stone and Black, J.: The Chief Justice and Justice Black issued a statement indicating they dissented from the Court's decision. *See also* **Discrimination in Grand or Petit Jury Selection**

Alabama

The State of Alabama is a capital punishment jurisdiction. The State reenacted its death penalty law after the United States Supreme Court decision in *Furman v. Georgia,* 408 U.S. 238 (1972), on March 5, 1976.

Alabama has a three-tier legal system. The State's legal system is composed of a supreme court, court of appeals and courts of general jurisdiction. The Alabama Supreme Court is presided over by a chief justice and eight associate justices. The Alabama Court of Criminal Appeals is composed of a presiding judge and four judges. The courts of general jurisdiction in the State are called Circuit Courts. Capital offenses against the State of Alabama are tried in the Circuit Courts.

Alabama's capital punishment statute is triggered if a person commits a homicide under the following special circumstances:

1. With intent to cause the death of another person, he or she causes the death of that person or of another person; or
2. Under circumstances manifesting extreme indifference to human life, he or she recklessly engages in conduct which creates a grave risk of death to a person other than him/herself, and thereby causes the death of another person; or
3. He or she commits or attempts to commit arson in the first degree, burglary in the first or second degree, escape in the first degree, kidnapping in the first degree, rape in the first degree, robbery in any degree, sodomy in the first degree or any other felony clearly dangerous to human life and, in the course of and in furtherance of the crime that he or she is committing or attempting to commit, or in immediate flight therefrom, he or she, or another participant if there be any, causes the death of any person.

Capital murder in Alabama is punishable by death or life imprisonment without parole. A capital prosecution in Alabama is bifurcated into a guilt phase and penalty phase. A jury is used at both phases of a capital trial. It is required that, at the penalty phase, at least 10 of 12 jurors must agree that a death sentence is appropriate before it can be imposed. If the penalty phase jury is unable to reach a verdict, the trial judge is required to declare a mistrial and convene another penalty phase jury. The decision of a penalty phase jury is not binding on the trial court under the laws of Alabama. The trial court may accept or reject the jury's determination on punishment, and impose whatever sentence he or she believes the evidence established.

In order to impose a death sentence upon a defendant under Alabama law, it is required that the prosecutor establish the existence of at least one of the following statutory aggravating circumstances at the penalty phase:

1. The capital offense was committed by a person under sentence of imprisonment;
2. The defendant was previously convicted of another capital offense or a felony involving the use or threat of violence to the person;
3. The defendant knowingly created a great risk of death to many persons;

William H. Pryor, Alabama Attorney General in 2000. His office represents the State in capital punishment appellate proceedings. (Alabama Attorney General Office)

4. The capital offense was committed while the defendant was engaged or was an accomplice in the commission of, or an attempt to commit, or flight after committing, or attempting to commit, rape, robbery, burglary or kidnapping;
5. The capital offense was committed for the purpose of avoiding or preventing a lawful arrest or effecting an escape from custody;
6. The capital offense was committed for pecuniary gain;
7. The capital offense was committed to disrupt or hinder the lawful exercise of any governmental function or the enforcement of laws; or
8. The capital offense was especially heinous, atrocious or cruel compared to other capital offenses.

Although the Federal Constitution will not permit jurisdictions to prevent capital felons from presenting all relevant mitigating evidence at the penalty phase, Alabama has provided the following statutory mitigating circumstances that permit the jury (or judge) to reject imposition of the death penalty:

1. The defendant has no significant history of prior criminal activity;
2. The capital offense was committed while the defendant was under the influence of extreme mental or emotional disturbance;
3. The victim was a participant in the defendant's conduct or consented to it;
4. The defendant was an accomplice in the capital offense committed by another person and his participation was relatively minor;
5. The defendant acted under extreme duress or under the substantial domination of another person;

ALABAMA EXECUTIONS 1976–1999

96.8% 579   3.2% 19

■ ALABAMA EXECUTIONS
■ ALL OTHER EXECUTIONS

EXECUTIONS BY ALABAMA 1930–1999

96.5% 4303   3.5% 154

■ ALABAMA
■ ALL OTHER JURISDICTIONS

6. The capacity of the defendant to appreciate the criminality of his conduct or to conform his conduct to the requirements of law was substantially impaired; and
7. The age of the defendant at the time of the crime.

Under Alabama's capital punishment statute, a sentence of death is automatically reviewed by the Alabama Supreme Court. Alabama uses the electric chair to carry out death sentences. The State's death row facility for men is located in Atmore, Alabama; while the facility maintaining female death row inmates is located in Wetumpka, Alabama.

Pursuant to the laws of Alabama the Governor has authority to grant clemency in capital cases. Capital felons who have their death sentences commuted to life imprisonment are eligible for a pardon from the State's Board of Pardons and Parole, if the Board obtains sufficient evidence to indicate that the inmate is innocent of the crime and unanimously approves the pardon with the Governor.

From the start of modern capital punishment in 1976, through 1999, Alabama executed 19 capital felons. During this period Alabama did not execute any female capital felons, al-

though 2 of its death row inmates during this period were females. In 1999 the State had 10 juveniles on death row. The State permits capital punishment to be imposed on persons 16 years old or older. A total of 178 capital felons were on death row in Alabama in 1999. The 1999 death row population in the State was listed as: 78 black inmates; 94 white inmates; and 6 unidentified inmates. Alabama does not prohibit the execution of mentally retarded capital felons.

Executions by Alabama 1976–1999

Name	Race	Date of Execution	Method
John Evans	White	April 22, 1983	Electrocution
Arthur Lee Jones	Black	March 21, 1986	Electrocution
Wayne Ritter	White	August 28, 1987	Electrocution
Michael Lindsey	Black	May 26, 1989	Electrocution
Horace Dunkins	Black	July 14, 1989	Electrocution
Herbert Richardson	Black	August 18, 1989	Electrocution
Arthur Julius	Black	November 17, 1989	Electrocution
Wallace Thomas	Black	July 13, 1990	Electrocution
Larry Heath	White	March 20, 1992	Electrocution
Cornelius Singleton	Black	November 20, 1992	Electrocution
Willie Clisby	Black	April 28, 1995	Electrocution
Varnall Weeks	Black	May 12, 1995	Electrocution
Edward Horsley	Black	February 16, 1996	Electrocution
Billy Wayne Waldrop	White	January 10, 1997	Electrocution
Walter Hill	Black	May 2, 1997	Electrocution
Henry Hays	White	June 6, 1997	Electrocution
Steven Thompson	White	May 8, 1998	Electrocution
Brian K. Baldwin	Black	June 18, 1999	Electrocution
Victor Kennedy	Black	August 6, 1999	Electrocution

Alaska The death penalty is not carried out by the State of Alaska. The last execution in Alaska was in 1949. The State abolished the punishment in 1957.

Albania The death penalty is authorized in the country of Albania. Albania utilizes firing squad and hanging as methods of execution. However, the nation has not carried out an execution in over a decade. Albania's legal system is in an impasse and the nation does not have a constitution.

Prior to massive political reforms in the 1990s, Albania had a harsh penal code. The pre–1990 penal code listed a total of 34 offenses punishable by death. Further, defendants could not use attorneys because the private practice of law in Albania had been banned in 1967.

In 1990, following widespread public unrest, steps were taken to liberalize the penal code. The number of offenses punishable by death was reduced to 11. The new code exempted women from the death penalty. The legal status of lawyers was restored, so that defendants could retain counsel. *See also* **International Capital Punishment Nations**

Alberty v. United States *Court:* United States Supreme Court; *Case Citation:* Alberty v. United States, 162 U.S. 499 (1896); *Argued:* Not reported; *Decided:* April 20, 1896; *Opinion of the Court:* Justice Brown; *Concurring Opinion:* None; *Dissenting Opinion:* None; *Appellate Defense Counsel:* Wm. M. Cravens argued and briefed; *Appellate Prosecution Counsel:* Mr. Whitney argued and briefed; *Amicus Curiae Brief Supporting*

Prosecutor: None; *Amicus Curiae Brief Supporting Defendant:* None

Issue Presented: Whether the trial court committed error by instructing the jury to infer the defendant's guilt from evidence of his flight from the jurisdiction of the court?

Case Holding: The trial court committed error by instructing the jury to infer the defendant's guilt from evidence of his flight from the jurisdiction of the court, therefore the judgment against him could not stand.

Factual and procedural background of case: The defendant, Alberty, was convicted of capital murder and sentenced to death by the United States. The defendant appealed to the United States Supreme Court, alleging that the trial court committed error by instructing the jury to infer guilt from evidence of his flight from the jurisdiction of the court. The United States Supreme Court granted certiorari to consider the issue.

Opinion of the Court by Justice Brown: Justice Brown held that it was error to instruct the jury to infer the defendant's guilt from evidence that he temporarily fled the county where the crime occurred. The opinion addressed the matter as follows:

> ... [I]t was especially misleading for the court to charge the jury that, from the fact of absconding, they might infer the fact of guilt, and that flight "is a silent admission by the defendant that he is unwilling or unable to face the case against him. It is in some sense ... a confession; and it comes in with the other incidents, the corpus delicti being proved, from which guilt may be cumulatively inferred." While, undoubtedly, the flight of the accused is a circumstance proper to be laid before the jury, as having a tendency to prove his guilt, at the same time ... there are so many reasons for such conduct consistent with innocence that it scarcely comes up to the standard of evidence tending to establish guilt, but this and similar evidence has been allowed upon the theory that the jury will give it such weight as it deserves, depending upon the surrounding circumstances.
>
> ... [I]t is not universally true that a man who is conscious that he has done a wrong will pursue a certain course not in harmony with the conduct of a man who is conscious of having done an act which is innocent, right, and proper, since it is a matter of common knowledge that men who are entirely innocent do sometimes fly from the scene of a crime through fear of being apprehended as the guilty parties, or from an unwillingness to appear as witnesses. Nor is it true as an accepted axiom of criminal law that "the wicked flee when no man pursueth, but the righteous are as bold as a lion." Innocent men sometimes hesitate to confront a jury; not necessarily because they fear that the jury will not protect them, but because they do not wish their names to appear in connection with criminal acts, are humiliated at being obliged to incur the popular odium of an arrest and trial, or because they do not wish to be put to the annoyance or expense of defending themselves.

The judgment of the Federal trial court was reversed and a new trial awarded.

Alcohol or Drug Abuse *see* Intoxication Defense; Intoxication Mitigator

Alcorta v. Texas
Court: United States Supreme Court; *Case Citation:* Alcorta v. Texas, 355 U.S. 28 (1957); *Argued:* October 23, 1957; *Decided:* November 12, 1957; *Opinion of the Court:* Per Curiam; *Concurring Opinion:* None; *Dissenting Opinion:* None; *Appellate Defense Counsel:* Fred A. Semaan and Raul Villarreal argued; Fred A. Semaan on brief; *Appellate Prosecution Counsel:* Roy R. Barrera and Hubert W. Green, Jr. argued; Will Wilson on brief; *Amicus Curiae Brief Supporting Prosecutor:* Not reported; *Amicus Curiae Brief Supporting Defendant:* Not reported.

Issue Presented: Whether the defendant was denied due process of law because of false testimony given by the prosecutor's star witness?

Case Holding: The defendant was denied due process of law because of false testimony given by the prosecutor's star witness.

Factual and procedural background of case: The defendant, Alvaro Alcorta, was charged with the capital murder of his wife by the State of Texas. During the trial the defendant admitted killing his wife, but contended that he killed her in a heat of passion, after discovering her embracing a man called Castilleja. The alleged paramour, Castilleja, testified at trial and denied having any relationship with the defendant's wife. The jury rejected the defense and convicted the defendant of capital murder. The defendant was sentenced to death. The Texas Court of Criminal Appeals affirmed the conviction and sentence.

The defendant filed a habeas corpus petition in a State trial court. During a hearing on the petition Castilleja confessed to having had sexual intercourse with the defendant's wife on several occasions. He also testified that he had informed the prosecutor of the affair before the trial and that the prosecutor had told him he should not volunteer any information about it. The prosecutor admitted that these statements were true. The trial court denied relief. The Texas Court of Criminal Appeals affirmed the denial of relief. In doing so, the appellate court rejected the defendant's claim that his conviction violated due process of law. The United States Supreme Court granted certiorari to consider the issue.

Opinion of the Court was delivered Per Curiam: The per curiam opinion held that the defendant was denied due process of law because of Castilleja's false testimony at trial, and the prosecutor's conduct in letting him testify falsely. The opinion reasoned as follows:

> A hearing was held on the petition for habeas corpus. Castilleja was called as a witness. He confessed [to] having sexual intercourse with [the defendant's] wife on five or six occasions within a relatively brief period before her death. He testified that he had informed the prosecutor of this before trial and the prosecutor had told him he should not volunteer any information about such intercourse but if specifically asked about it to answer truthfully. The prosecutor took the stand and admitted that these statements were true. He conceded that he had not told [the defendant] about Castilleja's illicit intercourse with his wife. He also admitted that he had not included this information in a written statement taken from Castilleja prior to the trial but instead had noted it in a separate record....
>
> Under ... general principles ... [the defendant] was not accorded due process of law. It cannot seriously be disputed that

Castilleja's testimony, taken as a whole, gave the jury the false impression that his relationship with [the defendant's] wife was nothing more than that of casual friendship. This testimony was elicited by the prosecutor who knew of the illicit intercourse between Castilleja and [the defendant's] wife. Undoubtedly Castilleja's testimony was seriously prejudicial to [the defendant]. It tended squarely to refute his claim that he had adequate cause for a surge of "sudden passion" in which he killed his wife. If Castilleja's relationship with [the defendant's] wife had been truthfully portrayed to the jury, it would have, apart from impeaching his credibility, tended to corroborate [the defendant's] contention that he had found his wife embracing Castilleja. If [the defendant's] defense had been accepted by the jury, as it might well have been if Castilleja had not been allowed to testify falsely, to the knowledge of the prosecutor, his offense would have been reduced to "murder without malice" precluding the death penalty now imposed upon him.

The judgment of the Texas Court of Criminal Appeals was reversed. *See also* **Actual Innocence Claim**

Aldridge v. United States
Court: United States Supreme Court; *Case Citation:* Aldridge v. United States, 283 U.S. 308 (1931); *Argued:* March 16, 1931; *Decided:* April 20, 1931; *Opinion of the Court:* Chief Justice Hughes; *Concurring Opinion:* None; *Dissenting Opinion:* Justice McReynolds; *Appellate Defense Counsel:* James Francis Reilly argued and briefed; *Appellate Prosecution Counsel:* Leo A. Rober argued and briefed; *Amicus Curiae Brief Supporting Prosecutor:* None; *Amicus Curiae Brief Supporting Defendant:* None.

Issue Presented: Whether the trial court committed reversible error in refusing a request to ask the prospective jury, during jury selection, if they had racial prejudices that would prevent them from fairly deciding the case because the defendant was black and the victim was white?

Case Holding: The trial court committed reversible error in refusing a request to ask the prospective jury, during jury selection, if they had racial prejudices that would prevent them from fairly deciding the case because the defendant was black and the victim was white.

Factual and procedural background of case: The defendant, Alfred Scott Aldridge was convicted of capital murder and sentenced to death by the District of Columbia. The District of Columbia Court of Appeals affirmed the judgment. In doing so, the appellate court rejected the defendant's argument that the trial court committed error in refusing to ask the prospective jurors, during jury selection, if racial prejudices would prevent them from fairly deciding the case because the defendant was black and the victim was white. The United States Supreme Court granted certiorari to consider the issue.

Opinion of the Court by Chief Justice Hughes: The Chief Justice held that it was reversible error for the trial court to refuse to inquire into racial prejudice when asked by the defendant. The opinion reasoned as follows:

> The right to examine jurors on the voir dire as to the existence of a disqualifying state of mind has been upheld with respect to other races than the black race, and in relation to religious and other prejudices of a serious character....
>
> ... Despite the privileges accorded to [blacks], we do not

think that it can be said that the possibility of such prejudice is so remote as to justify the risk in forbidding the inquiry. And this risk becomes most grave when the issue is of life or death.

> The argument is advanced on behalf of the government that it would be detrimental to the administration of the law in the courts of the United States to allow questions to jurors as to racial or religious prejudices. We think that it would be far more injurious to permit it to be thought that persons entertaining a disqualifying prejudice were allowed to serve as jurors and that inquiries designed to elicit the fact of disqualification were barred. No surer way could be devised to bring the processes of justice into disrepute.

The judgment of the Court of Appeals was reversed and the case remanded for a new trial.

Dissenting opinion by Justice McReynolds: Justice McReynolds dissented from the Court's decision on the grounds that the record did not disclose any unfairness to the defendant in failing to make inquiries into racial prejudice. He expressed his opinion as follows:

> Nothing is revealed by the record which tends to show that any juror entertained prejudice which might have impaired his ability fairly to pass upon the issues. It is not even argued that considering the evidence presented there was room for reasonable doubt of guilt....
>
> Two local courts could not conclude that there was adequate reason for holding the accused man had suffered deprivation of any substantial right through refusal by the trial judge to ask prospective jurors something relative to racial prejudice. And certainly I am unable to affirm that they were wrong....
>
> Unhappily, the enforcement of our criminal laws is scandalously ineffective. Crimes of violence multiply; punishment walks lamely. Courts ought not to increase the difficulties by magnifying theoretical possibilities. It is their province to deal with matters actual and material; to promote order and not to hinder it by excessive theorizing of or by magnifying what in practice is not really important. *See also* **Race-Qualified Jury**

Alexander v. United States
Court: United States Supreme Court; *Case Citation:* Alexander v. United States, 138 U.S. 353 (1891); *Argued:* Not reported; *Decided:* February 2, 1891; *Opinion of the Court:* Justice Brown; *Concurring Opinion:* None; *Dissenting Opinion:* None; *Justice Taking No Part in Decision:* Justice Gray; *Appellate Defense Counsel:* A. H. Garland argued; Heber J. May on brief; *Appellate Prosecution Counsel:* United States Solicitor General William Howard Taft argued and briefed; *Amicus Curiae Brief Supporting Prosecutor:* None; *Amicus Curiae Brief Supporting Defendant:* None.

Issue Presented: Whether it was error for the Federal District Court to force an attorney who was consulted by the defendant, to reveal the communication given by the defendant?

Case Holding: It was error for the Federal District Court to force an attorney who was consulted by the defendant, to reveal the communication given by the defendant, because the attorney-client privilege protected such communication from disclosure.

Factual and procedural background of case: The defendant, Alexander, was prosecuted for capital murder by the United States. The offense occurred "at the Creek Nation in [Native American] country." The trial was held in a Federal

District Court in the State of Arkansas. The defendant was convicted and sentenced to death. The defendant appealed to the United States Supreme Court, arguing that it was error for trial court to force an attorney he consulted to reveal to the jury confidential communication between them.

Opinion of the Court by Justice Brown: Justice Brown held that it was error for the trial court to force the attorney to disclose communication provided by the defendant. The opinion stated that the common law attorney-client privilege prohibited disclosure of confidential communication between an attorney and client, unless the client consented to such disclosure. It was also said that neither the payment of a fee nor the pendency of litigation was necessary to invoke the privilege. The opinion found that the defendant consulted with an attorney about the disappearance of the murder victim (the defendant's business partner) and that such communication was protected by the attorney-client privilege, even though the attorney did not represent the defendant in the subsequent murder prosecution. Justice Brown wrote that "[w]hatever facts, therefore, are communicated by a client to a counsel solely on account of that relation, such counsel are not at liberty, even if they wish, to disclose; and the law holds their testimony incompetent."

Justice Brown acknowledged that the attorney-client privilege did not protect communication made to an attorney in furtherance of a scheme to commit a crime. However, he wrote that the defendant did not consult the attorney for the purpose of committing a future crime. It was said that "[h]ad the interview in this case been held for the purpose of preparing his defense, or even for devising a scheme to escape the consequences of his crime, there could be no doubt of its being privileged, although he had made the same statement that his partner was missing and he had not heard from him." The judgment of the District Court was reversed and the case remanded for a new trial. *See also* **Attorney-Client Privilege**

Alford Plea

In the context of capital punishment, an Alford Plea is a protestation by a defendant that he or she is innocent, but will plead guilty to avoid the death penalty. The United States Supreme Court has found that an Alford Plea does not violate the Federal Constitution. *See also* **Guilty Plea; North Carolina v. Alford**

Algeria

Algeria imposes the death penalty as punishment for criminal offenses. The method of execution used by Algeria is the firing squad. It was reported that more than 100 persons were under sentence of death in 1992. The legal system of the nation is based on French and Islamic law. A constitution was adopted by Algerians on December 7, 1996.

The Algerian judiciary is generally independent of executive or military control. The court structure of Algeria is divided into a Supreme Court and 48 provincial (trial) courts. The Supreme Court's review of lower court decisions is limited to questions of procedure, not questions of legal dispute. When overruled, lower court decisions are returned to the lower courts for retrial.

Provincial courts have original jurisdiction over felony offenses. Criminal charges are instituted by the Chamber of Accusation, which serves as a grand jury. Arrested suspects must be informed of the nature of charges against them. No bail system exists in Algeria, but courts have discretion to release suspects on their own recognizance.

A criminal trial is presided over by a panel of three judges and four lay jurors. Defendants usually have access to legal counsel. The Algerian Bar Association provides free legal services to defendants who are unable to pay for legal services. Defendants have the right to confront witnesses and present evidence. Trials are public and defendants have the right to appeal. *See also* **International Capital Punishment Nations**

Alibi Defense

The defense of alibi is an affirmative defense. A capital felon offering such a defense has the burden of proving alibi usually by a preponderance of the evidence. When a defendant presents an alibi defense, the prosecutor must prove the defendant's presence at the scene of the crime beyond a reasonable doubt. *See also* **Affirmative Defenses**

Allen Charge *see* **Deadlocked Jury**

Allison v. United States

Court: United States Supreme Court; *Case Citation:* Allison v. United States, 160 U.S. 203 (1895); *Argued:* Not reported; *Decided:* December 16, 1895; *Opinion of the Court:* Chief Justice Fuller; *Concurring Opinion:* None; *Dissenting Opinion:* None; *Appellate Defense Counsel:* W. M. Cravens argued and briefed; *Appellate Prosecution Counsel:* Mr. Whitney argued and briefed; *Amicus Curiae Brief Supporting Prosecutor:* None; *Amicus Curiae Brief Supporting Defendant:* None.

Issue Presented: Whether the trial court erroneously instructed the jury on how to receive the defendant's evidence of self-defense?

Case Holding: The trial court erroneously instructed the jury on how to receive the defendant's evidence of self-defense, therefore the judgment against him could not stand.

Factual and procedural background of case: The defendant, John Allison, was convicted of capital murder and sentenced to death by the United States. The defendant appealed to the United States Supreme Court, contending that the trial court improperly instructed the jury on how to interpret his evidence of self-defense. The United States Supreme Court granted certiorari to consider the issue.

Opinion of the Court by Chief Justice Fuller: The Chief Justice held that the trial court incorrectly instructed the jury on the defendant's evidence of self-defense. The opinion explained as follows:

> ... The hypothesis upon which the defense rested on the trial was that John Allison had a gun with him on the morning of the tragedy, in order to hunt deer, and that his stopping at [the place where the victim was at], was accidental. His testimony to this effect was corroborated, and was not contradicted....

Justice and the law demanded that, so far as reference was made to the evidence, that which was favorable to the accused should not be excluded. His guilt or innocence turned on a narrow hinge, and great caution should have been used not to complicate and confuse the issue. But the [jury instruction] ignored the evidence tending to show that defendant had not armed himself at all, but had a gun with him for purposes of sport; ... and invited the jury to contemplate the spectacle of [the defendant] hunting up [the victim] with the deliberately preconceived intention of murdering him, unrelieved by allusion to defensive matter, which threw a different light on the transaction.

If [the] defendant were in the right at the time of the killing, the inquiry as to how he came to be armed was immaterial, or, at least, embraced by that expression. If there were evidence — and as to this the record permits no doubt — tending to establish that defendant carried his gun that morning for no purpose of offense or defense, then [the jury instruction] of the court was calculated to darken the light cast on the homicide by the attendant circumstances as defendant claimed them to be; and of this he had just cause to complain....

... [T]hreats [by the victim] were recent, and were communicated, and were admissible in evidence as relevant to the question whether defendant had reasonable cause to apprehend an attack fatal to life, or fraught with great bodily injury; and hence was justified in acting on a hostile demonstration, and one of much less pronounced character than if such threats had not preceded it.... The logical inference was that these threats excited apprehension, and another and inconsistent inference could not be arbitrarily substituted. If [the] defendant, to use the graphic language of the court, hunted [the victim] up and shot him down merely because he had made the threats, speculation as to his mental processes was uncalled for. If [the] defendant committed the homicide because of the threats, in the sense of acting upon emotions aroused by them, then some basis must be laid by the evidence other than the threats themselves before a particular emotion different from those they would ordinarily inspire under the circumstances could be imputed as a motive for the fatal shot.

The judgment of the Federal trial court was reversed and the case remanded for a new trial. *See also* **Self-Defense**

Allocution   At common law, it was deemed essential in capital cases that inquiry be made of the defendant, before judgment was passed, whether he or she had anything to say why the sentence of death should not be pronounced. The right of allocution at the sentencing stage is deemed of such substantial value to the accused that a judgment will be reversed if the record does not show that it was accorded to him or her. This rule of the common law applies to the court of original jurisdiction which pronounced the sentence, and not to an appellate court reviewing a sentence. That is, a defendant does not have a right to be personally present or make a personal statement during appellate proceedings.

All courts afford a capital defendant a narrowly defined right to make a personal brief unsworn statement in mitigation to the factfinder. Before a capital defendant speaks a trial court will instruct him or her outside the presence of the jury, regarding (1) the limited scope of the right to allocution at the penalty phase, (2) the fact that his or her statement is subject to the court's supervision, and (3) that should the statement go beyond the boundaries permitted he or she will be subject

to corrective action by the court, including reopening the proceeding for cross-examination. *See also* **Fielden v. Illinois; Requesting Death; Schwab v. Berggren**

Alternate Jurors *see* **Jury Selection**

Alternative Methods of Execution *see* **Execution Option Jurisdictions**

Amadeo v. Zant   *Court:* United States Supreme Court; *Case Citation:* Amadeo v. Zant, 486 U.S. 214 (1988); *Argued:* March 28, 1988; *Decided:* May 31, 1988; *Opinion of the Court:* Justice Marshall; *Concurring Opinion:* None; *Dissenting Opinion:* None; *Appellate Defense Counsel:* Stephen B. Bright argued; Palmer Singleton, Robert L. McGlasson, and William M. Warner on brief; *Appellate Prosecution Counsel:* Susan V. Boleyn argued; Michael J. Bowers, Marion O. Gordon and William B. Hill, Jr. on brief; *Amicus Curiae Brief Supporting Prosecutor:* None; *Amicus Curiae Brief Supporting Defendant:* 1.

Issue Presented: Whether the factual findings of the Federal District Court were clearly erroneous as support for its conclusion that the defendant successfully established good cause for his failure to raise in the State trial court a constitutional challenge to the composition of the jurors that convicted and sentenced him to death?

Case Holding: The factual findings of the Federal District Court were not clearly erroneous as support for its conclusion that the defendant successfully established good cause for his failure to raise in the State trial court a constitutional challenge to the composition of the jurors that convicted and sentenced him to death.

Factual and procedural background of case: The defendant, Tony B. Amadeo, was convicted of capital murder and sentenced to death by a jury in the Superior Court of Putnam County, Georgia. While the defendant's direct appeal was pending before the Georgia Supreme Court, a Federal District judge, in an independent civil action, concluded that the master list from which jurors were called in Putnam County was systematically compiled so as to exclude minorities and women from jury service. As a result of the Federal judge's findings and order prohibiting use of the Putnam County master jury list, the defendant, on his direct appeal, raised a challenge to the composition of the Putnam County jurors that had convicted and sentenced him. The Georgia Supreme Court rejected the argument as coming too late to be raised, and affirmed the defendant's conviction and sentence.

After exhausting his state post-conviction remedies, the defendant filed a writ of habeas corpus in a Federal District Court on the basis of the jury composition issue. The District Court granted the defendant habeas relief, after finding the defendant had established good cause for his failure to raise the jury challenge in the trial court, as well as having demonstrated sufficient prejudice to excuse the procedural default. A Federal Court of Appeals reversed the District Court's decision, on the basis that evidence of the systemic jury discrimination was readily discoverable in public records, and that the defendant's lawyers had made a tactical decision not to mount a jury challenge. The appellate court concluded that the defendant had not established good cause for his failure to raise the constitutional challenge in accordance with Georgia procedural law. The United States Supreme Court granted certiorari to consider the issue.

Opinion of the Court by Justice Marshall: Justice Marshall ruled that the factual findings upon which the District Court based its conclusion that the defendant had established good cause for his procedural default were not clearly erroneous and should not have been set aside by the Court of Appeals. The opinion noted that although a tactical or intentional decision to forgo a procedural opportunity in State court normally cannot constitute good cause, the failure of counsel to raise a constitutional issue reasonably unknown to him or her is a situation in which the good cause requirement is met. It was further said that showing that the factual or legal basis for a claim was not reasonably available to counsel or that some interference by public officials made compliance impracticable, constitutes good cause.

The opinion found that the facts determined by the District Court permitted that court's legal conclusion that the defendant had established good cause for his procedural default. The facts before the District Court indicated that the evidence of jury discrimination was not reasonably discoverable because it was concealed by officials. Justice Marshall held that the Court of Appeals offered factual, rather than legal grounds for its reversal of the District Court's order. However, it was said that a Federal appellate court may set aside a trial court's factfindings only if they are "clearly erroneous," and must give due regard to the trial court's opportunity to judge the credibility of the witnesses. Justice Marshall stated that the record viewed in its entirety established that the Court of Appeals failed properly to apply the clearly erroneous standard. The Court of Appeals identified no evidence in the record that contradicted the District Court's conclusions about the concealment of evidence of jury discrimination. The judgment of the Court of Appeals was reversed. *See also* **Procedural Default of Constitutional Claims**

American Bar Association The American Bar Association (ABA) is the premier national organization of the legal profession. The ABA was founded in 1878, with a goal of promoting the growth and advancement of the Anglo-American legal system. With more than 400,000 members, the ABA is the largest voluntary professional association in the world. The work of the ABA has included providing accreditation for law schools, continuing legal education for lawyers, general information about the law, programs to assist judges and lawyers in their work, and initiatives to advance the legal system. The ABA has been instrumental in developing models for all areas of the law.

The ABA has taken an active role in seeking changes in areas of the capital punishment system that it considers un-

fair. In 1983, the ABA issued a resolution opposing, in principle, the imposition of the death penalty upon any defendant for an offense committed while under the age of eighteen. In 1988, a resolution was made by the ABA opposing discrimination in capital sentencing on the basis of the race of either the victim or the defendant; and supporting enactment of legislation to eliminate any racial discrimination in capital sentencing. In 1989, the ABA passed a resolution urging that no person with mental retardation, as defined by the American Association on Mental Retardation, should be sentenced to death or executed; and supporting enactment of legislation barring the execution of mentally retarded defendants. In 1991, the ABA issued a resolution supporting, in principle, legislative measures which would prevent any disproportionate effects of Federal death penalty laws on Native Americans subject to Federal jurisdiction.

In 1997, the ABA adopted a resolution calling for a moratorium on executions until policies and procedures were put in place to ensure that death penalty cases were administered fairly, impartially and with minimal risk of executing innocent persons. The ABA has taken a position that procedural problems exist in the way capital punishment is carried out. It has not denounced capital punishment. The ABA has only expressed grave concerns with apparent inequities in the implementation of capital punishment. Some criticism has been launched at the ABA because the current capital punishment procedures used by most jurisdictions are patterned after a model previously endorsed by the ABA. *See also* **Moratorium on Capital Punishment**

American Civil Liberties Union The American Civil Liberties Union (ACLU) was founded by Roger Baldwin in 1920. It was the first public interest law firm of its kind. ACLU is a nonprofit public interest organization devoted exclusively to protecting the basic civil liberties of all Americans. ACLU is supported by annual dues and contributions from its members, and grants from private foundations and individuals. The stated mission of ACLU is to assure that the Federal constitutional Bill of Rights are preserved and enforced. It is widely recognized as the country's foremost advocate of individual rights.

Since 1978, Ira Glasser has served as the executive director of ACLU. Under Glasser's stewardship ACLU takes on almost 6,000 cases annually. ACLU carries out its work utilizing a staff of more than 60 attorneys, in collaboration with at least 2,000 volunteer attorneys. New York City serves as the national headquarters of ACLU. National projects that ACLU has been involved with include: AIDS, arts censorship, capital punishment, children's rights, education reform, lesbian and gay rights, immigrants' rights, national security, privacy and technology, prisoners' rights, reproductive freedom, voting rights, women's rights and workplace rights.

ACLU has taken the public position that the death penalty is cruel and unusual punishment. During the latter half of the 1990s, ACLU called for a moratorium on executions and an

Ira Glasser has headed the ACLU since 1978. Mr. Glasser has called for a moratorium on capital punishment. (American Civil Liberties Union)

end to capital punishment in the nation. It has taken the position that the death penalty is applied throughout the country in an inherently unfair manner. ACLU has cited specific aspects of capital punishment which it contends makes capital punishment unfair and cruel and unusual punishment: (1) murderers who have the economic means to retain private attorneys rarely receive a death sentence; (2) murderers whose victims were nonwhite rarely receive a sentence of death; (3) innocent people have been executed; and (4) the death penalty has no deterrent value.

ACLU has maintained a vigorous campaign to abolish capital punishment. It has filed amicus curiae briefs in courts throughout the nation, including the United States Supreme Court, raising and challenging countless capital punishment issues. It has kept up a relentless lobbying agenda in legislative chambers across the country, including Congress. ACLU has collaborated with national and international organizations that advocate the abolishment of capital punishment in the nation and worldwide. *See also* **Moratorium on Capital Punishment**

Amicus Curiae The phrase "amicus curiae" literally means "friend of the court." Usually when the outcome of a capital punishment case will have a significant impact, "outsiders" will seek to inform the appellate court of the legal outcome they believe the case should have. The vehicle by which a person, not a party to a criminal case, may intervene at the appellate level is through seeking permission to file an amicus curiae brief. Appellate courts have discretion to permit or deny amicus curiae briefs. As a practical matter, appellate courts will usually permit the filing of amicus curiae brief. One of the rare instances where an appellate court has refused to permit an amicus curiae brief to be filed in an important capital punishment case occurred in *Rosenberg v. United States*, 346 U.S. 273 (1953) where the United States Supreme Court refused to permit Dr. W.E.B. DuBois to file an amicus curiae brief on behalf of Ethel and Julius Rosenberg. *See also* **Appellate Rules of Procedure; Intervention by Next Friend**

Amnesty International In 1961, Amnesty International was formed. Amnesty was founded on the principle that people have fundamental rights that transcend national, cultural, religious, and ideological boundaries. It has worked to obtain prompt and fair trials for all prisoners, to end torture and executions, and to secure the release of prisoners of conscience.

Amnesty's earliest activity involved individual letter writing on behalf of prisoners of conscience. After the organization had investigated a prisoner's case and determined that he or she was indeed a prisoner of conscience, it would "adopt" this prisoner in the group and would write letters to officials in that prisoner's country asking for his or her release. The letter writing campaigns met with some success.

However, after a while group members grew restless and wanted to do more than just write reams of letters. During the late 1960s, group members became more active and began to form what were then called Adoption Groups, and in the 1980s, were renamed Local Groups, to focus additional efforts on an adopted prisoner and specific country or issue campaign.

Despite early mistakes and setbacks, and despite growing international opposition by human rights abusers, the methods, tools, and activities that formed Amnesty began to work and have an impact. In 1977, Amnesty was awarded the Nobel Peace Prize for its work. The organization has grown to over 1 million members in over 150 countries.

In 1999, Amnesty launched a vigorous campaign to abolish capital punishment in the United States. The reasons cited by Amnesty for seeking to abolish the death penalty in the United States include: (1) the punishment is cruel, inhuman and degrading; (2) the punishment is irrevocable and may be imposed on the innocent; (3) the punishment has not been shown to deter crime more effectively than other punishments; and (4) the punishment is frequently used based upon race and economic status. The work engaged in by Amnesty to end capital punishment in the United States includes lobbying State and Federal legislators, collaborating with other abolition groups and filing amicus briefs in appellate cases. *See also* **Moratorium on Capital Punishment**

Andersen v. Treat *Court:* United States Supreme Court; *Case Citation:* Andersen v. Treat, 172 U.S. 24 (1898); *Argued:* Not reported; *Decided:* November 14, 1898; *Opinion of the Court:* Chief Justice Fuller; *Concurring Opinion:* None; *Dissenting Opinion:* None; *Appellate Defense Counsel:* P. J. Morris argued; H. G. Miller on brief; *Appellate Prosecution Counsel:* United States Solicitor General Richards argued; W. H. White on brief; *Amicus Curiae Brief Supporting Prosecutor:* None; *Amicus Curiae Brief Supporting Defendant:* None.

Issue Presented: Whether the defendant was denied the right to counsel?

Case Holding: The defendant was not denied the right to counsel because the defendant did not request counsel.

Factual and procedural background of case: The defendant, John Andersen, was convicted of capital murder and sentenced to death by the United States. The United States Supreme Court affirmed the judgment in *Andersen v. United States*. Subsequently, the defendant filed a habeas corpus petition in a Federal trial court alleging that he was deprived of the right to counsel during his trial. The Federal trial court dismissed the petition. The United States Supreme Court granted certiorari to consider the issue.

Opinion of the Court by Chief Justice Fuller: The Chief Justice rejected the defendant's assertion that he was denied the right to counsel. The opinion indicated that the record did not support the defendant's assertion that the trial court forced his attorney to decline representation because the attorney was representing an accomplice in the case. The Chief Justice acknowledged that the defendant did not have counsel, but indicated that this was because the defendant did not request counsel. It was said that absent a request for counsel there was no requirement that counsel be assigned. The judgment of the Federal trial court was affirmed. *See also* **Andersen v. United States; Right to Counsel**

Andersen v. United States

Court: United States Supreme Court; *Case Citation:* Andersen v. United States, 170 U.S. 481 (1898); *Argued:* Not reported; *Decided:* May 9, 1898; *Opinion of the Court:* Chief Justice Fuller; *Concurring Opinion:* None; *Dissenting Statement:* Justice McKenna; *Appellate Defense Counsel:* George McIntosh argued and briefed; *Appellate Prosecution Counsel:* United States Solicitor General Richards argued; W. H. White on brief; *Amicus Curiae Brief Supporting Prosecutor:* None; *Amicus Curiae Brief Supporting Defendant:* None.

Issue Presented: Whether the defendant established self-defense as a legal excuse for the murder for which he was convicted and sentenced?

Case Holding: The defendant did not establish self-defense as a legal excuse for the murder for which he was convicted and sentenced, where the evidence indicated he killed the victim in order to avoid prosecution for another murder.

Factual and procedural background of case: The defendant, John Andersen, was convicted of capital murder and sentenced to death by the United States. The crime occurred onboard an American vessel on the high seas. Although the prosecution was for the murder of the vessel's cook, the defendant had also killed the ship's captain. During the trial the defendant asserted the defense of self-defense. The United States Supreme Court granted certiorari to consider the issue of self-defense.

Opinion of the Court by Chief Justice Fuller: The Chief Justice rejected the defendant's claim that he should have been acquitted on the ground of self-defense. The opinion reasoned as follows:

> It is true that a homicide committed in actual defense of life or limb is excusable, if it appear that the slayer was acting under a reasonable belief that he was in imminent danger of death or great bodily harm from the deceased, and that his act in causing death was necessary in order to avoid the death or great bodily harm which was apparently imminent. But where there is manifestly no adequate or reasonable ground for such belief, or the slayer brings on the difficulty for the purpose of killing the deceased, or violation of law on his part is the reason of

his expectation of an attack, the plea of self-defense cannot avail....

> The captain being dead, [the defendant] knew the [cook] would assume command, and that it would be his duty to arrest him and take him ashore for trial. The imminent danger which threatened him was the danger of the gallows. The inference is irresistible that to avert that danger he killed the [cook], cast the bodies into the sea, burned the ship, and took to the open boat. There can be no pretense that he was acting under a reasonable belief that he was in imminent danger of death or great bodily harm at the hands of the [cook].

The judgment of the Federal trial court was affirmed.

Dissenting statement by Justice McKenna: Justice McKenna issued a statement indicating he dissented from the Court's decision. *See also* **Andersen v. Treat; Self-Defense**

Anderson, Melanie

In July of 1994, Melanie Anderson and her boyfriend, Ronald Pierce, left their home in North Carolina and traveled to Pennsylvania to visit a relative of Pierce. While in Pennsylvania Anderson and Pierce made arrangements to bring back the two year old daughter of Pierce's relative. It was understood that Anderson and Pierce would keep the child for a few weeks.

On August 24, 1994, shortly after Anderson and Pierce returned to North Carolina, they took the child to a hospital. The child was unconscious and suffered severe injuries. The severity of the child's injuries required airlifting her immediately to the pediatric intensive care unit at another hospital. On August 25, 1994, the child died after life support was withdrawn.

Anderson gave hospital officials conflicting accounts of what happened to the child. Anderson initially reported that she heard a gasp in the bedroom of her home and found the child in the room making a gurgling sound. Anderson stated that she grabbed and shook the child. It was also alleged by Anderson that the child had slid on wet carpet, causing the bruises on her face.

Anderson later gave hospital officials a different version of what happened to the child. She reported that earlier in the evening, she had found the child outside, with a dog standing over her. Pierce joined Anderson in this version of what happened.

Anderson and Pierce told the police that a dog jumped on the child and knocked her down. Pierce stated that when he went outside, he found the child lying on the ground, unconscious and not breathing.

Anderson was indicted on January 30, 1995 for first degree murder and felonious child abuse. During Anderson's trial, in September of 1996, her former mother-in-law testified that some time after 11:00 P.M. August 24, 1994, Anderson called her and stated, "I've killed [the child]." Medical evidence during the trial revealed the following:

> The State's evidence tended to show that [the] child had numerous injuries extending all over her body, including bruises on her face, cheeks and jaw, chin, forehead, sides of her neck, collarbones, over the front of her chest, on her back, over her right flank, her buttocks, upper and lower legs, her eyelid, and

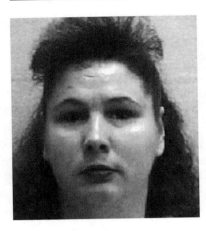

Melanie Anderson was sentenced to death for her role in the murder of a two year old child, while her accomplice and boyfriend, Ronald Pierce, received a life imprisonment sentence. (North Carolina Department of Corrections)

on her shins. Patches of her hair had been pulled out traumatically. [The child] had also suffered injuries caused by a blunt trauma to the mouth. There was evidence of forceful pinching and grabbing and human adult bite marks on [her] body. She had suffered a blunt trauma to her pubic area. Dr. Patrick E. Lantz, the forensic pathologist, found bruises in the forms of grab marks, belt marks, shoe marks, and marks from a radio antenna and a metal tray. [The child's] brain was swollen with a hemorrhage both over the surface of the brain in the lining as well as a subdural hematoma between the skull bone and the brain. There were retinal hemorrhages in the back of her eyes indicating that she had been shaken violently. Dr. Lantz opined that these injuries had been inflicted at various times, would have been painful, and would have required considerable force.

William Fisher, M.D., ... testified that he did not believe [the child's] injuries were caused by a dog, but instead by "some sort of a beating." Dr. Bowman testified that, based on her observations and on the history given to her by Pierce and [Anderson], she believed that [the child] had "been severely abused over a matter of days to weeks." Sybille Sabastian, a registered nurse ..., opined, based on her experience and her observations of [the child's] injuries, that [the child] "had been beaten." Sarah Sinal, M.D., an expert in pediatric medicine who saw [the child] in the pediatric intensive care unit ..., testified that, in her opinion, [the child] was "a victim of severe child abuse." She concluded that [the child] was a victim of the shaken-baby syndrome and the battered-child syndrome. Dr. Lantz testified that, in his opinion, [the child's] injuries were not caused by a dog, that the injuries were inflicted at various times, and that [the child] was a victim of battered-child syndrome.

Anderson was found guilty of first degree murder and felonious child abuse. Following a capital sentencing proceeding, the jury recommended a sentence of death for the first degree murder conviction, and the trial court entered judgment accordingly. The trial court also sentenced Anderson to three years imprisonment for felonious child abuse. She is on death row in North Carolina. Pierce was tried separately and convicted of capital murder, but received a sentence of life imprisonment. *See also* **Women and Capital Punishment**

Andorra   The nation of Andorra does not impose the death penalty. It was abolished by the country in 1990. *See also* **International Capital Punishment Nations**

Andres v. United States   *Court:* United States Supreme Court; *Case Citation:* Andres v. United States, 333 U.S. 740 (1948); *Argued:* February 5, 1948; *Decided:* April 26, 1948;

Opinion of the Court: Justice Reed; *Concurring Opinion:* Justice Frankfurter, in which Burton, J., joined; *Dissenting Opinion:* None; *Appellate Defense Counsel:* Oliver P. Soares argued and briefed; *Appellate Prosecution Counsel:* Vincent Kleinfeld argued and briefed; *Amicus Curiae Brief Supporting Prosecutor:* None; *Amicus Curiae Brief Supporting Defendant:* None.

Issue Presented: Whether the trial court's instruction to the jury that its verdict on guilt and punishment had to be unanimous was confusing and misleading?

Case Holding: The trial court's instruction to the jury that its verdict on guilt and punishment had to be unanimous was confusing and misleading.

Factual and procedural background of case: The defendant, Timoteo Mariano Andres, was convicted of capital murder in a United States District Court for the Territory of Hawaii and sentenced to death. The defendant appealed his conviction to a Federal Court of Appeals. In his appeal, the defendant argued that the trial court's instruction on a unanimous verdict was confusing and misleading to the jury. The appellate court rejected the argument and affirmed the conviction and sentence. The United States Supreme Court granted certiorari to consider the issue.

Opinion of the Court by Justice Reed: Justice Reed held that unanimity in a jury verdict was constitutionally required in Federal prosecutions. He wrote that "[i]n criminal cases this requirement of unanimity extends to all issues — character or degree of the crime, guilt and punishment — which are left to the jury." The opinion found that the statute under which the defendant was prosecuted required unanimity on the issue of guilt and punishment. It was said, however, that the manner in which the trial judge instructed the jury could be interpreted as not requiring unanimity on the issue of punishment. Justice Reed concluded "that the instructions given on this issue did not fully protect the [defendant]." The judgment of the Federal appellate court was reversed and the case remanded for a new trial.

Concurring opinion by Justice Frankfurter, in which Burton, J., joined: Justice Frankfurter concurred in the Court's decision. He wrote separately to express his view that trial court's should seek to use basic language when instructing juries, as a way of minimizing confusion and having cases reversed because of imprecise instructions. *See also* **Jury Unanimity**

Andrews v. Swartz   *Court:* United States Supreme Court; *Case Citation:* Andrews v. Swartz, 156 U.S. 272 (1895); *Argued:* Not reported; *Decided:* February 4, 1895; *Opinion of the Court:* Justice Harlan; *Concurring Opinion:* None; *Dissenting Opinion:* None; *Appellate Defense Counsel:* Geo. M. Shipman argued and briefed; *Appellate Prosecution Counsel:* Wm. A. Stryker argued and briefed; *Amicus Curiae Brief Supporting Prosecutor:* None; *Amicus Curiae Brief Supporting Defendant:* None.

Issue Presented: Whether the defendant was entitled to have his appeal heard by the appellate court of New Jersey?

Case Holding: The defendant was not entitled to have his appeal heard by the appellate court of New Jersey, because under that State's laws an appeal is discretionary.

Factual and procedural background of case: The defendant, Andrews, was convicted of capital murder and sentenced to death by the State of New Jersey. The defendant filed an appeal with the New Jersey Supreme Court. However, the appellate court declined to hear the appeal. The defendant next filed a petition for habeas corpus relief in a Federal District Court. The defendant alleged in the petition that his constitutional rights were violated by the State appellate court's refusal to hear his appeal. The Federal court dismissed the petition. The United States Supreme Court granted certiorari to consider the issue.

Opinion of the Court by Justice Harlan: Justice Harlan wrote that under the laws of New Jersey a conviction for a capital offense was not appealable as a right, but was discretionary with the State appellate court. The opinion disposed of the issue as follows:

> The contention of appellant is that such a statute is in violation of the constitution of the United States. If it were necessary, upon this appeal, to consider that question, we would only repeat what was said in *McKane v. Durston*, 153 U.S. 684 (1894): "An appeal from a judgment of conviction is not a matter of absolute right, independently of constitutional or statutory provisions allowing such appeal. A review by an appellate court of the final judgment in a criminal case, however grave the offense of which the accused is convicted, was not at common law, and is not now, a necessary element of due process of law. It is wholly within the discretion of the state to allow or not to allow such a review." "It is therefore clear that the right of appeal may be accorded by the state to the accused upon such terms as, in its wisdom, may be proper;" and "whether an appeal should be allowed, and, if so, under what circumstances or on what conditions, are matters for each state to determine for itself."

The judgment of the Federal District Court was affirmed.

Angola Angola does not utilize capital punishment. The nation abolished the punishment in 1992. *See also* **International Capital Punishment Nations**

Another Proximate Cause Mitigator The State of Maryland is the only capital punishment jurisdiction that utilizes "another proximate cause" as a statutory mitigating circumstance. This mitigator refers to some other factor which may have intervened to hasten the death of the victim, even though the defendant was convicted of murdering the victim. *See also* **Mitigating Circumstances**

Antigua and Barbuda Capital punishment is carried out in the island nation of Antigua and Barbuda. Antigua and Barbuda utilize hanging as the method of execution. The legal system used by the nation is based on English common law. Antigua and Barbuda adopted a constitution on November 1, 1981.

The constitution of Antigua and Barbuda sets forth the rights of citizens, including provisions to secure life, liberty, and the protection of person, property, and privacy, as well as freedom of speech, association, and worship.

The judicial branch of Antigua and Barbuda is relatively independent from the executive and legislative branches of government. The court structure consists of magistrate courts for minor offenses and High Courts for major offenses. Appeals from the High Courts are taken to the Supreme Court of the Organization of Eastern Caribbean States. Appointments or dismissals of judges to the Supreme Court must be unanimously approved by the heads of government that make up the Organization of Eastern Caribbean States. The prime minister of Antigua and Barbuda casts a vote for such appointment or dismissal. *See also* **International Capital Punishment Nations**

Antiterrorism and Effective Death Penalty Act of 1996 *see* **Habeas Corpus**

Apelt Brothers Michael Apelt and Rudi Apelt are brothers and German nationals. Michael was born on February 28, 1960, and Rudi's date of birth was August 1, 1963. The Apelt brothers were convicted of capital murder by the State of Arizona. Michael was sentenced to death on August 10, 1990, and Rudi received a death sentence on January 8, 1991.

The Apelt brothers came to the United States in August of 1988 with a specific plan. They intended to have Michael marry an American woman, obtain a large life insurance policy on the woman, kill her and collect the insurance proceeds.

The Apelt brothers arrived in the United States with Rudi's wife Susanne, and Michael's former girlfriend Anke Dorn. They landed in San Diego, California and took up lodging in a motel. Shortly after their arrival the Apelt brothers began visiting nightclubs in search of a wife for Michael. At one nightclub they met two women, Cheryl Rubenstein and Trudy Waters. Cheryl and Trudy lived in Phoenix, Arizona and were in San Diego to cater a party. During the course of the evening the bothers claimed to be wind surfing board manufacturers and Mercedes importers. Rudi denied being married. Before the brothers left the nightclub, the women gave them their addresses and phone numbers in Phoenix.

A few weeks after the nightclub encounter the Apelt brothers flew to Phoenix. Cheryl picked them up at the airport and took them to a hotel. After a couple of weeks, the brothers flew back to San Diego, picked up Anke Dorn and then returned to Phoenix. Rudi's wife, Susanne, returned to Germany.

Several months went by before the bothers stumbled into the situation they had been looking for. On October 6, they met Annette Clay at a bar. The brothers alleged to be international bankers who were staying at a Holiday Inn. Annette eventually gave Rudi her phone number. Rudi called her the following day and arranged to meet Annette and a friend she would bring along. That evening the brothers met Annette and her friend, Cindy Monkman. Michael spent the evening dancing with Cindy and telling her, "You're the woman I want to marry."

The Apelts saw Annette and Cindy several times during the next few weeks. The two women became suspicious of the brothers when Cindy discovered she was missing over $100 in cash after the Apelts visited her apartment. They placed a series of calls and learned that the brothers were not staying at a Holiday Inn, they were registered at a Motel 6. The two women went to the Motel 6 and discovered Anke Dorn.

The following day the Apelts met with Annette and Cindy. The brothers angrily told the two women that their meddling destroyed the brothers' "high security clearance" and cost them their jobs and work visas. They explained away Anke by saying she was a family friend whose husband was in the hospital. Annette and Cindy bought the story and apologized. After suggesting ways to make amends, which the brothers refused, Annette exclaimed, "What do you want us to do, marry you?" The Apelt brothers smiled and replied, "Yes."

Michael moved into Cindy's apartment and Rudi moved into Annette's apartment. Rudi lived with Annette less than a week before she discovered that the story regarding Anke was a lie. Annette threw Rudi out and did not see him again. Rudi moved into a motel with Anke.

After Rudi split up with Annette, Michael lied and told Cindy and Annette that Rudi had returned to Germany. On October 28, 1988, Cindy and Michael were secretly married in Las Vegas. Shortly afterwards Michael suggested they consult an insurance broker about a million dollar life insurance policy. Cindy was under the impression that Michael was wealthy and that purchasing a large insurance policy was a customary investment practice by Germans. They were able to obtain a $300,000 policy. Cindy wrote a check for the first month's premium.

Once the life insurance policy was obtained, the Apelt brothers plotted the death of Cindy. The plan was for Michael to drive her into the desert, while Rudi and Anke followed in a separate car. Once there she would be killed. The brothers executed their plan on the evening of December 23, 1988. Cindy's body was found in the early afternoon of December 24th. She had been stabbed five times. Her head was nearly severed from her body.

The police became suspicious of Michael's role in Cindy's death when they learned of the life insurance policy. The suspicion grew intense after Michael paid a homeless man to call his apartment and leave the following fake message: "Hear what I have to talk. I have cut through the throat of your wife and I stabbed and more frequently in the stomach in the back with a knife. If I don't get my stuff, your girl-

German born brothers (left to right) Michael and Rudi Apelt are on death row in Arizona for the murder of Michael's American born wife. (Arizona Department of Corrections)

friend is next and then your brother and last it is you. Do it now, if not, you see what happens. My eyes are everywhere." Michael gave the recorded message to the police, who immediately believed it was fake.

On January 6, 1989 the Apelt bothers and Anke went to police headquarters to report a fictitious story of several people coming to their apartment and threatening them. The police spoke with each of them separately. During the questioning of Anke the police threatened to prosecute her, but promised immunity if she would tell the truth. Anke confessed and the Apelts were immediately arrested.

Michael and Rudi were tried separately. Anke was granted immunity from prosecution in exchange for her testimony at both trials. The brothers were convicted of capital murder and sentenced to death. The death sentences were affirmed by the Arizona Supreme Court.

Appeal *see* **Appellate Review of Conviction and Death Sentence**

Appeal by Prosecutor *see* **Prosecutor**

Appeal in Forma Pauperis *see* **In Forma Pauperis**

Appellant
Appellant is the formal designation given to the party making an appeal. *See also* **Appellee**

Appellate Review of Conviction and Death Sentence
Appellate court review of the final judgment in a criminal case was not, at common law, a necessary element of due process of law. Consequently, in the case of *McKane v. Durston*, 153 U.S. 684 (1894), the United States Supreme Court held that the Constitution did not require States establish appellate courts to hear appeals of criminal convictions and sentences. The pronouncement in *McKane* has no practical meaning because all jurisdictions have established appellate courts to review criminal convictions and sentences.

The role of appellate courts is very limited. Unlike trial courts, appellate courts do not have jurisdiction to permit live witness testimony. Appellate courts may only review the record produced at the trial court level. Usually, appellate courts will permit attorneys to present oral arguments on the issues in a case. A defendant does not have a right to be present when attorneys make oral arguments to appellate courts.

Distinguishing Review Sentence from Appeal of Conviction: Prior to capital punishment being abolished by the United States Supreme Court in *Furman v. Georgia*, 408 U.S. 238 (1972) all capital punishment jurisdictions allowed capital felons to bring their conviction and sentence to appellate courts by way of an appeal (or writ of error, as it was sometimes called). When the Supreme Court resurrected the death penalty in *Gregg v. Georgia*, 428 U.S. 153 (1976) by approving of the capital punishment scheme Georgia created, one feature of Georgia's new procedures it approved of was the automatic review of every death sentence. Georgia's appellate review of death sentences was not the traditional appeal, which was not automatic and when taken, involved both conviction and sentence. In approving of this new review process, the Supreme Court did not hold that the Constitution required automatic review of death sentences. The Supreme Court indicated merely that the review process was constitutionally acceptable.

Gregg's acceptance of Georgia's automatic appellate review of death sentences was quickly adopted by other capital punishment jurisdictions. As it stands, Utah is the only capital punishment state that does not utilize an automatic death sentence appellate review process.

The automatic death sentence review process involves, ostensibly, only penalty phase sentencing issues. The question of whether a capital felon was erroneously found guilty of the offense is technically not part of appellate review of a sentence. The only issue at stake in the sentence review process, is whether a capital felon was sentenced to die in accordance with the law. Actual conviction or guilt phase issues are brought to the appellate level by way of the traditional appeal. In practice, however, what occurs is the consolidation of automatic sentencing issues with conviction appeal issues.

Appellate Review of a Death Sentence: Appellate review of a death sentence involves essentially two areas: (1) examination of aggravating and mitigating findings, and (2) determining whether death was the proper sentence.

1. *Review of penalty phase aggravating and mitigating findings.* Appellate courts engage in two types of aggravating circumstance review: (1) determine whether an aggravating circumstance is invalid because of vagueness and (2) determine whether an aggravating circumstance was actually proven to exist.

   All relevant mitigating evidence must be allowed into evidence at the penalty phase. Relevant mitigating evidence, for appellate review purposes, is divided into two issues: (1) evidence offered to establish the existence of a non-statutory mitigating circumstance and (2) evidence submitted to establish the existence of a statutory mitigating circumstance. Both issues are examined by appellate courts from the perspective that a determination was made that a mitigating circumstance was not established. Therefore, appellate review is concerned with examining whether evidence supported the existence of any mitigating circumstance.

2. *Determining whether death is the proper sentence.* Once an appellate court determines that at least one statutory aggravating circumstance was validly found by the fact-finder, and makes its statutory and non-statutory mitigating circumstance analysis, the next stage in the review process is triggered. At this stage the appellate court must determine whether the sentence of death was proper. This determination involves three separate issues: (1) did passion, prejudice or other arbitrary factor cause death to be imposed; (2) was the sentence excessive or dispropor-

tionate compared to other cases; and (3) making an independent weighing or sufficiency determination of aggravating and mitigating circumstances.

Appellate Review of a Capital Conviction: Review of a conviction involves traditional assignments of error. That is, for conviction review a defendant must point to specific matters involved with the guilt phase that he or she believes was wrongly decided against him or her. This could include assignments of error to pretrial issues such as suppression of evidence or dismissal of a charge.

Disposition by Appellate Court: Once an appellate court completes review of a conviction and death sentence, the case must be disposed of based upon the conclusions reached from the review process. A case may be disposed of in any of the following ways: (1) affirm conviction and sentence; (2) affirm conviction, but reverse sentence and remand for further proceedings; (3) affirm conviction, but reverse sentence and remand for imposition of life sentence; (4) affirm conviction, but reverse sentence and impose life sentence; (5) reverse conviction and sentence and remand for new trial; or (6) reverse conviction and sentence and remand for entry of acquittal. *See also* **Andrews v. Swartz; Bergemann v. Backer; Error; Kohl v. Lehlback**

Appellate Rules of Procedure

All appellate courts have special rules which must be followed in bringing a criminal case for appellate review. Although every appellate court has procedural nuances peculiar to it, appellate rules of procedure are, by and large, the same. The illustrative material that follows represents excerpts from the appellate rules of procedure of the Federal Fifth Circuit Court of Appeals.

a. *Filing the Notice of Appeal.* An appeal permitted by law as of right from a district court to a court of appeals must be taken by filing a notice of appeal with the clerk of the district court within the time allowed by law.

b. *Joint or Consolidated Appeals.* If two or more persons are entitled to appeal from a judgment or order of a district court and their interests are such as to make joinder practicable, they may file a joint notice of appeal, or may join in appeal after filing separate timely notices of appeal, and they may thereafter proceed on appeal as a single appellant. Appeals may be consolidated by order of the court of appeals upon its own motion or upon motion of a party, or by stipulation of the parties to the several appeals.

c. *Content of the Notice of Appeal.* A notice of appeal must specify the party or parties taking the appeal by naming each appellant in either the caption or the body of the notice of appeal. A notice of appeal also must designate the judgment, order, or part thereof appealed from, and must name the court to which the appeal is taken. An appeal will not be dismissed for informality of form or title of the notice of appeal, or for failure to name a party whose intent to appeal is otherwise clear from the notice.

d. *Serving the Notice of Appeal.* The clerk of the district court shall serve notice of the filing of a notice of appeal by mailing a copy to each party's counsel of record (apart from the appellant's). When a defendant appeals in a criminal case, the clerk of the district court shall also serve a copy of the notice of appeal upon the defendant, either by personal service or by mail addressed to the defendant.

e. *Appeal in a Criminal Case.* In a criminal case, a defendant shall file the notice of appeal in the district court within 10 days after the entry either of the judgment or order appealed from, or of a notice of appeal by the Government. A notice of appeal filed after the announcement of a decision, sentence, or order — but before entry of the judgment or order — is treated as filed on the date of and after the entry.

f. *Composition of the Record on Appeal.* The record on appeal consists of the original papers and exhibits filed in the district court, the transcript of proceedings, if any, and a certified copy of the docket entries prepared by the clerk of the district court.

g. *The Transcript; Duty of Appellant; Notice to Appellee.*

1. Within 10 days after filing the notice of appeal or entry of an order disposing of the last timely motion outstanding, whichever is later, the appellant shall order from the reporter a transcript of such parts of the proceedings not already on file as the appellant deems necessary, subject to local rules of the courts of appeals. The order shall be in writing and within the same period a copy shall be filed with the clerk of the district court.

2. If the appellant intends to urge on appeal that a finding or conclusion is unsupported by the evidence or is contrary to the evidence, the appellant shall include in the record a transcript of all evidence relevant to such finding or conclusion.

3. Unless the entire transcript is to be included, the appellant shall file a statement of the issues the appellant intends to present on the appeal, and shall serve on the appellee a copy of the order or certificate and of the statement. An appellee who believes that a transcript of other parts of the proceedings is necessary shall, within 10 days after the service of the order or certificate and the statement of the appellant, file and serve on the appellant a designation of additional parts to be included. Unless within 10 days after service of the designation the appellant has ordered such parts, and has so notified the appellee, the appellee may within the following 10 days either order the parts or move in the district court for an order requiring the appellant to do so.

4. At the time of ordering, a party must make satisfactory arrangements with the reporter for payment of the cost of the transcript.

h. *Statement When No Report Was Made or When the Transcript Is Unavailable.* If no report of the evidence or proceedings at a hearing or trial was made, or if a transcript is unavailable, the appellant may prepare a statement of the evidence or proceedings from the best available means, including the appellant's recollection. The statement shall be served on the appellee, who may serve objections or proposed amendments thereto within 10 days after service. Thereupon the statement and any objections or proposed amendments shall be submitted to the district court for settlement and approval and as settled and approved shall be included by the clerk of the district court in the record on appeal.

i. *Agreed Statement as the Record on Appeal.* In lieu of the record on appeal as defined in subdivision (a) of this rule, the parties may prepare and sign a statement of the case showing how the issues presented by the appeal arose and were decided in the district court and setting forth only so many of the facts averred and proved or sought to be proved as are essential to a decision of the issues presented. If the statement conforms to the truth, it, together with such additions as the court may consider necessary fully to present the issues raised by the appeal, shall be approved by the district court and shall then be certified to the court of appeals as the record on appeal and transmitted thereto by the clerk of the district court.

j. *Correction or Modification of the Record.* If any difference arises as to whether the record truly discloses what occurred in the district court, the difference shall be submitted to and settled by that court and the record made to conform to the truth. If anything material to either party is omitted from the record by error or accident or is misstated therein, the parties by stipulation, or the district court, either before or after the record is transmitted to the court of appeals, or the court of appeals, on proper suggestion or of its own initiative, may direct that the omission or misstatement be corrected, and if necessary that a supplemental record be certified and transmitted. All other questions as to the form and content of the record shall be presented to the court of appeals.

k. *Appellant's Brief.* The brief of the appellant must contain, under appropriate headings and in the order here indicated:

1. A table of contents, with page references, and a table of cases (alphabetically arranged), statutes and other authorities cited, with references to the pages of the brief where they are cited.

2. A statement of subject matter and appellate jurisdiction. The statement shall include: (i) a statement of the basis for subject matter jurisdiction in the district court or agency, with citation to applicable statutory provisions and with reference to the relevant facts to establish such jurisdiction; (ii) a statement of the basis for jurisdiction in the court of appeals, with citation to applicable statutory provisions and with reference to the relevant facts to establish such jurisdiction; the statement shall include relevant filing dates establishing the timeliness of the appeal or petition for review and (a) shall state that the appeal is from a final order or a final judgment

that disposes of all claims with respect to all parties or, if not, (b) shall include information establishing that the court of appeals has jurisdiction on some other basis.

3. A statement of the issues presented for review.

4. A statement of the case. The statement shall first indicate briefly the nature of the case, the course of proceedings, and its disposition in the court below. There shall follow a statement of the facts relevant to the issues presented for review, with appropriate references to the record.

5. A summary of argument. The summary should contain a succinct, clear, and accurate statement of the arguments made in the body of the brief. It should not be a mere repetition of the argument headings.

6. An argument. The argument must contain the contentions of the appellant on the issues presented, and the reasons therefor, with citations to the authorities, statutes, and parts of the record relied on. The argument must also include for each issue a concise statement of the applicable standard of review; this statement may appear in the discussion of each issue or under a separate heading placed before the discussion of the issues.

7. A short conclusion stating the precise relief sought.

l. *Appellee's Brief.* The brief of the appellee must conform to the requirements of outlined for the appellant, except that none of the following need appear unless the appellee is dissatisfied with the statement of the appellant:

1. the jurisdictional statement;
2. the statement of the issues;
3. the statement of the case;
4. the statement of the standard of review.

m. *Reply Brief.* The appellant may file a brief in reply to the brief of the appellee, and if the appellee has cross-appealed, the appellee may file a brief in reply to the response of the appellant to the issues presented by the cross appeal. No further briefs may be filed except with leave of court. All reply briefs shall contain a table of contents, with page references, and a table of cases (alphabetically arranged), statutes and other authorities cited, with references to the pages of the reply brief where they are cited.

n. *Brief of Amicus Curiae.* A brief of an amicus curiae may be filed only if accompanied by written consent of all parties, or by leave of court granted on motion or at the request of the court, except that consent or leave shall not be required when the brief is presented by the United States or an officer or agency thereof, or by a State, Territory or Commonwealth. The brief may be conditionally filed with the motion for leave. A motion for leave shall identify the interest of the applicant and shall state the reasons why a brief of an amicus curiae is desirable. Save as all parties otherwise consent, any amicus curiae shall file its brief within the time allowed the party whose position as to affirmance or reversal the amicus brief will support unless the court for cause shown shall grant leave

for a later filing, in which event it shall specify within what period an opposing party may answer. A motion of an amicus curiae to participate in the oral argument will be granted only for extraordinary reasons.

Appellee Appellee is the formal designation given to the party who responds to an appeal by the opposing party. *See also* **Appellant**

Application for Stay of Execution *see* Stay of Execution

Appointment of Experienced Counsel *see* Right to Counsel

Arave v. Creech *Court:* United States Supreme Court; *Case Citation:* Arave v. Creech, 507 U.S. 463 (1993); *Argued:* November 10, 1992; *Decided:* March 30, 1993; *Opinion of the Court:* Justice O'Connor; *Concurring Opinion:* None; *Dissenting Opinion:* Justice Blackmun, in which Stevens, J., joined; *Appellate Defense Counsel:* Cliff Gardner argued; Claude M. Stern on brief; *Appellate Prosecution Counsel:* Lynn E. Thomas argued; Larry Echo Hawk on brief; *Amicus Curiae Brief Supporting Prosecutor:* None; *Amicus Curiae Brief Supporting Defendant:* None.

Issue Presented: Whether the State of Idaho placed a constitutionally acceptable limiting construction on the statutory aggravating circumstance of "utter disregard for human life?"

Case Holding: The State of Idaho placed a constitutionally acceptable limiting construction on the statutory aggravating circumstance of "utter disregard for human life."

Factual and procedural background of case: The defendant, Thomas Eugene Creech, was charged by the State of Idaho with committing capital murder while he was incarcerated. The defendant entered a plea of guilty to the capital murder charge. During the penalty phase of the prosecution it was determined that the prosecutor established the statutory aggravating circumstance, that in committing the murder the defendant exhibited "utter disregard for human life." The trial court imposed a sentence of death. In affirming the conviction and sentence, the Idaho Supreme Court rejected the defendant's argument that the "utter disregard for human life" aggravating circumstance was unconstitutionally vague. The appellate court indicated that under its prior decisions the statutory aggravating circumstance was defined so that the phrase "utter disregard" was meant to be reflective of a "cold-blooded, pitiless slayer."

The defendant filed a habeas corpus petition in a Federal District Court. The District Court dismissed the petition. However, a Federal Court of Appeals reversed the District Court's ruling after concluding that the "utter disregard" circumstance was facially invalid and that the narrowing construction given by the Idaho Supreme Court was inadequate to cure the defect. The United States Supreme Court granted certiorari to consider the issue.

Opinion of the Court by Justice O'Connor: Justice O'-Connor held that in light of the narrowing definition given the "utter disregard" aggravating circumstance by the Idaho Supreme Court, the circumstance, on its face, meets constitutional standards.

The opinion held that to satisfy the Constitution, a capital sentencing scheme must channel the sentencer's discretion by clear and objective standards that provide specific and detailed guidance and make rationally reviewable the death sentencing process. Justice O'Connor indicated that in order to decide whether a particular aggravating circumstance meets those requirements, a Federal court must determine whether the statutory language defining the circumstance is itself too vague to guide the sentencer; if so, whether the State courts have further defined the vague terms; and, if so, whether those definitions are constitutionally sufficient, i.e., whether they provide some guidance.

Justice O'Connor found that it was not necessary for the Court to decide whether the statutory phrase "utter disregard for human life" itself passed constitutional muster, because the Idaho Supreme Court adopted a limiting construction, and that construction meets constitutional requirements. It was said that the limiting construction was sufficiently clear and objective. The opinion reasoned that in ordinary usage, the phrase "cold-blooded, pitiless slayer" refers to a killer who kills without feeling or sympathy. Thus, the phrase describes a defendant's state of mind or attitude toward his or her conduct and the victim. It was said that although determining whether a capital defendant killed without feeling or sympathy may be difficult, that did not mean that a State cannot, consistent with the Constitution, authorize sentencing judges to make the inquiry and to take their findings into account when deciding whether capital punishment is warranted. The judgment of the Court of Appeals was reversed.

Dissenting opinion by Justice Blackmun, in which Stevens, J., joined: Justice Blackmun dissented from the Court's decision. He believed that the limiting construction given the aggravating circumstance was itself unconstitutionally vague. Justice Blackmun wrote: "Confronted with an insupportable limiting construction of an unconstitutionally vague statute, the majority in turn concocts its own limiting construction of the state court's formulation. Like 'nonsense upon stilts,' however, the majority's reconstruction only highlights the deficient character of the nebulous formulation that it seeks to advance. Because the metaphor 'cold-blooded' by which Idaho defines its 'utter disregard' circumstance is both vague and unenlightening, and because the majority's recasting of that metaphor is not dictated by common usage, legal usage, or the usage of the Idaho courts, the statute fails to provide meaningful guidance to the sentencer, as required by the Constitution. Accordingly, I dissent."

Arbitrary and Capricious *see* Individualized Sentencing

Arcene, James *see* Juveniles

Argentina Argentina abolished capital punishment for ordinary crimes in 1984, but permits its use for exceptional offenses. The nation's legal system is a mixture of the United States and West European legal systems. Argentina has a constitution which was revised in August of 1994.

The judicial system of Argentina is divided into a federal court system and a provincial court system, with each headed by a Supreme Court. The federal Supreme Court is the highest court and court of last resort. Trials are public and defendants have the right to legal counsel and to call witnesses. A panel of judges, not lay jurors, decide guilt or innocence. *See also* **International Capital Punishment Nations**

Arizona The State of Arizona is a capital punishment jurisdiction. The State reenacted its death penalty law after the United States Supreme Court decision in *Furman v. Georgia*, 408 U.S. 238 (1972), on August 8, 1973.

Arizona has a three-tier legal system. The State's legal system is composed of a supreme court, court of appeals and courts of general jurisdiction. The Arizona Supreme Court is presided over by a chief justice, vice chief justice and three associate justices. The Arizona Court of Appeals is divided into two divisions. The first division is divided into five departments, with each department consisting of a panel of three judges. The second division is divided into two departments, with each department having a panel of three judges. The courts of general jurisdiction in the state are called Superior Courts. Capital offenses against the State of Arizona are tried in the Superior Courts.

Arizona's capital punishment statute is triggered if a person commits a homicide under the following special circumstances:

1. Intending or knowing that the person's conduct will cause death, such person causes the death of another with premeditation.
2. Acting either alone or with one or more other persons such person commits or attempts to commit a sexual offense, drug offense, kidnapping, burglary, arson, robbery, escape, child abuse, or unlawful flight from a pursuing law enforcement vehicle.
3. Intending or knowing that the person's

Janet Napolitano is the Arizona Attorney General. Her office represents the State in capital punishment appellate proceedings. (Arizona Attorney General Office)

conduct will cause death to a law enforcement officer, the person causes the death of a law enforcement officer who is in the line of duty.

Capital murder in Arizona is punishable by death or life imprisonment without parole. A capital prosecution in Arizona is bifurcated into a guilt phase and penalty phase. A jury is used only at the guilt phase of a capital trial. The trial judge presides over the penalty phase of a capital prosecution and determines the sentence without a jury.

In order to impose a death sentence upon a defendant under Arizona law, it is required that the prosecutor establish the existence of at least one of the following statutory aggravating circumstances at the penalty phase:

1. The defendant has been convicted of another offense in the United States for which under Arizona law a sentence of life imprisonment or death was imposable.
2. The defendant was previously convicted of a serious offense, whether preparatory or completed.
3. In the commission of the offense the defendant knowingly created a grave risk of death to another person or persons in addition to the victim of the offense.
4. The defendant procured the commission of the offense by payment, or promise of payment, of anything of pecuniary value.
5. The defendant committed the offense as consideration for the receipt, or in expectation of the receipt, of anything of pecuniary value.
6. The defendant committed the offense in an especially heinous, cruel or depraved manner.
7. The defendant committed the offense while in the custody of or on authorized or unauthorized release from the state department of corrections, a law enforcement agency or a county or city jail.
8. The defendant has been convicted of one or more other homicides, which were committed during the commission of the offense.
9. The defendant was an adult at the time the offense was committed or was tried as an adult and the victim was under fifteen years of age or was seventy years of age or older.
10. The murdered individual was an on duty peace officer who was killed in the course of performing his official duties and the defendant knew, or should have known, that the victim was a peace officer.

Although the Federal Constitution will not permit jurisdictions to prevent capital felons from presenting all relevant mitigating evidence at the penalty phase, Arizona has provided the following statutory mitigating circumstances that permit the judge to reject imposition of the death penalty:

1. The defendant's capacity to appreciate the wrongfulness of his conduct or to conform his conduct to the requirements of law was significantly impaired, but not so impaired as to constitute a defense to prosecution.
2. The defendant was under unusual and substantial duress, although not such as to constitute a defense to prosecution.
3. The defendant was legally accountable for the conduct of another, but his participation was relatively minor, although not so minor as to constitute a defense to prosecution.
4. The defendant could not reasonably have foreseen that his conduct in the course of the commission of the offense for which the defendant was convicted would cause, or would create a grave risk of causing, death to another person.
5. The defendant's age.

Under Arizona's capital punishment statute, a sentence of death is automatically reviewed by the Arizona Supreme Court. Arizona uses lethal injection to carry out death sentences. However, defendants sentenced prior to November 15, 1992, may elect between lethal gas or lethal injection as the means of execution. The State's death row facility for men is located in Florence, Arizona; while the facility maintaining female death row inmates is located in Perryville, Arizona.

Pursuant to the laws of Arizona the Governor has authority to grant clemency in capital cases. The Governor is required to obtain the consent of the State's Board of Pardons and Parole, before a capital sentence may be commuted.

From the start of modern capital punishment in 1976, through 1999, Arizona executed 19 capital felons. During this period Arizona did not execute any female capital felons, although one of its death row inmates during this period was a female. In 1999 the State had 3 juveniles on death row. The State permits capital punishment to be imposed on persons 16 years old or older. A total of 120 capital felons were on death row in Arizona in 1999. The 1999 death row population in the State was listed as: 13 black inmates; 84 white inmates; and 23 unidentified inmates. Arizona does not prohibit the execution of mentally retarded capital felons.

Executions by Arizona 1976–1999

Name	Race	Date of Execution	Method of Execution
Donald E. Harding	White	April 6, 1992	Lethal Gas
John G. Brewer	White	March 3, 1993	Lethal Injection
James Clark	White	April 14, 1993	Lethal Injection
Jimme Jeffers	White	September 13, 1995	Lethal Injection
Daren L. Bolton	White	June 19, 1996	Lethal Injection
Luis Mata	Hispanic	August 22, 1996	Lethal Injection
Randy Greenawalt	White	January 23, 1997	Lethal Injection
W. Lyle Woratzek	White	June 25, 1997	Lethal Injection
Jose J. Ceja	Hispanic	January 21, 1998	Lethal Injection
Jose Villafuerte	Hispanic	April 22, 1998	Lethal Injection
Arthur M. Ross	White	April 29, 1998	Lethal Injection
Douglas E. Gretzler	White	June 3, 1998	Lethal Injection
Jess J. Gillies	White	January 13, 1999	Lethal Injection
Darick Gerlaugh	N.A.	February 3, 1999	Lethal Injection
Karl LaGrand	White	February 24, 1999	Lethal Injection
Walter LaGrand	White	March 3, 1999	Lethal Gas
Robert W. Vickers	White	May 5, 1999	Lethal Injection
Michael Poland	White	June 17, 1999	Lethal Injection
Ignacio Ortiz	Hispanic	October 27, 1999	Lethal Injection

ARIZONA EXECUTIONS 1976–1999

96.8% 579

3.2% 19

■ ARIZONA EXECUTIONS
■ ALL OTHER EXECUTIONS

EXECUTIONS BY ARIZONA 1930–1999

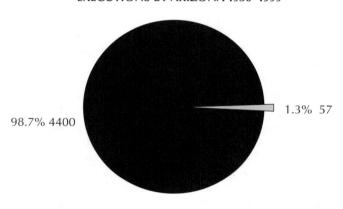

98.7% 4400

1.3% 57

■ ARIZONA
■ ALL OTHER JURISDICTIONS

Arizona v. Rumsey   *Court:* United States Supreme Court; *Case Citation:* Arizona v. Rumsey, 467 U.S. 203 (1984); *Argued:* April 23, 1984; *Decided:* May 29, 1984; *Opinion of the Court:* Justice O'Connor; *Concurring Opinion:* None; *Dissenting Opinion:* Justice Rehnquist, in which White, J., joined; *Appellate Defense Counsel:* James R. Rummage argued and briefed; *Appellate Prosecution Counsel:* William J. Schafer III argued; Robert K. Corbin on brief; *Amicus Curiae Brief Supporting Prosecutor:* None; *Amicus Curiae Brief Supporting Defendant:* 1.

Issue Presented: Whether the Double Jeopardy Clause prohibits the State of Arizona from sentencing the defendant to death after the life sentence he had initially received was set aside on appeal?

Case Holding: The Double Jeopardy Clause bars imposition of the death penalty upon reconviction after an initial conviction, set aside on appeal, has resulted in rejection of the death sentence.

Factual and procedural background of case: The defendant, Rumsey, was tried and convicted of capital murder by the State of Arizona. At a non-jury penalty phase, the trial judge found that no statutory aggravating circumstances or mitigating circumstances were present. Accordingly, the defendant was sentenced to life imprisonment. The Arizona Supreme Court found that the trial court had committed an error of law by misinterpreting the application of the "pecuniary gain" aggravating circumstance to contract killings. The appellate court set aside the life sentence and remanded the case for redetermination of aggravating and mitigating circumstances and for resentencing on the murder conviction.

On remand, the trial court held a new sentencing hearing. The trial court found that the "pecuniary gain" aggravating circumstance was present and that there was no mitigating circumstance sufficient to call for leniency. The defendant was sentenced to death. On appeal the Arizona Supreme Court held that under the United States Supreme Court's ruling in *Bullington v. Missouri,* the defendant's death sentence violated the Double Jeopardy Clause. The appellate court ordered that the death sentence be reduced to life imprisonment. The United States Supreme Court granted certiorari to consider the issue.

Opinion of the Court by Justice O'Connor: Justice O'Connor found that the case was controlled by *Bullington.* The opinion stated that "[i]n *Bullington v. Missouri* this Court held that the Double Jeopardy Clause applies to ... capital sentencing proceeding and thus bars imposition of the death penalty upon reconviction after an initial conviction, set aside on appeal, has resulted in rejection of the death sentence." It was noted that a capital penalty phase proceeding is comparable to a trial on the issue of guilt, thereby making the Double Jeopardy Clause relevant to such proceeding. Justice O'Connor ruled that the defendant's initial life sentence constituted an acquittal of the death penalty, and the trial court could not subsequently sentence him to death on a re-trial of the penalty phase proceeding. The judgment of the Arizona Supreme Court was therefore affirmed.

Dissenting opinion by Justice Rehnquist: Justice Rehnquist dissented from the majority opinion. He argued that the majority misconstrued the procedural posture of the case in order to reach its conclusion. The dissent outlined its argument as follows:

> Today the Court affirms the decision of the Arizona Supreme Court vacating the death sentence imposed on [the defendant] for a murder committed in the course of an armed robbery. Applying the interpretation given the Double Jeopardy Clause by a bare majority of this Court in *Bullington v. Missouri,* the Court concludes that in this case the first sentencing also amounted to an implied acquittal of [the defendant's] eligibility for the death penalty.... I do not believe that the reasoning underlying *Bullington* applies....
>
> The central premise of the Court's holding today is that the trial court's first finding — that there were no aggravating and no mitigating circumstances and therefore only a life sentence could be imposed — amounted to an "implied acquittal" on the merits of [the defendant's] eligibility for the death sentence, thereby barring the possibility of an enhanced sentence upon resentencing by virtue of the Double Jeopardy Clause. But the Court's continued reliance on the "implied acquittal" rationale

of *Bullington* is simply inapt. Unlike the jury's decision in *Bullington*, where the jury had broad discretion to decide whether capital punishment was appropriate, the trial judge's discretion in this case was carefully confined and directed to determining whether certain specified aggravating factors existed. It is obvious from the record that the State established at the first hearing that [the defendant] murdered his victim in the course of an armed robbery, a fact which was undisputed at sentencing. In no sense can it be meaningfully argued that the State failed to "prove" its case — the existence of at least one aggravating circumstance. It is hard to see how there has been an "implied acquittal" of a statutory aggravating circumstance when the record explicitly establishes the factual basis that such an aggravating circumstance existed. But for the trial judge's erroneous construction of governing state law, the judge would have been required to impose the death penalty....

The fact that in this case the legal error was ultimately corrected by the trial court did not mean that the State sought to marshal the same or additional evidence against a capital defendant which had proved insufficient to prove the State's "case" against him the first time. There is no logical reason for a different result here simply because the Arizona Supreme Court remanded the case to the trial court for the purpose of correcting the legal error, particularly when the resentencing did not constitute the kind of "retrial" which the *Bullington* Court condemned. Accordingly, I would reverse the decision of the Arizona Supreme Court in this case. *See also* **Bullington v. Missouri; Double Jeopardy Clause; Stroud v. United States**

Arkansas The State of Arkansas is a capital punishment jurisdiction. The State reenacted its death penalty law after the United States Supreme Court decision in *Furman v. Georgia*, 408 U.S. 238 (1972) on March 23, 1973.

Arkansas has a three-tier legal system. The State's legal system is composed of a supreme court, court of appeals and courts of general jurisdiction. The Arkansas Supreme Court is presided over by a chief justice and six associate justices. The Arkansas Court of Appeals is composed of a chief judge and eleven judges. The courts of general jurisdiction in the State are called Circuit Courts. Capital offenses against the State of Arkansas are tried in the Circuit Courts.

Arkansas' capital punishment statute is triggered if a person commits a homicide under the following special circumstances:

Members of the Arkansas Supreme Court: (standing left to right) Justice Ray Thornton, Justice Robert Brown, Justice Annabelle Imber, and Justice Lavenski Smith; (seated left to right) Justice Tom Glaze, Chief Justice W. H. Arnold, and Justice Donald Corbin. (Arkansas Supreme Court)

1. Acting alone or with one (1) or more other persons, he commits or attempts to commit rape, kidnapping, vehicular piracy, robbery, burglary, a felony violation of the Uniform Controlled Substances Act involving an actual delivery of a controlled substance, or escape in the first degree, and in the course of and in furtherance of the felony, or in immediate flight therefrom, he or an accomplice causes the death of any person under circumstances manifesting extreme indifference to the value of human life; or

2. Acting alone or with one (1) or more other persons, he commits or attempts to commit arson, and in the course of and in furtherance of the felony or in immediate flight therefrom, he or an accomplice causes the death of any person; or

3. With the premeditated and deliberated purpose of causing the death of any law enforcement officer, jailer, prison official, fire fighter, judge or other court official, probation officer, parole officer, any military personnel, or teacher or school employee, when such person is acting in the line of duty, he causes the death of any person; or

4. With the premeditated and deliberated purpose of causing the death of another person, he causes the death of any person; or

5. With the premeditated and deliberated purpose of causing the death of the holder of any public office filled by election or appointment or a candidate for public office, he causes the death of any person; or

6. While incarcerated in the Department of Correction or the Department of Community Punishment, he purposely causes the death of another person after premeditation and deliberation; or

7. Pursuant to an agreement that he cause the death of another person in return for anything of value, he causes the death of any person; or

8. He enters into an agreement whereby one person is to cause the death of another person in return for anything of value, and the person hired, pursuant to the agreement, causes the death of any person; or

9. Under circumstances manifesting extreme indifference to the value of human life, he knowingly causes the death of a person fourteen (14) years of age or younger at the time the murder was committed, provided that the defendant was eighteen (18) years of age or older at the time the murder was committed. It shall be an affirmative defense to any prosecution under this subdivision (a)(9) arising from the failure of the parent, guardian, or person standing in loco parentis to provide specified medical or surgical treatment, that the parent, guardian, or person standing in loco parentis relied solely on spiritual treatment through prayer in accordance with the tenets and practices of an established church or religious denomination of which he is a member; or

10. He purposely discharges a firearm from a vehicle at a person, or at a vehicle, conveyance, or a residential or commercial occupiable structure he knows or has good reason to believe to be occupied by a person, and thereby causes the death of another person under circumstances manifesting extreme indifference to the value of human life.

Capital murder in Arkansas is punishable by death or life imprisonment without parole. A capital prosecution in

Arkansas is bifurcated into a guilt phase and penalty phase. A jury is used at both phases of a capital trial. It is required that, at the penalty phase, jurors must unanimously agree that a death sentence is appropriate before it can be imposed. If the penalty phase jury is unable to reach a verdict, the trial judge is required to impose a sentence of life imprisonment.

In order to impose a death sentence upon a defendant under Arkansas law, it is required that the prosecutor establish the existence of at least one of the following statutory aggravating circumstances at the penalty phase:

1. The capital murder was committed by a person imprisoned as a result of a felony conviction;
2. The capital murder was committed by a person unlawfully at liberty after being sentenced to imprisonment as a result of a felony conviction;
3. The person previously committed another felony, an element of which was the use or threat of violence to another person or the creation of a substantial risk of death or serious physical injury to another person;
4. The person in the commission of the capital murder knowingly created a great risk of death to a person other than the victim or caused the death of more than one (1) person in the same criminal episode;
5. The capital murder was committed for the purpose of avoiding or preventing an arrest or effecting an escape from custody;
6. The capital murder was committed for pecuniary gain;
7. The capital murder was committed for the purpose of disrupting or hindering the lawful exercise of any government or political function;
8. (a) The capital murder was committed in an especially cruel or depraved manner.
   (b) For purposes of this subdivision (8), a capital murder is committed in an especially cruel manner when, as part of a course of conduct intended to inflict mental anguish, serious physical abuse, or torture upon the victim prior to the victim's death, mental anguish, serious physical abuse, or torture is inflicted. "Mental anguish" is defined as the victim's uncertainty as to his ultimate fate. "Serious physical abuse" is defined as physical abuse that creates a substantial risk of death or that causes protracted impairment of health, or loss or protracted impairment of the function of any bodily member or organ. "Torture" is defined as the infliction of extreme physical pain for a prolonged period of time prior to the victim's death.
   (c) For purposes of this subdivision (8), a capital murder is committed in an especially depraved manner when the person relishes the murder, evidencing debasement or perversion, or shows an indifference to the suffering of the victim and evidences a sense of pleasure in committing the murder; or
9. The capital murder was committed by means of a destructive device, bomb, explosive, or similar device which the person planted, hid, or concealed in any place, area, dwelling, building, or structure, or mailed or delivered, or caused to be planted, hidden, concealed, mailed, or delivered, and the person knew that his act or acts would create a great risk of death to human life.
10. The capital murder was committed against a person whom the defendant knew or reasonably should have known was especially vulnerable to the attack because of either a temporary or permanent severe physical or mental disability which would interfere with the victim's ability to flee or to defend himself.

Although the Federal Constitution will not permit jurisdictions to prevent capital felons from presenting all relevant mitigating evidence at the penalty phase, Arkansas has provided the following statutory mitigating circumstances that permit the jury to reject imposition of the death penalty:

1. The capital murder was committed while the defendant was under extreme mental or emotional disturbance;
2. The capital murder was committed while the defendant was acting under unusual pressures or influences or under the domination of another person;
3. The capital murder was committed while the capacity of the defendant to appreciate the wrongfulness of his conduct or to conform his conduct to the requirements of law was impaired as a result of mental disease or defect, intoxication, or drug abuse;
4. The youth of the defendant at the time of the commission of the capital murder;
5. The capital murder was committed by another person and the defendant was an accomplice and his participation relatively minor;
6. The defendant has no significant history of prior criminal activity.

Under Arkansas' capital punishment statute, a sentence of death is automatically reviewed by the Arkansas Supreme Court. Arkansas uses lethal injection to carry out death sentences. However, defendants committing capital murder before July 4, 1983, may choose between lethal injection or electrocution. The State's death row facility for men is located in Tucker, Arkansas; while the facility maintaining female death row inmates is located in Pine Bluff, Arkansas.

Pursuant to the laws of Arkansas the Governor has authority to grant clemency in capital cases. The State's Parole Board is permitted to make a nonbinding recommendation as to whether a death sentence should be commuted.

From the start of modern capital punishment in 1976, through 1999, Arkansas executed 21 capital felons. During this period Arkansas did not execute any female capital felons, although one of its death row inmates during this period was a female. In 1999 the State had one juvenile on death row. The State permits capital punishment to be imposed on persons 16 years old or older. A total of 42 capital felons were on death row in Arkansas in 1999. The 1999 death row population in the State was listed as: 23 black inmates; 17 white inmates; 1 Hispanic inmate and 1 unidentified inmate. Arkansas prohibits the execution of mentally retarded capital felons.

Executions by Arkansas 1976–1999

Name	Race	Date of Execution	Method of Execution
John Swindler	White	June 18, 1990	Electrocution
Ronald G. Simmons	White	June 25, 1990	Lethal Injection
Ricky R. Rector	Black	January 24, 1992	Lethal Injection
Stephen D. Hill	White	May 7, 1992	Lethal Injection
Charles E. Pickens	Black	May 11, 1994	Lethal Injection
Jonas Whitmore	White	May 11, 1994	Lethal Injection
Hoyt Clines	White	August 3, 1994	Lethal Injection
James Holmes	White	August 3, 1994	Lethal Injection
Darryl Richley	White	August 3, 1994	Lethal Injection
Richard Snell	White	April 19, 1995	Lethal Injection
Barry L. Fairchild	Black	August 31, 1995	Lethal Injection
William F. Parker	Black	August 8, 1996	Lethal Injection
Earl V. Denton	White	January 8, 1997	Lethal Injection
Paul Ruiz	Hispanic	January 8, 1997	Lethal Injection
Kirt Wainwright	Black	January 8, 1997	Lethal Injection
Eugene W. Perry	White	August 6, 1997	Lethal Injection
Wilburn A. Henderson	White	July 8, 1998	Lethal Injection
Johnie M. Cox	White	February 16, 1999	Lethal Injection
Marion A. Pruett	White	April 12, 1999	Lethal Injection
Mark Gardner	White	September 8, 1999	Lethal Injection
Alan Willett	White	September 8, 1999	Lethal Injection

ARKANSAS EXECUTIONS 1976–1999

96.5% 577   3.5% 21

■ ARKANSAS EXECUTIONS
■ ALL OTHER EXECUTIONS

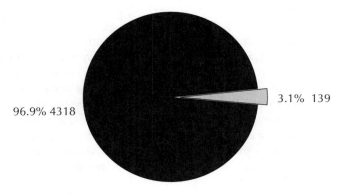

EXECUTIONS BY ARKANSAS 1930–1999

96.9% 4318   3.1% 139

■ ARKANSAS
■ ALL OTHER JURISDICTIONS

Armed Robbery *see* **Robbery; Robbery Aggravator**

Armenia Capital punishment is permitted in Armenia. Armenia uses the firing squad to carry out the death penalty. The death penalty may be imposed for first-degree murder, rape of a minor, treason, espionage, terrorism and certain military crimes. It was known that from 1991 to 1993, six defendants were sentenced to death. Armenia utilizes a civil law legal system. Armenians adopted a constitution on July 5, 1995.

The structure of the Armenian judiciary consists of District Courts and a Supreme Court. Criminal trials are conducted in District Courts. Judges for the District Courts are named by Armenia's president and confirmed by the parliament. The Supreme Court provides intermediate and final appellate review of criminal cases. The Supreme Court consists of 32 members. The Supreme Court uses a three-member panel for intermediate review and an 11-member presidium for final review. The full 32 member court provides plenary appellate review. *See also* **International Capital Punishment Nations**

Arnold v. North Carolina *Court:* United States Supreme Court; *Case Citation:* Arnold v. North Carolina, 376 U.S. 773 (1964); *Argued:* March 26, 1964; *Decided:* April 6, 1964; *Opinion of the Court:* Per Curiam; *Concurring Opinion:* None; *Dissenting Opinion:* None; *Appellate Defense Counsel:* J. Harvey Turner and Fred W. Harrison argued and briefed; *Appellate Prosecution Counsel:* Ralph Moody argued; T. W. Bruton on brief; *Amicus Curiae Brief Supporting Prosecutor:* Not reported; *Amicus Curiae Brief Supporting Defendant:* Not reported.

Issue Presented: Whether the defendants established that blacks were systematically excluded from the grand jury that indicted them?

Case Holding: The defendants established that blacks were systematically excluded from the grand jury that indicted them, therefore their convictions and sentences could not stand.

Factual and procedural background of case: This capital prosecution involved two defendants, Arnold and Dixon. The defendants were found guilty of capital murder and sentenced to death by the State of North Carolina. The North Carolina Supreme Court affirmed the judgments. In doing so, the appellate court rejected the defendants' contention that the judgments against them were invalid because blacks were systematically excluded from the grand jury that indicted them. The United States Supreme Court granted certiorari to consider the issue.

Opinion of the Court was delivered Per Curiam: The per curiam opinion found that the defendants established an unrebutted prima facie claim of racial discrimination in the selection of the grand jury that indicted them. It was said that the defendants presented evidence showing that blacks "comprise over 28 percent of persons on the tax records of the county, and over 30 percent of the persons on the poll tax list from which jurors are drawn, and that only one [black] served on a grand jury in 24 years[.]" The opinion concluded: "The judgment below must be reversed. The [evidence] in itself made out a prima facie case of the denial of the equal protection which the Constitution guarantees." *See also* **Discrimination in Grand or Petit Jury Selection**

Arraignment   Arraignment is a legal term used to describe a procedure for informing a defendant of the nature of the charges against him or her. Two types of an arraignment may occur in a criminal prosecution.

First if a defendant is charged with a crime by an indictment or information, he or she must be presented or arraigned in open court for the purpose of having the indictment or information read to him or her by a judge. At this arraignment a defendant must be called upon to enter a plea. If the defendant does not enter a plea, the judge must enter a plea of innocence. The defendant must also be given a copy of the indictment or information before being called upon to plead.

The second type of arraignment, also called initial appearance, occurs when a defendant is arrested on a complaint or without a warrant. A defendant arrested on a complaint or without a warrant has a right under due process of law, to be promptly presented to a neutral judicial officer and informed of his or her basic constitutional rights, as well as other procedural matters involved in the prosecution. At this arraignment a defendant may not be called upon to enter a plea (unless the arrest is for a misdemeanor only). All jurisdictions have outlined in criminal procedure rules the process that immediately follows an arrest of a suspect. The procedure used under the Federal Rules of Criminal Procedure, as illustrated below, fairly represents matters contained in most rules.

Federal Procedure for Initial Appearance:

a. *In General.* Except as otherwise provided in this rule, an officer making an arrest under a warrant issued upon a complaint or any person making an arrest without a warrant shall take the arrested person without unnecessary delay before the nearest available federal magistrate judge or, in the event that a federal magistrate judge is not reasonably available, before a state or local judicial officer authorized by law. If a person arrested without a warrant is brought before a magistrate judge, a complaint, satisfying the probable cause requirements of the law, shall be promptly filed. When a person, arrested with or without a warrant or given a summons, appears initially before the magistrate judge, the magistrate judge shall proceed in accordance with the applicable subdivisions of this rule.

b. *Misdemeanors and Other Petty Offenses.* If the charge against the defendant is a misdemeanor or other petty offense triable by a United States magistrate judge, the magistrate judge shall proceed in accordance with the law.

c. *Offenses Not Triable by the United States Magistrate Judge.* If the charge against the defendant is not triable by the United States magistrate judge, the defendant shall not

be called upon to plead. The magistrate judge shall inform the defendant of the complaint against the defendant and of any affidavit filed therewith, of the defendant's right to retain counsel or to request the assignment of counsel if the defendant is unable to obtain counsel, and of the general circumstances under which the defendant may secure pretrial release. The magistrate judge shall inform the defendant that the defendant is not required to make a statement and that any statement made by the defendant may be used against the defendant. The magistrate judge shall also inform the defendant of the right to a preliminary examination. The magistrate judge shall allow the defendant reasonable time and opportunity to consult counsel and shall detain or conditionally release the defendant as provided by statute or in these rules.

A defendant is entitled to a preliminary examination, unless waived, when charged with any offense, other than a petty offense, which is to be tried by a judge of the district court. If the defendant waives preliminary examination, the magistrate judge shall forthwith hold the defendant to answer in the district court. If the defendant does not waive the preliminary examination, the magistrate judge shall schedule a preliminary examination. Such examination shall be held within a reasonable time but in any event not later than 10 days following the initial appearance if the defendant is in custody and no later than 20 days if the defendant is not in custody, provided, however, that the preliminary examination shall not be held if the defendant is indicted or if an information against the defendant is filed in district court before the date set for the preliminary examination. With the consent of the defendant and upon a showing of good cause, taking into account the public interest in the prompt disposition of criminal cases, time limits specified in this subdivision may be extended one or more times by a federal magistrate judge. In the absence of such consent by the defendant, time limits may be extended by a judge of the United States only upon a showing that extraordinary circumstances exist and that delay is indispensable to the interests of justice.

See also **Arrest; Mallory v. United States; United States v. Carignan**

Arrest   An arrest refers to the physical custody and control of a person by a law enforcement agent. An arrest may occur in one of two ways: (1) pursuant to an arrest warrant or (2) without an arrest warrant. At common law an arrest for a felony offense could occur without a warrant even if the arresting officer did not see the arrestee commit the felony that resulted in the arrest. All that was required under the common law for a felony arrest was probable cause that a felony occurred and probable cause to believe that the arrestee committed the crime. The common law only permitted an arrest for a misdemeanor offense without a warrant, if the offense occurred in the presence of the arresting officer.

In the context of an arrest of a person for the suspected

commission of a capital offense, the issue of whether the arrest of the suspect was with or without a warrant may be critical. Certain rights are accorded to a person arrested without a warrant for a capital offense (and all felonies) that, if not provided, could result in a confession, incriminating statements or physical evidence being inadmissible at trial. For example, a capital felon arrested without a warrant has a constitutional right to be taken before a neutral judicial officer within 48 hours of his or her arrest (barring a medical emergency). This requirement is generally referred to as the prompt presentment rule. If the prompt presentment rule is violated and during its violation the arrestee gives a confession, the confession may be barred from use during the trial.

The procedure for issuing and executing an arrest warrant is fairly standard. The procedure used by Federal authorities under the Federal Rules of Criminal Procedure provides an illustration.

Federal Procedure for Arrest Warrant:

a. *Issuance.* If it appears from the complaint, or from an affidavit or affidavits filed with the complaint, that there is probable cause to believe that an offense has been committed and that the defendant has committed it, a warrant for the arrest of the defendant shall issue to any officer authorized by law to execute it. Upon the request of the attorney for the government a summons instead of a warrant shall issue. More than one warrant or summons may issue on the same complaint. If a defendant fails to appear in response to the summons, a warrant shall issue.

b. *Probable Cause.* The finding of probable cause may be based upon hearsay evidence in whole or in part.

c. *Form.*

　1. Warrant. The warrant shall be signed by the magistrate judge and shall contain the name of the defendant or, if the defendant's name is unknown, any name or description by which the defendant can be identified with reasonable certainty. It shall describe the offense charged in the complaint. It shall command that the defendant be arrested and brought before the nearest available magistrate judge.

　2. Summons. The summons shall be in the same form as the warrant except that it shall summon the defendant to appear before a magistrate at a stated time and place.

d. *Execution or Service; and Return.*

　1. By Whom. The warrant shall be executed by a marshal or by some other officer authorized by law. The summons may be served by any person authorized to serve a summons in a civil action.

　2. Territorial Limits. The warrant may be executed or the summons may be served at any place within the jurisdiction of the United States.

　3. Manner. The warrant shall be executed by the arrest of the defendant. The officer need not have the warrant at the time of the arrest but upon request shall show the warrant to the defendant as soon as possible. If the officer does not have the warrant at the time of the arrest, the officer shall then inform the defendant of the offense charged and of the fact that a warrant has been issued. The summons shall be served upon a defendant by delivering a copy to the defendant personally, or by leaving it at the defendant's dwelling house or usual place of abode with some person of suitable age and discretion then residing therein and by mailing a copy of the summons to the defendant's last known address.

　4. Return. The officer executing a warrant shall make return thereof to the magistrate judge or other officer before whom the defendant is brought. At the request of the attorney for the government any unexecuted warrant shall be returned to and canceled by the magistrate judge by whom it was issued. On or before the return day the person to whom a summons was delivered for service shall make return thereof to the magistrate judge before whom the summons is returnable. At the request of the attorney for the government made at any time while the complaint is pending, a warrant returned unexecuted and not canceled or summons returned unserved or a duplicate thereof may be delivered by the magistrate judge to the marshal or other authorized person for execution or service. *See also* **Arraignment; Elk v. United States**

Arson The crime of arson is a felony offense that was defined at common law as the unlawful burning of an occupied dwelling of another (modern statutes have broadened the definition). Arson, without more, cannot be used to inflict the death penalty. The Eighth Amendment of the United States Constitution prohibits this as cruel and unusual punishment. However, the crime of arson can play a role in a capital prosecution. If arson occurs during the commission of a homicide it may form the basis of a death-eligible offense, and therefore trigger a capital prosecution. *See also* **Arson Aggravator; Death-Eligible Offenses; Felony Murder Rule; Rape and Capital Punishment**

Arson Aggravator The crime of arson committed during the course of a homicide is a statutory aggravating

JURISDICTIONS USING ARSON AGGRAVATOR

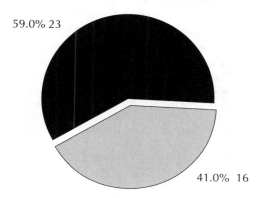

59.0% 23

41.0% 16

■ ARSON AGGRAVATOR JURISDICTIONS
▨ ALL OTHER JURISDICTIONS

circumstance in a majority of capital punishment jurisdictions. As a statutory aggravating circumstance, evidence of arson is used at the penalty phase of a capital prosecution for the factfinder to consider in determining whether to impose the death penalty. *See also* **Arson; Aggravating Circumstances; Felony Murder Rule**

Ashe v. Valotta

Court: United States Supreme Court; *Case Citation:* Ashe v. Valotta, 270 U.S. 424 (1926); *Argued:* March 5, 1926; *Decided:* March 15, 1926; *Opinion of the Court:* Justice Holmes; *Concurring Opinion:* None. *Dissenting Opinion:* None. *Appellate Defense Counsel:* George R. Wallace argued and briefed; *Appellate Prosecution Counsel:* James O. Campbell argued and briefed; *Amicus Curiae Brief Supporting Prosecutor:* None; *Amicus Curiae Brief Supporting Defendant:* None.

Issue Presented: Whether the State of Pennsylvania could prosecute the defendant in a single trial for two homicides and not afford him all the peremptory jury strikes he would be entitled to if the crimes were prosecuted separately?

Case Holding: The issue of the defendant's entitlement to peremptory jury strikes in a State prosecution is a matter controlled by State law and cannot be interfered with by Federal courts.

Factual and procedural background of case: The defendant, Valotta, was charged under separate indictments for the murder of two people by the State of Pennsylvania. The offenses were tried together. He was convicted of second degree murder on one indictment and capital murder on the other. The defendant was sentenced to death for the capital conviction. On appeal to the Pennsylvania Supreme Court the judgments were affirmed. The defendant filed a petition for habeas corpus relief in a Federal District Court. In the petition it was alleged that the defendant was denied due process of law in having a single trial on both offenses, because he was not given twenty peremptory jury strikes for each offense, which would have occurred if the offenses were tried separately. The Federal District Court agreed with the defendant and granted habeas relief. The United States Supreme Court granted certiorari to consider the issue.

Opinion of the Court by Justice Holmes: Justice Holmes ruled that the issue presented by the defendant was purely a State law matter that Federal courts could not interfere with. The opinion reasoned as follows:

> There is no question that the State Court had jurisdiction. But the much abused suggestion is made that it lost jurisdiction by trying the two indictments together. Manifestly this would not be true even if the trial was not warranted by law. But the Supreme Court of Pennsylvania has said that there was no mistake of law, and so far as the law of Pennsylvania was concerned it was most improper to attempt to go behind the decision of the Supreme Court, to construe statutes as opposed to it and to hear evidence that the practice of the State had been the other way. The question of constitutional power is the only one that could be raised, if even that were open upon this collateral attack, and as to that we cannot doubt that Pennsylvania could authorize the whole story to be brought out before the jury at

once, even though two indictments were involved, without denying due process of law. If any question was made at the trial as to the loss of the right to challenge twenty jurors on each indictment, the only side of it that would be open here, would be again the question of constitutional power. That Pennsylvania could limit the challenges on each indictment to ten does not admit doubt....

> There was not the shadow of a ground for interference with this sentence by habeas corpus.... In so delicate a matter as interrupting the regular administration of the criminal law of the State by this kind of attack too much discretion cannot be used, and it must be realized that it can be done only upon definitely and narrowly limited grounds.

The judgment of the Federal District Court was reversed. *See also* **Jury Selection**

Asians and Capital Punishment

The Asian ancestry population in America has historically been a minority group. The Asian population is of two types: Asian-Americans and Asian residents. While the number of Asians executed in Asian countries having the death penalty is extremely high, Asians in America have historically made up a negligible percentage of people executed in America. Ironically though, the first person executed in America by lethal gas was an Asian.

Jarturun Siripongs, a native of Thailand, was convicted by the State of California for killing two people. He was executed by lethal injection on February 9, 1999. (California Department of Corrections)

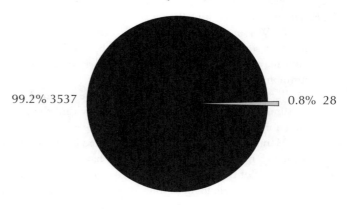

ASIANS ON DEATH ROW
On April 1, 1999

99.2% 3537   0.8% 28

■ ASIANS   ■ ALL OTHERS

Asians Executed 1976–1999

Name	Date of Execution	Jurisdiction	Method of Execution
Hai Hai Yuong	December 7, 1995	TX	Lethal Injection
Aua Lauti	November 4, 1997	TX	Lethal Injection
Tuan Nguyen	December 10, 1998	OK	Lethal Injection
Jaturin Siripongs	February 9, 1999	CA	Lethal Injection
Alvaro Calambro	April 6, 1999	NV	Lethal Injection

ASIANS EXECUTED 1976–1999

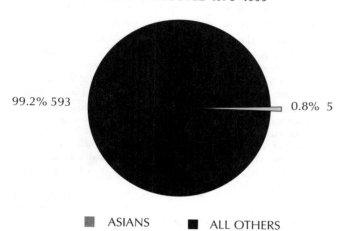

99.2% 593   0.8% 5

■ ASIANS   ■ ALL OTHERS

JURISDICTIONS USING ASSAULT AND BATTERY AGGRAVATOR

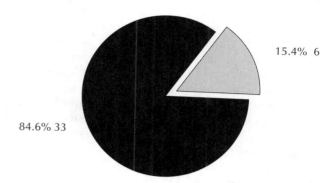

15.4% 6

84.6% 33

■ ASSAULT AND BATTERY AGGRAVATOR JURISDICTIONS
■ ALL OTHER JURISDICTIONS

Assault and Battery The crime of assault and battery refers to the physical injury of a victim that does not result in the victim's death. Assault and battery may constitute a misdemeanor or felony, depending upon the severity of the injury to the victim. Assault and battery, without more, cannot be used to inflict the death penalty. The Eighth Amendment of the United States Constitution prohibits this as cruel and unusual punishment. However, a felony assault and battery can play a role in a capital prosecution. If a felony assault and battery occurs during the commission of a homicide it may form the basis of a death-eligible offense, and therefore trigger a capital prosecution. *See also* **Assault and Battery Aggravator; Death-Eligible Offenses; Felony Murder Rule; Rape and Capital Punishment**

Assault and Battery Aggravator The crime of felony assault and battery committed during the course of a homicide is a statutory aggravating circumstance in six jurisdictions: Georgia, Kentucky, Missouri, Montana, Nebraska and Virginia. In these jurisdictions evidence of a prior criminal history of serious assaultive conduct is used at the penalty phase of a capital prosecution for the factfinder to consider in determining whether to impose the death penalty. *See also* **Assault and Battery; Aggravating Circumstances**

Assignment of Error Assignment of error is a legal term of art that refers to the designation of specific matters that are alleged to have been erroneously resolved at the trial court level. Assignment of error comes into play during the appellate phase of a criminal prosecution. A defendant is generally obligated to inform an appellate court the specific matters the defendant believes were resolved incorrectly at the trial. Examples of assignment of error include: (1) the trial court failed to suppress a confession; (2) the indictment did not provide adequate notice; (3) the jury was improperly instructed on self-defense.

As a general rule, appellate courts will deem any issue not raised or improperly raised, as waived or forfeited. That is, a defendant has an affirmative obligation to inform an appellate court of the matters he or she believed were wrongly resolved at the trial. In a few capital punishment jurisdictions legislators have imposed specific issues that appellate courts must examine in a capital case, regardless of whether the defendant raises the matter. This exception to waiver or forfeiture is unique to capital punishment.

Attorney-Client Privilege The attorney-client privilege is of common law origin. The attorney-client privilege prohibits disclosure of confidential communication between an attorney and client, unless the client consents to such disclosure. Creation of the privilege is not dependent upon the payment of a fee or the pendency of litigation. Whatever facts are communicated by a client to an attorney, solely because of that relationship, such counsel is not at liberty to disclose. The attorney-client privilege does not protect communication made to an attorney in furtherance of a scheme to commit a future crime. *See also* **Alexander v. United States**

Attorney General *see* Prosecutor; United States Attorney General

Atzerodt, George *see* Lincoln Assassination

Australia Australia abolished use of the death penalty for all crimes in 1985. *See also* **International Capital Punishment Nations**

Austria In 1968 Austria abolished capital punishment for all crimes. *See also* **International Capital Punishment Nations**

Authorized Release from Custody Aggravator

Authorized release from custody refers to an inmate who has been allowed to leave confinement for a stated period of time and for a specific reason, but must return to confinement according to the terms of release. An example of authorized release from custody would be an inmate who is allowed to leave confinement during the day to work for a private employer. In four jurisdictions, Arizona, Indiana, Washington and Wyoming, if an inmate commits murder while on authorized release, this fact may be used to impose the death penalty. *See also* **Aggravating Circumstances**

Automatic Review of Death Sentence *see* **Appellate Review of Conviction and Death Sentence**

Autrefois Acquit or Convict *see* **Double Jeopardy Clause**

Avery v. Alabama

Court: United States Supreme Court; *Case Citation:* Avery v. Alabama, 308 U.S. 444 (1940); *Argued:* December 7, 1939; *Decided:* January 2, 1940; *Opinion of the Court:* Justice Black; *Concurring Opinion:* None; *Dissenting Opinion:* None; *Appellate Defense Counsel:* L. S. Moore argued; John Foshee and Edward H. Saunders on brief; *Appellate Prosecution Counsel:* Thomas Seay Lawson argued and briefed; *Amicus Curiae Brief Supporting Prosecutor:* None; *Amicus Curiae Brief Supporting Defendant:* None.

Issue Presented: Whether the defendant was denied the right of effective assistance of counsel, because the trial court denied his attorneys' request to continue the trial date so that they could investigate the case and prepare a defense?

Case Holding: The defendant was not denied the right of effective assistance of counsel, because the trial court denied his attorneys' request to continue the trial date so that they could investigate the case and prepare a defense.

Factual and procedural background of case: The defendant, Avery, was charged with capital murder by the State of Alabama. He was appointed two attorneys to represent him. Prior to trial both attorneys requested the trial be continued to another date because they had not been given sufficient time to investigate the case and prepare a defense. The trial court denied a continuance. The defendant was convicted and sentenced to death. The Alabama Supreme Court affirmed the conviction and sentence. In doing so, the appellate court rejected the defendant's argument that the denial of a continuance had deprived him of the equal protection of the laws and due process of law by denying him the right of counsel, with the accustomed incidents of consultation and opportunity of preparation for trial. The United States Supreme Court granted certiorari to consider the issue.

Opinion of the Court by Justice Black: Justice Black ruled that the defendant was not deprived of effective assistance of counsel because of the trial court's decision not to continue the trial to another date. He set out the Court's position as follows:

> Since the Constitution nowhere specifies any period which must intervene between the required appointment of counsel and trial, the fact, standing alone, that a continuance has been denied, does not constitute a denial of the constitutional right to assistance of counsel. In the course of trial, after due appointment of competent counsel, many procedural questions necessarily arise which must be decided by the trial judge in the light of facts then presented and conditions then existing. Disposition of a request for continuance is of this nature and is made in the discretion of the trial judge, the exercise of which will ordinarily not be reviewed....
>
> But the denial of opportunity for appointed counsel to confer, to consult with the accused and to prepare his defense, could convert the appointment of counsel into a sham and nothing more than a formal compliance with the Constitution's requirement that an accused be given the assistance of counsel. The Constitution's guarantee of assistance of counsel cannot be satisfied by mere formal appointment.
>
> Under the particular circumstances appearing in this record, we do not think [the defendant] has been denied the benefit of assistance of counsel guaranteed to him by the Fourteenth Amendment. His appointed counsel, as the Supreme Court of Alabama recognized, have performed their full duty intelligently and well. Not only did they present [the defendant's] defense in the trial court, but ... they carried an appeal to the State Supreme Court. Their appointment and the representation rendered under it were not mere formalities.... [The defendant] has thus been afforded the assistance of zealous and earnest counsel from arraignment to final argument in this Court.

The judgment of the Alabama Supreme Court was affirmed. *See also* **Right to Counsel**

Azerbaijan

The death penalty was abolished by Azerbaijan in 1998. *See also* **International Capital Punishment Nations**

B

Bahamas

The laws of the Bahamas permit imposition of the death penalty. The method of execution used by Bahamas is hanging. It was known that in 1998, Bahamas executed two prisoners. The island nation's legal system is based on English common law. The constitution of the Bahamas was adopted July 10, 1973.

The Bahamian judicial structure consists of a Supreme Court (trial court) and a Court of Appeal (the highest court). The Court of Appeal consists of a president and two other justices. Under the constitution of Bahamas, a final appeal may be made to the Judicial Committee of the Privy Council in England. *See also* **International Capital Punishment Nations**

Bahrain Capital punishment is allowed in Bahrain. Bahrain uses the firing squad to carry out the death penalty. The legal system of Bahrain is based on several sources, which include customary tribal law, three separate doctrines of Islamic law, and civil law as embodied in codes, ordinances, and regulations. Bahrain adopted a constitution December 6, 1973.

Bahrain has been ruled by the Al-Khalifa extended family since the late 18th century. The nation has few democratic institutions and no political parties. Under the nation's constitution the Amir is confirmed as the hereditary ruler. The current Amir, Shaikh Isa Bin Sulman Al-Khalifa, governs the country with the assistance of his son as Crown Prince, a younger brother as Prime Minister, and an appointed cabinet of ministers.

According to the constitution, the judiciary is an independent and separate branch of government. However, in practice the Amir is at the pinnacle of the judicial system.

Bahrain has a dual court system that consists of civil and Shari'a (Islamic) courts. Shari'a courts have jurisdiction over domestic matters such as marriage, divorce, and inheritance. Civil courts consist of the Supreme Court of Appeal, trial courts and a special Security Court. The Supreme Court of Appeal is the highest appellate court in the country.

Defendants prosecuted in trial courts are provided with guarantees, such as public trials, the right to counsel (including legal aid if needed), and the right of appeal. Defendants charged with certain security offenses are tried in Security Court, which is composed of members of the Supreme Court of Appeal. Proceedings before the Security Court are held in secret and there is no right of judicial appeal. Defendants may be represented by counsel in Security Court proceedings. *See also* **International Capital Punishment Nations**

Bail *see* **Excessive Bail Clause**

Baldwin v. Alabama *Court:* United States Supreme Court; *Case Citation:* Baldwin v. Alabama, 472 U.S. 372 (1985); *Argued:* March 27, 1985; *Decided:* June 17, 1985; *Opinion of the Court:* Justice Blackmun; *Concurring Opinion:* Chief Justice Burger; *Dissenting Opinion:* Justice Brennan; *Dissenting Opinion:* Justice Stevens, in which Brennan and Marshall, JJ., joined; *Appellate Defense Counsel:* John L. Carroll argued and briefed; *Appellate Prosecution Counsel:* Edward E. Carnes argued; Charles A. Graddick on brief; *Amicus Curiae Brief Supporting Prosecutor:* None; *Amicus Curiae Brief Supporting Defendant:* None.

Issue Presented: Whether the Constitution permits a death penalty statute to allow a guilt phase jury to return a sentence of death, but the actual decision to impose such sentence is made by the trial judge after holding a penalty phase hearing?

Case Holding: The Constitution permits a guilt phase jury to return a sentence of death, so long as the actual decision to impose a death sentence is made after holding an independent penalty phase hearing in which a defendant is allowed to proffer mitigating circumstances.

Factual and procedural background of case: The defendant, Brian Keith Baldwin, was charged by the state of Alabama with committing capital murder in March of 1977 (a co-defendant was also charged). The defendant was tried before a jury. Pursuant to the death penalty statute of the State at that time, the jury found the defendant guilty of capital murder and fixed the punishment at death by electrocution. Under the State's laws the trial court then held an independent penalty phase hearing for the purpose of determining whether death should actually be imposed. At the penalty phase hearing the defendant was allowed to present mitigating evidence and the State was allowed to present aggravating circumstance evidence. After presentation of penalty phase evidence, the trial court weighed the evidence and determined that the aggravating circumstances outweighed the mitigating circumstances and imposed the death penalty.

The Alabama Court of Criminal Appeals affirmed the conviction and sentence. When the case went to the Supreme Court of Alabama the defendant argued that the State's death penalty statute was unconstitutional because it provided for a mandatory sentence by the jury, and that the trial court's sentence was unconstitutional because it was based in part upon consideration of the impermissible jury sentence. The Supreme Court of Alabama rejected the argument and held that even though the jury had no discretion regarding the sentence it would impose, the sentencing procedure was constitutionally valid because it was the trial judge who was the true sentencing authority. Almost simultaneous to this decision, in a different case, the United States Court of Appeals for the Eleventh Circuit ruled Alabama's capital sentencing scheme was facially unconstitutional. The United States Supreme Court granted certiorari to resolve this conflict.

Opinion of the Court by Justice Blackmun: Justice Blackmun noted Alabama's statute would have been unconstitutional, in view of the Court's precedents, if the jury's mandatory death sentence were dispositive. It was said that while the State's statute did not expressly preclude, and might seem to have authorized, the trial court to consider the jury's sentence in determining whether the death penalty was appropriate, the Alabama appellate courts interpreted the statute to mean that the trial court was to impose a sentence without regard to the jury's mandatory sentence. Justice Blackmun noted that the trial judge did not interpret the statute as requiring him to consider the jury's sentence, because he never mentioned the sentence as a factor in his deliberations. The opinion also rejected the defendant's contention that a trial judge's decision to impose the death penalty had to have been swayed by the fact that the jury returned a sentence of death.

The opinion noted favorably that if a trial court imposed a death sentence, the State's statute required the trial judge set forth in writing the factual findings from the trial and the sentencing hearing, including the aggravating and mitigating circumstances that formed the basis for the sentence. The statute further guided the trial judge's discretion by requiring that the death penalty be imposed only if the trial judge found specific statutory aggravating circumstances outweighed any statutory and non-statutory mitigating circumstances. The opinion went on to affirm the decision of the Alabama Supreme Court.

Concurring opinion by Chief Justice Burger: Chief Justice Burger believed that Alabama's statute did require the trial judge to consider the jury's sentence in determining the sentence actually to be imposed. He argued that the majority opinion should have addressed the constitutionality of the statute on this basis, and that if it had, the statute would pass constitutional muster. The Chief Justice did not believe that there was anything constitutionally impermissible about a trial judge considering the decision of the jury.

Dissenting opinion by Justice Brennan: Justice Brennan reiterated his longstanding position "that the death penalty is in all circumstances cruel and unusual punishment prohibited by the Eighth and Fourteenth Amendments[.]" He would therefore vacate the defendant's sentence on that ground.

Dissenting opinion by Justice Stevens, in which Brennan and Marshall, JJ., joined: Justice Stevens' dissent was based on two grounds. First, he argued that the State's statute did in fact require the trial court to consider the jury's decision. He contended that the majority opinion had no basis to say that the appellate courts of Alabama construed the statute as not requiring trial judges to consider the decision of juries. Next, Justice Stevens argued that "it is unrealistic to maintain that such a sentence from the jury does not enter the mind of the sentencing judge." For these reasons, Justice Stevens would have found the statute unconstitutional and vacated the defendant's death sentence.

Case Note: Alabama's death penalty statute was amended and no longer permits a guilt phase jury to render a death sentence. *See also* **Mandatory Death Penalty Statutes**

Ball v. United States (I) *Court:* United States Supreme Court; *Case Citation:* Ball v. United States, 140 U.S. 118 (1891); *Argued:* Not reported; *Decided:* April 27, 1891; *Opinion of the Court:* Chief Justice Fuller; *Concurring Opinion:* None; *Dissenting Opinion:* None; *Justices Taking No Part in Decision:* Justice Gray and Brewer, J.; *Appellate Defense Counsel:* John E. Kenna argued; C. J. Faulkner on brief; *Appellate Prosecution Counsel:* United States Solicitor General William Howard Taft argued and briefed; *Amicus Curiae Brief Supporting Prosecutor:* None; *Amicus Curiae Brief Supporting Defendant:* None.

Issue Presented: Whether the indictment against the defendants was fatally defective because it failed to allege the time and place of the charged murder?

Case Holding: The indictment against the defendants was fa-

tally defective because it failed to allege the time and place of the charged murder, therefore the judgments against them could not stand.

Factual and procedural background of case: The defendants, John C. Ball, Robert E. Boutwell and Millard F. Ball, were charged with capital murder by the United States. The crime occurred near Texas, "in the Chickasaw Nation, in [Native American] country." The defendants were tried together. The jury acquitted Millard, but convicted John and Robert. Both defendants were sentenced to death. In their appeal to the United States Supreme Court the defendants argued that their convictions were void because the indictment against them was insufficient to charge them with murder.

Opinion of the Court by Chief Justice Fuller: Before addressing the issue raised by the defendants, the Chief Justice discussed a technical error in the record of the case. It was said that the record nowhere disclosed that the defendants were present when the sentences were pronounced by the trial court. The Chief Justice wrote that "[a]t common law no judgment for corporal punishment could be pronounced against a man in his absence, and in all capital felonies it was essential that it should appear of record that the defendant was asked before sentence if he had anything to say why it should not be pronounced." The opinion found that the technical error alone was fatal only as to the sentences, but not the convictions.

In turning to the defendants' argument that the indictment was fatally defective, the Chief Justice indicated that the Court agreed with them. The Chief Justice wrote: "[The indictment] fails to aver either the time or place of the death. By the common law, both time and place were required to be alleged. It was necessary that it should appear that the death transpired within a year and a day after the [fatal blow], and the place of death equally with that of the [fatal blow] had to be stated, to show jurisdiction in the court." The opinion went on to reverse the judgments and award a new trial. *See also* **Ball v. United States (II); Grand Jury**

Ball v. United States (II) *Court:* United States Supreme Court; *Case Citation:* Ball v. United States, 163 U.S. 662 (1896); *Argued:* Not reported; *Decided:* May 25, 1896; *Opinion of the Court:* Justice Gray; *Concurring Opinion:* None; *Dissenting Opinion:* None; *Appellate Defense Counsel:* C. H. Smith argued and briefed; *Appellate Prosecution Counsel:* Mr. Dickinson argued and briefed; *Amicus Curiae Brief Supporting Prosecutor:* None; *Amicus Curiae Brief Supporting Defendant:* None.

Issue Presented: Whether principles of double jeopardy prohibited a second prosecution of the defendants for the same offense?

Case Holding: Principles of double jeopardy prohibited a second prosecution of Millard F. Ball because he was acquitted in his first trial; however the remaining two defendants could be prosecuted a second time because judgments were found against them in the first trial and reversed on appeal.

Factual and procedural background of case: The

defendants, John C. Ball, Robert E. Boutwell and Millard F. Ball, were charged with capital murder by the United States. The crime occurred near Texas, "in the Chickasaw Nation, in [Native American] country." The defendants were tried together. The jury acquitted Millard, but convicted John and Robert. Both defendants were sentenced to death. The United States Supreme Court reversed the judgments and awarded a new trial because the indictment against the defendants was fatally defective.

On remand, the grand jury returned an indictment against all three defendants. To this indictment all three defendants filed motions to quash the indictment based on double jeopardy principles. The trial court rejected the motions. The jury returned a verdict of guilty of capital murder against all three defendants. The trial court sentenced all three defendants to death. The defendants appealed to the United States Supreme Court arguing double jeopardy principles precluded a second prosecution of them. The United States Supreme Court granted certiorari to consider the issue.

Opinion of the Court by Justice Gray: Justice Gray held that "Millard F. Ball's acquittal by the verdict of the jury could not be deprived of its legitimate effect by the subsequent reversal by this court of the judgment against the other defendants upon the writ of error sued out by them only." In finding that Millard could not be prosecuted after his initial acquittal, Justice Gray explained:

> ... [A] general verdict of acquittal upon the issue of not guilty to an indictment undertaking to charge murder, and not objected to before the verdict as insufficient in that respect, is a bar to a second indictment for the same killing.
>
> The constitution of the United States, in the fifth amendment, declares, "nor shall any person be subject to be twice put in jeopardy of life or limb." The prohibition is not against being twice punished, but against being twice put in jeopardy; and the accused, whether convicted or acquitted, is equally put in jeopardy at the first trial. An acquittal before a court having no jurisdiction is, of course, like all the proceedings in the case, absolutely void, and therefore no bar to subsequent indictment and trial in a court which has jurisdiction of the offense....
>
> As to the defendant who had been acquitted by the verdict duly returned and received, the court could take no other action than to order his discharge. The verdict of acquittal was final, and could not be reviewed, on error or otherwise, without putting him twice in jeopardy, and thereby violating the constitution.

The opinion then turned to the claim by defendants John C. Ball and Robert E. Boutwell, that double jeopardy principles barred a second prosecution of them. Justice Gray found that both defendants could be reprosecuted. He wrote: "[T]heir plea of former conviction cannot be sustained, because upon [an appeal made] by themselves, the judgment and sentence against them were reversed, and the indictment ordered to be dismissed. [I]t is quite clear that a defendant who procures a judgment against him upon an indictment to be set aside may be tried anew upon the same indictment, or upon another indictment, for the same offense of which he had been convicted." The judgment against Millard F. Ball was reversed and affirmed as to the other defendants. *See also* **Ball v. United States (I); Double Jeopardy Clause**

Bangladesh Bangladesh imposes the death penalty. Bangladesh utilizes the firing squad and hanging to carry out the death penalty. Bangladesh's legal system is based on English common law. The nation's constitution was first adopted on December 16, 1972.

The constitution of Bangladesh provides for an independent judiciary. However, under a special provision of the constitution, some lower courts are part of the executive branch of government and are subject to its influence. The judicial system is composed of a Supreme Court District Courts, Magistrate Courts and Village Courts. The Supreme Court is divided into two sections: the High Court and the Appellate Court. The High Court hears original cases and reviews cases from the lower courts. The Appellate Court has jurisdiction to hear appeals of judgments, decrees, orders, or sentences of the High Court. Decisions by the Appellate Court are binding on all other courts.

Criminal trials are open to the public. A defendant has the right to be represented by counsel, to call witnesses, and to appeal verdicts. Government-funded defense attorneys are rarely provided. In rural areas of the country, defendants usually do not receive legal representation. In urban areas, legal counsel is generally available if defendants are able to afford the expense.

The laws of Bangladesh permit defendants to be tried in absentia, although this is rarely done. The most famous absentia trial involved the prosecution of defendants charged with the 1975 killing of President Sheikh Mujibur Rahman. Fourteen of the defendants involved had fled the country. Twelve of the defendants that fled the country were convicted and many were sentenced to death. *See also* **International Capital Punishment Nations**

Barbados Capital punishment is allowed in Barbados. Barbados uses hanging as the method of execution. Barbados utilizes the English common law legal system. The nation's constitution was adopted on November 30, 1966.

Barbados' judiciary includes the Supreme Court, which consists of a High Court and a Court of Appeal. Appeals from decisions made by the High Court may be made to the Court of Appeal. The highest appeal is to the Judicial Committee of the Privy Council in England.

The constitution of Barbados provides that persons charged with criminal offenses be given a fair trial. Criminal defendants have the right to counsel, including appointed counsel for indigent defendants. The law presumes defendants innocent until proven guilty. *See also* **International Capital Punishment Nations**

Barclay v. Florida *Court:* United States Supreme Court; *Case Citation:* Barclay v. Florida, 463 U.S. 939 (1983); *Argued:* March 30, 1983; *Decided:* July 6, 1983; *Plurality Opinion:* Justice Rehnquist announced the Court's judgment and delivered an opinion, in which Burger, C. J., and White and O'Connor, JJ., joined; *Concurring Opinion:* Justice Stevens, in which

Powell, J., joined; *Dissenting Opinion:* Justice Marshall, in which Brennan, J., joined; *Dissenting Opinion:* Justice Blackmun; *Appellate Defense Counsel:* James M. Nabrit III argued; Kenneth Vickers, Jack Greenberg, Joel Berger, John Charles Boger, Deborah Fins, James S. Liebman, and Anthony G. Amsterdam on brief; *Appellate Prosecution Counsel:* Wallace E. Allbritton argued; Jim Smith on brief; *Amicus Curiae Brief Supporting Prosecutor:* None; *Amicus Curiae Brief Supporting Defendant:* None.

Issue Presented: Whether a State may constitutionally impose the death penalty when one of the aggravating circumstances relied upon by the trial judge to support the sentence was not among those established by the State's death penalty statute?

Case Holding: A death sentence is not constitutionally invalid because of the consideration of an improper aggravating circumstance, if an appellate court performs an analysis that removes the improper factor and finds that with the improper factor removed, the sentence of death is supported by the remaining permissible aggravating factors.

Factual and procedural background of case: The defendant, Elwood Barclay, was convicted by a Florida jury of committing first-degree murder on June 17, 1974. (A co-defendant was also convicted and sentenced to death.) As required by the Florida death penalty statute, a separate sentencing hearing was held before the same jury. The jury rendered an advisory sentence recommending that Barclay be sentenced to life imprisonment. The trial judge, after receiving a presentence report, decided to sentence the defendant to death. The trial judge made written findings of fact concerning aggravating and mitigating circumstances as required by Florida law. The trial judge found that several of the aggravating circumstances set out in the statute were present. He found that Barclay had knowingly created a great risk of death to many persons, had committed the murder while engaged in a kidnapping, had endeavored to disrupt governmental functions and law enforcement, and the murder had been especially heinous, atrocious, or cruel.

The Florida Supreme Court initially affirmed the sentence and conviction, but subsequently reversed the sentence and remanded for a new penalty phase hearing. The defendant was again sentenced to death. One of the issues the defendant raised on a second appeal was that the trial judge improperly found that his prior criminal record was an aggravating circumstance. The Florida Supreme Court found that consideration of the improper aggravating factor was harmless error, in light of the remaining valid aggravating circumstances. The United States Supreme Court granted certiorari to consider the constitutionality of a death sentence when an invalid factor is considered in the sentencing decision.

Plurality opinion in which Justice Rehnquist announced the Court's judgment and in which Burger, C. J., and White and O'Connor, JJ., joined: Justice Rehnquist ruled that the determination of whether the defendant's sentence must be vacated depended on the function of the finding of aggravating circumstances under Florida law and on the reason why

the aggravating factor was invalid. It was observed that the trial judge's consideration of the defendant's criminal record as an aggravating circumstance was improper as a matter of Florida law. The death penalty statute of Florida set out statutory aggravating circumstances that may be considered, and expressly precluded consideration of non-statutory aggravating circumstances. The prior criminal record of a capital felon did not fall within the definition of any statutory aggravating circumstance provided by statute.

The plurality opinion noted that the Florida Supreme Court had developed a body of case law to address the situation wherein an invalid aggravating circumstance was considered in imposing the death penalty. If the trial court found that some mitigating circumstances existed, the case will generally be remanded for resentencing. However, if the trial court properly found that there are no mitigating circumstances, the Florida Supreme Court applied harmless error analysis. In such a case, a reversal of the death sentence will not occur if the Florida Supreme Court determined the error was harmless. In determining whether consideration of an invalid aggravating circumstance was harmless, the appellate court removes the invalid factor and considers whether the remaining aggravating circumstances were sufficient to sustain the death sentence. If so, the sentence is affirmed. If not, the sentence is reversed and a new sentencing hearing is ordered.

Justice Rehnquist held that the harmless error analysis used by the Florida Supreme Court comported with constitutional standards, and that its application was constitutionally sound in the defendant's case. The judgment of the Florida Supreme Court was therefore affirmed.

Concurring opinion by Justice Stevens, in which Powell, J., joined: Justice Stevens noted that the Florida rule that statutory aggravating factors must be exclusive afforded greater protection than the federal Constitution required. It was said that although a death sentence may not rest solely on non-statutory aggravating factors, the Constitution did not prohibit consideration of factors not directly related to either statutory aggravating factors, as long as that information is relevant to the character of the defendant or the circumstances of the crime.

Dissenting opinion by Justice Marshall, in which Brennan, J., joined: Justice Marshall started out his dissent by noting that he continued to adhere to his position that the death penalty is in all circumstances cruel and unusual punishment forbidden by the Eighth and Fourteenth Amendments. He would, therefore, vacate the defendant's death sentence on that basis alone.

The dissent went further and argued that the Florida Supreme Court conducted a perfunctory review of the death sentence in the case. Justice Marshall believed that the "Florida Supreme Court's perfunctory analysis focused on the death sentence imposed on petitioner's codefendant[.]" He contended that the review procedures used by the Florida Supreme Court in the case did not pass constitutional muster. The dissent reasoned succinctly: "First, the trial judge's reliance on aggravating circumstances not permitted under the Florida death penalty scheme is constitutional error that cannot be harmless. Second, the Florida Supreme Court's failure to conduct any meaningful review of the death sentence deprived petitioner of a safeguard that the Court has deemed indispensable to a constitutional capital sentencing scheme." For these reasons Justice Marshall would have reversed the defendant's death sentence.

Dissenting opinion by Justice Blackmun: Justice Blackmun, in brief fashion, stated that "[t]he errors and missteps — intentional or otherwise — come close to making a mockery of the Florida statute and are too much for me to condone." He believed that the Florida Supreme Court did not properly review the case and would, therefore, reverse the defendant's death sentence.

Barefoot v. Estelle

Court: United States Supreme Court; *Case Citation:* Barefoot v. Estelle, 463 U.S. 880 (1983); *Argued:* April 26, 1983; *Decided:* July 6, 1983; *Opinion of the Court:* Justice White; *Concurring Opinion:* Justice Stevens; *Dissenting Opinion:* Justice Marshall, in which Brennan, J., joined; *Dissenting Opinion:* Justice Blackmun, in which Brennan and Marshall, JJ., joined; *Appellate Defense Counsel:* Will Gray argued; Carolyn Garcia on brief; *Appellate Prosecution Counsel:* Douglas M. Becker argued; Jim Mattox and David R. Richards on brief; *Amicus Curiae Brief Supporting Prosecutor:* 2; *Amicus Curiae Brief Supporting Defendant:* 4.

Issues Presented: (1) Whether the Court of Appeals correctly denied a stay of execution of the defendant's death sentence pending appeal of the District Court's judgment?

(2) Whether the District Court erred on the merits in rejecting the petition for habeas corpus filed by the defendant?

Case Holdings: (1) The Court of Appeals correctly denied a stay of execution of the defendant's death sentence pending appeal of the District Court's judgment.

(2) The District Court did not err on the merits in rejecting the petition for habeas corpus filed by the defendant.

Factual and procedural background of case: The defendant, Thomas Barefoot, was convicted of capital murder by the State of Texas. During the penalty phase proceeding, one of the questions submitted to the jury, as required by a Texas statute, was whether there was a probability that the defendant would commit further criminal acts of violence and would constitute a continuing threat to society. The prosecutor introduced evidence by two psychiatrists who testified that there was such a probability. The defendant was sentenced to death. On appeal, the Texas Court of Criminal Appeals rejected the defendant's contention that such use of psychiatric testimony at the sentencing hearing was unconstitutional, and affirmed the conviction and sentence.

After exhausting state post-conviction remedies, the defendant filed a petition for habeas corpus in a Federal District Court raising the same claim with respect to the use of psychiatric testimony. The District Court rejected the claim and denied relief. The District Court did, however, issue a certificate of probable cause, which was required in order for the defendant to appeal. While in the process of preparing his appeal, the defendant's execution date was arising. The defendant filed an application for stay of execution with the Texas Court of Criminal Appeals, but it denied the stay of execution. Shortly thereafter, a Federal Court of Appeals also denied a stay of execution. The United States Supreme Court granted certiorari to consider the propriety of denying a stay of execution.

Opinion of the Court by Justice White: Justice White first addressed the defendant's claim that the Court of Appeals should have granted his application for stay of execution pending appeal. The opinion concluded that the Court of Appeals did not err in refusing to stay the defendant's death sentence.

It was reasoned by Justice White that although the Court of Appeals did not formally affirm the District Court's judgment, there was no question that the Court of Appeals ruled on the merits of the appeal in the course of denying the stay. It was said that the parties, as directed, filed briefs and presented oral arguments, thus making it clear that whether a stay would be granted depended on the probability of success on the merits. Justice White noted that although the Court of Appeals moved swiftly to deny the stay, this did not mean that its treatment of the merits was cursory or inadequate.

Justice White went on to set out procedural guidelines for handling applications for stays of execution on habeas corpus appeals pursuant to a District Court's issuance of a certificate of probable cause:

1. A certificate of probable cause requires more than a showing of the absence of frivolity of the appeal. The petitioner must make a substantial showing of the denial of a federal right, the severity of the penalty in itself not sufficing to warrant automatic issuance of a certificate.

2. When a certificate of probable cause is issued, the petitioner must be afforded an opportunity to address the merits, and the Court of Appeals must decide the merits.

3. A Court of Appeals may adopt expedited procedures for resolving the merits of habeas corpus appeals, notwithstanding the issuance of a certificate of probable cause, but local rules should be promulgated stating the manner in which such cases will be handled and informing counsel that the merits of the appeal may be decided on the motion for a stay.

4. Where there are second or successive federal habeas corpus petitions, it is proper for the District Court to expedite consideration of the petition, even where it cannot be concluded that the petition should be dismissed because it fails to allege new or different grounds for relief.

5. Stays of execution are not automatic pending the filing and consideration of a petition for certiorari from the Supreme Court to a Court of Appeals which has denied a writ of habeas corpus. Applications for stays must contain the information and materials necessary to make a careful assessment of the merits and so reliably to determine whether a plenary review and a stay are warranted. A stay of execution should first be sought from the Court of Appeals.

The opinion then turned to the issue of whether the District Court correctly denied relief to the defendant. Justice White ruled that the District Court did not err on the merits in denying the defendant's habeas corpus petition.

The opinion held that there was no merit to the defendant's

argument that psychiatrists, individually and as a group, are incompetent to predict with an acceptable degree of reliability that a particular criminal will commit other crimes in the future and so represent a danger to the community. Justice White stated that to accept such an argument would call into question predictions of future behavior that are constantly made in other contexts. Moreover, he wrote that despite the view of the American Psychiatric Association supporting the defendant's view, there was no convincing evidence that such testimony is almost entirely unreliable and that the factfinder and the adversary system will not be competent to uncover, recognize, and take due account of its shortcomings. The judgment of the District Court was affirmed.

Concurring opinion by Justice Stevens: Justice Stevens acknowledged that procedural errors were made by the Court of Appeals, but that "since this Court has now reviewed the merits of [the defendant's] appeal, and since I agree with the ultimate conclusion that the judgment of the District Court must be affirmed, I join the Court's judgment."

Dissenting opinion by Justice Marshall in which Brennan, J., joined: Justice Marshall dissented strongly against the majority in this case. In doing so he accused the majority of fabricating matters to cover up the procedural errors of the Court of Appeals. The dissent stated its position as follows:

> I cannot subscribe to the Court's conclusion that the procedure followed by the Court of Appeals in this case was "not inconsistent with our cases." Nor can I accept the notion that it would be proper for a court of appeals to adopt special "summary procedures" for capital cases. On the merits, I would vacate [the defendant's] death sentence....
>
> I frankly do not understand how the Court can conclude that the Court of Appeals' treatment of this case was "tolerable." If, as the Court says, the Court of Appeals was "obligated to decide the merits of the appeal," it most definitely failed to discharge that obligation, for the court never ruled on [the defendant's] appeal. It is simply false to say that "the Court of Appeals ruled on the merits of the appeal." The record plainly shows that the Court of Appeals did no such thing. It neither dismissed the appeal as frivolous nor affirmed the judgment of the District Court. The Court of Appeals made one ruling and one ruling only: it refused to stay [the defendant's] execution. Had this Court not granted a stay, [the defendant] would have been put to death without his appeal ever having been decided one way or the other.
>
> The Court is flatly wrong in suggesting that any defect was merely technical because the Court of Appeals could have "verif[ied] the obvious by expressly affirming the judgment of the District Court" at the same time it denied a stay. The Court of Appeals' failure to decide [the defendant's] appeal was no oversight. The court simply had no authority to decide the appeal on the basis of the papers before it....
>
> The Court offers no justification for the procedure followed by the Court of Appeals because there is none. A State has no legitimate interest in executing a prisoner before he has obtained full review of his sentence. A stay of execution pending appeal causes no harm to the State apart from the minimal burden of providing a jail cell for the prisoner for the period of time necessary to decide his appeal. By contrast, a denial of a stay on the basis of a hasty finding that the prisoner is not likely to succeed on his appeal permits the State to execute him prior to full review of a concededly substantial constitutional challenge to his

sentence. If the court's hurried evaluation of the appeal proves erroneous, as is entirely possible when difficult legal issues are decided without adequate time for briefing and full consideration, the execution of the prisoner will make it impossible to undo the mistake.

> Once a federal judge has decided, as the District Judge did here, that a prisoner under sentence of death has raised a substantial constitutional claim, it is a travesty of justice to permit the State to execute him before his appeal can be considered and decided. If a prisoner's statutory right to appeal means anything, a State simply cannot be allowed to kill him and thereby moot his appeal....
>
> In view of the irreversible nature of the death penalty and the extraordinary number of death sentences that have been found to suffer from some constitutional infirmity, it would be grossly improper for a court of appeals to establish special summary procedures for capital cases. The only consolation I can find in today's decision is that the primary responsibility for selecting the appropriate procedures for these appeals lies, as the Court itself points out, with the courts of appeals. Notwithstanding the profoundly disturbing attitude reflected in today's opinion, I am hopeful that few circuit judges would ever support the adoption of procedures that would afford less consideration to an appeal in which a man's life is at stake than to an appeal challenging an ordinary money judgment.

Dissenting opinion by Justice Blackmun, in which Brennan and Marshall, JJ., joined: Justice Blackmun dissented from the majority decision. He focused his dissent on the psychiatric evidence proffered at the defendant's penalty phase hearing:

> I agree with most of what Justice Marshall has said in his dissenting opinion. I, too, dissent, but I base my conclusion also on evidentiary factors that the Court rejects with some emphasis. The Court holds that psychiatric testimony about a defendant's future dangerousness is admissible, despite the fact that such testimony is wrong two times out of three. The Court reaches this result — even in a capital case — because, it is said, the testimony is subject to cross-examination and impeachment. In the present state of psychiatric knowledge, this is too much for me. One may accept this in a routine lawsuit for money damages, but when a person's life is at stake — no matter how heinous his offense — a requirement of greater reliability should prevail. In a capital case, the specious testimony of a psychiatrist, colored in the eyes of an impressionable jury by the inevitable untouchability of a medical specialist's words, equates with death itself....
>
> The American Psychiatric Association (APA), participating in this case as amicus curiae, informs us that "[t]he unreliability of psychiatric predictions of long-term future dangerousness is by now an established fact within the profession." The APA's best estimate is that two out of three predictions of long-term future violence made by psychiatrists are wrong. The Court does not dispute this proposition, and indeed it could not do so; the evidence is overwhelming.... Neither the Court nor the State of Texas has cited a single reputable scientific source contradicting the unanimous conclusion of professionals in this field that psychiatric predictions of long-term future violence are wrong more often than they are right....
>
> It is impossible to square admission of this purportedly scientific but actually baseless testimony with the Constitution's paramount concern for reliability in capital sentencing. Death is a permissible punishment in Texas only if the jury finds beyond a reasonable doubt that there is a probability the defendant will commit future acts of criminal violence. The admission of unreliable psychiatric predictions of future violence,

offered with unabashed claims of "reasonable medical certainty" or "absolute" professional reliability, creates an intolerable danger that death sentences will be imposed erroneously. *See also* **Lonchar v. Thomas; Stay of Execution**

Barfield, Velma Margie   Velma Margie Barfield was executed for capital murder of Stuart Taylor by the state of North Carolina on November 2, 1984. Barfield was the first woman executed by lethal injection and the first woman executed after the United States Supreme Court lifted the moratorium on capital punishment in the case of *Gregg v. Georgia*, 428 U.S. 153 (1976).

Barfield and Taylor had been going together. On occasion, Barfield stayed with Taylor at his home in St. Pauls, North Carolina. On January 31, 1978, Taylor became ill and had violent vomiting and diarrhea. Taylor's illness continued for two days before Barfield took him to a local hospital where he was treated. At the time he was examined by an emergency room physician, Taylor was complaining of nausea, vomiting and diarrhea, as well as general pain in his muscles, chest and abdomen. After receiving intravenous fluids and vitamins, as well as other treatment, Taylor was released from the hospital and Barfield took him back to his home in St. Pauls where she fed him.

The day after Taylor returned home he became violently ill and was rushed back to the hospital in an ambulance. While he was in the hospital emergency room, Taylor was given intravenous fluids. A tracheotomy was performed but he died in the emergency room approximately one hour after he was brought in. Taylor's family requested that an autopsy be performed.

The autopsy of Taylor revealed his blood had an arsenic level of .13 milligrams percent. His liver had an arsenic level of one milligram percent. These findings led physicians to conclude that Taylor died from acute arsenic poisoning.

On March 10, 1978, police officers talked with Barfield. The conversation between Barfield and the police involved a number of Taylor's checks that had been forged. Barfield denied forging the checks during this interrogation. She then proceeded to deny that she was in any way involved with Taylor's death.

On March 13, 1978, Barfield returned to police headquarters. During this interrogation she made a lengthy statement. In her statement, she admitted that she had forged some checks on Taylor's account, which he found out about when his bank statements came in the mail. Upon finding out about the forgeries, Taylor talked with her and threatened to turn her in to the authorities. Barfield indicated she purchased a bottle of Terro Ant Poison and put some of the poison in Taylor's tea and later put more of the substance in Taylor's beer. She stated that she gave Taylor the poison because she was afraid that he would turn her in for forgery. Barfield concluded her confession by revealing that she had given poison to three other persons besides Taylor and that they too had died.

During Barfield's trial for the murder of Taylor evidence revealed that she poisoned John Henry Lee, an 80 year old man that she lived with and worked for as a housekeeper and nurse's aide in early 1977. Though no autopsy was performed at the time of Lee's death, his body was exhumed pursuant to a court order and an autopsy was performed. Toxicological screenings revealed that Lee's liver contained an arsenic level of 2.8 milligrams percent and the muscle tissue contained an arsenic level of 0.3 milligrams percent. Medical testimony concluded that Lee's death was caused by arsenic poisoning.

Velma Margie Barfield was the first woman executed by lethal injection and the first woman executed after the 1976 decision by the United States Supreme Court lifting the moratorium on capital punishment. She was executed by the state of North Carolina on November 2, 1984. (North Carolina Department of Corrections)

The trial evidence showed Barfield had poisoned Dolly Taylor Edwards. In early 1976, Barfield moved into the home of Edwards as a live-in helper. Edwards died on March 1, 1977. Though no autopsy was performed on the body of Edwards at the time of her death, pursuant to a court order her body was exhumed and an autopsy was performed. During the autopsy, toxicological screenings were conducted on samples of Edwards' liver tissue and muscle tissue. In the liver tissue, there was found an arsenic level of 0.4 milligrams percent. In the muscle tissue, there was found an arsenic level of .08 milligrams percent. Medical testimony concluded that Edwards' death was caused by arsenic poisoning.

Finally, trial evidence revealed that Barfield had poisoned her mother, Lillie McMillan Bullard. Her mother died on December 30, 1974. Pursuant to a court order the body of her mother was exhumed for an autopsy. Medical testimony revealed that Bullard's hair sample had an arsenic concentration of .6 milligrams percent; that muscle tissue had an arsenic level of .3 milligrams percent; and that skin samples had an arsenic level of .1 milligrams percent. It was concluded that Bullard's death was caused by arsenic poisoning.

Although Barfield did not admit any involvement in the death of her husband, Jennings L. Barfield, his body was exhumed pursuant to a court order and an autopsy was performed. Toxicological screenings indicated that varying levels of arsenic were present in his body tissue. Medical testimony concluded that the cause of Mr. Barfield's death was arsenic poisoning. *See also* **Women and Capital Punishment**

Battery *see* **Assault and Battery**

Beck v. Alabama   *Court:* United States Supreme Court; *Case Citation:* Beck v. Alabama, 447 U.S. 625 (1980); *Argued:* February 20, 1980; *Decided:* June 20, 1980; *Opinion of the Court:* Justice Stevens; *Concurring Statement:* Justice Brennan; *Concurring Statement:* Justice Marshall; *Dissenting Opinion:* Justice Rehnquist, in which White, J., joined; *Appellate Defense Counsel:* David Klingsberg argued; John A. Herfort, Jay Wishingrad, and John L. Carroll on brief; *Appellate Prosecution Counsel:* Edward E. Carnes argued; Charles A. Graddick on brief; *Amicus Curiae Brief Supporting Prosecutor:* None; *Amicus Curiae Brief Supporting Defendant:* None.

Issue Presented: Whether a sentence of death may constitutionally be imposed after a jury verdict of guilt of a capital offense, when the jury was not permitted to consider a verdict of guilt of a lesser included non-capital offense for which evidence was presented to support such a verdict?

Case Holding: The death sentence may not constitutionally be imposed after a jury verdict of guilt of a capital offense where the jury was not permitted to consider a verdict of guilt of a lesser included offense, for which evidence was presented to support such a verdict.

Factual and procedural background of case: The defendant, Beck, was charged with capital murder by the State of Alabama. At the time of the prosecution Alabama's death penalty statute provided that the trial judge was prohibited from giving the guilt phase jury the option of convicting the defendant of any lesser included offense. Instead, the jury had to either convict the defendant of the capital crime or acquit him.

During the trial the defendant presented evidence tending to show that he was guilty of a lesser included offense to capital murder. However, because of Alabama's statute, the trial court refused to instruct the jury that they could return a verdict of guilt of a lesser included offense. The defendant was convicted of capital murder and sentenced to death. The Alabama appellate courts upheld the conviction and death sentence, after rejecting the defendant's contention that the statutory prohibition on lesser included offense instructions violated the Federal Constitution. The United States Supreme Court granted certiorari to consider the issue.

Opinion of the Court by Justice Stevens: Justice Stevens held that a death sentence may not constitutionally be imposed after a jury verdict of guilt of a capital offense where the jury was not permitted to consider a verdict of guilt of a lesser included offense. The opinion reasoned that providing the jury with the option of convicting on a lesser included offense gave assurances that the jury would accord the defendant the full benefit of the reasonable doubt standard. It was said that when the evidence establishes that the defendant is guilty of a serious and violent offense, but leaves some doubt as to an element justifying conviction of a capital offense, the failure to give the jury such a lesser included instruction inevitably enhances the risk of an unwarranted conviction. Justice Stevens

ruled that such a risk could not be tolerated in a case in which the defendant's life was at stake. Accordingly, the judgment of the Alabama Supreme Court was reversed.

Concurring statement by Justice Brennan: Justice Brennan issued a concurring statement indicating that although he joined the Court's opinion, he "continue[d] to believe that the death penalty is, in all circumstances, contrary to the Eighth Amendment's prohibition against imposition of cruel and unusual punishments."

Concurring statement by Justice Marshall: Justice Marshall's concurring statement indicated that he "continue[d] to believe that the death penalty is, under all circumstances, cruel and unusual punishment prohibited by the Eighth and Fourteenth Amendments."

Dissenting opinion by Justice Rehnquist, in which White, J., joined: Justice Rehnquist indicated in his dissent that he could not join the majority decision because the issue it resolved was not properly before the Court. The dissent pointed out that while the defendant presented the issue to the Alabama Court of Criminal Appeals, he did not present the issue to the Alabama Supreme Court. Justice Rehnquist wrote: "I do not believe it suffices, under the jurisdiction granted to us by the Constitution and by Congress, to brush this matter off as the Court does in [a] footnote ... on the grounds that [the defendant] presented his claim 'in some fashion' to the Supreme Court of Alabama[.]"

Beets, Betty Lou   Betty Lou Beets was born on March 12, 1937. By the time Betty Lou was 47 years old she had been married five times. On August 6, 1983, a boat belonging to Betty Lou's fifth husband, Jimmy Beets, was found drifting empty on a Texas lake called Cedar Creek Lake. The boat was retrieved by strangers in the area. After searching the boat they found a fishing license bearing Jimmy Beets' name. Authorities were notified and an investigation followed. After going through a telephone book authorities made contact with Jimmy Beets' home and spoke with Betty Lou. Shortly after speaking with law enforcement officials Betty Lou came to the lake and identified the boat as belonging to her husband.

An extended search was made in the lake in an effort to find Jimmy Beets' body, but authorities were not successful. No immediate suspicion of foul play was directed at Betty Lou, although authorities quickly learned that she had a $110,000 life insurance policy on her husband. Without locating Jimmy Beets' body Betty Lou could not collect the life insurance money until seven years had passed from the date of her husband's disappearance.

Two years after Jimmy Beets disappeared authorities received information that linked Betty Lou to the disappearance of her husband. On June 8, 1985, Betty Lou was arrested and a search warrant issued that permitted authorities to dig up the ground around her home. Pursuant to the execution of the search warrant, physical remains of the bodies of Jimmy Beets and Doyle Wayne Barker, another former husband of Betty Lou, were found at different locations near her home. Jimmy

Betty Lou Beets was executed by the State of Texas for the murder of her husband. (Texas Department of Criminal Justice)

Beets' remains were found buried in a "wishing well," which was located in the front yard of the residence. Barker's remains were found buried under a storage shed located in the backyard of the residence. Two bullets were recovered from Jimmy Beets' remains. The remains of the two bodies were transported to the Dallas Forensic Science Laboratory where they were subsequently identified as being the remains of the bodies of Jimmy Beets and Barker.

Betty Lou was indicted for the capital murder of Jimmy Beets. During the trial her son, Robert Franklin Branson, testified against her. According to Branson he was living with his mother and Jimmy Beets in 1983. Branson stated that on August 6, 1983, his mother told him that she was going to kill Jimmy Beets that evening. Branson testified that he left the home for two hours because he did not want to be present when the crime occurred. After Branson returned to the residence he assisted Betty Lou in placing Jimmy Beets' body in the "wishing well." Branson testified that the next day he took Jimmy Beets' boat onto the lake to make it appear as though Jimmy Beets fell into the lake and drowned. Robbie testified that he knew of Barker, but had only seen him one time, and that he did not live with his mother and Barker when she and Barker were married and lived together.

There was also trial testimony against Betty Lou by her daughter, Shirley Stegner. Shirley testified that several weeks after Jimmy Beets' reported disappearance, Betty Lou confided in her that he was buried in the "wishing well." Shirley also testified that in October of 1981, when her mother and Barker were married and living together, Betty Lou told her that she was going to kill Barker. Approximately three days later, Betty Lou told Shirley "that she waited until [Barker] went to sleep and then she got the gun and covered it with a pillow and pulled the trigger and when she pulled the trigger, the pillow [interfered] with the firing pin, so she hesitated for a minute, afraid that [Barker] was going to wake up, and she cocked the gun again and fired and shot him in the head." Shirley testified that she assisted her mother in disposing of Barker's body.

Betty Lou was found guilty of murdering Jimmy Beets and was sentenced to death. On direct appeal, the Texas Court of Criminal Appeals affirmed the conviction and sentence. Betty Lou was executed by lethal injection on February 24, 2000. She became the first woman executed in the 21st century. *See also* **Women and Capital Punishment**

Belarus Capital punishment is carried out in Belarus. Belarus uses the firing squad as the method of execution. In 1998, Belarus executed 33 defendants. Its legal system is based on civil law. Belarus' constitution became effective on November 17, 1996.

Belarus has a government in which nearly all power is concentrated in the president. Since his election in 1994, President Aleksandr Lukashenko has consolidated power steadily in the executive branch through authoritarian means. Consequently, the judiciary is not independent.

The criminal justice system has three tiers: district courts, regional courts, and a Supreme Court. In 1994, a Constitutional Court was established to adjudicate serious constitutional issues. The Constitutional Court has no means to enforce its decisions.

Generally defendants are not entitled to a jury trial. The only exception occurs in capital offense cases. Defendants charged with capital crimes may demand trial by jury. Criminal defendants have a right to a public trial, right to counsel, and a right to confront witnesses. The law establishes a presumption of innocence. Both the defendant and prosecutor have the right to appeal. The prosecutor may appeal an acquittal and obtain a retrial on the same charge. *See also* **International Capital Punishment Nations**

Belgium Belgium officially abolished capital punishment in 1996. *See also* **International Capital Punishment Nations**

Belize Belize imposes the death penalty. Belize utilizes hanging as the method of execution. Its legal system is based on English law. The nation's constitution was adopted on September 21, 1981.

The Belizean legal system is composed of magistrate courts, Supreme Court (trial court), and Court of Appeal. In cases involving the interpretation of the nation's constitution, appeals may be taken to the Judicial Committee of the Privy Council in England.

Defendants have constitutional rights to presumption of innocence, protection against self-incrimination, double jeopardy, legal counsel, a public trial, and appeal. Legal counsel for indigent defendants is provided by the government only for capital offenses. Trial by jury is mandatory in capital cases. *See also* **International Capital Punishment Nations**

Bell v. Ohio *Court:* United States Supreme Court; *Case Citation:* Bell v. Ohio, 438 U.S. 637 (1978); *Argued:* January 17, 1978; *Decided:* July 3, 1978; *Plurality Opinion:* Chief Justice Burger announced the Court's judgment and delivered an opinion, in which Stewart, Powell and Stevens, JJ., joined; *Concurring Statement:* Justice Blackmun; *Concurring Statement:* Justice Marshall; *Concurring and Dissenting Statement:* Justice White; *Dissenting Statement:* Justice Rehnquist; *Justice Taking No Part in Decision:* Justice Brennan; *Appellate Defense Counsel:* H. Fred Hoefle argued; Jack Greenberg, James M. Nabrit III, Joel Berger, David E. Kendall and Anthony G.

Amsterdam on brief; *Appellate Prosecution Counsel:* Leonard Kirschner argued; Simon L. Leis, Jr., Fred J. Cartolano, William P. Whalen, Jr., and Claude N. Crowe on brief; *Amicus Curiae Brief Supporting Prosecutor:* 1; *Amicus Curiae Brief Supporting Defendant:* 1.

Issue Presented: Whether the Ohio death penalty statute violated the Constitution because it prevented the penalty phase three-panel judges from considering relevant non-statutory mitigating evidence?

Case Holding: The Ohio death penalty statute violated the Constitution because it prevented the penalty phase three-panel judges from considering relevant non-statutory mitigating evidence.

Factual and procedural background of case: The defendant, Willie Lee Bell, was convicted of capital murder by the State of Ohio. Under the death penalty statute of the State, the defendant was limited to presenting mitigating circumstances delineated in the statute. During the penalty phase, a three-judge panel sentenced the defendant to death, after refusing to consider the particular circumstances of his crime and aspects of his character and record as mitigating factors. The Ohio Supreme Court affirmed the conviction and sentence, and rejected the defendant's contention that he had a constitutional right to have non-statutory mitigating circumstances presented and considered. The United States Supreme Court granted certiorari to consider the issue.

Plurality opinion in which Chief Justice Burger announced the Court's judgment and in which Stewart, Powell and Stevens, JJ., joined: The Chief Justice found that the Constitution accorded the defendant the right to present and have considered, all relevant mitigating evidence. The opinion stated in summary fashion: "For the reasons stated in ... our opinion in *Lockett v. Ohio*, we have concluded that 'the Eighth and Fourteenth Amendments require that the sentencer, in all but the rarest kind of capital case, not be precluded from considering, as a mitigating factor, any aspect of a defendant's character or record and any of the circumstances of the offense that the defendant proffers.' We also concluded that '[t]he Ohio death penalty statute does not permit the type of individualized consideration of mitigating factors,' that is required by the Eighth and Fourteenth Amendments. We therefore agree with Bell's contention." The judgment of Ohio Supreme Court was reversed.

Concurring statement by Justice Blackmun: Justice Blackmun issued a statement indicating he concurred in the Court's judgment for the reasons stated in his concurring opinion in *Lockett*.

Concurring statement by Justice Marshall: Justice Marshall issued a statement indicating he concurred in the Court's judgment for the reasons stated in his concurring opinion in *Lockett*.

Concurring and dissenting statement by Justice White: Justice White issued a statement indicating he concurred and dissented in the Court's decision for the reasons stated in his concurring and dissenting opinion in *Lockett*.

Dissenting statement by Justice Rehnquist: Justice Rehnquist issued a statement indicating he dissented in the Court's decision for the reasons stated in his concurring and dissenting opinion in *Lockett*. See also **Lockett v. Ohio; Mitigating Circumstances**

Bench Conference   A bench conference refers to a meeting at the judge's bench, with the parties and the judge, during a jury trial. The purpose of a bench conference is to permit an issue to be discussed with and resolved by the judge without the jury hearing the issue. A defendant has a constitutional right to be personally present at a bench conference.

Bench Trial   A capital offender may waive the right to trial by jury, but nonetheless have a trial. A trial without a jury is called a bench trial. The factfinder in a bench trial is the presiding judge. In a capital prosecution the issue of a bench trial involves two separate trial proceedings: (1) guilt phase proceeding and (2) penalty phase proceeding.

1. *Guilt Phase Proceeding.* All capital punishment jurisdictions afford a capital offender the privilege of waiving the right to trial by jury at the guilt phase and having a guilt phase bench trial instead. A guilt phase bench trial is deemed a privilege because the United States Supreme Court held in *Singer v. United States*, 380 U.S. 24 (1965), that there was no constitutional right to a guilt phase bench trial.

   A guilt phase bench trial usually will not occur unless three factors are met: (1) the capital felon validly waives his or her right to trial by jury, (2) the prosecutor consents to trial by the bench, and (3) the judge agrees to holding a bench trial. Two jurisdictions, Connecticut and Ohio, require that a capital punishment guilt phase bench trial be presided over by a three-judge panel. In all other jurisdictions a single judge sits as factfinder in a guilt phase bench trial.

2. *Penalty Phase Proceeding.* The United States Supreme Court has held that there is no constitutional right to have a jury preside over the penalty phase of a capital prosecution. Jurisdictions have responded to the issue in different ways.

   In capital punishment jurisdictions that allow participation of penalty phase juries, a capital felon can waive the jury and have the trial judge preside over the penalty phase. In several jurisdictions a penalty phase jury is prohibited per se. Under the statutes of Arizona, Colorado, Idaho, Montana, and Nebraska, a capital offender cannot have a jury participate at the penalty phase under any circumstance. These five jurisdictions adhere to common law principles that vest all sentencing decisions in the trial judge. In *State v. Gallegos*, 916 P.2d 1056 (Ariz. 1996) the Arizona Supreme Court ruled that a defendant is not denied equal protection of the law because of the denial of penalty phase jury.

   Nebraska allows a three-judge panel to preside over the penalty phase, if the presiding judge makes a request that

On July 7, 1984 a Nebraska three-judge panel imposed a death sentence on John Joubert. Joubert had pled guilty to two capital murders. He was executed by electrocution on July 17, 1996. (Sarpy County Sheriff)

two additional judges participate in the proceeding. Nevada and Ohio require a three-judge panel preside over the penalty phase, if a capital felon's guilt was determined by a plea or at a guilt phase bench trial. Colorado requires a three-judge panel preside over the penalty phase under all circumstances. The death penalty may not be imposed in the three-judge panel jurisdictions unless the verdict is unanimous by the judges.

Five capital punishment jurisdictions, Indiana, Kentucky, New Mexico, Oklahoma, and Wyoming, require the trial judge alone decide a defendant's punishment if his or her guilt was determined by a plea or at a guilt phase bench trial. *See also* **Jury Trial**

Benin Capital punishment is permitted in Benin. Benin uses the firing squad to carry out the death penalty. The legal system of Benin is based on French civil law and customary law. The constitution of Benin was adopted on December 2, 1990.

Benin is a democracy headed by President Mathieu Kerekou, who was inaugurated on April 4, 1996. The nation has a unicameral legislature. Benin's constitution provides for an independent judiciary.

The judicial structure of Benin includes a civilian court system that operates on the national and provincial levels. The nation has a Supreme Court that is the last resort in all administrative and judicial matters. There is also a Constitutional Court that is charged with passing on the constitutionality of laws and disputes between the president and the National Assembly, and with resolving disputes regarding presidential and National Assembly elections.

Under the constitution of Benin a defendant has a right to a public trial. A defendant enjoys the presumption of innocence, has the right to be present at trial, the right to representation by retained or appointed legal counsel, and the right to confront witnesses. *See also* **International Capital Punishment Nations**

Benson v. United States *Court:* United States Supreme Court; *Case Citation:* Benson v. United States, 146 U.S. 325 (1892); *Argued:* Not reported; *Decided:* December 5, 1892;

Opinion of the Court: Justice Brewer; *Concurring Opinion:* None; *Dissenting Opinion:* None; *Appellate Defense Counsel:* A. L. Williams argued; Leland J Webb and Wm. Dillon brief; *Appellate Prosecution Counsel:* United States Assistant Attorney General Parker argued and briefed; *Amicus Curiae Brief Supporting Prosecutor:* None; *Amicus Curiae Brief Supporting Defendant:* None.

Issue Presented: Whether the United States had jurisdiction to prosecute the defendant for murder committed on the Fort Leavenworth military reservation?

Case Holding: The United States had jurisdiction to prosecute the defendant for murder committed on the Fort Leavenworth military reservation, even though the crime occurred on a portion of the reservation that was not used for military purposes.

Factual and procedural background of case: The defendant, Benson, was charged by the United States with committing capital murder on the Fort Leavenworth military reservation, in Kansas. At the trial the defendant unsuccessfully argued that the Federal Government did not have jurisdiction over the area in which the crime occurred, and therefore could not prosecute him. The defendant was convicted and sentenced to death by a Federal District Court. The United States Supreme Court granted certiorari to consider the issue of jurisdiction.

Opinion of the Court by Justice Brewer: Justice Brewer held that the Fort Leavenworth military reservation was within the territorial boundaries of the state of Kansas, and was not excepted from the jurisdiction of the State when the State was admitted to the Union. However, it was said in 1875 the legislature of the state of Kansas passed an act which relinquished jurisdiction to the United States over the territory of the Fort Leavenworth military reservation. Justice Brewer noted that it was "competent for the legislature of a state to cede exclusive jurisdiction over places needed by the general government in the execution of its powers, the use of the places being, in fact, as much for the people of the state as for the people of the United States generally[.]"

The decision rejected the defendant's argument that jurisdiction over the area only passed to such portions of the reserve as were actually used for military purposes by the Federal Government. The defendant had contended that the crime charged was committed on land used solely for farming purposes. Justice Brewer responded: "But in matters of that kind the courts follow the action of the political department of the government. The entire tract had been legally reserved for military purposes. The character and purposes of its occupation having been officially and legally established by that branch of the government which has control over such matters, it is not open to the courts, on a question of jurisdiction, to inquire what may be the actual uses to which any portion of the reserve is temporarily put." The judgment of the Federal District Court was affirmed. *See also* **Jurisdiction**

Bergemann v. Backer *Court:* United States Supreme Court; *Case Citation:* Bergemann v. Backer, 157 U.S. 655

(1895); *Argued:* Not reported; *Decided:* April 1, 1895; *Opinion of the Court:* Justice Harlan; *Concurring Opinion:* None; *Dissenting Opinion:* None; *Appellate Defense Counsel:* Wm. D. Daly argued and briefed; *Appellate Prosecution Counsel:* Joshua S. Salmon argued and briefed; *Amicus Curiae Brief Supporting Prosecutor:* None; *Amicus Curiae Brief Supporting Defendant:* None.

Issue Presented: Whether the defendant was entitled to habeas relief as a result of the New Jersey Supreme Court's refusal to hear his appeal?

Case Holding: The defendant was not entitled to habeas relief as a result of the New Jersey Supreme Court's refusal to hear his appeal, because the Constitution does not require States create appellate courts.

Factual and procedural background of case: The defendant, August Bergemann, was convicted of capital murder and sentenced to death by the State of New Jersey. The defendant filed an appeal with the New Jersey Supreme Court, but the appellate court refused to hear the case. The defendant then filed a petition for habeas corpus relief in a Federal District Court, alleging his constitutional rights were violated because the State appellate court refused to hear his appeal. The petition was dismissed. The United States Supreme Court granted certiorari to consider the issue.

Opinion of the Court by Justice Harlan: Justice Harlan held that the defendant did not have a right under the Federal Constitution to have his case reviewed by the State appellate court. It was said that appellate review of a criminal case was not required by the Constitution. Justice Harlan observed that to the degree a State provides appellate review, is a matter firmly controlled by the State. The opinion concluded "that the refusal of the courts of New Jersey to grant the accused [an appeal] ... constituted no reason for interference in his behalf by a writ of habeas corpus issued by a court of the United States." The judgment of the Federal District Court was affirmed.

Bermuda Capital punishment is on the law books of Bermuda, although the punishment has not been invoked for many years. The method of execution used by Bermuda is hanging. The nation's legal system is based on English law. Bermuda's constitution was adopted on June 8, 1968. *See also* **International Capital Punishment Nations**

Best Evidence Rule *see* Rules of Evidence

Beyond a Reasonable Doubt *see* Burden of Proof at Guilt Phase

Bhutan The death penalty is imposed in Bhutan. The legal system is based on Indian law and English common law. Bhutan does not have a written constitution, though it uses a 1953 Royal decree for the constitution of the National Assembly. The Wangchuk royal family has ruled the country since 1907. The judiciary of Bhutan is not independent of the nation's king.

The criminal code of Bhutan is based on the Tsa Yig, a code established by the *shabdrung* in the 17th century. In 1998, the government formed a special committee to review the country's basic laws and propose changes.

The judicial system is composed of a High Court, district courts and magistrate courts. The High Court is the supreme court of the nation. However, decisions from the High Court may be appealed to the king.

Criminal trials are conducted in open hearings. For offenses against the government, state- appointed prosecutors file charges and prosecute cases. In other instances, the relevant organization or department of government files charges and conducts the prosecution. Defendants are presented with written charges in languages that they understand. In cases where defendants cannot write their own defense, judicial officers are assigned to assist defendants. The nation does not have trained lawyers. However, the government has implemented a program to provide trained legal representation. *See also* **International Capital Punishment Nations**

Biddle v. Perovich *Court:* United States Supreme Court; *Case Citation:* Biddle v. Perovich, 274 U.S. 480 (1927); *Argued:* May 2, 1927; *Decided:* May 31, 1927; *Opinion of the Court:* Justice Holmes; *Concurring Opinion:* None; *Dissenting Opinion:* None; *Justice Taking No Part in Decision:* Chief Justice Taft; *Appellate Defense Counsel:* George T. McDermott argued and briefed; *Appellate Prosecution Counsel:* William D. Mitchell argued; Robert P. Reeder on brief; *Amicus Curiae Brief Supporting Prosecutor:* None; *Amicus Curiae Brief Supporting Defendant:* None.

Issue Presented: Whether the President had authority to commute the defendant's death sentence to life imprisonment without the consent of the defendant?

Case Holding: The President had authority to commute the defendant's death sentence to life imprisonment without consent of the defendant.

Factual and procedural background of case: The defendant, Vuko Perovich, was convicted of capital murder and sentenced to death by the United States. An appeal was filed on behalf of the defendant to the United States Supreme Court, alleging that the conviction was invalid because the prosecutor failed to prove the identity of the victim of the crime. The Supreme Court affirmed the judgment in *Perovich v. United States.*

On June 5, 1909, President Taft executed a document commuting the defendant's sentence to imprisonment for life in a penitentiary. The defendant eventually filed a petition for habeas corpus relief in a Federal District Court, alleging that the commutation of his sentence and removal to a penitentiary were without his consent. The District Court agreed and granted habeas relief. An appeal was taken by the government to a Federal Court of Appeals. The Court of Appeals thereafter certified the following question to the United States Supreme Court: Did the President have authority to commute the sentence of the defendant from death to life imprisonment?

Opinion of the Court by Justice Holmes: Justice Holmes observed that the answer to the certified question was entangled in the defendant's contention that the President could not commute the sentence without the defendant's consent. Both the certified question and the defendant's contention were addressed as follows:

> We will not go into history, but we will say a word about the principles of pardons in the law of the United States. A pardon in our days is not a private act of grace from an individual happening to possess power. It is a part of the Constitutional scheme. When granted it is the determination of the ultimate authority that the public welfare will be better served by inflicting less than what the judgment fixed. Just as the original punishment would be imposed without regard to the prisoner's consent and in the teeth of his will, whether he liked it or not, the public welfare, not his consent determines what shall be done. So far as a pardon legitimately cuts down a penalty it affects the judgment imposing it. No one doubts that a reduction of the term of an imprisonment or the amount of a fine would limit the sentence effectively on the one side and on the other would leave the reduced term or fine valid and to be enforced, and that the convict's consent is not required.
>
> When we come to the commutation of death to imprisonment for life it is hard to see how consent has any more to do with it than it has in the cases first put. Supposing that Perovich did not accept the change, he could not have got himself hanged against the Executive order. Supposing that he did accept, he could not affect the judgment to be carried out. The considerations that led to the modification had nothing to do with his will. The only question is whether the substituted punishment was authorized by law — here, whether the change is within the scope of the words of the Constitution, article 2, 2:
>
> > "The President ... shall have Power to grant Reprieves and Pardons for Offences against the United States, except in Cases of Impeachment."
>
> We cannot doubt that the power extends to this case. By common understanding imprisonment for life is a less penalty than death.... The opposite answer would permit the President to decide that justice requires the diminution of a term or a fine without consulting the convict, but would deprive him of the power in the most important cases and require him to permit an execution which he had decided ought not to take place unless the change is agreed to by one who on no sound principle ought to have any voice in what the law should do for the welfare of the whole.

The certified question was answered in the affirmative.

Case note: Chief Justice Taft, who took no part in the case, was the President who commuted the defendant's death sentence. *See also* **Certified Question; Clemency; Perovich v. United States**

Bifurcation of Guilt and Penalty Phases *see* Trial Structure

Bill of Attainder Clause

In Article I, Section 9.3 of the Federal Constitution it is expressly stated that "[n]o Bill of Attainder ... shall be passed." The Bill of Attainder Clause has been interpreted as prohibiting legislatures from enacting laws that impose capital punishment without any conviction within the ordinary course of a judicial proceeding.

Capital felons have unsuccessfully argued that when jurisdictions enact legislation providing for alternative methods of execution, such laws violate the Bill of Attainder Clause. This argument has always been made in the context of a pending constitutional attack on the existing method of execution used by a jurisdiction. That is, capital felons contend that by enacting legislation creating an alternative method of execution while a capital felon has a pending challenge to the constitutionality of the existing method of execution, the new law effectively moots the pending constitutional challenge on the existing method of execution. Courts have consistently ruled that this reasoning stretches the meaning and intent of the Bill of Attainder Clause and, therefore, has been uniformly rejected. *See also* **Ex Post Facto Clause**

Bill of Particulars

A bill of particulars is a legal device that a defendant will utilize when he or she needs detailed information about the crime charged against him or her. In practice, a charging instrument will only set out the bare facts that puts a defendant on notice of the charge against him or her. Details such as exact dates, places, type of instrument used or victim identification, are matters which a defendant may request through a bill of particulars.

Bill of Rights

The first ten amendments to the United States Constitution are called the Bill of Rights. The Bill of Rights enumerates basic Anglo-American civil liberties that cannot be infringed upon by the government. In 1791 the States ratified the Bill of Rights. As originally interpreted by the United States Supreme Court, the Bill of Rights applied only to the Federal government. However, through use of the Fourteenth Amendment, the Supreme Court has made most of the provisions in the Bill of Rights applicable to the States. In capital prosecutions many of the provisions in the Bill of Rights have been used to affirm and reverse capital convictions and sentences.

Amendment I. Congress shall make no law respecting an establishment of religion, or prohibiting the free exercise thereof; or abridging the freedom of speech, or of the press, or the right of the people peaceably to assemble, and to petition the Government for a redress of grievances.

Amendment II. A well regulated Militia, being necessary to the security of a free State, the right of the people to keep and bear Arms, shall not be infringed.

Amendment III. No Soldier shall, in time of peace be quartered in any house, without the consent of the Owner, nor in time of war, but in a manner to be prescribed by law.

Amendment IV. The right of the people to be secure in their persons, houses, papers, and effects, against unreasonable searches and seizures, shall not be violated, and no Warrants shall issue, but upon probable cause, supported by Oath or affirmation, and particularly describing the place to be searched, and the persons or things to be seized.

Amendment V. No person shall be held to answer for a capital, or otherwise infamous crime, unless on a presentment or indictment of a Grand Jury, except in cases arising in the land or naval forces, or in the Militia, when in actual service in time of War or public danger; nor shall any person be subject for the same offence to be twice put in jeopardy of life or limb; nor shall be compelled in any criminal case to be a witness against himself, nor be deprived of life, liberty, or property, without due process of law; nor shall private property be taken for public use, without just compensation.

Amendment VI. In all criminal prosecutions, the accused shall enjoy the right to a speedy and public trial, by an impartial jury of the State and district wherein the crime shall have been committed, which district shall have been previously ascertained by law, and to be informed of the nature and cause of the accusation; to be confronted with the witnesses against him; to have compulsory process for obtaining witnesses in his favor, and to have the Assistance of Counsel for his defense.

Amendment VII. In Suits at common law, where the value in controversy shall exceed 20 dollars, the right of trial by jury shall be preserved, and no fact tried by a jury, shall be otherwise re-examined in any Court of the United States, than according to the rules of the common law.

Amendment VIII. Excessive bail shall not be required, nor excessive fines imposed, nor cruel and unusual punishments inflicted.

Amendment IX. The enumeration in the Constitution, of certain rights, shall not be construed to deny or disparage others retained by the people.

Amendment X. The powers not delegated to the United States by the Constitution, nor prohibited by it to the States, are reserved to the States respectively, or to the people. *See also* **Fourteenth Amendment**

Billy the Kid *see* McCarty, Henry

Binding Authority

A new principle of law announced by an appellate court constitutes precedent and binding authority on all lower courts. Binding authority means that a lower court must follow a principle of law announced by a higher court.

In order for an appellate court's decision to have binding authority on a lower court, the lower court must come within the jurisdiction of the appellate court. For example, a new principle of law announced by the Georgia Supreme Court is not binding on the trial courts of Texas, because the Texas trial courts are not under the jurisdiction of the Georgia Supreme Court. If a Texas trial court decided to follow a rule of law announced by the Georgia Supreme Court, it would do so because it found the rule of law to be persuasive authority.

The only appellate court in the nation whose decisions can be binding authority on all courts in the country, is the United States Supreme Court. However, the United State Supreme Court's nation-wide authority only comes into play when it makes a ruling grounded in the Federal Constitution. A decision by the United States Supreme Court that is not based on the Constitution has binding authority only on Federal courts.

Binding/Nonbinding Jury Sentencing Determination

Although a majority of capital punishment jurisdictions permit the use of a jury at the penalty phase, the actual decision made by a capital penalty phase jury is not constitutionally required to be followed by the trial judge. That is, the Federal Constitution does not prohibit a trial judge from overriding a jury's recommendation to sentence a capital felon to life imprisonment, and impose a sentence of death instead. As a general rule, it is only when facts suggesting a sentence of death are so clear and convincing, that virtually no reasonable person could differ on a sentence of death, may a trial judge override a jury's recommendation of life imprisonment and impose death.

An Indiana jury recommended life imprisonment for Benny Saylor during the penalty phase of his capital prosecution. However, the trial judge rejected the recommendation and sentenced him to death on February 17, 1994. (Indiana Department of Corrections)

While there is no constitutional right to have a penalty phase jury's decision followed, a majority of jurisdictions that utilize penalty phase juries require that judges impose the verdict returned by the jury. These jurisdictions are called binding jurisdictions. Five jurisdictions, Alabama, Delaware, Florida, Indiana, and Ohio permit trial judges to override the penalty phase jury's verdict and impose a different sentence. These jurisdictions are called nonbinding jurisdictions. *See also* **Harris v. Alabama; Spaziano v. Florida**

Bind Over *see* Preliminary Hearing

Bird v. United States (I)

Court: United States Supreme Court; *Case Citation:* Bird v. United States, 180 U.S. 356 (1901); *Argued:* January 21, 1901; *Decided:* February 25, 1901; *Opinion of the Court:* Justice Shiras; *Concurring Opinion:* None; *Dissenting Opinion:* None; *Appellate Defense Counsel:* L. T. Michener argued; W. W. Dudley on brief; *Appellate Prosecution Counsel:* Mr. Beck argued and briefed; *Amicus Curiae Brief Supporting Prosecutor:* None; *Amicus Curiae Brief Supporting Defendant:* None.

Issue Presented: Whether the trial court properly instructed the jury on the law of self-defense?

Case Holding: The trial court did not properly instruct the jury on the law of self-defense, therefore the judgment against the defendant could not stand.

Factual and procedural background of case: The defendant, Homer Bird, was convicted of capital murder and sentenced to death by the United States. The defendant filed an appeal with the United States Supreme Court, alleging that the trial court improperly instructed the jury on the law of self-defense. The United States Supreme Court granted certiorari to consider the issue.

Opinion of the Court by Justice Shiras: Justice Shiras noted that the issue of whether the defendant killed the victim was not in dispute. The question was whether the killing was justified as self-defense. Justice Harlan found that the following instruction given by the trial court on the issue of self-defense was erroneous:

> The court instructs the jury, if they believe from the evidence beyond a reasonable doubt that the defendant Homer Bird, on the 27th day of September, 1898, at a point on the Yukon river, about 2 miles below the coal mine known as Camp Dewey and about 85 miles above Anvik and within the district of Alaska, shot and killed one J. H. Hurlin, and that said killing was malicious, premeditated, and wilful, and that said killing was not in the necessary defense of the defendant's life or to prevent the infliction upon him of great bodily harm, then it is your duty to find the defendant guilty as charged in the indictment.

Justice Shiras pointed out that the jury instruction was only a partial statement of the law. The instruction should also have said "that if the defendant believed, and had reason to believe, that the killing was necessary for the defense of his life or to prevent the infliction upon him of great bodily harm, then he was not guilty." Justice Shiras concluded that "[i]t is well settled that the defendant has a right to a full statement of the law from the court, and that a neglect to give such full statement, when the jury consequently fall into error, is sufficient reason for reversal." The judgment of the Federal District Court was reversed and the case remanded for a new trial. *See also* **Bird v. United States (II); Jury Instructions**

Bird v. United States (II)
Court: United States Supreme Court; *Case Citation:* Bird v. United States, 187 U.S. 118 (1902); *Argued:* October 14, 1902; *Decided:* November 17, 1902; *Opinion of the Court:* Justice McKenna; *Concurring Opinion:* None; *Dissenting Opinion:* None; *Appellate Defense Counsel:* L. T. Michener argued; W. W. Dudley on brief; *Appellate Prosecution Counsel:* Mr. Beck argued; Charles H. Robb on brief; *Amicus Curiae Brief Supporting Prosecutor:* None; *Amicus Curiae Brief Supporting Defendant:* None.

Issue Presented: Whether the trial court committed error in refusing to instruct the jury on accomplice liability principles?

Case Holding: The trial court did not commit error in refusing to instruct the jury on accomplice liability principles, because no evidence was presented which warranted such an instruction.

Factual and procedural background of case: The defendant, Homer Bird, was convicted of capital murder and sentenced to death by the United States. The defendant filed an appeal with the United States Supreme Court. The Supreme Court reversed the judgment and awarded a new trial, because the trial court improperly instructed the jury on the defense of self-defense. At the defendant's second trial he was again convicted and sentenced to death. The defendant filed a second appeal with the United States Supreme Court, alleging the trial court committed error in refusing to instruct the jury on accomplice liability principles. The United States Supreme Court granted certiorari to consider the issue.

Opinion of the Court by Justice McKenna: Justice McKenna held that the trial court correctly refused to instruct the jury on accomplice liability principles. The opinion pointed out that two witnesses were present when the defendant killed the victim. Both witnesses testified against the defendant. Consequently, the defendant sought to make the two witnesses accomplices, in order to discredit their testimony. Justice McKenna found that the defendant's own testimony precluded a jury instruction on accomplice liability principles, because his defense was self-defense. The opinion concluded that "[a]ssuming, without deciding, that the instruction requested expressed the law correctly, it was nevertheless rightly refused, because there were no facts in the case to justify it." The judgment of the Federal trial court was affirmed. *See also* **Bird v. United States (I); Jury Instructions**

Bittaker, Lawrence *see* Murder Mack

Black, Hugo L.
Hugo L. Black served as an associate justice of the United States Supreme Court from 1937 to 1971. While on the Supreme Court Black was known as a moderate who maintained an intractable belief that the Bill of Rights were intended to curtail the authority of States over their citizens.

Black was born in Harlan, Alabama on February 27, 1886. His higher education began at a medical college, but he soon lost interest and enrolled at the University of Alabama Law School, where he graduated in 1906. Black's early legal career was spent in private practice and as a prosecutor. In 1917 he joined the Army and rose to the rank of captain before resigning his commission. After leaving the Army Black resumed a private law practice until his election to the United States Senate in 1926. Eleven years later, in 1937, President Franklin D. Roosevelt nominated Black to the Supreme Court.

While on the Supreme Court Black wrote a number of capital punishment opinions. The capital punishment opinion by Black which best exemplified his belief in the supremacy of the Bill of Rights over States, was *Chambers v. Florida*. The decision in *Chambers* involved several African American defendants who were sentenced to death for capital murder. The defendants argued on appeal that their confessions were extracted in violation of the Constitution. Black, writing for the Court, agreed with the defendants. In reversing the judgments against the defendants, Black wrote:

> The scope and operation of the Fourteenth Amendment have been fruitful sources of controversy in our constitutional history. However, in view of its historical setting and the wrongs which

called it into being, the due process provision of the Fourteenth Amendment — just as that in the Fifth — has led few to doubt that it was intended to guarantee procedural standards adequate and appropriate, then and thereafter, to protect, at all times, people charged with or suspected of crime by those holding positions of power and authority. Tyrannical governments had immemorially utilized dictatorial criminal procedure and punishment to make scape goats of the weak, or of helpless political, religious, or racial minorities and those who differed, who would not conform and who resisted tyranny. The instruments of such governments were in the main, two. Conduct, innocent when engaged in, was subsequently made by fiat criminally punishable without legislation. And a liberty loving people won the principle that criminal punishments could not be inflicted save for that which proper legislative action had already by "the law of the land" forbidden when done. But even more was needed. From the popular hatred and abhorrence of illegal confinement, torture and extortion of confessions of violations of the "law of the land" evolved the fundamental idea that no man's life, liberty or property be forfeited as criminal punishment for violation of that law until there had been a charge fairly made and fairly tried in a public tribunal free of prejudice, passion, excitement and tyrannical power. Thus, as assurance against ancient evils, our country, in order to preserve "the blessings of liberty", wrote into its basic law the requirement, among others, that the forfeiture of the lives, liberties or property of people accused of crime can only follow if procedural safeguards of due process have been obeyed.

Black resigned from the Supreme Court on September 17, 1971, after serving one of the longest tenures in the Court's history. Within eight days of his resignation Black died.

Capital Punishment Opinions Written by Black

Case Name	Opinion of the Court	Concurring Opinion	Dissenting Opinion	Concurring and Dissenting
Adamson v. California			✓	
Avery v. Alabama	✓			
Brown v. Allen			✓	
Chambers v. Florida	✓			
Eubanks v. Louisiana	✓			
Green v. United States	✓			
Jackson v. Denno				✓
Leyra v. Denno	✓			
Lisenba v. California			✓	
McGautha v. California		✓		
Patton v. Mississippi	✓			
Phyle v. Duffy	✓			
Pierre v. Louisiana	✓			
Robinson v. United States	✓			
Rosenberg v. United States			✓	
Solesbee v. Balkcom	✓			
Stein v. New York			✓	
Stewart v. United States	✓			
White v. Texas	✓			
Williams v. New York	✓			

Blackmun, Harry A. Harry A. Blackmun served as an associate justice of the United States Supreme Court from 1970 to 1994. Blackmun started out on the Supreme Court with a conservative philosophy that eventually was transformed into a liberal ideology and interpretation of the Constitution, with respect to individual liberties and rights.

Blackmun was born in Nashville, Illinois, on November 12, 1908. His family would eventually move to St. Paul, Minnesota, where Blackmun met his childhood friend Warren Earl Burger (former Supreme Court chief justice). Blackmun attended Harvard University, where he obtained a degree in mathematics. In 1932 he graduated from Harvard Law School.

After leaving law school he was a clerk briefly for a Federal Court of Appeals judge, before going into private practice. During his years in private practice Blackmun managed to find time to teach law courses at St. Paul College of Law and at the University of Minnesota Law School. In 1959 President Dwight D. Eisenhower nominated Blackmun to the Federal Court of Appeals for the Eighth Circuit. As an appeals court judge Blackmun horned a reputation as a conservative jurist. In 1970 President Richard M. Nixon nominated Blackmun for a position on the Supreme Court.

During Blackmun's tenure on the Supreme Court he issued a significant number of capital punishment opinions. Blackmun approached capital punishment cases in three stages of his judicial development in this area. In the first stage he was conservative and leaned toward the government's position. In the second stage he shifted toward the center and began to question blanket denial of basic constitutional rights to capital defendants. Near the end of his judicial career Blackmun swung to the left and denounced capital punishment as a violation of the Constitution. Examples of Blackmun's shift away from his conservative philosophy include *McCleskey v. Kemp*, where he argued in dissent that "[t]he Court today sanctions the execution of a man despite his presentation of evidence that establishes a constitutionally intolerable level of racially based discrimination leading to the imposition of his death sentence." He dissented tersely in *Barclay v. Florida*, a case questioning the Florida Supreme Court's review of a death sentence, by writing that "[t]he errors and missteps — intentional or otherwise — come close to making a mockery of the Florida statute and are too much for me to condone." Finally, in *Walton v. Arizona*, a case involving restrictions on evidence by capital defendants at the penalty phase, Blackmun wrote in dissent: "In my view, two Arizona statutory provisions, pertinent here, run afoul of the established Eighth Amendment principle that a capital defendant is entitled to an individualized sentencing determination which involves the consideration of all relevant mitigating evidence. The first is the requirement that the sentencer may consider only those mitigating circumstances proved by a preponderance of the evidence. The second is the provision that the defendant bears the burden of establishing mitigating circumstances 'sufficiently substantial to call for leniency.' I also conclude that Arizona's 'heinous, cruel or depraved' aggravating circumstance, as construed by the Arizona Supreme Court, provides no meaningful guidance to the sentencing authority and, as a consequence, is unconstitutional." Blackmun died March 4, 1999.

Capital Punishment Opinions Written by Blackmun

Case Name	Opinion of the Court	Plurality Opinion	Concurring Opinion	Dissenting Opinion	Concurring and Dissenting
Arave v. Creech				✓	
Baldwin v. Alabama	✓				
Barclay v. Florida				✓	
Barefoot v. Estelle				✓	
Bullington v. Missouri	✓				
Burger v. Kemp				✓	
Cabana v. Bullock				✓	
California v. Brown				✓	
California v. Ramos				✓	
Clemons v. Mississippi					✓
Coleman v. Thompson				✓	
Darden v. Wainwright				✓	
Dawson v. Delaware			✓		
Dugger v. Adams				✓	
Furman v. Georgia				✓	
Godinez v. Moran				✓	
Gray v. Mississippi	✓				
Herrera v. Collins				✓	
Lewis v. Jeffers				✓	
Lockett v. Ohio			✓		
McCleskey v. Kemp				✓	
McFarland v. Scott	✓				
McKoy v. North Carolina			✓		
Mills v. Maryland	✓				
Moore v. Illinois	✓				
Roberts v. Louisiana (II)				✓	
Romano v. Oklahoma				✓	
Sawyer v. Whitley			✓		
Schiro v. Farley				✓	
Simmons v. South Carolina		✓			
Spaziano v. Florida	✓				
Sumner v. Shuman	✓				
Tuilaepa v. California				✓	
Victor v. Nebraska					✓
Walton v. Arizona				✓	
Witherspoon v. Illinois				✓	

Bolivia Bolivia's constitution of 1961 abolished capital punishment. However, capital punishment was restored in October 1971, for terrorism, kidnapping, and crimes against government and security personnel. In 1981 the death penalty was extended to drug trafficking. Bolivia abolished capital punishment for ordinary crimes in 1997, but still retains the death penalty for exceptional crimes. Bolivia uses the firing squad as the method of execution. A death sentence may not be carried out until the nation's president decides against commutation. The president may commute the death penalty to 30 years at hard labor. Its legal system is based on Spanish law and the Napoleonic Code. The constitution of Bolivia was revised in August of 1994.

The judicial system of Bolivia consists of a Supreme Court of Justice and Superior District Courts. The Supreme Court of Justice is composed of a president and 11 justices. The legal system in Bolivia does not provide for trial by jury. Defendants are presumed innocent until proven guilty, have a right to a public trial, a right to retained or appointed legal counsel, the right to confront witnesses, to present evidence, to appeal a judicial decision, and may be granted bail. *See also* **International Capital Punishment Nations**

Bonin, William *see* **Freeway Killer**

Booth v. Maryland *Court:* United States Supreme Court; *Case Citation:* Booth v. Maryland, 482 U.S. 496 (1987); *Argued:* March 24, 1987; *Decided:* June 15, 1987; *Opinion of the Court:* Justice Powell; *Concurring Opinion:* None; *Dissenting Opinion:* Justice White, in which Rehnquist, C. J., and O'Connor and Scalia, JJ., joined; *Dissenting Opinion:* Justice Scalia, in which Rehnquist, C. J., and White and O'Connor, JJ., joined; *Appellate Defense Counsel:* George E. Burns, Jr. argued; Alan H. Murrell and Julia Doyle Bernhardt on brief; *Appellate Prosecution Counsel:* Charles O. Monk II argued; J. Joseph Curran, Jr. and Valerie V. Cloutier on brief; *Amicus Curiae Brief Supporting Prosecutor:* 1; *Amicus Curiae Brief Supporting Defendant:* 1.

Issue Presented: Whether use of victim impact statements by the prosecutor during the penalty phase violated the Constitution?

Case Holding: Use of victim impact statements by the prosecutor during the penalty phase violated the Constitution, because such information served only to inflame the decisionmaking process of the jury.

Factual and procedural background of case: The defendant, John Booth, was convicted of two capital murders by the State of Maryland. During the penalty phase the jury was allowed to consider victim impact statements, which concerned the hardship caused on family members by the victims' death. The jury sentenced the defendant to death. The Maryland Court of Appeals affirmed the judgment. In doing so, the appellate court rejected the defendant's contention that use of the victim impact statements violated the Federal Constitution. The United States Supreme Court granted certiorari to consider the issue.

Opinion of the Court by Justice Powell: Justice Powell held that the introduction of the victim impact statements at the penalty phase violated the Eighth Amendment. It was said that such information was irrelevant to a capital sentencing decision. Justice Powell found that admission of victim impact statements created a constitutionally unacceptable risk that the jury might impose the death penalty in an arbitrary and capricious manner. It was reasoned that such information might be wholly unrelated to the blameworthiness of a particular defendant, and could cause the sentencing decision to turn on irrelevant factors such as the degree to which the victim's family was willing and able to articulate its grief, or the relative worth of the victim's character. It was concluded that the admission of family members' emotionally charged opinions and characterizations of the crimes could serve no other purpose than to inflame the jury and divert it from deciding the case on the relevant evidence concerning the crime and the defendant. Such admission was therefore inconsistent with the rational decisionmaking required in capital cases. The judgment of the Maryland Court of Appeals was reversed, to the extent that it affirmed the capital sentence.

Dissenting opinion by Justice White, in which Rehnquist, C. J., and O'Connor and Scalia, JJ., joined: Justice White dissented from the Court's decision. He argued that victim impact statements represented a constitutionally acceptable manner of letting the jury know the full extent of the harm caused by the defendant. Justice White stated his position as follows:

> The Court's judgment is based on the premises that the harm that a murderer causes a victim's family does not in general reflect on his blameworthiness, and that only evidence going to blameworthiness is relevant to the capital sentencing decision. Many if not most jurors, however, will look less favorably on a capital defendant when they appreciate the full extent of the harm he caused, including the harm to the victim's family. There is nothing aberrant in a juror's inclination to hold a murderer accountable not only for his internal disposition in committing the crime but also for the full extent of the harm he caused; many if not most persons would also agree, for example, that someone who drove his car recklessly through a stoplight and unintentionally killed a pedestrian merits significantly more punishment than someone who drove his car recklessly through the same stoplight at a time when no pedestrian was there to be hit. I am confident that the Court would not overturn a sentence for reckless homicide by automobile merely because the punishment exceeded the maximum sentence for reckless driving; and I would hope that the Court would not overturn the sentence in such a case if a judge mentioned, as relevant to his sentencing decision, the fact that the victim was a mother or father. But if punishment can be enhanced in noncapital cases on the basis of the harm caused, irrespective of the offender's specific intention to cause such harm, I fail to see why the same approach is unconstitutional in death cases. If anything, I would think that victim impact statements are particularly appropriate evidence in capital sentencing hearings: the State has a legitimate interest in counteracting the mitigating evidence which the defendant is entitled to put in, by reminding the sentencer that just as the murderer should be considered as an individual, so too the victim is an individual whose death represents a unique loss to society and in particular to his family.

Dissenting opinion by Justice Scalia, in which Rehnquist, C. J., and White and O'Connor, JJ., joined: Justice Scalia dissented from the Court's decision. He stated his objections as follows:

> ... The Court's opinion does not explain why a defendant's eligibility for the death sentence can (and always does) turn upon considerations not relevant to his moral guilt. If a bank robber aims his gun at a guard, pulls the trigger, and kills his target, he may be put to death. If the gun unexpectedly misfires, he may not. His moral guilt in both cases is identical, but his responsibility in the former is greater. Less than two months ago, we held that two brothers who planned and assisted in their father's escape from prison could be sentenced to death because in the course of the escape their father and an accomplice murdered a married couple and two children. Had their father allowed the victims to live, the brothers could not be put to death; but because he decided to kill, the brothers may. The difference between life and death for these two defendants was thus a matter "wholly unrelated to the[ir] blameworthiness." But it was related to their personal responsibility, i. e., to the degree of harm that they had caused. In sum, the principle upon which the Court's opinion rests — that the imposition of capital punishment is to be determined solely on the basis of moral guilt — does not exist, neither in the text of the Constitution, nor in the historic practices of our society, nor even in the opinions of this Court.

Case note: The decision in the case was short lived, as the Court eventually overruled the opinion and held that victim impact statements may be introduced during the penalty phase. *See also* **California v. Brown; Payne v. Tennessee; South Carolina v. Gathers**

Bosnia-Herzegovina   In 1997 Bosnia-Herzegovina abolished capital punishment for ordinary crimes, but retained the punishment for exceptional offenses. The firing squad is used by Bosnia-Herzegovina to carry out the death penalty. The legal system of Bosnia-Herzegovina is based on the civil law system. The 1995 Dayton Accords provided for creation of Bosnia and Herzegovina as a single nation (they had previously been one of the republics of Yugoslavia). The Dayton Accords established a constitution for the nation that includes a central government with a bicameral legislature, a three-member presidency (consisting of a Bosniak, a Serb, and a Croat), and a constitutional court.

The judicial structure of the nation consists of municipal courts (which have original jurisdiction in most criminal cases), cantonal courts (which have appellate jurisdiction), and three federal courts (Constitutional, Supreme, and Human Rights). Defendants have the right to a public trial and the right to legal counsel. *See also* **International Capital Punishment Nations**

"Born to Raise Hell" *see* **Speck, Richard**

Boston Strangler   Thirteen women were sexually assaulted and murdered in the Boston area between June of 1962 and January of 1964. As the murders surfaced the media drew the public's attention to the crimes by calling the killer the "Boston Strangler." The identity of the Boston Strangler was unknown to authorities until the arrest of Albert DeSalvo in November of 1964.

DeSalvo was born on September 3, 1931 in Chelsea, Massachusetts. Although DeSalvo developed a juvenile record while

Albert DeSalvo confessed to being the infamous Boston Stranger. (Cambridge Police)

growing up, he was not considered a dangerous youth. Upon reaching adulthood he joined the Army in 1948. DeSalvo left the Army in 1956 and returned to Massachusetts with a German wife.

After DeSalvo returned to civilian life he had several arrests for breaking and entering during the period 1957 and 1960. In spite of his encounters with the law, DeSalvo maintained steady employment and appeared to be a devoted family man. The appearance of hardworking family man was torn asunder in 1964, after DeSalvo was arrested on sexual assault charges. While in custody DeSalvo confessed to being the infamous Boston Strangler.

Although authorities believed DeSalvo was the Boston Strangler, he was not prosecuted for the capital murders (his confession was taken under circumstances that would not permit its use at a trial). Instead, on January 10, 1967, DeSalvo was prosecuted for a series of sexual assault crimes. He was convicted of the sexual assault crimes and sentenced to life in prison. DeSalvo was stabbed to death while in prison in November of 1973.

Botched Execution Implementing the death penalty is not an exact science. Mistakes are made wherein a capital felon is not put to death after the method of death is inflicted. When this occurs, authorities may make a second or subsequent attempt at executing the capital felon. The crucial constitutional issue involved in making subsequent attempts to carry out an execution, involves the reason for the initial failure. So long as the initial or any subsequent failure is due to an honest mistake, further attempts may ensue. The Federal Constitution prohibits authorities from purposely tormenting a capital felon by intentionally botching an initial attempt at execution. *See also* **Francis v. Resweber**

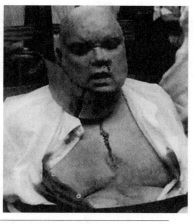

The botched electrocution execution of Allen Davis by the State of Florida on July 8, 1999, was a factor in causing the State to enact legislation in January 2000, that gives condemned defendants an option of death by lethal injection or electrocution. Allen bleed profusely from his nose during the execution. (Florida Department of Corrections)

BOTCHED EXECUTIONS 1976–1999

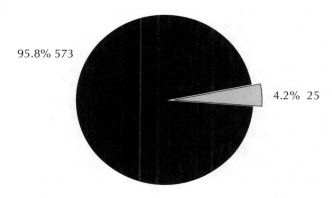

95.8% 573

4.2% 25

■ BOTCHED EXECUTIONS
■ EXECUTIONS CORRECTLY PERFORMED

Botched Executions 1976–1999

Name	Date of Execution	State	Execution Method	Problem
John Evans	4/22/83	AL	electrocution	electrocuted twice
Jimmy L. Gray	9/2/83	MS	lethal gas	beat head on steel pole
Alpha O. Stephens	12/12/84	GA	electrocution	electrocuted twice
Stephen P. Morin	3/13/85	TX	lethal injection	unable to find vein
William E. Vandiver	10/16/85	IN	electrocution	electrocuted three times
Randy Woolls	8/20/86	TX	lethal injection	unable to find vein
Elliott Johnson	6/24/87	TX	lethal injection	unable to find vein
Raymond Landry	12/13/88	TX	lethal injection	syringe popped out of vein
Stephen McCoy	5/24/89	TX	lethal injection	insufficient dose of drugs
Horace F. Dunkins	7/14/89	AL	electrocution	electrocuted twice
Jesse J. Tafero	5/4/90	FL	electrocution	headpiece caught fire
Wilbert L. Evans	10/17/90	VA	electrocution	blood burst from face
Derick L. Peterson	8/22/91	VA	electrocution	electrocuted twice
Rickey R. Rector	1/24/92	AR	lethal injection	unable to find vein
Robyn L. Parks	3/10/92	OK	lethal injection	too much drug used
Billy W. White	4/23/92	TX	lethal injection	unable to find vein
Justin L. May	5/7/92	TX	lethal injection	too much drug used
John W. Gacy	5/10/94	IL	lethal injection	tube clogged
Emmitt Foster	5/3/95	MO	lethal injection	straps on inmate too tight
Tommie Smith	7/18/96	IN	lethal injection	unable to find vein
Pedro Medina	3/25/97	FL	electrocution	headpiece caught fire
Scott Carpenter	5/8/97	OK	lethal injection	too much drug used
Michael Elkins	6/13/97	SC	lethal injection	unable to find vein
Joseph Cannon	4/23/98	TX	lethal injection	syringe popped out
Allen L. Davis	7/8/99	FL	electrocution	blood poured from nose

Botswana Botswana imposes capital punishment. Botswana uses hanging as the method of carrying out the death penalty. Its legal system is based on Roman-Dutch law and local customary law. The constitution of Botswana was made effective September 30, 1966. Botswana is a multiparty democracy. Constitutional power is shared between an executive, unicameral legislature, and judiciary.

The judicial structure of Botswana consists of both civil and customary court systems. The civil court system is composed of a Court of Appeal, High Court, and Magistrate Court. Under Botswana's constitution every defendant is entitled to due process, the presumption of innocence, and freedom from arbitrary arrest. Defendants charged with noncapital offenses are released on their own recognizance. Detention without bail is mandated in capital cases. Defendants have the right to counsel and, in capital cases, indigent defendants have the right to appointed counsel. *See also* **International Capital Punishment Nations**

Boulden v. Holman *Court:* United States Supreme Court; *Case Citation:* Boulden v. Holman, 394 U.S. 478 (1969); *Argued:* February 26, 1969; *Decided:* April 2, 1969; *Opinion of the Court:* Justice Stewart; *Concurring Statement:* Justice Black; *Concurring and Dissenting Opinion:* Justice Harlan, in which Burger, C.J., and Marshall, J., joined; *Justice Taking No Part in Decision:* Justice Fortas; *Appellate Defense Counsel:* William B. Moore, Jr. argued and briefed; *Appellate Prosecution Counsel:* David W. Clark argued; MacDonald Gallion on brief; *Amicus Curiae Brief Supporting Prosecutor:* None; *Amicus Curiae Brief Supporting Defendant:* None.

Issue Presented: Whether the defendant's confession was properly introduced into evidence by the prosecutor?

Case Holding: The defendant's confession was properly introduced into evidence by the prosecutor. However, because of an issue not raised in the lower courts involving a *Witherspoon v. Illinois* jury selection violation, the defendant's conviction would be set aside and the case remanded.

Factual and procedural background of case: The defendant, Boulden, was convicted of capital murder and sentenced to death by the State of Alabama. The Alabama Supreme Court affirmed the conviction and sentence. The defendant filed a habeas corpus petition in a Federal District Court alleging that his conviction was invalid because the prosecutor introduced into evidence his unlawfully obtained confession. After a full hearing the District Court found the confession voluntary. A Federal Court of Appeals affirmed. The United States Supreme Court granted certiorari to consider the issue.

Opinion of the Court by Justice Stewart: Justice Stewart found that the confession was voluntary and therefore admissible into evidence. However, the opinion found that an issue raised for the first time by the defendant, involving jury selection, warranted reversing and remanding the case.

At the time the defendant's case was brought to the Court, the Court rendered its decision in *Witherspoon v. Illinois,* wherein it was held that a sentence of death could not be carried out if the jury that imposed or recommended the sentence was chosen by excluding potential jurors for "cause" simply because they voiced general objections to the death penalty or expressed conscientious or religious scruples against its infliction. Justice Stewart found that *Witherspoon* was violated in the defendant's case.

During jury selection in the defendant's case, Alabama had a statute which expressly required rejection of potential jurors that had a fixed opinion against capital punishment. As a result of this statute the trial court removed 15 potential jurors. Justice Stewart wrote that under *Witherspoon's* standard the most that could be demanded of potential jurors is that they be willing to consider all of the penalties provided by law, and that they not be irrevocably committed, before the trial has begun, to vote against the penalty of death regardless of the facts and circumstances that might emerge in the course of the proceedings. The opinion indicated that if a potential juror was excluded on any broader basis than the *Witherspoon* standard, the death sentence cannot be carried out. In view of the *Witherspoon* violation, the Court reversed the judgment of the Court of Appeals and remanded the case to the District Court for a full evidentiary hearing on the *Witherspoon* violation.

Concurring Statement Justice Black: Justice Black issued a statement concurring in the Court's opinion and judgment.

Concurring and dissenting opinion by Justice Harlan, in which Burger, C.J., and Marshall, J., joined: Justice Harlan issued an opinion concurring in the Court's decision to remand the case for a *Witherspoon* hearing. However, he dissented from the Court's ruling that the confession was voluntary. Justice Harlan believed that the issue of the defendant's confession was not thoroughly reviewed by the lower courts and that, consequently, the Court should have remanded that issue as well. *See also* **Witherspoon v. Illinois**

Boyde v. California *Court:* United States Supreme Court; *Case Citation:* Boyde v. California, 494 U.S. 370 (1990); *Argued:* November 28, 1989; *Decided:* March 5, 1990; *Opinion of the Court:* Chief Justice Rehnquist; *Concurring Opinion:* None; *Dissenting Opinion:* Justice Marshall, J., in which Brennan, Blackmun and Stevens, JJ., joined; *Appellate Defense Counsel:* Dennis A. Fischer argued; John M. Bishop on brief; *Appellate Prosecution Counsel:* Frederick R. Millar, Jr. argued; John K. Van de Kamp, Richard B. Iglehart, Harley D. Mayfield, and Jay M. Bloom on brief; *Amicus Curiae Brief Supporting Prosecutor:* 2; *Amicus Curiae Brief Supporting Defendant:* 1.

Issue Presented: Whether two standard capital punishment penalty phase jury instructions used by California were ambiguous and prevented the jury from considering relevant evidence in violation of the Constitution?

Case Holding: When a capital defendant makes a claim that a jury instruction is ambiguous and therefore subject to erroneous interpretation, the test to be used is whether there is a reasonable likelihood that the jury has applied the instruction in a way that prevents the consideration of constitutionally relevant evidence.

Factual and procedural background of case: The defendant, Richard Boyde, was found guilty by a jury in the murder of Dickie Gibson on January 15, 1981. During the penalty phase the trial court read instructions to the jury that included two standard capital punishment jury instructions. One instruction listed 11 factors that the jury "shall" consider in determining whether to impose a sentence of death or life imprisonment, the last of which was the so-called "unadorned version" that read: "Any other circumstance which extenuates the gravity of the crime even though it is not a legal excuse for the crime."

The second jury instruction told the jury to consider all applicable aggravating and mitigating circumstances, and directed that it "shall" impose a sentence either of death or of life imprisonment depending upon whether the aggravating circumstances outweighed the mitigating circumstances or vice versa. The jury imposed the death sentence.

The California Supreme Court affirmed the conviction and sentence. In doing so, it rejected the defendant's contention that the aforementioned jury instructions were ambiguous and violated the Constitution. The United States Supreme Court granted certiorari to consider the issue.

Opinion of the Court by Chief Justice Rehnquist: Chief Justice Rehnquist held that the mandatory nature of the language of the jury instruction did not prevent the jury from making an individualized assessment of the appropriateness of death penalty. The instructions satisfied the Constitution insofar as they permitted the jury to consider all relevant mitigating evidence. The decision ruled that there was no constitutional basis for the defendant's contention that the jury must have unfettered discretion to decline to impose the death penalty even if it decides that the aggravating circumstances outweigh the mitigating circumstances. The Chief Justice indicated that "States are free to structure and shape consideration of mitigating evidence to achieve a more rational and equitable administration of the death penalty."

Focusing on the specific issue presented by the case, the opinion ruled that when a claim is made by a capital defendant that a jury instruction is ambiguous and therefore subject to erroneous interpretation, the test to be used is whether there is a reasonable likelihood that the jury has applied the instruction in a way that prevents the consideration of constitutionally relevant evidence. It was said that "[a]lthough a defendant need not establish that the jury was more likely than not to have been impermissibly inhibited by the instruction, a capital sentencing proceeding does not violate the Eighth Amendment if there is only a possibility of such an inhibition."

Applying the "reasonable likelihood" test to the facts of the case, the Chief Justice found that there was no showing by the defendant that there was a reasonable likelihood that the jurors interpreted the trial court's instructions to preclude consideration of mitigating evidence proffered by him. The in-

structions directed the jury to consider any other circumstance that might excuse a crime. It was said that "reasonable jurors surely would not have felt constrained by the ... instruction to ignore all of Boyde's unobjected-to penalty-phase evidence ... particularly since the jury was also instructed that it 'shall consider all of the evidence ... received during any part of the trial.'" The decision of the California Supreme Court was affirmed.

Dissenting opinion by Justice Marshall, in which Brennan, Blackmun and Stevens, JJ., joined: Justice Marshall pointed out that "[i]t is a bedrock principle of our capital punishment jurisprudence that, in deciding whether to impose a sentence of death, a sentencer must consider not only the nature of the offense but also the 'character and propensities of the offender.'" The dissent interpreted the majority's opinion as holding that the defendant's death sentence must be affirmed even if the penalty phase jury reasonably could have believed that it could not consider mitigating evidence regarding his character and background.

The dissent rejected the majority's adoption and use of a "reasonable likelihood" test to analyze the issue presented. It was said that the majority's approach "is inconsistent with our longstanding focus, in reviewing challenged instructions in all criminal contexts, on whether a juror could reasonably interpret the instructions in an unconstitutional manner. By adopting its unprecedented standard, the majority places too much of the risk of error in capital sentencing on the defendant." The dissent concluded that under traditional jury instruction analysis, the defendant's death sentence would have been reversed.

Boykin v. Alabama

Court: United States Supreme Court; *Case Citation:* Boykin v. Alabama, 395 U.S. 238 (1969); *Argued:* March 4, 1969; *Decided:* June 2, 1969; *Opinion of the Court:* Justice Douglas; *Concurring Opinion:* None; *Dissenting Opinion:* Justice Harlan, in which Black, J., joined; *Appellate Defense Counsel:* E. Graham Gibbons argued; Stephen A. Hopkins on brief; *Appellate Prosecution Counsel:* David W. Clark argued; MacDonald Gallion on brief; *Amicus Curiae Brief Supporting Prosecutor:* None; *Amicus Curiae Brief Supporting Defendant:* 1.

Issue Presented: Whether the defendant's guilty pleas to capital offenses were constitutionally void because the trial record failed to disclose that the guilty pleas were made intelligently and voluntarily?

Case Holding: The defendant's guilty pleas to capital offenses were constitutionally void because the trial record failed to disclose that the guilty pleas were made intelligently and voluntarily.

Factual and procedural background of case: The defendant, Boykin, was indicted by the State of Alabama on five counts of robbery. The maximum punishment for robbery was the death penalty. The defendant plead guilty to each robbery charge. Under State law it was required that a jury fix punishment when a defendant entered a guilty plea. A jury imposed the death penalty for each charge. The Alabama Supreme Court affirmed the convictions and sentences. The United States Supreme Court granted certiorari to consider the voluntariness of the defendant's guilty pleas.

Opinion of the Court by Justice Douglas: Justice Douglas held that the Constitution required the record to reflect an affirmative showing that a guilty plea was intelligently and voluntarily made. It was said that this stringent requirement was necessary because several constitutional rights are involved when a plea of guilty is entered, including (1) the privilege against compulsory self-incrimination, (2) the right to trial by jury, and (3) the right to confront one's accusers. Justice Douglas stated that relinquishment of these rights could not be presumed from a silent record. The opinion concluded that the defendant's guilty pleas constituted reversible error because the record did not disclose that the defendant voluntarily and understandingly entered his pleas of guilty. The judgment of the Alabama Supreme Court was reversed.

Dissenting opinion by Justice Harlan, in which Black, J., joined: Justice Harlan dissented from the Court's decision. He argued that the Court was wrong to constitutionalize the requirement that a trial record must reflect that a guilty plea was intelligently and voluntarily made. Justice Harlan wrote that "[t]he Court .... in effect fastens upon the States, as a matter of federal constitutional law, the rigid prophylactic requirements of Rule 11 of the Federal Rules of Criminal Procedure." It was further contended that "the Court does all this at the behest of a [defendant] who has never at any time alleged that his guilty plea was involuntary or made without knowledge of the consequences." Justice Harlan concluded: "I would hold that ... Boykin is not entitled to outright reversal of his conviction simply because of the 'inadequacy' of the record pertaining to his guilty plea. Further, I would not vacate the judgment below and remand for a state-court hearing on voluntariness. For even if it is assumed for the sake of argument that [the defendant] would be entitled to such a hearing if he had alleged that the plea was involuntary, a matter which I find it unnecessary to decide, the fact is that he has never made any such claim. Hence, I consider that [the defendant's] present arguments relating to his guilty plea entitle him to no federal relief."

Case note: Under modern capital punishment jurisprudence, the death penalty may not be imposed for robbery without an accompanying homicide. *See also* **Guilty Plea; Rape and Capital Punishment**

Bracy v. Gramley

Court: United States Supreme Court; *Case Citation:* Bracy v. Gramley, 520 U.S. 899 (1997); *Argued:* April 14, 1997; *Decided:* June 9, 1997; *Opinion of the Court:* Chief Justice Rehnquist; *Concurring Opinion:* None; *Dissenting Opinion:* None; *Appellate Defense Counsel:* Not reported; *Appellate Prosecution Counsel:* Not reported; *Amicus Curiae Brief Supporting Prosecutor:* Not reported; *Amicus Curiae Brief Supporting Defendant:* Not reported.

Issue Presented: Whether the defendant established "good cause" to conduct discovery during his habeas corpus proceeding, for the purpose of showing that his trial judge was biased against him?

Case Holding: In showing that his trial judge was convicted of taking bribes from criminal defendants, the defendant established "good cause" to conduct discovery during his habeas corpus proceeding.

Factual and procedural background of case: The defendant, William Bracy, was convicted and sentenced to death for capital murder by the State of Illinois. The defendant's conviction and sentence were affirmed on direct appeal by the Illinois Supreme Court.

Subsequent to the defendant's conviction and sentence, the judge who presided over his trial was convicted of Federal charges for taking bribes from criminal defendants. After the trial judge's conviction, the defendant filed a habeas corpus petition in a Federal District Court. In the petition the defendant alleged that his trial judge had an interest in his conviction in order to deflect suspicion that the judge was taking bribes in other murder cases, and that this interest violated the fair trial guarantee of the Due Process Clause. The defendant also filed a motion requesting "discovery" to obtain evidence to substantiate his allegations. The District Court denied relief on the motion to conduct discovery. A Federal Court of Appeals affirmed. In doing so, the appellate court ruled that the defendant had not shown "good cause" for discovery to prove his claim, as required by habeas corpus rules. The United States Supreme Court granted certiorari to consider the issue.

Opinion of the Court by Chief Justice Rehnquist: The Chief Justice ruled that the defendant made a sufficient factual showing under the habeas corpus rules to establish "good cause" for discovery on his claim of actual judicial bias in his case. It was said that due process requires a fair trial before a judge without actual bias against the defendant or an interest in the outcome of his or her particular case. The Chief Justice reasoned that if the defendant established his claim that the trial judge had a bias against defendants who did not pay bribes to him, then that would establish a violation of due process. The opinion indicated that the proffered evidence already asserted by the defendant overcame the usual presumption that public officials have properly discharged their official duties. The Chief Justice noted that the trial judge's conviction proved that he was thoroughly corrupt. Additionally, it was shown that the lawyer appointed to the defendant was a former law partner of the judge. The judgment of the Court of Appeals was reversed and the case remanded for the defendant to engage in discovery. *See also* **Discovery; Habeas Corpus Procedural Rules**

Brady v. Maryland

Court: United States Supreme Court; *Case Citation:* Brady v. Maryland, 373 U.S. 83 (1963); *Argued:* March 18–19, 1963; *Decided:* May 13, 1963; *Opinion of the Court:* Justice Douglas; *Concurring Opinion:* Justice White; *Dissenting Opinion:* Justice Harlan, in which Black, J., joined; *Appellate Defense Counsel:* E. Clinton Bamberger, Jr.

argued; John Martin Jones, Jr. on brief; *Appellate Prosecution Counsel:* Thomas W. Jamison III argued; Thomas B. Finan and Robert C. Murphy on brief; *Amicus Curiae Brief Supporting Prosecutor:* None; *Amicus Curiae Brief Supporting Defendant:* None.

Issues Presented: (1) Whether the defendant was denied due process of law when the prosecutor withheld exculpatory evidence during his trial? (2) Whether the defendant was denied equal protection when the Maryland Court of Appeals restricted his new trial to the issue of punishment?

Case Holdings: (1) The defendant was denied due process of law when the prosecutor withheld exculpatory evidence during his trial. (2) The defendant was not denied equal protection when the Maryland Court of Appeals restricted his new trial to the issue of punishment.

Factual and procedural background of case: The defendant, Brady, was convicted of capital murder and sentenced to death by the State of Maryland. After the defendant's conviction and sentence were affirmed by the Maryland Court of Appeals, the defendant learned that the prosecutor withheld information that indicated the defendant's accomplice actually committed the murder. During the defendant's trial he admitted to be being present when the murder occurred, but that an accomplice did the actual killing.

The defendant filed a habeas corpus petition with the trial court alleging his constitutional rights were violated by the prosecutor's suppression of exculpatory evidence. The trial court denied relief. On appeal the Maryland Court of Appeals held that suppression of the evidence by the prosecutor denied the defendant due process of law. The appellate court reversed the death sentence, but not the conviction, and ordered a retrial on issue of punishment. The United States Supreme Court granted certiorari to consider the issue.

Opinion of the Court by Justice Douglas: Justice Douglas held that the Court agreed with the Maryland Court of Appeals that suppression of the exculpatory evidence was a violation of the Due Process Clause. It was ruled that suppression by the prosecutor of evidence favorable to an accused who has requested it, violates due process where the evidence is material either to guilt or to punishment, irrespective of the good faith or bad faith of the prosecutor. Justice Douglas wrote that "[s]uch a contrivance by a State to procure the conviction and imprisonment of a defendant is as inconsistent with the rudimentary demands of justice as is the obtaining of a like result by intimidation."

Turning to the issue of the proper relief the defendant was entitled to, the opinion held that when the Maryland Court of Appeals restricted defendant's new trial to the issue of punishment only, it did not deny him due process or equal protection of the laws. Justice Douglas reasoned that the suppressed evidence could not have reduced the defendant's offense below murder in the first degree. The judgment of the Maryland Court of Appeals was affirmed.

Concurring opinion by Justice White: Justice White concurred in the Court's judgment. He believed, however, that the

Court should not have addressed the due process issue because the Maryland Court of Appeals did not indicate if the violation was against Federal constitutional due process or State constitutional due process. Justice White wrote: "It certainly is not the case, as it may be suggested, that without [the Federal due process issue] we would have only a state law question, for assuming the court below was correct in finding a violation of [the defendant's] rights in the suppression of evidence, the federal question he wants decided here still remains, namely, whether denying him a new trial on guilt as well as punishment deprives him of equal protection. There is thus a federal question to deal with in this Court, wholly aside from the due process question involving the suppression of evidence."

Dissenting opinion by Justice Harlan, in which Black, J., joined: Justice Harlan dissented from the Court's decision. He argued that the only issue that was properly before the Court was the defendant's claim that it was a violation of equal protection of the law to limit his relief to retrial on punishment. Justice Harlan also contended that the resolution of this issue by the Maryland Court of Appeals was not so clear that the Court should defer to it. He was of the opinion that the judgment should be reversed and the case remanded for further consideration of the equal protection claim.

Case note: The decision in this case had a tremendous impact on capital prosecutions, as well as criminal prosecutions in general. The decision placed an affirmative duty upon prosecutors and the police to disclose all evidence that tended to show the defendant's innocence, as well as evidence that a defendant could use to impeach the testimony of witnesses. A *Brady* violation, as it is called, will usually result in a defendant obtaining a new trial. *See also* **Exculpatory Evidence; Kyles v. Whitley; Strickler v. Greene**

Bram v. United States
Court: United States Supreme Court; *Case Citation:* Bram v. United States, 168 U.S. 532 (1897); *Argued:* Not reported; *Decided:* December 13, 1897; *Opinion of the Court:* Justice White; *Concurring Opinion:* None; *Dissenting Opinion:* Justice Brewer, in which Fuller, C.J., and Brown, J., joined; *Appellate Defense Counsel:* Asa P. French argued; James E. Cotter on brief; *Appellate Prosecution Counsel:* United States Assistant Attorney General Boyd argued and briefed; *Amicus Curiae Brief Supporting Prosecutor:* None; *Amicus Curiae Brief Supporting Defendant:* None.

Issue Presented: Whether the defendant's confession was voluntarily given?

Case Holding: The defendant's confession was not voluntarily given, even though physical force was not used against him, as it was enough that he was in a situation that precluded him from exercising free will.

Factual and procedural background of case: The defendant, Bram, was indicted for capital murder by the United States. The offense was committed on the high seas. During the trial of the case the defendant sought to exclude his confession on the grounds that it was involuntarily made. The trial court found the confession was voluntary and admitted it into evidence. They jury convicted the defendant of capital murder and he was sentenced to death The United States Supreme Court granted certiorari to consider the issue the defendant's confession.

Opinion of the Court by Justice White: Justice White held that the defendant's confession was not voluntarily given. The opinion pointed out that "[i]n criminal trials, in the courts of the United States, wherever a question arises whether a confession is incompetent because not voluntary, the issue is controlled by that portion of the fifth amendment to the constitution of the United States commanding that no person 'shall be compelled in any criminal case to be a witness against himself.'" Justice White noted that "a confession, in order to be admissible, must be free and voluntary; that is, must not be extracted by any sort of threats or violence, nor obtained by any direct or implied promises, however slight, nor by the exertion of any improper influence. It was also ruled that "[a] confession can never be received in evidence where the prisoner has been influenced by any threat or promise; for the law cannot measure the force of the influence used, or decide upon its effect upon the mind of the prisoner, and therefore excludes the declaration if any degree of influence has been exerted." The circumstances surrounding the defendant's involuntary confession were given as follows:

> Before analyzing the statement of the police detective as to what took place between himself and the accused, it is necessary to recall the exact situation. The crime had been committed on the high seas. [A co-suspect], Brown, immediately after the homicide, had been arrested by the crew in consequence of suspicion aroused against him, and had been by them placed in irons. As the vessel came in sight of land, and was approaching Halifax, the suspicions of the crew having been also directed to Bram, he was arrested by them, and placed in irons. On reaching port, these two suspected persons were delivered to the custody of the police authorities of Halifax, and were there held in confinement, awaiting the action of the United States consul, which was to determine whether the suspicions which had caused the arrest justified the sending of one or both of the prisoners into the United States for formal charge and trial. Before this examination had taken place, the police detective caused Bram to be brought from jail to his private office; and, when there alone with the detective, he was stripped of his clothing, and either while the detective was in the act of so stripping him, or after he was denuded, the conversation offered as a confession took place....
>
> The fact, then, is that the language of the accused, which was offered in evidence as a confession, was made use of by him as a reply to the statement of the detective that Bram's co-suspect had charged him with the crime; and, although the answer was in the form of a denial, it was doubtless offered as a confession, because of an implication of guilt which it was conceived the words of the denial might be considered to mean. But the situation of the accused, and the nature of the communication made to him by the detective, necessarily overthrow any possible implication that his reply to the detective could have been the result of a purely voluntary mental action; that is to say, when all the surrounding circumstances are considered in their true relations, not only is the claim that the statement was voluntary overthrown, but the impression is irresistibly produced that it must necessarily have been the result of either hope or fear, or both, operating on the mind.

> It cannot be doubted that, placed in the position in which the accused was when the statement was made to him that the other suspected person had charged him with crime, the result was to produce upon his mind the fear that, if he remained silent, it would be considered an admission of guilt, and therefore render certain his being committed for trial as the guilty person; and it cannot be conceived that the converse impression would not also have naturally arisen that, by denying, there was hope of removing the suspicion from himself. If this must have been the state of mind of one situated as was the prisoner when the confession was made, how, in reason, can it be said that the answer which he gave, and which was required by the situation, was wholly voluntary, and in no manner influenced by the force of hope or fear? To so conclude would be to deny the necessary relation of cause and effect.

The judgment of the Federal District Court was reversed and a new trial ordered.

Dissenting opinion by Justice Brewer, in which Fuller, C.J., and Brown, J., joined: Justice Brewer dissented from the Court's decision. He argued that the circumstances of surrounding the confession did not cause it to be involuntary. Justice Brewer expressed his thoughts as follows: "The fact that the defendant was in custody and in irons does not destroy the competency of a confession. Confinement or imprisonment is not in itself sufficient to justify the exclusion of a confession, if it appears to have been voluntary, and was not obtained by putting the prisoner in fear or by promises." *See also* **Right to Remain Silent**

Brandeis, Louis D.

Louis D. Brandeis served as an associate justice on the United States Supreme Court from 1916 to 1939. While on the Supreme Court Brandeis was known as a progressive jurist who interpreted the Constitution in a manner that gave the greatest protection to individual freedoms from government encroachment.

Brandeis was born in Louisville, Kentucky on November 13, 1856. Although he did not obtain an undergraduate college degree, Brandeis was considered a brilliant student of life. He enrolled in Harvard Law School and received a law degree in 1877. After law school Brandeis embarked on a legal career that, while making him wealthy, brought him immense respect as an intellectual vanguard within the nation's legal community. He wrote articles and books along the way and became affectionately known as the "People's Lawyer."

In 1916 President Woodrow Wilson withstood political controversy to nominate Brandeis as the first Jewish American member of the Supreme Court. While on the Supreme Court Brandeis wrote a number of progressive thinking dissenting opinions that would eventually be adopted as the constitutional law of the nation. Brandeis was only known to have written one capital punishment case while on the bench (it is possible that he wrote more but did not indicate the punishment received by defendants in other criminal decisions authored by him).

In the case of *Ziang v. United States*, Brandeis was called upon to determine whether a defendant's confession and incriminating statements were obtained in violation of the

Constitution. The defendant in *Ziang* was interrogated by the police for thirteen days, before being formally arrested and arraigned. During that period the police obtained a confession and incriminating statements which were used to convict the defendant of capital murder and obtain a sentence of death. Brandeis rejected the government's contention that the confession and incriminating statements were voluntary because of the absence of physical injury or threats. He wrote: "In the federal courts, the requisite of voluntariness is not satisfied by establishing merely that the confession was not induced by a promise or a threat. A confession is voluntary in law if, and only if, it was, in fact, voluntarily made. A confession may have been given voluntary, although it was made to police officers, while in custody, and in answer to an examination conducted by them. But a confession obtained by compulsion must be excluded whatever may have been the character of the compulsion, and whether the compulsion was applied in a judicial proceeding or otherwise." Brandeis granted the defendant a new trial. On October 5, 1941 Brandeis died.

B.R.A.V.E.   B.R.A.V.E., Be Ready Against Violence Everywhere, is a Des Moines, Iowa nonprofit group that was founded in 1993 by Deborah M. Zimmer and Julie A. Turner. The organization was established as a vehicle for helping people defend themselves against violent crime. The primary work of B.R.A.V.E. is to increase safety awareness, provide violence prevention information, as well teaching basic self defense techniques. The group provides violence prevention seminars throughout the Midwest.

Brazil   Brazil abolished the death penalty for ordinary crimes in 1979, but retained its application for exceptional offenses. Its legal system is based on Roman codes. Brazil's constitution was adopted on October 5, 1988. Brazil is a constitutional federal republic composed of 26 states and a federal district. The federal political structure consists of an executive branch, legislative branch, and judicial branch.

The judicial system is composed of federal, state, and municipal courts. The federal court system includes a Supreme Court, Superior Court of Justice (appeal court), and Regional Federal Courts (trial courts). Each state has a State Supreme Court. The governor, with approval by the State Assembly, appoints the judges to the court. Each state has lower courts called District Courts. Defendants are entitled to retained or appointed counsel and must be made fully aware of the charges against them. Trials are open to the public. Juries decide only cases of crimes

against life; judges try all others. *See also* **International Capital Punishment Nations**

Brennan, William J., Jr.   William J. Brennan, Jr., served as an associate justice on the United States Supreme Court from 1956 to 1990. While on the Supreme Court Brennan was known as an expansive interpreter of the Constitution, with respect to individual liberties and rights.

Brennan was born in Newark, New Jersey on April 25, 1906. He received a bachelor of science degree from the Wharton School of Finance and Commerce, at the University of Pennsylvania. After he receiving a scholarship to attend Harvard University Law School, Brennan studied law under Felix Frankurter. Both the student of law and professor of law would eventually serve on the Supreme Court together.

After graduating near the top of his law school class in 1931, Brennan spent a few years in private practice before World War II broke out. While in the Army he rose to the rank of colonel. Brennan returned home after the war and picked up his legal practice. By 1949 he found himself appointed as a New Jersey trial court judge. His outstanding service as a trial judge earned Brennan an appointment to the New Jersey Supreme Court in 1952.

After four years of service on New Jersey's highest court, Brennan was tapped by President Dwight D. Eisenhower in 1956 to serve on the United States Supreme Court. Throughout

Capital Punishment Opinions Written by Brennan*

Case Name	Opinion of the Court	Concurring Opinion	Dissenting Opinion	Concurring and Dissenting
Baldwin v. Alabama			✓	
Butler v. McKellar			✓	
California v. Brown			✓	
Clemons v. Mississippi				✓
Coker v. Georgia		✓		
Demosthenes v. Baal			✓	
Ferguson v. Georgia	✓			
Furman v. Georgia		✓		
Gardner v. Florida				✓
Gregg v. Georgia			✓	
Heath v. Alabama			✓	
Heckler v. Chaney		✓		
Hildwin v. Florida			✓	
Irvin v. Dowd (I)	✓			
McCleskey v. Kemp			✓	
McGautha v. California			✓	
Mills v. Maryland		✓		
North Carolina v. Alford			✓	
Penry v. Lynaugh				✓
Pulley v. Harris			✓	
Rose v. Hodges			✓	
Saffle v. Parks			✓	
South Carolina v. Gathers	✓			
Stanford v. Kentucky			✓	
Strickland v. Washington				✓
Tison v. Arizona			✓	
Turner v. Murray				✓
Wainwright v. Goode			✓	
Wainwright v. Witt			✓	
Walton v. Arizona			✓	

*Does not include capital punishment memorandum opinions and written statements.

his tenure on the nation's highest court, Brennan interpreted the Constitution so as to provide the greatest degree of liberty and rights to individuals. In the area of capital punishment Brennan staunchly held the position that the Constitution prohibited governments from inflicting death as punishment under any circumstances. The anti–death penalty position taken by Brennan would eventually lead him to be one of two justices to issue the greatest number of capital punishment dissenting opinions, memorandums and statements, than any other person to ever sit on the Supreme Court. Justice Thurgood Marshall shared this distinction with Brennan.

The anti–death penalty banner that was proudly worn by Brennan was articulated best in his concurring opinion in *Furman v. Georgia*, the 1972 decision that temporarily halted executions in the nation. Brennan wrote in *Furman*: "Today death is a uniquely and unusually severe punishment. When examined by the principles applicable under the Cruel and Unusual Punishments Clause, death stands condemned as fatally offensive to human dignity. The punishment of death is therefore cruel and unusual, and the States may no longer inflict it as a punishment for crimes." Brennan's rejection of the death penalty as offensive to human dignity was underscored by his concern that the death penalty was inflicted almost exclusively on the poor and in large measure upon minorities. On July 24, 1997 Brennan died.

Brewer, David Josiah

David Josiah Brewer served as an associate justice on the United States Supreme Court from 1890 to 1910. While on the Supreme Court Brewer was known as a liberal interpreter of the Constitution, with respect to individual liberties and rights.

Brewer was born in Turkey, where his father worked as a missionary, on June 20, 1837. Brewer received an undergraduate degree from Yale in 1856. He went on to Albany Law School where he obtained a law degree in 1858. A few years after law school Brewer ventured west and settled in Kansas. While in Kansas he served in various judicial positions before being elected to the Kansas Supreme Court in 1870. Brewer would eventually serve as a Federal judge before President William H. Harrison nominated him to the Federal Supreme Court in 1890.

Brewer wrote a number of capital punishment opinions while on the Supreme Court. His reputation for liberally construing the Constitution when individual rights were involved, did not carry over into capital punishment cases. Brewer revealed a conservative trend in favor of the government when writing capital punishment opinions. An example of his conservative approach to the Constitution in capital punishment cases may be cleaned from the decision in *Perovich v. United States*. In *Perovich* the defendant contended that due process of law was violated when the jury convicted him of capital

murder, even though no direct proof of the identify of the person murdered was given. Brewer wrote in *Perovich* as follows: "While it is true there was no witness to the homicide and the identification of the body found in the cabin was not perfect, owing to its condition, caused by fire, yet, taking all the circumstances together, there was clearly enough to warrant the jury in finding that the partially burned body was that of [the named victim] and that he had been killed by the defendant." Brewer died in office on March 28, 1910.

Capital Punishment Opinions Written by Brewer

Case Name	Opinion of the Court	Dissenting Opinion	Concurring and Dissenting
Benson v. United States	✓		
Bram v. United States		✓	
Brown v. New Jersey	✓		
Davis v. United States (II)	✓		
Hardy v. United States	✓		
In Re Medley		✓	
Johnson v. United States	✓		
Lewis v. United States		✓	
Nofire v. United States	✓		
Perovich v. United States	✓		
Sparf v. United States			✓
Storti v. Massachusetts	✓		
Thiede v. Utah	✓		
Westmoreland v. United States	✓		
Wheeler v. United States	✓		

Breyer, Stephen G.

Stephen G. Breyer was appointed to the United States Supreme Court in 1994. Early opinions by Breyer have evidenced a pragmatic and moderate judicial philosophy.

Breyer was born in San Francisco on August 15, 1938. Prior to attending Harvard Law School, Breyer obtained an A.B. degree from Stanford University and a B.A. degree from Oxford University. Breyer received his law degree from Harvard in 1964.

Prior to his elevation to the Supreme Court, Breyer engaged in a variety of legal work. He clerked for Supreme Court Justice Arthur J. Goldberg after leaving law school. Breyer left his clerkship position after two years and became an assistant U.S. Attorney General. During his employment with the Attorney General's office, Breyer managed to teach courses at Harvard Law School. Breyer was as an aide to Senator Edward M. Kennedy during the 1970s, as well as chief counsel for the Senate Judiciary Committee. President Jimmy Carter nominated Breyer to the U.S. Court of Appeals for the First Circuit, but he was confirmed by the Senate under the administration of President Ronald Reagan. As a Court of Appeals Judge, Breyer was viewed as a moderate.

In 1994 President Clinton selected Breyer to fill a vacancy on the Supreme Court. The Senate confirmed the nomination on July 29, 1994. Breyer wrote a few opinions in capital punishment cases during his early years on the Supreme Court. Only one of the early opinions was written for the Supreme Court. In that opinion, *Lonchar v. Thomas*, Breyer would not allow a Federal Court of Appeals to discard procedural rules and impose equitable principles in order to expedite the execution of a prisoner. The decision in *Lonchar* suggested Breyer may be committed to maintaining a moderate course in viewing the Constitution in the context of capital punishment.

The dissenting opinion by Breyer in *Buchanan v. Angelone* supports the early indication that he will maintain a moderate position in capital punishment cases. In *Buchanan* Breyer wrote that he believed the majority on the Supreme Court was wrong in assuming that the jury did not misinterpret a jury instruction in the case. In a patient and scholarly tone Breyer cautioned the majority that "[t]o uphold the instructions given here is to 'risk that the death penalty will be imposed in spite of factors which may call for a less severe penalty.'" The facts in the case were not overwhelming in suggesting the jury may have misapplied the trial court's instructions. However, because some evidence existed to support the issue, Breyer believed the best course was not to allow the defendant to be executed under such circumstances.

Capital Punishment Opinions Written by Breyer

Case Name	Opinion of the Court	Concurring Opinion	Dissenting Opinion
Buchanan v. Angelone			✓
Calderon v. Ashmus		✓	
Lilly v. Virginia			✓
Lonchar v. Thomas	✓		

British Democratic Dictatorship Party
The British Democratic Dictatorship Party (BDDP) is a political group existing in England. The BDDP was founded in 1983. The chairman of BDDP, Dr. Richard Turner, has been an outspoken proponent of capital punishment. Although England abolished the death penalty for all crimes in 1998, BDDP has maintained a platform advocating capital punishment.

Dr. Turner has written extensively on the merits of capital punishment and has, in many ways, grafted his pro–death penalty ideology as a centerpiece of BDDP. The BDDP takes the position that prison is nothing more than a "hotel" for capital offenders that wastes taxpayers money. The party advocates public executions as a source of revenue. The BDDP does not hold a seat in Parliament, but has actively sought such representation. The membership of BDDP is estimated at between 1,500 to 4,200.

As head of the BDDP, Dr. Richard Turner has taken a strong position in favor of capital punishment and hopes to have the punishment reinstated in England. (Richard Turner)

Brooks, Charlie *see* Lethal Injection

Brothers *see* Apelt Brothers; Gutierrez Brothers; Lagrand Brothers; Poland Brothers

Brown, Debra Denise *see* Coleman and Brown

Brown, Henry B.
Henry Billings Brown served as an associate justice on the United States Supreme Court from 1890 to 1906. While on the Supreme Court Brown was known as a conservative interpreter of the Constitution.

Brown was born on March 2, 1836, in South Lee, Massachusetts. He received an undergraduate degree from Yale University in 1856. Brown studied law at both Yale and Harvard and was eventually admitted to the bar in Michigan in 1859. While in Michigan, Brown entered private practice for a short time, lectured on the law, published a legal journal, served as an assistant United States Attorney, and served as a State judge.

President Benjamin H. Harrison nominated Brown to the Supreme Court in 1890. Brown wrote several capital punishment opinions while on the Supreme Court. His opinions reflected a strict application of constitutional and nonconstitutional principles. For example, in *Alexander v. United States* he applied fundamental law which precluded forcing an attorney to disclose communication given by a client. In *Alberty v. United States* Brown wrote that basic legal doctrines prohibited a trial court from instructing the jury to infer a defendant's guilt from evidence of his flight from the jurisdiction of the court. Brown died in 1913.

Capital Punishment Opinions Written by Brown

Case Name	Opinion of the Court	Dissenting Opinion
Alberty v. United States	✓	
Alexander v. United States	✓	
Crumpton v. United States	✓	
Davis v. Burke	✓	
Ex Parte Johnson	✓	
Isaacs v. United States	✓	

Brown, John
John Brown was born in 1800, in Torrington, Connecticut. He grew to become a staunch opponent of American enslavement of blacks. During his early years Brown moved about the country, settling in Ohio, Pennsylvania, Massachusetts, and New York. During these years Brown fathered twenty children. He pursued various occupations including farmer, tanner, land speculator and wool merchant. While living in Pennsylvania in 1834, Brown began a project to help educate free blacks. Brown moved to a black community in North Elba, New York, in 1849. This community had been established as a result of the philanthropy of Gerrit Smith, who donated land to free black families willing to clear and farm the land. In 1851, Brown helped establish the League

John Brown was hanged on December 2, 1859, in Charles Town, Virginia. (Harper Ferry National Historical Park)

of Gileadites, an organization that worked to protect escaped slaves from slave catchers.

Brown moved to the Kansas Territory in 1855. While there he became the leader of an antislavery group that sought revenge upon a proslavery attack against the antislavery town of Lawrence. Brown went to a proslavery town and killed five of its settlers. The Kansas Territory events helped propel Brown as a nationally famous irreconcilable foe of slavery.

Brown's intractable position on slavery led him to plan an insurrection to overthrow slavery. In October 1859, Brown led a small group of men to a United States arsenal and armory at Harpers Ferry, Virginia (now West Virginia). Brown's plan was to take control of the armory for weapons. On October 16, 1859, Brown put his plan in motion and, along with 21 confederates (5 blacks and 16 whites), raided the Federal armory at Harper's Ferry. The plot failed. On the morning of October 18, town citizens and a small group of United States soldiers led by Robert E. Lee, broke down the door of the armory. Ten of Brown's men, including two of his sons, were killed in the ensuing battle. Brown was wounded and quickly captured. He was taken to Charles Town, Virginia where he was charged with various crimes, including treason and murder. Brown was tried, convicted and sentenced to death by the Commonwealth of Virginia. On December 2, 1859 Brown was hanged in Charles Town.

Brown v. Allen *Court:* United States Supreme Court; *Case Citation:* Brown v. Allen, 344 U.S. 443 (1953); *Argued:* April 29, 1952; reargued October 13, 1952; *Decided:* February 9, 1953; *Opinion of the Court:* Justice Reed; *Concurring Opinion:* Justice Jackson; *Concurring Statement:* Justice Burton and Clark, J.; *Dissenting Opinion:* Justice Black, in which Douglas, J., joined; *Dissenting Opinion:* Justice Frankfurter, in which Black and Douglas, JJ., joined; *Appellate Defense Counsel in Case No. 32:* Hosea V. Price argued; Herman L. Taylor on brief; *Appellate Defense Counsel in Case No. 22:* Herman L. Taylor argued and briefed; *Appellate Defense Counsel in Case No. 20:* O. John Rogge and Murray A. Gordon argued; Herman L. Taylor on brief; *Appellate Prosecution Counsel in Case No 32:* R. Brookes Peters argued; Harry McMullan on brief; *Appellate Prosecution Counsel in Case No. 22:* E. O. Brogden, Jr. argued; Harry McMullan on brief; *Appellate Prosecution Counsel in Case No. 20:* Ralph Moody argued; Harry Mc-

Mullan on brief; *Amicus Curiae Brief Supporting Prosecutor:* None; *Amicus Curiae Brief Supporting Defendant:* None.

Issue Presented: Whether any weight is to be given to the United States Supreme Court's former refusal of certiorari in a case, when a lower Federal court receives the case again in a habeas corpus proceeding?

Case Holding: No weight is to be given to the United States Supreme Court's former refusal of certiorari in a case, when a lower Federal court receives the case again in a habeas corpus proceeding.

Factual and procedural background of case: This case represented a consolidation of three cases presenting the same issues for resolution. In case No. 32 the defendant, Brown, was convicted of rape by a North Carolina jury and sentenced to death. In case No. 22 the defendant, Speller, was convicted of rape by a North Carolina jury and sentenced to death. Case No. 20 involved two defendants who were convicted of murder by a North Carolina jury and sentenced to death.

All four defendants were black. They each had exhausted their State post-conviction remedies. On direct appeal to the United States Supreme Court, certiorari was refused for each defendant. All four defendants filed a habeas corpus petition in a Federal District Court alleging that their confessions were involuntary and that blacks were systematically excluded from serving on their juries. The District Court denied relief to each defendant, and in doing so, gave weight to the fact that the Supreme Court had previously denied certiorari to each case. A Federal Court of Appeals affirmed. The United States Supreme Court granted certiorari.

Opinion of the Court by Justice Reed: Justice Reed held that a denial of certiorari by the Court (with no statement of reasons therefor) to review a decision of a State court affirming a conviction in a criminal prosecution, should be given no weight by a Federal court in passing upon a defendant's petition for habeas relief. It was said that although in each of the cases presented, the District Court erroneously gave consideration to the Court's prior denial of certiorari, it affirmatively appeared from the record that the error could not have affected the result, and such error may be and was disregarded as harmless.

In turning to the merits of the claims made by the defendants, Justice Reed found that the defendants' constitutional rights were not violated, either by their confessions or in the selection of jurors. The opinion held that: "Our Constitution requires that jurors be selected without inclusion or exclusion because of race. There must be neither limitation nor representation for color. By that practice, harmony has an opportunity to maintain essential discipline, without that objectionable domination which is so inconsistent with our constitutional democracy." The judgments of the Court of Appeals were affirmed.

Concurring opinion by Justice Jackson: Justice Jackson concurred in the Court's decision. He wrote separately to indicate the circumstances under which he believed a lower Federal court should entertain a habeas petition. Justice Jackson stated that habeas petitions should be reviewed on the merits only if: (1) the petition raises a jurisdictional question involving federal law on which the state law allowed no access to its courts, either by habeas corpus or appeal from the conviction; or (2) the petition shows that although the law allows a remedy, the defendant was actually improperly obstructed from making a record upon which the question could be presented. He concluded: "There may be circumstances so extraordinary that I do not now think of them which would justify a departure from this rule, but the run-of-the-mill case certainly does not."

Concurring statement by Justice Burton and Clark, J.: Justices Burton and Clark issued a concurring statement indicating that they believed no weight should be accorded a denial of certiorari.

Dissenting opinion by Justice Black, in which Douglas, J., joined: Justice Black dissented from the Court's decision. In doing so, he stated his position as follows: "In denying habeas corpus in all the cases, the District Court felt constrained to give and did give weight to our prior denials of certiorari. So did the Court of Appeals. I agree with the Court that this was error but disagree with its holding that the error was harmless. It is true that after considering our denials of certiorari as a reason for refusing habeas corpus, the district judge attempted to pass upon the constitutional questions just as if we had not declined to review the convictions. But the record shows the difficulty of his attempt to erase this fact from his mind and I am not willing to act on the assumption that he succeeded in doing so. Both the jury and confession questions raised in these death cases have entirely too much record support to refuse relief on such a questionable assumption. I would therefore reverse and remand all the cases for the district judge to consider and appraise the issues free from his erroneous belief that this Court decided them against petitioners by denying certiorari."

Dissenting opinion by Justice: Frankfurter, in which Black and Douglas, JJ., joined: Justice Frankfurter dissented from the Court's decision. He believed the Court was in error in finding the lower courts did not prejudice the cases by giving weight to the Court's denial of certiorari. Justice Frankfurter wrote:

> The Court is holding today that a denial of certiorari in habeas corpus cases is without substantive significance. The Court of Appeals sustained denials of applications for writs of habeas corpus chiefly because it treated our denial of a petition for certiorari from the original conviction in each of these cases as a review on the merits and a rejection of the constitutional claims asserted by these petitioners. In short, while the only significance of the denials of certiorari was a refusal to review, the Court of Appeals for all practical purposes, though disavowing the full technical import of res judicata, treated substantively empty denials as though this Court had examined and approved the holdings of the Supreme Court of North Carolina....
>
> I cannot protest too strongly against affirming a decision of the Court of Appeals patently based on the ground that that court was foreclosed on procedural grounds from considering the

merits of constitutional claims, when we now decide that the court was wrong in believing that it was so foreclosed. The affirmance by this Court of the District Court's denial of writs of habeas corpus in these cases is all the more vulnerable in that this Court, without guidance from the Court of Appeals, proceeds to consider the merits of the constitutional claim. This Court concludes that there was not a systematic discrimination.... If this Court deemed it necessary to consider the merits, the merits should equally have been open to the Court of Appeals. As I have already indicated, that court is far better situated than we are to assess the circumstances of jury selection in North Carolina and to draw the appropriate inferences. *See also* **Smith v. Baldi**

Brown v. Mississippi
Court: United States Supreme Court; *Case Citation:* Brown v. Mississippi, 297 U.S. 278 (1936); *Argued:* January 10, 1936; *Decided:* February 17, 1936; *Opinion of the Court:* Chief Justice Hughes; *Concurring Opinion:* None; *Dissenting Opinion:* None; *Appellate Defense Counsel:* Earl Brewer argued; J. Morgan Stevens on brief; *Appellate Prosecution Counsel:* W. D. Conn argued; W. H. Maynard on brief; *Amicus Curiae Brief Supporting Prosecutor:* None; *Amicus Curiae Brief Supporting Defendant:* None.

Issue Presented: Whether the confessions given by the defendants were obtained in violation of the Federal Constitution?

Case Holding: The confessions given by the defendants were obtained in violation of the Federal Constitution, therefore the judgments against them could not stand.

Factual and procedural background of case: This case involved three defendants, Ed Brown, Henry Shields and a defendant named only as Ellington. The defendants were convicted of capital murder and sentenced to death by the State of Mississippi. The Mississippi Supreme Court affirmed the judgments. In doing so, the appellate court rejected the defendants' contention that their confessions were involuntary. The United States Supreme Court granted certiorari to consider the issue.

Opinion of the Court by Chief Justice Hughes: The Chief Justice held that the confessions given by the defendants were obtained in violation of the Constitution. The opinion set out the circumstances of the confessions as follows:

> On [the night of the murder] one Dial, a deputy sheriff, accompanied by others, came to the home of Ellington, one of the defendants, and requested him to accompany them to the house of the deceased, and there a number of white men were gathered, who began to accuse the defendant of the crime. Upon his denial they seized him, and with the participation of the deputy they hanged him by a rope to the limb of a tree, and, having let him down, they hung him again, and when he was let down the second time, and he still protested his innocence, he was tied to a tree and whipped, and, still declining to accede to the demands that he confess, he was finally released, and he returned with some difficulty to his home, suffering intense pain and agony. The record of the testimony shows that the signs of the rope on his neck were plainly visible during the so-called trial. A day or two thereafter the said deputy, accompanied by another, returned to the home of the said defendant and arrested him, and departed with the prisoner towards the jail in an

adjoining county, but went by a route which led into the state of Alabama; and while on the way, in that state, the deputy stopped and again severely whipped the defendant, declaring that he would continue the whipping until he confessed, and the defendant then agreed to confess to such a statement as the deputy would dictate, and he did so, after which he was delivered to jail.

The other two defendants, Ed Brown and Henry Shields, were also arrested and taken to the same jail. On Sunday night, April 1, 1934, the same deputy, accompanied by a number of white men, one of whom was also an officer, and by the jailer, came to the jail, and the two last named defendants were made to strip and they were laid over chairs and their backs were cut to pieces with a leather strap with buckles on it, and they were likewise made by the said deputy definitely to understand that the whipping would be continued unless and until they confessed, and not only confessed, but confessed in every matter of detail as demanded by those present; and in this manner the defendants confessed to the crime, and, as the whippings progressed and were repeated, they changed or adjusted their confession in all particulars of detail so as to conform to the demands of their torturers. When the confessions had been obtained in the exact form and contents as desired by the mob, they left with the parting admonition and warning that, if the defendants changed their story at any time in any respect from that last stated, the perpetrators of the outrage would administer the same or equally effective treatment.

After setting forth the facts surrounding the defendants' confessions, the Chief Justice went on to explain the legal basis for reversing the judgments:

> The state is free to regulate the procedure of its courts in accordance with its own conceptions of policy, unless in so doing it offends some principle of justice so rooted in the traditions and conscience of our people as to be ranked as fundamental. The state may abolish trial by jury. It may dispense with indictment by a grand jury and substitute complaint or information. But the freedom of the state in establishing its policy is the freedom of constitutional government and is limited by the requirement of due process of law. Because a state may dispense with a jury trial, it does not follow that it may substitute trial by ordeal. The rack and torture chamber may not be substituted for the witness stand. The state may not permit an accused to be hurried to conviction under mob domination—where the whole proceeding is but a mask—without supplying corrective process. The state may not deny to the accused the aid of counsel. Nor may a state, through the action of its officers, contrive a conviction through the pretense of a trial which in truth is but used as a means of depriving a defendant of liberty through a deliberate deception of court and jury by the presentation of testimony known to be perjured. And the trial equally is a mere pretense where the state authorities have contrived a conviction resting solely upon confessions obtained by violence. The due process clause requires that state action, whether through one agency or another, shall be consistent with the fundamental principles of liberty and justice which lie at the base of all our civil and political institutions. It would be difficult to conceive of methods more revolting to the sense of justice than those taken to procure the confessions of these [defendants], and the use of the confessions thus obtained as the basis for conviction and sentence was a clear denial of due process....

> Coercing the supposed state's criminals into confessions and using such confessions so coerced from them against them in trials has been the curse of all countries. It was the chief iniquity, the crowning infamy of the Star Chamber, and the Inquisition, and other similar institutions. The Constitution recognized the evils that lay behind these practices and prohibited them in this country. ... The duty of maintaining constitutional rights of a person on trial for his life rises above mere rules of procedure, and wherever the court is clearly satisfied that such violations exist, it will refuse to sanction such violations and will apply the corrective.

The judgments of the Mississippi Supreme Court were reversed. *See also* **Right to Remain Silent**

Brown v. New Jersey *Court:* United States Supreme Court; *Case Citation:* Brown v. New Jersey, 175 U.S. 172 (1899); *Argued:* October 30, 1899; *Decided:* November 20, 1899; *Opinion of the Court:* Justice Brewer; *Concurring Statement:* Justice Harlan; *Dissenting Opinion:* None; *Appellate Defense Counsel:* William D. Daly argued; Joseph M. Noonan on brief; *Appellate Prosecution Counsel:* James S. Erwin argued and briefed; *Amicus Curiae Brief Supporting Prosecutor:* None; *Amicus Curiae Brief Supporting Defendant:* None.

Issue Presented: Whether use of a struck jury deprived the defendant of due process of law?

Case Holding: Use of a struck jury did not deprive the defendant of due process of law and did not present an issue cognizable under the Constitution.

Factual and procedural background of case: The defendant, James K. Brown, was indicted for capital murder by the State of New Jersey. The jury used in the defendant's trial was selected under a seldom used statute providing for a "struck jury." The procedure for using a "struck jury" involved compiling a list of 96 names of potential jurors, and letting the defendant and prosecutor each strike 24 names from the list. The remaining 48 names formed the pool from which the 12 person jury was ultimately chosen.

The jury selected for the defendant's case found him guilty and he was sentenced to death. The New Jersey Supreme Court affirmed the judgment. In doing so, the appellate court rejected the defendant's argument that the "struck jury" procedure denied him due process of law. The United States Supreme Court granted certiorari to consider the issue.

Opinion of the Court by Justice Brewer: Justice Brewer held that New Jersey's statutory provision for a struck jury was a State matter that the Constitution could not be used to interfere with. The opinion reasoned as follows:

> In providing for a trial by a struck jury, impaneled in accordance with the provisions of the New Jersey statute, no fundamental right of the defendant is trespassed upon. The manner of selection is one calculated to secure an impartial jury, and the purpose of criminal procedure is not to enable the defendant to select jurors, but to secure an impartial jury. The accused cannot complain if he is still tried by an impartial jury. He can demand nothing more. The right to challenge is the right to reject, not to select, a juror. If from those who remain an impartial jury is obtained, the constitutional right of the accused is maintained.... Within any and all definitions, trial by a struck jury in the manner prescribed must, when authorized by a statute valid under the Constitution of the state, be adjudged due process. A struck jury was not unknown to the common law, though, as urged by counsel for [the defendant], it may never have been resorted to in trials for murder. But if appropriate for

and used in criminal trials for certain offenses, it could hardly be deemed essentially bad when applied to other offenses. It gives the defendant a reasonable opportunity to ascertain the qualifications of proposed jurors, and to protect himself against any supposed prejudices in the mind of any particular individual called as a juror. Whether better or no than any other method, it is certainly a fair and reasonable way of securing an impartial jury, was provided for by the laws of the state, and that is all that due process in this respect requires.

The judgment of the New Jersey Supreme Court was affirmed.

Concurring statement by Justice Harlan: Justice Harlan issued a statement indicating he concurred in the Court's judgment. *See also* **Jury Selection**

Brown v. United States (I)

Court: United States Supreme Court; *Case Citation:* Brown v. United States, 150 U.S. 93 (1893); *Argued:* Not reported; *Decided:* November 6, 1893; *Opinion of the Court:* Justice Jackson; *Concurring Opinion:* None; *Dissenting Opinion:* None; *Appellate Defense Counsel:* A. H. Garland argued and briefed; *Appellate Prosecution Counsel:* Mr. Whitney argued and briefed; *Amicus Curiae Brief Supporting Prosecutor:* None; *Amicus Curiae Brief Supporting Defendant:* None.

Issue Presented: Whether it was reversible error to admit during the defendant's trial evidence of an unrelated conspiracy to commit murder?

Case Holding: It was reversible error to admit during the defendant's trial evidence of an unrelated conspiracy to commit murder.

Factual and procedural background of case: The defendant, John Brown, was indicted by the United States for the murder of two deputy marshals "at the Cherokee Nation, in [Native American] Territory." The victims were killed while searching for an escaped prisoner. The victims erroneously believed the defendant was the person they were searching for and attempted to arrest him when they were killed.

During the defendant's trial the prosecutor was allowed to present evidence that the defendant had been part of an unrelated conspiracy to murder the husband of a woman named Mrs. Hitchcock. The jury eventually convicted the defendant of killing both deputy marshals and he was sentenced to death. The defendant appealed to the United States Supreme Court, arguing that the testimony of the alleged conspiracy to murder Mrs. Hitchcock's husband was prejudicial and should not have been allowed into evidence. The United States Supreme Court granted certiorari to consider the issue.

Opinion of the Court by Justice Jackson: Justice Jackson held that it was reversible error to admit the testimony of the alleged conspiracy. The opinion reasoned as follows:

> … [T]he court improperly admitted the … evidence tending to establish a conspiracy between the [defendant] and [Mrs. Hitchcock] and others to kill her husband. It was furthermore objectionable because there was no evidence in the case tending to show that the defendant or his alleged co-conspirators killed either of the [deputy marshals] under the mistaken supposition that either one of them was Hitchcock. In the admission of the statements and declarations of Mrs. Hitchcock, the

court assumed that the acts and declarations of one co-conspirator after the completion or abandonment of a criminal enterprise constituted proof against the defendant of the existence of the conspiracy. This is not a sound proposition of law.

Justice Jackson indicated that, assuming a conspiracy had existed, the evidence was not admissible because only those acts and declarations of a conspiracy are admissible which are done and made while the conspiracy is pending, and in furtherance of its object. It was said that "[a]fter the conspiracy has come to an end, whether by success or by failure, the admissions of one conspirator by way of narrative of past facts are not admissible in evidence against the others." The judgment of the Federal District Court was reversed and a new trial awarded. *See also* **Brown v. United States (II)**

Brown v. United States (II)

Court: United States Supreme Court; *Case Citation:* Brown v. United States, 159 U.S. 100 (1895); *Argued:* Not reported; *Decided:* June 3, 1895; *Opinion of the Court:* Justice Harlan; *Concurring Opinion:* None; *Dissenting Statement:* Justice Brewer and Brown, J.; *Appellate Defense Counsel:* Wm. M. Cravens argued and briefed; *Appellate Prosecution Counsel:* Mr. Whitney argued; Wm. H. Pope on brief; *Amicus Curiae Brief Supporting Prosecutor:* None; *Amicus Curiae Brief Supporting Defendant:* None.

Issue Presented: Whether the trial court erroneously instructed the jury on the lesser included offense of manslaughter?

Case Holding: The trial court erroneously instructed the jury on the lesser included offense of manslaughter, therefore the conviction and sentence could not stand.

Factual and procedural background of case: The defendant, John Brown, was indicted by the United States for the murder of two deputy marshals "at the Cherokee Nation, in [Native American] Territory." The victims were killed while searching for an escaped prisoner. The victims erroneously believed the defendant was the person they were searching for and attempted to arrest him when they were killed. The jury eventually convicted the defendant of killing both deputy marshals and he was sentenced to death. The defendant appealed to the United States Supreme Court, which reversed the judgment and awarded a new trial.

On remand the defendant was again convicted of both murders. The trial court sentenced the defendant to death for one of the murderers, but held the sentence on the second conviction in abeyance pending the defendant's appeal. The defendant appealed to the United States Supreme Court contending that the trial court erroneously instructed the jury on the lesser included offense of manslaughter. The United States Supreme Court granted certiorari to consider the issue.

Opinion of the Court by Justice Harlan: Justice Harlan found that the instruction given to the jury on murder and manslaughter was erroneous and misleading. It was said that "[t]here was some evidence before the jury which, if credited, would have justified a verdict against the defendant for manslaughter only." However, it was said by Justice Harlan that the trial court's instruction did not allow the jury to properly consider the evidence on manslaughter. The opinion addressed the matter as follows:

> ... [T]he jury might well have inferred, from the instruction ..., that they were at liberty to return a verdict of murder because of the way or mode in which the killing was done, even if they believed that, apart from the way in which the life of the deceased was taken, the facts made a case of manslaughter, not of murder. We do not think that a verdict of guilty of manslaughter or murder should have turned alone upon an inquiry as to the way in which the killing was done. The inquiry, rather, should have been whether, at the moment the defendant shot, there were present such circumstances, taking all of them into consideration, including the mode of killing, as made the taking of the life of the deceased manslaughter, and not murder.

The judgment of the Federal District Court was reversed and a new trial awarded.

Dissenting statement by Justice Brewer and Brown, J.: Justices Brewer and Brown issued a statement indicating they dissented from the Court's decision. *See also* **Brown v. United States (I); Lesser Included Offense Instruction**

Brunei   Capital punishment stands on the law books of Brunei, but the punishment has not been utilized with any degree of frequency. The method of execution used by Brunei is hanging. The nation's legal system is based on English common law and Shari'a (Islamic) law. The constitution of Brunei came into existence on September 29, 1959, but some provisions have been suspended since December of 1962. *See also* **International Capital Punishment Nations**

Buchalter v. New York   *Court:* United States Supreme Court; *Case Citation:* Buchalter v. New York, 319 U.S. 427 (1943); *Argued:* May 7–10, 1943; *Decided:* June 1, 1943; *Opinion of the Court:* Justice Roberts; *Concurring Statement:* Justice Black; *Dissenting Opinion:* None; *Justice Taking No Part in Decision:* Justice Murphy and Jackson, J.; *Appellate Defense Counsel in Case No. 606:* J. Bertram Wegman argued; I. Maurice Wormser on brief; *Appellate Defense Counsel in Case No. 610:* Arthur Garfield Hays argued; John Schulman on brief; *Appellate Defense Counsel in Case No. 619:* Sidney Rosenthal argued and briefed; *Appellate Prosecution Counsel:* Solomon A. Klein argued and on briefed; *Amicus Curiae Brief Supporting Prosecutor:* None; *Amicus Curiae Brief Supporting Defendant:* None.

Issue Presented: Whether the defendants were denied due process of law because of widespread pretrial publicity of their trial?

Case Holding: The defendants were not denied due process of law because of widespread pretrial publicity of their trial.

Factual and procedural background of case: This case involved the prosecution of three defendants for capital murder by the State of New York. The defendants were: Louis "Lepke" Buchalter, case No. 606; Emanuel Weiss, case No. 610; and Louis Capone, case No. 619. The defendants were members of an organized crime syndicate called Murder, Inc. All three

defendants were convicted and sentenced to death. The New York Court of Appeals affirmed the judgments. In doing so, the appellate court found that the defendants were not denied due process of law because of widespread pretrial publicity surrounding their trial. The United States Supreme Court granted certiorari to consider the issue.

Opinion of the Court by Justice Roberts: Justice Roberts found that the defendants trial was not held in violation of due process principles. The opinion addressed the due process doctrine as follows: "The due process clause of the Fourteenth Amendment requires that action by a state through any of its agencies must be consistent with the fundamental principles of liberty and justice which lie at the base of our civil and political institutions, which not infrequently are designated as the 'law of the land.' Where this requirement has been disregarded in a criminal trial in a state court this court has not hesitated to exercise its jurisdiction to enforce the constitutional guarantee. But the Amendment does not draw to itself the provisions of state constitutions or state laws. It leaves the states free to enforce their criminal laws under such statutory provisions and common law doctrines as they deem appropriate; and does not permit a party to bring to the test of a decision in this court every ruling made in the course of a trial in a state court."

The opinion found that the defendants failed to show actual bias by the jury that presided at their trial. Justice Roberts held that "[t]hough the statute governing the selection of the jurors and the court's rulings on challenges are asserted to have worked injustice in the impanelling of a jury such assertion raises no due process question requiring review by this court." The opinion concluded that "it is not asking too much that the burden of showing essential unfairness be sustained by him who claims such injustice and seeks to have the result set aside, and that it be sustained not as a matter of speculation but as a demonstrable reality." The judgments of the New York Court of Appeals were affirmed.

Concurring statement by Justice Black: Justice Black issued a statement indicating he concurred in the Court's opinion. *See also* **Murder, Inc.; Pretrial Publicity**

Buchanan v. Angelone   *Court:* United States Supreme Court; *Case Citation:* Buchanan v. Angelone, 522 U.S. 269 (1998); *Argued:* November 3, 1997; *Decided:* January 21, 1998; *Opinion of the Court:* Chief Justice Rehnquist; *Concurring Opinion:* Justice Scalia; *Dissenting Opinion:* Justice Breyer, in which Stevens and Ginsburg, JJ., joined; *Appellate Defense Counsel:* Not reported; *Appellate Prosecution Counsel:* Not reported; *Amicus Curiae Brief Supporting Prosecutor:* Not reported; *Amicus Curiae Brief Supporting Defendant:* Not reported.

Issue Presented: Whether the Constitution requires that a capital penalty phase jury be instructed on the concept of mitigating evidence generally, or on particular statutory mitigating factors?

Case Holding: The Constitution does not require that a

capital penalty phase jury be instructed on the concept of mitigating evidence generally, or on particular statutory mitigating factors, when the jury is instructed to consider all relevant mitigating evidence.

Factual and procedural background of case: The defendant, Douglas Buchanan, was convicted of capital murder by a Virginia jury. During the penalty phase the defendant requested the trial judge instruct the jury on particular statutory mitigating factors and a general instruction on the concept of mitigating evidence. The trial judge refused the request. The jury returned a verdict of death and the trial judge imposed that sentence. The Virginia Supreme Court affirmed the conviction and sentence. The defendant filed a petition for habeas corpus in a Federal District Court, alleging that the trial judge committed constitutional error in refusing to instruct the penalty phase jury on particular statutory mitigating factors and a general instruction on the concept of mitigating evidence. The District Court dismissed the petition and denied relief. A Federal Court of Appeals affirmed. The United States Supreme Court granted certiorari to consider the issue.

Opinion of the Court by Chief Justice Rehnquist: The Chief Justice ruled that the absence of instructions on the concept of mitigation and on particular statutorily defined mitigating factors did not violate the Constitution. It was said that during the penalty phase the State may shape and structure the jury's consideration of mitigating evidence, so long as restrictions on the sentencing determination do not preclude the jury from giving effect to any such evidence. The opinion pointed out that the determinative standard is whether there is a reasonable likelihood that the jury applied its instructions in a way that prevented consideration of constitutionally relevant evidence. The Chief Justice concluded that the instructions given in the case did not violate the latter constitutional principles. It was said that the trial judge directed the jurors to base their decision on all the evidence and to impose a life sentence if they believed the evidence so warranted. Therefore, there was not a reasonable likelihood that the jurors understood the instructions to preclude consideration of relevant mitigating evidence. The judgment of the Court of Appeals was affirmed.

Concurring opinion by Justice Scalia: Justice Scalia concurred in the Court's decision. He believed that there was "no reasonable likelihood that the jurors in [the defendant's] case understood the challenged instructions to preclude consideration of relevant mitigating evidence." Justice Scalia also wrote that he did not believe the Constitution required sentencing juries be given discretion to consider mitigating evidence.

Dissenting opinion by Justice Breyer, in which Stevens and Ginsburg, JJ., joined: Justice Breyer dissented from the Court's decision, on the grounds that he believed the instructions given by the trial judge indicated that there was a reasonable likelihood that the jury understood and applied the instructions in a way that prevented it from considering relevant mitigating evidence. He argued that "[t]o uphold the instructions given here is to 'risk that the death penalty will be imposed in spite of factors which may call for a less severe penalty.'"

Case note: Virginia executed Douglas Buchanan by lethal injection on March 18, 1998.

Buenoano, Judias V.

Judias (Judy) V. Buenoano was executed for capital murder by the state of Florida on March 30, 1998. The method of execution used was electrocution. The victim of Buenoano's capital conviction and death sentence was her husband James Goodyear.

The media dubbed Buenoano the "black widow" because of the murder of her husband, a boyfriend and attempted murder of her fiancé. In between the murders and attempted murder, Buenoano murdered her nineteen year old son. In March of 1984 a Florida jury convicted Buenoano of drowning her son, and she was sentenced to life imprisonment. In October of 1984 a Florida jury convicted her of the attempted murder of her fiancé, and she was sentenced to imprisonment for a term of years. In November of 1985 she was found guilty by an Orlando jury for the murder of her husband, and sentenced to death.

During Buenoano's trial for the murder of Goodyear, evidence was presented which chronicled the murderous trail she left as her legacy. Trial testimony indicated that upon Goodyear's return to Florida in September of 1971, from a tour of duty in Vietnam, he began suffering from nausea, vomiting and diarrhea. He endured the symptoms for two weeks before being hospitalized at a naval hospital in Orlando on September 13, 1971. While hospitalized Goodyear suffered fluid overload and pulmonary congestion, and died as a consequence of cardiovascular collapse and renal failure on September 16, 1971. At the time of his death there was no suspicion of foul play.

Authorities stumbled upon the true cause of Goodyear's death through Buenoano's relationship with John Gentry. In 1981 Buenoano and Gentry began living together and later became engaged. In November of 1982, Gentry caught a cold and Buenoano began treating him with vitamins. After experiencing extreme nausea and vomiting, Gentry checked into a hospital on December 15, 1982. He recovered and returned home. On the day he returned home Buenoano began treating him with vitamins again. Gentry's nausea and vomiting returned. Gentry decided to have the vitamins

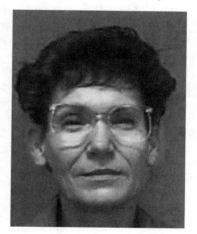

Judias V. Buenoano used poison to kill her husband and a boyfriend. She poisoned her son and eventually drowned him. Her last poison victim, a fiancé, survived and helped send her to the electric chair in 1998. (Florida Department of Corrections)

chemically analyzed. The test results revealed that the vitamins contained paraformaldehyde, a class III poison.

Suspicion did not immediately center on Buenoano as a result of poison being found in the vitamins. As a result, Buenoano took the next step and had a bomb placed in Gentry's car. Gentry survived the blast. Authorities then launched a full scale investigation into Buenoano. It was learned that the name "Buenoano" was actually taken on by her and represented a rough Spanish adaptation for "Goodyear." Authorities realized that Buenoano changed her name in order to distance herself from the death of her husband.

In 1984 Goodyear's body was exhumed. A forensic toxicologist reported that the level of arsenic found in Goodyear's liver, kidneys, hair and nails indicated chronic exposure to arsenic poison. Medical experts opined that Goodyear's death was the result of chronic arsenic poisoning occurring over a period of time.

Trial evidence indicated that Buenoano's son died from drowning on May 13, 1980. His body was eventually exhumed by authorities. It was discovered that her son, who had been paralyzed, was poisoned with arsenic and that the arsenic may have caused his paralysis. Eventually authorities prosecuted Buenoano for the murder of her son, on the theory that she pushed him out of a canoe.

There was also trial evidence showing that Bobby Joe Morris, the man whom Buenoano lived with immediately after Goodyear's death, became ill and died after exhibiting symptoms of vomiting, nausea and fever. Morris' body was exhumed in 1984. Tissue analysis of Morris' remains revealed acute arsenic poisoning. Buenoano was not prosecuted for Morris' death.

Other trial evidence showed that Buenoano collected the benefits from various life insurance policies on Goodyear's life totaling $33,000. Buenoano also received $62,000 in dependency compensation from the Veterans Administration. After Morris' death Buenoano received insurance money from three separate policies on his life totaling $23,000. After her son's death Buenoano collected $125,000 in life insurance proceeds. Buenoano also owned a life insurance policy on Gentry's life totaling $510,000. *See also* **Women and Capital Punishment**

Bulgaria   Bulgaria abolished capital punishment in 1998. *See also* **International Capital Punishment Nations**

Bullington v. Missouri   *Court:* United States Supreme Court; *Case Citation:* Bullington v. Missouri, 451 U.S. 430 (1981); *Argued:* January 14, 1981; *Decided:* May 4, 1981; *Opinion of the Court:* Justice Blackmun; *Concurring Opinion:* None; *Dissenting Opinion:* Justice Powell, in which Burger, C. J., and White and Rehnquist, JJ., joined; *Appellate Defense Counsel:* Richard H. Sindel argued; Gail Gaus on brief; *Appellate Prosecution Counsel:* James J. Cook argued and briefed; *Amicus Curiae Brief Supporting Prosecutor:* None; *Amicus Curiae Brief Supporting Defendant:* None.

Issue Presented: Whether the Double Jeopardy Clause pro-

hibits the State from seeking the death penalty at a second trial of a defendant, when a defendant is granted a new trial and the jury rejected imposition of the death penalty at the first trial?

Case Holding: When a capital penalty phase jury rejects imposition of the death penalty and imposes a lesser punishment on a defendant, at a new trial granted to the defendant, the Double Jeopardy Clause prohibits the State from seeking the death penalty at the new trial.

Factual and procedural background of case: In December 1977, the defendant, Robert Bullington, was indicted by the state of Missouri for capital murder. The guilt phase of the defendant's trial resulted in a verdict of guilty of capital murder. The penalty phase jury rejected the death penalty and returned a verdict fixing his punishment at life imprisonment. However, the defendant was granted a new trial. Before the new trial was held the prosecutor announced it would once again seek the death penalty. The defendant filed a motion with the trial court requesting the prosecutor be prohibited from seeking the death penalty at the second trial based on federal Constitutional double jeopardy grounds. The trial court granted the motion and barred the prosecutor from seeking the death penalty. The prosecutor requested a writ of prohibition from the Missouri Court of Appeals to prohibit the trial court from preventing him from seeking the death penalty at the second trial. The Missouri Court of Appeals denied the prosecutor's request for a writ of prohibition. However, the Missouri Supreme Court ultimately granted the prosecutor a writ of prohibition against the trial court. The United States Supreme Court thereafter granted certiorari to consider the issue.

Opinion of the Court by Justice Blackmun: The initial task that Justice Blackmun undertook was to limit the application of *Stroud v. United States*, 251 U.S. 15 (1919). The decision in *Stroud* concerned a defendant who was convicted of first-degree murder and sentenced to life imprisonment. However, the conviction in *Stroud* was reversed and a new trial was granted. At the second trial the defendant was again convicted, but the punishment imposed was the death penalty. The defendant in *Stroud* argued to the United States Supreme Court that the Double Jeopardy Clause prohibited the jury from imposing the death penalty at the second trial. In a unanimous decision in that case, it was "held that the Double Jeopardy Clause of the Fifth Amendment did not bar the imposition of the death penalty when Stroud at his new trial was again convicted."

Rather than overrule *Stroud*, Justice Blackmun distinguished it from Bullington's case. The opinion noted that when the *Stroud* decision was rendered capital punishment prosecutions did not involve independent guilt phase and penalty phase stages. During the *Stroud* era of capital punishment, which extended to 1972, capital prosecutions were basically unitary proceedings, with no elaborate penalty phase proceeding. However, under modern capital punishment it has been found that the Constitution requires utilization of a penalty phase proceeding for the purpose of allowing capital defendants to present mitigating evidence. With this distinction in view, Justice Blackmun found that *Stroud* was not controlling on the outcome of Bullington's case.

The opinion noted that capital punishment penalty phase proceedings have the hallmarks of a trial on guilt or innocence. It was said that the general rule which holds that a defendant may not be retried if he or she obtains a reversal of his or her conviction on the ground that the evidence was insufficient to convict, is relevant to capital sentencing schemes. Under modern capital sentencing requirements a sentence of life imprisonment by a penalty phase jury means that the jury has acquitted a defendant of whatever was necessary to impose the death sentence. Under such a scheme double jeopardy principles bar consideration of the death penalty upon a second trial. The judgment of the Missouri Supreme Court was reversed.

Dissenting opinion by Justice Powell, in which Burger, C. J., and White and Rehnquist, JJ., joined: Justice Powell argued that the decision in the case was controlled by *Stroud* and its progeny. The dissent observed that "[s]ince *Stroud*, it has been settled that a defendant whose conviction is reversed may receive a more severe sentence upon retrial than he received at his first trial." Justice Powell believed that the double jeopardy principles used for considering an acquittal on guilt or innocence as absolutely final, simply do not apply equally to a sentencing decision. It was said that "[t]he possibility of a higher sentence is acceptable under the Double Jeopardy Clause[.]" Therefore, Justice Powell would have affirmed the decision of the Missouri Supreme Court. *See also* **Double Jeopardy Clause; Stroud v. United States**

Bundy, Theodore

Theodore Bundy was executed for three capital murders by the state of Florida on January 24, 1989. The method of execution used was electrocution. The victims of Bundy's capital convictions were Lisa Levy, Margaret Bowman and Kimberly Leach.

Although Bundy was convicted and sentenced to death for killing three persons, authorities believed he was a serial killer who was responsible for the sex-related deaths of more than 36 women. Before his execution Bundy confirmed what authorities knew, but could not prove, by confessing to killing 30 women from 1973 to 1978: 11 murders in the State of Washington, 8 in Utah, 3 in Colorado, 2 in Oregon, 3 in Florida, 2 in Idaho and 1 in California. Through media coverage Bundy became America's most famous sexual serial killer.

The facts leading up to the murder of Bowman and Levy began on January 7, 1978, when Bundy rented a room near the Florida State University campus. (On December 30, 1977 Bundy had escaped confinement in Colorado while awaiting murder charges.) Bundy stalked the University area for a week before making his planned attack on female students at a sorority house.

On January 15, 1978, at approximately 3:00 A.M. a student resident at the sorority house arrived and heard the sounds of

someone running down a flight of stairs. When the student approached the front entrance hall, she saw a man leaving the building with a large stick in his right hand. The man was later identified by the student as Bundy.

After the student proceeded to her room she informed her roommate of what she saw while entering the sorority house. Within moments another student entered the room bleeding and bruised. The police and an ambulance were summoned. Authorities quickly discovered that

Theodore Bundy was executed by the State of Florida for killing three women, but prior to his execution he confessed to having killed 30 women. (Florida Department of Corrections)

Levy and Bowman had been killed and two other students had been severely beaten. Levy and Bowman were killed by strangulation after receiving severe beatings with a limb of a tree branch. Bowman's skull was crushed and literally torn open.

During Bundy's trial for Kimberly's murder the following facts came out. On February 9, 1978, twelve year old Kimberly was reported missing from her junior high school in Lake City, Florida. Two months later her partially decomposed body was located in a wooded area near the Suwanee River. The child had been strangled and sexually assaulted.

By chance Bundy was stopped by a police officer in Pensacola on February 15, 1978, when the officer realized the vehicle Bundy was driving had been reported stolen. As the officer attempted to arrest Bundy for possession of a stolen vehicle, he struck the officer and fled. The officer fired at Bundy before pursuing and capturing him.

Authorities were able to connect Bundy to the deaths of Levy and Bowman based upon teeth marks left on Levy that matched Bundy's teeth prints. Authorities were able to connect Bundy to the murder of Kimberly based upon an eyewitness who had seen Bundy with the child. Bundy's trial for the murder of Levy and Bowman was separate from his prosecution for the murder of Kimberly. Bundy defended himself during both trials.

Burden of Proof at Guilt Phase

The doctrine of burden of proof is concerned with the degree of evidence that the law requires to be produced in order to persuade the factfinder of the truth of an allegation. If proffered evidence does not rise to the level required by the law, then the burden has not been sustained and the allegation is deemed not proven. Burden of proof, as a general proposition, means having the obligation of proffering a specific level of evidence to persuade a factfinder of the truth of an allegation.

At the guilt phase of a trial the Federal Constitution has been interpreted as requiring prosecutors prove beyond a reasonable doubt every element of a charged offense. This burden can never shift to a defendant. The significance in having the prosecutor prove a defendant's guilt beyond a reasonable doubt is best understood through the presumption of innocence doctrine.

Anglo-American jurisprudence affords a person charged with a crime a presumption of innocence. The presumption of innocence is a conclusion drawn by the law in favor of the defendant. The burden of proof is never upon the defendant to establish his or her innocence, or to disprove the facts necessary to establish the crime for which he or she is charged. The burden of proof is on the prosecution from the beginning to the end of the trial, and applies to every element necessary to constitute the crime. What this means is that a defendant is not obligated to present any evidence at trial in order to be acquitted of a crime. For example: (1) if the prosecutor presents no evidence during a trial a defendant must be set free; (2) if evidence by a prosecutor only shows that a defendant might have committed a charged crime, the defendant must be acquitted; (3) if a the prosecutor's evidence only establishes that a defendant probably committed a charged crime, a verdict of acquittal must be rendered. In each of the latter three situations the presumption of innocence combined with the beyond a reasonable doubt standard in order to render an acquittal.

Capital felons frequently challenge their convictions based upon alleged erroneous instructions to juries on the meaning of "beyond a reasonable doubt." Occasionally this challenge has proven successful, but in most instances it has failed. This is primarily true because the Federal Constitution does not dictate that any particular form of words be used in advising the jury of the government's burden of proof at the guilt phase, so long as, taken as a whole, the instructions correctly convey the concept of reasonable doubt. The proper inquiry into the constitutional validity of a jury instruction on the meaning of "beyond a reasonable doubt," is not whether the instruction "could have" been applied unconstitutionally, but whether there was a reasonable likelihood that the jury in fact applied it unconstitutionally. *See also* **Affirmative Defenses; Cage v. Louisiana; Burden of Proof at Penalty Phase; Victor v. Nebraska**

Burden of Proof at Penalty Phase   The issue of burden of proof at the penalty phase of a capital prosecution is not simplistic for several reasons. First, the Federal Constitution does not require the burden of proof be imposed upon the prosecutor at the penalty phase. The primary reason is that no presumption of innocence exists for a defendant at the penalty phase; his or her guilt has been determined at the guilt phase. Second, the penalty phase only involves evidence of aggravating circumstances and mitigating circumstances. The prosecutor has the burden of presenting aggravating circumstances and the defendant has the burden of presenting miti-

gating circumstances. As a result both parties having the burden of presenting some evidence on their respective issue, a mechanism must be used for the jury to determine how to interpret the evidence of both parties. Third, each jurisdiction is free to device any mechanism it desires, within the limits of due process of law, for determining the interpretation to give to proven mitigating and aggravating circumstances.

The material in this section will unravel the complex nature of burden of proof at the penalty phase under three broad headings: (1) establishing the existence of aggravators and mitigators, (2) comparing proven aggravators and mitigators, and (3) determining the result of comparing proven aggravators and mitigators.

1. *Establishing the Existence of Aggravators and Mitigators*

a. *Proving statutory aggravating circumstances exist.* In the case of *Woratzeck v. Lewis*, 863 F.Supp. 1079 (D.Ariz. 1994) the Federal District Court of Arizona enumerated three key points regarding statutory aggravating circumstances. First, the District Court pointed out that "[a]n aggravating factor in the penalty phase of a capital proceeding is not an element of the offense." Second, it was pointed out "that the federal constitution does not require that aggravating factors in a capital sentencing proceeding be proven beyond a reasonable doubt." The final point made by *Woratzeck* is that "the Supreme Court ... has [not] determined what burden of proof must be satisfied when proving the existence of aggravating factors."

Whenever the Constitution is deemed silent on an issue, jurisdictions are generally free to address the matter as they deem appropriate. Capital punishment jurisdictions have responded to the Constitution's silence on the standard of proof needed to establish the existence of statutory aggravating circumstances. The majority of capital punishment jurisdictions require by statute that the existence of statutory aggravating circumstances be proven beyond a reasonable doubt.

One capital punishment jurisdiction, California, does not require statutory aggravating circumstances be proven beyond a reasonable doubt. However, as explained by the California supreme court in *People v. Davenport*, 221 Cal.Rptr. 794 (1985), California does require a heightened standard of proof for "other crimes" that are used as statutory aggravating circumstances. Excluding California's heightened standard of proof for other crimes, it does not statutorily impose any standard of proof on establishing the existence of statutory aggravating circumstances. The factfinder is instructed merely to "consider" evidence submitted to show statutory aggravating circumstances exist.

b. *Proving mitigating circumstances exist.* In the capital case of *Walton v. Arizona*, 497 U.S. 639 (1990) the United States Supreme Court held that "a defendant's constitutional rights are not violated by placing on him the burden of proving mitigating circumstances sufficiently

JURISDICTIONS STATUTORILY REQUIRING AGGRAVATORS BE PROVEN BEYOND A REASONABLE DOUBT

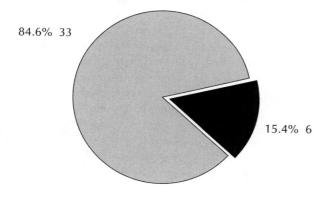

84.6% 33

15.4% 6

■ STATUTORY JURISDICTIONS

■ ALL OTHER JURISDICTIONS

substantial to call for leniency." The potential harshness of imposing a burden of proof on capital felons was ameliorated by other Supreme Court rulings which held that requiring jury unanimity on the determination of whether a mitigating circumstance existed was unconstitutional. Therefore, if only one penalty phase juror finds that a capital felon carried his or her burden of proof on the existence of a mitigating circumstance, then the circumstance is deemed proven.

No capital punishment jurisdiction requires capital felons prove the existence of mitigating circumstances beyond a reasonable doubt. A minority of capital punishment jurisdictions require by statute that capital felons prove the existence of mitigating circumstances by a preponderance of evidence. One capital punishment jurisdiction, Alabama, provides by statute that the prosecutor must disprove the existence of mitigating circumstances by a preponderance of evidence. The statutes of a majority of capital punishment jurisdictions do not provide any standard of proof for establishing the existence of mitigating circumstances. This statutory silence means that capital felons merely have to raise the issue of mitigating circumstances, i.e., present some evidence on the issue. Only one jurisdiction, Colorado, explicitly provides by statute that a capital felon merely has to raise the issue of mitigating circumstances.

2. *Comparing Proven Aggravators and Mitigators.* Determining the existence of mitigating and statutory aggravating circumstances does not end the burden of proof process. Once the existence hurdle is overcome, a second process is triggered: mitigating and statutory aggravating circumstances must be compared with each other. The comparison process is carried out in one of two manners: (a) weighing or (b) non-weighing.

a. *Weighing jurisdictions.* The Utah supreme court described the weighing process in *State v. Wood*, 648 P.2d 71 (Utah 1981) as follows:

[This] standard[] require[s] that the sentencing body compare the totality of the mitigating against the totality of the aggravating factors, not in terms of the relative numbers of the aggravating and the mitigating factors, but in terms of their respective substantiality and persuasiveness. Basically, what the sentencing authority must decide is how … persuasive the totality of the mitigating factors are when compared against the totality of the aggravating factors. The sentencing body [is] making the judgment that aggravating [or mitigating] factors "outweigh," or are more [persuasive] than, the mitigating [or aggravating] factors[.]

Wood points out that the weighing process does not involve determining if more mitigating circumstances exist than statutory aggravating circumstances. Mere tallying is not the purpose of the weighing process. It matters not that, for example, five statutory aggravating circumstances were proven to exist, but only one mitigating circumstance is found to exist. The factfinder could still determine the mitigating circumstance outweighed the five statutory aggravating circumstances.

The United States Supreme Court noted in *Harris v. Alabama*, 115 S.Ct. 1031 (1995), that no "specific method for balancing mitigating and aggravating factors in a capital sentencing proceeding is constitutionally required." The "balancing" referred to in *Harris* is the weighing process. The result of *Harris'* pronouncement is that capital punishment jurisdictions may devise weighing processes as they see fit. This discretion has led to the development of two classes of weighing jurisdictions: (i) no standard of proof jurisdictions and (ii) standard of proof jurisdictions.

i. No standard of proof jurisdictions. There are two types of weighing jurisdictions that do not impose a standard of proof on the weighing process.

First, the statutes in nine capital punishment jurisdictions require statutory aggravating circumstances outweigh mitigating circumstances. Under this process the prosecutor has the burden of showing that statutory aggravating circumstances are more creditable than mitigating circumstances. However, no standard of proof is imposed on the prosecutor. That is, in weighing mitigating and statutory aggravating circumstances, the factfinder is free to use its own judgment as to why statutory aggravating circumstances appear more creditable than mitigating circumstances.

Second, the statutes in twelve capital punishment jurisdictions require mitigating circumstances outweigh statutory aggravating circumstances. Under this process the capital felon is given the burden of establishing that mitigating circumstances are more creditable than statutory aggravating circumstances. The burden on the capital felon under this weighing process is lessened by the fact that no specific standard of proof is imposed upon the capital felon. The factfinder uses its own judgment in determining why more credibility should be given to mitigating circumstances.

ii. Standard of proof jurisdictions. There are two types of weighing jurisdictions that impose a standard of proof on the weighing process.

First, in two capital punishment jurisdictions, Delaware and Maryland, statutory aggravating circumstances are required to outweigh mitigating circumstances by a preponderance of evidence. These jurisdictions impose the burden of proof on the prosecutor. More significantly, the prosecutor is required to persuade the factfinder by a preponderance of evidence that the statutory aggravating circumstances outweigh the mitigating circumstances.

Second, in six capital punishment jurisdictions statutory aggravating circumstances must outweigh mitigating circumstances beyond a reasonable doubt. Under this process the prosecutor is strapped with the burden of proving beyond a reasonable doubt that the statutory aggravating circumstances outweigh the mitigating circumstances.

b. *Non-weighing jurisdictions.* The South Carolina supreme court held in *State v. Bellamy*, 359 S.E.2d 63 (S.C. 1987) that the penalty phase jury should not be instructed to weigh statutory aggravating circumstances against mitigating circumstances. Instead, the jury had to be instructed to merely consider the mitigating and statutory aggravating circumstances. The holding in *Bellamy* was in accord with a ruling by the Supreme Court in *Zant v. Stephens*, 462 U.S. 862 (1983), that the Constitution does not require weighing mitigating and statutory aggravating circumstances. The decision in *Zant* fostered what are called non-weighing capital punishment jurisdictions. There are nine non-weighing capital punishment jurisdictions.

In non-weighing jurisdictions the factfinder is not instructed or guided on how to compare mitigating and statutory aggravating circumstances. As explained in *Bellamy*, the factfinder in a non-weighing jurisdiction is instructed to merely consider the proffered circumstances for sufficiency. The non-weighing process has developed along three different lines.

First, there are seven non-weighing jurisdictions that require nothing more than the penalty phase factfinder determine whether sufficient mitigating circumstances exist to warrant leniency. The method for making this "sufficiency determination" is left up to the factfinder. Additionally, this particular non-weighing process does not have a standard of proof for measuring sufficiency. The factfinder is allowed to determine for itself what constitutes sufficiency. The burden of proving sufficiency is on the capital felon.

Second, one capital punishment jurisdiction, Washington, utilizing the non-weighing process requires the factfinder determine whether sufficient mitigating circumstances do not exist beyond a reasonable doubt. In making its sufficiency determination under this process the factfinder is provided with a standard of proof for measuring sufficiency. The beyond a reasonable doubt standard of proof is used. The burden of proof is placed on the prosecutor. The prosecutor must persuade the factfinder that mitigating circumstances are not sufficient beyond a reasonable doubt.

Finally, one capital punishment jurisdiction, Connecticut, requires only that the factfinder determine if at least one mitigating circumstance was proven to exist. Nothing else is required under this process.

3. *Determining the Result of Comparing Proven Aggravators and Mitigators.* In *Boyde v. California*, 494 U.S. 370 (1990) the United States Supreme Court held that there was no constitutional requirement that a penalty phase jury must be instructed that it can decline to impose the death penalty, even if it decided that statutory aggravating circumstances outweighed mitigating circumstances. The *Boyde* holding has been interpreted to mean that, once a weighing or sufficiency determination has been made that is favorable to the prosecutor, the constitution permits the death penalty to be imposed. Nothing further is constitutionally required. The *Boyde* decision has promoted two types of jurisdictions: (a) death automatic jurisdictions and (b) death discretionary jurisdictions.

a. *Death automatic jurisdictions.* A majority of all capital punishment jurisdictions require that death must be imposed, once a weighing or sufficiency determination is made that is favorable to the prosecutor. There are seventeen weighing capital punishment jurisdictions that require the death penalty be imposed, if the weighing process is favorable to the prosecutor. In three non-weighing jurisdictions no discretion is given to the factfinder once a pro-prosecutor determination is made. The death penalty must be imposed once a sufficiency determination is made that is favorable to the prosecutor.

b. *Death discretionary jurisdictions.* Notwithstanding a weighing or sufficiency determination that is favorable to the prosecutor, a large majority of all capital punishment jurisdictions provide discretion to the factfinder. The factfinder can refuse to impose the death penalty even though the weighing or sufficiency determination was favorable to the prosecutor.

In 15 weighing capital punishment jurisdictions the factfinder may reject imposing the death penalty on the capital felon, even though the weighing process called for imposition of the death penalty. In four non-weighing capital punishment jurisdictions the factfinder is given death discretion once it makes a sufficiency determination that is favorable to the prosecutor. In these jurisdictions the capital felon may be spared the death penalty, notwithstanding the fact that the sufficiency determination called for death. *See also* **Burden of Proof at Guilt Phase; Presumption of Innocence of Aggravators**

Burger v. Kemp *Court:* United States Supreme Court; *Case Citation:* Burger v. Kemp, 483 U.S. 776 (1987); *Argued:* March 30, 1987; *Decided:* June 26, 1987; *Opinion of the Court:* Justice Stevens; *Concurring Opinion:* None; *Dissenting Opinion:* Justice Blackmun, in which Brennan, Marshall and Powell, JJ., joined; *Dissenting Opinion:* Justice Powell, in which Brennan, J., joined; *Appellate Defense Counsel:* Joseph M. Nursey argued; Millard C. Farmer on brief; *Appellate Prosecution Counsel:* William B. Hill, Jr. argued; Michael J. Bowers, Marion O. Gordon and Susan v. Boleyn on brief; *Amicus Curiae Brief Supporting Prosecutor:* None; *Amicus Curiae Brief Supporting Defendant:* None.

Issue Presented: Whether the defendant received ineffective assistance of counsel based upon an alleged conflict of interest and failure to present mitigating evidence at the penalty phase?

Case Holding: The defendant failed to establish a conflict of interest by his counsel and failed to show that his counsel's decision not to put on the sparse available mitigating evidence was an unreasonable decision.

Factual and procedural background of case: The defendant, Christopher Burger, was convicted and sentenced for capital murder by the State of Georgia. A co-defendant was involved in the murder and was tried separately. Counsel for the defendant and counsel for the co-defendant worked in the same law firm. Although the defendant was able to have his death sentence reversed by the Georgia Supreme Court, the defendant was subsequently resentenced to death.

After exhausting state collateral remedies, the defendant filed a habeas corpus petition in a Federal District Court. The defendant alleged ineffective assistance of counsel on the ground that his attorney had a conflict of interest in representing him while his law party represented the co-defendant; and that his attorney failed to present any mitigating circumstances at either penalty phase hearing he had. The District Court dismissed the petition. A Court of Appeals ultimately affirmed. The United States Supreme Court granted certiorari to consider the issues.

Opinion of the Court by Justice Stevens: Justice Stevens ruled that there was no merit to the defendant's ineffective assistance claim based on defense counsel's alleged conflict of interest. The opinion found that even assuming that law partners are to be considered as one attorney in determining such a claim, permitting a single attorney to represent co-defendants is not per se violative of constitutional guarantees of effective assistance of counsel. It was said that any overlap or shared work by the attorneys did not so infect the legal representation as to constitute an active representation of competing interests.

The opinion also rejected the defendant's ineffective assistance claim on the ground that his attorney failed to develop and present any mitigating evidence at either of the two sentencing hearings. It was said that the evidence that might have been presented would have disclosed that the defendant had an exceptionally unhappy and unstable childhood. Based on interviews with the defendant, his mother, and others, defense counsel decided that the defendant's interest would not be served by presenting such evidence. Justice Stevens held that this decision was supported by reasonable professional judgment. The judgment of the Court of Appeals was affirmed.

Dissenting opinion by Justice Blackmun, in which Brennan, Marshall and Powell, JJ., joined: Justice Blackmun dissented from the majority opinion. He wrote: "In *Strickland v. Washington*, this Court set forth the standards that are to govern a court's consideration of a criminal defendant's claims that he has been denied his Sixth Amendment right to effective assistance of counsel. Burger presents two such claims in this case. I believe each claim meets those specified standards for establishing a constitutional violation. Each therefore calls for a grant of the federal habeas corpus relief sought by [him]. Accordingly, I dissent from the Court's judgment that denies such relief."

Dissenting opinion by Justice Powell, in which Brennan, J., joined: Justice Powell dissented on the basis that the defendant established one of his claims. He wrote: "I would reverse the judgment of the Court of Appeals on the ground that counsel unreasonably failed to investigate and present to the sentencing jury available mitigating evidence that would have raised a substantial question whether the sentence of death should have been imposed.... I therefore do not reach the question whether there was a conflict of interest resulting from the fact that two law partners represented Burger and [his co-defendant] in their separate trials." *See also* **Right to Counsel; Strickland v. Washington**

Burger, Warren Earl Warren Earl Burger served as chief justice of the United States Supreme Court from 1969 to 1986. While on the Supreme Court Burger was known as a centrist who never strayed to the left or right in his interpretation of the Constitution.

Burger was born in St. Paul, Minnesota on September 17, 1907. The humble background of his family caused Burger to resort to nontraditional means for obtaining an education. As a result of financial difficulties he was unable to accept a scholarship that would have taken him to Princeton University. Instead, Burger worked as an insurance agent while taking undergraduate extension courses from the University of Minnesota. He eventually received a law degree from St. Paul College of Law in 1931, while taking night law school classes.

Burger's career as a private attorney was modest and uneventful. His path to the Supreme Court did not begin in earnest until his appointment in 1952 as an assistant United States Attorney General. That position landed him an appointment in 1956 as an appellate judge on the Court of Appeals for the District of Columbia. In 1969 President Richard M. Nixon appointed Burger as chief justice of the Supreme Court.

During Burger's tenure as chief justice he wrote a number of opinions in capital punishment cases. The centrist legal philosophy that became Burger's legacy was evident in capital punishment cases in the manner in which he voted, however, his written opinions in this area tended to lean toward the conservative side of the legal spectrum. This was never more evident than in Burger's dissenting opinion in *Furman v. Georgia.* The decision in *Furman* halted executions in the nation on the grounds that juries were permitted to arbitrarily determine who would receive a death sentence. Burger addressed the issue in his dissenting opinion as follows: "The selectivity of juries in imposing the punishment of death is properly viewed as a refinement on, rather than a repudiation of, the statutory authorization for that penalty.... Given the general awareness that death is no longer a routine punishment for the crimes for which it is made available, it is hardly surprising that juries have been increasingly meticulous in their imposition of the penalty. But to assume from the mere fact of relative infrequency that only a random assortment of pariahs are sentenced to death, is to cast grave doubt on the basic integrity of our jury system." Burger died on June 25, 1995.

Capital Punishment Opinions Written by Burger

Case Name	Opinion of the Court	Plurality Opinion	Concurring Opinion	Dissenting Opinion
Ake v. Oklahoma			✓	
Baldwin v. Alabama			✓	
Bell v. Ohio		✓		
Cabana v. Bullock			✓	
Coker v. Georgia				✓
Darden v. Wainwright			✓	
Dobbert v. Florida			✓	
Eddings v. Oklahoma				✓
Estelle v. Smith	✓			
Furman v. Georgia				✓
Godfrey v. Georgia				✓
Hopper v. Evans	✓			
Lockett v. Ohio		✓		
Schick v. Reed	✓			

Burglary   The crime of burglary was defined by the common law as breaking and entering the dwelling of another, at night, with the intent to commit a felony. Most jurisdictions have expanded the common law definition of burglary to include its commission during the day and in structures other than a dwelling. Burglary, without more, cannot be used to inflict the death penalty. The Eighth Amendment of the United States Constitution prohibits this as cruel and unusual punishment. However, the crime of burglary can play a role in a capital prosecution. If burglary occurs during the commission of a homicide it may form the basis of a death-eligible offense, and therefore trigger a capital prosecution. *See also* **Burglary Aggravator; Death-Eligible Offenses; Felony Murder Rule; Rape and Capital Punishment**

Burglary Aggravator   The crime of burglary committed during the course of a homicide is a statutory aggravating circumstance in a majority of capital punishment jurisdictions. As a statutory aggravating circumstance, evidence of burglary is used at the penalty phase of a capital prosecution for the factfinder to consider in determining whether to im-

pose the death penalty. *See also* **Aggravating Circumstances; Burglary; Felony Murder Rule**

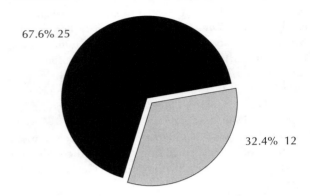

JURISDICTIONS USING BURGLARY AGGRAVATOR

67.6% 25

32.4% 12

■ BURGLARY AGGRAVATOR JURISDICTIONS

■ ALL OTHER JURISDICTIONS

Burkina Faso   Capital punishment is carried out in the nation of Burkina Faso. The firing squad is used by Burkina Faso to carry out the death penalty. Its legal system is based on French civil law system and customary law. The nation's constitution came into existence on June 2, 1991. The political structure of Burkina Faso consists of an executive branch, bicameral legislative branch and judicial branch.

Under the nation's constitution the judicial system is composed of a Supreme Court, two Courts of Appeal, and 10 provincial (trial) courts. There is also a High Court of Justice, with authority to try the president and senior government officials for treason and other serious crimes. In addition to the constitutional courts, customary or traditional courts, presided over by village chiefs, handle many local problems, such as divorce and inheritance disputes. Defendants are constitutionally entitled to public trials, access to counsel, bail, and appeal. *See also* **International Capital Punishment Nations**

Burma   Capital punishment is carried out in Burma (Myanmar). Burma uses hanging as the method of carrying out the death penalty. Burma uses a legal system that has remnants of the British-era legal system. The nation's constitution was adopted on January 3, 1974, but has been suspended since September 18, 1988.

The court system is composed of trial courts and a Supreme Court. Defendants have the right to a public trial, to legal counsel, and cross examine witnesses. *See also* **International Capital Punishment Nations**

Burns v. Wilson   *Court:* United States Supreme Court; *Case Citation:* Burns v. Wilson, 346 U.S. 137 (1953); *Argued:*

February 5, 1953; *Decided:* June 15, 1953; *Plurality Opinion:* Chief Justice Vinson announced the Court's judgment and delivered an opinion, in which Reed, Burton and Clark, JJ., joined; *Concurring Opinion:* Justice Minton; *Concurring Statement:* Justice Jackson; *Dissenting Opinion:* Justice Douglas, in which Black , J., joined; *Dissenting Opinion:* Justice Frankfurter; *Appellate Defense Counsel:* Robert L. Carter and Frank D. Reeves argued; Thurgood Marshall, Charles W. Quick and Herbert O. Reid on brief; *Appellate Prosecution Counsel:* Solicitor General Cummings argued; Oscar H. Davis, Beatrice Rosenberg and Walter Kiechel, Jr. on brief; *Amicus Curiae Brief Supporting Prosecutor:* None; *Amicus Curiae Brief Supporting Defendant:* None.

Issue Presented: Whether Federal courts may review anew, in habeas corpus proceedings, the decision of military courts?

Case Holding: Federal courts must defer to the decisions reached by military courts in proceedings that fairly and fully addressed issues raised by defendants in habeas corpus petitions.

Factual and procedural background of case: The defendants, Robert Burns, Calvin Dennis and Herman Dennis, were tried separately by court martial for murder and rape. They were each found guilty and sentenced to death. After exhausting all remedies available to them under the Articles of War, the defendants applied to a Federal District Court for writs of habeas corpus, alleging that they had been subjected to illegal detention; that coerced confessions had been extorted from them; that they had been denied counsel of their choice and denied effective representation; that the military authorities had suppressed evidence favorable to them; procured perjured testimony against them; and that their trials were conducted in an atmosphere of terror and vengeance, conducive to mob violence instead of fair play. The District Court denied relief summarily without taking evidence. A Federal Court of Appeals affirmed. The United States Supreme Court granted certiorari to consider the issue.

Plurality opinion in which Chief Justice Vinson announced the Court's judgment and in which Reed, Burton and Clark, JJ., joined: The Chief Justice held that the defendants received a fair trial and review of their cases by military courts. The opinion indicated that the statute which vests Federal courts with jurisdiction over applications for habeas corpus from persons confined by the military courts, is the same statute which vests Federal courts with jurisdiction over the applications of persons confined by the civil courts. However, the Chief Justice was of the opinion that in military habeas corpus, the inquiry and the scope of matters open for review by Federal courts was more narrow than in civil law cases. He wrote that the law which governed a civil court in the exercise of its jurisdiction over military habeas corpus applications could not be assimilated to the law which governed the exercise of that power in other instances.

It was said that military law, like State law, was a jurisprudence which existed separate and apart from the law which governed the Federal judicial process. The Chief Justice noted

that historically the Court had played no role in the development of military law and exerted no supervisory power over the courts which enforce military law. He reasoned that the rights of persons in the armed forces must be conditioned to meet certain overriding demands of discipline and duty, and civil courts are not the agencies which must determine the precise balance to be struck in that adjustment.

The Chief Justice believed that in military habeas corpus cases, even more than in State habeas corpus cases, it would be in disregard of the statutory scheme if the Federal civil courts failed to give deference to prior military review proceedings. He stated that Congress had provided that military court martial determinations were final and binding upon all courts. The opinion stated further that the mere fact of habeas jurisdiction by Federal courts over military court martial proceedings, did not mean that when a military decision dealt fully and fairly with an allegation raised in a habeas petition, it was still open to a Federal civil court to grant habeas simply to re-evaluate the evidence.

The opinion recognized the seriousness of the allegations raised by the defendants, but found that the military courts fully and fairly considered the claims. Accordingly, the Chief Justice indicated that it was not the duty of the civil courts simply to repeat that process. He wrote that habeas review must be limited to determining whether the military gave fair consideration to each claim raised. The opinion concluded that military courts gave fair consideration to each of the claims raised by the defendants in their habeas petition. The judgment of the Court of Appeals was affirmed.

Concurring opinion by Justice Minton: Justice Minton concurred in the Court's judgment. In his concurrence it was said that Federal civil courts are not empowered to protect the constitutional rights of military defendants, except for limited habeas review of jurisdiction over offenses. Justice Minton wrote more specifically as follows:

> This grant to set up military courts is as distinct as the grant to set up civil courts. Congress has acted to implement both grants. Each hierarchy of courts is distinct from the other. We have no supervisory power over the administration of military justice, such as we have over civil justice in the federal courts. Due process of law for military personnel is what Congress has provided for them in the military hierarchy in courts established according to law. If the court is thus established, its action is not reviewable here. Such military court's jurisdiction is exclusive but for the exceptions contained in the statute, and the civil courts are not mentioned in the exceptions.
>
> If error is made by the military courts, to which Congress has committed the protection of the rights of military personnel, that error must be corrected in the military hierarchy of courts provided by Congress. We have but one function, namely, to see that the military court has jurisdiction, not whether it has committed error in the exercise of that jurisdiction.

Concurring statement by Justice Jackson: Justice Jackson issued a statement indicating he concurred in the Court's judgment.

Dissenting opinion by Justice Douglas: Justice Douglas dissented from the Court's decision. He believed that some deference should be accorded to military determinations, but he wrote that he did not believe such deference extended to refusal to examine factual determinations made by military courts. Justice Douglas expressed his views as follows:

> ... [T]he Court gives binding effect to the ruling of the military tribunal on the constitutional question, provided it has given fair consideration to it....
>
> If the military agency has fairly and conscientiously applied the standards of due process formulated by this Court, I would agree that a rehash of the same facts by a federal court would not advance the cause of justice. But where the military reviewing agency has not done that, a court should entertain the petition for habeas corpus. In the first place, the military tribunals in question are federal agencies subject to no other judicial supervision except what is afforded by the federal courts. In the second place, the rules of due process which they apply are constitutional rules which we, not they, formulate....
>
> I think [the defendants] are entitled to a judicial hearing on the circumstances surrounding their confessions....
>
> Congress has [constitutional authority] ... "[t]o make Rules for the Government and Regulation of the land and naval Forces." The rules which Congress has made relative to trials for offenses by military personnel are contained in the Uniform Code of Military Justice. Those rules do not provide for judicial review. But it is clear from our decisions that habeas corpus may be used to review some aspects of a military trial....
>
> If a prisoner is coerced by torture or other methods to give the evidence against him, if he is beaten or slowly "broken" by third-degree methods, then the "trial" before the military tribunal becomes an empty ritual. The real trial takes place in secret where the accused without benefit of counsel succumbs to physical or psychological pressures. A soldier or sailor convicted in that manner has been denied due process of law; and, like the accused in criminal cases he should have relief by way of habeas corpus....
>
> The undisputed facts in this case make a prima facie case that our rule on coerced confessions expressed in *Watts v. Indiana* was violated here. No court has considered the question whether repetitious questioning over a period of 5 days while the accused was held incommunicado without benefit of counsel violated the Fifth Amendment.
>
> There has been at no time any considered appraisal of the facts surrounding these confessions in light of our opinions. Before these men go to their death, such an appraisal should be made.

Dissenting opinion by Justice Frankfurter: Justice Frankfurter dissented from the Court's decision not to have the parties reargue the case. He was not prepared to rule for or against the defendants, because he believed further consideration of the case was required by the Court. Justice Frankfurter also expressed doubts about the Court's position to the degree of deference to be accorded military decisions. He concluded his dissent by stating: "It is my view that this is not just a case involving individuals. Issues of far-reaching import are at stake which call for further consideration. They were not explored in all their significance in the submissions made to the Court.... The short of it is that I believe this case should be set down for reargument."

Case note: The position taken by Justice Douglas' dissent would eventually become the law, through a 1983 legislative enactment by Congress which gave the Supreme Court authority to have discretionary direct review of military capital punishment cases. *See also* **Loving v. United States; Military Death Penalty Law**

Burton, Harold Hitz Harold Hitz Burton served as an associate justice on the United States Supreme Court from 1944 to 1958. While on the Supreme Court Burton was known as a moderate conservative interpreter of the Constitution.

Burton was born in Jamaica Plains, Massachusetts on June 22, 1888. He graduated from Bowdoin College in 1909. In 1912 Burton received a law degree from Harvard Law School. Upon graduation from law school he established a private law practice in Cleveland. Burton's law practice was interrupted by World War I, when he joined the Army and served in the infantry. Burton rose to the rank of captain before leaving the Army.

After the war Burton launched a political career that included being elected twice as mayor of Cleveland and, in 1940, being elected to the United States Senate. In 1944 President Harry S Truman nominated Burton to the Supreme Court. While on the Supreme Court Burton is known to have authored only a few capital punishment opinions. The opinion which best illustrated his views of capital punishment and the Constitution was his dissent in *Francis v. Resweber*.

The issue in *Francis* was whether or not the Constitution permitted a State to attempt a second execution of a defendant, after the first attempt failed. Burton argued that it was cruel and unusual punishment to attempt a second execution of a defendant. He stated his position on the issue as follows: "Although the failure of the first attempt, in the present case, was unintended, the reapplication of the electric current will be intentional. How many deliberate and intentional reapplications of electric current does it take to produce a cruel, unusual and unconstitutional punishment? While five applications would be more cruel and unusual than one, the uniqueness of the present case demonstrates that, today, two separated applications are sufficiently 'cruel and unusual' to be prohibited. If five attempts would be 'cruel and unusual,' it would be difficult to draw the line between two, three, four and five." Burton died on October 28, 1964.

Capital Punishment Opinions Written by Burton

Case Name	Opinion of the Court	Dissenting Opinion
Darcy v. Handy	✓	
Francis v. Resweber		✓
Taylor v. Alabama	✓	

Burundi The death penalty is used in Burundi. Burundi utilizes the firing squad and hanging as methods of carrying out the death penalty. The nation has a legal system which is based on German and Belgian civil codes and customary law. Burundi's constitution was adopted March 13, 1992. In July of 1996, a military coup ousted the government of President Sylvestre Ntibantunganya. The self-proclaimed interim president, Major Pierre Buyoya, replaced Burundi's constitution with the Transitional Constitutional Act. This new constitution changed the structure of the government.

Under Burundi's new constitution the judicial system is divided into civil and criminal courts with a Supreme Court at the apex. The public generally does not have access to court proceedings. Defendants are presumed innocent, have a right to counsel, and have the right to appeal. *See also* **International Capital Punishment Nations**

Bus Hijacking Aggravator

The crime of bus hijacking committed during the course of a homicide is a statutory aggravating circumstance in Illinois and Missouri. As a statutory aggravating circumstance, evidence of bus hijacking is used at the penalty phase of a capital prosecution for the factfinder to consider in determining whether to impose the death penalty. *See also* **Aggravating Circumstances**

Bush v. Kentucky

Court: United States Supreme Court; *Case Citation:* Bush v. Kentucky, 107 U.S. 110 (1883); *Argued:* Not reported; *Decided:* January 29, 1883; *Opinion of the Court:* Justice Harlan; *Concurring Opinion:* None; *Dissenting Opinion:* Chief Justice Waite, in which Gray, J., joined; *Dissenting Statement:* Justice Field; *Appellate Defense Counsel:* L. P. Tarleton, Jr. argued and briefed; *Appellate Prosecution Counsel:* I. D. Hunt argued; W. C. P. Breckinridge on brief; *Amicus Curiae Brief Supporting Prosecutor:* None; *Amicus Curiae Brief Supporting Defendant:* None.

Issue Presented: Whether the defendant's conviction and sentence violated the Constitution because the laws of Kentucky expressly precluded blacks from serving on grand and petit juries?

Case Holding: The defendant's conviction and sentence violated the Constitution because the laws of Kentucky expressly precluded blacks from serving on grand and petit juries.

Factual and procedural background of case: The defendant, John Bush, was convicted of capital murder and sentenced to death by the State of Kentucky. On appeal, the Kentucky Supreme Court affirmed the judgment. The defendant then filed a motion in a Federal District Court requesting the case be removed to Federal court, on the grounds that the laws of Kentucky excluded blacks from the grand and petit juries. The Federal court agreed with the defendant and ordered his release. Subsequently, the State of Kentucky charged the defendant a second time with the same offense. The defendant was again convicted and sentenced to death. The State appellate court affirmed the judgment. In doing so, the appellate court rejected the defendant's contention that the judgment was invalid because blacks were systematically excluded from serving on grand and petit juries under the laws of the State. The United States Supreme Court granted certiorari to consider the issue.

Opinion of the Court by Justice Harlan: Justice Harlan ruled that the defendant's conviction could not stand because the laws of Kentucky expressly precluded blacks from serving on grand and petit juries. The opinion reasoned as follows:

... In several cases heretofore decided in this court we have had occasion to consider the general question whether the four-

teenth amendment, and the laws passed by congress for the enforcement of its provisions, do not prohibit any discrimination, in the selection of grand and petit jurors, against citizens of African descent because of their race or color....

[We have said] that a denial to citizens of African descent, because of their race, of the right or privilege accorded to white citizens, of participating as jurors in the administration of justice, is a discrimination against the former inconsistent with the amendment, and within the power of congress, by appropriate legislation, to prevent; that to compel a [defendant] to submit to a trial before a jury drawn from a panel from which is excluded, because of their color, every man of his race, however well qualified by education and character to discharge the functions of jurors, is a denial of the equal protection of the laws; and that such exclusion of the black race from juries, because of their color, is not less forbidden by law than would be the exclusion from juries, in the states where the blacks have the majority, of the white race, because of their color. It [has also been said] that the presumption should be indulged, in the first instance, that the state recognizes, as is its plain duty, an amendment of the federal constitution, from the time of its adoption, as binding on all of its citizens and every department of its government, and to be enforced within its limits, without reference to any inconsistent provisions in its own constitution or statutes....

We are of opinion that ... in the absence of any evidence that the selection of grand jurors ... was in fact made without discrimination against [black] citizens, because of their race, it should be assumed that the jury commissioners then appointed followed the statutes of Kentucky so far as they restricted the selections of grand jurors to citizens of the white race.

The judgment of the Kentucky Supreme Court was reversed.

Dissenting opinion by Chief Justice Waite, in which Gray, J., joined: The Chief Justice dissented from the Court's decision. It was said by the Chief Justice that the Court wrongly assumed that Kentucky authorities failed to follow the Court's prior decision which held that racial discrimination in jury selection was prohibited by the Constitution. The Chief Justice wrote: "In my opinion it is not to be presumed that the courts or the officers of Kentucky neglected or refused to follow the rulings in *Strauder v. West Virginia* after the judgment in that case was pronounced by this court. The court of appeals promptly recognized the authority of that case, and, in the absence of any proof to the contrary, it seems to me we must assume the inferior courts also did."

Dissenting statement by Justice Field: Justice Field issued a statement indicating he dissented from the Court's judgment. *See also* **Discrimination in Grand or Petit Jury Selection**

Butler, Pierce

Pierce Butler served as an associate justice of the United States Supreme Court from 1923 to 1939. While on the Supreme Court Butler was known as a conservative who was philosophically opposed to government regulation of the economy.

Butler was born in Dakota County, Minnesota on March 17, 1866. He received two undergraduate degrees from Carleton College in 1887. Butler did not receive a formal education in the law. He was a legal apprentice for a law firm in St. Paul. He would eventually be admitted to the Minnesota bar in 1888. As a private attorney Butler established a national reputation representing railroad companies. In 1922 President Warren G. Harding nominated Butler to the Supreme Court.

While on the Supreme Court Butler was known to issue only one opinion in a capital punishment case. Butler wrote a dissenting opinion in *Powell v. Alabama.* The decision in *Powell* involved seven African American defendants (dubbed the Scottsboro Boys) who were convicted of rape and sentenced to death by the State of Alabama. The majority on the Supreme Court held that the judgments could not stand because the defendants were denied the right to counsel. Butler, taking a conservative view of the record in the case, disagreed with the majority. In doing so, Butler argued that two attorneys had volunteered to represent the defendants and that any lack of an adequate opportunity to prepare a defense was not made at the trial court level, therefore the issue was waived. Butler's dissent concluded tersely: "Their silence requires a finding that the claim is groundless for if it had any merit they would be bound to support it." Butler died on November 16, 1939.

Butler v. McKellar *Court:* United States Supreme Court; *Case Citation:* Butler v. McKellar, 494 U.S. 407 (1990); *Argued:* October 30, 1989; *Decided:* March 5, 1990; *Opinion of the Court:* Chief Justice Rehnquist; *Concurring Opinion:* None; *Dissenting Opinion:* Justice Brennan, in which Marshall, Blackmun and Stevens, JJ., joined; *Appellate Defense Counsel:* John H. Blume argued; David I. Bruck and Dale T. Cobb, Jr. on brief; *Appellate Prosecution Counsel:* Donald J. Zelenka argued; T. Travis Medlock on brief; *Amicus Curiae Brief Supporting Prosecutor:* None; *Amicus Curiae Brief Supporting Defendant:* None.

Issue Presented: Whether a new constitutional rule could apply to the defendant's conviction and sentence after his conviction became final?

Case Holding: A new constitutional rule could not apply to the defendant's conviction and sentence after his conviction became final.

Factual and procedural background of case: The defendant, Horace Butler, was convicted and sentenced to death for capital murder by the State of South Carolina. The South Carolina Supreme Court affirmed the conviction and sentence. After exhausting State post-conviction remedies, the defendant filed a petition for habeas corpus in a Federal District Court. The habeas petition was dismissed. The defendant appealed to a Federal Court of Appeals. While the case was pending before the Court of Appeals the United States Supreme Court issued an opinion in a non-capital case, *Arizona v. Roberson,* 486 U.S. 675 (1988), in which it held that the Fifth Amendment bars police initiated interrogation following a suspect's request for counsel in the context of a separate investigation. The Court of Appeals rejected the argument. It held that the defendant was not entitled to the retroactive benefit of *Roberson.* The United States Supreme Court granted certiorari to consider the issue.

Opinion of the Court by Chief Justice Rehnquist: The Chief Justice ruled that the defendant was not entitled to the benefits of *Roberson.* It was said that *Roberson* announced a new rule that was not dictated by a precedent existing at the time the defendant's conviction became final, and was therefore inapplicable to his collateral attack on his conviction and sentence.

The opinion noted that for *Roberson's* new rule to apply retroactively to the defendant's case, the new rule had to fit into one of the two exceptions to the general prohibition on retroactive application. The Chief Justice indicated that the first exception, for a rule that placed an entire category of primary conduct beyond the reach of criminal law or prohibited imposition of a certain type of punishment for a class of defendants because of their status or offense, was clearly inapplicable. The proscribed conduct in the case is capital murder, the prosecution of which was not prohibited by the *Roberson* rule. It was also determined that the *Roberson* rule did not establish any principle that would come within the second exception — which involved a watershed rule of criminal procedure implicating a criminal proceeding's fundamental fairness and accuracy. The opinion reasoned that the scope of the second exception was limited to those new procedures without which the likelihood of an accurate conviction was seriously diminished. It was said that a violation of *Roberson's* prophylactic protection might actually increase the likelihood of obtaining an accurate conviction. The decision of the Court of Appeals was affirmed.

Dissenting opinion by Justice Brennan, in which Marshall, Blackmun and Stevens, JJ., joined: Justice Brennan dissented from the Court's decision. He believed that the Court misinterpreted and misapplied legal principles to reach a desired end. Justice Brennan wrote:

> Today, under the guise of fine-tuning the definition of "new rule," the Court strips state prisoners of virtually any meaningful federal review of the constitutionality of their incarceration. A legal ruling sought by a federal habeas petitioner is now deemed "new" as long as the correctness of the rule, based on precedent existing when the petitioner's conviction became final, is "susceptible to debate among reasonable minds." Put another way, a state prisoner can secure habeas relief only by showing that the state court's rejection of the constitutional challenge was so clearly invalid under then-prevailing legal standards that the decision could not be defended by any reasonable jurist. With this requirement, the Court has finally succeeded in its thinly veiled crusade to eviscerate Congress' habeas corpus regime....
>
> It is Congress and not this Court who is "responsible for defining the scope of the writ." Yet the majority, whose Members often pride themselves on their reluctance to play an "activist" judicial role by infringing upon legislative prerogatives, does not hesitate today to dismantle Congress' extension of federal habeas to state prisoners. Hereafter, federal habeas relief will be available in only the most egregious cases, in which state courts have flouted applicable Supreme Court precedent that cannot be distinguished on any arguable basis. I must dissent from this curtailment of the writ's capacity for securing individual liberty. *See also* **Retroactive Application of a New Constitutional Rule**

C

Cabana v. Bullock *Court:* United States Supreme Court; *Case Citation:* Cabana v. Bullock, 474 U.S. 376 (1986); *Argued:* November 5, 1985; *Decided:* January 22, 1986; *Opinion of the Court:* Justice White; *Concurring Opinion:* Chief Justice Burger; *Dissenting Opinion:* Justice Blackmun, in which Brennan and Marshall, JJ., joined; *Dissenting Opinion:* Justice Stevens, in which Brennan, J., joined; *Dissenting Statement:* Justice Brennan; *Appellate Defense Counsel:* Joseph T. McLaughlin argued; Henry Weisburg and Daniel Levin on brief; *Appellate Prosecution Counsel:* Marvin L. White, Jr. argued; Edwin Lloyd Pittman, Amy D. Whitten and William S. Boyd III on brief; *Amicus Curiae Brief Supporting Prosecutor:* 1; *Amicus Curiae Brief Supporting Defendant:* 1.

Issue Presented: Whether a violation of *Enmund v. Florida* requires a new sentencing hearing before a jury?

Case Holding: A violation of *Enmund v. Florida* does not require a new sentencing hearing before a jury, because a trial judge or appellate court may determine the issue from the record in a case.

Factual and procedural background of case: The defendant, Crawford Bullock, was convicted of capital murder and sentenced to death by the State of Mississippi. The facts of the case revealed that the defendant held the victim while an accomplice actually beat the victim to death. The judgment against the defendant was affirmed by the Mississippi Supreme Court. The defendant subsequently filed a habeas corpus petition in a Federal District Court, which denied relief. The defendant appealed to a Federal Court of Appeals. The Court of Appeals reversed the sentence, on the ground that the defendant's sentence was invalid under the intervening decision by the United States Supreme Court in *Enmund v. Florida*, which held that the Constitution forbids the imposition of the death penalty on "one ... who aids and abets a felony in the course of which a murder is committed by others but who does not himself kill, attempt to kill, or intend that a killing take place or that lethal force will be employed." The United States Supreme Court granted certiorari to consider the issue.

Opinion of the Court by Justice White: Justice White held that the Court of Appeals "was correct in concluding that neither the jury's verdict of guilt nor its imposition of the death sentence necessarily reflected a finding that [the defendant] killed, attempted to kill, or intended to kill." The opinion found that the Court of Appeals committed error in not remanding the case to the courts of Mississippi for a determination of the defendant's mental state during the crime. Justice White wrote as follows:

> The proper course for a federal court faced with a habeas corpus petition raising an *Enmund* claim when the state courts have failed to make any finding regarding the *Enmund* criteria is to

take steps to require the State's own judicial system to make the factual findings in the first instance. Therefore, it is Mississippi, not the federal habeas corpus court, that should first provide [the defendant] with a reliable determination as to whether he killed, attempted to kill, or intended that a killing take place or that lethal force be used.

> Here, the District Court should be directed to issue the habeas corpus writ vacating [the defendant's] death sentence but to leave to the State the choice of either imposing a sentence of life imprisonment or reimposing the death sentence after obtaining a determination from its own courts of the factual question whether respondent killed, attempted to kill, intended to kill, or intended that lethal force would be used.

> The proceeding that the state courts must provide Bullock need not take the form of a new sentencing hearing before a jury.... [T]he Eighth Amendment does not require that a jury make the findings required by *Enmund*. Moreover, the sentence currently in force may stand provided only that the requisite findings are made in an adequate proceeding before some appropriate tribunal — be it an appellate court, a trial judge, or a jury. A new hearing devoted to the identification and weighing of aggravating and mitigating factors is thus, as far as we are concerned, unnecessary.

The judgment of the Court of Appeals was modified so as to require the case be returned to the State for a determination of the defendant's mental state at the time of the crime.

Concurring opinion by Chief Justice Burger: The Chief Justice concurred in the Court's decision. He wrote separately to indicate that he believed the case did not have to be returned to the courts of Mississippi because, "the Mississippi Supreme Court's opinion makes it clear that *Enmund's* concerns have been fully satisfied in this case." The Chief Justice believed that language in the decision by the State appellate court implicitly indicated that the State appellate court believed the defendant intended the victim be killed.

Dissenting opinion by Justice Blackmun, in which Brennan and Marshall, JJ., joined: Justice Blackman dissented from the Court's decision. He believed that an *Enmund* determination could only be made by a jury before a defendant was sentenced. Justice Blackman also indicated that he believed the Court's decision weakened the constitutional concerns *Enmund* sought to protect. He wrote as follows:

> The central message of *Enmund* is that the death penalty cannot constitutionally be imposed without an intensely individual appraisal of the "personal responsibility and moral guilt" of the defendant.... Put simply, *Enmund* establishes a constitutionally required factual predicate for the valid imposition of the death penalty....

> The question of how to cure this constitutional violation remains. The Court holds that an adequate remedy for the absence of *Enmund* findings can be supplied by "any court that has the power to find the facts and vacate the sentence." I believe that, in this case, only a new sentencing proceeding before a jury can guarantee the reliability which the Constitution demands. But the Court's decision today goes beyond a simple determination

of how to cure an error that has already occurred. It tells the States, in effect, that it is no error for a jury or a trial judge to say that a defendant should die without first considering his personal responsibility and moral guilt, as *Enmund* requires. By turning the jury or trial court's determination into what can be viewed only as a preliminary stage in the capital sentencing process, the Court's holding poses the threat of diffusing the sentencer's sense of responsibility.... The Court thus ignores both the proper institutional roles of trial and appellate courts and the pragmatic and constitutional concerns with reliability that underlie those roles. In short, the Court's holding rests on an improper equation of the wholly dissimilar functions of finding facts and of vacating a sentence because no facts have been found. *Enmund* established a clear constitutional imperative that a death sentence not be imposed by a sentencer who fails to make one of the *Enmund* findings. The Court confuses this imperative with the guarantee it purports to make today that a death sentence will not be carried out before someone makes an *Enmund* finding....

Here, Bullock had a legitimate expectation that the sentencing jury would consider his personal responsibility and moral guilt before deciding to send him to die. Under *Enmund*, the only way to guarantee that such consideration has been given is to require the sentencer to determine that the defendant either killed, or attempted to kill, or intended to kill. That a jury might or could have made such a determination hardly provides a guarantee that this jury did. Because I believe every defendant is entitled to that guarantee, I would vacate the death sentence and remand the case with instructions to provide Bullock with a sentencing hearing before a jury. Inasmuch as the majority refuses to take this essential step, I dissent.

Dissenting statement by Justice Stevens, in which Brennan, J., joined: Justice Stevens dissented from the Court's decision. He believed that the Court of Appeals was correct in deciding to return the case for a new penalty phase proceeding before a jury. Justice Stevens wrote as follows: "... I believe that the decision whether a death sentence is the only adequate response to the defendant's moral culpability must be made by a single decisionmaker, be it the trial court or the jury. The State of Mississippi has wisely decided that the jury is the decisionmaker that is best able to express the conscience of the community on the ultimate question of life or death.... It follows, in my view, that a Mississippi jury has not determined that a death sentence is the only response that will satisfy the outrage of the community, and that a new sentencing hearing must be conducted if [defendant] is ultimately to be sentenced to die. In accordance with this reasoning, I would affirm the judgment of the Court of Appeals."

Dissenting statement by Justice Brennan: Justice Brennan issued a statement indicating he dissented from the Court's decision. *See also* **Enmund v. Florida**

Cage v. Louisiana
Court: United States Supreme Court; *Case Citation:* Cage v. Louisiana, 498 U.S. 39 (1990); *Argued:* Not reported; *Decided:* November 13, 1990; *Opinion of the Court:* Per Curiam; *Concurring Opinion:* None; *Dissenting Opinion:* None; *Appellate Defense Counsel:* Not reported; *Appellate Prosecution Counsel:* Not reported; *Amicus Curiae Brief Supporting Prosecutor:* Not reported; *Amicus Curiae Brief Supporting Defendant:* Not reported.

Issue Presented: Whether the trial court correctly defined "reasonable doubt" to the jury? *Case Holding:* The trial court did not correctly define "reasonable doubt" to the jury, because its definition allowed a conviction based on less evidence than the Constitution required to sustain a conviction.

Factual and procedural background of case: The defendant, Cage, was convicted of capital murder and sentenced to death by the State of Louisiana. The Louisiana Supreme Court affirmed the judgment. In doing so, the appellate court rejected the defendant's argument that the trial court incorrectly defined "reasonable doubt" to the jury. The trial court had instructed the jury that reasonable doubt was "such doubt as would give rise to a grave uncertainty" and "an actual substantial doubt." The United States Supreme Court granted certiorari to consider the issue.

Opinion of the Court was delivered Per Curiam: The per curiam opinion held that the trial court incorrectly defined "reasonable doubt." The opinion reasoned as follows: "In construing the instruction, we consider how reasonable jurors could have understood the charge as a whole. The charge did at one point instruct that, to convict, guilt must be found beyond a reasonable doubt; but it then equated a reasonable doubt with a 'grave uncertainty' and an 'actual substantial doubt,' and stated that what was required was a 'moral certainty' that the defendant was guilty. It is plain to us that the words 'substantial' and 'grave,' as they are commonly understood, suggest a higher degree of doubt than is required for acquittal under the reasonable doubt standard. When those statements are then considered with the reference to 'moral certainty,' rather than evidentiary certainty, it becomes clear that a reasonable juror could have interpreted the instruction to allow a finding of guilt based on a degree of proof below that required by the Due Process Clause." The judgment of the Louisiana Supreme Court was reversed. *See also* **Victor v. Nebraska**

Calderon v. Ashmus
Court: United States Supreme Court; *Case Citation:* Calderon v. Ashmus, 523 U.S. 740 (1998); *Argued:* March 24, 1998; *Decided:* May 26, 1998; *Opinion of the Court:* Chief Justice Rehnquist; *Concurring Opinion:* Justice Breyer, in which Souter, J., joined; *Dissenting Opinion:* None; *Appellate Defense Counsel:* Not reported; *Appellate Prosecution Counsel:* Not reported; *Amicus Curiae Brief Supporting Prosecutor:* Not reported; *Amicus Curiae Brief Supporting Defendant:* Not reported.

Issue Presented: Whether California's constitutional rights were violated by injunctive and declaratory relief granted to a class of death row inmates against the State?

Case Holding: The issue presented need not be resolved because Federal courts did not have jurisdiction over the type of class action brought by the death row inmates.

Factual and procedural background of case: This case originated as a class action suit brought in a Federal District Court by a death row inmate, Troy Ashmus, against various California officials. The suit was brought to prevent California from creating legislation that would enable it to qualify for the expedited habeas corpus death penalty provisions under the Federal Antiterrorism and Effective Death Penalty Act of 1996 (AEDP Act). The class which Ashmus represented included all death row inmates in California whose convictions were affirmed on direct appeal after June 6, 1989.

The District Court issued a declaratory judgment holding that California did not presently qualify for the expedited habeas procedures under the AEDP Act, therefore the AEDP Act did not apply to any class members. The District Court also issued a preliminary injunction enjoining California from seeking to obtain the benefits of the AEDP Act in any State or Federal proceeding involving any of the class members. A Court of Appeals affirmed, after rejecting the State's claim that the Eleventh Amendment barred the class action and that the injunction violated the State's First Amendment rights. The United States Supreme Court granted certiorari to consider the issue.

Opinion of the Court by Chief Justice Rehnquist: The Chief Justice indicated that the Court did not need to reach the merits of the State's position, because the dispositive issue in the case was whether the class action involved the type of "case or controversy" constitutionally required to give Federal courts jurisdiction. It was determined by the Chief Justice that the class action brought was not a justiciable case under the authority of Article III of the Constitution. The opinion indicated that Federal courts have jurisdiction to enter declaratory judgments in cases where the controversy would admit of specific relief through a decree of a conclusive character, as distinguished from an opinion advising what the law would be upon a hypothetical set of facts. It was found that the class action only sought to have an advance ruling on the AEDP Act, vis-a-vis California. The opinion concluded that if class members file habeas petitions and the State asserts the benefits the AEDP Act, they could litigate California's compliance with the AEDP Act at that time. The judgment of the Court of Appeals was reversed.

Concurring opinion by Justice Breyer, in which Souter, J., joined: Justice Breyer concurred in the Court's decision. He indicated that he believed some members of the class should be permitted "to obtain a relatively expeditious judicial answer to the [the AEDP Act] question and thereby provide legal guidance for others. That is because, in at least some cases, whether a petitioner can or cannot amend, say, a 'bare bones' habeas petition (filed within 180 days) will likely depend upon whether California does, or does not, qualify as an 'opt-in' State." *See also* **Felker v. Turpin; Habeas Corpus**

Calderon v. Coleman

Court: United States Supreme Court; *Case Citation:* Calderon v. Coleman, 119 S.Ct. 500 (1998); *Argued:* Not reported; *Decided:* December 14, 1998; *Opinion of the Court:* Per Curiam; *Concurring Opinion:* None; *Dissenting Opinion:* Justice Stevens, in which Souter, Ginsburg, and Breyer, JJ., joined; *Appellate Defense Counsel:* Not reported; *Appellate Prosecution Counsel:* Not reported; *Amicus Curiae Brief Supporting Prosecutor:* Not reported; *Amicus Curiae Brief Supporting Defendant:* Not reported.

Issue Presented: Whether the Court of Appeals applied the correct review standard in reaching the conclusion that the defendant's death sentence was imposed in violation of the Constitution?

Case Holding: The Court of Appeals applied the wrong review standard in reaching the conclusion that the defendant's death sentence was imposed in violation of the Constitution.

Factual and procedural background of case: The defendant, Russell Coleman, was convicted of capital murder by a California jury. Under California law, during the penalty phase, the trial court was required to instruct the jury that a sentence of life imprisonment without the possibility of parole may be commuted by the Governor to a sentence that includes the possibility of parole. (This instruction, known as the "Briggs instruction," was incorporated into the California Penal Code as a result of a 1978, voter initiative popularly known as the Briggs Initiative.) At the penalty phase of the defendant's prosecution the trial judge gave the jury the Briggs instruction. The trial court also instructed the jury that it was not to consider the Governor's commutation power in reaching a verdict. The jury returned a verdict of death. The California Supreme Court affirmed the defendant's conviction and sentence. In doing so, the appellate court found that it was error to give the Briggs instruction, because it violated the State's constitution, but that the error was not prejudicial because of the trial court's instruction that the jury was not to consider the Governor's commutation authority in reaching a verdict.

The defendant then filed a habeas corpus petition in a Federal District Court arguing that the Briggs instruction violated the Federal Constitution. The District Court acknowledged that the United States Supreme Court had ruled in *California v. Ramos* that the Briggs instruction did not violate the Federal Constitution. Nevertheless, the District Court found the Briggs instruction in the defendant's case violated the Constitution, because it failed to inform the jury that the Governor's commutation authority was limited, insofar as the Governor needed the concurrence of four judges on the California Supreme Court in order to commute the defendant's sentence. The District Court vacated the defendant's death sentence. A Federal Court of Appeals affirmed after concluding that there was a "reasonable likelihood" that the Briggs instruction mislead the jury. The United States Supreme Court granted certiorari to consider the issue.

Opinion of the Court was delivered Per Curiam: The per curiam opinion indicated that the Court would not determine whether, consistent with the decision in *Ramos*, the Briggs instruction violated the Constitution because the State did not ask the Court to do so. Instead, the State argued that the Court of Appeals applied the wrong review standard to the issue. The opinion agreed with the State. It was said that the review standard used by the Court of Appeals, "reasonable likelihood," was used for determining whether constitutional error prevented a jury from considering relevant error. The opinion ruled that harmless error analysis was the proper review standard for the defendant's claim. Under this standard it had to be shown that the error had a substantial and injurious effect or influence in determining the jury's verdict. The judgment of the Court of Appeals was reversed and the case remanded for harmless error analysis.

Dissenting opinion by Justice Stevens, in which Souter, Ginsburg, and Breyer, JJ., joined: Justice Stevens dissented from the Court's decision. He argued that the Court misread the Court of Appeals' written decision, and that the Court of Appeals did in fact apply harmless error analysis to the case. Justice Stevens contended that, while the decision of the Court of Appeals did not use the magic words "harmless error," the substance of its analysis was consistent with harmless error analysis. *See also* **California v. Ramos; Clemency; Harmless Error Rule; Ohio Adult Parole Authority v. Woodard; Rose v. Hodges; Schick v. Reed**

Calderon v. Thompson
Court: United States Supreme Court; *Case Citation:* Calderon v. Thompson, 523 U.S. 538 (1998); *Argued:* December 9, 1997; *Decided:* April 29, 1998; *Opinion of the Court:* Justice Kennedy; *Concurring Opinion:* None; *Dissenting Opinion:* Justice Souter, in which Stevens, Ginsburg, and Breyer, JJ., joined; *Appellate Defense Counsel:* Not reported; *Appellate Prosecution Counsel:* Not reported; *Amicus Curiae Brief Supporting Prosecutor:* Not reported; *Amicus Curiae Brief Supporting Defendant:* Not reported.

Issue Presented: Whether the Court of Appeals abused its discretion in recalling an order denying all habeas relief to the defendant, on the grounds that a miscarriage of justice would result from the order?

Case Holding: The Court of Appeals abused its discretion in recalling an order denying all habeas relief to the defendant, because no miscarriage of justice would result from the order.

Factual and procedural background of case: The State of California convicted the defendant, Thomas M. Thompson, of capital murder and sentenced him to death. The defendant exhausted State post-conviction remedies without success. He filed several habeas corpus petitions in Federal court. During the review of one of the Federal petitions a Federal District Court vacated his death sentence, but a Court of Appeals reversed the decision. Eventually the Court of Appeals issued an order denying all habeas relief. Subsequent to the Court of Appeals' order, the State issued a death warrant setting an execution date. However, two days before the execution the Court of Appeals recalled its order denying all habeas relief. The Court of Appeals indicated that the order was the result of an internal procedural misunderstanding and that the decision would lead to a miscarriage of justice if not recalled. The Court of Appeals granted the defendant habeas relief based upon an earlier claim that he made alleging actual innocence due to ineffective assistance of counsel. The United States Supreme Court granted certiorari to consider the issue.

Opinion of the Court by Justice Kennedy: Justice Kennedy held that a Court of Appeals' inherent power to recall an order, subject to review for an abuse of discretion, is a power of last resort, to be held in reserve against grave, unforeseen circumstances. He indicated that the Court of Appeals' recall decision rested on doubtful of grounds. It was said that the promptness with which a court acts to correct its mistakes was evidence of the adequacy of its grounds for reopening a case. Justice Kennedy expressed concern that it was just two days before the scheduled execution that the court recalled a judgment on which all authorities had placed heavy reliance. The opinion concluded that the recall was a grave abuse of discretion.

It was ruled that unless a Court of Appeals acts to avoid a miscarriage of justice as defined by the Court's habeas jurisprudence, the Court of Appeals abuses its discretion when it recalls an order to revisit the merits of an earlier decision denying habeas relief. Justice Kennedy found that the Court's miscarriage of justice standard was not met in the case. Under the Court's standard a defendant asserting actual innocence of the underlying conviction must show "it is more likely than not" that no reasonable juror would have convicted him or her in light of the new evidence presented in the habeas petition. However, a defendant challenging his or her death sentence in particular must show "by clear and convincing evidence" that no reasonable juror would have found him or her eligible for the death penalty in light of the new evidence. The opinion found that the defendant's actual innocence claim failed under either standard. Justice Kennedy reasoned that the evidence presented by the defendant did not meet the "more likely than not" showing necessary to vacate his conviction, nor did it establish the "clear and convincing" showing necessary to vacate his sentence of death. Therefore, the judgment of the State would not result in a miscarriage of justice. The judgment of the Court of Appeals was reversed.

Dissenting opinion by Justice Souter, in which Stevens, Ginsburg, and Breyer, JJ., joined: Justice Souter dissented from the Court's decision on the grounds that it erected a new and more stringent standard for reviewing the decision to recall an order by a Court of Appeals. He argued that the traditional abuse of discretion standard of review was jettisoned "for the sake of solving a systemic problem that does not exist." Justice Souter believed that the recall order was based on tenuous grounds, but that such grounds passed muster under traditional abuse of discretion review.

Case note: California executed Thomas M. Thompson by lethal injection on July 14, 1998.

Caldwell v. Mississippi
Court: United States Supreme Court; *Case Citation:* Caldwell v. Mississippi, 472 U.S. 320 (1985); *Argued:* February 25, 1985; *Decided:* June 11, 1985; *Opinion of the Court:* Justice Marshall; *Concurring Opinion:* Justice O'Connor; *Dissenting Opinion:* Justice Rehnquist, in which Burger, C. J., and White, J., joined; *Justice Taking No Part in the Decision:* Justice Powell; *Appellate Defense Counsel:* E. Thomas Boyle argued and briefed; *Appellate Prosecution*

Counsel: William S. Boyd III argued; Edwin Lloyd Pittman, and Marvin L. White, Jr. on brief; *Amicus Curiae Brief Supporting Prosecutor:* 1; *Amicus Curiae Brief Supporting Defendant:* 1.

Issue Presented: Whether a capital sentence is constitutionally valid when the prosecutor leads the sentencing jury to believe that responsibility for determining the appropriateness of a death sentence rests not with the jury, but with the appellate court which later reviews the case?

Case Holding: A capital sentence is not constitutionally valid when the prosecutor leads the sentencing jury to believe that responsibility for determining the appropriateness of a death sentence rests not with the jury, but with the appellate court which later reviews the case.

Factual and procedural background of case: The defendant, Caldwell, was convicted and sentenced to death for capital murder by the State of Mississippi. During the closing arguments of the penalty phase of the prosecution, defense counsel referred to the defendant's youth, family background, and poverty, as well as to general character evidence, and asked the jury to show mercy. In response to defense counsel's pleas for mercy, the prosecutor urged the jury not to view itself as finally determining whether the defendant would die, because a death sentence would be reviewed for correctness by the Mississippi Supreme Court.

On appeal, the Mississippi Supreme Court affirmed the conviction and sentence. In doing so, the appellate court rejected the defendant's contention that the federal Constitution precluded the prosecutor's closing argument to the jury that the ultimate responsibility for a death sentence was made the appellate court. The United States Supreme Court granted certiorari to consider the issue.

Opinion of the Court by Justice Marshall: Justice Marshall found the prosecutor's closing remarks presented too great a risk that a death sentence was returned, merely because the jury believed the State appellate court would make the real decision. He stated his position and the disposition of the case as follows:

> In evaluating the prejudicial effect of the prosecutor's argument, we must ... recognize that the argument offers jurors a view of their role which might frequently be highly attractive. A capital sentencing jury is made up of individuals placed in a very unfamiliar situation and called on to make a very difficult and uncomfortable choice. They are confronted with evidence and argument on the issue of whether another should die, and they are asked to decide that issue on behalf of the community. Moreover, they are given only partial guidance as to how their judgment should be exercised, leaving them with substantial discretion. Given such a situation, the uncorrected suggestion that the responsibility for any ultimate determination of death will rest with others presents an intolerable danger that the jury will in fact choose to minimize the importance of its role. Indeed, one can easily imagine that in a case in which the jury is divided on the proper sentence, the presence of appellate review could effectively be used as an argument for why those jurors who are reluctant to invoke the death sentence should nevertheless give in.
>
> This problem is especially serious when the jury is told that

the alternative decisionmakers are the justices of the state supreme court. It is certainly plausible to believe that many jurors will be tempted to view these respected legal authorities as having more of a "right" to make such an important decision than has the jury. Given that the sentence will be subject to appellate review only if the jury returns a sentence of death, the chance that an invitation to rely on that review will generate a bias toward returning a death sentence is simply too great....

This Court has always premised its capital punishment decisions on the assumption that a capital sentencing jury recognizes the gravity of its task and proceeds with the appropriate awareness of its "truly awesome responsibility." In this case, the State sought to minimize the jury's sense of responsibility for determining the appropriateness of death. Because we cannot say that this effort had no effect on the sentencing decision, that decision does not meet the standard of reliability that the Eighth Amendment requires. The sentence of death must therefore be vacated. Accordingly, the judgment is reversed to the extent that it sustains the imposition of the death penalty, and the case is remanded for further proceedings.

Concurring opinion by Justice O'Connor: Justice O'Connor concurred in the Court's judgment. She expressed concerns about the impact the prosecutor's remarks may have had on the jury. Justice O'Connor wrote: "Laypersons cannot be expected to appreciate without explanation the limited nature of appellate review, especially in light of the reassuring picture of 'automatic' review evoked by the sentencing court and the prosecutor in this case. Although the subsequent remarks of the prosecutor ... may have helped to restore the jurors' sense of the importance of their role, I agree with the Court that they failed to correct the impression that the appellate court would be free to reverse the death sentence if it disagreed with the jury's conclusion that death was appropriate. I believe the prosecutor's misleading emphasis on appellate review misinformed the jury concerning the finality of its decision, thereby creating an unacceptable risk that 'the death penalty [may have been] meted out arbitrarily or capriciously,' or through 'whim ... or mistake[.]'"

Dissenting opinion by Justice Rehnquist, in which Burger, C. J., and White, J., joined: Justice Rehnquist dissented from the majority opinion in the case. He argued that the majority gave too great an emphasis to the remarks of the prosecutor, in view of the evidence which indicated the death sentence was appropriate. The dissent stated its position as follows:

> The Court holds that under the Eighth Amendment it is "constitutionally impermissible to rest a death sentence on a determination made by a sentencer who has been led to believe that the responsibility for the appropriateness of the defendant's death rests elsewhere." Even if I were to agree with this proposition in the abstract, I do not believe that under the circumstances of this case it can properly be applied to justify the overturning of [the defendant's] death sentence....
>
> [Our precedents] teach that a death sentence need not be vacated in every case where the procedures by which it is imposed are in some way flawed. If the prosecutor in this case actually had argued to the jury that it should go ahead and impose the death sentence because it did not really matter — the appellate court would correct any "mistake" the jury might make in choice of sentence — and if the trial judge had not corrected such an argument, I might well agree that the process afforded did not

comport with some constitutional norm related to procedural fairness. But despite the Court's sweeping characterization the argument here fell far short of telling the jury that it would not be responsible for imposing the death penalty. Admittedly, some of the remarks early in the prosecutor's rebuttal indicated that the jury's decision was not "final" because it was subject to appellate review. But viewed in its entirety, it is evident that the thrust of the prosecutor's argument was that the jury was not solely responsible for [the defendant's] sentence. In addition to appellate review, the prosecutor referred to the decision of the Mississippi Legislature to allow capital punishment, to the rules that the jury must follow in determining the appropriate sentence, and to the jury's ultimate responsibility under the law to render a "fair verdict," "without passion, without prejudice, without sympathy."

This Court should avoid turning every perceived departure from what it conceives to be optimum procedure in a capital case into a ground for constitutional reversal. In this case the State of Mississippi proved four aggravating factors, including that [the defendant] previously had been convicted of four crimes involving threat of violence to a person. The jury was instructed to find the facts based upon the evidence and to apply those facts to the law as charged; at the sentencing proceeding it was told that it must find that the aggravating factors outweighed the mitigating factors, and the prosecutor's argument stressed these aspects of the jury's singular duty. There is no indication in the record that the jury returned the death sentence on any basis other than the evidence adduced, nor is there any reason to question the jury's conclusion. Under those circumstances I do not think that the Eighth Amendment or any other provision of the Constitution requires that [the defendant's] death sentence be overturned. I would affirm the judgment of the Mississippi Supreme Court.

California   The State of California is a capital punishment jurisdiction. The State reenacted its death penalty law after the United States Supreme Court decision in *Furman v. Georgia*, 408 U.S. 238 (1972) in 1977. In November of 1978 California voters approved Proposition 7 reaffirming the death penalty.

California has a three-tier legal system. The State's legal system is composed of a supreme court, court of appeals and courts of general jurisdiction. The California Supreme Court is presided over by a chief justice and six associate justices. The California Courts of Appeals are divided into six districts, with one or more divisions. The divisions are composed of a presiding justice and two or more associate justices. The courts of general jurisdiction in the State are called Superior Courts. Capital offenses against the State of California are tried in the Superior Courts.

California's capital punishment statute is triggered if a person commits a homicide under the following special circumstances:

Members of the California Supreme Court: (seated left to right) Justice Stanley Mosk, Chief Justice Ronald M. George, Justice Joyce L. Kennard; (standing left to right) Justice Ming W. Chin, Justice Marvin R. Baxter, Justice Kathryn M. Wedegar, Justice Janice R. Brown. (California Supreme Court)

By means of a destructive device or explosive; knowing use of ammunition designed primarily to penetrate metal or armor; poison; lying in wait; torture; or by any other kind of willful, deliberate, and premeditated killing; or which is committed in the perpetration of, or attempt to perpetrate, arson, rape, carjacking, robbery, burglary, mayhem, kidnapping, train wrecking; or any murder which is perpetrated by means of discharging a firearm from a motor vehicle, intentionally at another person outside of the vehicle with the intent to inflict death.

Capital murder in California is punishable by death, life imprisonment without parole, or confinement in the state prison for a term of 25 years. A capital prosecution in California is bifurcated into a guilt phase and penalty phase. A jury is used at both phases of a capital trial. It is required that, at the penalty phase, the jury must unanimously agree that a death sentence is appropriate before it can be imposed. If the penalty phase jury is unable to reach a verdict, the trial judge is required to impanel a second penalty phase jury to decide the defendant's fate. If the second jury cannot reach a unanimous verdict, the trial judge is required to impanel a third penalty phase jury to decide the defendant's fate. If the third jury cannot reach a unanimous verdict, the trial judge is required to impose a punishment of confinement in prison for a term of 25 years. A unanimous decision by the penalty phase jury is binding on the trial court under the laws of California.

In order to impose a death sentence upon a defendant under California law, it is required that the prosecutor establish the existence of at least one of the following statutory aggravating circumstances at the penalty phase:

1. The murder was intentional and carried out for financial gain.
2. The defendant was convicted previously of murder in the first or second degree.
3. The defendant has been convicted in the current prosecution of more than one offense of murder in the first or second degree.
4. The murder was committed by means of a destructive device, bomb, or explosive planted, hidden, or concealed in any place, area, dwelling, building, or structure, and the defendant knew, or reasonably should have known, that his or her act or acts would create a great risk of death to one or more human beings.
5. The murder was committed for the purpose of avoiding or preventing a lawful arrest, or perfecting or attempting to perfect, an escape from lawful custody.
6. The murder was committed by means of a destructive device, bomb, or explosive that the defendant mailed or delivered, attempted to mail or deliver, or caused to be mailed or delivered, and the defendant knew, or reasonably should have known, that his or her act or acts would create a great risk of death to one or more human beings.
7. The victim was a peace officer.
8. The victim was a federal law enforcement officer or agent.
9. The victim was a firefighter.
10. The victim was a witness to a crime who was intentionally killed for the purpose of preventing his or her testimony in any criminal or juvenile proceeding.

11. The victim was a prosecutor or assistant prosecutor or a former prosecutor or assistant prosecutor of any local or state prosecutor's office.

12. The victim was a judge or former judge of any court of record in the local, state, or federal system.

13. The victim was an elected or appointed official or former official of the federal government, or of any local or state government.

14. The murder was especially heinous, atrocious, or cruel, manifesting exceptional depravity.

15. The defendant intentionally killed the victim while lying in wait.

16. The victim was intentionally killed because of his or her race, color, religion, nationality, or country of origin.

17. The murder was committed while the defendant was engaged in, or was an accomplice in, the commission of, attempted commission of, or the immediate flight after committing, or attempting to commit, the following felonies:

    (a) robbery, (b) kidnapping, (c) rape, (d) sodomy, (e) performance of a lewd or lascivious act upon the person of a child under the age of 14 years, (f) oral copulation, (g) burglary, (h) arson, (i) train wrecking, (j) mayhem, (k) rape with an instrument, or (l) carjacking.

18. The murder was intentional and involved the infliction of torture.

19. The defendant intentionally killed the victim by the administration of poison.

20. The victim was a juror in any court of record in the local, state, or federal system.

21. The murder was intentional and perpetrated by means of discharging a firearm from a motor vehicle, intentionally at another person or persons outside the vehicle with the intent to inflict death.

Although the Federal Constitution will not permit jurisdictions to prevent capital felons from presenting all relevant mitigating evidence at the penalty phase, California has provided the following statutory mitigating circumstances that permit the jury to reject imposition of the death penalty:

a. The circumstances of the crime of which the defendant was convicted.

b. The presence or absence of criminal activity by the defendant which involved the use or attempted use of force or violence or the express or implied threat to use force or violence.

c. The presence or absence of any prior felony conviction.

d. Whether or not the offense was committed while the defendant was under the influence of extreme mental or emotional disturbance.

e. Whether or not the victim was a participant in the defendant's homicidal conduct or consented to the homicidal act.

f. Whether or not the offense was committed under circumstances which the defendant reasonably believed to be a moral justification or extenuation for his conduct.

g. Whether or not defendant acted under extreme duress or under the substantial domination of another person.

h. Whether or not at the time of the offense the capacity of the defendant to appreciate the criminality of his conduct or to conform his conduct to the requirements of law was impaired as a result of mental disease or defect, or the affects of intoxication.

Bill Lockyer is the California Attorney General. His office represents the State in capital punishment appellate proceedings. (California Attorney General Office)

i. The age of the defendant at the time of the crime.

j. Whether or not the defendant was an accomplice to the offense and his participation in the commission of the offense was relatively minor.

Under California's capital punishment statute, a sentence of death is automatically reviewed by the California Supreme Court. California uses the lethal gas and lethal injection to carry out death sentences. The State's death row facility for men is located in San Quentin, California; while the facility maintaining female death row inmates is located in Chowchilla, California.

Pursuant to the laws of California the Governor has authority to grant clemency in capital cases. If a capital felon has two prior felony convictions, the Governor must obtain the recommendation of the State's Supreme Court in order to grant clemency.

From the start of modern capital punishment in 1976, through 1999, California executed 7 capital felons. During this period California did not execute any female capital felons, although 10 of its death row inmates during this period were females. The State does not permit capital punishment to be imposed on persons 17 years old or younger. A total of 536 capital felons were on death row in California in 1999. The 1999 death row population in the State was listed as: 191 black inmates; 217 white inmates; 101 Hispanic inmates; and 27 unidentified inmates. California does not prohibit the execution of mentally retarded capital felons.

Executions by California 1976–1999

Name	Race	Date of Execution	Method of Execution
Robert A. Harris	White	April 21, 1992	Lethal Gas
David Mason	White	August 24, 1993	Lethal Gas

Name	Race	Date of Execution
William G. Bonin	White	February 23, 1996
Keith D. Williams	White	May 3, 1996
Thomas Thompson	White	July 14, 1998
Jaturun Siripongs	Asian	February 9, 1999
Manuel Babbitt	Black	May 4, 1999

Method of Execution
Lethal Injection
Lethal Injection
Lethal Injection
Lethal Injection
Lethal Injection

CALIFORNIA EXECUTIONS 1976–1999

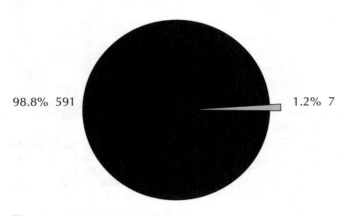

98.8% 591   1.2% 7

■ CALIFORNIA EXECUTIONS
■ ALL OTHER EXECUTIONS

EXECUTIONS BY CALIFORNIA 1930–1999

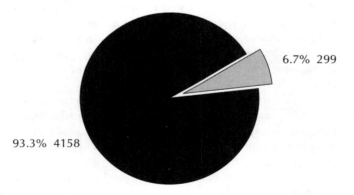

6.7% 299

93.3% 4158

■ CALIFORNIA
■ ALL OTHER JURISDICTIONS

California Coalition for Alternatives to the Death Penalty

The California Coalition for Alternatives to the Death Penalty (CCADP) is a group of organizations and individuals who work for the abolition of the death penalty everywhere. CCADP does a variety of work on behalf of death row inmates and other prisoners. The organization works closely with the National Coalition to Abolish the Death Penalty.

California v. Brown

Court: United States Supreme Court; *Case Citation:* California v. Brown, 479 U.S. 538 (1987); *Argued:* December 2, 1986; *Decided:* January 27, 1987;

Opinion of the Court: Chief Justice Rehnquist; *Concurring Opinion:* Justice O'Connor; *Dissenting Opinion:* Justice Brennan, in which Marshall and Stevens, JJ., joined; *Dissenting Opinion:* Justice Blackmun, in which Marshall, J., joined; *Appellate Defense Counsel:* Monica Knox argued and briefed; *Appellate Prosecution Counsel:* Jay M. Bloom argued; John K. Van de Kamp, Steve White, and Harley D. Mayfield on brief; *Amicus Curiae Brief Supporting Prosecutor:* 1; *Amicus Curiae Brief Supporting Defendant:* 1.

Issue Presented: Whether an instruction informing jurors that they must not be swayed by mere sentiment, conjecture, sympathy, passion, prejudice, public opinion or public feeling during the penalty phase of a capital murder trial violates the Constitution?

Case Holding: The Constitution is not violated by the giving of an antisympathy instruction to a capital penalty phase jury.

Factual and procedural background of case: A California guilt phase jury convicted the defendant, Albert Brown, of capital murder. During the penalty phase the defendant presented the testimony of several family members, who recounted the defendant's peaceful nature and expressed disbelief that he was capable of such a brutal crime. The defendant also presented the testimony of a psychiatrist, who stated that the defendant killed the victim because of his shame and fear over sexual dysfunction. The defendant testified, stating that he was ashamed of his prior criminal conduct and asked the jury for mercy.

The trial court instructed the penalty phase jury to consider and weigh the aggravating and mitigating circumstances, but cautioned that the jury must not be swayed by mere sentiment, conjecture, sympathy, passion, prejudice, public opinion or public feeling. The defendant was sentenced to death. On automatic appeal, the California Supreme Court reversed the defendant's death sentence, on the grounds that the antisympathy instruction violated federal constitutional law by denying the defendant the right to have sympathy factors raised by the evidence considered by the jury when determining the appropriate penalty. The United States Supreme Court granted certiorari to determine whether the California Supreme Court correctly interpreted federal constitutional law.

Opinion of the Court by Chief Justice Rehnquist: Chief Justice Rehnquist held that the instruction did not violate the constitutional requirement that capital punishment jurors are not to be given unbridled discretion and that defendants be allowed to introduce any relevant mitigating evidence.

The opinion found that the California Supreme Court improperly focused solely on the word "sympathy" in the instruction. It was said that a reasonable jury would be unlikely to single out the word "sympathy," and would most likely interpret the admonition to avoid basing a decision on mere sympathy as a directive to ignore only the sort of sympathy that was not rooted in the aggravating and mitigating evidence introduced during the penalty phase.

The opinion noted that by limiting the jury's sentencing considerations to actual evidence, the instruction served the useful purpose of cautioning the jury against reliance on extraneous emotional factors, and thereby fosters the constitutional need for reliability in death sentence determinations and ensures the availability of meaningful judicial review. Chief Justice Rehnquist reversed the decision of the California Supreme Court and remanded the case for the California Supreme Court to consider whether the jury was adequately informed of its obligation to consider all of the mitigating evidence introduced by the defendant.

Concurring opinion by Justice O'Connor: Justice O'Connor indicated that she joined with judgment of the majority opinion "[b]ecause the individualized assessment of the appropriateness of the death penalty is a moral inquiry into the culpability of the defendant, and not an emotional response to the mitigating evidence[.]" She cautioned, however, that jury instructions must clearly inform the jury that they are to consider any relevant mitigating evidence about a defendant's background and character, or about the circumstances of the crime.

Dissenting opinion by Justice Brennan, in which Marshall and Stevens, JJ., joined: Justice Brennan indicated he would affirm the California Supreme Court, because that court reasonably interpreted the jury instruction as diverting the jury from its constitutional duty to consider all mitigating evidence introduced by a defendant at the penalty phase. It said that a sentencing instruction is invalid if it prevents the jury from considering, as a mitigating factor, any aspect of a defendant's character or record that was proffered by a defendant as a basis for a sentence less than death. The dissenting opinion summarized its position as follows:

> The California Supreme Court in this case has provided an eminently reasonable interpretation of the State's antisympathy instruction. The language of the instruction on its face prohibits a jury from relying on sympathy in determining whether to sentence a defendant to death. The defendant literally staked his life in this case on the prospect that a jury confronted with evidence of his psychological problems and harsh family background would react sympathetically, and any instruction that would preclude such a response cannot stand. Furthermore, even acceptance of the State's attenuated interpretation of other instructions does not mean that these provisions cure the problem with the antisympathy instruction, but leads only to the conclusion that the jury was confronted with contradictory instructions, a state of affairs that we have declared intolerable.

Dissenting opinion by Justice Blackmun, in which Marshall, J., joined: Justice Blackman indicated that a penalty phase jury's ability to respond with mercy towards a defendant is a particularly valuable aspect of the capital sentencing procedure. "When, however, a jury member is moved to be merciful to the defendant, an instruction telling the juror that he or she cannot be 'swayed' by sympathy well may arrest or restrain this humane response, with truly fatal consequences for the defendant. This possibility I cannot accept, in light of the special role of mercy in capital sentencing and the stark finality of the death sentence." For these reasons, Justice Blackmun

would have affirmed the California Supreme Court's decision.
See also **Victim Impact Evidence**

California v. Ramos

Court: United States Supreme Court; *Case Citation:* California v. Ramos, 463 U.S. 992 (1983); *Argued:* February 22, 1983; *Decided:* July 6, 1983; *Opinion of the Court:* Justice O'Connor; *Concurring Opinion:* None; *Dissenting Opinion:* Justice Marshall, in which Brennan and Blackmun, JJ., joined; *Dissenting Opinion:* Justice Blackmun; *Dissenting Opinion:* Justice Stevens; *Appellate Defense Counsel:* Ezra Hendon argued and briefed; *Appellate Prosecution Counsel:* Harley D. Mayfield argued; George Deukmejian, Robert Philibosian, Daniel J. Kremer and Jay M. Bloom on brief; *Amicus Curiae Brief Supporting Prosecutor:* None; *Amicus Curiae Brief Supporting Defendant:* None.

Issue Presented: Whether the Constitution permits a capital penalty phase jury to be instructed regarding a Governor's power to commute a sentence of life without possibility of parole, to one with parole?

Case Holding: The Constitution permits a capital penalty phase jury to be instructed regarding a Governor's power to commute a sentence of life without possibility of parole, to one with parole.

Factual and procedural background of case: The defendant, Marcelino Ramos, was convicted of capital murder by a California jury. Under California law, during the penalty phase, the trial court was required to instruct the jury that a sentence of life imprisonment without the possibility of parole may be commuted by the Governor to a sentence that includes the possibility of parole. (This instruction, known as the "Briggs instruction," was incorporated into the California Penal Code as a result of a 1978, voter initiative popularly known as the Briggs Initiative.) At the penalty phase of the defendant's prosecution the trial judge gave the jury the Briggs Instruction. The jury returned a verdict of death. The California Supreme Court affirmed defendant's conviction, but reversed the death penalty after concluding that the Briggs Instruction violated the Federal Constitution. The United States Supreme Court granted certiorari to consider the issue.

Opinion of the Court by Justice O'Connor: Justice O'Connor held that the Constitution did not prohibit an instruction permitting a capital sentencing jury to consider the Governor's power to commute a life sentence without possibility of parole. It was reasoned that the possible commutation of a life sentence does not impermissibly inject an element too speculative for the jury's consideration. The opinion held that by bringing to the jury's attention the possibility that the defendant may be returned to society, the Briggs instruction invited the jury to assess whether the defendant is someone whose probable future behavior made it undesirable that he be permitted to return to society, thus focusing the jury on the defendant's probable future dangerousness.

It was said in the opinion that giving the Briggs instruction did result in any diminution in the reliability of the sentencing decision. The Briggs instruction gave the jury accurate information of which both the defendant and his counsel are aware, and it did not preclude the defendant from offering any evidence or argument regarding the Governor's power to commute a life sentence.

Justice O'Connor rejected the argument that the Briggs instruction deflected the jury's focus from its central task of undertaking an individualized sentencing determination. She wrote that in the sense that the instruction focused attention on the defendant's future dangerousness, the jury's deliberation was individualized. The Briggs instruction simply placed before the jury an additional element to be considered, along with many other factors, in determining which sentence was appropriate under the circumstances of the defendant's case.

The opinion also ruled that the Briggs instruction was not unconstitutional because it failed to also inform the jury of the Governor's power to commute a death sentence. It was said that, assuming arguendo, the Briggs instruction had the impermissible effect of skewing the jury toward imposing the death penalty, an instruction on the Governor's power to commute death sentences as well as life sentences would not restore neutrality or increase the reliability of the sentencing choice. Justice O'Connor reasoned that advising jurors that a death verdict is theoretically modifiable, and thus not final, may incline them to approach their sentencing decision with less appreciation for the gravity of their choice and for the moral responsibility reposed in them as sentencers. Therefore, an instruction disclosing the Governor's power to commute a death sentence may operate to the defendant's distinct disadvantage. The judgment of the California Supreme Court was reversed.

Dissenting opinion by Justice Marshall, in which Brennan and Blackmun, JJ., joined: Justice Marshall dissented from the decision of the majority on the basis that he "could not agree that a State may tip the balance in favor of death by informing the jury that the defendant may eventually be released if he is not executed." He believed the Briggs instruction was unconstitutional for three reasons: (1) it was misleading; (2) it invited speculation and guesswork; and (3) it injected into the capital sentencing process a factor that beared no relation to the nature of the offense or the character of the defendant.

Dissenting opinion by Justice Blackmun: Justice Blackmun indicated that he dissented from the majority decision because it redefined the issue presented by the case and improperly focused on the dangerousness of the defendant. He concluded: "The issue actually presented is an important one, and there may be arguments supportive of the instruction. The Court, however, chooses to present none. Instead, it approves the Briggs Instruction by substituting an intellectual sleight of hand for legal analysis. This kind of appellate review compounds the original unfairness of the instruction itself, and thereby does the rule of law disservice. I dissent."

Dissenting opinion by Justice Stevens: Justice Stevens argued in his dissent that the majority was wrong in disturbing the California Supreme Court's decision. His dissent reasoned as follows:

Even if one were to agree with the Court's conclusion that the instruction does not violate the defendant's procedural rights, it would nevertheless be fair to ask what harm would have been done to the administration of justice by state courts if the California court had been left undisturbed in its determination. It is clear that omission of the instruction could not conceivably prejudice the prosecutor's legitimate interests. Surely if the character of an offense and the character of the offender are such that death is the proper penalty, the omission of a comment on the Governor's power to commute a life sentence would not preclude the jury from returning the proper verdict. If it were true that this instruction may make the difference between life and death in a case in which the scales are otherwise evenly balanced, that is a reason why the instruction should not be given — not a reason for giving it. For the existence of the rarely exercised power of commutation has absolutely nothing to do with the defendant's culpability or his capacity for rehabilitation. The Governor's power to commute is entirely different from any relevant aggravating circumstance that may legitimately impel the jury toward voting for the death penalty. The Briggs Instruction has no greater justification than an instruction to the jury that if the scales are evenly balanced, you should remember that more murders have been committed by people whose names begin with the initial "S" than with any other letter.

No matter how trivial the impact of the instruction may be, it is fundamentally wrong for the presiding judge at the trial — who should personify the evenhanded administration of justice — to tell the jury, indirectly to be sure, that doubt concerning the proper penalty should be resolved in favor of the most certain method of preventing the defendant from ever walking the streets again.

See also **Calderon v. Coleman; Clemency; Ohio Adult Parole Authority v. Woodard; Rose v. Hodges; Schick v. Reed**

Calton v. Utah *Court:* United States Supreme Court; *Case Citation:* Calton v. Utah, 130 U.S. 83 (1889); *Argued:* January 2, 1889; *Decided:* March 11, 1889; *Opinion of the Court:* Justice Harlan; *Concurring Opinion:* None; *Dissenting Opinion:* None; *Appellate Defense Counsel:* John H. Mitchell argued and briefed; *Appellate Prosecution Counsel:* Assistant Attorney General Maury argued and briefed; *Amicus Curiae Brief Supporting Prosecutor:* None; *Amicus Curiae Brief Supporting Defendant:* None.

Issue Presented: Whether due process of law was violated because the trial court failed to instruct the jury that it could return a recommendation of life imprisonment?

Case Holding: Due process of law was violated because the trial court failed to instruct the jury that it could return a recommendation of life imprisonment.

Factual and procedural background of case: The defendant, Calton, was convicted of capital murder and sentenced to death by the Territory of Utah. The Utah Supreme Court affirmed the judgment. In doing so, the appellate court rejected the defendant's argument that the trial court committed reversible error in failing to instruct the jury that it could return a verdict recommendation of life imprisonment. The United States Supreme Court granted certiorari to consider the issue.

Opinion of the Court by Justice Harlan: Justice Harlan held that it was reversible error for the trial court to fail to instruct the jury that it could recommend life imprisonment, even though the defendant was found guilty of first degree murder. The opinion reasoned as follows: "If their attention had been called to [the fact that they could recommend life imprisonment], it may be that they would have made such a recommendation, and thereby enabled the court to reduce the punishment to imprisonment for life. We are of opinion that the court erred in not directing the attention of the jury to this matter. The [Territory's law] evidently proceeds upon the ground that there may be cases of murder in the first degree, the punishment for which by imprisonment for life at hard labor will suffice to meet the ends of public justice. Its object could only have been met through a recommendation by the jury that the lesser punishment be inflicted, and it is not to be presumed that they were aware of their right to make such recommendation." The judgment of the Utah Supreme Court was reversed and a new trial awarded.

Cambodia The death penalty was abolished in Cambodia in 1989. *See also* **International Capital Punishment Nations**

Cameras in Courtroom *see* **Public Trial**

Cameras in Execution Chamber *see* **Public Viewing of Execution**

Cameroon Cameroon employs capital punishment. Cameroon utilizes the firing squad and hanging as methods of carrying out the death penalty. The legal structure of Cameroon is strongly influenced by the French legal system, although in some provinces certain aspects of the Anglo-Saxon tradition apply. Cameroon's constitution was adopted on May 20, 1972. The nation's constitution provides for an independent judiciary; however, the judiciary is part of the executive branch and is subordinate to the Ministry of Justice.

The court system includes a Supreme Court, courts of appeal in each of the nation's ten provinces, and trial courts. Traditional or customary courts exist in rural areas of the country. Most traditional courts permit appeal of their decisions to the modern court system. Under the constitution trials are open to the public. Defendants are presumed innocent, have the right to retained or appointed counsel, right to bail, and the right to appeal. *See also* **International Capital Punishment Nations**

Campaign to End the Death Penalty The Campaign to End the Death Penalty (CEDP) is a Chicago based national organization that was founded in 1995. The CEDP stresses grassroots organizing and regularly organizes to win support for prisoners on death row. The organization launched a successful campaign in the latter part of the 1990s to prevent the reimposition of the death penalty in Massachusetts. It has also engaged in work to defeat efforts to bring capital punishment to Washington D.C. and Iowa.

Campbell, Charles Charles Campbell was executed for capital murder by the state of Washington on May 27, 1994. The method of execution used was hanging. The victims of Campbell's capital murder were Renae Wicklund, Shannah Wicklund and Barbara Hendrickson.

The record in this case indicated that prior to the murders, Campbell had previous contacts with the victims. In 1974, Campbell assaulted and sodomized Renae. Campbell held a knife to the throat of Renae's infant daughter Shannah and threatened to harm her if Renae did not submit. Afterwards, Renae ran to the home of her neighbor Hendrickson for help. In 1976, Campbell was convicted of the 1974 sexual assault and sodomy of Renae. Both Renae and Hendrickson had testified at trial against Campbell.

In 1982, Campbell was an inmate at Everett Work Release Facility. On April 14, 1982, Renae, her 8-year-old daughter Shannah, and Hendrickson, were found dead in Renae's home. Evidence produced at trial indicated Renae had been the first victim. She was found nude on her bedroom floor. Shannah, the second victim, had been attacked in the dining room, then dragged into her mother's bedroom and killed. Hendrickson, the third victim, had also been attacked in the dining room and killed in the hallway.

All three victims had been beaten and assaulted prior to death. The right earlobes of Renae and Hendrickson had been torn. The autopsy revealed Renae had received extensive blunt trauma beating on her head, back, and upper chest area. Her jaw and nose were broken and she had been strangled. Her neck had a 7 inch incision across the front, which severed both carotid arteries. She had bled to death from the neck cut. After her death, a blunt object was used to tear a 1 inch cut into the upper end of the vaginal wall. Shannah had also been strangled and suffered a 7½ inch cut across her upper neck, inflicted by extending her backward and elevating the chin. Hendrickson had a 7 inch upper neck cut and died of a massive hemorrhage.

A few days after the murders, Campbell was charged with three counts of aggravated first degree murder. The prosecution's case was overwhelmingly strong, relying upon numerous witnesses and abundant evidence linking Campbell to the crimes. Campbell's girl friend, Judith Dirks, testified Campbell visited her on the morning of April 14. He had been drinking and drank a 6-pack of beer at her home. Dirks testified that on April 15 she noticed her butcher knife was missing. Dirks also stated Campbell felt a resentment toward Renae and had driven by her home while on work release.

Another witness, Tim Fowler, testified that while riding home from school on the bus at 3 P.M. on April 14, he saw a red car parked in an inlet in the woods near the crime scene. Tim's brother, Mike Fowler, testified he saw the car parked in the woods around 3:15–3:20 P.M. Tim's dad, Jim Fowler, testified that at 3:40 P.M. that afternoon he saw the same car backed into the woods. The type of car described by the witnesses was very similar to the one owned by Campbell.

Eleven-year-old Josette Frase, a next door neighbor of

Renae, testified at trial that at about 3:30 P.M. on April 14, she saw a man wiggle around in the bushes by her house and then walk down a gravel road. She testified he was tall, had dark brown curly hair, and was wearing a blue sports jacket with a yellow stripe running across the middle. She identified Campbell in court and at a lineup, as the man she saw.

The jury determined the evidence was proof beyond a reasonable doubt of Campbell's guilt and convicted him of three counts of capital murder. He was subsequently sentenced to death.

Canada   Canada abolished the death penalty for ordinary crimes in 1976, and abolished the punishment completely in 1998. *See also* **International Capital Punishment Nations**

Canadian Coalition Against the Death Penalty

The Canadian Coalition Against the Death Penalty (CCADP) is a nonprofit human rights organization that was founded in 1998. Its primary focus is the abolition of the death penalty in the United States. CCADP has chapters in Ontario and Quebec. Its membership includes activists, professionals, crime victims and their families, persons working within the justice system opposed to capital punishment, persons opposed to capital punishment on religious and moral grounds, and other concerned citizens opposed to capital punishment.

Dave Parkinson, left, and Tracy Lamourie, right, founded the Canadian Coalition Against the Death Penalty in 1998. (Dave Parkinson and Tracy Lamourie)

CCADP was founded by its executive officers, Tracy Lamourie and Dave Parkinson. They are both Toronto residents and have a long history of activism in human rights and social issues. Through their guidance CCADP provides emotional and practical support to inmates, their families and families of murder victims. It also raises funds for legal defense fees for inmates, makes arrangements for Canadian nationwide bookstores to be admitted on the prison mailing list in order to purchase reading and educational material to send to inmates, and it seeks and provides penpals for inmates.

Capacity Substantially Impaired Mitigator   The "capacity substantially impaired mitigator" is a statutory mitigating circumstance. Under this mitigator a capital felon must present evidence that his or her capacity to appreciate the wrongfulness of his or her conduct, or to conform that conduct to the requirements of the law was substantially impaired at the time of the commission of the capital offense. Courts have held that the capacity substantially impaired mitigator is stated in the disjunctive, so that proof of incapacity as to either ability to "appreciate" or "conform" establishes this mitigator.

Usually the capacity substantially impaired mitigator is

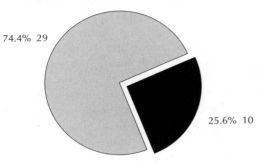

JURISDICTIONS USING CAPACITY
SUBSTANTIALLY IMPAIRED MITIGATOR

74.4% 29

25.6% 10

■ CAPACITY SUBSTANTIALLY IMPAIRED MITIGATOR JURISDICTIONS
■ ALL OTHER JURISDICTIONS

satisfied only by evidence of a mental disease or psychological defect. Character or personality disorders alone generally are not sufficient to find that a capital defendant's ability to appreciate the criminality of his or her conduct, or to conform that conduct to the requirements of law was substantially impaired.

Courts generally permit voluntary intoxication or drug addiction to be used in an effort to establish the capacity substantially impaired mitigator. In order to satisfy this mitigator by a showing of intoxication or drug use, substantial evidence must be proffered which shows that intoxication or drug use at the time of the commission of a capital offense was of such degree as to substantially impair the defendant's capacity to appreciate the criminality of his or her conduct or to conform that conduct to the requirements of the law. It has been held that if the alcohol or drug impairment does not rise to the level of the statutory mitigator, trial courts should still consider whether such impairment constitutes a non-statutory mitigator, when viewed in the light of a capital defendant's alleged history of alcohol or drug abuse. *See also* **Intoxication Defense; Intoxication Mitigator; Mitigating Circumstances**

Capano, Thomas   Thomas Capano, a wealthy and influential Delaware lawyer, was convicted by a jury on January 17, 1999, of the capital murder of his mistress, Anne Marie Fahey. On March 16, 1999, the 49 year old Capano was sentenced to death by Superior Court Judge William Swain Lee. The penalty phase jury had recommended the death penalty by a vote of 10–2.

The tragic fate of Fahey and Capano began in 1996 when she tried to end their affair. They had been seeing each for three years. Capano, who was married — but separated, was a deputy attorney general and Fahey was employed as an aide to the Governor of Delaware.

On June 27, 1996 Capano and Fahey were seen together having dinner in a Philadelphia restaurant. Later that evening 30 year old Fahey was murdered by Capano at his home. For over a year Capano denied any knowledge of what happened to Fahey. However, in November of 1997, Capano's younger brother, Gerard, went to authorities and told them that on June 28, 1996 he and Capano dumped Fahey's body from his boat 70 miles off the New Jersey coast. Another brother, Louis, also admitted to helping Capano conceal evidence. In the face of condemning evidence from his own family, Capano still denied killing Fahey. Capano admitted at trial to dumping Fahey's body in the Atlantic Ocean, but said she was killed by his other mistress, Deborah MacIntyre, after she found them together. Capano's theory was that MacIntyre accidentally shot Fahey in a jealous rage, and that he got rid of the body to protect her. MacIntyre denied being at Capano's house the night Fahey died.

Without a body or a murder weapon, prosecutors relied on a mound of circumstantial evidence to convict Capano of planning and killing Fahey because she wanted to end their affair.

Cape Verde

Capital punishment was abolished in Cape Verde in 1981. *See also* **International Capital Punishment Nations**

Capital Crime *see* Death-Eligible Offenses; Murder; Types of Crimes

Capital Felon

Capital felon is the legal term or phrase used to designate a person charged with or convicted of committing a crime that carries the punishment of death.

Capital Punishment

Capital punishment refers to the infliction of death as the legal punishment for a crime. It is the most severe form of punishment inflicted under Anglo-American jurisprudence. Under the Cruel and Unusual Punishment Clause of the Eighth Amendment, the method of inflicting capital punishment and the crimes so punishable are restricted. *See also* **Death-Eligible Offenses; Rape and Capital Punishment**

Capital Punishment in Colonial America *see* Pre-Furman Capital Punishment

Capital Punishment Jurisdictions

The United States Supreme Court decision in *Furman v. Georgia*, 408 U.S. 238 (1972) placed a moratorium on capital punishment, until procedures were developed that would minimize arbitrary imposition of the punishment. The moratorium was lifted with the Supreme Court's approval of Georgia's new capital punishment procedures in *Gregg v. Georgia*, 428 U.S. 153 (1976).

Subsequent to the decision in *Gregg*, thirty-eight states and the Federal government enacted new capital punishment procedures. The United States Supreme Court invalidated the death penalty statutes in a few States that made capital punishment mandatory (the affected States amended their statutes). Massachusetts had its new death penalty procedures judicially invalidated by the Massachusetts Supreme Judicial Court in *Commonwealth v. Colon-Cruz*, 470 N.E.2d 116

Capital Punishment Jurisdictions 1999

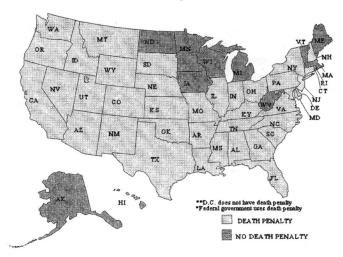

**D.C. does not have death penalty
*Federal government uses death penalty

☐ DEATH PENALTY
■ NO DEATH PENALTY

(1984). The Massachusetts legislature did not pass legislation to amend the statute, though efforts were made. *See also* **Impact of the Furman Decision**

Cardona, Ana Marie

Ana Marie Cardona who was sentenced to death on April 1, 1992, by the state of Florida for the murder of her three year old son, Lazaro Figueroa. Cardona was born in Cuba on November 26, 1961.

Cardona's journey to death row began after the death of her common law spouse Fidel Figueroa. Fidel was an alleged Miami drug kingpin who was killed in 1987. Cardona lived a life of luxury while Fidel was alive. Fidel's death turned Cardona's life upside down.

A month after Fidel's death, Cardona gave birth to Lazaro on September 18, 1987. The initial months after Fidel's death and Lazaro's birth were not difficult for Cardona, because she "inherited" $100,000 from Fidel's estate. This money, however, was quickly depleted by Cardona. When the money ran out Cardona took up residence in cheap motels with a female lover named Olivia Mendoza. It was during Cardona's relationship with Mendoza that Lazaro became a scapegoat for Cardona's financial woes.

Cardona beat, choked, starved, confined, emotionally abused and systematically tortured Lazaro. The child spent

A Florida jury found Ana Marie Cardona guilty of brutally beating her three year old child to death. The trial evidence revealed she beat the child in the head with a baseball bat. Cardona is on Florida's death row. (Florida Department of Corrections)

much of the time tied to a bed, left in a bathtub with the hot or cold water running, or locked in a closet. To avoid changing Lazaro's diaper for as long as possible, Cardona would wrap duct tape around the child's diaper to hold in the excrement. The end for Lazaro came on the last day of October 1990, when Cardona severely beat Lazaro with a baseball bat. After splitting the child's head open, Cardona locked him in the closet where he had been confined for the last two months. The next day another beating ensued with the baseball bat. This beating killed the child. Cardona and Mendoza took Lazaro to a Miami Beach residence and abandoned him in some bushes. On November 2, 1990, the battered body of the child was found.

When Cardona learned that the child's body had been found she and Mendoza fled to the Orlando area and then to St. Cloud, where they were later arrested. Cardona told police that the child had fallen off the bed and injured himself. When she could not revive him, she took the child to a Miami Beach residence and left him on a doorstep so the people who owned the house could help him. Mendoza concurred in the story. Both women were charged with aggravated child abuse and first degree murder. Mendoza eventually admitted her role in the abuse, pled guilty to second degree murder and aggravated child abuse, and agreed to testify against Cardona.

During Cardona's trial the medical examiner testified that Lazaro did not die from one particular injury, rather, he died from months of child abuse and neglect. The medical examiner detailed the injuries as follows:

> Due to repeated injury, the muscle between the elbow and shoulder of Lazaro's left arm had turned to bone, rendering the arm useless. The child had deep bruises on his left hand and palm that were consistent with defensive wounds. Lazaro's right forearm was fractured, in a manner also consistent with a defensive wound. The child's left leg, which was much thicker than the right, was engorged with blood. His feet and toes also had extensive deep bruises. Some of the child's toenails had been crushed. There were other deep blunt trauma bruises to the child's chest and buttocks. Lazaro's left eye was bruised and there was a laceration on his right eye. There were cigarette burns on the child's cheek and pressure sores all over his body, from being forced to lie in bed for extended periods. The inside of the child's lips was obliterated by scar tissue and his front teeth had been knocked out. There were lacerations to the scalp, the most recent of which was an open festering wound that had allowed meningitis bacteria to invade the child's brain through a skull fracture. The blow that caused that fracture also crushed the child's olfactory nerve. A later blow to the head had sheared the nerves connecting the spinal cord to the rear of the child's brain.

The guilt phase jury found Cardona guilty of both offenses and at the conclusion of the penalty phase, recommended death by a vote of eight to four. The trial court followed the recommendation and imposed a death sentence. The Florida Supreme Court affirmed the judgment. *See also* **Women and Capital Punishment**

Cardozo, Benjamin N.

Benjamin N. Cardoza served as an associate justice of the United States Supreme Court from 1932 to 1938. While on the Supreme Court Cardoza was known as a moderate, who had left of center underpinnings in his interpretation of the Constitution.

Cardoza was born on May 24, 1870 in New York City. Cardoza attended Columbia College where he earned an undergraduate degree in 1889 and a master's degree in 1890. He received a law degree from Columbia Law School in 1891. Cardoza engaged in a private legal practice for over two decades before joining the judiciary. He served as both a trial judge and a judge on New York's highest court. In 1932 President Herbert Hoover nominated Cardoza as the second Jewish American to sit on the Supreme Court.

While on the Supreme Court Cardoza is known to have written only two capital punishment opinions. In *Snyder v. Massachusetts* the Supreme Court was asked to decide whether the Federal Constitution required a defendant be permitted to accompany a jury to view the crime scene. Cardoza, writing for the Court, held in *Snyder* that: "We consider a bare inspection and nothing more, a view where nothing is said by any one to direct the attention of the jury to one feature or another. The Fourteenth Amendment does not assure to a defendant the privilege to be present at such a time. There is nothing he could do if he were there, and almost nothing he could gain."

Cardoza's opinion in *Palko v. Connecticut* provided his greatest legacy in the area of capital punishment, and criminal law in general. In *Palko* the Supreme Court was asked to decide whether the double jeopardy principles contained in the Fifth Amendment were applicable to States. Cardoza, in a far-reaching decision, held that the double jeopardy principles of the Fifth Amendment were applicable against the Federal government, but had no application to States. The ruling by Cardoza in *Palko* would eventually be overruled in *Benton v. Maryland*, 395 U.S. 784 (1969). Cardoza died in 1938.

Carjacking Aggravator

The crime of carjacking involves forcibly taking a vehicle from its owner or possessor. The crime of carjacking has been elevated to a statutory aggravating circumstance when accompanied by murder. Four capital punishment jurisdictions, California, Illinois, Indiana and Maryland, have made this crime a statutory aggravating circumstance that permits the imposition of a death sentence. *See also* **Aggravating Circumstances**

Carpenter, David *see* Trailside Killer

Carter v. Texas

Court: United States Supreme Court; *Case Citation:* Carter v. Texas, 177 U.S. 442 (1900); *Argued:* March 16, 1900; *Decided:* April 16, 1900; *Opinion of the Court:* Justice Gray; *Concurring Opinion:* None; *Dissenting Opinion:* None; *Appellate Defense Counsel:* Wilford H. Smith argued; E. M. Hewlett on brief; *Appellate Prosecution Counsel:* T. S. Smith argued and briefed; *Amicus Curiae Brief Supporting Prosecutor:* None; *Amicus Curiae Brief Supporting Defendant:* None.

Issue Presented: Whether the defendant may be deprived of

the right to have an evidentiary hearing to challenge an indictment on the ground that blacks were systematically excluded from the grand jury that returned the indictment?

Case Holding: The defendant may not be deprived of the right to have an evidentiary hearing to challenge an indictment on the ground that blacks were systematically excluded from the grand jury that returned the indictment, when the challenge is timely and properly made.

Factual and procedural background of case: The defendant, Seth Carter, was indicted for capital murder by a grand jury in the State of Texas. Prior to trial the defendant requested a hearing to challenge the indictment on the ground that blacks were systematically excluded from the grand jury that returned the indictment against him. The trial court denied the request to hold an evidentiary hearing. The defendant was ultimately convicted and sentenced to death. On appeal, the Texas Court of Criminal Appeals affirmed the judgment. In doing so, the appellate court rejected the defendant's contention that he was entitled to an evidentiary hearing to challenge the indictment because of alleged racial discrimination in the selection of the grand jury members. The United States Supreme Court granted certiorari to consider the issue.

Opinion of the Court by Justice Gray: Justice Gray noted that "[w]henever by any action of a state, whether through its legislature, through its courts, or through its executive or administrative officers, all persons of the African race are excluded, solely because of their race or color, from serving as grand jurors in the criminal prosecution of a person of the African race, the equal protection of the laws is denied to him, contrary to the Fourteenth Amendment of the Constitution of the United States." The opinion held that when a defendant does not have an adequate opportunity to challenge the composition of a grand jury before it returns an indictment, the proper procedure is to permit a meaningful opportunity to challenge the indictment before trial. Justice Gray found that the defendant was improperly denied a meaningful opportunity to challenge the indictment through an evidentiary hearing. In ultimately granting the defendant a new trial, the opinion supported the Court's decision as follows:

> It thus clearly appears by the record that the defendant, having duly and distinctly alleged, in his motion to quash [the indictment], that all persons of the African race were excluded, because of their race and color, from the grand jury which found the indictment, asked leave of the court to introduce witnesses, and offered to introduce witnesses, to prove and sustain that allegation; and that the court refused to hear any evidence upon the subject, and overruled the motion, without investigating whether the allegation was true or false.
>
> The defendant having offered to introduce witnesses to prove the allegations in the motion to quash, and the court having declined to hear any evidence upon the subject, it is quite clear that the omission [of the record] to give the names of the witnesses whom the defendant proposed or intended to call, or to state their testimony in detail, cannot deprive the defendant of the benefit of [challenge to the indictment] And the assumption, in the final opinion of the state [appellate] court, that no evidence was tendered by the defendant in support of the allega-

tions in the motion to quash, is plainly disproved by ... what took place in the trial court.

The necessary conclusion is that the defendant has been denied a right duly set up and claimed by him under the Constitution and laws of the United States; and therefore the judgment is reversed, and the case is remanded for further proceedings not inconsistent with this opinion. *See also* **Discrimination in Grand or Petit Jury Selection**

Carver v. United States

Court: United States Supreme Court; *Case Citation:* Carver v. United States, 160 U.S. 553 (1896); *Argued:* Not reported; *Decided:* January 13, 1896; *Opinion of the Court:* Chief Justice Fuller; *Concurring Opinion:* None; *Dissenting Opinion:* None; *Appellate Defense Counsel:* Wm. M. Cravens argued and briefed; *Appellate Prosecution Counsel:* Mr. Dickinson argued and briefed; *Amicus Curiae Brief Supporting Prosecutor:* None; *Amicus Curiae Brief Supporting Defendant:* None.

Issue Presented: Whether it was error for the trial court to admit into evidence statements made by the victim prior to her death?

Case Holding: It was not error for the trial court to admit into evidence the statement made by the victim two days after she was shot, but it was reversible error to admit the statement made by the victim a few weeks after she was shot.

Factual and procedural background of case: The defendant, Frank Carver, was convicted of capital murder and sentenced to death by the United States. The defendant appealed to the United States Supreme Court, contending the trial court improperly allowed into evidence statements made by the victim prior to her death. The United States Supreme Court granted certiorari to consider the issue.

Opinion of the Court by Chief Justice Fuller: The Chief Justice wrote that two different statements attributed to the victim were introduced into evidence. Both statements concerned the circumstances surrounding the victim being shot by the defendant. The first statement was made two days after the victim was shot by the defendant. The second statement was made a few weeks after the victim was shot. It was said that the first statement was admissible as a dying declaration, because the victim believed she was going to die at that time. However, the Chief Justice ruled that the second statement was not admissible as a dying declaration, because the victim believed she was going to recover from the wound (but did not). The opinion explained the law on the issue as follows: "It has been held that a declaration is admissible if made while hope lingers, if it is afterwards ratified when hope is gone, or if made when the person is without hope, though afterwards he regains confidence. But the repetition of a dying declaration cannot itself be admitted as a reiteration of the alleged facts if made when hope has been regained." The judgment of the Federal trial court was reversed and the case remanded for a new trial. *See also* **Hearsay; Hearsay Exceptions**

Case-in-Chief *see* **Trial Structure**

Casey, James P. *see* **Vigilance Committee of San Francisco**

Cassell v. Texas *Court:* United States Supreme Court; *Case Citation:* Cassell v. Texas, 339 U.S. 282 (1950); *Argued:* November 10, 1949; *Decided:* April 24, 1950; *Plurality Opinion:* Justice Reed announced the Court's judgment and delivered an opinion, in which Vinson, C.J., and Black and Clark JJ., joined; *Concurring Opinion:* Justice Frankfurter, in which Burton and Minton, JJ., joined; *Concurring Opinion:* Justice Clark; *Dissenting Opinion:* Justice Jackson; *Justice Taking No Part in Decision:* Justice Douglas; *Appellate Defense Counsel:* Chris Dixie argued; L. N. D. Wells, Jr. and W. J. Durham on brief; *Appellate Prosecution Counsel:* Joe R. Greenhill argued; Price Daniel and E. Jacobson on brief; *Amicus Curiae Brief Supporting Prosecutor:* None; *Amicus Curiae Brief Supporting Defendant:* None.

Issue Presented: Whether the defendant established his claim of racial discrimination in the selection of the grand jury that indicted him?

Case Holding: The defendant established his claim of racial discrimination in the selection of the grand jury that indicted him, therefore the judgment against him could not stand.

Factual and procedural background of case: The defendant, Cassell, was convicted of capital murder and sentenced to death by the State of Texas. The Texas Court of Criminal Appeals affirmed the judgment. In doing so, the appellate court rejected the defendant's contention the judgment against him was invalid because blacks were excluded from the grand jury that indicted him. The United States Supreme Court granted certiorari to consider the issue.

Plurality opinion in which Justice Reed announced the Court's judgment and in which Vinson, C.J., and Black and Clark, JJ., joined: Justice Reed found that the defendant had established racial discrimination in the selection of the grand jury that indicted him. The opinion cited the following evidence tendered on the issue by the defendant: "The jury commissioners testified that no [blacks] were selected for the grand jury because they chose jurymen only from people with whom they were personally acquainted and they knew no [blacks] who were eligible and available for grand jury service. It also appeared from the record that, from 1942, until [the defendant's] indictment in 1947, there had been 21 grand juries on none of which was there more than one [black], that of the 252 members 17 (or 6.7 percent) were [black], and that about 15.5 percent of the population of the county and 6.5 percent of the eligible voters were [black]."

Justice Reed pointed out that the statistical evidence proffered by the defendant did not "establish a prima facie case of discrimination." It was said that the statistical evidence showed that blacks did participate overall in the grand jury process. Justice Reed noted that the Constitution did not require proportional representation, it prohibited racial discrimination. The plurality opinion explained: "We have recently written why proportional representation of races on a

jury is not a constitutional requisite. Succinctly stated, our reason was that the Constitution requires only a fair jury selected without regard to race. Obviously the number of races and nationalities appearing in the ancestry of our citizens would make it impossible to meet a requirement of proportional representation. Similarly, since there can be no exclusion of [blacks] as a race and no discrimination because of color, proportional limitation is not permissible."

Although the statistical evidence did not provide a prima facie showing of racial discrimination, Justice Reed found the testimony of the jury commissioners provided evidence of racial discrimination in the selection of the grand jury that indicted the defendant. Justice Reed wrote on this issue as follows: "The existence ... of discrimination ... does not depend upon systematic exclusion continuing over a long period and practiced by a succession of jury commissioners. Since the issue must be whether there has been discrimination in the selection of the jury that has indicted [the defendant], it is enough to have direct evidence based on the statements of the jury commissioners in the very case. Discrimination may be proved in other ways than by evidence of long-continued unexplained absence of [blacks] from many panels. The statements of the jury commissioners that they chose only whom they knew, and that they knew no eligible [black] in an area where [blacks] made up so large a proportion of the population, prove the intentional exclusion that is discrimination in violation of [the defendant's] constitutional rights." The judgment of the Texas Court of Criminal Appeals was reversed.

Concurring opinion by Justice Frankfurter, in which Burton and Minton, JJ., joined: Justice Frankfurter concurred in the Court's judgment. He wrote separately primarily to express his opinion on the issue of racial proportionality in jury service:

It has been settled law since 1880 that the Civil War Amendments barred the States from discriminating because of race in the selection of juries, whether grand or petty. As a result, a conviction cannot stand which is based on an indictment found by a grand jury from which [blacks] were kept because of discrimination. We ought not to reverse a course of decisions of long standing directed against racial discrimination in the administration of justice. But discrimination in this context means purposeful, systematic non-inclusion because of color. It does not mean an absence of proportional representation of the various racial components of the relevant political unit from which a grand jury is drawn or an isolated instance of disparity among such components. Assuming that the grand jury pool fairly enough reflects the racial composition of the community, there is no basis for a claim of constitutional discrimination if without design it comes to pass that a particular grand jury has no representation of a particular race. The Civil War Amendments did not deprive the States of their power to define qualifications for grand jury service relevant to the functions of a grand jury, nor did they turn matters that are inherently incommensurable into mere matters of arithmetic. The Constitution has not withdrawn the administration of criminal justice, of which the jury system is a part, from the States. It does command that no State purposefully make jury service turn on color.

Concurring opinion by Justice Clark: Justice Clark concurred in the Court's judgment. He wrote separately to state that he believed the Court's prior precedents may have been wrong in requiring reversal of a judgment because of racial discrimination in selection of a grand jury. However, he was not willing to retreat from the Court's precedents, as he wrote: "I think we must adhere to the settled course of decision by this Court with respect to such exclusion."

Dissenting opinion by Justice Jackson: Justice Jackson dissented from the Court's decision. He argued that racial discrimination in grand jury selection did not affect a defendant's guilt or innocence, and should therefore not be a basis for reversing a judgment. Justice Jackson expressed his thoughts as follows:

> In setting aside this conviction, the Court is moved by a desire to enforce equality in that realm where, above all, it must be enforced — in our judicial system. But this conviction is reversed for errors that have nothing to do with the defendant's guilt or innocence, or with a fair trial of that issue. This conflicts with another principle important to our law, viz., that no conviction should be set aside for errors not affecting substantial rights of the accused.
>
> This Court has never weighed these competing considerations in cases of this kind. The use of objections to the composition of juries is lately so much resorted to for purposes of delay, however, and the spectacle of a defendant putting the grand jury on trial before he can be tried for a crime is so discrediting to the administration of justice, that it is time to examine the basis for the practice....
>
> The [right of blacks] to be selected for grand jury service is unquestionable and should be directly and uncompromisingly enforced. But I doubt if any good purpose will be served in the long run by identifying the right of the most worthy [blacks] to serve on grand juries with the efforts of the least worthy to defer or escape punishment for crime. I cannot believe that those qualified for grand jury service would fail to return a true bill against a murderer because he is a [black]. But unless they would, this defendant has not been harmed.
>
> I would treat this as a case where the irregularity is not shown to have harmed this defendant, and affirm the conviction.

See also **Discrimination in Grand or Petit Jury Selection**

Catholics Against Capital Punishment
Catholics Against Capital Punishment (CACP) is a Virginia based organization that was founded in 1992. CACP seeks to promote greater awareness of Catholic Church teachings that characterize capital punishment as inappropriate and unacceptable in today's world. It does this in three ways: (1) by communicating such teachings to federal and state lawmakers, urging them to oppose proposed legislation imposing or extending the use of the death penalty, and to work for repeal of such laws currently on the books; (2) by encouraging members of the Catholic hierarchy and clergy in the United States to speak out more forcefully against capital punishment; and (3) by mobilizing the support of the Catholic laity to oppose capital punishment through its newsletter, *CACP News Notes*, and disseminating news of Catholic-oriented anti–death penalty efforts.

Central African Republic
Capital punishment is allowed by the Central African Republic, but the punishment has not been used in more than a decade. The Central African Republic utilizes the firing squad to carry out the death penalty. The nation's legal system is based on French law. The Central African Republic underwent many political changes during the 1990s. In 1994 a new constitution providing for multiparty democracy was approved by a national referendum. Under the new constitution the government is divided into an executive branch, legislative branch, and judicial branch.

Legislation implementing the new judiciary was enacted in 1996. New courts of justice were created in 1997. Under the laws of the Central African Republic defendants are presumed innocent, have the right to legal counsel, to public trial, to be present at their trials, and to confront witnesses. Court proceedings are broadcast on national radio. *See also* **International Capital Punishment Nations**

Certified Question
Very often a court will encounter a legal issue that it is uncertain of how to resolve. When this occurs a court may seek an answer on how to resolve the matter by submitting a "certified question" to another court. Generally, certified questions come from trial courts and are submitted to appellate courts. However, occasionally appellate courts submit certified questions to other appellate courts. For example, a Federal appellate court may submit a certified question to the highest court of a State, where the issue needing to be resolved involves interpretation of the law of that State. Also, in a jurisdiction having a three tier legal system, a mid-level appellate court may submit a certified question to the highest appellate court in the jurisdiction. For example, a Federal appellate court may submit a certified question to the United States Supreme Court.

The use of certified questions occurs before the merits of the underlying case has been resolved. In every instance, the answer to a certified question is needed to properly resolve the merits of the underlying case. Certified questions are used more frequently in civil litigation than criminal litigation. However, occasionally legal issues arise in criminal cases that are ripe for certified questions. *See also* **Biddle v. Perovich; Ex Parte Milligan; Gooch v. United States; United States v. Bevins; United States v. Klintock; United States v. Palmer; United States v. Pirates; United States v. Smith; Zant v. Stephens (I); Zant v. Stephens (II)**

Certiorari, Writ of
The writ of certiorari is an appellate device that is used to address the merits of a case. This writ is used when review by an appellate court is discretionary, as opposed to an appeal of right. In practice, a party will submit a petition for appeal. If the appellate court decides to hear the appeal, based on the merits of the petition, it will issue a writ of certiorari ordering the full record in the case to be produced.

Chad
The death penalty is used in the nation of Chad. The firing squad is used by Chad as the method of execution.

Its legal system is based on French civil law and customary law. Chad endured tremendous political upheaval during the 1990s. In 1996, Idriss Deby was elected president. He had previously strong-armed his way to the presidency in 1990. Also in 1996, the people of Chad adopted a new constitution.

The judicial system has a Court of Appeals and operates with trial courts located in provincial capitals. The traditional or customary system of law presided over by local chiefs and sultans has been preserved for property and family affairs and for cases of local petty crime. Decisions of the customary courts are subject to appeal to the regular courts.

Although the nation's constitution mandates an independent judiciary, it was reported that the judiciary is ineffective, underfunded, overburdened, and subject to executive interference. Criminal trials are said to be totally lacking in fundamental due process. Persons accused of crimes have been known to endure up to several years of incarceration before being formally charged or tried. *See also* **International Capital Punishment Nations**

Challenge for Cause *see* Jury Selection

Chamber *see* Execution Chamber

Chambers v. Florida
Court: United States Supreme Court; *Case Citation:* Chambers v. Florida, 309 U.S. 227 (1940); *Argued:* January 4, 1940; *Decided:* February 12, 1940; *Opinion of the Court:* Justice Black; *Concurring Opinion:* None; *Dissenting Opinion:* None; *Justice Taking No Part in Decision:* Justice Murphy; *Appellate Defense Counsel:* Leon A. Ransom argued; S. D. McGill on brief; *Appellate Prosecution Counsel:* Tyrus A. Norwood argued and brief; *Amicus Curiae Brief Supporting Prosecutor:* None; *Amicus Curiae Brief Supporting Defendant:* None.

Issue Presented: Whether the confessions given by the defendants were obtained in violation of the Due Process Clause?

Case Holding: The confessions given by the defendants were obtained in violation of the Due Process Clause, and therefore the judgments against them could not stand.

Factual and procedural background of case: This case involved the prosecution of four defendants, Chambers, Williamson, Woodward and Davis, for capital murder by the State of Florida. Defendants Williamson, Woodward and Davis pleaded guilty to capital murder. Chambers was found guilty by a jury. All four defendants were sentenced to death. The Florida Supreme Court affirmed the judgments. In doing so, the appellate court rejected the argument by the defendants that their confessions were taken in violation of the Federal Constitution. The United States Supreme Court granted certiorari to consider the issue.

Opinion of the Court by Justice Black: Justice Black held that the confessions given by the defendants were obtained in violation of the Constitution. In describing the circumstances of the confessions, the opinion stated:

> For five days [the defendants] were subjected to interroga-

tions.... Over a period of five days they steadily refused to confess and disclaimed any guilt. The very circumstances surrounding their confinement and their questioning without any formal charges having been brought, were such as to fill [the defendants] with terror and frightful misgivings.

> These are the confessions utilized by the State to obtain the judgments upon which [the defendants] were sentenced to death. No formal charges had been brought before the confessions. Two days thereafter, [the defendants] were indicted [and] arraigned.... When Chambers was tried, his conviction rested upon his confession and testimony of the other three confessors.... And from arrest until sentenced to death, [the defendants] were never — either in jail or in court — wholly removed from the constant observation, influence, custody and control of those whose persistent pressure brought about the .... confessions.

Justice Black relied upon the Due Process Clause to reject the method used to obtain the confessions. The opinion outlined the contours of the Due Process Clause and the conduct requiring its creation as follows:

> The scope and operation of the Fourteenth Amendment have been fruitful sources of controversy in our constitutional history. However, in view of its historical setting and the wrongs which called it into being, the due process provision of the Fourteenth Amendment — just as that in the Fifth — has led few to doubt that it was intended to guarantee procedural standards adequate and appropriate, then and thereafter, to protect, at all times, people charged with or suspected of crime by those holding positions of power and authority. Tyrannical governments had immemorially utilized dictatorial criminal procedure and punishment to make scape goats of the weak, or of helpless political, religious, or racial minorities and those who differed, who would not conform and who resisted tyranny. The instruments of such governments were in the main, two. Conduct, innocent when engaged in, was subsequently made by fiat criminally punishable without legislation. And a liberty loving people won the principle that criminal punishments could not be inflicted save for that which proper legislative action had already by "the law of the land" forbidden when done. But even more was needed. From the popular hatred and abhorrence of illegal confinement, torture and extortion of confessions of violations of the "law of the land" evolved the fundamental idea that no man's life, liberty or property be forfeited as criminal punishment for violation of that law until there had been a charge fairly made and fairly tried in a public tribunal free of prejudice, passion, excitement and tyrannical power. Thus, as assurance against ancient evils, our country, in order to preserve "the blessings of liberty," wrote into its basic law the requirement, among others, that the forfeiture of the lives, liberties or property of people accused of crime can only follow if procedural safeguards of due process have been obeyed.

> The determination to preserve an accused's right to procedural due process sprang in large part from knowledge of the historical truth that the rights and liberties of people accused of crime could not be safely entrusted to secret inquisitorial processes. The testimony of centuries, in governments of varying kinds over populations of different races and beliefs, stood as proof that physical and mental torture and coercion had brought about the tragically unjust sacrifices of some who were the noblest and most useful of their generations. The rack, the thumbscrew, the wheel, solitary confinement, protracted questioning and cross questioning, and other ingenious forms of entrapment of the helpless or unpopular had left their wake of mutilated bodies and shattered minds along the way to the cross, the guillotine, the stake and the hangman's noose. And they

who have suffered most from secret and dictatorial proceedings have almost always been the poor, the ignorant, the numerically weak, the friendless, and the powerless....

We are not impressed by the argument that law enforcement methods such as those under review are necessary to uphold our laws. The Constitution proscribes such lawless means irrespective of the end. And this argument flouts the basic principle that all people must stand on an equality before the bar of justice in every American court. Today, as in ages past, we are not without tragic proof that the exalted power of some governments to punish manufactured crime dictatorially is the handmaid of tyranny. Under our constitutional system, courts stand against any winds that blow as havens of refuge for those who might otherwise suffer because they are helpless, weak, outnumbered, or because they are non-conforming victims of prejudice and public excitement. Due process of law, preserved for all by our Constitution, commands that no such practice as that disclosed by this record shall send any accused to his death. No higher duty, no more solemn responsibility, rests upon this Court, than that of translating into living law and maintaining this constitutional shield deliberately planned and inscribed for the benefit of every human being subject to our Constitution — of whatever race, creed or persuasion.

The judgments of the Florida Supreme Court were reversed.

See also **Due Process Clause; Right to Remain Silent**

Change of Venue *see* Venue

Chaplain *see* Spiritual Advisor

Character Evidence *see* Rules of Evidence

Charging the Jury *see* Jury Instructions

Chase, Salmon P.
Salmon P. Chase served as chief justice of the United States Supreme Court from 1864 to 1873. While on the Supreme Court Chase was known for his a liberal interpretation of the Fourteenth Amendment as a tool to restrict States from infringing upon the rights of African Americans.

Chase was born in Cornish, New Hampshire, on January 13, 1808. He graduated from Dartmouth College in 1826. After graduating from college Chase moved to Washington, D.C., where he worked as a legal apprentice for a prosecuting attorney. He would eventually pass the bar in Washington, before moving to Cincinnati, Ohio to start a private practice.

While in Ohio Chase launched a political career that took him to the United States Senate for two terms. In between his Senate election Chase was elected Governor of Ohio. In 1861 President Abraham Lincoln nominated Chase to be Secretary of the Treasury. In 1864 Lincoln nominated Chase as chief justice of the Supreme Court.

While on the Supreme Court Chase was known to have written only two capital punishment decisions. In *Twitchell v. Pennsylvania* the defendant was convicted of capital murder and sentenced to death by the State of Pennsylvania. On appeal the defendant contended that the indictment returned against him failed to adequately inform him of the nature of the charge against him and therefore violated the Sixth

Amendment. Writing for the Court, Chase ruled that the requirements of the Sixth Amendment were not applicable to States. This decision in decades to follow would be overruled.

Chase also wrote a concurring opinion in *Ex Parte Milligan.* The defendant in *Milligan* was a civilian who was convicted of murder by the Army and sentenced to death. The Supreme Court ruled that the military did not have jurisdiction to prosecute the defendant, because he was a civilian unconnected with military service. Chase agreed with the Court's decision in the case, but noted that he believed that under certain circumstances Congress could authorize the military to prosecute civilians unconnected with military service. Chase died on May 7, 1873.

Chessman v. Teets
Court: United States Supreme Court; *Case Citation:* Chessman v. Teets, 354 U.S. 156 (1957); *Argued:* May 13, 1957; *Decided:* June 10, 1957; *Opinion of the Court:* Justice Harlan; *Concurring Opinion:* None; *Dissenting Opinion:* Justice Douglas, in which Clark, J., joined; *Dissenting Statement:* Justice Burton; *Justice Taking No Part in Decision:* Chief Justice Warren; *Appellate Defense Counsel:* George T. Davis argued; Rosalie S. Asher on brief; *Appellate Prosecution Counsel:* William M. Bennett argued; Edmund G. Brown, Arlo E. Smith and Clarence A. Linn on brief; *Amicus Curiae Brief Supporting Prosecutor:* None; *Amicus Curiae Brief Supporting Defendant:* None.

Issue Presented: Whether the procedure used to reproduce the defendant's trial transcript, after the court reporter died, violated the defendant's due process rights?

Case Holding: The procedure used to reproduce the defendant's trial transcript, after the court reporter died, violated the defendant's due process rights.

Factual and procedural background of case: The defendant, Caryl Chessman, was convicted of kidnaping and sentenced to death by the State of California. Shortly after the defendant's sentence, the court reporter of the trial died. Consequently, the transcript of the trial had to be reproduced by another court reporter, from the shorthand notes of the deceased court reporter. The defendant, who represented himself during the trial, did not have direct input or counsel representation during the proceedings that determined how the transcript would be reproduced. Once the transcript was reproduced, the defendant appealed his conviction and sentence. The California Supreme Court affirmed the conviction and sentence. The defendant filed a habeas corpus petition in a Federal District Court arguing his due process rights were violated by the way the trial transcript issue was resolved. The District Court dismissed the petition. A Federal Court of Appeals affirmed. The United States Supreme Court granted certiorari to consider the issue.

Opinion of the Court by Justice Harlan: Justice Harlan ruled that the defendant's due process rights were violated in the manner in which the trial transcript issue was settled. The opinion stated:

[The defendant] was entitled to be represented either in person or by counsel throughout the proceedings for the settlement of the trial record. [The defendant's] refusal to be represented by counsel at the trial did not constitute a waiver of his right to counsel at the settlement proceedings. The hearings before a federal judge in the habeas corpus proceedings, at which [the defendant] was personally present and represented by counsel, did not cure the lack of procedural due process in the state proceedings. Consistently with procedural due process, the State Supreme Court's affirmance of [the defendant's] conviction upon a seriously disputed record, whose accuracy [the defendant] had no voice in determining, cannot be allowed to stand. A valid appeal to the Constitution, even by a guilty man, does not come too late because courts were not earlier able to enforce what the Constitution demands. The judgments of the Federal District Court and Court of Appeals are vacated, and the case is remanded to the District Court for entry of such orders as may be appropriate allowing the State a reasonable time within which to take further proceedings not inconsistent with this Court's opinion, failing which [the defendant] shall be discharged.

Dissenting opinion by Justice Douglas, in which Clark, J., joined: Justice Douglas dissented from the Court's decision. He believed due process was not denied the defendant in the settlement of trial transcript. Justice Douglas wrote as follows:

> My dissent is based on the conviction that, in substance, the requirements of due process have been fully satisfied, that to require more is to exalt a technicality. To say that the settlement in this case was ex parte is to be technically accurate. But it is not to state the whole story. Chessman was not present in court when the record was settled. Nor was he represented there by a lawyer, for he had over and again refused to allow a state-appointed lawyer to represent him. Chessman, however, played an active role in the process of the settlement of the record. The early draft prepared by Fraser, the new reporter, was sent to him for his suggestions. That Chessman went over this draft with a fine-tooth comb is evident from a reading of 200-odd corrections which he prepared. Of these proposals, about 80 were adopted and the rest refused....
>
> ... To order, after this long delay, a new record seems to me a futility. It must be remembered that Chessman was convicted on May 21, 1948 — over nine years ago. It is difficult to see how, after that long lapse of time, the memory of any participant (if he is still alive) would be sharp enough to make any hearing meaningful. We meddle mischievously with the law when we issue the writ today. We do not act to remedy any injustice that has been demonstrated. When the whole history of the case is considered, we seize upon a technicality to undo what has been repeatedly sustained both by the California Supreme Court and by this Court. I would guard the ancient writ jealously, using it only to prevent a gross miscarriage of justice.

Dissenting statement by Justice Burton: Justice Burton issued a dissenting statement indicating he believed "the State of California has accorded to [the defendant] due process of law within the meaning of the Constitution of the United States."

Case note: The State of California executed Caryl Chessman in the gas chamber on May 3, 1960. Under modern capital punishment jurisprudence the death penalty may not be imposed for the crime of kidnapping without an accompanying homicide. *See also* **Rape and Capital Punishment**

Chicago Labor Riots of 1886

During the 1880s, Chicago was the site of numerous international labor organizations that advocated the destruction of capitalism and the redistribution of wealth equally to all. The supporters of these organizations were anarchists. From about 1883 to 1886 a great deal of labor violence and unrest occurred in Chicago over wages and working conditions. On May 1, 1886, the violence and unrest reached a critical point when anarchists launched a general strike in Chicago.

On May 3, 1886, bitter fighting erupted at a factory in Chicago and two laborers were killed. The killings sparked a hastily planned protest meeting by the anarchists on May 4, in Chicago's Haymarket Square. The planned protest was initially under control with the mayor of Chicago present, along with scores of police. Once the mayor left the protest turned violent.

After the mayor's departure the police ordered the crowd to disperse. As the crowd began to shuffle out of the area a bomb exploded. Police reacted to the bomb explosion by firing indiscriminately into the crowd. By the time matters were brought under control 66 police officers were wounded, 7 of whom would later die.

The police arrested eight anarchists who were present at the protest and believed to be responsible for setting off the bomb. The eight anarchists arrested were George Engel, Samuel Fielden, Adolph Fischer, Louis Lingg, Oscar W. Neebe, Albert R. Parsons, Michael Schwab and August Spies. The authorities charged all eight anarchists with the murder of only one police officer — officer Mathias J. Degan.

All of the anarchists were prosecuted together on June 21, 1886. The trial was marred by national and international publicity. The jury, as expected, convicted each of the anarchists. Engel, Fielden, Fischer, Lingg, Parsons, Schwab and Spies were all sentenced to death. Neebe was sentenced to 15 years imprisonment. After the anarchists exhausted State and Federal appeals, four of the anarchists, Spies, Parsons, Fischer and Engel, were executed on November 11, 1887. One anarchist, Lingg, committed suicide while awaiting execution. Prior to the executions the governor of Illinois commuted the death sentences of Fielden and Schwab to life imprisonment. In June of 1893 the governor of Illinois granted a pardon to Neebe, Fielden and Schwab. *See also* **Ex Parte Spies; Fielden v. Illinois; Schwab v. Berggren**

The anarchists who were executed were, clockwise: A.R. Parsons, Adolph Fischer, George Engel, and August Spies. Louis Lingg is in the center. Lingg committed suicide shortly before he was scheduled to be executed. (Chicago Public Library)

Chief Justice

The administrative head of an appellate court is referred to as chief justice (chief judge or presiding judge in a few jurisdictions). In some jurisdictions the position of chief justice is rotating, while in others it is permanent. A chief justice's vote among members of an appellate court carries no greater weight than any other member.

Child Abuse Mitigator Courts accept child abuse evidence proffered by capital felons at the penalty phase as being relevant non-statutory mitigating evidence. Child abuse, for penalty phase purposes, generally occurs when a capital felon is of such tender years that violent beating or repeated beatings by an adult could have a tendency to affect the child's moral capacity by predisposing him or her toward committing violence in later years. The child abuse mitigator may be used by a jury or judge to reject imposition of the death penalty. *See also* **Family Background Mitigator; Mitigating Circumstances**

"Child Killers" Known to the media as the "Child Killers," Debra Jean Milke, James Styers and Roger Scott, were convicted of capital murder by the State of Arizona for the 1989 death of four year old Christopher Milke. The Child Killers were sentenced to death.

Debra was the mother of Christopher. Prior to the child's murder, he lived in a Phoenix apartment with his mother and her male companion, Styers. Debra worked at an insurance agency and Styers was an unemployed and disabled veteran. Debra and Christopher's father were divorced, and Debra had legal custody of him.

In September of 1989 Debra took out a $5,000 life insurance policy on Christopher as part of her employee benefit plan. The policy named Debra as the beneficiary. At some point between the time she bought the policy and the time of Christopher's death, Debra and Styers discussed the policy and the benefits.

On the morning of December 2, 1989, Styers took Christopher from the apartment. Styers told Christopher they were going to a mall to see Santa Claus. While en route to the mall Styers picked up Scott. Later in the day, at about 2:45 P.M., Styers telephoned Debra and told her that Christopher was missing. Debra called her father in Florence, Arizona, and told him that Christopher was missing. Eventually the Phoenix police were notified. Debra was interviewed several times throughout the night. The next morning she went to Florence with relatives that had driven over upon learning that Christopher was missing.

The police interviewed Styers and Scott separately. Initially the two men gave consistent stories. They both said that Christopher walked away from them at the mall and could not be found. The intensity of the interviews broke Scott. He confessed to having taken part in the child's death. Scott led the police out into the desert where the child's body was found shot to death. A Phoenix police detective flew to Florence to interview Debra. She was told that her son had been found shot to death in the desert and that she was under arrest.

Debra told the detective that she was upset with Christopher because she felt he was going to turn out like his father — a convict, alcoholic, and drug user. Debra stated that she verbalized these fears to Styers. After doing so, she decided it would be best for Christopher to die. She stated that she had a hard time telling Styers what she wanted, but she finally told him, and he agreed to help. Debra and Styers discussed the plan several times and included Scott on at least one occasion. Ultimately, they decided that Styers and Scott would take Christopher, kill him, and then report him missing, but Debra was not to know how Christopher was killed. Debra denied that insurance money was her motivation, but admitted that it may have been Styers' and Scott's because Styers knew of the policy.

At separate trials Debra, Styers and Scott were each convicted of capital murder. The death penalty was imposed on each. The Child Killers are on Arizona's death row waiting to be executed.

Chile Capital punishment is used in Chile. Chile's constitution became effective on March 11, 1981. Chile abolished the death penalty in 1930, but reinstituted the punishment for certain crimes in 1937. Chile uses the firing squad to carry out the death penalty. Its legal system is a based on Spanish law, with French and Austrian law influences. Chile is a multiparty democracy with a constitution that provides for an executive branch, bicameral legislative branch, and judicial branch.

The judicial system has a Supreme Court, courts of appeal, and trial courts. The Supreme Court consists of 17 members, who select a president from their number for a three-year term. Chile has sixteen courts of appeal. The majority of the courts have four members, although the two largest courts have 13 and 25 members respectively.

In September 1997, legislation was signed into law creating the office of attorney general, as well as national and regional prosecutors. This law displaces the former system that used judges to investigate and prosecute defendants. Under Chile's criminal justice system defendants are not presumed innocent nor do they have a right to trial by jury. Criminal trials are inquisitorial rather than adversarial. Defendants have the right to legal counsel. *See also* **International Capital Punishment Nations**

China China imposes the death penalty. China utilizes the firing squad and lethal injection to carry out the death penalty. China's legal system is a complex amalgam of ancient customary law and statutory law. The nation adopted a constitution in 1993. China is an authoritarian state in which the Chinese Communist Party is the ultimate source of power. The nation's constitution provides for an independent judiciary; however, in practice the judicial system is subject to the policy decisions of the Communist Party.

China's judicial system is divided into four levels: Supreme People's Court, Higher People's Courts (provinces, autonomous regions, and special municipalities), Intermediate

People's Courts (prefectures, autonomous prefectures, and municipalities), and Basic People's Courts (autonomous counties, towns, and municipal districts). Under Chinese law all trials are supposed to be held in public, but in practice, many trials are not. Defendants are presumed guilty under Chinese law and therefore must prove their innocence. Defendants do not have a right to trial by jury. The conviction rate in criminal cases has been reported at being over 90 percent. This result is attributed to the fact that trials in China are little more than sentencing hearings. Although an appeal process exists, rarely are convictions overturned.

In 1997, China enacted a new criminal law code. Under the new code, death penalty offenses were reduced from over 70 to around 60. Also during the latter part of the 1990s, China adopted criminal procedure rules and implemented measures to provide adequately trained lawyers. China's new criminal code sets out the following provisions addressing capital punishment:

> *Article 48.* The death penalty is only to be applied to criminal elements who commit the most heinous crimes. In the case of a criminal element who should be sentenced to death, if immediate execution is not essential, a two-year suspension of execution may be announced at the same time the sentence of death is imposed.
>
> Except for judgments made by the Supreme People's Court according to law, all sentences of death shall be submitted to the Supreme People's Court for approval. Sentences of death with suspension of execution may be decided or approved by a High People's Court.
>
> *Article 49.* The death penalty is not to be applied to persons who have not reached the age of eighteen at the time the crime is committed or to women who are pregnant at the time of adjudication.

Tremendous international criticism has been launched at China because of the lack of due process in its criminal justice system, particularly in death penalty cases. It was reported that China executed 4,367 prisoners in 1996, 1,876 in 1997, and 1,067 prisoners in 1998. The case of Zhao Binyi provides an example of the type of capital punishment case routinely prosecuted by China and condemned by the international community. In May 1997, Zhao Binyi was executed after being convicted of fraud involving only $6,000.

Credible reports have surfaced alleging that organs from some executed prisoners are removed, sold, and transplanted. Chinese officials have confirmed that executed prisoners are among the sources of organs for transplant, but maintain that consent is required from prisoners or their relatives before organs are removed. *See also* **International Capital Punishment Nations**

Choosing Method of Execution *see* Execution Option Jurisdictions

CIA Murders   On the morning of January 25, 1993, a random shooting spree occurred outside the Federal Central Intelligence Agency (CIA) headquarters in Langley, Virginia. The shooting was carried out by Mir Aimal Kasi, a 29 year old

Pakistanian, using an AK-47 assault rifle. Kasi killed two people and wounded three others. The two victims killed in the incident were Frank Darling, a 28 year old covert operative for the CIA, and Lansing Bennett, a 66 year old physician and intelligence analyst. The three victims wounded in the attack— Nicholas Starr, Calvin Morgan, and Stephen Williams—were also employees of the CIA.

Mir Aimal Kasi, a Pakistanian, was sentenced to death for the 1993, murder of two CIA employees. (U.S. Department of Justice/FBI)

After the shooting Kasi fled to his home in the Pakistani city of Quetta. Kasi was captured in a Pakistani hotel in 1997 by Federal Bureau of Investigation (FBI) agents. Kasi confessed to the crimes on the flight back to the United States. On November 14, 1997 a jury in Fairfax County, Virginia found Kasi guilty of capital murder. On January 23, 1998 the trial judge imposed the jury's recommended sentence of death. At his sentencing hearing Kasi described his actions as retaliation for United States policies that he said hurt Islamic nations.

In June of 1999, the United States Supreme Court rejected an appeal by Kasi. In that failed appeal, Kasi alleged that his seizure by FBI agents in Pakistan violated international treaties, that his confession was illegally obtained and other constitutional rights were violated. The Virginia Supreme Court, which had earlier upheld Kasi's conviction, ruled that he lacked the legal right to claim his seizure violated the Federal Constitution because he was captured overseas. The rejection of Kasi's appeal by the United States Supreme Court was an affirmation of the State high court ruling.

Kasi's lawyers contended in their brief to the United States Supreme Court that the FBI agents never told him that he had the right to contact a representative of the Pakistani consulate and the United States never requested his extradition from Pakistan. They also claimed that the Virginia courts violated Kasi's constitutional rights by failing to force the FBI and the CIA to produce documents that could contain evidence raising doubts about his guilt. These issues were presumptively meritless due to the United States Supreme Court's refusal to hear Kasi's appeal. Kasi is on death row in a Virginia maximum security prison. *See also* **Foreign Nationals and Capital Punishment**

Circumstantial Evidence   Two types of evidence may be used to obtain conviction of a defendant: direct or circumstantial. Examples of direct evidence include a confession, eyewitness testimony and a videotaped recording of the crime. Most criminal convictions are obtained without the use of direct evidence.

All courts accept circumstantial evidence as an alternative method of proof in obtaining a criminal conviction. Circumstantial evidence is inferential evidence that is fluid and case specific. This is because circumstantial evidence is any relevant fact from which a jury may reasonably "infer" a defendant's guilt.

At the guilt phase of a capital prosecution, circumstantial evidence must rise to the level of establishing beyond a reasonable doubt every element of the offense charged against the defendant. At the penalty phase of a capital prosecution circumstantial evidence plays a minimal role, because a defendant's guilt has already been determined.

Citizens Against Homicides
Citizens Against Homicides (CAH) is a California based nonprofit organization. A primary activity of CAH is to engage in peaceful protests when designated murderers seek parole. CAH has taken the position that community safety is best served by not releasing murderers. CAH produces a monthly newsletter that profiles murder victims.

Citizens United for Alternatives to the Death Penalty
Citizens United for Alternatives to the Death Penalty (CUADP) is a Florida based national nonprofit organization. The organization was formed for the purpose of working to end the death penalty in the United States. The executive director of CUADP is Abraham J. Bonowitz.

As executive director of CUADP, Abraham J. Bonowitz has subjected himself to incarceration for peaceful, but aggressive protests against capital punishment. (Abraham J. Bonowitz)

Under the leadership of Bonowitz, CUADP engages in direct action to educate the public about the need to abolish capital punishment. To this end, Bonowitz has personally subjected himself on the frontline of CUADP's struggle. He has been arrested on numerous occasions in large cities across the country during peaceful, but aggressive campaigns to awaken the public to the "evils" of capital punishment. Most recently, in 1997, Bonowitz was arrested along with other anti–death penalty activists for unfurling a banner in front of the United States Supreme Court which read, "Stop Executions!"

Ciucci v. Illinois
Court: United States Supreme Court; *Case Citation:* Ciucci v. Illinois, 356 U.S. 571 (1958); *Argued:* March 13, 1958; *Decided:* May 19, 1958; *Opinion of the Court:* Per Curiam; *Concurring Opinion:* None; *Dissenting Opinion:* Justice Douglas, in which Warren, C.J., and Brennan, J., joined; *Dissenting Statement:* Justice Black; *Appellate Defense Counsel:* George N. Leighton argued; Loring B. Moore and William R. Ming, Jr. on brief; *Appellate Prosecution Counsel:* William C. Wines argued; Latham Castle and Theodore G. Maherason brief; *Amicus Curiae Brief Supporting Prosecutor:* None; *Amicus Curiae Brief Supporting Defendant:* None.

Issue Presented: Whether due process of law was violated by separately prosecuting the defendant for four murders until a death sentence was obtained in the third trial?

Case Holding: Due process of law was not violated by separately prosecuting the defendant for four murders until a death sentence was obtained in the third trial.

Factual and procedural background of case: The defendant, Ciucci, was charged by the State of Illinois with murdering his wife and three children. The defendant was prosecuted separately for each murder. In the first two prosecutions the defendant was found guilty and sentenced to life imprisonment for each conviction. In the third trial the defendant was found guilty and sentenced to death. The defendant appealed the death sentence conviction. The Illinois Supreme Court affirmed the conviction and death sentence. In doing so, the appellate court rejected the defendant's argument that due process of law prohibited the prosecutor from successively prosecuting him for the sole purpose of obtaining a death sentence. The United States Supreme Court granted certiorari to consider the issue.

Opinion of the Court was delivered Per Curiam: The per curiam opinion found that due process of law was not violated by the repeated prosecution of the defendant. It was said that: "The State was constitutionally entitled to prosecute these individual offenses singly at separate trials, and to utilize therein all relevant evidence, in the absence of proof establishing that such a course of action entailed fundamental unfairness."

The opinion noted that the defendant raised another argument, but that the record on the issue was not submitted to the Court, therefor the issue would not be addressed. The judgment of the Illinois Supreme Court was affirmed.

Dissenting opinion by Justice Douglas, in which Warren, C.J., and Brennan, J., joined: Justice Douglas dissented from the Court's decision. He believed the successive prosecutions of the defendant were motivated by the desire to obtain a death sentence and that such a course violated due process principles. Justice Douglas wrote:

This case presents an instance of the prosecution being allowed to harass the accused with repeated trials and convictions on the same evidence, until it achieves its desired result of a capital verdict....

In my view the Due Process Clause of the Fourteenth Amendment prevents this effort by a State to obtain the death penalty. No constitutional problem would have arisen if [the defendant] had been prosecuted in one trial for as many murders as there were victims. But by using the same evidence in multiple trials the State continued its relentless prosecutions until it got the result it wanted. It in effect tried the accused for four murders three consecutive times, massing in each trial the horrible details of each of the four deaths. This is an unseemly and oppressive use of a criminal trial that violates the concept of due process contained in the Fourteenth Amendment, whatever its ultimate scope is taken to be.

Dissenting statement by Justice Black: Justice Black issued a dissenting statement indicating that he believed "the Fourteenth Amendment bars a State from placing a defendant twice in jeopardy for the same offense."

Clark, Tom C.

Tom C. Clark served as an associate justice of the United States Supreme Court from 1949 to 1967. While on the Supreme Court Clark was known as a conservative who shifted to the center during his last years on the Court.

Clark was born in Dallas, Texas on September 23, 1899. In the early 1920s Clark attended the University of Texas, where he studied law and eventually received a degree. After college Clark joined his father's law firm for a short period of time. His legal career shifted into full gear when he left private practice and began a long service as a State and Federal government attorney in various aspects of the law. From 1945 to 1949 Clark served as United States Attorney General under President Harry S. Truman. In 1949 President Truman appointed Clark to the Supreme Court.

While on the Supreme Court Clark wrote a number of capital punishment opinions. His capital punishment cases, for the most part, reflected the conservative philosophy that Clark was known for during much of his time on the bench. For example, in *Leland v. Oregon* the issue confronting the Supreme Court was whether or not Oregon could force defendants to prove insanity beyond a reasonable doubt. Clark, writing for the Court, held that "[w]e are ... reluctant to interfere with Oregon's determination of its policy with respect to the burden of proof on the issue of sanity since we cannot say that policy violates generally accepted concepts of basic standards of justice." In *Stroble v. California*, Clark was reluctant to disturb a capital conviction. In that case Clark held that the defendant was not denied due process of law as a result of his confession, interrogation without counsel, or pretrial publicity. A decision issued in Clark's later years on the bench which reflected his a shift in his judicial philosophy was *Coleman v. Alabama*. In *Coleman* the defendant contended he was denied a fair trial because African Americans were excluded from the grand jury that indicted him and the petit jury that convicted him. The actual issue brought to the Supreme Court in *Coleman* was that the Alabama courts denied him the opportunity to present evidence to prove his claim of jury discrimination. Clark, writing for the Court, agreed with the defendant and

Capital Punishment Opinions Written by Clark

Case Name	Opinion of the Court	Concurring Opinion	Dissenting Opinion
Cassell v. Texas		✓	
Coleman v. Alabama (I)	✓		
Crooker v. California	✓		
Ferguson v. Georgia		✓	
Irvin v. Dowd (II)	✓		
Jackson v. Denno			✓
Leland v. Oregon	✓		
Payne v. Arkansas			✓
Reece v. Georgia	✓		
Rideau v. Louisiana			✓
Rosenberg v. United States		✓	
Sims v. Georgia (I)	✓		
Stewart v. United States			✓
Stroble v. California	✓		
Thomas v. Arizona	✓		
Williams v. Georgia			✓

reversed and remanded the case for a full evidentiary hearing to so that the defendant could present evidence on his claim of jury discrimination. Clark died on June 13, 1977.

Clarke, John Hessin

John Hessin Clarke served as an associate justice of the United States Supreme Court from 1916 to 1922. While on the Supreme Court Clarke was known as a liberal interpreter of the Constitution.

Clarke was born on September 18, 1857, in Lisbon, Ohio. He received an undergraduate degree from Western Reserve College in 1877, and a masters degree from the school in 1880. Clarke did not receive a formal legal education. He studied as a legal apprentice with his father, who was a lawyer, and in 1878 passed the Ohio bar.

Most of Clarke's adult life was spent practicing law. He developed a good reputation and became quite successful with several firms. In 1914 President Woodrow Wilson appointed Clarke as a Federal District Court judge in Ohio. Two years later, President Wilson appointed him to the Supreme Court.

During Clarke's relatively brief tenure on the Supreme Court he was known to have written only one capital punishment opinion. In *Valdez v. United States*, Clarke wrote a dissenting opinion. The primary issue in Valdez was whether the absence of the defendant during the trial judge's visit to the crime scene denied him due process of law. The majority on the Supreme Court held that the defendant was not denied due process. Clarke disagreed with the majority and wrote: "It has long been familiar, textbook, law, that a viewing of the premises where the crime is alleged to have been committed is part of the trial.... It is very clear to my mind ... that the viewing of the scene of the murder by the judge without the presence of the accused requires that it be reversed and a new trial granted." Clarke died in 1945.

Class and Capital Punishment

Opponents of capital punishment have argued that it is a poor person's punishment, that is rarely imposed on influential or wealthy people. Although statistical evidence supports the claim that the vast number of defendant's receiving capital punishment are at the lower end of the nation's socio-economic ladder, proponents of capital punishment contend that such statistics do not tell the whole story. It has been argued by proponents of capital punishment that the less privileged in society simply commit the overwhelming number of capital crimes. Therefore, statistics must necessarily reflect the reality of who actually commits capital offenses.

Characteristics of Death Row Inmates 1994

Characteristic	Percentage
Male	98.6%
Female	1.4
White	56.9
Black	41.4
Other races	1.7
8th grade or less	15.3
9th to 11th grade	37.1
Diploma/GED	37.4
Some college	10.2
Total death row population	2,890

Source: Bureau of Justice Statistics, Capital Punishment (1996).

Clemency As a general matter, executive clemency refers to granting a specific form of leniency from a conviction and sentence. Executive clemency is a matter of grace, not of right. No defendant has a right to obtain executive clemency. Power of executive clemency in the United States derived from the practice as it had existed in England. Such power has traditionally rested in governors or the President. Historically courts have been hesitant to review challenges to the exercise of executive clemency power. Courts have held that death penalty statutes which expressly prohibit commutation of death sentences do not violate the Federal constitution. Between the period 1977–1999, a total of 41 death row inmates had their death sentences commuted to life imprisonment, as a result of executive clemency.

Jurisdictions vary as to the autonomy granted chief executive officers in making executive clemency decisions. A few jurisdictions attach no strings to the chief executive officer's authority in this area, while others require involvement of a board. The following statutes illustrate how capital punishment jurisdictions address the matter.

Governor Jeb Bush of Florida has the authority to grant clemency on the advice of the State's Board of Executive Clemency. (Governor's Office)

Texas Code Annotated-C.C.P. Art. 48.01: In all criminal cases, except treason and impeachment, the Governor shall have power, after convic-

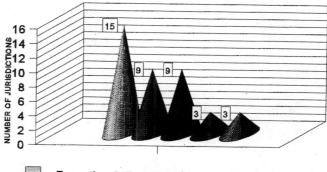
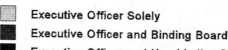

CLEMENCY AUTHORITY

- Executive Officer Solely
- Executive Officer and Binding Board
- Executive Officer and Non-binding Board
- Board Solely
- Board and Executive Officer

tion, on the written signed recommendation and advice of the Board of Pardons and Paroles, or a majority thereof, to grant reprieves and commutations of punishments and pardons.... The Governor shall have the power to grant one reprieve in any capital case for a period not to exceed 30 days; and shall have power to revoke conditional pardons[.]

Washington Code Annotated § 8.01.120: Whenever a prisoner has been sentenced to death, the governor shall have power to commute such sentence to imprisonment for life at hard labor; and in all cases in which the governor is authorized to grant pardons or commute sentence of death, he may, upon the petition of the person convicted, commute a sentence or grant a pardon, upon such conditions, and with such restrictions, and under such limitations as he may think proper.... The governor may also, on good cause shown, grant respites or reprieves from time to time as he may think proper.

730 Illinois Comp. Stat. Ann. § 5/3-3-13: a. Petitions seeking pardon, commutation or reprieve shall be addressed to the Governor and filed with the Prisoner Review Board. The petition shall be in writing and signed by the person under conviction or by a person on his behalf. It shall contain a brief history of the case and the reasons for executive clemency.

b. Notice of the proposed application shall be given by the Board to the committing court and the state's attorney of the county where the conviction was had.

c. The Board shall, if requested and upon due notice, give a hearing to each application, allowing representation by counsel, if desired, after which it shall confidentially advise the Governor by a written report of its recommendations which shall be determined by majority vote. The Board shall meet to consider such petitions no less than 4 times each year.

d. The Governor shall decide each application and communicate his decision to the Board which shall notify the petitioner.

Executive clemency may manifest itself in three ways: (1) reprieve (sometimes called "respite"), (2) commutation, or (3) pardon. Each type of executive clemency has its own unique consequence for a capital felon.

1. *Executive Reprieve.* A reprieve merely postpones an execution temporarily. Capital felon reprieves usually occur in one of two contexts. First, if a capital felon has filed a habeas corpus or other type of petition with a court, but

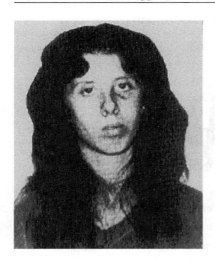

Judith Ann Neelley had her death sentence commuted to life imprisonment by the governor of Alabama. (Alabama Department of Corrections)

the court refuses to grant a stay while the matter is before it, the capital felon can request an executive reprieve while the court evaluates the matter. Second, if a capital felon requests a pardon or commutation, an executive reprieve may be granted while the application for pardon or commutation is under review.

2. *Executive Commutation.* The court in *State ex rel. Maurer v. Steward*, 644 N.E.2d 369 (Ohio 1994) defined commutation as "the change of a punishment to which a person has been condemned into a less severe one." Most capital punishment jurisdictions limit commutation of a death sentence to that of life imprisonment. In theory, when this limitation is not imposed, a capital felon can have his or her death sentence commuted to time served—which would mean immediate release.

However, as a practical matter commutations are always confined to life imprisonment. Usually commutations are made with a condition that the capital felon will not seek parole. Commutations may also take on any other conditions deemed appropriate and in compliance with general laws. A violation of a condition of commutation can, in theory, result in the death penalty being reinstated and carried out.

3. *Executive Pardon.* It was pointed out in *Ex Parte May*, 717 S.W.2d 84 (Tex.Cr.App. 1986) that, unlike commutation and reprieve, "a pardon may be granted by proper authority at any time—even before a criminal charge has been lodged against the offender." The court in *State ex rel. Maurer v. Steward*, 644 N.E.2d 369 (Ohio 1994) made the following observations regarding a pardon:

A pardon discharges the individual designated from all or some specified penal consequences of his crime. It may be full or partial, absolute or conditional.

A full and absolute pardon releases the offender from the entire punishment prescribed for his offense, and from all the disabilities consequent on his conviction.

Pardons for capital felons waiting to be executed have been rare. This is because of the nature of a pardon—it allows the immediate release of the capital felon. Defendants who receive sentences less than death, are usually the beneficiaries of pardons. *See also* **Biddle v. Perovich; Calderon v. Coleman; California v. Ramos; Ex Parte Wells; Lamber v. Barrett (I);**

Ohio Adult Parole Authority v. Woodard; Rose v. Hodges; Schick v. Reed

Clemons v. Mississippi   *Court:* United States Supreme Court; *Case Citation:* Clemons v. Mississippi, 494 U.S. 738 (1990); *Argued:* November 28, 1989; *Decided:* March 28, 1990; *Opinion of the Court:* Justice White; *Concurring and Dissenting Opinion:* Justice Brennan; *Concurring and Dissenting Opinion:* Justice Blackmun, in which Brennan, Marshall, and Stevens, JJ., joined; *Appellate Defense Counsel:* Kenneth S. Resnick argued and briefed; *Appellate Prosecution Counsel:* Marvin L. White, Jr. argued; Mike Moore on brief; *Amicus Curiae Brief Supporting Prosecutor:* 1; *Amicus Curiae Brief Supporting Defendant:* 1.

Issue Presented: Whether it is constitutionally impermissible for a State appellate court to uphold a death sentence imposed by a jury that has relied in part on an invalid aggravating circumstance?

Case Holding: The Constitution does not prevent a State appellate court from upholding a death sentence that is based in part on an invalid or improperly defined aggravating circumstance, either by reweighing of the aggravating and mitigating evidence or by harmless error review.

Factual and procedural background of case: The defendant, Chandler Clemons, was convicted by a Mississippi jury of committing capital murder on April 17, 1987. At the penalty phase hearing the trial court instructed the jury, among other things, that, in deciding whether to impose the death penalty, it should consider the following statutory aggravating circumstances: (1) that the murder was committed during the course of a robbery for pecuniary gain, and (2) that it was an "especially heinous, atrocious or cruel" killing. The jury, finding that both aggravating factors were present and that they outweighed any mitigating circumstances, sentenced the defendant to death.

On appeal, the Mississippi Supreme Court upheld the death sentence. The state appellate court acknowledged that the "especially heinous" statutory aggravating factor was constitutionally invalid because it was vague. However, it was held that the case did not require reversal, since the appellate court had previously given the factor a constitutionally acceptable limiting construction. The appellate court declared that, beyond a reasonable doubt, the jury's verdict would have been the same without the "especially heinous" factor. The United States Supreme Court granted certiorari to address the issue of what the Constitution requires when an aggravating circumstance is invalid.

Opinion of the Court by Justice White: The defendant argued that under State law only a jury has the authority to impose a death sentence, therefore he had a constitutional right to have the jury assess the consequences of an invalid statutory aggravating circumstance that was used to impose the death penalty against him.

In rejecting this argument, Justice White observed that nothing in the Constitution requires the jury, as opposed to the appellate court, to impose the death sentence after the appellate court has invalidated one of two or more statutory aggravating circumstances found by the jury. Therefore, it is constitutionally permissible for an appellate court to reweigh the aggravating and mitigating evidence in order to uphold a death sentence that is based in part on an invalid or improperly defined statutory aggravating circumstance.

Justice White noted that nothing in appellate court weighing or reweighing is at odds with the constitutional standards of fairness, nor is such a process inherently unreliable and likely to result in arbitrary imposition of the death penalty. It was said that appellate courts can and do give each defendant an individualized and reliable sentencing determination based on his or her circumstances, background, and crime. It was pointed out that even if a particular State's law made weighing of aggravating and mitigating circumstances an exclusive jury function, it would still be constitutionally permissible for any State appellate court to apply harmless error analysis to the jury's consideration of an invalid aggravating circumstance.

Although the opinion found that appellate courts could engage in harmless error analysis, or weighing or reweighing aggravating and mitigating factors, Justice White found that it was not clear from the record in the case that the Mississippi Supreme Court correctly employed reweighing analysis. Therefore, the opinion vacated the judgment and remanded the case for reconsideration and reweighing of aggravating and mitigating factors by the Mississippi Supreme Court.

Concurring and dissenting opinion by Justice Brennan: Justice Brennan wrote succinctly that he concurred solely in the majority's decision to vacate the judgment.

Justice Brennan gave two grounds for dissenting. First, he wrote that because of his adherence to the "view that the death penalty is in all circumstances cruel and unusual punishment prohibited by the Eighth and Fourteenth Amendments, I would direct that the proceedings on remand be circumscribed so as to preclude the reimposition of the death sentence." Second, he indicated in dissent that he did not believe a State court could "save a death sentence by 'reweighing' aggravating and mitigating circumstances."

Concurring and dissenting opinion by Justice Blackmun, in which Brennan, Marshall, and Stevens, JJ., joined: In his concurrence Justice Blackmun wrote that he agreed with the majority that the Mississippi Supreme Court failed to articulate a satisfactory basis for affirming the defendant's death sentence. He therefore concurred in the majority's decision that the judgment must be vacated.

Justice Blackmun dissented "from the majority's strong and gratuitous suggestion that the Mississippi Supreme Court … may 'salvage' Clemons' death sentence by performing its own weighing of aggravating and mitigating circumstances." Justice Blackmun did not believe that it was appropriate for an appellate court to engage in reweighing of aggravating and mitigating circumstances to determine whether a sentence of death is appropriate. He wrote that "[t]he logical implication of the majority's approach is that no trial-level sentencing procedure need be conducted at all. Instead, the record of a capital trial (including a sentencing hearing conducted before a court reporter) might as well be shipped to the appellate court, which then would determine the appropriate sentence in the first instance." *See also* **Appellate Review of Conviction and Death Sentence; Barclay v. Florida; Harmless Error Rule; Invalid Aggravator**

Cleveland State University Racial Murders In 1982, Frank G. Spisak, Jr., brought terror to the campus of Cleveland State University through a series of random murders. Spisak was a native of Ohio who grew up to be a transvestite known as "Ann Spisak." Ridiculed because of his lifestyle, Spisak turned to reading works about Adolph Hitler. Through his readings about Hitler, Spisak found a new identity as a race hater.

Spisak's mind proved to be far too weak for the literature he read concerning Hitler. In time he believed he was the leader destined to make America a nation of "Arayans" only. On February 1, 1982, Spisak set out to start his leadership role as the purifier of America. On that day he visited the campus of Cleveland State University and found his first victim, an African American minister named Reverend Horace Rickerson. Spisak followed Reverend Rickerson into a library restroom and shot him dead.

Spisak's next victim was a maintenance supervisor at Cleveland State University named Timothy Sheehan. Spisak wrongly believed that Sheehan was a Jewish professor at the University. On August 27, 1982, Spisak followed Sheehan into University restroom and shot him dead.

On the night of August 29, 1982, Spisak set out to find another victim on the University campus. Spisak drove around the area of the campus until he found a victim, Brian Warford, a young black man who was sitting at a bus stop. Spisak parked his car, walked over to Warford and shot him dead.

In addition to the three murders on the University campus, Spisak had also attacked and injured several other victims. The police were baffled by the murders and attempted murders. They had no clue whatsoever as to the identity of the perpetrator. A break in the case did not come until after authorities arrested Spisak on September 4, 1982. The arrest resulted from a report that a man fired a gun from a window. The police arrived at the scene, arrested Spisak and confiscated several weapons from him. He was charged with discharging a weapon within the city

Frank G. Spisak, Jr. went on a racial killing spree in 1982, and killed two African-Americans and a person he thought was Jewish. (Ohio Department of Corrections)

limits and for possession of unregistered handguns. Spisak posted bond a few hours after his arrest.

On September 5, 1982, the police received an anonymous call from a woman with information about the University murders. The woman told the police that the guns that were confiscated from Spisak had been used in the killings at the University. Tests were immediately performed on the weapons, and comparisons were made with the pellets and casings found in connection with the murders. After conducting this investigation, the police obtained a warrant for Spisak's arrest. He was eventually arrested at the home of a friend. He was found hiding in a basement crawl space.

Spisak was indicted for the University murders. The case went to trial on June 7, 1983. On July 15, the jury convicted Spisak of the murders. On July 19, he was sentenced to death. Spisak is on death row in Ohio.

Clifford, Nathan Nathan Clifford served as an associate justice of the United States Supreme Court from 1858 to 1881. While on the Supreme Court Clifford was known as a conservative interpreter of the Constitution who favored States' rights.

Clifford was born in Rumney, New Hampshire, on August 18, 1803. Although Clifford received some formal education during his youth, he was largely self-educated. Clifford served for a time as a legal apprentice and was able to pass the bar in 1827. After passing the bar Clifford moved to Maine where he began a law practice in the town of Newfield. Clifford eventually entered politics and served in Maine's House of Representatives, State attorney general and two terms in the United States House of Representatives. President James Polk appointed Clifford as United States Attorney General in 1846. President James Buchanan nominated Clifford to the Supreme Court in December of 1857, and he assumed his seat in 1858.

While on the Supreme Court Clifford was known to have written only a few capital punishment opinions. In spite of the paucity of capital punishment opinions by Clifford, his opinion for the Supreme Court in *Wilkerson v. Utah* became one of the major capital punishment cases decided by the Court. The primary issue in *Wilkerson* was whether or not death by firing squad was a cruel and unusual punishment. After the opinion in the case analyzed the history of death by firing squad, Clifford concluded that "[c]ruel and unusual punishments are forbidden by the Constitution, but ... the punishment of shooting as a mode of executing the death penalty for the crime of murder in the first degree is not included in that category, within the meaning of the eighth amendment." Clifford died on July 25, 1881.

Capital Punishment Opinions Written by Clifford

Case Name	Opinion of the Court	Dissenting Opinion
Coleman v. Tennessee		✓
Wiggins v. Utah		✓
Wilkerson v. Utah	✓	

Closing Argument *see* **Trial Structure**

Coalition of Arizonans to Abolish the Death Penalty The Coalition of Arizonans to Abolish the Death Penalty (CAADP) is composed of a group of organizations and individuals pledged to end the death penalty in Arizona. The purpose of CAADP is to further a cohesive effort to abolish the death penalty in the state of Arizona, with an emphasis on the legislative process and community education. The organization advocates the use of prayer, public education, dialog, constitutional recourse, and public and legislative action.

Co-Defendant The term "co-defendant" is used when a prosecution involves more than one defendant. A defendant and co-defendant may be tried together or separately. Although a defendant and co-defendant are charged with the exact same offense, the disposition of the case against each may be different. *See also* **Co-Defendant Spared Death Penalty Mitigator**

Co-Defendant Spared Death Penalty Mitigator It is not unusual for equally culpable co-defendants to receive different sentences for the same offense. This situation occurs most often when a defendant agrees to testify against a co-defendant in exchange for lighter punishment. This situation can result in a capital felon being sentenced to life in prison, while his or her co-defendant is sentenced to death. Two capital punishment jurisdictions, New Hampshire and the Federal government, have made "co-defendant spared death penalty" a statutory mitigating circumstance. Some courts preclude evidence of this issue on the grounds that it is not relevant to individualized capital punishment sentencing. *See also* **Individualized Sentencing; Mitigating Circumstances**

Coker v. Georgia *Court:* United States Supreme Court; *Case Citation:* Coker v. Georgia, 433 U.S. 584 (1977); *Argued:* March 28, 1977; *Decided:* June 29, 1977; *Plurality Opinion:* Justice White announced the Court's judgment and delivered an opinion, in which Stewart, Blackmun, and Stevens, JJ., joined; *Concurring Opinion:* Justice Brennan; *Concurring Opinion:* Justice Marshall; *Concurring and Dissenting Opinion:* Justice Powell; *Dissenting Opinion:* Chief Justice Burger, in which Rehnquist, J., joined; *Appellate Defense Counsel:* David E. Kendall argued; E. Kontz Bennett, Jr., Jack Greenberg, James M. Nabrit III, Peggy C. Davis, and Anthony G. Amsterdam on brief; *Appellate Prosecution Counsel:* B. Dean Grindle, Jr. argued; Arthur K. Bolton, Robert S. Stubbs II, Richard L. Chambers, John C. Walden, Harrison Kohler, and Dewey Hayes on brief; *Amicus Curiae Brief Supporting Prosecutor:* None; *Amicus Curiae Brief Supporting Defendant:* 1.

Issue Presented: Whether the Constitution permits imposition of the death penalty for the crime of rape?

Case Holding: The sentence of death for the crime of rape is grossly disproportionate and excessive punishment and is therefore forbidden by the Eighth Amendment as cruel and unusual punishment.

Factual and procedural background of case: The defendant, Ehrlich Anthony Coker, escaped from a Georgia prison and, on September 2, 1974, while in the course of committing an armed robbery and other offenses, raped a woman. He was convicted of rape, armed robbery, and the other offenses and sentenced to death on the rape charge. The defendant argued that the federal Constitution prohibited imposition of the death penalty for the crime of rape. The Georgia Supreme Court rejected the argument and affirmed the death sentence. The United States Supreme Court granted certiorari to address the issue.

Plurality opinion in which Justice White announced the Court's judgment and in which Stewart, Blackmun, and Stevens, JJ., joined: Justice White's plurality opinion noted that the Eighth Amendment prohibited not only those punishments that are barbaric, but also those that are excessive in relation to the crime committed. The opinion observed that although rape deserves serious punishment, the death penalty is an excessive penalty for the rapist who, unlike the murderer, does not unjustifiably take human life. It was said that objective evidence demonstrated that death is a disproportionate penalty for rape. The opinion pointed out that Georgia was the only state to still authorize capital punishment for rape of a woman. The opinion indicated that only two states still permitted imposition of the death penalty for rape of a child. The judgment of the Georgia Supreme Court upholding the death sentence was reversed.

Concurring opinion by Justice Brennan: Justice Brennan wrote that he maintained his belief that the death penalty is in all circumstances cruel and unusual punishment prohibited by the Constitution and, therefore, concurred in the judgment setting aside the death sentence.

Concurring opinion by Justice Marshall: Justice Marshall wrote that his views had not changed, insofar as he believed that the Constitution precluded imposition of the death penalty. He, therefore, concurred in the judgment.

Concurring and dissenting opinion by Justice Powell: Justice Powell concurred in the judgment based on the facts of the case. He wrote that there was no evidence that the defendant's "offense was committed with excessive brutality or that the victim sustained serious or lasting injury."

Justice Powell dissented from the plurality's position "that capital punishment always — regardless of the circumstances — is a disproportionate penalty for the crime of rape." He believed that the death penalty may be constitutionally permissible "for the crime of aggravated rape."

Dissenting opinion by Chief Justice Burger: Chief Justice Burger argued that, while the Constitution prohibits imposing the death penalty for minor crimes, "rape is not a minor crime[.]" He believed that the Constitution permitted states to create statutes imposing death for the crime of rape.

Case note: The decision in the case had a significant impact upon death penalty crimes. Except for treason and espionage (one jurisdiction retains rape of a child as a capital crime), all offenses that have the death penalty as an authorized punishment require a homicide also occur. *See also* **Rape and Capital Punishment**

Coleman and Brown Alton Coleman received a death sentence from the States of Ohio, Illinois and Indiana. Debra Denise Brown received a death sentence from the States of Indiana and Ohio (Ohio was reversed and life sentence imposed). In 1984 Coleman and Brown set out together on a journey across mid–America that resulted in a trail that left eight dead bodies.

Coleman was born in November 6, 1955, and Brown was born on November 11, 1962. At some point during the early 1980s the two met in Waukegan, Illinois and became lovers. By the time they met Coleman had already developed a violent criminal past that included confinement at Joliet State Prison.

The murder spree embarked upon by Coleman and Brown started on May 29, 1984, with the disappearance of nine year old Vernita Wheat. The child was taken from her home in Kenosha, Wisconsin and brought to Waukegan by Coleman and Brown. On June 19 Wheat's corpse was found in an abandoned building.

On June 18 Coleman and Brown appeared in Gary, Indiana. While there they kidnapped seven year old Tamika Turks and her aunt. Tamika was beaten, raped and strangled to death. The aunt was raped and bludgeoned, but miraculously survived.

Brown and Coleman needed transportation to leave Indiana. To obtain a vehicle they kidnapped Donna Williams and took her car on June 19. Eventually Williams' body was discovered on July 11. She had been strangled to death with panty hose.

The next victims for Coleman and Brown were targeted on July 7. On that date they managed to convince Virginia Temple to let them spend the night at her home with her 10 year old daughter, Rochelle. Before leaving the home, Coleman and Brown raped and murdered mother and daughter.

Coleman and Brown left Indiana bound for Ohio. On July 11, while in Cincinnati, they find their next victim, 15 year old Tonnie Storey. Tonnie's raped and strangled body was discovered on July 19. Upon leaving Cincinnati, Coleman and Brown drifted to Norwood. On July 13, while in Norwood, the duo

Debra Denise Brown joined Alton Coleman in 1984, and went on a killing binge that resulted in the deaths of eight people. (Ohio Department of Corrections)

beat to death Marlene Walters and attempted to kill her husband, but he survived. The Walters' car was stolen by Coleman and Brown.

Upon leaving Ohio, Coleman and Brown journey to Indianapolis. When they arrived there they needed another vehicle. They obtained one from their next victim, 77 year old Eugene Scott. Scott's body was found shot and stabbed to death.

Coleman and Brown ended up in Evanston, Illinois, where an anonymous tip to the police brought their reign of terror to an end. Upon being captured, Coleman and Brown were prosecuted for the Ohio murders of Walters and Storey. They received death sentences for both murders. However, Brown's sentence was reversed on appeal and she was given life sentences. The State of Indiana prosecuted the duo for the murder of Turks. They both received the death penalty for the crime. Illinois prosecuted Coleman for the murder of Wheat. He received a death sentence for that murder. Authorities eventually decided not to continue prosecuting the duo, though the evidence of guilt was available. Coleman sits on death row in Ohio and Brown is being held on her life sentences in Ohio.

Coleman v. Alabama (I)   *Court:* United States Supreme Court; *Case Citation:* Coleman v. Alabama, 377 U.S. 129 (1964); *Argued:* March 25, 1964; *Decided:* May 4, 1964; *Opinion of the Court:* Justice Clark; *Concurring Opinion:* None; *Dissenting Opinion:* None; *Appellate Defense Counsel:* Michael C. Meltsner argued; Jack Greenberg and Orzell Billingsley, Jr. on brief; *Appellate Prosecution Counsel:* Leslie Hall argued; Richmond M. Flowers on brief; *Amicus Curiae Brief Supporting Prosecutor:* None; *Amicus Curiae Brief Supporting Defendant:* None.

Issue Presented: Whether the defendant was entitled to present evidence on his claim of racial discrimination in the selection of the grand jury that indicted him and the petit jury that presided at his trial?

Case Holding: The defendant was entitled to present evidence on his claim of racial discrimination in the selection of the grand jury that indicted him and the petit jury that presided at his trial, because the trial court ruled on the merits of the issue without affording him such an opportunity.

Factual and procedural background of case: The defendant, Coleman, was convicted of capital murder and sentenced to death by a Alabama jury. The defendant filed a motion for a new trial asserting for the first time deprivation of his constitutional rights through systematic exclusion of blacks from the grand jury that indicted him and petit jury that presided at his trial. The trial judge denied the motion because the issue was not raised before trial. The Alabama Supreme Court affirmed the conviction and sentence. The United States Supreme Court granted certiorari to consider the issue.

Opinion of the Court by Justice Clark: Justice Clark ruled that the defendant's conviction and sentence had to be reversed because he was not presented an opportunity to present evidence on his claim of grand and petit jury discrimi-

nation. The opinion rejected the State's claim that the defendant waived the issue by not presenting it before trial. It was said that the trial court actually accepted the motion, but refused to take evidence on the issue. Justice Clark found that once the trial court accepted the motion on its merits, due process required that the defendant be afforded an opportunity to present evidence on his claim. The opinion pointed out that the Alabama Supreme Court affirmed the judgment by indicating the defendant failed to present any evidence on his jury discrimination claim. The judgment of the Alabama Supreme Court was reversed and the case remanded for an evidentiary hearing on the defendant's jury discrimination claim. *See also* **Coleman v. Alabama (II); Discrimination in Grand or Petit Jury Selection; Sims v. Georgia (II); Whitus v. Georgia**

Coleman v. Alabama (II)   *Court:* United States Supreme Court; *Case Citation:* Coleman v. Alabama, 389 U.S. 22 (1967); *Argued:* Not reported; *Decided:* October 16, 1967; *Opinion of the Court:* Per Curiam; *Concurring Opinion:* None; *Dissenting Opinion:* None; *Appellate Defense Counsel:* Jack Greenberg, Michael Meltsner and Orzell Billingsley on brief; *Appellate Prosecution Counsel:* McDonald Gallion and Leslie Hall on brief; *Amicus Curiae Brief Supporting Prosecutor:* Not reported; *Amicus Curiae Brief Supporting Defendant:* Not reported.

Issue Presented: Whether the State rebutted the defendant's prima facie case of racial discrimination in the selection of the grand and petit juries involved in his prosecution?

Case Holding: The State failed to rebut the defendant's prima facie case of racial discrimination in the selection of the grand and petit juries involved in his prosecution.

Factual and procedural background of case: The defendant, Coleman, was convicted of capital murder and sentenced to death by a Alabama jury. The defendant filed a motion for a new trial asserting for the first time deprivation of his constitutional rights through systematic exclusion of blacks from the grand jury that indicted him and petit jury that presided at his trial. The trial judge denied the motion because the issue was not raised before trial. The Alabama Supreme Court affirmed the conviction and sentence. The United States Supreme Court reversed the judgment in *Coleman v. Alabama (I)*, and remanded the case for an evidentiary hearing on the defendant's jury discrimination claim. On remand the defendant was afforded an evidentiary hearing on his claim. The trial court found that the defendant failed to prove his claim. The Alabama Supreme Court affirmed. The United States Supreme Court granted certiorari to consider the issue.

Opinion of the Court was delivered Per Curiam: The per curiam opinion found that no black had served on the grand jury that indicted the defendant, and no black served on the jury which presided at his trial. It was further found that up to the time of the defendant's trial, no black had ever served on a grand jury panel in the county where he was prosecuted and few, if any, blacks had served on petit jury panels. The opinion held that such evidence made out a prima facie case of the denial of equal protection which the Constitution guaranteed. It was said that the State failed to rebut the prima facie case of discrimination. The judgment of the Alabama Supreme Court was reversed. *See also* **Coleman v. Alabama (I); Discrimination in Grand or Petit Jury Selection; Sims v. Georgia (II); Whitus v. Georgia**

Coleman v. Tennessee

Court: United States Supreme Court; *Case Citation:* Coleman v. Tennessee, 97 U.S. 509 (1879); *Argued:* Not reported; *Decided:* October Term, 1878; *Opinion of the Court:* Justice Field; *Concurring Opinion:* None; *Dissenting Opinion:* Justice Clifford; *Appellate Defense Counsel:* Henry S. Foote argued; Leonidas C. Houk on brief; *Appellate Prosecution Counsel:* J. B. Heiskell argued and briefed; *Amicus Curiae Brief Supporting Prosecutor:* None; *Amicus Curiae Brief Supporting Defendant:* None.

Issue Presented: Whether double jeopardy principles barred the State of Tennessee from prosecuting the defendant for an offense that he was prosecuted for by the United States military?

Case Holding: Double jeopardy principles did not bar the State of Tennessee from prosecuting the defendant for an offense that he was prosecuted for by the United States military, but under the rules of war such prosecution by the State could not occur.

Factual and procedural background of case: The defendant, Coleman, was a soldier in the Union Army in 1865. The Union Army prosecuted him for committing capital murder of a civilian on March 7, 1865. The murder occurred in Tennessee, which was an insurgent State at the time, and under the jurisdiction of the Union Army. The defendant was found guilty by a military tribunal and sentenced to death. The President, however, did not confirm the defendant's execution as required by law.

In 1874, the State of Tennessee indicted the defendant for the capital murder in which the military had previously convicted and sentenced him. The defendant was found guilty and sentenced to death. The Tennessee Supreme Court affirmed the judgment. In doing so, the appellate court rejected the defendant's contention that double jeopardy principles prohibited the State from prosecuting him. The United States Supreme Court granted certiorari to consider the issue.

Opinion of the Court by Justice Field: Justice Field held that double jeopardy principles did not bar the defendant's prosecution by the State of Tennessee. He ruled that the prosecution was barred by the rules of war recognized by international law. The opinion reasoned: "When the armies of the United States were in the territory of insurgent States, banded together in hostility to the national government and making war against it, ... the military tribunals [of the United States] had, under the laws of war, ... exclusive jurisdiction to try and punish offenses of every grade committed by persons in the military service. Officers and soldiers of the armies of the Union were not subject during the war to the laws of the enemy.... They were answerable only to their own government, and only by its laws, as enforced by its armies, could they be punished." The opinion concluded that, because Tennessee was an insurgent State at the time of the offense, it did not have jurisdiction to prosecute the defendant. The judgment of the Tennessee Supreme Court was reversed.

Dissenting opinion by Justice Clifford: Justice Clifford dissented from the Court's decision. He argued that Tennessee did not lose its sovereign authority to enforce its criminal laws merely because of military occupation by the Union army. Justice Clifford reasoned that, the issue raised by the defendant before the State courts, i.e., double jeopardy, was the sole dispositive issue in the case. He contended that double jeopardy principles did not prevent the State from enforcing its laws concurrently with the Federal Government through its military. Justice Clifford also believed that because the President never authorized the defendant's execution, the military judgment became a nullity, which supported the conclusion that double jeopardy did not bar the prosecution. *See also* **Double Jeopardy Clause; Jurisdiction; Military Death Penalty Law**

Coleman v. Thompson

Court: United States Supreme Court; *Case Citation:* Coleman v. Thompson, 501 U.S. 722 (1991); *Argued:* February 25, 1991; *Decided:* June 24, 1991; *Opinion of the Court:* Justice O'Connor; *Concurring Opinion:* Justice White; *Dissenting Opinion:* Justice Blackmun, in which Marshall and Stevens, JJ., joined; *Appellate Defense Counsel:* John H. Hall argued; Daniel J. Goldstein and Richard G. Price on brief; *Appellate Prosecution Counsel:* Donald R. Curry argued; Mary Sue Terry, H. Lane Kneedler, Stephen D. Rosenthal and Jerry P. Slonaker on brief; *Amicus Curiae Brief Supporting Prosecutor:* 31; *Amicus Curiae Brief Supporting Defendant:* None.

Issue Presented: Whether Federal courts may review Federal habeas corpus claims that were defaulted on by a defendant in a State habeas corpus proceeding?

Case Holding: Federal courts may not review Federal habeas corpus claims that were defaulted on by a defendant in a State habeas corpus proceeding, unless the defendant can demonstrate (1) cause for the default; (2) actual prejudice as a result of the alleged violation of federal law; or (3) that failure to consider the claims will result in a fundamental miscarriage of justice.

Factual and procedural background of case: The defendant, Roger Keith Coleman, was convicted and sentenced to death for capital murder by the State of Virginia. On direct appeal, the Virginia Supreme Court affirmed the conviction and sentence. The defendant then filed a petition for habeas corpus in a State trial court. The State trial court dismissed the habeas petition. He then appealed the dismissal of the habeas petition to the Virginia Supreme Court. The appellate court dismissed the habeas appeal on the grounds that the defendant did not file the appeal within the time frame provided by State law.

The defendant next filed a habeas petition in a Federal District Court, alleging claims that were brought in his State habeas petition. The District Court dismissed the petition on the grounds that the defendant had procedurally defaulted the claims because of the dismissal of his petition. A Federal Court of Appeals affirmed the dismissal by the District Court, after finding the defendant had not shown cause to excuse the default of the claims at the State level. The United States Supreme Court granted certiorari to consider the issue.

Opinion of the Court by Justice O'Connor: Justice O'Connor held that the defendant's claims presented for the first time in the State habeas proceeding were not subject to review in a Federal habeas proceeding. It was reasoned in the opinion that because of the requirement that States have the first opportunity to correct their own mistakes, Federal habeas courts generally may not review a State court's denial of a defendant's constitutional claim, if the State court's decision rests on a State procedural default that is independent of the Federal claims and is adequate to support the defendant's continued custody.

It was ruled that in all cases in which a State prisoner has defaulted his or her federal claims in a State court pursuant to an independent and adequate state procedural rule, Federal habeas review of the claims is barred unless the defendant can demonstrate (1) cause for the default; (2) actual prejudice as a result of the alleged violation of federal law; or (3) that failure to consider the claims will result in a fundamental miscarriage of justice.

Justice O'Connor rejected the defendant's contention that it was his attorney's error that led to the late filing of his State habeas appeal. She indicated that this did not establish good cause for excusing the default. She reasoned that, because there is no constitutional right to an attorney in State post-conviction proceedings, a defendant cannot claim constitutionally ineffective assistance of counsel in such proceedings. Thus, since any attorney error that lead to the default of the defendant's claims could not constitute "cause," he was barred from bringing the claims in a Federal habeas proceeding. The decision of the Court of Appeals was affirmed.

Concurring opinion by Justice White: Justice White concurred in the Court's opinion. His concurrence addressed the defendant's argument that the Virginia Supreme Court occasionally allowed untimely filed appeals to be considered on the merits. He wrote:

> The predicate for this argument is that, on occasion, the Virginia Supreme Court waives the untimeliness rule. If that were true, the rule would not be an adequate and independent state ground barring direct or habeas review. The filing of briefs and their consideration would do no more than buttress the claim that the rule is not strictly enforced.
>
> Petitioner argues that the Virginia court does, in fact, waive the rule on occasion, but I am not now convinced that there is a practice of waiving the rule when constitutional issues are at stake, even fundamental ones. The evidence is too scanty to permit a conclusion that the rule is no longer an adequate and independent state ground barring federal review. The fact that

merits briefs were filed and were considered by the court, without more, does not justify a different conclusion.

Dissenting opinion by Justice Blackmun, in which Marshall and Stevens, JJ., joined: Justice Blackmun dissented from the Court's opinion. He believed the Court wrongly elevated the rights of States over the constitutional rights of defendants. The dissent argued as follows:

> … One searches the majority's opinion in vain … for any mention of … Coleman's right to a criminal proceeding free from constitutional defect or his interest in finding a forum for his constitutional challenge to his conviction and sentence of death…. Rather, displaying obvious exasperation with the breadth of substantive federal habeas doctrine and the expansive protection afforded by the Fourteenth Amendment's guarantee of fundamental fairness in state criminal proceedings, the Court today continues its crusade to erect petty procedural barriers in the path of any state prisoner seeking review of his federal constitutional claims. Because I believe that the Court is creating a Byzantine morass of arbitrary, unnecessary, and unjustifiable impediments to the vindication of federal rights, I dissent.
>
> The Court cavalierly claims that "[t]his is a case about federalism," and proceeds without explanation to assume that the purposes of federalism are advanced whenever a federal court refrains from reviewing an ambiguous state court judgment. Federalism, however, has no inherent normative value: it does not, as the majority appears to assume, blindly protect the interests of States from any incursion by the federal courts. Rather, federalism secures to citizens the liberties that derive from the diffusion of sovereign power. "Federalism is a device for realizing the concepts of decency and fairness which are among the fundamental principles of liberty and justice lying at the base of all our civil and political institutions." In this context, it cannot lightly be assumed that the interests of federalism are fostered by a rule that impedes federal review of federal constitutional claims.

Case note: Virginia executed Roger Keith Coleman by electrocution on May 20, 1992. *See also* **Amadeo v. Zant; Dugger v. Adams; Procedural Default of Constitutional Claims; Smith v. Murray**

Collateral Attack *see* Habeas Corpus

Colombia
Colombia abolished the death penalty in 1910. *See also* **International Capital Punishment Nations**

Colorado
The State of Colorado is a capital punishment jurisdiction. The State reenacted its death penalty law after the United States Supreme Court decision in *Furman v. Georgia*, 408 U.S. 238 (1972) on January 1, 1975.

Colorado has a three-tier legal system. The State's legal system is composed of a supreme court, court of appeals and courts of general jurisdiction. The Colorado Supreme Court is presided over by a chief justice and six associate justices. The Colorado Court of Appeals is composed of a chief judge and fifteen judges. The courts of general jurisdiction in the State are called District Courts. Capital offenses against the State of Colorado are tried in the District Courts.

Colorado's capital punishment statute is triggered if a person commits a homicide under the following special circumstances:

Ken Salazar is the Colorado Attorney General. His office represents the State in capital punishment appellate proceedings. (Colorado Attorney General Office)

a. After deliberation and with the intent to cause the death of a person other than himself, he causes the death of that person or of another person; or

b. Acting either alone or with one or more persons, he commits or attempts to commit arson, robbery, burglary, kidnapping, sexual assault, or the crime of escape and, in the course of or in furtherance of the crime that he is committing or attempting to commit, or of immediate flight therefrom, the death of a person, other than one of the participants, is caused by anyone; or

c. By perjury or subornation of perjury he procures the conviction and execution of any innocent person; or

d. Under circumstances evidencing an attitude of universal malice manifesting extreme indifference to the value of human life generally, he knowingly engages in conduct which creates a grave risk of death to a person, or persons, other than himself, and thereby causes the death of another; or

e. He or she commits unlawful distribution, dispensation, or sale of a controlled substance to a person under the age of eighteen years on school grounds, and the death of such person is caused by the use of such controlled substance; or

f. The person knowingly causes the death of a child who has not yet attained twelve years of age and the person committing the offense is one in a position of trust with respect to the victim.

Capital murder in Colorado is punishable by death or life imprisonment without parole. A capital prosecution in Colorado is bifurcated into a guilt phase and penalty phase. A jury is used at the guilt phase of a capital trial, but the penalty phase is presided over by a three judge panel. It is required that, at the penalty phase, the three judge panel must unanimously agree that a death sentence is appropriate before it can be imposed. If the penalty phase panel of judges are unable to reach a unanimous verdict, the defendant must be sentenced to imprisonment for life.

In order to impose a death sentence upon a defendant under Colorado law, it is required that the prosecutor establish the existence of at least one of the following statutory aggravating circumstances at the penalty phase:

a. The murder was committed by a person under sentence of imprisonment for a felony; or

b. The defendant was previously convicted of a felony; or

c. The defendant intentionally killed any of the following persons while such person was engaged in the course of the performance of such person's official duties, and the defendant knew or reasonably should have known that such victim was such a person engaged in the performance of such person's official duties, or the victim was intentionally killed in retaliation for the performance of the victim's official duties:

I. A peace officer or former peace officer; or

II. A firefighter; or

III. A judge, referee, or former judge or referee of any court of record in the state or federal system or in any other state court system or a judge or former judge in any municipal court in this state or in any other state; or

IV. An elected state, county, or municipal official; or

V. A federal law enforcement officer or agent or former federal law enforcement officer or agent; or

d. The defendant intentionally killed a person kidnapped or being held as a hostage by the defendant or by anyone associated with the defendant; or

e. The defendant has been a party to an agreement to kill another person in furtherance of which a person has been intentionally killed; or

f. The defendant committed the offense while lying in wait, from ambush, or by use of an explosive or incendiary device; or

g. The defendant committed a felony and, in the course of or in furtherance of such or immediate flight therefrom, the defendant intentionally caused the death of a person other than one of the participants; or

h. The murder was committed for pecuniary gain; or

i. In the commission of the offense, the defendant knowingly created a grave risk of death to another person in addition to the victim of the offense; or

j. The defendant committed the offense in an especially heinous, cruel, or depraved manner; or

k. The murder was committed for the purpose of avoiding or preventing a lawful arrest or prosecution or effecting an escape from custody.

l. The defendant unlawfully and intentionally, knowingly, or with universal malice manifesting extreme indifference to the value of human life generally, killed two or more persons during the commission of the same criminal episode; or

m. The defendant intentionally killed a child who has not yet attained twelve years of age; or

n. The defendant committed the murder against the victim because of the victim's race, color, ancestry, religion, or national origin.

Although the Federal Constitution will not permit

jurisdictions to prevent capital felons from presenting all relevant mitigating evidence at the penalty phase, Colorado has provided the following statutory mitigating circumstances that permit the three judge panel to reject imposition of the death penalty:

a. The age of the defendant at the time of the crime; or

b. The defendant's capacity to appreciate wrongfulness of the defendant's conduct or to conform the defendant's conduct to the requirements of law was significantly impaired, but not so impaired as to constitute a defense to prosecution; or

c. The defendant was under unusual and substantial duress, although not such duress as to constitute a defense to prosecution; or

d. The defendant was a principal in the offense which was committed by another, but the defendant's participation was relatively minor, although not so minor as to constitute a defense to prosecution; or

e. The defendant could not reasonably have foreseen that the defendant's conduct in the course of the commission of the offense for which the defendant was convicted would cause, or would create a grave risk of causing, death to another person; or

f. The emotional state of the defendant at the time the crime was committed; or

g. The absence of any significant prior conviction; or

h. The extent of the defendant's cooperation with law enforcement officers or agencies and with the office of the prosecuting district attorney; or

i. The influence of drugs or alcohol; or

j. The good faith, although mistaken, belief by the defendant that circumstances existed which constituted a moral justification for the defendant's conduct; or

k. The defendant is not a continuing threat to society; or

l. Any other evidence which in the court's opinion bears on the question of mitigation.

Under Colorado's capital punishment statute, a sentence of death is automatically reviewed by the Colorado Supreme Court. Colorado uses lethal injection to carry out death sentences. The State's death row facility for men and women are located in Cannon City, Colorado.

Pursuant to the laws of Colorado the Governor has authority to grant clemency in capital cases. Commutation may be life imprisonment or a term of not less than twenty years at hard labor.

From the start of modern capital punishment in 1976, through 1999, Colorado executed one capital felon. During this period Colorado did not have any female death row inmates. The State does not permit capital punishment to be imposed on persons 17 years old or younger. A total of 3 capital felons were on death row in Colorado in 1999. The 1999 death row population in the State was listed as: 2 black inmates; 0 white inmates; and 1 unidentified inmate. Colorado prohibits the execution of mentally retarded capital felons.

Executions by Colorado 1976–1999

Name	Race	Date of Execution	Method of Execution
Gary L. Davis	White	October 13, 1997	Lethal Injection

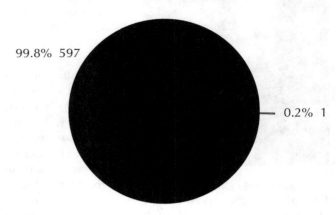

COLORADO EXECUTIONS 1976–1999

99.8% 597

0.2% 1

■ COLORADO EXECUTIONS
■ ALL OTHER EXECUTIONS

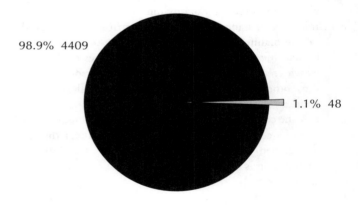

EXECUTIONS BY COLORADO 1930–1999

98.9% 4409

1.1% 48

■ COLORADO
■ ALL OTHER JURISDICTIONS

Common Design Rule   The common design rule (also known as concert of action theory) is an adaptation of the felony murder rule. Under the common design rule when two or more persons act in concert in the commission of a felony, and a victim is killed by one of the felons, the intent of the actual killer is transferred to the co-felon. Some courts have held that criminal liability for murder under the common design rule will not attach unless the defendant has the requisite specific intent to commit murder.

In general, proof of a common design to commit an unlawful act which results in death may be inferred from circumstances such as: (1) presence at the scene of the crime without opposition or disapproval, (2) continued close association with the perpetrator after the criminal act, (3) failure to inform authorities of the killing, or (4) concealment or destruction of evidence after the crime. *See also* **Felony Murder Rule**

Common Law and Capital Punishment

Anglo-American jurisprudence owes its understanding and acceptance of the death penalty to the common law of England. The phrase "common law" and all of its implications stem from England. The actual use of the phrase has been traced back to the 13th century, during the reign of Edward I (1272–1307). During that period of time two types of legal systems existed in England. The island nation had a temporal legal system and an ecclesiastical or religious legal system. The legal principles that fall under the phrase common law were developed by judges in the temporal courts of England.

The common law recognized two types of criminal offenses: misdemeanor and felony. While numerous factors distinguished the two types of offenses, the ultimate difference resided in the fact that a convicted misdemeanant was not called upon to relinquish his or her life, but a convicted felon could be punished with death.

Common Law Nonfatal Criminal Punishment. If one compared the nonfatal criminal punishments that are permitted by Anglo-American jurisprudence today, with the nonfatal criminal punishments under the common law, the two would appear as different as night and day. Some of the milder forms of nonfatal criminal punishment under the common law included confinement, hard labor, banishment, the pillory, stocks and the dunking stool. More drastic forms of punishment included plucking out eyes, castration, cutting off feet, hands, noses, ears, upper lips and scalping. Additionally, convicted prisoners would also be mercilessly whipped or branded with hot irons on their cheeks or hands.

Common Law Capital Offenses. The common law created only a few felony offenses, which included: murder, arson, larceny, robbery, burglary, rape, treason and petty treason. The limited number of felony offenses under the common law help explain why the common law adopted the rule that all felony offenses were to be punished with death. Unfortunately for Englanders however, the number of felony offenses in England expanded beyond what the common law created. As a result of parliamentary statutes, the number of felony offenses in England grew to 263 by the year 1822. Moreover, the common law rule that all felony offenses were to be punished with death, was made applicable to each of the 263 felonies that developed in England.

The tragedy of imposing the death penalty on all felony offenses was sarcastically commented upon by the great English jurist, Blackstone. It was pointed out by Blackstone that, as a result of misguided intentions by parliament, it had become a capital offense (1) to tear down the mound of a fish pond and allow fish to escape; (2) to chop down a cherry tree that was in an orchard; and (3) to be publicly seen with a gypsy for one month.

Common Law Methods of Capital Punishment. The methods by which the death penalty was carried out under the common law represents a journey into the underworld. Many of the capital offenses under the common law had their own special execution methods. A male defendant convicted of treason or the felony crime of falsifying, had to be dragged by horse to the place of execution and hung. A conviction for sodomy carried a penalty of death by being buried alive. A convicted heretic had to be burned alive. A conviction for a routine crime like murder, rape, arson, robbery or burglary was punished by simple hanging. However, if any of the latter offenses was found to be especially vicious, the defendant was beheaded.

The crime of treason by a female was punished initially under the common law by burning alive the defendant. However, in the year 1790 this method was halted and the punishment became strangulation and burning of the corpse. For the crime of high treason (affecting the Crown directly) a defendant was punished by quartering, disemboweling and beheading. In certain egregious murder prosecutions a convicted defendant would be publicly dissected while alive.

Commutation of Sentence *see* Clemency

Comoros

The island nation of Comoros imposes the death penalty. Comoros uses the firing squad to carry out the death penalty. Its legal system is based on French law and Islamic law. Comoros' constitution was adopted on October 20, 1996.

The Comorian judicial system is composed of a Supreme Court and local courts. Under the laws of Comoros trials are open to the public. Defendants have a right to counsel, but this right is meaningless because there are very few lawyers in the country and the government does not provide free legal counsel.

Two capital cases illustrate the grave situation in Comoros. In 1996, a man was charged with killing a pregnant woman. He was prosecuted in a lay criminal court. His trial took two days and he was represented by a paralegal. The defendant was found guilty, sentenced to death and executed. In 1997, another man was prosecuted for a similar crime. He, too, was represented by a paralegal in a lay criminal court. This defendant was also found guilty, sentenced to death and executed. Both defendants had unsuccessfully appealed their convictions. *See also* **International Capital Punishment Nations**

Competency Hearing *see* Insanity

Competency of the Defendant to be a Witness

The disqualification of a defendant as a witness in his or her own trial characterized a principle of law under the common law for centuries. The remote origins of this principle are traced to the contest for judicial hegemony between the developing common law jury trial, and the older modes of trial such as compurgation and wager of law. Under those old forms, a defendant's oath itself was a means of decision in a case. The jury trial replaced judgment by oath, with judgment of the jury based upon the testimony of witnesses. A result of this change, was that a defendant was deemed incapable of being a witness at his or her trial. In time the principal justification for the rule was the potential untrustworthiness of the defendant's testimony.

By the sixteenth century it became necessary for a defendant to conduct his or her own defense, a defendant was neither allowed to call witnesses nor permitted the assistance of counsel. In the seventeenth century rules changed and a defendant was permitted to call witnesses in his or her behalf. The common law drew a distinction between the accused and his or her witnesses — the defendant's witnesses gave evidence, but the defendant did not.

Disqualification for interest was entrenched in the common law when the United States was formed. The early courts in America followed the common law and held that defendants were deemed incompetent as witnesses in their own trial. In the early nineteenth century American courts began to abandon the disqualification rule. In 1859 Maine created the first statute to permit a defendant to give sworn evidence in the trial of a few crimes. This statute was followed by Maine in 1864, with the enactment of a general competency statute for criminal defendants. Within 20 years most of the States had followed Maine's lead. Before the end of the century every State except Georgia had abolished the common law disqualification rule. Georgia retained the rule well into the 1960s.

The greatest negative impact of the disqualification rule was manifested in capital prosecutions, where defendants could not testify to their own defense. Legal historians believe the disqualification rule resulted in countless death sentences being imposed on innocent defendants. *See also* **Ferguson v. Georgia**

Competency to Stand Trial *see* Insanity

Competent Court *see* Jurisdiction

Complaint
A complaint is a criminal charging instrument that is used primarily in jurisdictions that prosecute felony offenses by grand jury indictment. A complaint is usually drawn up by a magistrate based upon statements by an affiant, that arise to probable cause to believe that a crime was committed and that a named defendant committed the crime. A complaint is used to initiate proceedings, but is eventually replaced by an indictment. *See also* **Grand Jury**

Complicity *see* Conspiracy

Compulsory Process Clause
Under the Sixth Amendment of the Federal Constitution it states that a defendant shall "have compulsory process for obtaining witnesses in his favor." The Compulsory Process Clause guarantees a defendant the right to have a witness subpoenaed to appear for examination at trial.

Two types of subpoenas exist. A "subpoena ad testificandum" is an ordinary subpoena that compels the presence of a witness. The second type of subpoena is called a "subpoena duces tecum," and it is used to compel a person having documents to bring them to trial.

Under modern capital punishment jurisprudence the Compulsory Process Clause has taken on an added dimension. It is now the source of constitutional authority to compel the attendance of witnesses at both, the guilt phase and penalty phase of a capital prosecution. *See also* **Bill of Rights**

Compulsory Self-Incrimination *see* Right to Remain Silent

Concurrent Jurisdiction *see* Dual Sovereignty

Concert of Action Theory *see* Common Design Rule

Concurrent Sentences
Concurrent sentences refers to the imposition of two or more sentences that are served simultaneously. *See also* **Consecutive Sentences**

Concurring Opinion
A concurring opinion is a written opinion by an appellate court judge that agrees with the decision reached by the majority of the court, but for reasons that are different than that used by the majority opinion. *See also* **Dissenting Opinion**

Conditional Plea *see* Guilty Plea

Confession of Error
Under the doctrine of "confession of error," a prosecutor concedes to an appellate court that an assignment of trial error by the defendant actually occurred. Generally when confession of error is made the prosecutor will urge a new trial be permitted. Occasionally, however, prosecutors will request the appellate court find that the error was harmless and, therefore, the conviction and sentence should be affirmed. *See also* **Williams v. Georgia**

Confession *see* Right to Remain Silent

Confrontation Clause
The Confrontation Clause of the Sixth Amendment of the Federal Constitution requires a defendant be permitted to confront witnesses against him or her. The purpose of the Confrontation Clause is to ensure the reliability of evidence against a defendant, by subjecting the evidence to rigorous testing in a criminal trial through cross examination of an adverse witness. The Confrontation Clause generally forbids the introduction of hearsay into a trial unless the evidence falls within a firmly rooted hearsay exception or otherwise possesses particularized guarantees of trustworthiness. *See also* **Bill of Rights; Hearsay; Lilly v. Virginia**

Congo (Democratic Republic) The Democratic Republic of Congo imposes the death penalty. Its legal system is based on Belgian civil law and customary law. Congo utilizes the firing squad and hanging as the method of execution. It was reported that in 1998, the nation executed 100 prisoners.

In 1997, the government of Congo was overthrown. The new government was headed by President Laurent Desire Kabila. The political organs of government in Congo are in transition, as different factions sort out implementation of a new constitution.

The judicial system is composed of a Supreme Court, appellate courts, trial courts, and a Court of State Security. The criminal code of Congo is based on Belgian and customary law. Under the legal code defendants have a right to a speedy public trial, the presumption of innocence, and legal counsel at all stages of proceedings. The law provides for court appointed counsel in capital cases. Defendants have the right to appeal in all cases except those involving national security, armed robbery, and smuggling. The latter offenses are adjudicated by the Court of State Security. *See also* **International Capital Punishment Nations**

Congo (Republic) The Republic of Congo has capital punishment on its law books, but the punishment is infrequently used. Congo utilizes the firing squad and beheading as methods of execution. The nation's legal system is based on French law and customary law. Its constitution was approved in March of 1992, but is being redrafted.

The judicial system of Congo consists of local courts, courts of appeal, a Supreme Court, and traditional courts. Rights afforded defendants under Congo's laws include: public trial, presumption of innocence, counsel, confront witnesses, and appeal. *See also* **International Capital Punishment Nations**

Connecticut The State of Connecticut is a capital punishment jurisdiction. The State reenacted its death penalty law after the United States Supreme Court decision in *Furman v. Georgia*, 408 U.S. 238 (1972) on October 1, 1973.

Connecticut has a three-tier legal system. The State's legal system is composed of a supreme court, court of appeals and courts of general jurisdiction. The Connecticut Supreme Court is presided over by a chief justice and six associate justices. The Connecticut Appellate Court is composed of a chief judge and eight judges. The courts of general jurisdiction in the State are called Superior Courts. Capital offenses against the State of Connecticut are tried in the Circuit Courts.

Connecticut's capital punishment statute is triggered if a person commits a homicide under the following special circumstances:

(1) murder of a law enforcement officer, correctional officer or fireman; (2) murder committed by a defendant who is hired to commit the same for pecuniary gain, or murder committed by one who is hired by the defendant to commit the same for pecuniary gain; (3) murder committed by one who has previously been convicted of intentional murder, or of murder committed in the course of commission of a felony; (4) murder committed by one who was, at the time of commission of the murder, under sentence of life imprisonment; (5) murder by a kidnapper of a kidnapped person during the course of the kidnapping or before such person is able to return or be returned to safety; (6) the illegal sale, for economic gain, of cocaine, heroin or methadone to a person who dies as a direct result of the use by him of such cocaine, heroin or methadone; (7) murder committed in the course of the commission of sexual assault in the first degree; (8) murder of two or more persons at the same time or in the course of a single transaction; or (9) murder of a person under sixteen years of age.

Capital murder in Connecticut is punishable by death or life imprisonment without parole. A capital prosecution in Connecticut is bifurcated into a guilt phase and penalty phase. A jury is used at both phases of a capital trial. It is required that, at the penalty phase, that the jury unanimously agree that a death sentence is appropriate before it can be imposed. If the penalty phase jury is unable to reach a verdict, the trial judge is required to impose a sentence of life imprisonment without parole.

In order to impose a death sentence upon a defendant under Connecticut law, it is required that the prosecutor establish the existence of at least one of the following statutory aggravating circumstances at the penalty phase:

(1) the defendant committed the offense during the commission or attempted commission of, or during the immediate flight from the commission or attempted commission of, a felony and he had previously been convicted of the same felony; or (2) the defendant committed the offense after having been convicted of two or more state or federal offenses, or one or more state offenses and one or more federal offenses for each of which a penalty of more than one year imprisonment may be imposed, which offenses were committed on different occasions and which involved the infliction of serious bodily injury upon another person; or (3) the defendant committed the offense and in such commission knowingly created a grave risk of death to another person in addition to the victim of the offense; or (4) the defendant committed the offense in an especially heinous, cruel or depraved manner; or (5) the defendant procured the commission of the offense by payment, or promise of payment, of anything of pecuniary value; or (6) the defendant committed the offense as consideration for the receipt, or in expectation of the receipt, of anything of pecuniary value; or (7) the defendant committed the offense with an assault weapon.

Although the Federal Constitution will not permit jurisdictions to prevent capital felons from presenting all relevant mitigating evidence at the penalty phase, Connecticut has provided the following statutory mitigating circumstances that permit the jury (or judge) to reject imposition of the death penalty:

(1) the defendant was under the age of eighteen years; or (2) his mental capacity was significantly impaired or his ability to conform his conduct to the requirements of law was significantly impaired but not so impaired in either case as to constitute a defense to prosecution; or (3) his participation in such offense was relatively minor, although not so minor as to constitute a defense to prosecution; or (4) he could not reasonably have foreseen that his conduct in the course of commission of the offense of which he was convicted would cause, or would create a grave risk of causing, death to another person.

Under Connecticut's capital punishment statute, a sentence

of death is automatically reviewed by the Connecticut Supreme Court. Connecticut uses lethal injection to carry out death sentences. The State's death row facility is located in Somers, Connecticut.

Pursuant to the laws of Connecticut, its Board of Pardons has full authority to grant clemency in capital cases. The State's Governor only has authority to grant temporary reprieves.

From the start of modern capital punishment in 1976, through 1999, Connecticut did not execute any capital felon. A total of 5 capital felons were on death row in Connecticut in 1999. The 1999 death row population in the State was listed as: 3 black inmates; and 2 white inmates. The State does not permit capital punishment to be imposed on persons 17 years old or younger. Connecticut does not prohibit the execution of mentally retarded capital felons.

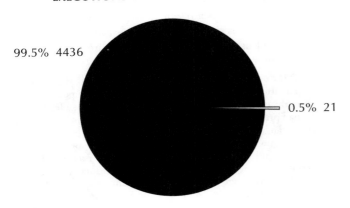

EXECUTIONS BY CONNECTICUT 1930–1999

99.5% 4436

0.5% 21

■ CONNECTICUT
■ ALL OTHER JURISDICTIONS

Consecutive Sentences   When one sentence is required to be served before a second and subsequent sentence begins to run, the sentences are called consecutive sentences. *See also* **Concurrent Sentences**

Consent *see* **Victim's Consent Mitigator**

Conspiracy   A conspiracy occurs when two or more persons agree to commit some unlawful or criminal act. *See also* **Law of Parties**

Constitution   A constitution represents the will of the people expressed through specific principles voted upon by them to regulate certain matters pertaining to their collective existence. The Federal Constitution is the supreme constitution in the United States. Each of the States have constitutions, but they are subordinate to the Federal Constitution.

Constitution Party   The Constitution Party is a national political party. It has fielded candidates for local, statewide and national offices, including Presidential candidates. The national chairman of the organization, James N. Clymer, has taken an active and vigorous position on crime in general and the death penalty in particular. In speaking for the Constitution Party, Clymer has stated that, "We favor the right of states and localities to execute criminals convicted of capital crimes and to require restitution for the victims of crime." The pro–death penalty position of the party has been seen by some as a vehicle for giving the party greater credibility and visibility.

As national chairman of the Constitution Party, James N. Clymer supports use of the death penalty. (Constitution Party)

Constitutional Error *see* **Appellate Review of Conviction and Death Sentence; Procedural Default of Constitutional Claims**

Constitutionality of the Death Penalty   The infliction of death as punishment for murder has never been found by the United States Supreme Court to violate the Federal Constitution per se. In *Furman v. Georgia*, 408 U.S. 238 (1972), the Supreme Court placed a moratorium on the death penalty because the procedures used by all capital punishment jurisdictions allowed the punishment to be imposed arbitrarily. When the Supreme Court lifted the moratorium in *Gregg v. Georgia*, 428 U.S. 153 (1976), it specifically held that "the infliction of death as a punishment for murder is not without justification and thus is not unconstitutionally severe." *See also* **Furman v. Georgia; Gregg v. Georgia**

Continuing Threat Aggravator *see* **Future Dangerousness Aggravator**

Continuing Threat Mitigator *see* **Future Dangerousness Mitigator**

Cook Islands   Capital punishment is permitted in the Cook Islands for extreme crimes. Its legal system is based on New Zealand law and English common law. The nation's constitution was adopted on August 4, 1965. *See also* **International Capital Punishment Nations**

Cook v. United States   *Court:* United States Supreme Court; *Case Citation:* Cook v. United States, 138 U.S. 157 (1891); *Argued:* Not reported; *Decided:* January 26, 1891;

Opinion of the Court: Justice Harlan; *Concurring Opinion:* None; *Dissenting Opinion:* None; *Appellate Defense Counsel:* Jos. Frease argued; Wm. R. Day, John F. Dillon, Geo. R. Peck and W. H. Rossington on brief; *Appellate Prosecution Counsel:* United States Attorney General Miller argued; United States Solicitor General Taft on brief; *Amicus Curiae Brief Supporting Prosecutor:* None; *Amicus Curiae Brief Supporting Defendant:* None.

Issues Presented: (1) Whether the United States had criminal jurisdiction over territory called the "Public Land Strip"? (2) Whether prejudicial hearsay statements were admitted into evidence against the defendants?

Case Holdings: (1) The United States had criminal jurisdiction over territory called the "Public Land Strip," therefore the defendants were properly charged in the Federal District Court in Texas. (2) Prejudicial hearsay statements were admitted into evidence against the defendants, therefore the convictions and death sentences obtained against them could not stand.

Factual and procedural background of case: The case involved the prosecution of Cook and other unnamed defendants. The United States charged the defendants with committing capital murder on territory called the "Public Land Strip." The territory was adjacent to the north eastern part of Texas. The defendants were prosecuted in a Federal District Court in Texas, found guilty and sentenced to death. The United States Supreme Court granted certiorari to consider two claims made by the defendants: (1) that on the date of the murder the Public Land Strip was not within the jurisdiction of any particular Federal or State district, and that no court of the United States had jurisdiction to try the offense; and (2) prejudicial hearsay statements were admitted into evidence against them.

Opinion of the Court by Justice Harlan: Justice Harlan examined the history of the Public Land Strip and concluded that the United States had exerted jurisdiction over the territory, and that jurisdiction over the offense was proper in the court that prosecuted the defendants. The opinion stated: "Upon a careful scrutiny of the act of 1889, giving full effect to all of its clauses, according to the reasonable meaning of the words used, yet interpreting it in the light of the previous history of the Public Land Strip, and of the information communicated to congress by public officers, we do not doubt that congress intended to bring that strip ... for limited judicial purposes, to the eastern district of Texas; thus enabling the general government to protect its own interests, as well as the rights of individuals."

In turning to the hearsay argument, Justice Harlan ruled that the hearsay statements introduced against the defendants were prejudicial. The hearsay statements involved a report of the murder for which the defendants were prosecuted. The report contained confessions purported to be made by the defendants. Witnesses testified that the report was inaccurate and that the defendants did not make the confessions alleged in the report. Justice Harlan pointed out that in spite of the unreliability of the report, the trial judge admitted damaging

portions of it and instructed the jury to consider it as substantive evidence. The opinion in the case added that "[t]he representatives of the government, in this court, frankly concede, as it was their duty to do, that this action of the court below was so erroneous as to entitle the defendants to a reversal." The judgment of the District Court was reversed and a new trial awarded. *See also* **Hearsay; Jurisdiction**

Cooperation with Authorities Mitigator   Four capital punishment jurisdictions, Colorado, New Jersey, New Mexico, and North Carolina, provide by statute that cooperation with authorities is a statutory mitigating circumstance. This mitigating circumstance involves two types of cooperation: (1) cooperation by a capital felon with authorities investigating the murder for which the capital felon was charged, and (2) cooperation with authorities concerning a felony offense for which the capital felon was not charged with or suspected of committing.

Many defendants have unsuccessfully challenged this statutory mitigating circumstance as being unconstitutional, in that it purportedly "allows for imposition of the death penalty based upon the exercise of the right to remain silent." *State v. Compton*, 726 P.2d 837 (N.M. 1986). This is to say that the statutory mitigating circumstance indirectly punishes a capital felon who remains silent and does not cooperate in bringing about his or her own conviction. This situation, it is contended, violates a capital felon's constitutional right to remain silent.

On the other hand capital felons also demand the right to take advantage of this statutory mitigating circumstance. In the case of *State v. Bacon*, 390 S.E.2d 327 (N.C. 1990) the defendant argued that the trial court committed error by failing to instruct the penalty phase jury that his cooperation in helping authorities apprehend another capital felon was a statutory mitigating circumstance. The North Carolina Supreme Court agreed with the defendant in *Bacon* and reversed his death sentence. *See also* **Mitigating Circumstances**

Cooper v. Oklahoma   *Court:* United States Supreme Court; *Case Citation:* Cooper v. Oklahoma, 517 U.S. 314 (1996); *Argued:* January 17, 1996; *Decided:* April 16, 1996; *Opinion of the Court:* Justice Stevens; *Concurring Opinion:* None; *Dissenting Opinion:* None; *Appellate Defense Counsel:* Not reported; *Appellate Prosecution Counsel:* Not reported; *Amicus Curiae Brief Supporting Prosecutor:* Not reported; *Amicus Curiae Brief Supporting Defendant:* Not reported.

Issue Presented: Whether the Due Process Clause permits a State to require a defendant prove incompetency to stand trial by clear and convincing evidence?

Case Holding: The Due Process Clause does not permit a State to require a defendant prove incompetency to stand trial by clear and convincing evidence.

Factual and procedural background of case: The defendant, Byron Keith Cooper, was charged with capital murder by the State of Oklahoma. Prior to trial the defendant argued that he was incompetent and could not be tried. Under Oklahoma's laws a defendant was presumed to be competent to stand trial unless the defendant proved his or her incompetence by "clear and convincing evidence." Applying that standard to the defendant, the trial judge found the defendant competent to be tried. The defendant was convicted and sentenced to death.

On appeal, the Oklahoma Court of Criminal Appeals affirmed the conviction and sentence. In doing so, the appellate court rejected the defendant's argument that the State's presumption of competence, combined with its clear and convincing evidence standard, placed such an onerous burden on him as to violate due process. The United States Supreme Court granted certiorari to consider the issue.

Opinion of the Court by Justice Stevens: Justice Stevens held that Oklahoma's clear and convincing evidence standard for proving incompetency to stand trial violated due process. The opinion noted that the law was clear that the prosecuting attorney must prove a defendant's guilt. It was further said that prior precedent by the Court established that a State may presume that the defendant is competent and require him or her to prove incompetence by a preponderance of the evidence. Justice Stevens indicated that such a presumption did not offend due process. However, he wrote, Oklahoma's standard would permit a criminal trial after a defendant has shown that he or she was more likely than not incompetent.

The opinion found that Oklahoma's rule had no roots in historical practice. Both early English and American cases suggested that the common law standard of proof was preponderance of the evidence. Justice Stevens stated that the common law standard was used by 46 States and the Federal courts. Consequently, the Court was convinced that Oklahoma's heightened standard was not necessary to vindicate the State's interest in prompt and orderly disposition of criminal cases.

Justice Stevens stated that Oklahoma's rule did not exhibit fundamental fairness in its operation. He observed that although it was normally within a State's power to establish the procedures through which its laws are given effect, the power to regulate procedural burdens was subject to proscription under the Due Process Clause when the procedures did not sufficiently protect a fundamental constitutional right. It was concluded that Oklahoma's "clear and convincing evidence" standard violated the defendant's right not to be prosecuted while incompetent. The judgment of the Oklahoma Court of Criminal Appeals was reversed. *See also* **Insanity**

Cora, Charles *see* **Vigilance Committee of San Francisco**

Coram Nobis   The term "coram nobis" is Latin and means "our court." A writ of coram nobis is a common law device that permits a trial court to set aside its own judgment in a criminal case, because of an error of fact not apparent on the record. This device is distinguished from an appeal, which enables an appellate court to review an error of law committed by a trial court. The writ of coram nobis brings the error of fact directly before the trial court.

From a procedural standpoint, when the judgment of the trial court has already been affirmed by the judgment of an appellate court, then the trial court is bound by the mandate of the appellate court. Under such circumstances, it is appropriate to require a defendant to secure, from the appellate court, permission to file a petition for writ of coram nobis in the trial court where he or she seeks an order setting aside the judgment already affirmed by the appellate court. *See also* **Lane v. Brown; Taylor v. Alabama**

Corpus Delicti   The phrase corpus delicti refers to the body of the crime. It is not constitutionally required that the body of a murdered victim actually be found and identified in order to sustain a capital murder conviction and death sentence. The corpus delicti can be established by circumstantial evidence. It has been held that the corpus delicti cannot be established by the mere statement of a witness, but such statement, taken in connection with other facts, might be used to show that a person was murdered. *See also* **Isaacs v. United States; Perovich v. United States**

Correctional Institution *see* **Death Row**

Correction Officer Aggravator   Almost a majority of capital punishment jurisdictions have recognized the dangerous work performed by penal correction officers and made the killing of a correction officer a statutory aggravating circumstance. Under the correction officer aggravator a convicted capital felon may be sentenced to death, if the penalty phase jury finds the victim of the offense was a correctional officer killed while performing his or her duties. *See also* **Aggravating Circumstances**

JURISDICTIONS USING CORRECTION OFFICER AGGRAVATOR

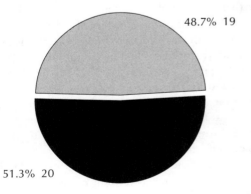

48.7% 19

51.3% 20

■ CORRECTION OFFICER AGGRAVATOR JURISDICTIONS

■ ALL OTHER JURISDICTIONS

Cost of Capital Punishment   Numerous studies have been conducted which have all concluded that prosecution of a capital felon is more expensive than any other type of criminal prosecution. In one study done of North Carolina it was found that it cost the State $2.16 million per execution above the costs of a non-death penalty murder case where the highest sentence was imprisonment for life. It was estimated that the death penalty costs California $90 million annually above the costs of all prosecutions. It was calculated that from 1973–1988, Florida spent an average of $3.2 million per execution to execute 18 prisoners. The figures for Texas indicated that it spent an average of $2.3 million per death penalty case, which was about three times the cost of imprisoning someone for 40 years. A study in Kansas indicated that a capital prosecution cost $116,700 more than a non-capital murder trial.

Numerous factors make the cost of prosecuting capital felons more expensive than any other type of criminal case. Additional costs have been traced to complex pretrial motions, lengthy jury selections, and expenses for expert witnesses. Holding separate guilt phase and penalty phase proceedings factor tremendously in the increased costs. Once a defendant is convicted and sentenced to death, costs continue to incur through years of legal battles in appellate courts.

Costa Rica Costa Rica abolished the death penalty in 1877. *See also* **International Capital Punishment Nations**

Côte D'Ivoire Capital punishment is on the law books in Côte d'Ivoire but has not been used in more than a decade. Côte d'Ivoire uses the firing squad to carry out the death penalty. Its legal system is based on French civil law and customary law. The nation's constitution was adopted on November 3, 1960.

The judicial system of Côte d'Ivoire consists of Supreme Court, Court of Appeals and trial courts. In rural areas of the country traditional institutions frequently administer justice at the village level, handling domestic and land disputes in accordance with customary law.

In criminal prosecutions defendants have the right to public trial, enjoy a presumption of innocence, and may appeal convictions. The law allows defendants to have legal representation, but only in capital cases may court appointed counsel be provided. *See also* **International Capital Punishment Nations**

Count The term "count" is used to designate a single charged offense in an indictment that contains several charged offenses. Principles of due process of law require setting out separately and distinctly each charge in an indictment, so as to give a defendant fair notice of each offense that was brought against him or her.

Court Appointed Counsel The United States Supreme Court recognized in *Powell v. Alabama*, 287 U.S. 45 (1932) the constitutional right to counsel in capital cases. (Thirty years later the right to counsel was extended to all criminal proceedings where incarceration was possible.) The constitutional right to counsel in capital cases means that, if a capital defendant cannot afford to retain counsel, the prosecuting ju-risdiction must appoint an attorney to represent the defendant.

It is unquestioned that capital prosecutions present the most difficult criminal cases to defend. Capital prosecutions are more complex than any noncapital prosecution. As a result of the complexity of a capital prosecution, it is imperative that experienced counsel represent a capital felon and that adequate financial resources be made available for the defense. All studies that have evaluated capital prosecutions concluded that inexperienced counsel and inadequate financial resources were the norm. This situation exists because the overwhelming majority of capital defendants are poor and must obtain court appointed counsel.

Examples of inexperienced legal counsel for capital defendants include the following. The attorney appointed for Larry Heath by Alabama filed a six page brief in the appeal before the Alabama Court of Criminal Appeal, and a one page brief in the appeal to the Alabama Supreme Court. The attorney also failed to show up for oral argument at the Alabama Supreme Court. Heath was eventually executed on March 20, 1992. During the Texas capital trial of Jesus Romero, his court appointed attorney did not call any witnesses at the penalty phase of the trial. Romero was executed on May 20, 1992. In the case of John Young, who was executed by Georgia on March 10, 1985, it was learned that his court appointed counsel was on illegal drugs during his trial (the attorney was subsequently disbarred).

In a study done of Mississippi court appointed attorneys, it was found that 83 percent of the attorneys appointed in capital cases indicated they would refuse any subsequent appointment because of inadequate financial resources. It is generally recognized that a properly conducted capital trial should take a month or more to complete. A random sampling of capital trials in Louisiana for the period 1978–1987 revealed the average length of a trial was three days. Another study of Louisiana revealed that in 85 percent of the capital trials held between 1976–1994, defense counsel failed to present the type of mitigating evidence during the penalty phase that is essential for obtaining a life sentence.

Studies have shown that one of the primary factors that determine whether a capital defendant will receive the death penalty is the nature of the legal representation, i.e., court appointed counsel or retained counsel. A defendant convicted of a capital offense will, more likely than not, receive a death sentence if he or she is represented by court appointed counsel. On the other hand, studies have shown that a defendant convicted of a capital offense, but was represented by retained counsel, will more likely than not receive a life sentence. In a Georgia study it was shown that the odds of a capital defendant with court appointed counsel receiving the death were 2.6 times higher than a capital defendant with retained counsel.

A few capital punishment jurisdictions have begun to address the problem of inexperienced counsel and inadequate financial resources. Statutes and court rules have been promulgated in a few capital punishment jurisdictions that require legal counsel have a minimum number of years experience, and make available greater financial resources. The material below involving Montana and Arizona provides examples of how some jurisdictions have responded to the problem.

Montana Supreme Court Proposed Standards for Competency of Counsel for Indigent Persons in Death Penalty Cases:

I. Trial Phase

1. a. In any case in which death is a potential punishment, the prosecutor shall file with this Court, within 60 days after arraignment, a statement indicating whether the prosecutor believes that sufficient evidence exists to establish by the appropriate standard of proof one or more of the statutory aggravating factors necessary to impose the death penalty under Montana law, and whether the prosecutor intends to seek the death penalty upon a conviction in the case.

   b. The prosecutor shall not identify in the notice the aggravating factor or factors believed to be present or the evidence on which the prosecutor will rely to prove an aggravating factor, but upon request by the defense the prosecutor shall identify to defense counsel the aggravating factor(s) the prosecutor believes are present and the evidence supporting the existence of the aggravating factor(s).

   c. The prosecutor may withdraw the notice provided in this standard at any time.

   d. If the prosecutor does not indicate a belief that the death penalty may be appropriate in a notice filed within 60 days after arraignment as provided by this standard, but later acquires evidence that, together with any other evidence, leads the prosecutor to conclude that sufficient evidence exists to establish, to the appropriate standard of proof, one or more of the statutory aggravating factors necessary to impose the death penalty upon a conviction in the case, the prosecutor may file the notice provided in this section, only with leave of court, after consideration of the cause for the delay and any prejudice to the defendant.

2. Upon establishment of indigency as provided [by law], and identification of a case as one in which the prosecutor believes sufficient evidence exists to show that one or more statutory aggravating factors, can be proved to the appropriate standard of proof, the Court shall appoint two counsel to represent the defendant.

3. In selecting appointed counsel, the Court shall secure sufficient information from counsel to be appointed, either in writing or on the record, to satisfy the Court that counsel possess the following minimum qualifications:

   a. Both appointed attorneys must be members in good standing of the State Bar of Montana or admitted to practice before the court pro hac vice.

   b. Both counsel must have completed or taught, in the two-year period prior to appointment or within 90 days after the appointment, a continuing legal education course or courses, approved for credit by the appropriate authority under the rules adopted by the Montana Supreme Court, at least 12 hours of which deal with subjects related to the defense of persons accused or convicted of capital crimes.

   c. Counsel, either individually or in combination, must have had significant experience within the past 5 years in the trial of criminal cases to conclusion, including a capital case or a case involving charges of or equivalent to deliberate homicide under Montana law.

   d. The nature and volume of the workload of both appointed counsel is such that they will have the ability to spend the time necessary to defend a capital case.

   e. Counsel are familiar with and have a copy of the current American Bar Association standards for the defense of capital cases. By adoption of this provision, the Court does not hold that adherence to the guidelines is required as a condition of providing effective assistance of counsel, or that failure to adhere to the guidelines gives rise to an inference of ineffective assistance of counsel.

II. Appeal Phase

1. If a defendant is sentenced to death and is determined by the Court to be indigent, the Court shall appoint two attorneys to represent the defendant on direct appeal.

2. In selecting appointed counsel for appeal, the Court shall secure sufficient information from counsel to be appointed, either in writing or on the record, to satisfy the Court that counsel possess sufficient appellate experience to provide adequate representation to the defendant on appeal and the following minimum qualifications:

   a. Both appointed attorneys must be members in good standing of the State Bar of Montana or admitted to practice before the court pro hac vice.

   b. Both counsel must have completed or taught, in the two-year period prior to appointment or within 90 days after the appointment, a continuing legal education course or courses, approved for credit by the appropriate authority under the rules adopted by the Montana Supreme Court, at least 12 hours of which deal with subjects related to the defense of persons accused or convicted of capital crimes.

   c. Counsel, either individually or in combination, must have had significant experience within the past 5 years in the appeal of criminal cases, including a capital case or a case involving charges of or equivalent to deliberate homicide under Montana law.

   d. The nature and volume of the workload of both appointed counsel is such that they will have the ability to spend the time necessary to appeal a capital case.

   e. Counsel are familiar with and have a copy of the current American Bar Association standards for the defense of capital cases. By adoption of this provision, the Court does not hold that adherence to the guidelines is required as a condition of providing effective assistance of counsel, or that failure to adhere to the guidelines gives rise to an inference of ineffective assistance of counsel.

III. Post Conviction Phase. The following standards shall apply to counsel appointed by the district court to represent indigent petitioners in postconviction proceedings, who are sentenced to death.

1. The court shall follow the procedure [for] appointing counsel in state postconviction cases.

2. The district court shall appoint two counsel. One of the appointed counsel may be an attorney who has been admitted pro hac vice. Lead counsel shall satisfy all of the following:

   a. He or she must be an active member in good standing of the Montana State Bar or be admitted pro hac vice.

   b. He or she must have at least 5 years criminal trial, criminal appellate, or state or federal postconviction experience, which experience may have been obtained in Montana or in another jurisdiction.

   c. He or she must have completed or taught, in the two-year period prior to appointment or within 90 days after the appointment, a continuing legal education course or courses, approved for credit by the appropriate authority under the rules adopted by the Montana Supreme Court, at least 12 hours of which deal with subjects related to the defense of persons accused or convicted of capital crimes.

3. In addition, the appointed counsel, either individually or in combination, shall have the following qualifications obtained in Montana or another jurisdiction:

   a. Experience as counsel for either the defendant or the state in the trial of one deliberate homicide case;

   b. Experience as counsel for either the defendant or the state in the trial of three felony cases;

   c. Experience as counsel for either the defendant or the state in the direct appeal of three felony convictions; and

   d. Experience as counsel for either the petitioner or the state in three cases involving claims for state postconviction or federal habeas corpus review.

4. As used in this Order, "trial" means a case concluded with a judgment of acquittal under [law], or submission to the trial court or jury for decision and verdict.

IV. Effect of Failure to Adhere to Standards. No error or omission in the procedure outlined in the trial or appellate standards shall constitute a ground for relief from a conviction or sentence unless the defendant shows that the standards were not followed in a material way and that counsel's performance fell so far below the standard of reasonably effective counsel, and was sufficiently prejudicial to the defense of the defendant, as to constitute a denial of effective assistance of counsel as guaranteed by the Sixth and Fourteenth Amendments to the United States Constitution or Article II, Section 24 of the Montana Constitution.

Any failure to adhere to the standards for appointment of postconviction counsel may not serve as a basis for a claim for postconviction relief.

Arizona Code § 13-4041 Fee of Counsel:

A. Except pursuant to subsection G of this section, if counsel is appointed by the court to represent the defendant in either a criminal proceeding or insanity hearing on appeal, the county in which the court from which the appeal is taken presides shall pay counsel, except that in those appeals where the defendant is represented by a public defender or other publicly funded office, compensation shall not be set or paid. Compensation for services rendered on appeal shall be in an amount as the supreme court in its discretion deems reasonable, considering the services performed.

B. After the supreme court has affirmed a defendant's conviction and sentence in a capital case, the supreme court, or if authorized by the supreme court, the presiding judge of the county from which the case originated shall appoint counsel to represent the capital defendant in the state post-conviction relief proceeding. Counsel shall meet the following qualifications:

   1. Membership in good standing of the state bar of Arizona for at least five years immediately preceding the appointment.

   2. Practice in the area of state criminal appeals or post-conviction proceedings for at least three years immediately preceding the appointment.

   3. No previous representation of the capital defendant in the case either in the trial court or in the direct appeal, unless the defendant and counsel expressly request continued representation and waive all potential issues that are foreclosed by continued representation.

C. The supreme court shall establish and maintain a list of qualified candidates. In addition to the qualifications prescribed in subsection B of this section, the supreme court may establish by rule more stringent standards of competency for the appointment of post-conviction counsel in capital cases. The supreme court may refuse to certify an attorney on the list who meets the qualifications established under subsection B of this section or may remove an attorney from the list who meets the qualifications established under subsection B of this section if the supreme court determines that the attorney is incapable or unable to adequately represent a capital defendant. The court shall appoint counsel pursuant to subsection B of this section from the list.

D. Notwithstanding subsection C of this section, the court may appoint counsel pursuant to subsection B of this section from outside the list of qualified candidates if either:

   1. No counsel meets the qualifications under subsections B and C of this section.

   2. No qualified counsel is available to serve.

E. Before filing a petition, the capital defendant may personally appear before the trial court and waive counsel. If the trial court finds that the waiver is knowing and voluntary, appointed counsel may withdraw. The time limits in which to file a petition shall not be extended due solely to the change from appointed counsel to self-representation.

F. If at any time the trial court determines that the capital defendant is not indigent, appointed counsel shall no longer be compensated by public monies and may withdraw.

G. Unless counsel is employed by a publicly funded office, counsel appointed to represent a capital defendant in state post-conviction relief proceedings shall be paid an hourly rate of not to exceed one hundred dollars per hour for up to two hundred hours of work, whether or not a petition is filed. Monies shall not be paid to court appointed counsel unless either:

1. A petition is timely filed.

2. If a petition is not filed, a notice is timely filed stating that counsel has reviewed the record and found no meritorious claim.

H. On a showing of good cause, the trial court shall compensate appointed counsel from county funds in addition to the amount of compensation prescribed by subsection G of this section by paying an hourly rate in an amount that does not exceed one hundred dollars per hour. The attorney may establish good cause for additional fees by demonstrating that the attorney spent over two hundred hours representing the defendant in the proceedings. The court shall review and approve additional reasonable fees and costs. If the attorney believes that the court has set an unreasonably low hourly rate or if the court finds that the hours the attorney spent over the two hundred hour threshold are unreasonable, the attorney may file a special action with the Arizona supreme court.

I. The county shall request reimbursement for fees it incurs pursuant to subsections G, H and J of this section arising out of the appointment of counsel to represent an indigent capital defendant in a state post-conviction relief proceeding. The state shall pay fifty per cent of the fees incurred by the county out of monies appropriated to the supreme court for these purposes. The supreme court shall approve county requests for reimbursement after certification that the amount requested is owed.

J. The trial court may authorize additional monies to pay for investigative and expert services that are reasonably necessary to adequately litigate those claims that are not precluded by [law]. *See also* **Right to Counsel**

Court of Appeals *see* **Appellate Review of Conviction and Death Sentence**

Courts of General Jurisdiction *see* **Jurisdiction**

Courts of Limited Jurisdiction *see* **Jurisdiction**

Craemer v. Washington *Court:* United States Supreme

Court; *Case Citation:* Craemer v. Washington, 168 U.S. 124 (1897); *Argued:* Not reported; *Decided:* October 25, 1897; *Opinion of the Court:* Chief Justice Fuller; *Concurring Opinion:* None; *Dissenting Opinion:* None; *Appellate Defense Counsel:* Jas. Hamilton Lewis argued and briefed; *Appellate Prosecution Counsel:* W. C. Jones argued and briefed; *Amicus Curiae Brief Supporting Prosecutor:* None; *Amicus Curiae Brief Supporting Defendant:* None.

Issue Presented: Whether the defendant was convicted of a crime other than capital murder when the jury returned a general verdict of guilty as charged?

Case Holding: The defendant was not convicted of a crime other than capital murder when the jury returned a general verdict of guilty as charged, because the defendant was only charged with capital murder.

Factual and procedural background of case: The defendant, Henry Craemer, was convicted of capital murder and sentenced to death by the State of Washington. The Washington Supreme Court affirmed the judgment, and the United States Supreme Court refused to hear an appeal. Subsequently, the defendant filed a petition for habeas corpus relief in a Federal District Court. In the petition, the defendant alleged that the jury convicted him of second degree murder or manslaughter, but not capital murder, therefore he could not be executed for a noncapital conviction. The District Court dismissed the petition and denied relief. The United States Supreme Court granted certiorari to consider the issue.

Opinion of the Court by Chief Justice Fuller: The Chief Justice found that the defendant was not entitled to habeas relief. It was said that the jury returned a general verdict of "guilty as charged." The opinion noted that the defendant was "charged" by an information with capital (first degree) murder. The Chief Justice indicated that no charge of second degree murder or manslaughter was lodged against the defendant, therefore it was clear that the jury found him guilty of capital murder. Therefore, it was concluded "that the rendition of the judgment complained of involved no violation of the constitution of the United States." The judgment of the Washington Supreme Court was affirmed.

Criminal Justice Legal Foundation The Criminal Justice Legal Foundation is a California based victim oriented nonprofit organization, created for the purpose of seeking to assure that convicted criminal defendants swiftly receive the punishment they have been given. The Foundation utilizes attorneys to introduce legal arguments in criminal cases before appellate courts to encourage precedent-setting decisions which recognize the rights of victims to justice. The Foundation has obtained some success in judicial decisions that paved the way for reducing the length and complexity of appeals.

The Foundation takes the position that violent crime is the result of a deterioration in basic social values. It also believes that the criminal justice system has transformed from an institution that encouraged lawful behavior to one that now permits flagrant violations of the law. A central theme of the

Foundation is to restore law enforcement's ability to assure that crime does not pay. The Foundation produces a quarterly newsletter, Advisory, to report on its activities.

Criminal Justice System *see* Adversarial Criminal Justice System

Criminal Record *see* Future Dangerousness Mitigator; Prior Felony or Homicide Aggravator

Croatia Croatia abolished the death penalty in 1990. *See also* International Capital Punishment Nations

Crooker v. California

Court: United States Supreme Court; *Case Citation:* Crooker v. California, 357 U.S. 433 (1958); *Argued:* April 2, 1958; *Decided:* June 30, 1958; *Opinion of the Court:* Justice Clark; *Concurring Opinion:* None; *Dissenting Opinion:* Justice Douglas, in which Warren, C.J., and Black and Brennan, JJ., joined; *Appellate Defense Counsel:* Robert W. Armstrong argued and briefed; *Appellate Prosecution Counsel:* William E. James argued; Edmund G. Brown, William B. McKesson and Fred N. Whichello on brief; *Amicus Curiae Brief Supporting Prosecutor:* None; *Amicus Curiae Brief Supporting Defendant:* 1.

Issue Presented: Whether the defendant was denied due process of law as a result of his confession being given after he requested counsel?

Case Holding: The defendant was not denied due process of law as a result of his confession being given after he requested counsel, because under the totality of the circumstances he was not prejudiced.

Factual and procedural background of case: The defendant, Crooker, was convicted of capital murder and sentenced to death by the State of California. The California Supreme Court affirmed the judgment. In doing so, the appellate court rejected the defendant's argument that he was denied due process of law because his confession was involuntary and made after he had requested counsel. The United States Supreme Court granted certiorari to consider the issue.

Opinion of the Court by Justice Clark: Justice Clark held that the defendant's confession was not involuntary. The opinion pointed out that the defendant was a former law student and understood his right to remain silent. Justice Clark found that no coercion, intimidation or physical assault was used to obtain the confession. It was also said that the fact that the confession was given after the defendant requested counsel, did not invalidate the confession. Justice Clark indicated that the totality of the circumstances did not reveal any prejudice because the confession was obtained after counsel was requested. The judgment of the California Supreme Court was affirmed.

Dissenting opinion by Justice Douglas, in which Warren, C.J., and Black and Brennan, JJ., joined: Justice Douglas dissented from the Court's decision. He believed the Consti-

tution required the confession be held inadmissible because it was given after the defendant requested counsel. Justice Douglas wrote as follows: When [the defendant] was first arrested, and before any real interrogation took place, he asked that his attorney be present.... This demand for an attorney was made over and again prior to the time a confession was extracted from the accused. Its denial was in my view a denial of that due process of law guaranteed the citizen by the Fourteenth Amendment."

Case note: The position taken by the dissent would eventually be adopted by the Supreme Court. *See also* **Right to Counsel; Right to Remain Silent**

Cross Examination of Witness *see* Examination of Witness

Cross v. Burke

Court: United States Supreme Court; *Case Citation:* Cross v. Burke, 146 U.S. 82 (1892); *Argued:* Not reported; *Decided:* November 14, 1892; *Opinion of the Court:* Chief Justice Fuller; *Concurring Opinion:* None; *Dissenting Opinion:* None; *Appellate Defense Counsel:* C. Maurice Smith argued; Joseph Shillington on brief; *Appellate Prosecution Counsel:* Mr. Aldrich argued and briefed; *Amicus Curiae Brief Supporting Prosecutor:* None; *Amicus Curiae Brief Supporting Defendant:* None.

Issue Presented: Whether the United States Supreme Court had jurisdiction to hear an appeal from a habeas corpus proceeding in the courts of the District of Columbia?

Case Holding: The United States Supreme Court did not have jurisdiction to hear an appeal from a habeas corpus proceeding in the courts of the District of Columbia, because Congress did not grant such authority.

Factual and procedural background of case: The defendant, William D. Cross, was convicted of capital murder and sentenced to death by the District of Columbia. The Court of Appeals of the District of Columbia affirmed the judgment. The defendant filed a petition for appeal with the United States Supreme Court, challenging his conviction and sentence. The government filed a motion to dismiss the petition on the grounds that the Supreme Court did not have appellate jurisdiction over the case. The Supreme Court agreed and dismissed the petition for appeal in *Cross v. United States.*

The defendant next filed a habeas corpus petition in a trial court for the District of Columbia, which was dismissed. The appellate court of the District of Columbia affirmed. The United States Supreme Court granted an appeal. The government filed a motion to dismiss the petition on the grounds that the Supreme Court did not have appellate jurisdiction over the case.

Opinion of the Court by Chief Justice Fuller: The Chief Justice noted that the Court had previously ruled that Congress had limited its jurisdiction to hear a direct criminal appeal from a court in the District of Columbia. The motion to dismiss filed by the government asked the Court to determine if it had "jurisdiction over the judgments of that court on habeas corpus?" In examining the applicable statute, the Chief Justice found that Congress did not give it authority to entertain a habeas appeal directly from a court in the District of Columbia. The appeal was therefor dismissed. *See also* **Cross v. United States; In Re Cross; Jurisdiction**

Cross v. United States

Court: United States Supreme Court; *Case Citation:* Cross v. United States, 145 U.S. 571 (1892); *Argued:* Not reported; *Decided:* May 16, 1892; *Opinion of the Court:* Chief Justice Fuller; *Concurring Opinion:* None; *Dissenting Opinion:* None; *Appellate Defense Counsel:* C. Maurice Smith argued; Joseph Shillington on brief; *Appellate Prosecution Counsel:* Mr. Aldrich argued and briefed; *Amicus Curiae Brief Supporting Prosecutor:* None; *Amicus Curiae Brief Supporting Defendant:* None.

Issue Presented: Whether the United States Supreme Court had jurisdiction to review a criminal case prosecuted in a trial court of the District of Columbia and initially reviewed by the appellate court of the District of Columbia?

Case Holding: The United States Supreme Court did not have jurisdiction to review a criminal case prosecuted in a trial court of the District of Columbia and initially reviewed by the appellate court of the District of Columbia, because Congress limited review to the appellate court of the District of Columbia or the United States Supreme Court, but not both.

Factual and procedural background of case: The defendant, William D. Cross, was convicted of capital murder and sentenced to death by the District of Columbia. The Court of Appeals of the District of Columbia affirmed the judgment. The defendant filed a petition for appeal with the United States Supreme Court, challenging his conviction and sentence. The government filed a motion to dismiss the petition on the grounds that the Court did not have appellate jurisdiction over the case.

Opinion of the Court by Chief Justice Fuller: The Chief Justice ruled that the Court was not given appellate jurisdiction over criminal cases that were reviewed by the appellate court for the District of Columbia. The opinion found that by statute a prosecution in a trial court of the District of Columbia could be reviewed by the Court or the appellate court of the District of Columbia, but not both. Chief Justice Fuller wrote: "The obvious object was to secure a review by some other court than that which passed upon the case at [the trial level]. Such review by two other courts was not within the intention [of the statute]." The petition for appeal was thereby dismissed. *See also* **Cross v. Burke; In Re Cross; Jurisdiction**

Crossley v. California

Court: United States Supreme Court; *Case Citation:* Crossley v. California, 168 U.S. 640 (1898); *Argued:* Not reported; *Decided:* January 3, 1898; *Opinion of the Court:* Chief Justice Fuller; *Concurring Opinion:* None; *Dissenting Opinion:* None; *Appellate Defense Counsel:* Not represented; *Appellate Prosecution Counsel:* W. F. Fitzgerald argued; W. H. Anderson on brief; *Amicus Curiae Brief Supporting Prosecutor:* None; *Amicus Curiae Brief Supporting Defendant:* None.

Issue Presented: Whether the State of California had jurisdiction to prosecute the defendant for a murder committed during the transportation of United States mail?

Case Holding: The State of California had jurisdiction to prosecute the defendant for a murder committed during the transportation of United States mail, because the crime occurred within the borders of the State.

Factual and procedural background of case: The defendant, Worden Crossley, was convicted of capital murder and sentenced to death by the State of California. The California Supreme Court affirmed the judgment. The defendant next filed a habeas corpus petition with a Federal District Court. In the petition the defendant alleged that California did not have jurisdiction to prosecute the offense, because the crime was a Federal offense. It was said that the victim, a train engineer, was killed when the defendant derailed a train exclusively engaged in the carrying or transportation of the mail of the United States. The defendant asserted that such conduct constituted an obstruction or stopping of the transmission of United States mail, and was a restraint and retarding of the interstate commerce of the United States. The District Court denied relief and dismissed the petition. The United States Supreme Court granted certiorari to consider the issue.

Opinion of the Court by Chief Justice Fuller: The Chief Justice ruled that the defendant's argument was without merit. It was said that California had a right to prosecute the defendant for a murder committed within the jurisdiction of the State. The opinion pointed out: "[I]t is settled law that the same act may constitute an offense against the United States and against a state, subjecting the guilty party to punishment under the laws of each government, and may embrace two or more offenses. There is no statute of the United States under which [the defendant] could, on the alleged facts, have been prosecuted for murder in the courts of the United States. He was convicted of that crime in the administration of the laws of California; and the conviction has been sustained by the highest court of the state." The judgment of the Federal District Court was affirmed. *See also* **Dual Sovereignty**

Cruel and Unusual Punishment Clause

Under the common law capital punishment was carried out in a variety of agonizing and painful ways. The cruelty of death under the common law was adopted by the American Colonists. However, with the ratification of the Eighth Amendment to the Federal Constitution, the death knell was sounded for the common law's barbaric methods of execution. The Eighth Amendment provides: "nor cruel and unusual punishments inflicted."

Origin of the Eighth Amendment. The Eighth Amendment became a part of the Constitution in 1791. The history of this amendment, however, does not begin with its insertion into the Federal Constitution. The birth of the Eighth Amendment reaches back to the shores of England and the English Bill of Rights of 1689.

The tenth clause of the English Bill of Rights provided the following: "nor cruel and unusual punishments inflicted." It was pointed out by Supreme Court Justice Thurgood Marshall that scholars are in debate over "[w]hether, the English Bill of Rights prohibition against cruel and unusual punishments is properly read as a response to excessive or illegal punishments, as a reaction to barbaric and objectionable modes of punishment, or both[.]" While there is no unanimous agreement as to why the English Rill of Rights included a clause prohibiting cruel and unusual punishments, there is no dissent to the fact that the Eighth Amendment owes its existence to the English Bill of Rights.

The Eighth Amendment did not leap directly from the English Bill of Rights into the Constitution. The precise language used in the Eighth Amendment first appeared in America on June 12, 1776, in Virginia's Declaration of Rights. A Virginia delegate named George Mason was responsible for taking the tenth clause of the English Bill of Rights and placing it into Virginia's Declaration of Rights. Delegate Mason was also a strong advocate, at the Constitutional Convention, for placing the tenth clause into the Federal Constitution as the Eighth Amendment. Delegate Mason's foresight eventually paid off and in 1791 the tenth clause, with slight modifications, became the constitution's Eighth Amendment.

Interpreting the Cruel and Unusual Punishment Clause. In the case of *Trop v. Dulles*, 356 U.S. 86 (1958), the Supreme Court expounded upon the framework in which it viewed the Cruel and Unusual Punishment Clause. In succinct fashion the Supreme Court stated in *Trop* that: "The basic concept underlying the [Clause] is nothing less than the dignity of man. While the State has the power to punish, the [Clause] stands to assure that this power be exercised within the limits of civilized standards. Fines, imprisonment and even execution may be imposed depending upon the enormity of the crime, but any technique outside the bounds of these traditional penalties is constitutionally suspect."

While *Trop* set out the general framework in which the Supreme Court views the Cruel and Unusual Punishment Clause, it was Justice William Brennan's concurring opinion in *Furman v. Georgia*, 408 U.S. 238 (1972), that first pulled together the principles of law the Supreme Court historically relied upon to decide whether or not a particular punishment was cruel and unusual. Justice Brennan found the following principles of law guided the Supreme Court's interpretation of the Cruel and Unusual Punishment Clause: (1) the punishment must not be so severe as to be degrading to the dignity of human beings; (2) a government cannot arbitrarily inflict a severe punishment; (3) a severe punishment must not be unacceptable to contemporary society; and (4) a severe punishment must not be excessive. *See also* **Bill of Rights; Excessive Bail Clause**

Crumpton v. United States
Court: United States Supreme Court; *Case Citation:* Crumpton v. United States, 138 U.S. 361 (1891); *Argued:* January 16, 1891; *Decided:* February 2, 1891; *Opinion of the Court:* Justice Brown; *Concurring Opinion:* None; *Dissenting Opinion:* None; *Appellate Defense Counsel:* A. H. Garland argued and briefed; *Appellate Prosecution Counsel:* United States Solicitor General argued and briefed; *Amicus Curiae Brief Supporting Prosecutor:* None; *Amicus Curiae Brief Supporting Defendant:* None.

Issues Presented: (1) Whether the evidence was sufficient to sustain the defendant's conviction? (2) Whether the prosecutor made prejudicial remarks to the jury during closing argument? (3) Whether the trial court was obligated to delay the trial so that the defendant could subpoena certain witnesses?

Case Holdings: (1) The evidence was sufficient to sustain the defendant's conviction, and to the extent the evidence was conflicting, it was for the jury to resolve such conflict. (2) The prosecutor did not make prejudicial remarks to the jury during closing argument, and to the extent remarks were improper, defense counsel failed to properly preserve the issue for review by interposing an objection. (3) The trial court was not obligated to delay the trial so that the defendant could subpoena certain witnesses, when the defendant waited until the last day of trial to seek to subpoena the witnesses.

Factual and procedural background of case: The defendant, Crumpton, was charged by the United States with committing capital murder "at the Cherokee Nation, in [Native American] country." The defendant was tried in a Federal District Court in Arkansas. A jury convicted the defendant and he was sentenced to death. The defendant appealed to the United States Supreme Court alleging (1) the evidence was insufficient to sustain the conviction; (2) defense counsel failed to object to improper remarks by the prosecutor; and (3) the trial court committed error in not delaying the trial so that the defendant could subpoena certain witnesses.

Opinion of the Court by Justice Brown: Justice Brown ruled none of the defendant's assignments of error had merit. The opinion found that the evidence was sufficient to establish that the defendant committed the crime, though such evidence was circumstantial. It was said that "[t]he weight of this evidence and the extent to which it was contradicted or explained away by witnesses on behalf of the defendant, were questions exclusively for the jury, and not reviewable [by the Court]."

The opinion observed that, while the prosecutor made a closing argument comment to the jury that was slightly inappropriate, defense counsel failed to properly object and preserve the issue for review. Justice Brown wrote: "There is no doubt that, in the excitement of an argument, counsel do sometimes make statements which are not fully justified by the evidence. This is not such an error, however, as will necessarily vitiate the verdict or require a new trial. It is the duty of the defendant's counsel at once to call the attention of the court to the objectionable remarks, and request its interposition, and, in case of refusal, to note an exception."

In dispensing with the defendant's third issue, Justice Brown found that the defendant waited until the last day of trial to ask the court to permit him to subpoena certain witnesses. The opinion noted: "It would probably have delayed the trial a number of days to send the [subpoena] into [Native American] Territory, make service of it there, and bring in these witnesses to testify. Whether the trial should be delayed for the production of these witnesses was clearly a matter of discretion and not reviewable[.]" The judgment of the District Court was affirmed.

Cuba The death penalty is allowed in Cuba. Cuba uses the firing squad as the method of carrying out the death penalty. It was known that in 1998, Cuba executed five prisoners. Its legal system is based on Spanish law and American law. The nation's constitution was adopted on February 24, 1976.

Cuba is a totalitarian state controlled by President Fidel Castro. President Castro exercises control over all aspects of Cuban life through the Communist Party. The judiciary is completely subordinate to the government and to the Communist Party. The nation's constitution explicitly subordinates the judiciary to the National Assembly of the People's Power and the Council of State, which is headed by President Castro.

The judicial system of Cuba consists of municipal courts, provincial courts, and a Supreme Court. Under the laws of Cuba criminal defendants do not have a right to trial by jury. Generally trials are public, but when state security is allegedly involved proceedings are not public. Defendants have a right to legal counsel. The laws recognize the right of appeal from municipal courts, but limits appeals in provincial courts to cases involving maximum prison terms or the death penalty. Appeals in death penalty cases are automatic. A death sentence must ultimately be affirmed by the Council of State. *See also* **International Capital Punishment Nations**

Curtis, Benjamin R. Benjamin R. Curtis served as an associate justice of the United States Supreme Court from 1851 to 1857. While on the Supreme Court Curtis was viewed as a liberal interpreter of the Constitution.

Curtis was born on November 4, 1809 in Watertown, Massachusetts. He received an undergraduate degree from Harvard College in 1829, and a law degree from Harvard Law School in 1832. Curtis entered private practice after law school. During his years of practice he became politically active with the Whig Party. In 1851 his political activities earned him a seat in the Massachusetts House of Representatives. A few months after his election to State office, President Millard Fillmore nominated Curtis to the Supreme Court.

Curtis is known to have written only one capital punishment opinion while on the Supreme Court. In *Ex Parte Wells* Curtis wrote a dissenting opinion. The issue in *Wells* was whether or not the President had authority to pardon the defendant's death sentence upon the condition that the defendant remain in prison for life. The majority on the Supreme Court held that the President had such authority. Curtis dissented from the Court's decision on a technical matter. He wrote that the trial court's ruling on the President's conditional pardon was not a collateral matter that the Court had authority to review. Curtis died on September 15, 1874.

Custodial Interrogation *see* **Right to Remain Silent**

Cyanide Gas *see* **Lethal Gas**

Cyprus Cyprus abolished the death penalty for ordinary crimes in 1983, but permits the punishment for premeditated murder, high treason, piracy, and certain capital offenses under military law. The method of execution used in Cyprus is hanging. Its legal system is based on English common law. The nation's constitution was adopted on August 16, 1960.

Politically the island nation of Cyprus is two countries. The island has been divided since Turkish military intervention in 1974, following a coup d'etat backed by Greece. The southern part of the island is under the control of the government of the Republic of Cyprus. The northern part is ruled by a Turkish Cypriot administration. The two parts are separated by a buffer zone patrolled by United Nations forces.

The judicial system in the Republic of Cyprus consists of district courts, assize courts, and a Supreme Court. The structure of the court system under the Turkish Cypriot administration is similar to that of the Republic of Cyprus, insofar as having district courts, assize courts, and a Supreme Court. In both parts of the island defendants have the right to be present at their trials, to be represented by retained or appointed counsel, to confront witnesses, to have a jury, to present evidence in their own defense, and to appeal. *See also* **International Capital Punishment Nations**

Czech Republic The death penalty was abolished in the Czech Republic in 1990. *See also* **International Capital Punishment Nations**

Czolgosz, Leon *see* **McKinley's Assassination**

D

Daily Routine of Death Row Inmates *see* **Death Row**

Dakota Executions

On December 26, 1862 the largest mass execution in the history of the nation occurred. On that date 38 Dakota Native Americans were hung in Mankato, Minnesota. At that time the Dakota people comprised seven distinct Native American ethic groups that were also called Sioux Native Americans.

The events which led to the mass execution involved matters pertaining to longstanding abuses of the Dakota people by unscrupulous Federal government agents and treaty violations by the United States. This situation left the Dakota people dying in poverty. On August 17, 1862 the desperate plight of the people turned to war against the Federal government. The first incident of war involved the killing of five settlers in Acton, Minnesota. From this incident an all out war was declared against the United States by the Dakota leaders. The war lasted less than a month, as the Dakota people did not have the resources to sustain a war against the nation.

Rather than treat the defeated Dakota people as belligerents of war, a military decision was made to prosecute them as pure criminals. A five member military commission was appointed to preside over the prosecution. Criminal charges of rape, robbery and murder were brought against 392 Dakota men. On September 28, 1862 the trials began. When the last trial was held on November 3, the commission had convicted 323 defendants. The commission sentenced 303 convicted defendants to death, while 20 were sentenced to imprisonment, and 69 were acquitted. None of the defendants had legal counsel.

President Abraham Lincoln was called upon to review the 303 death sentences. On December 6, the President issued a decision commuting the sentences of all but 39 defendants. On December 23, President Lincoln suspended the sentence of one of the 39 defendants.

A scaffold was erected by soldiers that would allow the 38 defendants to be executed simultaneously. On December 26, the 38 defendants were assembled on the scaffold. An order was given and the men swung from gallows as the crowd cheered.

Several years after the mass execution, two other Dakota men were prosecuted for crimes committed in 1862. A military commission convicted the two defendants in December of 1864. On November 11, 1865 the two defendants were hung at Fort Snelling. *See also* **Native Americans and Capital Punishment; Military Death Penalty Law**

In 1862, the United States Army convicted 323 Dakota (Sioux) Native Americans of crimes during a war with the nation. Thirty-eight defendants were hung at the largest mass execution in the history of the nation. (Minnesota Historical Society)

Darcy v. Handy

Court: United States Supreme Court; *Case Citation:* Darcy v. Handy, 351 U.S. 454 (1956); *Argued:* May 1–2, 1956; *Decided:* June 11, 1956; *Opinion of the Court:* Justice Burton; *Concurring Opinion:* None; *Dissenting Opinion:* Justice Harlan, in which Frankfurter and Douglas, JJ., joined; *Appellate Defense Counsel:* Charles J. Margiotti argued; Morton Witkin on brief; *Appellate Prosecution Counsel:* Frank P. Lawley, Jr. argued; Herbert B. Cohen and Donald W. Van Artsdalen on brief; *Amicus Curiae Brief Supporting Prosecutor:* None; *Amicus Curiae Brief Supporting Defendant:* None.

Issue Presented: Whether the defendant was tried under such prejudicial circumstances and improper influences that he was denied due process of law?

Case Holding: The defendant failed to produce evidence to establish that he was tried under such prejudicial circumstances and improper influences that he was denied due process of law.

Factual and procedural background of case: The defendant, Darcy, was convicted of capital murder and sentenced to death by the State of Pennsylvania. The Pennsylvania Supreme Court affirmed the conviction and sentence. The defendant filed a habeas corpus petition in a Federal District Court alleging pretrial publicity denied him a fair trial. The District Court dismissed the petition. A Federal Court of appeals affirmed. The United States Supreme Court granted certiorari to consider the issue.

Opinion of the Court by Justice Burton: Justice Burton held that the defendant was not denied a fair trial. It was said that the burden was on the defendant to show such essential unfairness as vitiates his trial, and the burden had to be sustained by more than speculation. The opinion found that the most that was shown by the defendant was that, in certain respects, opportunity for prejudice existed. The evidence failed to support the defendant's claim that the news coverage of the crime and of the proceedings prior to his trial created such an atmosphere of hysteria and prejudice as precluded a fair trial. The opinion concluded: "While this Court stands ready to correct violations of constitutional rights, it also holds that 'it is not asking too much that the burden of showing essential unfairness be sustained by him who claims such injustice and seeks to have the result set aside, and that it be sustained not as a matter of speculation but as a demonstrable reality.' 'If the mere opportunity for prejudice or corruption is to raise a presumption that they exist, it will be hard to maintain jury trial under the conditions of the present day.'" The judgment of the Court of Appeals was affirmed.

Dissenting opinion by Justice Harlan, in which Frankfurter and Douglas, JJ., joined: Justice Harlan dissented from the Court's decision. He believed the defendant was denied a fair trial because the judge who presided over the trials of the defendant's two co-defendants was present as a spectator. Justice Harlan noted that this judge had publicly proclaimed his satisfaction with the death sentences given to the defendant's co-defendants. The dissent also pointed out that the spectator judge was highly respected in the community and that his views had to have had an impact on the defendant's trial. *See also* **Pretrial Publicity**

Darden v. Wainwright   *Court:* United States Supreme Court; *Case Citation:* Darden v. Wainwright, 477 U.S. 168 (1986); *Argued:* January 13, 1986; *Decided:* June 23, 1986; *Opinion of the Court:* Justice Powell; *Concurring Opinion:* Chief Justice Burger; *Dissenting Opinion:* Justice Blackmun, in which Brennan, Marshall and Stevens, JJ., joined; *Dissenting Statement:* Justice Brennan; *Appellate Defense Counsel:* Robert Augustus Harper, Jr. argued and briefed; *Appellate Prosecution Counsel:* Richard W. Prospect argued; Jim Smith on brief; *Amicus Curiae Brief Supporting Prosecutor:* None; *Amicus Curiae Brief Supporting Defendant:* None.

Issues Presented: (1) Whether the exclusion for cause of a member of the venire panel violated the defendant's constitution rights? (2) Whether the prosecutor's closing argument during the guilt phase rendered the defendant's trial fundamentally unfair? (3) Whether the defendant was denied effective assistance of counsel at the penalty phase of his trial?

Case Holdings: (1) The exclusion for cause of a member of the venire panel did not violate the defendant's constitutional rights. (2) The prosecutor's closing argument during the guilt phase did not render the defendant's trial fundamentally unfair. (3) The defendant was not denied effective assistance of counsel at the penalty phase of his trial.

Factual and procedural background of case: The State of Florida convicted the defendant, Darden, of capital murder and sentenced him to death. The Florida Supreme Court affirmed the conviction and sentence. The defendant filed a petition for habeas corpus relief in a Federal District Court. The defendant asserted three primary arguments in federal court. First, that his constitutional rights were violated when the trial judge excluded for "cause," a potential juror who responded affirmatively to the trial judge's voir dire question,

"Do you have any moral or religious, conscientious moral or religious principles in opposition to the death penalty so strong that you would be unable without violating your own principles to vote to recommend a death penalty regardless of the facts?" Second, the defendant contended that the prosecutor's closing argument during the guilt phase of the trial rendered the trial fundamentally unfair and deprived the sentencing determination of the reliability required by the Eighth Amendment. Third, the defendant contended that he received ineffective assistance of counsel at the penalty phase, because his attorney was not prepared to adequately represent him at that stage of the prosecution.

The District Court denied relief. A Court of Appeals reversed on the claim of improper exclusion of a member of the venire. The United States Supreme Court, in a memorandum order, vacated the Court of Appeals' judgment, and remanded for reconsideration in light of its decision in *Wainwright v. Witt.* On remand, the Court of Appeals denied relief to the defendant. The United States Supreme Court granted certiorari to consider the merits of the issues in the case.

Opinion of the Court by Justice Powell: Justice Powell first addressed the defendant's issue involving the excluded potential juror. He stated that the record of the jury voir dire, viewed in its entirety, revealed that the trial court's decision to exclude the juror for cause was proper. It was said that the juror's response to the trial judge's question established that the juror's views on capital punishment would prevent or substantially impair the performance of his duties as a juror in accordance with his instructions and his oath.

The opinion indicated that the record also supported the rejection of the defendant's contention as to the prosecutor's closing argument. Justice Powell wrote that the prosecutor's closing argument included improper remarks that indicated that the defendant was on a weekend furlough from an earlier prison sentence when the capital murder occurred; implying that the death penalty would be the only guarantee against a future similar act. The prosecutor also referred to the defendant as an animal. Justice Powell ruled that the relevant question is whether the comments so infected the trial with unfairness as to make the resulting conviction a denial of due process. Viewed under this standard, he wrote, the prosecutor's comments did not deprive the defendant of a fair trial. The comments did not manipulate or misstate the evidence, or implicate other specific rights of the defendant.

With respect to the defendant's claim of ineffective assistance of counsel at the penalty phase of the trial, Justice Powell found that he failed to satisfy the first part of the two-part test for determining ineffective representation: that his trial counsels' performance fell below an objective standard of reasonableness. It was said that there was no merit to the defendant's contention that defense counsel devoted only the time between the close of the guilt phase of trial and the start of the penalty phase — approximately one-half hour — to prepare the case in mitigation. Justice Powell found that the record indicated that a great deal of time and effort went into the defense of the case; with a significant portion of that time being devoted to preparation for the penalty phase. The judgment of the Court of Appeals was affirmed.

Concurring opinion by Chief Justice Burger: In his concurring opinion, the Chief Justice was concerned with what he perceived to be mischaracterizations of the case in Justice Blackmun's dissenting opinion. The Chief Justice wrote:

> I concur fully in the opinion for the Court and write separately only to address the suggestion in Justice Blackmun's dissent that the Court rejects Darden's ... claim because of its "impatience with the progress of Darden's constitutional challenges to his conviction." ...
>
> The dissent's suggestion that this Court is motivated by impatience with Darden's constitutional claims is refuted by the record; the 13 years of judicial proceedings in this case manifest substantial care and patience. Our rejection of Darden's claims in this the fourth time he has sought review in this Court is once again based on a thoughtful application of the law to the facts of the case. At some point there must be finality.

Dissenting opinion by Justice Blackmun, in which Brennan, Marshall and Stevens, JJ., joined: Justice Blackmun argued in his dissenting opinion that the Court incorrectly resolved the issue of the prosecutor's remarks and the exclusion of a juror for cause. He wrote as follows:

> Although the Constitution guarantees a criminal defendant only "a fair trial [and] not a perfect one," this Court has stressed repeatedly in the decade since *Gregg v. Georgia*, that the Eighth Amendment requires a heightened degree of reliability in any case where a State seeks to take the defendant's life. Today's opinion, however, reveals a Court willing to tolerate not only imperfection but a level of fairness and reliability so low it should make conscientious prosecutors cringe.
>
> The Court's discussion of Darden's claim of prosecutorial misconduct is noteworthy for its omissions. Despite the fact that earlier this Term the Court relied heavily on standards governing the professional responsibility of defense counsel in ruling that an attorney's actions did not deprive his client of any constitutional right, today it entirely ignores standards governing the professional responsibility of prosecutors in reaching the conclusion that the summations of Darden's prosecutor[] did not deprive him of a fair trial....
>
> ...I simply do not believe the evidence in this case was so overwhelming that this Court can conclude, on the basis of the written record before it, that the jury's verdict was not the product of the prosecutor[']s misconduct. The three most damaging pieces of evidence — the identifications of Darden by [two witnesses] and the ballistics evidence — are all sufficiently problematic that they leave me unconvinced that a jury not exposed to [the prosecutor's] egregious summation would necessarily have convicted Darden....
>
> Even if Darden had been convicted fairly, however, I believe his death sentence should be vacated because of the improper exclusion for cause of a member of the venire who was qualified to serve....
>
> Prior to the voir dire of individual venire members, the trial judge announced his intention to excuse, not only any potential juror whose religious or moral principles made him unable to impose the death penalty, but also any potential juror who, if he did follow the court's instructions, "would be going against his principles" This standard is essentially indistinguishable from the standard employed by Illinois and expressly disapproved by this Court[.]
>
> I believe this Court must do more than wring its hands when a State uses improper legal standards to select juries in capital cases and permits prosecutors to pervert the adversary process. I therefore dissent.

Dissenting statement by Justice Brennan: Justice Brennan issued a dissenting statement indicating that he joined Justice Blackmun's dissent, and adhered to his position "that the death penalty is in all circumstances cruel and unusual punishment prohibited by the Eighth and Fourteenth Amendments[.]" *See also* **Jury Selection; Right to Counsel**

Davis, David

David Davis served as an associate justice of the United States Supreme Court from 1862 to 1877. While on the Supreme Court Davis was known as a moderate in his interpretation of the Constitution.

Davis was born on March 9, 1815, in Sassafras Neck, Maryland. At age 13 Davis enrolled in Kenyon College and went on to graduate. He subsequently took legal courses at New Haven Law School. Davis eventually moved to Illinois where he passed the bar in 1835 and began a legal practice. During the ensuing years he was elected to the Illinois House of Representatives and as a trial court judge. Davis was active as a campaign manager for Abraham Lincoln. After Lincoln's election to the Presidency he appointed Davis to the Supreme Court in 1862.

Davis is known to have written only one capital punishment opinion while on the Supreme Court. In the case of *Ex Parte Milligan*, Davis wrote the opinion for the Court. The two issues facing the Court in *Milligan* concerned whether the President had authority to suspend habeas corpus and whether the military had jurisdiction to prosecute the defendant, who was a civilian. Davis wrote that the President did not have authority to suspend habeas corpus. He also held that the military was without authority to prosecute the defendant for capital crimes because he was not in the military. Davis died on June 26, 1886.

Davis v. Burke

Court: United States Supreme Court; *Case Citation:* Davis v. Burke, 179 U.S. 399 (1900); *Argued:* December 3, 1900; *Decided:* December 17, 1900; *Opinion of the Court:* Justice Brown; *Concurring Opinion:* None; *Dissenting Opinion:* None; *Appellate Defense Counsel:* James H. Hawley argued; George Ainslie on brief; *Appellate Prosecution Counsel:* Samuel H. Hays argued; W. E. Borah on brief; *Amicus Curiae Brief Supporting Prosecutor:* None; *Amicus Curiae Brief Supporting Defendant:* None.

Issue Presented: Whether the effect of the repeal and amendment of Idaho's death penalty law prevented the defendant from being executed?

Case Holding: The effect of the repeal and amendment of Idaho's death penalty law did not present a Federal question, because the matter was resolved on State law grounds by the State's appellate court.

Factual and procedural background of case: The defendant, Jack Davis, was convicted of capital murder and sentenced to death by the State of Idaho. The Idaho Supreme Court affirmed the judgment. Subsequently, the State's death penalty statute was amended to require executions be carried out in the State penitentiary. In a proceeding brought before the State appellate court, it was determined that the defendant had to be executed under the law that was in place at the time of the commission of his offense, which meant execution in the yard of a county jail. The defendant shortly thereafter filed a habeas corpus petition in a Federal District Court. In the petition the defendant alleged that he was being unlawfully held because he could not be executed under the new law and, since the old law was repealed, he could not be executed at all. The District Court dismissed the petition. The United States Supreme Court granted certiorari to consider the issue.

Opinion of the Court by Justice Brown: Justice Brown held that "[t]he question whether [the defendant] shall be executed ... by the warden of the penitentiary, or ... by the sheriff, or whether he shall escape punishment altogether, was determined adversely to him by the supreme court of the state and involves no question of due process of law under the 14th Amendment." The judgment of the District Court was affirmed.

Davis v. Georgia
Court: United States Supreme Court; *Case Citation:* Davis v. Georgia, 429 U.S. 122 (1976); *Argued:* Not reported; *Decided:* December 6, 1976; *Opinion of the Court:* Per Curiam; *Concurring Opinion:* None; *Dissenting Opinion:* Justice Rehnquist, in which Burger, C.J. and Blackmun, J., joined; *Appellate Defense Counsel:* Not reported; *Appellate Prosecution Counsel:* Not reported; *Amicus Curiae Brief Supporting Prosecutor:* Not reported; *Amicus Curiae Brief Supporting Defendant:* Not reported.

Issue Presented: Whether a death sentence may be deemed constitutionally valid where one prospective juror was excluded from the jury for cause for merely expressing scruples against the death penalty, rather than being irrevocably committed to vote against it?

Case Holding: Unless a venireperson is irrevocably committed, before the trial has begun, to vote against the penalty of death regardless of the facts and circumstances that might emerge in the course of the proceedings, he or she cannot be excluded for cause.

Factual and procedural background of case: The defendant, Davis, was convicted and sentenced to death by the State of Georgia. On appeal, the Georgia Supreme Court found that one prospective juror had been excluded for "cause" in violation of the United States Supreme Court's ruling in *Witherspoon v. Illinois.* The appellate court nevertheless affirmed the conviction and death sentence, reasoning that the erroneous exclusion of one death-scrupled juror did not deny the defendant a jury representing a cross section of the community. It was further said that: "The rationale of *Witherspoon* and its progeny is not violated where merely one of a qualified class or group is excluded where it is shown, as here, that others of such group were qualified to serve. This record is completely void of any evidence of a systematic and intentional exclusion of a qualified group of jurors so as to deny the [defendant] a

jury of veniremen representing a cross section of the community." The United States Supreme Court granted certiorari to address the issue.

Opinion of the Court was delivered Per Curiam: The per curiam opinion observed that "[t]he *Witherspoon* case held that 'a sentence of death cannot be carried out if the jury that imposed or recommended it was chosen by excluding veniremen for cause simply because they voiced general objections to the death penalty or expressed conscientious or religious scruples against its infliction.'" It was said that the record in the case indicated that a *Witherspoon* violation occurred in the selection of jurors to preside over the defendant's case. "Accordingly, the ... judgment is reversed, and the case is remanded[.]"

Dissenting opinion by Justice Rehnquist, in which Burger, C.J. and Blackmun, J., joined: Justice Rehnquist dissented from the Court's judgment. He believed that the Court misread the decision in *Witherspoon.* The dissent reasoned as follows:

> As is clear from the most cursory reading, *Witherspoon v. Illinois,* does not inexorably lead to the result this Court now reaches. Indeed, much of the language in that opinion would support the reasoning, and the result, reached by the Supreme Court of Georgia. The extension of *Witherspoon* to cover the case where a sole venireman is excluded in violation of its test deserves plenary consideration, not a per se rule that precludes application of even the harmless-error test. There is no indication that the Supreme Court of Georgia was wrong when it observed that the "record is completely void of any evidence of a systematic and intentional exclusion of a qualified group of jurors so as to deny the appellant a jury of veniremen representing a cross section of the community[.]"
>
> ... Finally, the defect in this case is not that a juror was improperly excluded because she was not irrevocably opposed to the death penalty; rather, the defect is a failure to question sufficiently to determine whether or not she was irrevocably opposed. It is not inconceivable that a hearing with the excluded juror could be conducted now to finish the aborted questioning and determine whether she would have, in fact, been excludable for cause.
>
> The effects of the arguably improper exclusion, in short, are too murky to warrant summary reversal of the sentence imposed. *See also* **Jury Selection; Witherspoon v. Illinois**

Davis v. United States (I)
Court: United States Supreme Court; *Case Citation:* Davis v. United States, 160 U.S. 469 (1895); *Argued:* Not reported; *Decided:* December 16, 1895; *Opinion of the Court:* Justice Harlan; *Concurring Opinion:* None; *Dissenting Opinion:* None; *Appellate Defense Counsel:* Not represented; *Appellate Prosecution Counsel:* Mr. Dickinson argued and briefed; *Amicus Curiae Brief Supporting Prosecutor:* None; *Amicus Curiae Brief Supporting Defendant:* None.

Issue Presented: Whether it was correct for the trial court to instruct the jury that it could convict the defendant even if it had a reasonable doubt concerning his sanity at the time of the crime?

Case Holding: It was incorrect for the trial court to instruct the jury that it could convict the defendant even if it had a reasonable doubt concerning his sanity at the time of the crime.

Factual and procedural background of case: The defendant, Dennis Davis, was charged with capital murder by the United States. During the trial the defendant raised the defense of insanity. The defendant put on evidence through witnesses to show that at the time of the crime he was not mentally competent. The jury rejected the defense and convicted the defendant. The trial court sentenced the defendant to death. The defendant appealed to the United States Supreme Court, alleging that the trial court improperly instructed the jury on the defense of insanity. The United States Supreme Court granted certiorari to consider the issue.

Opinion of the Court by Justice Harlan: Justice Harlan agreed with that the defendant that the trial court incorrectly instructed the jury on the defense of insanity. The opinion examined the issue as follows:

> ... [T]he court below instructed the jury that the defense of insanity could not avail the accused unless it appeared affirmatively to the reasonable satisfaction of the jury that he was not criminally responsible for his acts. The fact of killing being clearly proved, the legal presumption, based upon the common experience of mankind that every man is sane, was sufficient, the court in effect said, to authorize a verdict of guilty, although the jury might entertain a reasonable doubt upon the evidence whether the accused, by reason of his mental condition, was criminally responsible for the killing in question. In other words, if the evidence was in equilibria as to the accused being sane,— that is, capable of comprehending the nature and effect of his acts,— he was to be treated just as he would be if there were no defense of insanity, or if there were an entire absence of proof that he was insane....
>
> We are unable to assent to the doctrine that in a prosecution for murder, the defense being insanity, and the fact of the killing with a deadly weapon being clearly established, it is the duty of the jury to convict where the evidence is equally balanced on the issue as to the sanity of the accused at the time of the killing. On the contrary, he is entitled to an acquittal of the specific crime charged if, upon all the evidence, there is reasonable doubt whether he was capable in law of committing crime....
>
> One who takes human life cannot be said to be actuated by malice aforethought, or to have deliberately intended to take life, ... unless at the time he had sufficient mind to comprehend the criminality or the right and wrong of such an act. Although the killing of one human being by another human being with a deadly weapon is presumed to be malicious until the contrary appears, yet, in order to constitute a crime, a person must have intelligence and capacity enough to have a criminal intent and purpose; and if his reason and mental powers are either so deficient that he has no will, no conscience, or controlling mental power, or if, through the overwhelming violence of mental disease, his intellectual power is for the time obliterated, he is not a responsible moral agent, and is not punishable for criminal acts. Neither in the adjudged cases nor in the elementary treatises upon criminal law is there to be found any dissent from these general propositions. All admit that the crime of murder necessarily involves the possession by the accused of such mental capacity as will render him criminally responsible for his acts....

The judgment of the Federal trial court was reversed and the case remanded for a new trial. *See also* **Davis v. United States (II); Insanity Defense**

Davis v. United States (II) *Court:* United States Supreme Court; *Case Citation:* Davis v. United States, 165 U.S. 373 (1897); *Argued:* Not reported; *Decided:* February 15, 1897; *Opinion of the Court:* Justice Brewer; *Concurring Opinion:* None; *Dissenting Opinion:* None; *Appellate Defense Counsel:* Not represented; *Appellate Prosecution Counsel:* Mr. Dickinson argued and briefed; *Amicus Curiae Brief Supporting Prosecutor:* None; *Amicus Curiae Brief Supporting Defendant:* None.

Issue Presented: Whether the trial court committed error in refusing to instruct the jury on manslaughter?

Case Holding: The trial court did not commit error in refusing to instruct the jury on manslaughter, because no evidence was presented to suggest a conviction for any crime less than murder.

Factual and procedural background of case: The defendant, Dennis Davis, was convicted of capital murder and sentenced to death by the United States. The United States Supreme Court reversed the judgment and ordered a new trial because the trial court improperly instructed the jury on the defense of insanity. At the second trial the defendant was again convicted and sentenced to death. A second appeal was filed with the United States Supreme Court, wherein the defendant contended the trial court erred in failing to instruct the jury on manslaughter. The United States Supreme Court granted certiorari to consider the issue.

Opinion of the Court by Justice Brewer: Justice Brewer pointed out that at the second trial the defendant again raised the defense of insanity. It was said that "[o]n the second trial the court charged the law in accordance with the rule laid down by this court,— quoting the very language of our opinion,— and also defined what was meant by insanity, in language which, under the circumstances of this case, was in no degree prejudicial to the rights of the defendant."

In turning the issue presented by the appeal, Justice Brewer found that the trial court did not commit error in refusing to instruct the jury on manslaughter. The opinion reasoned as follows: "[U]nder the evidence there was no occasion for any statement of the law on this. There was no testimony to reduce the offense, if any there was, below the grade of murder. If the defendant was sane, and responsible for his actions, there was nothing upon which any suggestion of any inferior degree of homicide could be made, and therefore the court was under no obligation (indeed, it would simply have been confusing the minds of the jury) to give any instruction upon a matter which was not really open for their consideration." The judgment of the Federal trial court was affirmed. *See also* **Davis v. United States (I)**

Dawson v. Delaware *Court:* United States Supreme Court; *Case Citation:* Dawson v. Delaware, 503 U.S. 159 (1992); *Argued:* November 12, 1991; *Decided:* March 9, 1992; *Opinion of the Court:* Chief Justice Rehnquist; *Concurring Opinion:* Justice Blackmun; *Dissenting Opinion:* Justice Thomas; *Appellate Defense Counsel:* Bernard J. O'Donnell argued; Brian J. Bartley on brief; *Appellate Prosecution Counsel:* Richard E. Fairbanks, Jr. argued; Charles M. Oberly III, Gary A. Myers and Loren C. Meyers on brief; *Amicus Curiae Brief Supporting Prosecutor:* 1; *Amicus Curiae Brief Supporting Defendant:* 1.

Issue Presented: Whether the First and Fourteenth Amendments prohibit the introduction in a capital sentencing proceeding of the fact that the defendant was a member of a prison gang, where the evidence had no relevance to the issues being decided in the proceeding?

Case Holding: The First and Fourteenth Amendments prohibit the introduction in a capital sentencing proceeding of the fact that the defendant was a member of a prison gang, where the evidence had no relevance to the issues being decided in the proceeding.

Factual and procedural background of case: A Delaware jury convicted the defendant, David Dawson, of committing capital murder during an escape from prison. At the penalty phase the prosecutor introduced evidence that the defendant was a member of a violent prison gang. The defendant was sentenced to death. The Delaware Supreme Court affirmed the conviction and sentence, after rejecting the defendant's claim that introduction of evidence of his prison gang membership violated his First and Fourteenth Amendment rights. The United States Supreme Court granted certiorari to consider the issue.

Opinion of the Court by Chief Justice Rehnquist: The Chief Justice held that the defendant's First and Fourteenth Amendment rights were violated by the admission of evidence of his prison gang membership, because the evidence had no relevance to the issues being decided in the proceeding. It was said that the Constitution did not erect a per se barrier to the admission of evidence concerning a defendant's associations at a sentencing hearing simply because those associations are protected by the First Amendment. However, the Chief Justice found that the evidence in the defendant's case proved only the prison gang's and the defendant's abstract beliefs, not that the gang had committed any unlawful act. Thus, it was concluded that such evidence was not relevant to help prove any aggravating circumstance. The judgment of the Delaware Supreme Court was reversed.

Concurring opinion by Justice Blackmun: Justice Blackmun concurred with the Court's opinion and judgment. He wrote separately to note his understanding that the Court did not require application of harmless error review on remand. Justice Blackmun believed that harmless error analysis was inappropriate for a First Amendment violation.

Dissenting opinion by Justice Thomas: Justice Thomas dissented from the majority's decision. He argued that the prosecutor was entitled to introduce evidence of the defendant's prison gang membership, in order to rebut evidence that the defendant proffered which showed "that he had earned good time credits while in prison."

Day, William R.

William R. Day served as an associate justice of the United States Supreme Court from 1903 to 1922. While on the Supreme Court Day was known as a moderate in his interpretation of the Constitution.

Day was born in Ravenna, Ohio on April 17, 1849. He received an undergraduate degree from the University of Michigan in 1870. After attending the University's law school for a year, Day moved to Canton, Ohio where he was admitted to the bar in 1872. As a result of Day's political activities President William McKinley appointed him Secretary of State in 1898. A year later President McKinley appointed Day as an appellate judge for the Sixth Circuit Court of Appeals. In 1903 President Theodore Roosevelt appointed Day to the Supreme Court.

Day was known to have written only a few capital punishment opinions while on the Supreme Court. His most noteworthy of capital punishment opinion was *Stroud v. United States*. In *Stroud* the Supreme Court was asked to determine whether the Double Jeopardy Clause prohibited reprosecution of a capital defendant for the same capital offense, when the first judgment is reversed. Day wrote that successive prosecutions, where there has been a reversal of the initial judgment, did not violate double jeopardy principles. Day died on July 9, 1923.

Capital Punishment Opinions Written by Day

Case Name	Opinion of the Court	Concurring Opinion	Dissenting Opinion
Franklin v. South Carolina	✓		
Rogers v. Peck	✓		
Stroud v. United States	✓		

Deadlocked Jury

In the context of capital punishment, a deadlocked jury is one that is unable to reach a verdict on a defendant's guilt or punishment. In the case of *Allen v. United States*, 164 U.S. 492 (1896), the United States Supreme Court approved of an instruction to use when a jury is deadlocked. The instruction, called an *Allen* charge, advises the jury to give deference to each other's opinions and informs the minority holdout to reconsider the reasonableness of their position, in light of the position taken by the majority. The *Allen* charge was in great favor for some time, but has been increasingly rejected by State and Federal courts as intruding too much on the deliberation process.

During the guilt phase of a capital trial if the jury is deadlocked and unable to reach a verdict, the trial court will declare a mistrial. A defendant may be reprosecuted after a mistrial caused by a deadlocked jury.

It is not uncommon for a penalty phase jury to be hopelessly deadlocked and unable to reach a verdict on the sentence. The United States Supreme Court has not declared that the Federal Constitution requires a particular procedure be used or disposition rendered, when a penalty phase jury is deadlocked. The Constitution's silence on this issue means that capital punishment jurisdictions have the discretion to determine the resolution of this issue as they deem fair.

A majority of capital punishment jurisdictions that utilize penalty phase juries, require that a capital felon be sentenced to prison for life by the trial judge, if the jury is deadlocked. Alabama and California depart from the majority position, as shown by the statutes below.

> *Alabama Code § 13A-5-46(g):* If the jury is unable to reach [a] verdict recommending a sentence ... the trial court may declare a mistrial of the sentence hearing. Such a mistrial shall not affect the conviction. After such a mistrial or mistrials another sentence hearing shall be conducted before another jury, selected according to the laws and rules governing the selection of a jury for the trial of a capital case.

> *California Penal Code § 190.4(b):* If [the] defendant was convicted by the court sitting without a jury the trier of fact at the penalty hearing shall be a jury[.] If the ... jury ... has been unable to reach a unanimous verdict as to what the penalty shall be, the court shall dismiss the jury and shall order a new jury impaneled[.] If such new jury is unable to reach a unanimous verdict ... the court ... shall either order a new jury or impose a punishment of confinement in state prison for a term of life without the possibility of parole.

Two other capital punishment jurisdictions do not follow the majority rule on disposition of a capital case when the penalty phase jury is deadlocked. Under Indiana's death penalty statute the trial judge is required to determine the punishment when a penalty phase jury is deadlocked. The capital offense statute of Nevada requires a three-judge panel be selected to determine a capital felon's punishment when a penalty phase jury is deadlocked.

JURISDICTIONS REQUIRING LIFE IMPRISONMENT WHEN PENALTY PHASE JURY DEADLOCKED

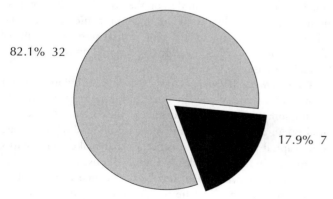

82.1% 32

17.9% 7

■ LIFE IMPRISONMENT JURISDICTIONS

■ ALL OTHER JURISDICTIONS

Death Automatic Jurisdictions *see* Burden of Proof at the Penalty Phase

Death Chamber *see* Execution Chamber

Death Discretionary Jurisdictions *see* Burden of Proof at the Penalty Phase

Death-Eligible Offenses As a result of the Supreme Court's interpretation of the Cruel and Unusual Punishment Clause, capital punishment today does not resemble its common law counterpart. A principle alteration has been the drastic reduction in the number of crimes punishable as capital offenses. Crimes that are punishable with death are called death-eligible offenses. The distinguishing feature of death-eligible offenses is that they are created with *special circumstances.*

An underlying premise of special circumstances is that not every murder justifies capital punishment consideration. That is, in keeping with constitutional requirements, special circumstances seek to limit the class of murders that will be exposed to death penalty prosecution. In an effort to pull out a subclass of death-eligible murders from among all murders, legislators have singled out specific factors or conduct that may appear in some murders. These specific factors or conduct are called special circumstances and form the basis of all death-eligible offenses. As a result of forming the basis of death-eligible offenses, a special circumstance actually constitutes an element of the capital offense. As an element of an offense, the constitution requires a death-eligible special circumstance be proven at the guilt phase beyond a reasonable doubt. Illustrations of death-eligible offenses follow.

Murder-Without-More: The phrase murder-without-more refers to the killing of a single human being. A majority of capital punishment jurisdictions authorize death penalty consideration for the crime of murder-without-more. A variety of names are used to describe this offense: first-degree murder, murder, deliberate homicide, and aggravated murder.

The special circumstance that is used to make murder-without-more a death-eligible offense is the mental state of a defendant at the time of the commission of the murder. Capital punishment jurisdictions differ on how they describe the mental state. The following are the words that are found in statutes: intentional, willful, deliberate, premeditated, malice, and prior calculation and design.

Homicide in the Commission of Another Offense: A majority of capital punishment jurisdictions make it a death-eligible offense for anyone causing the death of another during the course of committing a crime. This offense is nothing more than felony murder. A few capital punishment jurisdictions do not refer to the offense as such, though they adhere to the principles attendant to felony murder. The justification for making homicide during the commission of a crime, a death-eligible offense, is to try and deter the taking of life when homicide is not the motive of a crime.

Victim-Specific Murder: Almost a majority of capital punishment jurisdictions provide that victim-specific murder is a death-eligible offense. Victim-specific murder refers to the intentional killing of an individual who has been officially recognized by a statute, such as a law enforcement officer, prison official, fire fighter, judge, probation officer or parole officer. Victim-specific murder statutes seek to provide additional protection for the lives of individuals whose occupations expose them to potential revenge by criminals.

Murder-for-Hire: A large minority of capital punishment jurisdictions allow imposition of the death penalty for a homicide committed pursuant to a contract, i.e., exchange of something of pecuniary value for killing another.

Len Bias Murder: On June 18, 1986 University of Maryland basketball standout Len Bias signed a lucrative contract to play professional basketball with the Boston Celtics. On June 19, 1986 Len Bias was found dead after allegedly ingesting cocaine. The nation was stunned over the way in which the basketball world had lost a promising superstar.

Before national outrage reached its peak over the death of Len Bias, another tragedy struck the sports world. On June 27, 1986 Cleveland Browns defensive back Don Rogers was found dead after allegedly ingesting cocaine.

After the death of Bias and Rogers, a national call rang out demanding special punishment for drug pushers if death resulted from the use of their drugs. All jurisdictions responded to this call, one way or another, by toughening their drug laws. Three states, Colorado, Connecticut and Florida, took the ultimate step by enacting specific death-eligible offenses for deaths that occur from the use of illegal drugs.

Drive-by-Shooting Murder: At the height of the Prohibition Era, traffickers in the sale of illegal alcohol were famous for taking the life of competitors by firing machine guns and pistols from vehicles. This brazen public method of handling disputes lost its luster and subsided as a national problem in the 1940s.

Drive-by-shooting resurfaced as a national problem during the 1990s. The perpetrators of this deadly resurrection are not bootleggers, however. Drug dealers took up this brazen method of handling disputes between themselves. An unfortunate side effect of the current drive-by-shooting problem is that innocent bystanders (too often these bystanders are children) have been gun-downed. A minority of capital punishment jurisdictions have responded to drive-by-shooting murder, by making it a death-eligible offense.

Specific-Device Murder: Specific-device murder refers to a homicide committed by means of a prohibited weapon or instrument, such as a bomb or outlawed handgun. A significant minority of capital punishment jurisdictions have addressed specific-device murder by making this crime a death-eligible offense.

Hostage/Human-Shield Murder: Hostage-murder refers to causing the death of a victim who was seized against his or her will, for the purpose of obtaining some political goal (or freedom) in exchange for the release of the hostage. The human-shield offense refers to the killing of a person who was used as protection from bullets. One jurisdiction, Utah, has specifically provided that hostage-murder and human-shield murder are death-eligible offenses. The Federal system has made hostage-murder a death eligible-offense.

Multiple-Victim Murder: Multiple-victim murder refers to the willful and deliberate killing of more than one person as part of the same act or transaction. A minority of capital punishment jurisdictions provide that multiple-victim murder is a death-eligible offense.

Drug-Trafficking Murder: Drug-trafficking murder occurs when the offender has the specific intent to kill or to inflict great bodily harm while engaged in the distribution, exchange, sale, or purchase of a controlled dangerous substance. A minority of capital punishment jurisdictions have made drug-trafficking murder an independent death-eligible offense.

Murder-on-the-Run: Murder-on-the-run occurs when a homicide is committed by a person while escaping or attempting to escape from lawful custody. A significant minority of capital punishment jurisdictions have responded to homicides committed by escaped inmates by making murder-on-the-run a death-eligible offense.

Grave-Risk Murder: The capital offense of grave-risk murder is triggered when unintended victims are endangered by a capital felon's conduct. A minority of capital punishment jurisdictions have made grave-risk murder a death-eligible offense.

Perjury/Subornation of Perjury Murder: The offense of perjury may be defined as giving false testimony, while under oath, in a matter that involves a felony offense. Subornation of perjury, on the other hand, involves inducing another person to testify falsely, while under oath, in a matter that involves a felony or misdemeanor offense. Colorado and Nebraska have made perjury murder and subornation of perjury murder death-eligible offenses.

Forced-Suicide Murder: The death-eligible offense of forced-suicide murder is distinguishable from the crime of assisted suicide, though both produce the same result. Assisted suicide involves intentionally or knowingly making an instrument available for someone who wants to voluntarily commit suicide. Forced-suicide murder, on the other hand, involves intentionally compelling someone to commit suicide, when the victim does not want to die. One capital punishment jurisdiction, Delaware, has made forced-suicide murder a death-eligible offense.

Gang-Status Murder: Gang-status murder involves killing someone as a rite of passage into a criminal organization, or killing someone in order to advance in the hierarchy of a criminal organization. At present, the state of Washington is the only capital punishment jurisdiction that makes gang-status murder an independent death-eligible offense.

Perpetrator-Status Murder: Not infrequently homicide is committed by someone who is on parole or probation, or has had a previous homicide conviction, or is incarcerated at the time of the commission of the homicide. In any of the latter situations the perpetrator has a legally recognizable status, i.e., parolee, probationer, ex-offender or inmate. The crime of perpetrator-status murder has as its focal point, the particular status of the perpetrator at the time of the commission of a murder. The significance of status, in this context, is that it implies that the person is a threat to society. A large minority of capital punishment jurisdictions have singled out particular statuses and created death-eligible perpetrator-status murder offenses.

Torture-Murder: Torture-murder refers to the infliction of severe physical or mental pain upon a homicide victim while he or she remains alive and conscious. A minority of capital punishment jurisdictions have isolated torture-murder and made it a death-eligible offense.

Lying-in-Wait Murder: The elements of lying-in-wait murder are: (1) concealment of purpose, (2) substantial period of watching and waiting for an opportune time to act, and (3) immediately thereafter, a surprise attack on an unsuspecting victim from a position of advantage. A minority of capital punishment jurisdictions have isolated lying-in-wait murder and made it a death-eligible offense.

Victim-Age Murder: The age of the victim of homicide, adolescent or senior citizen, has begun to carve out a path as a distinct death-eligible offense. A minority of capital punishment jurisdictions currently have some form of a death-eligible victim-age murder statute. *See also* **Aggravating Circumstances; Rape and Capital Punishment**

Death Penalty Charging Discretion *see* **Prosecutor**

Death Penalty Focus of California
Death Penalty Focus of California (DPFC) was founded in 1988. It is a nonprofit organization dedicated to the abolition of capital punishment in California through grassroots organizing, research, and the dissemination of information about the death penalty and its alternatives. DPFC publishes and distribute a quarterly newsletter, *The Sentry*, which provides comprehensive information and editorials on the death penalty on a local, national and international scale. The organization distributes thousands of pieces of educational materials, such as the California Death Penalty fact sheet, and a brochure called Myths and Facts About California's Death Penalty. The staff of DPFC participate in numerous speaking engagements before community groups, schools, church groups, legal and other professional organizations.

Death Penalty Information Center
The Death Penalty Information Center is a Washington, D.C., based nonprofit organization that was founded in 1990. The primary work of the Center is to serve the media and the public with analysis and information on issues concerning capital punishment. The Center prepares in-depth reports, issues press releases, conducts briefings for journalists, and serves as a resource to those working on this issue. The Center is widely quoted and consulted by all those concerned with the death penalty. The executive director of the Center, Richard C. Dieter, is an attorney who has written and spoken extensively on this subject.

Since its founding, the Center's reports on issues related to the death penalty have received wide attention. The major reports have included:

Chattahoochee Judicial District: The Buckle of the Death Belt, concerning racism in the administration of capital punishment (1991); *Killing Justice: Government Misconduct and the*

Death Penalty, detailing abuses by prosecutors in pursuing the death penalty (1992); *Millions Misspent: What Politicians Don't Say About the High Costs of the Death Penalty*, concerning the exorbitant expense of capital punishment (1994); *The Future of the Death Penalty in the U.S.A.: Texas-Sized Crisis*, pointing to the severe problems in the implementation of the death penalty in Texas and foreshadowing a similar crisis in the rest of the country (1994); *On the Front Line: Law Enforcement Views on the Death Penalty*, providing the results of a national survey of police chiefs and their view that the death penalty is not an effective law enforcement tool (1995); *With Justice for Few: The Growing Crisis in Death Penalty Representation*, illustrating the recurrent problem of unprepared and unqualified attorneys handling the most important cases (1995); *Killing for Votes: The Dangers of Politicizing the Death Penalty Process*, exposes the political use of the death penalty by judges and prosecutors (1996); *Innocence and the Death Penalty: The Increasing Danger of Executing the Innocent*, an examination of prisoners released from death row due to evidence of their innocence (1997); *The Death Penalty in Black & White: Who Lives, Who Dies, Who Decides*, contains the results of two new studies which underscore the continuing injustice of racism in the application of the death penalty (1998).

Death Penalty Institute of Oklahoma
Death Penalty Institute of Oklahoma (DPIO) is a nonprofit organization with a focus on public education about capital punishment. Specifically, DPIO serves the media and the public with analysis and information on issues concerning capital punishment in Oklahoma. The information is presented to the public through its quarterly newsletter and public speaking engagements.

Death Penalty Notice *see* **Notice of Intent to Seek the Death Penalty**

Death Penalty Statutes *see* **Aggravating Circumstances; Death-Eligible Offenses; Mitigating Circumstances**

Death Row
Death row is a phrase used to describe the place of incarceration of defendants sentenced to death. All death row facilities are maintained in maximum security prisons. For obvious reasons, intense security is the operating principle for maintaining death row inmates.

Age of Death Row Inmates December 31, 1997

Age	Number	Percent
17 or younger	0	0
18–19	14	0.4
20–24	275	8.2
25–29	497	14.9
30–34	578	17.3
35–39	727	21.8
40–44	521	15.6
45–49	354	10.6
50–54	216	6.5

Age	Number	Percent
55–59	88	2.6
60 or older	65	1.9

Source: Bureau of Justice Statistics, Capital Punishment Table 8 (1997).

The North Block death row at San Quentin State Prison. (California Department of Corrections)

Although life on death row necessarily varies among institutions, a few generalizations can be made regarding the conditions of death row. Inmates on death row are isolated from the main population of a prison. This isolation includes, for much of the time, keeping death row inmates locked in their cells and away from each other. Institutions do not place more than one death row inmate to a cell.

Time on Death Row 1977–97

Year of Execution	Average time from sentence to execution (in months)
1977–83	51
1984	74
1985	71
1986	87
1987	86
1988	80
1989	95
1990	95
1991	116
1992	114
1993	113
1994	122
1995	134
1996	125
1997	133

Source: Bureau of Justice Statistics, Capital Punishment Table 12 (1997).

Death row cells generally comprise one or more wings in a prison. Each cell has a bed, a lavatory, commode, and a mounted writing table. Some institutions permit death row inmates to have cigarettes, food, radios and televisions in their cells. Most institutions have death watch cells to incarcerate death row inmates after an authorized official signs a death warrant setting the day and time for the execution. A death watch cell is usually larger than a regular death row cell. The death watch cell is usually adjacent to the execution chamber. The inmate remains in the death watch cell until receiving a stay or until escorted to the execution chamber. An inmate on death watch status is allowed a legal and social phone call while on death watch.

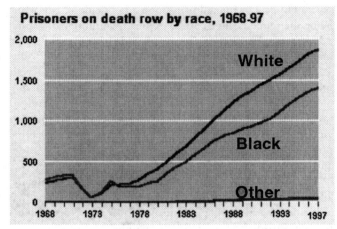

SOURCE: Bureau of Justice Statistics, Capital Punishment (1997)

Death row inmates are served food three times a day. Some institutions require the meals be served in the cells, while others permit death row inmates to eat in dining halls. Most institutions do not permit them to leave their cells except for medical reasons, exercise, or for scheduled visits with outside visitors. Institutions provide a visiting area inside the prison where inmates and visitors may see and talk to each other, but have no physical contact. Death row inmates may receive mail.

Institutions do not assign prison jobs to death row inmates, other than a requirement that they keep their cells clean. Death row inmates have at least one hour per day for exercise. They are escorted in groups to outdoor or indoor exercise areas.

Florida Death Row Information
Death Row and Death Watch Cells: A Death Row cell is 6 × 9 × 9.5 feet high. Florida State Prison also has Death Watch cells to incarcerate inmates awaiting execution after the Governor signs a death warrant for them. A Death Watch cell is 12 × 7 × 8.5 feet high.

Meals: Death Row inmates are served meals three times a day: at 5:00 A.M., from 10:30 A.M. to 11:00 A.M. and from 4:00 P.M. to 4:30 P.M. Food is prepared by Florida State Prison personnel and is transported in insulated carts to the cells. Inmates are allowed plates

Death watch cell at North Carolina's Central Prison. (North Carolina Department of Corrections)

and spoons to eat their meals. Prior to execution, an inmate may request a last meal. To avoid extravagance, the food to prepare the last meal must cost no more than $20 and must be purchased locally.

Visitors: Visitors are allowed every weekend from 9 A.M. to 3 P.M. All visitors must be approved by prison officials before being placed on the inmate visitor list. Visitors traveling over

200 miles may visit both Saturday and Sunday. Members of the news media may request Death Row inmate interviews through the Department of Corrections. Inmates must agree to being interviewed. Because of safety and security concerns, the news media may not interview any prison personnel who are involved in executions except for official Department of Corrections spokesmen.

Showers: The inmates may shower every other day.

Security: Death Row inmates are counted at least once an hour. They are escorted in handcuffs and wear them everywhere except in their cells, the exercise yard and the shower. They are in their cells at all times except for medical reasons, exercise, social or legal visits or media interviews. When a death warrant is signed the inmate is put under Death Watch status and is allowed a legal and social phone call.

Mail, Magazines and Entertainment: Inmates may receive mail every day except holidays and weekends. They may have cigarettes, snacks, radios and black and white televisions in their cells. They do not have cable television or air-conditioning and they are not allowed to be with each other in a common room. They can watch church services on closed circuit television. While on Death Watch, inmates may have radios and black and white televisions positioned outside their cell bars.

Clothing: Death Row inmates can be distinguished from other inmates by their orange t-shirts. Their pants are the same blue colored pants worn by regular inmates.

Mabel Bassett Correctional Center houses female death row inmates for the State of Oklahoma. (Oklahoma Department of Corrections)

at the other end. Each cell has a bed, a lavatory, commode, and a wall-mounted writing table.

When correction officers begin the prison's count of inmates at six in the morning, the day begins on death row. The death row population spends nearly all their time in either their cells or the adjacent dayroom. They may stay in their dayroom from 7:00 A.M. until 11:00 P.M. While in the dayroom, they may view television.

Confined to their cellblock, death row inmates are not assigned jobs in the prison like other inmates. However, they are required to keep their cells and dayrooms clean.

The death row inmates have at least one hour per day for exercise and showers. Correction officers escort death row inmates in groups from each cellblock wing to outdoor exercise areas, weather permitting, two days a week where the inmates can play basketball, walk or jog. Correction officers also escort the death row inmates by cellblock to the dining halls for each meal.

Death row inmates may receive one visit a week with a maximum of two visitors. There is a visiting area inside the prison where inmates and visitors may see and talk to each other, but they have no physical contact.

Death row inmates may participate in a one-hour Christian worship service each Sunday, or Islamic worship services for one hour each Friday. A Bible study class is also conducted by the prison's chaplain for 90 minutes each Tuesday morning.

Death Row April 1999

Jurisdiction	Inmates on Death Row	Jurisdiction	Inmates on Death Row	Jurisdiction	Inmates on Death Row
Alabama	178	Kentucky	39	Ohio	192
Arizona	120	Louisiana	82	Oklahoma	151
Arkansas	42	Maryland	17	Oregon	26
California	536	Mississippi	65	Pennsylvania	225
Colorado	3	Missouri	84	South Carolina	69
Connecticut	5	Montana	6	South Dakota	2
Delaware	19	Nebraska	9	Tennessee	104
Florida	390	Nevada	86	Texas	437
Georgia	123	New Hampshire	0	Utah	11
Idaho	22	New Jersey	16	Virginia	37
Illinois	156	New Mexico	4	Washington	17
Indiana	45	New York	2	Wyoming	2
Kansas	2	North Carolina	212	Federal	21

Source: Death Penalty Information Center, Death Row (1999).

North Carolina Death Row Information

The Division of Prisons houses male death row inmates in Central Prison and female death row inmates at the North Carolina Correctional Institution for Women. Both prisons are located in Raleigh.

The men are housed in cellblocks of the maximum security building at Central Prison. One correction officer in a control center watches the inmates at all times. Each cellblock is divided into two wings, each with 16 single cells in two tiers with eight cells on top and eight cells on the bottom. The cells open into a dayroom area that has a television at one end, stainless steel tables in the middle and showers

Death row for females at Central California Women's Facility. (California Department of Corrections)

If a death row inmate violates Division of Prisons' regulations, the inmate is placed in a segregation cellblock outside of the death row area. He must eat his meals in his cell and is separated from other death row inmates for his daily hour of exercise and shower.

Conditions are similar for women inmates on death row. The women are housed in a cellblock of the maximum security building at the North Carolina Correctional Institution for Women. Each of the single cells has a bed, lavatory and commode. The seven cells are side by side down a corridor. At the front of the cellblock is a dayroom with a television, table and chairs. This is where the women eat their meals. This room also serves as the visiting area, and all visits are supervised by correctional staff. As a group, the women inmates are given at least an hour daily for exercise and showers. Volunteers provide Sunday worship services on death row. Chaplains are available for counseling.

When a death row inmate exhausts all appeals and the secretary of correction sets an execution date, that inmate — male or female — is moved into the death watch area of Central Prison three to seven days prior to the execution date. The death watch area is adjacent to the execution chamber and is located in the prison's custody control building.

The inmate moves all personal belongings from the death row cell to one of the four cells in the death watch area. Each cell has a bed, lavatory, commode and a wall-mounted writing table.

The cells are side by side and open into a dayroom where there is a table, a television and shower. With the exception of 15 minutes allowed for a shower, the inmate spends the entire day in the cell. A correction sergeant and a correction officer are stationed just outside the cell in the dayroom 24 hours a day.

The inmate may receive visits from his attorney, chaplains, psychologists and others authorized by the Division of Prisons and may receive non-contact family visits in the prison's regular visiting area. An inmate on death watch is not allowed contact with other inmates. The inmate remains in the death watch area until receiving a stay or until escorted to the execution chamber.

Death-Qualified Jury *see* Jury Selection

Death Warrant
A death warrant is an order signed by an authorized official that sets the day and time for a capital felon's death. Once a death warrant is issued it must be followed by prison officials, unless they receive a written judicial or executive order stopping the execution. *See also* **Lamber v. Barrett (II)**

The Supreme Court of South Carolina

The State,	Respondent
v.	
J. D. Gleaton,	Appellant.

Lexington County
The Honorable Julius Baggett
The Honorable Rodney Peeples

ORDER

TO THE HONORABLE MICHAEL W. MOORE, DIRECTOR, DEPARTMENT OF CORRECTIONS:

This is to notify you that the sentence of death imposed in the case of The State v. J. D. Gleaton, from which an appeal has been taken has been affirmed and finally disposed of by the Supreme Court and the remittitur has been sent down to the Clerk of the Court of General Sessions of Lexington County.

IT IS, THEREFORE, required of you by Section 17-25-370 of the Code of Laws of South Carolina to execute the judgment and sentence of death imposed on said defendant on the fourth Friday after the service upon you or receipt of this notice.

Let a copy of this notice be served immediately upon the appellant J. D. Gleaton.

[signature]
CLERK

Death warrant ordering the execution of J. D. Gleaton, who was executed by the State of South Carolina on December 4, 1998. (Clerk's Office, South Carolina Supreme Court)

Death Watch Cell *see* Death Row

Default *see* Procedural Default Of Constitutional Claims

Delaware
The State of Delaware is a capital punishment jurisdiction. The State reenacted its death penalty law after the United States Supreme Court decision in *Furman v. Georgia*, 408 U.S. 238 (1972) on March 29, 1974.

M. Jane Brady is the Delaware Attorney General. Her office represents the State in capital punishment appellate proceedings. (Delaware Attorney General Office)

Delaware has a two-tier legal system. The State's legal system is composed of a supreme court and courts of general jurisdiction. The Delaware Supreme Court is presided over by a chief justice and four associate justices. The courts of general jurisdiction in the State are called Superior Courts. Capital offenses against the State of Delaware are tried in the Superior Courts.

Delaware's capital punishment statute is triggered if a person commits a homicide under the following special circumstances:

1. The person intentionally causes the death of another person;
2. In the course of and in furtherance of the commission or attempted commission of a felony or immediate flight therefrom, the person recklessly causes the death of another person;
3. The person intentionally causes another person to commit suicide by force or duress;
4. The person recklessly causes the death of a law-enforcement officer, corrections employee or fire fighter while such officer is in the lawful performance of duties;
5. The person causes the death of another person by the use of or detonation of any bomb or similar destructive device;
6. The person, with criminal negligence, causes the death of another person in the course of and in furtherance of the commission or attempted commission of any degree of rape, unlawful sexual intercourse in the first or second degree, kidnapping, arson in the first degree, robbery in the first degree, burglary in the first degree, or immediate flight therefrom;
7. The person causes the death of another person in order to

avoid or prevent the lawful arrest of any person, or in the course of and in furtherance of the commission or attempted commission of escape in the second degree or escape after conviction.

Capital murder in Delaware is punishable by death or life imprisonment without parole. A capital prosecution in Delaware is bifurcated into a guilt phase and penalty phase. A jury is used at both phases of a capital trial. It is not required that, at the penalty phase, the jury must unanimously agree that a death sentence is appropriate before it can be imposed. This is because the decision of a penalty phase jury is not binding on the trial court under the laws of Delaware. The trial court may accept or reject the jury's determination on punishment, and impose whatever sentence he or she believes the evidence established.

In order to impose a death sentence upon a defendant under Delaware law, it is required that the prosecutor establish the existence of at least one of the following statutory aggravating circumstances at the penalty phase:

a. The murder was committed by a person in, or who has escaped from, the custody of a law-enforcement officer or place of confinement.

b. The murder was committed for the purpose of avoiding or preventing an arrest or for the purpose of effecting an escape from custody.

c. The murder was committed against any law enforcement officer, corrections employee or firefighter, while such victim was engaged in the performance of official duties.

d. The murder was committed against a judicial officer, a former judicial officer, Attorney General, former Attorney General, Assistant or Deputy Attorney General or former Assistant or Deputy Attorney General, State Detective or former State Detective, Special Investigator or former Special Investigator, during, or because of, the exercise of an official duty.

e. The murder was committed against a person who was held or otherwise detained as a shield or hostage.

f. The murder was committed against a person who was held or detained by the defendant for ransom or reward.

g. The murder was committed against a person who was a witness to a crime and who was killed for the purpose of preventing the witness's appearance or testimony in any grand jury, criminal or civil proceeding involving such crime, or in retaliation for the witness' appearance or testimony in any grand jury, criminal or civil proceeding involving such crime.

h. The defendant paid or was paid by another person or had agreed to pay or be paid by another person or had conspired to pay or be paid by another person for the killing of the victim.

i. The defendant was previously convicted of another murder or manslaughter or of a felony involving the use of, or threat of, force or violence upon another person.

j. The murder was committed while the defendant was engaged in the commission of, or attempt to commit, or flight after committing or attempting to commit any degree of rape, unlawful sexual intercourse, arson, kidnapping, robbery, sodomy or burglary.

k. The defendant's course of conduct resulted in the deaths of 2 or more persons where the deaths are a probable consequence of the defendant's conduct.

l. The murder was outrageously or wantonly vile, horrible or inhuman in that it involved torture, depravity of mind, use of an explosive device or poison or the defendant used such means on the victim prior to murdering the victim.

m. The defendant caused or directed another to commit murder or committed murder as an agent or employee of another person.

n. The defendant was under a sentence of life imprisonment, whether for natural life or otherwise, at the time of the commission of the murder.

o. The murder was committed for pecuniary gain.

p. The victim was pregnant.

q. The victim was severely handicapped or severely disabled.

r. The victim was 62 years of age or older.

s. The victim was a child 14 years of age or younger, and the murder was committed by an individual who is at least 4 years older than the victim.

t. At the time of the killing, the victim was or had been a nongovernmental informant or had otherwise provided any investigative, law enforcement or police agency with information concerning criminal activity, and the killing was in retaliation for the victim's activities as a nongovernmental informant or in providing information concerning criminal activity to an investigative, law enforcement or police agency.

u. The murder was premeditated and the result of substantial planning. Such planning must be as to the commission of the murder itself and not simply as to the commission or attempted commission of any underlying felony.

v. The murder was committed for the purpose of interfering with the victim's free exercise or enjoyment of any right, privilege or immunity protected by the First Amendment to the United States Constitution, or because the victim has exercised or enjoyed said rights, or because of the victim's race, religion, color, disability, national origin or ancestry.

Delaware does not provide by statute any mitigating circumstances to the imposition of the death penalty. Even though the State does not provide statutory mitigating circumstances, the United States Supreme Court has ruled that all relevant mitigating evidence must be allowed at the penalty phase.

Under Delaware's capital punishment statute, a sentence of death is automatically reviewed by the Delaware Supreme Court. Delaware uses lethal injection to carry out death sentences. Defendants who committed capital murder before June 13, 1986, may choose between lethal injection and hanging as the method of execution. The State's death row facility for men is located in Smyrna, Delaware; while the facility maintaining female death row inmates is located in Claymont, Delaware.

Pursuant to the laws of Delaware the Governor has authority to grant clemency in capital cases. The Governor must obtain the consent of the State's Board of Pardons in order to grant clemency.

From the start of modern capital punishment in 1976, through 1999, Delaware executed 10 capital felons. During this period Delaware did not have any female capital felons. A total of 19 capital felons were on death row in the State in 1999. The 1999 death row population in the State was listed as: 10 black inmates and 9 white inmates. In 1999 the State did not have any juveniles on death row. The State permits capital punishment to be imposed on persons 16 years old or older. Delaware does not prohibit the execution of mentally retarded capital felons.

Executions by Delaware 1976–1999

Name	Race	Date of Execution	Method of Execution
Steven B. Pennell	White	March 14, 1992	Lethal Injection
James "Red Dog" Allen	N.A.	March 3, 1993	Lethal Injection
Kenneth DeShields	Black	August 31, 1993	Lethal Injection
Andre Deputy	Black	June 23, 1994	Lethal Injection
Nelson Shelton	White	March 17, 1995	Lethal Injection
Billy Bailey	White	January 25, 1996	Hanging
William Flamer	Black	January 30, 1996	Lethal Injection
James Clark, Jr.	White	April 19, 1996	Lethal Injection
David Lawrie	White	April 23, 1999	Lethal Injection
Willie Sullivan	Black	September 24, 1999	Lethal Injection

DELAWARE EXECUTIONS 1976–1999

98.3% 588   1.7% 10

■ DELAWARE EXECUTIONS

■ ALL OTHER EXECUTIONS

Deliberation *see* Jury Deliberation

Delo v. Lashley

Court: United States Supreme Court; *Case Citation:* Delo v. Lashley, 507 U.S. 272 (1993); *Argued:* Not reported; *Decided:* March 8, 1993; *Opinion of the Court:* Per Curiam; *Concurring Opinion:* None; *Dissenting Opinion:*

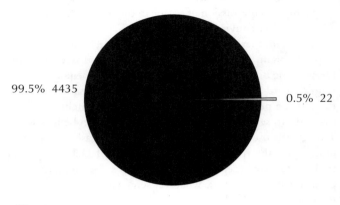

EXECUTIONS BY DELAWARE 1930–1999

99.5% 4435   0.5% 22

■ DELAWARE

■ ALL OTHER JURISDICTIONS

Justice Stevens, in which Blackmun, J., joined; *Appellate Defense Counsel:* Not reported; *Appellate Prosecution Counsel:* Not reported; *Amicus Curiae Brief Supporting Prosecutor:* Not reported; *Amicus Curiae Brief Supporting Defendant:* Not reported.

Issue Presented: Whether the Constitution requires a penalty phase jury be instructed on a mitigating circumstance for which no evidence was presented?

Case Holding: The Constitution does not require a penalty phase jury be instructed on a mitigating circumstance when no evidence was presented on the matter.

Factual and procedural background of case: The defendant, Frederick Lashley, was convicted of capital murder by a jury in the state of Missouri. During the penalty phase of the trial defense counsel requested the trial court instruct the jury on the mitigating circumstance of "no significant prior criminal history," i.e., that the defendant had no significant criminal history. However, no evidence was presented to the jury on the defendant's prior criminal record, so the trial judge refused to give the requested instruction. The defendant was sentenced to death. In affirming the conviction and sentence, the Missouri Supreme Court ruled that Missouri law required mitigating circumstance instructions to be supported by some evidence, before they are given to a jury. Subsequently a federal Court of Appeals vacated the death sentence, after holding that the Constitution required that, if the State failed to come forward with evidence of a criminal history, the trial court had to instruct the jury on the mitigating circumstance. The United States Supreme Court granted certiorari to consider the issue.

Opinion of the Court was delivered Per Curiam: The per curiam opinion noted that the Constitution required juries be given instructions on all relevant mitigating circumstances for which evidence was introduced. However, it was ruled that State courts are not obligated by the Constitution to give juries mitigating circumstance instructions when no evidence is offered to support them. The judgment of the Court of Appeals was reversed.

Dissenting opinion by Justice Stevens, in which Blackmun, J., joined: The dissent argued that the majority refused to address one of the critical, dispositive, issues presented by the defendant. The defendant contended during the penalty phase the Constitution erected a "presumption of innocence" in having committed any other crime. Therefore, when the State does not present any evidence of a criminal history, the law presumes the defendant is innocent of having committed any other crime. As a result of this presumption, the trial court is required to instruct the penalty phase jury on the mitigating circumstance even though the defendant did not present any evidence on the issue. It was reasoned by Justice Stevens that: "The mitigating factor in question corresponds precisely to the presumption of innocence. When the trial record reveals no prior criminal history at all, the presumption serves as 'a prima facie case, and in that sense it is, temporarily, the substitute or equivalent for evidence,' that a criminal defendant is blameless in spite of his indictment, and that, even after conviction of one crime, he is presumptively innocent of all other crimes." Therefore, Justice Stevens would affirm the Court of Appeals decision.

Case note: Although the decision in the case was a per curiam opinion, it has had a significant impact on the penalty phase of capital prosecutions. The decision placed a burden on capital defendants to come forward with some evidence on all relevant mitigating circumstances, or else they will not have the jury instructed to consider the matter for which no evidence was proffered. The decision has been criticized along the lines of Justice Stevens' dissent. *See also* **Bell v. Ohio; Eddings v. Oklahoma; Hitchcock v. Dugger; Lockett v. Ohio; Mitigating Circumstances; Skipper v. South Carolina**

Demonstrative Evidence

Demonstrative evidence refers to evidence presented at a trial solely to help demonstrate some issue in dispute, but is not to be used by the jury in determining a defendant's guilt or innocence. For example, a prosecutor or defendant may use a map to show the location of an event in helping the jury understand some issue in the trial, but the map would not constitute evidence for the jury to consider during its deliberations.

Demosthenes v. Baal

Court: United States Supreme Court; *Case Citation:* Demosthenes v. Baal, 495 U.S. 731 (1990); *Argued:* Not reported; *Decided:* June 3, 1990; *Opinion of the Court:* Per Curiam; *Concurring Opinion:* None; *Dissenting Opinion:* Justice Brennan, in which Marshall, J. joined; *Dissenting Statement:* Justice Blackmun and Stevens, J.; *Appellate Defense Counsel:* Not reported; *Appellate Prosecution Counsel:* Not reported; *Amicus Curiae Brief Supporting Prosecutor:* Not reported; *Amicus Curiae Brief Supporting Defendant:* Not reported.

Issue Presented: Whether the defendant's parents made a proper showing that the defendant was not competent to give up his rights to seek post-conviction relief from his death sentence?

Case Holding: The defendant's parents failed to make a proper showing that the defendant was not competent to give up his rights to seek post-conviction relief from his death sentence.

Factual and procedural background of case: The defendant, Thomas Baal, plead guilty to capital murder and was sentenced to death by a Nevada court. On direct appeal, the Nevada Supreme Court affirmed the conviction and sentence. The defendant initiated State post-conviction habeas corpus proceedings, but subsequently withdrew his request for post-conviction relief. A hearing was held by a State court to determine his competency to make the decision not to continue the proceedings and to determine if he was aware of his impending execution and the reason for it. The court reviewed psychiatric reports and other evidence and held that the defendant was sane and had made an intelligent waiver of his right to pursue post-conviction relief.

A few hours before the defendant's scheduled execution, his parents filed a petition for Federal habeas corpus relief as his "next friend," contending that the defendant was not competent to waive Federal review of his conviction and sentence. A Federal District Court denied their application for a stay of execution, holding that it had no jurisdiction to entertain the petition. The District Court found that, based on the record before the State court, the defendant was legally competent. A Federal Court of Appeals reversed, ruling that the defendant's parents had made a minimum showing of his incompetence warranting a basis for a full evidentiary hearing by the District Court. The State of Nevada asked the United States Supreme Court to vacate the order of the Court of Appeals granting a stay of the execution of the defendant.

Opinion of the Court was delivered Per Curiam: The per curiam opinion ruled that no adequate basis for the exercise of Federal power existed in the case. It was said that the prerequisite for litigating as a "next friend," is that the real party in interest be unable to litigate his or her own cause due to mental incapacity. The opinion held that this prerequisite was not satisfied where an evidentiary hearing shows that a defendant has given a knowing, intelligent, and voluntary waiver of his or her right to proceed. The Court found the prerequisite was not satisfied in the case. The reasoning and conclusion of the Court were stated as follows:

> A state court's determinations on the merits of a factual issue are entitled to a presumption of correctness on federal habeas review. A federal court may not overturn such determinations unless it concludes that they are not "fairly supported by the record." We have held that a state court's conclusion regarding a defendant's competency is entitled to such a presumption. In this case, the state court's conclusion that Baal was competent to waive his right to further proceedings was "fairly supported by the record." Three psychiatrists who examined Baal had determined he was competent; a psychiatrist who had the opportunity to observe and talk to Baal testified that Baal was competent at the hearing; and the trial court concluded that Baal

was competent after both observing Baal and questioning him extensively on the record. Accordingly, under [the] presumption of correctness, the state court's factual finding as to Baal's competence is binding on a federal habeas court.

We realize that last minute petitions from parents of death row inmates may often be viewed sympathetically. But federal courts are authorized by the federal habeas statutes to interfere with the course of state proceedings only in specified circumstances. Before granting a stay, therefore, federal courts must make certain that an adequate basis exists for the exercise of federal power. In this case, that basis was plainly lacking. The State is entitled to proceed without federal intervention. Accordingly, we grant the State's motion to vacate the stay entered by the Court of Appeals.

Dissenting opinion by Justice Brennan, in which Marshall, J. joined: Justice Brennan dissented from the Court's decision to vacate the stay. He believed the record in the case was insufficiently developed for the Court to interfere with the ruling of the Court of Appeals. Justice Brennan stated his position as follows:

The Court today vacates a stay of execution that the United States Court of Appeals for the Ninth Circuit had entered so that it might consider the case in an orderly fashion. For the second time within the span of only a few weeks, this Court has seen fit to interfere with the administration of justice by the lower federal courts by vacating a stay issued in the sound discretion of judges who are much more familiar with the cases than we are. I find this development unfortunate and distressing.

The Court's action in the instant case is particularly unwise. The Court of Appeals issued the stay so that it could consider Mr. Baal's first federal habeas petition, filed on his behalf by his parents in their capacity as next friends. It is wholly inappropriate to deny the court an opportunity to consider the case at such an early stage of the collateral review process....

The fact that a state court held an evidentiary hearing one week ago and determined that Mr. Baal was competent offers no support for the Court's action today.... A state court's determination of subsidiary facts may enjoy a presumption of correctness in whatever federal hearing is held. This does not answer the antecedent question, however, whether an evidentiary hearing in federal court is warranted on the basis of the factual allegations made in the federal habeas petition. In addition, of course, the state court's findings would receive deference only if the state hearing provided a full and fair opportunity for resolution of the issue. Because the proceedings in this case have been so hurried, it is not at all clear that the state hearing was "full and fair" and that the findings are supported by the record.

Dissenting statement by Justice Blackmun and Stevens, J.: Justices Blackman and Stevens issued a joint dissenting statement indicating they would deny the application to vacate the stay.

Case note: The State of Nevada executed Thomas Baal by lethal injection on June 3, 1990. *See also* **Intervention by Next Friend; Rosenburg v. United States; Whitmore v. Arkansas**

Denmark
Denmark abolished the death penalty for ordinary crimes in 1933, and in 1978 it outlawed the death penalty for all crimes. *See also* **International Capital Punishment Nations**

Deposition
A deposition refers to testimony given out-of-court, but under conditions that would permit its use at trial.

A deposition may be through video recording or transcribed testimony. The use of deposition testimony in criminal trials is discouraged, though situations arise where it becomes necessary. The primary impediment to deposition testimony at a criminal trial, proffered by the prosecutor, is that a defendant has a constitutional right to confront his or her accusers in open court.

The basic rules for conducting depositions are fairly standard. The guidelines for depositions used in Federal rules of criminal procedure provide an illustration of the deposition process.

Federal Deposition Rules:

a. *When Taken.* Whenever due to exceptional circumstances of the case it is in the interest of justice that the testimony of a prospective witness of a party be taken and preserved for use at trial, the court may upon motion of such party and notice to the parties order that testimony of such witness be taken by deposition and that any designated book, paper, document, record, recording, or other material not privileged, be produced at the same time and place. If a witness is detained pursuant to Federal law, the court on written motion of the witness and upon notice to the parties may direct that the witness' deposition be taken. After the deposition has been subscribed the court may discharge the witness.

b. *Notice of Taking.* The party at whose instance a deposition is to be taken shall give to every party reasonable written notice of the time and place for taking the deposition. The notice shall state the name and address of each person to be examined. On motion of a party upon whom the notice is served, the court for cause shown may extend or shorten the time or change the place for taking the deposition. The officer having custody of a defendant shall be notified of the time and place set for the examination and shall, unless the defendant waives in writing the right to be present, produce the defendant at the examination and keep the defendant in the presence of the witness during the examination, unless, after being warned by the court that disruptive conduct will cause the defendant's removal from the place of the taking of the deposition, the defendant persists in conduct which is such as to justify exclusion from that place. A defendant not in custody shall have the right to be present at the examination upon request subject to such terms as may be fixed by the court, but a failure, absent good cause shown, to appear after notice and tender of expenses in accordance with subdivision (c) of this rule shall constitute a waiver of that right and of any objection to the taking and use of the deposition based upon that right.

c. *Payment of Expenses.* Whenever a deposition is taken at the instance of the government, or whenever a deposition is taken at the instance of a defendant who is unable to bear the expenses of the taking of the deposition, the court may direct that the expense of travel and subsistence of the defendant and the defendant's attorney for attendance at the examination and the cost of the transcript of the deposition shall be paid by the government.

d. *How Taken.* Subject to such additional conditions as the court shall provide, a deposition shall be taken and filed in the manner provided in civil actions except as otherwise provided in these rules, provided that (1) in no event shall a deposition be taken of a party defendant without that defendant's consent, and (2) the scope and manner of examination and cross-examination shall be such as would be allowed in the trial itself. The government shall make available to the defendant or the defendant's counsel for examination and use at the taking of the deposition any statement of the witness being deposed which is in the possession of the government and to which the defendant would be entitled at the trial.

e. *Use.* At the trial or upon any hearing, a part or all of a deposition, so far as otherwise admissible under the rules of evidence, may be used as substantive evidence if the witness is unavailable, or the witness gives testimony at the trial or hearing inconsistent with that witness' deposition. Any deposition may also be used by any party for the purpose of contradicting or impeaching the testimony of the deponent as a witness. If only a part of a deposition is offered in evidence by a party, an adverse party may require the offering of all of it which is relevant to the part offered and any party may offer other parts.

f. *Objections to Deposition Testimony.* Objections to deposition testimony or evidence or parts thereof and the grounds for the objection shall be stated at the time of the taking of the deposition.

g. *Deposition by Agreement Not Precluded.* Nothing in this rule shall preclude the taking of a deposition, orally or upon written questions, or the use of a deposition, by agreement of the parties with the consent of the court.

Desalvo, Albert *see* Boston Strangler

Deterrence Theory of Capital Punishment *see* Justifications for Capital Punishment

Direct Examination of Witness *see* Examination of Witness

Directed Verdict *see* Acquittal

Discovery
The term "discovery" is a legal technical word. Discovery is a legal device that permits a defendant and prosecutor to learn the nature of the evidence each will present at trial before the trial begins. The basic idea behind discovery is that neither party should be surprised about what evidence will be introduced at trial. Discovery also serves as a mechanism for encouraging plea agreements. That is, a defendant will be more willing to enter a plea agreement if he or she learns before trial that the prosecutor has strong evidence against him or her. Also, a prosecutor is more likely to seek dismissal of charges if it is learned that the defendant has strong evidence to show his or her innocence.

Generally discovery must occur before trial. However, in capital prosecutions discovery may occur at the guilt phase and the penalty phase. Unlike typical criminal prosecutions, the penalty phase of a capital prosecutions utilizes witnesses and other evidence. Consequently, courts permit discovery to occur for the penalty phase.

The basic rules for conducting discovery are fairly uniform. The discovery rules used in Federal prosecutions provide an illustration of the discovery process.

Federal Discovery Rules:

a. **Governmental Disclosure of Evidence**

1. *Information Subject to Disclosure.*

A. Statement of Defendant. Upon request of a defendant the government must disclose to the defendant and make available for inspection, copying, or photographing: any relevant written or recorded statements made by the defendant, or copies thereof, within the possession, custody, or control of the government, the existence of which is known, or by the exercise of due diligence may become known, to the attorney for the government; that portion of any written record containing the substance of any relevant oral statement made by the defendant whether before or after arrest in response to interrogation by any person then known to the defendant to be a government agent; and recorded testimony of the defendant before a grand jury which relates to the offense charged. The government must also disclose to the defendant the substance of any other relevant oral statement made by the defendant whether before or after arrest in response to interrogation by any person then known by the defendant to be a government agent if the government intends to use that statement at trial. Upon request of a defendant which is an organization such as a corporation, partnership, association or labor union, the government must disclose to the defendant any of the foregoing statements made by a person who the government contends (1) was, at the time of making the statement, so situated as a director, officer, employee, or agent as to have been able legally to bind the defendant in respect to the subject of the statement, or (2) was, at the time of the offense, personally involved in the alleged conduct constituting the offense and so situated as a director, officer, employee, or agent as to have been able legally to bind the defendant in respect to that alleged conduct in which the person was involved.

B. Defendant's Prior Record. Upon request of the defendant, the government shall furnish to the defendant such copy of the defendant's prior criminal record, if any, as is within the possession, custody, or control of the government, the existence of which is known, or by the exercise of due diligence may become known, to the attorney for the government.

C. Documents and Tangible Objects. Upon request of the defendant the government shall permit the defendant to inspect and copy or photograph books, papers, documents, photographs, tangible objects, buildings or places, or copies or portions thereof, which are within the possession, custody or control of the government, and which are material to the preparation of the defendant's defense or are intended for use by the government as evidence in chief at the trial, or were obtained from or belong to the defendant.

D. Reports of Examinations and Tests. Upon request of a defendant the government shall permit the defendant to inspect and copy or photograph any results or reports of physical or mental examinations, and of scientific tests or experiments, or copies thereof, which are within the possession, custody, or control of the government, the existence of which is known, or by the exercise of due diligence may become known, to the attorney for the government, and which are material to the preparation of the defense or are intended for use by the government as evidence in chief at the trial.

E. Expert Witnesses. At the defendant's request, the government shall disclose to the defendant a written summary of testimony the government intends to use during its case in chief at trial. If the government requests discovery and the defendant complies, the government shall, at the defendant's request, disclose to the defendant a written summary of testimony the government intends to use at trial on the issue of the defendant's mental condition. The summary provided under this subdivision shall describe the witnesses' opinions, the bases and the reasons for those opinions, and the witnesses' qualifications.

2. *Information Not Subject to Disclosure.* Except as provided by this rule, this rule does not authorize the discovery or inspection of reports, memoranda, or other internal government documents made by the attorney for the government or any other government agent investigating or prosecuting the case. Nor does the rule authorize the discovery or inspection of statements made by government witnesses or prospective government witnesses except as otherwise provided by statute.

3. *Grand Jury Transcripts.* Except as provided by other rules, this rule does not relate to discovery or inspection of recorded proceedings of a grand jury.

b. **The Defendant's Disclosure of Evidence.**

1. *Information Subject to Disclosure.*

A. Documents and Tangible Objects. If the defendant requests disclosure under this rule, upon compliance with such request by the government, the defendant, on request of the government, shall permit the gov-

ernment to inspect and copy or photograph books, papers, documents, photographs, tangible objects, or copies or portions thereof, which are within the possession, custody, or control of the defendant and which the defendant intends to introduce as evidence in chief at the trial.

B. Reports of Examinations and Tests. If the defendant requests disclosure under this rule, upon compliance with such request by the government, the defendant, on request of the government, shall permit the government to inspect and copy or photograph any results or reports of physical or mental examinations and of scientific tests or experiments made in connection with the particular case, or copies thereof, within the possession or control of the defendant, which the defendant intends to introduce as evidence in chief at the trial or which were prepared by a witness whom the defendant intends to call at the trial when the results or reports relate to that witness' testimony.

C. Expert Witnesses. Under the following circumstances. the defendant shall, at the government's request, disclose to the government a written summary of testimony that the defendant intends to use as evidence at trial: (i) if the defendant requests disclosure under this rule and the government complies, or (ii) if the defendant has given notice of an intent to present expert testimony on the defendant's mental condition. This summary shall describe the witnesses' opinions, the bases and reasons for those opinions, and the witnesses' qualifications.

2. *Information Not Subject to Disclosure.* Except as to scientific or medical reports, this subdivision does not authorize the discovery or inspection of reports, memoranda, or other internal defense documents made by the defendant, or the defendant's attorneys or agents in connection with the investigation or defense of the case, or of statements made by the defendant, or by government or defense witnesses, or by prospective government or defense witnesses, to the defendant, the defendant's agents or attorneys.

c. **Continuing Duty to Disclose.** If, prior to or during trial, a party discovers additional evidence or material previously requested or ordered, which is subject to discovery or inspection under this rule, such party shall promptly notify the other party or that other party's attorney or the court of the existence of the additional evidence or material.

d. **Regulation of Discovery.**

1. *Protective and Modifying Orders.* Upon a sufficient showing the court may at any time order that the discovery or inspection be denied, restricted, or deferred, or make such other order as is appropriate. Upon motion by a party, the court may permit the party to make such showing, in whole or in part, in the form of a written statement to be inspected by the judge alone. If the court

enters an order granting relief following such an ex parte showing, the entire text of the party's statement shall be sealed and preserved in the records of the court to be made available to the appellate court in the event of an appeal.

2. *Failure to Comply with a Request.* If at any time during the course of the proceedings it is brought to the attention of the court that a party has failed to comply with this rule, the court may order such party to permit the discovery or inspection, grant a continuance, or prohibit the party from introducing evidence not disclosed, or it may enter such other order as it deems just under the circumstances. The court may specify the time, place and manner of making the discovery and inspection and may prescribe such terms and conditions as are just. *See also* **Bracy v. Gramley; Brady v. Maryland; Strickler v. Greene**

Discretion to Seek the Death Penalty *see* **Prosecutor**

Discretionary Review *see* **Certiorari, Writ of**

Discrimination in Grand or Petit Jury Selection
A criminal defendant is denied the equal protection of the laws guaranteed by the Fourteenth Amendment of the Federal Constitution if he or she is indicted by a grand jury or tried by a petit jury from which members of his or her race, gender or religion have been excluded because of their race, gender or religion. Procedures used to select grand or petit juries may not systematically exclude persons because of their race, gender or religion. A claim of discrimination in grand or petit jury selection cannot be sustained on bare allegations. A defendant must present evidence in support of the claim.

During the early history of the development of capital punishment jurisprudence, the United States Supreme Court was called upon on numerous occasions to address the issue of racial discrimination in the composition of grand and petit juries. Beginning with the decision in *Strauder v. West Virginia*, 100 U.S. 303 (1879), the Supreme Court has been inflexible in holding that, because of the finality of capital punishment prosecutions, racial discrimination cannot be tolerated in the selection of grand or petit juries. *See also* **Akins v. Texas; Arnold v. North Carolina; Bush v. Kentucky; Carter v. Texas; Cassell v. Texas; Coleman v. Alabama (I); Coleman v. Alabama (II); Eubanks v. Louisiana; Franklin v. South Carolina; Gibson v. Mississippi; Hale v. Kentucky; Hill v. Texas; In Re Jugiro; In Re Wood; Jury Selection; Martin v. Texas; Murray v. Louisiana; Neal v. Delaware; Patton v. Mississippi; Pierre v. Louisiana; Race-Qualified Jury; Rogers v. Alabama; Reece v. Georgia; Shepherd v. Florida; Sims v. Georgia (II); Smith v. Mississippi; Strauder v. West Virginia; Swain v. Alabama; Thomas v. Texas; Whitus v. Georgia; Williams v. Georgia; Williams v. Mississippi**

Disposal of Executed Corpse
There are five statutorily recognized dispositions for the bodies of executed capital felons. Each disposition is presented below.

1. *Permit Relatives to Take the Corpse:* Fifteen capital punishment jurisdictions provide by statute that the corpse of an executed felon is to be turned over to a requesting relative. Six of those jurisdictions go so far as to pay the cost of shipping the corpse to a requesting relative, at the last residence of the capital felon.

2. *Permit a Friend to Take the Corpse:* The statutes in eleven capital punishment jurisdictions provide that the corpse of an executed felon may be turned over to a requesting friend. In this situation the corpse would only be given to a friend of the capital felon, if no relative made a request for the corpse.

3. *An Entity Designated by the Capital Felon:* Currently only two capital punishment jurisdictions provide by statute that the corpse of an executed felon may be turned over to an entity designated by the capital felon prior to execution. This type of disposal contemplates having the corpse sent to a medical facility for research.

4. *Unclaimed Corpse Donated to Medical Center:* The statutes in five capital punishment jurisdictions provide that the corpse of a capital felon may be turned over to a medical center for research. This type of disposal is only triggered if neither relatives nor friends of the capital felon request the corpse.

5. *Unclaimed Corpse Buried by the Jurisdiction:* If no claim is made for the corpse of an executed capital felon, the statutes in fourteen capital punishment jurisdictions provide for burial by the jurisdiction. These statutes also provide that the cost of burial is borne by the jurisdiction.

Disrupting Government Function Aggravator
The 1995 Oklahoma bombing incident can be viewed from many perspectives. One of those perspectives includes disruption of a governmental function. That is, the deaths that occurred in the bombing resulted from efforts to disrupt the federal governmental operations that took place in the building that was bombed. Seven capital punishment jurisdictions, Alabama, Arkansas, Florida, Mississippi, Nebraska, North Carolina, and Utah, have made disruption of a government function a statutory aggravating circumstance when death results therefrom. Consequently, in those jurisdictions the death penalty may be imposed if this aggravator is found to exist in the commission of a capital offense. *See also* **Aggravating Circumstances**

Dissenting Opinion
When a justice on an appellate court does not agree with the outcome of a case, as decided by the majority on the appellate court, he or she may issue a dissenting opinion. A dissenting opinion expresses the individual view of a justice on how the majority should have decided a case. Dissenting opinions are not binding or controlling

JURISDICTIONS USING DISRUPTING GOVERNMENT FUNCTION AGGRAVATOR

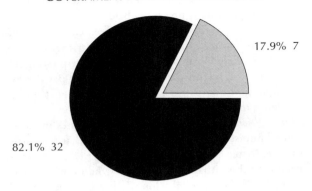

17.9% 7

82.1% 32

■ DISRUPTING GOVERNMENT FUNCTION JURISDICTIONS
■ ALL OTHER JURISDICTIONS

authority on any lower court. It is not uncommon, however, for a dissenting opinion to be adopted in later case by the majority on an appellate court. *See also* **Concurring Opinion**

District of Columbia The death penalty is not carried out by the District of Columbia. The last execution in the District of Columbia was in 1957.

Djibouti Capital punishment is on the law books in the nation of Djibouti, but the death penalty has not been used in more than 10 years. The firing squad is used by Djibouti to carry out the death penalty. Its legal system is a mixture of French civil law, Islamic law and customary law. The nation's constitution was adopted on September 4, 1992.

The judicial system of Djibouti comprises trial courts, appeal courts, and a Supreme Court. Defendants have the right to public trials, they are presumed innocent, have the right to retained or appointed counsel. There is no right to trial by jury. *See also* **International Capital Punishment Nations**

DNA Evidence DNA is the abbreviation for deoxyribonucleic acid. DNA is the genetic material present in the nucleus of cells in all living organisms. DNA has been referred to as the "blueprint of life," because it contains all of the information required to make an organism grow and develop. Researchers have found that the majority of the DNA is identical from one human to another, but there are locations in the DNA that have been found to differ from one individual to another, with the exception of twins. These locations are the regions of DNA that are used to compare the DNA obtained from an unknown evidence sample, to the DNA of a known individual in DNA identification testing.

There are three basic types of DNA tests: (1) Restriction Fragment Length Polymorphism Testing; (2) Polymerase Chain Reaction Testing — Nuclear DNA; and (3) Polymerase Chain Reaction Testing — Mitochondrial DNA. While there are different types of DNA testing done, a few basic steps are performed regardless of the type of test used. The general procedure includes: (1) isolating the DNA from an evidence sample containing DNA of unknown origin; (2) processing the DNA so that test results may be obtained; (3) determination of the DNA test results from specific regions of the DNA; and (4) comparison and interpretation of the test results to determine whether the known individual is excluded as the source of the DNA or is included as a possible source of the DNA.

DNA samples may be taken from: liquid blood or bloodstains; liquid saliva or saliva stains; liquid semen or dried semen stains; pieces of tissue or skin; fingernails; plucked and shed hairs; bone; teeth; fingernails; tissues from internal organs (including brain).

In 1986 the first known use of DNA to solve a criminal identification occurred in Narborough, England. Authorities there had arrested a 17 year old mentally disturbed youth for a rape/murder incident. Approximately 3 months after the youth confessed to the crime, authorities used DNA testing to apprehend the true perpetrator. DNA was first introduced into evidence in a United States court in 1986. In little more than a decade DNA testing has become the foremost forensic technique for identifying criminals, eliminating suspects, and freeing innocently convicted defendants.

Death Row Inmates Released Due to DNA Evidence

Name	Year Released	Years on Death Row	State
Kirk Bloodsworth	1993	9	MD
Rolando Cruz	1995	10	IL
Al Hernandez	1995	10	IL
Vern Jimerson	1996	11	IL
Dennis Williams	1996	17	IL
Robert Miller	1998	10	OK
Ron Williamson	1999	11	OK
Ronald Jones	1999	10	IL

Source: Death Penalty Information Center, Innocence (1999).

Dobbert v. Florida *Court:* United States Supreme Court; *Case Citation:* Dobbert v. Florida, 432 U.S. 282 (1977); *Argued:* March 28, 1977; *Decided:* June 17, 1977; *Opinion of the Court:* Justice Rehnquist; *Concurring Opinion:* Chief Justice Burger; *Dissenting Opinion:* Justice Stevens, in which Brennan and Marshall, JJ., joined; *Dissenting Statement:* Justice Brennan and Marshall, J.; *Appellate Defense Counsel:* Louis O. Frost, Jr. argued and briefed; *Appellate Prosecution Counsel:* Charles W. Musgrove argued; Robert L. Shevin on brief; *Amicus Curiae Brief Supporting Prosecutor:* None; *Amicus Curiae Brief Supporting Defendant:* 1.

Issue Presented: Whether procedural changes to Florida's death penalty law which were not enacted at the time of the commission of the defendant's capital crime, could be applied to the defendant consistent with the Ex Post Facto Clause?

Case Holding: Procedural changes to Florida's death penalty law which were not enacted at the time of the commission of the defendant's capital crime, may be applied to the defendant consistent with the Constitution.

Factual and procedural background of case: The State of

Florida convicted the defendant, Ernest Dobbert, of capital murder. During the penalty phase of the prosecution, the jury recommended life imprisonment, but the trial judge rejected the recommendation and imposed a sentence of death. On appeal to the Florida Supreme Court, the defendant contended that his conviction and sentence violated the Ex Post Facto Clause of the Federal Constitution, on the grounds that the death penalty statute under which he was prosecuted was not enacted at the time of the commission of his offense. Specifically, the defendant argued that under the old law, which was invalid under *Furman v. Georgia*, the trial judge could not reject a jury's decision on punishment. The State appellate court rejected the defendant's claim and affirmed the conviction and sentence. The United States Supreme Court granted certiorari to consider the issue.

Opinion of the Court by Justice Rehnquist: Justice Rehnquist held that the defendant's conviction and sentence did not violate the Ex Post Facto Clause. The opinion reasoned that the changes in the death penalty statute between the time of the murder and the time of the trial were procedural and on the whole ameliorative. It was said that the new statute simply altered the methods employed in determining whether the death penalty was to be imposed, but there was no change in the quantum of punishment attached to the crime. Further, Justice Rehnquist indicated that the existence of the earlier statute at the time of the murder served as an operative fact to "warn" the defendant of the penalty which Florida would seek to impose on him if he were convicted of murder. The opinion pointed out that this was sufficient compliance with the ex post facto provision of the Constitution, notwithstanding the subsequent invalidation of the statute. Justice Rehnquist concluded that "[e]ven though it may work to the disadvantage of a defendant, a procedural change is not ex post facto." The judgment of the Florida Supreme Court was affirmed.

Concurring opinion by Chief Justice Burger: The Chief Justice concurred in the Court's decision. The concurring opinion stated: "A crucial factor in this case, for me, is that, as the Court's opinion recites, when [the defendant] committed the crime, a Florida statute permitted the death penalty for the offense. [The defendant] was at least constructively on notice that this penalty might indeed follow his actions. During the time which elapsed between the commission of the offense and the trial, the statute was changed to provide different procedures for determining whether death was an appropriate punishment. But these new procedures, taken as a whole, were, if anything, more favorable to the [defendant]; consequently the change cannot be read otherwise than as the Court's opinion suggests."

Dissenting opinion by Justice Stevens, in which Brennan and Marshall, JJ., joined: Justice Stevens dissented from the majority opinion on the grounds that the Court's decision was reached after altering the meaning of the Ex Post Facto Clause. The dissent argued as follows:

> The Court holds that Florida may apply this law to [the defendant] without violating the Ex Post Facto Clause. In its view,

the unconstitutional law which was on the Florida statute books at the time of the offense "clearly indicated Florida's view of the severity of murder and of the degree of punishment which the legislature wished to impose upon murderers." The Court concludes that the "fair warning" provided by the invalid statute "was sufficient compliance with the ex post facto provision of the United States Constitution."

This conclusion represents a clear departure from the test the Court has applied in past cases construing the Ex Post Facto Clause....

... Fair warning cannot be the touchstone, for two reasons. First, "fair warning" does not provide a workable test for deciding particular cases. Second, ... fair notice is not the only important value underlying the constitutional prohibition; the Ex Post Facto Clause also provides a basic protection against improperly motivated or capricious legislation. It ensures that the sovereign will govern impartially and that it will be perceived as doing so. The Court's "fair warning" test, if it extends beyond this case, would allow government action that is just the opposite of impartial. If that be so, the "fair warning" rationale will defeat the very purpose of the Clause....

Because a logical application of the Court's "fair warning" rationale would lead to such manifestly intolerable results, I assume that this case will ultimately be regarded as nothing more than an archaic gargoyle. It is nevertheless distressing to witness such a demeaning construction of a majestic bulwark in the framework of our Constitution.

Dissenting statement by Justice Brennan and Marshall, J.: Justices Brennan and Marshall issued a joint dissenting statement indicating that they adhered to their "views that the death penalty is in all circumstances cruel and unusual punishment prohibited by the Eighth and Fourteenth Amendments[.]"

Case note: Florida executed Ernest Dobbert by electrocution on September 7, 1984. *See also* **Ex Post Facto Clause; Kring v. Missouri; Holden v. Minnesota**

Dobbs v. Zant

Court: United States Supreme Court; *Case Citation:* Dobbs v. Zant, 506 U.S. 357 (1993); *Argued:* Not reported; *Decided:* January 19, 1993; *Opinion of the Court:* Per Curiam; *Concurring Opinion:* Justice Scalia, in which Thomas joined; *Dissenting Opinion:* None; *Appellate Defense Counsel:* Not reported; *Appellate Prosecution Counsel:* Not reported; *Amicus Curiae Brief Supporting Prosecutor:* Not reported; *Amicus Curiae Brief Supporting Defendant:* Not reported.

Issue Presented: Whether the "law of the case doctrine" prevents a Federal appellate court from revisiting a previously decided issue when manifest injustice would result from failing to revisit the issue?

Case Holding: The "law of the case doctrine" does not prevent a Federal appellate court from revisiting a previously decided issue when manifest injustice would result from failing to do so.

Factual and procedural background of case: The defendant, Wilburn Dobbs, was convicted and sentenced to death for capital murder by the State of Georgia. After the defendant exhausted his State post-conviction remedies, he filed a habeas corpus petition in a Federal District Court. The defendant alleged ineffective assistance of counsel at the penalty phase of his trial. In rejecting the defendant's claim, the District Court was forced to rely upon representations by defense counsel regarding his trial performance, because the penalty phase transcript was not available. A Federal Court of Appeals affirmed the District Court's decision.

After the Court of Appeals affirmed the denial of relief, the defendant located a transcript of the penalty phase proceedings which contradicted defense counsel's account of what occurred at the proceeding. At the time of the discovery of the transcript, the Court of Appeals was reviewing another matter presented to it by the defendant. Consequently, the defendant motioned the Court of Appeals to supplement the appellate record with the transcript. The Court of Appeals denied his motion to supplement the appellate record with the transcript. The Court of Appeals reasoned that the "law of the case doctrine" prevented it from revisiting its prior rejection of the ineffective assistance claim. The United States Supreme Court granted certiorari to consider the issue.

Opinion of the Court was delivered Per Curiam: The per curiam opinion held that the Court of Appeals erred by refusing to consider the sentencing hearing transcript. It was said that the transcript was no doubt relevant, because it called into serious question the factual predicate on which the lower courts relied in deciding the defendant's ineffective assistance claim. The Court rejected the assertion that the law of the case doctrine precluded the Court of Appeals from revisiting the issue. It was said that the manifest injustice exception to the law of the case doctrine allowed the Court of Appeals to revisit the issue. The judgment of the Court of Appeals was reversed.

Concurring opinion by Justice Scalia, in which Thomas joined: Justice Scalia concurred in the Court's judgment. He wrote as follows: "Today's judgment reverses the decision below on the grounds that, in deciding not to apply the 'manifest injustice' exception to the law of the case, the Court of Appeals wrongfully failed to consider a newly discovered transcript from [the defendant's] trial. The judgment is correct, but the judgment is also not worth making, serving no purpose but to extend the scandalous delay in the execution of a death sentence lawfully pronounced more than 18 years ago." *See also* **Law of the Case Doctrine**

Dominica The death penalty is permitted in the island nation of Dominica. Dominica uses hanging as the method of execution. Its legal system is based on English common law. The nation's constitution was adopted on November 3, 1978. Dominica is a parliamentary democracy and a member of the Commonwealth of Nations. The structure of the government includes an executive branch, unicameral legislative branch, and judicial branch.

The judicial system is composed of a high court and magistrate courts. Appeals may be made to the Supreme Court of the Organization of Eastern Caribbean States and to the Judicial Committee of the Privy Council in England. Under the laws of Dominica criminal trials are public, defendants are presumed innocent, are allowed legal counsel, and have the right to appeal. Free legal counsel is provided to the indigent defendants only in capital cases. *See also* **International Capital Punishment Nations**

Dominican Republic The Dominican Republic abolished the death penalty in 1966. *See also* **International Capital Punishment Nations**

Double-Counting Aggravators Courts prohibit double-counting of certain statutory aggravating circumstances when both factors relate to the same aspect of the crime. For example, it is improper for the trial court to utilize both a felony murder aggravator and a pecuniary gain aggravator when the murder occurred during a robbery. The reason is that the same evidence would support the "monetary" aspect of both aggravators.

Some courts prohibit giving the jury instructions on statutory aggravating circumstances that relate to the same aspect of the crime, and require the prosecutor to make an election between the aggravators the jury will consider. The general approach of most courts, however, is simply to give the jury a list of relevant statutory aggravating circumstances from which to choose, in making their assessment as to whether death is the proper sentence in light of any mitigating circumstances presented in the case. The trial judge must set out in his or her final order the statutory aggravating circumstances found to exist without double-counting. Criticism has been launched against this procedure because it still permits the jury to double-count, even though the trial court removes the double-counting in the sentencing judgment order.

When requested, a capital felon is entitled to a limiting instruction advising the jury not to double-count the weight of multiple aggravating circumstances supported by a single aspect of the crime. Courts have held that the same facts may be used to support more than one statutory aggravating circumstance as long the facts reveal different characteristics of the crime. *See also* **Aggravating Circumstances**

Double Jeopardy Clause The Fifth Amendment to the Federal Constitution declares that no person shall "be subject for the same offence to be twice put in jeopardy of life or limb[.]" The constitutional prohibition against double jeopardy was designed to protect an individual from being subjected to the hazards of trial and possible conviction more than once for an alleged offense. Under the common law double jeopardy was grounded in the plea of autrefois acquit or convict (former acquittal or conviction), which represented the universal maxim that no person was to be brought into jeopardy of his or her life more than once for the same offense.

The principle of autrefois was part of the legal tradition of the American Colonists. The Massachusetts Body of Liberties of 1641, a compilation of legal principles taken from the common law and English statutes, provided: "No man shall be twise sentenced by Civill Justice for one and the same Crime, offence, or Trespasse," and that "Everie Action betweene partie and partie, and proceedings against delinquents in Criminall causes shall be briefly and distinctly entered on the Rolles of every Court by the Recorder thereof. That such actions be not afterwards brought againe to the vexation of any man."

Although the Colonists were aware of principles against double jeopardy from the common law and English Statutes, New York was the lone jurisdiction to propose an amendment to the Constitution that included a prohibition against double jeopardy. The bill of rights adopted at the New York convention, and transmitted to Congress included a declaration that, "no Person ought to be put twice in Jeopardy of Life or Limb for one and the same Offence, nor, unless in case of impeachment, be punished more than once for the same Offence."

James Madison was influenced by New York's double jeopardy clause when he drafted the constitutional amendments to be proposed to the States. The words Madison introduced into the House of Representatives were: "No person shall be subject, except in cases of impeachment, to more than one punishment or one trial for the same offence[.]" The double jeopardy principle worded by Madison caused some concern. Representatives feared that, as proposed by Madison, double jeopardy might be taken to prohibit a second trial of a defendant who had his or her conviction reversed on appeal. Representative Benson of New York argued that the double jeopardy principle had to express the idea "that no man's life should be more than once put in jeopardy for the same offence; yet it was well known, that they were entitled to more than one trial." The provision that was ratified as part of the Fifth Amendment, was substantially in the language used by Representative Benson.

Under Anglo-American jurisprudence the Double Jeopardy Clause has been interpreted as protecting against (1) a second prosecution for the same offense after acquittal, (2) a second prosecution for the same offense after conviction, and (3) multiple punishments for the same offense.

Under double jeopardy principles when the same criminal act or transaction constitutes a violation of two distinct statutory provisions, the test to be applied to determine whether there are two offenses or only one, is whether each provision requires proof of an additional fact which the other does not. If additional proof is not required, then the two offenses are the same and double jeopardy may prohibit dual punishment.

A capital penalty phase proceeding has been deemed comparable to a trial on the issue of guilt, thereby making the Double Jeopardy Clause relevant to such proceeding. *See also* **Bill of Rights; Retrials and the Death Penalty**

Douglas, William O.
William O. Douglas served as an associate justice of the United States Supreme Court from 1939 to 1975. While on the Supreme Court Douglas was known as a progressive thinker who sought to expand the reach of the Constitution for the protection of individual freedoms from government control.

Douglas was born in Maine, Minnesota on October 16, 1898. Douglas graduated from Whitman College in 1920. He went on to attend Columbia Law School where he graduated in 1925. Douglas' resume included teaching at the law schools of Columbia and Yale, as well as an appointment to the Securities and Exchange Commission. In 1939 President Franklin D. Roosevelt nominated Douglas to the Supreme Court.

While on the Supreme Court Douglas wrote numerous capital punishment opinions. The capital punishment opinion that he was best known for involved his dissent in *Rosenberg v. United States*. The *Rosenberg* case brought about a great deal of controversy for Douglas because he granted a stay of execution of the death sentences of Julius and Ethal Rosenberg, based upon an appeal by a person not involved in the case. The majority on the Supreme Court lifted the stay. Douglas dissented and defended his decision to issue the temporary stay. He also argued strenuously in *Rosenberg* that the trial court in the case did not have authority to impose death sentences in the case. He denounced the majority for denying relief to the defendants on the grounds that the issue argued on appeal was never raised previously: "A suggestion is made that the question comes too late, that since the Rosenbergs did not raise this question on appeal, they are barred from raising it now. But the question of an unlawful sentence is never barred. No man or woman should go to death under an unlawful sentence merely because his lawyer failed to raise the point. It is that function among others that the Great Writ serves." Douglas died on January 18, 1980.

Capital Punishment Opinions Written by Douglas

Case Name	Opinion of the Court	Concurring Opinion	Dissenting Opinion
Boykin v. Alabama	✓		
Brady v. Maryland	✓		
Burns v. Wilson			✓
Chessman v. Teets			✓
Ciucci v. Illinois			✓
Crooker v. California			✓
Furman v. Georgia		✓	
Harris v. South Carolina		✓	
Kawakita v. United States	✓		
Malinski v. New York	✓		
McGautha v. California			✓
Rosenberg v. United States			✓
Spano v. New York		✓	
Stein v. New York			✓
Stroble v. California			✓
Turner v. Pennsylvania		✓	
United States v. Carignan		✓	
Watts v. Indiana		✓	
Witherspoon v. Illinois		✓	

Drive-by-Shooting Aggravator
In five capital punishment jurisdictions, California, Illinois, Indiana, Louisiana, and Washington, drive-by-shooting that results in the death

of the victim is a statutory aggravating circumstance. As such, the death penalty may be imposed if the penalty phase jury determines that the victim was killed as a result of the defendant shooting from inside a moving vehicle. This aggravator was prompted by a rash of drug related drive-by-shootings. *See also* **Aggravating Circumstances**

Drug-Trafficking Aggravator
The proliferation of illegal drugs in the nation has brought the 1930s style gang-warfare back onto the American stage. A minority of capital punishment jurisdictions, Florida, Illinois, Indiana, Louisiana, Pennsylvania, South Carolina, South Dakota and the Federal government, have responded to drug related killings by making murder committed during the course of drug-trafficking a statutory aggravating circumstance. In these jurisdictions if the penalty phase jury determines a defendant committed murder during the course of trafficking in drugs, the death penalty may be imposed. *See also* **Aggravating Circumstances**

JURISDICTIONS USING DRUG-TRAFFICKING AGGRAVATOR

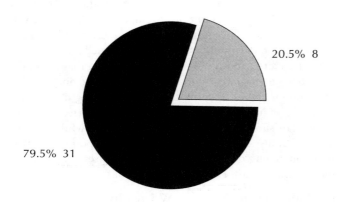

20.5% 8

79.5% 31

■ DRUG-TRAFFICKING AGGRAVATOR JURISDICTIONS
■ ALL OTHER JURISDICTIONS

Dual Sovereignty
Under the dual sovereignty doctrine when a defendant in a single act violates the law of two sovereign jurisdictions, he or she has committed two distinct offenses and may be prosecuted by both jurisdictions. For constitutional purposes, the United States and each of the fifty States are sovereign jurisdictions. A political subdivision of a State is not a sovereign jurisdiction.

In the context of capital punishment, the dual sovereignty doctrine permits the death penalty to be imposed on a defendant in two jurisdictions for the murder of one victim. This may occur where sufficient acts take place in both jurisdictions concerning the murder, though the victim actually dies in only one of the jurisdictions. *See also* **Crossley v. California; Heath v. Alabama**

Due Process Clause
The phrase "due process" appears in the Fifth and Fourteenth Amendments to the Federal Constitution. Due process, as it appears in the Fifth Amendment,

was ratified on December 15, 1791. Due process, as it appears in the Fourteenth Amendment, was ratified on July 9, 1868. The Fifth Amendment Due Process Clause is applicable only against the Federal government. The Fourteenth Amendment Due Process Clause is applicable against the States.

The Fifth Amendment Due Process Clause provides that no person shall "be deprived of life, liberty, or property, without due process of law." The Fourteenth Amendment Due Process Clause provides that "nor shall any State deprive any person of life, liberty, or property, without due process of law." The legal significance of the Fourteenth Amendment Due Process Clause is that through it almost all of the "Bill of Rights" have been imposed upon the States.

As a general matter, due process of law refers to fundamental fairness in the treatment of citizens by the government. In the context of criminal law, due process of law requires governments utilize fundamentally fair procedures in prosecuting persons accused of committing criminal offenses. *See also* **Bill of Rights; Fourteenth Amendment**

Dugan, Eva
Eva Dugan was born in 1878. She was hanged on February 21, 1930 by the State of Arizona for the murder of a Tucson rancher named Andrew J. Mathis. Dugan is the only woman ever executed by Arizona.

Dugan worked as a housekeeper for Mathis in January 1927. She was fired by him after only a few weeks of employment. Shortly after Mathis fired Dugan he disappeared, along with Dugan. Although authorities suspected foul play in the disappearance of Mathis, they had no leads on what happened to him. Eventually Pima County Sheriff Jim McDonald began sending missing person notices on Dugan and Mathis throughout the country. Slowly reports came in revealing that Dugan had sold Mathis' car in Kansas City, Missouri. A background check of Dugan revealed that she had been married at least five times. All of her husbands disappeared under mysterious circumstances and were never located. Sheriff McDonald learned that Dugan had a daughter living in White Plains, New York and a father residing in California, however, neither had seen Dugan for several years.

Sheriff McDonald eventually located Dugan in White Plains, where she was working at a hospital. Extradition pro-

Eva Dugan's execution by hanging was botched, which resulted in her being accidentally decapitated. (Arizona Department of Corrections)

ceedings were begun and on March 4, 1927 she was returned to Pima County, Arizona. Dugan was initially prosecuted solely for the theft of Mathis' car and was convicted of the charge and sentenced to prison. About nine months after Dugan's conviction for auto theft, Mathis' corpse was accidentally discovered buried in a shallow grave on his Tucson ranch.

Dugan was immediately charged with Mathis' murder. The evidence against her was circumstantial and she denied committing the crime. However, after a short trial she was convicted of the crime and sentenced to death. Dugan sat on death row for two years before she was publicly executed before an audience of 70 onlookers on February 21, 1930. It was reported that the execution was botched and her body separated from her head. *See also* **Women and Capital Punishment**

Dugger v. Adams *Court:* United States Supreme Court; *Case Citation:* Dugger v. Adams, 489 U.S. 401 (1989); *Argued:* November 1, 1988; *Decided:* February 28, 1989; *Opinion of the Court:* Justice White; *Concurring Opinion:* None; *Dissenting Opinion:* Justice Blackmun, in which Brennan, Marshall, and Stevens, JJ., joined; *Appellate Defense Counsel:* Ronald J. Tabak argued; Larry Helm Spalding and Mark Olive on brief; *Appellate Prosecution Counsel:* Margene A. Roper argued; Robert A. Butterworth on brief; *Amicus Curiae Brief Supporting Prosecutor:* 1; *Amicus Curiae Brief Supporting Defendant:* 1.

Issue Presented: Whether the Florida Supreme Court's determination that the defendant's failure to raise an issue in State court on direct appeal and initial habeas proceeding resulted in a default of the issue, precluded Federal courts from addressing the defaulted issue?

Case Holding: The Florida Supreme Court's determination that the defendant's failure to raise an issue in State court on direct appeal and initial habeas proceeding resulted in a default of the issue, precluded Federal courts from addressing the defaulted issue.

Factual and procedural background of case: The State of Florida charged the defendant, Aubrey Dennis Adams, with capital murder. During jury selection for the trial, the trial judge instructed the prospective jurors on their responsibility for the sentence they would recommend, stating that the court, not the jury, was responsible for sentencing and that the jury had merely an advisory role. Defense counsel did not object to these instructions. The jury found the defendant guilty of capital murder and recommended the death sentence, which the trial judge imposed.

The Florida Supreme Court affirmed the conviction and sentence on direct appeal. The defendant did not raise the issue of the trial judge's instruction to the prospective jurors during jury selection. The defendant subsequently filed unsuccessful State and Federal habeas corpus petitions, in which he also failed to raise the issue of the trial judge's instruction to the prospective jurors. Thereafter, it was held by the United States Supreme Court in *Caldwell v. Mississippi*, that the Eighth Amendment prohibited prosecutors from misinforming the jury in a capital case as to their role. Based on *Cald-*

well, the defendant filed another State trial court habeas petition challenging for the first time the instruction given by the trial judge. He contended that the instruction violated the Eighth Amendment by misinforming the jury of its sentencing role under Florida law. The State trial court denied relief. On appeal the Florida Supreme Court refused to address this argument because the defendant had failed to raise it on direct appeal.

Subsequently, the defendant filed another Federal habeas petition raising for the first time in Federal court his *Caldwell* claim. The Federal District Court held that the claim was procedurally barred. However, a Federal Court of Appeals reversed, holding that the claim was so novel at the time of defendant's trial, sentencing, and appeal that its legal basis was not reasonably available and that therefore he had established cause for his procedural default. The Court Appeals found the instruction violated the Eighth Amendment. The United States Supreme Court granted certiorari to consider the issue.

Opinion of the Court by Justice White: Justice White held that the defendant's claim was procedurally defaulted and that he was not entitled to relief. The opinion stated the Courts reasoning as follows:

> [The defendant] offers no excuse for his failure to challenge the remarks on state-law grounds, and we discern none that would amount to good cause in a federal habeas corpus proceeding. Had [the defendant] objected at the time and asserted error under state law, and had the trial or appellate court sustained his objection, the error would have been corrected in the state system. Had his objection been overruled and that ruling sustained on appeal, we would very likely know that the instruction was an accurate reflection of state law. In either event, it is doubtful that the later decision in *Caldwell* would have provoked the filing of a second habeas corpus petition. In these circumstances, the fact that it turns out that the trial court's remarks were objectionable on federal as well as state grounds is not good cause for his failure to follow Florida procedural rules....
>
> Neither do we hold that whenever a defendant has any basis for challenging particular conduct as improper, a failure to preserve that claim under state procedural law bars any subsequently available claim arising out of the same conduct. Indeed, [the defendant] here could have challenged the improper remarks by the trial judge at the time of his trial as a violation of due process. Rather, what is determinative in this case is that the ground for challenging the trial judge's instructions — that they were objectionable under state law — was a necessary element of the subsequently available *Caldwell* claim. In such a case, the subsequently available federal claim does not excuse the procedural default.

The judgment of the Court of Appeals was reversed.

Dissenting opinion by Justice Blackmun, in which Brennan, Marshall, and Stevens, JJ., joined: Justice Blackmun strongly dissented from the majority's decision in the case. He argued that the *Caldwell* claim was not barred from consideration in a Federal habeas proceeding. The dissent argued its position as follows:

> Although this Court repeatedly has ruled that the Eighth Amendment prohibits the arbitrary or capricious imposition of the death penalty, the Court today itself arbitrarily imposes procedural obstacles to thwart the vindication of what apparently is a meritorious Eighth Amendment claim.

In this case, the Eleventh Circuit determined that ... Aubrey Dennis Adams was sentenced to death in violation of the Eighth Amendment, as interpreted in *Caldwell v. Mississippi*. This Court now reverses that determination, not because it finds the death sentence valid, but because [the defendant] was late in presenting his claim to the Florida courts. In other words, this Court is sending a man to a presumptively unlawful execution because he or his lawyers did not raise his objection at what is felt to be the appropriate time for doing so.

I would understand, and accept, the Court's decision if the federal courts lacked authority to remedy the unconstitutional death sentence. But, manifestly, that is not the case. In reversing the judgment of the Court of Appeals, the majority relegates to a footnote its discussion of established doctrines that, upon full consideration, might entitle [the defendant] to an affirmance, not a reversal, of that judgment. Thus, the majority not only capriciously casts aside precedent to reinstate an unconstitutionally "unreliable" death sentence purely for procedural reasons, but also compounds that capriciousness by issuing an opinion in which decisive issues receive only dismissive consideration....

Even if, somehow, I could be convinced that the Florida Supreme Court's reliance on the [defendant's] procedural default was "adequate," within the meaning of this Court's precedents, I would still conclude that the Court of Appeals properly reached the merits of [the defendant's] *Caldwell* claim. I have no quarrel with the majority's determination that [the defendant] cannot show "cause" for his procedural default. "That determination, however, does not end our inquiry."

Rather, ... we must consider whether the failure to examine the merits of the *Caldwell* claim in this habeas action would result in a fundamental miscarriage of justice. The majority believes that no such injustice would occur. Again, I disagree....

[The defendant's] *Caldwell* claim is precisely the kind of claim that remains reviewable in a federal habeas action even though [the defendant] cannot establish cause for his procedural default. In holding otherwise, the Court sends [the defendant] to an execution that not only is presumptively unlawful, but is presumptively inaccurate as well. Nothing in the habeas corpus precedents of this Court calls for this consummately capricious result.

Case note: Florida executed Aubrey Dennis Adams by electrocution on May 4, 1989. *See also* **Caldwell v. Mississippi; Procedural Default of Constitutional Claims**

Duncan v. Missouri
Court: United States Supreme Court; *Case Citation:* Duncan v. Missouri, 152 U.S. 377 (1894); *Argued:* Not reported; *Decided:* March 12, 1894; *Opinion of the Court:* Chief Justice Fuller; *Concurring Opinion:* None; *Dissenting Opinion:* None; *Appellate Defense Counsel:* Emanuel M. Hewlett argued and briefed; *Appellate Prosecution Counsel:* R. F. Walker argued and briefed; *Amicus Curiae Brief Supporting Prosecutor:* None; *Amicus Curiae Brief Supporting Defendant:* None.

Issue Presented: Whether application to the defendant of changes in the appellate procedure of Missouri's high court violated ex post facto principles?

Case Holding: Application to the defendant of changes in the appellate procedure of Missouri's high court did not violate ex post facto principles.

Factual and procedural background of case: The defendant, Harry Duncan, was convicted of capital murder and sentenced to death by the State of Missouri. The defendant appealed the judgment to a special division of the Missouri Supreme Court, which had been established by the State constitution after the commission of the defendant's crime. The special appellate division affirmed the judgment. The defendant next sought review by the full membership of the appellate court, on the grounds that application of the new appellate procedure to him violated the Ex Post Facto Clause of the Federal Constitution. The full appellate court refused to review the case. The United States Supreme Court granted certiorari to consider the issue.

Opinion of the Court by Chief Justice Fuller: The Chief Justice initially explained that "[t]he amendment to the constitution of the state of Missouri provided for the separation of the supreme court into two divisions for the transaction of business, and that, when a federal question was involved, the cause, on the application of the losing party, should be transferred to the full court for decision." In turning to the substantive issue of ex post facto, the opinion explained: "It may be said, generally speaking, that an ex post facto law is one which imposes a punishment for an act which was not punishable at the time it was committed; or an additional punishment to that then prescribed; or changes the rules of evidence by which less or different testimony is sufficient to convict than was then required; or, in short, in relation to the offense or its consequences, alters the situation of a party to his disadvantage, but the prescribing of different modes of procedure, and the abolition of courts and creation of new ones, leaving untouched all the substantial protections with which the existing law surrounds the person accused of crime, are not considered within the constitutional inhibition."

In addition to finding the Ex Post Facto Clause had no application to the defendant's case, the Chief Justice found the issue was waived because the defendant did not present it to the special appellate court of the State. The judgment of the Missouri Supreme Court was affirmed. *See also* **Ex Post Facto Clause**

Duress *see* **Extreme Duress Mitigator**

Durham Rule *see* **Insanity Defense**

E

Echols, Damien Wayne *see* **West Memphis Cult Murders**

Ecuador Ecuador abolished capital punishment in 1906. *See also* **International Capital Punishment Nations**

Eddings v. Oklahoma *Court:* United States Supreme Court; *Case Citation:* Eddings v. Oklahoma, 455 U.S. 104 (1982); *Argued:* November 2, 1981; *Decided:* January 19, 1982; *Opinion of the Court:* Justice Powell; *Concurring Statement:* Justice Brennan; *Concurring Opinion:* Justice O'Connor; *Dissenting Opinion:* Chief Justice Burger, in which White, Blackmun and Rehnquist, JJ., joined; *Appellate Defense Counsel:* Jay C. Baker argued and briefed; *Appellate Prosecution Counsel:* David W. Lee argued; Jan Eric Cartwright and Tomilou Gentry Liddell on brief; *Amicus Curiae Brief Supporting Prosecutor:* 1; *Amicus Curiae Brief Supporting Defendant:* 2.

Issue Presented: Whether refusal by a trial court to consider relevant mitigating evidence proffered at the penalty phase of a capital prosecution violates the Constitution?

Case Holding: Refusal by a trial court to consider relevant mitigating evidence proffered at the penalty phase of a capital prosecution violates the Constitution.

Factual and procedural background of case: The defendant, Monty Lee Eddings, was convicted in an Oklahoma trial court of capital murder and was sentenced to death. At the time of the offense the defendant was 16 years old, but he was tried as an adult. At the penalty phase of the prosecution the defendant presented, as mitigating circumstances, evidence of a turbulent family history, of beatings by a harsh father, and of serious emotional disturbance.

In imposing the death sentence, the trial judge refused, as a matter of law, to consider in mitigation the circumstances of the defendant's unhappy upbringing and emotional disturbance, and found that the only mitigating circumstance was his youth, which circumstance was held to be insufficient to outweigh the aggravating circumstances found. The Oklahoma appellate courts affirmed the conviction and sentence. The United States Supreme Court granted certiorari to consider the punishment in view of the defendant's age. However, the Court only addressed the issue of the trial court's refusal to consider certain mitigating evidence.

Opinion of the Court by Justice Powell: Justice Powell ruled that in view of the Court's decision in *Lockett v. Ohio*, that all relevant mitigating evidence must be considered during a capital penalty phase proceeding, the defendant's death sentence must be vacated as it was imposed without the type of individualized consideration of mitigating factors required by the Constitution. Justice Powell outlined the Court's reasoning as follows:

... Just as the State may not by statute preclude the sentencer from considering any mitigating factor, neither may the sentencer refuse to consider, as a matter of law, any relevant mitigating evidence. In this instance, it was as if the trial judge had instructed a jury to disregard the mitigating evidence Eddings proffered on his behalf. The sentencer, and the Court of Criminal Appeals on review, may determine the weight to be given relevant mitigating evidence. But they may not give it no weight by excluding such evidence from their consideration.

Nor do we doubt that the evidence Eddings offered was relevant mitigating evidence. Eddings was a youth of 16 years at the time of the murder. Evidence of a difficult family history and of emotional disturbance is typically introduced by defendants in mitigation. In some cases, such evidence properly may be given little weight. But when the defendant was 16 years old at the time of the offense there can be no doubt that evidence of a turbulent family history, of beatings by a harsh father, and of severe emotional disturbance is particularly relevant.

The trial judge recognized that youth must be considered a relevant mitigating factor. But youth is more than a chronological fact. It is a time and condition of life when a person may be most susceptible to influence and to psychological damage. Our history is replete with laws and judicial recognition that minors, especially in their earlier years, generally are less mature and responsible than adults. Particularly "during the formative years of childhood and adolescence, minors often lack the experience, perspective, and judgment" expected of adults.

Even the normal 16-year-old customarily lacks the maturity of an adult. In this case, Eddings was not a normal 16-year-old; he had been deprived of the care, concern, and paternal attention that children deserve. On the contrary, it is not disputed that he was a juvenile with serious emotional problems, and had been raised in a neglectful, sometimes even violent, family background. In addition, there was testimony that Eddings' mental and emotional development were at a level several years below his chronological age. All of this does not suggest an absence of responsibility for the crime of murder, deliberately committed in this case. Rather, it is to say that just as the chronological age of a minor is itself a relevant mitigating factor of great weight, so must the background and mental and emotional development of a youthful defendant be duly considered in sentencing.

We are not unaware of the extent to which minors engage increasingly in violent crime. Nor do we suggest an absence of legal responsibility where crime is committed by a minor. We are concerned here only with the manner of the imposition of the ultimate penalty: the death sentence imposed for the crime of murder upon an emotionally disturbed youth with a disturbed child's immaturity.

The Court's opinion vacated the judgment of the Oklahoma Supreme Court, insofar as the sentence of death and remanded the case for resentencing.

Concurring statement by Justice Brennan: Justice Brennan issued a concurring statement which read: "I join the Court's opinion without, however, departing from my view that the death penalty is in all circumstances cruel and unusual punishment prohibited by the Eighth and Fourteenth Amendments."

Concurring opinion by Justice O'Connor: Justice O'-Connor concurred in the Court's decision. The focus of her concurrence was on the arguments proffered by Chief Justice Burger's dissenting opinion in the case. Justice O'Connor wrote:

> I disagree with the suggestion in the dissent that remanding this case may serve no useful purpose. Even though the [defendant] had an opportunity to present evidence in mitigation of the crime, it appears that the trial judge believed that he could not consider some of the mitigating evidence in imposing sentence. In any event, we may not speculate as to whether the trial judge and the Court of Criminal Appeals actually considered all of the mitigating factors and found them insufficient to offset the aggravating circumstances, or whether the difference between this Court's opinion and the trial court's treatment of the [defendant's] evidence is "purely a matter of semantics," as suggested by the dissent. [Our precedents] require us to remove any legitimate basis for finding ambiguity concerning the factors actually considered by the trial court.
>
> The Chief Justice may be correct in concluding that the Court's opinion reflects a decision by some Justices that they would not have imposed the death penalty in this case had they sat as the trial judge. I, however, do not read the Court's opinion either as altering this Court's opinions establishing the constitutionality of the death penalty or as deciding the issue of whether the Constitution permits imposition of the death penalty on an individual who committed a murder at age 16. Rather, by listing in detail some of the circumstances surrounding the petitioner's life, the Court has sought to emphasize the variety of mitigating information that may not have been considered by the trial court in deciding whether to impose the death penalty or some lesser sentence.

Dissenting opinion by Chief Justice Burger: The Chief Justice dissented from the Court's decision. He argued that the Court decided the case on an issue for which review was not granted. The dissent went further to indicate the futility in requiring a new sentencing hearing:

> To be sure, neither the Court of Criminal Appeals nor the trial court labeled Eddings' family background and personality disturbance as "mitigating factors." It is plain to me, however, that this was purely a matter of semantics associated with the rational belief that "evidence in mitigation" must rise to a certain level of persuasiveness before it can be said to constitute a "mitigating circumstance." In contrast, the Court seems to require that any potentially mitigating evidence be described as a "mitigating factor"—regardless of its weight; the insubstantiality of the evidence is simply to be a factor in the process of weighing the evidence against aggravating circumstances. Yet if this is all the Court's opinion stands for, it provides scant support for the result reached. For it is clearly the choice of the Oklahoma courts—a choice not inconsistent with *Lockett* or any other decision of this Court—to accord relatively little weight to Eddings' family background and emotional problems as balanced against the circumstances of his crime and his potential for future dangerousness....
>
> Whether the Court's remand will serve any useful purpose remains to be seen, for [the defendant] has already been given an opportunity to introduce whatever evidence he considered relevant to the sentencing determination. Two Oklahoma courts have weighed that evidence and found it insufficient to offset the aggravating circumstances shown by the State. The Court's opinion makes clear that some Justices who join it would not have imposed the death penalty had they sat as the sentencing authority. Indeed, I am not sure I would have done so. But the Constitution does not authorize us to determine whether sentences imposed by state courts are sentences we consider "appropriate"; our only authority is to decide whether they are constitutional under the Eighth Amendment. *See also* **Bell v. Ohio; Delo v. Lashley; Hitchcock v. Dugger; Lockett v. Ohio; Mitigating Circumstances; Skipper v. South Carolina**

Effective Assistance of Counsel *see* **Right to Counsel**

Egypt   Capital punishment is permitted in Egypt. Egypt uses hanging and the firing squad to carry out the death penalty. It was reported that in 1998, Egypt executed 48 prisoners. Its legal system is a mixture of English common law, Islamic law and the Napoleonic codes. The nation's constitution was adopted on September 11, 1971. Under the constitution of Egypt the nation is a social democracy in which Islam is the state religion. The judiciary is independent; however, cases that involve national security or terrorism may be handled by military or State Security Emergency courts, in which constitutional protections may not be observed.

Egypt has three levels of courts: primary courts, appeal courts, and the Court of Cassation (the highest court). Defendants have the right to retained or appointed counsel, public trials, and bail. Juries are not used in the judicial system. Felonies that are punishable by imprisonment or the death penalty are heard by three judges. Appeals may be taken to the Court of Cassation. Capital crimes that carry a possible death sentence include murder, felony-murder, arson or the use of explosives that caused death, rape, treason, and endangerment of state security. The Court of Cassation and the president review each death sentence. *See also* **International Capital Punishment Nations**

Eighth Amendment *see* **Bill of Rights; Cruel and Unusual Punishment Clause; Excessive Bail Clause**

El Salvador   El Salvador abolished capital punishment for ordinary crimes in 1983, but permits the punishment for exceptional crimes. The method of execution used by El Salvador is the firing squad. Its legal system is based on civil and Roman law, with traces of English common law. El Salvador adopted a constitution on December 20, 1983. El Salvador is a democracy with an executive branch, unicameral legislature branch and judicial branch.

The court structure of El Salvador consists of trial courts, appellate courts, and a Supreme Court. Under the nation's constitution, defendants have the right to a presumption of innocence, protection from self-incrimination, retained or appointed legal counsel, jury trials, freedom from coercion, and compensation for damages due to judicial error. *See also* **International Capital Punishment Nations**

Elected Official Aggravator   The public is periodically reminded of the danger politicians face with incidents like

the attempted assassination of former President Ronald Reagan, former Governor George Wallace, and the assassinations of former President John F. Kennedy and his brother, former Senator Robert Kennedy. A minority of capital punishment jurisdictions have taken a hard stand against the murder of politicians by making the killing of an elected official a statutory aggravating circumstance. The jurisdictions include: California, Colorado, Florida, Kentucky, Missouri, Ohio, Pennsylvania, Utah, and the Federal government. In these jurisdictions if the penalty phase jury finds that the victim of the defendant's capital murder was an elected official, the death penalty may be imposed. *See also* **Aggravating Circumstances**

JURISDICTIONS USING ELECTED OFFICIAL AGGRAVATOR

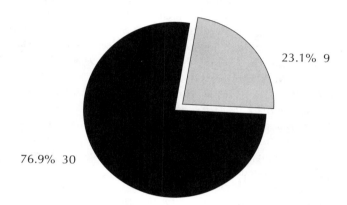

23.1% 9

76.9% 30

■ ELECTED OFFICIAL AGGRAVATOR JURISDICTIONS

■ ALL OTHER JURISDICTIONS

Electrocution   The use of electricity to execute the death penalty dates back to the late 19th century. On January 6, 1885, the governor of New York gave the annual *State of the State Address* to the New York legislature. In that *Address* the governor made the following observation and suggestion:

> The present mode of executing criminals by hanging has come down to us from the dark ages, and it may well be questioned whether the science of the present day cannot provide a means for taking the life of such as are condemned to die in a less barbarous manner. I commend this suggestion to the consideration of the legislature.

As a result of prompting by the governor, the legislature assembled a commission to determine "the most humane and practical method known to modern science of carrying into effect the sentence of death in capital cases."

The New York commission evaluated several possible methods of execution, including lethal injection. Eventually the commission was persuaded by Thomas Edison's proposal to use DC current as the most efficient method for execution. The commission reported back that execution by electricity was the most humane method of imposing the death penalty. The New York legislature heeded the advice and in 1888, signed into law the first electrocution death penalty statute. The statute by its terms went into effect January 1, 1889. One

year later, on August 6, 1890, William Kemmler became the first person executed by electrocution when New York executed him for the crime of murder.

Electrocution Jurisdictions: As of January 2000, only twelve capital punishment jurisdictions employed electrocution as a method of execution. Six of those jurisdictions, Florida, Kentucky, Ohio, South Carolina, Tennessee, and Utah, provide electrocution as a capital felon option. Two jurisdictions, Arkansas and Illinois, utilize electrocu-tion solely as a single fall-

Florida's electric chair is known as "Ol' Sparky." (Florida Department of Corrections)

back option. One jurisdiction, Oklahoma, utilizes electrocution as part of its dual fallback option. Two jurisdictions, Alabama and Nebraska utilize electrocution exclusively. Georgia utilizes electrocution for defendants sentenced to death prior to May 2000.

JURISDICTIONS WHERE ELECTROCUTION IS ALLOWED

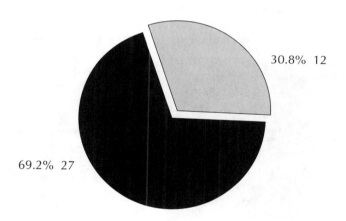

30.8% 12

69.2% 27

■ ELECTROCUTION JURISDICTIONS

■ NON-ELECTROCUTION JURISDICTIONS

Constitutionality of Electrocution: The constitutionality of execution by electrocution was answered by the United States Supreme Court in *In re Kemmler*, 136 U.S. 436 (1890). In *Kemmler* the Supreme Court held that death by electrocution did not violate the Federal Constitution. The decision in *Kemmler* has withstood countless challenges for over one hundred years.

The two major criticisms of death by electrocution are that death is slow and the punishment disfigures the victim. Both

EXECUTIONS PERFORMED BY ELECTROCUTION 1976–1999

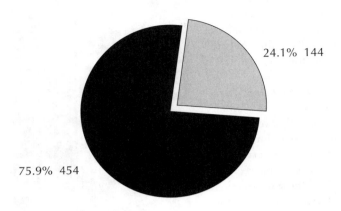

24.1% 144

75.9% 454

- ■ ELECTROCUTION
- ■ ALL OTHER METHODS

criticisms stem from executions that are not carried out properly. When done correctly, death by electrocution is relatively quick and disfigurement minimal. However, when problems arise such as too much electrical current or not enough electrical current, the victim will suffer needlessly.

Electrocution Protocol: The electric chair apparatus consists of a wooden chair, attached leg electrodes, a leather and sponge helmet with electrode, a drip pan, a plexiglass seat and a non-incremental restraint system. The chair is connected to an electrical power supply. The leg electrodes, which are fabricated onto the leg stock, are composed of solid brass. The helmet consists of an outer helmet of leather and an inner helmet of copper mesh and sponge. The chair design includes a removable drip pan. The straps used include two ankle straps, two wrist straps and one chest harness.

The condemned inmate is led to the chair and strapped in. One of the leg electrodes will be attached to a shaved leg. The helmet will be attached to the head (a leather strap may also be fastened to the condemned inmate's face). A hood will then be placed over the head of the condemned. The actual switch used ranges from a lever, switch or a three button system where three people will push each button (only one of them will

The actual execution of Allen Davis by the State of Florida on July 8, 1999. Davis began bleeding from the nose during his execution, and his mask popped off. (Florida Department of Corrections)

push the real button). The condemned inmate will be given two sequences of electrical shocks. The initial voltage of electricity will be not less than 2200 volts for ten seconds; a five second interval must occur; followed by 750 volts or more for 22 seconds. The process is then repeated once. Actual voltage used is calculated by the weight of the condemned inmate. The heavier the inmate, the more voltage required. If the initial sequence is performed correctly, a physician will examine the condemned to proclaim him or her as heart dead. *See also* **Execution Option Jurisdictions; In Re Kemmler; Methods of Execution**

Elements of a Crime *see* **Actus Reus; Mens Rea**

Elk v. United States *Court:* United States Supreme Court; *Case Citation:* Elk v. United States, 177 U.S. 529 (1900); *Argued:* February 26, 1900; *Decided:* April 30, 1900; *Opinion of the Court:* Justice Peckham; *Concurring Opinion:* None; *Dissenting Opinion:* None; *Appellate Defense Counsel:* Thos. B. McMartin argued; S. B. Van Buskirk on brief; *Appellate Prosecution Counsel:* Mr. Boyd argued and briefed; *Amicus Curiae Brief Supporting Prosecutor:* None; *Amicus Curiae Brief Supporting Defendant:* None.

Issue Presented: Whether it was error for the trial court to instruct the jury that the defendant did not have a right to resist being arrested?

Case Holding: It was error for the trial court to instruct the jury that the defendant did not have a right to resist being arrested, because the police officers did not have an arrest warrant and the matter involved a misdemeanor that was not committed in their presence.

Factual and procedural background of case: The defendant, John Bad Elk, was indicted for capital murder by the United States. Both the defendant and the victim were Native American police officers. The crime occurred on a reservation in South Dakota. At the time of the killing the victim and several other police officers were attempting to arrest the defendant. During the trial the judge instructed the jury that the arrest was lawful and that the defendant did not have a right to resist. The defendant was convicted and sentenced to death. The defendant appealed to the United States Supreme Court, arguing that the trial judge committed error in instructing the jury that he did not have a right to resist the attempted arrest. The United States Supreme Court granted certiorari to consider the issue.

Opinion of the Court by Justice Peckham: Justice Peckham held that it was reversible error for the trial court to instruct the jury that the defendant did not have a right to resist the attempted arrest. The opinion reasoned as follows:

> At common law, if a party resisted arrest by an officer without warrant and who had no right to arrest him, and if in the course of that resistance the officer was killed, the offense of the party resisting arrest would be reduced from what would have been murder if the officer had had the right to arrest, to manslaughter. What would be murder if the officer had the right to arrest might be reduced to manslaughter by the very fact that

he had no such right. So an officer, at common law, was not authorized to make an arrest without a warrant, for a mere misdemeanor not committed in his presence. If the officer had no right to arrest, the other party might resist the illegal attempt to arrest him, using no more force than was absolutely necessary to repel the assault constituting the attempt to arrest.

We do not find any statute of the United States or of the state of South Dakota giving any right to these men to arrest an individual without a warrant, on a charge of misdemeanor not committed in their presence. Marshals and their deputies have in each state ... the same powers in executing the laws of the United States as sheriffs and their deputies in such state may have by law in executing the laws thereof. This certainly does not give any power to an officer at the Pine Ridge agency to arrest a person without warrant, even though charged with the commission of a misdemeanor. These policemen were not marshals nor deputies of marshals, and the statutes have no application to them.

It is plain from this review of the subject that the charge of the court below, that the policemen had the right to arrest this [defendant], without warrant, and that, in order to accomplish such arrest, they had the right to show and use their pistols so far as was necessary for that purpose, and that the [defendant] had no right to resist such arrest, was erroneous. That it was a material error, it seems to us, is equally plain. It placed the transaction in a false light before the jury, and denied to the [defendant] those rights which he clearly had.... He, of course, had no right to unnecessarily injure, much less to kill, his assailant; but where the officer is killed in the course of the disorder which naturally accompanies an attempted arrest that is resisted, the law looks with very different eyes upon the transaction, when the officer had the right to make the arrest, from what it does if the officer had no such right. What might be murder in the first case might be nothing more than manslaughter in the other, or the facts might show that no offense had been committed.

The judgment of the trial court was reversed and the case remanded for a new trial.

Engel, George *see* Chicago Labor Riots of 1886

England

England abolished the death penalty for ordinary crimes in 1973. The nation's Crime and Disorder Act of 1998 removed the death penalty for the only remaining civilian crimes of treason and piracy. Pursuant to the Human Rights Act of 1998, five offences that were under England's military code were abolished. *See also* **International Capital Punishment Nations**

Enmund v. Florida

Court: United States Supreme Court; *Case Citation:* Enmund v. Florida, 458 U.S. 782 (1982); *Argued:* March 23, 1982; *Decided:* July 2, 1982; *Opinion of the Court:* Justice White; *Concurring Statement:* Justice Brennan; *Dissenting Opinion:* Justice O'Connor, in which Burger, C. J., and Powell and Rehnquist, JJ., joined; *Appellate Defense Counsel:* James S. Liebman argued; William C. McLain, Jack Greenberg, James M. Nabrit III, Joel Berger, John Charles Boger, Deborah Fins, and Anthony G. Amsterdam on brief; *Appellate Prosecution Counsel:* Lawrence A. Kaden argued; Jim Smith, George R. Georgieff and Raymond L. Marky on brief; *Amicus Curiae Brief Supporting Prosecutor:* 2

Amicus Curiae Brief Supporting Defendant: None. *Issue Presented:* Whether a sentence of death is a valid penalty under the Constitution for defendant who neither took life, attempted to take life, nor intended to take life?

Case Holding: The Constitution prohibits imposition of the death penalty upon a defendant who neither took life, attempted to take life, nor intended to take life.

Factual and procedural background of case: The defendant, Earl Enmund, (and a co-defendant) was convicted by a Florida court of committing felony murder on April 1, 1975, in which two people were killed during the course of a robbery. The evidence showed that the defendant was a lookout and was not present when the murders occurred, and did not know that killings would take place. The defendant was sentenced to death.

On appeal to the Florida Supreme Court, the defendant contended that the federal constitution prohibited imposition of the death penalty against him because he neither took life, attempted to take life, nor intended to take life. The Florida Supreme Court affirmed. The appellate court held that the mere fact that the defendant was the person in a car parked at the home where the crimes occurred was enough under Florida law to make him a constructive aider and abettor and hence a principal in first-degree murder upon whom the death penalty could be imposed. The appellate court found that it was thus irrelevant that the defendant did not himself kill and was not present at the killings, or whether he intended that the victims be killed or anticipated that lethal force might be used to effectuate the robbery or escape. The United States Supreme Court granted certiorari to address the issue of whether imposition of the death penalty upon the defendant was constitutionally permissible.

Opinion of the Court by Justice White: Justice White indicated that the current judgments of legislatures, juries, and prosecutors weigh heavily on the side of rejecting capital punishment for the crime at issue. It was observed that only a small minority of States allow the death penalty to be imposed solely because the defendant somehow participated in the robbery in the course of which a murder was committed, but did not take or attempt or intend to take life, or intend that lethal force be employed. He wrote that the evidence was overwhelming that American juries have repudiated imposition of the death penalty against persons who did not take or attempt or intend to take life, or intend that lethal force be employed.

Justice White noted that while robbery is a serious crime deserving serious punishment, it is not a crime "so grievous an affront to humanity that the only adequate response may be the penalty of death." He believed the death penalty was an excessive penalty for the robber, who, as such, does not take human life. The opinion held that the focus must be on a defendant's culpability, not on those who committed the robbery and killings. When a robbery defendant did not kill or intend to kill, his or her culpability is different from that of the robbers who killed, and it is impermissible for the State to treat them alike and attribute to the defendant the culpability of those who killed.

The opinion ruled that neither deterrence of capital crimes nor retribution is a sufficient justification for executing the defendant. It is was said that it was highly unlikely that the threat of the death penalty for murder will measurably deter one such as the defendant, who does not kill or intend to kill. As to retribution, it was said that this depended on the degree of the defendant's culpability, which must be limited to his participation in the robbery. Putting him to death to avenge two killings that he did not commit or intend to commit or cause would not measurably contribute to the retribution end of ensuring that the criminal gets his or her just deserts. The decision of the Florida Supreme Court was, therefore, reversed.

Concurring statement by Justice Brennan: Justice Brennan issued a concurring statement indicating his longstanding "view that the death penalty is in all circumstances cruel and unusual punishment prohibited by the Eighth and Fourteenth Amendments."

Dissenting opinion by Justice O'Connor, in which Burger, C. J., and Powell and Rehnquist, JJ., joined: Justice O'Connor argued in her dissent that "[t]oday the Court holds that the Eighth Amendment prohibits a State from executing a convicted felony murderer." She believed that such a decision was not supported by the analysis in prior cases and that it "interferes with state criteria for assessing legal guilt by recasting intent as a matter of federal constitutional law."

The dissent urged that the determination of what conduct made a defendant a "principal or merely an accessory before the fact" was a matter uniquely within the authority of the States. She reasoned that "the intent-to-kill requirement is crudely crafted; it fails to take into account the complex picture of the defendant's knowledge of his accomplice's intent and whether he was armed, the defendant's contribution to the planning and success of the crime, and the defendant's actual participation during the commission of the crime. Under the circumstances, the determination of the degree of blameworthiness is best left to the sentencer, who can sift through the facts unique to each case." The dissent concluded "that the death penalty is not disproportionate to the crime of felony murder, even though the defendant did not actually kill or intend to kill his victims."

Case note: The majority decision was profound in its impact on the common law doctrine of felony murder. Prior to the decision, all co-defendants convicted of felony murder were subject to the same punishment. The result of the majority's decision, and a subsequent case, was that of creating different categories of felony murder, one of which allows a defendant to escape the death penalty. *See also* **Felony Murder Rule; Mens Rea; Tison v. Arizona**

Equal Justice USA   Equal Justice USA was founded in Maryland in 1990. It is a nonprofit organization created specifically to advocate for human rights in the nation's legal system. The organization has made abolishment of the death penalty a priority goal.

In 1993, the organization launched a campaign to aid death row inmate Mumia Abu-Jamal. As a result of the organization's work Mumia has become the most recognized death row inmate in the world.

In 1997, Equal Justice USA launched its "Moratorium Now!" campaign to bring about a moratorium on capital punishment. The organization has gained national support that is being used to apply pressure at all levels of government. *See also* **Abu-Jamal, Mumia**

Equal Protection Clause   The Equal Protection Clause is part of the Fourteenth Amendment to the Federal Constitution, which was ratified on July 9, 1868. The Equal Protection Clause provides that no State shall "deny to any person within its jurisdiction the equal protection of the laws." The thrust of the Equal Protection Clause is a prohibition against unlawful discriminatory treatment of persons.

Although the Equal Protection Clause is regularly invoked by defendants in capital punishment cases, the Clause has not been called upon to play a large role in capital punishment jurisprudence. The area where the Equal Protection Clause played a prominent role in capital punishment involved the selection of grand and petit juries. During the first half of the 20th century the United States Supreme Court was frequently called upon to use the Equal Protection Clause to reverse judgments because grand or petit juries where selected in a racially discriminatory manner. *See also* **Discrimination in Grand or Petit Jury Selection; Fourteenth Amendment**

Equatorial Guinea   Equatorial Guinea imposes capital punishment. Equatorial Guinea utilizes the firing squad and hanging as methods of carrying out the death penalty. Its legal system is based on Spanish civil law and customary law. The nation's constitution was adopted on November 17, 1991.

The court system of Equatorial Guinea is composed of provincial courts, two appeal courts, and a Supreme Court. There are also traditional courts in rural areas, in which tribal elders adjudicate minor civil and criminal matters. Criminal defendants have the right to legal counsel and appeal. *See also* **International Capital Punishment Nations**

Eritrea   Eritrea has capital punishment on its law books. Eritrea became an independent state in 1993, following a referendum in which its citizens voted for independence from Ethiopia. The nation is still in political infancy. Its legal system is functioning under customary law. The nation's constitution was replaced in May of 1997.

The judicial system of Eritrea consists of village courts, subregional courts, regional courts, and a High Court that serves as an appellate court. Under the laws of the nation minor offenses are brought to village courts and subregional courts. More serious crimes are argued before regional courts. Cases involving murder, rape, and other serious felonies are heard by the High Court. All courts except the High Court are presided over by a single judge. In the High Court panels of three judges hear cases. Defendants have access to retained legal counsel. *See also* **International Capital Punishment Nations**

Error It is commonly understood in the legal community that no trial is ever error free. Consequently, appellate courts recognize two types of trial court errors: harmless error and prejudicial error. An error is deemed harmless if it is found to have no impact on the outcome of the trial. If an appellate court cannot conclude that there was no reasonable likelihood that an error affected the outcome of a trial, the error is deemed prejudicial and the judgment reversible. *See also* **Appellate Review of Conviction and Death Sentence; Harmless Error Rule**

Error, Writ of *see* **Certiorari, Writ of**

Escape The crime of escape may constitute a felony or misdemeanor offense, depending upon the circumstances and jurisdiction. Escape may involve fleeing from capture or custody. The crime of escape, without more, cannot be used to inflict the death penalty. The Eighth Amendment of the United States Constitution prohibits this as cruel and unusual punishment. However, the crime of escape can play a role in a capital prosecution. If escape occurs during the commission of a homicide it may form the basis of a death-eligible offense, and therefore trigger a capital prosecution. *See also* **Death-Eligible Offenses; Escape Aggravator; Felony-Murder Rule; Rape and Capital Punishment**

Escape Aggravator A person incarcerated or in the custody of a law enforcement officer, who flees from such confinement or custody, commits the offense of escape. A majority of capital punishment jurisdictions have made this offense a statutory aggravating circumstance when it accompanies murder. The death penalty may be imposed when this statutory aggravator is proven to exist at the penalty phase. *See also* **Aggravating Circumstances**

JURISDICTIONS USING ESCAPE AGGRAVATOR

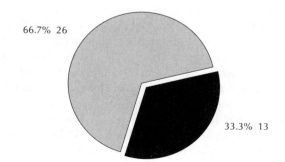

66.7% 26

33.3% 13

■ ESCAPE AGGRAVATOR JURISDICTIONS
■ ALL OTHER JURISDICTIONS

Espinosa v. Florida *Court:* United States Supreme Court; *Case Citation:* Espinosa v. Florida, 505 U.S. 1079 (1992); *Argued:* Not reported; *Decided:* June 29, 1992; *Opinion of the Court:* Per Curiam; *Concurring Opinion:* None; *Dissenting Statement:* Chief Justice Rehnquist and White, J.; *Dissenting Statement:* Justice Scalia; *Appellate Defense Counsel:* Not reported; *Appellate Prosecution Counsel:* Not reported; *Amicus Curiae Brief Supporting Prosecutor:* Not reported; *Amicus Curiae Brief Supporting Defendant:* Not reported.

Issue Presented: Whether the "especially wicked, evil, atrocious or cruel" aggravating circumstance used at the penalty phase of the defendant's trial was constitutionally vague?

Case Holding: The "especially wicked, evil, atrocious or cruel" aggravating circumstance used at the penalty phase of the defendant's trial was constitutionally vague and therefore required his death sentence be vacated, notwithstanding the fact that the jury only provided a non-binding sentence recommendation to the trial court.

Factual and procedural background of case: The defendant, Henry Jose Espinosa, was convicted of capital murder by the State of Florida. During the penalty phase the trial court instructed the jury that it could find as an aggravating factor that the murder was "especially wicked, evil, atrocious or cruel." The jury returned a recommendation that the defendant be sentenced to death. The trial court imposed a death sentence. On appeal, the Florida Supreme Court affirmed the conviction and sentence, after rejecting the defendant's argument that the "especially wicked, evil, atrocious or cruel" factor was constitutionally vague and left the jury with insufficient guidance when to find the existence of the aggravating factor. The United States Supreme Court granted certiorari to consider the issue.

Opinion of the Court was delivered Per Curiam: The per curiam opinion held that the defendant's death sentence was invalid because the "especially wicked, evil, atrocious or cruel" aggravating factor was constitutionally vague. The opinion rejected the State's argument that because the jury only provided a non-binding recommendation, the error was harmless insofar as the trial court properly found other valid aggravating factors in which to impose the death sentence. It was noted that under Florida death penalty law the trial judge is required to give weight and deference to the recommendation of the jury, therefore, the Court would presume the jury's consideration of the invalid aggravator impacted the trial court's ultimate decision to impose the death penalty. The judgment of the Florida Supreme Court was reversed.

Dissenting statement by Chief Justice Rehnquist and White, J.: The Chief Justice and Justice White issued a joint dissenting statement indicating the Court should have held a full hearing on the case, instead of addressing it summarily.

Dissenting statement by Justice Scalia: Justice Scalia provided a dissenting statement indicating he dissented for the reasons set out in his concurring and dissenting opinion in *Sochor v. Florida. See also* **Invalid Aggravator**

Espionage The death penalty statutes of the Federal government make espionage, without more, an offense for which the death penalty may be imposed. Prior to the United States Supreme Court decision in *Coker v. Georgia*, 433 U.S. 584 (1977), the Federal Constitution did not bar imposition of the death penalty when death to a victim did not occur. However, *Coker* invalidated as a capital offense, rape of an adult woman that does not result in death. Courts have interpreted *Coker* as barring imposition of the death penalty for all crimes that do not result in a homicide. Under decisions decided prior to *Coker* the Supreme Court permitted the death penalty to be imposed for espionage, without an accompanying homicide. Commentators have suggested that in the wake of *Coker*, the death penalty may not be imposed for espionage without a resulting death.

Nazi Spies

In 1942, American soil was invaded by eight Nazi spies who were sent by Germany to destroy critical cites in the nation. George John Dasch, Richard Quirin, Ernest Peter Burger, Heinrich Harm Heinck, Edward John Kerling, Werner Thiel, Herman Otto Neubauer, and Herbert Hans Haupt, were all born in Germany, though each had lived in the United States. They returned, separately, to Germany between 1933 and 1941.

After the declaration of war between the United States and Germany, the eight men received training at a sabotage school near Berlin, Germany, where they were instructed in the use of explosives and in methods of secret writing. At the conclusion of their training they proceeded from Germany to a seaport in Occupied France. Upon arrival in Occupied France, Dasch, Burger, Heinck and Quirin boarded a German submarine which proceeded across the Atlantic to Amagansett Beach on Long Island, New York. The four men were there landed from the submarine on June 13, 1942. They carried with them a supply of explosives. After burying their German

The eight Nazi spies: (top left to right) *George John Dasch, Herman Otto Neubauer, Richard Quirin, and Heinrich Harm Heinck;* (bottom left to right) *Edward John Kerling, Herbert Hans Haupt, Werner Thiel, and Ernest Peter Burger. (U.S. Department of Justice/FBI)*

military uniforms, the four men proceeded in civilian dress to New York City.

The remaining four men, Kerling, Thiel, Neubauer, and Haupt boarded another German submarine from Occupied France, which carried them across the Atlantic to Ponte Vedra Beach, Florida. On June 17, 1942, they came ashore carrying a supply of explosives. After burying their German uniforms, they proceeded in civilian dress to Jacksonville, Florida.

By June 27, 1942 all eight spies were captured by agents of the Federal Bureau of Investigation (FBI). The FBI learned that the men came to the United States to destroy war industries and war facilities. They were captured before they could carry out any act of sabotage.

The swift capture of the spies was due to the ostensible defection of one of them — Dasch. On June 14, Dasch contacted the FBI from New York and stated that he had entered the country as a war saboteur. Dasch made a promise to phone the FBI again when he arrived in Washington, D.C. On June 19, Dasch kept his word and called the FBI. Shortly after the phone conversation Dasch was arrested. After light interrogation, Dasch gave the FBI all the information needed to capture the other spies.

President Franklin D. Roosevelt signed an order on July 2, 1942, appointing a Military Commission to prosecute the defendants for offenses against the law of war and the Articles of War. The Military Commission was comprised of seven Army officers. The spies were appointed military legal counsel. The trial was held from July 8, to August 4, 1942. When the trial ended all of the defendants were found guilty and sentenced to death.

President Roosevelt intervened and commuted the sentence of Dasch to 30 years and that of Burger to life imprisonment. The remaining spies were executed at the District of Columbia Jail on August 8, 1942. In April of 1948, President Harry S. Truman granted clemency to Dasch and Burger on condition of deportation. They were eventually taken to the American Zone of Germany and released. *See also* **Coker v. Georgia; Ex Parte Quirin; Rape and Capital Punishment; Rosenberg v. United States**

Estelle v. Smith *Court:* United States Supreme Court; *Case Citation:* Estelle v. Smith, 451 U.S. 454 (1981); *Argued:* October 8, 1980; *Decided:* May 18, 1981; *Opinion of the Court:* Chief Justice Burger; *Concurring Statement:* Justice Brennan; *Concurring Statement:* Justice Marshall; *Concurring Opinion:* Justice Stewart, in which Powell, J., joined; *Concurring Opinion:* Justice Rehnquist; *Dissenting Opinion:* None; *Appellate Defense Counsel:* Joel Berger argued; John F. Simmons, Jack Greenberg, James M. Nabrit III, John Charles Boger, and Anthony G. Amsterdam on brief; *Appellate Prosecution Counsel:* Anita Ashton argued; Mark White, John W. Fainter, Jr., Ted L. Hartley, W. Barton Boling and Douglas M. Becker on brief; *Amicus Curiae Brief Supporting Prosecutor:* None; *Amicus Curiae Brief Supporting Defendant:* 1.

Issue Presented: Whether the prosecutor's use of psychiatric testimony at the penalty phase of the defendant's capital murder trial to establish his future dangerousness violated the defendant's constitutional rights?

Case Holding: The defendant's Fifth and Sixth Amendment rights were violated by the prosecutor's use of psychiatric testimony at the penalty phase of the defendant's capital murder trial to establish his future dangerousness.

Factual and procedural background of case: The defendant, Ernest Benjamin Smith, was indicted in Texas for capital murder. Prior to trial the court ordered a psychiatric examination, to determine the defendant's competency to stand trial. A psychiatrist conducted the examination at the jail where the defendant was being held, and determined that the defendant was competent. Thereafter, the defendant was tried by a jury and convicted of capital murder. One of the statutory issues the penalty phase jury had to resolve was the future dangerousness of the defendant, i.e., whether there was a probability that he would commit criminal acts of violence that would constitute a continuing threat to society. At the sentencing hearing, the doctor who had conducted the pretrial psychiatric examination was allowed to testify for the prosecutor over defense counsel's objection that the doctor's name did not appear on the list of witnesses the prosecutor planned to use at the penalty phase. The doctor testified that the defendant would be a danger to society. The jury then returned a sentence of death.

The Texas Court of Criminal Appeals affirmed the conviction and death sentence. After unsuccessfully seeking a writ of habeas corpus in State courts, the defendant petitioned for such relief in a Federal District Court. That court vacated the death sentence because it found constitutional error in admitting the doctor's testimony at the penalty phase. A Federal Court of Appeals affirmed the District Court's ruling. The United States Supreme Court granted certiorari to consider the issue.

Opinion of the Court by Chief Justice Burger: The Chief Justice held that the admission of the doctor's testimony at the penalty phase violated the defendant's Fifth Amendment privilege against compelled self-incrimination, and his Sixth Amendment right to the assistance of counsel.

Addressing the issue of the defendant's right to remain silent, Chief Justice Burger found that the defendant was not advised before the pretrial psychiatric examination that he had a right to remain silent and that any statement he made could be used against him at a capital sentencing proceeding. The opinion held that there was no basis for distinguishing between the guilt and penalty phases of the defendant's trial, so far as the protection of the Fifth Amendment privilege was concerned. It was said that the prosecutor's attempt to establish the defendant's future dangerousness, by relying on the unwarned statements the defendant made to the examining doctor, infringed the Fifth Amendment just as much as would have any effort to compel the defendant to testify against his will at the sentencing hearing.

The Chief Justice indicated that merely because the defendant's statements were made in the context of a psychiatric examination did not automatically remove them from the reach of the Fifth Amendment. He reasoned that the considerations calling for the accused to be warned prior to custodial interrogation apply with no less force to a pretrial psychiatric examination. The opinion ruled that an accused who neither initiated a psychiatric evaluation nor attempted to introduce any psychiatric evidence, may not be compelled to respond to a psychiatrist if his or her statements can be used against him or her at a capital sentencing proceeding. When faced with a court ordered psychiatric inquiry, the defendant's statements to the doctor were not given freely and voluntarily without any compelling influences and, as such, could only be used by the prosecutor at the penalty phase if the defendant had been apprised of his rights and had freely and knowingly decided to waive them.

As to the defendant's Sixth Amendment right to the assistance of counsel, the Chief Justice found that such right already had attached when the doctor examined the defendant in jail. It was said that defense counsel was not notified in advance that the psychiatric examination would encompass the issue of the defendant's future dangerousness. Therefore, the defendant was denied the assistance of his counsel in making the significant decision of whether to submit to the examination and to what end the psychiatrist's findings could be employed. The judgment of the Court of Appeals was affirmed.

Concurring statement by Justice Brennan: Justice Brennan issued a concurring statement indicating that he joined the Court's opinion and that he maintained his "position that the death penalty is in all circumstances unconstitutional."

Concurring statement by Justice Marshall: Justice Marshall issued a statement concurring in the Court's decision and pointing out that he continued to adhere to his "consistent view that the death penalty is under all circumstances cruel and unusual punishment forbidden by the Eighth and Fourteenth Amendments."

Concurring opinion by Justice Stewart, in which Powell, J., joined: Justice Powell concurred in the Court's judgment. He wrote that the case was correctly decided on the Sixth Amendment claim, and that as a result, he would not have reached nor decided the Fifth Amendment issue.

Concurring opinion by Justice Rehnquist: Justice Rehnquist issued an opinion concurring in the Court's judgment. He indicated that the Court should not have went beyond resolving the Sixth Amendment claim. Justice Rehnquist stated that he was not convinced that any Fifth Amendment rights were implicated by the psychiatric examination of the defendant. He wrote: "Even if there are Fifth Amendment rights involved in this case, [the defendant] never invoked these rights when confronted with [the psychiatrist's] questions. The Fifth Amendment privilege against compulsory self-incrimination is not self-executing." *See also* **Powell v. Texas; Right to Counsel; Right to Remain Silent; Satterwhite v. Texas**

Estonia Estonia abolished capital punishment in 1998. *See also* **International Capital Punishment Nations**

Ethiopia Ethiopia utilizes the death penalty. Ethiopia uses the firing squad as the method of carrying out the death penalty. Its legal system is based largely on customary law. Ethiopia adopted a constitution in December of 1994.

The court structure of Ethiopia consists a federal and state (regional) system. The federal system is composed of a Supreme Court, High Court, and District Courts. The federal Supreme Court and High Court adjudicate cases involving federal law, transregional issues, and national security. Both courts hear original and appeal cases. The state system is composed of district courts, zonal courts, high court, and supreme court.

The laws of Ethiopia recognize religious and customary courts. Both parties to a dispute must agree before a customary or religious court may hear a case. Shari'a (Islamic) courts have authority to hear religious and family cases involving Muslims.

Under the laws of Ethiopia defendants have the right to be released on bail, the right to a public trial, a speedy trial, and the right to retained or appointed counsel. *See also* **International Capital Punishment Nations**

Eubanks v. Louisiana *Court:* United States Supreme Court; *Case Citation:* Eubanks v. Louisiana, 356 U.S. 584 (1958); *Argued:* April 30–May 1, 1958; *Decided:* May 26, 1958; *Opinion of the Court:* Justice Black; *Concurring Opinion:* None; *Dissenting Opinion:* None; *Appellate Defense Counsel:* Herbert J. Garon argued; Leopold Stahl on brief; *Appellate Prosecution Counsel:* Michael E. Culligan argued; Jack P. F. Gremillion, Leon D. Hubert, Jr. and William P. Schuler on brief; *Amicus Curiae Brief Supporting Prosecutor:* None; *Amicus Curiae Brief Supporting Defendant:* None.

Issue Presented: Whether the defendant established that his conviction and sentence were invalid because blacks were systematically excluded from the grand jury that indicted him?

Case Holding: The defendant established that his conviction and sentence were invalid because blacks were systematically excluded from the grand jury that indicted him.

Factual and procedural background of case: The defendant, Eubanks, was convicted of capital murder and sentenced to death by the State of Louisiana. The Louisiana Supreme Court affirmed the judgment. In doing so, the appellate court rejected the defendant's contention that his conviction and sentence were invalid because blacks were systematically excluded from the grand jury that indicted him. The United States Supreme Court granted certiorari to consider the issue.

Opinion of the Court by Justice Black: Justice Black found that the judgment against the defendant could not stand. The opinion noted that "[i]n an unbroken line of cases stretching back almost 80 years this Court has held that a criminal defendant is denied the equal protection of the laws guaranteed by the Fourteenth Amendment if he is indicted by a grand jury or tried by a petit jury from which members of his race have been excluded because of their race." Justice Black noted that from 1936 to 1954, the county (parish) in which the defen-

dant was indicted selected 432 persons to serve on grand juries. Out of that number only one grand juror was black. The opinion indicted that "this lone exception apparently resulted from the mistaken impression that the juror was white." In contrast, the opinion found that blacks had been well represented on Federal grand juries from the county during the same period. It was concluded that uniform and long-continued exclusion of blacks from grand juries shown by the record in the case could not be attributed to chance, accident, or to the fact that no sufficiently qualified blacks have ever been included in the lists submitted to the various local judges for selection as grand jurors. The judgment of the Louisiana Supreme Court was reversed. *See also* **Discrimination in Grand or Petit Jury Selection**

Evidence Rules *see* **Hearsay; Hearsay Exceptions; Rules of Evidence**

Examination of Witness A witness in a criminal trial may be questioned through direct examination or cross examination. Direct examination and cross examination have technical meanings in the law.

Direct examination refers to presenting the witness with open ended questions that generally require more than a yes or no response. For example, "Where were you on the night of April 1, 2000?" Under cross examination a witness may be presented with questions that require only a yes or no answer. For example, "On the night of April 1, 2000, you were at the decedent's home, correct?"

Direct examination is done by the party calling the witness to testify. Cross examination is performed by the party who did not call the witness to testify. An exception for direct examination questioning occurs when a witness called becomes adverse or hostile to the party calling him or her. That is, when a witness adversely changes the testimony the party expected the witness to give.

In capital prosecutions the rigid demands of direct and cross examination are generally adhered to during the guilt phase. However, the requirements are generally relaxed during the penalty phase.

Excessive Bail Clause The Eighth Amendment to the Federal Constitution states that "[e]xcessive bail shall not be required." The Excessive Bail Clause has been interpreted as not constitutionally requiring bail be established in criminal cases. The United States Supreme Court has ruled that the Excessive Bail Clause only requires that bail not be excessive, if it is imposed. Because there is no Federal Constitutional right to have bail set, jurisdictions are free to deny bail outright. Some jurisdictions prohibit bail from being set in capital prosecutions. While others allow courts to set bail. When bail is allowed in capital cases, the amount of the bail will generally be in an amount that cannot be posted by the defendant. *See also* **Bill of Rights**

Excessive Punishment *see* Cruel and Unusual Punishment Clause

Exclusionary Rule

The exclusionary rule is a legal device adopted by the United States Supreme Court for violations of the Fourth Amendment's prohibition against unreasonable searches and seizures. Under the exclusionary rule evidence obtained in violation of the Fourth Amendment may be excluded from evidence during a defendant's trial. The exclusionary rule extends to evidence obtained as a result of information learned from the unlawfully obtained evidence. This extension is called "fruits of the poisonous tree." Some courts have used the exclusionary rule to prohibit the use of unlawfully seized evidence during the penalty phase of a capital prosecution.

One exception to the exclusionary rule is the independent source rule. Under the latter rule if authorities learn of incriminating evidence from a source independent of unlawfully obtained evidence, the new incriminating evidence may be used at trial. *see* **Bill of Rights**

Exculpatory Evidence

The United States Supreme Court has held in *Brady v. Maryland*, 373 U.S. 83 (1963) that the Constitution provides a defendant with the right to have a prosecutor reveal all material evidence that may tend to show the defendant's innocence or that could be used by a defendant to attack the credibility of a witness. Failure of prosecutors to abide by this constitutional right is called a *Brady* violation, and may result in a conviction being reversed. There are three essential components of a *Brady* violation: (1) withheld evidence must be favorable to the defendant, either because it is exculpatory, or because it is impeaching; (2) the evidence must have been suppressed by the prosecutor, either willfully or inadvertently; and (3) prejudice must have been caused to the defendant. *See also* **Brady v. Maryland; Discovery**

Executing a Capital Felon More Than Once *see* Botched Execution; Francis v. Resweber

Execution Before Expiration of Prior Prison Sentence

Capital offenses are occasionally committed by persons while incarcerated on noncapital convictions. An argument that periodically surfaces in this regard, is the claim that the previous prison sentence must be served before the defendant may be executed. This argument has never prevailed. The United States Supreme Court has ruled that the Constitution does not prohibit executing a capital felon before he or she has served the full term of a previous prison sentence. *See also* **Kelley v. Oregon**

Execution Methods *see* Electrocution; Firing Squad; Hanging; Lethal Gas; Lethal Injection

Execution Chamber

The place wherein an execution occurs is called the execution chamber. Modern methods of execution created execution chambers. When hanging and firing squad were the exclusive means of executing condemned prisoners, and executions were public, there was no practical need for special chambers to perform the executions.

During the early history of execution chambers, some prisons maintained execution chambers in small buildings built inside prison walls, but separate from inmate buildings. Today execution chambers are generally found inside the prison building that maintains death row inmates.

Top: *Lethal injection execution chamber at San Quentin State Prison. (California Department of Corrections)* Bottom: *Lethal gas execution chamber at North Carolina's Central Prison. (North Carolina Department of Corrections)*

Execution Option Jurisdictions

The phrase "execution option jurisdictions" refers to capital punishment jurisdictions that have statutes which provide more than one method of execution. In jurisdictions that provide alternative methods of execution for capital felons to choose from, oftentimes capital felons will attack such options as infringing upon their religious beliefs. That is, capital felons contend that their religious beliefs prevent them from choosing a method of death. This argument has never found firm footing with courts. The reason that this argument invariably fails is that, when a capital felon has religious qualms about choosing a method of execution, the death penalty statutes provide for the method to be used in such situations. Therefore, a capital felon does not have to violate religious beliefs by choosing a method.

Three types of execution option jurisdictions exist: (1) capital felon option, (2) federal option, and (3) fallback option.

Capital Felon Option: Capital felon option jurisdictions permit capital murderers to choose the method of their execution. There are eleven capital felon option jurisdictions. Capital felon option jurisdictions provide two methods of execution. The statutes in these jurisdictions provide that if a capital felon refuses to select a method of execution, or fails to select a method within a specified time period, then a statutory "default" method of execution will be used. That is, one of the two methods of execution is designated as the method to use if either of the latter two events occur. Capital felons have on average ten days, prior to the week of the scheduled execution, to select an execution method. There are four categories of capital felon option jurisdictions. Each category is presented seriatim below.

1. *Lethal injection-lethal gas jurisdictions.* North Carolina, California and Missouri permit capital felons to select between lethal injection and lethal gas, as the method of execution. North Carolina provides that lethal gas is the default method of execution, i.e., failure to select or untimely selecting a method will result in execution by lethal gas. California provides that lethal injection is the default method of execution. Missouri's death penalty statute fails to set out a default method of execution.

2. *Electrocution-lethal injection jurisdictions.* Six capital punishment jurisdictions, Florida, Kentucky, Ohio, South Carolina, Tennessee and Virginia, allow capital felons to select between electrocution and lethal injection as the method of execution. The default method of execution in Ohio is electrocution. Lethal injection is the default method of execution in Florida, South Carolina and Virginia. The death penalty statutes in Kentucky and Tennessee do not set out a default method of execution.

3. *Hanging-lethal injection jurisdictions.* The states of Montana and Washington provide that capital felons may choose between hanging and lethal injection as the method of execution. Both jurisdictions utilize hanging as the default method of execution.

4. *Firing squad-lethal injection jurisdictions.* Only one jurisdiction, Utah, provides the execution option of firing squad and lethal injection. The default method of execution in this jurisdiction is lethal injection.

Federal Option: Under the 1988 Federal death penalty law lethal injection was designated as the method of execution for offenses under that statute. However, under the 1994 Federal death penalty law the method of execution is chosen as follows:

> **18 U.S.C.A. § 3597(a):** A person who has been sentenced to death ... shall be committed to the custody of the Attorney General until exhaustion of the procedures for appeal of the judgment of conviction and for review of the sentence. When the sentence is to be implemented, the Attorney General shall release the person sentenced to death to the custody of a United States marshal, who shall supervise implementation of the sentence in the manner prescribed by the law of the State in which the sentence is imposed. If the law of the State does not provide for implementation of a sentence of death, the court shall designate another State, the law of which does provide for the implementation of a sentence of death, and the sentence shall be implemented in the latter State in the manner prescribed by such law.

As the above statute shows, execution under the 1994 Federal death penalty law may take one of two paths. If the state in which the capital sentence was obtained is a capital punishment jurisdiction, then whatever method of execution provided by that state will be imposed upon the capital felon. However, if the capital sentence was obtained in a non-capital punishment jurisdiction, the capital felon will be transported to a judicially determined capital punishment jurisdiction and executed according to the laws of that state.

Fallback Option: A minority of capital punishment jurisdictions have hedged their execution statutes by providing fallback option execution methods. That is, if a designated method of execution is ruled unconstitutional, an alternative method of execution is provided for by statute. There are two types of fallback option jurisdictions: (1) single fallback option and (2) dual fallback option.

1. *Single fallback option.* A single fallback option jurisdiction is one that has provided only a single alternative method of execution, should the primary method be found invalid. The illustration below sets out single fallback option jurisdictions and the fallback option provided by each jurisdiction.

Single Fallback Option Jurisdictions

Fallback Options

Jurisdiction	Lethal injection	Lethal gas	Firing squad	Hanging	Electrocution
Arkansas					✓
California	✓	✓			
Delaware				✓	
Idaho			✓		
Illinois					✓
Mississippi		✓			
New Hampshire			✓		
Ohio					✓
South Carolina					✓
Wyoming	✓				

Source: Louis J. Palmer, Jr., *Organ Transplants from Executed Prisoners* p. 89, Table 5 (1999).

It will be noted that California is not a pure single fallback option jurisdiction. California's statute provides that lethal injection or lethal gas is the fallback option. What California has done is simply provided that if either method of execution is found invalid, then the remaining method of execution becomes the fallback option.

2. *Dual fallback option.* A dual fallback option jurisdiction is one that has provided a fallback option for its fallback option. Currently Oklahoma is the only dual fallback option jurisdiction. Oklahoma provides that electrocution is its initial fallback option. However, should this option be invalidated, its second fallback option, firing squad, is the method of execution.

Executioner

Under modern capital punishment the role of the executioner varies with the method of execution used and the jurisdiction employing the method. For example, lethal injection involves injecting two or three (depending on the jurisdiction) chemicals in a condemned prisoner. Some jurisdictions employ a single person to perform the task, while others use a different person to inject each chemical.

The statutes in most jurisdictions require specially selected and trained correction officers to carry out the death penalty. However, prior to the year 2000, when Florida used only the electric chair to carry out the death penalty, its laws required a private individual be employed to carry out executions. Florida paid the executioner $150 for each execution.

The identity of capital punishment executioners is not made public for security reasons. Several challenges have been made by capital felons seeking to learn the identity of executioners. However, courts have been consistent in holding that capital felons do not have a constitutional right to know the identity of their executioners.

Prior to the shroud of secrecy engulfing executioners under modern capital punishment, executioners enjoyed some notoriety (albeit mostly negative). Robert G. Elliott was one of the most well-known executioners. In addition to executing 357 prisoners, Elliott performed the unusual feat of executing six prisoners by electrocution on the same day. He executed three prisoners in New York and three prisoners in Massachusetts.

One of the more tragic tails of executioners was that of John Hurlbert. He was the executioner at New York's Sing Sing Prison during the 1920s. Hurlbert executed over 120 prisoners in the electric chair at Sing Sing. The pressures of constantly executing prisoners took a tragic toll on

During the 1930s and 1940s, Robert G. Elliott was the executioner for several states, including New York, New Jersey and Massachusetts. (New York State Library)

Hurlbert. He unexpectedly resigned his job as executioner in 1926. Three years after Hurlbert left his job as executioner, the depression that had engulfed him drove to him to commit suicide in the basement of his home. *See also* **Identity of Executioner**

Executive Clemency *see* **Clemency**

Exhaustion of State Remedies Doctrine

Federal courts have power to grant writs of habeas corpus for the purpose of inquiring into the cause of restraint of liberty of any person in custody under the authority of a State in violation of the Federal Constitution. However, under the doctrine of exhaustion of State remedies, Federal courts will not, except in cases of peculiar urgency, exercise habeas corpus jurisdiction by a discharge of the person in advance of a final determination of his or her case in the courts of the State. This includes all appellate remedies in the State courts and direct appeal for certiorari in the United States Supreme Court.

The doctrine of exhaustion of State remedies is frequently invoked in capital punishment cases, when defendants seek Federal habeas intervention before exhausting all State avenues of legal redress.

State courts also utilize a version of the exhaustion of remedies doctrine. At the State level defendant's are generally prohibited from bringing collateral constitutional issues, such as ineffective assistance of counsel, on direct appellate review. Alleged collateral errors are usually deferred for habeas corpus or coram nobis proceedings, which follow direct appeals. *See also* **Habeas Corpus; Irvin v. Dowd (I)**

Ex Parte Bollman (I)

Court: United States Supreme Court; *Case Citation:* Ex Parte Bollman, 8 U.S. 75 (1807); *Argued:* Not reported; *Decided:* February 13, 1807; *Opinion of the Court:* Chief Justice Marshall; *Concurring Opinion:* None; *Dissenting Opinion:* Justice Johnson; *Justices Taking No Part in Decision:* Justice Cushing and Chase, J.; *Appellate Defense Counsel:* C. Lee and Mr. Harper argued and briefed; *Appellate Prosecution Counsel:* C. A. Rodney on brief; *Amicus Curiae Brief Supporting Prosecutor:* None; *Amicus Curiae Brief Supporting Defendant:* None.

Issue Presented: Whether the United States Supreme Court had authority to issue a writ of habeas corpus upon a motion by the defendants, who were in jail awaiting prosecution?

Case Holding: The United States Supreme Court had authority to issue a writ of habeas corpus upon a motion by the defendants, who were in jail awaiting prosecution.

Factual and procedural background of case: This case involved two defendants, Erick Bollman and Samuel Swartwout. The defendants were charged separately with the capital crime of treason by the United States. The defendants were held without bail pending prosecution. The defendants filed a motion with the United States Supreme Court, requesting the Court issue a writ of habeas corpus ordering that they be brought before the Court, and that a writ of certiorari be issued bringing the records in their cases to the Court. The defendants requested such relief for the purpose of having the Court ordering them released on bail or dismissing the charges against them.

Opinion of the Court by Chief Justice Marshall: The Chief Justice held that the Court had the authority by an act of Congress to issue a writ of habeas corpus commanding the defendants be brought before the Court. The opinion reasoned as follows:

> The decision that the individual shall be imprisoned must always precede the application for a writ of habeas corpus, and this writ must always be for the purpose of revising that decision, and therefore appellate in its nature....
>
> If at any time the public safety should require the suspension of the powers vested by this act in the courts of the United States, it is for the legislature to say so.

The motion prayed for by the defendants was granted.

Dissenting opinion by Justice Johnson: Justice Johnson dissented from the decision of the Court. He argued that the Court was without authority to issue a writ of habeas corpus. Justice Johnson stated his position as follows: "Let it be remembered that I am not disputing the power of the individual judges who compose this court to issue the writ of habeas corpus. This application is not made to us at chambers, but to us holding the supreme court of the United States — a creature of the constitution, and possessing no greater capacity to receive jurisdiction or power than the constitution gives it." *See also* **Ex Parte Bollman (II)**

Ex Parte Bollman (II)

Court: United States Supreme Court; *Case Citation:* Ex Parte Bollman, 8 U.S. 108 (1807); *Argued:* February 16–20, 1807; *Decided:* February 21, 1807; *Opinion of the Court:* Chief Justice Marshall; *Concurring Opinion:* None; *Dissenting Opinion:* None; *Appellate Defense Counsel:* C. Lee, F. S. Key, Mr. Martin and Mr. Harper argued and briefed; *Appellate Prosecution Counsel:* C. A. Rodney and Mr. Jones argued and briefed; *Amicus Curiae Brief Supporting Prosecutor:* None; *Amicus Curiae Brief Supporting Defendant:* None.

Issue Presented: Whether the conduct alleged against the defendants established probable cause that they committed treason against the United States?

Case Holding: The conduct alleged against the defendants did not establish probable cause that they committed treason against the United States, therefore they must be discharged from custody.

Factual and procedural background of case: This case involved two defendants, Erick Bollman and Samuel Swartwout. The defendants were charged separately with the capital crime of treason by the United States. The defendants were held without bail pending prosecution. The defendants filed a motion with the United States Supreme Court, requesting the Court issue a writ of habeas corpus ordering that they be brought before the Court, and that a writ of certiorari be issued bringing the records in their cases to the Court. The defendants requested such relief for the purpose of the Court ordering them released on bail or dismissing the charges against

them. The Court granted the relief sought and the defendants were brought before the Court, along with the records in the proceedings.

Opinion of the Court by Chief Justice Marshall: Chief Justice Marshall held that the charges of treason against the defendants had to be dismissed. It was said that treason against the United States, as defined by statute, required an actual levying of war against the nation. The Chief Justice found that the records in the case did not establish probable cause that the defendants engaged in treason as defined by law. The opinion reasoned as follows:

> To constitute that specific crime for which the prisoners now before the court have been committed, war must be actually levied against the United States. However flagitious may be the crime of conspiring to subvert by force the government of our country, such conspiracy is not treason. To conspire to levy war, and actually levy war, are distinct offense. The first must be brought into operation by the assemblage of men for a purpose treasonable in itself, or the fact of levying war cannot have been committed....
>
> It is not the intention of the court to say that no individual can be guilty of this crime who has not appeared in arms against his country. On the contrary, if war be actually levied, that is, if a body of men be actually assembled for the purpose of effecting by force a treasonable purpose, all those who perform any part, however minute, or however remote from the scene of action, and who are actually leagued in the general conspiracy, are to be considered as traitors. But there must be actual assembling of men for the treasonable purpose, to constitute a levying of war....
>
> ... In the case now before the court, a design to overturn the government of the United States in New Orleans by force, would have been unquestionably a design which, if carried into execution, would have been treason, and the assemblage of a body of men for the purpose of carrying it into execution would amount to levying war against the United States; but no conspiracy for this object, no enlisting of men to effect it, would be an actual levying of war....
>
> That both of the prisoners were engaged in a most culpable enterprise against the dominions of a power at peace with the United States ... cannot [be] doubt[ed]. But no part of this crime was committed in the district of Columbia is apparent. It is therefore the unanimous opinion of the court that they cannot be tried in this district.

The defendants were ordered discharged from custody. *See also* **Ex Parte Bollman (I)**

Ex Parte Crow Dog

Court: United States Supreme Court; *Case Citation:* Ex Parte Crow Dog, 109 U.S. 556 (1883); *Argued:* November 26, 1883; *Decided:* December 17, 1883; *Opinion of the Court:* Justice Matthews; *Concurring Opinion:* None; *Dissenting Opinion:* None; *Appellate Defense Counsel:* A. J. Plowman argued and briefed; *Appellate Prosecution Counsel:* United States Solicitor General argued and briefed; *Amicus Curiae Brief Supporting Prosecutor:* None; *Amicus Curiae Brief Supporting Defendant:* None.

Issue Presented: Whether the courts of the Territory of Dakota had jurisdiction over the defendant, a member of the Brule Sioux tribe whose victim was also a member of the same tribe?

Case Holding: The courts of the Territory of Dakota did

not have jurisdiction over the defendant, a member of the Brule Sioux tribe whose victim was also a member of the same tribe, because under Federal laws and treaties with Native Americans crimes by and against Native Americans must be prosecuted under the laws and customs of Native Americans.

Factual and procedural background of case: The defendant, Kan-Gi-Shun-Ca (aka Crow Dog), was convicted of capital murder and sentenced to death by the Territory of Dakota. The Dakota Territory Supreme Court affirmed the judgment. In doing so, the appellate court rejected the defendant's contention that the courts of the Dakota Territory did not have jurisdiction over the offense committed by him. The United States Supreme Court granted certiorari to consider the issue.

Opinion of the Court by Justice Matthews: Justice Matthews ruled that the courts established by the Federal Government for the Territory of Dakota did not have jurisdiction to prosecute the defendant for capital murder. The opinion held that under Federal statutes and treaties with Native Americans, crimes committed by Native Americans against other Native Americans had to be prosecuted by Native Americans. It was noted that the defendant was a member of the Brule Sioux tribe and the victim was also a member of the same tribe. Justice Matthews concluded that jurisdiction to prosecute the defendant resided exclusively with the Brule Sioux tribe. The opinion justified its position as follows:

> ... [This] is a case of life and death. It is a case where, against an express exception in the law itself, that law, by argument and inference only, is sought to be extended over aliens and strangers; over the members of a community separated by race, by tradition, by the instincts of a free ... life, from the authority and power which seeks to impose upon them the restraints of an external and unknown code, and to subject them to the responsibilities of civil conduct, according to rules and penalties of which they could have no previous warning; which judges them by a standard made by others and not for them, which takes no account of the conditions which should except them from its exactions, and makes no allowance for their inability to understand it. It tries them, not by their peers, nor by the customs of their people, nor the law of their land, but by [people] of a different race, according to the law of a social state of which they have imperfect conception, and which is opposed to the traditions of their history [and] to the habits of their lives....
>
> To ... uphold the jurisdiction exercised in this case, would be to reverse in this instance the general policy of the government towards the [Native Americans], as declared in many statutes and treaties, and recognized in many decisions of this court, from the beginning to the present. To justify such a departure, in such a case, requires a clear expression of the intention of Congress, and that we have not been able to find.

The judgment of the Dakota Territory Supreme Court was reversed. *See also* **Jurisdiction**

Ex Parte Gon-shay-ee   *Court:* United States Supreme Court; *Case Citation:* Ex Parte Gon-shay-ee; *Argued:* Not reported; *Decided:* April 15, 1889; *Opinion of the Court:* Justice Miller; *Concurring Opinion:* None; *Dissenting Opinion:* None; *Appellate Defense Counsel:* S. F. Phillips argued; W. H. Lamarand and J. G. Zachry on brief; *Appellate Prosecution Counsel:*

Mr. Jenks argued and briefed; *Amicus Curiae Brief Supporting Prosecutor:* None; *Amicus Curiae Brief Supporting Defendant:* None.

Issue Presented: Whether the Federal District Court of the Territory of Arizona had jurisdiction to prosecute the defendant for committing capital murder in violation of Federal law?

Case Holding: The Federal District Court of the Territory of Arizona did not have jurisdiction to prosecute the defendant for committing capital murder in violation of Federal law, because the defendant was a Native American who had to be tried under the laws of the Territory of Arizona.

Factual and procedural background of case: The defendant, Gon-shay-ee, was convicted of capital murder and sentenced to death by the United States. The crime and prosecution occurred in the Territory of Arizona. The defendant was a member of the Apache tribe and the victim was an American citizen. The defendant appealed to the United States Supreme Court, arguing that the Federal District Court did not have jurisdiction to prosecute him for violating a Federal law.

Opinion of the Court by Justice Miller: Justice Miller held that the District Court did not have jurisdiction to prosecute the defendant for violating federal law. The opinion pointed out that Federal trial courts were given two types of jurisdiction. Federal trial courts were authorized to preside over offenses committed against Federal law. Under this jurisdiction trial courts applied Federal law to criminal prosecutions. The Federal trial courts also had jurisdiction to preside over offenses committed in violation of the laws of the territory in which they sat. Under this jurisdiction, Federal trial courts had to apply the laws of the territory in which they sat.

The opinion indicated that Congress had enacted a statute which gave Federal trial courts authority to prosecute Native Americans for a certain class of offenses, including murder, regardless of where the offense occurred. However, this statute required Federal trial courts apply the law of the territory where the offense occurred, not Federal law. Justice Miller found that the trial court had authority to prosecute the defendant under the laws of the Territory of Arizona. However, the trial court invoked the laws of the United States. Consequently, the conviction and sentence were reversed. *See also* **Jurisdiction**

Ex Parte Gordon   *Court:* United States Supreme Court; *Case Citation:* Ex Parte Gordon, 66 U.S. 503 (1861); *Argued:* Not reported; *Decided:* December Term, 1861; *Opinion of the Court:* Chief Justice Taney; *Concurring Opinion:* None; *Dissenting Opinion:* None; *Appellate Defense Counsel:* Mr. Dean argued and briefed; *Appellate Prosecution Counsel:* Not represented; *Amicus Curiae Brief Supporting Prosecutor:* None; *Amicus Curiae Brief Supporting Defendant:* None.

Issue Presented: Whether the United States Supreme Court could, upon a motion by the defendant, issue a writ of prohibition halting his execution and issue a writ of certiorari commanding the record in the case be brought to the Court for review?

Case Holding: The United States Supreme Court did not have authority, upon a motion by the defendant, to issue a writ of prohibition halting his execution or to issue a writ of certiorari commanding the record in the case be brought to the Court for review.

Factual and procedural background of case: The defendant, Nathaniel Gordon, was convicted of piracy (violating the African Slave Trade Act) and sentenced to death by the United States. A death warrant was issued for his execution. The defendant filed a motion with the United States Supreme Court seeking a writ of prohibition halting his execution and a writ of certiorari to have the record in the case brought to the Court.

Opinion of the Court by Chief Justice Taney: The Chief Justice held that the Court was not empowered to grant the type of relief sought by the defendant from the Court. The opinion stated:

> ... [I]n criminal cases, the proceedings and judgment of the Circuit Court cannot be revised or controlled here, in any form of proceeding, either by [appeal] or prohibition, and, consequently, we have no authority to examine them by a certiorari....
>
> But this motion asks the court to do even more than exercise an appellate power where none is given by law, for the case has now passed out of the hands of the court, and the [death] warrant is in the hands of the marshal commanding him to execute the judgment of the court. The Circuit Court itself has not now the power to recall it, and, certainly, it would be without precedent in any judicial proceeding to prohibit a ministerial officer from performing a duty which the Circuit Court had a lawful right to command, ... and in a case, too, where no appellate power is given to this court to revise or control in any respect the judgment or proceedings of the Circuit Court. We are not aware of any case in which a similar motion has heretofore been made in this court in a criminal case.

The defendant's motion for relief was denied and the case dismissed.

Ex Parte Johnson

Court: United States Supreme Court; *Case Citation:* Ex Parte Johnson, 167 U.S. 120 (1897); *Argued:* Not reported; *Decided:* May 10, 1897; *Opinion of the Court:* Justice Brown; *Concurring Opinion:* None; *Dissenting Opinion:* None; *Appellate Defense Counsel:* John J. Weed argued and briefed; *Appellate Prosecution Counsel:* Mr. Conrad argued and briefed; *Amicus Curiae Brief Supporting Prosecutor:* None; *Amicus Curiae Brief Supporting Defendant:* None.

Issues Presented: (1) Whether the defendant's conviction and sentence were valid even though the Federal court prosecuting him did not have jurisdiction to prosecute capital offenses after the defendant's crime was committed? (2) Whether the judgment against the defendant was valid when he was unlawfully brought within the jurisdiction of the court?

Case Holdings: (1) The defendant's conviction and sentence were valid even though the Federal court prosecuting him did not have jurisdiction to prosecute capital offenses after the defendant's crime was committed. (2) The judgment against the defendant was valid because, even though he was unlawfully brought within the jurisdiction of the court, a criminal court does not lose jurisdiction over a defendant merely because custody was obtained illegally.

Factual and procedural background of case: The defendant, Johnson, was indicted by the Federal Southern District Court of Native American Territory, in Texas, for the capital crime of rape. The defendant was convicted and sentenced to death. Subsequently, an indictment was handed down against the defendant for the same offense by the Federal Eastern District Court, in Texas. The defendant was turned over to authorities representing the Eastern District Court. The defendant filed a petition for habeas corpus relief in the United States Supreme Court. The defendant alleged that the Southern District Court judgment was void, because it did not have jurisdiction over the offense, and because he was unlawfully brought before the court. The defendant wanted to be prosecuted by the Eastern District Court, because of the possibility of obtaining a sentence of life imprisonment. The United States Supreme Court granted certiorari to consider the issues.

Opinion of the Court by Justice Brown: Justice Brown noted that the Eastern District Court was newly created after the defendant committed the offense. Prior to its creation the Southern District Court had jurisdiction over the offense. The opinion reasoned that, while the Southern District Court no longer retained jurisdiction to prosecute capital offenses, it had such authority when it prosecuted the defendant.

The opinion rejected the defendant's contention that he should be released because he was improperly brought before the Southern District Court. Justice Brown held that even if the defendant had been unlawfully abducted and brought before the Southern District Court, such conduct would not invalidate the judgment. The opinion presented the law on this issue as follows:

> ... If the [defendant] was in the actual custody of the marshal ... his subsequent indictment and trial were valid, though in the first instance he might have been illegally arrested.... Indeed, there are many authorities which go to the extent of holding that in criminal cases a forcible abduction is no sufficient reason why the party should not answer when brought within the jurisdiction of the court which has the right to try him for such an offense, and presents no valid objection to his trial in such court. Although it has been frequently held that, if a defendant in a civil case be brought within the process of the court by a trick or device, the service will be set aside, and he will be discharged from custody. The law will not permit a person to be kidnapped or decoyed within the jurisdiction for the purpose of being compelled to answer to a mere private claim, but in criminal cases the interests of the public override that which is, after all, a mere privilege from arrest. But in this case there was nothing of the kind. The crime was committed and the prisoner arrested within the territory, and within the local jurisdiction of the territorial court. Had he been arrested without warrant by the marshal, or even by a private individual, and detained in custody ..., he might then have been indicted, although, perhaps, [a civil lawsuit] might have lain against the person so arresting him for false imprisonment.

The defendant's petition for relief was denied.

Case note: Under modern capital punishment jurisprudence the death penalty may not be imposed for the crime of rape, without an accompanying homicide. *See also* **Rape and Capital Punishment**

Ex Parte Milligan

Court: United States Supreme Court; *Case Citation:* Ex Parte Milligan, 71 U.S. 2 (1866); *Argued:* Not reported; *Decided:* December Term, 1866; *Opinion of the Court:* Justice Davis; *Concurring Opinion:* Chief Justice Chase, in which Wayne, Swayne and Miller, JJ., joined; *Dissenting Opinion:* None; *Appellate Defense Counsel:* J. E. McDonald argued; J. S. Black, J. Garfield and David D. Field on brief; *Appellate Prosecution Counsel:* United States Attorney General Speed argued; B. F. Butler on brief; *Amicus Curiae Brief Supporting Prosecutor:* None; *Amicus Curiae Brief Supporting Defendant:* None.

Issues Presented: (1) Whether the District Court had authority to entertain the defendant's habeas corpus petition when the President had suspended habeas relief? (2) Whether the military had jurisdiction to prosecute the defendant?

Case Holdings: (1) The District Court had authority to entertain the defendant's habeas corpus petition although the President had suspended habeas relief, because the Constitution does not permit indefinite suspension of habeas relief. (2) The military did not have jurisdiction to prosecute the defendant, because he was a civilian unconnected with military service.

Factual and procedural background of case: The defendant, Lambdin P. Milligan, was arrested at his Indiana home on October 21, 1864, by military personnel. The defendant was subsequently prosecuted by a military tribunal for unnamed capital crimes. He was found guilty and sentenced to death. The President signed a death warrant ordering the defendant's execution. The defendant filed a habeas corpus petition in a Federal District Court, alleging that the military tribunal did not have jurisdiction to prosecute him because he was never in the military. The District Court was uncertain as to how to proceed with the petition and, therefore, certified dispositive questions to the United States Supreme Court. The certified questions included: Did the District Court have authority to entertain the habeas petition, in view of the President's suspension of habeas corpus? Did the military have jurisdiction to prosecute the defendant? The United States Supreme Court granted certiorari to consider the questions.

Opinion of the Court by Justice Davis: Justice Davis acknowledged that the President, with congressional authorization, suspended habeas corpus by Proclamation on September 15, 1863. It was said that such suspension was not absolute in view of the constitutional prohibition against suspending habeas corpus. Justice Davis indicated that habeas corpus relief could not be indefinitely denied a prisoner. The opinion pointed out that procedurally, the suspension for prisoners had to be for a brief period of confinement, after which the Constitution required prisoners seeking habeas relief be afforded an opportunity to obtain release. Justice Davis found

that the District Court had authority to entertain the defendant's habeas petition. The opinion concluded on this issue:

> … The suspension of the privilege of the writ of habeas corpus does not suspend the writ itself. The writ issues as a matter of course; and on the return made to it the court decides whether the party applying is denied the right of proceeding any further with it.
>
> If the military trial of Milligan was contrary to law, then he was entitled, on the facts stated in his petition, to be discharged from custody[.]

In turning to the question of the military's jurisdiction, Justice Davis ruled that the military did not have jurisdiction to prosecute the defendant. It was said that no authority existed which could give the military authority to prosecute civilians unconnected with military service. Justice Davis wrote: "Congress could grant no such power; and to the honor of our national legislature be it said, it has never been provoked by the state of the country even to attempt its exercise. One of the plainest constitutional provisions was, therefore, infringed when Milligan was tried by a court not ordained and established by Congress[.]"

Justice Davis rebuffed arguments by the government that the defendant could be prosecuted by the military because he was a prisoner of war. To this it was said: "It is not easy to see how he can be treated as a prisoner of war, when he lived in Indiana for the past twenty years, was arrested there, and had not been, during the late troubles, a resident of any of the states in rebellion. If in Indiana he conspired with bad men to assist the enemy, he is punishable for it in the courts of Indiana; but, when tried for the offense, he cannot plead the rights of war; for he was not engaged in legal acts of hostility against the government, and only such persons, when captured, are prisoners of war. If he cannot enjoy the immunities attaching to the character of a prisoner of war, how can he be subject to their pains and penalties?" The District Court was, therefore, instructed to dispose of the case consistent with the rulings of the Court's opinion.

Concurring opinion by Chief Justice Chase, in which Wayne, Swayne and Miller, JJ., joined: The Chief Justice concurred in the Court's decision. He disagreed, however, with the Court's position that the military could never prosecute civilians unconnected with the military. The Chief Justice believed that Congress could, in times of emergency, authorize the military to prosecute civilians unconnected with military service. *See also* **Certified Question; Habeas Corpus; Military Death Penalty Law**

Ex Parte Quirin

Court: United States Supreme Court; *Case Citation:* Ex Parte Quirin, 317 U.S. 1 (1942); *Argued:* July 29–30, 1942; *Decided:* July 31, 1942; *Opinion of the Court:* Chief Justice Stone; *Concurring Opinion:* None; *Dissenting Opinion:* None; *Justice Taking No Part in Decision:* Justice Murphy; *Appellate Defense Counsel:* Colonel Kenneth C. Royall argued and briefed; *Appellate Prosecution Counsel:* Francis B. Biddle argued and briefed; *Amicus Curiae Brief Supporting*

Prosecutor: None; *Amicus Curiae Brief Supporting Defendant:* None.

Issue Presented: Whether the detention and prosecution of the defendants as spies by a Military Commission, appointed by Order of the President, is in conformity to the laws and Constitution of the United States?

Case Holding: The detention and prosecution of the defendants as spies by a Military Commission, appointed by Order of the President, is in conformity to the laws and Constitution of the United States.

Factual and procedural background of case: The defendants, Richard Quirin, Ernest Peter Burger, Heinrich Harm Heinck, Edward John Kerling, Werner Thiel, Herman Otto Neubauer, and Herbert Hans Haupt, were all born in Germany, though each had lived in the United States. The defendants returned to Germany between 1933 and 1941. After the declaration of war between the United States and Germany, the defendants received training at a sabotage school near Berlin, Germany, where they were instructed in the use of explosives. The defendants secretly returned to the United States with instructions to destroy war industries and war facilities (an eighth spy, George John Dasch, accompanied them but was not part of the proceeding before the United States Supreme Court). They were eventually captured by agents of the Federal Bureau of Investigation. After their capture the President, by Order of July 2, 1942, appointed a Military Commission and directed it to try the defendants and Dasch for offenses against the law of war and the Articles of War (the offenses were punishable with death). The President's order also stated that the men were to be access to the courts.

The Commission met on July 8, 1942, and proceeded with the trial. During the course of the trial the defendants filed a habeas corpus petition in a Federal District Court, challenging the authority of the President to have them prosecuted. The District Court dismissed the petition. The United States Supreme Court convened a special session to consider the issue.

Opinion of the Court by Chief Justice Stone: The Chief Justice ruled that the President was not prohibited by the Constitution from empowering a military commission to prosecute the defendants. It was said that "the detention and trial of [the defendants] — ordered by the President in the declared exercise of his powers as Commander in Chief of the Army in time of war and of grave public danger — are not to be set aside by the courts without the clear conviction that they are in conflict with the Constitution or laws of Congress constitutionally enacted." The Chief Justice found that "[b]y his Order creating the present Commission he has undertaken to exercise the authority conferred upon him by Congress, and also such authority as the Constitution itself gives the Commander in Chief, to direct the performance of those functions which may constitutionally be performed by the military arm of the nation in time of war." The opinion went on to justify the Court's decision as follows:

By the Articles of War, Congress has provided rules for the government of the Army. It has provided for the trial and punishment, by courts martial, of violations of the Articles by members of the armed forces and by specified classes of persons associated or serving with the Army. But the Articles also recognize the "military commission" appointed by military command as an appropriate tribunal for the trial and punishment of offenses against the law of war not ordinarily tried by court martial. Articles 38 and 46 authorize the President, with certain limitations, to prescribe the procedure for military commissions. Articles 81 and 82 authorize trial, either by court martial or military commission, of those charged with relieving, harboring or corresponding with the enemy and those charged with spying. And Article 15 declares that "the provisions of these articles conferring jurisdiction upon courts-martial shall not be construed as depriving military commissions ... or other military tribunals of concurrent jurisdiction in respect of offenders or offenses that by statute or by the law of war may be triable by such military commissions ... or other military tribunals." Article 2 includes among those persons subject to military law the personnel of our own military establishment. But this, as Article 12 provides, does not exclude from that class "any other person who by the law of war is subject to trial by military tribunals" and who under Article 12 may be tried by court martial or under Article 15 by military commission....

An important incident to the conduct of war is the adoption of measures by the military command not only to repel and defeat the enemy, but to seize and subject to disciplinary measures those enemies who in their attempt to thwart or impede our military effort have violated the law of war. It is unnecessary for present purposes to determine to what extent the President as Commander in Chief has constitutional power to create military commissions without the support of Congressional legislation. For here Congress has authorized trial of offenses against the law of war before such commissions. We are concerned only with the question whether it is within the constitutional power of the national government to place [the defendants] upon trial before a military commission for the offenses with which they are charged. We must therefore first inquire whether any of the acts charged is an offense against the law of war cognizable before a military tribunal, and if so whether the Constitution prohibits the trial. We may assume that there are acts regarded in other countries, or by some writers on international law, as offenses against the law of war which would not be triable by military tribunal here, either because they are not recognized by our courts as violations of the law of war or because they are of that class of offenses constitutionally triable only by a jury. It was upon such grounds that the Court denied the right to proceed by military tribunal in Ex parte Milligan. But as we shall show, these [defendants] were charged with an offense against the law of war which the Constitution does not require to be tried by jury....

By universal agreement and practice the law of war draws a distinction between the armed forces and the peaceful populations of belligerent nations and also between those who are lawful and unlawful combatants. Lawful combatants are subject to capture and detention as prisoners of war by opposing military forces. Unlawful combatants are likewise subject to capture and detention, but in addition they are subject to trial and punishment by military tribunals for acts which render their belligerency unlawful. The spy who secretly and without uniform passes the military lines of a belligerent in time of war, seeking to gather military information and communicate it to the enemy, or an enemy combatant who without uniform comes secretly through the lines for the purpose of waging war by destruction of life or property, are familiar examples of belligerents who are generally deemed not to be entitled to the status of prisoners of war, but to be offenders against the law of war subject to trial and punishment by military tribunals.

But [the defendants] insist that even if the offenses with which they are charged are offenses against the law of war, their trial is subject to the requirement of the Fifth Amendment that no person shall be held to answer for a capital or otherwise infamous crime unless on a presentment or indictment of a grand jury, and that such trials … must be by jury in a civil court....

Presentment by a grand jury and trial by a jury of the vicinage where the crime was committed were at the time of the adoption of the Constitution familiar parts of the machinery for criminal trials in the civil courts. But they were procedures unknown to military tribunals, which are not courts in the sense of the Judiciary Article, and which in the natural course of events are usually called upon to function under conditions precluding resort to such procedures. As this Court has often recognized, it was not the purpose or effect of [the Constitution], read in the light of the common law, to enlarge the then existing right to a jury trial. The object was to preserve unimpaired trial by jury in all those cases in which it had been recognized by the common law and in all cases of a like nature as they might arise in the future, but not to bring within the sweep of the guaranty those cases in which it was then well understood that a jury trial could not be demanded as of right....

We need not inquire whether Congress may restrict the power of the Commander in Chief to deal with enemy belligerents. For the Court is unanimous in its conclusion that the [Constitution] could not at any stage of the proceedings afford any basis for issuing the writ [of habeas corpus]....

The judgment of the District Court was affirmed. *See also* **Espionage; Military Death Penalty Law**

Ex Parte Spies

Court: United States Supreme Court; *Case Citation:* Ex Parte Spies, 123 U.S. 131 (1887); *Argued:* Not reported; *Decided:* November 2, 1887; *Opinion of the Court:* Chief Justice Waite; *Concurring Opinion:* None; *Dissenting Opinion:* None; *Appellate Defense Counsel:* Moses Salomon and B. F. Butler argued; W. P. Black, Roger A. Pryor and Randolph Tucker on brief; *Appellate Prosecution Counsel:* Geo. Hunt argued and briefed; *Amicus Curiae Brief Supporting Prosecutor:* None; *Amicus Curiae Brief Supporting Defendant:* None.

Issues Presented: (1) Whether the jury statute of the State of Illinois deprived the defendants of a fair trial, because it did not disqualify jurors who had prior knowledge of a case? (2) Whether defendant Spies was forced to testify against himself, because the prosecutor cross examined him about matters he did not testify to?

Case Holdings: (1) The jury statute of the State of Illinois did not deprive the defendants of a fair trial, because it did not disqualify jurors who had prior knowledge of a case, in view of the statute's requirement that such jurors give an oath that they can fairly and impartially decide the issues in the case. (2) Defendant Spies was not forced to testify against himself when the prosecutor cross examined him about matters he did not testify to, because the issues brought out were pertinent to the case.

Factual and procedural background of case: This case involved the prosecution of eight defendants by the State of Illinois for the capital murder of a police officer. The defendants were August Spies, Michael Schwab, Samuel Fielden, Albert R. Parsons, Adolph Fischer, George Engel, Louis Lingg, and Oscar W. Neebe. All of the defendants were found guilty by a jury. Seven of the defendants were sentenced to death. One defendant, Neebe, was sentenced to 15 years imprisonment. The Illinois Supreme Court affirmed the judgments. In doing so, the appellate court rejected the defendants' contention that they were deprived of a fair trial because of a State statute that allowed biased jurors to be impanelled; and an argument by defendant Spies that he was forced to testify against himself. The United States Supreme Court granted certiorari to consider the issues.

Opinion of the Court by Chief Justice Waite: The Chief Justice addressed the defendants' attack on the State's jury statute as follows. Under the statute a juror could not be disqualified because he or she had formed an opinion about a case based upon rumor or media reports, if upon oath the juror stated that he or she believed he or she could fairly and impartially render a verdict in accordance with the law. The Chief Justice ruled that the statute did not violate the Constitution. It was said that several States had statutes with similar language and that such statutes had never been invalidated by any State appellate court. The Chief Justice wrote: "[W]e agree entirely with the supreme court of Illinois in its opinion in this case that the statute on its face … is not repugnant to … the constitution[.]"

In turning to defendant Spies' contention that he was forced to testify against himself, the Chief Justice disagreed. It was said that Spies voluntarily took the stand and testified on his own behalf. The opinion indicated that once Spies took the stand "he became bound to submit to a proper cross examination under the law[.]" The prosecutor cross examined Spies about matters he testified to, and about other matters relevant to the case. The Chief Justice concluded: "It is not contended that the subject to which the cross examination related was not pertinent to the issue to be tried; and whether a cross examination must be confined to matters pertinent to the testimony [given], or may be extended to the matters in issue, is certainly a question of state law, as administered in the courts of the state, and not of federal law." The judgment of the Illinois Supreme Court was affirmed. *See also* **Chicago Labor Riots of 1886; Fielden v. Illinois; Schwab v. Berggren**

Ex Parte Wells

Court: United States Supreme Court; *Case Citation:* Ex Parte Wells, 59 U.S. 307 (1855); *Argued:* Not reported; *Decided:* December Term, 1855; *Opinion of the Court:* Justice Wayne; *Concurring Opinion:* None; *Dissenting Opinion:* Justice McLean; *Dissenting Opinion:* Justice Curtis, in which Campbell, J., joined; *Appellate Defense Counsel:* Charles L. Jones argued and briefed; *Appellate Prosecution Counsel:* United States Attorney General Cushing argued and briefed; *Amicus Curiae Brief Supporting Prosecutor:* None; *Amicus Curiae Brief Supporting Defendant:* None.

Issue Presented: Whether the President had authority to pardon the defendant's death sentence upon the condition that the defendant remain in prison for life?

Case Holding: The President had authority to pardon the defendant's death sentence upon the condition that the defendant remain in prison for life, because pardons may be absolute as well as conditional.

Factual and procedural background of case: The defendant, William Wells, was convicted of capital murder and sentenced to death by the District of Columbia. On the date set for his execution President Fillmore granted him a pardon upon the condition that he be imprisoned for life. The defendant accepted the conditional pardon. Subsequently, the defendant filed a habeas corpus petition in a trial court for the District of Columbia. In the petition the defendant contended that the President could not grant a conditional pardon and that the pardon had to be absolute. The trial court denied relief. The United States Supreme Court granted certiorari to consider the issue.

Opinion of the Court by Justice Wayne: Justice Wayne ruled that the President had authority to grant a conditional pardon. He wrote: "Such a thing as a pardon without a designation of its kind is not known in the law. Time out of mind, in the earliest books of the English law, every pardon has its particular denomination. They are general, special or particular, conditional or absolute[.]" Justice Wayne continued: "[T]he language used in the constitution, conferring the power to grant reprieves and pardons, must be construed with reference to its meaning at the time of its adoption. At the time of our separation from Great Britain, that power had been exercised by the king, as the chief executive…. Hence, when the words to grant pardons were used in the constitution, they conveyed to the mind the authority as exercised by the English crown…. In the convention which framed the constitution, no effort was made to define or change its meaning, although it was limited in cases of impeachment." The opinion concluded that the President's authority to grant conditional pardons was consistent with law. The judgment of the trial court was affirmed.

Dissenting opinion by Justice McLean: Justice McLean dissented from the Court's decision. He argued that the power of the President was different from that of English Kings, insofar as the President's authority was constitutionally and statutorily limited. Justice McLean urged that the President should not have authority to reduce a death sentence to life imprisonment, absent a statute authorizing life imprisonment as a lesser penalty.

Dissenting opinion by Justice Curtis, in which Campbell, J., joined: Justice Curtis dissented from the Court's opinion. He believed the Court lacked jurisdiction to hear the case. Justice Curtis was of the opinion that, for the Court to have jurisdiction, the trial court had to deny habeas relief on an attack of the original death sentence. He believed that the trial court's ruling on the President's conditional pardon was not a collateral matter that the Court had authority to review. *See also* **Clemency**

Expiration of Execution Date   Generally statutes establish the time in which an execution should be carried out.

However, under modern capital punishment law an execution will rarely be carried out during a time period fixed by statute, because defendants usually file numerous appeals. The United States Supreme Court has held that when an execution is not carried out in the time required by statute, because of appeals by a defendant, the Constitution is not violated because the execution occurs outside the time set out by statute. *See also* **In Re Cross**

Explosives Aggravator   The term "explosives" refers to any type of device that causes an incendiary-like explosion. Unlike a single shot from a gun, the use of explosives to commit a murder carries the high potential that the effects of the blast will harm many. A large minority of capital punishment jurisdictions have sought to deter the use of explosives by designating the use of explosives as a statutory aggravating circumstance. If the penalty phase jury in those jurisdictions find that explosives were used in the commission of capital murder the death penalty may be imposed. *See also* **Aggravating Circumstances**

JURISDICTIONS USING EXPLOSIVES AGGRAVATOR

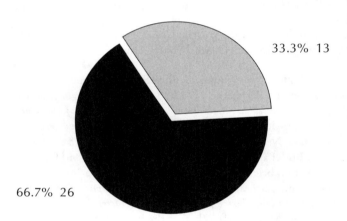

33.3% 13

66.7% 26

■ EXPLOSIVES AGGRAVATOR JURISDICTIONS

■ ALL OTHER JURISDICTIONS

Ex Post Facto Clause   In Article I, Section 9 of the Federal Constitution it is expressly stated that "[n]o … ex post facto Law shall be passed." There are four distinct classes of laws embraced by the Ex Post Facto Clause: (1) every law that makes an action done before the passing of the law, and which was innocent when done, criminal, and punishes such action; (2) every law that aggravates the crime of makes it greater than it was when committed; (3) every law that changes the punishment and inflicts a greater punishment than was annexed to the crime when committed; and (4) every law that alters the legal rules of evidence, and receives less or different testimony than the law required at the time of the commission of the offense in order to convict the offender.

A frequent issue raised in capital prosecutions involves

changing the method of execution. Capital felons have contended that when the method of execution changes after the commission of their crimes, the Ex Post Facto Clause prevents the new method of execution from being applied to them. The argument is further extended by the assertion that since the initial method of execution was repealed, their executions cannot be carried out because no valid law exists stating the method of execution. Courts have consistently and unanimously rejected this argument. Whatever method of execution is provided for by statute when it is time to execute a capital felon, may be imposed regardless of when the method was authorized.

An issue that frequently arises which capital felons have prevailed on, involves changing the standard for considering penalty phase evidence at the appellate level. For example, some legislators have altered the way in which appellate courts must treat penalty phase evidence when an invalid aggravating factor has been introduced. The initial post–*Furman v. Georgia*, 408 U.S. 238 (1972) death penalty statutes in a few jurisdictions required setting aside the death sentence in such circumstances and awarding a new sentencing hearing. However, legislators decided to change this method and permit appellate courts to remove the invalid factor and reweigh the evidence to see if the death sentence should be affirmed. Courts have found that such a change, while procedural, is substantive in effect and cannot be imposed retroactively under ex post facto principles. *See also* **Bill of Attainder Clause; Dobbert v. Florida; Duncan v. Missouri; Holden v. Minnesota; In Re Medley; Kring v. Missouri; Malloy v. South Carolina; McNulty v. California; Rooney v. North Dakota; Thompson v. Missouri**

Extradition Extradition refers to the involuntary or voluntary removal of a suspect from one jurisdiction to another jurisdiction for criminal prosecution. Two contentions are frequently raised regarding extradition.

First, usually when a capital murder suspect is apprehended in a state that does not have capital punishment, he or she will argue against being extradited to the demanding state because of the prospect of being put to death if found guilty. Under modern capital punishment jurisprudence noncapital punishment states will not refuse to extradite a capital murder suspect to a capital punishment state for prosecution. On the international level during the late 1990s, Israel refused to extradite Samuel Sheinbein to Maryland to face a capital murder prosecution. Sheinbein and another suspect (the other suspect committed suicide in a Maryland jail while awaiting prosecution) were accused by Maryland of killing and dismembering the body of 19 year old Alfredo Enrique Tello in 1997. Sheinbein, 17 years old at the time, fled the United States to Israel. The highest court in Israel refused to permit Sheinbein to be extradited to Maryland because he would face a capital punishment prosecution. Sheinbein was eventually prosecuted in Israel for the Maryland murder and sentenced to prison.

The second extradition argument that finds frequent use, involves defendants sentenced to death in one State, but temporarily extradited to another State for prosecution on other charges. In this situation defendants have argued that the State which imposed the death sentence no longer has jurisdiction to impose the death penalty, as a result of the temporary extradition. Courts unanimously have held that authority to carry out the death penalty is not lost by a State that temporarily extradites a defendant for further prosecution.

Extreme Duress Mitigator A majority of capital punishment jurisdictions have provided that being under extreme duress or substantial domination of another is a statutory mitigating circumstance that may preclude imposition of the death penalty. Courts have defined the extreme duress mitigator to refer to any (1) illegal confinement, (2) legal confinement used for illegal purposes, (3) threats of bodily or other harm, or (4) other means amounting to or tending to coerce the will of the capital defendant and actually induces him or her to commit the crime contrary to his or her will. Low intelligence of a capital defendant and his or her susceptibility to influences of others are relevant to the determination of the existence of the extreme duress mitigator. Courts have rejected impulse control problems as sufficient evidence, standing alone, to establish the extreme duress mitigator. *See also* **Mitigating Circumstances**

JURISDICTIONS USING EXTREME DURESS MITIGATOR

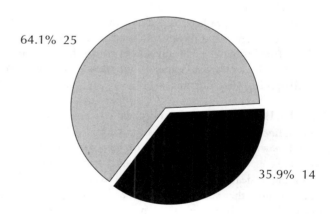

64.1% 25

35.9% 14

■ EXTREME DURESS MITIGATOR JURISDICTIONS

■ ALL OTHER JURISDICTIONS

Extreme Mental or Emotional Disturbance Mitigator A majority of capital punishment jurisdictions provide that "extreme mental or emotional disturbance," at the time of the commission of murder, is a statutory mitigating circumstance that may preclude imposition of the death penalty. This statutory mitigating circumstance does not refer to or include mental retardation or mental impairment due to a foreign substance. Its meaning lies somewhere between mental retardation and mental impairment due to a foreign substance. It does not reach insanity, because that is a defense to a prosecution.

Some guidance in fashioning an understanding of this statutory mitigating circumstance was provided by the Kentucky Supreme Court in *McClellan v. Commonwealth*, 715 S.W.2d 464 (Ky. 1986) The *McClellan* court held that:

> Extreme emotional disturbance is a temporary state of mind so enraged, inflamed, or disturbed as to overcome one's judgment, and to cause one to act uncontrollably from the impelling force of the extreme emotional disturbance rather than from evil or malicious purposes; it is not a mental disease in itself[.]

The definition provided by *McClellan* raises more questions than it answers. However, the definition does nail home the point that mental or emotional disturbance is not a mental disease. *See also* **Mentally Retarded Mitigator; Mitigating Circumstances**

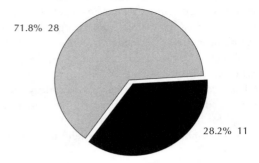

JURISDICTIONS USING EXTREME MENTAL OR
EMOTIONAL DISTURBANCE MITIGATOR

71.8% 28

28.2% 11

■ MENTAL OR EMOTIONAL DISTURBANCE
   MITIGATOR JURISDICTIONS

■ ALL OTHER JURISDICTIONS

F

Family and Friends' Testimony

Capital felons have consistently argued that they have a right to introduce, during the penalty phase, testimony and petition letters from relatives and friends indicating death is not appropriate in their particular cases. It has been urged by capital felons that such evidence is mitigating and relevant. Some courts have rejected such evidence as being irrelevant. Other courts, however, permit such evidence as non-statutory mitigating evidence. *See also* **Mitigating Circumstances**

Family Background Mitigator

Courts are unanimous in finding that evidence of a capital felon's family background may be relevant penalty phase non-statutory mitigating evidence. However, a difficult family background is not mitigating in death penalty analysis unless the capital defendant can show that something in his or her background impacted his or her behavior in committing the offense. If such evidence is produced, the penalty phase jury may recommend against the death penalty. *See also* **Mitigating Circumstances**

Father and Son *see* **Herreras**

Faulder, Joseph Stanley

Joseph Stanley Faulder became the first Canadian executed in the United States in almost fifty years, when the State of Texas executed him by lethal injection on June 17, 1999. Faulder was born in Canada on October 19, 1937. While living in Canada he served three years in Stoney Mountain Prison, Manitoba for auto theft. After his release in 1959 he was subsequently imprisoned in the British Columbia Prison for several years for an unknown offense.

Faulder eventually drifted to the United States, settling in Texas. His occupation was that of an auto mechanic. On July 8, 1975 Faulder and an accomplice, Linda Summers broke into the Gladewater home of 75 year old Inez Phillips. The home was robbed and Phillips was brutally stabbed to death by Faulder.

It was not until 1977 that Texas authorities apprehended Faulder. At the time he was being held by Colorado officials on unrelated charges. Faulder was extradited to Texas. While in custody Faulder confessed to the crime. In October of 1977 Faulder was charged with capital murder and Summers was charged with conspiracy to commit burglary. Faulder was convicted and sentenced to death

Joseph Stanley Faulder was the first known Canadian executed for crimes in the United States since Stanley Buckowski of Toronto, was executed by lethal gas on May 9, 1952 by the State of California. (Texas Department of Criminal Justice)

in 1978. The Texas Court of Criminal Appeals reversed the judgment in 1979, after finding Faulder's confession had been obtained under duress. In July of 1981 Faulder was tried a second time and again convicted and sentenced to death. All appeals failed to overturn the second judgment.

Faulder's case had sparked an international outcry and strained relations between Canada and the United States. Canada, which abolished the death penalty in 1976, tried to stop Faulder's execution on the grounds that diplomatic protocol established by the Vienna Convention had been violated, since it learned of Faulder's case after he had been imprisoned on death row for 15 years. Canadian protests had no impact on Texas officials. On June 17, 1999, Faulder was executed by lethal injection. Five members of the Phillips family were present at the execution. *See also* **Foreign Nationals and Capital Punishment**

Federal Bureau of Investigation

The Federal Bureau of Investigation (FBI) is the leading criminal investigative agency in the nation. The FBI was created at the request of President Theodore Roosevelt in 1909. In its earliest beginnings the agency was simply called Bureau of Investigation. It was not until July 1, 1935 that a Congressional enactment gave the agency its present name.

The FBI was an inefficient and unorganized agency until J. Edgar Hoover took over initially as acting director on May 10, 1924 and subsequently on December 10, 1924 as permanent director of the agency. Through Hoover's stewardship the FBI developed into a powerful and effective national criminal investigative agency. Hoover was singlehandedly responsible for expanding the investigative authority of the agency, increasing its staff manifold, and obtaining field offices throughout the nation. Hoover initiated recruitment policies that assured the agency of hiring only highly educated individuals. A training facility was established by Hoover that became the model for all law enforcement agencies in the nation, as well as a model for the international community.

Many of the high profile capital punishment cases investigated by the FBI were done under Hoover's watch as director. Hoover spearheaded the FBI investigation of the 1932 Lindbergh baby kidnapping, the 1933 Kansas City Massacre, the 1942 German spy invasion, the 1950 espionage prosecution of the Rosenbergs, the 1955 bombing of Flight 629, and the 1956 Weinberger kidnapping. Hoover died in office on May 2, 1972. Subsequent to his death, Congress enacted a law barring future FBI directors from holding office longer than 10 years.

The FBI has maintained its elite and highly respected status as an investigative agency after Hoover's passing. The single most prominent post–Hoover capital punishment case investigated by the FBI was that of the 1998 Oklahoma bombing, which sent Timothy McVeigh to death row. *See also* **Espionage; Flight 629; Kansas City Massacre; Lindbergh Kidnapping; Oklahoma Bombing; Rosenberg, Julius and Ethel; Weinberger Kidnapping**

J. Edgar Hoover is credited with building the FBI into the foremost criminal investigation agency in the world. (National Archives)

Federal Government

The Federal Government is a capital punishment jurisdiction. The Federal Government reenacted its death penalty law after the United States Supreme Court decision in *Furman v. Georgia*, 408 U.S. 238 (1972) in 1988.

The Federal Government has a three-tier criminal legal system. The Federal Government's criminal legal system is composed of a supreme court, courts of appeal and courts of general jurisdiction. The Federal Supreme Court is presided over by a chief justice and eight associate justices. The Federal Courts of Appeal are divided into eleven circuits. Each circuit consists of three or more States. The courts of general jurisdiction for Federal Government are called District Courts. Capital offenses against the Federal Government are tried in the District Courts.

The Federal Government's capital punishment statutes are triggered if a person commits a homicide under the following special circumstances:

1. Murder perpetrated by poison, lying in wait, or any other kind of willful, deliberate, malicious, and premeditated killing; or committed in the perpetration of, or attempt to perpetrate, any arson, escape, murder, kidnapping, treason, espionage, sabotage, aggravated sexual abuse or sexual abuse, burglary, or robbery;
2. Murder involving the smuggling of aliens;
3. Death resulting from destruction of aircraft, motor vehicles, or related facilities;
4. Drug related drive-by shooting murder;
5. Murder committed at an airport serving international civil aviation;
6. Retaliatory murder of a law enforcement official's immediate family member;
7. Civil rights offenses resulting in death;
8. Murder of a member of Congress, an executive official, or Supreme Court Justice;
9. Murder by an escaped Federal prisoner already sentenced to life imprisonment;
10. Death resulting from offenses involving transportation of explosives, destruction of government property, or destruction of property related to foreign or interstate commerce;
11. Murder committed during drug trafficking crime;
12. Murder committed in a Federal Government facility;
13. Genocide;
14. Murder of a Federal judge or law enforcement official;
15. Murder of a foreign official;
16. Murder by a Federal prisoner;
17. Murder of a United States national in a foreign country;
18. Murder of a State or local law enforcement official or other person aiding in a Federal investigation;

19. Murder of a State correctional officer;
20. Murder during a kidnaping;
21. Murder during a hostage taking;
22. Murder of a court officer or juror;
23. Murder with the intent of preventing testimony by a witness, victim, or informant;
24. Retaliatory murder of a witness, victim or informant;
25. Mailing of injurious articles with intent to kill or resulting in death;
26. Assassination or kidnaping resulting in the death of the President or Vice President;
27. Murder for hire;
28. Murder involved with a racketeering offense;
29. Willful wrecking of a train resulting in death;
30. Bank robbery related murder or kidnaping;
31. Murder related to a carjacking;
32. Murder related to rape or child molestation;
33. Murder related to sexual exploitation of children;
34. Murder committed during an offense against maritime navigation;
35. Murder committed during an offense against a maritime fixed platform;
36. Terrorist murder of a United States national in another country;
37. Murder by the use of a weapon of mass destruction;
38. Murder involving torture;
39. Murder related to a continuing criminal enterprise;
40. Death resulting from aircraft hijacking;
41. Espionage;
42. Treason;
43. Trafficking in large quantities of drugs; or
44. Attempting, authorizing or advising the killing of any officer, juror, or witness in cases involving a continuing criminal enterprise.

Capital murder under Federal law is punishable by death or life imprisonment. A capital prosecution by the Federal Government is bifurcated into a guilt phase and penalty phase. A jury is used at both phases of a capital trial. It is required that, at the penalty phase, the jury unanimously agree that a death sentence is appropriate before it can be imposed. If the penalty phase jury is unable to reach a verdict, the trial judge is required to impose a sentence of life imprisonment. The decision of a penalty phase jury is binding on the trial court under the laws of the Federal Government.

The Federal Government provides specific statutory aggravating circumstances for capital murder committed under its statute for (1) espionage or treason, (2) pure homicide or (3) drug offense. In order to impose a death sentence upon a defendant under Federal law, it is required that the prosecutor establish the existence of at least one of the following statutory aggravating circumstances at the penalty phase, premised upon a conviction for (1) espionage or treason, (2) pure homicide or (3) drug offense:

Aggravating Circumstances for Espionage and Treason:

1. The defendant has previously been convicted of another offense involving espionage or treason for which a sentence of either life imprisonment or death was authorized by law.
2. In the commission of the offense the defendant knowingly created a grave risk of substantial danger to the national security.
3. In the commission of the offense the defendant knowingly created a grave risk of death to another person.

Aggravating Circumstances for Homicide:

1. Death resulted during the commission of another crime.
2. The defendant had a previous conviction of violent felony involving firearm.
3. The defendant had a previous conviction of offense for which a sentence of death or life imprisonment was authorized.
4. The defendant has previously been convicted of 2 or more Federal or State offenses, punishable by a term of imprisonment of more than 1 year, committed on different occasions, involving the infliction of, or attempted infliction of, serious bodily injury or death upon another person.
5. The defendant created a grave risk of death to additional persons.
6. The defendant committed the offense in an especially heinous, cruel, or depraved manner in that it involved torture or serious physical abuse to the victim.
7. The defendant procured the commission of the offense by payment, or promise of payment, of anything of pecuniary value.
8. The defendant committed the offense as consideration for the receipt, or in the expectation of the receipt, of anything of pecuniary value.
9. The defendant committed the offense after substantial planning and premeditation to cause the death of a person or commit an act of terrorism.
10. The defendant has previously been convicted of 2 or more State or Federal offenses punishable by a term of imprisonment of more than one year, committed on different occasions, involving the distribution of a controlled substance.
11. The victim was particularly vulnerable due to old age, youth, or infirmity.
12. The defendant had previously been convicted of a drug offense for which a sentence of 5 or more years may be imposed or had previously been convicted of engaging in a continuing criminal enterprise.
13. The defendant committed the offense in the course of engaging in a continuing criminal enterprise that involved the distribution of drugs to persons under the age of 21.
14. The defendant committed the offense against:
    A. the President of the United States, the President-elect, the Vice President, the Vice President-elect, the Vice President-designate, or, if there is no Vice President, the officer next in order of succession to the office of the President of the United States, or any person who

is acting as President under the Constitution and laws of the United States;

    B. a chief of state, head of government, or the political equivalent, of a foreign nation;

    C. a foreign official if the official is in the United States on official business; or

    D. a Federal public servant who is a judge, a law enforcement officer, or an employee of a United States penal or correctional institution.

15. The defendant had a prior conviction of sexual assault or child molestation.

Aggravating Circumstances for Drug Offense Death Penalty Statute:

1. The defendant has previously been convicted of another Federal or State offense resulting in the death of a person, for which a sentence of life imprisonment or death was authorized by statute.

2. The defendant has previously been convicted of two or more Federal or State offenses, each punishable by a term of imprisonment of more than one year, committed on different occasions, involving the importation, manufacture, or distribution of a controlled substance or the infliction of, or attempted infliction of, serious bodily injury or death upon another person.

3. The defendant has previously been convicted of another Federal or State offense involving the manufacture, distribution, importation, or possession of a controlled substance for which a sentence of five or more years of imprisonment was authorized by statute.

4. In committing the offense, or in furtherance of a continuing criminal enterprise of which the offense was a part, the defendant used a firearm or knowingly directed, advised, authorized, or assisted another to use a firearm to threaten, intimidate, assault, or injure a person.

5. The offense, or a continuing criminal enterprise of which the offense was a part, involved distribution to a person under 21 which was committed directly by the defendant.

6. The offense, or a continuing criminal enterprise of which the offense was a part, involved distribution near a school which was committed directly by the defendant.

7. The offense, or a continuing criminal enterprise of which the offense was a part, involved using minors which was committed directly by the defendant.

8. The offense involved the importation, manufacture, or distribution of a controlled substance, mixed with a potentially lethal adulterant, and the defendant was aware of the presence of the adulterant.

Although the Federal Constitution will not permit jurisdictions to prevent capital felons from presenting all relevant mitigating evidence at the penalty phase, The Federal Government has provided the following statutory mitigating circumstances that permit the jury to reject imposition of the death penalty:

1. The defendant's capacity to appreciate the wrongfulness of the defendant's conduct or to conform conduct to the requirements of law was significantly impaired, regardless of whether the capacity was so impaired as to constitute a defense to the charge.

2. The defendant was under unusual and substantial duress, regardless of whether the duress was of such a degree as to constitute a defense to the charge.

3. The defendant is punishable as a principal in the offense, which was committed by another, but the defendant's participation was relatively minor, regardless of whether the participation was so minor as to constitute a defense to the charge.

4. Another defendant or defendants, equally culpable in the crime, will not be punished by death.

5. The defendant did not have a significant prior history of other criminal conduct.

6. The defendant committed the offense under severe mental or emotional disturbance.

7. The victim consented to the criminal conduct that resulted in the victim's death.

8. Other factors in the defendant's background, record, or character or any other circumstance of the offense that mitigate against imposition of the death sentence.

Under the Federal Government's capital punishment statutes, a sentence of death must be appealed for review by a Federal Court of Appeals. The Federal Government uses lethal injection to carry out death sentences. Under Federal law a Federal prisoner may be executed by the method authorized in the State where the offense occurred. The Federal death row facility is located in Terre Haute, Indiana. Pursuant to Federal laws the President has exclusive authority to grant clemency in capital cases.

From the start of modern capital punishment in 1976, through 1999, the Federal Government has not executed any capital felon. The last Federal execution occurred in 1963. A total of 21 capital felons were on Federal death row in 1999. The 1999 Federal death row population was: 14 black inmates; 5 white inmates; 1 Hispanic inmate; and 1 Asian inmate. The Federal Government does not permit capital punishment to be imposed on persons 17 years old or younger. The Federal Government does not prohibit the execution of mentally retarded capital felons.

Executions by Federal Government 1930–1999

Name	Race	Date of Execution	Method of Execution	Place of Execution
Carl Panzaran	White	September 5, 1930	Hanging	Kansas
George Barrett	White	March 24, 1936	Electrocution	Indiana
Arthur Gooch	White	June 19, 1936	Hanging	Oklahoma
Earl Gardner	N.A.	July 12, 1936	Hanging	Arizona
Anthony Chebatoria	White	July 8, 1938	Hanging	Michigan
Henry Seadlund	White	July 14, 1938	Hanging	Illinois
Robert Suhay	White	August 12, 1938	Hanging	Kansas

Name	Race	Date of Execution	Method of Execution	Place of Execution
Glenn Applegate	White	August 12, 1938	Hanging	Kansas
James Dalhover	White	November 18, 1938	Electrocution	Indiana
Nelson Charles	N.A.	November 10, 1939	Hanging	Arkansas
Hebert Haupt	White	August 8, 1942	Electrocution	D.C.
Heinrich Heinck	White	August 8, 1942	Electrocution	D.C.
Edward Keiling	White	August 8, 1942	Electrocution	D.C.
Herman Neubauer	White	August 8, 1942	Electrocution	D.C.
Richard Quirin	White	August 8, 1942	Electrocution	D.C.
Werner Thiel	White	August 8, 1942	Electrocution	D.C.
Clyde Arwood	White	August 14, 1943	Electrocution	Tennessee
Henry Ruhl	White	April 27, 1945	Lethal Gas	Wyoming
Austin Nelson	Black	March 1, 1948	Hanging	Arkansas
David J. Watson	Black	September 15, 1948	Electrocution	Florida
Samuel R. Shockley	White	December 3, 1948	Lethal Gas	California
Meran E. Thompson	White	December 3, 1948	Lethal Gas	California
Carlos R. Ochoa	Hispanic	December 10, 1948	Lethal Gas	California
Eugene LaMoore	Black	April 14, 1950	Hanging	Arkansas
Julius Rosenberg	White	June 19, 1953	Electrocution	New York
Ethel Rosenberg	White	June 19, 1953	Electrocution	New York
Carl A. Hall	White	December 18, 1953	Lethal Gas	Missouri
Bonnie B. Heady	White	December 18, 1953	Lethal Gas	Missouri
Gerhard A. Puff	White	August 12, 1954	Electrocution	New York
Arthur R. Brown	White	February 24, 1956	Lethal Gas	Missouri
George Krull	White	August 21, 1957	Electrocution	Georgia
Michael Krull	White	August 21, 1957	Electrocution	Georgia
Victor Feguer	White	March 15, 1963	Hanging	Iowa

EXECUTIONS BY FEDERAL GOVERNMENT 1930–1999

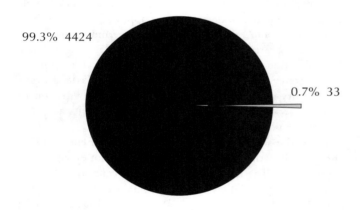

99.3% 4424

0.7% 33

- ▪ FEDERAL GOVERNMENT
- ▪ ALL OTHER JURISDICTIONS

Felder, Sammie *see* **Last 20th Century Execution**

Felker v. Turpin   *Court:* United States Supreme Court; *Case Citation:* Felker v. Turpin, 518 U.S. 651 (1996); *Argued:* June 3, 1996; *Decided:* June 28, 1996; *Opinion of the Court:* Chief Justice Rehnquist; *Concurring Opinion:* Justice Stevens, in which Souter and Breyer, JJ., joined; *Concurring Opinion:* Justice Souter, in which Stevens and Breyer, JJ., joined; *Dissenting Opinion:* None; *Appellate Defense Counsel:* Not reported; *Appellate Prosecution Counsel:* Not reported; *Amicus Curiae Brief Supporting Prosecutor:* Not reported; *Amicus Cu-*

riae Brief Supporting Defendant: Not reported.

Issues Presented: (1) Whether the provisions of the Antiterrorism and Effective Death Penalty Act of 1996 applied to petitions for habeas corpus filed as original matters in the United States Supreme Court? (2) Whether application of the Antiterrorism and Effective Death Penalty Act of 1996 unconstitutionally suspended habeas relief?

Case Holdings: (1) The Antiterrorism and Effective Death Penalty Act of 1996 did not preclude the Court from entertaining an application for habeas corpus relief filed as an original matter with the Court. (2) Application of the Antiterrorism and Effective Death Penalty Act of 1996 did not unconstitutionally suspend habeas relief.

Factual and procedural background of case: The defendant, Ellis Wayne Felker, was convicted of capital murder and sentenced to death by the State of Georgia. After the defendant exhausted unsuccessfully State post-conviction remedies, he filed a petition for Federal habeas corpus relief. The Federal courts denied relief.

While the defendant was awaiting execution, the President of the United States signed into law the Antiterrorism and Effective Death Penalty Act of 1996 (AEDP Act). The AEDP Act changed the procedures involved with State death row inmates' ability to seek Federal habeas relief. Pursuant to the AEDP Act, Federal courts must dismiss a habeas petition of a State prisoner that constitutes the prisoner's second or successive Federal habeas application if the claim presented was also presented in a prior application. The AEDP Act also required a prisoner seeking to file a second or successive habeas petition to first a motion in a Federal Court of Appeals requesting permission to file a second or successive habeas petition in a Federal District Court. The AEDP Act prohibited review of a Court of Appeals' decision to deny or grant a prisoner authorization to file a second or successive habeas petition.

After the AEDP Act was signed into law, the defendant filed a motion in a Court of Appeals seeking permission to file a second Federal habeas petition. The Court of Appeals denied the request. The defendant appealed the denial to the United States Supreme Court. The Supreme Court granted certiorari to consider the constitutionality of the AEDP Act.

Opinion of the Court by Chief Justice Rehnquist: The Chief Justice ruled that the AEDP Act did not preclude the Court from entertaining an application for habeas corpus relief filed as an original matter with the Court. It was said that the AEDP Act barred consideration of original habeas petitions in the Courts of Appeals. The Chief Justice reasoned that although the AEDP Act precluded the Court from reviewing, by appeal or certiorari, a Court of Appeals' decision on a request to file a second or successive habeas petition, the AEDP Act did not mention the Court's original habeas jurisdiction.

The opinion held that the AEDP Act did not violate Article I, Section 9, Clause 2 of the Constitution, which provides that "[t]he Privilege of the Writ of Habeas Corpus shall not be suspended." It was said that the new restrictions on a second or successive habeas petition constituted a restraint on what was called in habeas practice "abuse of the writ." The Chief Justice wrote that the doctrine of abuse of the writ referred to a complex and evolving body of equitable principles designed to limit frivolous use of habeas corpus. The opinion found that the restrictions imposed by the AEDP Act were consistent with the doctrine of abuse of the writ and therefore did not amount to a suspension of habeas corpus.

The Chief Justice concluded that the defendant's petition for an original writ of habeas corpus with the Court was baseless, because the defendant failed to establish "exceptional circumstances" justifying habeas relief. It was said that the claims made by the defendant did not materially differ from numerous other claims made by him previously.

The Court denied the defendant's petition for writ of certiorari from the Court of Appeals because of lack of jurisdiction to review the decision under the AEDP Act; and denied the defendant's petition for an original writ of habeas corpus with the Court.

Concurring opinion by Justice Stevens, in which Souter and Breyer, JJ., joined: Justice Stevens concurred in the Court's decision. He wrote that he agreed with the Court that the AEDP Act did not divest it of authority to grant habeas relief on an original petition with the Court. He also believed that the Court did not go far enough in addressing the Court's jurisdiction to entertain appeals that were precluded under the AEDP Act. Justice Stevens believed that the AEDP Act did not divest the Court of jurisdiction to review interlocutory orders issued by appellate courts involving second or successive habeas petitions.

Concurring opinion by Justice Souter, in which Stevens and Breyer, JJ., joined: Justice Souter concurred in the Court's decision. He agreed with the Court that the AEDP Act was constitutional, based upon the issues presented. However, Justice Souter believed that if Congress attempted to foreclose other avenues of review of lower court rulings on habeas petitions, a different outcome might result concerning the constitutionality of the AEDP Act.

Case note: Ellis Wayne Felker was executed by electrocution on November 15, 1996, by the State of Georgia. *See also* **Calderon v. Ashmus; Habeas Corpus; Stewart v. Martinez-Villareal**

Felony *see* **Types of Crimes**

Felony Murder Rule The felony murder rule is a common law doctrine that makes it easier for a prosecutor to obtain a murder conviction, when a victim is killed during the commission of another felony offense. If a capital felon commits a homicide during the course of committing a non-homicide felony offense, this conduct constitutes a special circumstance that would trigger a death penalty prosecution in a majority of capital punishment jurisdictions. In other words, a non-homicide felony combined with a homicide forms a death-eligible offense.

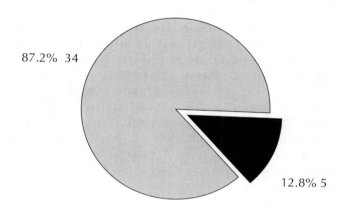

JURISDICTIONS WHERE FELONY MURDER IS A DEATH-ELIGIBLE OFFENSE

87.2% 34

12.8% 5

■ FELONY MURDER JURISDICTIONS
■ ALL OTHER JURISDICTIONS

Under the felony murder rule, a person who commits a felony is liable for any homicide that occurs during the commission of that felony, regardless of whether he or she commits, attempts to commit, or intended to commit that murder. The doctrine thus imposes liability on capital felons for killings committed by co-felons during a felony.

The common law did not make a distinction in punishment for co-defendants convicted of felony murder. That is, even though a victim's death may have actually been caused by a single defendant, under the common law all defendants involved in the underlying felony were subjected to the same punishment that was provided for the defendant who actually killed the victim.

The compact and simplistic punishment interpretation given to the felony murder rule was fragmented and complicated, as a result of decisions reached by the United States Supreme Court in two separate cases. Both cases involved the issue of whether the Cruel and Unusual Punishment Clause prohibited imposition of capital punishment for felony murder convictions. In addressing this issue the Supreme Court dissected the felony murder rule into three distinct new doctrines: (1) felony murder simpliciter, (2) felony murder aggravatus, and (3) felony murder supremus or traditional felony murder.

Felony Murder Simpliciter: The first case to begin the dissection of the felony murder rule was *Enmund v. Florida*, 458 U.S. 782 (1982). Under the traditional felony murder rule, the defendant and a confederate in *Enmund* were convicted of committing two murders during the course of a robbery in a home. The defendant was convicted of the two murders in spite of the fact that he did not actually kill the victims, and was not present in the home at the time of the killings. The defendant was the driver of the get-away car.

In its analysis of the facts of *Enmund*, the Supreme Court approved of the defendant's convictions based upon the application of the felony murder rule. The Supreme Court viewed the defendant's role in the crime, driver of the get-away car, as sufficient to convict him for homicides committed during the course of the robbery. However, the Supreme Court was disturbed by the punishment the defendant received. In order to rescue the defendant from the death penalty, the Supreme Court created an exception to the punishment component of the common law felony murder rule. The Supreme Court held in *Enmund* that the Cruel and Unusual Punishment Clause prohibits imposition of the death penalty upon a defendant "who aids and abets a felony in the course of which a murder is committed by others[,] but who does not himself kill, attempt to kill, or intend that a killing take place or that lethal force will be employed." This exception to the traditional felony murder rule is known as the felony murder simpliciter doctrine.

Felony Murder Aggravatus: Several years after the *Enmund* decision, the Supreme Court was asked to apply the felony murder simpliciter doctrine to invalidate the death sentences imposed upon two brothers in *Tison v. Arizona*, 481 U.S. 137 (1987). The defendants in *Tison* took part in killing four people during the course of helping their father escape from prison.

The defendants in *Tison* asked the Supreme Court to overturn their death sentences, on the grounds that the sentences were an unconstitutional imposition of capital punishment for felony murder simpliciter. The Supreme Court analyzed the conduct of the brothers under the elements of felony murder simpliciter and concluded that their conduct fell outside of the felony murder simpliciter doctrine.

The Supreme Court next analyzed the conduct of the defendants under the elements of felony murder supremus or traditional felony murder, which it described as "[a] category of felony murderers for which *Enmund* explicitly finds the death penalty permissible under the Eighth Amendment." The elements of felony murder supremus are: (1) the defendant actually killed, (2) attempted to kill, or (3) intended to kill. It was concluded by the Supreme Court that the conduct of the brothers in *Tison* did not fall within the elements of felony murder supremus.

The Supreme Court then reduced the conduct of the brothers down to two factors: (1) their participation in the felonies was major and (2) their mental state was one of reckless indifference to the value of human life. Although this conduct

did not satisfy the elements of felony murder simpliciter nor felony murder supremus, the Supreme Court determined that it was nevertheless a midrange level of felony murder. This midrange felony murder is the felony murder aggravatus doctrine.

After reducing the conduct of the brothers to felony murder aggravatus, the Supreme Court then concluded that the Cruel and Unusual Punishment Clause did not prohibit imposition of the death penalty for felony murder aggravatus. *See also* **Enmund v. Florida; Tison v. Arizona**

Female Serial Killer *see* **Wuornos, Aileen**

Ferguson v. Georgia

Court: United States Supreme Court; *Case Citation:* Ferguson v. Georgia, 365 U.S. 570 (1961); *Argued:* November 14–15, 1960; *Decided:* March 27, 1961; *Opinion of the Court:* Justice Brennan; *Concurring Opinion:* Justice Frankfurter, in which Clark, J., joined; *Concurring Opinion:* Justice Clark, in which Frankfurter, J., joined; *Dissenting Opinion:* None; *Appellate Defense Counsel:* Paul James Maxwell argued and briefed; *Appellate Prosecution Counsel:* Dan Winn argued; Eugene Cook, John T. Ferguson, John T. Perrin and Robert J. Noland on brief; *Amicus Curiae Brief Supporting Prosecutor:* None; *Amicus Curiae Brief Supporting Defendant:* None.

Issue Presented: Whether Georgia's statute prohibiting the defendant from testifying under oath, and limiting the defendant to giving only an unsworn written statement, violated the Constitution?

Case Holding: The question of the constitutionality of that part of Georgia's statute prohibiting the defendant from giving testimony under oath was not properly before the Court and would not be answered. However, that part of Georgia's statute which limited the defendant to giving only an unsworn written statement violated the Constitution.

Factual and procedural background of case: The defendant, Ferguson, was charged with capital murder by the State of Georgia. At the time of his prosecution, Georgia had a statute which prohibited defendants from testifying on their own behalf. Defendants could only offer unsworn written statements. During the defendant's trial defense counsel called the defendant as a witness to give unsworn testimony, but the trial court precluded the defendant from actually testifying. The jury convicted the defendant and sentenced him to death. The Georgia Supreme Court affirmed the conviction and sentence. In doing so, the appellate court rejected the defendant's contention that he was denied his constitutional right to effective assistance of counsel, because defense counsel could not question him on the witness stand. The United States Supreme Court granted certiorari to consider the issue.

Opinion of the Court by Justice Brennan: Justice Brennan observed that Georgia was the only State to retain the common law rule that a person charged with a criminal offense was incompetent to testify under oath in his or her own behalf at his or her trial. It was said that Georgia had two distinct disqualification rules. Under one rule a defendant could not give testimony under oath. Under the second rule, a defendant could give a written unsworn statement, but could not give live unsworn testimony. During the defendant's trial he sought to testify under the rule regarding unsworn statements.

Because the defendant invoked the unsworn statement rule, Justice Brennan did not believe the Court had jurisdiction to render a decision on the constitutionality of Georgia's rule which prohibited sworn testimony by a defendant. The opinion, therefore, limited its holding to the second rule. Justice Brennan held that the part of the Georgia statute which denied the defendant the right to give live "unsworn" testimony and be questioned by his counsel, denied the defendant his constitutional right to effective assistance of his counsel. The judgment of the Supreme Court of Georgia was reversed.

Concurring opinion by Justice Frankfurter, in which Clark, J., joined: Justice Frankfurter concurred in the Court's judgment. However, he believed the Court had authority to reach the issue of whether Georgia could constitutionally bar defendants from giving sworn testimony on their own behalf. Justice Frankfurter also believed that in addressing the sworn testimony disqualification rule, the Court should find the rule unconstitutional.

Concurring opinion by Justice Clark, in which Frankfurter, J., joined: Justice Clark concurred in the Court's decision. He wrote separately to indicate that he believed the Court should have addressed and resolved the sworn testimony disqualification rule. Justice Clark pointed out that by allowing that rule to remain intact, the Court created the anomalous situation where defendants could give unsworn live testimony that prosecutors could not cross examine them on.
See also **Competency of the Defendant to be a Witness**

Ferrell, Rodrick *see* **Vampire Clan Murders**

Field, Stephen J.

Stephen J. Field served as an associate justice of the United States Supreme Court from 1863 to 1897. While on the Supreme Court Field was known as a conservative who interpreted the Constitution to advance the interest of private industry over government interference.

Field was born on November 4, 1816, in Haddam, Connecticut. He attended Williams College where he graduated in 1833. Field went on to study law as an apprentice to his brother in New York City. After spending several years in private practice in New York City, Field ventured out west to California. His journey to California proved successful in 1857 when he was elected to the State's highest court. In 1863 President Abraham Lincoln nominated Field to the Supreme Court.

While on the Supreme Court Field was known to have written only a few capital punishment opinions. The capital punishment opinion authored by Field which had some impact on constitutional jurisprudence was *Coleman v. Tennessee*. In that case the Supreme Court was asked to decide whether double

jeopardy principles barred the State of Tennessee from prosecuting the defendant for a capital offense that he was prosecuted for by the United States military. Writing for the Court in *Coleman*, Field held that double jeopardy principles did not bar the State of Tennessee from prosecuting the defendant for an offense that he was prosecuted for by the United States military, but under the rules of war such prosecution by the State could not occur. Field died on April 9, 1899.

Capital Punishment Opinions Written by Field

Case Name	Opinion of the Court	Concurring Opinion	Dissenting Opinion
Coleman v. Tennessee	✓		
In Re Wood		✓	
Neal v. Delaware			✓

Fielden, Samuel *see* **Chicago Labor Riots of 1886; Fielden v. Illinois**

Fielden v. Illinois

Court: United States Supreme Court; *Case Citation:* Fielden v. Illinois, 143 U.S. 452 (1892); *Argued:* Not reported; *Decided:* February 29, 1892; *Opinion of the Court:* Justice Harlan; *Concurring Opinion:* None; *Dissenting Opinion:* None; *Appellate Defense Counsel:* Benjamin F. Butler argued; Moses Salomon on brief; *Appellate Prosecution Counsel:* George Hunt argued; E. S. Smith on brief; *Amicus Curiae Brief Supporting Prosecutor:* None; *Amicus Curiae Brief Supporting Defendant:* None.

Issue Presented: Whether the defendant had a constitutional right to be present in person when the State appellate court affirmed his death sentence?

Case Holding: The defendant did not have a constitutional right to be present in person when the State appellate court affirmed his death sentence, because such right was only afforded at the trial court level when the original sentence was pronounced.

Factual and procedural background of case: The defendant, Samuel Fielden, was prosecuted, along with seven other defendants, for the capital murder of a police officer by the State of Illinois. The other defendants were August Spies, Michael Schwab, Albert R. Parsons, Adolph Fischer, George Engel, Louis Lingg, and Oscar W. Neebe. All of the defendants were found guilty by a jury. Fielden and six of the other defendants were sentenced to death. One defendant, Neebe, was sentenced to 15 years imprisonment. The Illinois Supreme Court affirmed all of the judgments. In *Ex Parte Spies*, the United States Supreme Court affirmed all of the judgments.

The defendant, Fielden, had his sentence commuted to life imprisonment by the governor of Illinois (Schwab's sentence was also commuted to life imprisonment). Subsequently, the defendant filed a habeas corpus petition in a Federal District Court, alleging his constitutional rights were violated because he was not present when the State appellate court affirmed the original death sentence, therefore his detention under the commutation was unlawful. The petition was dismissed. The

United States Supreme Court granted certiorari to consider the issue.

Opinion of the Court by Justice Harlan: Justice Harlan initially addressed the defendant's contention that the Illinois Supreme Court should have amended its ruling affirming the death sentence to reflect that the defendant was not present during the appellate proceedings. The opinion stated "that no right secured to the [defendant] by the constitution of the United States was violated by the refusal of the supreme court of Illinois to allow the proposed amendment of its record."

The opinion then addressed the defendant's argument that he had a constitutional right to be present during the State appellate proceedings. Justice Harlan indicated that no such right existed at the appellate level, and ruled that the issue was moot because the Court previously ruled in a companion case, *Schwab v. Berggren,* that there was no right for a defendant to be present at appellate proceedings. The judgment of the District Court was affirmed. *See also* **Allocution; Chicago Labor Riots of 1886; Ex Parte Spies; Schwab v. Berggren**

Fifth Amendment *see* **Bill of Rights; Right to Remain Silent**

Fiji Capital punishment was abolished for ordinary crimes in Fiji in 1979, but the punishment is still possible for exceptional crimes. Fiji has a democratic government consisting of an executive branch, legislative branch, and judicial branch. Its legal system is based on British law. The nation's new constitution took effect July 28, 1998.

The judicial system is composed of magistrate courts, High Court, Court of Appeal, and Supreme Court. Defendants have the right to bail, a public trial and to counsel. *See also* **International Capital Punishment Nations**

Fikes v. Alabama *Court:* United States Supreme Court; *Case Citation:* Fikes v. Alabama, 352 U.S. 191 (1957); *Argued:* December 6, 1956; *Decided:* January 14, 1957; *Opinion of the Court:* Chief Justice Warren; *Concurring Opinion:* Justice Frankfurter, in which Brennan, J., joined; *Dissenting Opinion:* Justice Harlan, in which Reed and Burton, JJ., joined; *Appellate Defense Counsel:* Jack Greenberg argued; Peter A. Hall and Orzell Billingsley on brief; *Appellate Prosecution Counsel:* Robert Straub argued; John Patterson on brief; *Amicus Curiae Brief Supporting Prosecutor:* None; *Amicus Curiae Brief Supporting Defendant:* None.

Issue Presented: Whether the defendant's confession was involuntary based upon long periods of isolation, even though no physical force was used against him?

Case Holding: The defendant's confession was involuntary based upon long periods of isolation, even though no physical force was used against him.

Factual and procedural background of case: The defendant, Fikes, was convicted of burglary with intent to commit rape and was sentenced to death by the State of Alabama. The Alabama Supreme Court affirmed the conviction and sentence.

In doing so, the appellate court rejected the defendant's contention that his confession was involuntary. The United States Supreme Court granted certiorari to consider the issue.

Opinion of the Court by Chief Justice Warren: The Chief Justice held that the defendant's confession was involuntary. The opinion outlined the Court's justification for its ruling as follows:

> Here the prisoner was ... certainly of low mentality, if not mentally ill. He was first arrested by civilians, lodged in jail, and then removed to a state prison far from his home. We do not criticize the decision to remove the prisoner before any possibility of violence might mature, but [the defendant's] location and the conditions of his incarceration are facts to be weighed in connection with the issue before us. For a period of a week, he was kept in isolation, except for sessions of questioning. He saw no friend or relative. Both his father and a lawyer were barred in attempts to see him. The protections to be afforded to a prisoner upon preliminary hearing were denied him, contrary to the law of Alabama. He was questioned for several hours at a time over the course of five days preceding the first confession, and again interrogated at length before the written confession was secured.

The judgment of the Alabama Supreme Court was reversed.

Concurring opinion by Justice Frankfurter, in which Brennan, J., joined: Justice Frankfurter concurred in the Court's decision. He wrote separately to stress his belief that physical force was not the only method of rendering a confession involuntary. Justice Frankfurter wrote: "For myself, I cannot see the difference, with respect to the 'voluntariness' of a confession, between the subversion of freedom of the will through physical punishment and the sapping of the will appropriately to be inferred from the circumstances of this case — detention of the accused virtually incommunicado for a long period; failure to arraign him in that period; horse-shedding of the accused at the intermittent pleasure of the police until confession was forthcoming. No single one of these circumstances alone would in my opinion justify a reversal. I cannot escape the conclusion, however, that in combination they bring the result below the Plimsoll line of 'due process.'"

Dissenting opinion by Justice Harlan, in which Reed and Burton, JJ., joined: Justice Harlan dissented from the Court's decision. He believed that the tactics used to obtain the defendant's confession were allowed by due process. He wrote: "In this instance I do not think it can be said that the procedures followed in obtaining [the defendant's] confessions violated constitutional due process. The elements usually associated with cases in which this Court has been constrained to act are, in my opinion, not present here in constitutional proportions, separately or in combination. Concededly, there was no brutality or physical coercion. And psychological coercion is by no means manifest. While the total period of interrogation was substantial, the questioning was intermittent; it never exceeded two or three hours at a time, and all of it took place during normal hours[.]"

Case note: Under modern capital punishment jurisprudence the death penalty may not be imposed for the crime of burglary with intent to commit rape, without an accompanying homicide. *See also* **Right to Remain Silent; Rape and Capital Punishment**

Film Depictions of Capital Punishment

With the inception of big screen movies and television, film producers have had a fascination with capital punishment. The film industry has never taken a fixed position on capital punishment. Movies have appeared which depict the death penalty as a necessary punishment or as a senseless and primitive form of public revenge. Anti–death penalty films tend to center around innocent defendants being sentenced to death, whereas pro–death penalty films have generally involved characters whom everyone could hate. Between these two extremes there have appeared films that simply tell the story of real life defendants who received the death penalty.

The film industry's love affair with the death penalty has made the industry the primary medium in which most of the American public obtains its understanding and knowledge about the death penalty. This fact has raised opposing critics. Anti–death penalty proponents have argued that the film industry has a duty not to depict capital punishment as a necessary form of punishment. On the other side, pro–death penalty adherents contend that the film industry should not portray capital punishment as a system that executes innocent defendants.

Some of the noteworthy American and international films depicting capital punishment appear below.

Capital Punishment Films: *The Public Enemy*, starring James Cagney (1931). Ruthless gangster sentenced to death. *20,000 Years in Sing Sing*, starring Spencer Tracy (1932). Gangster commits murder while in prison gets death sentence. *Illegal*, starring Edward G. Robinson (1955). Story of a prosecutor who had an innocent person executed. *Hold Back Tomorrow*, directed by Hugo Haas (1955). Tale of death row inmate's final day before execution. *Time Without Pity*, directed by Joseph Losey (1956). Depicting efforts to save innocent man from execution. *Compulsion*, starring Orson Welles (1959). Based on true story involving unsuccessful 1924, capital prosecution of Nathan Leopold and Richard Loeb. *Murder, Inc.*, starring Peter Falk (1960). True story of the life and execution of gangster Louis "Lepke" Buchalter. *Why Must I Die*, directed by Roy Del Ruth (1960). Tale of efforts to save a woman hours before her execution. *Chiamate 22-22 Tenente Sheridan*, directed by Giorgio Bianchi (1960). Italian film showing efforts to save a woman on death row during the last 24 hours before her execution. *The Boston Strangler*, starring Tony Curtis and Henry Fonda (1968). True story of man confessing to be the Boston Strangler. *Aspen*, starring Sam Elliot (1977). Tale of innocent man sentenced to death. *Le Pull-over Rouge*, directed by Michel Drach (1979). French film created with helping abolish death penalty in France through its depiction of the true story of an execution of an innocent man. *I Want to Live*, starring Martin Balsam (1983). Tale of a woman on death row. *A Short Film About Killing*, starring Miroslaw Baka (1987). Polish film of man on death row. *Rampage*, directed by William Friedkin (1988). Story of a prosecutor's efforts to obtain the death penalty for a man who killed a family. *The Thin Blue Line*, directed by Errol Morris (1988). Documentary tale of man wrongfully sentenced to death. *Let Him Have It*, directed by Peter Medak (1991). English film condemning capital punishment through execution of innocent man. *Reflections on a Crime*, directed by Jon Purdy (1994). Depiction of last hours of a woman on death row. *Just Cause*, starring Sean Connery (1995). Depicting authorities rejecting evidence that proves a death row inmate's innocence. *Dead Man Walking*, starring Sean Penn (1995). Depicting man's life on death row. *Last Dance*, starring Sharon Stone (1996). Tale of woman's life on death row. *Beyond the Call*, starring Sissy Spacek (1996). Tale of a man's life on death row. *Last Rights*, directed by Kevin Dowling (1998). Story of a death row inmate's fight to prevent a second attempt to execute him. *A Letter from Death Row*, starring Martin Sheen (1998). Death row inmate struggles to prove his innocence. *The Green Mile*, starring Tom Hanks (1999). Tale of death row through the eyes of prison guards. *True Crime*, directed by and starring Clint Eastwood (1999). Tale of struggle to save an innocent man from being executed. *In the Name of the People*, starring Richard Thomas (2000). Story of interaction between death row inmate and the family of his victim. *See also* **Literary Depictions of Capital Punishment**

Finland

Finland abolished the death penalty for ordinary crimes in 1949, and completely abolished the punishment for all crimes in 1972. *See also* **International Capital Punishment Nations**

Finley v. California

Court: United States Supreme Court; *Case Citation:* Finley v. California, 222 U.S. 28 (1911); *Argued:* October 26, 1911; *Decided:* November 6, 1911; *Opinion of the Court:* Justice McKenna; *Concurring Opinion:* None; *Dissenting Opinion:* None; *Appellate Defense Counsel:* C. C. Calhoun argued; James N. Sharp, H. G. W. Dinkelspiel, Samuel T. Bush and G. C. Ringolsky on brief; *Appellate Prosecution Counsel:* U. S. Webb argued; E. B. Power on brief; *Amicus Curiae Brief Supporting Prosecutor:* None; *Amicus Curiae Brief Supporting Defendant:* None.

Issue Presented: Whether principles of equal protection permit the mandatory imposition of the death penalty upon a prisoner who commits murder while serving a life sentence, even though a prisoner serving less than a life sentence would not face a mandatory sentence of death for committing murder?

Case Holding: Principles of equal protection permit the mandatory imposition of the death penalty upon a prisoner who commits murder while serving a life sentence, even though a prisoner serving less than a life sentence would not face a mandatory sentence of death for committing murder, because no other effective punishment exists for a prisoner already serving a life sentence.

Factual and procedural background of case: The

defendant, James W. Finley, was convicted of capital murder and sentenced to death by the State of California. At the time of the defendant's offense he was serving a life sentence in the State penitentiary. The defendant was prosecuted under a State statute which made a sentence of death automatic for anyone committing murder while serving a life sentence. In the defendant's appeal to the California Supreme Court he argued that the statute under which he was prosecuted denied him equal protection of the laws, because it did not apply to anyone who was serving a prison sentence that was less than life imprisonment. The State appellate court rejected the argument and affirmed the judgment. The United States Supreme Court granted certiorari to consider the issue.

Opinion of the Court by Justice McKenna: Justice McKenna held that the State's statute provided a proper basis for having a different classification between prisoners serving life sentences in the state prison and prisoners serving lesser terms. It was said that a clear distinction existed between prisoners serving life sentences and those who were not. With respect to prisoners serving life sentences, Justice McKenna observed that "there could be no extension of the term of imprisonment as a punishment for crimes they might commit[.]" On the other hand, prisoners who were serving less than life sentences faced the possibility of receiving a life sentence for crimes committed while incarcerated. Therefore, it was reasoned, a deterrent existed for the prisoner serving less than a life sentence, whereas no such deterrent existed, other than death, for a prisoner serving a life sentence. The judgment of the California Supreme Court was affirmed. *See also* **In Custody Aggravator**

Firefighter Aggravator

Firefighter Aggravator   The work of firefighters is inherently dangerous. The danger is not lessened because of fire being accidentally set or purposely started. Firefighters have died in both. A large minority of capital punishment jurisdictions have responded to the death of firefighters caused by fires intentionally set, by making the death of a firefighter a statutory aggravating circumstance. The penalty phase jury may impose the death penalty if it is found that a defendant caused the death of a firefighter while he or she was performing his or her duties. *See also* **Aggravating Circumstances**

Firing Squad

Firing Squad   Death by firing squad is traced to military tradition. Mutiny and desertion were among the offenses that the military punished with death by firing squad. The common law did not accept or reject execution by firing squad. Common law judges simply never resorted to this method of execution.

The exact date that execution by firing squad was adopted by civilian law, in the United States, is uncertain. Records reflect, however, that by the 1850s death by firing squad was a part of civilian law in the nation.

The most publicized firing squad execution in the last half of the 20th century, was the January 17, 1977 execution of Gary Gilmore by the state of Utah. Gilmore was executed for having killed Ben Bushnell and Max Jensen. Two issues made Gilmore's execution noteworthy.

First, Gilmore refused to appeal his conviction. However, his attorneys filed a state court appeal without his permission. Gilmore demanded the appeal be withdrawn. The appeal eventually reached the United States Supreme Court in the name of Gilmore's mother, who sought to halt his execution. The Supreme Court refused to stay the execution and denied the appeal in a memorandum opinion. However, a separate opinion was written by Chief Justice Warren Burger. In *Gilmore v. Utah*, 429 U.S. 238 (1972) Chief Justice Burger summed up the matter as follows:

> This case may be unique in the annals of the Court. Not only does Gary Mark Gilmore request no relief himself, but on the contrary he has expressly and repeatedly stated since his conviction in the Utah courts that he had received a fair trial and had been well treated by the Utah authorities. Nor does he claim to be innocent of the crime for which he was convicted. Indeed, his only complaint against Utah or its judicial process ... has been with respect to the delay on the part of the State in carrying out the sentence.

The second issue making Gilmore's case significant, was the fact that the constitutionality of Utah's death penalty statute was still not determined. Utah had enacted a new death penalty statute in response to the moratorium placed on capital punishment by *Furman v. Georgia*, 408 U.S. 238 (1972). Although the Supreme Court had approved of lifting the moratorium in *Gregg v. Georgia*, 428 U.S. 153 (1976), no express determination had been made about the validity of Utah's new death penalty statute at the time of Gilmore's prosecution. Chief Justice Burger explained the problem as follows in *Gilmore*:

> ... [Gilmore's attorneys] informed the trial court that they had advised Gilmore ... that the constitutionality of the Utah death penalty statute had not yet been reviewed by either the Utah Supreme Court or the United States Supreme Court, and that in their view there was a chance that the statute would eventually

JURISDICTIONS USING FIREFIGHTER AGGRAVATOR

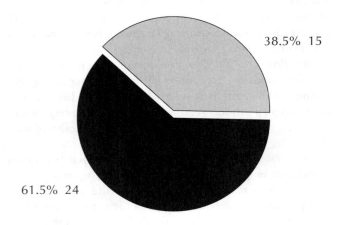

38.5% 15

61.5% 24

■ FIREFIGHTER AGGRAVATOR JURISDICTIONS
■ ALL OTHER JURISDICTIONS

be held unconstitutional. The trial court itself advised Gilmore ... that the constitutional issue had not yet been resolved, and that both counsel for the State and Gilmore's own counsel would attempt to expedite an appeal to avoid unnecessary delay. Gilmore stated that he did not "care to languish in prison for another day," that the decision was his own....

Subsequent to Gilmore's execution Utah's death penalty statute was found constitutional by a Federal Court of Appeals in the case of *Andrew v. Shulsen*, 802 F.2d 1256 (10th Cir. 1986).

Firing Squad Jurisdictions: As of January 2000, only three capital punishment jurisdictions, Utah, Idaho and Oklahoma allowed execution by firing squad. In Utah the firing squad is one of two methods of execution that a capital felon may choose from. Idaho utilizes the firing squad as its fallback option in the event its primary option is invalidated. Oklahoma provides for the use of a firing squad as dual fallback option.

JURISDICTIONS WHERE FIRING SQUAD IS ALLOWED

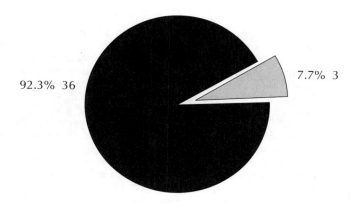

92.3% 36   7.7% 3

■ FIRING SQUAD JURISDICTIONS

■ NON-FIRING SQUAD JURISDICTIONS

Constitutionality of Firing Squad: The constitutionality of execution by firing squad was answered by the United States Supreme Court in *Wilkerson v. Utah*, 99 U.S. 130 (1878). In Wilkerson the Supreme Court held that "[c]ruel and unusual punishments are forbidden by the Constitution, but the ... punishment of shooting as a mode of executing the death penalty ... is included in that category[.]" The decision in *Wilkerson* has stood unassailable for over 120 years.

A major criticism of death by firing squad is that death is slow. A capital felon executed by firing squad literally has to bleed to death while in agony from the wounds.

Firing Squad Protocol: The general procedure for carrying out death by firing squad involves the use of a five-person firing squad. The members of the firing squad use rifles (pistols have been known to be used), some of which have blanks. The use of blanks is done so that the firing squad team will not know who actually killed the prisoner.

The execution is carried out on prison grounds in an area not accessible to view by other prisoners or the public. The prisoner is strapped to a chair facing the firing squad. A hood

EXECUTIONS PERFORMED BY FIRING SQUAD 1976–1999

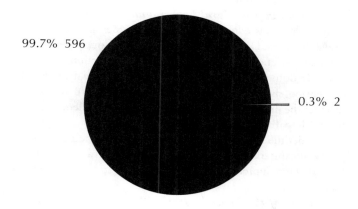

99.7% 596   0.3% 2

■ FIRING SQUAD

■ ALL OTHER METHODS

is placed over the prisoner's head. A circular target is placed on the torso of the prisoner. A designated official gives a synchronized count, while the firing squad takes aim at from thirty to forty feet away from the prisoner. When the designated official shouts "Fire," the prisoner is put to death. *See also* **Execution Option Jurisdictions; Methods of Execution; Wilkerson v. Utah**

First Execution of the 21st Century

Oklahoma holds the distinction of carrying out the first execution in the 21st century. It did so when Malcom Johnson was executed by the State on January 6, 2000. Johnson, an African American, was executed by lethal injection. Johnson was convicted of the 1981 rape and murder of a 76 year old woman. *See also* **Last Execution of the 20th Century**

Fischer, Adolph *see* Chicago Labor Riots of 1886

Fisher v. United States

Court: United States Supreme Court; *Case Citation:* Fisher v. United States, 328 U.S. 463 (1946); *Argued:* December 5, 1945; *Decided:* June 10, 1946; *Opinion of the Court:* Justice Reed; *Concurring Opinion:* None; *Dissenting Opinion:* Justice Frankfurter; *Dissenting Opinion:* Justice Murphy, in which Frankfurter and Rutledge, JJ., joined; *Dissenting Opinion:* Justice Rutledge; *Justice Taking No Part in Decision:* Justice Jackson; *Appellate Defense Counsel:* Charles H. Houston argued and briefed; *Appellate Prosecution Counsel:* Charles B. Murray argued and briefed; *Amicus Curiae Brief Supporting Prosecutor:* None; *Amicus Curiae Brief Supporting Defendant:* None.

Issue Presented: Whether it was error for the trial court of the District of Columbia to refuse to instruct the jury on the defendant's mental deficiency so as to allow for a sentence less than death?

Case Holding: The Court declined to impose a non-constitutional rule upon the District of Columbia, because the issue was one of local concern.

Factual and procedural background of case: The defendant, Fisher, was convicted of capital murder and sentenced to death by the District of Columbia. The Court of Appeals for the District of Columbia affirmed the conviction and sentence. In doing so, the appellate court rejected the defendant's contention that it was error for the trial court to refuse to instruct the jury that they should consider the evidence of the his psychopathic aggressive tendencies, low emotional response and borderline mental deficiency to determine whether he was guilty of capital murder or murder in the second degree. The United States Supreme Court granted certiorari to consider the issue.

Opinion of the Court by Justice Reed: Justice Reed held that the relief sought by the defendant was for the Court to declare that mental deficiency which does not show legal irresponsibility should be a relevant factor in determining whether an accused is guilty of capital murder or murder in the second degree. It was said that for the "Court to force the District of Columbia to adopt such a requirement for criminal trials would involve a fundamental change in the common law theory of responsibility." Justice Reed ruled that the Court was not prepared to force an evidentiary rule on the courts of the District of Columbia. The opinion concluded: "We express no opinion upon whether the theory for which [the defendant] contends should or should not be made the law of the District of Columbia. Such a radical departure from common law concepts is more properly a subject for the exercise of legislative power or at least for the discretion of the courts of the District. The administration of criminal law in matters not affected by Constitutional limitations or a general federal law is a matter peculiarly of local concern." The judgment of the Court of appeals was affirmed.

Dissenting opinion by Justice Frankfurter: Justice Frankfurter dissented from the Court's decision. He believed the defendant was entitled to have the jury instructed on his mental deficiency. Justice Frankfurter wrote: "Men ought not to go to their doom because this Court thinks that conflicting legal conclusions of an abstract nature seem to have been 'nicely balanced' by the Court of Appeals for the District of Columbia. The deference which this Court pays to that Court's adjudications in ordinary cases involving issues essentially of minor or merely local importance seems out of place when the action of this Court, no matter how phrased, sustains a death sentence at the seat of our Government as a result of a trial over which this Court, by direction of Congress, has the final reviewing power. This Court cannot escape responsibility for the death sentence if it affirms the judgment. One can only hope that even more serious consequences will not follow, which would be the case if the Court's decision were to give encouragement to doctrines of criminal law that have only obscurantist precedents of the past to recommend them."

Dissenting opinion by Justice Murphy, in which Frankfurter and Rutledge, JJ., joined: Justice Murphy dissented from the Court's decision in the case. He believed that the Court was wrong in refusing to address the issue, and wrong in refusing to adopt the position taken by the defendant. Justice Murphy stated his argument thus:

> As this case reaches us, we are not met with any question as to whether [the defendant] killed an individual. That fact is admitted. Our sole concern here is with the charge given to the jury concerning the elements entering into the various degrees of murder for which [the defendant] could be convicted.
>
> The rule that this Court ordinarily will refrain from reviewing decisions dealing with matters of local law in the District of Columbia is a sound and necessary one. But it is not to be applied without discretion. Like most rules, this one has its exceptions. And those exceptions are grounded primarily in considerations of public policy and of sound administration of justice.
>
> Here we have more than an exercise in statutory construction or in local law. It is a capital case involving not a question of innocence or guilt but rather a consideration of the proper standards to be used in judging the degree of guilt. What the Court says and decides here today will affect the life of the [defendant] as well as the lives of countless future criminals in the District and in the various states....
>
> The issue here is narrow yet replete with significance. Stated briefly, it is this: May mental deficiency not amounting to complete insanity properly be considered by the jury in determining whether a homicide has been committed with the deliberation and premeditation necessary to constitute first degree murder? The correct answer, in my opinion, was given by this Court more than sixty years ago ... when it said, "But when a statute establishing different degrees of murder requires deliberate premeditation in order to constitute murder in the first degree, the question whether the accused is in such a condition of mind, by reason of drunkenness or otherwise, as to be capable of deliberate premeditation, necessarily becomes a material subject of consideration by the jury."
>
> More precisely, there are persons who, while not totally insane, possess such low mental powers as to be incapable of the deliberation and premeditation requisite to statutory first degree murder. Yet under the rule adopted by the court below, the jury must either condemn such persons to death on the false premise that they possess the mental requirements of a first degree murderer or free them completely from criminal responsibility and turn them loose among society. The jury is forbidden to find them guilty of a lesser degree of murder by reason of their generally weakened or disordered intellect.
>
> Common sense and logic recoil at such a rule. And it is difficult to marshal support for it from civilized concepts of justice or from the necessity of protecting society. When a man's life or liberty is at stake he should be adjudged according to his personal culpability as well as by the objective seriousness of his crime. That elementary principle of justice is applied to those who kill while intoxicated or in the heat of passion; if such a condition destroys their deliberation and premeditation the jury may properly consider that fact and convict them of a lesser degree of murder. No different principle should be utilized in the case of those whose mental deficiency is of a more permanent character.

Dissenting opinion by Justice Rutledge: In setting out his dissent from the Court's decision in the case, Justice Rutledge stated the following: "Because I think the charge was deficient in not including the requested instruction or one substantially similar, thus in my opinion failing to meet the standard set by Congress in the Code, and because the effect of this deficiency was magnified by the failure to point up the instructions given in some more definite relation to the evidence, I think the judgment should be reversed."

Case note: The position taken by the dissenting justices eventually was adopted by the Court under modern capital punishment. It is a constitutional violation under modern capital punishment to refuse to instruct a penalty phase jury on mitigating evidence of a defendant's mental disease that is short of insanity. *See also* **Mitigating Circumstances**

Flight 629

Flight 629 took off from Stapleton Airport, Denver, Colorado, bound for Seattle, Washington at 6:52 P.M. on November 1, 1955. The plane was carrying 39 passengers and five crew members. Within 11 minutes of the plane's departure it exploded. All 44 persons aboard were instantly killed.

Shortly after the explosion the Federal Bureau of Investigation (FBI) launched an investigation into the cause of the explosion. Wreckage from the plane was recovered and analyzed. It was determined that the explosion was not due to a malfunction of the plane. Further investigation of the wreckage lead to the conclusion that a bomb was placed in the rear cargo pit of the plane.

The next phase of the investigation involved obtaining a background check on each of the 44 individual victims. During this phase investigators found a considerable quantity of personal effects of a passenger named Daisie E. King. Through the personal effects of King authorities learned that she had a son, Jack Gilbert Graham.

Graham was born on January 23, 1932. He was married, with two infant children, and lived in Denver. His mother had been living in his home before her death. Graham was initially interviewed by authorities on November 10, 1955. Subsequent interviews followed as authorities began to mount suspicion toward Graham. The authorities became particularly suspicious toward him after his wife informed them that Graham had given his mother a wrapped Christmas gift before she boarded the plane. In a separate interview with Graham, he told authorities his wife was mistaken and that he had intended to buy his mother a tool set for Christmas but could not find the right kind.

On November 13 FBI Agents were sent to make a search of Graham's home. During the search a small roll of copper wire

Jack Gilbert Graham committed the first aerial mass murder in the nation's history. (Colorado State Archives)

with yellow insulation was located in a shirt belonging to Graham. The wire appeared to be the type used in detonating primer caps. Authorities also found a travel insurance policy on the life of King, dated November 1, 1955. The policy paid $37,500 and named Graham as the beneficiary. The policy was found hidden in a small cedar chest in one of the bedrooms at Graham's home.

Graham was summoned to FBI headquarters and questioned intensely. Eventually he confessed. Graham told authorities that he had used a time bomb composed of 25 sticks of dynamite, two electric primer caps, a timer, and a six-volt battery. On November 17 Graham was charged with the murder of his mother by the State of Colorado.

The trial started on April 16, 1956 and lasted several weeks. On May 5, after deliberating for less than two hours, the jury found Graham guilty of murder. He was sentenced to death. Graham's attorneys filed a motion for a new trial. However, on May 15 Graham informed the trial judge that he did not want a new trial and that he did not want his case appealed. Graham's attorneys filed an appeal, against his wishes, but the State high court affirmed the judgment. Graham was executed by lethal gas at Colorado State Penitentiary on January 11, 1957. *See also* **Mass Murder**

Florida

The State of Florida is a capital punishment jurisdiction. The State reenacted its death penalty law after the United States Supreme Court decision in *Furman v. Georgia*, 408 U.S. 238 (1972), on December 8, 1972.

Florida has a three-tier legal system. The State's legal system is composed of a supreme court, courts of appeal and courts of general jurisdiction. The Florida Supreme Court is presided over by a chief justice and six associate justices. The Florida District Courts of Appeal are divided into five districts. Each district has a chief judge and eight or more judges. The courts of general jurisdiction in the State are called Circuit Courts. Capital offenses against the State of Florida are tried in the Circuit Courts.

Florida's capital punishment statute is triggered if a person

Members of the Florida Supreme Court (seated left to right): *Justice Leander J. Shaw, Jr., Chief Justice Major B. Harding, and Justice Charles T. Wells;* (standing left to right) *Justice R. Fred Lewis, Justice Harry Lee Anstead, Justice Barbara J. Pariente, and Justice Peggy A. Quince. (Florida Supreme Court)*

commits a homicide under the following special circumstances:

1. When perpetrated from a premeditated design to effect the death of the person killed or any human being;
2. When committed by a person engaged in the perpetration of, or in the attempt to perpetrate, any: (a) drug trafficking offense; (b) arson; (c) sexual battery; (d) robbery; (e) burglary; (f) kidnaping; (g) escape; (h) aggravated child abuse; (i) aggravated abuse of an elderly person or disabled adult; (j) aircraft piracy; (k) unlawful throwing, placing, or discharging of a destructive device or bomb; (l) carjacking; (m) home-invasion robbery; (n) aggravated stalking; (o) murder of another human being; or
3. Which resulted from the unlawful distribution of cocaine or opium or any synthetic or natural salt, compound, derivative, or preparation of opium by a person 18 years of age or older, when such drug is proven to be the proximate cause of the death of the user.

Capital murder in Florida is punishable by death or life imprisonment without parole. A capital prosecution in Florida is bifurcated into a guilt phase and penalty phase. A jury is used at both phases of a capital trial. It is required that, at the penalty phase, a majority of the jury must agree that a death sentence is appropriate before it can be imposed. If the penalty phase jury is unable to reach a verdict, the trial judge is required to sentence the defendant to life imprisonment. The decision of a penalty phase jury is not binding on the trial court under the laws of Florida. The trial court may accept or reject the jury's determination on punishment, and impose whatever sentence he or she believes the evidence established.

In order to impose a death sentence upon a defendant under Florida law, it is required that the prosecutor establish the existence of at least one of the following statutory aggravating circumstances at the penalty phase:

a. The capital felony was committed by a person previously convicted of a felony and under sentence of imprisonment or placed on community control or on felony probation.
b. The defendant was previously convicted of another capital felony or of a felony involving the use or threat of violence to the person.
c. The defendant knowingly created a great risk of death to many persons.
d. The capital felony was committed while the defendant was engaged, or was an accomplice, in the commission of, or an attempt to commit, or flight after committing or attempting to commit, any: robbery; sexual battery; aggravated child abuse; abuse of an elderly person or disabled adult resulting in great bodily harm, permanent disability, or permanent disfigurement; arson; burglary; kidnaping; aircraft piracy; or unlawful throwing, placing, or discharging of a destructive device or bomb.
e. The capital felony was committed for the purpose of avoiding or preventing a lawful arrest or effecting an escape from custody.
f. The capital felony was committed for pecuniary gain.
g. The capital felony was committed to disrupt or hinder the lawful exercise of any governmental function or the enforcement of laws.
h. The capital felony was especially heinous, atrocious, or cruel.
i. The capital felony was a homicide and was committed in a cold, calculated, and premeditated manner without any pretense of moral or legal justification.
j. The victim of the capital felony was a law enforcement officer engaged in the performance of his or her official duties.
k. The victim of the capital felony was an elected or appointed public official engaged in the performance of his or her official duties if the motive for the capital felony was related, in whole or in part, to the victim's official capacity.
l. The victim of the capital felony was a person less than 12 years of age.
m. The victim of the capital felony was particularly vulnerable due to advanced age or disability, or because the defendant stood in a position of familial or custodial authority over the victim.
n. The capital felony was committed by a criminal street gang member.

Although the Federal Constitution will not permit jurisdictions to prevent capital felons from presenting all relevant mitigating evidence at the penalty phase, Florida has provided the following statutory mitigating circumstances that permit the jury (or judge) to reject imposition of the death penalty:

a. The defendant has no significant history of prior criminal activity.
b. The capital felony was committed while the defendant was under the influence of extreme mental or emotional disturbance.
c. The victim was a participant in the defendant's conduct or consented to the act.
d. The defendant was an accomplice in the capital felony committed by another person and his or her participation was relatively minor.
e. The defendant acted under extreme duress or under the substantial domination of another person.
f. The capacity of the defendant to appreciate the criminality of his or her conduct or to conform his or her conduct to the requirements of law was substantially impaired.
g. The age of the defendant at the time of the crime.
h. The existence of any other factors in the defendant's background that would mitigate against imposition of the death penalty.

Florida has a separate statute that provides for determining whether to impose the death penalty upon a defendant convicted of capital murder while committing specific drug trafficking offenses. Under the drug trafficking death penalty statute, in order to impose a death sentence upon a defendant, it is required that the prosecutor establish the existence of at least one of the following statutory aggravating circumstances at the penalty phase:

a. The capital felony was committed by a person under a sentence of imprisonment.

b. The defendant was previously convicted of another capital felony or of a state or federal offense involving the distribution of a controlled substance that is punishable by a sentence of at least 1 year of imprisonment.

c. The defendant knowingly created grave risk of death to one or more persons such that participation in the offense constituted reckless indifference or disregard for human life.

d. The defendant used a firearm or knowingly directed, advised, authorized, or assisted another to use a firearm to threaten, intimidate, assault, or injure a person in committing the offense or in furtherance of the offense.

e. The offense involved the distribution of controlled substances to persons under the age of 18 years, the distribution of controlled substances within school zones, or the use or employment of persons under the age of 18 years in aid of distribution of controlled substances.

f. The offense involved distribution of controlled substances known to contain a potentially lethal adulterant.

g. The defendant:

1. Intentionally killed the victim;

2. Intentionally inflicted serious bodily injury which resulted in the death of the victim; or

3. Intentionally engaged in conduct intending that the victim be killed or that lethal force be employed against the victim, which resulted in the death of the victim.

h. The defendant committed the offense as consideration for the receipt, or in the expectation of the receipt, of anything of pecuniary value.

i. The defendant committed the offense after planning and premeditation.

j. The defendant committed the offense in a heinous, cruel, or depraved manner in that the offense involved torture or serious physical abuse to the victim.

Under Florida's capital drug trafficking sentencing statute the following statutory mitigating circumstances are set out:

a. The defendant has no significant history of prior criminal activity.

b. The capital felony was committed while the defendant was under the influence of extreme mental or emotional disturbance.

c. The defendant was an accomplice in the capital felony committed by another person, and the defendant's participation was relatively minor.

d. The defendant was under extreme duress or under the substantial domination of another person.

e. The capacity of the defendant to appreciate the criminality of her or his conduct or to conform her or his conduct to the requirements of law was substantially impaired.

f. The age of the defendant at the time of the offense.

g. The defendant could not have reasonably foreseen that her or his conduct in the course of the commission of the offense would cause or would create a grave risk of death to one or more persons.

h. The existence of any other factors in the defendant's background that would mitigate against imposition of the death penalty.

Under Florida's capital punishment statute, a sentence of death is automatically reviewed by the Florida Supreme Court. Florida permits capital felons to choose between death by lethal injection or the electric chair. Florida instituted this option in January of 2000. The State's death row facility for men is located in Starke, Florida; while the facility maintaining female death row inmates is located in Pembroke Pines, Florida.

Pursuant to the laws of Florida the Governor has authority to grant clemency in capital cases. The Governor must obtain the consent of the State's Board of Executive Clemency in order to grant clemency.

From the start of modern capital punishment in 1976, through 1999, Florida executed 44 capital felons. During this period Florida executed one female capital felon. A total of 390 capital felons were on death row in Florida in 1999. The 1999 death row population in the State was listed as: 138 black inmates; 213 white inmates; and 39 unidentified inmates. In 1999 Florida had four female capital felons on death row. The State had 6 juveniles on death row in 1999. By statute the State permits capital punishment to be imposed on persons 16 years old or older, however, the Florida Supreme Court ruled in a 1999 decision that under the State's constitution the minimum age for receiving a capital sentence was 17. Florida does not prohibit the execution of mentally retarded capital felons.

Executions by Florida 1976–1999

Name	Race	Date of Execution	Method of Execution
John Spenkelink	White	May 25, 1979	Electrocution
Robert Sullivan	White	November 30, 1983	Electrocution
Anthony Antone	White	January 26, 1984	Electrocution
Arthur Goode	White	April 5, 1984	Electrocution
James Adams	Black	May 10, 1984	Electrocution
Carl Shriner	White	June 20, 1984	Electrocution
David Washington	Black	July 13, 1984	Electrocution
Ernest Dobbert	White	September 7, 1984	Electrocution
James D. Henry	Black	September 20, 1984	Electrocution
Timothy Palmes	White	November 8, 1984	Electrocution
James Raulerson	White	January 30, 1985	Electrocution
Johnny P. Witt	White	March 6, 1985	Electrocution
Marvin Francois	Black	May 29, 1985	Electrocution
Daniel Thomas	Black	April 15, 1986	Electrocution
David Funchess	Black	April 22, 1986	Electrocution
Ronald Straight	White	May 20, 1986	Electrocution

Name	Race	Date of Execution	Method of Execution
Beauford White	Black	August 28, 1987	Electrocution
Willie Darden	Black	March 15, 1988	Electrocution
Jeffrey Daugherty	White	November 7, 1988	Electrocution
Theodore Bundy	White	January 24, 1989	Electrocution
Aubrey Adams	White	May 4, 1989	Electrocution
Jesse Tafero	White	May 4, 1990	Electrocution
Anthony Bertolotti	Black	July 27, 1990	Electrocution
James Hamblen	White	September 21, 1990	Electrocution
Raymond R. Clark	White	November 19, 1990	Electrocution
Roy A. Harich	White	April 24, 1991	Electrocution
Bobby M. Francis	Black	June 25, 1991	Electrocution
Nollie Martin	White	May 12, 1992	Electrocution
Edward D. Kennedy	Black	July 21, 1992	Electrocution
Robert Henderson	White	April 21, 1993	Electrocution
Larry J. Johnson	White	May 5, 1993	Electrocution
Michael Durocher	White	August 25, 1993	Electrocution
Roy A. Stewart	White	April 20, 1994	Electrocution
Bernard Bolender	White	July 18, 1995	Electrocution
Jerry White	Black	December 4, 1995	Electrocution
Philip Atkins	White	December 5, 1995	Electrocution
John E. Bush	Black	October 21, 1996	Electrocution
John Mills, Jr.	Black	December 6, 1996	Electrocution
Pedro Medina	Hispanic	March 25, 1997	Electrocution
Gerald Stano	White	March 23, 1998	Electrocution
Leo Jones	Black	March 25, 1998	Electrocution
Judy Buenoano	White	March 30, 1998	Electrocution
Daniel Remeta	N.A.	March 31, 1998	Electrocution
Allen L. Davis	White	July 8, 1999	Electrocution

FLORIDA EXECUTIONS 1976–1999

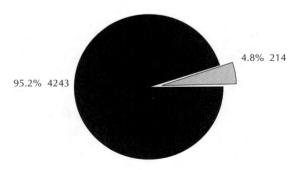

7.4% 44

92.6% 554

■ FLORIDA EXECUTIONS
■ ALL OTHER EXECUTIONS

EXECUTIONS BY FLORIDA 1930–1999

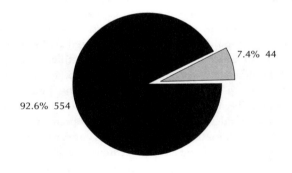

4.8% 214

95.2% 4243

■ FLORIDA
■ ALL OTHER JURISDICTIONS

Ford v. Wainwright *Court:* United States Supreme Court; *Case Citation:* Ford v. Wainwright, 477 U.S. 399 (1986); *Argued:* April 22, 1986; *Decided:* June 26, 1986; *Opinion of the Court:* Justice Marshall; *Concurring Opinion:* Justice Powell; *Concurring and Dissenting Opinion:* Justice O'Connor, in which White, J., joined; *Dissenting Opinion:* Justice Rehnquist, in which Burger, C. J., joined; *Appellate Defense Counsel:* Richard H. Burr III argued; Richard L. Jorandby, Craig S. Barnard, and Laurin A. Wollan, Jr. on brief; *Appellate Prosecution Counsel:* Joy B. Shearer argued; Jim Smith on brief; *Amicus Curiae Brief Supporting Prosecutor:* None; *Amicus Curiae Brief Supporting Defendant:* 3.

Issue Presented: Whether the Eighth Amendment prohibits the execution of a death row inmate while he or she is insane?

Case Holding: The Eighth Amendment prohibits the execution of a death row inmate while he or she is insane.

Factual and procedural background of case: The defendant, Alvin Bernard Ford, was convicted by the state of Florida of capital murder in 1974, and sentenced to death. There was no suggestion that he was incompetent at the time of his offense, at trial, or at sentencing. However, subsequently he began to manifest changes in behavior, indicating a mental disorder. This led to extensive separate examinations by two psychiatrists at his counsel's request, one of whom concluded that the defendant was not competent to be put to death. Defense counsel then invoked a Florida statute governing the determination of a death row inmate's competency. In compliance with statutory procedures, the Governor of Florida appointed three psychiatrists, who together interviewed the defendant for 30 minutes. The Governor's order directed that the attorneys should not participate in the examination in any adversarial manner. Each psychiatrist filed a separate report with the Governor, to whom the statute delegated the final decision. The reports reached conflicting diagnoses but were in accord that the defendant was competent to be executed.

Defense counsel attempted to submit to the Governor other written materials, including the reports of the two psychiatrists who had previously examined the defendant, but the Governor's office refused to inform defense counsel whether the submission would be considered. The Governor subsequently signed a death warrant without explanation or statement.

After unsuccessfully seeking a hearing in State court to determine anew the defendant's competency, defense counsel filed a habeas corpus proceeding in Federal District Court, seeking an evidentiary hearing. The federal court denied the petition without a hearing, and the Federal Court of Appeals affirmed. The United States Supreme Court granted certiorari to address the issue.

Opinion of the Court by Justice Marshall: Justice Marshall concluded that the Eighth Amendment prohibited the State from inflicting the death penalty upon a prisoner who is insane. The conclusion was justified, in part, by the position taken by the common law. The common law barred executing an insane prisoner because such an execution had questionable retributive value, presented no example to others and therefore had no deterrence value. The majority opinion found that the common law rationale "have no less logical, moral, and practical force at present."

The opinion also indicated that Florida's statutory procedures for determining a condemned inmate's sanity provided inadequate assurance of accuracy. The first defect in Florida's procedures was its failure to include the defendant in the truth-seeking process. It was said that any procedure that precluded a defendant or defense counsel from presenting material relevant to the issue of sanity or bars consideration of that material by the factfinder was necessarily inadequate. The opinion noted that a related flaw in the procedures was the denial of any opportunity to challenge or impeach the findings of the state appointed psychiatrists, thus creating a significant possibility that the ultimate decision made in reliance on such experts will be distorted. Justice Marshall found the most striking defect in the procedures was the placement of the ultimate decision wholly within the Executive Branch of state government. The opinion concluded that the Governor, who appointed the experts and ultimately decided whether the State would be able to carry out the death sentence, could not be said to have the neutrality that is necessary for reliability in the factfinding proceedings.

As a result of the defendant being denied a factfinding procedure "adequate to afford a full and fair hearing" on the issue of insanity, the opinion held that the defendant was entitled to an evidentiary hearing in the Federal District Court on the question of his competence to be executed. The judgment of the Court of Appeals was reversed, and the case was remanded for further proceedings consistent with the opinion.

Concurring opinion by Justice Powell: Justice Powell indicated that he agreed that the Constitution barred executing a defendant who was insane. He indicated, however, that he "would not require the kind of full-scale 'sanity trial' that Justice Marshall appears to find necessary." He believed that the States could satisfy constitutional due process by providing an impartial officer or board to receive evidence and argument from the inmates, including expert psychiatric evidence. Beyond these requirements, Justice Powell believed the States retained substantial discretion to create appropriate procedures.

Justice Powell believed that the test for whether an inmate is insane for constitutional purposes, is whether the inmate is aware of his or her impending execution and of the reason for it. He believed the defendant's claim fell within this definition, and that because the defendant's claim was not adjudicated fairly, he was entitled to have his claim adjudicated on remand by the Federal District Court.

Concurring and dissenting opinion by Justice O'Connor: Justice O'Connor indicated that she agreed with the majority opinion insofar as finding that Florida did not provide minimal procedural protections required by due process. But, she "would vacate the judgment and remand to the Court of Appeals with directions that the case be returned to the Florida system so that a hearing can be held in a manner consistent with the requirements of the Due Process Clause. I cannot agree, however, that the federal courts should have any role whatever in the substantive determination of a defendant's competency to be executed."

Justice O'Connor wrote that she was "in full agreement with Justice Rehnquist's conclusion that the Eighth Amendment does not create a substantive right not to be executed while insane. Accordingly, I do not join the Court's reasoning or opinion."

Dissenting opinion by Justice Rehnquist, in which Burger, C. J., joined: Justice Rehnquist argued that the majority was wrong in giving constitutional backing to the issue of an inmate's sanity at the time of execution. He believed that "[c]reating a constitutional right to a judicial determination of sanity before that sentence may be carried out, whether through the Eighth Amendment or the Due Process Clause, needlessly complicates and postpones still further any finality in this area of the law."

It was reasoned by Justice Rehnquist that: "The defendant has already had a full trial on the issue of guilt, and a trial on the issue of penalty; the requirement of still a third adjudication offers an invitation to those who have nothing to lose by accepting it to advance entirely spurious claims of insanity. A claim of insanity may be made at any time before sentence and, once rejected, may be raised again; a prisoner found sane two days before execution might claim to have lost his sanity the next day, thus necessitating another judicial determination of his sanity and presumably another stay of his execution."

Case note: The decision in the case did not have a major impact in spite of rendering the first decision by the United States Supreme Court that the Constitution barred executing an insane defendant. The reason for the lack of an impact by the opinion was due to an observation made in Justice Rehnquist's dissent: "[N]o State sanctions execution of the insane." All jurisdictions had followed the common law rule (by statute or judicial decision) barring execution of insane prisoners. *See also* **Insanity While Awaiting Execution; Mentally Retarded Capital Felon; Penry v. Lynaugh**

Foreign Nationals and Capital Punishment

For the purpose of capital punishment, a foreign national is a defendant having citizenship in another country, but is a resident in the United States. The critical issue that has consistently clouded capital prosecution of foreign nationals, is their right to communicate with their consular representatives in the United States. This right has unfortunately been routinely violated, so that consular representatives are rarely notified until long after foreign nationals have been prosecuted. In several

Abdul Hamin Awkal, a Lebanese foreign national, is on death row in Ohio for killing his wife and brother-in-law. (Ohio Department of Corrections)

instances foreign nations have sought to halt the execution of foreign nationals in the United States, because of the failure of local officials to notify consular representatives. In no instance has such pressure actually halted an execution.

FOREIGN NATIONALS ON DEATH ROW APRIL 1999

2.3% 83

97.72% 3482

■ FOREIGN NATIONALS
■ ALL OTHERS

Foreign Nationals Executed 1976–1999

Name	Date of Execution	Jurisdiction	Method of Execution	Nationality
Carlos Santana	March 23, 1993	TX	Lethal Injection	Dominican
Ramon Montoya	March 25, 1993	TX	Lethal Injection	Mexican
Nicholas Graham	April 7, 1995	GA	Electrocution	British
Pedro Medina	March 25, 1997	FL	Electrocution	Cuban
Irineo Montoya	June 18, 1997	TX	Lethal Injection	Mexican
Mario Murphy	September 17, 1997	VA	Lethal Injection	Mexican
Angel Breard	April 14, 1998	VA	Lethal Injection	Paraguayan
Jose Villafuerte	April 22, 1998	AZ	Lethal Injection	Honduran
Tuan Nguyen	December 10, 1998	OK	Lethal Injection	Vietnamese
Jaturun Siripongs	February 9, 1999	CA	Lethal Injection	Thailand
Karl LaGrand	February 24, 1999	AZ	Lethal Injection	Germany
Walter LaGrand	March 3, 1999	AZ	Lethal Gas	Germany
Alvaro Calambro	April 6, 1999	NV	Lethal Injection	Filippino
Joseph S. Faulder	June 17, 1999	TX	Lethal Injection	Canadian

Source: Death Penalty Information Center, Foreign Nationals (1999).

The United States ratified the Vienna Convention on Consular Relations in 1969. One of the provisions in this treaty expressly requires local officials to timely inform arrested foreign nationals of their right to consular assistance. Federal officials have been extremely relaxed in making certain local authorities comply with the treaty requirements.

FOREIGN NATIONALS EXECUTED 1976–1999

2.3% 14

97.7% 584

■ FOREIGN NATIONALS
■ ALL OTHER EXECUTIONS

At least one capital punishment jurisdiction has sought to recognize the consular notification right of foreign nationals. Florida has enacted a statute known as the "Recognition of International Treaties Act." This statute obligates Florida officials to assure that contact with consular representatives is timely made when a foreign national is arrested by the State:

> ***Fla. Code § 901.26 (3) Recognition of International Treaties Act:*** Wherever in the state a citizen of any sovereign nation to which the United States extends diplomatic recognition shall be arrested or detained for any reason whatsoever, the official who makes the arrest or detention shall immediately notify the nearest consul or other officer of the nation concerned or, if unknown, the Embassy in Washington, D.C., of the nation concerned or, if unknown, the nearest state judicial officer who shall in turn notify either of the above. Failure to give notice shall not be a defense in any criminal proceedings against any citizen of a sovereign nation and shall not be cause for the citizen's discharge from custody.

Former Jeopardy *see* **Double Jeopardy Clause**

Fourteenth Amendment   The Fourteenth Amendment was ratified on July 9, 1868. The amendment came at the end of the Civil War and was inspired as an effort allow Federal intervention whenever a State sought to intrude upon the citizenship rights of blacks. Section 1 of the Fourteenth Amendment provides:

> All persons born or naturalized in the United States, and subject to the jurisdiction thereof, are citizens of the United States and of the State wherein they reside. No State shall make or enforce any law which shall abridge the privileges or immunities of citizens of the United States; nor shall any State deprive any person of life, liberty, or property, without due process of law; nor deny to any person within its jurisdiction the equal protection of the laws.

For criminal prosecution purposes, the two major clauses in the Fourteenth Amendment are the Due Process Clause and Equal Protection Clause. Both of these clauses have been used, in conjunction with provisions of the Bill of Rights, to prevent jurisdictions from encroaching on the rights of capital felons and criminal defendants in general. *See also* **Due Process Clause; Equal Protection Clause**

Fourth Amendment *see* **Bill of Rights**

France France abolished the death penalty in 1981. *See also* **International Capital Punishment Nations**

Francis v. Resweber *Court:* United States Supreme Court; *Case Citation:* Francis v. Resweber, 329 U.S. 459 (1947); *Argued:* November 18, 1946; *Decided:* January 13, 1947; *Plurality Opinion:* Justice Reed announced the Court's judgment and delivered an opinion, in which Vinson, C.J., and Black and Jackson, JJ., joined; *Concurring Opinion:* Justice Frankfurter; *Dissenting Opinion:* Justice Burton, in which Douglas, Murphy and Rutledge, JJ., joined; *Appellate Defense Counsel:* James Skelly Wright argued and briefed; *Appellate Prosecution Counsel:* Michael E. Culligan argued; L. O. Pecot on brief; *Amicus Curiae Brief Supporting Prosecutor:* None; *Amicus Curiae Brief Supporting Defendant:* None.

Issue Presented: Whether the Constitution prohibits a second attempt to execute a prisoner, when the first attempt unintentionally fails?

Case Holding: The Constitution does not prevent a repeat attempt to execute a prisoner, when the initial attempt unintentionally fails.

Factual and procedural background of case: The defendant, Willie Francis, was convicted of murder by the State of Louisiana and sentenced to death by electrocution in September of 1945. The defendant was prepared for execution and on May 3, 1946, pursuant to a death warrant, was placed in the official electric chair of the State. The executioner threw the switch but, presumably because of some mechanical difficulty, death did not result. He was thereupon removed from the chair and returned to prison to await a second attempt at executing him. A new death warrant was issued by the Governor of Louisiana, fixing the second execution for May 9, 1946.

The defendant requested the Supreme Court of Louisiana prevent a second attempt to execute him on federal constitutional grounds. Execution of the sentence was stayed pending the defendant's challenge to a second attempt to execute him. The Supreme Court of Louisiana denied the defendant's request for judicial relief, after concluding there was no violation of state or federal law in attempting to execute him a second time. The United States Supreme Court granted certiorari to consider the issue.

Plurality opinion in which Justice Reed announced the Court's judgment and in which Vinson, C.J., and Black and Jackson, JJ., joined: Justice Reed indicated that, based on the record before the Court, "we must and do assume that the state officials carried out their duties under the death warrant in a careful and humane manner. Accidents happen for which no man is to blame."

The opinion addressed the defendant's argument that double jeopardy principles would be violated by a second attempt at executing him. Justice Reed noted that the Double Jeopardy Clause did not prevent a State from retrying a defendant whose conviction and sentence was set aside (for reasons other than insufficiency of evidence). The opinion then held: "For we see no difference from a constitutional point of view between a new trial for error of law at the instance of the state ... and an execution that follows a failure of equipment. When an accident, with no suggestion of malevolence, prevents the consummation of a sentence, the state's subsequent course in the administration of its criminal law is not affected on that account.... We find no double jeopardy here which can be said to amount to a denial of federal due process in the proposed execution."

Justice Reed also rejected the defendant's argument that attempting to execute him a second time was cruel and unusual punishment. It was said that: "Petitioner's suggestion is that because he once underwent the psychological strain of preparation for electrocution, now to require him to undergo this preparation again subjects him to a lingering or cruel and unusual punishment. Even the fact that petitioner has already been subjected to a current of electricity does not make his subsequent execution any more cruel in the constitutional sense than any other execution. The cruelty against which the Constitution protects a convicted man is cruelty inherent in the method of punishment, not the necessary suffering involved in any method employed to extinguish life humanely. The fact that an unforeseeable accident prevented the prompt consummation of the sentence cannot, it seems to us, add an element of cruelty to a subsequent execution. There is no purpose to inflict unnecessary pain nor any unnecessary pain involved in the proposed execution."

The final issue addressed in the plurality opinion was the defendant's contention that equal protection principles would be violated by a second attempt at executing him. Justice Reed wrote: "This suggestion ... is based on the idea that ... after an attempt at execution has failed, [it] would be a more severe punishment than is imposed upon others guilty of a like offense. That is, since others do not go through the strain of preparation for execution a second time or have not experienced a nonlethal current in a prior attempt at execution, as petitioner did, to compel petitioner to submit to execution after these prior experiences denies to him equal protection. Equal protection does not protect a prisoner against even illegal acts of officers in charge of him, much less against accidents during his detention for execution. Laws cannot prevent accidents nor can a law equally protect all against them. So long as the law applies to all alike, the requirements of equal protection are met." The opinion affirmed the decision of the Louisiana Supreme Court.

Concurring opinion by Justice Frankfurter: Justice Frankfurter agreed with the judgment in the case. His concurrence indicated that he believed the Constitution "did not withdraw the freedom of a State to enforce its own notions of fairness in the administration of criminal justice[.]" So long as the State did not find it abhorrent to twice attempt to execute a prisoner, the Constitution should not impose a different standard of decency on the State.

Dissenting opinion by Justice Burton, in which Douglas, Murphy and Rutledge, JJ., joined: The dissenting opinion indicated that in determining whether a second attempt at execution is unconstitutional, must be measured against a lawful electrocution. Justice Burton wrote: "The contrast is that between instantaneous death and death by installments.... Electrocution, when instantaneous, can be inflicted by a state in conformity with due process of law. The all-important consideration is that the execution shall be so instantaneous and substantially painless that the punishment shall be reduced, as nearly as possible, to no more than that of death itself. Electrocution has been approved only in a form that eliminates suffering."

It was argued that if state officials had intentionally placed the defendant in the electric chair five times, and each time applied electric current to his body in a manner not sufficient to kill him until the final time, such a form of torture would rival that of burning at the stake. The dissent followed up saying: "Although the failure of the first attempt, in the present case, was unintended, the reapplication of the electric current will be intentional. How many deliberate and intentional reapplications of electric current does it take to produce a cruel, unusual and unconstitutional punishment? While five applications would be more cruel and unusual than one, the uniqueness of the present case demonstrates that, today, two separated applications are sufficiently 'cruel and unusual' to be prohibited. If five attempts would be 'cruel and unusual,' it would be difficult to draw the line between two, three, four and five." The dissent would have granted the defendant relief from a second attempt at executing him.

Case note: Louisiana successfully executed Willie Francis by electrocution on May 9, 1947. *See also* **Botched Execution**

Frank v. Mangum
Court: United States Supreme Court; *Case Citation:* Frank v. Mangum, 237 U.S. 309 (1915); *Argued:* February 25–26, 1915; *Decided:* April 19, 1915; *Opinion of the Court:* Justice Pitney; *Concurring Opinion:* None; *Dissenting Opinion:* Justice Holmes, in which Hughes, J., joined; *Appellate Defense Counsel:* Louis Marshall argued; Henry C. Peeples and Henry A. Alexander on brief; *Appellate Prosecution Counsel:* Warren Grice argued; Hugh M. Dorsey on brief; *Amicus Curiae Brief Supporting Prosecutor:* None; *Amicus Curiae Brief Supporting Defendant:* None.

Issue Presented: Whether the defendant's conviction and death sentence were obtained in violation of due process of law because of mob intimidation during his trial?

Case Holding: The defendant's conviction and death sentence were not obtained in violation of due process of law.

Factual and procedural background of case: The defendant, Leo M. Frank, was convicted of capital murder and sentenced to death by the State of Georgia. The Supreme Court of Georgia affirmed the conviction and sentence. The defendant filed a habeas corpus petition in a Federal District Court alleging that his conviction was obtained in violation of the Constitution because: (1) of tremendous disorder in and about the courtroom during the trial; and (2) he was compelled, due to fear of mob violence, not to be present in the courtroom when the jury returned its verdict. The District Court denied relief. The United States Supreme Court granted certiorari to consider the issues.

Opinion of the Court by Justice Pitney: Justice Pitney indicated that if a trial was in fact dominated by a mob, so that the jury and judge are intimidated and there was an actual interference with the course of justice, due process of law would be violated. In reviewing the record in the case, and the decision of the Georgia Supreme Court, Justice Pitney ruled that the defendant's trial was not subject mob disturbance that amounted to a violation of due process. It was said that "[t]he Georgia courts ... proceeded upon the theory that Frank would have been entitled to ... relief had his charges been true, and they refused a new trial only because they found his charges untrue save in a few minor particulars not amounting to more than irregularities, and not prejudicial to the accused."

Turning to the issue of the defendant's absence from the trial when the jury returned its verdict, Justice Pitney wrote that under the common law it was the right of an accused to be present throughout the entire trial, from the commencement of the selection of the jury until the verdict was rendered and jury discharged. The opinion found, however, that the defendant waived his right to be present at trial when the jury returned its verdict. Justice Pitney agreed with the Georgia Supreme Court that "[t]he presence of the prisoner when the verdict is rendered is not so essential a part of the hearing that a rule of practice permitting the accused to waive it, and holding him bound by the waiver, amounts to a deprivation of due process of law." The judgment of the District Court was affirmed.

Dissenting opinion by Justice Holmes, in which Hughes, J., joined: Justice Holmes dissented from the opinion and judgment of the Court. He believed that due process of law was violated because of the intimidation caused by spectators. Justice Holmes wrote as follows:

> The only question before us is whether the petition shows on its face that the writ of habeas corpus should be denied, or whether the district court should have proceeded to try the facts. The allegations that appear to us material are these: The trial began on July 28, 1913, at Atlanta, and was carried on in a court packed with spectators and surrounded by a crowd outside, all strongly hostile to the [defendant]. On Saturday, August 23, this hostility was sufficient to lead the judge to confer in the presence of the jury with the chief of police of Atlanta and the colonel of the Fifth Georgia Regiment, stationed in that city, both of whom were known to the jury. On the same day, the evidence seemingly having been closed, the public press, apprehending danger, united in a request to the court that the proceedings should not continue on that evening. Thereupon

the court adjourned until Monday morning. On that morning, when the solicitor general entered the court, he was greeted with applause, stamping of feet and clapping of hands, and the judge, before beginning his charge, had a private conversation with the [defendant's] counsel in which he expressed the opinion that there would be "probable danger of violence" if there should be an acquittal or a disagreement, and that it would be safer for not only the [defendant] but his counsel to be absent from court when the verdict was brought in. At the judge's request they agreed that the [defendant] and [counsel] should be absent, and they kept their word. When the verdict was rendered, and before more than one of the jurymen had been polled, there was such a roar of applause that the polling could not go on until order was restored. The noise outside was such that it was difficult for the judge to hear the answers of the jurors, although he was only 10 feet from them. With these specifications of fact, the [defendant] alleges that the trial was dominated by a hostile mob and was nothing but an empty form.

We lay on one side the question whether the [defendant] could or did waive his right to be present at the polling of the jury. That question was apparent in the form of the trial and was raised by the application for a writ of error; and although, after the application to the full court, we thought that the writ ought to be granted, we never have been impressed by the argument that the presence of the prisoner was required by the Constitution of the United States. But habeas corpus cuts through all forms and goes to the very tissue of the structure. It comes in from the outside, not in subordination to the proceedings, and although every form may have been preserved, opens the inquiry whether they have been more than an empty shell. The argument for the [prosecutor] in substance is that the trial was in a court of competent jurisdiction, that it retains jurisdiction although, in fact, it may be dominated by a mob, and that the rulings of the state court as to the fact of such domination cannot be reviewed. But the argument seems to us inconclusive. Whatever disagreement there may be as to the scope of the phrase "due process of law," there can be no doubt that it embraces the fundamental conception of a fair trial, with opportunity to be heard. Mob law does not become due process of law by securing the assent of a terrorized jury. We are not speaking of mere disorder, or mere irregularities in procedure, but of a case where the processes of justice are actually subverted. In such a case, the Federal court has jurisdiction to issue the writ. The fact that the state court still has its general jurisdiction and is otherwise a competent court does not make it impossible to find that a jury has been subjected to intimidation in a particular case. The loss of jurisdiction is not general, but particular, and proceeds from the control of a hostile influence....

The single question in our minds is whether a petition alleging that the trial took place in the midst of a mob savagely and manifestly intent on a single result is shown on its face unwarranted, by the specifications, which may be presumed to set forth the strongest indications of the fact at the [defendant's] command. This is not a matter for polite presumptions; we must look facts in the face. Any judge who has sat with juries knows that, in spite of forms, they are extremely likely to be impregnated by the environing atmosphere. And when we find the judgment of the expert on the spot,—of the judge whose business it was to preserve not only form, but substance—to have been that if one juryman yielded to the reasonable doubt that he himself later expressed in court as the result of most anxious deliberation, neither prisoner nor counsel would be safe from the rage of the crowd, we think the presumption overwhelming that the jury responded to the passions of the mob. Of course we are speaking only of the case made by the petition, and whether it ought to be heard. Upon allegations of this gravity

in our opinion it ought to be heard, whatever the decision of the state court may have been, and it did not need to set forth contradictory evidence, or matter of rebuttal, or to explain why the motions for a new trial and to set aside the verdict were overruled by the state court. There is no reason to fear an impairment of the authority of the state to punish the guilty. We do not think it impracticable in any part of this country to have trials free from outside control. But to maintain this immunity it may be necessary that the supremacy of the law and of the Federal Constitution should be vindicated in a case like this. It may be that on a hearing a different complexion would be given to the judge's alleged request and expression of fear. But supposing the alleged facts to be true, we are of opinion that if they were before the supreme court, it sanctioned a situation upon which the courts of the United States should act; and if, for any reason, they were not before the supreme court, it is our duty to act upon them now, and to declare lynch law as little valid when practiced by a regularly drawn jury as when administered by one elected by a mob intent on death.

Case note: The prosecution of Leo M. Frank took place in an atmosphere of anti–Semitism. Frank was Jewish and the victim, Mary Phagan, was a Christian. The Governor of Georgia commuted Frank's sentence to life imprisonment in 1915. However, the commutation did not save Frank's life. A mob kidnapped Frank from prison and lynched him on August 16, 1915. It was reported that the mob consisted of 25 men, including a clergyman, two former State supreme court justices, and a former sheriff. In 1986, the State of Georgia posthumously granted Frank a pardon.

Frankfurter, Felix

Felix Frankfurter served as an associate justice of the United States Supreme Court from 1939 to 1962. While on the Supreme Court Frankfurter was known as a liberal constructionist of the Constitution in his early years, but forged a significant shift to the conservative side in later years.

Frankfurter was born in Vienna on November 15, 1882. His family immigrated to the United States when he was about 12 years old. Frankfurter received an undergraduate degree from New York's City College and obtained a law degree from Harvard Law School. After graduating from law school Frankfurter spent a number of years as an attorney for the Federal government. In 1914 he returned to Harvard Law School to teach. In 1939 President Franklin D. Roosevelt appointed Frankfurter to the Supreme Court.

Frankfurter issued a number of capital punishment opinions while on the Supreme Court. The capital punishment opinion which scholars cite the most was his dissent in *Rosenberg v. United States*. In that case the majority of the Supreme Court affirmed the death sentences handed down against Julius and Ethel Rosenberg. Frankfurter argued strenuously in dissent that under the law applicable to the case, the Atomic Energy Act, the trial judge was without authority to impose a death sentence, because the jury did not recommend a death sentence. Frankfurter wrote: "The Government having tried the Rosenbergs for a conspiracy, continuing from 1944 to 1950, to reveal atomic secrets among other things, it flies in the face of the charge made, the evidence adduced and the basis on which the conviction was secured now to contend that the terminal date of the Rosenberg conspiracy preceded the effective date of the Atomic Energy Act." Frankfurter died on February 22, 1965.

Capital Punishment Opinions Written by Frankfurter

Case Name	Opinion of the Court	Plurality Opinion	Concurring Opinion	Dissenting Opinion
Adamson v. California			✓	
Andres v. United States			✓	
Brown v. Allen				✓
Burns v. Wilson				✓
Cassell v. Texas			✓	
Ferguson v. Georgia			✓	
Fikes v. Alabama			✓	
Fisher v. United States				✓
Francis v. Resweber			✓	
Green v. United States				✓
Griffin v. United States	✓			
Harris v. South Carolina		✓		
Irvin v. Dowd (I)				✓
Irvin v. Dowd (II)			✓	
Leland v. Oregon				✓
Malinski v. New York			✓	
Mallory v. United States	✓			
Phyle v. Duffy			✓	
Rogers v. Richmond	✓			
Rosenberg v. United States				✓
Smith v. Baldi				✓
Solesbee v. Balkcom				✓
Stein v. New York				✓
Stewart v. United States				✓
Stroble v. California				✓
Taylor v. Alabama			✓	
Turner v. Pennsylvania		✓		
Watts v. Indiana		✓		
Williams v. Georgia	✓			

Franklin v. Lynaugh   *Court:* United States Supreme Court; *Case Citation:* Franklin v. Lynaugh, 487 U.S. 164 (1988); *Argued:* March 1, 1988; *Decided:* June 22, 1988; *Plurality Opinion:* Justice White announced the Court's judgment and delivered an opinion, in which Rehnquist, C. J., and Scalia and Kennedy, JJ., joined; *Concurring Opinion:* Justice O'Connor, in which Blackmun, J., joined; *Dissenting Opinion:* Justice Stevens, in which Brennan and Marshall, JJ., joined; *Appellate Defense Counsel:* Mark Stevens argued; Clarence Williams, Allen Cazier and George Scharmenon brief; *Appellate Prosecution Counsel:* William C. Zapalac argued; Jim Mattox, Mary F. Keller, Lou McCreary and Michael P. Hodge on brief; *Amicus Curiae Brief Supporting Prosecutor:* None; *Amicus Curiae Brief Supporting Defendant:* None.

Issue Presented: Whether the Constitution required the trial court to give certain jury instructions, relating to the consideration of mitigating evidence, that the defendant had requested in the sentencing phase of his capital trial?

Case Holding: The Constitution did not require the trial court to give certain jury instructions, relating to the consideration of mitigating evidence, that the defendant had requested in the sentencing phase of his capital trial.

Factual and procedural background of case: The defendant, Donald Franklin, was convicted of capital murder by the State of Texas. During the penalty phase of the trial the defendant requested the trial court give the jury five special questions, which, in essence, would have told the jury that any evidence they felt mitigated against the death penalty should be taken into account and could alone be enough to return a verdict less than death. The trial court refused to give the jury the proffered five defense instructions. Instead, the trial court instructed the jury, among other things, to arrive at their verdict based on all the evidence. The jury returned a verdict requiring imposition of the death penalty, which the trial court imposed. The Texas Court of Criminal Appeals affirmed the conviction and sentence.

The defendant filed a habeas corpus petition in a Federal District Court alleging that, absent his specially requested instructions, the jury was limited in its consideration of mitigating evidence in violation of the Eighth Amendment. The District Court rejected the argument and dismissed the petition. A Federal Court of Appeals affirmed the dismissal. The United States Supreme Court granted certiorari to consider the issue.

Plurality opinion in which Justice White announced the Court's judgment and in which Rehnquist, C.J., and Scalia and Kennedy, JJ., joined: Justice White ruled that the trial court's refusal to give the defendant's requested special instructions did not violate his Eighth Amendment right to present mitigating evidence. Neither the instructions actually given nor the Texas Special Issues precluded jury consideration of any relevant mitigating circumstances, or otherwise unconstitutionally limited the jury's discretion.

The opinion rejected the defendant's contention that the penalty phase jury was deprived of a sufficient opportunity to consider any "residual doubt" it might have harbored about his actual guilt in committing the crime. Justice White pointed out that the Court had never held that a capital defendant had a constitutional right to an instruction telling the jury to revisit the question of guilt as a basis for mitigation. It was said that lingering doubts over the defendant's guilt do not relate to his character, record or to the circumstances of the offense, which the sentencing jury must be given a chance to consider in mitigation. Justice White went further and indicated that even if the claimed right existed, the rejection of the defendant's proffered instructions did not impair that right, since the trial court placed no limitation on the defendant's opportunity to press the "residual doubts" issue to the sentencing jury. The judgment of the Court of Appeals was affirmed.

Concurring opinion by Justice O'Connor, in which Blackmun, J., joined: In her concurring opinion, Justice O'Connor concluded that the Texas capital sentencing procedure did not unconstitutionally prevent the jury from giving mitigating effect to any evidence relevant to the defendant's character, background or the circumstances of the offense. She noted that Texas' procedure did limit consideration of evidence of the defendant's good conduct while incarcerated during various points in his life, but the limitation had no practical or constitutional significance on the facts of the case, because the evidence had no relevance to any aspect of the defendant's character other than a lack of future dangerousness.

In addressing the defendant's residual doubt argument, Justice O'Connor wrote in her concurring opinion: "Although the capital sentencing procedure may have prevented the jury from giving effect to any 'residual doubts' it might have had about [the defendant's] guilt, that limitation did not violate the Eighth Amendment. Rather than being a fact about the defendant's character or background or the circumstances of the particular offense, 'residual doubt' is merely a lingering uncertainty about facts — a state of mind that exists somewhere between 'beyond a reasonable doubt' and 'absolute certainty' — and thus is not a mitigating circumstance under this Court's decisions, which have never required such a heightened burden of proof at capital sentencing."

Dissenting opinion by Justice Stevens, in which Brennan and Marshall, JJ., joined: Justice Stevens dissented primarily on the Courts determination that restrictions imposed on evidence of the defendant's past good conduct while incarcerated did not rise to a constitutional violation. Addressing what he perceived as being the significance of such evidence, Justice Stevens wrote: "In this case the mitigating evidence submitted by [the defendant] consisted of a stipulation indicating that during two periods of imprisonment aggregating about seven years he committed no disciplinary violations. That evidence militated against imposition of the death sentence in two quite different ways. Looking to the past, it suggested the possibility that [the defendant's] character was not without some redeeming features; a human being who can conform to strict prison rules without incident for several years may have virtues that can fairly be balanced against society's interest in killing him in retribution for his violent crime. Looking to the future, that evidence suggested that a sentence to prison, rather than to death, would adequately protect society from future acts of violence by [the defendant]. The evidence was admissible for both purposes."

The dissent argued that Texas' penalty phase procedures did not adequately allow for the jury to understand the significance of prior incarceration good conduct evidence. Justice Stevens contended that the proffered instructions by the defendant would have clarified the use of such evidence. He concluded that "[u]nder our cases, the substantial risk that the jury failed to perceive the full ambit of consideration to which evidence of [the defendant's] past good conduct was entitled requires us to vacate the death sentence and remand for resentencing."

Case note: Texas executed Donald Franklin by lethal injection on November 3, 1988. *See also* **Residual Doubt of Guilt**

Franklin v. South Carolina

Court: United States Supreme Court; *Case Citation:* Franklin v. South Carolina, 218 U.S. 161 (1910); *Argued:* April 20–21, 1910; *Decided:* May 31, 1910; *Opinion of the Court:* Justice Day; *Concurring Opinion:* None; *Dissenting Opinion:* None; *Appellate Defense Counsel:* John Adams argued; Jacob Moorer and Charles J. Bonaparte on brief; *Appellate Prosecution Counsel:* J. Fraser Lyon argued; D. S. Henderson, C. M. Efird and B. H. Moss on brief; *Amicus Curiae Brief Supporting Prosecutor:* None; *Amicus Curiae Brief Supporting Defendant:* None.

Issue Presented: Whether the defendant proved that blacks were systematically excluded from the grand jury that indicted him?

Case Holding: The defendant failed to prove that blacks were systematically excluded from the grand jury that indicted him, by merely making such an allegation without supporting evidence.

Factual and procedural background of case: The defendant, Pink Franklin, was convicted of capital murder and sentenced to death by the State of South Carolina. The South Carolina Supreme Court affirmed the conviction and sentence. In doing so, the appellate court rejected the defendant's argument that blacks were systematically excluded from the grand jury that indicted him. The United States Supreme Court granted certiorari to consider the issue.

Opinion of the Court by Justice Day: Justice Day ruled that blacks were not systematically excluded from the grand jury that indicted the defendant. It was said that under South Carolina law jury commissioners have discretion to exclude all persons from grand jury service who were not of "good moral character." The opinion found that the defendant did not produce any evidence to establish that jury commissioners exercised their discretion in a manner that systematically excluded blacks from grand jury service who were of good moral character. Justice Day wrote:

> We do not think there is anything in [the State's] statute having the effect to deny rights secured by the Federal Constitution. It gives to the jury commissioners the right to select electors of good moral character, such as they may deem qualified to serve as jurors, being persons of sound judgment and free from all legal exceptions. There is nothing in this statute which discriminates against individuals on account of race or color or previous condition, or which subjects such persons to any other or different treatment than other electors who may be qualified to serve as jurors. The statute simply provides for an exercise of judgment in attempting to secure competent jurors of proper qualifications.

The judgment of the South Carolina Supreme Court was affirmed. *See also* **Discrimination in Grand or Petit Jury Selection**

Freeway Killer

Between 1979 and 1980 California officials found the dead bodies of 14 teenaged boys along the

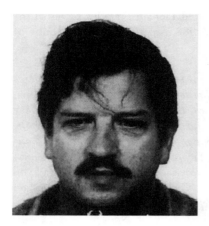

William George Bonin was executed after being found guilty of sodomizing and killing 14 youth in the State of California. (California Department of Corrections)

State's freeways. Ten of the bodies were found in Los Angeles County and four were found in Orange County. As the bodies were being discovered the media quickly alerted the public that a "freeway killer" was on the loose. All of the victims had been kidnapped, robbed and raped before being brutally murdered.

As a result of tireless investigative work, law enforcement officials captured the principal killer and his four accomplices in 1981. The principal killer, William George Bonin, was born January 8, 1947. Bonin had spent much of his life in and out of prison for sexual assaults on male adolescents. Beginning in 1979, Bonin convinced four young men, Vernon Robert Butts, Gregory Matthew Miley, William Ray Pugh, and James Michael Munro, to assist him in seducing and kidnapping young boys. Bonin usually only had one accomplice with him for each of the murders.

During the prosecution of Bonin, the main witness against him was his accomplice Miley. Miley testified that he was a sexual partner of Bonin. Miley described two of the murders as follows. On February 3, 1980, Bonin and Miley picked up a youth in Miley's van in Hollywood. According to Miley, Bonin and the youth had consensual sex in the van as Miley drove. When the sex ended Bonin whispered to Miley, "The kid's going to die," and then started to tie up the youth. Bonin asked the youth, "What does your dad want for you? How much do you think we can get for ransom? Maybe a couple thousand?" The youth replied, "I don't think that I can get that much." Bonin asked, "How much money do you have?" The youth answered, "About $6." Bonin then instructed Miley to take the money, which he did. Miley then stated, "Well, why don't you let the kid go?" Bonin responded, "No, man, he'll know the van and he'll know us." With Miley's help, Bonin proceeded to strangle the youth with a shirt and to crush his neck with a jack handle. The body was dumped from the van.

After doing the deed, Bonin said, "Well, I'm horny again. I need another one." Miley stated, "Oh, man, no way. I don't want to do it no more. I just want to go home." However, Bonin went ahead and eventually picked up another youth in Huntington Beach in the early afternoon of the same day, February 3. Bonin and the youth engaged in consensual sexual activity in the van. Soon, however, Bonin started to tie up the youth. Bonin asked, "What could you get for ransom? This is a kidnap." Bonin subsequently began to strangle the youth with a shirt and to crush his neck with a jack handle.

Bonin was prosecuted in Los Angeles County for 10 murders and sentenced to death for each on March 12, 1982. The co-defendants in that trial Miley, Pugh, and Munro received prison sentences (the fourth co-defendant, Butts, committed suicide while in jail). Bonin was subsequently prosecuted in Orange County for four murders and was sentenced to death for each on August 26, 1983. The two co-defendants in that trial, Miley and Munro, received prison sentences.

Bonin was executed by lethal injection February 23, 1996.

Frequency of Executions   Between 1976 and 1989, only 98 capital felons were executed in the United States. This figure reflected a willingness of appellate courts to allow capital felons to make repeated attacks on the judgments against them. However, beginning in the 1990s a trend set in to cut short the number of appeals. As a result, executions began to occur with greater frequency.

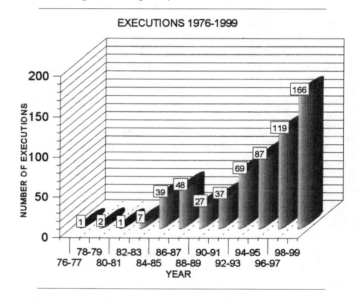

Opponents of capital punishment have condemned the efforts of courts and legislators to curb appellate rights of capital felons. The principal argument against expedited executions is that innocent people are more likely to be executed. However, this argument has not met with success in slowing down the pace of executions.

Frequency of Murder *see* **Murder**

Friends Committee to Abolish the Death Penalty
The Friends Committee to Abolish the Death Penalty (FCADP) is a national Quaker organization that was established in 1993. The mission of FCADP is to advocate for the abolition of the death penalty in the United States. FCADP is an action-oriented organization that believes the death penalty will not be abolished until committed individuals begin to use proactive and proven methods. The organization advocates assertive challenges to legislators, well-planned civil disobedience and massive public education.

Fruits of the Poisonous Tree *see* Exclusionary Rule

Fuller, Melville W.
Melville W. Fuller served as chief justice of the United States Supreme Court from 1888 to 1910. While on the Supreme Court Fuller was known for his conservative interpretation of the Constitution.

Fuller was born in Augusta, Maine on February 11, 1833. He graduated from Bowdoin College in 1853, and afterwards attending Harvard Law School briefly. Fuller's legal training, for the most part, was obtained as an apprentice in a law firm operated by relatives. In 1856 Fuller moved to Chicago to start his on law practice. After several decades of establishing an impressive law practice, Fuller was nominated by President Grover Cleveland in 1888 to be chief justice of the Supreme Court.

While on the Supreme Court Fuller wrote a number of capital punishment opinions. The opinion written by him which had the greatest impact on capital punishment jurisprudence was the decision in *In Re Kemmler*. The decision in *Kemmler* presented the Supreme Court with the first opportunity to determine whether death by electrocution was cruel and unusual punishment. Writing for the Court, Fuller held: "The enactment of this [punishment] was, in itself, within the legitimate sphere of the legislative power of the state, and in the observance of those general rules prescribed by our systems of jurisprudence; and the legislature of the state of New York determined that it did not inflict cruel and unusual punishment, and its courts have sustained that determination. We cannot perceive that the state has thereby abridged the privileges or immunities of the [defendant], or deprived him of due process of law." Fuller died in 1910.

Capital Punishment Opinions Written by Fuller

Case Name	Opinion of the Court	Concurring Opinion	Dissenting Opinion
Allison v. United States	✓		
Andersen v. Treat	✓		
Andersen v. United States	✓		
Ball v. United States (I)	✓		
Carver v. United States	✓		
Craemer v. Washington	✓		
Cross v. Burke	✓		
Cross v. United States	✓		
Crossley v. California	✓		
Duncan v. Missouri	✓		
Hickory v. United States	✓		
In Re Cross	✓		
In Re Durrant	✓		
In Re Kemmler	✓		
In Re Robertson	✓		
Kohl v. Lehlback	✓		
Lambert v. Barrett (I)	✓		
Lambert v. Barrett (II)	✓		
Mattox v. United States	✓		
McElvaine v. Brush	✓		
McNulty v. California	✓		
Minder v. Georgia	✓		
Starr v. United States	✓		
Thomas v. Texas	✓		
Wallace v. United States	✓		
Wilson v. United States	✓		

Furman v. Georgia
Court: United States Supreme Court; *Case Citation:* Furman v. Georgia, 408 U.S. 238 (1972); *Argued:* January 17, 1972; *Decided:* June 29, 1972; *Opinion of the Court:* Per Curiam; *Concurring Opinion:* Justice Douglas; *Concurring Opinion:* Justice Brennan; *Concurring Opinion:* Justice Stewart; *Concurring Opinion:* Justice White; *Concurring Opinion:* Justice Marshall; *Dissenting Opinion:* Chief Justice Burger; *Dissenting Opinion:* Justice Blackmun; *Dissenting Opinion:* Justice Powell; *Dissenting Opinion:* Justice Rehnquist; *Appellate Defense Counsel in Case No. 69-5003:* Anthony G. Amsterdam argued; B. Clarence Mayfield, Michael Meltsner, Jack Greenberg, James M. Nabrit III, Jack Himmelstein, and Elizabeth B. DuBois on brief; *Appellate Defense Counsel in Case No. 69-5030:* Jack Greenberg argued; Michael Meltsner, Anthony G. Amsterdam, James M. Nabrit III, Jack Himmelstein, and Elizabeth B. DuBois on brief; *Appellate Defense Counsel in Case No. 69-5031:* Melvyn Carson Bruder argued and briefed; *Appellate Prosecution Counsel in Case Nos. 69-5003 and 69-5030:* Dorothy T. Beasley argued; Arthur K. Bolton, Harold N. Hill, Jr., Courtney Wilder Stanton, and Andrew J. Ryan, Jr. on brief; *Appellate Prosecution Counsel in Case No. 69-5031:* Charles Alan Wright argued; Crawford C. Martin, Nola White, Alfred Walker, Robert C. Flowers, and Glenn R. Brown on brief; *Amicus Curiae Brief Supporting Prosecutors:* 4; *Amicus Curiae Brief Supporting Defendants:* 5.

Issue Presented: Whether the method by which the death penalty was imposed constituted cruel and unusual punishment in violation of the Eighth and Fourteenth Amendments?

Case Holding: The method by which the death penalty was imposed constituted cruel and unusual punishment in violation of the Eighth and Fourteenth Amendments.

Factual and procedural background of case: The opinion in the case consolidated three capital punishment cases. The defendant in case No. 69-5003 was convicted of murder in Georgia and was sentenced to death. The defendant in case No. 69-5030 was convicted of rape in Georgia and was sentenced to death. The defendant in case No. 69-5031 was convicted of rape in Texas and was sentenced to death. The defendants presented the same argument: The method used to impose the death penalty was arbitrary and capricious. The defendants contended that the Constitution prohibited imposition of capital punishment in an arbitrary and capricious manner. The United States Supreme Court granted certiorari to consider the matter.

Opinion of the Court was delivered Per Curiam: The per curiam opinion announcing the judgment of the Court was succinct. The opinion stated: "The Court holds that the imposition and carrying out of the death penalty in these cases constitute cruel and unusual punishment in violation of the

Eighth and Fourteenth Amendments. The judgment in each case is therefore reversed insofar as it leaves undisturbed the death sentence imposed, and the cases are remanded for further proceedings."

Concurring opinion by Justice Douglas: Justice Douglas was careful to restrict his concurrence to addressing the constitutionality of the method by which the death penalty was imposed upon the defendants. He did not address the constitutionality of the death penalty as punishment per se. The critical portions of Justice Douglas' concurrence are as follows:

In these three cases the death penalty was imposed, one of them for murder, and two for rape. In each the determination of whether the penalty should be death or a lighter punishment was left by the State to the discretion of the judge or of the jury. In each of the three cases the trial was to a jury. They are here on petitions for certiorari which we granted limited to the question whether the imposition and execution of the death penalty constitute "cruel and unusual punishment" within the meaning of the Eighth Amendment as applied to the States by the Fourteenth. I vote to vacate each judgment, believing that the exaction of the death penalty does violate the Eighth and Fourteenth Amendments.

That the requirements of due process ban cruel and unusual punishment is now settled. It is also settled that the proscription of cruel and unusual punishments forbids the judicial imposition of them as well their imposition by the legislature....

It has been assumed in our decisions that punishment by death is not cruel, unless the manner of execution can be said to be inhuman and barbarous....

It would seem to be incontestable that the death penalty inflicted on one defendant is "unusual" if it discriminates against him by reason of his race, religion, wealth, social position, or class, or if it is imposed under a procedure that gives room for the play of such prejudices.

There is evidence that the provision of the English Bill of Rights of 1689, from which the language of the Eighth Amendment was taken, was concerned primarily with selective or irregular application of harsh penalties and that its aim was to forbid arbitrary and discriminatory penalties of a severe nature....

The words "cruel and unusual" certainly include penalties that are barbaric. But the words, at least when read in light of the English proscription against selective and irregular use of penalties, suggest that it is "cruel and unusual" to apply the death penalty — or any other penalty — selectively to minorities whose numbers are few, who are outcasts of society, and who are unpopular, but whom society is willing to see suffer though it would not countenance general application of the same penalty across the board....

... Juris (or judges, as the case may be) have practically untrammeled discretion to let an accused live or insist that he die....

Former Attorney General Ramsey Clark has said, "It is the poor, the sick, the ignorant, the powerless and the hated who are executed." One searches our chronicles in vain for the execution of any member of the affluent strata of this society. The Leopolds and Loebs are given prison terms, not sentenced to death....

... [W]e deal with a system of law and of justice that leaves to the uncontrolled discretion of judges or juries the determination whether defendants ... should die or be imprisoned. Under [current] laws no standards govern the selection of the penalty. People live or die, dependant on the whim of one man or of 12....

Those who wrote the Eighth Amendment knew what price their forebears had paid for a system based, not on equal justice, but on discrimination. In those days the target was not the blacks or the poor, but the dissenters, those who opposed absolutism in government, who struggled for a parliamentary regime, and who opposed governments' recurring efforts to foist a particular religion on the people. But the tool of capital punishment was used with vengeance against the opposition and those unpopular with the regime. One cannot read this history without realizing that the desire for equality was reflected in the ban against "cruel and unusual punishments" contained in the Eighth Amendment.

In a Nation committed to equal protection of the laws there is no permissible "cast" aspect of law enforcement. Yet we know that the discretion of judges and juries in imposing the death penalty enables the penalty to be selectively applied, feeding prejudices against the accused if he is poor and despised, and lacking political clout, or if he is a member of a suspect or unpopular minority, and saving those who by social position may be in a more protected position. In ancient Hindu Law a Brahman was exempt from capital punishment, and under that law, "[g]enerally, in the law books, punishment increased in severity as social status diminished." We have, I fear, taken in practice the same position, partially as a result of making the death penalty discretionary and partially as a result of the ability of the rich to purchase the services of the most respected and most resourceful legal talent in the Nation.

The high service rendered by the "cruel and unusual" punishment clause of the Eighth Amendment is to require legislatures to write penal laws that are evenhanded, nonselective, and nonarbitrary, and to require judges to see to it that general laws are not applied sparsely, selectively, and spottily to unpopular groups....

Thus, these discretionary statutes are unconstitutional in their operation. They are pregnant with discrimination and discrimination is an ingredient not compatible with the idea of equal protection of the laws that is implicit in the ban on "cruel and unusual" punishments.

Concurring opinion by Justice Brennan: Justice Brennan's concurrence went to the point of concluding that the Constitution barred imposition of capital punishment per se. The critical features of his concurrence are stated as follows:

We have very little evidence of the Framers' intent in including the Cruel and Unusual Punishments Clause among those restraints upon the new Government enumerated in the Bill of Rights....

... Certainly they intended to ban torturous punishments, but the available evidence does not support the further conclusion that only torturous punishments were to be outlawed.... Nor did [the Framers] intend simply to forbid punishments considered cruel and unusual at the time. The "import" of the Clause is, indeed, indefinite, and for good reason. A constitutional provision is enacted, it is true, from an experience of evils, but its general language should not, therefore, be necessarily confined to the form that evil had theretofore taken. Time works changes, brings into existence new conditions and purposes. Therefore a principle to be vital must be capable of wider application than the mischief which gave it birth.

... At bottom, then, the Cruel and Unusual Punishments Clause prohibits the infliction of uncivilized and inhuman punishments. The State, even as it punishes, must treat its members with respect for their intrinsic worth as human beings. A punishment is cruel and unusual, therefore, if it does not comport with human dignity....

Death is truly an awesome punishment. The calculated killing of a human being by the State involves, by its very nature, a denial of the executed person's humanity. The contrast with the plight of a person punished by imprisonment is evident. An individual in prison does not lose the right to have rights. A prisoner retains, for example, the constitutional rights to the free exercise of religion, to be free of cruel and unusual punishments, and to treatment as a "person" for purposes of due process of law and the equal protection of the laws. A prisoner remains a member of the human family. Moreover, he retains the right of access to the courts. His punishment is not irrevocable.... [T]he finality of death precludes relief. An executed person has indeed lost the right to have rights....

The outstanding characteristic of our present practice of punishing criminals by death is the infrequency with which we resort to it. The evidence is conclusive that death is not the ordinary punishment for any crime.

There has been a steady decline in the infliction of this punishment in every decade since the 1930's, the earliest period for which accurate statistics are available. In the 1930's, executions averaged 167 per year; in the 1940's, the average was 128; in the 1950's, it was 72; and in the years 1960–1962, it was 48. There have been a total of 46 executions since then, 36 of them in 1963–1964. Yet our population and the number of capital crimes committed have increased greatly over the past four decades. The contemporary rarity of the infliction of this punishment is thus the end result of a long-continued decline. That rarity is plainly revealed by an examination of the years 1961–1970, the last 10-year period for which statistics are available. During that time, an average of 106 death sentences was imposed each year. Not nearly that number, however, could be carried out, for many were precluded by [a number of reasons]. On January 1, 1961, the death row population was 219; on December 31, 1970, it was 608; during that span, there were 135 executions. Consequently, had the 389 additions to death row also been executed, the annual average would have been 52. In short, the country might, at most, have executed one criminal each week. In fact, of course, far fewer were executed....

When a country of over 200 million people inflict an unusually severe punishment no more than 50 times a year, the inference is strong that the punishment is not being regularly and fairly applied. To dispel it would indeed require a clear showing of nonarbitrary infliction.

Although there are no exact figures available, we know that thousands of murders and rapes are committed annually in States where death is an authorized punishment for those crimes. However the rate of infliction is characterized—as "freakishly" or "spectacularly" rare, or simply as rare—it would take the purest sophistry to deny that death is inflicted in only a minute fraction of these cases. How much rarer, after all, could the infliction of death be?

When the punishment of death is inflicted in a trivial number of the cases in which it is legally available, the conclusion is virtually inescapable that it is being inflicted arbitrarily. Indeed, it smacks of little more than a lottery system.... Furthermore, our procedures in death cases ... actually sanction an arbitrary selection.... In other words, our procedures are not constructed to guard against the totally capricious selection of criminals for the punishment of death....

... Today death is a uniquely and unusually severe punishment. When examined by the principles applicable under the Cruel and Unusual Punishments Clause, death stands condemned as fatally offensive to human dignity. The punishment of death is therefore cruel and unusual, and the States may no longer inflict it as a punishment for crimes. Rather than kill an arbitrary handful of criminals each year, the States will confine them in prison....

Concurring opinion by Justice Stewart: Justice Stewart, like Justice Douglas, found that the method of imposition of the death penalty violated the Constitution, but was not prepared to find that the Constitution barred imposition of the death penalty per se. The central aspects of Justice Stewart's concurrence indicated the following:

The penalty of death differs from all other forms of criminal punishment, not in degree but in kind. It is unique in its total irrevocability. It is unique in its rejection of rehabilitation of the convict as a basic purpose of criminal justice. And it is unique, finally, in its absolute renunciation of all that is embodied in our concept of humanity....

Legislatures — state and federal — have sometimes specified that the penalty of death shall be the mandatory punishment for every person convicted of engaging in certain designated criminal conduct....

If we were reviewing death sentences imposed under these or similar laws, we would be faced with the need to decide whether capital punishment is unconstitutional for all crime and under all circumstances. We would need to decide whether a legislature — state or federal — could constitutionally determine that certain criminal conduct is so atrocious that society's interest in deterrence and retribution wholly outweighs any considerations of reform or rehabilitation of the perpetrator, and that, despite the inconclusive empirical evidence, only the automatic penalty will provide maximum deterrence.

On that score I would say only that I cannot agree that retribution is a constitutionally impermissible ingredient in the imposition of punishment. The instinct for retribution is part of the nature of man, and channeling that instinct in the administration of criminal justice serves an important purpose in promoting the stability of a society governed by law. When people begin to believe that organized society is unwilling or unable to impose upon criminal offenders the punishment they "deserve," then there are sown the seeds of anarchy — of self-help, vigilante justice, and lynch law.

The constitutionality of capital punishment in the abstract is not, however, before us in these cases. For the Georgia and Texas Legislatures have not provided that the death penalty shall be imposed upon all those who are found guilty of forcible rape. And the Georgia Legislature has not ordained that death shall be the automatic punishment for murder. In a word, neither State has made a legislative determination that forcible rape and murder can be deterred only by imposing the penalty of death upon all who perpetrate those offenses....

Instead, the death sentences now before us are the product of a legal system that brings them, I believe, within the very core of the Eighth Amendment's guarantee against cruel and unusual punishments, a guarantee applicable against the States through the Fourteenth Amendment. In the first place, it is clear that these sentences are "cruel" in the sense that they excessively go beyond, not in degree but in kind, the punishments that the state legislatures have determined to be necessary. In the second place, it is equally clear that these sentences are "unusual" in the sense that the penalty of death is infrequently imposed for murder, and that its imposition for rape is extraordinarily rare. But I do not rest my conclusion upon these two propositions alone.

These death sentences are cruel and unusual in the same way that being struck by lightning is cruel and unusual. For, of all the people convicted of rapes and murders in 1967 and 1968, many just us reprehensible as these, the petitioners are among a capriciously selected random handful upon whom the sentence of death has in fact been imposed.... [I] conclude that the Eighth and Fourteenth Amendments cannot tolerate the infliction of a sentence of death under legal systems that permit this unique penalty to be so wantonly and so freakishly imposed.

Concurring opinion by Justice White: Justice White, while finding the method used to impose the death penalty was unconstitutional, did not go so far as to find that the death penalty was barred by the Constitution per se. The essence of Justice White's concurrence said the following:

> … In joining the Court's judgments … I do not at all intimate that the death penalty is unconstitutional per se or that there is no system of capital punishment that would comport with the Eighth Amendment. That question, ably argued by several of my Brethren, is not presented by these cases and need not be decided.

> The narrower question to which I address myself concerns the constitutionality of capital punishment statutes under which (1) the legislature authorizes the imposition of the death penalty for murder or rape; (2) the legislature does not itself mandate the penalty in any particular class or kind of case (that is, legislative will is not frustrated if the penalty is never imposed), but delegates to judges or juries the decisions as to those cases, if any, in which the penalty will be utilized; and (3) judges and juries have ordered the death penalty with such infrequency that the odds are now very much against imposition and execution of the penalty with respect to any convicted murderer or rapist. It is in this context that we must consider whether the execution of these [defendants] would violate the Eighth Amendment.

> I begin with what I consider a near truism: that the death penalty could so seldom be imposed that it would cease to be a credible deterrent or measurably to contribute to any other end of punishment in the criminal justice system. It is perhaps true that no matter how infrequently those convicted of rape or murder are executed, the penalty so imposed is not disproportionate to the crime and those executed may deserve exactly what they received. It would also be clear that executed defendants are finally and completely incapacitated from again committing rape or murder or any other crime. But when imposition of the penalty reaches a certain degree of infrequency, it would be very doubtful that any existing general need for retribution would be measurably satisfied. Nor could it be said with confidence that society's need for specific deterrence justifies death for so few when for so many in like circumstances life imprisonment or shorter prison terms are judged sufficient, or that community values are measurably reinforced by authorizing a penalty so rarely invoked.

> Most important, a major goal of the criminal law — to deter others by punishing the convicted criminal — would not be substantially served where the penalty is so seldom invoked that it ceases to be the credible threat essential to influence the conduct of others. For present purposes I accept the morality and utility of punishing one person to influence another. I accept also the effectiveness of punishment generally and need not reject the death penalty as a more effective deterrent than a lesser punishment. But common sense and experience tell us that seldom-enforced laws become ineffective measures for controlling human conduct and that the death penalty, unless imposed with sufficient frequency, will make little contribution to deterring those crimes for which it may be exacted.

> The imposition and execution of the death penalty are obviously cruel in the dictionary sense. But the penalty has not been considered cruel and unusual punishment in the constitutional sense because it was thought justified by the social ends it was deemed to serve. At the moment that it ceases realistically to further these purposes, however, the emerging question is whether its imposition in such circumstances would violate the Eighth Amendment. It is my view that it would, for its imposition would then be the pointless and needless extinction of life with only marginal contributions to any discernible social or public

purposes. A penalty with such negligible returns to the State would be patently excessive and cruel and unusual punishment violative of the Eighth Amendment.

> It is also my judgment that this point has been reached with respect to capital punishment as it is presently administered under the statutes involved in these cases. Concededly, it is difficult to prove as a general proposition that capital punishment, however administered, more effectively serves the ends of the criminal law than does imprisonment. But however that may be, I cannot avoid the conclusion that as the statutes before us are now administered, the penalty is so infrequently imposed that the threat of execution is too attenuated to be of substantial service to criminal justice.

> … I can do no more than state a conclusion based on 10 years of almost daily exposure to the facts and circumstances of hundreds and hundreds of federal and state criminal cases involving crimes for which death is the authorized penalty. That conclusion, as I have said, is that the death penalty is exacted with great infrequency even for the most atrocious crimes and that there is no meaningful basis for distinguishing the few cases in which it is not. The short of it is that the policy of vesting sentencing authority primarily in juries — a decision largely motivated by the desire to mitigate the harshness of the law and to bring community judgment to bear on the sentence as well as guilt or innocence — has so effectively achieved its aims that capital punishment within the confines of the statutes now before us has for all practical purposes run its course.…

> … I add [finally] that past and present legislative judgment with respect to the death penalty loses much of its force when viewed in light of the recurring practice of delegating sentencing authority to the jury and the fact that a jury, in its own discretion and without violating its trust or any statutory policy, may refuse to impose the death penalty no matter what the circumstances of the crime. Legislative policy is thus necessarily defined not by what is legislatively authorized but by what juries and judges do in exercising the discretion so regularly conferred upon them. In my judgment what was done in these cases violated the Eighth Amendment.

Concurring opinion by Justice Marshall: Justice Marshall, like Justice Brennan, argued that the Constitution prohibited the imposition of the death penalty per se. The salient features of Justice Marshall's concurrence stated the following:

> The criminal acts with which we are confronted are ugly, vicious, reprehensible acts. Their sheer brutality cannot and should not be minimized. But, we are not called upon to condone the penalized conduct; we are asked only to examine the penalty imposed on each of the [defendants] and to determine whether or not it violates the Eighth Amendment.…

> Perhaps the most important principle in analyzing cruel and unusual punishment questions is one that is reiterated again and again in the prior opinions of the Court: i.e., the cruel and unusual language must draw its meaning from the evolving standards of decency that mark the progress of a maturing society. Thus, a penalty that was permissible at one time in our Nation's history is not necessarily permissible today.

> The fact, therefore, that the Court, or individual Justices, may have in the past expressed an opinion that the death penalty is constitutional is not now binding on us.…

> Capital punishment has been used to penalize various forms of conduct by members of society since the beginnings of civilization. Its precise origins are difficult to perceive, but there is some evidence that its roots lie in violent retaliation by members of a tribe or group, or by the tribe or group itself, against persons committing hostile acts toward group members. Thus,

infliction of death as a penalty for objectionable conduct appears to have its beginnings in private vengeance.

As individuals gradually ceded their personal prerogatives to a sovereign power, the sovereign accepted the authority to punish wrongdoing as part of its "divine right" to rule. Individual vengeance gave way to the vengeance of the state, and capital punishment became a public function. Capital punishment worked its way into the laws of various countries, and was inflicted in a variety of macabre and horrific ways....

It has often been noted that American citizens know almost nothing about capital punishment.... [E].g., that the death penalty is no more effective a deterrent than life imprisonment, that convicted murderers are rarely executed, but are usually sentenced to a term in prison; that convicted murderers usually are model prisoners, and that they almost always become law-abiding citizens upon their release from prison; that the costs of executing a capital offender exceed the costs of imprisoning him for life...; and that the death penalty may actually stimulate criminal conduct....

Regarding discrimination, it has been said that [it] is usually the poor, the illiterate, the underprivileged, the member of the minority group — the man who, because he is without means, and is defended by a court-appointed attorney — who becomes society's sacrificial lamb....

It ... is evident that the burden of capital punishment falls upon the poor, the ignorant, and the underprivileged members of society. It is the poor, and the members of minority groups who are least able to voice their complaints against capital punishment. Their impotence leaves them victims of a sanction that the wealthier, better-represented, just-as-guilty person can escape. So long as the capital sanction is used only against the forlorn, easily forgotten members of society, legislators are content to maintain the status quo, because change would draw attention to the problem and concern might develop. Ignorance is perpetuated and apathy soon becomes its mate, and we have today's situation.

Just as Americans know little about who is executed and why, they are unaware of the potential dangers of executing an innocent man. Our "beyond a reasonable doubt" burden of proof in criminal cases is intended to protect the innocent, but we know it is not fool-proof. Various studies have shown that people whose innocence is later convincingly established are convicted and sentenced to death....

No matter how careful courts are, the possibility of perjured testimony, mistaken honest testimony, and human error remain all too real. We have no way of judging how many innocent persons have been executed but we can be certain that there are some.... Surely there will be more as long as capital punishment remains part of our penal law....

In striking down capital punishment, this Court does not malign our system of government. On the contrary, it pays homage to it. Only in a free society could right triumph in difficult times, and could civilization record its magnificent advancement. In recognizing the humanity of our fellow beings, we pay ourselves the highest tribute. We achieve a major milestone in the long road up from barbarism ... by shunning capital punishment.

Dissenting opinion by Chief Justice Burger: The dissent by the Chief Justice presented the most comprehensive challenge to the judgment of the Court and the concurring opinions. The thrust of his arguments were presented as follows:

I conclude that the constitutional prohibition against "cruel and unusual punishments" cannot be construed to bar the imposition of the punishment of death....

If we were possessed of legislative power, I would either join with Mr. Justice Brennan and Mr. Justice Marshall or, at the very least, restrict the use of capital punishment to a small category of the most heinous crimes. Our constitutional inquiry, however, must be divorced from personal feelings as to the morality and efficacy of the death penalty, and be confined to the meaning and applicability of the uncertain language of the Eighth Amendment. There is no novelty in being called upon to interpret a constitutional provision that is less than self-defining, but, of all our fundamental guarantees, the ban on "cruel and unusual punishments" is one of the most difficult to translate into judicially manageable terms. The widely divergent views of the Amendment expressed in today's opinions reveal the haze that surrounds this constitutional command. Yet it is essential to our role as a court that we not seize upon the enigmatic character of the guarantee as an invitation to enact our personal predilections into law.

Although the Eighth Amendment literally reads as prohibiting only those punishments that are both "cruel" and "unusual," history compels the conclusion that the Constitution prohibits all punishments of extreme and barbarous cruelty, regardless of how frequently or infrequently imposed....

Counsel for petitioners properly concede that capital punishment was not impermissibly cruel at the time of the adoption of the Eighth Amendment. Not only do the records of the debates indicate that the Founding Fathers were limited in their concern to the prevention of torture, but it is also clear from the language of the Constitution itself that there was no thought whatever of the elimination of capital punishment. The opening sentence of the Fifth Amendment is a guarantee that the death penalty not be imposed "unless on a presentment or indictment of a Grand Jury." The Double Jeopardy Clause of the Fifth Amendment is a prohibition against being "twice put in jeopardy of life" for the same offense. Similarly, the Due Process Clause commands "due process of law" before an accused can be "deprived of life, liberty, or property." Thus, the explicit language of the Constitution affirmatively acknowledges the legal power to impose capital punishment; it does not expressly or by implication acknowledge the legal power to impose any of the various punishments that have been banned as cruel since 1791. Since the Eighth Amendment was adopted on the same day in 1791 as the Fifth Amendment, it hardly needs more to establish that the death penalty was not "cruel" in the constitutional sense at that time.

In the 181 years since the enactment of the Eighth Amendment, not a single decision of this Court has cast the slightest shadow of a doubt on the constitutionality of capital punishment. In rejecting Eighth Amendment attacks on particular modes of execution, the Court has more than once implicitly denied that capital punishment is impermissibly "cruel" in the constitutional sense....

Before recognizing such an instant evolution in the law, it seems fair to ask what factors have changed that capital punishment should now be "cruel" in the constitutional sense as it has not been in the past. It is apparent that there has been no change of constitutional significance in the nature of the punishment itself. Twentieth century modes of execution surely involve no greater physical suffering than the means employed at the time of the Eighth Amendment's adoption. And although a man awaiting execution must inevitably experience extraordinary mental anguish, no one suggests that this anguish is materially different from that experienced by condemned men in 1791, even though protracted appellate review processes have greatly increased the waiting time on "death row." To be sure, the ordeal of the condemned man may be thought cruel in the sense that all suffering is thought cruel. But if the Constitution proscribed every punishment producing severe emotional stress, then capital punishment would clearly have been impermissible in 1791.

However, the inquiry cannot end here. For reasons unrelated to any change in intrinsic cruelty, the Eighth Amendment prohibition cannot fairly be limited to those punishments thought excessively cruel and barbarous at the time of the adoption of the Eighth Amendment. A punishment is inordinately cruel, in the sense we must deal with it in these cases, chiefly as perceived by the society so characterizing it. The standard of extreme cruelty is not merely descriptive, but necessarily embodies a moral judgment. The standard itself remains the same, but its applicability must change as the basic mores of society change.... Nevertheless, the Court up to now has never actually held that a punishment has become impermissibly cruel due to a shift in the weight of accepted social values; nor has the Court suggested judicially manageable criteria for measuring such a shift in moral consensus.

The Court's quiescence in this area can be attributed to the fact that in a democratic society legislatures, not courts, are constituted to respond to the will and consequently the moral values of the people. For this reason, early commentators suggested that the "cruel and unusual punishments" clause was an unnecessary constitutional provision. As acknowledged in the principal brief for petitioners, "both in constitutional contemplation and in fact, it is the legislature, not the Court, which responds to public opinion and immediately reflects the society's standards of decency." Accordingly, punishments such as branding and the cutting off of ears, which were commonplace at the time of the adoption of the Constitution, passed from the penal scene without judicial intervention because they became basically offensive to the people and the legislatures responded to this sentiment....

The selectivity of juries in imposing the punishment of death is properly viewed as a refinement on, rather than a repudiation of, the statutory authorization for that penalty. Legislatures prescribe the categories of crimes for which the death penalty should be available, and, acting as "the conscience of the community," juries are entrusted to determine in individual cases that the ultimate punishment is warranted. Juries are undoubtedly influenced in this judgment by myriad factors. The motive or lack of motive of the perpetrator, the degree of injury or suffering of the victim or victims, and the degree of brutality in the commission of the crime would seem to be prominent among these factors. Given the general awareness that death is no longer a routine punishment for the crimes for which it is made available, it is hardly surprising that juries have been increasingly meticulous in their imposition of the penalty. But to assume from the mere fact of relative infrequency that only a random assortment of pariahs are sentenced to death, is to cast grave doubt on the basic integrity of our jury system.

It would, of course, be unrealistic to assume that juries have been perfectly consistent in choosing the cases where the death penalty is to be imposed, for no human institution performs with perfect consistency. There are doubtless prisoners on death row who would not be there had they been tried before a different jury or in a different State. In this sense their fate has been controlled by a fortuitous circumstance. However, this element of fortuity does not stand as an indictment either of the general functioning of juries in capital cases or of the integrity of jury decisions in individual cases. There is no empirical basis for concluding that juries have generally failed to discharge in good faith [their] responsibility ...- that of choosing between life and death in individual cases according to the dictates of community values....

Since there is no majority of the Court on the ultimate issue presented in these cases, the future of capital punishment in this country has been left in an uncertain limbo. Rather than providing a final and unambiguous answer on the basic constitutional question, the collective impact of the majority's ruling is to demand an undetermined measure of change from the various state legislatures and the Congress. While I cannot endorse the process of decisionmaking that has yielded today's result and the restraints that result imposes on legislative action, I am not altogether displeased that legislative bodies have been given the opportunity, and indeed unavoidable responsibility, to make a thorough re-evaluation of the entire subject of capital punishment. If today's opinions demonstrate nothing else, they starkly show that this is an area where legislatures can act far more effectively than courts.

The legislatures are free to eliminate capital punishment for specific crimes or to carve out limited exceptions to a general abolition of the penalty, without adherence to the conceptual strictures of the Eighth Amendment. The legislatures can and should make an assessment of the deterrent influence of capital punishment, both generally and as affecting the commission of specific types of crimes. If legislatures come to doubt the efficacy of capital punishment, they can abolish it, either completely or on a selective basis. If new evidence persuades them that they have acted unwisely, they can reverse their field and reinstate the penalty to the extent it is thought warranted. An Eighth Amendment ruling by judges cannot be made with such flexibility or discriminating precision.

Dissenting opinion by Justice Blackmun: The dissent by Justice Blackmun was concerned with the lack of justification for the majority's decision to use the constitution to invalidate the method by which the death penalty was imposed. He argued that no precedent for such a course was evident. The essence of Justice Blackmun's dissent stated the following:

The several concurring opinions acknowledge, as they must, that until today capital punishment was accepted and assumed as not unconstitutional per se under the Eighth Amendment or the Fourteenth Amendment....

Suddenly, however, the course of decision is now the opposite way, with the Court evidently persuaded that somehow the passage of time has taken us to a place of greater maturity and outlook. The argument, plausible and high-sounding as it may be, is not persuasive.... The Court has just decided that it is time to strike down the death penalty....

The Court has recognized, and I certainly subscribe to the proposition, that the Cruel and Unusual Punishments Clause may acquire meaning as public opinion becomes enlightened by a humane justice....

My problem, however, as I have indicated, is the suddenness of the Court's perception of progress in the human attitude since decisions of only a short while ago....

I do not sit on these cases, however, as a legislator, responsive, at least in part, to the will of constituents. Our task here, as must so frequently be emphasized and re-emphasized, is to pass upon the constitutionality of legislation that has been enacted and that is challenged. This is the sole task for judges. We should not allow our personal preferences as to the wisdom of legislative and congressional action, or our distaste for such action, to guide our judicial decision in cases such as these. The temptations to cross that policy line are very great. In fact, as today's decision reveals, they are almost irresistible.

I trust the Court fully appreciates what it is doing when it decides these cases the way it does today. Not only are the capital punishment laws of 39 States and the District of Columbia struck down, but also all those provisions of the federal statutory structure that permit the death penalty apparently are voided....

Although personally I may rejoice at the Court's result, I find it difficult to accept or to justify as a matter of history, of law, or of constitutional pronouncement. I fear the Court has overstepped. It has sought and has achieved an end.

Dissenting opinion by Justice Powell: Justice Powell's dissent displayed concern for the lack of precedent in the judgment of the majority, and the possible consequences of the majority's decision. Justice Powell presented the heart of his dissent as follows:

It is the judgment of five Justices that the death penalty, as customarily prescribed and implemented in this country today, offends the constitutional prohibition against cruel and unusual punishments. The reasons for that judgment are stated in five separate opinions, expressing as many separate rationales. In my view, none of these opinions provides a constitutionally adequate foundation for the Court's decision....

Whatever uncertainties may hereafter surface, several of the consequences of today's decision are unmistakably clear. The decision is plainly one of the greatest importance The Court's judgment removes the death sentences previously imposed on some 600 persons awaiting punishment in state and federal prisons throughout the country. At least for the present, it also bars the States and the Federal Government from seeking sentences of death for defendants awaiting trial on charges for which capital punishment was heretofore a potential alternative. The happy event for these countable few constitutes, however, only the most visible consequence of this decision. Less measurable, but certainly of no less significance, is the shattering effect this collection of views has on the root principles of stare decisis, federalism, judicial restraint and — most importantly — separation of powers....

In terms of the constitutional role of this Court, the impact of the majority's ruling is all the greater because the decision encroaches upon an area squarely within the historic prerogative of the legislative branch — both state and federal — to protect the citizenry through the designation of penalties for prohibitable conduct. It is the very sort of judgment that the legislative branch is competent to make and for which the judiciary is ill-equipped. Throughout our history, Justices of this Court have emphasized the gravity of decisions invalidating legislative judgments, admonishing the nine men who sit on this bench of the duty of self-restraint, especially when called upon to apply the expansive due process and cruel and unusual punishment rubrics. I can recall no case in which, in the name of deciding constitutional questions, this Court has subordinated national and local democratic processes to such an extent....

On virtually every occasion that any opinion has touched on the question of the constitutionality of the death penalty, it has been asserted affirmatively, or tacitly assumed, that the Constitution does not prohibit the penalty. No Justice of the Court, until today, has dissented from this consistent reading of the Constitution. The petitioners in these cases now before the Court cannot fairly avoid the weight of this substantial body of precedent merely by asserting that there is no prior decision precisely in point. Stare decisis, if it is a doctrine founded on principle, surely applies where there exists a long line of cases endorsing or necessarily assuming the validity of a particular matter of constitutional interpretation....

Members of this Court know, from the petitions and appeals that come before us regularly, that brutish and revolting murders continue to occur with disquieting frequency. Indeed, murders are so commonplace in our society that only the most sensational receive significant and sustained publicity. It could hardly be suggested that in any of these highly publicized murder cases — the several senseless assassinations or the too numerous shocking multiple murders that have stained this country's recent history — the public has exhibited any signs of "revulsion" at the thought of executing the convicted murderers. The public outcry, as we all know, has been quite to the contrary. Furthermore, there is little reason to suspect that the public's reaction would differ significantly in response to other less publicized murders. It is certainly arguable that many such murders, because of their senselessness or barbarousness, would evoke a public demand for the death penalty rather than a public rejection of that alternative. Nor is there any rational basis for arguing that the public reaction to any of these crimes would be muted if the murderer were "rich and powerful." The demand for the ultimate sanction might well be greater, as a wealthy killer is hardly a sympathetic figure. While there might be specific cases in which capital punishment would be regarded as excessive and shocking to the conscience of the community, it can hardly be argued that the public's dissatisfaction with the penalty in particular cases would translate into a demand for absolute abolition.

Dissenting opinion by Justice Rehnquist: Justice Rehnquist expressed concern about the usurpation of power he believed was represented in the judgment of the majority. The critical points of his dissent stated the following:

The Court's judgments today strike down a penalty that our Nation's legislators have thought necessary since our country was founded. My Brothers Douglas, Brennan, and Marshall would at one fell swoop invalidate laws enacted by Congress and 40 of the 50 state legislatures, and would consign to the limbo of unconstitutionality under a single rubric penalties for offenses as varied and unique as murder, piracy, mutiny, highjacking, and desertion in the face of the enemy. My Brothers Stewart and White, asserting reliance on a more limited rationale — the reluctance of judges and juries actually to impose the death penalty in the majority of capital cases — join in the judgments in these cases. Whatever its precise rationale, today's holding necessarily brings into sharp relief the fundamental question of the role of judicial review in a democratic society. How can government by the elected representatives of the people co-exist with the power of the federal judiciary, whose members are constitutionally insulated from responsiveness to the popular will, to declare invalid laws duly enacted by the popular branches of government?...

If there can be said to be one dominant theme in the Constitution, perhaps more fully articulated in the Federalist Papers than in the instrument itself, it is the notion of checks and balances. The Framers were well aware of the natural desire of office holders as well as others to seek to expand the scope and authority of their particular office at the expense of others. They sought to provide against success in such efforts by erecting adequate checks and balances in the form of grants of authority to each branch of the government in order to counteract and prevent usurpation on the part of the others.

... While overreaching by the Legislative and Executive Branches may result in the sacrifice of individual protections that the Constitution was designed to secure against action of the State, judicial over-reaching may result in sacrifice of the equally important right of the people to govern themselves. The Due Process and Equal Protection Clauses of the Fourteenth Amendment were "never intended to destroy the States' power to govern themselves."

Case note: The case was one of three opinions issued by the Court, on the same day, invalidating death penalty statutes.

Impact of the Furman Decision

From a legal technical perspective, the United States Supreme Court decision in *Furman v. Georgia*, 408 U.S. 238

(1972) merely invalidated the death penalty statutes of Georgia and Texas; as only those two States were represented in the consolidated cases. However, the practical effect of the decision was that of invalidating to death penalty statutes of all jurisdictions in the nation. The reason for this is that, procedurally all death penalty statutes mirrored the statutes of Georgia and Texas. (On the same day that the *Furman* decision was rendered the nation's highest court also issued terse opinions in *Stewart v. Massachusetts*, 408 U.S. 845 (1972) and *Moore v. Illinois*, 408 U.S. 786 (1972), which directly invalidated the death penalty procedures of Massachusetts and Illinois. Additionally, on the date *Furman* was decided, the Court issued a memorandum order that invalidated the death penalty in 121 cases that had been pending on its docket.)

Although two Justices writing in concurrence in *Furman*, Justices Marshall and Brennan, believed the constitution barred capital punishment per se, the decision in *Furman* did not extend that far. *Furman* left open the possibility of a resumption of capital punishment, provided the procedures used minimized arbitrary and capricious imposition of the punishment.

Immediately after the *Furman* decision was rendered many jurisdictions passed legislation that created death penalty statutes which provided mechanisms for limiting arbitrary and capricious imposition of capital punishment. The moratorium placed on capital punishment by *Furman* was lifted in 1976, when the United States Supreme Court reviewed and approved the new death penalty statutes of Georgia, Florida and Texas. As of January 2000, 38 States and the Federal government had new death penalty statutes.

The decision in *Furman* has altered capital punishment in several respects. First, as a result of *Furman* all capital prosecutions are now bifurcated into a guilt phase and penalty phase. This change has been instrumental in allowing capital defendants to proclaim their innocence, while also seeking mercy from imposition of the death penalty. Under pre–*Furman* unitary trials it was difficult for capital defendants to seek mercy while putting on evidence of innocence.

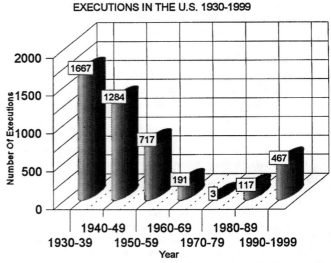

EXECUTIONS IN THE U.S. 1930-1999

Source: Bureau of Justice Statistics, Capital Punishment (1998).

Next, *Furman* has been instrumental in leading to a contrition in the types of crimes that the death penalty may be imposed upon. Under pre–*Furman* constitutional jurisprudence crimes such as robbery, burglary and rape were punishable with death. For all practical purposes, post–*Furman* constitutional jurisprudence has limited imposition of the death penalty to crimes involving a homicide.

Finally, actual executions have dramatically declined under the post-*Furman* era. During the peak period of executions prior to *Furman*, 1930–1939, there were 1,667 inmates executed. In contrast, during the peak period of executions after *Furman*, 1990–1999, there were only 467 inmates executed. *See also* **Capital Punishment Jurisdictions; Gregg v. Georgia; Jurek v. Texas; Moore v. Illinois; Pre-Furman Capital Punishment; Proffitt v. Florida; Rape and Capital Punishment; Stewart v. Massachusetts; Trial Structure**

Gabon   Gabon permits the imposition of the death penalty. The firing squad is the method of execution used in Gabon. The nation's legal system is based on French civil law and customary law. Gabon adopted a constitution on March 14, 1991.

The judicial system of Gabon is composed of trial courts, appellate courts, Supreme Court, Constitutional Court and a State Security Court. Criminal defendants have the right to a public trial and the right to legal counsel. Under the laws of

Gabon defendants are presumed guilty. This presumption oftentimes results in judges rendering an immediate verdict at the initial hearing if sufficient evidence is presented by the government. *See also* **International Capital Punishment Nations**

Gacy, John Wayne   During the period 1972 to 1978, John Wayne Gacy sodomized and killed 33 boys and young

John Wayne Gacy was executed after being found guilty of sodomizing and killing 33 boys and young men in the State of Illinois. (Chicago Police)

men in the State of Illinois. For a brief period Gacy held the distinction of being convicted of more murders than any other person in the history of the United States.

Gacy was born in Chicago on March 17, 1942. He dropped out of high school and wandered though several states before ending up in Waterloo, Iowa, with a wife in 1964. While living in Iowa Gacy presented himself as a likeable family man who enjoyed being around boys. The facade of Gacy's life crumbled in 1968, when he was charged with sodomizing 15 and 16 year old youth. He was sentenced to prison for 10 years. His wife divorced him while he was in prison. On June 18, 1970, Gacy was released on parole.

When Gacy left prison he returned to his native Chicago. Gacy began to pick up the pieces of his life when he returned home. His past did not haunt him and on June 1, 1972, Gacy married for a second time. At the time of his marriage, Gacy had already killed his first victim in January of 1972. Gacy's second marriage ended in a divorce in 1976.

Two years after Gacy's second marriage failed, the secret life he had been living during and after the marriage was exposed to a horrified public. Gacy's downfall started with the disappearance of 15 year old Robert Piest on December 11, 1978. Gacy had picked up Piest near a pharmacy in Des Plaines, Illinois. Piest had informed his mother that he was going to meet a "man" to discuss a summer job as a construction worker. Piest was never seen alive again.

When Piest was reported missing local police immediately suspected Gacy. Although witnesses could only give information about the vehicle Gacy drove at the time he picked up Piest, that was enough for the police to run a thorough background check on him. The background check revealed Gacy's pedophile history. Police were able to obtain a warrant to search Gacy's home, which was executed in his absence on December 13. Authorities were hoping to find Piest in the home, but did not. Numerous items were removed from the home however. After intense investigation into the items removed from Gacy's home, the police got a break. A ring that was removed from his home belonged to another teenager who had disappeared a year earlier. Armed with this evidence, the police apprehended Gacy and subjected him to interrogation.

Gacy broke down during interrogation. Initially he admitted to killing one person in self-defense, but later admitted that he had killed approximately 30 individuals, burying most of the bodies in a crawl space under his home and throwing some into the Des Plaines River. The authorities rushed to confirm Gacy's confession. Excavation was begun under the crawl space and the area surrounding Gacy's home. The digging uncovered 29 bodies. In addition, the police recovered four bodies from the Des Plaines and Illinois rivers, downstream from the place where Gacy told them he had thrown the bodies.

Gacy informed authorities that he would lure his victims into being handcuffed and would then sexually assault them. He described how he muffled their screams by stuffing socks or underwear into their mouths. Gacy reported that he would strangle his victims to death as he raped them.

Gacy was indicted for 33 murders. Twelve of the murders were committed after Illinois reenacted the death penalty, and therefore carried capital punishment. Gacy's trial on all 33 murders began on February 6, 1980. The jury in the case convicted Gacy of all 33 murders. He was sentenced to death for each of the 12 capital punishment murders, and sentenced to life imprisonment on each of the remaining murder convictions. Gacy was executed by lethal injection on May 10, 1994.

Gainesville Ripper Murders

In August of 1990, authorities in Gainesville, Florida, discovered the mutilated remains of five people. Because of the dismemberment of the bodies, the media dubbed the perpetrator the "Gainesville Ripper."

Investigation of the Gainesville Ripper murders led authorities to Danny Rolling. Rolling was born on May 26, 1954 in Shreveport, Louisiana. He was the troubled son of a police officer.

Rolling dropped out of high school and joined the air force at the age of 17. He was prematurely discharged in 1973, due to drug and alcohol abuse. After his discharge Rolling returned to Louisiana. He was married in 1974 and fathered a daughter during the marriage. The marriage ended in 1977.

After the breakup of his marriage Rolling embarked on a life of crime. In 1979, he was sentenced to six years in prison for the robbery of a store in Columbus, Georgia. He was also prosecuted for a second robbery in Alabama. Thus, after serving his Georgia sentence in 1982, Rolling was extradited Alabama to serve a ten year sentence.

Rolling Danny obtained early parole on his Alabama sentence and

Danny Rolling confessed to killing five people in Gainesville, Florida. (Florida Department of Corrections)

returned to Shreveport in 1984. Not long after being released Rolling was prosecuted for robbery in Mississippi in July of 1985. He received a 15 year sentence, but was released in 1988. After his release he again returned to Shreveport.

On November 6, 1989, authorities found three family members slaughtered in their Shreveport home. At the time of this incident authorities did not suspect Rolling of the crimes. In May of 1990, Rolling got into an argument with his father and shot him in the head and stomach. Rolling fled Louisiana and ended up in Gainesville, Florida.

Rolling's presence in Gainesville was felt when, on August 26, 1990, authorities found the decomposing bodies of roommates Sonja Larsen and Christina Powell. They were apparently killed two days earlier. Both victims had been mutilated, one with her nipples cut off, the other sodomized. On August 27, the decapitated body of 18-year-old Christa Hoyt was found slain at home. On August 28, the dead bodies of roommates Tracy Paules and Manuel Taboada were found in their apartment.

The five random murders sent Gainesville into a panic. Authorities were pressured into finding the perpetrator. During the investigation it was learned that similar murders had occurred in Shreveport. This knowledge was meaningless until Rolling was arrested for several robberies in the Gainesville area. A background check informed authorities that he was from Shreveport and was wanted for the attempted murder of his father. The Shreveport connection focused Gainesville authorities on Rolling as the perpetrator of the five mutilation deaths. Evidence began to reveal itself. Pubic hair and tools uncovered at Rolling's hideout placed him at the Gainesville murder scenes. Additionally, Rolling's DNA matched semen traces from the victims he had sodomized.

Rolling was first prosecuted for three robberies he committed in Tampa. In 1991, he was sentenced to three life terms plus 170 years in prison for the robberies. He was subsequently indicted for the Gainesville murders. Hoping to avoid the death penalty, Rolling decided to confess to the murders. On February 15, 1994, he entered a plea of guilty to each murder charge. On April 20, 1994, the trial court sentenced Rolling to death. He is now on death row in Florida.

Gambia

Capital punishment is on the law books in Gambia, but the punishment has not been enforced in over a decade. Its legal system is based on English common law, Islamic law and customary law. A new constitution was adopted by the nation on August 8, 1996.

Gambia's judicial system is composed of a Court of Appeal, high courts, and magistrate courts. Appeals may be taken to the Judicial Committee of the Privy Council in England (Gambia has considered ending the practice of allowing appeals in England). The judicial system also recognizes customary courts and Shari'a (Islamic) courts. Customary laws have jurisdiction over marriage and divorce for non–Muslims, inheritance, land tenure, and all other traditional and social relations. Shari'a courts have jurisdiction primarily over Muslim marriage and divorce matters.

Defendants have the right to public trials and retained legal counsel. Trials are public, and defendants have the right to an attorney at their own cost. In special situations trials may not be open to the public. For example the trial of three defendants in 1997 for complicity in a coup attempt was closed to the public. The three defendants were convicted of treason and sentenced to death. *See also* **International Capital Punishment Nations**

Gardner v. Florida

Court: United States Supreme Court; *Case Citation:* Gardner v. Florida, 430 U.S. 349 (1977); *Argued:* November 30, 1976; *Decided:* March 22, 1977; *Plurality Opinion:* Justice Stevens announced the Court's judgment and delivered an opinion, in which Stewart and Powell, JJ., joined; *Concurring Opinion:* Justice White; *Concurring and Dissenting Opinion:* Justice Brennan; *Concurring Statement:* Chief Justice Burger; *Concurring Statement:* Justice Blackmun; *Dissenting Opinion:* Justice Marshall; *Dissenting Opinion:* Justice Rehnquist; *Appellate Defense Counsel:* Charles H. Livingston argued; James A. Gardner, Jack Greenberg, James M. Nabrit III, Peggy C. Davis, and Anthony G. Amsterdam on brief; *Appellate Prosecution Counsel:* Wallace E. Allbritton argued; Robert L. Shevin on brief; *Amicus Curiae Brief Supporting Prosecutor:* None; *Amicus Curiae Brief Supporting Defendant:* None.

Issue Presented: Whether the defendant's due process rights were violated when the death sentence imposed against him was based, in part, on information that he had no opportunity to deny or explain?

Case Holding: The defendant's due process rights were violated when the death sentence imposed against him was based, in part, on information that he had no opportunity to deny or explain.

Factual and procedural background of case: The defendant, Gardner, was convicted of capital murder by a Florida jury. During the penalty phase the jury recommended life imprisonment as the punishment. The trial court, after reviewing an undisclosed part of a confidential presentence report, rejected the jury's recommendation and imposed a death sentence. The Florida Supreme Court affirmed the conviction and sentence without expressly discussing the defendant's contention that the trial court violated his constitutional rights by unilaterally considering the presentence report. The United States Supreme Court granted certiorari to consider the issue.

Plurality opinion in which Justice Stevens announced the Court's judgment and in which Stewart and Powell, JJ., joined: Justice Stevens held that the Due Process Clause required the defendant be given an opportunity to deny or explain the confidential information which was considered by the trial court in rendering the decision to impose the death penalty. The opinion ruled that no good cause was shown to warrant failing to disclose the confidential part of the presentence report to the defendant. The judgment of the Florida Supreme Court was reversed, with respect to the sentence, and the case was remanded for a new sentencing hearing.

Concurring opinion by Justice White: Justice White concurred in the Court's judgment. In doing so, he contended that the case should have been resolved under the Eighth Amendment and not on the due process ground. He wrote: "Here the sentencing judge indicated that he selected ... Gardner for the death penalty in part because of information contained in a presentence report which information was not disclosed to [the defendant] or to his counsel and to which [the defendant] had no opportunity to respond. A procedure for selecting people for the death penalty which permits consideration of such secret information relevant to the 'character and record of the individual offender,' fails to meet the 'need for reliability in the determination that death is the appropriate punishment[.]' This conclusion stems solely from the Eighth Amendment's ban on cruel and unusual punishments.... I thus see no reason to address in this case the possible application to sentencing proceedings — in death or other cases — of the Due Process Clause, other than as the vehicle by which the strictures of the Eighth Amendment are triggered in this case. For these reasons, I do not join the plurality opinion but concur in the judgment."

Concurring and dissenting opinion by Justice Brennan: Justice Brennan stated in his brief concurring and dissenting opinion: "I agree for the reasons stated in the plurality opinion that the Due Process Clause of the Fourteenth Amendment is violated when a defendant facing a death sentence is not informed of the contents of a presentence investigation report made to the sentencing judge. However, I adhere to my view that the death penalty is in all circumstances cruel and unusual punishment prohibited by the Eighth and Fourteenth Amendments. I therefore would vacate the death sentence, and I dissent from the Court's judgment insofar as it remands for further proceedings that could lead to its imposition."

Concurring Statement by Chief Justice Burger: The Chief Justice issued a statement indicating he concurred in the Court's judgment.

Concurring Statement by Justice Blackmun: Justice Blackmun issued a statement indicating he concurred in the Court's judgment.

Dissenting opinion by Justice Marshall: Justice Marshall argued in his dissent that the trial court failed to actually consider the merits of the evidence in rejecting the jury's recommendation. He also argued that the Florida Supreme Court failed to perform a constitutionally acceptable review of the defendant's death sentence. The dissent stated its position as follows:

> Last Term, this Court carefully scrutinized the Florida procedures for imposing the death penalty [in *Proffitt v. Florida*] and concluded that there were sufficient safeguards to insure that the death sentence would not be "wantonly" and "freakishly" imposed. This case, however, belies that hope. While I continue to believe that the death penalty is unconstitutional in all circumstances and therefore would remand this case for resentencing to a term of life, nevertheless, now that Florida may legally take a life, we must insist that it be in accordance with the standards enunciated by this Court. In this case I am ap-

palled at the extent to which Florida has deviated from the procedures upon which this Court expressly relied. It is not simply that the trial judge, in overriding the jury's recommendation of life imprisonment, relied on undisclosed portions of the presentence report. Nor is it merely that the Florida Supreme Court affirmed the sentence without discussing the omission and without concern that it did not even have the entire report before it. Obviously that alone is enough to deny due process and require that the death sentence be vacated as the Court now holds. But the blatant disregard exhibited by the courts below for the standards devised to regulate imposition of the death penalty calls into question the very basis for this Court's approval of that system....

> In the present case ... the Florida Supreme Court engaged in precisely the "cursory or rubber-stamp review" that the joint opinion in *Proffitt* trusted would not occur. The jury, after considering the evidence, recommended a life sentence[.] The judge, however, ignored the jury's findings. His statutorily required written findings consisted of [two brief paragraphs]. The Florida Supreme Court affirmed with two justices dissenting. The per curiam consisted of a statement of the facts of the murder, a verbatim copy of the trial judge's "findings," a conclusion that no new trial was warranted....

> ... [I]t is apparent that the State Supreme Court undertook none of the analysis it had previously proclaimed to be its duty. The opinion does not say that the Supreme Court evaluated the propriety of the death sentence. It merely says the trial judge did so. Despite its professed obligation to do so, the Supreme Court thus failed "to determine independently" whether death was the appropriate penalty. The Supreme Court also appears to have done nothing "to guarantee" consistency with other death sentences. Its opinion makes no comparison with the facts in other similar cases. Nor did it consider whether the trial judge was correct in overriding the jury's recommendation. There was no attempt to ascertain whether the evidence sustaining death was "so clear and convincing that virtually no reasonable person could differ." Indeed, it is impossible for me to believe that that standard can be met in this case....

> Clearly, this is not a case where the evidence suggesting death is "so clear and convincing that virtually no reasonable person could differ." Had the Florida Supreme Court examined the evidence in the manner this Court trusted it would, I have no doubt that the jury recommendation of life imprisonment would have been reinstated.

Dissenting opinion by Justice Rehnquist: Justice Rehnquist wrote a brief dissenting opinion indicating that due process analysis was inappropriate for the case. He believed that under Eighth Amendment analysis the death sentence was validly imposed against the defendant. He "would therefore affirm the judgment of the Supreme Court of Florida."

Garfield's Assassination

On July 2, 1881, President James Garfield was fatally shot by Charles Julius Guiteau. The assassination occurred as the President was about to depart for a vacation from the Baltimore and Potomac Railroad Station.

Guiteau was born on September 8, 1841, in Freeport, Illinois. He spent much of his adult life moving back and forth between Chicago and New York. Guiteau was married for about five years, before his wife divorced him because of abusive behavior. During the early 1860s, he was a practicing attorney in Chicago. However, he abandoned the practice of law and became an itinerant preacher in 1877.

A depiction of President James Garfield after being shot in the back and arm by Charles Julius Guiteau. (Library of Congress)

Guiteau took an active interest in national politics in 1880. He initially supported efforts to nominate President Ulysses S. Grant for a third term. However, when that movement failed he turned his support to Garfield. Guiteau performed grassroots work for Garfield's campaign in New York. After Garfield's election in 1881, Guiteau moved to Washington, D.C. in search of a political job as payment for his earlier campaign work.

When Guiteau arrived in Washington he was surprised to find that the President's staff did not know him from any of the other thousands of volunteer campaign workers. Guiteau made repeated requests for a political appointment, but was rejected. Guiteau felt betrayed by a President who did not know him. On July 2, 1881, Guiteau exacted his revenge by shooting the President in the arm and in the back.

Guiteau was immediately arrested after the shooting. His trial was lengthy, beginning on November 14, 1881, and ending on May 22, 1882. He was found guilty and sentenced to death. On June 30, 1882, Guiteau was hanged at the District of Columbia jail.

Gee Jon   *see*   Lethal Gas

Gender and Capital Punishment   *see*   Women and Capital Punishment

Georgia (Country)   Capital punishment was abolished by the nation of Georgia in 1997. *See also* **International Capital Punishment Nations**

Georgia   The State of Georgia is a capital punishment jurisdiction. The State reenacted its death penalty law after the United States Supreme Court decision in *Furman v. Georgia*, 408 U.S. 238 (1972) on March 28, 1973.

Georgia has a three-tier legal system. The State's legal system is composed of a supreme court, court of appeals and courts of general jurisdiction. The Georgia Supreme Court is presided over by a chief justice and six associate justices. The Georgia Court Appeals is composed of a chief judge and nine judges. The courts of general jurisdiction in the State are called Superior Courts. Capital offenses against the State of Georgia are tried in the Superior Courts.

Georgia's capital punishment statute is triggered if a person commits a homicide under the following special circumstances:

a. when he unlawfully and with malice aforethought, either express or implied, causes the death of another human being; or

b. when, in the commission of a felony, he causes the death of another human being irrespective of malice.

c. the death penalty may be imposed for the offenses of aircraft hijacking or treason in any case.

Capital murder in Georgia is punishable by death or life imprisonment without parole. A capital prosecution in Georgia is bifurcated into a guilt phase and penalty phase. A jury is used at both phases of a capital trial. It is required that, at the penalty phase, the jury unanimously agree that a death sentence is appropriate before it can be imposed. If the penalty phase jury is unable to reach a verdict, the trial judge is required to impose a sentence of life imprisonment without parole. The decision of a penalty phase jury is binding on the trial court under the laws of Georgia.

In order to impose a death sentence upon a defendant under Georgia law, it is required that the prosecutor establish the existence of at least one of the following statutory aggravating circumstances at the penalty phase:

1. the offense was committed by a person with a prior record of conviction for a capital felony;

2. the offense was committed while the offender was engaged in the commission of another capital felony or aggravated battery, or the offense of murder was committed while the offender was engaged in the commission of burglary or arson in the first degree;

3. the offender knowingly created a great risk of death to more than one person in a public place by means of a weapon or device which would normally be hazardous to the lives of more than one person;

4. the offender committed the offense for the purpose of receiving money or any other thing of monetary value;

5. the murder of a judicial officer, former judicial officer, district attorney or solicitor general, or former district attorney, solicitor, or solicitor general was committed during or because of the exercise of his or her official duties;

6. the offender caused or directed another to commit murder or committed murder as an agent or employee of another person;

7. the offense was outrageously or wantonly vile, horrible, or inhuman in that it involved torture, depravity of mind, or an aggravated battery to the victim;

8. the offense of murder was committed against any peace officer, corrections employee, or fireman while engaged in the performance of his official duties;

9. the offense was committed by a person in, or who has escaped from, the lawful custody of a peace officer or place of lawful confinement; or

10. the offense was committed for the purpose of avoiding, interfering with, or preventing a lawful arrest or custody in a place of lawful confinement, of himself or another.

Georgia does not provide by statute any mitigating circumstances to the imposition of the death penalty. Even though the State does not provide statutory mitigating circumstances, the United States Supreme Court has ruled that all relevant mitigating evidence must be allowed at the penalty phase.

Under Georgia's capital punishment statute, a sentence of death is automatically reviewed by the Georgia Supreme Court. In March 2000, Georgia switched to lethal injection to carry out the death penalty; it previously used electrocution. The State's death row facility for men is located in Jackson, Georgia; while the facility maintaining female death row inmates is located in Atlanta, Georgia.

Pursuant to the laws of Georgia the State's Board of Pardons and Parole has exclusive jurisdiction to grant or deny clemency.

From the start of modern capital punishment in 1976, through 1999, Georgia executed 23 capital felons. During this period Georgia did not execute any female capital felons, although one of its death row inmates during this period was a female. A total of 123 capital felons were on death row in Georgia in 1999. The 1999 death row population in the State was listed as: 56 black inmates; 65 white inmates; and 2 unidentified inmates. In 1999 the State had 2 juveniles on death row. The State permits capital punishment to be imposed on persons 17 years old or older. Georgia does not prohibit the execution of mentally retarded capital felons.

Executions by Georgia 1976–1999

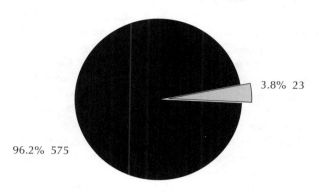

GEORGIA EXECUTIONS 1976–1999

3.8% 23

96.2% 575

■ GEORGIA EXECUTIONS
■ ALL OTHER EXECUTIONS

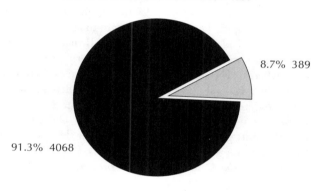

EXECUTIONS BY GEORGIA 1930–1999

8.7% 389

91.3% 4068

■ GEORGIA
■ ALL OTHER JURISDICTIONS

Name	Race	Date of Execution	Method of Execution
John E. Smith	White	December 15, 1983	Electrocution
Ivon Stanley	Black	July 12, 1984	Electrocution
Alpha O. Stephens	Black	December 12, 1984	Electrocution
Roosevelt Green	Black	January 9, 1985	Electrocution
Van R. Solomon	Black	February 20, 1985	Electrocution
John Young	Black	March 20 1985	Electrocution
Jerome Bowden	Black	June 24, 1986	Electrocution
Joseph Mulligan	Black	May 15, 1987	Electrocution
Richard Tucker	Black	May 19, 1987	Electrocution
William B. Tucker	White	May 28, 1987	Electrocution
Billy Mitchell	Black	September 1, 1987	Electrocution
Timothy McCorquodale	White	September 21, 1987	Electrocution
James Messer	White	July 28, 1988	Electrocution
Henry Willis	Black	May 18, 1989	Electrocution
Warren McCleskey	Black	September 25, 1991	Electrocution
Thomas D. Stevens	White	June 28, 1993	Electrocution
Christopher Burger	White	December 7, 1993	Electrocution
William H. Hance	Black	March 31, 1994	Electrocution
Nicholas Ingram	White	April 7, 1995	Electrocution
Darrell G. Devier	White	May 17, 1995	Electrocution
Larry Lonchar	White	November 14, 1996	Electrocution
Ellis W. Felker	White	November 15, 1996	Electrocution
David L. Cargill	White	June 10, 1998	Electrocution

Germany The death penalty was abolished by Germany in 1987. *See also* **International Capital Punishment Nations**

Ghana Ghana permits the imposition of the death penalty. The method of execution used by Ghana is the firing squad. Its legal system is based on English common law and customary law. Ghana approved a new constitution on April 28, 1992.

The judicial system of Ghana is composed of a Supreme Court, Appeals Court, High Court, and regional tribunals. The government also recognizes customary courts that preside over such matters as divorce, child custody, and property disputes. Under the laws of Ghana trials are public, defendants are presumed innocent, and have a right to appointed or retained counsel. *See also* **International Capital Punishment Nations**

Gibson v. Mississippi *Court:* United States Supreme Court; *Case Citation:* Gibson v. Mississippi, 162 U.S. 565 (1896); *Argued:* Not reported; *Decided:* April 13, 1896; *Opinion of the Court:* Justice Harlan; *Concurring Opinion:* None; *Dissenting Opinion:* None; *Appellate Defense Counsel:* E. M. Hewlett argued and briefed; *Appellate Prosecution Counsel:* Frank Johnston argued and briefed; *Amicus Curiae Brief Supporting Prosecutor:* None; *Amicus Curiae Brief Supporting Defendant:* None.

Issue Presented: Whether the defendant satisfied the requirements for removing his State capital murder prosecution into a Federal court?

Case Holding: The defendant did not satisfy the requirements for removing his State capital murder prosecution into a Federal court, because he failed to show that the laws or constitution of Mississippi authorized discrimination against blacks in selecting grand or petit juries.

Factual and procedural background of case: The defendant, John Gibson, was charged with capital murder by the State of Mississippi. The defendant sought to remove the prosecution into a Federal court on the grounds that blacks were systematically excluded from grand and petit juries in the county where he was being prosecuted. The request to remove the case to a Federal court was denied. The defendant was tried, convicted and sentenced to death. The Mississippi Supreme Court affirmed the judgment. The United States Supreme Court granted certiorari to consider the issue of removal of the case to a Federal court.

Opinion of the Court by Justice Harlan: Justice Harlan ruled that the request to remove the prosecution into a Federal court was properly denied. The opinion explained the Court's decision as follows: "We ... held, in *Neal v. Delaware*, that congress had not authorized a removal of the prosecution from the state court where jury commissioners or other subordinate officers had, without authority derived from the constitution and laws of the state, excluded [black] citizens from juries because of their race. In view of this decision, it is clear that the accused in the present case was not entitled to have the case removed into the circuit court of the United States, unless he was denied, by the constitution or laws of Mississippi, some of the fundamental rights of life or liberty that were guaranteed to other citizens resident in that state."

Justice Harlan indicated that neither the laws or constitution of Mississippi authorized discrimination against blacks in grand or petit jury selection. It was further said: "We do not overlook, in this connection, the fact that the petition for the removal of the cause into the federal court alleged that the accused, by reason of the great prejudice against him on account of his color, could not secure a fair and impartial trial in the county, and that he prayed an opportunity to subpoena witnesses to prove that fact. Such evidence, if it had been introduced, and however cogent, could not, as already shown, have entitled the accused to the removal sought; for the alleged existence of race prejudice, interfering with a fair trial, was not to be attributed to the constitution and laws of the state." The judgment of the Mississippi Supreme Court was affirmed. *See also* **Discrimination in Grand or Petit Jury Selection**

Gilmore, Gary *see* **Firing Squad**

Ginsburg, Ruth Bader Ruth Bader Ginsburg was appointed as an associate justice of the United States Supreme Court in 1993. Ginsburg's early opinions have indicated a moderate approach to constitutional interpretation.

Ginsburg was born in Brooklyn, New York on March 15, 1933. She received an undergraduate degree from Cornell University in 1954. Subsequently she attended Harvard Law School and Columbia Law School, where she obtained a law degree. After law school Ginsburg clerked for a Federal District Court judge before taking a teaching position at Rutgers University School of Law. Ginsburg left teaching in 1972 in order to take up a legal advocacy position with the Women's Rights Project of the American Civil Liberties Union. In 1993 President Bill Clinton appointed Ginsburg to the Supreme Court.

While on the Supreme Court for a relatively short time, Ginsburg quickly issued a number of opinions in capital punishment cases. The strongest indication of Ginsburg's understanding of the Constitution and capital punishment was provided in her dissenting opinion in *Jones v. United States* (II). One of the issues decided by the majority in *Jones* was that the penalty phase jury instructions were not so ambiguous as to require reversal of the defendant's death sentence. Ginsburg disagreed and wrote: "The Fifth Circuit's tolerance of error in this case, and this Court's refusal to face up to it, cannot be reconciled with the recognition ... that 'death is qualitatively different.' If the jury's weighing process is infected by the trial court's misperceptions of the law, the legitimacy of an ensuing death sentence should not hinge on defense counsel's shortfalls or the reviewing court's speculation about the decision the jury would have made absent the infection. I would vacate the jury's sentencing decision and remand the case for a new sentencing hearing[.]"

Capital Punishment Opinions Written by Ginsburg

Case Name	Opinion of the Court	Concurring Opinion	Dissenting Opinion
Gray v. Netherland			✓
Jones v. United States (II)			✓
Romano v. Oklahoma			✓
Simmons v. South Carolina		✓	
Victor v. Nebraska		✓	

Godfrey v. Georgia *Court:* United States Supreme Court; *Case Citation:* Godfrey v. Georgia, 446 U.S. 420 (1980); *Argued:* February 20, 1980; *Decided:* May 19, 1980; *Plurality Opinion:* Justice Stewart announced the Court's judgment and delivered an opinion, in which Blackmun, Powell and Stevens, JJ., joined; *Concurring Opinion:* Justice Marshall, in which Brennan, J., joined; *Dissenting Opinion:* Chief Justice Burger; *Dissenting Opinion:* Justice White, in which Rehnquist, J., joined; *Appellate Defense Counsel:* J. Calloway Holmes, Jr. argued; Gerry E. Holmes on brief; *Appellate Prosecution Counsel:* John W. Dunsmore, Jr. argued; Arthur K. Bolton, Robert S. Stubbs II, Don A. Langham and John C. Walden on brief; *Amicus Curiae Brief Supporting Prosecutor:* None; *Amicus Curiae Brief Supporting Defendant:* None.

Issue Presented: Whether the vague statutory aggravating circumstance of outrageously or wantonly vile, horrible or inhuman, was properly defined so as to sustain the defendant's death sentence?

Case Holding: The vague statutory aggravating circumstance of outrageously or wantonly vile, horrible or inhuman, was not properly defined so as to sustain the defendant's death sentence.

Factual and procedural background of case: The State of Georgia charged the defendant, Godfrey, with capital murder in the shooting deaths of his wife and mother-in-law. The jury convicted the defendant of both murders. During the penalty phase the trial judge instructed the jury that it could return death sentences if it found the murders were "outrageously or wantonly vile, horrible or inhuman." (This was a statutory aggravating circumstance.) The jury returned death sentences on both murder convictions. The Georgia Supreme Court affirmed the convictions and sentences, after rejecting the defendant's contention that the statutory aggravating circumstance was unconstitutionally vague. The United States Supreme Court granted certiorari to consider the issue.

Plurality opinion in which Justice Stewart announced the Court's judgment and in which Blackmun, Powell and Stevens, JJ., joined: Justice Stewart announced that it was the judgment of the Court that, in affirming the death sentences in the case, the Georgia Supreme Court adopted such a broad and vague construction of the statutory aggravating circumstance as to violate the Eighth and Fourteenth Amendments. It was said that if a State wishes to authorize capital punishment, it has a constitutional responsibility to tailor and apply its law in a manner that avoids the arbitrary and capricious infliction of the death penalty. Therefore, States must define the crimes for which death may be imposed in a way that obviates standardless sentencing discretion.

The opinion noted that in earlier decisions interpreting the statutory aggravating circumstance, the Georgia Supreme Court adequately limited the aggravator to mean torture, depravity of mind, or an aggravated battery to the victim. However, this limitation was not used in the defendant's case. The opinion indicated that the defendant did not torture or commit an aggravated battery upon his victims, or cause either of them to suffer any physical injury preceding their deaths. Justice Stewart concluded:

> Thus, the validity of the [defendant's] death sentences turns on whether, in light of the facts and circumstances of the murders that he was convicted of committing, the Georgia Supreme Court can be said to have applied a constitutional construction of the phrase "outrageously or wantonly vile, horrible or inhu-

man in that [they] involved ... depravity of mind[.]" We conclude that the answer must be no. The [defendant's] crimes cannot be said to have reflected a consciousness materially more "depraved" than that of any person guilty of murder. His victims were killed instantaneously. They were members of his family who were causing him extreme emotional trauma. Shortly after the killings, he acknowledged his responsibility and the heinous nature of his crimes. These factors certainly did not remove the criminality from the [defendant]. But, as was said in [previous decisions], it "is of vital importance to the defendant and to the community that any decision to impose the death sentence be, and appear to be, based on reason rather than caprice or emotion."

> That cannot be said here. There is no principled way to distinguish this case, in which the death penalty was imposed, from the many cases in which it was not. Accordingly, the judgment of the Georgia Supreme Court insofar as it leaves standing the [defendant's] death sentences is reversed, and the case is remanded to that court for further proceedings.

Concurring opinion by Justice Marshall, in which Brennan, J., joined: Justice Marshall stated in his concurring opinion that he continued to believe that the death penalty was prohibited by the Constitution. He noted that he agreed "with the plurality that the Georgia Supreme Court's construction of the provision at issue in this case is unconstitutionally vague[.]" The opinion concluded that, even under the prevailing view that the death penalty may, in some circumstances, constitutionally be imposed, it is not enough for a reviewing court to apply a narrowing construction to otherwise ambiguous statutory language. It was necessary that the jury be instructed on the proper, narrow construction of the statute.

Dissenting opinion by Chief Justice Burger: The Chief Justice believed that the Court was wrong to substitute its opinion for that of the Georgia Supreme Court. He believed the jury properly understood the common sense meaning to give the statutory aggravating circumstance and that the State's highest court correctly found the evidence existed to sustain the jury's decision. The Chief Justice concluded: "In short, I am convinced that the course the plurality embarks on today is sadly mistaken — indeed confused. It is this Court's function to insure that the rights of a defendant are scrupulously respected; and in capital cases we must see to it that the jury has rendered its decision with meticulous care. But it is emphatically not our province to second-guess the jury's judgment or to tell the states which of their 'hideous,' intentional murderers may be given the ultimate penalty. Because the plurality does both, I dissent."

Dissenting opinion by Justice White, in which Rehnquist, J., joined: Justice White argued in his dissenting opinion that the jury was properly instructed on the statutory aggravating circumstance, and that the evidence supported the jury's verdict. He further believed that the Court's decision was "an unwarranted invasion into the realm of state law[.]" Ultimately, Justice White indicated that to the extent any error may have occurred in the case, it was not "a genuine error of constitutional magnitude[.]"

Godinez v. Moran *Court:* United States Supreme Court; *Case Citation:* Godinez v. Moran, 509 U.S. 389 (1993); *Argued:* April 21, 1993; *Decided:* June 24, 1993; *Opinion of the Court:* Justice Thomas; *Concurring Opinion:* Justice Kennedy, in which Scalia, J., joined; *Dissenting Opinion:* Justice Blackmun, in which Stevens, J., joined; *Appellate Defense Counsel:* Cal J. Potter III argued; Edward M. Chikofsky on brief; *Appellate Prosecution Counsel:* David F. Sarnowski argued; Frankie Sue Del Papa and Brooke A. Nielsen on brief; *Amicus Curiae Brief Supporting Prosecutor:* 2; *Amicus Curiae Brief Supporting Defendant:* 3.

Issue Presented: Whether the competency standard for pleading guilty or waiving the right to counsel is higher than the competency standard for standing trial?

Case Holding: The competency standard for pleading guilty or waiving the right to counsel is no higher than the competency standard for standing trial.

Factual and procedural background of case: The defendant, Richard Allan Moran, was charged with three counts of capital murder by the State of Nevada. Initially the defendant pleaded not guilty. However, he informed that trial court that he wanted to discharge his attorneys and plead guilty to all three counts of capital murder. The trial court permitted the defendant to discharge his attorneys and plead guilty to three counts of capital murder. The defendant was ultimately sentenced to death.

The defendant subsequently sought State post-conviction relief, alleging that he was mentally incompetent to represent himself. A post-conviction hearing was held by the trial court and it found (1) that the defendant understood the nature of the criminal charges against him and was able to assist in his defense; (2) that he knowingly and intelligently waived his right to the assistance of counsel; and (3) that his guilty pleas were freely and voluntarily given. The trial court denied post-conviction relief and the Nevada Supreme Court affirmed.

The defendant next filed a petition for habeas corpus in a Federal District Court, but the petition was dismissed. However, a Federal Court of Appeals reversed. The Court of Appeals held that due process required the State trial court hold a hearing to evaluate and determine the defendant's competency before it accepted his decisions to waive counsel and plead guilty. It also found that the post-conviction hearing did not cure the error, because the trial court's ruling was premised on the wrong legal standard. It was said by the Court of Appeals that competency to waive constitutional rights requires a higher level of mental functioning than that required to stand trial. The appellate court reasoned that, while a defendant is competent to stand trial if he or she has a rational and factual understanding of the proceedings and is capable of assisting counsel, he or she is competent to waive counsel or plead guilty only if he or she has the capacity for reasoned choice among the available alternatives. The United States Supreme Court granted certiorari to consider the issue.

Opinion of the Court by Justice Thomas: Justice Thomas rejected the reasoning of the Court of Appeals. He held that the competency standard for pleading guilty or waiving the right to counsel is the same as the competency standard for standing trial. That standard was said to be, whether the defendant has sufficient present ability to consult with his or her lawyer with a reasonable degree of rational understanding and a rational as well as factual understanding of the proceedings against him or her.

It was said by Justice Thomas that there was no reason for the competency standard for pleading guilty or waiving the right to counsel to be higher than that for standing trial. He reasoned that the decision to plead guilty, though profound, is no more complicated than the sum total of decisions that a defendant may have to make during the course of a trial, such as whether to testify, whether to waive a jury trial, and whether to cross examine the prosecution's witnesses. Justice Thomas wrote that the decision to waive counsel did not require an appreciably higher level of mental functioning than the decision to waive other constitutional rights.

The opinion concluded that requiring that a criminal defendant be competent has a modest aim of seeking to ensure that he or she has the capacity to understand the proceedings and to assist counsel. The judgment of the Court of Appeals was reversed.

Concurring opinion by Justice Kennedy, in which Scalia, J., joined: Justice Kennedy wrote a concurring opinion indicating his agreement with the Court's decision. His concurring opinion stated the following:

> I am in full agreement with the Court's decision that the competency standard for pleading guilty and waiving the right to counsel is the same as the test of competency to stand trial....
>
> The Due Process Clause does not mandate different standards of competency at various stages of or for different decisions made during the criminal proceedings. That was never the rule at common law, and it would take some extraordinary showing of the inadequacy of a single standard of competency for us to require States to employ heightened standards.

Dissenting opinion by Justice Blackmun, in which Stevens, J., joined: Justice Blackmun dissented from the Court's decision. He believed that the defendant's behavior justified imposition of a higher standard for proving competency to waive counsel and plead guilty. Justice Blackmun presented his position as follows:

> Today, the majority holds that a standard of competence designed to measure a defendant's ability to consult with counsel and to assist in preparing his defense is constitutionally adequate to assess a defendant's competence to waive the right to counsel and represent himself. In so doing, the majority upholds the death sentence for a person whose decision to discharge counsel, plead guilty, and present no defense well may have been the product of medication or mental illness. I believe the majority's analysis is contrary to both common sense and longstanding case law....
>
> ... [T]he standard for competence to stand trial is specifically designed to measure a defendant's ability to "consult with counsel" and to "assist in preparing his defense." A finding that a defendant is competent to stand trial establishes only that he is capable of aiding his attorney in making the critical decisions required at trial or in plea negotiations. The reliability or even relevance of such a finding vanishes when its basic premise—

that counsel will be present — ceases to exist. The question is no longer whether the defendant can proceed with an attorney, but whether he can proceed alone and uncounseled. I do not believe we place an excessive burden upon a trial court by requiring it to conduct a specific inquiry into that question at the juncture when a defendant whose competency already has been questioned seeks to waive counsel and represent himself....

The record in this case gives rise to grave doubts regarding ... Moran's ability to discharge counsel and represent himself. Just a few months after he attempted to commit suicide, Moran essentially volunteered himself for execution: He sought to waive the right to counsel, to plead guilty to capital murder, and to prevent the presentation of any mitigating evidence on his behalf. The psychiatrists' reports supplied one explanation for Moran's self-destructive behavior: his deep depression. And Moran's own testimony suggested another: the fact that he was being administered simultaneously four different prescription medications....

To try, convict, and punish one so helpless to defend himself contravenes fundamental principles of fairness and impugns the integrity of our criminal justice system. I cannot condone the decision to accept, without further inquiry, the self-destructive "choice" of a person who was so deeply medicated and who might well have been severely mentally ill. I dissent.

Case note: Nevada executed Richard Allan Moran by lethal injection on March 30, 1996. *See also* **Guilty Plea; Insanity; Right to Counsel**

Goldberg, Arthur J.

Arthur J. Goldberg served as an associate justice of the United States Supreme Court from 1962 to 1965. While on the Supreme Court Goldberg was known as a liberal interpreter of the Constitution, particularly with respect to individual liberties and rights.

Goldberg was born in Chicago, Illinois on August 8, 1908. He was a 1929 graduate of Northwestern University Law School. Much of Goldberg's private law practice was spent representing labor organizations. He was able to gain national prominence as a result of his representation of labor groups. President John F. Kennedy appointed Goldberg as Secretary of Labor in 1961. In 1962 President Kennedy filled a vacancy on the Supreme Court by appointing Goldberg to the position.

Goldberg is known to have written only two capital punishment opinions while on the Supreme Court. In *Townsend v. Sain*, Goldberg issued a concurring opinion that was largely an attack on the dissenting opinion in the case. In *Swain v. Alabama*, Goldberg issued a scathing dissenting opinion. In *Swain* the defendant contended that his capital conviction was invalid because African Americans were systematically excluded from the grand jury that indicted him and the petit jury that convicted him. The majority rejected the contention on the grounds that the defendant failed to present sufficient proof of discrimination. Goldberg dissented harshly: "I deplore the Court's departure from its [precedents]. By affirming [the defendant's] conviction on this clear record of jury exclusion because of race, the Court condones the highly discriminatory procedures used in Talladega County under which [blacks] never have served on any petit jury in that county. By adding to the present heavy burden of proof required of defendants in these cases, the Court creates additional barriers to the elim-

ination of practices which have operated in many communities throughout the Nation to nullify the command of the Equal Protection Clause in this important area in the administration of justice." Goldberg resigned from the Supreme Court in 1965 in order to accept an appointment as United States ambassador to the United Nations. He died on January 19, 1990.

Gooch v. United States

Court: United States Supreme Court; *Case Citation:* Gooch v. United States, 297 U.S. 124 (1936); *Argued:* January 13, 1936; *Decided:* February 3, 1936; *Opinion of the Court:* Justice McReynolds; *Concurring Opinion:* None; *Dissenting Opinion:* None; *Appellate Defense Counsel:* W. F. Rampendahl argued and briefed; *Appellate Prosecution Counsel:* Homer S. Cummings argued; Gordon Dean on brief; *Amicus Curiae Brief Supporting Prosecutor:* None; *Amicus Curiae Brief Supporting Defendant:* None.

Issue Presented: Whether the Federal kidnaping statute allowed a conviction and death sentence under it to be sustained, where the kidnapping was for the purpose of preventing the defendant's arrest only and no monetary value was contemplated?

Case Holding: The Federal kidnaping statute allowed a conviction and death sentence under it to be sustained, where the kidnapping was for the purpose of preventing the defendant's arrest only and no monetary value was contemplated.

Factual and procedural background of case: The defendant, Gooch, was convicted of kidnaping and sentenced to death by the United States. The defendant appealed to a Federal Court of Appeals. The Court of Appeals thereafter certified the following question to the United States Supreme Court: Is holding an officer to avoid arrest within the meaning of the phrase, "held for ransom or reward or otherwise," under the Federal kidnaping statute?

Opinion of the Court by Justice McReynolds: Justice McReynolds held that the certified question had to be answered in the affirmative. The opinion set out the language of the applicable statute as follows:

Whoever shall knowingly transport or cause to be transported, or aid or abet in transporting, in interstate or foreign commerce, any person who shall have been unlawfully seized, confined, inveigled, decoyed, kidnaped, abducted, or carried away by any means whatsoever and held for ransom or reward or otherwise, except, in the case of a minor, by a parent thereof, shall, upon conviction, be punished (1) by death if the verdict of the jury shall so recommend, provided that the sentence of death shall not be imposed by the court if, prior to its imposition, the kidnaped person has been liberated unharmed, or (2) if the death penalty shall not apply nor be imposed the convicted person shall be punished by imprisonment in the penitentiary for such term of years as the court in its discretion shall determine.

Justice McReynolds rejected the defendant's contention that under the statute the words "ransom or reward" require some kind of pecuniary consideration or payment of something of value. In rejecting the argument the opinion reasoned as follows:

Holding an officer to prevent the captor's arrest is something done with the expectation of benefit to the transgressor. So also is kidnaping with purpose to secure money. These benefits, while not the same, are similar in their general nature and the desire to secure either of them may lead to kidnaping. If the word "reward," as commonly understood, is not itself broad enough to include benefits expected to follow the prevention of an arrest, they fall within the broad term, "otherwise." The words "except, in the case of a minor, by a parent thereof" emphasize the intended result of the enactment. They indicate legislative understanding that in their absence a parent, who carried his child away because of affection, might subject himself to condemnation of the statute.

The opinion concluded that the conviction and sentence under the statute were validly maintained.

Case note: Under modern capital punishment jurisprudence the death penalty may not be imposed for the crime of kidnaping, without an accompanying homicide. *See also* **Certified Question**

Gourko v. United States

Court: United States Supreme Court; *Case Citation:* Gourko v. United States, 153 U.S. 183 (1894); *Argued:* Not reported; *Decided:* April 16, 1894; *Opinion of the Court:* Justice Harlan; *Concurring Opinion:* None; *Dissenting Opinion:* None; *Appellate Defense Counsel:* Not represented; *Appellate Prosecution Counsel:* Mr. Conrad argued and briefed; *Amicus Curiae Brief Supporting Prosecutor:* None; *Amicus Curiae Brief Supporting Defendant:* None.

Issue Presented: Whether the trial court properly instructed the jury on how to interpret evidence showing the defendant armed himself after an altercation with the victim?

Case Holding: The trial court did not properly instruct the jury on how to interpret evidence showing the defendant armed himself after an altercation with the victim, therefore the judgment against him could not stand.

Factual and procedural background of case: The defendant, John Gourko, was convicted of capital murder and sentenced to death by the United States. The defendant appealed to the United States Supreme Court, alleging that the trial court committed error in failing to properly instruct the jury that it could return a verdict of manslaughter if it found he armed himself for self-defense only. The United States Supreme Court granted certiorari to consider the issue.

Opinion of the Court by Justice Harlan: Justice Harlan ruled that the trial court improperly instructed the jury on how to interpret the evidence of the defendant arming himself after an altercation with the victim. The opinion explained as follows:

> Assuming, for the purposes of the present inquiry, that the defendant was not entitled to an acquittal as having acted in self-defense, the vital question was as to the effect to be given to the fact that he armed himself with a deadly weapon after the angry meeting with [the victim]
>
> If he armed himself for the purpose of pursuing his adversary, or with the intention of putting himself in the way of his adversary, so as to obtain an opportunity to kill him, then he was guilty of murder. But if ... the defendant had reasonable grounds to believe, and in fact believed, that the deceased intended to take his life, or to inflict upon him great bodily harm, and, so believing, armed himself solely for necessary self-defense

in the event of his being pursued and attacked, ... then the defendant's arming himself ... did not have, in itself, the effect to convert his crime into that of murder.... [T]he jury were not authorized to find him guilty of murder because of his having deliberately armed himself, provided he rightfully so armed himself for purposes simply of self-defense, and if, independently of the fact of arming himself, the case tested by what occurred on the occasion of the killing was one of manslaughter only.

The judgment of the trial court was reversed and the cause remanded for a new trial.

Graham, Jack Gilbert *see* **Flight 629; Mass Murder**

Graham v. Collins

Court: United States Supreme Court; *Case Citation:* Graham v. Collins, 506 U.S. 461 (1993); *Argued:* October 14, 1992; *Decided:* January 25, 1993; *Opinion of the Court:* Justice White; *Concurring Opinion:* Justice Thomas; *Dissenting Opinion:* Justice Stevens; *Dissenting Opinion:* Justice Souter, in which Blackmun, Stevens, and O'Connor, JJ., joined; *Appellate Defense Counsel:* Michael E. Tigar argued; Jeffrey J. Pokorak on brief; *Appellate Prosecution Counsel:* Charles A. Palmer argued; Dan Morales, William C. Zapalac, Will Pryor, Mary F. Keller and Michael P. Hodge on brief; *Amicus Curiae Brief Supporting Prosecutor:* None; *Amicus Curiae Brief Supporting Defendant:* 1.

Issue Presented: Whether under the Texas death penalty scheme, the jury that sentenced the defendant to death was able to give effect to mitigating evidence of youth, family background, and positive character traits?

Case Holding: Because the issue presented by the defendant was brought after his conviction became final, the merit of the claim could not be reached insofar as granting relief to him would require creation of a new constitutional rule.

Factual and procedural background of case: The State of Texas convicted the defendant, Gary Graham, of capital murder and sentenced him to death. After unsuccessfully seeking post-conviction relief in the Texas state courts, the defendant filed a petition for habeas corpus relief in a Federal District Court. In the petition the defendant alleged that the three "special issues" his sentencing jury was required to answer under the State capital sentencing statute prevented the jury from giving effect to mitigating evidence of his youth, unstable family background, and positive character traits. The District Court denied relief and dismissed the petition. A Federal Court of Appeals affirmed the dismissal. The United States Supreme Court granted certiorari to consider the issue.

Opinion of the Court by Justice White: Justice White ruled that the defendant's claim was barred because the relief he sought would require announcement of a new rule of constitutional law. It was said that under the Court's precedents, a capital defendant whose conviction has become final, may not obtain relief in a Federal court if to do so required creation of or application of a new constitutional rule. The opinion pointed out that two narrow exceptions have been carved out from the general prohibition against applying a new constitutional rule to convictions that have become final. Justice White stated that a new rule may be applied retroactively if it (1) placed an entire category of primary conduct beyond the reach of criminal law or prohibited imposition of a certain type of punishment for a class of defendants because of their status or offense; or (2) was a watershed rule of criminal procedure implicating a criminal proceeding's fundamental fairness and accuracy.

The opinion indicated that a rule is new if it was not dictated by precedent existing at the time the defendant's conviction became final. Thus, the determinative question posed by the defendant was whether reasonable jurists hearing his claim before his conviction became final would have felt compelled by existing precedent to rule in his favor. Justice White found that it could not be said that reasonable jurists hearing the defendant's claim before his conviction became final would have felt that existing precedent dictated vacatur of his death sentence. It was reasoned that before the defendant's conviction became final, the Court approved of Texas' death penalty scheme as being constitutionally valid in *Jurek v. Texas*. Additionally, other decisions by the Court had embraced the *Jurek* opinion as providing adequate grounds for defendants to present mitigating evidence. The opinion also concluded that the new rule that the defendant sought would not fall within either of the two exceptions to the bar against retroactive application. The judgment of the Court of Appeals was affirmed.

Concurring opinion by Justice Thomas: Justice Thomas concurred in the Court's decision. He wrote separately to argue against the defendant's reliance upon the Court's decision in *Penry v. Lynaugh*, as precedent that dictated the new rule he sought. Justice Thomas believed that *Penry* did not foreshadow the rule sought by the defendant and he contended that, even if *Penry* dictated the new rule sought, he "believe[d] *Penry* was wrongly decided." In Justice Thomas' opinion, the relief sought by the defendant and the decision in *Penry* created a risk that sentencing decisions would become arbitrary.

Dissenting opinion by Justice Stevens: Justice Stevens dissented from the Court's opinion. He believed that the merits of the defendant's claim should have been addressed and a new rule created to provide relief. Justice Stevens also expressed his disagreement with Justice Thomas' concurring opinion that *Penry* did not foreshadow the relief sought by the defendant and that *Penry* was wrongly decided. "More specifically," he wrote, "I do not see how permitting full consideration of a defendant's mental retardation and history of childhood abuse, as in *Penry*, or of a defendant's youth, as in this case, in any way increases the risk of ... arbitrary decisionmaking."

Dissenting opinion by Justice Souter, in which Blackmun, Stevens, and O'Connor, JJ., joined: Justice Souter dissented from the majority's decision. He believed that the relief sought by the defendant did not require creation of a new rule, and that the relief sought was consistent with the Court's decision in *Penry*. Justice Souter stated his position as follows:

In *Penry v. Lynaugh* we concluded that a [defendant] did not seek the benefit of a "new rule" in claiming that the Texas special issues did not permit the sentencing jury in his case to give full mitigating effect to certain mitigating evidence, and we therefore held that the retroactivity doctrine ... did not bar the claim. The only distinctions between the claim in *Penry* and those presented here go to the kind of mitigating evidence presented for the jury's consideration, and the distance by which the Texas scheme stops short of allowing full effect to be given to some of the evidence considered. Neither distinction makes a difference under *Penry* or the prior law on which *Penry* stands. Accordingly, I would find no bar to the present claims, and would reach their merits: whether the mitigating force of [the defendant's] youth, unfortunate background, and traits of decent character could be considered adequately by a jury instructed only on the three Texas special issues. I conclude they could not be, and I would reverse the sentence of death and remand for resentencing. From the Court's contrary judgment, I respectfully dissent.

See also **Retroactive Application of a New Constitutional Rule**

Grand Jury

Grand Jury Depending upon the requirements of a particular jurisdiction, capital murder is prosecuted by an indictment or an information. An indictment is an instrument that is drawn up by a grand jury.

The origin of the grand jury is traditionally traced back to England, during the reign of King Henry II. Legal scholars report that in the year 1166, King Henry II created an institution called the Assize of Clarendon. The assize consisted of 12 men who were given the duty of informing the local sheriff, or an itinerant justice of the peace, of any criminal conduct in their community. The assize operated in this fashion until the end of the 14th century.

The assize split into two separate institutions by the end of the 14th century. One institution was called the petit jury (trial jury) and the other was called *le grande inquest* or grand jury. At its inception the grand jury had two purposes: (1) prevent unjust prosecutions and (2) initiate just prosecutions.

The grand jury was incorporated into Anglo-American jurisprudence by the Colonists. During the early development of the nation, all jurisdictions required felony prosecutions be initiated by the grand jury. The document used by the grand jury to initiate a prosecution was called an indictment. The grand jury may issue an indictment against a person only if it finds (1) probable cause existed that a crime was committed, and (2) probable cause that a named person committed the crime.

As a result of a decision by the United States Supreme Court in *Hurtado v. California*, 110 U.S. 516 (1884), which held that the Federal Constitution did not impose the use of grand juries on States, only a minority of jurisdictions now require felony offenses be prosecuted by a grand jury indictment.

The procedures involved with grand juries and indictments are generally consistent with that provided under the Federal Rules of Criminal Procedure. The federal requirements for grand juries and indictments are set out below.

Federal Grand Jury Requirements:

a. Summoning Grand Juries

    1. Generally. The court shall order one or more grand juries to be summoned at such time as the public interest requires. The grand jury shall consist of not less than 16 nor more than 23 members. The court shall direct that a sufficient number of legally qualified persons be summoned to meet this requirement.

    2. Alternate Jurors. The court may direct that alternate jurors may be designated at the time a grand jury is selected. Alternate jurors in the order in which they were designated may thereafter be impanelled as provided in this rule. Alternate jurors shall be drawn in the same manner and shall have the same qualifications as the regular jurors, and if impanelled shall be subject to the same challenges, shall take the same oath and shall have the same functions, powers, facilities and privileges as the regular jurors.

b. Objections to Grand Jury and to Grand Jurors

    1. Challenges. The attorney for the government or a defendant who has been held to answer in the district court may challenge the array of jurors on the ground that the grand jury was not selected, drawn or summoned in accordance with law, and may challenge an individual juror on the ground that the juror is not legally qualified. Challenges shall be made before the administration of the oath to the jurors and shall be tried by the court.

    2. Motion to Dismiss. A motion to dismiss the indictment may be based on objections to the array or on the lack of legal qualification of an individual juror, if not previously determined upon challenge. It shall be made in the manner prescribed by statute and shall be granted under the conditions prescribed in that statute. An indictment shall not be dismissed on the ground that one or more members of the grand jury were not legally qualified if it appears from the record kept that 12 or more jurors, after deducting the number not legally qualified, concurred in finding the indictment.

c. Foreperson and Deputy Foreperson. The court shall appoint one of the jurors to be foreperson and another to be deputy foreperson. The foreperson shall have power to administer oaths and affirmations and shall sign all indictments. The foreperson or another juror designated by the foreperson shall keep a record of the number of jurors concurring in the finding of every indictment and shall file the record with the clerk of the court, but the record shall not be made public except on order of the court. During the absence of the foreperson, the deputy foreperson shall act as foreperson.

d. Who May Be Present. Attorneys for the government, the witness under examination, interpreters when needed and, for the purpose of taking the evidence, a stenographer or operator of a recording device may be present while the grand jury is in session, but no person other than the jurors may be present while the grand jury is deliberating or voting.

e. Recording and Disclosure of Proceedings.

    1. Recording of Proceedings. All proceedings, except when the grand jury is deliberating or voting, shall be recorded stenographically or by an electronic recording device. An unintentional failure of any recording to reproduce all or any portion of a proceeding shall not affect the validity of the prosecution. The recording or reporter's notes or any transcript prepared therefrom shall remain in the custody or control of the attorney for the government unless otherwise ordered by the court in a particular case.

    2. General Rule of Secrecy. A grand juror, an interpreter, a stenographer, an operator of a recording device, a typist who transcribes recorded testimony, an attorney for the government, or any person to whom disclosure is made under this subdivision shall not disclose matters occurring before the grand jury, except as otherwise provided for in these rules. No obligation of secrecy may be imposed on any person except in accordance with this rule. A knowing violation of this rule may be punished as a contempt of court.

    3. Exceptions.

A. Disclosure otherwise prohibited by this rule of matters occurring before the grand jury, other than its deliberations and the vote of any grand juror, may be made to —

    i. an attorney for the government for use in the performance of such attorney's duty; and

    ii. such government personnel (including personnel of a state or subdivision of a state) as are deemed necessary by an attorney for the government to assist an attorney for the government in the performance of such attorney's duty to enforce federal criminal law.

B. Any person to whom matters are disclosed under this paragraph shall not utilize that grand jury material for any purpose other than assisting the attorney for the government in the performance of such attorney's duty to enforce federal criminal law. An attorney for the government shall promptly provide the district court, before which was impaneled the grand jury whose material has been so disclosed, with the names of the persons to whom such disclosure has been made, and shall certify that the attorney has advised such persons of their obligation of secrecy under this rule.

C. Disclosure otherwise prohibited by this rule of matters occurring before the grand jury may also be made —

    i. when so directed by a court preliminarily to or in connection with a judicial proceeding;

    ii. when permitted by a court at the request of the defendant, upon a showing that grounds may exist for a motion to dismiss the indictment because of matters occurring before the grand jury;

    iii. when the disclosure is made by an attorney for the government to another federal grand jury; or

iv. when permitted by a court at the request of an attorney for the government, upon a showing that such matters may disclose a violation of state criminal law, to an appropriate official of a state or subdivision of a state for the purpose of enforcing such law.

If the court orders disclosure of matters occurring before the grand jury, the disclosure shall be made in such manner, at such time, and under such conditions as the court may direct.

D. A petition for disclosure shall be filed in the district where the grand jury convened. Unless the hearing is ex parte, which it may be when the petitioner is the government, the petitioner shall serve written notice of the petition upon (i) the attorney for the government, (ii) the parties to the judicial proceeding if disclosure is sought in connection with such a proceeding, and (iii) such other persons as the court may direct. The court shall afford those persons a reasonable opportunity to appear and be heard.

E. If the judicial proceeding giving rise to the petition is in a federal district court in another district, the court shall transfer the matter to that court unless it can reasonably obtain sufficient knowledge of the proceeding to determine whether disclosure is proper. The court shall order transmitted to the court to which the matter is transferred the material sought to be disclosed, if feasible, and a written evaluation of the need for continued grand jury secrecy. The court to which the matter is transferred shall afford the aforementioned persons a reasonable opportunity to appear and be heard.

4. Sealed Indictments. The federal magistrate judge to whom an indictment is returned may direct that the indictment be kept secret until the defendant is in custody or has been released pending trial. Thereupon the clerk shall seal the indictment and no person shall disclose the return of the indictment except when necessary for the issuance and execution of a warrant or summons.

5. Closed Hearing. Subject to any right to an open hearing in contempt proceedings, the court shall order a hearing on matters affecting a grand jury proceeding to be closed to the extent necessary to prevent disclosure of matters occurring before a grand jury.

6. Sealed Records. Records, orders and subpoenas relating to grand jury proceedings shall be kept under seal to the extent and for such time as is necessary to prevent disclosure of matters occurring before a grand jury.

f. Finding and Return of Indictment. An indictment may be found only upon the concurrence of 12 or more jurors. The indictment shall be returned by the grand jury to a federal magistrate judge in open court. If a complaint or information is pending against the defendant and 12 jurors do not concur in finding an indictment, the foreperson shall so report to a federal magistrate judge in writing forthwith.

g. Discharge and Excuse. A grand jury shall serve until discharged by the court, but no grand jury may serve more than 18 months unless the court extends the service of the grand jury for a period of six months or less upon a determination that such extension is in the public interest. At any time for cause shown the court may excuse a juror either temporarily or permanently, and in the latter event the court may impanel another person in place of the juror excused.

Federal Indictment Requirements:

a. Use of Indictment. An offense which may be punished by death shall be prosecuted by indictment. An offense which may be punished by imprisonment for a term exceeding one year or at hard labor shall be prosecuted by indictment or, if indictment is waived, it may be prosecuted by information. Any other offense may be prosecuted by indictment or by information.

b. Waiver of Indictment. An offense which may be punished by imprisonment for a term exceeding one year or at hard labor may be prosecuted by information if the defendant, after having been advised of the nature of the charge and of the rights of the defendant, waives in open court prosecution by indictment.

c. Nature and Contents.

1. In General. The indictment shall be a plain, concise and definite written statement of the essential facts constituting the offense charged. It shall be signed by the attorney for the government. It need not contain a formal commencement, a formal conclusion or any other matter not necessary to such statement. Allegations made in one count may be incorporated by reference in another count. It may be alleged in a single count that the means by which the defendant committed the offense are unknown or that the defendant committed it by one or more specified means. The indictment shall state for each count the official or customary citation of the statute, rule, regulation or other provision of law which the defendant is alleged therein to have violated.

2. Criminal Forfeiture. No judgment of forfeiture may be entered in a criminal proceeding unless the indictment shall allege the extent of the interest or property subject to forfeiture.

3. Harmless Error. Error in the citation or its omission shall not be ground for dismissal of the indictment or for reversal of a conviction if the error or omission did not mislead the defendant to the defendant's prejudice.

d. Surplusage. The court on motion of the defendant may strike surplusage from the indictment. *See also* **Hurtado v. California; Prosecution by Information**

Gray, Horace Horace Gray served as an associate justice of the United States Supreme Court from 1881 to 1902. While on the Supreme Court Gray was known as a conservative interpreter of the Constitution who relied more on precedent, rather than creating groundbreaking new constitutional law.

Gray was born on March 24, 1828 in Boston, Massachusetts. He was educated at Harvard College and received a law degree from Harvard Law School in 1849. Gray spent several years in private practice before receiving an appointment to Massachusetts' Supreme Judicial Court in 1864. President Chester A. Arthur nominated Gray to the Supreme Court in 1881.

While on the Supreme Court Gray issued a few capital punishment opinions. His opinions in this area typified his conservative approach to the law. For example, in *Jones v. United States (I)* the Supreme Court was asked to determine whether the Federal government had authority to prosecute a murder offense that occurred on the Caribbean island of Navassa. Gray, writing for the Court, relied on precedent rather than establishing new law in order to affirm the Federal government's authority over the offense. Similarly in *Ball v. United States (II)* Gray stuck close to precedent in ruling that one of the defendants in the case could not be reprosecuted for murder because he had been acquitted in a former trial. He also relied on precedent in *Ball* to rule that the remaining defendants could be reprosecuted for murder because their former convictions were reversed on appeal. Ultimately Gray's conservative approach earned him the reputation of being the forgotten Supreme Court justice. Gray died on September 15, 1902.

Capital Punishment Opinions Written by Gray

Case Name	Opinion of the Court	Concurring and Dissenting
Ball v. United States (II)	✓	
Carter v. Texas	✓	
Hopt v. Utah (I)	✓	
Hopt v. Utah (III)	✓	
Jones v. United States (I)	✓	
Sparf v. United States		✓
Winston v. United States	✓	

Gray v. Mississippi

Court: United States Supreme Court; *Case Citation:* Gray v. Mississippi, 481 U.S. 648 (1987); *Argued:* November 12, 1986; *Decided:* May 18, 1987; *Opinion of the Court:* Justice Blackmun; *Concurring Opinion:* Justice Powell; *Dissenting Opinion:* Justice Scalia, in which Rehnquist, C. J., and White and O'Connor, JJ., joined; *Appellate Defense Counsel:* Andru H. Volinsky argued and briefed; *Appellate Prosecution Counsel:* Marvin L. White, Jr. argued; Edwin Lloyd Pittman and Amy D. Whitten on brief; *Amicus Curiae Brief Supporting Prosecutor:* 1; *Amicus Curiae Brief Supporting Defendant:* None.

Issue Presented: Whether exclusion of a potential juror for cause violated *Witherspoon v. Illinois* and its progeny?

Case Holding: The exclusion of the potential juror for cause violated *Witherspoon v. Illinois* and its progeny.

Factual and procedural background of case: The defendant, David Randolph Gray, was charged with capital murder by the State of Mississippi. During jury selection the trial judge, in eight instances, denied the prosecutor's motions to dismiss for cause venire members who expressed some degree

of doubt about the death penalty. The prosecutor used peremptory challenges to remove those eight panel members. When a ninth venire member, although initially somewhat confused in her response, stated that she could reach a guilty verdict and vote to impose the death penalty, the trial judge nevertheless excused her for cause on the motion of the prosecutor. The defendant was ultimately convicted by a jury and a sentence of death was imposed.

The Mississippi Supreme Court affirmed the defendant's conviction and death sentence. In doing so, the appellate court acknowledged that the juror excluded for cause was clearly qualified to be a juror, but concluded that her exclusion was harmless error that did not prejudice the defendant. The United States Supreme Court granted certiorari to consider the issue.

Opinion of the Court by Justice Blackmun: Justice Blackmun ruled that under the Court's decision in *Witherspoon v. Illinois* and its progeny the trial court was not authorized to exclude the juror for cause. It was said that a *Witherspoon* a violation constituted reversible constitutional error, and could not be subjected to harmless error review. Justice Blackmun rejected the Mississippi Supreme Court's attempt to find harmless error in the trial court's actions. He reasoned that the nature of the jury selection process defied any attempt to establish that an erroneous *Witherspoon* exclusion was harmless. The judgment of the Mississippi Supreme Court was reversed insofar as the death sentence.

Concurring opinion by Justice Powell: Justice Powell joined most of the Court's opinion and with its judgment. He agreed that the trial court erred in removing the juror for cause. He believed that the exclusion of the other jurors by means of peremptory challenges did not exacerbate the prejudice created by the trial court's erroneous exclusion the juror for cause. Justice Powell indicated that *Witherspoon* and its progeny did not restrict the traditional rights of prosecutors to remove peremptorily jurors believed to be unwilling to impose lawful punishment.

Dissenting opinion by Justice Scalia, in which Rehnquist, C. J., and White and O'Connor, JJ., joined: Justice Scalia dissented from the Court's judgment. He wrote: "The Court holds that [the defendant's] sentence must be vacated because [a juror] was improperly excluded for cause from the sentencing jury. I dissent because it is clear that she should in any event have been excluded on other grounds. The trial judge's error, if any, consisted of no more than giving the wrong reason for lawful action — which could not conceivably have affected the fairness of the sentence." *See also* **Jury Selection; Witherspoon v. Illinois**

Gray v. Netherland

Court: United States Supreme Court; *Case Citation:* Gray v. Netherland, 518 U.S. 152 (1996); *Argued:* April 15, 1996; *Decided:* June 20, 1996; *Opinion of the Court:* Chief Justice Rehnquist; *Concurring Opinion:* None; *Dissenting Opinion:* Justice Stevens; *Dissenting Opinion:* Justice Ginsburg, in which Stevens, Souter and Breyer, JJ., joined;

Appellate Defense Counsel: Not reported; *Appellate Prosecution Counsel:* Not reported; *Amicus Curiae Brief Supporting Prosecutor:* Not reported; *Amicus Curiae Brief Supporting Defendant:* Not reported.

Issue Presented: Whether creation of a requirement obligating prosecutors to give adequate notice of penalty phase evidence of uncharged crimes constitutes a new constitutional rule?

Case Holding: Creation of a requirement obligating prosecutors to give adequate notice of penalty phase evidence of uncharged crimes constitutes a new constitutional rule, and therefore may not be created and applied in the defendant's case.

Factual and procedural background of case: The defendant, Coleman Wayne Gray, was convicted of capital murder by the State of Virginia. During the penalty phase the defendant objected to the introduction of evidence by the prosecutor which linked the defendant to two other uncharged murders. The trial court permitted the evidence to be introduced. The jury sentenced the defendant to death. After exhausting his State post-conviction remedies unsuccessfully, the defendant filed a habeas corpus petition in a Federal District Court. In the petition the defendant alleged that the trial court committed error in allowing the prosecutor to introduce evidence of uncharged murders at the penalty phase, because he had inadequate notice about the evidence and that misrepresentations by the prosecutor mislead him about the evidence the prosecutor intended to present. The District Court granted habeas relief on the grounds that the defendant was denied due process when the prosecutor failed to provide adequate notice of the evidence concerning uncharged murders. A Federal Court of Appeals reversed the decision, after concluding that granting habeas relief would give the defendant the benefit of a new rule of Federal constitutional law, in violation of the non-retroactivity doctrine. The United States Supreme Court granted certiorari to consider the issue.

Opinion of the Court by Chief Justice Rehnquist: The Chief Justice ruled that recognition of the defendant's notice of evidence claim would require the adoption of a new constitutional rule, that would set guidelines for giving fair notice of penalty phase evidence. It was said that under the non-retroactivity doctrine, a defendant whose conviction had become final may not use a subsequently created constitutional rule to attack the conviction in a Federal habeas corpus proceeding, unless the new rule was foreshadowed by a prior decision of the Court. This prohibition also applied to preclude the creation of a new rule in a case actually being decided by the Court. The Chief Justice pointed out that two narrow exceptions were carved out from the general prohibition against applying a new constitutional rule to convictions that have become final. It was said that a new rule may be applied retroactively if it: (1) placed an entire category of primary conduct beyond the reach of criminal law or prohibited imposition of a certain type of punishment for a class of defendants because of their status or offense; or (2) was a watershed rule of criminal procedure implicating a criminal proceeding's fundamental fairness and accuracy.

The opinion held that none of the Court's prior decisions foreshadowed the rule which the defendant sought. It was also said that the requested new rule did not fall within either of the two exceptions to the non-retroactivity doctrine. However, the Court found that the defendant presented an adequate claim of being mislead by the prosecutor. The opinion therefore reversed the judgment of the Court of Appeals and remanded the case for consideration of the defendant's misrepresentation claim.

Dissenting opinion by Justice Stevens: Justice Stevens dissented from the Court's opinion. He argued that due process required the defendant be given adequate notice of the prosecutor's intent to introduce penalty phase evidence of uncharged crimes. Justice Stevens wrote: "The evidence tending to support the proposition that [the defendant] committed the [other] murders was not even sufficient to support the filing of charges against him. Whatever limits due process places upon the introduction of evidence of unadjudicated conduct in capital cases, they surely were exceeded here. Given the 'vital importance' that 'any decision to impose the death sentence be, and appear to be, based on reason rather than caprice or emotion', the sentencing proceeding would have been fundamentally unfair even if the prosecutors had given defense counsel fair notice of their intent to offer this evidence."

Dissenting opinion by Justice Ginsburg, in which Stevens, Souter and Breyer, JJ., joined: Justice Ginsburg dissented from the Court's decision. She believed that the rule sought by the defendant was not a new rule. Justice Ginsburg argued as follows:

> Basic to due process in criminal proceedings is the right to a full, fair, potentially effective opportunity to defend against the State's charges.... Gray was not accorded that fundamental right at the penalty phase of his trial for capital murder. I therefore conclude that no "new rule" is implicated in his petition for habeas corpus....
>
> There is nothing "new" in a rule that capital defendants must be afforded a meaningful opportunity to defend against the State's penalty phase evidence. As this Court affirmed more than a century ago: "Common justice requires that no man shall be condemned in his person or property without ... an opportunity to make his defence."
>
> ... I conclude that the District Court's decision vacating Gray's death sentence did not rest on a "new rule" of constitutional law. I would therefore reverse the judgment of the Court of Appeals, and respectfully dissent from this Court's decision.

Case note: Coleman Wayne Gray was executed by lethal injection on February 26, 1997, by the State of Virginia. *See also* **Retroactive Application of a New Constitutional Rule**

The Great Hanging
In 1862 Gainesville, Texas and its surrounding towns were the site of 42 hangings that were carried out by the confederate government of Texas. The defendants were convicted of treason and insurrection for alleged allegiance to Union forces. Legal historians have written that

most of the defendants hung were in fact innocent of the abolitionist sentiments for which they were prosecuted.

The Great Hanging, as it was later called, resulted from several years of building tension between those who enslaved blacks and those who were against the practice. As a result of a steady migration of people into the northern part of Texas, by 1860 less than 10 percent of the population owned slaves. Consequently many of the northern counties of Texas voted against secession from the Union. The anti-secession vote brought fear to slave owners. This fear reached a climax when certain individuals attempted to make the northern Texas area a new free State.

By September of 1862 rumors circulated that a Unionist plot was underway to seize the militia arsenals at Gainesville. In response, confederate authorities ordered the arrest of all able-bodied men who were not enlisted in the confederate military. More than 150 men were arrested on the morning of October 1. A "citizen's court" was convened to try the men on insurrection or treason charges. Initially seven men were convicted and hanged. Afterwards a decision was made to release the other prisoners. However, after two leading rebel figures were assassinated, the trials were started anew. Nineteen more men were convicted and hanged in Gainesville. Sixteen men were tried and hung in the surrounding towns of Sherman and Decatur.

Great Risk to Others Aggravator

The statutory aggravating circumstance called "great risk to others" seeks to punish with death those who, while committing murder, expose other persons to death or great bodily harm. To establish the great risk to others aggravator, the prosecutor must show that the capital felon created a grave risk of death to another person, in addition to the victim of the offense. The other person or persons need not suffer actual harm. If these circumstances are established at the penalty phase, the jury may impose death on the defendant. A majority of capital punishment jurisdictions use this aggravator. *See also* **Aggravating Circumstances**

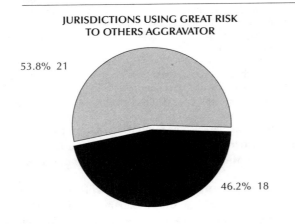

JURISDICTIONS USING GREAT RISK
TO OTHERS AGGRAVATOR

53.8% 21

46.2% 18

■ GREAT RISK TO OTHERS AGGRAVATOR JURISDICTIONS
■ ALL OTHER JURISDICTIONS

Greece   The death penalty was abolished in Greece in 1993. *See also* **International Capital Punishment Nations**

Green v. Georgia   *Court:* United States Supreme Court; *Case Citation:* Green v. Georgia, 442 U.S. 95 (1979); *Argued:* Not reported; *Decided:* May 29, 1979; *Opinion of the Court:* Per Curiam; *Concurring Statement:* Justice Brennan and Marshall, J.; *Dissenting Opinion:* Justice Rehnquist; *Appellate Defense Counsel:* Not reported; *Appellate Prosecution Counsel:* Not reported; *Amicus Curiae Brief Supporting Prosecutor:* Not reported; *Amicus Curiae Brief Supporting Defendant:* Not reported.

Issue Presented: Whether the Constitution prohibited Georgia from using its hearsay rules to preclude a defense witness' testimony at the penalty phase of the defendant's capital trial?

Case Holding: The Constitution prohibited Georgia from using its hearsay rules to preclude a defense witness' testimony at the penalty phase of the defendant's capital trial.

Factual and procedural background of case: The State of Georgia charged the defendant, Green, and a co-defendant with rape and murder. They were prosecuted separately. The defendant was found guilty of capital murder. During the penalty phase of the defendant's trial, he sought to introduce testimony from a witness who was going to state that the co-defendant admitted sole responsibility for killing the victim. The trial court refused to admit the testimony, ruling that it constituted inadmissible hearsay under Georgia law. The defendant was sentenced to death. The Georgia Supreme Court upheld the conviction and sentence, after rejecting the defendant's claim that he had a constitutional right to introduce the witness' testimony at the penalty phase. The United States Supreme Court granted certiorari to consider the issue.

Opinion of the Court was delivered Per Curiam: The per curiam opinion of the Court held that the defendant's constitutional rights were violated by the exclusion of the witness' testimony. The opinion reasoned:

Regardless of whether the proffered testimony comes within Georgia's hearsay rule, under the facts of this case its exclusion constituted a violation of the Due Process Clause of the Fourteenth Amendment. The excluded testimony was highly relevant to a critical issue in the punishment phase of the trial, and substantial reasons existed to assume its reliability. [The co-defendant] made his statement spontaneously to a close friend. The evidence corroborating the confession was ample, and indeed sufficient to procure a conviction of [the co-defendant] and a capital sentence. The statement was against interest, and there was no reason to believe that [the co-defendant] had any ulterior motive in making it. Perhaps most important, the State considered the testimony sufficiently reliable to use it against [the co-defendant], and to base a sentence of death upon it. In these unique circumstances, "the hearsay rule may not be applied mechanistically to defeat the ends of justice." Because the exclusion of [the witness'] testimony denied [the defendant] a fair trial on the issue of punishment, the sentence is vacated and the case is remanded for further proceedings not inconsistent with this opinion.

Concurring Statement by Justice Brennan and Marshall, J.: Justices Brennan and Marshall issued a joint statement concurring in the judgment, and indicating that they continue to "adher[e] to their view that the death penalty is in all circumstances cruel and unusual punishment prohibited by the Eighth and Fourteenth Amendments, would vacate the death sentence without remanding for further proceedings."

Dissenting opinion by Justice Rehnquist: Justice Rehnquist was strongly opposed to the Court's use of the Constitution to undermine the hearsay rules of Georgia. The dissenting opinion stated his position as follows:

> The Court today takes another step toward embalming the law of evidence in the Due Process Clause of the Fourteenth Amendment to the United States Constitution. I think it impossible to find any justification in the Constitution for today's ruling, and take comfort only from the fact that since this is a capital case, it is perhaps an example of the maxim that "hard cases make bad law."...
>
> Nothing in the United States Constitution gives this Court any authority to supersede a State's code of evidence because its application in a particular situation would defeat what this Court conceives to be "the ends of justice." The Court does not disagree that the testimony at issue is hearsay or that it fails to come within any of the exceptions to the hearsay rule provided by Georgia's rules of evidence. The Court obviously is troubled by the fact that the same testimony was admissible at the separate trial of [the defendant's] codefendant at the behest of the State. But this fact by no means demonstrates that the Georgia courts have not evenhandedly applied their code of evidence, with its various hearsay exceptions, so as to deny [the defendant] a fair trial. No practicing lawyer can have failed to note that Georgia's evidentiary rules, like those of every other State and of the United States, are such that certain items of evidence may be introduced by one party, but not by another. This is a fact of trial life, embodied throughout the hearsay rule and its exceptions. This being the case, the United States Constitution must be strained to or beyond the breaking point to conclude that all capital defendants who are unable to introduce all of the evidence which they seek to admit are denied a fair trial. I therefore dissent from the vacation of [the defendant's] sentence. *See also* **Hearsay; Hearsay Exceptions**

Green v. United States

Court: United States Supreme Court; *Case Citation:* Green v. United States, 355 U.S. 184 (1957); *Argued:* April 25, 1957; reargued October 15, 1957; *Decided:* December 16, 1957; *Opinion of the Court:* Justice Black; *Concurring Opinion:* None; *Dissenting Opinion:* Justice Frankfurter, in which Burton, Clark Harlan, JJ., joined; *Appellate Defense Counsel:* George Blow and George Rublee, II argued; Charles E. Ford on brief; *Appellate Prosecution Counsel:* Leonard B. Sand argued; Beatrice Rosenberg and Carl H. Imlay on brief; *Amicus Curiae Brief Supporting Prosecutor:* None; *Amicus Curiae Brief Supporting Defendant:* None.

Issue Presented: Whether the defendant's conviction for capital murder, on retrial from the reversal of his first conviction, violated double jeopardy principles because he was convicted of second degree murder in his first trial?

Case Holding: The defendant's conviction for capital murder, on retrial from the reversal of his first conviction, violated double jeopardy principles because he was convicted of second degree murder in his first trial.

Factual and procedural background of case: The defen-

dant, Everett Green, was indicted and tried for capital murder by the District of Columbia. The jury found him guilty of second degree murder and he was sentenced to imprisonment. On appeal, his conviction was reversed and the case was remanded for a new trial. On remand, the defendant was tried again for capital murder under the original indictment. He was convicted of capital murder and sentenced to death. The District of Columbia Court of Appeals affirmed the conviction and sentence. In doing so, the appellate court rejected the defendants contention the double jeopardy principles barred a conviction for capital murder. The United States Supreme Court granted certiorari to consider the issue.

Opinion of the Court by Justice Black: Justice Black ruled that the defendant's second trial for capital murder placed him in jeopardy twice for the same offense in violation of the Fifth Amendment. It was said that the defendant's jeopardy for the capital murder charge came to an end when the jury was discharged at the conclusion of his first trial, and he could not be retried for that offense. Justice Black reasoned that by making a successful appeal from his conviction of second degree murder, the defendant did not waive his constitutional defense of former jeopardy to a second prosecution on the capital murder charge. Further, he wrote that in order to secure the reversal of an erroneous conviction of one offense, a defendant need not surrender his or her valid defense of former jeopardy on a different offense for which he or she was not convicted and which was not involved in the appeal. Justice Black set out the contours of the legal justification for double jeopardy as follows:

> The underlying idea, one that is deeply ingrained in at least the Anglo-American system of jurisprudence, is that the State with all its resources and power should not be allowed to make repeated attempts to convict an individual for an alleged offense, thereby subjecting him to embarrassment, expense and ordeal and compelling him to live in a continuing state of anxiety and insecurity, as well as enhancing the possibility that even though innocent he may be found guilty. In accordance with this philosophy it has long been settled under the Fifth Amendment that a verdict of acquittal is final, ending a defendant's jeopardy, and even when "not followed by any judgment, is a bar to a subsequent prosecution for the same offence." Thus it is one of the elemental principles of our criminal law that the Government cannot secure a new trial by means of an appeal even though an acquittal may appear to be erroneous. Moreover it is not even essential that a verdict of guilt or innocence be returned for a defendant to have once been placed in jeopardy so as to bar a second trial on the same charge. This Court, as well as most others, has taken the position that a defendant is placed in jeopardy once he is put to trial before a jury so that if the jury is discharged without his consent he cannot be tried again. This prevents a prosecutor or judge from subjecting a defendant to a second prosecution by discontinuing the trial when it appears that the jury might not convict. At the same time jeopardy is not regarded as having come to an end so as to bar a second trial in those cases where "unforeseeable circumstances ... arise during [the first] trial making its completion impossible, such as the failure of a jury to agree on a verdict."

The judgment of the Court of Appeals was reversed.

Dissenting opinion by Justice Frankfurter, in which Burton, Clark Harlan, JJ., joined: Justice Frankfurter dissented from the Court's decision. He believed that when the defendant appealed his second degree murder conviction, and obtained a reversal, the defendant was subject to reprosecution on the original capital murder charge. Justice Frankfurter wrote: "Since the propriety of the original proceedings has been called in question by the defendant, a complete re-examination of the issues in dispute is appropriate and not unjust. In the circumstances of the present case, likewise, the reversal of [the defendant's] conviction was a sufficient reason to justify a complete new trial in order that both parties might have one free from errors claimed to be prejudicial." *See also* **Double Jeopardy Clause**

Gregg v. Georgia *Court:* United States Supreme Court; *Case Citation:* Gregg v. Georgia, 428 U.S. 153 (1976); *Argued:* March 31, 1976; *Decided:* July 2, 1976; *Plurality Opinion:* Justice Stewart announced the Court's judgment and delivered an opinion, in which Powell, and Stevens, JJ., joined; *Concurring Opinion:* Justice White, in which Burger, C. J., and Rehnquist, J., joined; *Concurring Statement:* Chief Justice Burger and Rehnquist, J.; *Concurring Statement:* Blackmun; *Dissenting Opinion:* Justice Brennan; *Dissenting Opinion:* Justice Marshall; *Appellate Defense Counsel:* G. Hughel Harrison argued and briefed; *Appellate Prosecution Counsel:* G. Thomas Davis argued; Arthur K. Bolton, Robert S. Stubbs II, Richard L. Chambers, John B. Ballard, Jr., and Bryant Huff on brief; *Amicus Curiae Brief Supporting Prosecutor:* 2; *Amicus Curiae Brief Supporting Defendant:* 2.

Issue Presented: Whether the imposition of the sentence of death for the crime of murder under the law of Georgia violates the Constitution?

Case Holding: The statutory capital punishment system of Georgia does not violate the Constitution.

Factual and procedural background of case: The defendant, Troy Gregg, was charged with committing capital murder on November 21, 1973, by the State of Georgia. The death penalty statute of Georgia required the defendant be prosecuted under a bifurcated procedure. The bifurcated procedure consisted of a guilt phase and a penalty phase. The death penalty statute also provided for a narrow category of crimes for which capital punishment could be prosecuted, and it listed aggravating and mitigating circumstances. The punishment of death under the statute could only be imposed if at least one of the statutory aggravating circumstances was proven to exist in the commission of the crime. It was also provided by the statute that upon conviction and sentence of death, the death sentence was automatically reviewed by the Georgia Supreme Court.

The defendant was convicted by a jury of capital murder at the guilt phase. At the penalty phase the jury found two statutory aggravating circumstances existed in the commission of the crime and returned a sentence of death. The Georgia Supreme Court affirmed the conviction and sentence of death. The United States Supreme Court granted certiorari to consider the constitutionality of Georgia's death penalty statute.

Plurality opinion in which Justice Stewart announced the Court's judgment and in which Powell and Stevens JJ., joined: Justice Stewart held that, as a general matter, the punishment of death for the crime of murder does not, under all circumstances, violate the Constitution. He indicated that the Eighth Amendment forbids the use of punishment that is excessive either because it involves the unnecessary and wanton infliction of pain, or because it is grossly disproportionate to the severity of the crime. It was noted that the existence of capital punishment was accepted by the Framers of the Constitution, and for nearly two centuries the Court recognized that capital punishment for the crime of murder is not invalid per se.

The opinion stated that retribution and the possibility of deterrence of capital crimes by prospective offenders are not impermissible considerations for a legislature to weigh in deciding whether the death penalty should be imposed. Justice Stewart wrote that capital punishment for the crime of murder cannot be viewed as invariably disproportionate to the severity of that crime.

It was said that the concerns expressed in *Furman v. Georgia*, that the death penalty not be imposed arbitrarily or capriciously, could be met by a carefully drafted statute that ensures that the sentencing authority is given adequate information and guidance, concerns which could best met by a system that provides for a bifurcated proceeding at which the sentencing authority is apprised of the information relevant to the imposition of sentence and provided with standards to guide its use of that information. Justice Stewart indicated that the Georgia death penalty statute under which the defendant was sentenced to death passed constitutional muster, because it provides for specific jury findings as to the circumstances of the crime or the character of the defendant, and requires the Georgia Supreme Court review the comparability of each death sentence with the sentences imposed on similarly situated defendants to ensure that the sentence of death in a particular case is not disproportionate. Accordingly, the judgment of the Georgia Supreme Court was affirmed.

Concurring opinion by Justice White, in which Burger, C. J., and Rehnquist, J., joined: In concurring in the Court's judgment, Justice White wrote that Georgia's new statutory scheme not only guided the jury in its exercise of discretion as to whether or not it will impose the death penalty, but also gave the Georgia Supreme Court the power and imposed the obligation to decide whether in fact the death penalty was being administered for any given class of crime in a discriminatory, standardless, or rare fashion. It was said that if the Georgia Supreme Court properly performed the task assigned to it under the Georgia death penalty statute, death sentences imposed for discriminatory reasons, wantonly or freakishly for any given category of crime will be set aside. The concurrence concluded that the death penalty may be carried out under the Georgia legislative scheme consistent with the *Furman* decision.

Concurring Statement by Chief Justice Burger and

Rehnquist, J.: Chief Justice Burger and Justice Rehnquist issued a joint statement that said: "We concur in the judgment and join the opinion of Mr. Justice White, agreeing with its analysis that Georgia's system of capital punishment comports with the Court's holding in *Furman v. Georgia*."

Concurring Statement by Blackmun: Justice Blackmun issued a statement which read: "I concur in the judgment."

Dissenting opinion by Justice Brennan: Justice Brennan wrote in dissent that: "The opinions of Mr. Justice Stewart, Mr. Justice Powell, and Mr. Justice Stevens today hold that 'evolving standards of decency' require focus not on the essence of the death penalty itself but primarily upon the procedures employed by the State to single out persons to suffer the penalty of death. Those opinions hold further that, so viewed, the [Constitution] invalidates the mandatory infliction of the death penalty but not its infliction under sentencing procedures that Mr. Justice Stewart, Mr. Justice Powell, and Mr. Justice Stevens conclude adequately safeguard against the risk that the death penalty was imposed in an arbitrary and capricious manner." The dissent rejected the judgment of the Court and the reasoning of the plurality opinion and concluded that "the punishment of death, for whatever crime and under all circumstances, is 'cruel and unusual' in violation of the Eighth and Fourteenth Amendments of the Constitution."

Dissenting opinion by Justice Marshall: Justice Marshall wrote in dissent that the Court was wrong in focusing on Georgia's procedures as a basis for affirming its death penalty statute. He argued that "[t]he death penalty ... is a cruel and unusual punishment prohibited by the Eighth and Fourteenth Amendments." Justice Marshall gave two reasons for believing that the death penalty was constitutionally invalid. "First, the death penalty is excessive. And second, the American people, fully informed as to the purposes of the death penalty and its liabilities, would in my view reject it as morally unacceptable."

Case note: The decision in the case was the first of three cases decided in 1976, wherein the Court approved of death penalty statutes. The decision in *Gregg* was significant because it marked the end of the moratorium on the death penalty that *Furman* imposed, and because it provided a constitutional blueprint for how States could reinstitute capital punishment. *See also* **Jurek v. Texas; Proffitt v. Florida**

Grenada

Capital punishment is on the law books of Grenada, but the punishment has not been used in recent memory. Grenada uses hanging as the method of execution. Its legal system is based on English common law. The nation's constitution was adopted on December 19, 1973.

The judiciary of Grenada is a part of the Eastern Caribbean legal system, having magistrate courts for minor offenses and High Courts for major offenses. Appeals from the High Courts are taken to the Supreme Court of the Organization of Eastern Caribbean States.

The laws of Grenada provide defendants with a right to a public trial, a presumption of innocence, the right to bail, the right against self-incrimination, the right to confront his or her accuser, and the right to appeal. Defendants also have the right to retain counsel, but may only obtain appointed counsel when charged with a capital offense. *See also* **International Capital Punishment Nations**

Griffin v. United States

Court: United States Supreme Court; *Case Citation:* Griffin v. United States, 336 U.S. 704 (1949); *Argued:* December 15–16, 1948; *Decided:* April 25, 1949; *Opinion of the Court:* Justice Frankfurter; *Concurring Opinion:* None; *Dissenting Opinion:* Justice Murphy, in which Vinson, C.J., and Douglas and Rutledge, JJ., joined; *Appellate Defense Counsel:* Francis J. Kelly argued and briefed; *Appellate Prosecution Counsel:* Charles B. Murray argued and briefed; *Amicus Curiae Brief Supporting Prosecutor:* None; *Amicus Curiae Brief Supporting Defendant:* None.

Issue Presented: Whether suppression of potentially exculpatory evidence by the prosecutor warrants a new trial for the defendant?

Case Holding: The issue presented could not be addressed because the Court of Appeals for the District of Columbia failed to make a ruling on whether the evidence would have been admissible at trial.

Factual and procedural background of case: The defendant, Baxter Griffin, was convicted of capital murder and sentenced to death by the District of Columbia. The Court of Appeals for the District of Columbia affirmed the conviction and sentence. The United States Supreme Court denied certiorari.

Shortly before the defendant's scheduled execution he discovered potentially exculpatory evidence that had been suppressed by the prosecutor. The defendant filed a motion with the trial court for a new trial based on the newly discovered evidence. The trial court denied the motion. The Court of Appeals summarily affirmed. The United States Supreme Court granted certiorari to consider the issue.

Opinion of the Court by Justice Frankfurter: Justice Frankfurter wrote that the suppressed evidence, a knife that was found in the victim's pocket, may have been relevant to the defendant's theory of self-defense. However, the Court was reluctant to reverse the judgment because the Court of Appeals did not rule upon the issue of the admissibility of the evidence at trial. Justice Frankfurter indicated that the evidence may have been admissible in a Federal court under Federal law, but the Court was not prepared to impose a Federal rule of evidence on the courts of the District of Columbia. The opinion concluded: "We must therefore remand the case to the Court of Appeals with instructions to decide, in the first instance, what rule should prevail in the District of Columbia. To do otherwise would constitute an unwarranted departure from a wise rule of practice in our consideration of cases coming here from the Court of Appeals of the District. There are cogent reasons why this Court should not undertake to decide questions of local law without the aid of some expression of the views of judges of the local courts who are familiar with the intricacies and trends of local law and practice. We do not ordinarily decide such questions without that aid where they may conveniently be decided in the first instance by the court whose special function it is to resolve questions of the local law of the jurisdiction over which it presides. Only in exceptional cases will this Court review a determination of such a question by the Court of Appeals for the District."

The judgment of the Court of Appeals was affirmed and the case remanded with instructions.

Dissenting opinion by Justice Murphy, in which Vinson, C.J., and Douglas and Rutledge, JJ., joined: Justice Murphy dissented from the Court's decision. He argued that the Court was wrong in not addressing the issue presented, merely because the Court of Appeals did not determine whether the evidence was admissible. Justice Murphy believed that the evidence was admissible and the Court should have so held. He wrote as follows:

> Self-limitation of our appellate powers may be a worthy thing, but it is not attractive to me when the behest of Congress is otherwise. Congress has given this Court the ultimate power to review District of Columbia trials. No matter how the decision is phrased, the Court's power in the premises is such that it is responsible for the evidence rule it asks the Court of Appeals to expound… We should declare the evidence admissible.
>
> If the evidence is admissible, a motion for a new trial should be granted. A contrary determination would be an abuse of discretion, for there is manifestly a reasonable possibility that the jury would lessen the verdict of first degree murder.

See also **Exculpatory Evidence**

Guatemala

Guatemala imposes the death penalty and uses lethal injection to carry it out. Its legal system is based on civil law. The nation's constitution became effective on January 14, 1986. Guatemala is a democratic republic with an executive branch, unicameral legislative branch and judicial branch.

The judicial system of Guatemala is composed of a Constitutional Court, a Supreme Court, appellate courts and trial courts. Defendants enjoy a presumption of innocence, the right to a public trial, the right to be present at trial, the right to retained or appointed counsel, and the right to bail. Trials are conducted before a three-judge panel without a jury. Guatemala permits private parties to participate in the prosecution of criminal cases as co-complainants. *See also* **International Capital Punishment Nations**

Guilty Plea

The Federal Constitution does not prohibit a court from accepting a defendant's plea of guilty to a capital offense. However, several Federal constitutional rights are implicated and waived when a defendant enters a valid plea of guilty, including the (1) privilege against compulsory self-incrimination, (2) right to trial by jury, and (3) right to confront one's accusers. For a guilty plea to be valid it is constitutionally required that the trial record reflect an affirmative showing that the guilty plea was intelligently and voluntarily made. The competency standard for pleading guilty is whether the defendant has sufficient present ability to consult with his or her lawyer with a reasonable degree of rational understanding, and a rational as well as factual understanding of the proceedings against him or her.

Westley A. Dodd pled guilty to three capital murder charges brought against him by the State of Washington. Dodd was executed by hanging on January 5, 1993. (Camas Police)

Generally prosecutors have discretion to enter into any type of constitutionally permissible plea agreement with a capital felon. However, a few courts have held that a prosecutor cannot enter a plea agreement wherein a defendant agrees to enter a plea of guilty to capital murder, in exchange for an agreement by the prosecutor to recommend life imprisonment to the penalty phase jury. Courts reason that so long as there is evidence of the existence of at least one statutory aggravating circumstance, a prosecutor is obligated to seek the death penalty once a valid capital offense conviction has been obtained.

Some courts have held that if a plea agreement is made whereby a capital defendant agrees to enter a plea of guilty to non-capital murder, but the agreement is broken, the prosecutor may not thereafter seek a capital murder conviction and sentence. It has been said that regardless of the propriety of increasing an offense charge following a breach of a plea agreement, imposition of the death penalty in such circumstances offends the constitutional principle that capital sentencing determinations require special treatment. When the predictable result of a breach of a plea agreement is the death penalty, imposition of that penalty is arbitrary and in violation of the federal constitution.

Prosecutors may seek the death penalty against capital felons who reject a plea agreement offer.

The basic procedural requirements used by all capital punishment jurisdictions for entering pleas follows the requirements found in the Federal Rules of Criminal Procedure, as shown below.

Pleas Under the Federal Rules

a. Alternatives

    1. In General. A defendant may plead not guilty, guilty, or nolo contendere. If a defendant refuses to plead or if a defendant corporation fails to appear, the court shall enter a plea of not guilty.

    2. Conditional Pleas. With the approval of the court and the consent of the government, a defendant may enter a conditional plea of guilty or nolo contendere, reserving in writing the right, on appeal from the judgment, to review of the adverse determination of any specified pretrial motion. A defendant who prevails on appeal shall be allowed to withdraw the plea.

b. Nolo Contendere. A defendant may plead nolo contendere only with the consent of the court. Such a plea shall be accepted by the court only after due consideration of the views of the parties and the interest of the public in the effective administration of justice.

c. Advice to Defendant. Before accepting a plea of guilty or nolo contendere, the court must address the defendant personally in open court and inform the defendant of, and determine that the defendant understands, the following:

1. the nature of the charge to which the plea is offered, the mandatory minimum penalty provided by law, if any, and the maximum possible penalty provided by law, including the effect of any special parole or supervised release term, the fact that the court is required to consider any applicable sentencing guidelines but may depart from those guidelines under some circumstances, and, when applicable, that the court may also order the defendant to make restitution to any victim of the offense; and

2. if the defendant is not represented by an attorney, that the defendant has the right to be represented by an attorney at every stage of the proceeding and, if necessary, one will be appointed to represent the defendant; and

3. that the defendant has the right to plead not guilty or to persist in that plea if it has already been made, the right to be tried by a jury and at that trial the right to the assistance of counsel, the right to confront and cross-examine adverse witnesses, and the right against compelled self-incrimination; and

4. that if a plea of guilty or nolo contendere is accepted by the court there will not be a further trial of any kind, so that by pleading guilty or nolo contendere the defendant waives the right to a trial; and

5. if the court intends to question the defendant under oath, on the record, and in the presence of counsel about the offense to which the defendant has pleaded, that the defendant's answers may later be used against the defendant in a prosecution for perjury or false statement.

d. Insuring That the Plea Is Voluntary. The court shall not accept a plea of guilty or nolo contendere without first, by addressing the defendant personally in open court, determining that the plea is voluntary and not the result of force or threats or of promises apart from a plea agreement. The court shall also inquire as to whether the defendant's willingness to plead guilty or nolo contendere results from prior discussions between the attorney for the government and the defendant or the defendant's attorney.

e. Plea Agreement Procedure.

1. In General. The attorney for the government and the attorney for the defendant or the defendant when acting pro se may engage in discussions with a view toward reaching an agreement that, upon the entering of a plea of guilty or nolo contendere to a charged offense or to a lesser or related offense, the attorney for the government will do any of the following:

A. move for dismissal of other charges; or

B. make a recommendation, or agree not to oppose the defendant's request, for a particular sentence, with the understanding that such recommendation or request shall not be binding upon the court; or

C. agree that a specific sentence is the appropriate disposition of the case.

The court shall not participate in any such discussions.

2. Notice of Such Agreement. If a plea agreement has been reached by the parties, the court shall, on the record, require the disclosure of the agreement in open court or, on a showing of good cause, in camera, at the time the plea is offered. If the agreement is of the type specified in subdivision (e)(1)(A) or (C), the court may accept or reject the agreement, or may defer its decision as to the acceptance or rejection until there has been an opportunity to consider the presentence report. If the agreement is of the type specified in subdivision (e)(1)(B), the court shall advise the defendant that if the court does not accept the recommendation or request the defendant nevertheless has no right to withdraw the plea.

3. Acceptance of a Plea Agreement. If the court accepts the plea agreement, the court shall inform the defendant that it will embody in the judgment and sentence the disposition provided for in the plea agreement.

4. Rejection of a Plea Agreement. If the court rejects the plea agreement, the court shall, on the record, inform the parties of this fact, advise the defendant personally in open court or, on a showing of good cause, in camera, that the court is not bound by the plea agreement, afford the defendant the opportunity to then withdraw the plea, and advise the defendant that if the defendant persists in a guilty plea or plea of nolo contendere the disposition of the case may be less favorable to the defendant than that contemplated by the plea agreement.

5. Time of Plea Agreement Procedure. Except for good cause shown, notification to the court of the existence of a plea agreement shall be given at the arraignment or at such other time, prior to trial, as may be fixed by the court.

6. Inadmissibility of Pleas, Plea Discussions, and Related Statements. Except as otherwise provided in this paragraph, evidence of the following is not, in any civil or criminal proceeding, admissible against the defendant who made the plea or was a participant in the plea discussions:

A. a plea of guilty which was later withdrawn;

B. a plea of nolo contendere;

C. any statement made in the course of any proceedings under this rule regarding either of the foregoing pleas; or

D. any statement made in the course of plea discussions with an attorney for the government which do not result in a plea of guilty or which result in a plea of guilty later withdrawn.

However, such a statement is admissible (i) in any proceeding wherein another statement made in the course of the same plea or plea discussions has been introduced and the statement ought in fairness be considered contemporaneously with it, or (ii) in a criminal proceeding for perjury or false statement if the statement was made by the defendant under oath, on the record, and in the presence of counsel.

f. Determining Accuracy of Plea. Notwithstanding the acceptance of a plea of guilty, the court should not enter a judgment upon such plea without making such inquiry as shall satisfy it that there is a factual basis for the plea.

g. Record of Proceedings. A verbatim record of the proceedings at which the defendant enters a plea shall be made and, if there is a plea of guilty or nolo contendere, the record shall include, without limitation, the court's advice to the defendant, the inquiry into the voluntariness of the plea including any plea agreement, and the inquiry into the accuracy of a guilty plea.

h. Harmless Error. Any variance from the procedures required by this rule which does not affect substantial rights shall be disregarded. *See also* **Boykin v. Alabama; Godinez v. Moran; Hallinger v. Davis; Nolo Contendere Plea; North Carolina v. Alford**

Guinea   Capital punishment is allowed in Guinea. Guinea uses the firing squad to carry out the death penalty. The nation's legal system is based on French civil law and customary law. Its constitution was adopted on December 23, 1990.

The judicial system is composed of trial courts, two Courts of Appeal, and a Supreme Court. The laws of Guinea also recognize customary courts. Defendants enjoy a presumption of innocence, the right to retain counsel (in felony cases counsel may be appointed), and the right to appeal a judicial decision. *See also* **International Capital Punishment Nations**

Guinea-Bissau   The death penalty was abolished in Guinea-Bissau in 1993. *See also* **International Capital Punishment Nations**

Guiteau, Charles Julius *see* **Garfield's Assassination**

Gusman v. Marrero   *Court:* United States Supreme Court; *Case Citation:* Gusman v. Marrero, 180 U.S. 81 (1901); *Argued:* December 3, 1900; *Decided:* January 7, 1901; *Opinion of the Court:* Justice McKenna; *Concurring Opinion:* None; *Dissenting Opinion:* None; *Justice Taking No Part in Decision:* Justice Harlan; *Appellate Defense Counsel:* A. A. Birney argued; A. L. Gusman on brief; *Appellate Prosecution Counsel:* Robert J. Perkins argued and briefed; *Amicus Curiae Brief Supporting Prosecutor:* None; *Amicus Curiae Brief Supporting Defendant:* None.

Issue Presented: Whether a stranger to a capital case may intervene on behalf of the defendant and litigate issues for the defendant?

Case Holding: A stranger to a capital case may not intervene on behalf of the defendant and litigate issues for the defendant.

Factual and procedural background of case: This case involved an undesignated petition filed in a Federal District Court by A. L. Gusman. Gusman filed the petition on behalf of Samuel Wright. The petition stated that Wright was convicted of assault with intent to commit rape and sentenced to death by the State of Louisiana. It was further alleged in the petition that Wright was prosecuted in violation of due process of law, because the grand jury that indicted Wright consisted of only twelve members, while the law of the State required that the grand jury consist of sixteen members. The State of Louisiana responded to the petition and asked the District Court to dismiss the matter as failing to allege any ground for relief. The District Court agreed and dismissed the petition. The United States Supreme Court granted certiorari to consider the issue.

Opinion of the Court by Justice McKenna: Justice McKenna held that Gusman failed to present any issue upon which he had standing to litigate. The opinion disposed of the case succinctly as follows: "The contention of [the State] is that this is not an application for habeas corpus nor for writ of mandamus, but is an ordinary action. [Gusman] not only concedes the fact, but takes pains to assert it. It follows necessarily that he has no cause of action. However friendly he may be to the doomed man and sympathetic for his situation; however concerned he may be lest unconstitutional laws be enforced, and however laudable such sentiments are,—the grievance they suffer and feel is not special enough to furnish a cause of action in a case like this." The judgment of the District Court was affirmed. *See also* **Intervention by Next Friend**

Gutierrez Brothers   Jose Gutierrez was born in Texas on October 14, 1960. About five years after Jose's birth his brother, Jessie, was born on April 30, 1965. Both brothers dropped out of high school and worked in construction.

On September 5, 1989, the Gutierrez brothers walked into a jewelry store in College Station, Texas and demanded the store clerk turn over jewelry. The store clerk, 42-year-old Dorothy McNew, attempted to flee into another office but was fatally shot by one of the brothers. With McNew lying dead on the floor the brothers rustled up over $500,000 in jewelry.

When the Gutierrez brothers left the scene of the crime they fled to Houston. Eight days after the crime, on September

The Gutierrez brothers, left to right, Jose and Jessie. The State of Texas executed Jessie on September 16, 1994, and executed Jose on November 18, 1999. (Texas Department of Criminal Justice)

13, authorities arrested both brothers. Only about $375,000 worth of the jewelry was recovered. The brothers were convicted of capital murder in 1990 and sentenced to death. On September 16, 1994 Jessie was executed by lethal injection. On November 18, 1999 Jose was executed by lethal injection.

Guyana Capital punishment is allowed in Guyana. Guyana uses hanging to carry out the death penalty. Its legal system is a mixture of English common law and Roman-Dutch law. The nation's constitution was adopted on October 6, 1980. Guyana is a democratic nation having an executive branch, unicameral legislative branch, and judicial branch.

The judicial system of Guyana is composed of a Supreme Court, an appeals court, and magistrate courts. Defendants have a right to public trials and the right to appeal. Defendants also have a right to retain counsel, but may obtain appointed counsel only in capital prosecutions. *See also* **International Capital Punishment Nations**

H

Habeas Corpus The term "habeas corpus" is Latin and means "you have the body." Habeas corpus is a writ or legal device designed to permit a person incarcerated to challenge his or her detention. Habeas corpus cannot be sought by a person who is not under confinement. The origin of habeas corpus is traceable to the common law. The English jurist, Blackstone, called habeas corpus the most celebrated writ in English law. American jurists have called habeas corpus "the Great Writ."

The legal history of habeas corpus in Anglo-American jurisprudence began with the founding of the nation. In Article I, Section 9, Clause 2, of the Federal Constitution it is proclaimed that "[t]he Privilege of the Writ of Habeas Corpus shall not be suspended, unless when in Cases of Rebellion or Invasion the public Safety may require it." Only once in the nation's history, during the Civil War, was habeas corpus suspended. That suspension was ultimately nullified by the United States Supreme Court in *Ex Parte Milligan*.

Congress codified habeas corpus in Section 14 of the Judiciary Act of 1789. The Judiciary Act authorized Federal courts to grant habeas corpus when prisoners were "in custody, under or by colour of the authority of the United States, or [were] committed for trial before some court of the same."

28 U.S.C.A. § 2255 Federal Habeas Statute for Person in Federal Custody: A prisoner in custody under sentence of a court established by Act of Congress claiming the right to be released upon the ground that the sentence was imposed in violation of the Constitution or laws of the United States, or that the court was without jurisdiction to impose such sentence, or that the sentence was in excess of the maximum authorized by law, or is otherwise subject to collateral attack, may move the court which imposed the sentence to vacate, set aside or correct the sentence.

Unless the motion and the files and records of the case conclusively show that the prisoner is entitled to no relief, the court shall cause notice thereof to be served upon the United States attorney, grant a prompt hearing thereon, determine the issues and make findings of fact and conclusions of law with respect thereto. If the court finds that the judgment was rendered with-out jurisdiction, or that the sentence imposed was not authorized by law or otherwise open to collateral attack, or that there has been such a denial or infringement of the constitutional rights of the prisoner as to render the judgment vulnerable to collateral attack, the court shall vacate and set the judgment aside and shall discharge the prisoner or resentence him or grant a new trial or correct the sentence as may appear appropriate.

A court may entertain and determine such motion without requiring the production of the prisoner at the hearing.

An appeal may be taken to the court of appeals from the order entered on the motion as from a final judgment on application for a writ of habeas corpus.

An application for a writ of habeas corpus in behalf of a prisoner who is authorized to apply for relief by motion pursuant to this section, shall not be entertained if it appears that the applicant has failed to apply for relief, by motion, to the court which sentenced him, or that such court has denied him relief, unless it also appears that the remedy by motion is inadequate or ineffective to test the legality of his detention.

A 1-year period of limitation shall apply to a motion under this section. The limitation period shall run from the latest of—

1. the date on which the judgment of conviction becomes final;

2. the date on which the impediment to making a motion created by governmental action in violation of the Constitution or laws of the United States is removed, if the movant was prevented from making a motion by such governmental action;

3. the date on which the right asserted was initially recognized by the Supreme Court, if that right has been newly recognized by the Supreme Court and made retroactively applicable to cases on collateral review; or

4. the date on which the facts supporting the claim or claims presented could have been discovered through the exercise of due diligence.

Except as provided in section 408 of the Controlled Substances Act, in all proceedings brought under this section, and any subsequent proceedings on review, the court may appoint counsel, except as provided by a rule promulgated by the Supreme Court pursuant to statutory authority. Appointment of counsel under this section shall be governed by section 3006A of title 18.

A second or successive motion must be certified as provided in section 2244 by a panel of the appropriate court of appeals to contain —

1. newly discovered evidence that, if proven and viewed in light of the evidence as a whole, would be sufficient to establish by clear and convincing evidence that no reasonable factfinder would have found the movant guilty of the offense; or

2. a new rule of constitutional law, made retroactive to cases on collateral review by the Supreme Court, that was previously unavailable.

The initial limitation on Federal courts to grant habeas corpus to persons confined by the Federal government, was expanded by Congress when it amended the Judiciary Act in 1867. Under this amendment Federal courts were authorized to grant habeas corpus "in all cases where any person may be restrained of his or her liberty in violation of the constitution, or of any treaty or law of the United States." The authority of Federal courts to grant habeas corpus relief to persons in State custody was not significantly exercised until well into 20th century, when the United States Supreme Court decided that Federal habeas relief was available to determine whether a State criminal process satisfied the due process requirements of the Fourteenth Amendment.

28 U.S.C. § 2254 Federal Habeas Statute for Person in State Custody: a. The Supreme Court, a Justice thereof, a circuit judge, or a district court shall entertain an application for a writ of habeas corpus in behalf of a person in custody pursuant to the judgment of a State court only on the ground that he is in custody in violation of the Constitution or laws or treaties of the United States.

b. 1. An application for a writ of habeas corpus on behalf of a person in custody pursuant to the judgment of a State court shall not be granted unless it appears that —

    A. the applicant has exhausted the remedies available in the courts of the State; or

    B. (i) there is an absence of available State corrective process; or (ii) circumstances exist that render such process ineffective to protect the rights of the applicant.

2. An application for a writ of habeas corpus may be denied on the merits, notwithstanding the failure of the applicant to exhaust the remedies available in the courts of the State.

3. A State shall not be deemed to have waived the exhaustion requirement or be estopped from reliance upon the requirement unless the State, through counsel, expressly waives the requirement.

c. An applicant shall not be deemed to have exhausted the remedies available in the courts of the State, within the meaning of this section, if he has the right under the law of the State to raise, by any available procedure, the question presented.

d. An application for a writ of habeas corpus on behalf of a person in custody pursuant to the judgment of a State court shall not be granted with respect to any claim that was adjudicated on the merits in State court proceedings unless the adjudication of the claim —

1. resulted in a decision that was contrary to, or involved an unreasonable application of, clearly established Federal law, as determined by the Supreme Court of the United States; or

2. resulted in a decision that was based on an unreasonable determination of the facts in light of the evidence presented in the State court proceeding.

e. 1. In a proceeding instituted by an application for a writ of habeas corpus by a person in custody pursuant to the judgment of a State court, a determination of a factual issue made by a State court shall be presumed to be correct. The applicant shall have the burden of rebutting the presumption of correctness by clear and convincing evidence.

2. If the applicant has failed to develop the factual basis of a claim in State court proceedings, the court shall not hold an evidentiary hearing on the claim unless the applicant shows that —

    A. the claim relies on —

        i. a new rule of constitutional law, made retroactive to cases on collateral review by the Supreme Court, that was previously unavailable; or

        ii. a factual predicate that could not have been previously discovered through the exercise of due diligence; and

    B. the facts underlying the claim would be sufficient to establish by clear and convincing evidence that but for constitutional error, no reasonable factfinder would have found the applicant guilty of the underlying offense.

f. If the applicant challenges the sufficiency of the evidence adduced in such State court proceeding to support the State court's determination of a factual issue made therein, the applicant, if able, shall produce that part of the record pertinent to a determination of the sufficiency of the evidence to support such determination. If the applicant, because of indigency or other reason is unable to produce such part of the record, then the State shall produce such part of the record and the Federal court shall direct the State to do so by order directed to an appropriate State official. If the State cannot provide such pertinent part of the record, then the court shall determine under the existing facts and circumstances what weight shall be given to the State court's factual determination.

g. A copy of the official records of the State court, duly certified by the clerk of such court to be a true and correct copy of a finding, judicial opinion, or other reliable written indicia showing such a factual determination by the State court shall be admissible in the Federal court proceeding.

h. Except as provided in section 408 of the Controlled Substances Act, in all proceedings brought under this section, and any subsequent proceedings on review, the court may appoint counsel for an applicant who is or becomes financially unable to afford counsel, except as provided by a rule promulgated by the Supreme Court pursuant to statutory authority. Appointment of counsel under this section shall be governed by section 3006A of title 18.

i. The ineffectiveness or incompetence of counsel during Federal or State collateral post-conviction proceedings shall not be a ground for relief in a proceeding arising under section 2254.

In addition to habeas corpus relief under Federal law, habeas corpus is provided directly by constitutions, statutes or court rules in every State. Both Federal and State laws provide limitations on the grounds upon which habeas corpus may be sought. Generally, a petition for habeas corpus relief must assert that (1) confinement is in violation of a constitutional right, (2) the court involved lacked jurisdiction to confine the petitioner, or (3) a sentence was imposed in excess of that provided for by law.

Habeas corpus may be used to challenge pretrial or post-conviction confinement. The greatest use of habeas comes at the post-conviction confinement stage. Except for the issue of post-conviction bail, all jurisdictions generally limit post-conviction use of habeas corpus until after direct review or appeal of the judgment imposing confinement. The requirement of exhausting direct review before resorting to habeas relief, launched the legal term "collateral attack" of judgment as the manner in which to describe the challenge to a judgment through habeas corpus.

Congress enacted significant changes to Federal habeas laws in 1996, through the Antiterrorism and Effective Death Penalty Act (AEDP Act). The AEDP Act provided for expedited review of habeas petitions, and limited the scope of review of the merits of habeas petitions. The AEDP Act also provided special procedures for habeas corpus relief sought by persons in State custody under a sentence of death.

The death penalty provisions of the AEDP Act were set out in 28 U.S.C. §§ 2261-2266. Those provisions provide for expedited review of habeas petitions of State death row inmates. The death penalty sections of the AEDP Act are only applicable in Federal habeas proceedings initiated by a State death row inmate if the State involved has "opted in" and qualified under either the procedures set out in § 2261 or § 2265. The requirement under § 2261 is that a State provide for the appointment of counsel to represent a death row inmate in a habeas proceedings. Under § 2265 a State is required to provide death row inmates with "unitary review" of direct appeal issues and collateral issues.

28 U.S.C. § 2261 Appointment of Counsel for Death Row Inmate: (a). This chapter shall apply to cases arising under section 2254 brought by prisoners in State custody who are subject to a capital sentence. It shall apply only if the provisions of subsections (b) and (c) are satisfied.

b. This chapter is applicable if a State establishes by statute, rule of its court of last resort, or by another agency authorized by State law, a mechanism for the appointment, compensation, and payment of reasonable litigation expenses of competent counsel in State post-conviction proceedings brought by indigent prisoners whose capital convictions and sentences have been upheld on direct appeal to the court of last resort in the State or have otherwise become final for State law purposes. The rule of court or statute must provide standards of competency for the appointment of such counsel.

c. Any mechanism for the appointment, compensation, and reimbursement of counsel as provided in subsection (b) must offer counsel to all State prisoners under capital sentence and must provide for the entry of an order by a court of record —

1. appointing one or more counsels to represent the prisoner upon a finding that the prisoner is indigent and accepted the offer or is unable competently to decide whether to accept or reject the offer;

2. finding, after a hearing if necessary, that the prisoner rejected the offer of counsel and made the decision with an understanding of its legal consequences; or

3. denying the appointment of counsel upon a finding that the prisoner is not indigent.

d. No counsel appointed pursuant to subsections (b) and (c) to represent a State prisoner under capital sentence shall have previously represented the prisoner at trial or on direct appeal in the case for which the appointment is made unless the prisoner and counsel expressly request continued representation.

e. The ineffectiveness or incompetence of counsel during State or Federal post-conviction proceedings in a capital case shall not be a ground for relief in a proceeding arising under section 2254. This limitation shall not preclude the appointment of different counsel, on the court's own motion or at the request of the prisoner, at any phase of State or Federal post-conviction proceedings on the basis of the ineffectiveness or incompetence of counsel in such proceedings.

In § 2262 of the AEDP Act, a Federal court must issue an order staying the death row inmate's execution pending review of the habeas petition. The stay of execution expires if the defendant (1) failed to file the habeas petition within the time frame provided by Federal law, (2) waived the right to pursue Federal habeas relief, or (3) failed to make a substantial showing of the denial of a Federal right. If a stay of execution is terminated because of any of the three reasons outlined in § 2262, no Federal court thereafter has the authority to enter a stay of execution in the case, unless a Federal Court of Appeals approves the filing of a second or successive habeas application.

Under § 2263 of the AEDP Act, the deadline for filing a habeas application is set out. The provision provides that any application for habeas relief must be filed in the appropriate Federal District Court not later than 180 days after final State court affirmance of the conviction and sentence on direct review or the expiration of the time for seeking such review. The filing deadline will be tolled (1) from the date that a petition for certiorari is filed in the United States Supreme Court, until the date of final disposition of the petition; (2) from the date on which the first petition for post-conviction review or other collateral relief is filed, until the final State court disposition of such petition; and (3) during an additional period not to exceed 30 days upon a showing of good cause for the failure to file the habeas corpus application untimely.

28 U.S.C. § 2265 State Unitary Review Procedure: a. For purposes of this section, a "unitary review" procedure means a State procedure that authorizes a person under sentence of death to raise, in the course of direct review of the judgment, such claims as could be raised on collateral attack. This chapter shall apply, as provided in this section, in relation to a State unitary review procedure if the State establishes by rule of its court of last resort or by statute a mechanism for the appointment, compensation, and payment of reasonable litigation expenses of competent counsel in the unitary review proceedings, including expenses relating to the litigation of collateral claims in the proceedings. The rule of court or statute must provide standards of competency for the appointment of such counsel.

b. To qualify under this section, a unitary review procedure must include an offer of counsel following trial for the purpose of representation on unitary review, and entry of an order, as provided in section 2261(c), concerning appointment of counsel or waiver or denial of appointment of counsel for that purpose. No counsel appointed to represent the prisoner in the unitary review proceedings shall have previously represented the prisoner at trial in the case for which the appointment is made unless the prisoner and counsel expressly request continued representation.

c. Sections 2262, 2263, 2264, and 2266 shall apply in relation to cases involving a sentence of death from any State having a unitary review procedure that qualifies under this section. References to State "post-conviction review" and "direct review" in such sections shall be understood as referring to unitary review under the State procedure. The reference in section 2262(a) to "an order under section 2261(c)" shall be understood as referring to the post-trial order under subsection (b) concerning representation in the unitary review proceedings, but if a transcript of the trial proceedings is unavailable at the time of the filing of such an order in the appropriate State court, then the start of the 180-day limitation period under section 2263 shall be deferred until a transcript is made available to the prisoner or counsel of the prisoner.

The scope of review of a habeas petition is set out in § 2264 of the AEDP Act. This provision states that a Federal District Court shall only consider claims that have been raised and decided on the merits in the State courts. Three exceptions to the review limitation is provided by the statute. A Federal District Court may address a "defaulted" claim if failure to raise the claim properly was (1) the result of State action in violation of the Constitution or laws of the United States; (2) the result of the United States Supreme Court's recognition of a new Federal right that is made retroactively applicable; or (3) based on a factual predicate that could not have been discovered through the exercise of due diligence in time to present the claim for State or Federal post-conviction review. An extension window of 30 days is provided for good cause. The statute expressly notes that failure of a District Court to comply with the time limitation shall not be a ground for granting relief from a conviction or sentence.

It is also provided under § 2264 of the AEDP Act, that a Federal Court of Appeals must hear and render a final determination of any appeal of a habeas order granting or denying relief not later than 120 days after the date on which the appellant reply brief is filed, or if no appellant reply brief is filed, not later than 120 days after the date on which the answering brief is filed. It is further provided that if a petition for rehearing is granted, the Court of Appeals shall hear and render a final determination of the appeal not later than 120 days after the date on which the order granting rehearing is entered. The statute expressly notes that failure of a Court of Appeals to comply with the time limitation shall not be the basis for granting relief from a conviction or sentence. *See also* **Calderon v. Ashmus; Exhaustion of State Remedies Doctrine; Ex Parte Milligan; Felker v. Turpin; Habeas Corpus Procedural Rules; McFarland v. Scott; Procedural Default of Constitutional Claims; Stewart v. Martinez-Villareal; Townsend v. Sain**

Habeas Corpus Procedural Rules

All capital punishment jurisdictions provide rules that govern the procedures of a habeas corpus proceeding. The habeas corpus rules promulgated by the United States Supreme Court, for use in Federal District Courts, embody the general procedural practice of most capital punishment jurisdictions. The Supreme Court has issued two sets of habeas corpus procedural rules. Separate habeas rules are provided for Federal prisoners and State prisoners. Only minor differences exist between the two sets of rules. The Federal habeas rules reproduced here are used in proceedings involving Federal death row inmates. The "comments" that follow each rule have been provided to assist in understanding the substance the rule.

Rule 1. Scope of Rules: These rules govern the procedure in the district court on a motion under 28 U.S.C. § 2255:

1. By a person in custody pursuant to a judgment of that court for a determination that the judgment was imposed in violation of the Constitution or laws of the United States, or that the court was without jurisdiction to impose such judgment, or that the sentence was in excess of the maximum authorized by law, or is otherwise subject to collateral attack; and

2. By a person in custody pursuant to a judgment of a state or other federal court and subject to future custody under a judgment of the district court for a determination that such future custody will be in violation of the Constitution or laws of the United States, or that the district court was without jurisdiction to impose such judgment, or that the sentence was in excess of the maximum authorized by law, or is otherwise subject to collateral attack.

Comment: Rule 1 provides that all of the rules which follow it are applicable to habeas corpus proceedings in Federal District Courts, that are initiated by defendants invoking the Federal statute applicable to persons held in custody by the Federal Government. The rule also indicates that a defendant must file a "motion" to begin the habeas proceeding. A motion is filed instead of a "petition," because the defendant's case would already be in the District Court where the habeas relief is sought. There is also a provision in the rule which makes the rules applicable to a defendant who is in the custody of a State, but is subject to a criminal judgment by the Federal Government. This latter situation arises when a defendant is prosecuted by both the Federal Government and a State.

Rule 2. Motion: a. Nature of application for relief. If the person is presently in custody pursuant to the federal judgment in question, or if not presently in custody may be subject to such custody in the future pursuant to such judgment, the application for relief shall be in the form of a motion to vacate, set aside, or correct the sentence.

b. Form of motion. The motion shall be in substantially the form annexed to these rules, except that any district court may by local rule require that motions filed with it shall be in a form prescribed by the local rule. Blank motions in the prescribed form shall be made available without charge by the clerk of the district court to applicants upon their request. It shall specify all the grounds for relief which are available to the movant and of which he has or, by the exercise of reasonable diligence, should have knowledge and shall set forth in summary form the facts supporting each of the grounds thus specified. It shall also state the relief requested. The motion shall be typewritten or legibly handwritten and shall be signed under penalty of perjury by the petitioner.

c. Motion to be directed to one judgment only. A motion shall be limited to the assertion of a claim for relief against one judgment only of the district court. If a movant desires to attack the validity of other judgments of that or any other district court under which he is in custody or may be subject to future custody, as the case may be, he shall do so by separate motions.

d. Return of insufficient motion. If a motion received by the clerk of a district court does not substantially comply with the requirements of Rule 2 or Rule 3, it may be returned to the movant, if a judge of the court so directs, together with a statement of the reason for its return. The clerk shall retain a copy of the motion.

Comment: Rule 2 provides guidelines for the substantive contents of a motion for habeas relief. The rule also cautions that a motion for habeas relief must challenge only one conviction judgment. A single conviction judgment may embody multiple offense convictions. If a motion is not filed in compliance with the rules, it may be denied on that ground.

Rule 3. Filing Motion:

a. Place of filing; copies. A motion under these rules shall be filed in the office of the clerk of the district court. It shall be accompanied by two conformed copies thereof.

b. Filing and service. Upon receipt of the motion and having ascertained that it appears on its face to comply with Rules 2 and 3, the clerk of the district court shall file the motion and enter it on the docket in his office in the criminal action in which was entered the judgment to which it is directed. He shall thereupon deliver or serve a copy of the motion together with a notice of its filing on the United States Attorney of the district in which the judgment under attack was entered. The filing of the motion shall not require said United States Attorney to answer the motion or otherwise move with respect to it unless so ordered by the court.

Comment: Rule 3 directs where a motion is to be filed. It also provides that the Clerk of the District Court is obligated to send a copy of the motion to the Federal prosecuting attorney. Under the rule the prosecuting attorney does not have to respond in writing to the motion until the court requires a response.

Rule 4. Preliminary Consideration by Judge:

a. Reference to judge; dismissal or order to answer. The original motion shall be presented promptly to the judge of the district court who presided at the movant's trial and sentenced him, or, if the judge who imposed sentence was not the trial judge, then it shall go to the judge who was in charge of that part of the proceedings being attacked by the movant. If the appropriate judge is unavailable to consider the motion, it shall be presented to another judge of the district in accordance with the procedure of the court for the assignment of its business.

b. Initial consideration by judge. The motion, together with all the files, records, transcripts, and correspondence relating to the judgment under attack, shall be examined promptly by the judge to whom it is assigned. If it plainly appears from the face of the motion and any annexed exhibits and the prior proceedings in the case that the movant is not entitled to relief in the district court, the judge shall make an order for its summary dismissal and cause the movant to be notified. Otherwise, the judge shall order the United States Attorney to file an answer or other pleading within the period of time fixed by the court or to take such other action as the judge deems appropriate.

Comment: Rule 4 authorizes a District Court judge to dis-

miss a habeas motion immediately if the motion and record in the case clearly reveal that the defendant is not entitled to relief from the court. If the motion and record of the case indicate grounds for possible relief by the court, the rule requires the judge to order the prosecuting attorney to file a response to the motion.

Rule 5. Answer and Contents:

a. Contents of answer. The answer shall respond to the allegations of the motion. In addition it shall state whether the movant has used any other available federal remedies including any prior post-conviction motions under these rules or those existing previous to the adoption of the present rules. The answer shall also state whether an evidentiary hearing was accorded the movant in a federal court.

b. Supplementing the answer. The court shall examine its files and records to determine whether it has available copies of transcripts and briefs whose existence the answer has indicated. If any of these items should be absent, the government shall be ordered to supplement its answer by filing the needed records. The court shall allow the government an appropriate period of time in which to do so, without unduly delaying the consideration of the motion.

Comment: Rule 6 is directed to the prosecuting attorney. It informs the prosecutor of the substantive matters that must be addressed in a response to a defendant's habeas motion.

Rule 6. Discovery:

a. Leave of court required. A party may invoke the processes of discovery available under the Federal Rules of Criminal Procedure or the Federal Rules of Civil Procedure or elsewhere in the usages and principles of law if, and to the extent that, the judge in the exercise of his discretion and for good cause shown grants leave to do so, but not otherwise. If necessary for effective utilization of discovery procedures, counsel shall be appointed by the judge for a movant who qualifies for appointment of counsel under 18 U.S.C. § 3006A(g).

b. Requests for discovery. Requests for discovery shall be accompanied by a statement of the interrogatories or requests for admission and a list of the documents, if any, sought to be produced.

c. Expenses. If the government is granted leave to take the deposition of the movant or any other person, the judge may as a condition of taking it direct that the government pay the expenses of travel and subsistence and fees of counsel for the movant to attend the taking of the deposition.

Comment: Rule 6 governs how the defendant and prosecutor are able to obtain information from each other that is not already in the record. Under the rule a party must obtain permission from the judge in order to conduct discovery of information not in the record. If the judge grants a party's request to engage in discovery, the discovery must take place within the framework of other rules that govern the discovery process. The rule also permits a judge to appoint an attorney for an indigent defendant, if doing so would assist the discovery process.

Rule 7. Expansion of Record:

a. Direction for expansion. If the motion is not dismissed summarily, the judge may direct that the record be expanded by the parties by the inclusion of additional materials relevant to the determination of the merits of the motion.

b. Materials to be added. The expanded record may include, without limitation, letters predating the filing of the motion in the district court, documents, exhibits, and answers under oath, if so directed, to written interrogatories propounded by the judge. Affidavits may be submitted and considered as a part of the record.

c. Submission to opposing party. In any case in which an expanded record is directed, copies of the letters, documents, exhibits, and affidavits proposed to be included shall be submitted to the party against whom they are to be offered, and he shall be afforded an opportunity to admit or deny their correctness.

d. Authentication. The court may require the authentication of any material under subdivision (b) or (c).

Comment: Rule 7 gives the judge authority to permit the record in the case to be expanded beyond that which was created during the actual prosecution. The expansion will generally occur when discovery has taken place.

Rule 8. Evidentiary Hearing:

a. Determination by court. If the motion has not been dismissed at a previous stage in the proceeding, the judge, after the answer is filed and any transcripts or records of prior court actions in the matter are in his possession, shall, upon a review of those proceedings and of the expanded record, if any, determine whether an evidentiary hearing is required. If it appears that an evidentiary hearing is not required, the judge shall make such disposition of the motion as justice dictates.

b. Function of the magistrate.

1. When designated to do so in accordance with 28 U.S.C. § 636(b), a magistrate may conduct hearings, including evidentiary hearings, on the motion, and submit to a judge of the court proposed findings and recommendations for disposition.

2. The magistrate shall file proposed findings and recommendations with the court and a copy shall forthwith be mailed to all parties.

3. Within ten days after being served with a copy, any party may serve and file written objections to such proposed findings and recommendations as provided by rules of court.

4. A judge of the court shall make a de novo determination of those portions of the report or specified proposed findings or recommendations to which objection is made. A judge of the court may accept, reject, or modify in whole or in part any findings or recommendations made by the magistrate.

c. Appointment of counsel; time for hearing. If an evidentiary hearing is required, the judge shall appoint counsel for a movant who qualifies for the appointment of counsel under 18 U.S.C. § 3006A(g) and the hearing shall be conducted as promptly as practicable, having regard for the need of counsel for both parties for adequate time for investigation and preparation. These rules do not limit the appointment of counsel under 18 U.S.C. § 3006A at any stage of the proceeding if the interest of justice so requires.

d. Production of statements at evidentiary hearing.

1. In general. Federal Rule of Criminal Procedure 26.2(a)-(d), and (f) applies at an evidentiary hearing under these rules.

2. Sanctions for failure to produce statement. If a party elects not to comply with an order under Federal Rule of Criminal Procedure 26.2(a) to deliver a statement to the moving party, at the evidentiary hearing the court may not consider the testimony of the witness whose statement is withheld.

Comment: Rule 8 authorizes a District Court judge to dispose of a habeas case on the merits with or without an evidentiary hearing. An evidentiary hearing is one in which witnesses may be called and testimony taken. If an evidentiary hearing is required, the judge must appoint counsel for an indigent defendant. The rule permits the judge to assign a Federal magistrate to preside over an evidentiary hearing.

Rule 9. Delayed or Successive Motions:

a. Delayed motions. A motion for relief made pursuant to these rules may be dismissed if it appears that the government has been prejudiced in its ability to respond to the motion by delay in its filing unless the movant shows that it is based on grounds of which he could not have had knowledge by the exercise of reasonable diligence before the circumstances prejudicial to the government occurred.

b. Successive motions. A second or successive motion may be dismissed if the judge finds that it fails to allege new or different grounds for relief and the prior determination was on the merits or, if new and different grounds are alleged, the judge finds that the failure of the movant to assert those grounds in a prior motion constituted an abuse of the procedure governed by these rules.

Comment: Rule 9 permits the court to dismiss a habeas motion if it is shown that the motion was brought untimely and the prosecutor is unduly prejudiced by the late filing. The court may also, under the rule, dismiss a second or subsequent habeas motion that fails to allege any issue that was not previously addressed on a prior motion, or if there is an assertion of new allegations that could have been alleged in a prior habeas proceeding.

Rule 10. Powers of Magistrates:
The duties imposed upon the judge of the district court by these rules may be performed by a United States magistrate pursuant to 28 U.S.C. § 636.

Comment: Rule 10 sets the scope of a Federal magistrate's

authority over a habeas proceeding coextensive with that of a District Court judge.

Rule 11. Time for Appeal: The time for appeal from an order entered on a motion for relief made pursuant to these rules is as provided in Rule 4(a) of the Federal Rules of Appellate Procedure. Nothing in these rules shall be construed as extending the time to appeal from the original judgment of conviction in the district court.

Comment: Rule 11 makes clear that the time for appealing a habeas decision is that which governs any type of appeal. The rule also cautions defendants that the habeas rules do not extend the time for appealing the underlying judgment in the case.

Rule 12. Rules of Criminal and Civil Procedure Applicability: If no procedure is specifically prescribed by these rules, the district court may proceed in any lawful manner not inconsistent with these rules, or any applicable statute, and may apply the Federal Rules of Criminal Procedure or the Federal Rules of Civil Procedure, whichever it deems most appropriate, to motions filed under these rules.

Comment: Rule 12 authorizes the District Court judge to use the court's inherent powers to formulate procedures to conduct a habeas proceeding when necessary. The rule also makes available other substantive procedural rules to assist the judge in conducting a habeas proceeding. *See also* **Bracy v. Gramley; Habeas Corpus; Lonchar v. Thomas; Townsend v. Sain**

Habitual Offender *see* Prior Felony or Homicide Aggravator

Haiti
The death penalty was abolished in Haiti in 1987. *See also* **International Capital Punishment Nations**

Hale v. Kentucky
Court: United States Supreme Court; *Case Citation:* Hale v. Kentucky, 303 U.S. 613 (1938); *Argued:* March 29, 1938; *Decided:* April 11, 1938; *Opinion of the Court:* Per Curiam; *Concurring Opinion:* None; *Dissenting Opinion:* None; *Justice Taking No Part in Decision:* Justice Cardozo; *Appellate Defense Counsel:* Charles H. Houston argued; Leon A. Ransom on brief; *Appellate Prosecution Counsel:* A. E. Funk argued and briefed; *Amicus Curiae Brief Supporting Prosecutor:* Not reported; *Amicus Curiae Brief Supporting Defendant:* Not reported.

Issue Presented: Whether the defendant established that blacks were systematically excluded from the grand jury that indicted him and the petit jury that convicted him?

Case Holding: The defendant established that blacks were systematically excluded from the grand jury that indicted him and the petit jury that convicted him, therefore his conviction and death sentence could not stand.

Factual and procedural background of case: The defendant, Hale, was convicted of capital murder and sentenced to death by the State of Kentucky. The Kentucky Supreme Court affirmed the judgment. In doing so, the appellate court rejected the defendant's contention that his conviction violated the Federal Constitution, because blacks were systematically excluded from the grand jury that indicted him and the petit jury that convicted him. The United States Supreme Court granted certiorari to consider the issue.

Opinion of the Court was delivered Per Curiam: The per curiam opinion held that the defendant established his claim of grand and petit jury discrimination. It was said "that the affidavits, which by the stipulation of the State were to be taken as proof, and were uncontroverted, sufficed to show a systematic and arbitrary exclusion of [blacks] from the jury lists solely because of their race or color, constituting a denial of the equal protection of the laws guaranteed to [the defendant] by the Fourteenth Amendment." The judgment of the Kentucky Supreme Court was reversed. *See also* **Discrimination in Grand or Petit Jury Selection**

Hallinger v. Davis
Court: United States Supreme Court; *Case Citation:* Hallinger v. Davis, 146 U.S. 314 (1892); *Argued:* Not reported; *Decided:* November 28, 1892; *Opinion of the Court:* Justice Shiras; *Concurring Statement:* Justice Harlan; *Dissenting Opinion:* None; *Appellate Defense Counsel:* B. F. Rice argued and briefed; *Appellate Prosecution Counsel:* C. H. Winfield argued and briefed; *Amicus Curiae Brief Supporting Prosecutor:* None; *Amicus Curiae Brief Supporting Defendant:* None.

Issue Presented: Whether due process of law required a jury determine the degree of guilt to assign to the defendant after he entered a plea of guilty to a homicide?

Case Holding: Due process of law did not require a jury determine the degree of guilt to assign to the defendant after he entered a plea of guilty to a homicide, therefore a two-judge panel used to ascertain the degree of his guilt was constitutionally acceptable.

Factual and procedural background of case: The defendant, Edward W. Hallinger, was indicted for capital murder by the State of New Jersey. The defendant entered a plea of guilty. Under the law of the State, a two-judge panel had to convene to determine what degree of guilt was to be attached to the defendant's plea of guilty. After holding a hearing and taking evidence, the two-judge panel determined that the defendant was guilty of murder in the first degree. The defendant was thereafter sentenced to death.

The defendant filed a habeas corpus petition in a Federal District Court, alleging that he was denied due process of law, because he was not permitted to have a jury determine the degree of guilt to assign to him. The District Court denied relief. The United States Supreme Court granted certiorari to consider the issue.

Opinion of the Court by Justice Shiras: Justice Shiras concluded that the defendant was not denied due process of law. The opinion dispensed with the contention as follows:

> The right of the accused to a trial was not affected, and we can therefore have no doubt that the proceeding to ascertain the degree of the crime where without a jury, in an indictment for murder, the defendant enters a plea of guilty, is constitutional

and valid. Statutes of like or similar import have been enacted in many of the states, and have never been held unconstitutional. On the other hand, they have been repeatedly and uniformly held to be constitutional....

... [W]e are readily brought to the conclusion that the [defendant], in voluntarily availing himself of the provisions of the statute and electing to plead guilty, was deprived of no right or privilege within the protection of the fourteenth amendment. The trial seems to have been conducted in strict accordance with the forms prescribed by the constitution and laws of the state, and with special regard to the rights of the accused thereunder. The court refrained from at once accepting his plea of guilty, assigned him counsel, and twice adjourned, for a period of several days, in order that he might be fully advised of the truth, force, and effect of his plea of guilty. Whatever may be thought of the wisdom of departing, in capital cases, from time-honored procedure, there is certainly nothing in the present record to enable this court to perceive that the rights of the [defendant], so far as the laws and constitution of the United States are concerned, have been in any wise infringed.

The judgment of the District Court was affirmed.

Concurring Statement by Justice Harlan: Justice Harlan issued a statement concurring in the Court's judgment and indicating he did not agree in all the reasoning of the opinion. *See also* **Guilty Plea**

Hands Off Cain

Hands Off Cain (HOC) is a nonprofit organization that was founded in Brussels, at the European Parliament in 1993. The organization was founded for the abolition of the death penalty worldwide by 2000. HOC engages in international campaigns against the death penalty. Its work includes lobbying government organs to introduce legislation to abolish the death penalty. HOC also provides support and coordinates the activities of local, national and international organizations, whose objective is to eliminate the death penalty from legal systems throughout the world.

Handicapped Person Aggravator

In 1985 religious extremists attacked a cruise ship called the Achille Lauro, off the Egyptian coast, and killed a helpless wheelchair-bound victim. Three capital punishment jurisdictions, Delaware, New Hampshire, and Wyoming, have sought to curb violence against handicapped persons by making the murder of a physically handicapped person a statutory aggravating circumstance. If evidence at the penalty phase establishes the victim was physically handicapped, the death penalty may be imposed by the jury. *See also* **Aggravating Circumstances**

Hanging

The common law accepted death by hanging as a legitimate method of execution. Hanging has also been a traditional part of Anglo-American jurisprudence as a result of its common law lineage. The American Colonists used hanging as a form of punishment and the practice continued after the American Revolution.

Hanging Jurisdictions: As of January 2000, only four capital punishment jurisdictions employed hanging as a method of execution. Two of those jurisdictions, Montana and Washington, provide hanging as a capital felon option. In both ju-

An unidentified prisoner is being prepared for execution, circa 1864. (National Archives)

risdictions, hanging is the default method of execution. The remaining two jurisdictions, Delaware and New Hampshire, utilize hanging solely as a single fallback option. That is, in the event the primary method of execution is invalidated, hanging would be used.

Constitutionality of Hanging: The constitutionality of execution by hanging was addressed in dicta by the United States Supreme Court in *Wilkerson v. Utah*, 99 U.S. 130 (1878). The decision in *Wilkerson* was directly concerned with the constitutionality of death by firing squad. However, the Supreme Court discussed hanging by analogy as a constitutionally

JURISDICTIONS WHERE HANGING IS ALLOWED

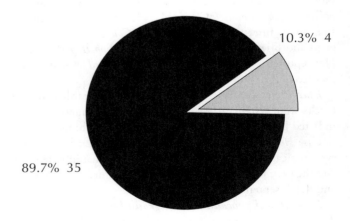

10.3% 4

89.7% 35

■ HANGING JURISDICTIONS
■ NON-HANGING JURISDICTIONS

EXECUTIONS PERFORMED BY HANGING 1976–1999

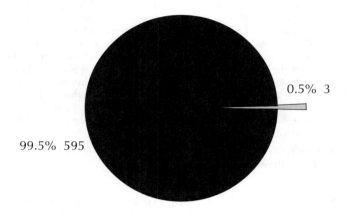

0.5% 3

99.5% 595

■ HANGING

■ ALL OTHER METHODS

acceptable method of execution. In the relatively recent decision of *Campbell v. Wood*, 18 F.3d 662 (1994), it was indicated on the merits that hanging did not violate the Constitution. However, in *Rupe v. Wood*, 863 F.Supp. 1307 (W.D. Wash. 1994) it was held that hanging was unconstitutional as a method of execution for the defendant in that case, because there was a substantial likelihood that he would be decapitated if hung, due to his weight (in excess of 400 lbs.).

Two principal arguments are waged in opposition to hanging as a method of execution. First, there is a risk that death will occur as a result of asphyxiation. This will happen if the execution is not properly done. Death by asphyxiation is slow and painful. As a result of the risk of asphyxiation and its attendant slow and agonizing pain, it is argued by some commentators that hanging should be prohibited as a method of execution.

Local officials are preparing to execute an unidentified prisoner, circa 1910. (Denver Public Library)

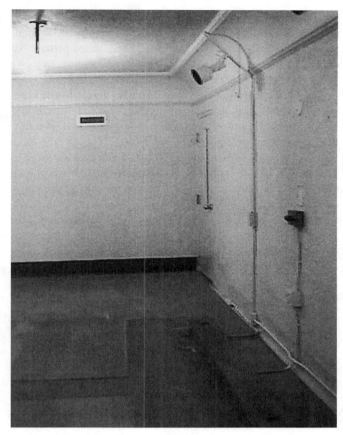

The gallows at the Washington State Penitentiary is located inside a room. A rope is dropped from the ceiling. The prisoner is placed on a section of the floor that has a trapdoor. A switch located on the wall of the room controls the trapdoor. (Washington Department of Corrections)

The second, and most profound, argument against hanging is that there is a risk of decapitation. If the hanging is done improperly the head of a capital felon could be torn from its trunk during the process. While decapitation was accepted and practiced under the common law as a method of execution, it has not been accepted by Anglo-American jurisprudence. Anti-hanging proponents contend that because of the risk of decapitation, hanging should not be used as a method of execution.

Hanging Protocol: Hanging has evolved as a method of execution. The early gallows are not like those used today. In the past the gallows was nothing more than a large tree from which the condemned prisoner was hanged. In time the tree was replaced by an outdoor scaffold from which the condemned prisoner would be dropped.

Under modern capital punishment hanging is now performed inside of a prison building. A special room with a trapdoor, and a ceiling fixture for a rope are used. The condemned prisoner is positioned on the trapdoor. The legs and arms of the condemned are fastened by restraints, and a hood placed over his or her head. If necessary (when a condemned has fainted), a metal frame is used to hold the condemned prisoner's body erect. A rope is lowered from the ceiling and placed around the condemned prisoner's neck. A button is then pushed to release the trapdoor and the condemned prisoner is dropped to his or her death.

When done correctly, the force of the drop and the stop caused by the length of the rope breaks the bones in the capital felon's neck and severs the spinal cord, causing him or her to go into shock and be rendered unconscious. At this point the capital felon strangles to death.

In carrying out a hanging the force of the drop is critical. The weight of the capital felon determines the force of the drop. Generally, the heavier the person is, the shorter the drop; and the lighter the person is, the longer the drop. A drop that is of too short a distance will result in the spinal cord not being severed and, in turn, the capital felon will not go into shock and will be conscious during the strangulation period. A drop that is too long a distance will result in decapitation. *See also* **Execution Option Jurisdictions; Methods of Execution**

Hardy v. United States

Court: United States Supreme Court; *Case Citation:* Hardy v. United States, 186 U.S. 224 (1902); *Argued:* April 28, 1902; *Decided:* June 2, 1902; *Opinion of the Court:* Justice Brewer; *Concurring Opinion:* None; *Dissenting Opinion:* None; *Appellate Defense Counsel:* Joseph F. Gould argued and briefed; *Appellate Prosecution Counsel:* Mr. Richards argued and briefed; *Amicus Curiae Brief Supporting Prosecutor:* None; *Amicus Curiae Brief Supporting Defendant:* None.

Issue Presented: Whether incriminating statements made by the defendant to a magistrate during a preliminary hearing were admissible at trial?

Case Holding: Incriminating statements made by the defendant to a magistrate during a preliminary hearing were admissible at trial, because the statements were voluntary and made after the defendant was warned against making any statements.

Factual and procedural background of case: The defendant, Fred Hardy, was convicted of capital murder and sentenced to death by the United States. The defendant appealed to the United States Supreme Court, alleging that it was error for the trial court to allow into evidence written and oral incriminating statements he made to a magistrate during his preliminary hearing. The United States Supreme Court granted certiorari to consider the issue.

Opinion of the Court by Justice Brewer: Justice Brewer held that the incriminating statements made by the defendant were voluntary and admissible against him at trial. The opinion set out the Court's reasoning as follows:

> ... So the question is whether voluntary statements made by a defendant before and after a preliminary examination are inadmissible in evidence because made to the magistrate who in fact conducted the preliminary examination. We know of no rule of evidence which excludes such testimony. Of course, statements which are obtained by coercion or threat or promise will be subject to objection. But, so far from anything of that

kind appearing, the defendant was cautioned that he was under no obligations to make a statement; that it would be used against him if he made one, and that there was a proper time for him to make one if he so desired. Without even a suggestion, he insisted on making, prior to the examination, a statement which was reduced to writing and by him signed and sworn to, and after the examination was over and he had been placed in jail, he had an interview with the magistrate and volunteered a further statement. Affirmatively and fully it appears that all that he said in the matter was said voluntarily, without any inducement or influence of any kind being brought to bear upon him.... The statements were properly admitted in evidence.

The judgment of the Federal trial court was affirmed. *See also* **Right to Remain Silent**

Harlan, John M.

John M. Harlan served as an associate justice of the United States Supreme Court from 1877 to 1911. While on the Supreme Court Harlan was known as a liberal interpreter of the Constitution, particularly in the undeveloped area of civil rights.

Harlan was born on June 1, 1833 in Boyle County, Kentucky. After graduating from Centre College, Harlan studied law at Transylvania University. In 1853 he was admitted to the bar in Kentucky. Harlan maintained a private practice until the Civil War broke out. During the war he was lieutenant colonel in the Union Army. After the war ended Harlan resumed his legal practice. In 1877 President Rutherford B. Hayes nominated Harlan to the Supreme Court.

Harlan wrote numerous capital punishment opinions while on the Supreme Court. His capital punishment writings provided mature constitutional reasoning that swung between moderate and liberal. For example, in *Hurtado v. California* Harlan dissented from the majority's decision to allow States to prosecute capital offenses without use of a grand jury indictment. Harlan argued that due process of law prohibited prosecution of capital crimes without an indictment. In *Holden v. Minnesota* Harlan wrote an opinion for the Court where he held that the Constitution did not bar enforcement of a death penalty statute that was repealed and reenacted after the date of the defendant's crime, but did not alter the substantive law existing at the time of the crime. In *Neal v. Delaware* Harlan reversed a capital conviction on the grounds that the defendant established that Delaware officials implemented the State's jury laws in such a manner as to systematically exclude African Americans from all jury service. Harlan died on October 14, 1911.

Capital Punishment Opinions Written by Harlan

Case Name	Opinion of the Court	Concurring Opinion	Dissenting Opinion
Andrews v. Swartz	✓		
Bergemann v. Backer	✓		
Brown v. United States (II)	✓		
Bush v. Kentucky	✓		
Calton v. Utah	✓		
Cook v. United States	✓		
Davis v. United States (I)	✓		
Fielden v. Illinois			✓

Case Name	Opinion of the Court	Concurring Opinion	Dissenting Opinion
Gibson v. Mississippi	✓		
Gourko v. United States	✓		
Holden v. Minnesota	✓		
Hopt v. Utah (II)	✓		
Hurtado v. California			✓
In Re Jugiro	✓		
In Re Wood	✓		
Martin v. Texas	✓		
Neal v. Delaware	✓		
Pointer v. United States	✓		
Rooney v. North Dakota	✓		
Schwab v. Berggren	✓		
Smith v. Mississippi	✓		
Sparf v. United States	✓		
St. Clair v. United States	✓		
Thompson v. Missouri	✓		

Harlan, John M. II   John M. Harlan II (grandson of former Justice Harlan) served as an associate justice of the United States Supreme Court from 1955 to 1971. While on the Supreme Court Harlan was known as a conservative interpreter of the Constitution.

Harlan was born in Chicago, Illinois on May 20, 1899. He graduated from Princeton University in 1920. He subsequently studied abroad at Oxford University on a Rhodes Scholarship. Upon returning to the United States Harlan enrolled in New York Law School, where he graduated in 1924. Harlan worked in private practice before taking a job as a Federal attorney. Through political connections Harlan was able to obtain President Dwight D. Eisenhower's nomination for the Supreme Court. The nomination occurred in 1954 and Senate confirmation followed in 1955.

Harlan wrote a number of capital punishment opinions while on the Supreme Court. His opinions were consistent in being conservative approaches to the Constitution. For example, in *Brady v. Maryland* Harlan dissented from the majority's decision to find that the defendant was entitled to a new sentencing hearing. Harlan argued that the issue was not properly before the Court and should have been sent back for resolution for the courts of Maryland. In *Boykin v. Alabama* Harlan dissented from the majority's decision to require trial records affirmatively show that a defendant voluntarily entered a guilty plea. Harlan argued that the Court was wrong to con-

Capital Punishment Opinions Written by Harlan

Case Name	Opinion of the Court	Concurring Opinion	Dissenting Opinion	Concurring and Dissenting
Boulden v. Holman				✓
Boykin v. Alabama			✓	
Brady v. Maryland			✓	
Chessman v. Teets	✓			
Darcy v. Handy			✓	
Fikes v. Alabama			✓	
Irvin v. Dowd (I)			✓	
Jackson v. Denno			✓	
Lane v. Brown		✓		
McGautha v. California	✓			
Spencer v. Texas	✓			

stitutionalize such a requirement. Harlan died on December 29, 1971.

Harmless Error Rule   Harmless error analysis is a standard of review used for determining the prejudicial impact of a constitutional error affecting a conviction or sentence in a case. The harmless error rule provides that any error, defect, irregularity or variance which does not affect substantial rights of a defendant shall be disregarded. Under this rule, if the prosecutor can prove beyond a reasonable doubt that a constitutional error did not contribute to the verdict, the error is harmless and the verdict may stand. *See also* **Calderon v. Coleman; Error; Jones v. United States (II); Satterwhite v. Texas**

Harris v. Alabama   *Court:* United States Supreme Court; *Case Citation:* Harris v. Alabama, 115 S.Ct. 1031 (1995); *Argued:* December 5, 1994; *Decided:* February 22, 1995; *Opinion of the Court:* Justice O'Connor; *Concurring Opinion:* None; *Dissenting Opinion:* Justice Stevens; *Appellate Defense Counsel:* Not reported; *Appellate Prosecution Counsel:* Not reported; *Amicus Curiae Brief Supporting Prosecutor:* Not reported; *Amicus Curiae Brief Supporting Defendant:* Not reported.

Issue Presented: Whether Alabama's capital sentencing statute is unconstitutional because it does not specify the weight the judge must give to the jury's recommendation?

Case Holding: The Constitution does not require the State to define the weight the sentencing judge must give to an advisory jury verdict.

Factual and procedural background of case: The defendant, Louise Harris, was convicted by an Alabama jury of capital murder. Under Alabama law capital sentencing authority is in the trial judge, but requires the judge to consider an advisory jury verdict. The penalty phase jury recommended that the defendant be imprisoned for life without parole, but the trial judge sentenced her to death upon concluding that the statutory aggravating circumstance found and considered outweighed all of the mitigating circumstances. The Alabama Court of Criminal Appeals affirmed the conviction and sentence. In doing so, the appellate court rejected the defendant's argument that Alabama's capital sentencing statute is unconstitutional because it does not specify the weight the judge must give to the jury's recommendation and thus permits the arbitrary imposition of the death penalty. The Alabama Supreme Court affirmed. The United States Supreme Court granted certiorari to address the defendant's constitutional claim.

Opinion of the Court by Justice O'Connor: Justice O'Connor noted that prior precedent of the Court held that the Constitution permits the trial judge, acting alone, to impose a capital sentence. Therefore, it was reasoned, the Constitution it is not offended when a State further requires the judge to consider a jury recommendation and trusts the judge to give it the proper weight. The opinion ruled that the hallmark of the analysis is not the particular weight a State chooses to place upon the jury's advice, but whether the scheme adequately channels the sentencer's discretion so as to prevent arbitrary results. It was said that the Constitution should not be used to micromanage tasks that properly rest within the State's discretion in administering its criminal justice system.

The opinion found unpersuasive statistical evidence demonstrating that there have been only 5 cases in which an Alabama judge rejected an advisory verdict of death, compared to 47 instances where the judge imposed a death sentence over a jury recommendation of life. It was said that these numbers do not tell the whole story because they do not indicate how many cases in which a jury recommendation of life was adopted would have ended differently had the judge not been required to consider the jury's advice. The opinion continued its reasoning and indicated that the statistics say little about whether the Alabama scheme is constitutional, a question which turns not solely on numerical tabulations of sentences, but rather on whether the punishment imposed is the result of properly guided discretion. Accordingly, the opinion affirmed the judgment of the Alabama Supreme Court.

Dissenting opinion by Justice Stevens: The dissent by Justice Stevens pointed out the following: "Alabama's capital sentencing statute is unique. In Alabama, unlike any other State in the Union, the trial judge has unbridled discretion to sentence the defendant to death — even though a jury has determined that death is an inappropriate penalty, and even though no basis exists for believing that any other reasonable, properly instructed jury would impose a death sentence." In view of the discretion given trial judges by Alabama's death penalty statute, Justice Stevens indicated he "would conclude that the complete absence of standards to guide the judge's consideration of the jury's verdict renders the statute invalid under the Eighth Amendment and the Due Process Clause of the Fourteenth Amendment."

Justice Stevens believed that "total reliance on judges to pronounce sentences of death is constitutionally unacceptable." He concluded: "The Court today casts a cloud over the legitimacy of our capital sentencing jurisprudence. The most credible justification for the death penalty is its expression of the community's outrage. To permit the state to execute a woman in spite of the community's considered judgment that she should not die is to sever the death penalty from its only legitimate mooring. The absence of any rudder on a judge's free-floating power to negate the community's will, in my judgment, renders Alabama's capital sentencing scheme fundamentally unfair and results in cruel and unusual punishment. I therefore respectfully dissent." See also **Binding/ Nonbinding Jury Sentencing Determination; Spaziano v. Florida**

Harris v. South Carolina   *Court:* United States Supreme Court; *Case Citation:* Harris v. South Carolina, 338 U.S. 68 (1949); *Argued:* November 16, 1948; *Decided:* June 27, 1949; *Plurality Opinion:* Justice Frankfurter announced the Court's judgment and delivered an opinion, in which Murphy and Rutledge, JJ., joined; *Concurring Opinion:* Justice Douglas; *Concurring Statement:* Justice Black; *Dissenting Opinion:* Justice Jackson; *Dissenting Statement:* Chief Justice Vinson and Reed and Burton, JJ.; *Appellate Defense Counsel:* Julian B. Salley, Jr. argued; Leonard A. Williamson on brief; *Appellate Prosecution Counsel:* B. D. Carter argued and briefed; *Amicus Curiae Brief Supporting Prosecutor:* None; *Amicus Curiae Brief Supporting Defendant:* None.

Issue Presented: Whether the defendant's confession was obtained in violation of due process of law, and thereby invalidated his conviction and death sentence?

Case Holding: The defendant's confession was obtained in violation of due process of law, therefore his conviction and death sentence were invalid.

Factual and procedural background of case: The defendant, Harris, was convicted of capital murder and sentenced to death by the State of South Carolina. The South Carolina Supreme Court affirmed the conviction and sentence. In doing so, the appellate court rejected the defendant's contention that his confession was obtained under circumstances which precluded its admission under the Due Process Clause of the Federal Constitution. The United States Supreme Court granted certiorari to consider the issue.

Plurality opinion in which Justice Frankfurter announced the Court's judgment and in which Murphy and Rutledge, JJ., joined: Justice Frankfurter outlined the following facts regarding the arrest of the defendant. It was said that the defendant was not informed of his rights under South Carolina law, such as the right to secure a lawyer, the right to request a preliminary hearing, or the right to remain silent. The opinion observed that the confession did not contain the usual statement that he was told that what he said might be used against him. Justice Frankfurter indicated that during the whole period of interrogation by the police, the defendant was denied the benefit of consultation with family and friends. The opinion also found relevant the fact that the defendant was illiterate. Under these facts, the opinion found the confession was not voluntarily given. Justice Frankfurter concluded:

> The trial judge in his charge told the jury that without the confession there was no evidence which would support a conviction and instructed them that they could consider the confession only if they found it to have been "voluntary." Upon appeal, the highest court of the State made a conscientious effort to measure the circumstances under which [the defendant's] confession was made against the circumstances surrounding confessions which we have held to be the product of undue pressure. It concluded that this confession was not so tainted. We are constrained to disagree. The systematic persistence of interrogation, the length of the periods of questioning, the failure to advise the [defendant] of his rights, the absence of friends or disinterested persons, and the character of the defendant constitute a complex of circumstances which invokes the same considerations which compelled our decisions in *Watts v. Indiana*. The judgment is accordingly reversed.

***Concurring opinion by Justice Douglas*:** Justice Douglas concurred in the Court's judgment. He found the conditions of the defendant's interrogation to be offensive to the Constitution. His concurring opinion outlined the details of the interrogations the defendant was subjected to, before he "broke" and confessed to the crime. Justice Douglas concluded:

> ... These interrogations had been held in a small room eight feet by eleven. Small groups of different officers conducted these interrogations, which went on and on in the heat of the days and nights. But during this time [the defendant] was denied counsel and access to family and friends.
>
> This is another illustration of the use by the police of the custody of an accused to wring a confession from him. The confession so obtained from literate and illiterate alike should [be] condemned.

Concurring Statement by Justice Black: Justice Black issued a statement indicating he concurred in the Court's judgment.

Dissenting opinion by Justice Jackson: Justice Jackson dissented from the Court's decision in the case. He referenced to his concurring and dissenting opinion written in a companion case, *Watts v. Indiana,* as the basis for his dissent. In *Watts,* Justice Jackson wrote that he believed involuntary confessions were not invalid under the Constitution. He believed such confessions assured the accuracy of convictions. Justice Jackson reasoned as follows in the dissenting part of his *Watts* opinion: "The seriousness of the Court's judgment is that no one suggests that any course held promise of solution of these murders other than to take the suspect into custody for questioning. The alternative was to close the books on the crime and forget it, with the suspect at large. This is a grave choice for a society in which two-thirds of the murders already are closed out as insoluble."

Dissenting statement by Chief Justice Vinson and Reed and Burton, JJ.: Chief Justice Vinson and Justices Reed and Burton issued a joint statement indicating they dissented from the Court's decision and believed the judgment should be affirmed.

Case note: This case was one of three cases decided by the Court, on the same day, involving involuntary confessions. In each of the cases the Court applied due process principals to invalidate the capital convictions. In subsequent decades the Court would apply the Fifth Amendment right to remain silent to review claims from State prisoners that their confessions were involuntary. *See also* **Right to Remain Silent; Turner v. Pennsylvania; Watts v. Indiana**

Haupt, Herbert Hans *see* Espionage

Hauptmann, Bruno Richard *see* Lindbergh Kidnapping

Hawaii The death penalty is not carried out by the State of Hawaii. There have been no executions in the state of Hawaii since its entry into the United States.

Hearsay Hearsay is a legal technical term that means a statement, other than one made by a declarant while testifying at trial or hearing, offered in evidence to prove the truth of the matter asserted by the statement. Under Anglo-American jurisprudence hearsay is generally not allowed at a trial or hearing. The basis of the hearsay exclusion is that the opposing party will not have had an opportunity to cross examine the declarant making the out-of-court statement. Thus, the veracity of an out-of-court statement is deemed questionable.

In capital prosecutions the hearsay rule is followed by all jurisdictions during the guilt phase. However, jurisdictions are split on the admissibility of hearsay during the penalty phase. Some jurisdictions generally permit hearsay at the penalty phase, while others apply the hearsay rule at the penalty phase. *See also* **Carver v. United States; Cook v. United States; Green v. Georgia; Hearsay Exceptions; Lilly v. Virginia**

Hearsay Exceptions The general rule barring hearsay evidence from a trial or hearing has exceptions. There are two general categories of exceptions to hearsay: (A) availability of declarant immaterial and (B) declarant unavailable. The exceptions to hearsay contained in the Federal Rules of Evidence, as shown below, represent the two general categories of exceptions which are followed by all jurisdictions.

A. *The following are not excluded by the hearsay rule, even though the declarant is available as a witness:*

1. Present sense impression. A statement describing or explaining an event or condition made while the declarant was perceiving the event or condition, or immediately thereafter.

2. Excited utterance. A statement relating to a startling event or condition made while the declarant was under the stress of excitement caused by the event or condition.

3. Then existing mental, emotional, or physical condition. A statement of the declarant's then existing state of mind, emotion, sensation, or physical condition (such as intent, plan, motive, design, mental feeling, pain, and bodily health), but not including a statement of memory or belief to prove the fact remembered or believed unless it relates to the execution, revocation, identification, or terms of declarant's will.

4. Statements for purposes of medical diagnosis or treatment. Statements made for purposes of medical diagnosis or treatment and describing medical history, or past or present symptoms, pain, or sensations, or the inception or general character of the cause or external source thereof insofar as reasonably pertinent to diagnosis or treatment.

5. Recorded recollection. A memorandum or record concerning a matter about which a witness once had knowledge but now has insufficient recollection to enable the witness to testify fully and accurately, shown to have been made or adopted by the witness when the matter was fresh in the witness' memory and to reflect that

knowledge correctly. If admitted, the memorandum or record may be read into evidence but may not itself be received as an exhibit unless offered by an adverse party.

6. Records of regularly conducted activity. A memorandum, report, record, or data compilation, in any form, of acts, events, conditions, opinions, or diagnoses, made at or near the time by, or from information transmitted by, a person with knowledge, if kept in the course of a regularly conducted business activity, and if it was the regular practice of that business activity to make the memorandum, report, record, or data compilation, all as shown by the testimony of the custodian or other qualified witness, unless the source of information or the method or circumstances of preparation indicate lack of trustworthiness. The term "business" as used in this paragraph includes business, institution, association, profession, occupation, and calling of every kind, whether or not conducted for profit.

7. Absence of entry in records properly kept. Evidence that a matter is not included in the memoranda reports, records, or data compilations, in any form, properly kept, to prove the nonoccurrence or nonexistence of the matter, if the matter was of a kind of which a memorandum, report, record, or data compilation was regularly made and preserved, unless the sources of information or other circumstances indicate lack of trustworthiness.

8. Public records and reports. Records, reports, statements, or data compilations, in any form, of public offices or agencies, setting forth (i) the activities of the office or agency, or (ii) matters observed pursuant to duty imposed by law as to which matters there was a duty to report, excluding, however, in criminal cases matters observed by police officers and other law enforcement personnel, or (iii) in civil actions and proceedings and against the Government in criminal cases, factual findings resulting from an investigation made pursuant to authority granted by law, unless the sources of information or other circumstances indicate lack of trustworthiness.

9. Records of vital statistics. Records or data compilations, in any form, of births, fetal deaths, deaths, or marriages, if the report thereof was made to a public office pursuant to requirements of law.

10. Absence of public record or entry. To prove the absence of a record, report, statement, or data compilation, in any form, or the nonoccurrence or nonexistence of a matter of which a record, report, statement, or data compilation, in any form, was regularly made and preserved by a public office or agency, evidence in the form of a certification, or testimony, that diligent search failed to disclose the record, report, statement, or data compilation, or entry.

11. Records of religious organizations. Statements of births, marriages, divorces, deaths, legitimacy, ancestry, relationship by blood or marriage, or other similar facts of personal or family history, contained in a regularly kept record of a religious organization.

12. Marriage, baptismal, and similar certificates. Statements of fact contained in a certificate that the maker performed a marriage or other ceremony or administered a sacrament, made by a clergyman, public official, or other person authorized by the rules or practices of a religious organization or by law to perform the act certified, and purporting to have been issued at the time of the act or within a reasonable time thereafter.

13. Family records. Statements of fact concerning personal or family history contained in family Bibles, genealogies, charts, engravings on rings, inscriptions on family portraits, engravings on urns, crypts, or tombstones, or the like.

14. Records of documents affecting an interest in property. The record of a document purporting to establish or affect an interest in property, as proof of the content of the original recorded document and its execution and delivery by each person by whom it purports to have been executed, if the record is a record of a public office and an applicable statute authorizes the recording of documents of that kind in that office.

15. Statements in documents affecting an interest in property. A statement contained in a document purporting to establish or affect an interest in property if the matter stated was relevant to the purpose of the document, unless dealings with the property since the document was made have been inconsistent with the truth of the statement or the purport of the document.

16. Statements in ancient documents. Statements in a document in existence twenty years or more the authenticity of which is established.

17. Market reports, commercial publications. Market quotations, tabulations, lists, directories, or other published compilations, generally used and relied upon by the public or by persons in particular occupations.

18. Learned treatises. To the extent called to the attention of an expert witness upon cross-examination or relied upon by the expert witness in direct examination, statements contained in published treatises, periodicals, or pamphlets on a subject of history, medicine, or other science or art, established as a reliable authority by the testimony or admission of the witness or by other expert testimony or by judicial notice. If admitted, the statements may be read into evidence but may not be received as exhibits.

19. Reputation concerning personal or family history. Reputation among members of a person's family by blood, adoption, or marriage, or among a person's associates, or in the community, concerning a person's birth, adoption, marriage, divorce, death, legitimacy, relationship by blood, adoption, or marriage, ancestry, or other similar fact of personal or family history.

20. Reputation concerning boundaries or general history.

Reputation in a community, arising before the controversy, as to boundaries of or customs affecting lands in the community, and reputation as to events of general history important to the community or State or nation in which located.

21. Reputation as to character. Reputation of a person's character among associates or in the community.

22. Judgment of previous conviction. Evidence of a final judgment, entered after a trial or upon a plea of guilty (but not upon a plea of nolo contendere), adjudging a person guilty of a crime punishable by death or imprisonment in excess of one year, to prove any fact essential to sustain the judgment, but not including, when offered by the Government in a criminal prosecution for purposes other than impeachment, judgments against persons other than the accused. The pendency of an appeal may be shown but does not affect admissibility.

23. Judgment as to personal, family or general history, or boundaries. Judgments as proof of matters of personal, family or general history, or boundaries, essential to the judgment, if the same would be provable by evidence of reputation.

B. *The following are not excluded by the hearsay rule if the declarant is unavailable as a witness:*

1. Former testimony. Testimony given as a witness at another hearing of the same or a different proceeding, or in a deposition taken in compliance with law in the course of the same or another proceeding, if the party against whom the testimony is now offered, or, in a civil action or proceeding, a predecessor in interest, had an opportunity and similar motive to develop the testimony by direct, cross, or redirect examination.

2. Statement under belief of impending death. In a prosecution for homicide or in a civil action or proceeding, a statement made by a declarant while believing that the declarant's death was imminent, concerning the cause or circumstances of what the declarant believed to be impending death.

3. Statement against interest. A statement which was at the time of its making so far contrary to the declarant's pecuniary or proprietary interest, or so far tended to subject the declarant to civil or criminal liability, or to render invalid a claim by the declarant against another, that a reasonable person in the declarant's position would not have made the statement unless believing it to be true. A statement tending to expose the declarant to criminal liability and offered to exculpate the accused is not admissible unless corroborating circumstances clearly indicate the trustworthiness of the statement.

4. Statement of personal or family history. A statement concerning the declarant's own birth, adoption, marriage, divorce, legitimacy, relationship by blood, adoption, or marriage, ancestry, or other similar fact of personal or family history, even though declarant had no means of acquiring personal knowledge of the matter stated; or a statement concerning the foregoing matters, and death also, of another person, if the declarant was related to the other by blood, adoption, or marriage or was so intimately associated with the other's family as to be likely to have accurate information concerning the matter declared. *See also* **Carver v. United States; Hearsay; Lilly v. Virginia**

Heath v. Alabama

Court: United States Supreme Court; *Case Citation:* Heath v. Alabama, 474 U.S. 82 (1985); *Argued:* October 9, 1985; *Decided:* December 3, 1985; *Opinion of the Court:* Justice O'Connor; *Concurring Opinion:* None; *Dissenting Opinion:* Justice Brennan, in which Marshall, J., joined; *Dissenting Opinion:* Justice Marshall, in which Brennan, J., joined; *Appellate Defense Counsel:* Ronald J. Allen argued and briefed; *Appellate Prosecution Counsel:* William D. Little argued; Charles A. Graddick on brief; *Amicus Curiae Brief Supporting Prosecutor:* None; *Amicus Curiae Brief Supporting Defendant:* None.

Issue Presented: Whether the Double Jeopardy Clause bars Alabama from trying the defendant for the capital offense of murder during a kidnaping after Georgia convicted him of murder based on the same homicide?

Case Holding: Successive prosecutions by two States for the same conduct are not barred by the Double Jeopardy Clause.

Factual and procedural background of case: In August 1981, the defendant, Larry Gene Heath, hired two men to kill his wife. In accordance with the defendant's plan, the two men kidnaped his wife from her home in Alabama. The murdered body of the defendant's wife was later found on the side of a road in Georgia. The defendant was prosecuted for murder by Georgia, and he pleaded guilty to murder in a Georgia trial court in exchange for a sentence of life imprisonment. Subsequently, the defendant was tried and convicted of capital murder and was sentenced to death in an Alabama trial court. The Alabama Court of Criminal Appeals and the Alabama Supreme Court affirmed the conviction and sentence. In doing so, both appellate courts rejected the defendant's claim that double jeopardy principles prohibited Alabama from prosecuting him. The United States Supreme Court granted certiorari to address the double jeopardy claim.

Opinion of the Court by Justice O'Connor: Justice O'Connor wrote that under the dual sovereignty doctrine, successive prosecutions by two States for the same conduct are not barred by the Double Jeopardy Clause, therefore Alabama was not barred from prosecuting the defendant.

The opinion explained the dual sovereignty doctrine as follows. The dual sovereignty doctrine provides that when a defendant in a single act violates the law of two sovereign jurisdictions, he or she has committed two distinct offenses for double jeopardy purposes. It was said that in applying the doctrine, the crucial determination is whether the two entities that seek successively to prosecute a defendant for the same course of conduct can be termed separate sovereigns. This determination turns on whether the prosecuting jurisdictions' powers to undertake criminal prosecutions derive from separate and independent sources. The opinion noted that it has been uniformly held that the States are separate sovereigns with respect to the Federal Government, because each State's power to prosecute derives from its inherent sovereignty. Thus, given the distinct sources of their powers to try a defendant, the opinion held that the States are no less sovereign with respect to each other than they are with respect to the Federal Government. The opinion affirmed the judgment of the Alabama Supreme Court.

Dissenting opinion by Brennan: Justice Brennan wrote that he believed double jeopardy principles prohibited successive prosecutions by different sovereigns for the same conduct. He would, therefore, reverse the judgment of the Alabama Supreme Court.

Dissenting opinion by Marshall: Justice Marshall argued that the dual sovereignty doctrine permitted the federal government and a State to prosecute a defendant for the same conduct. He drew a line there, however. Justice Marshall wrote: "The 'dual sovereignty' doctrine, heretofore used to permit federal and state prosecutions for the same offense, was born of the need to accommodate complementary state and federal concerns within our system of concurrent territorial jurisdictions. It cannot justify successive prosecutions by different States."

The dissent reasoned as follows: "Where two States seek to prosecute the same defendant for the same crime in two separate proceedings, the justifications found in the federal-state context for an exemption from double jeopardy constraints simply do not hold.... Thus, in contrast to the federal-state context, barring the second prosecution would still permit one government to act upon the broad range of sovereign concerns that have been reserved to the States by the Constitution. The compelling need in the federal-state context to subordinate double jeopardy concerns is thus considerably diminished in cases involving successive prosecutions by different States." Therefore, Justice Marshall would reverse the judgment of the Alabama Supreme Court. *See also* **Dual Sovereignty**

Heckler v. Chaney *Court:* United States Supreme Court; *Case Citation:* Heckler v. Chaney, 470 U.S. 821 (1985); *Argued:* December 3, 1984; *Decided:* March 20, 1985; *Opinion of the Court:* Justice Rehnquist; *Concurring Opinion:* Justice Brennan; *Concurring Opinion:* Justice Marshall; *Dissenting Opinion:* None; *Counsel for Petitioner:* Deputy Solicitor General Geller argued; Samuel A. Alito, Jr., Leonard Schaitman, John M. Rogers, Thomas Scarlett, and Michael P. Peskoe on brief; *Counsel for Respondents:* Steven M. Kristovich argued; David E. Kendall, Julius LeVonne Chambers, James M. Nabrit III, John Charles Boger, James S. Liebman, and Anthony G. Amsterdam on brief; *Amicus Curiae Brief Supporting Petitioner:* 1; *Amicus Curiae Brief Supporting Respondents:* 2.

Issue Presented: The extent to which determinations by the FDA not to exercise its enforcement authority over the use of drugs used in carrying out the death penalty may be judicially reviewed?

Case Holding: The FDA's decision not to exercise its enforcement authority over the use of drugs used in carrying out the death penalty is not judicially reviewable.

Factual and procedural background of case: The respondents in the case were prisoners who were convicted of capital offenses and sentenced to death by lethal injection of drugs. The respondents filed a claim with the Food and Drug Administration (FDA), alleging that use of the drugs to execute the death penalty violated Federal law. The respondents requested that the FDA take enforcement action to prevent such violations. The FDA refused the request. The respondents then filed a suit in a Federal District Court against the petitioner, Secretary of Health and Human Services, making the same claim and seeking the same enforcement actions. The District Court dismissed the suit on the grounds that Federal law did not indicate a Congressional intent to make the FDA's enforcement discretion reviewable by courts. A Federal Court of Appeals reversed. The appellate court indicated that Federal law only precluded judicial review of Federal agency action when it is precluded by statute, or is committed to agency discretion by law. It was said that the FDA's refusal to take enforcement action was reviewable by courts. The United States Supreme Court granted certiorari to address the matter.

Opinion of the Court by Justice Rehnquist: Justice Rehnquist observed that under Federal law judicial review of an administrative agency's decision is not allowed, if the enabling statute of the agency is written so that a court would have no meaningful standard against which to judge the agency's exercise of discretion. In such a situation, the opinion said, the enabling statute can be taken to have committed the decision making to the agency's judgment absolutely.

Justice Rehnquist ruled that an agency's decision not to take enforcement action is presumed immune from judicial review. Accordingly, such a decision is unreviewable unless Congress has indicated an intent to circumscribe agency enforcement discretion, and has provided meaningful standards for defining the limits of that discretion. The opinion concluded that, "[t]he fact that the drugs involved in this case are ultimately to be used in imposing the death penalty must not lead this Court or other courts to import profound differences of opinion over the meaning of the Eighth Amendment to the United States Constitution into the domain of administrative law." The judgment of the Court of Appeals was reversed.

Concurring opinion by Justice Brennan: Justice Brennan wrote in concurrence that he agreed with the ruling that individual decisions of the FDA not to take enforcement action in response to citizen requests are presumptively not reviewable. He added that "[t]his general presumption is based on the view that, in the normal course of events, Congress intends to allow broad discretion for its administrative agencies to make particular enforcement decisions, and there often may not exist readily discernible 'law to apply' for courts to conduct judicial review of nonenforcement decisions."

Concurring opinion by Justice Marshall: Justice Marshall concurred in the Court's judgment, but disapproved of its reasoning. He wrote that: "[T]he 'presumption of unreviewability' announced today is a product of that lack of discipline that easy cases make all too easy…. [T]his 'presumption of unreviewability' is fundamentally at odds with rule-of-law principles firmly embedded in our jurisprudence[.]" As an alternative reason for the Court's judgment, Justice Marshall wrote that the basis for the decision should be "that refusals to enforce, like other agency actions, are reviewable in the absence of a 'clear and convincing' congressional intent to the contrary, but that such refusals warrant deference when, as in this case, there is nothing to suggest that an agency with enforcement discretion has abused that discretion." *See also* **Lethal Injection**

Heinck, Heinrich Harm *see* Espionage

Heinous, Atrocious, Cruel or Depraved Aggravator

A large minority of capital punishment jurisdictions have designated murder that is heinous, atrocious, cruel or depraved, a statutory aggravating circumstance. When this conduct is established at the penalty phase, a death sentence may be imposed. Appellate courts have consistently reversed death sentences, however, when this aggravator has been used without a qualifying definition being given for its terms. Acceptable definitions have included the following. Cruelty refers to the infliction of pain and suffering in a wanton, insensitive or vindictive manner. Heinous and depraved refer to the mental state and attitude of a capital felon, such as acting in a cold-blooded manner. Atrocious refers to torture or serious physical abuse of the victim. *See also* **Aggravating Circumstances; Lewis v. Jeffers; Maynard v. Cartwright; Richmond v. Lewis; Shell v. Mississippi; Sochor v. Florida; Stringer v. Black ; Walton v. Arizona**

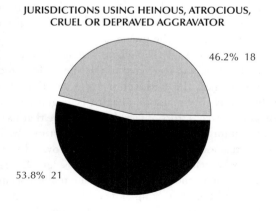

JURISDICTIONS USING HEINOUS, ATROCIOUS, CRUEL OR DEPRAVED AGGRAVATOR

46.2% 18

53.8% 21

■ HEINOUS, ATROCIOUS, CRUEL OR DEPRAVED JURISDICTIONS
■ ALL OTHER JURISDICTIONS

Henderson, Cathy Lynn In late January of 1994, the television show *America's Most Wanted*, profiled Cathy Lynn Henderson as a person wanted for kidnapping. Airing photographs of Henderson nationwide helped authorities locate and arrest her in Missouri. The kidnapping charge, however, expanded to include murder.

Henderson was born in Missouri on December 27, 1946. She eventually moved to Texas, where she resided in Travis County. Henderson hired herself out as a babysitter. On January 21, 1994 a couple left their three month old son with Henderson. The baby was never seen alive again. Henderson mysteriously disappeared with the child on the same day he was left with her.

As a result of her being profiled on *America's Most Wanted* television show, Henderson was identified in several states as she drove to Missouri. On February 1, Henderson was arrested by the Federal Bureau of Investigation in Kansas City, Missouri. Henderson informed authorities that she accidentally dropped the baby on his head and caused his death. She stated that she panicked and buried the body in a wooded area near Waco, Texas before fleeing to Missouri. The child's dead body was eventually found; he had sustained a fractured skull.

In May of 1995, Henderson was convicted of capital murder by a Travis County jury and sentenced to death. The Texas Court of Criminal Appeals affirmed the judgment. Henderson is on death row in Texas. *See also* **Women and Capital Punishment**

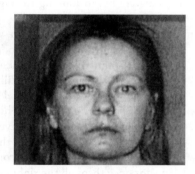

Cathy Lynn Henderson is on death row in Texas after being convicted of killing a three month old infant. (Texas Department of Criminal Justice)

Herold, David *see* Lincoln's Assassination

Herreras William Herrera, Sr. and William Herrera, Jr. are father and son. The Herreras are on death row together in an Arizona prison, having both been convicted of murdering a deputy sheriff.

William Sr. was born on October 31, 1946. William Jr. was born on May 1, 1968. William Sr. had two other younger sons, Mickel and Ruben. All of the Herreras lived in Phoenix Arizona. On June 30, 1988, William Sr. and his three sons took part in the murder of deputy sheriff Vernon Marconnet.

William Herrera, Jr., left, is on death row in Arizona with his father, William Herrera, Sr., right. (Arizona Department of Corrections)

The facts surrounding Marconnet's death were as follows. In the afternoon of June 30, William Sr., his three sons and a female companion named Mary Cardenas, went to a desert area in southwest Phoenix to drink beer and wine. They had driven two vehicles and parked them into some trees and shrubbery on the shoulder of a dirt road.

At about 5:20 that afternoon, a motorist drove by and saw the two vehicles. The motorist believed that one vehicle had forced the other off the road. Shortly after seeing the vehicles, the motorist flagged down Marconnet, who was cruising in his patrol car. The motorist conveyed his suspicions to Marconnet. Marconnet immediately proceeded to the area described by the motorist.

When Marconnet arrived at the scene he asked everyone for identification. William Sr. refused to comply and began cursing at the deputy. Marconnet proceeded to place William Sr. under arrest and put him in the backseat of the patrol car. Afterwards Marconnet went to a vehicle that Cardenas was sitting in and asked her to provide the vehicle registration. She immediately began looking through the glove compartment for the registration.

While Marconnet's attention was on Cardenas, Ruben opened the patrol car's backdoor and let his father out. William Sr. immediately approached Marconnet and a fight broke out. As William Sr. and William Jr. fought Marconnet, his gun fell to the ground. Mickel picked up the gun and, as he did, William Sr. commanded him to shoot. Mickel pulled the trigger and shot Marconnet. Everyone immediately fled the area leaving Marconnet lying on the ground dying.

When authorities found Marconnet he was dead. He had been shot once through the right eye. During the crime scene investigation authorities found an identification card bearing Ruben's name on it. All of the Herreras were tracked down and indicted for capital murder. Ruben entered a plea agreement that required him to testify against his father and brothers. Under the plea agreement Ruben received a ten year prison sentence.

William Jr. and Mickel were prosecuted together on September 5, 1989. A jury found them both guilty of capital murder. William Sr. was prosecuted on October 19, 1989. The jury also found him guilty of capital murder. On December 21, 1989, a penalty phase proceeding was held for all three of the Herreras. They were each sentenced to death. The Arizona Supreme Court affirmed the death sentence for William Sr. and William Jr. However, the State high court reversed Mickel's death sentence and imposed a sentence of life imprisonment. Mickel was given leniency because of his age at the time of the crime, 18; duress caused by his father's order that he shoot the deputy; and a borderline I.Q.

Herrera v. Collins

Court: United States Supreme Court; *Case Citation:* Herrera v. Collins, 506 U.S. 390 (1993); *Argued:* October 7, 1992; *Decided:* January 25, 1993; *Opinion of the Court:* Chief Justice Rehnquist; *Concurring Opinion:* Justice O'Connor, in which Kennedy, J., joined; *Concurring Opinion:* Justice Scalia, in which Thomas, J., joined; *Concurring Opinion:* Justice White; *Dissenting Opinion:* Justice Blackmun, in which Stevens and Souter, JJ., joined; *Appellate Defense Counsel:* Talbot D'Alemberte argued; Robert L. McGlasson, Phyllis L. Crocker, and Mark Evan Olive on brief; *Appellate Prosecution Counsel:* Margaret Portman Griffey argued; Dan Morales, Will Pryor, Mary F. Keller, Michael P. Hodge, Dana E. Parker and Joan C. Barton on brief; *Amicus Curiae Brief Supporting Prosecutor:* 1; *Amicus Curiae Brief Supporting Defendant:* None.

Issue Presented: Whether Federal habeas relief was available to the defendant on the basis of alleged newly discovered evidence of actual innocence 10 years after the defendant was convicted?

Case Holding: Claims of actual innocence based on newly discovered evidence have never been held to state a ground for Federal habeas relief, absent an independent constitutional violation occurring in the course of the underlying State criminal proceedings.

Factual and procedural background of case: The State of Texas convicted the defendant, Leonel Torres Herrera, of capital murder in the death of two police officers. The defendant was sentenced to death. The defendant unsuccessfully sought post-conviction relief in State and Federal courts. Ten years after his convictions, the defendant filed a second Federal habeas corpus petition in a Federal District Court. His ground for relief was that newly discovered evidence demonstrated that he was actually innocent of the murders and that his deceased brother killed the victims. The District Court granted a stay of execution so that the defendant could present his actual innocence claim and supporting evidence in a State court. A Federal Court of Appeals vacated the stay and held that the defendant's claim was not cognizable in a Federal habeas proceeding. The United States Supreme Court granted certiorari to consider the issue.

Opinion of the Court by Chief Justice Rehnquist: The Chief Justice ruled that the defendant's claim of actual innocence did not entitle him to Federal habeas relief. The opinion found that the defendant's constitutional claim for relief based upon his newly discovered evidence of innocence must be evaluated in light of the previous 10 years of proceedings in the case. It was said that where a defendant has been afforded a fair trial and convicted of the offense for which he or she was charged, the constitutional presumption of innocence disappears. The opinion ruled that Federal habeas courts do not sit to correct errors of fact, but to ensure that individuals are not imprisoned in violation of the Constitution. Thus, claims of actual innocence based on newly discovered evidence have never been held to state a ground for Federal habeas relief, absent an independent constitutional violation occurring in the course of the underlying State criminal proceedings.

It was indicated by the Chief Justice that the rule that a defendant, subject to defenses of abusive or successive use of the habeas writ, may have his or her federal constitutional claim considered on the merits if he or she makes a proper showing

of actual innocence is inapplicable to this case. It was reasoned that the defendant did not seek relief from a procedural error so that he may bring an independent constitutional claim challenging his conviction or sentence, but rather he argued that he is entitled to habeas relief because new evidence shows that his conviction is factually incorrect. The opinion said that to allow a Federal court to grant him typical habeas relief would, in effect, require a new trial 10 years after the first trial, not because of any constitutional violation at the first trial, but simply because of a belief that, in light of his newly found evidence, a jury might find him not guilty at a second trial.

The Chief Justice noted that the defendant was not left without a forum to raise his actual innocence claim. It was said that he may file a request for clemency under Texas law, which contains specific guidelines for pardons on the ground of innocence. The judgment of the Court of Appeals was affirmed.

Concurring opinion by Justice O'Connor, in which Kennedy, J., joined: Justice O'Connor concurred in the Court's opinion and judgment. She wrote separately to underscore her belief that the defendant was not actually innocent. She wrote as follows:

> As the Court explains, [the defendant] is not innocent in the eyes of the law.... He was tried before a jury of his peers, with the full panoply of protections that our Constitution affords criminal defendants. At the conclusion of that trial, the jury found [him] guilty beyond a reasonable doubt. [The defendant] therefore does not appear before us as an innocent man on the verge of execution. He is instead a legally guilty one who, refusing to accept the jury's verdict, demands a hearing in which to have his culpability determined once again.
>
> Consequently, the issue before us is not whether a State can execute the innocent. It is, as the Court notes, whether a fairly convicted and therefore legally guilty person is constitutionally entitled to yet another judicial proceeding in which to adjudicate his guilt anew, 10 years after conviction, notwithstanding his failure to demonstrate that constitutional error infected his trial. In most circumstances, that question would answer itself in the negative. Our society has a high degree of confidence in its criminal trials, in no small part because the Constitution offers unparalleled protections against convicting the innocent.

Concurring opinion by Justice Scalia, in which Thomas, J., joined: Justice Scalia concurred in the Court's opinion and judgment. He wrote separately to voice his disagreement with the dissenting opinion in the case. Justice Scalia wrote:

> We granted certiorari on the question whether it violates due process or constitutes cruel and unusual punishment for a State to execute a person who, having been convicted of murder after a full and fair trial, later alleges that newly discovered evidence shows him to be "actually innocent." I would have preferred to decide that question, particularly since, as the Court's discussion shows, it is perfectly clear what the answer is: there is no basis in text, tradition, or even in contemporary practice (if that were enough) for finding in the Constitution a right to demand judicial consideration of newly discovered evidence of innocence brought forward after conviction. In saying that such a right exists, the dissenters apply nothing but their personal opinions to invalidate the rules of more than two thirds of the States, and a Federal Rule of Criminal Procedure for which this Court itself is responsible. If the system that has been in place for 200 years (and remains widely approved) "shock[s]" the dissenters' consciences, perhaps they should doubt the calibration of their

consciences, or, better still, the usefulness of "conscience shocking" as a legal test.

Concurring opinion by Justice White: Justice White concurred in the Court's judgment. He indicated that he believed the defendant's claim, in and of itself, was not precluded from review by a Federal court. Justice White found that the defendant failed to make a minimal showing that would entitle him to have a Federal court address the merits of his claim. He wrote: "To be entitled to relief, [the defendant] would, at the very least, be required to show that, based on proffered newly discovered evidence and the entire record before the jury that convicted him, 'no rational trier of fact could [find] proof of guilt beyond a reasonable doubt.' For the reasons stated in the Court's opinion, [the defendant's] showing falls far short of satisfying even that standard, and I therefore concur in the judgment."

Dissenting Opinion Justice Blackmun, in which Stevens and Souter, JJ., joined: Justice Blackmun dissented from the Court's disposition of the case. He believed that the defendant's claim was cognizable in Federal court on its merits. Justice Blackmun wrote:

> Nothing could be more contrary to contemporary standards of decency, or more shocking to the conscience, than to execute a person who is actually innocent.
>
> I therefore must disagree with the long and general discussion that precedes the Court's disposition of this case.... Because I believe that, in the first instance, the District Court should decide whether [the defendant] is entitled to a hearing and whether he is entitled to relief on the merits of his claim, I would reverse the order of the Court of Appeals and remand this case for further proceedings in the District Court.

Case note: Texas executed Leonel Torres Herrera by lethal injection on May 12, 1993. *See also* **Actual Innocence Claim; Sawyer v. Whitley; Schlup v. Delo**

Hickory v. United States (I)

Court: United States Supreme Court; *Case Citation:* Hickory v. United States, 151 U.S. 303 (1894); *Argued:* Not reported; *Decided:* January 15, 1894; *Opinion of the Court:* Chief Justice Fuller; *Concurring Opinion:* None; *Dissenting Statement:* Justice Brewer; *Justice Taking No Part in Decision:* Justice Brown; *Appellate Defense Counsel:* A. H. Garland argued and briefed; *Appellate Prosecution Counsel:* Mr. Whitney argued and briefed; *Amicus Curiae Brief Supporting Prosecutor:* None; *Amicus Curiae Brief Supporting Defendant:* None.

Issue Presented: Whether the trial court erroneously instructed the jury on the defense of self-defense?

Case Holding: The trial court erroneously instructed the jury on the defense of self-defense, by informing the jury that the defense was inapplicable if the crime occurred without reflection and meditation.

Factual and procedural background of case: The defendant, Sam Hickory, was convicted and sentenced to death for capital murder by the United States. The victim of the crime was a United States deputy marshal, who attempted to arrest the defendant. The defendant appealed the judgment to the United States Supreme Court, on the grounds that the trial court erroneously instructed the jury on the defense of self-defense. The United States Supreme Court granted certiorari to consider the issue.

Opinion of the Court by Chief Justice Fuller: The Chief Justice held that the instruction given by the trial court on self-defense was improper. The instruction given by the trial court told the jury that "while premeditation may exist in a criminal sense upon the conception of an instant, the conclusion to kill in self-defense must be arrived at upon more serious deliberation, or it furnishes no excuse." The Chief Justice pointed out that "in the matter of self-defense, the deliberation of the slayer in respect of the greatness of the necessity to protect himself from death or great bodily harm, if material, would also be sufficient, although the conclusion to kill was arrived at instantaneously. The swiftness of thought in the latter case would no more exclude the element of deliberation than in the former, and whether the act was excusable or not could only be determined by all the facts and circumstances disclosed by the evidence." It was said that the instruction given by the trial court was tantamount to telling the jury not to consider the evidence of self-defense. The opinion concluded that "[i]n short, whether or not a particular homicide is committed in repulsion of an attack, and, if so, justifiably, are questions of fact, not necessarily dependent upon the duration or quality of the reflection by which the act may have been preceded." The judgment of the Federal trial court was reversed and the case remanded for a new trial.

Dissenting statement by Justice Brewer: Justice Brewer issued a statement indicating he dissented from the Court's decision. See also **Hickory v. United States (II); Self-Defense**

Hickory v. United States (II)
Court: United States Supreme Court; *Case Citation:* Hickory v. United States, 160 U.S. 408 (1896); *Argued:* Not reported; *Decided:* January 6, 1896; *Opinion of the Court:* Justice White; *Concurring Opinion:* None; *Dissenting Opinion:* None; *Appellate Defense Counsel:* Not represented; *Appellate Prosecution Counsel:* Mr. Whitney argued and briefed; *Amicus Curiae Brief Supporting Prosecutor:* None; *Amicus Curiae Brief Supporting Defendant:* None.

Issue Presented: Whether it was error for the trial court to instruct the jury to presume the defendant's guilt from testimony of his concealment of crime scene evidence?

Case Holding: It was error for the trial court to instruct the jury to presume the defendant's guilt from testimony of his concealment of crime scene evidence.

Factual and procedural background of case: The defendant, Sam Hickory, was convicted and sentenced to death for capital murder by the United States. The defendant appealed the judgment to the United States Supreme Court and the case was reversed and a new trial awarded. At the second trial the defendant was again convicted and sentenced to death. The defendant appealed again alleging that the trial court improperly instructed the jury to infer his guilt from testimony of his concealment of crime scene evidence. The United States Supreme Court granted certiorari to consider the issue.

Opinion of the Court by Justice White: Justice White held that the trial court's instruction on flight created an erroneous presumption of guilt. The opinion reasoned as follows:

> ... [The instruction] magnified and distorted the proving power of the facts on the subject of the concealment; it made the weight of the evidence depend not so much on the concealment itself as on the manner in which it was done. Considering the entire context of the charge, it practically instructed that the facts were ... conclusive proof of guilt. The statement that no one who was conscious of innocence would resort to concealment was substantially an instruction that all men who did so were necessarily guilty, thus ignoring the fundamental truth, evolved from the experience of mankind, that the innocent do often conceal through fear or other emotion.... Putting this language, in connection with the epithets applied to the acts of concealment and the vituperation which the charge contains, it is justly to be deduced that its effect was to instruct that the defendant was a murderer, and therefore the only province of the jury was to return a verdict of guilty.

The judgment of the Federal trial court was reversed and the case remanded for a new trial. *See also* **Hickory v. United States (I)**

Hildwin v. Florida
Court: United States Supreme Court; *Case Citation:* Hildwin v. Florida, 490 U.S. 638 (1989); *Argued:* Not reported; *Decided:* May 30, 1989; *Opinion of the Court:* Per Curiam; *Concurring Opinion:* None; *Dissenting Opinion:* Justice Brennan; *Dissenting Opinion:* Justice Marshall; *Appellate Defense Counsel:* Not reported; *Appellate Prosecution Counsel:* Not reported; *Amicus Curiae Brief Supporting Prosecutor:* Not reported; *Amicus Curiae Brief Supporting Defendant:* Not reported.

Issue Presented: Whether the Constitution requires specific findings authorizing the imposition of the death sentence be made by a jury?

Case Holding: The Constitution does not require that specific findings authorizing the imposition of the death sentence be made by a jury.

Factual and procedural background of case: The defendant, Paul C. Hildwin, Jr., was indicted for and convicted of first-degree murder by a Florida court. During the penalty phase the jury rendered a unanimous advisory sentence of death, and the trial judge imposed the death sentence, finding four aggravating circumstances and nothing in mitigation. The Florida Supreme Court affirmed the sentence. In doing so, the court rejected the defendant's argument that Florida's sentencing scheme violated the Constitution because it permitted the imposition of death without a specific finding by the jury that sufficient aggravating circumstances exist to qualify the defendant for capital punishment. The United States Supreme Court granted certiorari to address the matter.

Opinion of the Court was delivered Per Curiam: It was observed in the per curiam opinion that the Court had previously ruled that the Constitution does not require a jury be used during a capital penalty phase proceeding. Therefore, the opinion concluded, the Constitution does not require that the specific findings authorizing the imposition of the death sentence be made by a jury.

Dissenting opinion by Justice Brennan: Justice Brennan repeated his fundamental belief "that the death penalty is in all circumstances cruel and unusual punishment prohibited by the Eighth and Fourteenth Amendments[.]" Therefore, he would vacate the death sentence in this case

Dissenting opinion by Justice Marshall: Justice Marshall restated his longstanding belief "that the death penalty is in all circumstances cruel and unusual punishment prohibited by the Eighth and Fourteenth Amendments[.]" He would, therefore, vacate the death sentence in this case. Justice Marshall also criticized the Court for treating the case in a summary disposition, rather than fully developing the defendant's claim.

Hill, Joe

Joel Hagglund was born on October 7, 1879, in Gavle, Sweden. He immigrated to the United States in 1902, and changed his name to Joseph Hillstrom. Eventually the name changed again to simply Joe Hill.

The name Joe Hill has become a legend in the American labor movement. Two things made this so. First, Hill was a prolific songwriter, who wrote inspiring labor songs that are still sung today. Second, Hill was executed by the State of Utah for a murder labor union members believe to this day was a frame-up designed to silence Hill's leadership.

When Hill landed on the shores of Ellis Island in 1902, he found that his dream of American prosperity was not true. Life was hard, wages were low, and workers were without a voice. Hill traveled about the country finding work where he could and writing songs about the plight of workers as he went along.

In 1910, while in San Pedro, California, Hill joined a labor union called the Industrial Workers of the World (IWW). Over the next five years Hill helped make IWW a strong organization through his labor songs. The idea caught on that the most effective way to get workers to unite was through songs that expressed their common plight. This formula proved to be successful for IWW.

While still maintaining his membership in IWW, Hill moved to Utah in 1913, where he found employment in the Park City mines, near Murray, Utah. While in Utah Hill continued his active role with IWW and recruited workers as he wrote them songs that spoke of a better tomorrow through unity.

In 1914 Hill's life took a turn for the worse. He was accused of the murder of a Salt Lake City store owner named John A. Morrison. Hill was convicted of the crime and sentenced to death. An international battle was launched to prevent his execution. His supporters argued that he was the victim of an attempt by business owners to curtail the growing power of IWW. The voice of Hill's supporters caused President Woodrow Wilson to twice intervene in an attempt to prevent his execution. The American Federation of Labor and the Swedish government made valiant efforts to sway authorities in Utah. Hill's supporters failed. Hill was executed by firing squad at the Utah State Prison on November 19, 1915.

Hill's death did not silence his energy and belief in the labor movement. His most famous labor songs, The Preacher and

the Slave, The Rebel Girl and Casey Jones are still sung today. The labor movement went on to immortalize Hill in a song called, I Dreamed I Saw Joe Hill Last Night.

Hill v. Texas

Court: United States Supreme Court; *Case Citation:* Hill v. Texas, 316 U.S. 400 (1942); *Argued:* May 11, 1942; *Decided:* June 1, 1942; *Opinion of the Court:* Chief Justice Stone; *Concurring Opinion:* None; *Dissenting Opinion:* None; *Appellate Defense Counsel:* J. F. McCutcheon argued and briefed; *Appellate Prosecution Counsel:* Pat Coon, Jr. argued; Spurgeon E. Bell on brief; *Amicus Curiae Brief Supporting Prosecutor:* None; *Amicus Curiae Brief Supporting Defendant:* None.

Issue Presented: Whether the defendant made out a prima facie case of racial discrimination in the selection of the grand jury that indicted him?

Case Holding: The defendant made out a prima facie case of racial discrimination in the selection of the grand jury that indicted him, and the State of Texas failed to rebut the prima facie case, therefore the defendant's conviction and sentence could not stand.

Factual and procedural background of case: The defendant, Hill, was convicted of rape and sentenced to death by the State of Texas. The Texas Court of Criminal Appeals affirmed the judgment. In doing so, the appellate court rejected the defendant's contention that his conviction and sentence were invalid because blacks were excluded from the grand jury that indicted him. The United States Supreme Court granted certiorari to consider the issue.

Opinion of the Court by Chief Justice Stone: The Chief Justice held that the defendant made out a prima facie case of racial discrimination in the selection of the grand jurors that indicted him. The opinion set out the Court's reasoning as follows:

> An assistant district attorney for the county, who had lived in Dallas County for twenty-seven or twenty-eight years and had served for sixteen years as a judge of the criminal court in which [the defendant] was tried and convicted, testified that he never knew of a [black] being called to serve on a grand jury in the county. The district clerk of the county, whose duty it is to certify the grand jury list to the sheriff, knew of no citations issued for [blacks] to serve upon the grand jury.
>
> We think [the defendant] made out a prima facie case, which the state failed to meet, of racial discrimination in the selection of grand jurors which the equal protection clause forbids. As we pointed out in [a prior decision] chance or accident could hardly have accounted for the continuous omission of [blacks] from the grand jury lists for so long a period as sixteen years or more. The jury commissioners, although the matter was discussed by them, consciously omitted to place the name of any [black] on the jury list. They made no effort to ascertain whether there were within the county members of the [black] race qualified to serve as jurors, and if so who they were. They thus failed to perform their constitutional duty ... not to pursue a course of conduct in the administration of their office which would operate to discriminate in the selection of jurors on racial grounds. Discrimination can arise from the action of commissioners who exclude all [blacks] whom they do not know to be qualified and who neither know nor seek to learn whether there are in fact any

qualified to serve. In such a case discrimination necessarily results where there are qualified [blacks] available for jury service....

A prisoner whose conviction is reversed by this Court need not go free if he is in fact guilty, for Texas may indict and try him again by the procedure which conforms to constitutional requirements. But no state is at liberty to impose upon one charged with crime a discrimination in its trial procedure which the Constitution, and an Act of Congress passed pursuant to the Constitution, alike forbid. Nor is this Court at liberty to grant or withhold the benefits of equal protection, which the Constitution commands for all, merely as we may deem the defendant innocent or guilty.

The judgment of the Texas Court of Criminal Appeals was reversed.

Case note: Under modern capital punishment jurisprudence the death penalty may not be imposed for the crime of rape, without an accompanying homicide. *See also* **Discrimination in Grand or Petit Jury Selection; Rape and Capital Punishment**

Hispanics and Capital Punishment

Hispanics have historically been a minority population in the United States. Although Hispanic representation in prisons has generally been greater than its proportion to the majority population, this has not been the case for capital punishment. Historically Hispanics have maintained a relatively small percentage of the death row population.

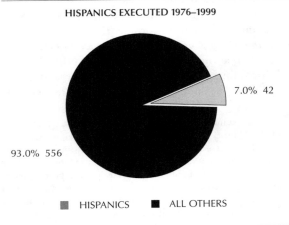

HISPANICS EXECUTED 1976–1999

7.0% 42

93.0% 556

■ HISPANICS ■ ALL OTHERS

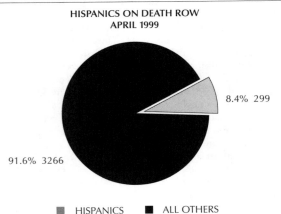

**HISPANICS ON DEATH ROW
APRIL 1999**

8.4% 299

91.6% 3266

■ HISPANICS ■ ALL OTHERS

Hitchock v. Dugger

Court: United States Supreme Court; *Case Citation:* Hitchcock v. Dugger, 481 U.S. 393 (1987); *Argued:* October 15, 1986; *Decided:* April 22, 1987; *Opinion of the Court:* Justice Scalia; *Concurring Opinion:* None; *Dissenting Opinion:* None; *Appellate Defense Counsel:* Craig S. Barnard argued; Richard L. Jorandby and Richard H. Burr III on brief; *Appellate Prosecution Counsel:* Sean Daly argued; Jim Smith and Richard Prospect on brief; *Amicus Curiae Brief Supporting Prosecutor:* 1; *Amicus Curiae Brief Supporting Defendant:* None.

Issue Presented: Whether the defendant's death sentence comports with the Constitution when the trial court refused to consider proffered mitigating evidence at the penalty phase?

Case Holding: The defendant's death sentence did not comport with the Constitution when the trial court refused to consider proffered mitigating evidence at the penalty phase.

Factual and procedural background of case: The defendant, Richard Hitchcock, was convicted of capital murder by the State of Florida. During the penalty phase the trial court instructed the jury that it was not to consider any mitigating evidence that was not enumerated under the State's death penalty statute. The defendant proffered mitigating circumstance evidence that was not listed in the State's death penalty statute. The jury recommended and the trial judge imposed the sentence of death.

The Florida Supreme Court affirmed the conviction and sentence. In doing so, the appellate court rejected the defendant's argument that the Federal Constitution prohibited exclusion and consideration of mitigating evidence at the penalty phase. Following unsuccessful State collateral proceedings, the defendant filed a habeas corpus petition in a Federal District Court seeking relief. The District Court dismissed the petition. A Federal Court of Appeals affirmed. The United States Supreme Court granted certiorari to consider the issue.

Opinion of the Court by Justice Scalia: Justice Scalia, writing for a unanimous Court, held that the defendant's death sentence was rendered in violation of the Constitution. The opinion reasoned and concluded as follows:

We think it could not be clearer that the advisory jury was instructed not to consider, and the sentencing judge refused to consider, evidence of nonstatutory mitigating circumstances, and that the proceedings therefore did not comport with the requirements of *Skipper v. South Carolina, Eddings v. Oklahoma,* and *Lockett v. Ohio.* [The prosecutor] has made no attempt to argue that this error was harmless, or that it had no effect on the jury or the sentencing judge. In the absence of such a showing our cases hold that the exclusion of mitigating evidence of the sort at issue here renders the death sentence invalid.... [T]he State is not precluded from seeking to impose a death sentence upon [the defendant], "provided that it does so through a new sentencing hearing at which [the defendant] is permitted to present any and all relevant mitigating evidence that is available."

We reverse the judgment and remand the case to the Court of Appeals. That court is instructed to remand to the District Court with instructions to enter an order granting the application for a writ of habeas corpus, unless the State within a reasonable period of time either resentences [the defendant] in a proceeding that comports with the requirements of *Lockett* or vacates the death sentence and imposes a lesser sentence consistent with law.

See also **Bell v. Ohio; Delo v. Lashley; Eddings v. Oklahoma; Lockett v. Ohio; Mitigating Circumstances; Skipper v. South Carolina**

Holberg, Brittany Marlowe

Brittany Marlowe Holberg is a Texas native who was born on January 1, 1973. In 1997 Holberg was profiled on the show *America's Most Wanted*, in connection with the murder of an 80-year-old Amarillo resident named A. B. Towery.

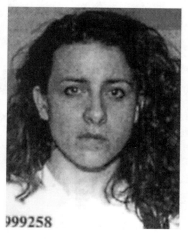

999258

Brittany Marlowe Holberg was convicted of capital murder by a Texas jury and sentenced to death. (Texas Department of Criminal Justice)

Police records indicated Holberg was a drug addict and prostitute who had an ongoing relationship with Towery. On November 13, 1996, Holberg went to the residence of Towery. While there she robbed him and viciously tortured him to death. Holberg struck Towery with a hammer and stabbed him nearly 60 times with a paring knife, butcher knife, grapefruit knife and a fork. A knife was left in his chest and a foot-long lamp pole had been shoved more than five inches down his throat.

After killing Towery, Holberg fled Texas and went to Memphis, Tennessee. With the help of the television show, *America's Most Wanted*, Holberg was captured in Memphis on February 17, 1997. Holberg was extradited back to Texas, where she was prosecuted in 1998 for capital murder. She was convicted and sentenced to death. She now sits on death row in Texas.

Holden v. Minnesota

Court: United States Supreme Court; *Case Citation:* Holden v. Minnesota, 137 U.S. 483 (1890); *Argued:* Not reported; *Decided:* December 8, 1890; *Opinion of the Court:* Justice Harlan; *Concurring Statement:* Justice Bradley; *Concurring Statement:* Justice Brewer; *Dissenting Opinion:* None; *Appellate Defense Counsel:* C. C. Willson argued and briefed; *Appellate Prosecution Counsel:* Moses E. Clapp argued; H. W. Childs on brief; *Amicus Curiae Brief Supporting Prosecutor:* None; *Amicus Curiae Brief Supporting Defendant:* None.

Issue Presented: Whether the Constitution prohibits enforcement of a death penalty statute that was repealed and reenacted after the date of the defendant's crime, but did not alter the substantive law existing at the time of the crime?

Case Holding: The Constitution does not bar enforcement of a death penalty statute that was repealed and reenacted after the date of the defendant's crime, but does not alter the substantive law existing at the time of the crime.

Factual and procedural background of case: The State of Minnesota charged the defendant, Clifton Holden, with committing capital murder on November 23, 1888. He was convicted and sentenced to death by hanging. The Minnesota Supreme Court affirmed the conviction and sentence. The governor of the State issued a death warrant requiring the defendant be put to death on June 27, 1890. After issuance of the death warrant, the defendant filed a habeas corpus petition in a federal District Court alleging that he was being detained in violation of the Constitution, because the law under which he was to be executed was enacted after the commission of his crime. The District Court denied relief. The United States Supreme Court granted certiorari to consider the matter.

Opinion of the Court by Justice Harlan: Justice Harlan noted that the State repealed and reenacted parts of its capital punishment statute on April 24, 1889, after the defendant's crime was committed. The new law added a provision requiring a convicted and sentenced capital felon be detained in solitary confinement until executed. The opinion indicated that based upon the change in law, the defendant presented two arguments. First, application of the solitary confinement provision to him violated the Ex Post Facto Clause. Second, that inasmuch as the new law had no saving clause as to previous capital punishment offenses, there was no statute in force after its enactment which prescribed the punishment of death for murder committed before the date of the new law's enactment. The defendant, wrote Justice Harlan, was in essence claiming that repeal of the old law "was an act of complete amnesty in respect to all offenses of murder in the first degree previously committed, making subsequent imprisonment therefor illegal."

Justice Harlan disagreed with the defendant's contention that repeal of the old statute represented amnesty. He pointed out that the new law only repealed provisions of the old law that were inconsistent with it, and that imposition of death by hanging under the new law was the same punishment under the old law. Therefore, "it is inaccurate to say that [the new] statute contained no saving clause whatever. By necessary implication, previous statutes that were consistent with its provisions were unaffected."

The opinion held that "[t]he only part of the act of 1889 that may be deemed ex post facto, if applied to offenses committed before its passage, ... is [the requirement] that, after the issue of the warrant of execution by the governor, 'the prisoner shall be kept in solitary confinement' in the jail[.]" Justice Harlan declined to address the constitutionality of the application of this new provision to the defendant, because "there is no proof in the record" that the defendant was being held in solitary confinement. The judgment of the lower court was affirmed.

Concurring Statement by Justice Bradley: Justice Bradley issued a statement concurring in the Court's judgment.

Concurring Statement by Justice Brewer: Justice Brewer issued a statement concurring in the Court's judgment. *See also* **Dobbert v. Florida; Ex Post Facto Clause; Kring v. Missouri**

Holmes, Dr. Henry H. *see* Mudgett, Herman

Holmes, Oliver Wendell, Jr.

Oliver Wendell Holmes, Jr., served as an associate justice of the United States Supreme Court from 1902 to 1932. While on the Supreme Court Holmes was known as a moderate and pragmatic interpreter of the Constitution.

Holmes was born in Boston, Massachusetts on March 8, 1841. He graduated from Harvard College in 1861. With the outbreak of the Civil War, Holmes enlisted in the Union Army as an officer. After the war he went on to graduate from Harvard Law School in 1866. In 1881 Holmes published his famous and influential book, "The Common Law." Holmes' legal career included teaching at Harvard Law School and serving on the Supreme Judicial Court of Massachusetts as chief justice. In 1902 President Theodore Roosevelt nominated Holmes to the Supreme Court.

While on the Supreme Court Holmes wrote a number of capital punishment opinions. The capital punishment opinion that carried the greatest influence was his dissent in *Frank v. Mangum*. The issue in *Frank* was whether the defendant's conviction and death sentence were obtained in violation of due process of law because of mob intimidation during his trial. The majority on the Supreme Court found that due process of law was not violated in the case. Holmes dissented strongly: "The argument for the [prosecutor] in substance is that the trial was in a court of competent jurisdiction, that it retains jurisdiction although, in fact, it may be dominated by a mob, and that the rulings of the state court as to the fact of such domination cannot be reviewed. But the argument seems to us inconclusive. Whatever disagreement there may be as to the scope of the phrase 'due process of law,' there can be no doubt that it embraces the fundamental conception of a fair trial, with opportunity to be heard. Mob law does not become due process of law by securing the assent of a terrorized jury. We are not speaking of mere disorder, or mere irregularities in procedure, but of a case where the processes of justice are actually subverted." Holmes died on March 6, 1935.

Capital Punishment Opinions Written by Holmes

Case Name	Opinion of the Court	Concurring Opinion	Dissenting Opinion
Ashe v. Valotta	✓		
Biddle v. Perovich	✓		
Frank v. Mangum			✓
Moore v. Dempsey	✓		
Rawlins v. Georgia	✓		
Rogers v. Alabama	✓		
Queenan v. Oklahoma	✓		

Homicide *see* Murder

Homicide Survivors

Homicide Survivors is an Arizona based pro-death penalty organization that provides free support services to family members of murder victims. Gail Leland is the executive officer of the organization. Leland founded Homicide Survivors (initially called Parents of Murdered Children) after the 1981 disappearance and murder of her 14-year-old son.

Leland's firsthand experience with being a family member of a murder victim provided her with insight

The murder of Gail Leland's son inspired her to start Homicide Survivors. (Gail Leland)

into the difficulties surviving family members face. She has taken her tragic experience and utilized it to help other surviving family members cope with the emotional trauma that follows the murder of a loved one.

Honduras

Honduras abolished capital punishment in 1956. *See also* **International Capital Punishment Nations**

Hopkins v. Reeves

Court: United States Supreme Court; *Case Citation:* Hopkins v. Reeves, 524 U.S. 88 (1998); *Argued:* February 23, 1998; *Decided:* June 8, 1998; *Opinion of the Court:* Justice Thomas; *Concurring Opinion:* None; *Dissenting Opinion:* Justice Stevens; *Appellate Defense Counsel:* Not reported; *Appellate Prosecution Counsel:* Not reported; *Amicus Curiae Brief Supporting Prosecutor:* Not reported; *Amicus Curiae Brief Supporting Defendant:* Not reported.

Issue Presented: Whether *Beck v. Alabama* required the trial court to instruct the guilt phase jury on offenses that were not lesser included offenses of capital felony murder under Nebraska law?

Case Holding: Beck v. Alabama did not require the trial court to instruct the guilt phase jury on offenses that were not lesser included offenses of capital felony murder under Nebraska law.

Factual and procedural background of case: The State of Nebraska charged the defendant, Randolph K. Reeves, with capital felony murder (murder committed during the course of a sexual assault). At the close of the guilt phase the defendant requested the trial court instruct the jury on the lesser included offenses of second degree murder and manslaughter. The trial court refused the request on the ground that the State Supreme Court consistently had held that those crimes were not lesser included offenses of felony murder. The defendant was convicted of capital felony murder and a three-judge panel sentenced him to death.

After exhausting his State post-conviction remedies, the defendant filed a habeas corpus petition in a Federal District

Court. The defendant alleged that the trial court's failure to give the requested instruction was unconstitutional under the United States Supreme Court decision in *Beck v. Alabama*, which had invalidated an Alabama law that prohibited lesser included offense instructions in capital cases. The District Court rejected the argument, bur granted relief on an unrelated due process claim. A Federal Court of Appeals disagreed with the basis of the District Court's ruling and found, instead, that in failing to give the requested instruction on lesser included offenses, the trial court had committed the same constitutional error that was condemned in *Beck*. The Court of Appeals granted relief on that basis. The United States Supreme Court granted certiorari to consider the issue.

Opinion of the Court by Justice Thomas: Justice Thomas ruled that *Beck* did not require State trial courts to instruct juries on offenses that were not lesser included offenses of the charged crime under State law. The opinion found that the facts of *Beck* were distinguishable from the defendant's case. It was said that the Alabama statute that was condemned in *Beck* had prohibited lesser included offense instructions in capital cases, but permitted lesser included offense instructions in non-capital cases. On the other hand, the opinion said, in the defendant's case when the Nebraska trial court declined to give the requested lesser included offense instruction, it merely followed the State Supreme Court's 100-year-old rule that second degree murder and manslaughter were not lesser included offenses of felony murder. Justice Thomas found that by ignoring the distinction, the Court of Appeals limited Nebraska's prerogative to structure its criminal law more severely than did the rule in *Beck*, for it required in effect that Nebraska create lesser included offenses to all capital crimes when no such lesser included offenses existed under State law. The judgment of the Court of Appeals was reversed.

Dissenting opinion by Justice Stevens: Justice Stevens dissented from the majority decision. He believed *Beck* was not distinguishable from the defendant's case and that the defendant was constitutionally entitled to the requested instruction. *See also* **Beck v. Alabama; Hopper v. Evans; Lesser Included Offense Instruction; Schad v. Arizona**

Hopper v. Evans

Court: United States Supreme Court; *Case Citation:* Hopper v. Evans, 456 U.S. 605 (1982); *Argued:* March 24, 1982; *Decided:* May 24, 1982; *Opinion of the Court:* Chief Justice Burger; *Concurring and Dissenting Statement:* Justice Brennan and Marshall, J.; *Appellate Defense Counsel:* John L. Carroll argued; Steven Alan Reiss on brief; *Appellate Prosecution Counsel:* Edward E. Carnes argued; Charles Graddick and Susan Beth Farmer on brief; *Amicus Curiae Brief Supporting Prosecutor:* None; *Amicus Curiae Brief Supporting Defendant:* None.

Issue Presented: Whether, after invalidation of a state law which precluded instructions on lesser included offenses in capital cases, a new trial is required in a capital case in which the defendant's own evidence negates the possibility that such an instruction might have been warranted?

Case Holding: Invalidation of a state law which precluded instructions on lesser included offenses in the defendant's capital case, did not require a new trial because the defendant's own evidence negated the possibility that such an instruction might have been warranted.

Factual and procedural background of case: The defendant, Evans, was convicted and sentenced to death for capital murder in an Alabama. At the time of the defendant's trial, an Alabama statute precluded jury instructions on lesser included offenses in capital cases. The Alabama Supreme Court affirmed the conviction and sentence on appeal.

Subsequently, a habeas corpus proceedings was brought in a Federal District Court seeking to have the conviction set aside on the ground that the defendant had been convicted and sentenced under a statute that unconstitutionally precluded consideration of lesser included offenses. The District Court denied relief. While the case was pending an appeal in a Federal Court of Appeals, the Alabama statute precluding lesser included offense instructions in capital cases was invalidated by the United States Supreme Court in the case of *Beck v. Alabama*. As a result of the *Beck* decision, the Court of Appeals granted relief and reversed the conviction and sentence. The Court of Appeals reasoned that, under *Beck*, the defendant had to be retried so that he might have the opportunity to introduce evidence of some lesser included offense. The United States Supreme Court granted certiorari to consider the issue.

Opinion of the Court by Justice Chief Justice Burger: The Chief Justice ruled that the Court of Appeals misread *Beck*. It was said that: "*Beck* held that due process requires that a lesser included offense instruction be given when the evidence warrants such an instruction. But due process requires that a lesser included offense instruction be given only when the evidence warrants such an instruction. The jury's discretion is thus channeled so that it may convict a defendant of any crime fairly supported by the evidence." The Chief Justice concluded that the Alabama preclusion statute did not prejudice the defendant in any way, and he was not entitled to a new trial, because his own evidence negated the possibility that a lesser included offense instruction might have been warranted. Accordingly, an instruction on a lesser included offense was not warranted. The judgment of the Court of Appeals was reversed.

Concurring and dissenting statement by Brennan and Marshall, JJ.: Justices Brennan and Marshall issued a statement concurring in part, and dissenting in part. The statement read: "We join the opinion of the Court to the extent that it reverses the judgment of the Court of Appeals invalidating [the defendant's] conviction. But we adhere to our view that the death penalty is in all circumstances cruel and unusual punishment prohibited by the Eighth and Fourteenth Amendments. Consequently, we would affirm the judgment of the Court of Appeals to the extent that it invalidates the sentence of death imposed upon [the defendant]." *See also* **Beck v. Alabama; Lesser Included Offense Instruction; Hopkins v. Reeves; Schad v. Arizona**

Hopt v. Utah (I) *Court:* United States Supreme Court; *Case Citation:* Hopt v. Utah, 104 U.S. 631 (1881); *Argued:* Not reported; *Decided:* October Term, 1881; *Opinion of the Court:* Justice Gray; *Concurring Opinion:* None; *Dissenting Opinion:* None; *Appellate Defense Counsel:* John R. McBride argued; J. G. Sutherland on brief; *Appellate Prosecution Counsel:* Not reported; *Amicus Curiae Brief Supporting Prosecutor:* None; *Amicus Curiae Brief Supporting Defendant:* None.

Issue Presented: Whether due process of law required the trial court to instruct the jury that if it found the defendant was intoxicated at the time of the murder, it had to return a verdict of guilty of second degree murder?

Case Holding: Due process of law required the trial court to instruct the jury that if it found the defendant was intoxicated at the time of the murder, it had to return a verdict of guilty of second degree murder.

Factual and procedural background of case: The defendant, Hopt, was convicted of capital murder and sentenced to death by the Territory of Utah. The Utah Supreme Court affirmed the judgment. In doing so, the appellate court rejected the defendant's argument that due process of law required the trial court to instruct the jury that, if it found he was intoxicated at the time of the crime he could only be convicted of murder in the second degree. The United States Supreme Court granted certiorari to consider the issue.

Opinion of the Court by Justice Gray: Justice Gray noted that at common law voluntary intoxication afforded no excuse, justification or extenuation of an offense committed under its influence. However, it was said that "when a statute establishing different degrees of murder requires deliberate premeditation in order to constitute murder in the first degree, the question whether the accused is in such a condition of mind, by reason of drunkenness or otherwise, as to be capable of deliberate premeditation, necessarily becomes a material subject of consideration by the jury." Justice Gray found that the evidence was sufficient to show that the defendant was drinking at the time of the offense, so as to warrant an instruction that intoxication could reduce the degree of murder to second degree. He held that "[t]he instruction requested by the defendant clearly and accurately stated the law applicable to the case; and the refusal to give that instruction ... necessarily prejudiced him with the jury." The judgment of the Utah Supreme Court was reversed and a new trial awarded. *See also* **Hopt v. Utah (II); Hopt v. Utah (III); Intoxication Defense**

Hopt v. Utah (II) *Court:* United States Supreme Court; *Case Citation:* Hopt v. Utah, 110 U.S. 574 (1884); *Argued:* Not reported; *Decided:* March 3, 1884; *Opinion of the Court:* Justice Harlan; *Concurring Opinion:* None; *Dissenting Opinion:* None; *Appellate Defense Counsel:* Thos. J. Marshall argued and briefed; *Appellate Prosecution Counsel:* Assistant Attorney General Maury argued and briefed; *Amicus Curiae Brief Supporting Prosecutor:* None; *Amicus Curiae Brief Supporting Defendant:* None.

Issue Presented: Whether it was constitutional error to require challenged jurors be questioned for bias outside the presence of the defendant?

Case Holding: It was constitutional error to require challenged jurors be questioned for bias outside the presence of the defendant.

Factual and procedural background of case: The defendant, Hopt, was convicted of capital murder and sentenced to death by the Territory of Utah. The Utah Supreme Court affirmed the judgment. The United States Supreme Court reversed the judgment in *Hopt v. Utah (I)* and awarded a new trial. Upon retrial the defendant was again found guilty of capital murder and sentenced to death. The Utah Supreme Court affirmed the judgment. In doing so, the appellate court rejected the defendant's contention that it was constitutional error for the trial court to require certain jurors challenged by the defendant to be questioned for bias out of the presence of the defendant. The United States Supreme Court granted certiorari to consider the issue.

Opinion of the Court by Justice Harlan: Justice Harlan held that it was constitutional error to require the challenged jurors be questioned out of the presence of the defendant. The opinion reasoned as follows: "The public has an interest in his life and liberty. Neither can be lawfully taken except in the mode prescribed by law. That which the law makes essential in proceedings involving the deprivation of life or liberty cannot be dispensed with.... [T]he legislature has deemed it essential to the protection of one whose life or liberty is involved in a prosecution for felony that he shall be personally present at the trial; that is at every stage of the trial when his substantial rights may be affected by the proceedings against him. If he be deprived of his life or liberty without being so present, such deprivation would be without that due process of law required by the constitution. For these reasons we are of opinion that it was error, which vitiated the verdict and judgment, to permit the trial of the challenges to take place in the absence of the accused." The judgment of the Utah Supreme Court was reversed and a new trial awarded. *See also* **Hopt v. Utah (I); Hopt v. Utah (III); Jury Selection**

Hopt v. Utah (III) *Court:* United States Supreme Court; *Case Citation:* Hopt v. Utah, 114 U.S. 488 (1885); *Argued:* January 28, 1885; *Decided:* April 20, 1885; *Opinion of the Court:* Justice Gray; *Concurring Opinion:* None; *Dissenting Statement:* Chief Justice Waite and Harlan, J.; *Appellate Defense Counsel:* R. N. Baskin argued; S. H. Snider and W. G. Van Horne on brief; *Appellate Prosecution Counsel:* Assistant Attorney General Maury argued and briefed; *Amicus Curiae Brief Supporting Prosecutor:* None; *Amicus Curiae Brief Supporting Defendant:* None.

Issue Presented: Whether the failure of the record in the case to report the jury instructions in the manner required by the laws of Utah, required the judgment against the defendant be reversed?

Case Holding: The failure of the record in the case to report the jury instructions in the manner required by the laws of Utah, required the judgment against the defendant be reversed.

Factual and procedural background of case: The defendant, Hopt, was convicted of capital murder and sentenced to death by the Territory of Utah. The Utah Supreme Court affirmed the judgment. The United States Supreme Court reversed the judgment in *Hopt v. Utah (I)* and awarded a new trial. Upon retrial the defendant was again found guilty of capital murder and sentenced to death. The Utah Supreme Court affirmed the judgment. The United States Supreme Court reversed the judgment in *Hopt v. Utah (II)* and awarded a new trial. Upon the third trial the defendant was again found guilty of capital murder and sentenced to death. The Utah Supreme Court affirmed the judgment. The United States Supreme Court granted certiorari to consider several issues assigned as error, but the Court decided to only address the issue of whether the record in the case complied with the requirements of Utah's laws.

Opinion of the Court by Justice Gray: Justice Gray observed that under the laws of Utah jury instructions must be reduced to writing before they are given, unless the parties consent to oral instructions. The opinion also pointed out that Utah required the record in the case contain in writing the instructions given to the jury or a written waiver of such recording by the defendant. It was said that "requiring the instructions to be in writing and recorded, is to secure an accurate and authentic report of the instructions, and to insure to the defendant the means of having them revised in an appellate court." Justice Gray found that the record in the case did not comply with the requirements of Utah's statutes. He wrote: "The record merely states that the court charged the jury, and does not state whether the charge was written or oral. If the charge was written, it should have been made part of the record, which has not been done. If it was oral, the consent of the defendant was necessary, and that consent does not appear of record, and cannot be presumed." As a result of this technical error, the judgment of the Utah Supreme Court was reversed and a new trial awarded.

Dissenting statement by Chief Justice Waite and Harlan, J.: The Chief Justice and Justice Harlan issued a statement dissenting from the Court's decision. *See also* **Hopt v. Utah (I)**; **Hopt v. Utah (II)**

Horn, Tom

Tom Horn was a born in Memphis, Missouri on November 21, 1860. He was raised on a farm and went on to become known in western lore as the last cowboy to go to the gallows.

Horn led a life for which the west was famous. He was an army scout at age 16. In 1886 he was involved in the historic battle against Geronimo. Horn tracked Geronimo and his band of warriors to their hideout in the Sierra Gordo, outside of Sonora, Mexico. It was Horn who, alone, rode into Geronimo's camp and negotiated the famed Native American's surrender. Geronimo's surrender ended the last epic war with Native Americans.

In 1890 Horn joined the Pinkerton Detective Agency and used his gun to capture bank robbers and train thieves throughout Colorado and Wyoming. Legend has it that Horn killed seventeen men as a Pinkerton agent.

Horn left Pinkerton in 1892 and hired his gun to the Wyoming Cattle Growers' Association. On July 18, 1901 Horn killed for the last time. On that date he set out to execute a contract to kill a rancher named Kels Nickell. Horn devised a plan to ambush Kels on the Powder River Road near Cheyenne, Wyoming. When a wagon appeared on the road Horn believed the driver was Kels. He fired a shot striking the driver, then fired a second shot that struck the driver in the back of the head—killing him. At the time Horn did not realize it, but the person he killed was not Kels, it was Kels' 14-year-old son Willie.

Horn fled to Denver after the killing. He was tracked by a Wyoming lawman named Joe Lefors. Although no hard evidence linked Horn to the killing, Lefors believed it was Horn. After Lefors reached Denver he engaged Horn in a saloon and got him drunk. While intoxicated Horn began talking about his last killing, believing the victim was Kels. After Horn's confession, Lefors immediately arrested him. Horn was taken back to Wyoming to stand trial.

Horn was convicted and sentenced to death. While awaiting execution Horn escaped from jail, but was quickly captured. On November 20, 1903 Horn mounted the gallows in Cheyenne and was sent swinging to his death.

Houston Military Riot of 1917

In 1917 the United States declared war on Germany. In preparation for the war, two military installations, Camp Logan and Ellington Field, were ordered constructed outside the Houston, Texas area. On July 27, 1917 a segregated battalion of African American soldiers were transported to the area to guard the construction site.

During their encampment in the Houston area the black soldiers encountered intense racial discrimination from the civilian population. On August 23, 1917, racial tension rose to a racial riot in Houston. The riot was sparked by a false report that local Houston police had killed a well-respected black soldier—corporal Charles Baltimore. Over a 100 black soldiers marched to Houston carrying loaded rifles. Chaos broke loose when the soldiers arrived. The soldiers killed 15 whites, including four policemen, and seriously wounded 12 others. Four black soldiers were killed.

By the early morning hours of August 24, civil authorities had regained control of Houston. The Army then turned to the black soldiers. Indictments were handed down for 118 soldiers. Between November 1, 1917, and March 26, 1918, the Army held three separate military trials in San Antonio. The military tribunals convicted 110 black soldiers. Nineteen soldiers were summarily hanged and the others sentenced to Federal prison for life. *See also* **Military Death Penalty Law**

Hughes, Charles E.

Charles E. Hughes served two separate terms on the United States Supreme Court. He was an associate justice from 1910–1916, and chief justice from 1930–1941. While on the Supreme Court Hughes was known as a moderate interpreter of the Constitution.

Hughes was born in Glen Falls, New York on April 11, 1862. He studied law at Columbia University Law School. His legal career included a lucrative private practice, teaching law at Columbia and Cornell. He was twice elected governor of New York. In 1910 President William Howard Taft nominated Hughes to the Supreme Court. Hughes ultimately resigned from the Court in 1916 to run for President. After losing in his bid at the presidency, Hughes returned to his private legal practice. Hughes was selected in 1921 by President Warren G. Harding to serve as Secretary of State. In 1938 President Calvin Coolidge nominated Hughes as chief justice of the Supreme Court.

Hughes was known to have written only a few capital punishment opinions while on the Supreme Court. Each of the opinions written by him were issued during his term as chief justice. The capital punishment opinions authored by Hughes revealed a liberal view of the Constitution. Each of the Hughes' capital punishment opinions were written for the majority of the Supreme Court. In each case Hughes reversed the death sentences. The opinion which had the most influence upon modern-day capital punishment was *Aldridge v. United States*. In *Aldridge* the defendant made the novel argument that the trial judge should have asked the jury if they would harbor any bias because the defendant was black and the victim was white. Hughes wrote that the trial court committed reversible error in refusing the request to ask the prospective jury if they had racial prejudices that would prevent them from fairly deciding the case because the defendant was black and the victim was white. Hughes died on August 27, 1948.

Capital Punishment Opinions Written by Hughes

Case Name	Opinion of the Court	Concurring Opinion	Dissenting Opinion
Aldridge v. United States	✓		
Brown v. Mississippi	✓		
Norris v. Alabama	✓		
Patterson v. Alabama	✓		

Human Rights Watch

Human Rights Watch (HRW) is an international organization that advocates human rights issues throughout the world. The organization investigates and exposes human rights violations and hold abusers accountable. Accountability is done through enlisting the public and the international community to support the cause of human rights for all.

The HRW has taken a public stance in total opposition to capital punishment anywhere in the world. The organization has targeted capital punishment in the United States and has aligned itself with other organizations to bring about the abolishment of the death penalty in the nation.

Specific work being conducted by HRW in the United States involves tracking death penalty cases and writing letters to clemency boards and governors asking that executions be halted and death sentences commuted. If a case presents a particularly egregious set of circumstance, e.g., the defendant is a juvenile, mentally impaired, or foreign nationals, HRW will bring its concerns to the national media and seek to raise the profile of the case.

Hungary

The death penalty was abolished in Hungary in 1990. *See also* **International Capital Punishment Nations**

Hung Jury *see* **Deadlocked Jury**

Hurtado v. California

Court: United States Supreme Court; *Case Citation:* Hurtado v. California, 110 U.S. 516 (1884); *Argued:* Not reported; *Decided:* March 3, 1884; *Opinion of the Court:* Justice Matthews; *Concurring Opinion:* None; *Dissenting Opinion:* Justice Harlan; *Appellate Defense Counsel:* A. L. Hart argued and briefed; *Appellate Prosecution Counsel:* John T. Carey argued and briefed; *Amicus Curiae Brief Supporting Prosecutor:* None; *Amicus Curiae Brief Supporting Defendant:* None.

Issue Presented: Whether the Constitution requires States prosecute capital offenses by grand jury indictment?

Case Holding: The Constitution does not impose upon States a requirement that capital offenses be prosecuted by grand jury indictment.

Factual and procedural background of case: Under the constitution of California adopted in 1879, all criminal offenses were permitted to be prosecuted by an information, rather than by grand jury indictment. On February 20, 1882, a California prosecutor drew up an information charging the defendant, Joseph Hurtado, with committing capital murder. The defendant was prosecuted under the information and a jury found him guilty of capital murder. The trial court imposed the sentence of death. The California Supreme Court affirmed.

The defendant subsequently went before the trial court and challenged his conviction and sentence on the grounds that the Due Process Clause of the Fourteenth Amendment required that he be prosecuted by grand jury indictment. The trial court rejected the argument. The California Supreme Court denied relief on this ground. The United States Supreme Court granted certiorari to consider the issue.

Opinion of the Court by Justice Matthews: Justice Matthews wrote that "[t]he proposition of law we are asked to affirm is that an indictment or presentment by a grand jury, as known to the common law of England, is essential to that 'due process of law,' when applied to prosecutions for felonies[.]" The opinion reasoned that "if an indictment or presentment by a grand jury is essential to due process of law in all cases of imprisonment for crime, it applies not only to felonies, but to misdemeanors and petty offenses, and the conclusion would be inevitable that informations as a substitute for indictments would be illegal in all cases."

The opinion noted that the Fifth Amendment imposed the use of grand jury indictment upon the federal government for infamous crimes. It was also observed that the Fifth Amendment contained a due process provision that was only applicable to the federal government. Justice Matthews thought it significant that the Fifth Amendment contained both due process and grand jury requirements, while the Fourteenth Amendment contained a due process provision but no grand jury provision. The opinion reasoned from this observation that: "The natural and obvious inference is that, in the sense of the constitution, 'due process of law' was not meant or intended to include ... the institution and procedure of a grand jury in any case. The conclusion is equally irresistible, that when the same phrase was employed in the [F]ourteenth [A]mendment to restrain the action of the states, it was used in the same sense and with no greater extent; and that if in the adoption of that amendment it had been part of its purpose to perpetuate the institution of the grand jury in all the states, it would have embodied, as did the [F]ifth [A]mendment, express declarations to that effect."

It was concluded by Justice Matthews that due process of law did not require States use grand jury indictments to prosecute capital offenses. "Due process of law ... resides in the right of the people to make their own laws, and alter them at their pleasure. For these reasons, finding no error therein, the judgment of the supreme court of California is affirmed."

Dissenting opinion by Justice Harlan: Justice Harlan wrote in dissent that he could not "agree that the state may, consistently, with due process of law require a person to answer for a capital offense, except upon the presentment or indictment of a grand jury[.]" The dissent believed that use of grand jury indictment was a basic component of due process. Justice Harlan asked rhetorically: "Does not the fact that the people of the original states required an amendment of the national constitution, securing exemption from prosecution for a capital offense, except upon the indictment or presentment of a grand jury, prove that, in their judgment, such an exemption was essential to protection against accusation and unfounded prosecution, and therefore was a fundamental principle in liberty and justice?"

Justice Harlan took issue with a suggestion by the majority opinion that progress in criminal procedure was pushing aside use of grand jury indictment to prosecute crimes. He wrote: "It is difficult ... to perceive anything in the system of prosecuting human beings for their lives, by information, which suggests that the state which adopts it has entered upon an era of progress and improvement in the law of criminal procedure." The dissent concluded that the judgment of the California Supreme Court should be reversed. *See also* **Grand Jury; Lem Woon v. Oregon; Prosecution by Information**

I

Iceland Capital punishment was abolished in Iceland in 1928. *See also* **International Capital Punishment Nations**

Idaho The State of Idaho is a capital punishment jurisdiction. The State reenacted its death penalty law after the United States Supreme Court decision in *Furman v. Georgia*, 408 U.S. 238 (1972), on July 1, 1973.

Idaho has a three-tier legal system. The State's legal system is composed of a supreme court, court of appeals and courts of general jurisdiction. The Idaho Supreme Court is presided over by a chief justice and four associate justices. The Idaho Court of Appeals is composed of a chief judge and two judges. The courts of general jurisdiction in the State are called District Courts. Capital offenses against the State of Idaho are tried in the District Courts.

Idaho's capital punishment statute is triggered if a person commits a homicide under the following special circumstances:

1. murder perpetrated by means of poison, lying in wait or torture; or
2. murder of any peace officer, executive officer, officer of the court, fireman, judicial officer or prosecuting attorney; or
3. murder committed by a person under a sentence for a prior murder, including such persons on parole or probation from such sentence; or
4. murder committed in the perpetration of, or attempt to perpetrate, aggravated battery on a child under twelve (12) years of age, arson, rape, robbery, burglary, kidnaping or mayhem; or
5. murder committed by a person incarcerated in a penal institution upon a person employed by the penal institution, another inmate or a visitor to the penal institution; or
6. murder committed by a person while escaping or attempting to escape from a penal institution.

Capital murder in Idaho is punishable by death or life imprisonment with the possibility of parole. A capital prosecution in Idaho is bifurcated into a guilt phase and penalty phase. A jury is used only at the guilt phase of a capital trial. The trial judge presides over the penalty phase of a capital prosecution and determines the sentence without a jury.

In order to impose a death sentence upon a defendant under Idaho law, it is required that the prosecutor establish the existence of at least one of the following statutory aggravating circumstances at the penalty phase:

A. the defendant was previously convicted of another murder;

B. at the time the murder was committed the defendant also committed another murder;

C. the defendant knowingly created a great risk of death to many persons;

D. the murder was committed for remuneration or the promise of remuneration or the defendant employed another to commit the murder for remuneration or the promise of remuneration;

E. the murder was especially heinous, atrocious or cruel, manifesting exceptional depravity;

F. the defendant exhibited utter disregard for human life;

G. the murder was committed in the perpetration of, or attempt to perpetrate, arson, rape, robbery, burglary, kidnapping or mayhem;

H. the defendant has exhibited a propensity to commit murder which will probably constitute a continuing threat to society;

I. the murder was committed against a former or present peace officer, executive officer, officer of the court, judicial officer or prosecuting attorney because of the exercise of official duty;

J. the murder was committed against a witness or potential witness in a criminal or civil legal proceeding because of such proceeding.

Idaho does not provide by statute any mitigating circumstances to the imposition of the death penalty. Even though the State does not provide statutory mitigating circumstances, the United States Supreme Court has ruled that all relevant mitigating evidence must be allowed at the penalty phase.

Under Idaho's capital punishment statute, a sentence of death is automatically reviewed by the Idaho Supreme Court. Idaho uses lethal injection or the firing squad (fallback option) to carry out death sentences. The State's death row facility for men is located in Boise, Idaho; while the facility maintaining female death row inmates is located in Pocatello, Idaho.

Pursuant to the laws of Idaho the State's Commission of Pardons and Paroles has authority to grant clemency. The State's Governor may grant temporary reprieves.

From the start of modern capital punishment in 1976, through 1999, Idaho executed one capital felon. During this period Idaho had one female capital felon on death row. A total of 22 capital felons were on death row in Idaho in 1999. The 1999 death row population in the State was listed as: 0 black inmates; 21 white inmates; and 1 unidentified inmate. In 1999 the State did not have any juveniles on death row. The State permits capital punishment to be imposed on persons 16 years old or older. Idaho does not prohibit the execution of mentally retarded capital felons.

Executions by Idaho 1976–1999

Name	Race	Date of Execution	Method of Execution
Keith Wells	White	January 6, 1994	Lethal Injection

IDAHO EXECUTIONS 1976–1999

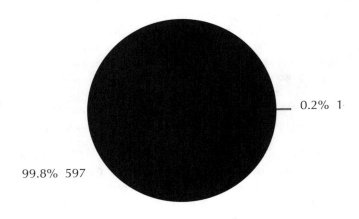

0.2% 1

99.8% 597

■ IDAHO EXECUTIONS

■ ALL OTHER EXECUTIONS

EXECUTIONS BY IDAHO 1930–1999

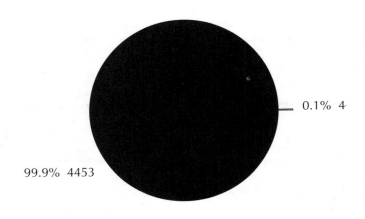

0.1% 4

99.9% 4453

■ IDAHO

■ ALL OTHER JURISDICTIONS

Identity of Executioner *see* **Executioner**

Illegally Obtained Evidence *see* **Exclusionary Rule**

Illinois The State of Illinois is a capital punishment jurisdiction. The State reenacted its death penalty law after the United States Supreme Court decision in *Furman v. Georgia*, 408 U.S. 238 (1972), on July 1, 1974.

Illinois has a three-tier legal system. The State's legal system is composed of a supreme court, court of appeals and courts of general jurisdiction. The Illinois Supreme Court is presided over by a chief justice and six associate justices. The Illinois Appellate Court is divided into five districts. Each district has at least three judges. The courts of general jurisdiction in the State are called Circuit Courts. Capital offenses against the State of Illinois are tried in the Circuit Courts.

Illinois' capital punishment statute is triggered if a person commits a homicide under the following special circumstances:

1. the defendant either intends to kill or do great bodily harm to the victim or another, or knows that his conduct will cause death to the victim or another; or
2. the defendant knows his conduct creates a strong probability of death or great bodily harm to the victim or another; or
3. the defendant is attempting or committing a forcible felony other than second degree murder.

Capital murder in Illinois is punishable by death or term of imprisonment. A capital prosecution in Illinois is bifurcated into a guilt phase and penalty phase. A jury is used at both phases of a capital trial. It is required that, at the penalty phase, the jury unanimously agree that a death sentence is appropriate before it can be imposed. If the penalty phase jury is unable to reach a verdict, the trial judge is required to impose a term of imprisonment. The decision of a penalty phase jury is binding on the trial court under the laws of Illinois.

In order to impose a death sentence upon a defendant under Illinois law, it is required that the prosecutor establish the existence of at least one of the following statutory aggravating circumstances at the penalty phase:

1. the murdered individual was a peace officer or fireman killed; or
2. the murdered individual was an employee of an institution or facility of the Department of Corrections, or any similar local correctional agency, or the murdered individual was an inmate at such institution or facility and was killed on the grounds thereof, or the murdered individual was otherwise present in such institution; or
3. the defendant has been convicted of murdering two or more individuals; or
4. the murdered individual was killed as a result of the hijacking of an airplane, train, ship, bus or other public conveyance; or
5. the defendant committed the murder pursuant to a contract, agreement or understanding by which he was to receive money or anything of value in return for committing the murder or procured another to commit the murder for money or anything of value; or
6. the murdered individual was killed in the course of another felony; or
7. the murdered individual was under 12 years of age and the death resulted from exceptionally brutal or heinous behavior indicative of wanton cruelty; or
8. the murdered individual was a witness; or
9. the defendant committed murder while trafficking in drugs; or
10. the defendant was incarcerated in an institution or facility of the Department of Corrections at the time of the murder; or

11. the murder was committed in a cold, calculated and premeditated manner pursuant to a preconceived plan, scheme or design to take a human life by unlawful means, and the conduct of the defendant created a reasonable expectation that the death of a human being would result therefrom; or
12. the murdered individual was a medical attendant employed by a municipality or other governmental unit; or
13. the defendant was a drug trafficking gang leader and the defendant counseled, commanded, induced, procured, or caused the intentional killing of the murdered person; or
14. the murder was intentional and involved the infliction of torture; or
15. the murder was committed as a result of the intentional discharge of a firearm by the defendant from a motor vehicle and the victim was not present within the motor vehicle; or
16. the murdered individual was 60 years of age or older and the death resulted from exceptionally brutal or heinous behavior indicative of wanton cruelty; or
17. the murdered individual was a disabled person and the defendant knew or should have known that the murdered individual was disabled; or
18. the murder was committed by reason of any person's activity as a community policing volunteer or to prevent any person from engaging in activity as a community policing volunteer.

Although the Federal Constitution will not permit jurisdictions to prevent capital felons from presenting all relevant mitigating evidence at the penalty phase, Illinois has provided the following statutory mitigating circumstances that permit the jury to reject imposition of the death penalty:

1. the defendant has no significant history of prior criminal activity;
2. the murder was committed while the defendant was under the influence of extreme mental or emotional disturbance, although not such as to constitute a defense to prosecution;
3. the murdered individual was a participant in the defendant's homicidal conduct or consented to the homicidal act;
4. the defendant acted under the compulsion of threat or menace of the imminent infliction of death or great bodily harm;
5. the defendant was not personally present during commission of the act or acts causing death.

Under Illinois' capital punishment statute, a sentence of death is automatically reviewed by the Illinois Supreme Court. Illinois uses lethal injection to carry out death sentences. The State's death row facilities for men are located in Tamms, Pontiac and Menard, Illinois; while the facility maintaining female death row inmates is located in Dwight, Illinois.

Pursuant to the laws of Illinois the Governor has authority to grant clemency in capital cases. The State's Prisoner Review Board makes nonbinding recommendation on clemency requests.

From the start of modern capital punishment in 1976, through 1999, Illinois executed 12 capital felons. During this period Illinois did not execute any female capital felons, although 3 of its death row inmates during this period were females. A total of 156 capital felons were on death row in Illinois in 1999. The 1999 death row population in the State was listed as: 97 black inmates; 52 white inmates; and 7 unidentified inmates. The State does not permit capital punishment to be imposed on persons 17 years old or younger. Illinois does not prohibit the execution of mentally retarded capital felons.

Executions by Illinois 1976–1999

Name	Race	Date of Execution	Method of Execution
Charles Walker	White	September 12, 1990	Lethal Injection
John W. Gacy	White	May 10, 1994	Lethal Injection
Hernando Williams	Black	March 22, 1995	Lethal Injection
James Free	White	March 22, 1995	Lethal Injection
Girvies Davis	Black	May 17, 1995	Lethal Injection
Charles Albanese	White	September 20, 1995	Lethal Injection
George D. Vecchio	White	November 22, 1995	Lethal Injection
Raymond L. Stewart	Black	September 18, 1996	Lethal Injection
Walter Stewart	Black	November 19, 1997	Lethal Injection
Durlyn Eddmonds	Black	November 19, 1997	Lethal Injection
Lloyd W. Hampton	White	January 21, 1998	Lethal Injection
Andrew Kokoraleis	White	March 17, 1998	Lethal Injection

ILLINOIS EXECUTIONS 1976–1999

2.0% 12

98.0% 586

■ ILLINOIS EXECUTIONS
■ ALL OTHER EXECUTIONS

EXECUTIONS BY ILLINOIS 1930–1999

2.3% 102

97.7% 4355

■ ILLINOIS
■ ALL OTHER JURISDICTIONS

Illinois Coalition Against the Death Penalty

The Illinois Coalition Against the Death Penalty (ICADP) was founded in 1976, to fight for the abolition of the death penalty in Illinois. ICADP provides research and technical support for attorneys working on capital cases and acts as a link between prisoners and the outside world. The organization also tracks State and Federal legislation and lobbies on behalf of any initiative that will abolish or curtail the death penalty's reach and effect. ICADP publishes a quarterly newsletter, maintains an active speakers bureau, holds conferences, gathers statistics, and maintains a comprehensive resource file for students and other interested individuals. Its members also monitor the conditions of Illinois' death row through monthly inspection visits, distributes donated typewriters and paper supplies and books to inmates, and supplies information to inmates and their families.

Incarceration *see* Death Row

Incompetent *see* Insanity

In Custody Aggravator

James Rich was convicted of committing murder while incarcerated in a North Carolina prison. Rich was executed on March 26, 1999. (North Carolina Department of Corrections)

The term "custody" refers to incarceration in prison or jail. A majority of capital punishment jurisdictions have made murder committed by a defendant in custody a statutory aggravating circumstance. In those jurisdictions if it is proven at the penalty phase that a murder was committed by a defendant in custody, the death penalty may be imposed. *See also* **Aggravating Circumstances**

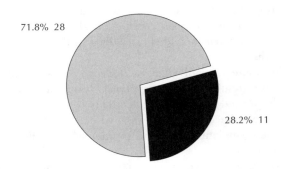

JURISDICTIONS USING IN CUSTODY AGGRAVATOR

71.8% 28

28.2% 11

■ IN CUSTODY AGGRAVATOR JURISDICTIONS
■ ALL OTHER JURISDICTIONS

Independent Source Rule *see* **Exclusionary Rule**

India India imposes capital punishment. India uses hanging to carry out the death penalty. Its legal system is based on English common law. The country's constitution was adopted on January 26, 1950.

India's judicial system is composed of district courts, High Courts, and a Supreme Court. Defendants have a right to a public trial (except in limited circumstances), the right to counsel and the right to appeal. *See also* **International Capital Punishment Nations**

Indiana The State of Indiana is a capital punishment jurisdiction. The State reenacted its death penalty law after the United States Supreme Court decision in *Furman v. Georgia*, 408 U.S. 238 (1972), on May 1, 1973.

Indiana has a three-tier legal system. The State's legal system is composed of a supreme court, court of appeals and courts of general jurisdiction. The Indiana Supreme Court is presided over by a chief justice and four associate justices. The Indiana Court of Appeals is divided into five districts. Each district has at least three judges. The courts of general jurisdiction in the State are called Circuit Courts (the State also has courts of general jurisdiction that are called Superior Courts). Capital offenses against the State of Indiana are tried in the Circuit Courts.

Indiana's capital punishment statute is triggered if a person commits a homicide under the following special circumstances:

1. knowingly or intentionally kills another human being;
2. kills another human being while committing or attempting to commit arson, burglary, child molesting, consumer product tampering, criminal deviate conduct, kidnapping, rape, robbery, or carjacking;
3. kills another human being while committing or attempting to commit a drug offense; or
4. knowingly or intentionally kills a fetus that has attained viability.

Capital murder in Indiana is punishable by death or life imprisonment without parole. A capital prosecution in Indiana is bifurcated into a guilt phase and penalty phase. A jury is used at both phases of a capital trial. It is required that, at the penalty phase, the jury unanimously agree that a death sentence is appropriate before it can be imposed. If the penalty phase jury is unable to reach a verdict, the trial judge is required to declare a mistrial and hold a new penalty phase hearing without a jury. The decision of a penalty phase jury is not binding on the trial court under the laws of Indiana. The trial court may accept or reject the jury's determination on punishment, and impose whatever sentence he or she believes the evidence established.

In order to impose a death sentence upon a defendant under Indiana law, it is required that the prosecutor establish the existence of at least one of the following statutory aggravating circumstances at the penalty phase:

1. The defendant committed the murder by intentionally killing the victim while committing or attempting to commit any of the following: (A) arson; (B) burglary; (C) child molesting; (D) criminal deviate conduct; (E) kidnaping; (F) rape; (G) robbery; (H) carjacking; (I) criminal gang activity; (J) dealing in cocaine or a narcotic drug.
2. The defendant committed the murder by the unlawful detonation of an explosive with intent to injure person or damage property.
3. The defendant committed the murder by lying in wait.
4. The defendant who committed the murder was hired to kill.
5. The defendant committed the murder by hiring another person to kill.
6. The victim of the murder was a corrections employee, probation officer, parole officer, community corrections worker, home detention officer, fireman, judge, or law enforcement officer.
7. The defendant has been convicted of another murder.
8. The defendant has committed another murder, at any time, regardless of whether the defendant has been convicted of that other murder.
9. The defendant was at the time of the crime: (A) under the custody of the department of correction; (B) under the custody of a county sheriff; (C) on probation after receiving a sentence for the commission of a felony; or (D) on parole.
10. The defendant dismembered the victim.
11. The defendant burned, mutilated, or tortured the victim while the victim was alive.
12. The victim of the murder was less than twelve (12) years of age.
13. The victim was a victim of any of the following offenses for which the defendant was convicted: (A) battery; (B) kidnaping; (C) criminal confinement; (D) a sex crime.
14. The victim of the murder was listed by the state or known by the defendant to be a witness against the defendant and the defendant committed the murder with the intent to prevent the person from testifying.
15. The defendant committed the murder by intentionally discharging a firearm: (A) into an inhabited dwelling; or (B) from a vehicle.
16. The victim of the murder was pregnant and the murder resulted in the intentional killing of a fetus that has attained viability.

Although the Federal Constitution will not permit jurisdictions to prevent capital felons from presenting all relevant mitigating evidence at the penalty phase, Indiana has provided the following statutory mitigating circumstances that permit the jury (or judge) to reject imposition of the death penalty:

1. The defendant has no significant history of prior criminal conduct.
2. The defendant was under the influence of extreme mental

or emotional disturbance when the murder was committed.

3. The victim was a participant in or consented to the defendant's conduct.

4. The defendant was an accomplice in a murder committed by another person, and the defendant's participation was relatively minor.

5. The defendant acted under the substantial domination of another person.

6. The defendant's capacity to appreciate the criminality of the defendant's conduct or to conform that conduct to the requirements of law was substantially impaired as a result of mental disease or defect or of intoxication.

7. The defendant was less than eighteen years of age at the time the murder was committed.

8. Any other circumstances appropriate for consideration.

Under Indiana's capital punishment statute, a sentence of death is automatically reviewed by the Indiana Supreme Court. Indiana uses lethal injection to carry out death sentences (switched from electrocution in 1995). The State's death row facility for men is located in Michigan City, Indiana; while the facility maintaining female death row inmates is located in Indianapolis, Indiana.

Pursuant to the laws of Indiana the Governor has authority to grant clemency in capital cases. The Governor is re-

Executions by Indiana 1976–1999

Name	Race	Date of Execution	Method of Execution
Steven Judy	White	March 9, 1981	Electrocution
William Vandiver	White	October 16, 1985	Electrocution
Gregory Resnover	Black	December 8, 1994	Electrocution
Tommie Smith	Black	July 18, 1996	Lethal Injection
Gary Burris	Black	November 20, 1997	Lethal Injection
Robert A. Smith	White	January 29, 1998	Lethal Injection
D. H. Fleenor	White	December 9, 1999	Lethal Injection

INDIANA EXECUTIONS 1976–1999

98.8% 591   1.2% 7

■ INDIANA EXECUTIONS
■ ALL OTHER EXECUTIONS

EXECUTIONS BY INDIANA 1930–1999

98.9% 4409   1.1% 48

■ INDIANA
■ ALL OTHER JURISDICTIONS

quired to obtain the consent of the State's Parole Board, before clemency may be granted.

From the start of modern capital punishment in 1976, through 1999, Indiana executed 7 capital felons. During this period Indiana did not execute any female capital felons, although one of its death row inmates during this period was a female. A total of 45 capital felons were on death row in Indiana in 1999. The 1999 death row population in the State was listed as: 16 black inmates; 28 white inmates; and 1 unidentified inmate. In 1999 the State did not have any juvenile on death row. The State permits capital punishment to be imposed on persons 16 years old or older. Indiana prohibits the execution of mentally retarded capital felons.

Indictment *see* **Grand Jury**

Indigent Defendant *see* **In Forma Pauperis**

Individualized Sentencing   A cornerstone of modern capital punishment is the Federal constitutional requirement of individualized sentencing. The basic underlying premise of individualized sentencing is that imposition of capital punishment must, at minimum, be based upon the gravity of the offense, character of the offender and the need to protect the public. Under this formula the factfinder must consider all relevant mitigating and aggravating evidence in making the determination of whether to impose a sentence of death.

Courts have held that the purpose behind individualized sentencing is not served where the factfinder decides not to impose the death penalty purely out of a personal sense of mercy and in disregard of the presence of aggravating circumstances. Nor is the purpose of individualized sentencing served where the factfinder ignores the presence of mitigating circumstances for personal reasons in order to render a death sentence. Individualized sentencing strikes a delicate balance that demands the factfinder deliberate on a slate that only has superimposed upon it evidence of relevant mitigating and aggravating circumstances. A sentence of death imposed for any reason other than that the penalty is particularized to circumstances of the crime and defendant offends the Federal Constitution and is invalid.

Included in the scheme of individualized sentencing is the persistent theme that a capital felon's social, economic and educational background, personality, character, propensities and tendencies be given evidentiary expression and consideration. These factors may prove mitigating or aggravating, or both. In the final analysis, individualized sentencing seeks to place the whole person before the factfinder, not an abstract notion or preconceived idea of the capital felon.

Individualized sentencing also requires the factfinder consider all the circumstances surrounding the capital crime for which the defendant was convicted. This evidence can be aggravating or mitigating, or both. Courts permit evidence of whether capital punishment would have a deterrent effect based upon the particular case before the factfinder. The factfinder may draw inferences from evidence received during the guilt phase.

Although the death penalty may be imposed upon a capital defendant convicted as a party to capital murder, it may not be imposed upon him or her for deliberate conduct of another or future dangerousness of another. The punishment must be imposed in view of the individual conduct of the capital felon whose fate is being determined by the penalty phase jury. *See also* **Aggravating Circumstances; Mitigating Circumstances**

Indonesia

Indonesia imposes capital punishment. The firing squad is used by Indonesia to carry out the death penalty. Its legal system is based on Roman-Dutch law and customary law. Indonesia's constitution was restored on July 5, 1959.

The judicial system is composed of district courts, High Courts and a Supreme Court. Defendants do not have a right to trial by jury in Indonesia. Guilt or innocence is determined by a panel of judges. The laws of Indonesia provide defendants with the right to retained or appointed counsel. Defendants do not have the right to remain silent and may be compelled to testify against themselves. Both the defense and the prosecution may appeal. *See also* **International Capital Punishment Nations**

Informant Aggravator

In the context of criminal law, an informant is a person who provides information to the police that implicates a defendant in a crime. Two capital punishment jurisdictions, Delaware and Pennsylvania, have made the killing of an informant a statutory aggravating circumstance. In these jurisdictions the death penalty may be imposed if evidence establishes at the penalty phase, that the killing occurred because of the informant's cooperation with the police. *See also* **Aggravating Circumstances**

In Forma Pauperis

Under the doctrine of in forma pauperis an indigent defendant is permitted to have access to legal services, materials and legal assistance, without having to personally pay the cost of such services and assistance. The in forma pauperis doctrine has constitutional underpinnings, insofar as equal protection principles demand that poor defendants have similar access to legal services as do defendants having personal financial resources.

Information *see* Prosecution by Information

Informing Jury of How Death Is Imposed

Capital felons have argued that evidence of how capital punishment is carried out is relevant mitigating evidence, that is required by the Federal Constitution to be introduced at the penalty phase. However, courts have consistently ruled that evidence of how capital punishment is imposed is irrelevant and that the Federal Constitution does not require introduction of such evidence. The proper focus of the penalty phase is on the capital felon's character, record, and the circumstances of the offense for which he or she was convicted. *See also* **Mitigating Circumstances**

Initial Appearance *see* Arraignment

Injunction

An injunction is a legal order issued by a court restraining a person from performing certain conduct. Capital felons will occasionally resort to seeking an injunction as a remedy. For example, if a jurisdiction changes the method of execution after a capital felon's conviction and death sentence, he or she may seek an injunction to prevent use of the new method of execution.

Innocent *see* Actual Innocence Claim

In Re Cross

Court: United States Supreme Court; *Case Citation:* In Re Cross, 146 U.S. 271 (1892); *Argued:* Not reported; *Decided:* December 5, 1892; *Opinion of the Court:* Chief Justice Fuller; *Concurring Opinion:* None; *Dissenting Opinion:* None; *Appellate Defense Counsel:* C. Maurice Smith argued; Joseph Shillington on brief; *Appellate Prosecution Counsel:* Not represented; *Amicus Curiae Brief Supporting Prosecutor:* None; *Amicus Curiae Brief Supporting Defendant:* None.

Issue Presented: Whether the defendant could be executed after the time for execution set by law had passed?

Case Holding: The defendant could be executed after the time for execution set by law had passed, because the delay in carrying out the execution was caused by appeals initiated by the defendant.

Factual and procedural background of case: The defendant, William D. Cross, was convicted of capital murder and sentenced to death by the District of Columbia. The Court of Appeals of the District of Columbia affirmed the judgment. The defendant filed a petition for appeal with the United States Supreme Court, challenging his conviction and sentence. The government filed a motion to dismiss the petition on the grounds that the Supreme Court did not have appellate jurisdiction over the case. The Supreme Court agreed and dismissed the petition for appeal in *Cross v. United States.*

The defendant next filed a habeas corpus petition in a trial court for the District of Columbia, which was dismissed. The appellate court of the District of Columbia affirmed. The United States Supreme Court granted an appeal. The government filed a motion to dismiss the petition on the grounds that the Supreme Court did not have appellate jurisdiction over the case. The Supreme Court agreed and dismissed the petition for appeal in *Cross v. Burke.*

The defendant then filed an application for habeas corpus relief directly with the Supreme Court, contending that he could not be executed because the time for execution required by law had expired.

Opinion of the Court by Chief Justice Fuller: The Chief Justice ruled that the defendant's argument was without merit. It was said that the time of execution was not part of the sentence of death unless made so by statute. The Chief Justice found that under the laws of the District of Columbia, promulgated by Congress, "if the time for execution had passed, in any case, the court could make a new order." The opinion reasoned: "Unquestionably, congress did not intend that the execution of a sentence should not be carried out, if judgment were affirmed on [appeal], except where the appellate court was able to announce a result within the time allowed for the application for the [appeal] to be made. The postponements were rendered necessary by reason of delays occasioned by the acts of the condemned in his own interest, and the position that he thereby became entitled to be set at large cannot be sustained." The defendant's application for habeas relief was denied. *See also* **Cross v. Burke; Cross v. United States**

In Re Durrant   *Court:* United States Supreme Court; *Case Citation:* In Re Durrant, 169 U.S. 39 (1898); *Argued:* Not reported; *Decided:* January 7, 1898; *Opinion of the Court:* Chief Justice Fuller; *Concurring Opinion:* None; *Dissenting Opinion:* None; *Appellate Defense Counsel:* Louis P. Boardman argued and briefed; *Appellate Prosecution Counsel:* Not represented; *Amicus Curiae Brief Supporting Prosecutor:* None; *Amicus Curiae Brief Supporting Defendant:* None.

Issue Presented: Whether the State trial court could set an imminent execution date before the United States Supreme Court issued its mandate affirming a Federal District Court's denial of habeas relief to the defendant?

Case Holding: The State trial court could set an imminent execution date before the United States Supreme Court issued its mandate affirming a Federal District Court's denial of habeas relief to the defendant, although the better practice would be to wait for the mandate to be issued.

Factual and procedural background of case: The defendant, Durrant, was convicted of capital murder and sentenced to death by the State of California. The California Supreme Court affirmed the judgment on appeal. The defendant sub-

sequently filed a habeas corpus petition in a Federal District Court. The habeas petition was dismissed. The defendant thereafter appealed the habeas dismissal to the United States Supreme Court. The Supreme Court summarily denied the habeas appeal. However, before the Supreme Court sent its mandate to the Federal District Court affirming the dismissal, the State trial court set an execution date for the defendant. The defendant thereafter motioned the Supreme Court to grant him habeas relief because the State intended to execute him before the mandate was sent to the Federal District Court.

Opinion of the Court by Chief Justice Fuller: The Chief Justice referred to the Court's decision in the case of *In Re Jugiro*, in order to hold that the State trial court could set an execution date even though its mandate affirming the denial of habeas relief had not been sent to the Federal District Court. The opinion held succinctly: "The judgment of this court affirming [the federal] order was rendered, as we know from our own records, and we have decided that if the state court, after judgment here, proceeds before our mandate issues, its action, though not to be commended, is not void." The defendant's motion for relief was denied and the case dismissed. *See also* **In Re Jugiro; Mandate**

In Re Jugiro   *Court:* United States Supreme Court; *Case Citation:* In Re Jugiro, 140 U.S. 291 (1891); *Argued:* April 10, 1891; *Decided:* May 11, 1891; *Opinion of the Court:* Justice Harlan; *Concurring Opinion:* None; *Dissenting Opinion:* None; *Justice Taking No Part in Decision:* Justice Gray; *Appellate Defense Counsel:* Roger M. Sherman on brief; *Appellate Prosecution Counsel:* Isaac H. Maynard argued; Charles F. Tabor on brief; *Amicus Curiae Brief Supporting Prosecutor:* None; *Amicus Curiae Brief Supporting Defendant:* None.

Issues Presented: (1) Whether New York could set an execution date for the defendant before the United States Supreme Court filed its mandate in a Federal District Court affirming the District Court's denial of habeas relief to the defendant? (2) Whether the defendant's conviction and sentence were invalid because of his claim that Japanese residents were systematically excluded from the grand jury that indicted him and the petit jury that convicted him?

Case Holdings: (1) New York could set an execution date for the defendant before the United States Supreme Court filed its mandate in a Federal District Court affirming the District Court's denial of habeas relief to the defendant, although it would have been more appropriate to wait for the mandate to be filed. (2) The merits of the defendant's jury discrimination claim could not be addressed by Federal courts because the defendant failed to raise the issue before the courts of New York.

Factual and procedural background of case: The defendant, Shibuya Jugiro, was convicted of capital murder and sentenced to death by the State of New York. The New York Court of Appeals affirmed the judgment. The defendant filed a habeas corpus petition in a Federal District Court challenging his conviction and sentence. The District Court dismissed the petition. The United States Supreme Court, by memorandum order, affirmed the District Court's decision. Subsequently, a death warrant was issued fixing the date of the defendant's execution. The defendant thereafter filed another habeas corpus petition in a Federal District Court. In the petition the defendant alleged that he could not be executed because the United States Supreme Court had not sent a mandate to the District Court affirming the District Court's decision. The defendant also alleged, for the first time, that his conviction and sentence were invalid because Japanese residents were systematically excluded from the grand jury that indicted him and the petit jury that convicted him. The District Court dismissed the petition. The United States Supreme Court granted certiorari to consider the issues.

Opinion of the Court by Justice Harlan: Justice Harlan held that New York did not have to postpone the execution because the Court had not sent a mandate to the District Court officially affirming its decision on the defendant's first habeas proceeding. The opinion acknowledged that "it would have been more appropriate and orderly if the state court had deferred [setting the execution date] until our mandate was issued[.]" However, the Court was not willing to concede that mere filing of the mandate of affirmance with the District Court was "absolutely necessary before the state court [could] proceed in the execution of the judgment of conviction."

In turning to the defendant's jury discrimination claim, the Court held that the resolution of the issue was controlled by its decision in the case of *In Re Wood*. The *Wood* decision held that a claim of jury discrimination by a State could not be raised for the first time in a Federal habeas proceeding. In order for Federal courts to have jurisdiction to address the merits of a jury discrimination claim, *Wood* required the appropriate State courts to have addressed the issue first. Justice Harlan found that the defendant failed to present his jury discrimination claim to the courts of New York. The opinion also stated: "The criminal laws of New York [made] no discrimination against [the defendant] because of his nativity or race. They accord[ed] to him when upon trial for his life or liberty the same rights and privileges that are accorded, under like circumstances, to native or naturalized citizens of this country." The judgment of the District Court was affirmed. *See also* **Discrimination in Grand or Petit Jury Selection; In Re Durrant; In Re Wood; Mandate; Procedural Default of Constitutional Claims**

In Re Kemmler
Court: United States Supreme Court; *Case Citation:* In Re Kemmler, 136 U.S. 436 (1890); *Argued:* Not reported; *Decided:* May 19, 1890; *Opinion of the Court:* Chief Justice Fuller; *Concurring Opinion:* None; *Dissenting Opinion:* None; *Appellate Defense Counsel:* Roger Sherman argued and briefed; *Appellate Prosecution Counsel:* Charles. F. Tabor argued and briefed; *Amicus Curiae Brief Supporting Prosecutor:* None; *Amicus Curiae Brief Supporting Defendant:* None.

Issue Presented: Whether imposition of the death penalty by a current of electricity violates the Constitution as cruel and unusual punishment?

Case Holding: The use of electricity to execute a sentence of death does not violate the Constitution.

Factual and procedural background of case: The defendant, William Kemmler, was indicted for capital murder by the State of New York in 1889. He was convicted and sentenced to death by electrocution. After unsuccessfully challenging his conviction and sentence on direct appeal, the defendant filed a habeas corpus petition arguing that death by electrocution violated the federal Constitution as cruel and unusual punishment. The courts of New York rejected the claim. The United States Supreme Court granted certiorari to consider the matter.

Opinion of the Court by Chief Justice Fuller: The Chief Justice wrote that "[d]ifficulty would attend the effort to define with exactness the extent of the constitutional provision which provides that cruel and unusual punishments shall not be inflicted; but it is safe to affirm that punishments of torture, ... and all others in the same line of unnecessary cruelty, are forbidden by that amendment to the constitution." Elaborating on this theme, the opinion observed: "Punishments are cruel when they involve torture or a lingering death; but the punishment of death is not cruel within the meaning of that word as used in the constitution. It implies there something inhuman and barbarous, something more than the mere extinguishment of life."

It was noted by the Chief Justice that "[t]he courts of New York held that the mode [of punishment] adopted in this instance might be said to be unusual because it was new, but that it could not be assumed to be cruel in the light of that common knowledge which has stamped certain punishments as such; that it was for the legislature to say in what manner sentence of death should be executed; that this [form of punishment] was ... passed in the effort to devise a more humane method of reaching the result[.]"

Ultimately the Chief Justice determined that death by electrocution was a matter that was in the sphere of the State of New York to decide, insofar as such punishment was not shown to be in violation of the Constitution. The opinion concluded: "The enactment of this [punishment] was, in itself, within the legitimate sphere of the legislative power of the state, and in the observance of those general rules prescribed by our systems of jurisprudence; and the legislature of the state of New York determined that it did not inflict cruel and unusual punishment, and its courts have sustained that determination. We cannot perceive that the state has thereby abridged the privileges or immunities of the [defendant], or deprived him of due process of law." The judgment of New York's highest court was affirmed. *See also* **Electrocution**

In Re Medley
Court: United States Supreme Court; *Case Citation:* In Re Medley, 134 U.S. 160 (1890); *Argued:* Not reported; *Decided:* March 3, 1890; *Opinion of the Court:* Justice Miller; *Concurring Opinion:* None; *Dissenting Opinion:* Justice Brewer, in which Bradley, J., joined; *Appellate Defense Counsel:* A. T. Britton argued; Henry Wise Garnett and W. V. R.

Berry on brief; *Appellate Prosecution Counsel:* H. M. Teller argued and briefed; *Amicus Curiae Brief Supporting Prosecutor:* None; *Amicus Curiae Brief Supporting Defendant:* None.

Issue Presented: Whether the defendant's conviction and sentence were invalid because he was prosecuted under a statute that was not in existence at the time of his crime?

Case Holding: The defendant's conviction and sentence were invalid because he was prosecuted under a statute that was not in existence at the time of his crime.

Factual and procedural background of case: The defendant, James J. Medley, was convicted of capital murder and sentenced to die by the State of Colorado. The Colorado Supreme Court affirmed the judgment. The defendant subsequently filed a habeas corpus petition directly with the United States Supreme Court. In the petition the defendant alleged that he was convicted and sentenced under a statute that was not in existence at the time of the commission of his crime, therefore the judgment against him violated the Ex Post Facto Clause.

Opinion of the Court by Justice Miller: Justice Miller found that the defendant's conviction and sentence violated the Ex Post Facto Clause. The opinion stated that "it may be said that any law which was passed after the commission of the offense for which the party is being tried is an ex post facto law when it inflicts a greater punishment than the law annexed to the crime at the time it was committed or which alters the situation of the accused to his disadvantage; and that no one can be criminally punished in this country except according to a law prescribed for his government by the sovereign authority before the imputed offense was committed, or by some law passed afterwards, by which the punishment is not increased." Justice Miller determined that two provisions of the statute under which the defendant was prosecuted were not in existence at the time of his crime.

One of the provisions disapproved of by the Court involved detaining the defendant in solitary confinement until he was executed. Under the law at the time of the defendant's crime "[t]he prisoner was to be kept in the county jail under the control of the sheriff of the county, who was the officer charged with the execution of the sentence of the court." Justice Miller ruled "that the solitary confinement to which the prisoner was subjected by the [new] statute ..., was an additional punishment of the most important and painful character, and is therefore forbidden by [the Ex Post Facto Clause] of the constitution of the United States."

The opinion also disapproved of a provision under the new law which gave the warden the authority to fix the day and time of execution. Under the law at the time of the defendant's crime, the trial court had the authority to fix the day and time of execution. "It is obvious that it confers upon the warden of the penitentiary a power which had heretofore been solely confided to the court and is therefore a departure from the law as it stood when the crime was committed." It was concluded by Justice Miller that "this new power of fixing any day and hour during a period of a week for the execution is a new and

important power conferred on that officer, and is a departure from the law as it existed at the time the offense was committed, and with its secrecy must be accompanied by an immense mental anxiety amounting to a great increase of the offender's punishment."

Because of the two constitutionally objectionable provisions of the State's new statute, Justice Miller held that "[t]hese considerations render it our duty to order the release of the prisoner from the custody of the warden of the penitentiary of Colorado, as he is now held by him under the judgment and order of the court." The judgment of the Colorado Supreme Court was reversed and the defendant ordered released.

Dissenting opinion by Justice Brewer, in which Bradley, J., joined: Justice Brewer dissented from the Court's decision. He wrote: "The substantial punishment imposed by each statute is death by hanging. The differences between the two, as to the manner in which this sentence of death shall be carried into execution, are trifling.... Yet, on account of these differences, a convicted murderer is to escape the death he deserves, and be turned loose in society." *See also* **Ex Post Facto Clause**

In Re Robertson
Court: United States Supreme Court; *Case Citation:* In Re Robertson, 156 U.S. 183 (1895); *Argued:* Not reported; *Decided:* January 22, 1895; *Opinion of the Court:* Chief Justice Fuller; *Concurring Opinion:* None; *Dissenting Opinion:* None; *Appellate Defense Counsel:* L. W. Anderson on brief; *Appellate Prosecution Counsel:* Not represented; *Amicus Curiae Brief Supporting Prosecutor:* None; *Amicus Curiae Brief Supporting Defendant:* None.

Issue Presented: Whether the defendant's appeal was properly before the United States Supreme Court?

Case Holding: The defendant's appeal was not properly before the United States Supreme Court, because it was not requested by any Justice nor concurred in by any Justice.

Factual and procedural background of case: The defendant, William Robertson, was convicted of capital murder and sentenced to death by the State of Virginia. The Virginia Supreme Court affirmed the judgment. The defendant then appealed to the United States Supreme Court, which denied review. However, by some mistake the case was placed on the Supreme Court's docket as being accepted.

Opinion of the Court by Chief Justice Fuller: The Chief Justice held that the case was not properly before the Court and application for appeal had to be denied. The opinion explained: "Applications to this court for [appeal] are not entertained, unless at the request of one of the members of the court, concurred in by his associates. In this case there seems to have been some misunderstanding on the part of counsel as to the practice, in view of which, and considering that this is a capital case, and that the day appointed for the execution of the sentence is very near, we have examined the application, and are of opinion that the [issue presented] is not a federal question, and that no federal question appears, upon the record, to have been presented to the supreme court of appeals of Virginia[.]" The appeal was dismissed.

In Re Wood *Court:* United States Supreme Court; *Case Citation:* In Re Wood, 140 U.S. 278 (1891); *Argued:* April 10, 1891; *Decided:* May 11, 1891; *Opinion of the Court:* Justice Harlan; *Concurring Opinion:* Justice Field; *Dissenting Opinion:* None; *Justice Taking No Part in Decision:* Justice Gray; *Appellate Defense Counsel:* R. J. Haire argued and briefed; *Appellate Prosecution Counsel:* Isaac H. Maynard argued; Charles F. Tabor on brief; *Amicus Curiae Brief Supporting Prosecutor:* None; *Amicus Curiae Brief Supporting Defendant:* None.

Issue Presented: Whether the defendant's conviction and death sentence were void because blacks were systematically excluded from the grand jury that indicted him and the petit jury that convicted him?

Case Holding: The jury discrimination issue could not be addressed by Federal courts because the defendant failed to raise the issue in the State courts of New York.

Factual and procedural background of case: The defendant, Joseph Wood, was convicted of capital murder and sentenced to death by the State of New York. The New York Court of Appeals affirmed the judgment. The defendant filed a habeas corpus petition in a Federal District Court, alleging that his conviction violated the Federal Constitution because blacks were systematically excluded from the grand jury that indicted him and the petit jury that convicted him. The District Court rejected the petition. The United States Supreme Court granted certiorari to consider the issue.

Opinion of the Court by Justice Harlan: Justice Harlan indicated that under the Court's precedent, *Neal v. Delaware*, States were prohibited from systematically excluding blacks from grand or petit juries. It was said that the rule observed in *Neal* could not be invoked by the defendant, because the issue of jury discrimination was never presented to the courts of New York by the defendant. Justice Harlan made clear that, if a defendant desired to raise a claim of unlawful jury discrimination by a State, the defendant must first raise the issue in a State court in order for a Federal court to examine the matter in a habeas corpus proceeding. The judgment of the District Court was affirmed.

Concurring opinion by Justice Field: Justice Field concurred in the Court's judgment. He wrote that it was his view that the Constitution did not prohibit States from excluding blacks from grand or petit juries. Justice Field argued that States were free to determine the qualifications required to participate in grand or petit juries. *See also* **Discrimination in Grand or Petit Jury Selection; In Re Jugiro; Procedural Default of Constitutional Claims**

Insanity Insanity is a legal term of art that varies in meaning, depending upon the jurisdiction. As a general matter, insanity is a condition of the mind which negatives the necessary mens rea or culpability prong of an offense. In the eyes of the law insanity may be temporary, permanent or partial.

The issue of insanity may present itself at various stages of a capital murder prosecution. The issue may arise before trial, during the guilt phase, at the penalty phase, as a defense, or

while awaiting execution. The United States Constitution requires that a defendant be competent throughout all stages of the prosecution. If a determination is made by the trial judge at any stage of the prosecution that the defendant may not be competent to assist his or her counsel, nor understand the nature of the proceedings, the proceedings must come to a halt. The trial court is obligated, upon a proper showing of possible incompetency, to order a psychiatric examination of the defendant. Usually defense counsel will seek an independent evaluation in conjunction with the evaluation done at the behest of the court. Prosecutors generally will rely upon the testing done by the court ordered psychiatric examination.

After a defendant has undergone psychiatric evaluations a competency hearing will be held. At that proceeding the court will hear evidence from all psychiatrists involved. The two key constitutional issues the court is concerned with during the hearing, is whether the defendant is capable of understanding the nature of the proceedings against him or her and is able to assist his or her counsel in his or her defense. If the evidence shows that the defendant understands the nature of the proceedings and is able to assist in his or her defense, the prosecution will proceed. Conversely, if the evidence shows that the defendant does not understand the nature of the proceedings and is unable to assist in his or her defense, the defendant will be remanded to a correctional facility for treatment aimed at restoring his or her mental competency. Should the defendant remain mentally incompetent after a brief period of treatment, a civil commitment proceeding must occur in order to legally confine the defendant for however long it takes to restore his or her sanity.

The United States Supreme Court has disapproved, on constitutional due process grounds, imposing upon a defendant the burden of proving competency to "stand trial" by clear and convincing evidence. This high standard has been deemed constitutionally unfair because it would permit an "insane" person to stand trial. The highest burden of proof that may be constitutionally imposed upon a defendant claiming incompetency to stand trial, is the preponderance of the evidence standard of proof.

A problem that very often arises in the area of a defendant's competency to stand trial, is the issue of forced use of antipsychotic drugs to enable the defendant to be prosecuted. It has been held by the United States Supreme Court that forced administration of antipsychotic medication during the defendant's trial may violate a defendant's constitutional right to a fair trial. In order for a State to force a defendant to use an antipsychotic drug during a trial, the State must show that the treatment was medically appropriate and, considering less intrusive alternatives, essential for the defendant's own safety or the safety of others. Additionally, the State may justify such treatment if medically appropriate, by showing that an adjudication of guilt or innocence could not be obtained by using less intrusive means. *See also* **Cooper v. Oklahoma; Ford v. Wainwright; Godinez v. Moran; Insanity Defense; Insanity While Awaiting Execution; Riggins v. Nevada**

Insanity Defense The insanity defense is an affirmative defense. Capital punishment jurisdictions vary in the burden of proof imposed on a capital felon asserting the insanity defense. Most jurisdictions impose a preponderance of the evidence burden. However, the United States Supreme Court has approved of requiring a defendant prove insanity beyond a reasonable doubt. Notwithstanding the burden placed on a defendant, the prosecutor must still prove guilt beyond a reasonable doubt.

The issue of insanity as a defense is centered on the defendant's state of mind precisely at the time of the commission of the offense. If during the guilt phase of trial the prosecutor fails to show beyond a reasonable doubt that a defendant was sane at the time the offense was being committed, then a verdict of not guilty by reason of insanity must be returned by the trial factfinder. The ultimate result of acquittal that follows a successful assertion of the insanity defense caused two capital punishment jurisdictions, Idaho and Montana, to actually abolish the defense by statute.

The first step in a capital punishment prosecution wherein the defendant asserts the insanity defense, is for the trial court to make a determination as to whether the defendant is competent for trial purposes. To make this determination the trial court will order a psychiatric evaluation of the defendant. The evaluation at this stage is for the purpose of determining whether the defendant is competent to stand trial. As a practical matter, the overwhelming majority of defendants who assert the insanity defense are found to be competent for trial purposes. The statutory procedure for determining sanity used by Colorado illustrates the procedure generally used by all jurisdictions.

> **Colo. Rev. Stat. Ann. § 16-8-105.5 Insanity Defense Procedure:** 1. When a plea of not guilty by reason of insanity is accepted, the court shall forthwith commit the defendant for a sanity examination, specifying the place and period of commitment.
>
> 2. Upon receiving the report of the sanity examination, the court shall immediately set the case for trial. Every person is presumed to be sane; but, once any evidence of insanity is introduced, the people have the burden of proving sanity beyond a reasonable doubt.
>
> 3. When the affirmative defense of not guilty by reason of insanity has been raised, the jury shall be given special verdict forms containing interrogatories. The trier of fact shall decide first the question of guilt as to felony charges that are before the court. If the trier of fact concludes that guilt has been proven beyond a reasonable doubt as to one or more of the felony charges submitted for consideration, the special interrogatories shall not be answered. Upon completion of its deliberations on the felony charges as previously set forth in this subsection (3), the trier of fact shall consider any other charges before the court in a similar manner; except that it shall not answer the special interrogatories regarding such charges if it has previously found guilt beyond a reasonable doubt with respect to one or more felony charges. The interrogatories shall provide for specific findings of the jury with respect to the affirmative defense of not guilty by reason of insanity. When the court sits as the trier of fact, it shall enter appropriate specific findings with respect to the affirmative defense of not guilty by reason of insanity.
>
> 4. If the trier of fact finds the defendant not guilty by reason of insanity, the court shall commit the defendant to the custody of the department of human services until such time as the defendant is found eligible for release. The executive director of the department of human services shall designate the state facility at which the defendant shall be held for care and psychiatric treatment and may transfer the defendant from one facility to another if in the opinion of the director it is desirable to do so in the interest of the proper care, custody, and treatment of the defendant or the protection of the public or the personnel of the facilities in question.

Legal Definitions of Insanity: The most perplexing issue involving the insanity defense has been that of finding a workable legal definition for the defense. Numerous definitions for legal insanity have been crafted by judges, legislators and commentators on the law. The most reported upon legal definitions of insanity include the M'Naghten rule, Durham rule, Irresistible Impulse test, and the Substantial Capacity test.

M'Naghten Rule. The M'Naghten rule was imported to the United States from England. This test for insanity was developed in an English judicial decision styled *M'Naghten's Case*, 8 Eng. Rep. 718 (1843). Under the M'Naghten rule a trial court instructs the jury that the defendant may be found not guilty by reason of insanity if the evidence shows that, at the time of committing the act, the defendant was suffering under such a defect of reason, from disease of the mind, as not to know the nature and quality of the act he or she was doing; or, if he or she did know it, that he or she did not know what he or she was doing was wrong.

When the M'Naghten rule first hit the legal shores of the United States, it was quickly adopted by almost every court in the nation. Time, however, proved the test to be cumbersome and unworkable.

Durham Rule. The Durham rule represented the initial break with the unworkable M'Naghten rule. The Durham rule was fashioned in the case of *Durham v. United States*, 214 F.2d 862 (D.C. Cir. 1954). Under the Durham rule the jury is instructed by the trial court that in order to find the defendant not guilty by reason of insanity, the evidence must establish that the defendant was suffering from a diseased or defective mental condition at the time of the commission of the act charged; and that there was a causal relation between such disease or defective condition and the act. The Durham rule has never been widely adopted.

Irresistible Impulse Test. The Irresistible Impulse test was developed by courts as an alternative to the M'Naghten rule. In the final analysis, the Irresistible Impulse test is broader than the M'Naghten Rule. The Irresistible Impulse test is defined as an impulse to commit a criminal act which cannot be resisted, because a mental disease has destroyed a defendant's freedom of will, power of self-control and choice of actions. Under this test a defendant may avoid criminal responsibility for his or her conduct, even though he or she is capable of distinguishing between right and wrong and is fully aware of the nature and quality of his or her conduct, provided he or she establishes that he or she was unable to refrain from acting. A number of courts utilize this test.

Substantial Capacity Test. The Substantial Capacity test was developed by the American Law Institute in 1962 and set out under § 4.01 of the Model Penal Code. Under the Substantial Capacity test a defendant is not responsible for criminal conduct if at the time of such conduct, as a result of mental disease or defect, he or she lacks substantial capacity either to appreciate the wrongfulness of his or her conduct or to conform his or her conduct to the requirement of the law. The Substantial Capacity test has been widely adopted. As illustrated below, the Federal government has adopted a version of the substantial capacity test.

18 U.S.C.A. § 17 Federal Insanity Defense Reform Act of 1984: a. Affirmative Defense.— It is an affirmative defense to a prosecution under any Federal statute that, at the time of the commission of the acts constituting the offense, the defendant, as a result of a severe mental disease or defect, was unable to appreciate the nature and quality or the wrongfulness of his acts. Mental disease or defect does not otherwise constitute a defense.

b. Burden of Proof.— The defendant has the burden of proving the defense of insanity by clear and convincing evidence.

Bifurcation of Guilt and Insanity Issues: A few capital punishment jurisdictions have, by statute, instituted a bifurcated trial of the issue of guilt and insanity. The legislatures in Arizona, California, Colorado, and Wyoming created a procedure requiring bifurcated trials whenever a defendant raises the insanity defense. In Arizona and Wyoming the statutes were found unconstitutional by the supreme courts of each state. The basic idea behind such statutes is simple. First, a trial on the issue of the defendant's guilt is held. Second, if the defendant is found guilty, a trial on the issue of insanity is held. The statutory bifurcation procedures utilized by California, as shown below, illustrates how the matter proceeds.

Cal. Penal Code § 1026(a) Bifurcated Trial of Guilt and Insanity Defense: When a defendant pleads not guilty by reason of insanity, and also joins with it another plea or pleas, the defendant shall first be tried as if only such other plea or pleas had been entered, and in that trial the defendant shall be conclusively presumed to have been sane at the time the offense is alleged to have been committed. If the jury shall find the defendant guilty, or if the defendant pleads only not guilty by reason of insanity, then the question whether the defendant was sane or insane at the time the offense was committed shall be promptly tried, either before the same jury or before a new jury in the discretion of the court. In that trial, the jury shall return a verdict either that the defendant was sane at the time the offense was committed or was insane at the time the offense was committed. If the verdict or finding is that the defendant was sane at the time the offense was committed, the court shall sentence the defendant as provided by law. If the verdict or finding be that the defendant was insane at the time the offense was committed, the court, unless it shall appear to the court that the sanity of the defendant has been recovered fully, shall direct that the defendant be confined in a state hospital for the care and treatment of the mentally disordered or any other appropriate public or private treatment facility approved by the community program director, or the court may order the defendant placed on outpatient status.

Civil Commitment: Although being found not guilty by reason of insanity acquits a defendant of the offense, this does not mean that the defendant will freely leave the courtroom upon hearing the verdict of the factfinder. A defendant found not guilty by reason of insanity will usually be confined to a secure mental institution under the civil commitment laws of the jurisdiction. This is accomplished through a post-acquittal civil commitment proceeding wherein a determination is made as to whether the defendant is a substantial danger to him/herself or society, by reason of a mental defect that is short of insanity. The procedure used by Utah, as shown below, illustrates the basic procedure used by all jurisdictions.

Utah Code Ann. § 77-16a-302 Persons Found Not Guilty by Reason of Insanity: 1. Upon a verdict of not guilty by reason of insanity, the court shall conduct a hearing within ten days to determine whether the defendant is currently mentally ill. The defense counsel and prosecutors may request further evaluations and present testimony from those examiners.

2. After the hearing and upon consideration of the record, the court shall order the defendant committed to the department if it finds by clear and convincing evidence that:

    a. the defendant is still mentally ill; and

    b. because of that mental illness the defendant presents a substantial danger to himself or others.

3. The period of commitment described in Subsection (2) may not exceed the period for which the defendant could be incarcerated had he been convicted and received the maximum sentence for the crime of which he was accused. At the time that period expires, involuntary civil commitment proceedings may be instituted.

See also **Affirmative Defenses; Bifurcation of Guilt and Penalty Phases; Davis v. United States (I); Diminished Capacity; Insanity; Insanity While Awaiting Execution; Leland v. Oregon; Mens Rea; Mentally Ill Defense; Queenan v. Oklahoma; Trifurcated Trial**

Insanity While Awaiting Execution

The common law prohibited execution of a defendant who had become insane prior to execution. This common law proscriptive rule was adopted by Anglo-American jurisprudence. In addition to the common law rule against executing an insane capital felon, the federal constitution has been interpreted to bar execution of an insane capital felon, on the grounds of being cruel and unusual punishment. Even though the common law and federal constitution bar executing an insane capital felon, a majority of capital punishment jurisdictions have codified this prohibition.

Capital punishment jurisdictions differ on the disposition of a convicted capital felon who has become insane prior to being executed. Some jurisdictions confine the capital felon until he or she returns to sanity and then executes him or her. Other jurisdictions require the capital felon's sentence be reduced to life imprisonment without parole. The procedure used by Mississippi is illustrated below.

Miss. Code Ann. § 99-19-57(a) Procedure When Convicted Capital Felon Becomes Insane:

a. If it is believed that a convict under sentence of death has become insane since the judgment of the court, the following shall be the exclusive procedural and substantive procedure. The convict, or a person acting as his next friend, or the commissioner of corrections may file an appropriate application seeking post conviction relief with the Mississippi Supreme Court.

JURISDICTIONS CODIFYING BAR AGAINST EXECUTING INSANE CAPITAL FELON

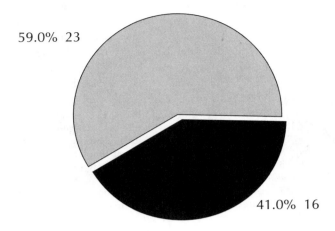

59.0% 23

41.0% 16

■ JURISDICTIONS WITH STATUTE

■ NON-STATUTE JURISDICTIONS

If it is found that the convict is insane, as defined in this subsection, the court shall suspend the execution of the sentence. The convict shall then be committed to the forensic unit of the Mississippi State Hospital at Whitfield. The order of commitment shall require that the convict be examined and a written report be furnished to the court at that time and every month thereafter stating whether there is a substantial probability that the convict will become sane under this subsection within the foreseeable future and whether progress is being made toward that goal. If at any time during such commitment the appropriate official at the state hospital shall consider the convict is sane under this subsection, such official shall promptly notify the court to that effect in writing, and place the convict in the custody of the commissioner of corrections. The court shall thereupon conduct a hearing on the sanity of the convict. The finding of the circuit court is a final order appealable under the terms and conditions of the Mississippi Uniform Post-Conviction Collateral Relief Act.

b. For the purposes of this subsection, a person shall be deemed insane if the court finds the convict does not have sufficient intelligence to understand the nature of the proceedings against him, what he was tried for, the purpose of his punishment, the impending fate which awaits him, and a sufficient understanding to know any fact which might exist which would make his punishment unjust or unlawful and the intelligence requisite to convey such information to his attorneys or the court.

See also **Ford v. Wainwright; Insanity; Mentally Retarded Capital Felon; Nobles v. Georgia; Phyle v. Duffy; Solesbee v. Balkcom**

Instructions to Jury *see* Jury Instructions

Intent to Kill *see* Mens Rea

Intermediate Courts of Appeal

There are two types of appellate courts: intermediate and final. A majority of capital punishment jurisdictions have both intermediate and final courts of appeal. Capital punishment jurisdictions that do not have intermediate appellate courts include: Delaware, Montana, Nevada, New Hampshire, New Jersey, South Dakota, and Wyoming.

The issue of whether a jurisdiction has an intermediate appellate court has significance in those jurisdictions that permit direct capital appeals, or capital habeas corpus appeals to be reviewed by intermediate appellate courts. Involvement of an intermediate appellate court will slow done the process between sentence and execution.

INTERMEDIATE APPELLATE COURT JURISDICTIONS

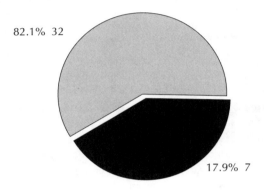

82.1% 32

17.9% 7

■ JURISDICTIONS WITH INTERMEDIATE APPELLATE COURTS

■ NON-INTERMEDIATE APPELLATE COURT JURISDICTIONS

International Capital Punishment Nations

A decisive trend was set in motion during the last decade of the 20th century which saw the international community moving away from capital punishment. At the end of the 20th century there were 70 nations that had abolished capital punishment completely, while 123 nations still retained the punishment in their legal codes. (A large minority of the nations still retaining capital punishment have severely restricted the circumstances when it may be imposed or have not imposed the punishment in over a decade. Some authorities prefer to include such nations with true non-capital punishment nations, but such inclusion is inaccurate and misleading.)

Nations That Permit Capital Punishment

Afghanistan	Bolivia	Congo (Republic)
Albania	Bosnia-Herzegov-	Cook Islands
Algeria	ina	Côte d'Ivoire
Antigua and Bar-	Botswana	Cuba
buda	Brazil	Cyprus
Argentina	Brunei Darussalam	Djibouti
Armenia	Burkina Faso	Dominica
Bahamas	Burundi	El Salvador
Bahrain	Cameroon	Egypt
Bangladesh	Central African	Equatorial Guinea
Barbados	Republic	Eritrea
Belarus	Chad	Ethiopia
Belize	Chile	Fiji
Benin	China	Gabon
Bermuda	Comoros	Gambia
Bhutan	Congo (D.R.)	Ghana

Nations That Permit Capital Punishment (cont.)

Grenada	Mauritania	South Korea
Guatemala	Mexico	Sri Lanka
Guinea	Mongolia	Sudan
Guyana	Morocco	Suriname
India	Myanmar	Swaziland
Indonesia	Nauru	Syria
Iran	Niger	Taiwan
Iraq	Nigeria	Tajikistan
Israel	North Korea	Tanzania
Jamaica	Oman	Thailand
Japan	Pakistan	Togo
Jordan	Papua New	Tonga
Kazakstan	Guinea	Trinidad and To-
Kenya	Peru	bago
Kuwait	Philippines	Tunisia
Kyrgyzstan	Qatar	Turkey
Laos	Russia	Uganda
Latvia	Rwanda	Ukraine
Lebanon	St. Christopher-	United Arab Emi-
Lesotho	Nevis	rates
Liberia	St. Lucia	United States
Libya	St. Vincent-	Uzbekistan
Madagascar	Grenadines	Viet Nam
Malawi	Saudi Arabia	Yemen
Malaysia	Senegal	Yugoslavia (Serbia)
Maldives	Sierra Leone	Zambia
Mali	Singapore	Zimbabwe
Malta	Somalia	

A prominent impetus for the trend toward international abolishment of capital punishment has been international agreements calling for such abolishment. The three major international agreements calling for the abolishment of capital punishment that have been ratified by nations are: (1) the Second Optional Protocol to the International Covenant on Civil and Political Rights; (2) the Protocol No. 6 to the European Convention for the Protection of Human Rights and Fundamental Freedoms; and (3) the Protocol to the American Convention on Human Rights to Abolish the Death Penalty.

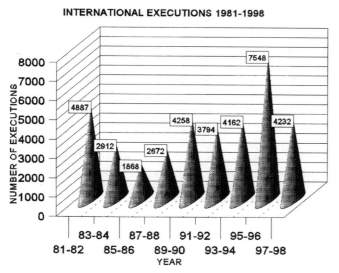

INTERNATIONAL EXECUTIONS 1981-1998

Source: Amnesty International Report May 4, 1999.

NATIONS WITH HIGHEST EXECUTIONS IN 1998

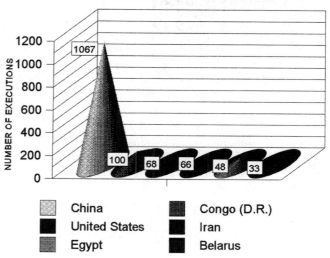

China
United States
Egypt
Congo (D.R.)
Iran
Belarus

Source: Death Penalty Information Center, International (1999).

Intervention by Next Friend   There have been incidents where death row inmates request death and terminate the appeal process. In such situations the rules of criminal procedure permit relatives, such as parents of the condemned inmate, to seek to intervene on behalf of the inmate as a "next friend." A prerequisite for litigating as a "next friend," is that the real party in interest (the inmate) be unable to litigate his or her own cause due to mental incapacity, lack of access to court, or other similar disability. Courts uniformly hold that this prerequisite is not satisfied where an evidentiary hearing shows that the inmate has given a knowing, intelligent, and voluntary waiver of his or her right to challenge a death sentence. *See also* **Demosthenes v. Baal; Gusman v. Marrero; Rosenberg v. United States; Whitmore v. Arkansas**

Intoxication Defense   Under the common law voluntary intoxication afforded no excuse, justification or extenuation of an offense committed under its influence. All jurisdictions follow the common law, insofar as not permitting the intoxication defense to exonerate a defendant of criminal responsibility. However, jurisdictions do permit intoxication to be used as a defense to reduce capital murder to a lesser included homicide. *See also* **Affirmative Defenses; Hopt v. Utah (I); Intoxication Mitigator**

Intoxication Mitigator   Courts generally hold that voluntary intoxication or drug use is a weak mitigating factor. Nevertheless, courts permit intoxication or drug use to be used as a non-statutory mitigating circumstance at the penalty phase, when it is relevant and there has been a showing of a history of alcohol or drug abuse. Courts generally permit evidence of alcohol or drug use to be used in an attempt to satisfy the "capacity substantially impaired" statutory mitigating circumstance. *See also* **Capacity Substantially Impaired Mitigator; Intoxication Defense; Mitigating Circumstances**

Invalid Aggravator Statutory aggravating circumstances permit imposition of the death penalty, therefore, statutory aggravating circumstances must be constitutionally valid. That is, statutory aggravators cannot be vague in their meaning or have an overinclusive application. Statutory aggravating circumstances are not unconstitutionally vague if they have some common sense core of meaning that the factfinder is capable of understanding.

When faced with a "vagueness" challenge to a statutory aggravating circumstance, courts must determine whether the aggravator is vague on its face and, if so, whether appellate case law decisions have adequately defined the aggravator so as to provide guidance for the penalty phase factfinder. If a particular statutory aggravating circumstance leaves the factfinder without sufficient guidance for determining its evidentiary presence or absence, it will be constitutionally vague and invalid.

Infrequently a jurisdiction will have a statutory aggravating circumstance that is constitutionally invalid for one reason or another. If a capital felon is sentenced to death based upon presentation of only one statutory aggravating circumstance, and that aggravator is found to be constitutionally invalid, the death sentence must be vacated. On the other hand, where multiple aggravators have been used, and only one is found to be invalid, the general rule is that a death sentence supported by multiple aggravating circumstances need not always be set aside if one aggravator is found to be invalid. This rule is predicated on the fact that even after elimination of the invalid aggravator, the death sentence rests on firm ground. However, the existence of a valid aggravator does not always excuse a constitutional error in the admission of an invalid aggravator. If it is shown that evidence used to support an incurable invalid aggravator played a substantial role in the decision to impose the death penalty, the presence of other valid aggravators will not sustain the punishment.

Appellate courts in "weighing" jurisdictions may accomplish review of a death sentence involving an invalid statutory aggravating circumstance in one of two ways. First, such courts may jettison the improper aggravator and reweigh the remaining valid aggravators against the mitigating circumstances. Second, weighing jurisdiction appellate courts may cure the taint caused by a jury's reliance on an invalid aggravator by providing a constitutionally acceptable definition to the invalid aggravator, and reweighing all aggravators (including the previous invalid one) against any mitigating circumstances. *See also* **Espinosa v. Florida; Sochor v. Florida; Aggravating Circumstances; Tuggle v. Netherland; Zant v. Stephens (I); Zant v. Stephens (II)**

Involuntary Confession *see* Right to Remain Silent

Iowa The death penalty was abolished in Iowa in 1965.

Iran Iran imposes capital punishment. Iran uses the firing squad, stoning, and hanging to carry out the death penalty. In 1998, Iran executed 66 prisoners. Its legal system is based on Islamic law. Iran's constitution was adopted on December 3, 1979.

Iran has two primary court systems: regular courts which try criminal cases; and Islamic Revolutionary Courts, which try offenses against internal or external security, narcotics crimes, and official corruption. Iran's Supreme Court has limited authority to review cases.

Defendants have the right to a public trial, may choose their own lawyer, and have the right of appeal. There is no jury system in Iran. Trials are adjudicated by panels of judges. Defendants do not have the right to confront their accusers. *See also* **International Capital Punishment Nations**

Iraq Capital punishment is carried out in Iraq. Iraq carries out the death penalty through hanging and the firing squad. Its legal system is based on Islamic law and civil law. Iraq's constitution became in effect on July 16, 1970.

The judiciary in Iraq is not independent. The president may override any court decision. There are two judicial systems in Iraq: regular courts which try criminal offenses; and special security courts, which try cases involving espionage, treason, political dissent, smuggling, currency exchange violations, and drug trafficking. In addition to trial level courts, Iraq has a Court of Appeal and Court of Cassation (the highest court).

Trials in the regular courts are public and defendants have the right to retained or appointed counsel. There is no jury system. Iraq uses a panel of three judges to try cases. Defendants have the right to appeal. *See also* **International Capital Punishment Nations**

Ireland Ireland abolished capital punishment in 1990. *See also* **International Capital Punishment Nations**

Irrelevant Evidence *see* Relevant Evidence

Irresistible Impulse Test *see* Insanity Defense

Irvin v. Dowd (I) *Court:* United States Supreme Court; *Case Citation:* Irvin v. Dowd, 359 U.S. 394 (1959); *Argued:* January 15, 1959; *Decided:* May 4, 1959; *Opinion of the Court:* Justice Brennan; *Concurring Statement:* Justice Stewart; *Dissenting Opinion:* Justice Frankfurter; *Dissenting Opinion:* Justice Harlan, in which Frankfurter, Clark and Whittaker, JJ., joined; *Appellate Defense Counsel:* James D. Lopp and Theodore Lockyear, Jr. argued; James D. Nafe on brief; *Appellate Prosecution Counsel:* Richard M. Givan argued; Edwin K. Steers on brief; *Amicus Curiae Brief Supporting Prosecutor:* None; *Amicus Curiae Brief Supporting Defendant:* None.

Issue Presented: Whether the doctrine of exhaustion of State remedies precluded the defendant from bringing a Federal habeas corpus proceeding?

Case Holding: The doctrine of exhaustion of State remedies did not preclude the defendant from bringing a Federal habeas corpus proceeding, because his Federal constitutional claim was addressed by the Indiana Supreme Court on direct appeal.

Factual and procedural background of case: The defendant, Irvin, was convicted of capital murder and sentenced to death by the State of Indiana. The defendant escaped from custody immediately after judgment was pronounced against him. While the defendant was an escapee, his defense counsel motioned the trial court for a new trial. The trial court, in denying the motion, noted that the defendant was an escapee when the motion was made and denied. After his capture and return to custody, the defendant filed an appeal to the Indiana Supreme Court. The only issue raised by the defendant was that it was error for the trial court to deny his motion for a new trial. The appellate court affirmed the conviction and sentence. In doing so, the appellate court ruled the motion for new trial was correctly denied because the defendant was an escapee at the time it was made, and that it was correctly denied because the trial did not deprive him of any constitutional right. Subsequently, the defendant filed a petition for habeas corpus relief in a Federal District Court. The District Court dismissed the petition on the ground that the defendant had not exhausted his State court remedies, as required under Federal habeas law. A Federal Court of Appeals affirmed. The United States Supreme Court granted certiorari to consider the issue.

Opinion of the Court by Justice Brennan: Justice Brennan held that the defendant's habeas petition was properly before the District Court. He wrote that a reasonable interpretation of the decision by the Indiana Supreme Court, revealed that the State appellate court determined that there was no merit to the defendant's constitutional claim. It was said that the doctrine of exhaustion of State remedies, which was codified in Federal habeas law, did not bar resort to Federal habeas corpus by the defendant because he obtained a decision on his constitutional claim, even though the State appellate court could have based its decision on another State ground. Justice Brennan ruled that the Court would not reach the question of whether Federal habeas corpus would have been available to the defendant had the Indiana Supreme Court rested its decision on the State escape ground. The judgment of the Court of Appeals was reversed and the case remanded.

Concurring Statement by Justice Stewart: Justice Stewart issued a statement concurring in the judgment and the opinion of the Court.

Dissenting opinion by Justice Frankfurter: Justice Frankfurter dissented from the Court's decision. He believed the Indiana Supreme Court did not decide the defendant's federal claim, though it gave the matter passing comments. He argued that the decision was based solely on State grounds:

> Even the most benign or latitudinarian attitude in reading state court opinions precludes today's decision. It is not questioned that the Indiana Supreme Court discussed two issues, one

indisputably a rule of local law and the other a claim under the Fourteenth Amendment. That court discussed the claim under the Fourteenth Amendment rather summarily, after it had dealt extensively with the problem of local law.... What this Court is therefore saying, in effect, is that it interprets the discussion of the Fourteenth Amendment problem which follows the elaborate and potentially conclusive discussion of the state issue not as resting the case on two grounds, state and federal, but as a total abandonment of the state ground, a legal erasing of the seven-page discussion of state law. Concededly, if a state court rests a decision on both an adequate state ground and a federal ground, this Court is without jurisdiction to review the superfluous federal ground. For while state courts are subject to the Supremacy Clause of the United States Constitution, they are so subject only if that Clause becomes operative, and they need not pass on a federal issue if a relevant rule of state law can dispose of the litigation.

Dissenting opinion by Justice Harlan, in which Frankfurter, Clark and Whittaker, JJ., joined: Justice Harlan dissented from the Court's decision. He agreed with the Court that the Indiana Supreme Court addressed the defendant's constitutional claim. Justice Harlan disagreed, however, with the Court's decision to remand the case to determine whether the State appellate court correctly resolved the defendant's constitutional claim. He expressed his concerns as follows:

> I think that the Court's disposition of the matter, which contemplates the overturning of [the defendant's] conviction without the necessity of further proceedings in the state courts if his constitutional contentions are ultimately federally sustained, rests upon an impermissible interpretation of the opinion of the State Supreme Court, and that a different procedural course is required if state and federal concerns in this situation are to be kept in proper balance....
>
> Were we to conclude that the Indiana Supreme Court was correct in its premise that [the defendant's] constitutional points are without merit, the judgment of the Court of Appeals dismissing the writ of habeas corpus should of course be affirmed. If, on the other hand, we should decide that [the defendant] was in fact deprived of due process at trial, I would hold the case and give [the defendant] a reasonable opportunity to seek, through such avenues as may be open to him, a determination by the Indiana Supreme Court as to whether, in light of such a decision, it would nevertheless hold that [the defendant's] failure to comply with the State's procedural rules required affirmance of his conviction. Should no such avenues be open to [the defendant] in Indiana, it would then be time enough to decide what final disposition should be made of this case. *See also* **Exhaustion of State Remedies Doctrine; Habeas Corpus; Irvin v. Dowd (II)**

Irvin v. Dowd (II)   *Court:* United States Supreme Court; *Case Citation:* Irvin v. Dowd, 366 U.S. 717 (1961); *Argued:* November 9, 1960; *Decided:* June 5, 1961; *Opinion of the Court:* Justice Clark; *Concurring Opinion:* Justice Frankfurter; *Dissenting Opinion:* None; *Appellate Defense Counsel:* James D. Lopp and Theodore Lockyear, Jr. argued; James D. Nafe on brief; *Appellate Prosecution Counsel:* Richard M. Givan argued; Edwin K. Steers on brief; *Amicus Curiae Brief Supporting Prosecutor:* None; *Amicus Curiae Brief Supporting Defendant:* None.

Issue Presented: Whether the defendant was denied a fair trial because of pretrial publicity?

Case Holding: The defendant was denied a fair trial because of pretrial publicity and must be released, if the State of Indiana did not seek to retry him again.

Factual and procedural background of case: The defendant, Irvin, was able to get the United States Supreme Court to remand his case in *Irvin v. Dowd (I)*, for the purpose of making a determination of his claim that he was denied a fair trial in violation of the Fourteenth Amendment. A Federal Court of Appeals reviewed the issue and found the following facts regarding the defendant's prosecution.

Six highly publicized unsolved murders had been committed in the area of Vanderburgh County, Indiana. Shortly after the defendant was arrested for one of the murders, the prosecutor and local police officials issued press releases, which were intensively publicized, stating that the defendant had confessed to the six murders. As a result of the widespread negative and prejudicial publicity, defense counsel moved the trial court to change the venue of the trial to nearby Gibson County. The motion was granted and the trial was set for prosecution in Gibson County. However, defense counsel soon discovered that the widespread publicity had prejudiced the people of Gibson County against the defendant. Therefore, defense counsel motioned the trial court to change venue once again. The trial court refused the motion.

During jury selection in Gibson County 430 persons were summoned as potential jurors. The trial court had to remove for "cause," 268 of the potential jurors after they had expressed fixed opinions as to the guilt of the defendant. Out of the 12 jurors chosen, 8 of them admitted that they thought the defendant was guilty, but each indicated that, notwithstanding such opinion, they could render an impartial verdict. The jury convicted the defendant and sentenced him to death.

The Federal Court of Appeals found on remand that the defendant received a fair trial by an impartial jury and denied habeas relief. The United States Supreme Court granted certiorari to consider the issue.

Opinion of the Court by Justice Clark: Justice Clark held that the defendant was not accorded a fair and impartial trial, to which he was entitled under the Due Process Clause of the Fourteenth Amendment. It was said that the right to jury trial guarantees to the criminally accused a fair trial by a panel of impartial and indifferent jurors. Justice Clark wrote: "A fair trial in a fair tribunal is a basic requirement of due process. In the ultimate analysis, only the jury can strip a man of his liberty or his life.... His verdict must be based upon the evidence developed at the trial. This is true, regardless of the heinousness of the crime charged, the apparent guilt of the offender or the station in life which he occupies....The theory of the law is that a juror who has formed an opinion cannot be impartial."

It was said by Justice Clark that the Constitution was not monolithic in the face of modern communication and the impact of such communication in communities. Justice Clark conceded that absolute ignorance of the facts of a crime by jurors in most instances is not possible. The opinion stated: "It is not required, however, that the jurors be totally ignorant of the facts and issues involved. In these days of swift, widespread and diverse methods of communication, an important case can be expected to arouse the interest of the public in the vicinity, and scarcely any of those best qualified to serve as jurors will not have formed some impression or opinion as to the merits of the case. This is particularly true in criminal cases. To hold that the mere existence of any preconceived notion as to the guilt or innocence of an accused, without more, is sufficient to rebut the presumption of a prospective juror's impartiality would be to establish an impossible standard. It is sufficient if the juror can lay aside his impression or opinion and render a verdict based on the evidence presented in court."

The opinion went on to lay out the type of pretrial prejudice that was generated against the defendant:

> Here the build-up of prejudice is clear and convincing. An examination of the then current community pattern of thought as indicated by the popular news media is singularly revealing. For example, [the defendant's] first motion for a change of venue from Gibson County alleged that the awaited trial of [the defendant] had become the cause celebre of this small community—so much so that curbstone opinions, not only as to [the defendant's] guilt but even as to what punishment he should receive, were solicited and recorded on the public streets by a roving reporter, and later were broadcast over the local stations. A reading of the 46 exhibits which [the defendant] attached to his motion indicates that a barrage of newspaper headlines, articles, cartoons and pictures was unleashed against him during the six or seven months preceding his trial. The motion further alleged that the newspapers in which the stories appeared were delivered regularly to approximately 95 percent of the dwellings in Gibson County and that, in addition, the ... radio and TV stations, which likewise blanketed that county, also carried extensive newscasts covering the same incidents. These stories revealed the details of his background, including a reference to crimes committed when a juvenile, his convictions for arson almost 20 years previously, for burglary and by a court-martial on AWOL charges during the war. He was accused of being a parole violator. The headlines announced his police line-up identification, that he faced a lie detector test, had been placed at the scene of the crime and that the six murders were solved.... [T]hey announced his confession to the six murders.... They reported [the defendant's] offer to plead guilty if promised a 99-year sentence, but also the determination, on the other hand, of the prosecutor to secure the death penalty, and that [the defendant] had confessed to 24 burglaries. One story dramatically relayed the promise of a sheriff to devote his life to securing [the defendant's] execution by the State of Kentucky, where petitioner is alleged to have committed one of the six murders, if Indiana failed to do so. Another characterized [the defendant] as remorseless and without conscience but also as having been found sane by a court-appointed panel of doctors. In many of the stories [the defendant] was described as the "confessed slayer of six," a parole violator and fraudulent-check artist. Petitioner's court-appointed counsel was quoted as having received "much criticism over being Irvin's counsel" and it was pointed out, by way of excusing the attorney, that he would be subject to disbarment should he refuse to represent Irvin.

The judgment of the Court of Appeals was reversed and the case remanded with instructions that the defendant was to be released, if the State did not seek to retry him again.

Concurring opinion by Justice Frankfurter: Justice Frankfurter concurred in the Court's decision. He wrote separately only to share his observations about the growing problem caused by media coverage of criminal cases. It was said by him: "Not a Term passes without this Court being importuned to review convictions, had in States throughout the country, in which substantial claims are made that a jury trial has been distorted because of inflammatory newspaper accounts — too often, as in this case, with the prosecutor's collaboration — exerting pressures upon potential jurors before trial and even during the course of trial, thereby making it extremely difficult, if not impossible, to secure a jury capable of taking in, free of prepossessions, evidence submitted in open court. Indeed such extraneous influences, in violation of the decencies guaranteed by our Constitution, are sometimes so powerful that an accused is forced, as a practical matter, to forego trial by jury." *See also* **Irvin v. Dowd (I); Pretrial Publicity; Venue**

Isaacs v. United States

Court: United States Supreme Court; *Case Citation:* Isaacs v. United States, 159 U.S. 487 (1895); *Argued:* Not reported; *Decided:* November 11, 1895; *Opinion of the Court:* Justice Brown; *Concurring Opinion:* None; *Dissenting Opinion:* None; *Appellate Defense Counsel:* Not represented; *Appellate Prosecution Counsel:* No argument; United States Assistant Attorney General Dickinson on brief; *Amicus Curiae Brief Supporting Prosecutor:* None; *Amicus Curiae Brief Supporting Defendant:* None.

Issue Presented: Whether defendant's confession to committing murder was sufficient to establish the corpus delicti or that a person had actually been murdered?

Case Holding: The defendant's confession to committing murder was not sufficient to establish the corpus delicti or that a person had actually been murdered, but combined with other evidence, such confession could help establish that a person had been murdered.

Factual and procedural background of case: The defendant, Isaacs, was convicted of capital murder and sentenced to death by the United States. During the trial evidence only established that Mike P. Cushing, or an unknown white man was murdered by the defendant. The corpus delicti or body of the crime was never actually found and identified. On appeal to the United States Supreme Court, the defendant argued that his conviction could not stand based upon only his confession to having killed a man.

Opinion of the Court by Justice Brown: Justice Brown held that the corpus delicti cannot be established by the mere statement of a defendant, but that such statement, taken in connection with other facts, might be used to show that a person was murdered. It was said in the opinion that "[t]he fact that a crime was committed, or the fact that the man charged in the indictment, either as Mike P. Cushing, or an unknown white man, was murdered, must be proven by evidence outside of the confession of the defendant; and that, whenever that state of case is established, then you may take the declarations of the defendant as tending to show his guilt."

The opinion held that there was abundant evidence in the case, outside of the defendant's confession, not only that a man had been murdered, but considerable evidence that he was a white man. It was concluded that "[t]he fact that the murdered man was a white man had no bearing upon the question of the corpus delicti, or of the fact that the defendant murdered him, and bore only upon the jurisdiction of the court." The judgment of the lower court was therefore affirmed. *See also* **Corpus Delicti**

Israel

Israel abolished capital punishment for ordinary crimes in 1954, but retains the authority to impose capital punishment for exceptional and extreme offenses. Israel authorizes execution by hanging. Its legal system is a mixture of English common law, British Mandate regulations, and Jewish, Christian and Moslem authoritative principles. Israel has no formal constitution.

The judicial system is composed of trial courts and a High Court of Justice. Israeli law provides for the right to representation by counsel. Trials are generally public. Cases involving national security may be partly or wholly closed to the public. *See also* **International Capital Punishment Nations**

Italy

Italy abolished capital punishment for ordinary crimes in 1947, and completely abolished the punishment in 1994. *See also* **International Capital Punishment Nations**

Itow v. United States

Court: United States Supreme Court; *Case Citation:* Itow v. United States, 233 U.S. 581 (1914); *Argued:* April 8, 1914; *Decided:* May 11, 1914; *Opinion of the Court:* Chief Justice White; *Concurring Opinion:* None; *Dissenting Opinion:* None; *Appellate Defense Counsel:* J. H. Cobb argued and briefed; *Appellate Prosecution Counsel:* Mr. Adkins argued; Karl W. Kirchwey on brief; *Amicus Curiae Brief Supporting Prosecutor:* None; *Amicus Curiae Brief Supporting Defendant:* None.

Issue Presented: Whether the United States Supreme Court could hear a direct appeal from a Federal District Court?

Case Holding: The United States Supreme Court could not hear a direct appeal from a Federal District Court, because Congress changed the law and required Federal Courts of Appeals hear direct appeals from Federal District Courts.

Factual and procedural background of case: The defendant, O. Itow, was convicted of capital murder and sentenced to death by the United States. The defendant filed a direct appeal with the United States Supreme Court. The government moved to dismiss the case on the grounds of lack of jurisdiction.

Opinion of the Court by Chief Justice White: The Chief Justice ruled that the Court did not have jurisdiction to hear the case on direct appeal. It was said that, as a result of statutory changes, Federal Courts of Appeals had to first pass upon cases tried in Federal District Courts before they could be brought to the Supreme Court. The Chief Justice noted that the statutory amendments "changed the general rule of the prior law by taking capital cases out of the class which could come, because they were capital cases, directly to this court, and by bringing such cases within the final reviewing power of the circuit court of appeals[.]" The case was dismissed for lack of jurisdiction. *See also* **Jurisdiction**

J

Jackson, Howell E.

Howell E. Jackson served as an associate justice of the United States Supreme Court from 1893 to 1895. Jackson's brief tenure on the Supreme Court did not enable him to establish a meaningful constitutional philosophy.

Jackson was born in Paris, Tennessee on April 8, 1832. He received an undergraduate degree from West Tennessee College in 1849, and a law degree from Cumberland University in 1856. Jackson was elected to the United States Senate in 1881. He accepted a Federal court of appeals judicial position in 1886. President Benjamin Harrison appointed Jackson to the Supreme Court in 1893.

Jackson was known to have written only one capital punishment opinion. In *Brown v. United States (I)* Jackson, writing for the Supreme Court, reversed the defendant's convictions for two murders after ruling that the trial court committed reversible error by admitting evidence during the trial of an unrelated conspiracy to commit murder. Jackson died on August 8, 1895.

Jackson, Robert H.

Robert H. Jackson served as an associate justice of the United States Supreme Court from 1941 to 1951. While on the Supreme Court Jackson was known as a moderate in his interpretation of the Constitution.

Jackson was born on February 13, 1892 in Spring Creek, Pennsylvania. Jackson would eventually settle in New York after obtaining a law degree from Albany Law School in 1913. Jackson developed a successful private practice before accepting various Federal attorney positions. President Franklin D. Roosevelt appointed Jackson to the Supreme Court in 1941.

While on the Supreme Court Jackson issued a number of capital punishment opinions. The capital punishment opinion for which he was most known was *Stein v. New York*. The decision in *Stein* involved three defendants who were sentenced to death. The defendants asked the Supreme Court to rule that New York's procedure of requiring the jury to determine whether a confession was voluntary violated the Constitution. Jackson, writing for the Court, rejected the argument. He wrote: "The Fourteenth Amendment does not forbid jury trial of the issue. The states are free to allocate functions as between judge and jury as they see fit." The decision in *Stein* would eventually be overruled by *Jackson v. Denno*. Jackson died on October 9, 1954.

Capital Punishment Opinions Written by Jackson

Case Name	Opinion of the Court	Concurring Opinion	Dissenting Opinion
Brown v. Allen		✓	
Cassell v. Texas			✓
Harris v. South Carolina			✓
Rosenberg v. United States		✓	
Shepherd v. Florida		✓	
Stein v. New York	✓		
Turner v. Pennsylvania			✓

Jackson v. Denno

Court: United States Supreme Court; *Case Citation:* Jackson v. Denno, 378 U.S. 368 (1964); *Argued:* December 9–10, 1963; *Decided:* June 22, 1964; *Opinion of the Court:* Justice White; *Concurring and Dissenting Opinion:* Justice Black, in which Clark, J., joined; *Dissenting Opinion:* Justice Clark; *Dissenting Opinion:* Justice Harlan, in which Clark and Stewart, JJ., joined; *Appellate Defense Counsel:* Daniel G. Collins argued and briefed; *Appellate Prosecution Counsel:* William I. Siegel argued; Edward S. Silver on brief; *Amicus Curiae Brief Supporting Prosecutor:* None; *Amicus Curiae Brief Supporting Defendant:* None.

Issue Presented: Whether the New York rule of requiring the jury to determine the voluntariness of a confession violated due process of law?

Case Holding: The New York rule of requiring the jury to determine the voluntariness of a confession violated due process of law, as such decision should be determined by the trial judge.

Factual and procedural background of case: The defendant, Jackson, was charged with capital murder by the State of New York. The defendant gave two confessions, which he disputed on substantive and voluntariness grounds at trial. Under New York law the issue of the voluntariness of a confession had to be decided by the jury. Consequently, the trial court told the jury to disregard the confession entirely if it was found involuntary, and to determine the guilt or innocence solely from other evidence; or, if it found the confession voluntary, it was to determine its truth or reliability and weigh it accordingly. The jury found the defendant guilty of capital murder and he was sentenced to death.

The New York Court of Appeals affirmed the conviction and sentence, and the United States Supreme Court denied certiorari. The defendant filed a habeas corpus petition in a Federal District Court alleging that the New York procedure for determining voluntariness of a confession was unconstitutional. The District Court denied the petition. A Federal Court of Appeals affirmed. The United States Supreme Court granted certiorari to consider the issue.

Opinion of the Court by Justice White: Justice White ruled that the New York procedure for determining voluntariness of a confession did not provide an adequate and reliable determination of the voluntariness of the confession and did not adequately protect the defendant's right not to be convicted through the use of a coerced confession. The opinion pointed out that it was a deprivation of due process of law to base a conviction, in whole or in part, on a coerced confession, regardless of its truth, and even though there may be sufficient other evidence to support the conviction.

Justice White stated that the defendant had a constitutional right to a fair hearing and reliable determination of the voluntariness of his confession. He wrote that it was impossible to tell whether the trial jury found the confession voluntary and relied on it, or involuntary and ignored it. It was said that the defendant was entitled to a State court hearing on the issue of the voluntariness of the confession by the trial judge and not by the jury trying his guilt or innocence.

The judgment of the Court of Appeals was reversed and the case remanded so that New York courts could either determine the voluntariness of the confession at a hearing or simply grant a new trial. If a hearing was held and it was determined that the confession was voluntary and admissible in evidence, a new trial was not necessary; but if it was determined at the hearing that the confession was involuntary, a new trial, at which the confession would be excluded, was required.

Concurring and dissenting opinion by Justice Black, in which Clark, J., joined: Justice Black concurred with the Court's decision insofar as the new trial option. He believed the last confession was unconstitutionally obtained and required a new trial. Justice Black dissented from the Court's decision to find New York's procedure for determining the voluntariness of a confession unconstitutional. He questioned the Court's authority to invalidate the procedure and believed that having a judge, rather than a jury, determine voluntariness did not provide any great benefit to defendants. He wrote: "The New York rule does now and apparently always has put on the State the burden of convincing the jury beyond a reasonable doubt that a confession is voluntary. Whatever might be a judge's view of the voluntariness of a confession, the jury in passing on a defendant's guilt or innocence is, in my judgment, entitled to hear and determine voluntariness of a confession along with other factual issues on which its verdict must rest."

Dissenting opinion by Justice Clark: Justice Clark dissented from the Court's decision. He argued that the issue of "the constitutionality of New York's rule [was] not ripe for decision here[.]" Justice Clark indicated that in his judgment the facts of the case did not properly bring the constitutionality of the rule before the Court. Justice Clark also believed that the Court was wrong in fashioning the new rule and having it applied retroactively to the defendant's case. He believed that the proper course was simply to order a new trial.

Dissenting opinion by Justice Harlan, in which Clark and Stewart, JJ., joined: Justice Harlan dissented from the Court's decision. He argued that it was wrong for the Court to invalidate the New York procedure because that procedure had previously been expressly approved by the Court in the capital case of *Stein v. New York*. Justice Clark also questioned the authority of the Court to invalidate a procedure that had such a long history in the New York criminal justice system. He wrote: "My disagreement with the majority does not concern the wisdom of the New York procedure. It may be that in the abstract the problems which are created by leaving to the jury the question of coercion should weigh more heavily than traditional use of the jury system. Be as it may, the states are free to allocate functions as between judge and jury as they see fit. I, like the Court in *Stein*, believe that this Court has no authority to strike down as unconstitutional procedures so long established and widely approved by state judiciaries, regardless of our personal opinion as to their wisdom." This principle, alone here relevant, was founded on a solid constitutional approach the loss of which will do serious disservice to the healthy working of our federal system in the criminal field." *See also* **Right to Remain Silent; Sims v. Georgia (I); Sims v. Georgia (II); Stein v. New York**

Jamaica The death penalty is on the law books of Jamaica. Jamaica uses hanging as the method of carrying out the death penalty. Its legal system is based on English common law. The constitution of the nation was adopted on August 6, 1962.

Criminal cases are prosecuted in three types of courts in Jamaica. Magistrate courts try misdemeanor offense. All felonies, except those involving firearms, are tried in a Supreme Court. Other felony offenses are tried in a Gun Court. Defendants have a right to appointed counsel only for "serious" crimes. Defendants have the right to appeal a conviction in any of the trial level courts to the Court of Appeal, which is the highest court. Under the constitution of Jamaica, the Court of Appeal may refer cases to the Judicial Committee of the Privy Council in England. *See also* **International Capital Punishment Nations**

Japan Capital punishment is recognized in Japan. Hanging is the method of execution used by the nation. In 1998, Japan executed six prisoners. Its legal system is modeled after European civil law and American law. Japan's constitution was adopted on May 3, 1947.

The judicial system in Japan is composed of District Courts, High Courts, and a Supreme Court. Cases are tried in the District Court and may be appealed to the High Court and Supreme Court. Both the defendant and the prosecutor may appeal. Defendants have a right to a speedy and public trial. There is no trial by jury in Japan. Defendants have the right to retained or appointed counsel, and the right not to be compelled to testify against themselves. Japan's laws protect defendants from the retroactive application of criminal laws. *See also* **International Capital Punishment Nations**

Jasper County Dragging Murder

On the night of June 7, 1998, Lawrence Russell Brewer, John William King, and Shawn Allen Berry engaged in murderous conduct in Jasper County, Texas that shook the nation. On that night the trio chained a man, James Byrd, Jr., to the back of a pickup truck and dragged his body for three miles. When the dragging ended, Byrd's head had been ripped off his body.

Byrd was murdered because he was an African American. The trio kidnapped and killed Byrd because they believed their conduct would inspire racial unrest and racial war in the nation.

Law enforcement officials had little difficulty in apprehending the trio. They were each prosecuted separately for capital murder. King was tried first. He was convicted and on February 25, 1999, a jury sentenced him death. Brewer's trial was next. He was convicted and on September 23, 1999, a jury sentenced him to death. Berry was then tried. He was also convicted, but on November 18, 1999, the jury recommended life imprisonment.

The killers of James Byrd, Jr.: (left to right) John William King, Shawn Allen Berry, and Lawrence Russell Brewer. King and Brewer received death sentences. Berry was sentenced to life imprisonment. (Jasper County Sheriff)

Jennings, Patricia

On November 5, 1990, Patricia Jennings was sentenced to death by the State of North Carolina, after having been convicted of the capital murder of her husband, William Henry Jennings. At the time of his death, William was 80 years old.

Patricia and William met in June of 1983. She was 40 years old at the time and was employed as a nurse in a nursing home located in Wilson, North Carolina. William, who was a retired businessman, was summoned to the nursing home as a consultant for an alcoholic patient. Despite their age differences, Patricia and William developed a warm relationship during his consultation visits at the nursing home. Four years later, in February of 1987, Patricia and William were married.

Six months after their marriage, William visited his financial consultant for the purpose of transferring half of his assets, which then totaled about $150,000, to Patricia. A separate account was opened for Patricia and the assets were transferred to her.

In time, William became a victim of spousal abuse. William consulted an attorney in May of 1989 and disclosed the abuse

he was receiving from Patricia. William told the attorney that Patricia had physically beaten him, dragged him across the room, and stomped him with her cowboy boots. He also told the attorney that Patricia had tried to have him committed.

On September 19, 1989, Patricia and William were staying at a hotel in Wilson. At about 9:30 P.M., that evening Patricia called the hotel desk clerk requesting medical assistance. When emergency medical personnel arrived they found William lying naked on the floor and Patricia applying CPR on him. She was wearing a black nightgown and brown cowboy boots at the time. Patricia informed the medical team that William had fell and had been on the floor for about ten minutes.

Patricia Jennings was given a death sentence for killing her 80-year-old husband. (North Carolina Department of Corrections)

William was taken to a local hospital where he was pronounced dead. Based upon medical evidence of injuries to William, Patricia was indicted for capital murder.

During the trial evidence indicated that William was tortured and beaten to death. Testimony established that William had been dead for six to eight hours before he was brought to the hospital. The State's chief medical examiner testified that William had sustained multiple bruises and scrapes on various parts of his head, scalp, face, neck, legs, arms and hands. William had also sustained a large bruise in the mesentery of the abdominal cavity, the tissue which holds in and supports the intestines and contains blood vessels to the intestines. It was determined by the chief medical examiner that a blunt force impact to the abdominal wall caused the tears in the mesentery, and that blood loss from those tears caused William's death. The medical examiner opined that the injury was consistent with a kick or stomp to the abdomen, not a fall.

Patricia testified at the trial and denied beating William. She alleged that he fell several times in the hotel bathroom. The jury rejected Patricia's version of events and found her guilty of capital murder. Patricia is now on death row in North Carolina. *See also* **Women and Capital Punishment**

Johnson v. Mississippi

Court: United States Supreme Court; *Case Citation:* Johnson v. Mississippi, 486 U.S. 578 (1988); *Argued:* April 25, 1988; *Decided:* June 13, 1988; *Opinion of the Court:* Justice Stevens; *Concurring Opinion:* Justice White, in which Rehnquist, C. J., joined; *Concurring Statement:* Justice Brennan, in which Marshall, J., joined; *Concurring Statement:* Justice O'Connor; *Dissenting Opinion:* None; *Appellate Defense Counsel:* Floyd Abrams argued; Laurence T. Sorkin, Marshall Cox, Anthony Paduano, and Clive A. Stafford Smith on brief; *Appellate Prosecution Counsel:* Marvin

L. White, Jr. argued; Mike Moore on brief; *Amicus Curiae Brief Supporting Prosecutor:* None; *Amicus Curiae Brief Supporting Defendant:* 4.

Issue Presented: Whether the reversal of the defendant's prior rape conviction by a New York court rendered his Mississippi death sentence unconstitutional, because the death sentence was imposed in part due to the prosecutor's use of the rape conviction to establish the "prior felony conviction" statutory aggravating circumstance?

Case Holding: The reversal of the defendant's prior rape conviction by a New York court rendered his Mississippi death sentence unconstitutional, because the death sentence was imposed in part due to the prosecutor's use of the rape conviction to establish the "prior felony conviction" statutory aggravating circumstance.

Factual and procedural background of case: The defendant, Samuel Johnson, was convicted of capital murder by the State of Mississippi. During the penalty phase the prosecutor produced evidence on three statutory aggravating circumstances. One of the aggravating circumstances involved concerned prior felony conviction. The prosecutor introduced evidence showing that the defendant had previously been convicted of rape by the State of New York. The jury found all three aggravating circumstances were proven and sentenced the defendant to death. The Mississippi Supreme Court affirmed the conviction and death sentence.

Subsequent to the State appellate court's decision affirming the judgment, the New York Court of Appeals issued an opinion reversing the defendant's rape conviction. The defendant then filed a petition for habeas corpus relief with the Mississippi Supreme Court, arguing that his sentence was constitutionally infirm because it was based on a prior felony conviction which was overturned. The appellate court rejected the petition. The United States Supreme Court granted certiorari to consider the issue.

Opinion of the Court by Justice Stevens: Justice Stevens wrote that by allowing the defendant's death sentence to stand despite the fact that it was based in part on the vacated New York conviction, the Mississippi Supreme Court violated the Eighth Amendment's prohibition against cruel and unusual punishment. It was said that the New York conviction did not provide any legitimate support for the defendant's sentence. Justice Stevens found that reversal of the rape conviction deprived the prosecutor's sole piece of evidence as to the most significant aggravating circumstance proven against the defendant. It was said that the fact that the defendant served time in prison pursuant to the invalid rape conviction did not make the conviction itself relevant, or prove that the defendant was guilty of the crime. The opinion concluded that the New York conviction clearly prejudiced the defendant. The judgment of the Mississippi Supreme Court was reversed, insofar as setting aside the sentence.

Concurring opinion by Justice White, in which Rehnquist, C. J., joined: Justice White concurred briefly in the Court's opinion. He wrote: "I join the Court's opinion, agree-

ing that the death sentence cannot stand, given the introduction of inadmissible and prejudicial evidence at the hearing before the jury. That evidence, however, was irrelevant to the other two aggravating circumstances found to be present, and I note that the case is remanded for further proceedings not inconsistent with the Court's opinion. It is left to the Mississippi Supreme Court to decide whether a new sentencing hearing must be held or whether that court should itself decide the appropriate sentence without reference to the inadmissible evidence, thus undertaking to reweigh the two untainted aggravating circumstances against the mitigating circumstances."

Concurring Statement by Justice Brennan, in which Marshall, J., joined: Justice Brennan issued a concurring statement indicating that, while he joined the Court's judgment, he "would direct that the resentencing proceedings be circumscribed such that the State may not reimpose the death sentence."

Concurring Statement by Justice O'Connor: Justice O'Connor issued a statement indicating that she concurred in the Court's judgment. *See also* **Prior Felony or Homicide Aggravator**

Johnson v. Texas

Court: United States Supreme Court; *Case Citation:* Johnson v. Texas, 509 U.S. 350 (1993); *Argued:* April 26, 1993; *Decided:* June 24, 1993; *Opinion of the Court:* Justice Kennedy; *Concurring Opinion:* Justice Scalia; *Concurring Opinion:* Justice Thomas; *Dissenting Opinion:* Justice O'Connor, in which Blackmun, Stevens, and Souter, JJ., joined; *Appellate Defense Counsel:* Michael E. Tigar argued; Robert C. Owen and Jeffrey J. Pokorak on brief; *Appellate Prosecution Counsel:* Dana E. Parker argued; Dan Morales, Will Pryor, Mary F. Keller and Michael P. Hodge on brief; *Amicus Curiae Brief Supporting Prosecutor:* 1; *Amicus Curiae Brief Supporting Defendant:* None.

Issue Presented: Whether the penalty phase special issues used by Texas adequately allowed the jury to consider the defendant's age as a mitigating factor?

Case Holding: The penalty phase special issues used by Texas adequately allowed the jury to consider the defendant's age as a mitigating factor.

Factual and procedural background of case: The State of Texas prosecuted the defendant, Dorsey Johnson, for capital murder committed when he was 19 years old. A jury found him guilty of the crime. During the penalty phase of the prosecution, the trial court instructed the jury to answer two special issues required by statute at that time: (1) whether the defendant's conduct was committed deliberately and with the reasonable expectation that death would result, and (2) whether there was a probability that he would commit criminal acts of violence that would constitute a continuing threat to society. The jury was also instructed that, in determining each of those issues, it could take into consideration all the evidence submitted to it, whether aggravating or mitigating, in either phase of the trial. A unanimous jury answered yes to both special issues, and the trial court sentenced the defendant to death.

On appeal to the Texas Court of Criminal Appeals, the defendant argued that the special issues did not allow the penalty phase jury to give adequate mitigating effect to evidence of his youth and that under the United States Supreme Court decision in *Penry v. Lynaugh* a separate instruction was required on the question of his age. The appellate court rejected the argument and affirmed the conviction and sentence. The United States Supreme Court granted certiorari to consider the issue.

Opinion of the Court by Justice Kennedy: Justice Kennedy ruled that the Texas death penalty procedures used in the case were consistent with the requirements of the Constitution and the Court's precedents. The opinion indicated although a penalty phase jury cannot be precluded from considering, as a mitigating factor, any aspect of the defendant's character or record and any of the circumstances of the particular offense that the defendant proffers as a basis for a sentence less than death, States are free to structure and shape consideration of mitigating evidence in an effort to achieve a more rational and equitable administration of the death penalty. Justice Kennedy stated that other cases decided by the Court involving Texas' death penalty statute found that it adequately allowed for penalty phase juries to consider the youth of defendants as mitigating evidence.

It was said that the special issues used in the defendant's case allowed for adequate consideration of his youth. The opinion ruled that there was no reasonable likelihood that the jury would have found itself foreclosed from considering the relevant aspects of the defendant's youth, since it was told to consider all mitigating evidence. Justice Kennedy concluded that for the Court to find a constitutional defect in the defendant's sentence, it would have to overrule *Jurek v. Texas*, which approved of Texas' death penalty system, by requiring a further instruction whenever a defendant introduced mitigating evidence that had some arguable relevance beyond the special issues used. The opinion indicated the Court was not prepared to overrule precedent. The judgment of the Texas Court of Criminal Appeals was affirmed.

Concurring opinion by Justice Scalia: Justice Scalia concurred in the Court's decision. He wrote that the Court's decision was consistent with and a clarification of prior decisions.

Concurring opinion by Justice Thomas: Justice Thomas concurred in the decision of the Court. He indicated that the decision was "simply a clarification (and I think a plainly correct one) of this Court's opinions[.]" It was also said by Justice Thomas that "[b]ecause [the defendant's] youth had mitigating relevance to the second special issue, ... this case is readily distinguishable from *Penry*, and does not compel its reconsideration."

Dissenting opinion by Justice O'Connor, in which Blackmun, Stevens, and Souter, JJ., joined: Justice O'Connor dissented from the Court's decision. She believed that *Penry* controlled the case and that a special instruction was required to inform the penalty phase jury to consider evidence of the defendant's youth as mitigating circumstances and not aggra-vating circumstances. Justice O'Connor stated her position as follows:

> [The defendant] was 19 years old when he committed the murder that led to his death sentence. Today, the Court upholds that sentence, even though the jurors who considered Johnson's case were not allowed to give full effect to his strongest mitigating evidence: his youth. The Court reaches this result only by invoking a highly selective version of stare decisis and misapplying our habeas precedents to a case on direct review....
>
> By all accounts, [the defendant] was not a model youth. As an adolescent, he frequently missed school, and when he did attend, he often was disruptive. He was drinking and using drugs by the time he was 16, habits that had intensified by the time he was 19. Johnson's father testified that the deaths of Johnson's mother and sister in 1984 and 1985 had affected Johnson deeply, but he primarily attributed Johnson's behavior to drug use and youth. A jury hearing this evidence easily could conclude, as Johnson's jury did, that the answer to the second Texas special question — whether it was probable that Johnson "would commit criminal acts of violence that would constitute a continuing threat to society," was yes. It is possible that the jury thought Johnson might outgrow his temper and violent behavior as he matured, but it is more likely that the jury considered the pattern of escalating violence to be an indication that Johnson would become even more dangerous as he grew older. Even if the jurors viewed Johnson's youth as a transient circumstance, the dangerousness associated with that youth would not dissipate until sometime in the future, and it is reasonably likely that the jurors still would have understood the second question to require an affirmative answer. Thus, to the extent that Johnson's youth was relevant at all to the second Texas special issue, there is a reasonable likelihood that it was an aggravating factor.

Case note: Texas executed Dorsey Johnson by lethal injection on June 4, 1997.

Johnson v. United States

Court: United States Supreme Court; *Case Citation:* Johnson v. United States, 157 U.S. 320 (1895); *Argued:* Not reported; *Decided:* March 25, 1895; *Opinion of the Court:* Justice Brewer; *Concurring Opinion:* None; *Dissenting Opinion:* None; *Appellate Defense Counsel:* Not reported; *Appellate Prosecution Counsel:* Mr. Whitney argued and briefed; *Amicus Curiae Brief Supporting Prosecutor:* None; *Amicus Curiae Brief Supporting Defendant:* None.

Issue Presented: Whether the defendant's conviction and sentence were invalid as a result of the prosecutor's failure to prove a motive for the crime?

Case Holding: The defendant's conviction and sentence were not invalid as a result of the prosecutor's failure to prove a motive for the crime, because motive is not an element of a crime.

Factual and procedural background of case: The defendant, Willie Johnson, was convicted of capital murder and sentenced to death by the United States. The defendant appealed the judgment against him to the United States Supreme Court, contending that his conviction was invalid because there was no proof of motive for the killing. The United States Supreme Court granted certiorari to consider the issue.

Opinion of the Court by Justice Brewer: Justice Brewer found that the judgment rendered against the defendant was valid, even though the prosecutor failed to establish any motive for the killing. The opinion addressed the issue as follows:

> ... There was nothing in the evidence disclosing previous hostility to the deceased on the part of Johnson, or any reason or motive for the murderous attack. Thereupon, the defendant's counsel asked an instruction that where the evidence shows that the defendant did not commit the actual killing, and when it is uncertain whether he did participate in it, then the jury may regard the absence of any proof of motive for the killing, in finding their verdict. This instruction the court gave, but added to it the observation that the absence or presence of motive is not a necessary requisite to enable the jury to find the guilt of a party, because it is frequently impossible for the government to find a motive.
>
> In thus qualifying the instruction the learned judge committed no error The jury were, in effect, told that they had a right to consider the absence of any proof of motive, but that such proof was not essential to enable them to convict.

The judgment of the Federal District Court was affirmed.

Johnson, William

William Johnson served as an associate justice of the United States Supreme Court from 1804 to 1834. While on the Supreme Court Johnson was known as a conservative interpreter of the Constitution who espoused absolute Federal supremacy in matters involving Federal-State relations.

Johnson was born in Charleston, South Carolina on December 27, 1771. Following his graduation from Princeton in 1790, Johnson worked as a legal apprentice before being admitted to the South Carolina bar in 1793. Johnson served in the State legislature and on the State supreme court, before President Thomas Jefferson appointed him to the Supreme Court in 1804.

While on the Supreme Court Johnson was known to have issued only two capital punishment opinions. The case of *United States v. Pirates* involved certified questions from a lower court. Johnson wrote the opinion for the Supreme Court. In responding to one of the questions certified, Johnson answered by stating that a foreign defendant who murdered another foreigner aboard an American ship may be prosecuted under the Piracy Act, because national character was lost when piracy was entered into. In the case of *Ex Parte Bollman (I)* the issue addressed by the Supreme Court was whether it had authority to issue a writ of habeas corpus commanding condemned defendants be brought before the Court. The majority ruled that the Court had such authority. Johnson issued a dissenting opinion. He argued that, while the justices had authority in their individual capacity to issue the writ, the Constitution did not confer such authority on the Court collectively. Johnson died in 1834.

Joint Venture Theory

The joint venture theory is a version of the felony murder rule. To convict a defendant for murder under the joint venture theory, the prosecutor must prove (1) the defendant was present at the scene of the crime, (2) the defendant had knowledge another intended to commit a crime, and (3) by agreement the defendant was willing and available to help the confederate if necessary.

The theory of joint venture murder requires more than mere knowledge of planned criminal conduct or a failure to take affirmative steps to prevent it, rather, a defendant must intend that the victim be killed or know that there is a substantial likelihood of the victim being killed. A joint venturer may be prosecuted for murder if he or she intended that the victim be killed or knew that there was a substantial likelihood that the victim would be killed. Unlike a felony murder rule prosecution, the joint venture theory requires that each participant share the requisite mental state of the principal. *See also* **Felony Murder Rule**

Jones v. United States (I)

Court: United States Supreme Court; *Case Citation:* Jones v. United States, 137 U.S. 202 (1890); *Argued:* Not reported; *Decided:* November 24, 1890; *Opinion of the Court:* Justice Gray; *Concurring Opinion:* None; *Dissenting Opinion:* None; *Appellate Defense Counsel:* Archibald Stirling, Jr. argued; E. J. Waring and John Henry Keene, Jr. on brief; *Appellate Prosecution Counsel:* United States Attorney General Miller argued and briefed; *Amicus Curiae Brief Supporting Prosecutor:* None; *Amicus Curiae Brief Supporting Defendant:* None.

Issue Presented: Whether the United States had jurisdiction over the territory in which the defendant committed murder?

Case Holding: The United States had jurisdiction over the territory in which the defendant committed murder, therefore his prosecution for the offense by the Federal Government was valid.

Factual and procedural background of case: The defendant, Henry Jones, was prosecuted for capital murder by the United States. The offense charged was committed on an island in the Caribbean sea called Navassa. The defendant was taken to be prosecuted in a Federal District Court sitting in Maryland. A jury found the defendant guilty and he was sentenced to death. The defendant prosecuted an appeal to the United States Supreme Court, alleging that his conviction was invalid because the United States did not have jurisdiction over Navassa island.

Opinion of the Court by Justice Gray: Justice Gray ruled that under the Constitution a crime committed within any State must be tried in that State, but that a crime not committed within any state of the Union may be tried at such place as Congress may by law have directed. It was said that Congress directed that the trial of all offenses committed upon the high seas, or elsewhere, out of the jurisdiction of any particular state or district, shall be in the Federal district where the offender is found, or into which he or she is first brought. Justice Gray indicated that offenses committed "elsewhere" included murder committed on any land within the exclusive jurisdiction of the United States, and not within any judicial district, as well as murder committed on the high seas.

The opinion held that the island of Navassa was, at the time of the murder, under the sole and exclusive jurisdiction of the United States, and out of the jurisdiction of any particular State or district of the United States. Justice Gray noted: "Who is the sovereign, de jure or de facto, of a territory, is not a judicial, but a political question, the determination of which by the legislative and executive departments of any government conclusively binds the judges, as well as all other officers, citizens, and subjects of that government. This principle has always been upheld by this court, and has been affirmed under a great variety of circumstances." The judgment of the District Court was affirmed. *See also* **Jurisdiction**

Jones v. United States (II)

Court: United States Supreme Court; *Case Citation:* Jones v. United States, 119 S.Ct. 2090 (1999); *Argued:* February 22, 1999; *Decided:* June 21, 1999; *Opinion of the Court:* Justice Thomas; *Concurring Opinion:* None; *Dissenting Opinion:* Justice Ginsburg, in which Stevens, Souter and Breyer, JJ., joined; *Appellate Defense Counsel:* Not reported; *Appellate Prosecution Counsel:* Not reported; *Amicus Curiae Brief Supporting Prosecutor:* Not reported; *Amicus Curiae Brief Supporting Defendant:* Not reported.

Issues Presented: (1) Whether the defendant was entitled to an instruction as to the effect of jury deadlock on the issue of punishment? (2) Whether there was a reasonable likelihood that the penalty phase jury was led to believe that the defendant would receive a court imposed sentence less than life imprisonment in the event that they could not reach a unanimous sentence recommendation? (3) Whether the submission to the penalty phase jury of two allegedly duplicative, vague, and overbroad non-statutory aggravating factors was harmless error?

Case Holdings: (1) The Constitution does not require the penalty phase jury be instructed as to the effect of a jury deadlock on the issue of punishment. (2) There was no reasonable likelihood that the penalty phase jury was led to believe that the defendant would receive a court imposed sentence less than life imprisonment in the event that they could not reach a unanimous sentence recommendation. (3) The two non-statutory aggravating circumstances were not duplicative, vague, or overbroad; assuming, arguendo, that they were duplicative, vague, and overbroad, submission of them to the jury was harmless error beyond a reasonable doubt.

Factual and procedural background of case: The defendant, Louis Jones, was convicted of capital murder and sentenced to death by the United States. On appeal to the Fifth Circuit Court of Appeals, the defendant argued his sentence should be reversed because the trial court committed error in (1) refusing his request to instruct the penalty phase jury as to the consequences of jury deadlock; (2) providing the penalty phase jury with confusing instructions led them to believe that the defendant would receive a court imposed sentence less than life imprisonment in the event that they could not reach a unanimous sentence recommendation; and (3) providing the penalty phase jury with instructions on two duplicative, vague, and overbroad non-statutory aggravating factors. The Court of Appeals rejected the arguments and affirmed the conviction and sentence. The United States Supreme Court granted certiorari to consider the three issues.

Opinion of the Court by Justice Thomas: Justice Thomas ruled that the Constitution did not require that a penalty phase jury be instructed as to the consequences of their failure to agree on a punishment. It was said that such an instruction had no bearing on the jury's role in the sentencing process. The opinion stated that the jury system's very object is to secure unanimity, and the Government has a strong interest in having the jury express the conscience of the community on the ultimate life or death question. Justice Thomas reasoned that a jury instruction of the sort the defendant suggested might well undermine this strong governmental interest. In addition, he wrote that Congress chose not to require such an instruction be given. Under the Federal death penalty statute the trial judge was required to impose the sentence when the jury, after retiring for deliberations, reports itself as unable to reach a unanimous verdict.

Next, Justice Thomas held that there was no reasonable likelihood that the jury was led to believe that the defendant would receive a court imposed sentence less than life imprisonment, in the event they could not recommend unanimously a sentence of death or life imprisonment without the possibility of release. The opinion noted that this issue was not properly preserved at the trial court level, therefore the claim of error was subject to a limited appellate review under the plain error rule. Under such review, relief is not granted unless there has been (1) error, (2) that is plain, and (3) affects substantial rights. Justice Thomas found the defendant's argument fell short of satisfying the first requirement, for no error occurred. It was said that the proper standard for reviewing claims that allegedly ambiguous instructions caused jury confusion was whether there was a reasonable likelihood that the jury applied the challenged instruction in a way that violates the Constitution. It was determined that there was no such likelihood in the case.

Finally, Justice Thomas held that the two non-statutory aggravating circumstances were not duplicative, vague, or overbroad. It was said that assuming, arguendo, that the two factors were vague, overbroad, or duplicative, submission of them to the penalty phase jury was harmless error beyond a reasonable doubt. The opinion found that the jury would have reached the same result without the allegedly erroneous non-statutory aggravating factors. The judgment of the Court of Appeals was affirmed.

Dissenting opinion by Justice Ginsburg, in which Stevens, Souter and Breyer, JJ., joined: Justice Ginsburg dissented from the Court's decision. Her dissent targeted the majority's ruling on the defendant's claim that it was error for the trial court to (1) provide the penalty phase jury with confusing instructions led them to believe that the defendant would receive a court imposed sentence less than life imprisonment in the event that they could not reach a unanimous sentence recommendation and (2) provide the penalty phase jury with instructions on two duplicative, vague, and overbroad non-statutory aggravating factors. Justice Ginsburg argued that the defendant's asserted grounds of error were proven. In summary, she concluded: "The Fifth Circuit's tolerance of error in this case, and this Court's refusal to face up to it, cannot be reconciled with the recognition ... that 'death is qualitatively different.' If the jury's weighing process is infected by the trial court's misperceptions of the law, the legitimacy of an ensuing death sentence should not hinge on defense counsel's shortfalls or the reviewing court's speculation about the decision the jury would have made absent the infection. I would vacate the jury's sentencing decision and remand the case for a new sentencing hearing[.]" *See also* **Harmless Error Rule; Plain Error Rule**

Jordan Jordan recognizes capital punishment. Jordan uses hanging and the firing squad to carry out the death penalty. In 1998, Jordan executed nine prisoners. Its legal system is based on Islamic law and French codes. Jordan's constitution was adopted on January 8, 1952.

Jordan is a constitutional monarchy that was ruled by King Hussein bin Talal from 1952 until his death in February 1999. The constitution of Jordan places a high degree of executive and legislative authority in the king, who determines domestic and foreign policy. The actual daily affairs of the government are managed by a prime minister and a cabinet, all of whom are appointed by the king. The king also appoints the 40 members that make up the Senate. The legislative branch has an 80-member Chamber of Deputies, who are elected every four years. The constitution of Jordan provides for the independence of the judiciary. However, in practice the judiciary is subject to pressure from the executive branch.

The judicial system consists of trial courts, the Court of Cassation, and the State Security Court. The State Security Court prosecutes cases involving sedition, armed insurrection, financial crimes, drug trafficking, and offenses against the king. Shari'a (Islamic) courts have jurisdiction over domestic relations matters involving Muslims.

Criminal trials are generally open to the public. Defendants are entitled to legal counsel, may cross examine witnesses, and have the right to appeal. Indigent defendants facing the death penalty have the right to appointed counsel.

Prosecutions in the State Security Court are usually closed to the public. A panel of three judges preside over State Security Court prosecutions. Defendants in the State Security Court have the right to appeal their sentences to the Court of Cassation. Appeals are automatic for cases involving the death penalty. *See also* **International Capital Punishment Nations**

Judge-Made Law *see* Common Law and Capital Punishment

Judge Trial *see* Bench Trial

Judge Aggravator The responsibility of judges for imposing sentences upon convicted defendants carries with it the potential for reprisal. A large minority of jurisdictions have responded to the potential danger judges are exposed to, by making the murder of a judge a statutory aggravating circumstance. If a penalty phase jury in a capital prosecution determines that a judge was killed because of the performance of his or her official duties, the death penalty may be imposed. *See also* **Aggravating Circumstances**

JURISDICTIONS USING JUDGE AGGRAVATOR

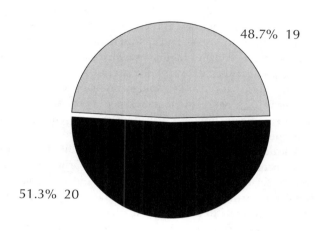

48.7% 19

51.3% 20

■ JUDGE AGGRAVATOR JURISDICTIONS

■ ALL OTHER JURISDICTIONS

Jurek v. Texas *Court:* United States Supreme Court; *Case Citation:* Jurek v. Texas, 428 U.S. 262 (1976); *Argued:* March 30, 1976; *Decided:* July 2, 1976; *Plurality Opinion:* Justice Stevens announced the Court's judgment and delivered an opinion, in which Stewart and Powell JJ., joined; *Concurring Opinion:* Justice White, in which Burger, C. J., and Rehnquist, J., joined; *Concurring Statement:* Justice Blackmun; *Concurring Statement:* Chief Justice Burger; *Dissenting Statement:* Justice Brennan; *Dissenting Statement:* Justice Marshall; *Appellate Defense Counsel:* Anthony G. Amsterdam argued; Jack Greenberg, James M. Nabrit III, and Peggy C. Davis on brief; *Appellate Prosecution Counsel:* John L. Hill argued; Bert W. Pluymen and Jim D. Vollers on brief; *Amicus Curiae Brief Supporting Prosecutor:* 2; *Amicus Curiae Brief Supporting Defendant:* 1.

Issue Presented: Whether the imposition of the sentence of death for the crime of murder under the law of Texas violates the Constitution?

Case Holding: The imposition of the sentence of death for the crime of murder under the law of Texas does not violate the Constitution.

Factual and procedural background of case: The defendant, Jerry Lane Jurek, was convicted of murder and sentenced to death by the State of Texas. The defendant was prosecuted under a new death penalty statute enacted by the State in the wake of the United States Supreme Court's decision in *Furman v. Georgia.*

Under the new law the death penalty was limited to homicides committed under specific circumstances. Under the new statute a capital prosecution was divided into a guilt phase and penalty phase. Pursuant to this bifurcation, a capital felon's guilt was first determined. At the second stage the punishment was determined. During the penalty phase the jury was required to answer the following three questions: (1) whether the conduct of the defendant causing the death was committed deliberately and with the reasonable expectation that the death would result; (2) whether it is probable that the defendant would commit criminal acts of violence constituting a continuing threat to society; and (3) if raised by the evidence, whether the defendant's conduct was an unreasonable response to the provocation, if any, by the deceased. If the jury finds that the State has proved beyond a reasonable doubt that the answer to each of the three questions is affirmative, then the death sentence is imposed; if it finds that the answer to any question is negative a sentence of life imprisonment results.

The defendant challenged the constitutionality of the Texas death penalty statute. The Texas Court of Criminal Appeals found that the death penalty procedures did not violate the federal Constitution. The United States Supreme Court granted certiorari to address the matter.

Plurality opinion in which Justice Stevens announced the Court's judgment and in which Stewart and Powell, JJ., joined: Justice Stevens observed that, as a general matter, "[t]he imposition of the death penalty is not per se cruel and unusual punishment in violation of the Eighth and Fourteenth Amendments." After reviewing in detail the procedures used under Texas' new death penalty statute, it was found that the procedures do not violate the Constitution.

The opinion looked upon favorably at the limited circumstances in which a defendant would be subject to a capital prosecution. It was noted that, while the statute did not specifically address mitigating circumstances, the statute had been construed to embrace the jury's consideration of such circumstances. Justice Stevens found the procedures guided and focused the jury's objective consideration of the particularized circumstances of the individual offense and the individual offender before it could impose a sentence of death. Such procedures thus eliminated the arbitrariness and caprice of the system invalidated in *Furman*. The judgment of the Texas Court of Criminal Appeals was, therefore, affirmed.

Concurring opinion by Justice White, in which Burger, C.J., and Rehnquist, J., joined: Justice White concurred in the Court's judgment. In doing so he wrote "that under the revised Texas law the substantive crime of murder is narrowly defined and when murder occurs in one of the five circumstances detailed in the statute, the death penalty must be imposed if the jury makes the certain additional findings against the defendant." The concurrence was satisfied that the new law removed "unconstitutionally arbitrary or discretionary statutory features[.]

Concurring Statement by Justice Blackmun: Justice Blackmun issued a concurring statement stating succinctly: "I concur in the judgment."

Concurring Statement by Chief Justice Burger: Chief Justice Burger issued a concurring statement stating succinctly: "I concur in the judgment."

Dissenting statement by Justice Brennan: Justice Brennan issued a statement referencing to his dissent in *Gregg v. Georgia* as the basis for his dissent in this case.

Dissenting statement by Justice Marshall: Justice Marshall issued a statement referencing to his dissent in *Gregg v. Georgia* as the basis for his dissent in this case.

Case note: The decision in this case was significant because it was one of three decisions rendered by the Court in 1976, which had the effect of lifting the moratorium placed on capital punishment in the United States by the 1972 decision in *Furman v. Georgia. See also* **Gregg v. Georgia; Proffitt v. Florida**

Jurisdiction The term "jurisdiction" has several meanings in criminal law. The term is used to refer to a sovereign government, i.e., a State or the Federal government. Jurisdiction is also used to refer to the specific authority of a court to decide a criminal matter presented to it. In order for any court to address the merits of a criminal matter, the court must have authority over the defendant and the subject matter.

Authority over a defendant requires that alleged unlawful conduct by the defendant must have occurred within the judicial area that the court has authority over. Subject matter jurisdiction requires a court have specific authority over the substantive issue presented. Trial courts have general jurisdiction over criminal matters. Appellate courts have limited jurisdiction. *See also* **Benson v. United States; Coleman v. Tennessee; Cook v. United States; Cross v. Burke; Cross v. United States; Ex Parte Crow Dog; Ex Parte Gon-Shay-Ee; Ex Parte Johnson; Itow v. United States; Jones v. United States (I); Lamber v. Barrett (I); Nofire v. United States; St. Clair v. United States; United States v. Bevins; Wynne v. United States**

Juror Aggravator Jurors in criminal prosecutions are vulnerable to potential threats, as a result of their participation

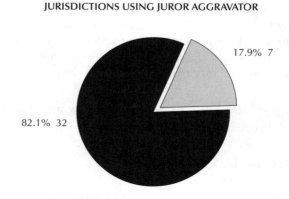

JURISDICTIONS USING JUROR AGGRAVATOR

17.9% 7

82.1% 32

■ JUROR AGGRAVATOR JURISDICTIONS
■ ALL OTHER JURISDICTIONS

in trials. A minority of capital punishment jurisdictions have decided to make the murder of a juror a statutory aggravating circumstance. In these jurisdictions if a capital penalty phase jury finds that the victim was killed as a result of his or her participation in a jury, the death penalty may be imposed on the defendant. *See also* **Aggravating Circumstances**

Jury *see* Jury Selection

Jury Deadlock *see* Deadlocked Jury

Jury Deliberation

The phase "jury deliberation" refers to the sequestration of a jury for the purpose of deciding issues presented to it during a trial. During jury deliberation no one is allowed in the jury room.

In capital punishment prosecutions two distinct jury deliberations occur. First, the jury must deliberate to determine whether a defendant is guilty of a capital offense. This deliberation occurs at the guilt phase. Second, if the guilt phase jury renders a verdict finding the defendant guilty of capital murder, the jury must then hear evidence on the issue of punishment. This occurs at the penalty phase. Once the penalty phase jury has heard the evidence on the issue of punishment it will retire to deliberate on the punishment the defendant should receive.

Jury Instructions

Jury instructions embody the law which jurors must apply to the evidentiary facts presented during a prosecution. The trial judge has the exclusive authority to give jury instructions. However, the actual instructions given may incorporate legal principles proffered by the defendant and the prosecutor.

In capital prosecutions separate jury instructions must be given to the guilt phase jury and penalty phase jury. The jury instructions given at the guilt phase encompass legal doctrines concerned with determining guilt or innocence. The penalty phase jury instructions embody legal principles associated with determining whether to impose a sentence of death or grant mercy and impose a sentence of life imprisonment. *See also* **Bird v. United States (I); Bird v. United States (II); Non-Discrimination Jury Instruction**

Jury Override *see* Binding/Nonbinding Jury Sentencing Determination

Jury Selection

In determining who will be a juror in a trial, the defendant has a right, along with the prosecutor, to challenge persons summoned as potential jurors. The challenge and removal of prospective jurors are done in two ways: (1) for cause, and (2) by peremptory strikes.

Removal for Cause: Removal of a prospective juror for "cause" is done by the trial judge. In order to remove a prospective juror for "cause," it must be shown that the juror has a bias or prejudice which prevents him or her from fairly and impartially deciding the issues in the case.

Peremptory Strike: Removal of a juror by a peremptory strike is done by the defendant and prosecutor independently. Both the defendant and prosecutor will have a limited number of peremptory strikes which they may use to remove potential jurors for any reason (other than for racial or gender reasons).

Voir Dire: In order to utilize peremptory strikes and challenges for cause, potential jurors are questioned. The questioning process is called voir dire examination. The right of challenge comes from the common law, and has always been held essential to the fairness of trial by jury. Under Anglo-American jurisprudence, it is constitutional error to conduct jury selection out of the presence of the defendant.

Death-Qualified Jury: Selecting jurors for capital prosecutions presents greater difficulties than the selection process in non-capital cases. In non-capital prosecutions jury selection merely involves selecting a fair and impartial panel. In capital prosecutions the jury selection involves selecting a fair, impartial and death-qualified panel. The death-qualified component of jury selection in capital cases is the factor which imposes greater stress in the jury selection process.

Two unique legal principles have developed and become a part of the process of selecting a jury to decide the facts in a capital offense prosecution. The two legal principles in question were developed for the purpose of having a death-qualified jury preside over the trial of a capital punishment prosecution. A death-qualified jury is one that can fairly and impartially hear the evidence of a capital offense prosecution and return a verdict that serves the interests of justice.

The first death-qualified jury principle was developed by the United States Supreme Court in *Witherspoon v. Illinois*, 391 U.S. 510 (1968) and refined in *Wainwright v. Witt*, 469 U.S. 412 (1985). The *Witherspoon-Wainwright* principle holds that a trial court may exclude from a venire panel, any potential juror who has acknowledged that he or she is opposed to the death penalty. The second death-qualified jury principle was announced by the United States Supreme Court in *Morgan v. Illinois*, 112 S.Ct. 2222 (1992). Under the *Morgan* principle a trial judge may exclude from the venire panel, any potential juror who has made known that he or she would automatically vote for imposition of the death penalty, regardless of the evidence in the case.

Courts have held that jurors in capital prosecutions have an obligation to apply the law which mandates death under certain circumstances. Jurors may not ignore their oath or affirmation and obligation to apply the law by choosing to reject the death penalty due to moral opposition to capital punishment. Consequently, the Federal Constitution does not prohibit the removal for "cause" of prospective jurors whose opposition to the death penalty is so strong that it would prevent or substantially impair the performance of their duties as jurors at the penalty phase of the trial. This is so even though death-qualification may produce juries somewhat more conviction-prone than non-death-qualified juries. However, a sentence of death cannot be carried out if the jury that imposed or recommended the sentence was chosen by excluding potential jurors for "cause," simply because they voiced general objections to the death penalty or expressed conscientious or religious scruples against its infliction.

The standard for determining when a prospective juror may be excused for cause due to his or her views on capital punishment, is whether the juror's views would prevent or substantially impair the performance of his or her duties as a juror in accordance with his or her instructions and oath.

Federal Jury Selection Process: The rules governing the Federal jury selection process, as illustrated below, represents the manner in which other jurisdictions provide for the process.

a. *Examination.* The court may permit the defendant or the defendant's attorney and the attorney for the government to conduct the examination of prospective jurors or may itself conduct the examination. In the latter event the court shall permit the defendant or the defendant's attorney and the attorney for the government to supplement the examination by such further inquiry as it deems proper or shall itself submit to the prospective jurors such additional questions by the parties or their attorneys as it deems proper.

b. *Peremptory Challenges.* If the offense charged is punishable by death, each side is entitled to 20 peremptory challenges. If the offense charged is punishable by imprisonment for more than one year, the government is entitled to 6 peremptory challenges and the defendant or defendants jointly to 10 peremptory challenges. If the offense charged is punishable by imprisonment for not more than one year or by fine or both, each side is entitled to 3 peremptory challenges. If there is more than one defendant, the court may allow the defendants additional peremptory challenges and permit them to be exercised separately or jointly.

c. *Alternate Jurors.* The court may direct that not more than 6 jurors in addition to the regular jury be called and impanelled to sit as alternate jurors. Alternate jurors in the order in which they are called shall replace jurors who, prior to the time the jury retires to consider its verdict, become or are found to be unable or disqualified to perform their duties. Alternate jurors shall be drawn in the same manner, shall have the same qualifications, shall be subject to the same examination and challenges, shall take the same oath and shall have the same functions, powers, facilities and privileges as the regular jurors. An alternate juror who does not replace a regular juror shall be discharged after the jury retires to consider its verdict. Each side is entitled   to 1 peremptory challenge in addition to those otherwise allowed by law if 1 or 2 alternate jurors are to be impanelled, 2 peremptory challenges if 3 or 4 alternate jurors are to be impanelled, and 3 peremptory challenges if 5 or 6 alternate jurors are to be impanelled. The additional peremptory challenges may be used against an alternate juror only, and the other peremptory challenges allowed by these rules may not be used against an alternate juror. *See also* **Discrimination in Grand or Petit Jury Selection; Morgan v. Illinois; Race-Qualified Jury; Wainwright v. Witt; Witherspoon v. Illinois**

Jury Trial   The Sixth Amendment to the Federal Constitution provides that "[i]n all criminal prosecutions, the accused shall enjoy the right to ... an impartial jury[.]" Qualifications have been made to the constitutional right to trial by jury. In capital prosecutions the qualifications may be viewed in terms of the guilt phase and penalty phase.

Guilt Phase Jury Right: The determination of a capital offender's guilt may not occur without a jury unless he or she validly waives the constitutional right to trial by jury. The United States Supreme Court has ruled that, any offense carrying a penalty greater than six months incarceration must be presided over by a jury, unless a defendant validly waives the right to trial by jury.

All capital punishment jurisdictions require that a jury in a capital prosecution consist of 12 members. This requirement is not required by the Federal Constitution. The United States Supreme Court has held that the use of a 12-person jury in a criminal prosecution is not constitutionally required. The Supreme Court has indicated that a jury of less than six persons would violate the Constitution.

Penalty Phase Jury Right: The United States Supreme Court indicated in *Walton v. Arizona*, 497 U.S. 639 (1990), that the Federal Constitution does not extend a right to have a jury preside over the penalty phase of a capital prosecution. However, a majority of capital punishment jurisdictions do in fact permit jury participation at the penalty phase of capital prosecutions. In jurisdictions that permit the use of a jury at the penalty phase, defendants do not have a right to have separate juries determine guilt and punishment. That is, the jury determining guilt presides over the penalty phase.

Five jurisdictions, Arizona, Colorado, Idaho, Montana, and Nebraska, prohibit the use of juries at the penalty phase of capital prosecutions. In Colorado it is required that a three-judge panel preside over the penalty phase. Nebraska grants discretion to the trial judge to request assistance of two other judges during the penalty phase. The States of Arizona, Idaho

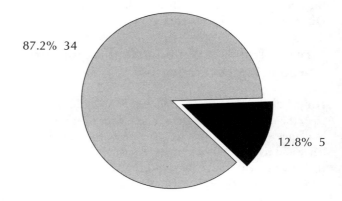

THE USE OF A JURY AT THE PENALTY PHASE

87.2% 34

12.8% 5

■ JURISDICTIONS ALLOWING PENALTY PHASE JURY

■ JURISDICTIONS PROHIBITING PENALTY PHASE JURY

and Montana only permit the trial judge to preside over the penalty phase.

Additionally, in two jurisdictions that permit the use of a jury at the penalty phase, Nevada and Ohio, use of a jury is prohibited if the conviction was obtained through a guilty plea or at a bench trial. In either situation, Nevada and Ohio require that a three-judge panel preside over the penalty phase. *See also* **Bench Trial; Bill of Rights; Walton v. Arizona**

Jury Unanimity   The United States Supreme Court has held that there is no constitutional right to have a defendant's guilt determined by a unanimous verdict when a 12-person jury is used. However, the Supreme Court has indicated that if a six person jury is used to determine a defendant's guilt, a verdict of guilty must be unanimous.

It is not constitutionally required that a penalty phase jury return a unanimous punishment verdict. In a majority of jurisdictions that use penalty phase juries, however, it is statutorily required that the punishment verdict be unanimous. *See also* **Andres v. United States; McKoy v. North Carolina; Mills v. Maryland**

Jury View   The purpose of a jury view is merely to acquaint the jury with a crime scene in order to enable them better to understand trial testimony. As a general rule, observations during a jury view are not part of the trial and should not be considered as evidence. *See also* **Snyder v. Massachusetts; Valdez v. United States**

Justice Against Crime   Justice Against Crime (JAC) is a California based organization that advocates reform of the criminal justice system to benefit victims of crime and to punish criminals. The organization was founded by George H. Cullins, whose daughter was a victim of capital murder. JAC actively proposes laws that seek to bring about greater safety for citizens. A primary focus of JAC is to bring about an expeditious execution of lawfully imposed punishments.

Justice for All   Justice for All (JFA) is a Houston based nonprofit organization. JFA was founded in July 1993. Its purpose is to advocate for change in the criminal justice system. JFA takes the position that the criminal justice system is inadequate in protecting the lives and property of citizens. The organizational strategy of JFA is to seek legislative changes in laws.

Justifications for Capital Punishment   The two primary theories that are used to justify imposition of capital punishment are: deterrence theory and retribution theory.

Deterrence Theory: Under the deterrence theory it is posited that certain types of criminal conduct stands as being so reprehensible and detrimental to the existence of society, that all means must be used to deter members of society from taking part in it. Criminal conduct which intentionally and unlawfully takes the life of a human being has been deemed

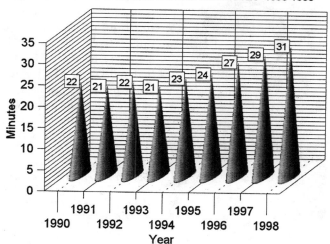

FREQUENCY OF MURDER IN THE U.S. IN MINUTES 1990–1998

Source: U.S. Department of Justice, Federal Bureau of Investigation, *Uniform Crime Reports* (1990–1999).

sufficiently reprehensible and detrimental to the existence of society, to warrant imposing the death penalty as a means of deterring people from engaging in such conduct.

Opponents of the deterrence theory have argued that capital punishment, per se, does not deter people from committing murder. It is further argued that by killing murderers under the guise of deterrence, society actually reinforces the idea that intentionally taking human life is not morally wrong.

Retribution Theory: The retribution theory of capital punishment is grounded in revenge. Under this theory, loved ones of victims of murder deserve to obtain the maximum degree of revenge against murderers. It is contended that no greater degree of revenge can be extracted from murderers than that of killing them. Opponents of the retribution theory argue that retribution is a primitive instinct that has no place in civilized society.

Juvenile Offenses   Juvenile adjudications are generally not permitted to be introduced as evidence during the guilt phase of a capital prosecution. However, for purposes of the penalty phase of a capital prosecution, courts have held that a prior juvenile adjudication constitutes a conviction, and may be used as an aggravating circumstance against a capital felon who has a previous juvenile adjudication. *See also* **Aggravating Circumstances**

Juveniles   During the period of 1776 through 1972, there were approximately 277 executions in the United States of persons under 18 years of age at the time of the commission of their capital offense. There were four such executions in the American Colonies during the period 1642–1775.

The youngest known person to commit a capital offense and be executed in the nation was a Native American named James Arcene. Arcene was ten years old when he committed capital murder. He was executed by the Federal Government on June 26, 1885, at the age of 23.

The youngest known persons to be actually be executed in the nation were three 12-year-old juveniles named Hannah Ocuish, Alfred and Clem. The last juvenile under the age of 16 to be executed in the nation was 15-year-old James Lewis, who was executed in 1947.

Floyd Loveless was 17 years old when the State of Nevada executed him on September 29, 1944. (Nevada State Library and Archives)

Juveniles Between the Ages 12–15 When Executed

Name	Date Executed	Age When Executed	Jurisdiction
Alfred	July 16, 1858	12	Alabama
Brad Beard	December 17, 1897	14	Alabama
Willie Bell	November 29, 1892	15	Georgia
John Berry	June 16, 1899	15	Maryland
Milbry Brown	October 7, 1892	14	South Carolina
Clem	May 11, 1787	12	Virginia
Jim Conelm	February 3, 1888	14	Louisiana
Susan Eliza	February 7, 1868	13	Kentucky
James Guild	November 28, 1828	13	New Jersey
Irving Hanchett	May 6, 1910	15	Florida
Henry	April 20, 1866	15	Alabama
Buck High	May 29, 1907	15	Georgia
Perry Homer	November 7, 1884	15	Georgia
James Lewis, Jr.	July 23, 1947	15	Mississippi
Hannah Ocuish	December 20, 1786	12	Connecticut
Samuel Orr	December 11, 1873	15	Missouri
George Stinney, Jr.	June 16, 1944	14	South Carolina
Jack Thomasson	July 6, 1877	15	Georgia

Source: Victor L. Streib, *Death Penalty for Juveniles* (1987).

An age limit for prosecuting and executing juveniles for capital offenses was constitutionally imposed on the nation in 1988. The United States Supreme Court ruled in the case of *Thompson v. Oklahoma*, 487 U.S. 815 (1988), that the Constitution prohibited the execution of a person who was under 16 years of age at the time of the commission of his or her capital offense. The result of the ruling in *Thompson* marked a break with traditional capital punishment jurisprudence in America.

A year after the decision in *Thompson*, the United States Supreme Court handed down a ruling in *Stanford v. Kentucky*, 492 U.S. 361 (1989). The Supreme Court held in *Stanford* that the imposition of capital punishment on an individual for a capital crime committed at 16 or 17 years of age did not constitute cruel and unusual punishment under the Constitution. The ruling in *Stanford* was consistent with traditional capital punishment jurisprudence in the nation. During the period of 1776 through 1972, there were 34 juveniles put to death in the nation who were 16 years old at the time of execution. For this same period, 81 juveniles were executed who were 17 years old at the time of execution.

EXECUTION OF CAPITAL FELONS WHO WERE UNDER 18 WHEN THEY COMMITTED MURDER 1976–1999

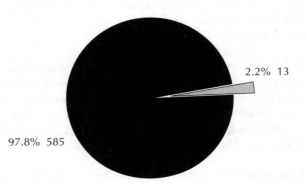

2.2% 13

97.8% 585

■ EXECUTED FOR MURDER COMMITTED WHILE UNDER 18
■ ALL OTHER EXECUTIONS

As of June 1999, there were 70 capital felons on death row who committed their crimes while under the age of 18. This population represented less than three percent of the total death row population for that time period. All of the death row inmates in this population group were male. *See also* **Stanford v. Kentucky; Thompson v. Oklahoma**

K

Kansas The State of Kansas is a capital punishment jurisdiction. The State reenacted its death penalty law after the United States Supreme Court decision in *Furman v. Georgia*, 408 U.S. 238 (1972), on April 22, 1994.

Kansas has a three-tier legal system. The State's legal system is composed of a supreme court, court of appeals and courts of general jurisdiction. The Kansas Supreme Court is presided over by a chief justice and six associate justices. The Kansas Court of Appeals is composed of a chief judge and nine judges. The courts of general jurisdiction in the State are called District Courts. Capital offenses against the State of Kansas are tried in the District Courts.

Kansas' capital punishment statute is triggered if a person commits a homicide under the following special circumstances:

1. intentional and premeditated killing of any person in the commission of kidnaping, when the kidnaping was committed with the intent to hold such person for ransom;

2. intentional and premeditated killing of any person pursuant to a contract or agreement to kill such person or being a party to the contract or agreement pursuant to which such person is killed;

3. intentional and premeditated killing of any person by an inmate or prisoner confined in a state correctional institution, community correctional institution or jail or while in the custody of an officer or employee of a state correctional institution, community correctional institution or jail;

4. intentional and premeditated killing of the victim of one of the following crimes in the commission of rape or criminal sodomy;

5. intentional and premeditated killing of a law enforcement officer;

6. intentional and premeditated killing of more than one person as a part of the same act or transaction or in two or more acts or transactions connected together or constituting parts of a common scheme or course of conduct; or

7. intentional and premeditated killing of a child under the age of 14 in the commission of kidnaping, when the kidnaping was committed with intent to commit a sex offense upon or with the child or with intent that the child commit or submit to a sex offense.

Capital murder in Kansas is punishable by death or imprisonment for a term of years. A capital prosecution in Kansas is bifurcated into a guilt phase and penalty phase. A jury is used at both phases of a capital trial. It is required that, at the penalty phase, the jury unanimously agree that a death sentence is appropriate before it can be imposed. If the penalty phase jury is unable to reach a verdict, the trial judge is required to impose a sentence for a term of years. The decision of a penalty phase jury is binding on the trial court under the laws of Kansas.

In order to impose a death sentence upon a defendant under Kansas law, it is required that the prosecutor establish the existence of at least one of the following statutory aggravating circumstances at the penalty phase:

1. The defendant was previously convicted of a felony in which the defendant inflicted great bodily harm, disfigurement, dismemberment or death on another.

2. The defendant knowingly or purposely killed or created a great risk of death to more than one person.

3. The defendant committed the crime for the defendant's self or another for the purpose of receiving money or any other thing of monetary value.

4. The defendant authorized or employed another person to commit the crime.

5. The defendant committed the crime in order to avoid or prevent a lawful arrest or prosecution.

6. The defendant committed the crime in an especially heinous, atrocious or cruel manner.

7. The defendant committed the crime while serving a sentence of imprisonment on conviction of a felony.

8. The victim was killed while engaging in, or because of the victim's performance or prospective performance of, the victim's duties as a witness in a criminal proceeding.

Although the Federal Constitution will not permit jurisdictions to prevent capital felons from presenting all relevant mitigating evidence at the penalty phase, Kansas has provided the following statutory mitigating circumstances that permit the jury to reject imposition of the death penalty:

1. The defendant has no significant history of prior criminal activity.

2. The crime was committed while the defendant was under the influence of extreme mental or emotional disturbances.

3. The victim was a participant in or consented to the defendant's conduct.

4. The defendant was an accomplice in the crime committed by another person, and the defendant's participation was relatively minor.

5. The defendant acted under extreme distress or under the substantial domination of another person.

6. The capacity of the defendant to appreciate the criminality of the defendant's conduct or to conform the defendant's conduct to the requirements of law was substantially impaired.

7. The age of the defendant at the time of the crime.

8. At the time of the crime, the defendant was suffering from post-traumatic stress syndrome caused by violence or abuse by the victim.

9. A term of imprisonment is sufficient to defend and protect the people's safety from the defendant.

Under Kansas' capital punishment statute, a sentence of death is automatically reviewed by the Kansas Supreme Court. Kansas uses lethal injection to carry out death sentences. The State's death row facility for men is located in El Dorado, Kansas; while the facility maintaining female death row inmates is located in Topeka, Kansas.

Pursuant to the laws of Kansas the Governor has exclusive authority to grant clemency in capital cases. The Governor may commute a death sentence to life imprisonment without parole.

From the start of modern capital punishment in 1976, through 1999, Kansas did not execute any capital felon. A total of two capital felons were on death row in Kansas in 1999. The 1999 death row population in the State was listed as: no black inmates and two white inmates. The State does not permit capital punishment to be imposed on persons 17 years old or younger. Kansas prohibits the execution of mentally retarded capital felons.

EXECUTIONS BY KANSAS 1930–1999

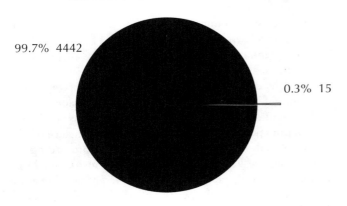

99.7% 4442

0.3% 15

■ KANSAS

■ ALL OTHER JURISDICTIONS

Kansas City Massacre

The Kansas City Massacre involved the June 17, 1933 attempt to free a captured Federal prisoner named Frank Nash. Three men directly participated in the attempted rescue: Charles Arthur "Pretty Boy" Floyd, Vernon Miller and Adam Richetti.

Nash was a career criminal. In 1913 the State of Oklahoma sentenced Nash to life imprisonment for a murder conviction. He was eventually pardoned. In 1920 Nash was sentenced to 25 years imprisonment for burglary, but was again pardoned. In 1924 the Federal government sentenced Nash to 25 years imprisonment for assaulting a mail custodian. Nash escaped from federal detention on October 19, 1930. A massive investigation was launched by the Federal Bureau of Investigation (FBI) to capture Nash.

It was not until June 16, 1933, that Nash was captured by the FBI. Nash was apprehended in a store in Hot Springs, Arkansas by two FBI Agents, Frank Smith and F. Joseph Lackey, and a local Oklahoma Police Chief named Otto Reed. After Nash's capture arrangements were made to transport him by train to Kansas City, Missouri. Law enforcement agents were not aware of it, but a planned attempt to free Nash was waiting to be executed by Floyd, Richetti and Miller when the FBI arrived in Kansas City on June 17.

Floyd was about 29 years old at the time of the Kansas City Massacre. He had an extensive criminal record that began with his arrest in St. Louis, Missouri on September 16, 1925 for highway robbery. Floyd pleaded guilty and was sentenced to prison. He was released on March 7, 1929. On May 20, 1930, Floyd was arrested in Toledo, Ohio on a bank robbery charge and was sentenced to 12 to 15 years in prison. However, while enroute to the penitentiary Floyd escaped and was a fugitive when the Kansas City Massacre took place.

Richetti was about 23 years old at the time of the Kansas City Massacre. His first arrest occurred on August 7, 1928, for a robbery in Hammond, Indiana. Richetti was sentenced to prison for one to ten years for the crime. He was paroled in 1930. On March 9, 1932, Richetti was arrested for bank rob-

bery in Sulphur, Oklahoma. While out on bond for the crime Richetti illegally fled Oklahoma. At the time of the Kansas City Massacre Richetti was a fugitive.

Miller was about 37 and a native of South Dakota. He was a World War I veteran who became a policeman in 1920. He was elected county sheriff in 1922. After serving one year as sheriff, Miller embarked on a life of crime. On April 4, 1923, he was arrested for embezzling public funds. Miller was convicted of the crime and sentenced from two to ten years in prison. After his release Miller had various arrests, but no convictions, for petty crimes. It was believed that Miller was a hired gunman for New York crime boss Louis "Lepke" Buchalter.

On the morning of June 17, Miller, Floyd and Richetti drove to the railroad station to wait on Nash's arrival. The train arrived with Nash being escorted by agents Lackey and Smith and sheriff Reed. When they departed the train they were met by two other FBI agents and two local policemen. Upon leaving the railroad station they all walked to two waiting cars. Before they could leave, however, they were ambushed by Miller, Floyd and Richetti. Machine gun fire tore through the air striking officers and Nash. When the shooting ended the two local policemen were killed, sheriff Reed was killed, one FBI agent was killed and two were wounded. Nash was also killed in the battle by his rescuers.

Miller, Floyd and Richetti escaped from the crime scene unscathed. A massive investigation was immediately launched after the murders. Miller fled to Chicago, then to New York, and back to Chicago. On October 31, 1933, the FBI learned of his presence in Chicago, but he escaped capture. On November 29, 1933, the FBI found Miller's corpse in a ditch on the outskirts of Detroit, Michigan. He had been beaten and strangled. It was reported that he was killed by mobsters.

Floyd and Richetti made their way to Toledo, Ohio, after the massacre. They eventually traveled to Buffalo, New York, in September of 1933. In October of 1934 they decided to drive out to Oklahoma, accompanied by two female companions. Their car ran off the road and was damaged near Wellsville, Ohio. The two men decided to let their female companions drive the car into Wellsville to be repaired, while they waited along side the road.

Word quickly spread to the local police that two suspicious looking men were seen on the roadside near the outskirts of town. A routine investigation was made by the local police

The FBI hunted down Adam Richetti (left) and Charles Arthur "Pretty Boy" Floyd (right) after the Kansas City massacre. Floyd was gunned down by the FBI. Richetti was captured and later executed. (U.S. Department of Justice/FBI)

chief. However, when he came upon Floyd and Richetti they fired at him. A gun battle ensued. Richetti was captured, but Floyd escaped.

The FBI were called in and an intensive search for Floyd was made. On October 22, a squad of four FBI Agents led by Melvin Purvis, along with five local Ohio police officers, spotted Floyd in a car behind a barn near Clarkson, Ohio. Floyd leaped from the car with a pistol, shots were fired and he was wounded. Floyd surrendered. He died while waiting on an ambulance.

Richetti was returned to Kansas City, where he was indicted on four counts of first degree murder on March 1, 1935. On June 17, he was found guilty and sentenced to death. He was executed by lethal gas on October 7, 1938.

Kasi, Mir Aimal *see* Cia Murders

Kawakita v. United States

Court: United States Supreme Court; *Case Citation:* Kawakita v. United States, 343 U.S. 717 (1952); *Argued:* April 2–3, 1952; *Decided:* June 2, 1952; *Opinion of the Court:* Justice Douglas; *Concurring Opinion:* Justice None; *Dissenting Opinion:* Chief Justice Vinson, in which Black and Burton, JJ., joined; *Justice Taking No Part in Decision:* Justice Frankfurter and Clark, J.; *Appellate Defense Counsel:* Morris Lavine and A. L. Wirin argued; Fred Okrand on brief; *Appellate Prosecution Counsel:* Oscar H. Davis argued; Beatrice Rosenberg on brief; *Amicus Curiae Brief Supporting Prosecutor:* None; *Amicus Curiae Brief Supporting Defendant:* None.

Issue Presented: Whether the defendant renounced his United States citizenship and became expatriated by reason of acts committed in Japan during World War II, and therefore could not be convicted of treason against the United States?

Case Holding: The defendant did not renounce his United States citizenship and become expatriated by reason of acts committed in Japan during World War II, and therefore he could be convicted of treason against the United States.

Factual and procedural background of case: The defendant, Kawakita, was convicted of treason and sentenced to death by the United States. In an appeal to a Federal Court of Appeals, the defendant contended that he was not a citizen of the United States and therefore could not be convicted of treason against the nation. The relevant facts on the appeal showed that the defendant was born in the United States in 1921, to Japanese parents who were citizens of Japan. He was thus a citizen of the United States by birth and, by reason of Japanese law, a national of Japan. In 1939, the defendant went to Japan with his father to visit his grandfather. He traveled on a United States passport and, to obtain it, he took the customary oath of allegiance. In 1940, he registered with an American consul in Japan as an American citizen. The defendant remained in Japan, but his father returned to the United States.

In March of 1941, the defendant entered Meiji University in Japan and took a commercial course and military training. In April of 1941, he renewed his United States passport, once more taking the oath of allegiance to the United States. Dur-ing this period he was registered as an alien with the Japanese police. When war broke out between the United States and Japan, the defendant was still a student at Meiji University. He completed his schooling in 1943, at which time it was impossible for him to return to the United States. In 1943, he registered in the Koseki, a family census register. The defendant did not join the Japanese Army. Rather, he obtained employment as an interpreter with the Oeyama Nickel Industry Company, where he worked until Japan's surrender. He was hired to interpret communications between the Japanese and the prisoners of war who were assigned to work at a mine and in a factory owned by his employer. The treasonable acts for which he was convicted involved his conduct toward American prisoners of war.

In December of 1945, the defendant went to the United States consul at Yokohama and applied for registration as an American citizen. He stated under oath that he was a United States citizen and had not done various acts amounting to expatriation. He was issued a passport and returned to the United States in 1946. Shortly thereafter he was recognized by a former American prisoner of war, whereupon he was arrested, tried and convicted of treason.

In his appeal to the Court of Appeals the defendant argued that he had renounced or abandoned his United States citizenship and was expatriated. The defendant contended that he had expatriated himself by his acts and conduct beginning in 1943, with the entry of his name in the Koseki. Prior to that time he had been registered by the police as an alien. However, after that time he was considered by Japanese authorities as a Japanese. He had his name removed as an alien; he changed his registration at the University from American to Japanese and his address from California to Japan; he used the Koseki entry to get a job at the Oeyama camp; he went to China on a Japanese passport; he accepted labor draft papers from the Japanese government; and he faced the east each morning and paid his respects to the Emperor. The Court of Appeals rejected the expatriation evidence and affirmed the conviction and sentence. The United States Supreme Court granted certiorari to consider the issue.

Opinion of the Court by Justice Douglas: Justice Douglas held that the evidence was sufficient to support the finding of the jury that the defendant had not renounced or lost his American citizenship at the time of the overt acts of treason. It was said that in view of the defendant's dual nationality, it could not be said as a matter of law that his action in registering in the Koseki and changing his registration from American to Japanese amounted to a renunciation of American citizenship within the meaning of the Nationality Act. Justice Douglas wrote that in view of the conflict between the defendant's statements at his trial that he felt no loyalty to the United States from March 1943 to late 1945, and his actions after Japan's defeat (when he applied for registration as an American citizen and for an American passport), the question whether he had renounced his American citizenship was peculiarly for the jury to determine.

The opinion reasoned that notwithstanding his dual nationality and his residence in Japan, the defendant owed allegiance to the United States and could be punished for treasonable acts voluntarily committed. Justice Douglas noted that the definition of treason contained in the Constitution provided no territorial limitation, therefore an American citizen living beyond the territorial limits of the United States could be guilty of treason against the United States. It was said that an American citizen owes allegiance to the United States wherever he or she may reside.

In turning to the substantive elements of the crime, the opinion found that each of the overt acts of which the defendant was convicted was properly proven by two witnesses. Both witnesses established that the defendant gave aid and comfort to the enemy. It was said that the overt act of abusing American prisoners for the purpose of getting more work out of them in producing war materials for the enemy, qualified as an overt act within the constitutional standard of treason, since it gave aid and comfort to the enemy. The opinion found that the other overt act, cruelty to American prisoners of war, gave aid and comfort to the enemy by helping to make all the prisoners fearful, docile and subservient, reducing the number of guards needed, and requiring less watching — all of which encouraged the enemy and advanced the enemy's interests. The judgment of the Court of Appeals was affirmed.

Dissenting opinion by Chief Justice Vinson, in which Black and Burton, JJ., joined: The Chief Justice dissented from the Court's opinion. He believed that, beginning in March of 1943, the defendant "[a]s a matter of law, ... expatriated himself as well as that can be done." The Chief Justice argued that the defendant's "statements that he was still a citizen of the United States — made in order to obtain a United States passport after Japan had lost the War — cannot restore citizenship renounced during the War." *See also* **Treason**

Kazakhstan

Capital punishment is carried out in Kazakhstan. Kazakhstan uses the firing squad to carry out the death penalty. Its legal system is based on civil law. The nation's constitution was adopted on August 30, 1995.

The judicial system of Kazakhstan is composed of local courts, provincial courts, and a Supreme Court. Trials are public, defendants enjoy a presumption of innocence, are protected from self-incrimination, have the right to retained or appointed counsel, and have the right to appeal. *See also* **International Capital Punishment Nations**

Keizo v. Henry

Court: United States Supreme Court; *Case Citation:* Keizo v. Henry, 211 U.S. 146 (1908); *Argued:* October 29, 1908; *Decided:* November 16, 1908; *Opinion of the Court:* Justice Moody; *Concurring Opinion:* None; *Dissenting Opinion:* None; *Appellate Defense Counsel:* Duane E. Fox argued; Arthur S. Browne and A. S. Humphreys on brief; *Appellate Prosecution Counsel:* Charles R. Hemenway argued; M. F. Prosser on brief; *Amicus Curiae Brief Supporting Prosecutor:* None; *Amicus Curiae Brief Supporting Defendant:* None.

Issue Presented: Whether the defendant was denied due process of law because eight members of the grand jury that indicted him may not have been citizens.?

Case Holding: The issue raised by the defendant may not be brought on a habeas petition to the United States Supreme Court, when the matter could have been properly brought in a direct appeal.

Factual and procedural background of case: The defendant, Morita Keizo, was indicted by the territory of Hawaii for capital murder. Prior to trial the defendant requested the indictment be dismissed because eight members of the grand jury that indicted him were not citizens of the United States or the territory of Hawaii. It was subsequently determined that the eight grand jurors were citizens of Hawaii only by virtue of judgments of naturalization in a circuit court of the territory. The trial court therefore denied the request to dismiss the indictment. The defendant was thereafter tried, convicted and sentenced to death. The Hawaii Supreme Court affirmed the judgment.

A few days before the defendant's scheduled execution he filed a petition for habeas corpus relief with the Hawaii Supreme Court, alleging once again that eight members of the grand jury were not citizens and that the judgment against him was therefore void. The appellate court dismissed the petition. The United States Supreme Court granted certiorari to consider the issue.

Opinion of the Court by Justice Moody: Justice Moody held that the defendant waived the merits of his argument by failing to appeal the initial ruling by the Hawaii Supreme Court affirming the judgment against him. The opinion reasoned as follows:

> The principal question argued before us by counsel is, whether the eight members of the grand jury, whose qualifications were questioned, were naturalized by courts having the authority to naturalize aliens. But we find no occasion to decide or consider this question. If the [defendant] desired the judgment of this court upon it, he should have brought [an appeal] to the judgment of the supreme court of the territory which passed upon it in affirming the judgment of conviction in the trial court. He may not lie by, as he did in this case, until the time for the execution of the judgment comes near, and then seek to raise collaterally, by habeas corpus, questions not affecting the jurisdiction of the court which convicted him, which were open to him in the original case, and, if properly presented then, could ultimately have come to this court upon [appeal].... [N]o court may properly release a prisoner under conviction and sentence of another court, unless for want of jurisdiction of the cause or person, or for some other matter rendering its proceedings void. Where a court has jurisdiction, mere errors which have been committed in the course of the proceedings cannot be corrected upon a writ of habeas corpus, which may not, in this manner, usurp the functions of [an appeal]. These well-settled principles are decisive of the case before us. Disqualifications of grand jurors do not destroy the jurisdiction of the court in which an indictment is returned, if the court has jurisdiction of the cause and of the person, as the trial court had in this case. The indictment, though voidable, if the objection is seasonably taken, as it was in this case, is not void. The objection may be waived, if it is not made at all or delayed too long. This is but another form of saying that the indictment is a sufficient

foundation for the jurisdiction of the court in which it is returned, if jurisdiction otherwise exists. That court has the authority to decide all questions concerning the constitution, organization, and qualification of the grand jury, and, if there are errors in dealing with these questions, like all other errors of law committed in the course of the proceedings, they can only be corrected by [appeal].

The judgment of the Hawaii Supreme Court was affirmed. *See also* **Procedural Default of Constitutional Claims**

Kelley v. Oregon

Court: United States Supreme Court; *Case Citation:* Kelley v. Oregon, 273 U.S. 589 (1927); *Argued:* March 9, 1927; *Decided:* April 11, 1927; *Opinion of the Court:* Chief Justice Taft; *Concurring Opinion:* None; *Dissenting Opinion:* None; *Appellate Defense Counsel:* Will R. King argued and briefed; *Appellate Prosecution Counsel:* John H. Carson argued and briefed; *Amicus Curiae Brief Supporting Prosecutor:* None; *Amicus Curiae Brief Supporting Defendant:* None.

Issue Presented: Whether the defendant had a constitutional right to serve out a prior imprisonment sentence before he could be executed for another crime?

Case Holding: The defendant did not have a constitutional right to serve out a prior imprisonment sentence before he could be executed for another crime.

Factual and procedural background of case: The defendant, Ellsworth Kelley, was indicted for capital murder by the State of Oregon. At the time of the crime the defendant was an inmate at a State penitentiary serving a 20-year sentence. The killing occurred during the defendant's attempt to escape from prison. The defendant was tried, convicted and sentenced to death. The Oregon Supreme Court affirmed the judgment. In doing so, the appellate court rejected the defendant's claim that he could not be executed until after he served his previous imprisonment sentence. The United States Supreme Court granted certiorari to consider the issue.

Opinion of the Court by Chief Justice Taft: The Chief Justice held that the defendant did not have a constitutional right to serve out the remainder of his prison sentence before he could be executed. The opinion stated the Court's reasoning succinctly as follows: "A prisoner may certainly be tried, convicted, and sentenced for another crime, committed either prior to or during his imprisonment, and may suffer capital punishment and be executed during the term. The penitentiary is no sanctuary, and life in it does not confer immunity from capital punishment provided by law. He has no vested constitutional right to serve out his unexpired sentence." The judgment of the Oregon Supreme Court was affirmed.

Kemmler, William *see* Electrocution; In Re Kemmler

Kennedy, Anthony M.

Anthony M. Kennedy was appointed as an associate justice of the United States Supreme Court in 1988. While on the Supreme Court Kennedy has been known as a conservative interpreter of the Constitution.

Kennedy was born on July 28, 1936, in Sacramento, California. He received an undergraduate degree from Stanford University in 1958, and a law degree from Harvard University Law School in 1961. Kennedy's legal career included a private practice, teaching at McGeorge School of Law, and 13 years as an appellate judge on the Ninth Circuit Court of Appeals. In 1988 President Ronald Reagan appointed Kennedy to the Supreme Court.

While on the Supreme Court Kennedy has written a number of capital punishment opinions. His writings in this area of the law have shown a consistent conservative philosophy that favors the government over capital defendants. For example, in *Tuilaepa v. California* two defendants challenged a penalty phase statutory factor as vague and misleading. Kennedy, writing for the Supreme Court, sidestepped legal analysis of the merits of the issue and held that constitutional vagueness review was deferential and therefore a factor is not unconstitutional if it has some common sense core meaning that criminal juries should be capable of understanding. The problem legal analysts have found with *Tuilaepa's* reasoning is that the decision turned a blind eye to the real issue presented by the defendants, i.e., in addition to a possible common sense understanding the statutory factor left ajar the door for a jury to reach an irrational conclusion.

Capital Punishment Opinions Written by Kennedy

Case Name	Opinion of the Court	Concurring Opinion	Dissenting Opinion
Calderon v. Thompson	✓		
Godinez v. Moran		✓	
Johnson v. Texas	✓		
Loving v. United States	✓		
McKoy v. North Carolina		✓	
Mu'Min v. Virginia			✓
Murray v. Giarratano		✓	
Riggins v. Nevada		✓	
Saffle v. Parks	✓		
Sawyer v. Smith	✓		
Stringer v. Black	✓		
Tuilaepa v. California	✓		
Victor v. Nebraska		✓	

Kentucky

The State of Kentucky is a capital punishment jurisdiction. The State reenacted its death penalty law after the United States Supreme Court decision in *Furman v. Georgia*, 408 U.S. 238 (1972), on January 1, 1975.

Kentucky has a three-tier legal system. The State's legal system is composed of a supreme court, court of appeals and courts of general jurisdiction. The Kentucky Supreme Court is presided over by a chief justice and six associate justices. The Kentucky Court of Appeals is composed of a chief judge and 13 judges. The courts of general jurisdiction in the State are called Circuit Courts. Capital offenses against the State of Kentucky are tried in the Circuit Courts.

Kentucky's capital punishment statute is triggered if a person commits a homicide under the following special circumstances:

a. With intent to cause the death of another person, he causes the death of such person or of a third person.

b. Including, but not limited to, the operation of a motor vehicle under circumstances manifesting extreme indifference to human life, he wantonly engages in conduct which creates a grave risk of death to another person and thereby causes the death of another person.

c. Kidnapping when the victim is not released alive or when the victim is released alive but subsequently dies as a result thereof.

Capital murder in Kentucky is punishable by death, life imprisonment without parole, or imprisonment for a term of years. A capital prosecution in Kentucky is bifurcated into a guilt phase and penalty phase. A jury is used at both phases of a capital trial. It is required that, at the penalty phase, the jury unanimously agree that a death sentence is appropriate before it can be imposed. If the penalty phase jury is unable to reach a verdict, the trial judge is required to impose a sentence of life imprisonment without parole or a term of years. The decision of a penalty phase jury is binding on the trial court under the laws of Kentucky.

In order to impose a death sentence upon a defendant under Kentucky law, it is required that the prosecutor establish the existence of at least one of the following statutory aggravating circumstances at the penalty phase:

1. The offense of murder or kidnapping was committed by a person with a prior record of conviction for a capital offense, or the offense of murder was committed by a person who has a substantial history of serious assaultive criminal convictions;

2. The offense of murder or kidnapping was committed while the offender was engaged in the commission of arson in the first degree, robbery in the first degree, burglary in the first degree, rape in the first degree, or sodomy in the first degree;

3. The offender by his act of murder, armed robbery, or kidnapping knowingly created a great risk of death to more than one person in a public place by means of a destructive device, weapon, or other device which would normally be hazardous to the lives of more than one person;

4. The offender committed the offense of murder for himself or another, for the purpose of receiving money or any other thing of monetary value, or for other profit;

5. The offense of murder was committed by a person who was a prisoner and the victim was a prison employee engaged at the time of the act in the performance of his duties;

6. The offender's act or acts of killing were intentional and resulted in multiple deaths;

7. The offender's act of killing was intentional and the victim was a state or local public official or police officer, sheriff, or deputy sheriff engaged at the time of the act in the lawful performance of his duties; and

8. The offender murdered the victim when an emergency protective order or a domestic violence order was in effect, or when any other order designed to protect the victim from the offender, such as an order issued as a condition of a bond, conditional release, probation, parole, or pretrial diversion, was in effect.

Although the Federal Constitution will not permit jurisdictions to prevent capital felons from presenting all relevant mitigating evidence at the penalty phase, Kentucky has provided the following statutory mitigating circumstances that permit the jury to reject imposition of the death penalty:

1. The defendant has no significant history of prior criminal activity;

2. The capital offense was committed while the defendant was under the influence of extreme mental or emotional disturbance even though the influence of extreme mental or emotional disturbance is not sufficient to constitute a defense to the crime;

3. The victim was a participant in the defendant's criminal conduct or consented to the criminal act;

4. The capital offense was committed under circumstances which the defendant believed to provide a moral justification or extenuation for his conduct even though the circumstances which the defendant believed to provide a moral justification or extenuation for his conduct are not sufficient to constitute a defense to the crime;

5. The defendant was an accomplice in a capital offense committed by another person and his participation in the capital offense was relatively minor;

6. The defendant acted under duress or under the domination of another person even though the duress or the domination of another person is not sufficient to constitute a defense to the crime;

7. At the time of the capital offense, the capacity of the defendant to appreciate the criminality of his conduct to the requirements of law was impaired as a result of mental illness or retardation or intoxication even though the impairment of the capacity of the defendant to appreciate the criminality of his conduct or to conform the conduct to the requirements of law is insufficient to constitute a defense to the crime; and

8. The youth of the defendant at the time of the crime.

Under Kentucky's capital punishment statute, a sentence of death is automatically reviewed by the Kentucky Supreme Court. Kentucky uses lethal injection to carry out death sentences. Defendants sentenced before March 31, 1998, have a choice of execution by lethal injection or electrocution. The State's death row facility for men is located in Eddyville, Kentucky; while the facility maintaining female death row inmates is located in Pee Wee Valley, Kentucky.

Pursuant to the laws of Kentucky the Governor has exclusive authority to grant clemency in capital cases. The Governor may commute a capital sentence to life imprisonment without parole.

From the start of modern capital punishment in 1976, through 1999, Kentucky executed 2 capital felons. During this period Kentucky did not have any female capital felons. A total of 39 capital felons were on death row in Kentucky in 1999. The 1999 death row population in the State was listed as: eight black inmates and 31 white inmates. In 1999 the State had one juvenile on death row. The State permits capital punishment to be imposed on persons 16 years old or older. Kentucky prohibits the execution of mentally retarded capital felons.

Executions by Kentucky 1976–1999

Name	Race	Date of Execution	Method of Execution
Harold McQueen	White	July 1, 1997	Electrocution
Edward L. Harper	White	May 25, 1999	Lethal Injection

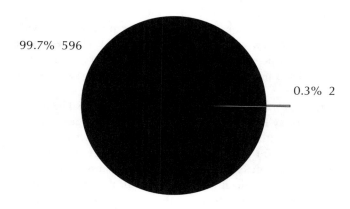

EXECUTIONS BY KENTUCKY 1976–1999

99.7% 596

0.3% 2

◼ KENTUCKY EXECUTIONS

◼ ALL OTHER EXECUTIONS

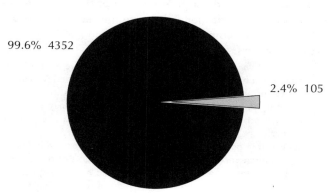

EXECUTIONS BY KENTUCKY 1930–1999

99.6% 4352

2.4% 105

◼ KENTUCKY

◼ ALL OTHER JURISDICTIONS

Kentucky Coalition to Abolish the Death Penalty

The Kentucky Coalition to Abolish the Death Penalty (KCADP) was founded in Kentucky in the late 1970s, shortly after the State reenacted a new death penalty statute. KCADP is a statewide nonprofit organization of over 30 religious and civic organizations. The mission of KCADP is the abolishment of the death penalty in Kentucky.

Through the leadership of its chairman, Rev. Patrick Delahanty, KCADP vigorously lobbied and obtained Kentucky legislation in 1990 which abolished the imposition of the death penalty on mentally retarded capital felons. The KCADP was also instrumental in getting the State legislature to pass the 1998 Racial Justice Act. This legislation allows a capital felon to introduce at trial statistical evidence that shows racial bias in the imposition of the death penalty.

In 1998, KCADP launched its ABOLITION 2000 campaign. This project is a grass roots educational effort to make facts about executions known to all Kentuckians. The organization hopes that through the campaign it will be able to mount enough pressure to force Kentucky legislators to repeal the State's death penalty statute.

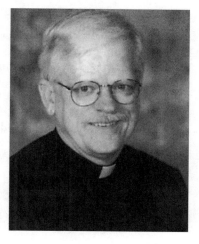

Rev. Patrick Delahanty is chairman of the KCADP. Rev. Delahanty worked tirelessly in lobbying the Kentucky legislature to enact a law in 1990, which abolished imposition of the death penalty on mentally retarded capital felons. (Patrick Delahanty)

Kenya Kenya recognizes capital punishment. Hanging is the method of execution used by Kenya to carry out the death penalty. Its legal system is a mixture of English common law, Islamic law and customary law. The nation's first constitution was adopted on December 12, 1963.

The court system of Kenya consists of Magistrate Courts, High Courts, and a Court of Appeals. Trials are open to the public. Judges preside alone over all cases. There is no jury system. Defendants enjoy a presumption of innocence, have the right to confront witnesses, to present evidence, and have a right to retain counsel. Defendants have the right to appointed legal counsel in capital cases only. *See also* **International Capital Punishment Nations**

Kerling, Edward John *see* Espionage

Kidnapping The crime of kidnapping is a felony offense that is generally defined as the unlawful abduction of another person for ransom. Kidnapping, without more, cannot be used to inflict the death penalty. The Eighth Amendment of the United States Constitution prohibits this as cruel and unusual punishment. However, the crime of kidnapping can play a role in a capital prosecution. If kidnapping occurs during the commission of a homicide it may form the basis of a death-eligible offense, and therefore trigger a capital prosecution. *See also* **Rape and Capital Punishment; Death-Eligible Offenses; Felony Murder Rule; Kidnapping Aggravator**

Kidnapping Aggravator The crime of kidnapping committed during the course of a homicide is a statutory aggravating circumstance in a majority of capital punishment jurisdictions. As a statutory aggravating circumstance, evidence of kidnapping is used at the penalty phase of a capital prosecution for the factfinder to consider in determining whether to impose the death penalty. *See also* **Aggravating Circumstances; Felony Murder Rule; Kidnapping**

JURISDICTIONS USING KIDNAPPING AGGRAVATOR

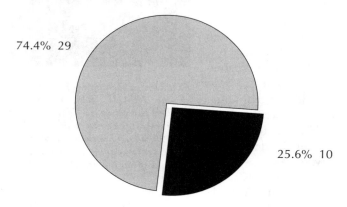

74.4% 29

25.6% 10

■ KIDNAPPING AGGRAVATOR JURISDICTIONS

■ ALL OTHER JURISDICTIONS

Kintpuash, Jack In the fall of 1872, a group of Modoc Native Americans under the leadership of Jack Kintpuash left the Klamath Reservation in Oregon and moved into northeastern California. During their journey they killed several people at Lost River. The Modocs were pursued by an Army unit, and retreated into the lava beds region of northeastern California near Lake Tule.

The Modoc War became a national concern in April 1873, when Kintpuash killed General E. R. S. Canby, an army negotiator, during peace negotiations. Two months later the Army was able to overtake the Modocs and force a surrender. Kintpuash was summarily tried for the killing and General Canby, found guilty and sentenced to death. Kintpuash was executed October 3, 1873.

Jack Kintpuash was executed by the United States Army shortly after the Modoc War ended. (National Archives)

Kiribati Capital punishment is not carried out in Kiribati. *See also* **International Capital Punishment Nations**

Kohl v. Lehlback *Court:* United States Supreme Court;

Case Citation: Kohl v. Lehlback, 160 U.S. 293 (1895); *Argued:* Not reported; *Decided:* December 23, 1895; *Opinion of the Court:* Chief Justice Fuller; *Concurring Opinion:* None; *Dissenting Opinion:* None; *Appellate Defense Counsel:* Arthur English argued and briefed; *Appellate Prosecution Counsel:* E. W. Crane argued and briefed; *Amicus Curiae Brief Supporting Prosecutor:* None; *Amicus Curiae Brief Supporting Defendant:* None.

Issues Presented: (1) Whether the defendant was entitled to habeas relief due to the State appellate court's refusal to hear his appeal? (2) Whether the defendant was entitled to habeas relief due to an alien taking part in his trial as a juror?

Case Holdings: (1) The defendant was not entitled to habeas relief due to the State appellate court's refusal to hear his appeal, because the Constitution does not require States provide appellate review of criminal judgments. (2) The defendant was not entitled to habeas relief due to an alien taking part in his trial as a juror, because the issue was never presented to a State court.

Factual and procedural background of case: The defendant, Henry Kohl, was convicted of capital murder and sentenced to death by the State of New Jersey. The defendant filed an appeal, but the New Jersey Supreme Court refused to hear the case. The defendant then filed a petition for habeas corpus relief in a Federal District Court. In the habeas petition the defendant argued he was unlawfully confined because the State appellate court refused his appeal, and because a foreign citizen was a member of the jury that convicted him. The Federal court dismissed the petition. The United States Supreme Court granted certiorari to consider the issue.

Opinion of the Court by Chief Justice Fuller: The Chief Justice held that under a prior decision of the Court it was ruled that the Constitution did not require States provide appellate review of criminal cases. The opinion addressed the matter as follows:

> In *McKane v. Durston*, 153 U.S. 684 (1894) we held that an appeal to a higher court from a judgment of conviction is not a matter of absolute right, independently of constitutional or statutory provisions allowing it, and that a state may accord it to a person convicted of crime upon such terms as it thinks proper.... [T]he refusal of the courts of New Jersey to grant [an appeal] to a person convicted of murder, or to stay the execution of a sentence, will not itself warrant a court of the United States in interfering in his behalf by writ of habeas corpus....
>
> ... At all events, inasmuch as the right of review in an appellate court is purely a matter of state concern, we can neither anticipate nor overrule the action of the state courts in that regard, since a denial of the right altogether would constitute no violation of the constitution of the United States.

The Chief Justice turned to the defendant's argument that an alien sat on the jury that convicted him. The opinion noted that under the laws of New Jersey it was required that every juror be a citizen of the State. It was also pointed out that at common law an alien could not sit on a jury. The Chief Justice went on to point out that the defendant was not entitled to habeas relief because of a noncitizen participating in his trial as a juror. The opinion found that the issue was never presented to the trial court. The Chief Justice reasoned that the error in having an alien on the jury was waived by the defendant's failure to present it to a State court. The judgment of the Federal court was affirmed.

Kokoraleis, Andrew *see* Ripper Crew Cult Murders

Korea, North
Capital punishment is recognized in North Korea. North Korea uses the firing squad and hanging to carry out the death penalty. North Korea is a dictatorship under the absolute rule of the Korean Workers' Party. Kim Il Sung, as head of the party, ruled the nation until his death in 1994. His son, Kim Jong Il, was named general secretary of the party in October 1997.

Under North Korea's legal system an independent judiciary and individual rights do not exist. In practice the Public Security Ministry dispenses with trials in political cases and refers defendants to the Ministry of State Security for imposition of punishment. In non-political cases lawyers appear to be assigned to defendants. However, the role of the defendant's counsel is that of persuading the defendant to confess guilt. *See also* International Capital Punishment Nations

Korea, South
Capital punishment is permitted in South Korea. South Korea uses hanging as the method of carrying out the death penalty. Its legal system is a mixture of European law and American law. The nation adopted its constitution on February 25, 1988. South Korea is a republic that has an executive branch, unicameral legislative branch, and judicial branch.

The judicial system of South Korea consists of trial courts, appeals courts, Supreme Court, and Constitutional Court. Trials are open to the public, but there is no trial by jury. Defendants enjoy the presumption of innocence, protection against self-incrimination, freedom from retroactive laws and double jeopardy, the right to a speedy trial, and the right of appeal. Death sentences are appealed automatically. *See also* International Capital Punishment Nations

Kring v. Missouri
Court: United States Supreme Court; *Case Citation:* Kring v. Missouri, 107 U.S. 221 (1883); *Argued:* Not reported; *Decided:* April 2, 1883; *Opinion of the Court:* Justice Miller; *Concurring Opinion:* None; *Dissenting Opinion:* Justice Matthews, in which Waite, C.J., and Bradley and Gray, JJ., joined; *Appellate Defense Counsel:* L. D. Seward argued; Jeff Chandleron on brief; *Appellate Prosecution Counsel:* S. F. Phillips argued and briefed; *Amicus Curiae Brief Supporting Prosecutor:* None; *Amicus Curiae Brief Supporting Defendant:* None.

Issue Presented: Whether application of a new State constitutional amendment to the defendant's case, which amendment permitted prosecuting him for capital murder, violated the Ex Post Facto Clause of the Federal Constitution?

Case Holding: Application of a new State constitutional amendment to the defendant's case, which amendment permitted prosecuting him for capital murder, violated the Ex Post Facto Clause of the Federal Constitution.

Factual and procedural background of case: The defendant, Kring, was charged with capital murder by the State of Missouri. The defendant entered a plea of guilty, however, to second degree murder and was sentenced to 25 years imprisonment. The defendant challenged the sentence in the State appellate courts on the ground that he had an understanding with the prosecutor that, in pleading guilty to second degree murder, he would be sentenced to not more than 10 years imprisonment. The Missouri Supreme Court reversed the judgment and remanded the case.

On remand, the defendant refused to withdraw his guilty plea and demanded to be sentenced to no more than 10 years in prison. The trial court entered an order setting aside the guilty plea and ordering a general not guilty plea be placed on the record. The defendant was tried by a jury, found guilty and sentenced to death. On appeal the defendant argued to the Missouri Supreme Court that, under the law which existed at the time the crime was committed, he could not be tried nor convicted of an offense greater than second degree murder, once he plead guilty to that offense. The appellate court agreed with the defendant, but ruled that a subsequent amendment to the State's constitution permitted him to be prosecuted for capital murder after withdrawal of his guilty plea to second degree murder. The appellate court rejected the defendant's argument that the Ex Post Facto Clause of the Federal Constitution prohibited retroactive application of the change in the law. The United States Supreme Court granted certiorari to consider the issue.

Opinion of the Court by Justice Miller: Justice Miller ruled that application of the State constitutional amendment to the defendant's case violated the Ex Post Facto Clause. The opinion indicated that there were four distinct classes of laws embraced by the Ex Post Facto Clause: (1) every law that makes an action done before the passing of the law, and which was innocent when done, criminal, and punishes such action; (2) every law that aggravates the crime or makes it greater than it was when committed; (3) every law that changes the punishment and inflicts a greater punishment than was annexed to the crime when committed; and (4) every law that alters the legal rules of evidence, and receives less or different testimony than the law required at the time of the commission of the offense in order to convict the offender.

The opinion further held that any law passed after the commission of an offense which in relation to that offense, or its consequences, alters the situation of a defendant to his or her disadvantage, is an ex post facto law. Justice Miller proclaimed that no one can be criminally punished in the nation, except according to a law prescribed for the government before the imputed offense was committed and which existed as a law at the time. The opinion concluded: "Tested by these criteria, the provision of the constitution of Missouri which denies to [the defendant] the benefit which the previous law gave him of acquittal of the charge of murder in the first degree, on conviction of murder in the second degree, is, as to his case, an ex post facto law within the meaning of the constitution of the United States, and for the error of the supreme court of Missouri, in holding otherwise, its judgment is reversed, and the case is remanded to it, with direction to reverse the judgment of the criminal court of St. Louis[.]"

Dissenting opinion by Justice Matthews, in which Waite, C.J., and Bradley and Gray, JJ., joined: Justice Matthews dissented from the Court's decision. He contended that the new constitutional amendment did not alter the crime for which the defendant was charged and therefore it could be applied to him. Justice Matthews wrote: "That law did not operate upon the offense to change its character; nor upon its punishment to aggravate it; nor upon the evidence which, according to the law in force at the time of its commission, was competent to prove or disprove it. It operated upon a transaction between the prisoner and the prosecution, which might or might not have taken place[.]" *See also* **Dobbert v. Florida; Ex Post Facto Clause; Holden v. Minnesota**

Kuwait Kuwait recognizes capital punishment. Kuwait carries out the death penalty using hanging and the firing squad. In 1998, Kuwait executed six prisoners. Its legal system is based on Islamic law and civil law. Kuwait promulgated a constitution on November 11, 1962. Kuwait has been ruled by Amirs (princes) from the Al-Sabah family for over 200 years. The constitution and laws of Kuwait provide for judicial independence, but the Amir appoints all judges.

The court system consists of trial courts, a High Court of Appeal, and a Court of Cassation. Defendants have a right to retained counsel and, when indigent, must be appointed counsel in felony prosecutions. Both defendants and prosecutors may appeal trial court verdicts. *See also* **International Capital Punishment Nations**

Kyles v. Whitley *Court:* United States Supreme Court; *Case Citation:* Kyles v. Whitley, 514 U.S. 419 (1995); *Argued:* November 7, 1994; *Decided:* April 19, 1995; *Opinion of the Court:* Justice Souter; *Concurring Opinion:* Justice Stevens, in which Ginsburg and Breyer, JJ., joined; *Dissenting Opinion:* Justice Scalia, in which Rehnquist, C. J., and Kennedy and Thomas, JJ., joined; *Appellate Defense Counsel:* Not reported; *Appellate Prosecution Counsel:* Not reported; *Amicus Curiae Brief Supporting Prosecutor:* Not reported; *Amicus Curiae Brief Supporting Defendant:* Not reported.

Issue Presented: Whether the prosecutor's suppression of exculpatory evidence of the defendant's possible innocence required reversal of the defendant's conviction and death sentence?

Case Holding: The prosecutor's suppression of exculpatory evidence of the defendant's possible innocence required reversal of the defendant's conviction and death sentence, and a new trial.

Factual and procedural background of case: The State of Louisiana charged the defendant, Curtis Lee Kyles, with cap-

ital murder. After the defendant's first trial ended in a hung jury, he was tried again. At the second trial the defendant was convicted and sentenced to death. The Louisiana Supreme Court affirmed the conviction and sentence.

The defendant next filed a habeas corpus petition in a State trial court. In the habeas petition the defendant alleged that the prosecutor withheld exculpatory evidence. The State trial court denied relief, and the State appellate court affirmed. He then sought relief on federal habeas in a District Court, claiming that his conviction was obtained in violation of the United States Supreme Courts decision in *Brady v. Maryland*, which held that the suppression by the prosecution of evidence favorable to an accused violates due process where the evidence is material either to guilt or to punishment. The District Court denied relief, and a Federal Court of Appeals affirmed the denial. The United States Supreme Court granted certiorari to consider the issue.

Opinion of the Court by Justice Souter: Justice Souter held that suppression of the evidence violated *Brady v. Maryland*. The opinion found that because the net effect of the suppressed evidence favoring the defendant raised a reasonable probability that its disclosure would have produced a different result at trial, the conviction could not stand and the defendant was is entitled to a new trial. It was said that a review of the suppressed statements of eyewitnesses — whose testimony identifying the defendant as the killer was the essence of the prosecutor's case — revealed that their disclosure not only would have resulted in a markedly weaker case for the prosecution and a markedly stronger one for the defense, but also would have substantially reduced or destroyed the value of the prosecutor's two best witnesses.

The opinion noted that although not every item of the prosecutor's case would have been directly undercut if the suppressed evidence had been disclosed, it was significant that the physical evidence remaining unscathed would hardly have amounted to overwhelming proof that the defendant was the murderer. The judgment of the Court of Appeals was reversed.

Concurring opinion by Justice Stevens, in which Ginsburg and Breyer, JJ., joined: Justice Stevens concurred in the Court's opinion. He indicated that he was writing separately only for the purpose of addressing the dissent's argument that the Court's docket was too busy to have granted certiorari in the case. Justice Stevens wrote:

> ... Even aside from its legal importance, ... this case merits "favored treatment," for at least three reasons. First, the fact that the jury was unable to reach a verdict at the conclusion of the first trial provides strong reason to believe the significant errors that occurred at the second trial were prejudicial. Second, cases in which the record reveals so many instances of the state's failure to disclose exculpatory evidence are extremely rare. Even if I shared Justice Scalia's appraisal of the evidence in this case — which I do not — I would still believe we should independently review the record to ensure that the prosecution's blatant and repeated violations of a well-settled constitutional obligation did not deprive petitioner of a fair trial. Third, despite my high regard for the diligence and craftsmanship, of the author of the majority opinion in the Court of Appeals, my independent

review of the case left me with the same degree of doubt about [the defendant's] guilt expressed by the dissenting judge in that court.

Our duty to administer justice occasionally requires busy judges to engage in a detailed review of the particular facts of a case, even though our labors may not provide posterity with a newly minted rule of law.... I wish such review were unnecessary, but I cannot agree that our position in the judicial hierarchy makes it inappropriate. Sometimes the performance of an unpleasant duty conveys a message more significant than even the most penetrating legal analysis.

Dissenting opinion by Justice Scalia, in which Rehnquist, C. J., and Kennedy and Thomas, JJ., joined: Justice Scalia dissented from the Court's judgment. His dissent was centered upon what he believed to be a waste of time for the Court to have granted certiorari in the case. The dissent argued as follows: "The greatest puzzle of today's decision is what could have caused this capital case to be singled out for favored treatment. Perhaps it has been randomly selected as a symbol, to reassure America that the United States Supreme Court is reviewing capital convictions to make sure no factual error has been made. If so, it is a false symbol, for we assuredly do not do that. At, and during the week preceding, our February 24 Conference, for example, we considered and disposed of 10 petitions in capital cases, from seven States. We carefully considered whether the convictions and sentences in those cases had been obtained in reliance upon correct principles of federal law; but if we had tried to consider, in addition, whether those correct principles had been applied, not merely plausibly, but accurately, to the particular facts of each case, we would have done nothing else for the week. The reality is that responsibility for factual accuracy, in capital cases as in other cases, rests elsewhere — with trial judges and juries, state appellate courts, and the lower federal courts; we do nothing but encourage foolish reliance to pretend otherwise." *See also* **Brady v. Maryland; Exculpatory Evidence; Strickler v. Greene**

Kyrgyzstan The death penalty is carried out in Kyrgyzstan. Kyrgyzstan uses the firing squad to carry out the death penalty. In 1998, Kyrgyzstan executed four prisoners. Its legal system is based on civil law. Kyrgyzstan became an independent nation in 1991. The nations constitution was passed on May 5, 1993. Its republican form of government includes an executive branch, legislative branch, and judicial branch.

The judicial system of Kyrgyzstan includes trial courts, district and regional appellate courts, and a Supreme Court. Defendants are publicly tried before a judge and two assessors (citizens chosen from labor collectives). Defendants have a right to legal counsel, to cross examine witnesses, and to appeal. The court may render one of three decisions in a criminal case: innocent; guilty; or indeterminate (that is, the case is returned to the prosecutor for further investigation).

Kyrgyzstan also recognizes local elders courts. These courts exercise authority over petty crimes, such as robbery, hooliganism, or theft. In the past, local elders courts were known to exceed their authority by trying major crimes and even levying capital punishment. However, abuses such as stoning and death sentences are believed to have abated. *See also* **International Capital Punishment Nations**

L

LaGrand Brothers Walter LaGrand and Karl LaGrand were executed in 1999, for capital murder by the State of Arizona. The LaGrands were brothers. Walter was born on January 26, 1962, and Karl was on October 20, 1963. Both brothers were born in Augsburg, Germany. They moved to Arizona as children, after their mother married an American serviceman.

On the morning of January 7, 1982, the LaGrands left their home with a plan to rob the Valley National Bank in Marana, Arizona. The brothers arrived in Marana sometime before 8:00 A.M. Because the bank was closed they drove around Marana to pass time. They eventually stopped at a fastfood restaurant adjacent to the bank. However, the manager of the restaurant told them the place was closed. The LaGrands then drove off.

At 8:00 A.M. an employee of the bank, Dawn Lopez, arrived for work. Lopez noticed two vehicles parked in the bank's parking lot, one of which she did not recognize. As Lopez parked her car she observed the bank manager, Ken Hartsock, walking into the bank with another man whom she did not recognize. Lopez parked her car and walked toward the bank. As she moved passed the unknown vehicle, Walter LaGrand emerged from the car and asked her

Walter LaGrand** (left) **and his brother Karl LaGrand** (right) **were the first German citizens executed in the United States since World War II, when the State of Arizona executed them in 1999. (Arizona Department of Corections)

what time the bank opened. Lopez replied, "Ten o'clock." Lopez continued walking and went into the bank.

When Lopez entered the bank she saw Hartsock standing by the vault with Karl LaGrand. Karl told her to sit down and opened his jacket to reveal what appeared to be a gun (the gun was not real). Walter then entered the bank. Walter expressed impatience, before being told by Karl that Hartsock was unable to open the vault because he had only one-half of the vault combination.

The LaGrands then forced Lopez and Hartsock into an office where they bound their hands together with black electrical tape. Walter became agitated and accused Hartsock of lying, and then placed a letter opener to his throat, threatening to kill him if he was not telling the truth. Lopez and Hartsock were then gagged with bandannas.

At approximately 8:10 A.M. another bank employee, Wilma Rogers, arrived at the bank. Rogers immediately noticed an unknown vehicle in the parking lot and became suspicious. Rogers wrote down the license plate number of the unknown vehicle in the parking lot, and then went to a nearby grocery store to telephone the bank. The LaGrands allowed Lopez to answer the phone. Karl held the receiver to Lopez' ear and listened to the conversation. Rogers asked for Hartsock but Lopez denied that he was there. Rogers then told Lopez that her car headlights were still on, and that if she did not come out to turn them off she would call the sheriff. The LaGrands allowed Lopez to go outside to turn off her headlights, after warning her Hartsock would be killed if she did not return. Lopez left, but returned.

After Lopez returned she was again tied up. As Lopez was being bound Hartsock broke free and began fighting with the LaGrands. Hartsock was stabbed repeatedly before falling to the floor. Walter then turned to Lopez, who had also broken free, and stabbed her several times. The brothers then fled the bank and went to Tucson.

Lopez was able to call for help. When the police arrived at the bank Hartsock was dead. He had been stabbed 24 times. Lopez was rushed to a hospital where she recovered from her stab wounds.

Based upon the license plate number obtained by Rogers, the police were able to quickly locate the brothers in Tucson. They were arrested within hours of the attempted bank robbery.

The LaGrands were charged with capital murder in the death of Hartsock. They were tried together in 1984. The jury returned a verdict of guilty against both brothers. On December 14, 1984 the trial court sentenced both brothers to death.

While the LaGrands were on death row international efforts were made to prevent their executions. High level German officials and United Nations officials intervened in an attempt to rescue the brothers. German officials were particularly agitated because their American consulate was not informed about the brothers until nine years after their convictions. The Germans argued that the brothers were citizens of Germany and therefore the German consulate in America should have been notified when the brothers were arrested.

International pressure did not prevent Arizona from executed the brothers. On February 14, 1999, Karl became the first German citizen executed in the United States since World War II. The method of execution used was lethal injection. Walter was executed on March 3, 1999. The method of execution used was lethal gas. The LaGrand bothers were buried in the Arizona State Prison cemetery in Florence, Arizona. *See also* **Foreign Nationals and Capital Punishment**

Lamarca, Angelo *see* Weinberger Kidnapping

Lambert v. Barrett (I)
Court: United States Supreme Court; *Case Citation:* Lambert v. Barrett, 157 U.S. 697 (1895); *Argued:* Not reported; *Decided:* April 15, 1895; *Opinion of the Court:* Chief Justice Fuller; *Concurring Opinion:* None; *Dissenting Opinion:* None; *Appellate Defense Counsel:* John L. Semple argued and briefed; *Appellate Prosecution Counsel:* Wilson H. Jenkins argued and briefed; *Amicus Curiae Brief Supporting Prosecutor:* None; *Amicus Curiae Brief Supporting Defendant:* None.

Issue Presented: Whether the governor of New Jersey had authority to issue a reprieve of the defendant's execution and a subsequent death warrant for his execution?

Case Holding: The issue of whether the governor of New Jersey had authority to issue a reprieve of the defendant's execution and a subsequent death warrant for his execution, did not present a Federal question, therefore jurisdiction did not reside in Federal courts to address the matter.

Factual and procedural background of case: The defendant, Theodore Lambert, was convicted of capital murder and sentenced to death by the State of New Jersey. The New Jersey Supreme Court refused a direct appeal. Thereafter the governor of the State granted a reprieve. At the end of the reprieve the governor issued a death warrant for the defendant's execution. The defendant filed a petition for habeas corpus relief with the State appellate court which was refused. The defendant next filed a petition for habeas relief in a Federal District Court. In the petition the defendant alleged that the governor did not have authority to issue a reprieve of his execution. Consequently, since the initial execution date had passed, there was no authority in the governor to issue a death warrant for his execution. The Federal court dismissed the petition. The United States Supreme Court granted certiorari to consider the issue.

Opinion of the Court by Chief Justice Fuller: The Chief Justice ruled that the appeal had to be dismissed because it did not involve an issue for which the Court had jurisdiction over. The opinion reasoned as follows:

> ... The constitution of New Jersey provides that the governor shall have power "to grant reprieves to extend until the expiration of a time not exceeding ninety days, after conviction." The verdict was returned June 15th. Sentence was passed October 13th, and a reprieve for 30 days was granted December 4, 1894. [The defendant] contends that the word "conviction"

relates to the verdict of the jury, and not to the sentence of the court, and that, therefore, the governor had no power to grant the reprieve, nor subsequently to issue the warrant of execution. But the contention that [the defendant] cannot be made to pay the penalty for the crime of which he was adjudged guilty, because he was not executed at the time originally designated, by reason of the interposition of the governor at his instance, which [the defendant] alleges was, as matter of construction of the state constitution, unauthorized, was not sustained by the [state courts], to whom ... he applied, and their action is not open to review here. With the disposition of state questions by the appropriate state authorities, it is not the province of this court to interfere, and there is no basis for the suggestion of any violation of the constitution of the United States; the denial of due process of law; or deprivation of any right, privilege, or immunity secured to him by the constitution or laws of the United States.

The appeal was dismissed for lack of jurisdiction. *See also* **Clemency; Jurisdiction; Lambert v. Barrett (II)**

Lambert v. Barrett (II)

Court: United States Supreme Court; *Case Citation:* Lambert v. Barrett, 159 U.S. 660 (1895); *Argued:* Not reported; *Decided:* November 18, 1895; *Opinion of the Court:* Chief Justice Fuller; *Concurring Opinion:* None; *Dissenting Opinion:* None; *Appellate Defense Counsel:* John L. Semple argued and briefed; *Appellate Prosecution Counsel:* Wilson H. Jenkins argued and briefed; *Amicus Curiae Brief Supporting Prosecutor:* None; *Amicus Curiae Brief Supporting Defendant:* None.

Issue Presented: Whether the Constitution was violated because the governor of New Jersey issued a second death warrant against the defendant more than 90 days after the defendant's sentence?

Case Holding: The Constitution was not violated because the governor of New Jersey issued a second death warrant against the defendant more than 90 days after the defendant's sentence, as the matter was purely an issue of State law.

Factual and procedural background of case: The defendant, Theodore Lambert, was convicted of capital murder and sentenced to death by the State of New Jersey. The New Jersey Supreme Court refused a direct appeal. Thereafter the governor of the State granted a reprieve. At the end of the reprieve the governor issued a death warrant for the defendant's execution. The defendant filed a petition for habeas corpus relief with the State appellate court which was refused. The defendant next filed a petition for habeas relief in a Federal District Court. In the petition the defendant alleged that the governor did not have authority to issue a reprieve of his execution. Consequently, since the initial execution date had passed, there was no authority in the governor to issue a death warrant for his execution. The Federal court dismissed the petition. The United States Supreme Court granted certiorari to consider the issue. However, the Supreme Court determined that the matters raised by the defendant did not present a Federal question, therefore it did not have jurisdiction to decide matters brought in the appeal.

After the case was remanded to State court, the governor issued another death warrant setting a new execution date. The defendant thereafter filed a habeas petition in a State court, which petition was dismissed. The defendant then filed another habeas petition in the Federal District Court, arguing that the governor was without authority to issue a death warrant 90 days after his sentence. Further, that the second death warrant was in the nature of a new sentence, which could not be made without the presence of the defendant, and it placed him twice in jeopardy of his life in violation of the Federal Constitution. The Federal court dismissed the petition. The United States Supreme Court granted certiorari to consider the issue.

Opinion of the Court by Chief Justice Fuller: The Chief Justice held that the Constitution was not violated by the issuance of the second death warrant by the governor. The opinion addressed the matter as follows:

> The constitution of New Jersey provides that the governor may grant reprieves "to extend until the expiration of a time not exceeding 90 days after conviction"; and [under] the criminal procedure act of the state it is provided that when a reprieve is granted to any convict sentenced to the punishment of death, and he is not pardoned, it shall be the duty of the governor to issue his warrant to the sheriff of the proper county for the execution of the sentence at such time as is therein appointed and expressed. It is contended that, if there is no reprieve, there can be no warrant; that there was no authority to issue either, except within 90 days after conviction; and that [the defendant] must be brought before the trial court, and a new date be fixed for the execution. But these are matters for the determination of the state courts, and they appear to have been passed upon adversely to [the defendant]. That result involves no denial of due process of law, or the infraction of any provision of the constitution of the United States.

The judgment of the Federal District Court was affirmed. *See also* **Death Warrant; Lambert v. Barrett (I)**

Lambrix v. Singletary

Court: United States Supreme Court; *Case Citation:* Lambrix v. Singletary, 520 U.S. 771 (1997); *Argued:* January 15, 1997; *Decided:* May 12, 1997; *Opinion of the Court:* Justice Scalia; *Concurring Opinion:* None; *Dissenting Opinion:* Justice Stevens, in which Ginsburg and Breyer, JJ., joined; *Dissenting Opinion:* Justice O'Connor; *Appellate Defense Counsel:* Not reported; *Appellate Prosecution Counsel:* Not reported; *Amicus Curiae Brief Supporting Prosecutor:* Not reported; *Amicus Curiae Brief Supporting Defendant:* Not reported.

Issue Presented: Whether a death row inmate whose conviction became final before the decision in *Espinosa v. Florida* was rendered is foreclosed from relying on that decision in a Federal habeas corpus proceeding because the decision announced a new rule?

Case Holding: A death row inmate whose conviction became final before the decision in *Espinosa v. Florida* was rendered is foreclosed from relying on that decision in a Federal habeas corpus proceeding because the decision announced a new rule.

Factual and procedural background of case: The defendant, Cary Michael Lambrix, was convicted and sentenced to death for capital murder by the State of Florida. After his conviction and sentence were upheld on direct appeal and habeas corpus review by Florida courts, the defendant filed a habeas corpus petition in a Federal District Court. The District Court denied relief. The defendant appealed the denial to a Federal Court of Appeals. While the defendant's case was pending in the Court of Appeals, the United States Supreme Court rendered a decision in *Espinosa v. Florida*, which held that neither a trial court nor an advisory jury could weigh or consider an invalid statutory aggravating circumstance in deciding a capital defendant's sentence. The defendant argued to the Court of Appeals that *Espinosa* was applicable to his case, because the judge and advisory jury in his case weighed an invalid statutory aggravating circumstance in imposing his death sentence. The Court of Appeals affirmed the District Court's denial of relief, after ruling that *Espinosa* announced a new constitutional rule which could not be applied retroactively to his case. The United States Supreme Court granted certiorari to consider the issue.

Opinion of the Court by Justice Scalia: Justice Scalia held that a death row inmate whose conviction became final before *Espinosa* was decided was foreclosed from relying on that decision in a Federal habeas proceeding. It was said that in determining whether a new constitutional rule may be applied retroactively in a habeas proceeding a court must: (1) determine the date on which the defendant's conviction became final; (2) survey the legal landscape as it existed on that date to determine whether a State court then considering the defendant's claim would have felt compelled by existing precedent to conclude that the rule the defendant seeks was constitutionally required; and (3) if not, consider whether the relief sought falls within one of two narrow exceptions to nonretroactivity. The two narrow exceptions are that a new rule may be applied retroactively if it (1) placed an entire category of primary conduct beyond the reach of criminal law or prohibited imposition of a certain type of punishment for a class of defendants because of their status or offense; or (2) was a watershed rule of criminal procedure implicating a criminal proceeding's fundamental fairness and accuracy.

It was said that a survey of the legal landscape as of the date that the defendant's conviction became final revealed that *Espinosa* was not dictated by any existing precedent, and therefore it announced a new constitutional rule. Justice Scalia rejected the defendant's contention that the Court's decisions in *Baldwin v. Alabama* and *Godfrey v. Georgia* foreshadowed *Espinosa*. The opinion also ruled that *Espinosa's* new rule did not fall within either of the two narrow exceptions to the nonretroactivity doctrine. It was said that the first exception plainly had no application, since *Espinosa* did not decriminalize a class of conduct nor prohibit the imposition of capital punishment on a particular class of persons. Additionally, the second exception was inapplicable because *Espinosa* did not create a watershed rule of criminal procedure implicating a criminal proceeding's fundamental fairness and accuracy. The judgment of the Court of Appeals was affirmed.

Dissenting opinion by Justice Stevens, in which Gins- *burg and Breyer, JJ., joined:* Justice Stevens dissented from the Court's decision on the grounds that *Espinosa* did not create a new rule. He wrote in his dissent that: "Our decision in *Espinosa* did not create a new rule forbidding trial courts from curing a jury's error, rather it held that 'if a weighing State decides to place capital sentencing authority in two actors rather than one, neither actor must be permitted to weigh invalid aggravating circumstances.' This holding is a logical consequence of applying *Godfrey* to Florida's sentencing scheme."

Dissenting opinion by Justice O'Connor: Justice O'Connor dissented from the Court's decision on two grounds. First, she argued that the Court was wrong in not addressing the issue that the defendant's claim was barred because it was not raised timely in the State courts. Justice O'Connor contended that this issue had to be resolved before addressing the retroactivity issue. She indicated that the case should have been remanded to the Court of Appeals so that it could address the procedural default issue. As to the second ground of dissent, Justice O'Connor wrote that she agreed with Justice Stevens' position that *Espinosa* was not a new rule. *See also* **Baldwin v. Alabama; Espinosa v. Florida; Godfrey v. Georgia; Retroactive Application of a New Constitutional Rule**

Landmark Decision *see* **Binding Authority**

Lane v. Brown *Court:* United States Supreme Court; *Case Citation:* Lane v. Brown, 372 U.S. 477 (1963); *Argued:* January 16–17, 1963; *Decided:* March 18, 1963; *Opinion of the Court:* Justice Stewart; *Concurring Opinion:* Justice Harlan, in which Clark, J., joined; *Dissenting Opinion:* None; *Appellate Defense Counsel:* Nathan Levy argued; Joseph T. Helling on brief; *Appellate Prosecution Counsel:* William D. Ruckelshaus argued; Edwin K. Steers on brief; *Amicus Curiae Brief Supporting Prosecutor:* None; *Amicus Curiae Brief Supporting Defendant:* None.

Issue Presented: Whether the State of Indiana may constitutionally deny the defendant the right to have a free transcript of his coram nobis hearing for appeal purposes, solely because of his indigency?

Case Holding: The State of Indiana may not, consistent with the Constitution, deny the defendant the right to have a free transcript of his coram nobis hearing for appeal purposes, solely because of his indigency.

Factual and procedural background of case: The defendant, George Robert Brown, was convicted of capital murder and sentenced to death by the State of Indiana. After an unsuccessful appeal to the Indiana Supreme Court, the defendant filed a petition for a writ of coram nobis in the trial court. The trial court held a hearing on the petition, but denied relief. The defendant then requested a free copy of the transcript of the hearing for appeal purposes. The trial court denied the request for a free transcript. The defendant appealed the denial of free transcript to the Indiana Supreme Court. The appellate court ruled that the State did not have to provide the defendant with a free transcript even though he was indigent.

The defendant then filed a petition for habeas corpus relief with a Federal District Court, alleging that his Federal constitutional rights were violated by the State's refusal to provide him with a free transcript of his coram nobis hearing. The District Court held that Indiana deprived the defendant of a right secured by the Fourteenth Amendment by refusing him appellate review of the denial of a writ of error coram nobis solely because of his poverty. A Federal Court of Appeals affirmed. The United States Supreme Court granted certiorari to consider the issue.

Opinion of the Court by Justice Stewart: Justice Stewart observed that the rules of the Indiana Supreme Court expressly permit an appeal from the denial of a petition for a writ of coram nobis, but also require that a transcript be filed in order to confer jurisdiction upon the court to hear such an appeal. The opinion reasoned that a person with sufficient funds can appeal as of right to the Supreme Court of Indiana from the denial of a petition for a writ of coram nobis, but an indigent could be entirely cut off from any appeal at all. It was said that "the Court has held that a State with an appellate system which made available trial transcripts to those who could afford them was constitutionally required to provide means of affording adequate and effective appellate review to indigent defendants." Justice Stewart held that "once the State chooses to establish appellate review in criminal cases, it may not foreclose indigents from access to any phase of that procedure because of their poverty."

The opinion found that the State had deprived the defendant of a right secured by the Fourteenth Amendment by refusing him appellate review of the denial of his petition for a writ of coram nobis, solely because of his poverty. The opinion remanded the case to the District Court "so that appropriate orders may be entered ordering Brown's discharge from custody, unless within a reasonable time the State of Indiana provides him an appeal on the merits to the Supreme Court of Indiana from the denial of the writ of coram nobis."

Concurring opinion by Justice Harlan, in which Clark, J., joined: Justice Harlan concurred in the Court's decision. He expressed concern with the fact that the defendant's Public Defender counsel refused to assist in the appeal of the coram nobis petition, on the grounds that no issue of merit existed. Justice Harlan indicated that he believed the case should have been remanded with instructions to "the District Court to discharge the prisoner only if the Indiana Supreme Court fails, within a reasonable time, to accord him a review of the Public Defender's decision not to appeal the denial of coram nobis." *See also* **Coram Nobis; Transcript of Proceeding**

Lankford v. Idaho
Court: United States Supreme Court; *Case Citation:* Lankford v. Idaho, 500 U.S. 110 (1991); *Argued:* February 19, 1991; *Decided:* May 20, 1991; *Opinion of the Court:* Justice Stevens; *Concurring Opinion:* None; *Dissenting Opinion:* Justice Scalia, in which Rehnquist, C.J., and White and Souter, JJ., joined; *Appellate Defense Counsel:* Joan Marie Fisher argued; Timothy K. Ford on brief; *Appellate Prosecution Counsel:* Larry Echo Hawk argued; James T. Jones and Lynn E. Thomas on brief; *Amicus Curiae Brief Supporting Prosecutor:* None; *Amicus Curiae Brief Supporting Defendant:* None.

Issue Presented: Whether, at the time of the defendant's sentencing hearing, he and his counsel had adequate notice that the trial judge might sentence him to death?

Case Holding: The defendant's death sentence was imposed in violation of the Due Process Clause, because of inadequate notice that the trial judge was considering death as a possible sentence.

Factual and procedural background of case: On December 1, 1983, the State of Idaho charged the defendant, Bryan Lankford, with capital murder. During his arraignment the trial judge advised the defendant that the maximum punishment under State law that he could receive if convicted was life imprisonment or death. A jury found him guilty, and, prior to his sentencing hearing, the trial court entered an order requiring the State to provide notice whether it would seek the death penalty. The State filed a negative response, and there was no discussion of the death penalty as a possible sentence at the sentencing hearing, where both defense counsel and the prosecutor argued the merits of concurrent or consecutive, and fixed or indeterminate, sentence terms. At the conclusion of the sentencing, however, the trial judge sentenced the defendant to death.

In affirming the conviction and sentence, the Idaho Supreme Court rejected the defendant's claim that the trial court violated the Constitution by failing to give notice of its intention to consider imposing the death sentence, despite the State's notice that it was not seeking that penalty. The appellate court concluded that the express advice given the defendant at his arraignment, together with the terms of the Idaho Code, were sufficient notice to him that the death penalty might be imposed. The United States Supreme Court granted certiorari to consider the claim.

Opinion of the Court by Justice Stevens: Justice Stevens wrote that the sentencing process in the case violated the Due Process Clause because, at the time of the sentencing hearing, the defendant and his counsel did not have adequate notice that the judge might sentence him to death. The opinion noted that there was nothing in the record to indicate that the trial judge contemplated death as a possible sentence or to alert the parties that the real issue they should have been debating at the hearing was the choice between life and death.

It was said that if defense counsel had been given fair notice that the trial judge was contemplating a death sentence, presumably defense counsel would have advanced arguments at the sentencing hearing addressing the aggravating circumstances identified by the trial judge. No opportunity was presented for such a defense. The opinion held that it was unrealistic to assume that the notice provided by statute and the arraignment survived the State's response that it was not seeking the death penalty. Justice Stevens wrote that the trial judge's silence following that response had the practical effect of concealing from the parties the principal issues to be decided at the hearing. It was concluded that: "If notice is not given, and the adversary process is not permitted to function properly, there is an increased chance of error, and with that, the possibility of an incorrect result.... [The defendant's] lack of adequate notice that the judge was contemplating the imposition of the death sentence created an impermissible risk that the adversary process may have malfunctioned in this case. The judgment of the Idaho Supreme Court is reversed, and the case is remanded for further proceedings not inconsistent with this opinion."

Dissenting opinion by Justice Scalia, in which Rehnquist, C.J., and White and Souter, JJ., joined: Justice Scalia dissented from the majority opinion on the grounds that the defendant had adequate notice that he was subject to having the death penalty imposed against him. The dissent argued that the defendant knew that he had been convicted of capital murder and was told during his arraignment that he faced imprisonment for life or death. Justice Scalia concluded that: "Because Lankford has not established that his counsel had any basis reasonably to believe that the death penalty was, either legally or as a practical matter, out of the case — and indeed he has not even established that his counsel unreasonably believed that to be so — we have no cause to reverse the judgment of the Supreme Court of Idaho. In doing so, we seemingly adopt the topsy-turvy principle that the capital defendant cannot be presumed to know the law, but must be presumed to have detrimentally relied upon a misunderstanding of the law or a misinterpretation of the judge. I respectfully dissent."

Case note: The decision in the case is fact specific. That is, the decision did not hold that the Constitution required States provide defendants with notice (other than by statute) that the death penalty will be sought. The impact of the decision was limited to instances where a defendant has been misled into believing that he or she will not be subject to a sentence of death. *See also* **Notice of Intent to Seek Death Penalty**

Laos

Laos Capital punishment is recognized by Laos. Its legal system is based on French civil law and customary law. Laos promulgated a constitution on August 14, 1991. Laos is an authoritarian, one-party state ruled by the Laos People's Revolutionary Party. Although the nation's constitution provides for a system composed of executive branch, legislative branch, and judicial branch, in practice the Revolutionary Party governs the nation.

The judicial system of Laos consists of district courts, provincial courts, and a Supreme Court. Defendants have the right to public trials, the right to counsel, and enjoy a presumption of innocence. *See also* **International Capital Punishment Nations**

Larzelere, Gail Virginia

Larzelere, Gail Virginia On May 11, 1993 Virginia Gail Larzelere was sentenced to death by the State of Florida for masterminding the killing of her husband. Virginia was born on December 27, 1952. She was married to Dr. Norman Larzelere, a dentist, and she worked as the office manager for his dentistry practice. The couple had an adopted adult son named Jason.

On the afternoon of March 8, 1991, a masked gunman came into the Dr. Larzelere's dental office and shot him with a shotgun. Dr. Larzelere 'died within a short time after being shot.

Subsequent to the shooting Virginia and Jason were charged with the murder of Dr. Larzelere. Virginia's trial was held first. The prosecutor's theory was that Virginia and Jason conspired to kill Dr. Larzelere to obtain approximately $2 million in life insurance and $1 million in assets. To prove its theory, the prosecutor presented testimony from two of Virginia's former lovers. Both men testified that Virginia asked them to help her kill her husband. The prosecutor also called two other witnesses, Kristen Palmieri and Steven Heidle, who testified to a number of incriminating actions and statements made by Virginia regarding the murder. Palmieri and Heidle stated that Virginia told them that Jason committed the murder. Virginia gave Palmieri and Heidle the weapon used in the murder and told them to dispose of it.

Virginia Gail Larzelere was sentenced to death for conspiring to have her husband killed. The alleged co-conspirator, her adopted son, was acquitted of capital murder charges. (Florida Department of Corrections)

Additional evidence by the prosecutor showed that Virginia gave several conflicting versions of the murder to police, with differing descriptions of the gunman and the vehicle in which he left. A patient who was present at the time of the murder heard Dr. Larzelere call out just after he was shot, "Jason, is that you?" It was further established that within the six months preceding Dr. Larzelere's death, Virginia doubled the total amount payable on his life from over $1 million to over $2 million. In addition, evidence was introduced to show that Virginia gave false information and made false statements to obtain the policies. Further, soon after Dr. Larzelere's death, Virginia filed a fraudulent will, which left Dr. Larzelere's entire estate to her.

The jury found Virginia guilty as charged. During the penalty phase the jury recommended death by a seven-to-five vote. The trial judge sentenced Virginia to death. The Florida Supreme Court affirmed the judgment. Following Virginia's trial, Jason was tried but acquitted of all charges. *See also* **Women and Capital Punishment**

Last Execution of the 20th Century

Sammie Felder became the last person executed in the United States in the 20th century, when Texas executed him by lethal injection in December of 1999.

Felder, an African American, was born in Texas on August 23, 1945. Most of his adult life was spent in and out of prison. The crime which sent him to prison, never to be released alive, occurred on February 26, 1975. On that date Felder stabbed to death a paraplegic during a robbery. He was apprehended in Idaho and extradited back to Texas, where he confessed to the crime.

In 1976, Felder was convicted and sentenced to death. Eventually a Federal appellate court reversed the judgment, after finding Felder's confession was improperly obtained and admitted into evidence. Felder was retried in 1986, found guilty and sentenced to death a second time. On December 15, 1999 the State of Texas executed Felder by lethal injection. *See also* **First Execution of the 21st Century**

Last Meal

It is customary for a condemned inmate to be offered a last meal before execution. Records show that most inmates accept a last meal, though a few reject the offer. Prisons generally have a budget limit as to how much a condemned inmate may order for a last meal. Some prisons restrict the food to that provided in the prison, while others will allow meals to be purchased outside the prison.

LAST MEAL OF THE La-GRAND BROTHERS
Karl LaGrand executed by Arizona February 24, 1999
Two Bacon, Lettuce & Tomato sandwiches on white bread, Mayonnaise, 4 fried eggs, over-easy, Medium portion of hash-brown potatoes, 2 breakfast rolls, small portion of strawberry jelly. One half pint of pineapple sherbet ice cream, one 22 ounce of hot coffee, black, one medium slice of German chocolate cake with coconut-caramel icing, one 12 ounce cup of cold milk.
Walter LaGrand executed by Arizona March 3, 1999
Six fried eggs, cooked over-easy, 16 strips of bacon, one large portion of hash-browns, one pint of pineapple sherbet ice cream, one breakfast steak well done. One 16 ounce cup filled with ice, one 7UP, 1 Dr. Pepper, 1 Coke, one portion of hot sauce, one cup of coffee, two packets of sugar and four Rolaids tablets.

Last Statement

A ritual that has a long history in capital pun-

Dawud Abdullah Muhammad (aka David Junior Brown) gave the following last statement before his execution by the State of North Carolina on November 19, 1999: "Oh Allah, Oh Allah, condemn and lay a curse upon the killers of Dawud Abdullah Muhammad. Cursed be the people who did this injustice to me and cursed be the people who heard this and were pleased with it. Every true believer is a Hussain. Everywhere we go is Kabala. Everywhere we live is ashshura." (North Carolina Department of Corrections)

INMATE: Karla Faye Tucker   #   777

LAST STATEMENT:

Last statement of Karla Faye Tucker, who was executed by the State of Texas on February 3, 1998. (Texas Department of Corrections)

ishment, is that of asking a condemned person if he or she has a last statement to make before being executed. The last statement ritual has continued under modern capital punishment.

As a general matter, if a condemned person has a last statement to make, the statement will be transcribed verbatim by an official present during the execution. Occasionally a prisoner will make a lengthy last statement, in which case only a summary of the statement will be transcribed.

Latvia

The nation of Latvia maintains capital punishment, but abolished it for ordinary crimes in 1999. Latvia uses the firing squad to carry out the death penalty. Its legal system is based on civil law. Latvia first promulgated a constitution in 1922. Latvia regained its independence in 1991 after more than 50 years of being ruled by the former Soviet Union. The government consists of an executive branch, legislative branch, and judicial branch.

The judicial system of Latvia consists of trial courts, regional courts, and a Supreme Court. Defendants have a right to retained or appointed counsel, the right to confront witnesses, and a right to bail. Trials are generally public, but may be closed if state secrets might be revealed. Criminal cases are tried before a judge and two lay assessors. Defendants have the right to appeal. *See also* **International Capital Punishment Nations**

Law Enforcement Officer Aggravator The number of law enforcement officers killed in the line of duty has declined since the early 1970s. Between 1973–1979 there were 798 officers killed. During the entire decade of the 1980s there were 801 officers killed. For the period 1990–1998 there were 605 officers killed.

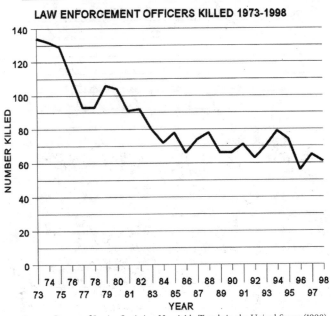

LAW ENFORCEMENT OFFICERS KILLED 1973-1998

Source: Bureau of Justice Statistics, Homicide Trends in the United States (1998).

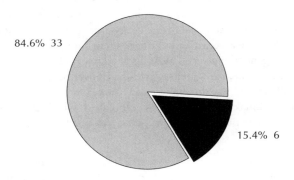

JURISDICTIONS USING LAW ENFORCEMENT OFFICER AGGRAVATOR

84.6% 33

15.4% 6

■ LAW ENFORCEMENT OFFICER AGGRAVATOR JURISDICTIONS
■ ALL OTHER JURISDICTIONS

The overwhelming majority of capital punishment jurisdictions have made the killing of a law enforcement officer a statutory aggravating circumstance. In these jurisdictions if it is determined at the penalty phase that the victim was a law enforcement officer killed in the performance of his or her duty, the death penalty may be imposed. *See also* **Aggravating Circumstances**

Law of Parties Various legal theories are available which permit a prosecutor to obtain a conviction of defendant for capital murder, even though he or she did not actually perform the act which resulted in the victim's death. One such legal theory is known as the law of parties.

Under the law of parties it is immaterial that the actual murder was not participated in by the defendant. Even where the actual killer is only convicted of a lesser included offense of murder, a co-defendant may be prosecuted for murder on the theory that he or she aided, abetted, counseled or procured the actual perpetrator to commit the homicide.

The law of parties does not apply at the penalty phase of a capital prosecution. At the penalty phase the jury is required to make its determination based solely on the conduct and perceived intent of the defendant and not the actions or intent of his or her co-defendants.

The law of parties is circumscribed by the limitation that the lethal force act must be (1) in furtherance of a crime, (2) in prosecution of a common design, or (3) an unlawful act the parties set out to accomplish. In determining whether a defendant should be prosecuted for murder as a party to a homicide, courts look at events occurring before, during and after the offense, as well as to the conduct of the parties which show an understanding and common design to kill the victim. The law of parties consists of four types of defendants: (1) principal in the first degree; (2) principal in the second degree; (3) accessory before the fact; and (4) accessory after the fact. Remarks about each follows.

Principal in the First Degree. A principal in the first degree is a defendant who, with the requisite mental state, actually performs the act which directly inflicts death upon a victim. Courts have held that a prosecution for murder may be sustained against a defendant as a principal in the first degree when the defendant and a co-defendant both shoot the victim, but it is not known which of the two actually fired the bullet that killed the victim. Moreover, where two or more persons take a direct part in a fatal beating of the victim, each participant may be prosecuted as principal in the first degree

Principal in the Second Degree. To be a principal in the second degree a defendant must (1) be present at the scene of the crime and (2) aid, abet, counsel, command or encourage the commission of the offense. The general rule is that one who aids and abets murder with the intent to assist the murder to completion may be prosecuted for capital murder. A principal in the second degree can be said to share the principal's intent to murder, when he or she knowingly intends to assist the principal in the commission of a crime and the murder is a natural and probable consequence of that crime. The Constitution does not prohibit jurisdictions from making a principal in the second degree equally responsible, as a matter of law, with a principal in the first degree.

A defendant may be convicted of first degree murder premised as a principal in the second degree, even though no other party was convicted of first degree murder. To establish a murder charge based on the theory of principal in the second degree, the prosecutor must show that (1) the defendant knew the crime was occurring, (2) the defendant associated him/herself with the effort to murder, (3) the defendant took part in murder as something he or she wished to bring about, and (4) the defendant committed some overt act to make the murder a success.

To prosecute a defendant for murder as a principal in the second degree, it is not necessary to prove an agreement between the defendant and another in advance of the criminal act or even at the time of the act. A defendant may be found constructively present and acting in concert with the principal in the first degree, if the defendant shared the criminal intent with the principal and the principal knew it.

Accessory Before the Fact. The general rule is that an accessory before the fact of murder may be prosecuted for murder. To be prosecuted as an accessory before the fact of murder (1) the defendant must have counseled, procured, commanded, encouraged, or aided the principal in killing the victim, (2) the principal must have murdered the victim, and (3) the defendant must not have been present when the killing occurred.

To successfully prosecute a defendant for murder as an accessory, the prosecutor must show the defendant had the intent to aid the principal and, in doing so, must have intended to commit the offense. A defendant may be prosecuted for first degree murder as an accessory before the fact, even though the principal pled guilty to second degree murder. A person who procures another to commit murder is an accessory before the fact of murder.

Accessory After the Fact. To sustain a charge of accessory after the fact, the prosecutor must show that (1) the principal committed murder, (2) the defendant aided the principal in evading arrest, punishment or escape, and (3) the defendant knew that principal committed the murder. An accessory after the fact may not constitutionally be punished with death.

Law of the Case Doctrine

The law of the case doctrine provides that when an appellate court renders a decision on a legal issue in a case and remands the case for further proceedings in a lower court, the appellate court will not revisit the issue previously decided by it, in any subsequent proceeding involving the case. Courts have recognized, in the context of capital punishment cases, a manifest injustice exception to the law of the case doctrine. Under this exception, an appellate court is obligated to revisit an issue it previously decided in the case in order to prevent a manifest injustice from occurring. *See also* **Dobbs v. Zant**

Lebanon

Capital punishment is recognized in Lebanon. Lebanon uses the firing squad and hanging to carry out the death penalty. In 1998, Lebanon executed two prisoners. Its legal system is a mixture of Ottoman law, canon law, Napoleonic code, and civil law. Lebanon promulgated its constitution on May 23, 1926. Lebanon is a parliamentary republic having an executive branch, legislative branch, and judicial branch.

The judicial system is composed of trial courts, Supreme Court, and Judicial Council (which tries national security offenses). Defendants have the right to counsel and the right to confront witnesses. *See also* **International Capital Punishment Nations**

Leland v. Oregon

Court: United States Supreme Court; *Case Citation:* Leland v. Oregon, 343 U.S. 790 (1952); *Argued:* January 29, 1952; *Decided:* June 9, 1952; *Opinion of the Court:* Justice Clark; *Concurring Opinion:* None; *Dissenting Opinion:* Justice Frankfurter, in which Black, J., joined; *Appellate Defense Counsel:* Thomas H. Ryan argued; Harold L. Davidson on brief; *Appellate Prosecution Counsel:* J. Raymond Carskadon and Charles Eugene Raymond argued; George Neuner on brief; *Amicus Curiae Brief Supporting Prosecutor:* None; *Amicus Curiae Brief Supporting Defendant:* None.

Issue Presented: Whether Oregon may constitutionally impose upon capital felons the burden of proving insanity, as an affirmative defense, beyond a reasonable doubt?

Case Holding: The Constitution is not offended by imposing upon capital felons the burden of proving insanity, as an affirmative defense, beyond a reasonable doubt.

Factual and procedural background of case: The defendant in the case, Leland, was charged by the State of Oregon with capital murder. He pleaded not guilty and gave notice of his intention to use the insanity defense. Under State law, the defendant was required to prove insanity beyond a reasonable doubt. The defendant was found guilty by a jury. The trial court sentenced the defendant to death.

One issue raised by the defendant on appeal to the Oregon Supreme Court, was that the federal Constitution prohibited requiring him to prove insanity beyond a reasonable doubt. The appellate court rejected the argument and affirmed the conviction and sentence. The United States Supreme Court granted certiorari to consider the defendant's claim.

Opinion of the Court by Justice Clark: Justice Clark recognized that Oregon was the only jurisdiction that required a capital felon prove insanity beyond a reasonable doubt. It was noted that most states require insanity be proven by the lower standard of preponderance of the evidence. The opinion found little constitutional significance in the different standards: "While there is an evident distinction between these two rules as to the quantum of proof required, we see no practical difference of such magnitude as to be significant in determining the constitutional question we face here. Oregon merely requires a heavier burden of proof. In each instance, in order to establish insanity as a complete defense to the charges preferred, the accused must prove that insanity. The fact that a practice is followed by a large number of states is not conclusive in a decision as to whether that practice accords with due process[.]"

Finding none of the defendant's arguments persuasive enough to impose the Constitution on this issue, Justice Clark wrote that "[w]e are therefore reluctant to interfere with Oregon's determination of its policy with respect to the burden of proof on the issue of sanity since we cannot say that policy violates generally accepted concepts of basic standards of justice." Of crucial significance to Justice Clark was the fact "that the burden of proof of guilt, and of all the necessary elements of guilt, was placed squarely upon the State. As the jury was told, this burden did not shift, but rested upon the State throughout the trial, just as, according to the instructions, [the defendant] was presumed to be innocent until the jury was convinced beyond a reasonable doubt that he was guilty." The opinion affirmed the judgment of the Oregon Supreme Court.

Dissenting opinion by Justice Frankfurter, in which Black, J., joined: Justice Frankfurter believed that constitutional due process prohibited Oregon from requiring the defendant prove insanity beyond a reasonable doubt. The dissent argued: "Because from the time that the law which we have inherited has emerged from dark and barbaric times, the conception of justice which has dominated our criminal law has refused to put an accused at the hazard of punishment if he fails to remove every reasonable doubt of his innocence in the minds of jurors. It is the duty of the Government to establish his guilt beyond a reasonable doubt. This notion— basic in our law and rightly one of the boasts of a free society—is a requirement and a safeguard of due process of law in the historic, procedural content of 'due process.' Accordingly there can be no doubt, I repeat, that a State cannot cast upon an accused the duty of establishing beyond a reasonable doubt that his was not the act which caused the death of another."

It was concluded by Justice Frankfurter that "it is a deprivation of life without due process to send a man to his doom if he cannot prove beyond a reasonable doubt that the physical events of homicide did not constitute murder because under the State's theory he was incapable of acting culpably." *See also* **Insanity Defense**

Lem Woon v. Oregon

Court: United States Supreme Court; *Case Citation:* Lem Woon v. Oregon, 229 U.S. 586 (1913); *Argued:* April 25, 1913; *Decided:* June 9, 1913; *Opinion of the Court:* Justice Pitney; *Concurring Opinion:* None; *Dissenting Opinion:* None; *Appellate Defense Counsel:* James E. Fenton argued; John F. Logan, Frank F. Freeman and Ralph E. Moody on brief; *Appellate Prosecution Counsel:* A. M. Crawford argued; Dan J. Malarkey and Walter H. Evans on brief; *Amicus Curiae Brief Supporting Prosecutor:* None; *Amicus Curiae Brief Supporting Defendant:* None.

Issue Presented: Whether the Federal Constitution required States to prosecute capital offenses by grand jury indictment?

Case Holding: The Federal Constitution does not require States to prosecute capital offenses by grand jury indictment.

Factual and procedural background of case: The defendant, Lem Woon, was charged with capital murder by the State of Oregon. The charge brought against the defendant was made in an information and not an indictment. However, prior to the defendant's trial an amendment to Oregon's constitution imposed a requirement that criminal prosecutions be made by grand jury indictment. The defendant was tried on the information and found guilty by a jury and sentenced to death. The Oregon Supreme Court affirmed the conviction and sentence. In doing so, the appellate court rejected the defendant's claim that due process of law required that he be prosecuted under an indictment. The United States Supreme Court granted certiorari to consider the issue.

Opinion of the Court by Justice Pitney: Justice Pitney ruled that the amendment to the State's constitution requiring prosecutions by indictment was to be applied prospectively, as was previously ruled by the Oregon Supreme Court. The opinion found that the issue of retroactive application of the amendment was purely a question of State law that did not invoke Federal constitutional law. The opinion also rejected the defendant's contention that, regardless of the amendment, he had a Federal constitutional right to be prosecuted by grand jury indictment. Justice Pitney wrote that "the 'due process of law' clause does not require the state to adopt the institution and procedure of a grand jury. *See also* **Grand Jury; Hurtado v. California; Prosecution by Information**

Lesotho

Lesotho recognizes capital punishment. Lesotho uses hanging as the method of carrying out the death penalty. Its legal system is based on English common law and Roman-Dutch law. Lesotho is a constitutional monarchy with King Letsie III as head of state. Lesotho promulgated its constitution on April 2, 1993. Under the constitution, the king fills only a ceremonial role. The government is run by Prime Minister Pakalitha Mosisili, in conjunction with a legislature and judiciary.

The judiciary consists of trial courts, a Court of Appeal and a High Court. Customary or traditional courts administer customary law in rural areas. Defendants have a right to a public trial, the right to bail, and the right to counsel. There is no right to trial by jury. Trials are presided over by a judge and two lay assessors. *See also* **International Capital Punishment Nations**

Lesser Included Offense Instruction

In a capital prosecution the death penalty cannot be imposed if the guilt phase jury was not permitted to consider a verdict of guilt of a lesser included offense that was supported by evidence. Lesser included offenses to capital murder include a conviction for any degree of noncapital murder (second or third degree murder), voluntary or involuntary manslaughter, or an attempt to commit murder or manslaughter. Constitutional due process requires that a lesser included offense instruction be given only when the evidence warrants such an instruction. If insufficient evidence is presented tending to establish a lesser included offense, then due process does not require an instruction on a lesser included offense.

Providing the jury with the option of convicting on a lesser included offense ensures that the jury will accord the defendant the full benefit of the reasonable doubt standard. When the evidence establishes that the defendant is guilty of a violent offense but leaves some doubt as to an element justifying conviction of a capital offense, the failure to give the jury such a lesser included offense instruction inevitably enhances the risk of an unwarranted conviction.

A few exceptions to the general rule requiring lesser included offense instructions be given have been carved out. One exception occurs in the context of a capital felon being prosecuted on alternative theories of murder, such as premeditated and felony murder. In this situation it has been held that a defendant is not entitled to a jury instruction on the lesser included offense under the felony murder theory, when the jury is instructed on the lesser included offense under the alternative theory. A second exception occurs when a State does not provide for lesser included offenses to any offense. There is no constitutional requirement of a lesser included offense instruction for capital murder in such situations. *See also* **Beck v. Alabama; Brown v. United States (II); Hopkins v. Reeves; Hopper v. Evans; Jury Instructions; Schad v. Arizona; Sparf v. United States**

Lethal Gas

The use of lethal gas as a method of execution is an early twentieth century Anglo-American jurisprudential phenomenon. The chemical agent used to carry out this method of execution is cyanide gas. Arizona was the first jurisdiction to actually have a gas chamber constructed.

Lethal gas was first used by Nevada. The first person to be executed by lethal gas was a condemned Nevada inmate named Gee Jon. He was executed, at age 29, on February 8, 1924. Gee Jon was born in China, but spent most of his life in the United States.

Gee Jon became the first person to be executed by lethal gas, when Nevada executed him on February 8, 1924. (Nevada State Library and Archives)

Lethal Gas Jurisdictions. As of January 2000, only five capital punishment jurisdictions provided for the use of lethal gas to execute the death penalty. Three jurisdictions, California, Missouri, and North Carolina, utilize lethal gas as a capital felon option. The two remaining jurisdictions, Mississippi and Wyoming, utilize lethal gas as a single fallback option. (Arizona allows inmates sentenced before 1992 to elect between lethal gas and lethal injection.)

Constitutionality of Lethal Gas. Several state appellate courts had, prior to 1983, addressed the issue of whether execution by lethal gas was a cruel and unusual method of punishment. The first such court to do so was the Nevada supreme court in the case of *State v. Gee Jon*, 211 P. 676 (Nev. 1923). This case involved two defendants, Gee Jon and Hughie Sing (Sing's sentence was eventually commuted to life imprisonment), who had been convicted and sentenced to death for

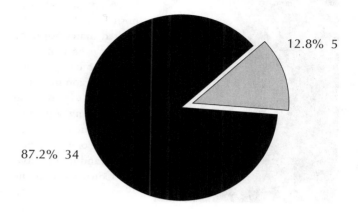

JURISDICTIONS WHERE LETHAL GAS IS ALLOWED

12.8% 5

87.2% 34

▧ LETHAL GAS JURISDICTIONS
■ NON-LETHAL GAS JURISDICTIONS

committing the crime of murder. At the time of their crime, the state of Nevada had but recently changed its method of execution to lethal gas.

The defendants challenged the use of lethal gas as cruel and unusual punishment. The court in *Gee Jon* rejected this argument. In doing so the court made the following observations.

> ... What has been the punishment for centuries for the crime of murder, of the character we know as murder in the first degree? It has been death. For the state to take the life of one who perpetrates a fiendish murder has from time immemorial been recognized as proper. The [statute] in question authorizes the taking of the life of a murderer as a penalty for the crime which he commits. It is the same penalty which has been exacted for ages — sanctioned in the old biblical law of "an eye for an eye and a tooth for a tooth." It is true that the penalty has been inflicted in different ways; for instance, by hanging, by shooting, and by electrocution; but in each case the method used has been to accomplish the same end, the death of the guilty party. Our statute inflicts no new punishment; it is the same old punishment, inflicted in a different manner, and we think it safe to say that in whatever way the death penalty is inflicted it must of necessity be more or less cruel.
>
> But we are not prepared to say that the infliction of the death penalty by the administration of lethal gas would of itself subject the victim to either pain or torture.... For many years animals have been put to death painlessly by the administration of poisonous gas.... No doubt gas may be administered so as to produce intense suffering. It is also true that one may be executed by hanging, shooting, or electrocution in such a bungling fashion as to produce the same result. But this is no argument against execution by either method.
>
> ... It may be said to be a scientific fact that a painless death may be caused by the administration of lethal gas.

Since 1983, three Federal appellate courts have addressed the issue of whether lethal gas is a cruel and unusual punishment. The federal appellate courts are split on this issue. Two appellate courts, *Gray v. Lucas*, 710 F.2d 1048 (5th Cir. 1983) and *Hunt v. Nuth*, 57 F.3d 1327 (4th Cir. 1995) concluded that lethal gas was not cruel and unusual punishment, while the third court, *Fierro v. Gomez*, 77 F.3d 301 (9th Cir. 1996),

Lethal gas chamber at San Quentin State Prison. (California Department of Corrections)

reversed, 117 S.Ct. 285 (1996), came to the opposite conclusion. The United States Supreme Court eventually vacated the court of appeals decision in *Fierro*, However, it did so without any guidance on the issue it reversed. In a terse one paragraph memorandum opinion, the Court vacated the *Fierro* decision and merely remanded the case with instructions that the appellate court reconsider its judgment in light of the fact that the jurisdiction in controversy (California) amended its death penalty statute so that lethal gas would be used only if requested by a capital felon.

EXECUTIONS PERFORMED BY LETHAL GAS 1976–1999

98.2% 587

1.8% 11

■ LETHAL GAS

■ ALL OTHER METHODS

Two arguments are offered against the use of lethal gas as a method of execution. First, it is asserted that cyanide gas induces excruciating pain. Capital felons have been known to urinate, defecate, vomit and drool while undergoing death by lethal gas. Second, and the primary threat to continued use of lethal gas, death by this method can take over ten minutes. It is argued that such a span of time amounts to pure torture.

Lethal Gas Protocol. In carrying out death by lethal gas the condemned inmate will have a heart monitor attached to his or her chest prior to the execution. The inmate is then led into the gas chamber where he or she is strapped into a large chair. The chair used will have holes in it to permit the gas to flow upwards. The gas chamber itself is air tight and has windows so the witnesses can view the execution. The heart monitor is

attached to an outside monitoring station so that the attending physician can declare the inmate dead.

Prison officials will place sulfuric acid in a large bowl below the inmate's chair. A small container of potassium cyanide is placed upon the sulfuric acid bowl. A switch located outside the gas chamber is used to empty the cyanide container into the bowl containing the sulfuric acid.

The effect of the cyanide gas will be to inhibit the body's ability to take in oxygen. The inmate will, in essence, strangle to death. The inmate will feel as if he or she is having a heart attack. Death usually occurs in 6 to 18 minutes.

After the execution ammonia gas will be pumped into the gas chamber to neutralize the cyanide gas. Prison officials wear gas masks when they enter the chamber to remove the body. *See also* **Methods of Execution**

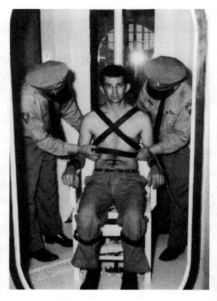

Walter Reppin is being strapped into the lethal gas chamber at the Colorado State Penitentiary in Canon City. Reppin's execution occurred on January 5, 1966. He was convicted of killing a taxi driver. (Denver Public Library)

Lethal Injection Lethal injection, as a method of execution, was not known to the common law. In the decision of *Ex Parte Granviel*, 561 S.W.2d 503 (Tex.Cr.App. 1978) the court noted that "[t]he intravenous injection of a lethal substance as a means of execution has not been heretofore utilized in this nation[.]" Injection of a barbiturate and a paralytic agent into the blood stream of a capital felon represents a new method of execution. Lethal injection, as this new method is called, is a child of the 1970s.

Oklahoma was the first jurisdiction to provide by statute for execution by lethal injection. It did so on May 10, 1977. The first State to actually execute a prisoner by lethal injection was Texas. It did

Lethal injection gurney. (California Department of Corrections)

so on December 7, 1982, when Charlie Brooks became the first inmate to die by lethal injection.

Lethal Injection Jurisdictions. As of March 2000, thirty-seven capital punishment jurisdictions utilize lethal injection as a method of carrying out the death penalty. The statutes in twelve of those jurisdictions provide for lethal injection as a capital felon option. The Federal government uses lethal injection for prosecutions under the 1988 Drug-Kingpin statute. The remaining lethal injection jurisdictions utilize this method exclusively. The statutes set out below illustrate how jurisdictions provide for the use of lethal injection.

> **Colorado Revised Statutes § 16-11-401 and 402:** The manner of inflicting the punishment of death shall be by the administration of a lethal injection.... For the purposes of this part ... "lethal injection" means a continuous intravenous injection of a lethal quantity of sodium thiopental or other equally or more effective substance sufficient to cause death....
>
> ... The execution shall be performed in the room or place by a person selected by the executive director and trained to administer intravenous injections. Death shall be pronounced by a licensed physician or a coroner according to accepted medical standards.

JURISDICTIONS WHERE LETHAL INJECTION IS ALLOWED

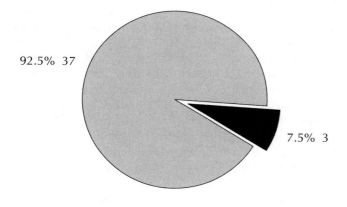

92.5% 37

7.5% 3

■ LETHAL INJECTION JURISDICTIONS

■ NON-LETHAL INJECTION JURISDICTIONS

Oregon Revised Statutes § 137.473: (1) The punishment of death shall be inflicted by the intravenous administration of a lethal quantity of an ultra-short-acting barbiturate in combination with a chemical paralytic agent and potassium chloride or other equally effective substances sufficient to cause death.... (2) The person who administers the lethal injection ... shall not thereby be considered to be engaged in the practice of medicine.

South Dakota Codified Laws § 23A-27A-32: ... The punishment of death shall be inflicted by the intravenous administration of a lethal quantity of an ultra-short-acting barbiturate in combination with a chemical paralytic agent and continuing the application thereof until the convict is pronounced dead by a licensed physician according to accepted standards of medical practice. An execution carried out by lethal injection shall be performed by a person selected by the warden and trained to administer the injection. The person administering the injection need not be a physician, registered nurse or licensed practical nurse.... Any infliction of the punishment of death by admin-

istration of the required lethal substance or substances in the manner required by this section may not be construed to be the practice of medicine and any pharmacist or pharmaceutical supplier is authorized to dispense the drugs to the warden without prescription, for carrying out the provisions of this section[.]

Two issues need to be highlighted regarding the above statutes. First, none of the statutes require that a medical professional administer the lethal drug. This issue has been a source of litigation by capital felons, who contend that the use of non-medical professionals increases the risk that death will be slow and agonizing.

A second matter involves the absence of a named ultra-short-acting barbiturate in the Oregon and South Dakota statutes. The Colorado statute designates (as an option) sodium thiopental as the lethal drug of choice. The majority of lethal injection jurisdictions follow Oregon and South Dakota in failing to name a specific lethal drug. This issue was litigated in *Ex Parte Granviel*, 561 S.W.2d 503 (Tex.Cr.App. 1978), where the defendant contended that failure to name a specific lethal drug made the death penalty statute vague and therefore constitutionally void. The defendant's position and the state's responses were set out in *Granviel* as follows:

> [The defendant] argues it cannot be ascertained from the statute what substance or substances can be used in the injection and that the statute fails to offer any hint as to which substance or substances would be permissible. The State points out that the ... electrocution statutes throughout the United States have not prescribed the use of a chair, the amount of voltage, the volume of amperage, the place of attachment of electrodes, or whether or not AC or DC current shall be used. The earlier hanging statutes did not, the State argues, prescribe the type of gallows, the height of the fall, the type of rope or type of knot used, etc. Likewise, the State says, the laws relating to execution by firing squads did not specify the number of executioners, the muzzle velocity of the rifles, the type of bullets, or the distance of the guns to the condemned. The State urges the earlier execution statutes were never in any greater detail than the statute under attack and that none of them had been declared unconstitutional on the basis of being vague.

The *Granviel* court rejected the defendant's vagueness challenge and held:

> While neither the exact substance to be injected nor the procedure surrounding the execution is expressly set forth in [the statute] we cannot conclude that failure to specify the exact substances and the procedure to be used render the statute unconstitutionally vague. The statute here, unlike penal statutes, was not intended to give fair notice of what specific behavior ... constitutes a criminal offense.... The context of the statute is a public statement of the general manner of execution. In this sense the statute is sufficiently definite....
>
> ... So long as the statute is sufficiently complete to accomplish the regulation of the particular matters falling within the Legislature's jurisdiction, the matters of detail that are reasonably necessary for the ultimate application, operation and enforcement of the law may be expressly delegated to the authority charged with the administration of the statute.

The position of the *Granviel* court was not that the issue of the type of lethal drug used was irrelevant. The opinion acknowledged that the issue of the drug of choice was highly relevant and important. However, the court believed that the drug of choice was a matter that could be delegated to administrative officials to determine.

Constitutionality of Lethal Injection. Lethal injection was devised as a method of execution because it is believed to be the most humane method of executing inmates. No attack on the constitutionality of lethal injection, per se, has ever succeeded. Even so, lethal injection has been criticized on various fronts, as being an unacceptable method of execution. It has been argued that utilizing a needle to interject death can be painful and necessitate surgery to impart the needle. It was reported that in a 1985 execution in Texas, it took a total of 23 attempts, covering a span of 40 minutes, to inject the needle in a capital felon.

Next, it has been argued that the drugs used do not always induce a quick and painless death. When death comes slow, it is contended that capital felons endure psychological trauma and in some instances physical pain.

EXECUTIONS PERFORMED BY LETHAL INJECTION 1976–1999

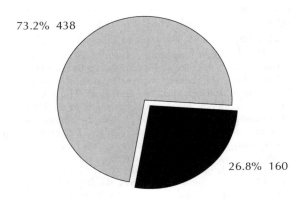

73.2% 438

26.8% 160

■ LETHAL INJECTION
■ ALL OTHER METHODS

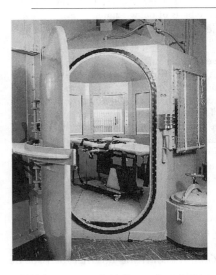

Lethal injection chamber at San Quentin State Prison. (California Department of Corrections)

The most thorny issue raised by opponents of lethal injection, is that the drugs used have not been approved by the Federal Food and Drug Administration (FDA) for the purpose in which they are being used. This issue was litigated in the United States Supreme Court in the case of *Heckler v. Chaney*, 470 U.S. 821 (1985). The Supreme Court rejected the challenge on procedural grounds, thereby keeping the debate alive.

Lethal Injection Protocol. An inmate executed by lethal injection is brought into the execution chamber a few minutes prior to the appointed time of execution. The inmate is placed on a gurney and his or her wrists and ankles are then strapped to the gurney. Cardiac monitor leads and a stethoscope are attached. Two sets of intravenous tubes are then inserted in each arm. Three commonly used drugs include: sodium pentothal (a sedative intended to put the inmate to sleep); pavulon (stops breathing and paralyzes the muscular system); and potassium chloride (causes the heart to stop). The sodium pentothal is injected first to put the inmate into a deep sleep. When the inmate is in a sedate mode, the other drugs are introduced into his or her body. (Some jurisdictions only use two drugs.) When done properly death by lethal injection is not painful and the inmate goes to sleep prior to the fatal effects of the pavulon and potassium chloride. *See also* **Heckler v. Chaney; Methods of Execution**

Lewis, James *see* Juveniles

Lewis v. Jeffers

Court: United States Supreme Court; *Case Citation:* Lewis v. Jeffers, 497 U.S. 764 (1990); *Argued:* February 21, 1990; *Decided:* June 27, 1990; *Opinion of the Court:* Justice O'Connor; *Concurring Opinion:* None; *Dissenting Opinion:* Justice Blackmun, in which Brennan, Marshall, and Stevens, JJ., joined; **Dissenting Statement:** Justice Brennan, in which Marshall, J., joined; *Appellate Defense Counsel:* James S. Liebman argued; Donald S. Klein and Frank P. Leto on brief; *Appellate Prosecution Counsel:* Gerald R. Grant argued; Robert K. Corbin and Jessica Gifford Funkhouser on brief; *Amicus Curiae Brief Supporting Prosecutor:* 1; *Amicus Curiae Brief Supporting Defendant:* None.

Issue Presented: Whether the construction given to the statutory aggravating circumstance "especially heinous, cruel or depraved manner," was vague as applied to the defendant?

Case Holding: The construction given to the statutory aggravating circumstance "especially heinous, cruel or depraved manner," was not vague as applied to the defendant.

Factual and procedural background of case: The defendant, Jimmie Wayne Jeffers, was convicted and sentenced to death for capital murder by the State of Arizona. On appeal to the Arizona Supreme Court the defendant argued that the statutory aggravating circumstance used to impose the death penalty, murder committed in an "especially heinous, cruel or depraved manner," was vague and unconstitutional. The appellate court rejected the argument and affirmed the conviction and sentence. In doing so, the appellate court noted its recent ruling that the infliction of gratuitous violence on the victim is among the factors to be considered in determining whether the murder was especially heinous and depraved. It found the presence of this factor in light of evidence that the defendant had climbed on top of the dead victim and hit her in the face several times, causing additional wounds and bleeding. The appellate court noted further that the apparent relish with which the defendant committed the murder is another relevant factor under its decisions, and concluded that the defendant's relish for his crime was evidenced by testimony that, while he was beating the dead victim, he called her a "bitch" and a "dirty snitch."

The defendant next filed a habeas corpus petition in a Federal District Court. The District Court denied relief. A Federal Court of Appeals granted relief to the defendant after finding that the "especially heinous, cruel or depraved manner" aggravating circumstance was unconstitutionally vague as applied to him. The United States Supreme Court granted certiorari to consider the issue.

Opinion of the Court by Justice O'Connor: Justice O'Connor ruled that the Court of Appeals erred in holding that the aggravating circumstance was vague. It was said that the construction given the aggravating circumstance by the State appellate court was approved by the Court in *Walton v. Arizona*. The opinion stressed that if a State has adopted a constitutionally narrow construction of a facially vague aggravating circumstance and has applied that construction to the facts of the particular case, the fundamental constitutional requirement of channeling and limiting the capital sentencer's discretion has been satisfied. The judgment of the Court of Appeals was reversed.

Dissenting opinion by Justice Blackmun, in which Brennan, Marshall, and Stevens, JJ., joined: Justice Blackmun dissented from the majority opinion in the case. He believed that the majority was wrong in relying on the decision in *Walton*, because in his opinion the *Walton* decision was wrongly decided. The dissent presented the argument as follows:

> I think it is important that we be frank about what is happening here. The death penalty laws of many States establish aggravating circumstances similar to the one at issue in this case. Since the statutory language defining these factors does not provide constitutionally adequate guidance, the constitutionality of the aggravating circumstances necessarily depends on the construction given by the State's highest court. We have expressed apparent approval of a limiting construction requiring "torture or serious physical abuse." This Court has not held that this is the only permissible construction of an aggravating circumstance of this kind, but, prior to today, we have never suggested that the aggravating factor can permissibly be construed in a manner that does not make reference to the suffering of the victim. The decision today will likely result in the execution of numerous inmates, in Arizona and elsewhere, who would not otherwise be put to death. Yet neither in this case nor in *Walton* has the Court articulated any argument in support of its decision. Nor has the majority undertaken any examination of the way in which this aggravating circumstance has been applied by the Arizona Supreme Court. Instead, the Court relies on a conspicuous bootstrap. Five Members have joined the majority opinion in *Walton*, which in a single sentence asserts without explanation that the majority cannot "fault" the Arizona Supreme Court's construction of the statutory term "depraved." In the present case, the same five Members proclaim themselves to be bound by this scrap of dictum. In any context, this would be a poor excuse for constitutional adjudication. In a capital case, it is deeply disturbing....
>
> ... The majority makes no effort to justify its holding that

the Arizona Supreme Court has placed constitutionally sufficient limitations on its "especially heinous ... or depraved" aggravating circumstance. Instead, the Court relies entirely on a sentence of dictum from today's opinion in *Walton*—an opinion which itself offers no rationale in support of the Court's conclusion. The dissenting opinion in *Walton* notes the Court's increasing tendency to review the constitutional claims of capital defendants in a perfunctory manner, but the Court's action in this case goes far beyond anything that is there observed.

Dissenting statement by Justice Brennan, in which Marshall, J., joined: Justice Brennan issued a statement referencing to his dissent in *Walton v. Arizona* as the basis for his dissent in this case. *See also* **Heinous, Atrocious, Cruel or Depraved Aggravator; Maynard v. Cartwright; Richmond v. Lewis; Shell v. Mississippi; Stringer v. Black; Walton v. Arizona**

Lewis v. United States

Court: United States Supreme Court; *Case Citation:* Lewis v. United States, 146 U.S. 370 (1892); *Argued:* Not reported; *Decided:* December 5, 1892; *Opinion of the Court:* Justice Shiras; *Concurring Opinion:* None; *Dissenting Opinion:* Justice Brewer; *Dissenting Statement:* Justice Brown; *Appellate Defense Counsel:* A. H. Garland argued; Hebe J. May on brief; *Appellate Prosecution Counsel:* United States Assistant Attorney General Parker argued and briefed; *Amicus Curiae Brief Supporting Prosecutor:* None; *Amicus Curiae Brief Supporting Defendant:* None.

Issue Presented: Whether the defendant had a right to be present when jurors were selected for his trial?

Case Holding: The defendant had a right to be present when jurors were selected for his trial, and a violation of that right invalidated his conviction and death sentence.

Factual and procedural background of case: The defendant, Alexander Lewis, was convicted of capital murder and sentenced to death by the United States. Federal jurisdiction was premised on the murder being committed on the lands of "the Cherokee Nation, in [Native American] country." During the selection of jurors for the trial, the trial court created two lists containing the names of 37 potential jurors. The trial court required the defendant and prosecutor to, independent of each other, make their "challenges" to the jury panel and without knowledge on the part of either as to what challenges had been made by the other. In his appeal to the United States Supreme Court, the defendant contended that his constitutional rights were violated by the method required for him to exercise his right to challenge potential jurors.

Opinion of the Court by Justice Shiras: Justice Shiras found that the defendant's rights were violated by the method imposed for selecting jurors. It was said that a leading principle that pervaded the entire law of criminal procedure was that, after an indictment was returned, nothing may be done in the absence of the defendant. The opinion held that "[i]t is the right of any one, when prosecuted on a capital or criminal charge, to be confronted with the accusers and witnesses; and it is within the scope of this right that he be present, not only when the jury are hearing his case, but at any subsequent stage when anything may be done in the prosecution by which he is to be affected." Justice Shiras noted that "the record in a capital case must show affirmatively the prisoner's presence in court, and that it was not allowable to indulge the presumption that everything was rightly done until the contrary appears."

The opinion concluded: "We do not think that the record affirmatively discloses that the [defendant] and the jury were brought face to face at the time the challenges were made, but we think that a fair reading of the record leads to the opposite conclusion, and that the [defendant] was not brought face to face with the jury until after the challenges had been made and the selected jurors were brought into the box to be sworn. Thus reading the record, and holding, as we do, that making of challenges was an essential part of the trial, and that it was one of the substantial rights of the [defendant] to be brought face to face with the jurors at the time when the challenges were made, we are brought to the conclusion that the record discloses an error for which the judgment of the court must be reversed." The judgment of the District Court was therefore reversed.

Dissenting opinion by Justice Brewer: Justice Brewer dissented from the Court's decision on the ground that the record was insufficient for the Court to make a ruling on the issue presented. He wrote: "Where the question is as to the inferences to be drawn from a record, it is well to have its very language before us. The entire record bearing upon the matters in controversy consists of a single journal entry and a portion of the bill of exceptions."

Dissenting statement by Justice Brown: Justice Brown issued a statement indicating he dissented from the Court's decision. *See also* **Jury Selection**

Leyra v. Denno *Court:* United States Supreme Court; *Case Citation:* Leyra v. Denno, 347 U.S. 556 (1954); *Argued:* April 28, 1954; *Decided:* June 1, 1954; *Opinion of the Court:* Justice Black; *Concurring Opinion:* None; *Dissenting Opinion:* Justice Minton, in which Reed and Burton, JJ., joined; *Justice Taking No Part in Decision:* Justice Jackson; *Appellate Defense Counsel:* Osmond K. Fraenkel argued; Frederick W. Scholem on brief; *Appellate Prosecution Counsel:* William I. Siegel argued; Nathaniel L. Goldstein, Wendell P. Brown, Samuel A. Hirshowitz and Edward S. Silver on brief; *Amicus Curiae Brief Supporting Prosecutor:* None; *Amicus Curiae Brief Supporting Defendant:* None.

Issue Presented: Whether the initial involuntary confession by the defendant tainted subsequent confessions, so as to preclude their use against the defendant?

Case Holding: The initial involuntary confession by the defendant tainted subsequent confessions, so as to preclude their use against the defendant.

Factual and procedural background of case: The defendant, Leyra, was arrested and charged with two capital murders by the State of New York. During his detention the defendant was interrogated extensively by police. The police brought in a psychiatrist with considerable knowledge of hypnosis and introduced him to the defendant as a "doctor" brought in to give him medical relief from a painful sinus condition. By skillful and suggestive questioning, threats and promises, the psychiatrist obtained a confession. The police were able to obtain additional confessions to the same crimes after the psychiatrist left.

At trial the prosecutor introduced the confession obtained by the psychiatrist. A jury convicted the defendant and he was sentenced to death. The New York Court of Appeals reversed the conviction on the ground that the confession was coerced. A second trial was held. At the second trial, the prosecutors introduced other confessions given to the police by the defendant. The defendant was again convicted and sentenced to death. The State appellate court affirmed the conviction and sentence. The defendant then filed a habeas corpus petition in a Federal District Court, alleging that the confessions used against him had been coerced. The District Court denied relief. A Federal Court of Appeals affirmed. The United States Supreme Court granted certiorari to consider the issue.

Opinion of the Court by Justice Black: Justice Black held that "[t]he use of confessions extracted in such a manner from a lone defendant unprotected by counsel is not consistent with the due process of law required by the Constitution[.]" He rejected the contention that the confessions were not tainted by the confession obtained by the psychiatrist. Justice Black wrote:

> The undisputed facts in this case are irreconcilable with [the defendant's] mental freedom "to confess to or deny a suspected participation in a crime," and the relation of the confessions made to the psychiatrist, the police captain and the state prosecutors is "so close that one must say the facts of one control the character of the other ...." All were simply parts of one continuous process. All were extracted in the same place within a period of about five hours as the climax of days and nights of intermittent, intensive police questioning. First, an already physically and emotionally exhausted suspect's ability to resist interrogation was broken to almost trance-like submission by use of the arts of a highly skilled psychiatrist. Then the confession [the defendant] began making to the psychiatrist was filled in and perfected by additional statements given in rapid succession to a police officer, a trusted friend, and two state prosecutors. We hold that use of confessions extracted in such ... is not consistent with due process of law....

The judgment of the Court of Appeals was reversed.

Dissenting opinion by Justice Minton, in which Reed and Burton, JJ., joined: Justice Minton dissented from the Court's decision. He believed the issue of the voluntariness of the confessions was a matter for the jury to decide. Justice Minton wrote:

> We are now asked to hold that the later confessions were involuntary as a matter of law and that [the defendant] was denied due process of law under the Fourteenth Amendment because the jury was allowed to consider the voluntariness of the subsequent confessions. It seems to me the very essence of due process to submit to a jury the question of whether these later confessions were tainted by the prior coercion and promises which led to the [initial] confession. I am familiar with no case in which this Court has ever held that an invalid confession ipso

facto invalidates all subsequent confessions as a matter of law. It does not seem to me a denial of due process for the State to allow the jury to say, under all the facts and circumstances in evidence and under proper instructions by the court, whether the subsequent confessions were tainted or were free and voluntary. *See also* **Right to Remain Silent**

Liberia   Liberia permits capital punishment. Liberia uses the firing squad and hanging to carry out the death penalty. Its legal system is based on Anglo-American law and customary law. The nation adopted its constitution on January 6, 1986.

The judicial system of Liberia consists of trial courts, appellate courts, and a Supreme Court. Under the laws of Liberia defendants have due process rights that include the right to counsel, to bail, and the right to confront witnesses. *See also* **International Capital Punishment Nations**

Libya   Capital punishment is allowed by Libya. Libya uses the firing squad and hanging to carry out the death penalty. The nation's legal system is based on Italian civil law and Islamic law. Its constitution was adopted on December 11, 1969. Libya has been ruled as a dictatorship by Colonel Mu'ammar Al-Qadhafi since 1969, when he led a military coup to overthrow the existing monarchy. In theory Libya is ruled by its people through a series of popular congresses, but in practice Colonel Qadhafi and his inner circle control political power. The judiciary is not independent of the government.

The judicial system consists of trial courts, appellate courts, and a Supreme Court. Special revolutionary courts exist to try political offenses. Although defendants have the right to counsel in Libya, the private practice of law is illegal. All lawyers must be members of the Secretariat of Justice. *See also* **International Capital Punishment Nations**

Liechtenstein   Capital punishment was officially abolished by Liechtenstein in 1987. *See also* **International Capital Punishment Nations**

Life Imprisonment   A defendant convicted of a capital offense does not have to be sentenced to death. The majority of capital punishment jurisdictions provide the alternative sentence of life imprisonment without parole, while a minority of jurisdictions permit the possibility of parole.

There are several ways in which a convicted capital felon may receive a sentence of life imprisonment with or without parole, instead of a sentence of death. First, the penalty phase factfinder may determine that the prosecutor failed to establish any statutory aggravating circumstances, in which case life imprisonment with or without parole is statutorily automatic. Second, the penalty phase factfinder, after finding at least one statutory aggravating circumstance exists, may nevertheless reject imposition of the death penalty and recommend or impose life imprisonment with or without parole. Third, the penalty phase factfinder may recommend the death penalty, but the trial judge may decide that based upon the

ALTERNATIVE TO DEATH SENTENCE PROVIDED BY JURISDICTIONS

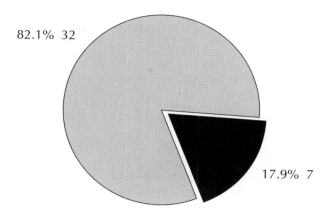

82.1% 32

17.9% 7

■ LIFE WITHOUT PAROLE JURISDICTIONS

■ LIFE WITH PAROLE JURISDICTIONS

evidence that a sentence of life imprisonment with or without parole is appropriate. Finally, appellate courts may impose life imprisonment with or without parole after finding an incurable prejudicial error occurred at the penalty phase when the capital felon was sentenced to death.

The argument has been made by capital felons, in life imprisonment without parole jurisdictions, that they have a right to have the penalty phase jury informed that if they are sentenced to life imprisonment, instead of death, they will not be eligible for parole. Capital felons argue that such information is a valid non-statutory mitigating circumstance for the jury to consider and that the Federal Constitution demands the penalty phase jury be informed about parole. Courts have responded, in general, that parole ineligibility is not a mitigating circumstance and, therefore, the Federal Constitution does not require penalty phase juries be informed about parole ineligibility. Notwithstanding the lack of a constitutional requirement, some courts have held that parole ineligibility is an appropriate matter for the penalty phase jury to consider in mitigation, when the prosecutor has argued the future dangerousness or continuing threat statutory aggravating circumstance.

A few capital punishment jurisdictions statutorily prohibit parole matters to be presented to the penalty phase jury. Capital felons sentenced to death in such jurisdictions have argued that their constitutional right to equal protection is violated by such statutes, because jurisdictions permit non-capital juries to be informed about parole matters. Courts addressing this argument have rejected it.

LIFESPARK   LIFESPARK is a non-profit organization located in Basel, Switzerland. The organization was founded in January of 1993. Barbara Haug, a Swiss nationalist, is the executive officer of LIFESPARK. Haug was appointed to the position in 1996. The primary impetus for the creation of the organization may be gleaned from this statement provided by LIFESPARK:

> Most of [the] world is moving swiftly toward complete rejection of the death penalty. But as country after country abolishes state-sanctioned killing, the USA continues to ignore this international trend. In a nation that many consider the standard bearer of human rights, over 3,500 men and women sit on death row. Nearly all of them are poor, many suffer from mental illness or mental retardation. A disproportionate number are people of color — some are innocent of the crimes for which they have been condemned to die.

The main initial focus of the group was on coordination of pen-friendship between death row inmates and European pen-pals. The scope of the organization expanded over time and it now seeks to build a powerful organization of anti–death penalty abolitionists. Internationally, LIFESPARK works with official humanitarian groups and religious bodies to develop and to promote anti–death penalty activism. At the grassroots level, the organization has linked with individuals and humanitarian groups, establishing relationships to foster a world-wide abolition effect by informing people on all issues of capital punishment.

LIFESPARK has taken part in numerous international anti–death penalty campaigns and initiatives, set up a support team to make available general information about the death penalty and specific information on scheduled executions. It has also initiated workshops, seminars and visits to schools. LIFESPARK has made financial support and legal help available to inmates on death row and coordinated visits on death row.

Lilly v. Virginia
Court: United States Supreme Court; *Case Citation:* Lilly v. Virginia, 119 S.Ct. 1887 (1999); *Argued:* March 29, 1999; *Decided:* June 10, 1999; *Plurality Opinion:* Justice Stevens announced the Court's judgment and delivered an opinion, in which Souter, Ginsburg, and Breyer, JJ., joined; *Concurring Opinion:* Justice Breyer; *Concurring Opinion:* Justice Scali; *Concurring Opinion:* Justice Thomas; *Concurring Opinion:* Chief Justice Rehnquist, in which O'Connor and Kennedy, JJ., joined; *Dissenting Opinion:* None; *Appellate Defense Counsel:* Not reported; *Appellate Prosecution Counsel:* Not reported; *Amicus Curiae Brief Supporting Prosecutor:* Not reported; *Amicus Curiae Brief Supporting Defendant:* Not reported.

Issue Presented: Whether the defendant's Sixth Amendment right to be confronted with the witnesses against him was violated by admitting into evidence at the guilt phase, a non-testifying accomplice's confession that contained statements which accused the defendant of committing murder?

Case Holding: The defendant's Sixth Amendment right to be confronted with the witnesses against him was violated by admitting into evidence at the guilt phase, a non-testifying accomplice's confession that contained statements which accused the defendant of committing murder.

Factual and procedural background of case: The defen-

dant, Benjamin Lilly, was charged with capital murder in the commission of a robbery by the State of Virginia. Two accomplices, Mark Lilly (defendant's brother) and Gary Barker, were also charged in the crime. The three men had separate trials. During the guilt phase of the defendant's trial the prosecutor called Mark Lilly as a witness against the defendant. Mark invoked his Fifth Amendment privilege against self-incrimination and refused to testify. Consequently, the prosecutor was allowed to introduce into evidence a written confession by Mark which implicated the defendant as the person who killed the robbery victim. Mark's confession was hearsay and inadmissible, but the trial court permitted its use under a hearsay exception for a declaration by an unavailable witness that is against the witness' penal interest. The jury convicted the defendant of capital murder and a sentence of death was imposed.

On appeal to the Virginia Supreme Court, the defendant argued that admission of Mark's confession violated the defendant's right to confront his accuser, as guaranteed under the Confrontation Clause of the Sixth Amendment. The appellate court rejected the argument and affirmed the conviction and sentence. The United States Supreme Court granted certiorari to consider the issue.

Plurality opinion in which Justice Stevens announced the Court's judgment and in which Souter, Ginsburg and Breyer, JJ., joined: Justice Stevens ruled that the admission of Mark's confession violated the defendant's Confrontation Clause rights. The opinion noted that the purpose of the Confrontation Clause is to ensure the reliability of evidence against a defendant, by subjecting it to rigorous testing in a criminal trial through cross examination of an adverse witness.

It was said that Mark's confession was inadmissible hearsay. The opinion pointed out that exceptions to the general exclusion of hearsay statements exist only where (1) the statements fall within a firmly rooted hearsay exception or (2) they contain particularized guarantees of trustworthiness such that adversarial testing would be expected to add little, if anything, to their reliability.

Justice Stevens indicated that hearsay statements are admissible under a firmly rooted hearsay exception when they fall within a hearsay category whose conditions have proven over time to remove all temptation to falsehood, and to enforce as strict an adherence to the truth as would the obligation of an oath and cross examination at a trial. One such firmly rooted hearsay exception involves statements that are against the declarant's penal or criminal interest. However, it was held that this exception cannot be extended to include admission of statements by an accomplice that shifts or spreads blame to a criminal defendant.

The opinion set aside the defendant's conviction and sentence and remanded the case for Virginia courts to consider whether the Confrontation Clause violation was harmless beyond a reasonable doubt.

Concurring opinion by Justice Breyer: Justice Breyer concurred in the Court's decision. He wrote separately to articulate concerns he had with Confrontation Clause analysis and hearsay analysis. He stated in the concurrence:

> As currently interpreted, the Confrontation Clause generally forbids the introduction of hearsay into a trial unless the evidence "falls within a firmly rooted hearsay exception" or otherwise possesses "particularized guarantees of trustworthiness."...
>
> Viewed in light of its traditional purposes, the current, hearsay-based Confrontation Clause test ... is both too narrow and too broad. The test is arguably too narrow insofar as it authorizes the admission of out-of-court statements prepared as testimony for a trial when such statements happen to fall within some well-recognized hearsay rule exception....
>
> At the same time, the current hearsay-based Confrontation Clause test is arguably too broad. It would make a constitutional issue out of the admission of any relevant hearsay statement, even if that hearsay statement is only tangentially related to the elements in dispute, or was made long before the crime occurred and without relation to the prospect of a future trial....
>
> We need not reexamine the current connection between the Confrontation Clause and the hearsay rule in this case, however, because the statements at issue violate the Clause regardless.

Concurring opinion by Justice Scalia: Justice Scalia indicated in his concurrence that a classic Confrontation Clause violation occurred in the case. He emphasized that "[s]ince the violation is clear, the case need be remanded only for a harmless-error determination."

Concurring opinion by Justice Thomas: Justice Thomas concurred in the Court's decision. His concurring opinion stressed his belief that the Confrontation Clause had limitations. He wrote: "Though I continue to adhere to my view that the Confrontation Clause 'extends to any witness who actually testifies at trial' and 'is implicated by extrajudicial statements only insofar as they are contained in formalized testimonial material, such as affidavits, depositions, prior testimony, or confessions,' I [believe] ... that the Clause does not impose a 'blanket ban on the government's use of accomplice statements that incriminate a defendant.' Such an approach not only departs from an original understanding of the Confrontation Clause but also freezes our jurisprudence by making trial court decisions excluding such statements virtually unreviewable...."

Concurring opinion by Chief Justice Rehnquist, in which O'Connor and Kennedy, JJ., joined: The Chief Justice concurred in the Court's judgment. He indicated that he was not prepared to give the Confrontation Clause the all-inclusive power intimated in the plurality opinion. The Chief Justice wrote: "This case ... does not raise the question whether the Confrontation Clause permits the admission of a genuinely self-inculpatory statement that also inculpates a codefendant.... A blanket ban on the government's use of accomplice statements that incriminate a defendant sweeps beyond this case's facts and this Court's precedents." *See also* **Confrontation Clause; Hearsay; Hearsay Exceptions**

Lincoln's Assassination

John Wilkes Booth was born in Bel Air, Maryland 1838. During the period 1860–1863 Booth was a successful actor of Shakespearean roles. However, the Civil War turned his life away from acting and into a diabolical plan to help the Confederate cause.

In 1864 Booth entered into a conspiracy with several others to abduct President Abraham Lincoln. The kidnapping conspiracy quickly died, but Booth's determination to avenge the Confederate loss of the war lived on. Eventually, Booth persuaded his conspirators to agree to killing President Lincoln, Vice President Andrew Johnson, Secretary of State William Seward, and General Ulysses S. Grant. The plan called for Secretary Seward and Vice President Johnson to be killed in their homes. President Lincoln and General Grant were to be killed during a theatrical performance at Ford's Theater in Washington, D.C.

On the night of April 14, 1865, Booth and his conspirators set their plan in motion. Secretary Seward was brutally attacked that evening in his home, but managed to survive. A conspirator stalked the residence of Vice President Johnson, but failed to make an attempt on his life. President Lincoln attended Ford's Theater, but General Grant did not. As the President sat in a box at the theater Booth shot him through the head. The President died 9 hours later.

Booth managed to escape from the theater with a broken leg, but was captured 12 days later in a barn near Bowling Green, Virginia. Booth was fatally shot while in the barn.

Immediately after the assassination authorities arrested hundreds of suspects. Eventually authorities narrowed down the suspects to eight people: Mary Surratt, David Herold, Lewis Paine, George Atzerodt, Edman Spangler, Michael O'Laughlin, Samuel Arnold, and Dr. Samuel Mudd. On May 1, 1865, President Johnson ordered the formation of a military commission to prosecute the conspirators. Paine was charged with conspiracy and the attempted assassination of Secretary Seward. Herold was charged with conspiracy, leading Paine to Secretary Seward's home, and assisting Booth to allude capture. Atzerodt was charged with conspiring to kill Vice President Johnson. Surratt was charged with conspiring with Booth and using her boardinghouse for the conspirators to meet. Dr. Mudd was charged with conspiring with Booth and

The execution of Lincoln's conspirators (left to right): *Mary Surratt, Lewis Paine, David Herold, and George Atzerodt. (National Archives)*

with aiding him after his escape. Arnold was charged with being part of Booth's earlier plot to kidnap President Lincoln. O'Laughlin was also charged with conspiracy to kidnap the President. Spangler was charged with helping Booth escape from Ford's Theatre.

The trial began on May 10, and lasted until June 30. It was held at the Old Arsenal Penitentiary (present-day Fort Mc-Nair). Judge Advocate General Joseph Holt of the United States Army presided over the trial. All of the defendants were found guilty. Surratt, Paine, Herold, and Atzerodt were sentenced to death. Mudd, Arnold, and O'Laughlin received life sentences. Spangler was sentenced to six years confinement.

On July 7, 1865 Surratt, Paine, Herold, and Atzerodt were hung by the neck until they were dead.

Lindbergh Kidnapping

On the evening of March 1, 1932, 20-month-old Charles Augustus Lindbergh, Jr., was kidnapped from the nursery on the second floor of his family's home near Hopewell, New Jersey. The child was the son of aviation pioneer and legend Charles Lindbergh and author Anne Morrow Lindbergh.

A ransom note demanding $50,000 was found on the nursery window sill. The local police were contacted. The ransom was paid on the night of April 2, 1932, in a New York cemetery. However, on May 12, 1932 the child was found dead from a skull fracture. His body was discovered in a wooded area about four miles from the Lindbergh home. A two year hunt for the murderer ensued. Eventually the investigation would be spearheaded by the Federal Bureau of Investigation.

Authorities got a break in the investigation when a man purchased $5 worth of gas from a Manhattan service station. The money had a serial number that matched one of the bills from the ransom money. An alert gas station attendant named Walter Lyle wrote down the vehicle license plate number of the man who gave him the money. The car was traced to its owner, Bruno Richard Hauptmann. On September 19, 1934 Hauptmann was arrested by New York authorities. He was eventually extradited to New Jersey in 1935 to stand trial for murder.

Hauptmann was a 35-year-old carpenter from Saxony, Germany. While in Germany he developed a criminal record that included robbery and time in prison. He illegally entered the United States as a stowaway on a German ship on July 13, 1923. Hauptmann remained in the country as an undetected illegal alien. He married a waitress named Anna Schoeffler on October 10, 1925. In 1933 the couple gave birth to a son.

Hauptmann's trial began on January 3, 1935, in Flemington, New Jersey. The evidence against him was circumstantial, but strong. Authorities found almost $14,000 from the ransom money in Hauptmann's garage. Shortly after the kidnapping he quit his job as a carpenter and began investing large sums of money on the stock exchange. Tool marks on the ladder used to climb into the Lindbergh home matched tools owned by Hauptmann. Wood in the ladder was found to match wood used as flooring in his attic. The telephone number and address of the ransom delivery drop person were found scrawled on a door frame inside a closet in his home. The handwriting on the ransom note matched samples of Hauptmann's handwriting. On February 13, 1935, the jury returned a verdict finding Hauptmann guilty of murder in the first degree. He was sentenced to death. On April 3, 1936, Hauptmann was electrocuted.

Bruno Richard Hauptmann was executed by the State of New Jersey on April 3, 1936. (New York City Police)

Lingg, Louis *see* Chicago Labor Riots of 1886

Lisenba v. California

Court: United States Supreme Court; *Case Citation:* Lisenba v. California, 314 U.S. 219 (1941); *Argued:* October 14–15, 1941; *Decided:* December 8, 1941; *Opinion of the Court:* Justice Roberts; *Concurring Opinion:* None; *Dissenting Opinion:* Justice Black, in which Douglas, J., joined; *Appellate Defense Counsel:* Morris Lavine argued and briefed; *Appellate Prosecution Counsel:* Everett W. Mattoon argued; Eugene D. Williams on brief; *Amicus Curiae Brief Supporting Prosecutor:* None; *Amicus Curiae Brief Supporting Defendant:* None.

Issue Presented: Whether the defendant's confessions were obtained and used in violation of the Constitution?

Case Holding: The defendant's confessions were not obtained or used in violation of the Constitution, even though the police used tactics that came close to the line of being constitutionally unacceptable.

Factual and procedural background of case: The defendant, Lisenba a.k.a. Robert James, was convicted of capital murder and sentenced to death by the State of California. The California Supreme Court affirmed the judgment. In doing so, the appellate court rejected the defendant's contention that his confessions were involuntary and therefore inadmissible at his trial. The United States Supreme Court granted certiorari to consider the issue.

Opinion of the Court by Justice Roberts: Justice Roberts held that the defendant's confessions were not obtained in violation of the Constitution, even though conduct used by the police in obtaining the confessions came close to the line of being constitutionally unacceptable. The opinion elaborated on due process principles involved in the use the confessions:

> The gravamen of [the defendant's] complaint is the unfairness of the use of his confessions, and what occurred in their

procurement is relevant only as it bears on that issue. On the other hand, the fact that the confessions have been conclusively adjudged by the decision below to be admissible under State law, notwithstanding the circumstances under which they were made, does not answer the question whether due process was lacking. The aim of the rule that a confession is inadmissible unless it was voluntarily made is to exclude false evidence. Tests are invoked to determine whether the inducement to speak was such that there is a fair risk the confession is false. These vary in the several states. This Court has formulated those which are to govern in trials in the federal courts. The Fourteenth Amendment leaves California free to adopt, by statute or decision, and to enforce such rule as she elects, whether it conform to that applied in the federal or in other state courts. But the adoption of the rule of her choice cannot foreclose inquiry as to whether, in a given case, the application of that rule works a deprivation of the [defendant's] life or liberty without due process of law. The aim of the requirement of due process is not to exclude presumptively false evidence, but to prevent fundamental unfairness in the use of evidence whether true or false. The criteria for decision of that question may differ from those appertaining to the State's rule as to the admissibility of a confession....

Like the Supreme Court of California, we disapprove the violations of law involved in the treatment of the [defendant], and we think it right to add that where a prisoner held incommunicado is subjected to questioning by officers for long periods, and deprived of the advice of counsel, we shall scrutinize the record with care to determine whether, by the use of his confession, he is deprived of liberty or life through tyrannical or oppressive means. Officers of the law must realize that if they indulge in such practices they may, in the end, defeat rather than further the ends of justice. Their lawless practices here took them close to the line. But on the facts as we [understood them], and in the light of the findings in the State courts, we cannot hold that the illegal conduct in which the law enforcement officers of California indulged by the prolonged questioning of the prisoner before arraignment, and in the absence of counsel, or their questioning ... coerced the confessions, the introduction of which is the infringement of due process of which the [defendant] complains. The [defendant] ... admits that no threats, promises, or acts of physical violence were offered him during this questioning or for eleven days preceding it. Counsel had been afforded full opportunity to see him and had advised him. He exhibited a self-possession, a coolness, and an acumen throughout his questioning, and at his trial, which negatives the view that he had so lost his freedom of action that the statements made were not his but were the result of the deprivation of his free choice to admit, to deny, or to refuse to answer.

The judgment of the California Supreme Court was affirmed.

Dissenting opinion by Justice Black, in which Douglas, J., joined: Justice Black dissented from the Court's decision. He argued that the confession was the result of coercion and compulsion. Justice Black outlined the facts upon which he dissented as follows:

Suspecting the defendant of murder they entered his home on Sunday, April 19, 1936, at 9 A.M. He was taken to a furnished house next door, in which the State's Attorney's office had installed a dictaphone. For the next forty-eight hours, or a little longer, the State's Attorney, his assistants, and investigators held James as their prisoner. He was so held not under indictment or warrant of arrest but by force. At about 4 A.M. Monday, one Southard, an investigator, "slapped" the defendant whose left ear was thereafter red and swollen. James was apparently kept at the State's Attorney's office during the daylight hours; the full extent to which he was questioned there is not clear. But on Monday and Tuesday nights, at the furnished house, with no one present but James and the officers, he was subjected to constant interrogation. The questioning officers divided themselves into squads, so that some could sleep while the others continued the questioning. The defendant got no sleep during the first forty-two hours after the officers seized him. And about 3:30 or 4 A.M. Tuesday morning, while sitting in the chair he occupied while being interrogated, at the very moment a question was being asked him, the defendant fell asleep. There he remained asleep until about 7 or 8 A.M. At about 11 A.M. the officers took him to jail and booked him on a charge of incest. During the entire forty-two hours defendant was held, he repeatedly denied any complicity in or knowledge of the murder of his wife.

The second episode during which the officers held defendant incommunicado, and which produced the confession, was on May 2 and in the early hours of May 3. About 11 A.M. on May 2 an investigator for the District Attorney took James from his cell to the chaplain's room of the jail. In the presence of an Assistant District Attorney he was confronted by [an accomplice] and told that [the accomplice] had made a confession implicating James in his wife's murder. James refused to talk and was then carried back to his cell. A short time later, under a purported order of court, the nature or authority of which does not appear, James was taken from the jail to his home, and then somewhere between 1 and 4 P.M. to the District Attorney's office. The doors were locked. From then until about midnight the District Attorney, his Assistants, and investigators, subjected James to constant interrogation. Upon asking for his attorney, James was told he was out of the city. He then asked for another but whatever efforts the officers made to satisfy this request were unsuccessful. He was again confronted with [the accomplice] but neither this nor the questioning had elicited an admission of any nature by midnight. At that time, according to the investigators, James said to one of them, "Can't we go out and get something to eat — if you fellows will take me out to eat now, I will tell you the story." He was taken out to eat by some of the officers, remained about an hour and a half, while at the restaurant made damaging admissions, and upon his return to the District Attorney's office, made the full statement which was used to bring about his conviction, completing it at about 3 A.M.

See also **Right to Remain Silent**

Literary Depictions of Capital Punishment
The print media has a long history of informing the American public about capital punishment. Hundreds of thousands of books have appeared which depict capital punishment from all perspectives. Such depictions include fictional and nonfictional accounts of capital punishment.

One of the areas most frequently written on is that of the actual life and murders of capital felons. Historically the public has had an unquenchable thirst for reading about the personalities that end up on death row. To some extent, literary tales of the life and times of capital felons has created a unique fraternity of celebrities. Death row inmates like Danny Rolling, Mumia Abu-Jamal, Richard Ramirez, and Aileen Carol Wuornos have garnered a flock of supporters and followers, as a result of literary accounts of the capital crimes they were sentenced to death for committing.

Listed below is a sampling of some of the literary work on specific capital felons and their crimes: Truman Capote, *In Cold Blood* (1966); Robert Graysmith, *The Sleeping Lady: The*

Trailside Murders Above the Golden Gate (1991); Paul Avrich, *Sacco & Vanzetti: The Anarchist Background* (1991); Burton B. Turkus and Sid Feder, *Murder, Inc.: The Story of the Syndicate* (1992); Joseph Harrington and Robert Burger, *Eye of Evil* (1993); Chris Anderson and Sharon McGehee, *Bodies of Evidence: The True Story of Judias Buenoano Florida's Serial Murderess* (1993); Dennis L. Breo and William J. Martin, *The Crime of the Century: Richard Speck and the Murder of Eight Nurses* (1993); Phyllis Chesler, *A Woman's Right to Self-Defense: The Case of Aileen Carol Wuornos* (1994); Polly Nelson, *Defending the Devil: My Story as Ted Bundy's Last Lawyer* (1994); Jim Thompson, *The Transgressors* (1994); Susan Kelly, *Boston Strangler: The Wrongful Conviction of Albert Desalvo and the True Story of Eleven Shocking Murders* (1995); John Gilmore and Rod Kenner, *The Garbage People: The Trip to Helter-Skelter and Beyond with Charlie Manson and the Family* (1995); Jaye Slade Fletcher, *Deadly Thrills: True Story of Chicago's Most Shocking Killers* (1995); John Grisham, *The Chamber* (1995); Danny Rolling and Sondra London, *The Making of a Serial Killer: The Real Story of the Gainesville Murders in the Killers Own Words* (1996); Philip Carlo, *The Night Stalker: The Life and Crimes of Richard Ramirez* (1996); Terry Sullivan and Peter T. Maiken, *Killer Clown: The John Wayne Gacy Murders* (1997); Mumia Abu-Jamal and Cornel West, *Death Blossoms: Reflections from a Prisoner of Conscience* (1997); Ernest J. Gaines, *A Lesson Before Dying* (1997); Andrew Klavan, *True Crime* (1997); Harold Schechter, *Depraved: The Shocking True Story of America's First Serial Killer* (1998); Harold Schechter, *Deranged: The Shocking True Story of America's Most Fiendish Killer* (1998); Norman Mailer, *Executioner's Song* (1998); Clifford L. Linedecker, *The Vampire Killers,* (1998); Donald A. Cabana, *Death at Midnight: The Confession of an Executioner* (1998); Stephen King, *The Green Mile* (1999); Sharyn McCrumb & Sharyn McCrub, *The Ballad of Frankie Silver* (1999). *See also* **Film Depictions of Capital Punishment**

Lithuania Lithuania abolished capital punishment in 1998. *See also* **International Capital Punishment Nations**

Livingston, Henry B. Henry B. Livingston served as an associate justice of the United States Supreme Court from 1807 to 1823. While on the Supreme Court Livingston was known as a conservative interpreter of the Constitution.

Livingston was born in New York City on November 25, 1757. He was educated at Princeton and was admitted to the New York bar in 1783. Livingston maintained a private legal practice for a number of years before being appointed a judge on the New York supreme court. In 1807 President Thomas Jefferson appointed Livingston to the Supreme Court.

While on the Supreme Court Livingston was known to have written only one capital punishment opinion. The case of *United States v. Smith* presented a certified question from a Federal trial court. The question presented was whether the defendant could be punished with death under the Piracy Act for plundering a ship. The majority in *Smith* answered the

question affirmatively. Livingston wrote a dissenting opinion. He argued that the Piracy Act provision under review violated the Constitution, because it defined piratical acts to mean anything that was on the law books involving the law of nations. Livingston died on March 18, 1823.

Local Government Executions Prior to the late 1800s all executions were carried out by local government officials, such as county sheriffs. A movement was begun in the late 1800s, to place the authority of carrying out executions exclusively in control of the State. This movement slowly swept the country until all jurisdictions placed responsibility for carrying out executions by the State (and Federal government). Under modern capital punishment law, no local government has authority to execute any prisoner. *See also* **McNulty v. California; Public Viewing of Execution**

Lockett v. Ohio *Court:* United States Supreme Court; *Case Citation:* Lockett v. Ohio, 438 U.S. 586 (1978); *Argued:* January 17, 1978; *Decided:* July 3, 1978; *Plurality Opinion:* Chief Justice Burger, announced the Court's judgment and delivered an opinion, in which Stewart, Powell and Stevens JJ., joined; *Concurring Opinion:* Justice Blackmun; *Concurring Opinion:* Justice Marshal; *Concurring and Dissenting Opinion:* Justice Whit; *Concurring and Dissenting Opinion:* Justice Rehnquist; *Justice Not Participating:* Justice Brennan; *Appellate Defense Counsel:* Anthony G. Amsterdam argued; Max Kravitz, Jack Greenberg, James M. Nabrit III, Joel Berger, David E. Kendall, and Peggy C. Davis on brief; *Appellate Prosecution Counsel:* Carl M. Layman III argued; Stephan M. Gabalac and James A. Rudgers on brief; *Amicus Curiae Brief Supporting Prosecutor:* None; *Amicus Curiae Brief Supporting Defendant:* None.

Issue Presented: Whether Ohio's death penalty statute violated the Constitution by limiting the sentencer's discretion to consider the circumstances of the crime and the record and character of the capital offender as mitigating factors?

Case Holding: The limited range of mitigating circumstances that may be considered by the sentencer under the Ohio death penalty statute violates the Eighth and Fourteenth Amendments.

Factual and procedural background of case: The defendant, Sandra Lockett, was convicted of capital murder and sentenced to death by an Ohio court. The defendant appealed and argued, among other matters, that Ohio's death penalty statute did not give the penalty phase three-judge panel a full opportunity to consider mitigating circumstances in capital cases as required by the Federal Constitution. The Ohio Supreme Court rejected the claim and affirmed the conviction and sentence. The United States Supreme Court granted certiorari to consider the case.

Plurality opinion in which Chief Justice Burger announced the Court's judgment and in which Stewart, Powell and Stevens JJ., joined: The plurality opinion pointed out that the Ohio death penalty statute limited mitigating circumstances that could be considered at the penalty phase of a capital prosecution, to only the three factors specified in the statute, and once it is determined that none of those factors is present, the statute mandates the death sentence. The Chief Justice explained that the need for treating each defendant in a capital case with the degree of respect due the uniqueness of the individual, is far more important than in noncapital cases, particularly in view of the unavailability of such post-conviction mechanisms in noncapital cases as probation, parole, and work furloughs.

The opinion concluded that: "There is no perfect procedure for deciding in which cases governmental authority should be used to impose death. But a statute that prevents the sentencer in all capital cases from giving independent mitigating weight to aspects of the defendant's character and record and to circumstances of the offense proffered in mitigation creates the risk that the death penalty will be imposed in spite of factors which may call for a less severe penalty. When the choice is between life and death, that risk is unacceptable and incompatible with the commands of the Eighth and Fourteenth Amendments." The judgment of the Ohio Supreme Court, insofar as affirming the death sentence, was reversed.

Concurring opinion by Justice Blackmun: Justice Blackmun wrote in his concurrence that he "would reverse the judgment of the Supreme Court of Ohio insofar as it upheld the imposition of the death penalty on [the defendant], but [he] would do so for a reason more limited than that which the plurality espouses, and for an additional reason not relied upon by the plurality."

The concurring opinion indicated that the death sentence should have been reversed on the grounds that (1) the Ohio death penalty statute was deficient in regard to the defendant, insofar as excluding consideration of her limited role in the crime as an aider and abettor, and (2) the criminal procedure rules of Ohio improperly gave the sentencing court full discretion to bar the death sentence in the interests of justice if a defendant pleads guilty or no contest, but no such discretion is given if the defendant goes to trial.

Concurring opinion by Justice Marshall: Justice Marshall concurred in the Court's judgment by indicating his longstanding belief that the Constitution prohibits imposition of the death penalty. He also added that: "When a death sentence is imposed under the circumstances presented here, I fail to understand how any of my Brethren — even those who believe that the death penalty is not wholly inconsistent with the Constitution — can disagree that it must be vacated. Under the Ohio death penalty statute, this [defendant] was sentenced to death for a killing that she did not actually commit or intend to commit. She was convicted under a theory of vicarious liability. The imposition of the death penalty for this crime totally violates the principle of proportionality embodied in the Eighth Amendment's prohibition."

Concurring and dissenting opinion by Justice White: Justice White concurred in the Court's judgment on the basis "that it violates the Eighth Amendment to impose the penalty

of death without a finding that the defendant possessed a purpose to cause the death of the victim." Justice White dissented from the plurality's conclusion "that the sentencer may constitutionally impose the death penalty only as an exercise of his unguided discretion after being presented with all circumstances which the defendant might believe to be conceivably relevant to the appropriateness of the penalty for the individual offender."

It was reasoned by Justice White in dissent that: "[T]he effect of the Court's decision today will be to compel constitutionally a restoration of the state of affairs at the time *Furman* was decided, where the death penalty is imposed so erratically and the threat of execution is so attenuated for even the most atrocious murders that 'its imposition would then be the pointless and needless extinction of life with only marginal contributions to any discernible social or public purposes.' By requiring as a matter of constitutional law that sentencing authorities be permitted to consider and in their discretion to act upon any and all mitigating circumstances, the Court permits them to refuse to impose the death penalty no matter what the circumstances of the crime. This invites a return to the pre–*Furman* days when the death penalty was generally reserved for those very few for whom society has least consideration."

Concurring and dissenting opinion by Justice Rehnquist: Justice Rehnquist concurred with the Court's resolution of meritless and nondispositive issues in the case that were decided against the defendant (not reproduced or discussed here). He dissented with the Court's decision to vacate the death sentence on the basis of the restriction Ohio's death penalty statute placed on mitigating circumstances. He wrote that "[s]ince all of [the defendant's] claims appear to me to be without merit, I would affirm the judgment of the Supreme Court of Ohio."

Case note: The decision in this case has had a tremendous impact on the penalty phase of capital prosecutions. The effect of the decision was to allow capital felons to introduce all relevant evidence at the penalty phase. Courts cannot exclude or limit any relevant mitigating evidence proffered by capital felons at the penalty phase, because under the decision in this case, to do so would violate the constitution. In subsequent decisions the Court has made clear that capital felons do not have a constitutional right to introduce or have the penalty phase jury instructed on nonrelevant mitigating evidence. *See also* **Bell v. Ohio; Delo v. Lashley; Eddings v. Oklahoma; Hitchcock v. Dugger; Mitigating Circumstances; Skipper v. South Carolina**

Lockhart v. Fretwell *Court:* United States Supreme Court; *Case Citation:* Lockhart v. Fretwell, 506 U.S. 364 (1993); *Argued:* November 3, 1992; *Decided:* January 25, 1993; *Opinion of the Court:* Chief Justice Rehnquist; *Concurring Opinion:* Justice O'Connor; *Concurring Opinion:* Justice Thomas; *Dissenting Opinion:* Justice Stevens, in which Blackmun, J., joined; *Appellate Defense Counsel:* Ricky R. Medlock argued and briefed; *Appellate Prosecution Counsel:* Winston Bryant argued; Clint Miller and J. Brent Standridge on brief; *Amicus Curiae Brief Supporting Prosecutor:* None; *Amicus Curiae Brief Supporting Defendant:* 4.

Issue Presented: Whether defense counsel's failure to make an objection at the defendant's sentencing proceeding—an objection that would have been supported by a decision which subsequently was overruled—constituted "prejudice" within the meaning of *Strickland v. Washington?*

Case Holding: Because the law which formed the basis of the defendant's ineffective assistance claim was overruled, so that the complained of deficient performance of his counsel no longer existed, the defendant suffered no prejudice from the deficient performance within the meaning of *Strickland v. Washington.*

Factual and procedural background of case: The defendant, Bobby Ray Fretwell, was convicted and sentenced to death for capital murder by the State of Arkansas. After exhausting State post-conviction remedies, the defendant filed a habeas corpus petition in a Federal District Court. The defendant alleged ineffective assistance of counsel at the penalty phase of his trial, on the grounds that his attorney did not object to the use of a statutory aggravating circumstance that was also used at the guilt phase as part of the capital offense. At the time of the defendant's trial, a Federal court had found such duplication unconstitutional (that decision was later overruled). The District Court granted habeas relief to the defendant, after concluding his counsel's failure to raise the objection amounted to prejudice under the United States Supreme Court decision in *Strickland v. Washington.* A Federal Court of Appeals affirmed the District Court's decision. The United States Supreme Court granted certiorari to consider the issue.

Opinion of the Court by Chief Justice Rehnquist: The Chief Justice ruled that defense counsel's failure to make the complained of objection during the sentencing proceeding did not constitute prejudice within the meaning of *Strickland.* The opinion noted that under *Strickland,* ineffective assistance of counsel requires proof of (1) deficient performance and (2) resulting prejudice. It was said that to show prejudice under *Strickland,* a defendant must demonstrate that counsel's errors are so serious as to deprive him or her of a trial whose result is unfair or unreliable, not merely that the outcome would have been different. The Chief Justice reasoned that unfairness or unreliability did not result unless defense counsel's ineffectiveness deprives the defendant of a substantive or procedural right to which the law entitles him or her. It was said that the defendant's sentencing proceeding was neither unfair nor unreliable, because the case in which he relied to show that his attorney had a basis to make an objection, was overruled. Therefore, the defendant suffered no prejudice from his counsel's deficient performance.

The opinion rejected the defendant's argument that prejudice is determined under the laws existing at the time of trial. The Chief Justice wrote that although contemporary assessment of defense counsel's conduct is used when determining the deficient performance component of the *Strickland* test, the prejudice component was not dependent upon analysis under the law existing at the time of the deficient performance. The decision of the Court of Appeals was reversed.

Concurring opinion by Justice O'Connor: Justice O'Connor concurred in the Court's decision. She believed that the defendant's claim had merit during his trial, because a judicial opinion existed at that time which supported an objection to the duplication of guilt phase offense elements with penalty phase statutory aggravating circumstances. However, she agreed with the Court's opinion that the force of the defendant's argument was lost because the judicial decision upon which the defendant relied was overruled, so that the complained of duplication was now constitutionally valid.

Concurring opinion by Justice Thomas: Justice Thomas concurred in the Court's decision. He indicated that the Court of Appeals wrongly based its decision on the belief that the courts of Arkansas would have been bound to follow the lower Federal court decision that had previously found unconstitutional the duplication of guilt phase offense elements with penalty phase aggravating circumstances. Justice Thomas wrote as follows: "The Supremacy Clause demands that state law yield to federal law, but neither federal supremacy nor any other principle of federal law requires that a state court's interpretation of federal law give way to a (lower) federal court's interpretation. In our federal system, a state trial court's interpretation of federal law is no less authoritative than that of the federal court of appeals in whose circuit the trial court is located. An Arkansas trial court is bound by this Court's (and by the Arkansas Supreme Court's and Arkansas Court of Appeals') interpretation of federal law, but if it follows [a federal court of appeals'] interpretation of federal law, it does so only because it chooses to, and not because it must."

Dissenting opinion by Justice Stevens, in which Blackmun, J., joined: Justice Stevens dissented from the majority's decision in the case. He argued against the Court's the new construction of the "prejudice" component of the *Strickland* test. Justice Stevens also indicated that he disapproved of the Court's creation of the new rule under *Strickland,* when all of the Court's precedents held that new constitutional rules would not be created or applied to capital cases that became final before the new rule was created. He believed the Court was using a double-standard in which the bar against retroactive application of a new rule applied to capital defendants, but did not apply to governments. *See also* **Right to Counsel**

Lonchar v. Thomas *Court:* United States Supreme Court; *Case Citation:* Lonchar v. Thomas, 517 U.S. 314 (1996); *Argued:* December 4, 1995; *Decided:* April 1, 1996; *Opinion of the Court:* Justice Breyer; *Concurring Opinion:* Chief Justice Rehnquist, in which Scalia, Kennedy and Thomas, JJ., joined; *Dissenting Opinion:* None; *Appellate Defense Counsel:* Not reported; *Appellate Prosecution Counsel:* Not reported; *Amicus Curiae Brief Supporting Prosecutor:* Not reported; *Amicus Curiae Brief Supporting Defendant:* Not reported.

Issue Presented: Whether a Federal court may deny a stay of execution and dismiss a first Federal habeas petition for general equitable reasons?

Case Holding: A Federal court may not deny a stay of execution and dismiss a first Federal habeas petition for general equitable reasons.

Factual and procedural background of case: The defendant, Larry Grant Lonchar, was convicted and sentenced to death for capital murder by the State of Georgia. The Georgia Supreme Court affirmed the conviction and sentence on direct appeal. The defendant subsequently filed a State habeas corpus petition, but had it withdrawn and dismissed. Shortly before his scheduled execution, the defendant filed another State habeas petition, which was denied. The defendant then filed his first habeas petition in a Federal District Court. The State argued against the District Court entering a stay of execution in the case, on the grounds that the defendant waited six years to file his first Federal habeas petition. The District Court issued the stay pending review of the petition, after determining that the Federal Habeas Corpus Rules permitted entry of the stay. A Federal Court of Appeals reversed, on the grounds that equitable doctrines of fairness in the case, and not the Federal Habeas Corpus Rules, applied. The United States Supreme Court granted certiorari to consider the issue.

Opinion of the Court by Justice Breyer: Justice Breyer held that the Court of Appeals erred in denying the stay and dismissing the defendant's petition for special ad hoc equitable reasons. It was said that under the Court's decision in *Barefoot v. Estelle*, the general rule is that when a District Court is faced with a request for a stay in a first Federal habeas case, if the District Court cannot dismiss the petition on the merits before the scheduled execution, it is obligated to address the merits and must issue a stay to prevent the case from becoming moot.

The opinion pointed out that Rule 9 of the Federal Habeas Corpus Rules permits dismissal of a first habeas petition, if the prosecuting authority has been prejudiced in its ability to respond due to the delay in filing the petition. It was noted that the District Court was not asked to, and did not, make a finding of prejudice in the case under Rule 9. It was concluded that the case should have been examined within the framework of the Federal Habeas Corpus Rules, not according to generalized equitable considerations outside that framework. The judgment of the Court of Appeals was reversed.

Concurring opinion by Chief Justice Rehnquist, in which Scalia, Kennedy and Thomas, JJ., joined: The Chief Justice concurred in the Court's decision. He wrote separately to note that he believed the Court's opinion confused the issue presented. The Chief Justice stated that the case involved in order reversing a stay of execution, and not dismissal of a petition for habeas relief.

Case note: Larry Grant Lonchar was executed by electrocution on November 14, 1996, by the State of Georgia. *See also* **Barefoot v. Estelle; Habeas Corpus Procedural Rules; Stay of Execution**

Louisiana The State of Louisiana is a capital punishment jurisdiction. The State reenacted its death penalty law after the United States Supreme Court decision in *Furman v. Georgia*, 408 U.S. 238 (1972), on July 2, 1973.

Louisiana has a three-tier legal system. The State's legal system is composed of a supreme court, courts of appeal and courts of general jurisdiction. The Supreme Court is presided over by a chief justice and seven associate justices. The Louisiana Courts of Appeal are divided into five circuits. Each circuit

Richard Ieyoub is the Louisiana Attorney General. His office represents the State in capital punishment appellate proceedings. (Louisiana Attorney General Office)

has a chief judge and at least seven judges. The courts of general jurisdiction in the State are called District Courts. Capital offenses against the State of Louisiana are tried in the District Courts.

Louisiana's capital punishment statute is triggered if a person commits a homicide under the following special circumstances:

1. When the offender has specific intent to kill or to inflict great bodily harm and is engaged in the perpetration or attempted perpetration of aggravated kidnapping, second degree kidnapping, aggravated escape, aggravated arson, aggravated rape, forcible rape, aggravated burglary, armed robbery, drive-by shooting, first degree robbery, or simple robbery.
2. When the offender has a specific intent to kill or to inflict great bodily harm upon a fireman or peace officer engaged in the performance of his lawful duties.
3. When the offender has a specific intent to kill or to inflict great bodily harm upon more than one person.
4. When the offender has specific intent to kill or inflict great bodily harm and has offered, has been offered, has given, or has received anything of value for the killing.
5. When the offender has the specific intent to kill or to inflict great bodily harm upon a victim under the age of twelve or sixty-five years of age or older.
6. When the offender has the specific intent to kill or to inflict great bodily harm while engaged in the distribution, exchange, sale, or purchase, or any attempt thereof, of a controlled dangerous substance.
7. When the offender has specific intent to kill and is engaged in ritualistic activities.

Capital murder in Louisiana is punishable by death or life

imprisonment without parole. A capital prosecution in Louisiana is bifurcated into a guilt phase and penalty phase. A jury is used at both phases of a capital trial. It is required that, at the penalty phase, the jury unanimously agree that a death sentence is appropriate before it can be imposed. If the penalty phase jury is unable to reach a verdict, the trial judge is required to sentence the defendant to life imprisonment without parole. The decision of a penalty phase jury is binding on the trial court under the laws of Louisiana.

In order to impose a death sentence upon a defendant under Louisiana law, it is required that the prosecutor establish the existence of at least one of the following statutory aggravating circumstances at the penalty phase:

1. The offender was engaged in the perpetration or attempted perpetration of aggravated rape, forcible rape, aggravated kidnapping, second degree kidnapping, aggravated burglary, aggravated arson, aggravated escape, assault by drive-by shooting, armed robbery, first degree robbery, or simple robbery.

2. The victim was a fireman or peace officer engaged in his lawful duties.

3. The offender has been previously convicted of an unrelated murder, aggravated rape, aggravated burglary, aggravated arson, aggravated escape, armed robbery, or aggravated kidnapping.

4. The offender knowingly created a risk of death or great bodily harm to more than one person.

5. The offender offered or has been offered or has given or received anything of value for the commission of the offense.

6. The offender at the time of the commission of the offense was imprisoned after sentence for the commission of an unrelated forcible felony.

7. The offense was committed in an especially heinous, atrocious or cruel manner.

8. The victim was a witness in a prosecution against the defendant, gave material assistance to the state in any investigation or prosecution of the defendant, or was an eye witness to a crime alleged to have been committed by the defendant or possessed other material evidence against the defendant.

9. The victim was a correctional officer or any employee of the Department of Public Safety and Corrections who, in the normal course of his employment was required to come in close contact with persons incarcerated in a state prison facility, and the victim was engaged in his lawful duties at the time of the offense.

10. The victim was under the age of twelve years or sixty-five years of age or older.

11. The offender was engaged in the distribution, exchange, sale, or purchase, or any attempt thereof, of a controlled dangerous substance.

12. The offender was engaged in ritualistic activities.

Although the Federal Constitution will not permit jurisdictions to prevent capital felons from presenting all relevant mitigating evidence at the penalty phase, Louisiana has provided the following statutory mitigating circumstances that permit the jury to reject imposition of the death penalty:

a. The offender has no significant prior history of criminal activity;

b. The offense was committed while the offender was under the influence of extreme mental or emotional disturbance;

c. The offense was committed while the offender was under the influence or under the domination of another person;

d. The offense was committed under circumstances which the offender reasonably believed to provide a moral justification or extenuation for his conduct;

e. At the time of the offense the capacity of the offender to appreciate the criminality of his conduct or to conform his conduct to the requirements of law was impaired as a result of mental disease or defect or intoxication;

f. The youth of the offender at the time of the offense;

g. The offender was a principal whose participation was relatively minor;

h. Any other relevant mitigating circumstance.

Under Louisiana's capital punishment statute, a sentence of death is automatically reviewed by the Louisiana Supreme Court. Louisiana uses lethal injection to carry out death sentences (electrocution was previously used). The State's death row facility for men is located in Angola, Louisiana; while the facility maintaining female death row inmates is located in St. Gabriel, Louisiana.

Pursuant to the laws of Louisiana the Governor has authority to grant clemency in capital cases. The Governor must obtain the consent of the State's Board of Pardons in order to grant clemency.

From the start of modern capital punishment in 1976, through 1999, Louisiana executed 25 capital felons. During this period Louisiana did not execute any female capital felons, although one of its death row inmates during this period was a female. A total of 82 capital felons were on death row in Louisiana in 1999. The 1999 death row population in the State was listed as: 57 black inmates; 22 white inmates; and 3 unidentified inmates. In 1999 the State had one juvenile on

Executions by Louisiana 1976–1999

Name	Race	Date of Execution	Method of Execution
Robert W. Williams	Black	November 30, 1983	Electrocution
John Taylor	Black	February 29, 1984	Electrocution
Elmo Sonnier	White	April 5, 1984	Electrocution
Timothy Baldwin	White	September 10, 1984	Electrocution
Ernest Knighton	Black	October 30, 1984	Electrocution
Robert L. Willie	White	December 28, 1984	Electrocution
David Martin	White	January 4, 1985	Electrocution
Benjamin Berry	White	June 7, 1987	Electrocution
Alvin Moore	Black	June 9, 1987	Electrocution
Jimmie Glass	White	June 12, 1987	Electrocution

Name	Race	Date of Execution	Method of Execution
Jimmy Wingo	White	June 16, 1987	Electrocution
Willie Celestine	Black	July 20, 1987	Electrocution
Willie Watson	Black	July 24, 1987	Electrocution
John Brogdon	White	July 30, 1987	Electrocution
Sterling Rault	White	August 24, 1987	Electrocution
Wayne Felde	White	March 15, 1988	Electrocution
Leslie Lowenfield	Black	April 13, 1988	Electrocution
Edward Byrne	White	June 14, 1988	Electrocution
Dalton Prejean	Black	May 18, 1990	Electrocution
Andrew L. Jones	Black	July 22, 1991	Electrocution
Robert Sawyer	White	March 5, 1993	Lethal Injection
Thomas L. Ward	Black	May 16, 1995	Lethal Injection
Antonio James	Black	March 1, 1996	Lethal Injection
John A. Brown, Jr.	White	April 24, 1997	Lethal Injection
Dobie G. Williams	Black	January 8, 1999	Lethal Injection

death row. The State permits capital punishment to be imposed on persons 16 years old or older. Louisiana does not prohibit the execution of mentally retarded capital felons.

LOUISIANA EXECUTIONS 1976–1999

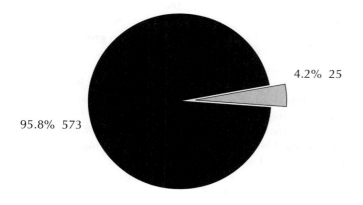

4.2% 25

95.8% 573

■ LOUISIANA EXECUTIONS

■ ALL OTHER EXECUTIONS

Louisiana Coalition to Abolish the Death Penalty

The Louisiana Coalition to Abolish the Death Penalty (LCADP) is composed of individuals and groups committed to the abolishment of capital punishment in Louisiana. The work of LCADP includes the dissemination of quality information about the death penalty through educational forums, public speaking, publications and resource materials. It produces a newsletter called *The Pilgrimage* and provides support for those on death row in Louisiana, their families and friends. It also maintains a commitment to the families of victims of violent crime.

Loving v. United States

Court: United States Supreme Court; *Case Citation:* Loving v. United States, 116 S.Ct. 1737 (1996); *Argued:* January 9, 1996; *Decided:* June 3, 1996; *Opinion of the Court:* Justice Kennedy; *Concurring Opinion:* Justice Stevens, in which Souter, Ginsburg and Breyer, JJ., joined; *Concurring Opinion:* Justice Scalia, in which O'Connor, J., joined; *Concurring Opinion:* Justice Thomas; *Dissenting Opinion:* None; *Appellate Defense Counsel:* Not reported; *Appellate Prosecution Counsel:* Not reported; *Amicus Curiae Brief Supporting Prosecutor:* Not reported; *Amicus Curiae Brief Supporting Defendant:* Not reported.

Issue Presented: Whether the doctrine of separation of powers required that Congress, and not the President, make the policy determination respecting the aggravating factors that warrant the death penalty in military prosecutions?

Case Holding: The doctrine of separation of powers did not require that Congress, instead of the President, make the policy determination respecting the aggravating factors that warrant the death penalty in military prosecutions.

Factual and procedural background of case: The defendant, Dwight J. Loving, was convicted of capital murder at a general military court martial and sentenced to death. The military commander who convened the court martial approved the conviction and sentence. At the appellate level, the United States Army Court of Military Review and the United States Court of Appeals for the Armed Forces affirmed the conviction and sentence. The military appellate courts rejected the defendant's contention that, Congress' grant of authority to the President to promulgate aggravating circumstances that allowed imposition of the death penalty violated the constitutional separation of powers doctrine. The United States Supreme Court granted certiorari to consider the issue.

Opinion of the Court by Justice Kennedy: The initial matter Justice Kennedy addressed was the application of *Furman v. Georgia* and its progeny to military capital punishment. It was said that counsel for the military did not contest the application of the Court's death penalty jurisprudence to court martials, at least in the context of a conviction for capital murder committed in peacetime within the United States. Justice Kennedy concluded the Court would assume, without deciding, that *Furman* and the case law resulting from it were applicable to the offense and sentence in the case. With the "assumption" in place, Justice Kennedy held that under the Eighth Amendment the military capital sentencing scheme must genuinely narrow the class of persons eligible for the death penalty and must reasonably justify the imposition of a more severe sentence on a defendant compared to others found guilty of murder. It was found that the constitutional narrowing was not achieved in the statute authorizing capital punishment for murder. However, it was found that the aggravating circumstances promulgated by the President satisfied the constitutional narrowing of the class of military defendants subject to capital punishment for murder.

In turning to the issue of the constitutional legitimacy of the President to promulgate aggravating circumstances used to impose the death penalty, Justice Kennedy held that the

President's congressionally authorized power to promulgate aggravating factors did not violate the separation of powers doctrine. The opinion pointed out that under the separation of powers doctrine, the Federal lawmaking function belonged to Congress and could not be conveyed to another branch of government. Justice Kennedy stated that the separation of powers doctrine did not mean, however, that only Congress could make a rule of prospective force. It was said that although Congress could not delegate the power to make laws, Congress may delegate to others the authority or discretion to execute the law under and in pursuance of its terms. The opinion rejected the defendant's argument that Congress lacked power to delegate to the President the authority to prescribe aggravating factors in military capital murder cases. Justice Kennedy concluded: "[I]t would be contrary to the respect owed the President as Commander in Chief to hold that he may not be given wide discretion and authority. Thus, in the circumstances presented here, Congress may delegate authority to the President to define the aggravating factors that permit imposition of a statutory penalty, with the regulations providing the narrowing of the death-eligible class that the Eighth Amendment requires." The judgment of the Court of Appeals of the Armed Forces was affirmed.

Concurring opinion by Justice Stevens, in which Souter, Ginsburg and Breyer, JJ., joined: Justice Stevens concurred in the Court's opinion and judgment. He wrote separately to underscore that the victims in the case were connected to the military, and that the Court was not deciding that the same constitutional standards would apply for capital military prosecutions where the victim was not connected to the military. Justice Stevens indicated that "[t]he question whether a 'service connection' requirement should obtain in capital cases is an open one[.]"

Concurring opinion by Justice Scalia, in which O'Connor, J., joined: Justice Scalia concurred in the Court's judgment. He wrote separately to express his view that the Court's opinion should not have made comparisons to "the historical sharing of power between Parliament and the English throne." Justice Scalia indicated that because England does not have a written constitution, "[o]ur written Constitution does not require us to trace out that history[.]"

Concurring opinion by Justice Thomas: Justice Thomas concurred in the Court's judgment. He wrote separately to point out his belief that the defendant did not present a legitimate issue, because the Court has never held that its constitutional capital punishment jurisprudence applied to military capital punishment. Justice Thomas wrote: "It is not clear to me that the extensive rules we have developed under the Eighth Amendment for the prosecution of civilian capital cases, including the requirement of proof of aggravating factors, necessarily apply to capital prosecutions in the military and this Court has never so held. I am therefore not certain that this case even raises a delegation question, for if Loving can constitutionally be sentenced to death without proof of aggravating factors, he surely cannot claim that the President vi-

olated the Constitution by promulgating aggravating factors that afforded more protection than that to which Loving is constitutionally entitled."

Case note: The commentary written on this case has emphasized the Court's delicate balance in not encroaching upon the authority of the military to enforce its capital punishment laws. The Court was able to walk this type rope by "assuming without deciding," that its constitutional capital jurisprudence applied to the military for the purposes of the disposing of the case. *See also* **Burns v. Wilson; Military Death Penalty Law**

Lowenfield v. Phelps   *Court:* United States Supreme Court; *Case Citation:* Lowenfield v. Phelps, 484 U.S. 231 (1988); *Argued:* October 14, 1987; *Decided:* January 13, 1988; *Opinion of the Court:* Chief Justice Rehnquist; *Concurring Opinion:* None; *Dissenting Opinion:* Justice Marshall, in which Brennan and Stevens, JJ., joined; *Appellate Defense Counsel:* David Klingsberg argued; Gary S. Guzy on brief; *Appellate Prosecution Counsel:* John M. Mamoulides argued; William J. Guste, Jr. and Dorothy A. Pendergast on brief; *Amicus Curiae Brief Supporting Prosecutor:* 2; *Amicus Curiae Brief Supporting Defendant:* None.

Issue Presented: Whether the Constitution prohibits use of a guilt phase death-eligible special circumstance as a penalty phase statutory aggravating circumstance?

Case Holding: The Constitution does not prohibit use of a guilt phase death-eligible special circumstance as a penalty phase statutory aggravating circumstance.

Factual and procedural background of case: The defendant, Leslie Lowenfield, was charged with killing five people by the State of Louisiana. The death-eligible special circumstance of the offenses was the "intent to kill or inflict great bodily harm upon more than one person." The jury returned guilty verdicts on three counts of first-degree murder. At the penalty phase the statutory aggravating circumstance relied upon by the prosecutor was "knowingly creating a risk of death or great bodily harm to more than one person." The penalty phase jury returned three death sentences after finding the existence of the statutory aggravating circumstance.

On appeal to the Louisiana Supreme Court the defendant argued that the guilt phase death-eligible special circumstance was the same factor used to impose the death sentences at the penalty phase, and that such duplication violated the Federal Constitution. The appellate court disagreed and affirmed the convictions and sentences. The defendant filed a habeas corpus petition in a Federal District Court seeking relief on the grounds asserted in State court. The District Court denied relief and dismissed the petition. A Federal Court of Appeals affirmed the dismissal. The United States Supreme Court granted certiorari to consider the issue.

Opinion of the Court by Chief Justice Rehnquist: The Chief Justice ruled that the Constitution did not prevent use of the guilt phase death-eligible special circumstance as a penalty phase statutory aggravating circumstance. The opinion reasoned as follows:

The use of "aggravating circumstances" is not an end in itself, but a means of genuinely narrowing the class of death-eligible persons and thereby channeling the jury's discretion. We see no reason why this narrowing function may not be performed by jury findings at either the sentencing phase of the trial or the guilt phase....

It seems clear to us ... that the narrowing function required for a regime of capital punishment may be provided in either of these two ways: The legislature may itself narrow the definition of capital offenses, as ... Louisiana ha[s] done, so that the jury finding of guilt responds to this concern, or the legislature may more broadly define capital offenses and provide for narrowing by jury findings of aggravating circumstances at the penalty phase....

Here, the "narrowing function" was performed by the jury at the guilt phase when it found defendant guilty of three counts of murder under the provision that "the offender has a specific intent to kill or to inflict great bodily harm upon more than one person." The fact that the sentencing jury is also required to find the existence of an aggravating circumstance in addition is no part of the constitutionally required narrowing process, and so the fact that the aggravating circumstance duplicated one of the elements of the crime does not make this sentence constitutionally infirm. There is no question but that the Louisiana scheme narrows the class of death-eligible murderers and then at the sentencing phase allows for the consideration of mitigating circumstances and the exercise of discretion. The Constitution requires no more.

The judgment of the Court of Appeals was affirmed.

Dissenting opinion by Justice Marshall, in which Brennan and Stevens, JJ., joined: Justice Marshall dissented from the majority opinion. He believed that the Constitution prohibited States from duplicating guilt phase death-eligible special circumstances in the guise of penalty phase statutory aggravating circumstances. The dissent stated its argument as follows:

> Adhering to my view that the death penalty is in all circumstances cruel and unusual punishment prohibited by the Eighth and Fourteenth Amendments, I would vacate the decision below insofar as it left undisturbed the death sentence imposed in this case.
>
> Even if I did not hold this view, I would vacate [the defendant's] sentence.... [T]he jury's sentence of death could not stand because it was based on a single statutory aggravating circumstance that duplicated an element of [the defendant's] underlying offense. This duplication prevented Louisiana's sentencing scheme from adequately guiding the discretion of the sentencing jury in this case and relieved the jury of the requisite sense of responsibility for its sentencing decision. As we have recognized frequently in the past, such failings may have the effect of impermissibly biasing the sentencing process in favor of death in violation of the Eighth and the Fourteenth Amendments....
>
> In sum, the application of the Louisiana sentencing scheme in cases like this one, where there is a complete overlap between aggravating circumstances found at the sentencing phase and elements of the offense previously found at the guilt phase, violates constitutional principles in ways that will inevitably tilt the sentencing scales toward the imposition of the death penalty. The State will have an easier time convincing a jury beyond a reasonable doubt to find a necessary element of a capital offense at the guilt phase of a trial if the jury is unaware that such a finding will make the defendant eligible for the death penalty at the sentencing phase. Then the State will have an even eas-

ier time arguing for the imposition of the death penalty, because it can remind the jury at the sentencing phase, as it did in this case, that the necessary aggravating circumstances already have been established beyond a reasonable doubt. The State thus enters the sentencing hearing with the jury already across the threshold of death eligibility, without any awareness on the jury's part that it had crossed that line. By permitting such proceedings in a capital case, the Court ignores our early pronouncement that "a State may not entrust the determination of whether a man should live or die to a tribunal organized to return a verdict of death."

Case note: The majority decision in the case had a tremendous impact on the creation of guilt phase death-eligible special circumstances that formed the basis of penalty phase statutory aggravating circumstances. Commentators have argued that the rate of death sentences returned by juries support Justice Marshall's dissenting argument, that such duplication unconstitutionally tilts the scales toward imposition of the death penalty.

Lundgren, Jeffrey *see* Ohio Cult Murders

Lurton, Horace H.

Horace H. Lurton served as an associate justice of the United States Supreme Court from 1910 to 1914. While on the Supreme Court Lurton was known as a conservative interpreter of the Constitution.

Lurton was born on February 26, 1844 in Newport, Kentucky. He received a law degree from Tennessee's Cumberland University Law School in 1867. In addition to having a successful private practice in Tennessee, Lurton was elected to the Tennessee supreme court in 1886. He also accepted an appointment as an appellate judge for the Sixth Circuit Court of Appeals and served as dean of Vanderbilt University Law School. In 1910 President William Howard Taft nominated Lurton to the Supreme Court.

While on the Supreme Court Lurton was known to have authored only one capital punishment opinion. In *Wynne v. United States* the Supreme Court was asked to decide whether the United States had jurisdiction to prosecute the defendant for murder committed in a harbor of the territory of Hawaii. Lurton, writing for the Court, held that the United States had jurisdiction over the offense. He wrote: "Unless, therefore, there was something in the legislation of Congress ... providing a government for the territory of Hawaii, which excluded the operation of [federal law], the jurisdiction of the courts of the United States over the bay here in question, in respect of the murder there charged to have been committed, was beyond question." Lurton died on July 12, 1914.

Luxembourg

Capital punishment was abolished in Luxembourg in 1979. *See also* **International Capital Punishment Nations**

Lying-in-Wait Aggravator

The common law recognized murder committed while lying-in-wait. The crime requires that a perpetrator secretly ambush an unsuspecting victim. Under modern capital punishment law four jurisdictions, California, Colorado, Indiana, and Montana, have made murder committed while lying-in-wait a statutory aggravating circumstance. In these jurisdictions if it is shown at the penalty phase that a murder was committed while the defendant was lying-in-wait, the death penalty may be imposed. *See also* **Aggravating Circumstances**

M

MacArthur Justice Center

The MacArthur Justice Center (MJC) is a nonprofit public interest law firm at the University of Chicago Law School. MJC is dedicated to fighting for human rights and social justice through litigation, with a particular emphasis on criminal cases that raise constitutional or other significant issues. MJC has been particularly active in capital cases. One of its attorneys represented and ultimately won the release of a death row inmate who was scheduled to be the first person executed in Illinois since 1962. MJC has submitted amicus briefs in several Illinois capital cases.

McCarty, Henry

Henry "Billy the Kid" McCarty (a.k.a. William H. Bonney) was born on November 23, 1859, in New York City. In the 1870s McCarty moved to Lincoln County, New Mexico. While in New Mexico McCarty hired on as a cowboy for a cattle rancher named J. H. Tunstall. In February of 1878, Tunstall was murdered by a rival cattle rancher. Tunstall's death started what became known as the Lincoln County War.

McCarty was one of the leading players in the Lincoln County War. During a three day shootout in July of 1878, McCarty shot to death Sheriff Bill Brady, who was trying to stop the shootout. McCarty fled the area after killing the sheriff.

In 1880 a new Lincoln County sheriff, Pat Garrett, and a posse trapped McCarty and four of his confederates in a shack at Stinking Springs. After a three fierce days of gun play, McCarty was captured on December 23, 1880.

McCarty was brought back to Lincoln County for trial in the death of sheriff Brady. McCarty was convicted by a jury of murder and was sentenced to be hanged. However, while awaiting execution McCarty escaped on April 28, 1881. During the escape he killed two guards.

Sheriff Garrett set out to capture McCarty and return him for execution. Legend has it that the sheriff had no intention of capturing McCarty — he was intent on killing him. On July 13, 1881 sheriff Garrett located McCarty in a hotel and shot him dead.

Legend has it that, while McCarty was charged with 12 murders by the time he was 18, he actually killed only four people in his life.

McCleskey v. Kemp

Court: United States Supreme Court; *Case Citation:* McCleskey v. Kemp, 481 U.S. 279 (1987); *Argued:* October 15, 1986; *Decided:* April 22, 1987; *Opinion of the Court:* Justice Powell; *Concurring Opinion:* None; *Dissenting Opinion:* Justice Brennan, in which Marshall, Blackmun and Stevens, JJ., joined; *Dissenting Opinion:* Justice Blackmun, in which Marshall, Stevens and Brennan, JJ., joined; *Dissenting Opinion:* Justice Stevens, in which Blackmun, J., joined; *Appellate Defense Counsel:* John Charles Boger argued; Julius L. Chambers, James M. Nabrit III, Vivian Berger, Robert H. Stroup, Timothy K. Ford, and Anthony G. Amsterdam on brief; *Appellate Prosecution Counsel:* Mary Beth Westmoreland argued; Michael J. Bowers, Marion O. Gordon, and William B. Hill, Jr. on brief; *Amicus Curiae Brief Supporting Prosecutor:* 2; *Amicus Curiae Brief Supporting Defendant:* 3.

Issue Presented: Whether statistical evidence establishes Georgia's capital punishment system is applied in a racially discriminatory manner and in violation of the Constitution?

Case Holding: Statistical evidence demonstrated some racial disparity in the application of Georgia's capital punishment system, but such disparity did not sufficiently rise to the level of a constitutional violation.

Factual and procedural background of case: The defendant, Warren McCleskey, was convicted of capital murder and sentenced to death in 1978, by a Georgia court. On direct appeal the Georgia Supreme Court affirmed and the United States Supreme Court denied certiorari. The defendant next filed for habeas corpus relief, but was denied by state and federal courts.

The defendant filed a second habeas corpus petition in a Federal District Court. In the second habeas claim the defendant alleged that the Georgia capital sentencing process was administered in a racially discriminatory manner in violation of the Constitution. In support of the claim, defendant proffered a statistical study, called the Baldus study, that revealed a disparity in the imposition of the death sentence in Georgia based on the murder victim's race and, to a lesser extent, the defendant's race. The study was based on over 2,000 murder cases that occurred in Georgia during the 1970s, and involves data relating to the victim's race, the defendant's race, and the various combinations of such persons' races. The study indicated that black defendants who killed white victims have the greatest likelihood of receiving the death penalty. The District Court rejected defendant's constitutional claim and denied him relief. A Court of Appeals affirmed the District Court's decision. The United States Supreme Court granted certiorari to address the matter.

Opinion of the Court by Justice Powell: Justice Powell indicated that the defendant alleged that, based on the Baldus study, racial discrimination existed in Georgia's capital punishment system in violation of the Equal Protection Clause and the Eighth Amendment. The opinion took up each constitutional claim separately.

As to the equal protection claim, Justice Powell ruled that the defendant offered no evidence specific to his own case that would support an inference that racial considerations played a part in his sentence, and that the Baldus study was insufficient to support an inference that any of the decision-makers in his case acted with discriminatory purpose. It was concluded that the Baldus study did not establish that the administration of the Georgia capital punishment system violated the Equal Protection Clause.

With respect to the defendant's Eighth Amendment claim, Justice Powell found that there was no merit to the contention that the Baldus study showed that Georgia's capital punishment system is arbitrary and capricious in application. The opinion held that the statistics did not prove that race entered into any capital sentencing decision or that race was a factor in the defendant's case. Justice Powell stated that the likelihood of racial prejudice shown by the study did not constitute the constitutional measure of an unacceptable risk of racial prejudice.

The majority opinion ruled that, at most, the Baldus study indicated a discrepancy that appears to correlate with race, but such discrepancy did not constitute a major systemic defect. It was said that any mode for determining guilt or punishment has its weaknesses and the potential for misuse. Justice Powell found that despite such imperfections, constitutional guarantees are met when the mode for determining guilt or punishment has been surrounded with safeguards to make it as fair as possible. It was concluded that the Baldus study did not demonstrate that the Georgia capital sentencing system violated the Eighth Amendment. Accordingly, the judgment of the Court of Appeals was affirmed.

Dissenting opinion by Justice Brennan, in which Marshall, Blackmun and Stevens, JJ., joined: Justice Brennan indicated that he would vacate the judgment of the Court of Appeals because the defendant established a constitutional violation. The thrust of the evidence relied upon by Justice Brennan to reach this conclusion was stated in his dissent as follows:

> The Baldus study indicates that, after taking into account some 230 nonracial factors that might legitimately influence a sentencer, the jury more likely than not would have spared McCleskey's life had his victim been black....
>
> Furthermore, even examination of the sentencing system as a whole, factoring in those cases in which the jury exercises little

discretion, indicates the influence of race on capital sentencing. For the Georgia system as a whole, race accounts for a six percentage point difference in the rate at which capital punishment is imposed. Since death is imposed in 11 percent of all white-victim cases, the rate in comparably aggravated black-victim cases is 5 percent. The rate of capital sentencing in a white-victim case is thus 120 percent greater than the rate in a black-victim case. Put another way, over half—55 percent—of defendants in white-victim crimes in Georgia would not have been sentenced to die if their victims had been black. Of the more than 200 variables potentially relevant to a sentencing decision, race of the victim is a powerful explanation for variation in death sentence rates—as powerful as nonracial aggravating factors such as a prior murder conviction or acting as the principal planner of the homicide.

> These adjusted figures are only the most conservative indication of the risk that race will influence the death sentences of defendants in Georgia. Data unadjusted for the mitigating or aggravating effect of other factors show an even more pronounced disparity by race. The capital sentencing rate for all white-victim cases was almost 11 times greater than the rate for black-victim cases. Furthermore, blacks who kill whites are sentenced to death at nearly 22 times the rate of blacks who kill blacks, and more than 7 times the rate of whites who kill blacks. In addition, prosecutors seek the death penalty for 70 percent of black defendants with white victims, but for only 15 percent of black defendants with black victims, and only 19 percent of white defendants with black victims. Since our decision upholding the Georgia capital sentencing system in *Gregg*, the State has executed seven persons. All of the seven were convicted of killing whites, and six of the seven executed were black. Such execution figures are especially striking in light of the fact that, during the period encompassed by the Baldus study, only 9.2 percent of Georgia homicides involved black defendants and white victims, while 60.7 percent involved black victims....

> The statistical evidence in this case thus relentlessly documents the risk that McCleskey's sentence was influenced by racial considerations. This evidence shows that there is a better than even chance in Georgia that race will influence the decision to impose the death penalty: a majority of defendants in white-victim crimes would not have been sentenced to die if their victims had been black. In determining whether this risk is acceptable, our judgment must be shaped by the awareness that "[t]he risk of racial prejudice infecting a capital sentencing proceeding is especially serious in light of the complete finality of the death sentence," and that "[i]t is of vital importance to the defendant and to the community that any decision to impose the death sentence be, and appear to be, based on reason rather than caprice or emotion." In determining the guilt of a defendant, a State must prove its case beyond a reasonable doubt. That is, we refuse to convict if the chance of error is simply less likely than not. Surely, we should not be willing to take a person's life if the chance that his death sentence was irrationally imposed is more likely than not. In light of the gravity of the interest at stake, petitioner's statistics on their face are a powerful demonstration of the type of risk that our Eighth Amendment jurisprudence has consistently condemned....

> It is tempting to pretend that minorities on death row share a fate in no way connected to our own, that our treatment of them sounds no echoes beyond the chambers in which they die. Such an illusion is ultimately corrosive, for the reverberations of injustice are not so easily confined. "The destinies of the two races in this country are indissolubly linked together," and the way in which we choose those who will die reveals the depth of moral commitment among the living.

Dissenting opinion by Justice Blackmun, in which

Marshall, Stevens and Brennan, JJ., joined: Justice Blackmun indicated in his dissent that "[t]he Court today sanctions the execution of a man despite his presentation of evidence that establishes a constitutionally intolerable level of racially based discrimination leading to the imposition of his death sentence."

A core concern expressed in the dissent was the Court's "departure from what seems to me to be well-developed constitutional jurisprudence." Justice Blackmun wrote: "The Court's assertion that the fact of McCleskey's conviction undermines his constitutional claim is inconsistent with a long and unbroken line of this Court's case law. The Court on numerous occasions during the past century has recognized that an otherwise legitimate basis for a conviction does not outweigh an equal protection violation. In cases where racial discrimination in the administration of the criminal justice system is established, it has held that setting aside the conviction is the appropriate remedy."

It was concluded by Justice Blackmum that it was necessary to impose guidelines to minimize abuse of discretion by prosecutors in making decisions about whether to seek the death penalty. He wrote that "the establishment of guidelines for [prosecutors] as to the appropriate basis for exercising their discretion at the various steps in the prosecution of a case would provide at least a measure of consistency."

Dissenting opinion by Justice Stevens, in which Blackmun, J., joined: Justice Stevens believed the defendant established a constitutional violation. In his dissent he wrote: "In this case it is claimed — and the claim is supported by elaborate studies which the Court properly assumes to be valid — that the jury's sentencing process was likely distorted by racial prejudice. The studies demonstrate a strong probability that McCleskey's sentencing jury, which expressed 'the community's outrage — its sense that an individual has lost his moral entitlement to live,' was influenced by the fact that McCleskey is black and his victim was white, and that this same outrage would not have been generated if he had killed a member of his own race. This sort of disparity is constitutionally intolerable. It flagrantly violates the Court's prior 'insistence that capital punishment be imposed fairly, and with reasonable consistency, or not at all.'"

Justice Stevens argued that correcting the problem posed by Georgia's death penalty system would not necessitate abolishing capital punishment by the State altogether. The dissent addressed the matter as follows: "The Court's decision appears to be based on a fear that the acceptance of McCleskey's claim would sound the death knell for capital punishment in Georgia. If society were indeed forced to choose between a racially discriminatory death penalty ... and no death penalty at all, the choice mandated by the Constitution would be plain. But the Court's fear is unfounded. One of the lessons of the Baldus study is that there exist certain categories of extremely serious crimes for which prosecutors consistently seek, and juries consistently impose, the death penalty without regard to the race of the victim or the race of the offender. If Georgia were to narrow the class of death-eligible defendants to those categories, the danger of arbitrary and discriminatory imposition of the death penalty would be significantly decreased, if not eradicated."

Macedonia Capital punishment is not carried out in Macedonia. *See also* **International Capital Punishment Nations**

McElvaine v. Brush *Court:* United States Supreme Court; *Case Citation:* McElvaine v. Brush, 142 U.S. 155 (1891); *Argued:* December 7, 1891; *Decided:* December 21, 1891; *Opinion of the Court:* Chief Justice Fuller; *Concurring Opinion:* None; *Dissenting Opinion:* None; *Appellate Defense Counsel:* George M. Curtis argued and briefed; *Appellate Prosecution Counsel:* Charles F. Tabor on brief; *Amicus Curiae Brief Supporting Prosecutor:* None; *Amicus Curiae Brief Supporting Defendant:* None.

Issue Presented: Whether detention in solitary confinement pending execution constituted cruel and unusual punishment within the meaning of the Federal Constitution?

Case Holding: Detention in solitary confinement pending execution did not constitute cruel and unusual punishment within the meaning of the Federal Constitution.

Factual and procedural background of case: The defendant, Charles McElvaine was convicted of capital murder and sentenced to death by the State of New York. On appeal, the New York Court of Appeals reversed the judgment and awarded a new trial. The defendant was tried a second time, convicted and sentenced to death. The State appellate court affirmed the second judgment. The defendant filed a habeas corpus petition in a Federal District Court, alleging that his detention in solitary confinement pending his execution constituted cruel and unusual punishment under the Federal Constitution. The District Court dismissed the petition. The United States Supreme Court granted certiorari to consider the issue.

Opinion of the Court by Chief Justice Fuller: The Chief Justice held that detention in solitary confinement while awaiting execution did not violate the Federal Constitution. The opinion rejected the defendant's contention that, because the death warrant did not specify holding him in solitary confinement, the State could not detain him in such a manner. The Chief Justice reasoned that it was an implied necessary administrative task to hold the defendant in solitary confinement pending execution, therefore the death warrant did not have to expressly provide for such detention. The judgment of the District Court was affirmed. *See also* **Death Row**

McFarland v. Scott *Court:* United States Supreme Court; *Case Citation:* McFarland v. Scott, 512 U.S. 849 (1994); *Argued:* March 29, 1994; *Decided:* June 30, 1994; *Opinion of the Court:* Justice Blackmun; *Concurring and Dissenting Opinion:* Justice O'Connor; *Dissenting Opinion:* Justice Thomas, in which Rehnquist, C.J., and Scalia, J., joined; *Appellate Defense*

Counsel: Not reported; *Appellate Prosecution Counsel:* Not reported; *Amicus Curiae Brief Supporting Prosecutor:* Not reported; *Amicus Curiae Brief Supporting Defendant:* Not reported.

Issue Presented: Whether a capital defendant must file a formal Federal habeas corpus petition in order to obtain appointment of counsel and to establish a Federal court's jurisdiction to enter a stay of execution?

Case Holding: A capital defendant is not required to file a formal Federal habeas corpus petition in order to obtain appointment of counsel and to establish a Federal court's jurisdiction to enter a stay of execution.

Factual and procedural background of case: The defendant, Frank McFarland, was convicted of capital murder by the State of Texas and sentenced to death. The Texas Court of Criminal Appeals affirmed the conviction and sentence. Subsequently, a Texas trial court scheduled the defendant's execution date. The defendant, on his own, filed a petition requesting that the trial court stay or withdraw his execution date to allow him time to obtain free legal counsel for a state habeas corpus proceeding. The trial court ultimately declined to disturb the execution date. The Texas Court of Criminal Appeals affirmed the decision.

The defendant next filed a "motion" in a Federal District Court, requesting appointment of counsel under the Federal habeas corpus statute and a stay of execution to give appointed counsel time to prepare and file a formal habeas corpus petition. The District Court denied the request after finding that, because no post-conviction proceeding had been initiated under the Federal habeas statute, the defendant was not entitled to appointment of counsel, and the court lacked jurisdiction to enter a stay of execution. A Federal Court of Appeals affirmed the District Court ruling, after concluding that Federal law expressly authorized Federal courts to stay State proceedings while a Federal habeas corpus proceeding is pending, but that no such proceeding was pending because the defendant's motion for stay and for appointment of counsel was not the equivalent of an application for habeas relief. The United States Supreme Court granted certiorari to consider the issue.

Opinion of the Court by Justice Blackmun: Justice Blackmun ruled that a capital defendant need not file a formal habeas corpus petition in order to invoke his or her right to counsel under the Federal habeas statute and to establish a Federal court's jurisdiction to enter a stay of execution. The opinion found that the language and purposes of the Federal habeas statute establish that the right to qualified appointed counsel adheres before the filing of a formal, legally sufficient habeas petition and includes a right to legal assistance in the preparation of such a petition. Therefore, the opinion reasoned, a post-conviction proceeding within the meaning of the statute is commenced by the filing of a death row defendant's motion requesting the appointment of counsel for his or her federal habeas proceeding. Justice Blackmun concluded that the defendant filed such a motion and was entitled to the ap-

pointment of a lawyer and a stay of execution. The decision of the Court of Appeals was reversed.

Concurring and dissenting opinion by Justice O'Connor: Justice O'Connor concurred in the Court's decision that the Federal habeas statute "entitles capital defendants pursuing federal habeas corpus relief to a properly trained attorney." However, Justice O'Connor dissented from the Court's decision that the Federal habeas statute "allows a district court to stay an execution pending counsel's preparation of an application for a writ of habeas corpus." She reasoned as follows: "In my view [the defendant] is not entitled under present law to a stay of execution while counsel prepares a habeas petition. The habeas statute provides in relevant part that '[a] justice or judge of the United States before whom a habeas corpus proceeding is pending, may ... stay any proceeding against the person detained in any State court.' While this provision authorizes a stay in the habeas context, it does not explicitly allow a stay prior to the filing of a petition, and our cases have made it clear that capital defendants must raise at least some colorable federal claim before a stay of execution may be entered."

Dissenting opinion by Justice Thomas, in which Rehnquist, C.J., and Scalia, J., joined: Justice Thomas dissented from the majority's decision. He did not believe that the Federal habeas statute authorized pre-petition appointment of counsel and stay of execution. He stated his position as follows: "Today the Court holds that a state prisoner under sentence of death may invoke a federal district court's jurisdiction to obtain appointed counsel ... and to obtain a stay of execution ... simply by filing a motion for appointment of counsel. In my view, the Court's conclusion is at odds with the terms of [the] statutory provisions. [The] statute allows a federal district court to take action, [appointing counsel or granting a stay], only after a habeas proceeding has been commenced."

Case note: Texas executed Frank McFarland by lethal injection on April 29, 1998.

McGautha v. California
Court: United States Supreme Court; *Case Citation:* McGautha v. California, 402 U.S. 183 (1971); *Argued:* November 9, 1970; *Decided:* May 3, 1971; *Opinion of the Court:* Justice Harlan; *Concurring Opinion:* Justice Black; *Dissenting Opinion:* Justice Douglas, in which Brennan and Marshall, JJ., joined; *Dissenting Opinion:* Justice Brennan, in which Douglas and Marshall, JJ., joined; *Appellate Defense Counsel in Case No. 203:* Herman F. Selvin argued and briefed; *Appellate Defense Counsel in Case No. 204:* John J. Callahan argued; Dan H. McCullough, William T. Burgess, William D. Driscoll and Gerald S. Lubitsky on brief; *Appellate Prosecution Counsel in Case No. 203:* Ronald M. George argued; Thomas C. Lynch and William E. James on brief; *Appellate Prosecution Counsel in Case No. 204:* Melvin L. Resnick argued; Harry Friberg and Alice L. Robie Resnick on brief; *Amicus Curiae Brief Supporting Prosecutor:* 2; *Amicus Curiae Brief Supporting Defendant:* 4.

Issues Presented: (1) Whether States may give juries absolute discretion in determining whether a defendant receives a death sentence or a sentence of life imprisonment? (2) Whether States may require in capital prosecutions that guilt and punishment be determined in a single proceeding?

Case Holdings: (1) States may give juries absolute discretion in determining whether a defendant receives a death sentence or a sentence of life imprisonment. (2) States may require in capital prosecutions that guilt and punishment be determined in a single proceeding.

Factual and procedural background of case: This case involved two defendants, McGautha and Crampton, who were prosecuted by different jurisdictions. McGautha was convicted of capital murder and sentenced to death by the State of California. Crampton was convicted of capital murder and sentenced to death by the State of Ohio. The judgments against both defendants were affirmed by the respective State appellate courts. Both defendants appealed to the United States Supreme Court, contending that their prosecutions violated due process of law because their respective juries had absolute discretion in selecting their punishment. Additionally, Crampton complained that he was denied due process of law because his guilt and punishment were determined in a single proceeding (McGautha had a bifurcated guilt and penalty phase trial). The United States Supreme Court granted certiorari and consolidated the cases to consider the issues presented.

Opinion of the Court by Justice Harlan: Justice Harlan initially addressed the issue of juries having absolute discretion to decide punishment. He wrote that the Constitution was not offended by giving juries such authority. The opinion reasoned as follows:

> Our function is not to impose on the States, ex cathedra, what might seem to us a better system for dealing with capital cases. Rather, it is to decide whether the Federal Constitution proscribes the present procedures of these two States in such cases....
>
> In light of history, experience, and the present limitations of human knowledge, we find it quite impossible to say that committing to the untrammeled discretion of the jury the power to pronounce life or death in capital cases is offensive to anything in the Constitution. The States are entitled to assume that jurors confronted with the truly awesome responsibility of decreeing death for a fellow human will act with due regard for the consequences of their decision and will consider a variety of factors, many of which will have been suggested by the evidence or by the arguments of defense counsel. For a court to attempt to catalog the appropriate factors in this elusive area could inhibit rather than expand the scope of consideration, for no list of circumstances would ever be really complete. The infinite variety of cases and facets to each case would make general standards either meaningless "boiler-plate" or a statement of the obvious that no jury would need.

The opinion next turned to Crampton's argument that due process required his guilt and punishment be determined in separate proceedings. Crampton contended that a unitary prosecution forced him to decide whether to put on evidence seeking mercy, while at the same time putting on evidence of his innocence. It was Crampton's position that a jury would inevitably convict a defendant who puts on evidence seeking mercy, while simultaneously proffering evidence of innocence. Crampton believed the Constitution prohibited requiring a defendant to make a choice between putting on or not putting on evidence seeking mercy. Justice Harlan disagreed with Crampton and stated the Court's position as follows:

> Crampton's argument for bifurcation runs as follows. He contends that under the Due Process Clause of the Fourteenth Amendment, he had a right to be heard on the issue of punishment and a right not to have his sentence fixed without the benefit of all the relevant evidence. Therefore, he argues, the Ohio procedure creates an intolerable tension between constitutional rights. Since this tension can be largely avoided by a bifurcated trial, [the defendant] contends that there is no legitimate state interest in putting him to the election, and that the single-verdict trial should be held invalid in capital cases....
>
> The criminal process, like the rest of the legal system, is replete with situations requiring "the making of difficult judgments" as to which course to follow. Although a defendant may have a right, even of constitutional dimensions, to follow whichever course he chooses, the Constitution does not by that token always forbid requiring him to choose. The threshold question is whether compelling the election impairs to an appreciable extent any of the policies behind the rights involved. Analysis of this case in such terms leads to the conclusion that [the defendant] has failed to make out his claim of a constitutional violation in requiring him to undergo a unitary trial.

The judgments against both defendants were affirmed.

Concurring opinion by Justice Black: Justice Black concurred in the Court's decision. He wrote separately to express his view that the Court did not have authority to restrict the States in the procedures used to prosecute capital offenders. Justice Black stated the following: "I concur in the Court's judgments and in substantially all of its opinion. However, in my view, this Court's task is not to determine whether the [defendants'] trials were "fairly conducted." The Constitution grants this Court no power to reverse convictions because of our personal beliefs that state criminal procedures are "unfair," "arbitrary," "capricious," "unreasonable," or "shocking to our conscience." Our responsibility is rather to determine whether [the defendants] have been denied rights expressly or impliedly guaranteed by the Federal Constitution as written. I agree with the Court's conclusions that the procedures employed by California and Ohio to determine whether capital punishment shall be imposed do not offend the Due Process Clause of the Fourteenth Amendment."

Dissenting opinion by Justice Douglas, in which Brennan and Marshall, JJ., joined: Justice Douglas dissented from the Court's decision. He wrote specifically on the issue of a unitary prosecution as follows:

> In my view the unitary trial which Ohio provides in first-degree murder cases does not satisfy the requirements of procedural Due Process under the Fourteenth Amendment.
>
> If a defendant wishes to testify in support of the defense of insanity or in mitigation of what he is charged with doing, he can do so only if he surrenders his right to be free from self-incrimination. Once he takes the stand he can be cross-examined not only as respects the crime charged but also on other misdeeds....
>
> If the right to be heard were to be meaningful, it would have

to accrue before sentencing; yet, except for allocution, any attempt on the part of the accused during the trial to say why the judgment of death should not be pronounced against him entails a surrender of his right against self-incrimination. It therefore seems plain that the single-verdict procedure is a burden on the exercise of the right to be free of compulsion as respects self-incrimination. For he can testify on the issue of insanity or on other matters in extenuation of the crime charged only at the price of surrendering the protection of the Self-Incrimination Clause of the Fifth Amendment made applicable to the States by the Fourteenth....

The unitary trial is certainly not "mercy" oriented. That is, however, not its defect. It has a constitutional infirmity because it is not neutral on the awesome issue of capital punishment. The rules are stacked in favor of death. It is one thing if the legislature decides that the death penalty attaches to defined crimes. It is quite another to leave to judge or jury the discretion to sentence an accused to death or to show mercy under procedures that make the trial death oriented. Then the law becomes a mere pretense, lacking the procedural integrity that would likely result in a fair resolution of the issues. In Ohio, the deficiency in the procedure is compounded by the unreviewability of the failure to grant mercy.

Dissenting opinion by Justice Brennan, in which Douglas and Marshall, JJ., joined: Justice Brennan dissented from the Court's decision. He wrote specifically on the issue of granting juries absolute discretion in determining punishment, as follows:

These cases test the viability of principles whose roots draw strength from the very core of the Due Process Clause. The question that [the defendants] present for our decision is whether the rule of law, basic to our society and binding upon the States by virtue of the Due Process Clause of the Fourteenth Amendment, is fundamentally inconsistent with capital sentencing procedures that are purposely constructed to allow the maximum possible variation from one case to the next, and provide no mechanism to prevent that consciously maximized variation from reflecting merely random or arbitrary choice. The Court does not, however, come to grips with that fundamental question. Instead, the Court misapprehends [the defendants'] argument and deals with the cases as if [the defendants] contend that due process requires capital sentencing to be carried out under predetermined standards so precise as to be capable of purely mechanical application, entirely eliminating any vestiges of flexibility or discretion in their use. This misapprehended question is then treated in the context of the Court's assumption that the legislatures of Ohio and California are incompetent to express with clarity the bases upon which they have determined that some persons guilty of some crimes should be killed, while others should live—an assumption that, significantly, finds no support in the arguments made by those States in these cases....

It is of critical importance in the present cases to emphasize that we are not called upon to determine the adequacy or inadequacy of any particular legislative procedure designed to give rationality to the capital sentencing process. For the plain fact is that the legislatures of California and Ohio, whence come these cases, have sought no solution at all. We are not presented with a State's attempt to provide standards, attacked as impermissible or inadequate. We are not presented with a legislative attempt to draw wisdom from experience through a process looking toward growth in understanding through the accumulation of a variety of experiences. We are not presented with the slightest attempt to bring the power of reason to bear on the considerations relevant to capital sentencing. We are faced with

nothing more than stark legislative abdication. Not once in the history of this Court, until today, have we sustained against a due process challenge such an unguided, unbridled, unreviewable exercise of naked power. Almost a century ago, we found an almost identical California procedure constitutionally inadequate to license a laundry. Today we hold it adequate to license a life. I would reverse [the defendants'] sentences of death.

Case note: Within a year of the Court's decision in this case, the position taken by the dissenting Justices was used to strike down capital punishment in the nation. *See also* **Furman v. Georgia**

McKenna, Joseph

Joseph McKenna served as an associate justice of the United States Supreme Court from 1898 to 1925. While on the Supreme Court McKenna was known as a conservative and pragmatic interpreter of the Constitution.

McKenna was born on August 10, 1843, in Philadelphia, Pennsylvania. His family background was humble and, consequently, McKenna was largely self-educated. He was able to study on his own to pass the bar in California, where his family had moved during his youth. McKenna's rise to prominence began when he was elected prosecutor of Solano county. He would eventually win a seat in the United States House of Representatives in 1885. President Benjamin Harris appointed McKenna as an appellate judge for the Ninth Circuit Court of Appeals in 1892. Subsequent to a brief term as United States Attorney General, McKenna was appointed to the Supreme Court by President William McKinley in 1897. He was confirmed by the Senate in 1898.

While on the Supreme Court McKenna issued a number of capital punishment opinions. His capital punishment opinions reflected a conservative pro-government philosophy. For example, in writing the opinion for the Court in *Valdez v. United States*, McKenna retreated from fundamental principles of due process in holding that the absence of a defendant during the trial judge's visit to the crime scene did not deny him due process of law. In *Bird v. United States II*, McKenna, again writing for the Court, upheld a murder conviction after ruling that the trial court did not commit error in refusing to instruct the jury on accomplice liability principles, though the defendant presented evidence on the issue. McKenna died on November 21, 1926.

Capital Punishment Opinions Written by McKenna

Case Name	Opinion of the Court	Concurring Opinion	Dissenting Opinion
Bird v. United States (II)	✓		
Finley v. California	✓		
Gusman v. Marrero	✓		
Ross v. Aguirre	✓		
Valdez v. United States	✓		
Williams v. Mississippi	✓		

McKinley's Assassination

On September 6, 1901, President William McKinley was attending the Pan American Exposition in Buffalo, New York. As the President stood with friends and well-wishers, a stranger walked up to him wearing a bandage around his right arm. The stranger was Leon

Depiction of Leon Czolgosz approaching and firing at President William McKinley on September 6, 1901. (Library of Congress)

Czolgosz. Leon extended his right arm, as if to greet the President. Instead, he fired two shots from a pistol concealed by the bandage. The shots struck the President in his abdomen. The President died two weeks later.

Ten days after the shooting, Leon was prosecuted for capital murder in New York. The trial took eight hours and 26 minutes. The jury returned a verdict of guilty. Leon was sentenced to death. On October 29, 1901, Leon was executed by electrocution at New York's Sing Sing Prison. After the execution, Leon's body was destroyed with quicklime and acid.

Prior to his execution, Leon stated that he killed the President because of a speech he had heard by "anarchist," Emma Goldman. Leon believed that it was his duty, in furtherance of the cause espoused by anarchists, to kill a representative of capitalist society. *See also* **Chicago Labor Riots of 1886**

McKoy v. North Carolina *Court:* United States Supreme Court; *Case Citation:* McKoy v. North Carolina, 494 U.S. 433 (1990); *Argued:* October 10, 1989 *Decided:* March 5, 1990; *Opinion of the Court:* Justice Marshall; *Concurring Opinion:* Justice Whit; *Concurring Opinion:* Justice Blackmu; *Concurring Opinion:* Justice Kennedy; *Dissenting Opinion:* Justice Scalia, in which Rehnquist, C. J., and O'Connor, J., joined; *Appellate Defense Counsel:* Malcolm Ray Hunter, Jr. argued; Gordon Widenhouse and Robert S. Mahler on brief; *Appellate Prosecution Counsel:* Joan H. Byers argued; Lacy H. Thornburg, J. Michael Carpenter, Steven F. Bryant and Barry S. McNeill on brief; *Amicus Curiae Brief Supporting Prosecutor:* 1; *Amicus Curiae Brief Supporting Defendant:* None.

Issue Presented: Whether the Constitution is violated by North Carolina's penalty phase requirement that the jury unanimously find the existence of a mitigating circumstance, before such circumstance may be considered by the jury?

Case Holding: North Carolina's mitigating circumstance unanimity requirement violates the Constitution by preventing the sentencer from considering all relevant mitigating evidence.

Factual and procedural background of case: The defendant, Dock McKoy, Jr., was convicted in a North Carolina court of capital murder. Under North Carolina's death penalty scheme it was required that the penalty phase jury unanimously agree that a mitigating circumstance was proven to exist by the defendant, before the jury could consider it in weighing aggravating circumstances against mitigating circumstances.

During the defendant's sentencing phase, the jury recom- mended the death penalty after finding unanimously: (1) the existence of two statutory aggravating circumstances; (2) the existence of two of eight possible mitigating circumstances; (3) that the mitigating circumstances found were insufficient to outweigh the aggravating circumstances found; and (4) that the aggravating circumstances found were sufficiently substantial to call for the imposition of the death penalty when considered with the mitigating circumstances found.

The North Carolina Supreme Court affirmed the conviction and sentence. In doing so, the appellate court rejected the defendant's claim that it was unconstitutional to require the jury unanimously find the existence of a mitigating circumstance. The United States Supreme Court granted certiorari to consider the issue.

Opinion of the Court by Justice Marshall: Justice Marshall determined that North Carolina's unanimity requirement violated the Constitution, by limiting jurors' consideration of relevant mitigating evidence and was contrary to the Court's decision in *Mills v. Maryland.* The opinion found unpersuasive the fact that the jury could opt for life imprisonment without finding any mitigating circumstances, because there was still a requirement that such a decision be based only on the circumstances it unanimously found. Justice Marshall indicated that the result of the unanimity requirement was that one holdout juror could prevent the others from giving effect to evidence they feel called for a lesser sentence. This situation violated the Constitution and the decision in *Mills.* Under *Mills* it is required that each juror be permitted to consider and give effect to mitigating evidence when deciding the ultimate question whether to vote for a death sentence. The opinion vacated the defendant's sentence and remanded the case to the North Carolina Supreme Court for further proceedings not inconsistent with the opinion.

Concurring opinion by Justice White: Justice White wrote a concurring opinion in which he articulated what he believed were the parameters of the majority opinion. It was said by Justice White: "There is nothing in the Court's opinion, as I understand it, that would invalidate on federal constitutional grounds a jury instruction that does not require unanimity with respect to mitigating circumstances but requires a juror to consider a mitigating circumstance only if he or she is convinced of its existence by a preponderance of the evidence. Under such an instruction, any juror must weigh in the balance any mitigating circumstance that in his or her mind is established by a preponderance of the evidence, whether or not any other jurors are likewise convinced. Neither does the Court's opinion hold or infer that the Federal Constitution forbids a State to place on the defendant the burden of persuasion with respect to mitigating circumstances. On this basis, I concur in the Court's opinion."

Concurring opinion by Justice Blackmun: Justice Blackmun's concurring opinion emphasized the consistency of the resolution of the case with prior precedent. He also indicated that North Carolina's unanimity requirement was inconsistent with fundamental principles. On this issue the concurrence stated: "[T]he North Carolina unanimity requirement ... represents an extraordinary departure from the way in which juries customarily operate. Juries are typically called upon to render unanimous verdicts on the ultimate issues of a given case. But it is understood that different jurors may be persuaded by different pieces of evidence, even when they agree upon the bottom line. Plainly there is no general requirement that the jury reach agreement on the preliminary factual issues which underlie the verdict."

Justice Blackmun also took issue with the State's contention that unanimity was required for both aggravating and mitigating circumstances, therefore any unfairness balanced itself out. He wrote: "The possibility that a single juror with aberrational views will thwart the majority therefore ... may work in favor of the capital defendant. But the injustice of a capital sentence in a case where 11 jurors believe that mitigation outweighs aggravation is hardly compensated for by the possibility that in some other case a defendant will escape the death penalty when 11 jurors believe death to be appropriate. The State's reliance on the 'symmetry' of its law seems to me to be the very antithesis of the constitutional command that the sentence be allowed to consider the 'character and record of the individual offender and the circumstances of the particular offense as a constitutionally indispensable part of the process of inflicting the penalty of death.'"

Concurring opinion by Justice Kennedy: Justice Kennedy concurred in the judgment by the majority. In his concurrence he noted that "[a]pplication of the death penalty on the basis of a single juror's vote is 'intuitively disturbing.'" Justice Kennedy believed that the unanimity requirement "represents imposition of capital punishment through a system that can be described as arbitrary or capricious." The opinion supported its position as follows: "A holdout juror incident can occur under North Carolina's statute if all jurors find an aggravating factor they agree to be of sufficient gravity to support a penalty of death, and 11 jurors find an outweighing mitigating factor that one juror refuses, for whatever reason, to accept. If the jurors follow their instructions, as we must assume they will, the 11 must disregard the mitigating circumstance. After the balancing step of the statute is performed, there can be only one result. The 'judgment is death even though eleven jurors think the death penalty wholly inappropriate.' Given the reasoned, moral judgment inherent in capital sentencing by the jury, the extreme arbitrariness of this potential result is evident."

Dissenting opinion by Justice Scalia, in which Rehnquist, C. J., and O'Connor, J., joined: Justice Scalia dissented on the basis that he did not believe the Constitution precluded North Carolina from requiring jury unanimity on mitigating circumstances. The dissent stated: "I think this scheme, taken as a whole, satisfies the due process and Eighth Amendment concerns enunciated by this Court. By requiring that the jury find at least one statutory aggravating circumstance, North Carolina has adequately narrowed the class of death-eligible murderers." *See also* **Jury Unanimity; Mills v. Maryland**

McLean, John

John McLean served as an associate justice of the United States Supreme Court from 1828 to 1861. While on the Supreme Court McLean was known as a moderate with progressive tendencies in his interpretation of the Constitution.

McLean was born in New Jersey on March 11, 1785. He did not have a formal education, but was able to obtain sporadic tutoring during his youth. McLean studied law as an apprentice to a court clerk in Ohio. He was admitted to the Ohio bar in 1807. McLean went on to operate a newspaper, serve two terms in the United States House of Representatives, win an election to the Ohio Supreme Court, and be appointed United States Postmaster General. In 1828 President Andrew Jackson appointed McLean to the Supreme Court.

Although McLean served one of the longest terms of any member of the Supreme Court, he was known to write only one capital punishment opinion. In *Ex Parte Wells* the Supreme Court was asked to decide whether the President had authority to pardon a defendant's death sentence upon the condition that the defendant remain in prison for life. The majority on the Court held that the President had such authority. McLean dissented. He argued that no statute gave the President such authority, therefore the Court should not interpret the Constitution as permitting that authority. McLean died on April 4, 1861.

McNulty v. California

Court: United States Supreme Court; *Case Citation:* McNulty v. California, 149 U.S. 645 (1893); *Argued:* Not reported; *Decided:* May 15, 1893; *Opinion of the Court:* Chief Justice Fuller; *Concurring Opinion:* None; *Dissenting Opinion:* None; *Appellate Defense Counsel:* Carroll Cook argued and briefed; *Appellate Prosecution Counsel:* W. H. H. Hart argued and briefed; *Amicus Curiae Brief Supporting Prosecutor:* None; *Amicus Curiae Brief Supporting Defendant:* None.

Issue Presented: Whether the repeal of a former death penalty procedure by the State of California prevented the defendant from being executed according to the repealed law?

Case Holding: The repeal of a former death penalty procedure by the State of California did not prevent the defendant from being executed according to the repealed law, and this issue being a purely State matter cannot be examined by a Federal court.

Factual and procedural background of case: The defendant, McNulty, was convicted of capital murder and sentenced to death by the State of California. The defendant appealed the judgment to the California Supreme Court. While the appeal was pending, the State made a procedural change to the manner in which the death penalty was carried out. Under the law of the State at the time of the commission of the defendant's crime, it was required that execution should be carried out not less than 30 nor more than 60 days after judgment, by the sheriff, within the walls or yard of a jail, or some convenient private place in the county. The new law required that the judgment should be executed in not less than 60 nor more than 90 days from the time of judgment, by the warden of one of the state prisons, within the walls thereof, and that the defendant should be delivered to such warden within 10 days from the judgment. The defendant contended to the State appellate court that the new law violated the Ex Post Facto Clause of the Federal Constitution, and that since the old law was repealed he could not be executed. The appellate court agreed that the new law could not apply to the defendant, but rejected the argument that he could not be executed under the repealed law that was in existence at the time of his crime. The United States Supreme Court granted certiorari to consider the issue.

Opinion of the Court by Chief Justice Fuller: The Chief Justice found that since the State appellate court found that the Federal Constitution prohibited application of the new procedure to the defendant, no Federal question was posed in the case for the Court to address. The opinion reasoned: "The contention of counsel is that the execution of [the defendant] as ordered would be without due process, because the amendments ... repealed the former law, and left no law under which he could be executed, since the amendments could not be enforced because of their being in violation of the constitution. But this argument amounts to no more than the assertion that the supreme court of the state erred as to the proper construction of the statutes of California, an inquiry it is not within our province to enter upon.... In our judgment the decision of the supreme court of California, that he should be punished under the law as it existed at the time of the commission of the crime of which he was convicted, involved no federal question whatever." The appeal was dismissed for lack of jurisdiction. *See also* **Ex Post Facto Clause**

McReynolds, James C.

James C. McReynolds served as an associate justice of the United States Supreme Court from 1914 to 1941. While on the Supreme Court McReynolds was known as an ultra conservative interpreter of the Constitution.

McReynolds was born in Elkton, Kentucky on February 3, 1862. He received an undergraduate degree from Vanderbilt University in 1882, and a law degree from the University of Virginia School of Law in 1884. McReynolds' legal career included private practice, teaching at Vanderbilt and United States Attorney General. In 1914 President Woodrow Wilson appointed McReynolds to the Supreme Court.

McReynolds wrote only a few capital punishment opinions while on the Supreme Court. The opinion which best illustrated McReynolds' ultra conservative reputation is *Malloy v. South Carolina*. In *Malloy* the defendant argued that constitutional ex post facto principles were violated by a change in South Carolina's laws, after he committed his offense, which changed the method of execution from hanging to electrocution. McReynolds, writing for the Court, rejected the defendant's argument. He wrote: "The constitutional inhibition of ex post facto laws was intended to secure substantial personal rights against arbitrary and oppressive legislative action, and

not to obstruct mere alteration in conditions deemed necessary for the orderly infliction of humane punishment." McReynolds died on August 24, 1946.

Capital Punishment Opinions Written by McReynolds

Case Name	Opinion of the Court	Concurring Opinion	Dissenting Opinion
Aldridge v. United States			✓
Gooch v. United States	✓		
Malloy v. South Carolina	✓		
Moore v. Dempsey			✓

McVeigh, Timothy James *see* Mass Murder; Oklahoma Bombing

Madagascar Madagascar recognizes capital punishment, but has not used the punishment within recent memory. Madagascar uses the firing squad to carry out the death penalty. Its legal system is based on French civil law and customary law. The nation's constitution was adopted on August 19, 1992.

The judicial system of Madagascar consists of trial courts, Court of Appeals, Supreme Court, and a High Constitutional Court. Trials are public, defendants have the right to counsel, to confront witnesses, and enjoy a presumption of innocence. Madagascar also recognizes customary or traditional courts known as dina tribunals. In practice, dina tribunals deal with criminal cases in rural areas. *See also* **International Capital Punishment Nations**

Magistrate *see* **Arraignment**

Maine The death penalty was abolished in Maine in 1887.

Majority Opinion Decisions rendered by appellate courts are not always unanimous. When a decision of an appellate court is handed down that has less than all the members, but more than half concurring in the result or in the reasoning used in the opinion, it is called a majority opinion. A majority opinion is binding on all lower courts. *See also* **Concurring Opinion; Plurality Opinion**

Malawi Malawi permits capital punishment. The legal system of the nation is based on English common law and customary law. The nation adopted its constitution on May 18, 1995. Malawi uses hanging to carry out the death penalty. In 1997, the president of Malawi, Bakili Muluzi, placed a moratorium on the death penalty and commuted the death sentences of all prisoners on death row. This unilateral action by President Muluzi did not affect the laws in the nation which permit capital punishment.

The judicial system of Malawi consists of a High Court and a Supreme Court of Appeal. Defendants have the right to a public trial but not to a trial by jury. However, in murder cases the High Court will use juries. Defendants have the right to legal counsel, the right to present and challenge evidence and witnesses, and the right of appeal. *See also* **International Capital Punishment Nations**

Malaysia Capital punishment is allowed in Malaysia. Malaysia uses hanging as the method of execution. Its legal system is based on English common law. The nation adopted its constitution on August 31, 1957.

The judicial system of Malaysia consists of High Courts, Court of Appeal, Federal Court, and Special Court (tries cases against the king and the sultans). Under the laws of Malaysia, trials are public, defendants have the right to counsel, the right to bail, enjoy the presumption of innocence and may appeal. A single judge presides over criminal trials. There are no jury trials. *See also* **International Capital Punishment Nations**

Maldives Maldives recognizes capital punishment, but the punishment has not been used in over a decade. Its legal system is a mixture of Islamic law and English common law. The nation's constitution was adopted on June 4, 1968. Maldives is composed of 1,190 islands scattered across the Indian Ocean. Less than 200 of the islands are inhabited. Maldives has a parliamentary form of government with an executive branch, unicameral legislative branch, and judicial branch.

The judiciary is subject to executive influence. Under a 1995 presidential decree, rulings by the High Court can be reviewed by a five-member advisory council appointed by the president. The president also has authority to affirm judgments, order a second hearing, or overturn judgments.

The judicial system is composed of trial courts and a High Court. Defendants do not have a right to trial by jury. Defendants have a right to retain counsel and to confront witnesses. *See also* **International Capital Punishment Nations**

Mali Capital punishment has not been officially abolished in Mali, but it has not been imposed in over a decade. Mali uses the firing squad to carry out the death penalty. Its legal system is based on French civil law and customary law. The nation's constitution was adopted on January 12, 1992.

The judicial system is composed of trial courts, Constitutional Court, High Court of Justice and Supreme Court. Trials are public, and defendants have the right to retained or appointed counsel. Defendants are presumed innocent, have the right to confront witnesses and to appeal. *See also* **International Capital Punishment Nations**

Malinski v. New York *Court:* United States Supreme Court; *Case Citation:* Malinski v. New York, 324 U.S. 401 (1945); *Argued:* December 4–5, 1944; *Decided:* March 26, 1945; *Opinion of the Court:* Justice Douglas; *Concurring Opinion:* Justice Frankfurter; *Concurring and Dissenting Opinion:* Justice Rutledge, in which Murphy, J., joined; *Concurring and Dissenting Opinion:* Justice Murphy; *Concurring and Dissent-*

ing Opinion: Chief Justice Stone, in which Roberts, Reed and Jackson, JJ., joined; *Appellate Defense Counsel:* John J. Fitzgerald and David F. Price argued and briefed; *Appellate Prosecution Counsel:* Solomon A. Klein argued and briefed; *Amicus Curiae Brief Supporting Prosecutor:* None; *Amicus Curiae Brief Supporting Defendant:* None.

Issues Presented: (1) Whether defendant Malinski's confession was involuntary? (2) Whether the case against co-defendant Rudish was prejudiced by the use of defendant Malinski's confession?

Case Holdings: (1) Defendant Malinski's confession was involuntary, therefore the judgment against him could not stand. (2) The case against co-defendant Rudish was not prejudiced by the use of defendant Malinski's confession, because the trial court used measures to insulate Rudish from the confession.

Factual and procedural background of case: The case involved two defendants, Malinski and Rudish, who were convicted of capital murder and sentenced to death by the State of New York. The New York Court of Appeals affirmed the judgments. In doing so, the appellate court rejected the constitutional challenge by Malinski that his confession was involuntary, and the constitutional challenge by Rudish that his conviction was tainted by Malinski's involuntary confession. The United States Supreme Court granted certiorari to consider the issues.

Opinion of the Court by Justice Douglas: Justice Douglas addressed the issue of Malinski's confession first. It was observed in the opinion that: "If all the attendant circumstances indicate that the confession was coerced or compelled, it may not be used to convict a defendant. And if it is introduced at the trial, the judgment of conviction will be set aside even though the evidence apart from the confession might have been sufficient to sustain the jury's verdict." Justice Douglas then moved to a description of Malinski's confession:

> Malinski was arrested while on his way to work on the morning of Friday, October 23, 1942. The police did not then arraign him but took him to a room in the Bossert Hotel in Brooklyn where he arrived about 8 A.M. He was immediately stripped and kept naked until about 11 A.M. At that time he was allowed to put on his shoes, socks and underwear and was given a blanket in which to wrap himself. He remained that way until about 6 P.M. Malinski claims he was beaten by the police during that period. The police denied this.... Sometime around 5:30 P.M. or 6:00 P.M., Malinski confessed to the police. After it was made Malinski was allowed to dress. Malinski was kept at the hotel that night and the next three days. The record does not show exactly how long and frequent the questioning was after the first confession. But it is clear that Malinski was questioned in the early hours of Saturday, the 24th and at other times during that day. He was further questioned on Sunday, the 25th, and taken ... from the hotel to the scene of the crime where he identified several places which had a relationship to the commission of the crime and where he pointed out how the crime was executed. On Monday, the 26th, he was taken from the hotel to the police garage where he identified the automobile used in the robbery. At about 5:00 P.M. on Monday he was taken to a police station and questioned. On Tuesday morning, October 27th, about 2 A.M. he made a confession at the police station. That

confession was introduced at the trial. Shortly thereafter — about 4:00 A.M. — he was booked and put in a cell and soon arraigned.

In view of the procedure used by the police to obtain a confession from Malinski, Justice Douglas ruled that the confession was involuntary.

Justice Douglas next turned to Rudish's contention that introduction of Malinski's confession was prejudicial to him. The opinion found that the manner in which the confession was used did not prejudice the case against Rudish. Justice Douglas explained the Court's position as follows:

> … [Rudish] did not confess to the police. He was tried jointly with Malinski, his counsel electing not to ask for a severance. We are asked to reverse as to Rudish because the confession of October 27th which was introduced in evidence against Malinski was prejudicial to Rudish. It is true that that confession referred to Rudish. But before that confession was offered in evidence the trial court with the complete approval of counsel for Rudish worked out a procedure for protecting Rudish, "X" was substituted for Rudish. The jury were plainly instructed that the confession was admitted against Malinski alone and that they were not to speculate concerning the identity of "X." When it came to the charge, the trial court submitted the case against Rudish separately from the one against Malinski. On this record the questions raised by Rudish involve matters of state procedure beyond our province to review. Since the case against him, both as tried and as sustained on review, was not dependent on Malinski's confession of October 27th, we think it inappropriate to vacate the judgment, though we assume that that confession was coerced. Whether our reversal of the judgment against Malinski would as a matter of state law affect that judgment against Rudish is not for us to say.

The opinion went on to reverse the judgment against Malinski, but affirmed the judgment against Rudish.

Concurring opinion by Justice Frankfurter: Justice Frankfurter concurred in the Court's opinion. He believed "that the judgment as to Malinski calls for reversal, leaving the disposition of Rudish's conviction in the light of such reversal to the New York Court of Appeals." Justice Frankfurter expressed his disfavor with the manner in which Malinski was interrogated as follows: "Considering the circumstances of Malinski's detention, the long and continuous questioning, the willful and wrongful delay in his arraignment and the opportunity that that gives for securing, by extortion, confessions such as were here introduced in evidence, the flagrant justification by the prosecutor of this illegality as a necessary police procedure, inevitably calculated to excite the jury — all these in combination are so below the standards by which the criminal law, especially in a capital case, should be enforced as to fall short of due process of law."

Concurring and dissenting opinion by Justice Rutledge, in which Murphy, J., joined: Justice Rutledge concurred in the Court's reversal of the judgment against Malinski. He dissented from the Court's decision to affirm the judgment against Rudish. Justice Rutledge wrote: "This is a capital case. Rudish has been sentenced to death. The written confession involved him. It was used in evidence against Malinski…. There could be no valid basis for admitting this confession

against Rudish in a separate trial. Due process does not permit one to be convicted upon his own coerced confession. It should not allow him to be convicted upon a confession wrung from another by coercion."

Concurring and dissenting opinion by Justice Murphy: Justice Murphy concurred in the Court's reversal of the judgment against Malinski. He dissented from the Court's decision to affirm the judgment against Rudish. Justice Murphy argued that it was "inconceivable … that the admission of these tainted confessions was without influence in the conviction of the co-defendant Rudish."

The ultimate catalyst in Justice Murphy's opinion was not the substantive issue of the confession. He used the opportunity to write about prejudicial remarks made by the prosecutor:

> … Malinski, as well as his co-defendant Rudish, is an American of Jewish ancestry. The prosecutor made certain remarks in his statement to the jury that may have been intended and were indicative of a desire to appeal to racial and religious bigotry. He spoke of Malinski as a "jerk from the East Side" and referred to his residence in "the lower east side of Manhattan, where your life is not worth a pretzel." This is a characterization of a territory containing a large proportion of Americans of like origin.
>
> Those clothed with authority in court rooms of this nation have the duty to conduct and supervise proceedings so that an accused person may be adjudged solely according to the dictates of justice and reason. This duty is an especially high one in capital cases. Instead of an attitude of indifference and carelessness in such matters, judges and officers of the court should take the initiative to create an atmosphere free from undue passion and emotionalism. This necessarily requires the exclusion of attacks or appeals made by counsel tending to reflect upon the race, creed or color of the defendant. Here the defendants' very lives were at stake and it was of the utmost importance that the trial be conducted in surroundings free from poisonous and dangerous irrelevancies that might inflame the jury to the detriment of the defendants. Brazen appeals relating to their race or faith had no relevance whatever to the grave issue facing the jury and could only be designed to influence the jury unfairly; and subtle and indirect attacks were even more dangerous and effective. Statements of this character are the direct antithesis of every principle of American justice and fair-play. They alone are enough to cast grave doubts upon the validity of the entire proceedings.

Concurring and dissenting opinion by Chief Justice Stone, in which Roberts, Reed and Jackson, JJ., joined: The Chief Justice concurred in the Court's decision affirming Rudish's judgment. He dissented from the Court's decision to reverse Malinski's judgment. The Chief Justice wrote:

> … Malinski, charged with murder, made several confessions of guilt, which were introduced in evidence at his trial. Two, made to the police, are alleged to have been coerced, the first on October 23rd and the other four days later on October 27th. During that time he admitted to the police other isolated facts which tended to fasten guilt upon him. Three friends of Malinski also testified that on several occasions shortly after the commission of the crime and long before his arrest, he voluntarily admitted to them and to his sister that he had committed the crime….
>
> It is not the function of this Court, in reviewing, on

constitutional grounds, criminal convictions by state courts, to weigh the evidence on which the jury has pronounced its verdict, also in the light of the arguments of counsel, or to sit as a superjury. We have, in appropriate cases, set aside state convictions as violating due process where we were able to say that the case was improperly submitted to the jury or that the unchallenged evidence plainly showed a violation of the constitutional rights of the accused. But we have not hitherto overturned the verdict of a state court jury by weighing the conflicting evidence on which it was based.

Judged by these standards, ... there was no denial of due process in submitting ... Malinski's confessions to the jury in the manner in which they were in fact submitted, and that there is no constitutional ground for setting aside the jury's verdict against him.

See also **Right to Remain Silent**

Mallory v. United States

Court: United States Supreme Court; *Case Citation:* Mallory v. United States, 354 U.S. 449 (1957); *Argued:* April 1, 1957; *Decided:* June 24, 1957; *Opinion of the Court:* Justice Frankfurter; *Concurring Opinion:* None; *Dissenting Opinion:* None; *Appellate Defense Counsel:* William B. Bryant argued; Joseph C. Waddy and William C. Gardner on brief; *Appellate Prosecution Counsel:* Edward L. Barrett, Jr. argued; Beatrice Rosenberg and Julia P. Cooper on brief; *Amicus Curiae Brief Supporting Prosecutor:* None; *Amicus Curiae Brief Supporting Defendant:* None.

Issue Presented: Whether the defendant's confession was obtained in violation of his right to prompt presentment before a magistrate after his arrest?

Case Holding: The defendant's confession was obtained in violation of his right to prompt presentment before a magistrate after his arrest.

Factual and procedural background of case: The defendant, Mallory, was arrested by the District of Columbia on a charge of rape. While in police custody the defendant confessed to the crime. The confession was given after interrogation that occurred before the defendant was taken before a magistrate and advised of his rights. Under the rules of criminal procedure applicable to the District of Columbia, the defendant had a right to be taken promptly to a magistrate after his arrest. The defendant was convicted of rape and sentenced to death. The District of Columbia Court of Appeals affirmed the conviction and sentence. In doing so, the appellate court found that the confession was admissible at trial even though the defendant was not promptly taken to a magistrate after his arrest. The United States Supreme Court granted certiorari to consider the issue.

Opinion of the Court by Justice Frankfurter: Justice Frankfurter ruled that failure to take the defendant to a magistrate after his arrest violated Rule 5 of the Federal Rules of Criminal Procedure, which required that an arrested person be taken before a committing magistrate without unnecessary delay. It was said that the requirement that arraignment of a defendant be without unnecessary delay was intended to interpose a neutral party between defendants and the prosecutorial system, for the purpose of informing defendants of their basic constitutional rights. The opinion outlined the defendant's detention as follows:

> The circumstances of this case preclude a holding that arraignment was "without unnecessary delay." [The defendant] was arrested in the early afternoon and was detained at headquarters within the vicinity of numerous committing magistrates. Even though the police had ample evidence from other sources than the [defendant] for regarding the [defendant] as the chief suspect, they first questioned him for approximately a half hour. When this inquiry of a nineteen-year-old lad of limited intelligence produced no confession, the police asked him to submit to a "lie-detector" test. He was not told of his rights to counsel or to a preliminary examination before a magistrate, nor was he warned that he might keep silent and "that any statement made by him may be used against him." After four hours of further detention at headquarters, during which arraignment could easily have been made in the same building in which the police headquarters were housed, [the defendant] was examined by the lie-detector operator for another hour and a half before his story began to waver. Not until he had confessed, when any judicial caution had lost its purpose, did the police arraign him.

The judgment of the District of Columbia Court of Appeals was reversed.

Case note: Under modern capital punishment jurisprudence the death penalty may not be imposed for the crime of rape without an accompanying homicide. *See also* **Arraignment; Rape and Capital Punishment**

Malloy v. South Carolina

Court: United States Supreme Court; *Case Citation:* Malloy v. South Carolina, 237 U.S. 180 (1915); *Argued:* March 5, 1915; *Decided:* April 5, 1915; *Opinion of the Court:* Justice McReynolds; *Concurring Opinion:* None; *Dissenting Opinion:* None; *Appellate Defense Counsel:* Charles L. Prince argued; W. F. Stevenson on brief; *Appellate Prosecution Counsel:* F. H. Dominick argued; Thomas H. Peeples on brief; *Amicus Curiae Brief Supporting Prosecutor:* None; *Amicus Curiae Brief Supporting Defendant:* None.

Issue Presented: Whether procedural changes in South Carolina's death penalty law could be applied to the defendant?

Case Holding: Procedural changes in South Carolina's death penalty law could be applied to the defendant, even though the procedures were not in existence at the time of the commission of the defendant's crime.

Factual and procedural background of case: The defendant, Joe Malloy, was convicted of capital murder and sentenced to death by the State of South Carolina. The South Carolina Supreme Court affirmed the judgment. In doing so, the appellate court rejected the defendant's claim that the application of new death penalty procedures to him violated ex post facto principles. The United States Supreme Court granted certiorari to consider the issue.

Opinion of the Court by Justice McReynolds: Justice McReynolds held that application to the defendant of new death penalty procedures did not violate the Ex Post Facto Clause. The opinion explained the Court's reasoning as follows:

> Under the South Carolina laws effective when the crime was committed the punishment for one found guilty of murder

without recommendation to mercy was death by hanging within the county jail, or its inclosure, in the presence of specified witnesses. The subsequent act prescribed electrocution as the method of producing death instead of hanging, fixed the place therefor within the penitentiary, and permitted the presence of more invited witnesses than had theretofore been allowed.

... The constitutional inhibition of ex post facto laws was intended to secure substantial personal rights against arbitrary and oppressive legislative action, and not to obstruct mere alteration in conditions deemed necessary for the orderly infliction of humane punishment....

The statute under consideration did not change the penalty — death — for murder, but only the mode of producing this, together with certain nonessential details in respect of surroundings. The punishment was not increased, and some of the odious features incident to the old method were abated.

The judgment of the South Carolina Supreme Court was affirmed. *See also* **Ex Post Facto Clause**

Malta

In 1971 Malta abolished capital punishment for ordinary crimes, but retains the punishment for exceptional crimes. Its legal system is based on English common law and Roman civil law. Malta's constitution was promulgated in 1964 and substantially amended on December 13, 1974.

The judicial system is composed of trial courts, Court of Criminal Appeal, and a Constitutional Court. Trials are public and are held before a judge and nine jurors. Defendants have the right to retained or appointed counsel, enjoy a presumption of innocence, may confront witnesses, and have the right to appeal. *See also* **International Capital Punishment Nations**

Mandamus

The writ of mandamus is a common law device used to compel an official to carry out a mandatory, nondiscretionay act. A petition for a writ of mandamus will not be issued by a court, if the act sought to be compelled is one that is not mandatory by law for an official to perform. Also, if a defendant has another legal remedy available, mandamus will not be granted. *See also* **Taylor v. Alabama**

Mandate

A mandate is legal term used to describe an order from an appellate court. When an appellate court makes a decision on a case appealed to it from a lower court, the appellate court will issue a mandate that embodies the appellate court's disposition of the case. A mandate is generally issued after an appellate court issues a written opinion of its decision.

An issue that capital felons frequently contested under premodern capital punishment law, was the setting of an imminent execution date by trial courts, before appellate courts issued their mandates. The United States Supreme Court ruled in a few early capital punishment cases that State trial courts could set imminent execution dates before it issued its mandate in appealed cases, although it believed the better practice would be to wait until its mandate was issued before setting an imminent execution date. *See also* **In Re Durrant; In Re Jugiro**

Mandatory Death Penalty Statutes

It is a common practice for legislatures to enact criminal offenses that carry mandatory penalties, that is, if a defendant is convicted of the offense he or she must be sentenced according to the requirements of the statute. Mandatory sentencing statutes remove the discretion of trial judges to determine the appropriate punishment for defendants on an individualized basis.

Mandatory death penalty statutes existed in all of the original 13 colonies prior to the Revolutionary War. Offenses that carried mandatory death sentences included: murder, arson, rape, robbery, burglary, sodomy, piracy and treason. The acceptance of mandatory death penalty statutes by the colonists was attributed to the common law and its insistence upon imposing the death penalty on all felony offenses.

Acceptance of mandatory death penalty statutes by the colonists slowly faded after the Revolutionary War ended. Over time many states repealed all mandatory death penalty statutes, while others limited the number of offenses that were subject to mandatory death sentences. The United States Supreme Court did not squarely address this issue until 1976. In two cases that it rendered written opinions, *Woodson v. North Carolina*, 428 U.S. 280 (1976) and *Roberts v. Louisiana*, 428 U.S. 325 (1976), the Supreme Court ruled that mandatory death penalty statutes violate the Federal Constitution because they do not allow for an individualized determination as to the appropriateness of the death penalty, based upon the character of the capital defendant and the circumstances of the crime.

At the same time that the decisions in *Woodson* and *Roberts* were rendered the Supreme Court issued memorandum decisions in 43 capital murder cases, which invalidated death sentences because they were imposed under mandatory death penalty statutes. The states and number of cases involved in the memorandum decisions were: North Carolina (34 cases); Oklahoma (6 cases); and Louisiana (3 cases). *See also* **Roberts v. Louisiana (I); Roberts v. Louisiana (II); Sumner v. Shuman; Woodson v. North Carolina**

Manson Family

Between July and August of 1969, the Manson Family killed nine people in the Los Angeles County area. The victims were: Sharon Tate, Leno and Rosemary LaBianca, Gary Hinman, Steve Parent, Abigail Folger, Voityck Frykowski, Jay Sebring, and Donald Shea.

The Manson Family were followers of Charles Manson. Authorities estimate that at one point the Manson Family numbered over 100 followers.

Manson was born in Cincinnati, Ohio on November 12, 1934. He spent all of his youth living with different relatives in various States. In time, the instability of his youth would send him to prison for much of his early adult life. Manson's initial troubles with the law involved only property crimes. On March 21, 1967, Manson was released from a long stretch in a California prison. This release started him along the path to a different type of crime — murder.

Manson took up residence in San Francisco upon his last

Charles Manson's death sentence was commuted to life imprisonment as a result of a decision of the California Supreme Court in People v. Anderson, *493 P.2d 880 (Cal. 1972), which invalidated the death penalty in California, and the United States Supreme Court decision in* Furman v. Georgia, *408 U.S. 238 (1972), which invalidated the death penalty in the nation. (Los Angeles Police)*

traveled to the Los Angeles area in an old school bus in search of someone to produce his songs. Eventually Manson and a couple of his followers moved into the Canyon Road home of Gary Hinman, a music teacher with connections to pop singing groups. Hinman introduced Manson to Dennis Wilson of the Beach Boys, but Manson was not able to get Wilson to take any of his songs seriously.

After failing to get his songs recognized through Hinman, Manson and his followers convinced a rancher named George Spahn to let them live on his ranch. Manson continued to try and meet influential people in the music business, but was unsuccessful in persuading anyone to take his work seriously. Eventually Manson became bitter. He decided to strike back violently at those he believed were responsible for stopping him from becoming a wealthy and famous song writer.

The first victim of Manson's bitterness was Hinman. Manson and four of his followers visited Hinman in early August of 1969, initially seeking money. When Hinman refused to provide them with money, Manson ordered one of his followers to kill him. The order was obeyed.

The next battle ground was at the Los Angeles home of a music industry executive that had rejected Manson. Manson had visited the home in March of 1969, but learned that the music executive had moved and leased the home to Sharon Tate and her husband Roman Polanski. Manson did not like the treatment he received on his visit. On August 8, Manson sent four of followers to exact revenge at the Tate residence.

release from prison. At this point in his life he believed he could make a living from writing songs. Manson mixed his song writing with drug use and began to attract followers, many of whom were very young women with troubled emotional lives. By supplying his followers with LSD and amphetamines, Manson quickly found that he could control them. The members of his new found family who would eventually kill people for him were: Charles Watson, Patricia Krenwinkel, Bruce Davis, Steve Grogan, Susan Denise Atkins, Robert Beausoleil, Leslie Van Houton, and Linda Kasabian.

In the spring of 1968, Manson and his family

When the four followers arrived they found Tate (who was pregnant) at home with four guests, Steve Parent, Abigail Folger, Voityck Frykowski, and Jay Sebring. When Manson's followers left the home Tate and her guests were dead — shot and stabbed to death.

On the night after the massacre at the Tate residence, Manson and some of his followers searched randomly for other victims. They eventually broke into the home of wealthy supermarket magnate Leno LaBianca and his wife Rosemary. Manson ordered three of his followers to kill the couple. The order was obeyed.

The final victim of Manson's quest for revenge was Donald Shea. He was a ranch hand on the ranch where Manson and his family were living. Shea was killed because he knew about the murders at the Tate residence.

Authorities were baffled by all of the killings. They were unable to find a suspect until after they arrested some of Manson's followers on auto theft charges. While they were locked up, one of Manson's followers began to brag to other inmates about taking part in the massacre at the Tate residence. Authorities learned of the bragging and turned their investigation on Manson (he was already in jail on a minor charge).

The investigation into Manson was fruitful. Authorities compiled enough evidence to bring murder charges against Manson and eight of his followers: Watson, Krenwinkel, Davis, Grogan, Atkins, Beausoleil, Houton, and Kasabian. Several trials were held during the period 1970 to 1972, which resulted in murder convictions and death sentences for Manson and his followers. However, as a result of a decision by the California Supreme Court in *People v. Anderson*, 493 P.2d 880 (Cal. 1972), which invalidated the death penalty in the State, and the United States Supreme Court decision in *Furman v. Georgia*, 408 U.S. 238 (1972), which invalidated the death penalty in the nation, the death sentences for Manson and his followers were commuted to life imprisonment.

Marshall, John John Marshall served as chief justice of the United States Supreme Court from 1801 to 1835. While on the Supreme Court Marshall was known as a forceful moderate interpreter of the Constitution.

Marshall was born in Virginia on September 24, 1755. His educational training was obtained primarily at home. Marshall practiced law in Virginia and was known to handle mostly appellate cases. He had a relatively uneventful political career that took him to Virginia's House of Delegates from 1782 to 1795. In 1798 Marshall was named an emissary to France. He served as a member of Congress from 1799 to 1800. In 1800 President John Adams appointed Marshall chief justice of the Supreme Court. He assumed that office on March 4, 1801.

Marshall was known to issue only a few capital punishment opinions as chief justice (in his capacity as a Supreme Court circuit judge he presided over a number of capital cases). The case of *United States v. Bevins* best illustrated the application of Marshall's moderate philosophy to capital punishment. The issue presented in *Bevins* was whether a Federal court in

Massachusetts had jurisdiction to prosecute the defendant for a murder committed on a military ship anchored in the Boston harbor. Marshall found that jurisdiction did not reside in the Federal court, because by statute such an offense had to be committed on waters outside the territory of any State. It was concluded by Marshall that the offense charged against the defendant in *Bevins* was "unquestionably within the original jurisdiction of Massachusetts[.]" Marshall died on July 6, 1835.

Capital Punishment Opinions Written by Marshall

Case Name	Opinion of the Court	Concurring Opinion	Dissenting Opinion
Ex Parte Bollman (I)	✓		
Ex Parte Bollman (II)	✓		
United States v. Bevins	✓		
United States v. Klintock	✓		
United States v. Palmer	✓		

Marshall, Thurgood Thurgood Marshall served as an associate justice of the United States Supreme Court from 1967 to 1991. While on the Supreme Court Marshall was known as a liberal interpreter of the Constitution, with respect to individual liberties and rights.

Marshall was born in Baltimore, Maryland on July 8, 1908. He obtained an undergraduate degree from Lincoln University and a law degree from Howard University School of Law in 1933. As an attorney Marshall took up the cause of civil rights and comprised an impressive record of legal victories that help dismantle racial segregation in the United States. He was also active in arguing a number of capital punishment cases before the Supreme Court.

Marshall was appointed as an appellate judge for the Second Circuit Court of Appeals in 1961. In 1965 he was appointed Solicitor General of the United States. President Lyndon B. Johnson appointed Marshall as the

Supreme Court Capital Punishment Cases in Which Marshall Was Appellate Counsel

Case Name	Won	Lost
Burns v. Wilson		✓
Patton v. Mississippi	✓	
Shepherd v. Florida	✓	
Taylor v. Alabama		✓
Watts v. Indiana	✓	

first African American on the Supreme Court in 1967.

While on the Supreme Court Marshall was an unrelenting opponent of capital punishment. The anti–death penalty position taken by Marshall would eventually lead him to be one of two justices to issue the greatest number of capital punishment dissenting opinions, memorandums and statements, than any other person to ever sit on the Supreme Court. Justice William Brennan shared this distinction with Marshall. The opinion which best captured Marshall's view of capital punishment was his concurring opinion in *Furman v. Georgia*, the case which temporarily halted executions in the nation. Marshall wrote in *Furman*:

> It ... is evident that the burden of capital punishment falls upon the poor, the ignorant, and the underprivileged members of society. It is the poor, and the members of minority groups who are least able to voice their complaints against capital punishment. Their impotence leaves them victims of a sanction that the wealthier, better-represented, just-as-guilty person can escape. So long as the capital sanction is used only against the forlorn, easily forgotten members of society, legislators are content to maintain the status quo, because change would draw attention to the problem and concern might develop. Ignorance is perpetuated and apathy soon becomes its mate, and we have today's situation....
>
> In striking down capital punishment, this Court does not malign our system of government. On the contrary, it pays homage to it. Only in a free society could right triumph in difficult times, and could civilization record its magnificent advancement. In recognizing the humanity of our fellow beings, we pay ourselves the highest tribute. We achieve a major milestone in the long road up from barbarism ... by shunning capital punishment.

Capital Punishment Opinions Written by Marshall*

Case Name	Opinion of the Court	Concurring Opinion	Dissenting Opinion	Concurring and Dissenting
Ake v. Oklahoma	✓			
Amadeo v. Zant	✓			
Barclay v. Florida			✓	
Barefoot v. Estelle			✓	
Boyde v. California			✓	
Caldwell v. Mississippi	✓			
California v. Ramos			✓	
Coker v. Georgia		✓		
Ford v. Wainwright	✓			
Furman v. Georgia		✓		
Gardner v. Florida			✓	
Godfrey v. Georgia		✓		
Gregg v. Georgia			✓	
Heath v. Alabama			✓	
Heckler v. Chaney		✓		
Hildwin v. Florida			✓	
Lockett v. Ohio		✓		
Lowenfield v. Phelps			✓	
McKoy v. North Carolina	✓			
Moore v. Illinois				✓
Mu'Min v. Virginia			✓	
Payne v. Tennessee			✓	
Poland v. Arizona			✓	
Ross v. Oklahoma			✓	
Satterwhite v. Texas		✓		
Sawyer v. Smith			✓	
Schick v. Reed			✓	
Shell v. Mississippi		✓		
Strickland v. Washington			✓	
Turner v. Murray				✓
Whitmore v. Arkansas			✓	
Zant v. Stephens (I)			✓	
Zant v. Stephens (II)			✓	

*Does not include capital punishment memorandum opinions and written statements.

Marshall died of heart failure in Washington, D.C. on January 25, 1993.

Marshall Islands
Capital punishment is not carried out by Marshall Islands. *See also* **International Capital Punishment Nations**

Martin v. Texas
Court: United States Supreme Court; *Case Citation:* Martin v. Texas, 200 U.S. 316 (1906); *Argued:* January 25, 1906; *Decided:* February 19, 1906; *Opinion of the Court:* Justice Harlan; *Concurring Opinion:* None; *Dissenting Opinion:* None; *Appellate Defense Counsel:* Watson E. Coleman argued; O. P. Easterwood and O. E. Smith on brief; *Appellate Prosecution Counsel:* C. K. Bell argued; Robert Vance Davidson and Claude Pollard on brief; *Amicus Curiae Brief Supporting Prosecutor:* None; *Amicus Curiae Brief Supporting Defendant:* None.

Issue Presented: Whether the defendant proved that blacks were systematically excluded from the grand jury that indicted him and the petit jury that convicted him?

Case Holding: The defendant failed to prove that blacks were systematically excluded from the grand jury that indicted him and the petit jury that convicted him, by merely asserting such allegations in written motions without any evidence to support the claim.

Factual and procedural background of case: The defendant, Rufus Martin, was indicted for capital murder by the State of Texas. Prior to trial the defendant motioned the trial court to dismiss the indictment on the ground that blacks were systematically excluded from the grand jury that indicted him. The motion was denied. After the jury was selected the defendant moved to quash the panel of jurors chosen to preside over his trial, on the ground that blacks were systematically excluded from the petit jury pool. The motion was denied. The defendant was tried, convicted and sentenced to death. The Texas Court of Criminal Appeals affirmed the conviction and sentence. The United States Supreme Court granted certiorari to consider the discrimination issue.

Opinion of the Court by Justice Harlan: Justice Harlan held that the defendant failed to prove that blacks were systematically excluded from the grand jury that indicted him and the petit jury that convicted him. The opinion stated that the defendant had to do more than make bare assertions of discrimination. He had to present evidence to support his allegations. The opinion stated: "What an accused is entitled to demand, under the Constitution of the United States, is that, in organizing the grand jury as well as in the impaneling of the petit jury, there shall be no exclusion of his race, and no discrimination against them, because of their race or color. Whether such discrimination was practiced in this case could have been manifested only by proof overcoming the denial on the part of the state of the facts set out in the written motions to quash. The absence of any such proof from the record in this case is fatal to the charge of the accused that his rights under the 14th Amendment were violated."

Justice Harlan made clear that the Court was intolerant with racial discrimination in grand and petit jury selection, as he wrote:

> For it is the settled doctrine of this court that whenever, by any action of a state, whether through its legislature, through its courts, or through its executive or administrative officers, all persons of the African race are excluded solely because of their race or color, from serving as grand jurors in the criminal prosecution of a person of the African race, the equal protection of the laws is denied to him, contrary to the 14th Amendment of the Constitution of the United States. So if, upon the hearing of the written motion to quash the panel of petit jurors, the facts stated in that motion had been proved, or if the opportunity to establish them by evidence had been denied to the accused, the judgment would be reversed.
>
> But the record before us makes no such case. Although the accused in each of his written motions prayed the court to hear evidence thereon, it does not appear that he introduced any evidence whatever to prove discrimination against his race because of their color, or made any actual offer of evidence in support of either motion. The reasonable inference from the record is that he did not offer any evidence on the charge of discrimination, but was content to rely simply on his verified written motions, although the facts stated in them were controverted by the state. The trial court, it must be assumed from the record, had nothing before it, when deciding the motions to quash, except the written motions and the written answers thereto.

The judgment of the Texas Court of Criminal Appeals was affirmed. *See also* **Coleman v. Alabama (I); Coleman v. Alabama (II); Discrimination in Grand or Petit Jury Selection; Sims v. Georgia (II); Whitus v. Georgia**

Martinsville Seven
Between the period February 2, 1951 to February 5, 1951, the largest number of executions in the nation for the crime of rape occurred. During that period the State of Virginia executed the so called "Martinsville Seven." The Martinsville Seven were: Joe Henry Hampton, Frank Hairston, Booker T. Millner, Howard Hairston, Francis De-Sales Grayson, John Clabon Taylor, and James Luther Hairston. All of the Martinsville Seven were African American.

The crime committed by the Martinsville Seven occurred on January 8, 1949, in the town of Martinsville, Virginia. On the afternoon of that day Ruby Stroud Floyd was abducted from the street by the men, dragged to a wooded area near railroad tracks, and raped. The crime was reported and the authorities arrested the seven men responsible. The men gave varying degrees of confessions against each other.

Trials were held for each of the seven men in mid–1949 (there were only six trials because two of the men were tried together). They were each convicted and sentenced to death. In spite of strong protests from members of the African American community, the Martinsville Seven were sent to their deaths in Virginia's electric chair.

Legal and social historians have criticized the execution of the Martinsville Seven on grounds other than innocence. The evidence, even without confessions, established that the men raped Floyd. The damaging indictment against the executions was the fact that between the period 1908–1950, the State of

Virginia executed 45 men for the crime of rape — all of whom were African American. Although white males were convicted of the crime of rape during that period, not one was ever put to death for the crime. It is for this reason that historians have called the execution of the Martinsville Seven a travesty of justice.

Maryland The State of Maryland is a capital punishment jurisdiction. The State reenacted its death penalty law after the United States Supreme Court decision in *Furman v. Georgia*, 408 U.S. 238 (1972), on July 1, 1975.

Maryland has a three-tier legal system. The State's legal system is composed of a court of appeals, special court of appeals and courts of general jurisdiction. The Maryland Court of Appeals is presided over by a chief judge and six associate judges. The Maryland Court of Special Appeals is composed of a chief judge and 12 associate judges. The courts of general jurisdiction in the State are called Circuit Courts. Capital offenses against the State of Maryland are tried in the Circuit Courts.

Maryland's capital punishment statute is triggered if a person commits a homicide under the following special circumstances:

1. Perpetrated by means of poison, or lying in wait, or by any kind of wilful, deliberate and premeditated killing.
2. Perpetration of, or attempt to perpetrate, arson in the first degree
3. All murder committed in the burning or attempting to burn any barn, tobacco house, stable, warehouse or other outhouse, not parcel of any dwelling house, having therein any tobacco, hay, grain, horses, cattle, goods, wares or merchandise.
4. All murder committed in the perpetration of, or attempt to perpetrate, any rape in any degree, sexual offense in the first or second degree, sodomy, mayhem, robbery, carjacking or armed carjacking, burglary in the first, second, or third degree, by means of destructive devices, kidnaping, or in the escape or attempt to escape from incarceration.

Capital murder in Maryland is punishable by death or life imprisonment without parole. A capital prosecution in Maryland is bifurcated into a guilt phase and penalty phase. A jury is used at both phases of a capital trial. It is required that, at the penalty phase, the jury unanimously agree that a death sentence is appropriate before it can be imposed. If the penalty phase jury is unable to reach a verdict, the trial judge is required to impose a sentence of life imprisonment without parole. The decision of a penalty phase jury is binding on the trial court under the laws of Maryland.

In order to impose a death sentence upon a defendant under Maryland law, it is required that the prosecutor establish the existence of at least one of the following statutory aggravating circumstances at the penalty phase:

1. One or more persons committed the murder of a law enforcement officer while in the performance of his duties;
2. The defendant committed the murder at a time when he was confined in any correctional institution;
3. The defendant committed the murder in furtherance of an escape or an attempt to escape from or evade the lawful custody, arrest, or detention of or by an officer or guard of a correctional institution or by a law enforcement officer;
4. The victim was taken or attempted to be taken in the course of a kidnaping or abduction or an attempt to kidnap or abduct;
5. The victim was an abducted child;
6. The defendant committed the murder pursuant to an agreement or contract for remuneration or the promise of remuneration to commit the murder;
7. The defendant engaged or employed another person to commit the murder and the murder was committed pursuant to an agreement or contract for remuneration or the promise of remuneration;
8. At the time of the murder, the defendant was under sentence of death or imprisonment for life;
9. The defendant committed more than one offense of murder in the first degree arising out of the same incident; or
10. The defendant committed the murder while committing or attempting to commit a carjacking, armed carjacking, robbery, arson in the first degree, rape or sexual offense in the first degree.

Although the Federal Constitution will not permit jurisdictions to prevent capital felons from presenting all relevant mitigating evidence at the penalty phase, Maryland has provided the following statutory mitigating circumstances that permit the jury to reject imposition of the death penalty:

1. The defendant has not previously (i) been found guilty of a crime of violence; (ii) entered a plea of guilty or nolo contendere to a charge of a crime of violence; or (iii) had a judgment of probation on stay of entry of judgment entered on a charge of a crime of violence.
2. The victim was a participant in the defendant's conduct or consented to the act which caused the victim's death.
3. The defendant acted under substantial duress, domination or provocation of another person, but not so substantial as to constitute a complete defense to the prosecution.
4. The murder was committed while the capacity of the defendant to appreciate the criminality of his conduct or to conform his conduct to the requirements of law was substantially impaired as a result of mental incapacity, mental disorder or emotional disturbance.
5. The youthful age of the defendant at the time of the crime.
6. The act of the defendant was not the sole proximate cause of the victim's death.
7. It is unlikely that the defendant will engage in further criminal activity that would constitute a continuing threat to society.
8. Any other facts which the jury or the court specifically sets forth in writing that it finds as mitigating circumstances in the case.

Under Maryland's capital punishment statute, a sentence of death is automatically reviewed by the Maryland Court of Appeals. Maryland uses lethal injection to carry out death sentences. Defendants who committed capital offenses before March 26, 1994 may elect between execution by lethal injection or lethal gas. The State's death row facility is located in Baltimore, Maryland.

Pursuant to the laws of Maryland the Governor has authority to grant clemency in capital cases. The Governor may commute a death sentence to any length of time he or she deems appropriate.

From the start of modern capital punishment in 1976, through 1999, Maryland executed three capital felons. During this period Maryland did not have any female capital felons on death row. A total of 17 capital felons were on death row in Maryland in 1999. The 1999 death row population in the State was listed as: 12 black inmates and five white inmates. The State does not permit capital punishment to be imposed on persons 17 years old or younger. Maryland prohibits the execution of mentally retarded capital felons.

Executions by Maryland 1976–1999

Name	Race	Date of Execution	Method of Execution
John Thanos	White	May 17, 1994	Lethal Injection
Flint G. Hunt	Black	July 2, 1997	Lethal Injection
Tyrone D. Gilliam	Black	November 16, 1998	Lethal Injection

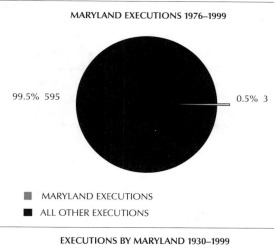

MARYLAND EXECUTIONS 1976–1999

99.5% 595   0.5% 3

■ MARYLAND EXECUTIONS
■ ALL OTHER EXECUTIONS

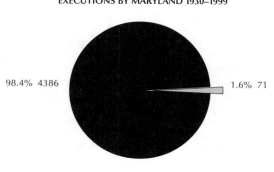

EXECUTIONS BY MARYLAND 1930–1999

98.4% 4386   1.6% 71

■ MARYLAND
■ ALL OTHER JURISDICTIONS

Maryland Coalition Against State Executions

The Maryland Coalition Against State Executions (MCASE) is composed of groups and individuals united to end the death penalty in Maryland. MCASE advocates education, legislative action, and public demonstration as means for bringing about the abolishment of capital punishment. It also produces a newsletter and sponsors weekly death penalty vigils at Maryland's death row prison.

Mass Executions *see* Dakota Executions

Mass Murder

The phrase "mass murder" is defined differently for various purposes. As used here, mass murder means the intentional and unlawful killing of 10 or more people in a single incident. There were relatively few mass murders in the United States during the 20th century. The majority of such incidents occurred after 1980. The single most devastating incident involved the Oklahoma bombing in 1995, when Timothy J. McVeigh killed 168 people.

MASS MURDER WEAPON 1927–1999

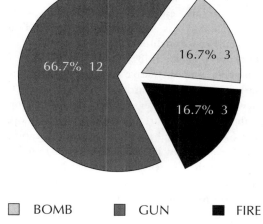

66.7% 12   16.7% 3   16.7% 3

□ BOMB   ■ GUN   ■ FIRE

As a general matter, people who commit mass murder escape legal punishment. This is because they either commit suicide or are killed by law enforcement officers. Only two mass murderers have actually been executed. Two others received death sentences and are on death row. *See also* **Flight 629; Oklahoma Bombing; Serial Killer**

Massachusetts

In 1984, the Massachusetts Supreme Court found that State's death penalty statute unconstitutional in *Commonwealth v. Colon-Cruz*, 470 N.E.2d 116 (Mass. 1984). The State has not amended the statute to correct the problems found with it by the appellate court. The last execution by the State was in 1947.

Matthews, Stanley

Stanley Matthews served as an associate justice of the United States Supreme Court from 1881 to 1889. While on the Supreme Court Matthews displayed a

Mass Murderers

Name	Date of Murders	Victims	Method of Killing	Place
Timothy J. McVeigh*	April 19, 1995	168	Bomb	Oklahoma
Julio Gonzalez	March 25, 1990	87	Fire	New York
Andrew Kehoe	May 18, 1927	45	Bomb	Michigan
Jack G. Graham†	November 1, 1955	44	Bomb	Airplane
David Burke	December 7, 1987	43	Gun	Airplane
Humberto Torre	Summer 1982	25	Fire	California
George Hennard	October 16, 1991	23	Gun	Texas
James Huberty	July 18, 1984	21	Gun	California
Charles Whitman	July 31, 1966	16	Gun	Texas
Ronald G. Simmons†	December 28, 1987	16	Gun	Arkansas
Pat Sherrill	August 20, 1986	14	Gun	Oklahoma
Eric Harris & Dylan Klebold	April 20, 1999	13	Gun	Oklahoma
George Banks*	September 25, 1982	13	Gun	Pennsylvania
Howard Unruh	September 6, 1949	13	Gun	New Jersey
Mark Barton	July 29, 1999	12	Gun	Georgia
James Ruppert	April 4, 1975	11	Gun	Ohio
R. Andrade & A. Lobos	May 3, 1993	10	Fire	California
James Pough	June 18, 1990	10	Gun	Florida

* On death row.   † Executed.

moderate philosophy on most issues, but embraced a few equal protection issues with a liberal disposition.

Matthews was born in Cincinnati, Ohio, on July 21, 1824. He was a graduate of Kenyon College. Matthews studied law as an apprentice and was admitted to the bar in Tennessee. Matthews' career path included the practice of law, newspaper editor and trial judge. In 1877 he was elected to the United States Senate as a representative of Ohio. In 1881 President James Garfield nominated Matthews to the Supreme Court.

Matthews wrote only a few capital punishment opinions while on the Supreme Court. However, one of his opinions, *Hurtado v. California*, had profound impact on capital punishment and criminal law in general. The issue raised in *Hurtado* was whether the Constitution permitted the State of California to use an information, rather than a grand jury indictment, to prosecute a defendant. Matthews, writing for the Court, held that the Constitution did not require States to use an indictment to commence a criminal prosecution. Mathews wrote: "The natural and obvious inference is that, in the sense of the constitution, 'due process of law' was not meant or intended to include … the institution and procedure of a grand jury in any case." Matthews died on March 22, 1889.

Capital Punishment Opinions Written by Matthews

Case Name	Opinion of the Court	Concurring Opinion	Dissenting Opinion
Ex Parte Crow Dog	✓		
Hurtado v. California	✓		
Kring v. Missouri			✓

Mattox v. United States

Court: United States Supreme Court; *Case Citation:* Mattox v. United States, 146 U.S. 140 (1892); *Argued:* Not reported; *Decided:* November 14, 1892; *Opinion of the Court:* Chief Justice Fuller; *Concurring Opinion:* None; *Dissenting Opinion:* None; *Appellate Defense Counsel:* J. W. Johnson argued and briefed; *Appellate Prosecution Counsel:* Mr. Maury argued and briefed; *Amicus Curiae Brief Supporting Prosecutor:* None; *Amicus Curiae Brief Supporting Defendant:* None.

Issue Presented: Whether improper contact with the jury was made during its deliberations?

Case Holding: Improper contact with the jury was made during its deliberations, therefore the judgment against the defendant could not stand.

Factual and procedural background of case: The defendant, Clyde Mattox, was convicted of capital murder and sentenced to death by the United States. The defendant appealed to the United States Supreme Court, alleging that improper contact with the jury deprived him of a fair trial. The United States Supreme Court granted certiorari to consider the issue.

Opinion of the Court by Chief Justice Fuller: The Chief Justice wrote that two types of improper contact with the jury was alleged by the defendant. It was said by the defendant the court bailiff improperly stated to the jury that the defendant had killed other people. The defendant also complained of the jury being given a newspaper reporting negatively about him. The Chief Justice found that the allegations by the defendant were substantiated by the record, and that the conduct complained of warranted a new trial. The opinion explained:

> It is vital in capital cases that the jury should pass upon the case free from external causes tending to disturb the exercise of deliberate and unbiased judgment. Nor can any ground of suspicion that the administration of justice has been interfered with be tolerated….
>
> Private communications, possibly prejudicial, between jurors and third persons, or witnesses, or the officer in charge, are absolutely forbidden, and invalidate the verdict, at least unless their harmlessness is made to appear….
>
> The jury in the case before us retired to consider of their verdict on the 7th of October, and had not agreed on the morning of the 8th, when the newspaper article was read to them. It is not open to reasonable doubt that the tendency of that article was injurious to the defendant. Statements that the defendant had been tried for his life once before; that the evidence against him was claimed to be very strong by those who had heard all the testimony; that the argument for the prosecution was such that the defendant's friends gave up all hope of any result but conviction; and that it was expected that the deliberations of the jury would not last an hour before they would return a verdict,— could have no other tendency. Nor can it be legitimately contended that the misconduct of the bailiff could have been otherwise than prejudicial. Information that this was the third person Clyde Mattox had killed, coming from the officer in charge, precludes any other conclusion.

The judgment of the Federal trial court was reversed and the cause remanded for a new trial. See also **Sequestration of Jury**

Mauritania Capital punishment is carried out in Mauritania. Mauritania uses the firing squad to carry out the death penalty. Its legal system is based on Islamic law. The constitution of Mauritania was adopted on July 12, 1991.

The judicial system includes trial courts, appellate courts, and a Supreme Court. Trials are public. Defendants enjoy a presumption of innocence, have the right to retained or appointed counsel, to bail, may confront witnesses, and may appeal their sentences. *See also* **International Capital Punishment Nations**

Mauritius Capital punishment was abolished by Mauritius in 1995. *See also* **International Capital Punishment Nations**

Maximum Security Prison *see* Death Row

Maxwell v. Bishop *Court:* United States Supreme Court; *Case Citation:* Maxwell v. Bishop, 398 U.S. 262 (1970); *Argued:* March 4, 1969; reargued May 4, 1970; *Decided:* June 1, 1970; *Opinion of the Court:* Per Curiam; *Concurring Opinion:* None; *Dissenting Statement:* Justice Black; *Justice Taking No Part in Decision:* Marshall; *Appellate Defense Counsel:* Anthony G. Amsterdam argued; Jack Greenberg, James M. Nabrit III, Norman C. Amaker, Michael Meltsner, Elizabeth DuBois, and George Howard, Jr. on brief; *Appellate Prosecution Counsel:* Don Langston argued; Joe Purcell on brief; *Amicus Curiae Brief Supporting Prosecutor:* 1; *Amicus Curiae Brief Supporting Defendant:* 6.

Issue Presented: Whether prospective jurors were unlawfully removed from the defendant's trial?

Case Holding: The issue of improper removal of potential jurors was raised for the first time in the Supreme Court, therefore the issue would be remanded for a hearing in the lower Federal courts.

Factual and procedural background of case: The defendant, Maxwell, was convicted of rape and sentenced to death by the State of Arkansas. The Arkansas Supreme Court affirmed the judgment. The defendant filed a habeas corpus petition in a Federal District Court alleging several constitutional procedural issues. The District Court rejected the petition. A Federal Court of Appeals affirmed. In seeking review by the United States Supreme Court, the defendant raised an issue in his appeal that was not presented to the lower Federal courts. The defendant alleged that several prospective jurors had been removed for cause from the jury panel in his case, merely because they voiced general objections to the death penalty. This issue was a matter that the Court held was impermissible in *Witherspoon v. Illinois*, a case decided after the defendant's trial. The Court granted certiorari to consider this belated issue.

Opinion of the Court was delivered Per Curiam: The per curiam opinion held that the defendant's claim that potential jurors were unlawfully removed from his case warranted full development by the lower courts. The opinion pointed out that under *Witherspoon*, "a sentence of death cannot be carried out if the jury that imposed or recommended it was chosen by excluding veniremen for cause simply because they voiced general objections to the death penalty or expressed conscientious or religious scruples against its infliction." It was said that "it cannot be supposed that once such people take their oaths as jurors they will be unable to follow conscientiously the instructions of a trial judge and to consider fairly the imposition of the death sentence in a particular case." Moreover, the opinion reasoned that "[u]nless a venireman states unambiguously that he would automatically vote against the imposition of capital punishment no matter what the trial might reveal, it simply cannot be assumed that that is his position." In view of the possible *Witherspoon* violation, the judgment of the Court of Appeals was reversed and the case was remanded to the District Court for a full evidentiary hearing on the issue.

Dissenting statement by Justice Black: Justice Black issued a statement indicating he dissented from the Court's decision because he believed *Witherspoon* was erroneously decided.

Case note: Under modern capital punishment jurisprudence the death penalty may not be imposed for the crime of rape, without an accompanying homicide. *See also* **Rape and Capital Punishment; Jury Selection; Witherspoon v. Illinois**

Maynard v. Cartwright *Court:* United States Supreme Court; *Case Citation:* Maynard v. Cartwright, 486 U.S. 356 (1988); *Argued:* April 19, 1988; *Decided:* June 6, 1988; *Opinion of the Court:* Justice White; *Concurring Statement:* Justice Brennan, in which Marshall, J., joined; *Dissenting Opinion:* None; *Appellate Defense Counsel:* Mandy Welch argued and briefed; *Appellate Prosecution Counsel:* Susan Stewart Dickerson argued; Robert H. Henry, David W. Lee, M. Caroline Emerson and Sandra D. Howard on brief; *Amicus Curiae Brief Supporting Prosecutor:* 15; *Amicus Curiae Brief Supporting Defendant:* 2.

Issue Presented: Whether the statutory aggravating circumstance, "especially heinous, atrocious, or cruel," was constitutionally vague as applied to the defendant?

Case Holding: The statutory aggravating circumstance, "especially heinous, atrocious, or cruel," was constitutionally vague as applied to the defendant.

Factual and procedural background of case: The defendant, Cartwright, was found guilty of capital murder by an Oklahoma jury. During the penalty phase the jury imposed the death penalty upon finding that two statutory aggravating circumstances, including the circumstance that the murder was "especially heinous, atrocious, or cruel," had been established, and that these circumstances outweighed the mitigating evidence. The Oklahoma Court of Criminal Appeals affirmed the conviction and sentence.

After exhausting State post-conviction remedies, the defendant filed a habeas corpus petition in a Federal District

Court. The District Court denied relief. However, a Federal Court of Appeals reversed, holding that the statutory aggravating circumstance, "especially heinous, atrocious, or cruel," was vague within the meaning of the Constitution. The appeal court also ruled that the Oklahoma courts had not adopted a limiting construction that cured the infirmity. The appellate court therefore enjoined the execution of the death sentence. The United States Supreme Court granted certiorari to consider the issue.

Opinion of the Court by Justice White: Justice White ruled that the statutory aggravating circumstance was unconstitutionally vague. The opinion rejected the State's contention that the death penalty should stand because the jury found another, unchallenged aggravating circumstance sufficient to sustain the sentence. It was said that Oklahoma had no procedure for attempting to save a death penalty when one of several aggravating circumstances found by the jury was held to be invalid or unsupported by evidence, it simply vacated the death sentence and automatically imposed a life imprisonment sentence. The judgment of the Court of Appeals was affirmed.

Concurring Statement by Justice Brennan, in which Marshall, J., joined: Justice Brennan issued a concurring statement joining the Court's opinion, but indicating he "would direct that the resentencing proceedings be circumscribed such that the State may not reimpose the death sentence." *See also* **Heinous, Atrocious, Cruel or Depraved Aggravator; Lewis v. Jeffers; Richmond v. Lewis; Shell v. Mississippi; Stringer v. Black; Walton v. Arizona**

Media Coverage of Execution *see* Public Viewing of Execution

Mens Rea   The phrase "mens rea" means guilty mind or mental state. Except for a few non-capital regulatory offenses, called strict liability offenses, all crimes must have a mens rea. The recognized criminal mens rea include: intentional (referred to in some statutes as felonious, wanton, purposeful or willful), knowing, reckless and negligent. Prosecutors are required to prove the mens rea of an offense beyond a reasonable doubt.

All capital offenses have "intentional" as the requisite mens rea that must be proven at the guilt phase of a trial in order to convict a defendant. Under traditional capital punishment jurisprudence mens rea played no role in the imposition of the death penalty. Traditional capital punishment required only that mens rea be proven in order to find a defendant guilty. Modern capital punishment law has carved out one exception to the general rule that mens rea is irrelevant for sentencing purposes.

Under modern capital punishment the death penalty cannot be imposed upon a defendant convicted of a capital offense involving co-defendants, if during the penalty phase it is shown that the defendant neither took life, attempted to take life, nor intended to take life. In this situation in order for the

death penalty to be imposed, a prosecutor is constitutionally required to establish at the penalty phase, that the defendant's mental state was one of reckless indifference to the value of human life. *See also* **Enmund v. Florida; Tison v. Arizona**

Mentally Ill Defense   The defense of guilty but mentally ill is a public policy response to societal frustration with criminal defendants who successfully assert the defense of insanity. The height of public disfavor with the result of a verdict of not guilty by reason of insanity reached its apogee in 1982, when John Hinckley was found not guilty by reason of insanity. Hinckley wounded President Ronald Reagan during an assassination attempt on the President's life in 1980. Hinckley's acquittal by reason of insanity spurred lawmakers around the nation to adopt the seldom previously used plea and verdict of guilty but mentally ill. A minority of capital punishment jurisdictions have adopted the plea and verdict of guilty but mentally ill.

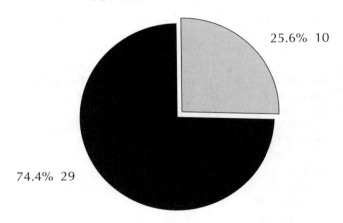

JURISDICTIONS ADOPTING GUILTY BUT MENTALLY ILL VERDICT

25.6% 10

74.4% 29

■ GUILTY BUT MENTALLY ILL JURISDICTIONS
■ ALL OTHER JURISDICTIONS

Capital punishment jurisdictions vary on the legal definition given to the phrase "mental illness" and the general requirements of the plea and verdict of guilty but mentally ill. Notwithstanding such differences, the result from a finding of guilty but mentally ill is the same in all capital punishment jurisdictions. That is, the capital felon may be sentenced to death.

South Carolina Code Ann. § 17-24-20: Guilty but Mentally Ill General Requirements

A. A defendant is guilty but mentally ill if, at the time of the commission of the act constituting the offense, he had the capacity to distinguish right from wrong or to recognize his act as being wrong as defined in Section 17-24-10(A), but because of mental disease or defect he lacked sufficient capacity to conform his conduct to the requirements of the law.

B. To return a verdict of "guilty but mentally ill" the burden of proof is upon the State to prove beyond a reasonable doubt to the trier of fact that the defendant committed the crime, and the burden of proof is upon the defendant to prove by a preponderance of evidence that when he committed the crime he was mentally ill as defined in subsection (A).

C. The verdict of guilty but mentally ill may be rendered only during the phase of a trial which determines guilt or innocence and is not a form of verdict which may be rendered in the penalty phase.

D. A court may not accept a plea of guilty but mentally ill unless, after a hearing, the court makes a finding upon the record that the defendant proved by a preponderance of the evidence that when he committed the crime he was mentally ill as provided in Section 17-24-20(A).

Capital punishment jurisdictions that utilize the plea and verdict of guilty but mentally ill also retain insanity as a defense. Unlike the insanity defense, which provides for acquittal, the defense of guilty but mentally ill will not remove a capital felon from the punishment prescribed by law. Capital felons found guilty but mentally ill are held criminally responsible and may be sentenced to death. Several state high court decisions have upheld the imposition of the death penalty upon capital felons who have been found guilty but mentally ill. *See also* **Insanity Defense**

Mentally Retarded Capital Felon

Much debate has taken place on the question of whether the Federal Constitution prohibits executing a capital felon who is mentally retarded. In *Penry v. Lynaugh*, 492 U.S. 302 (1989), the United States Supreme Court held that the constitution did not prohibit executing a person who was mentally retarded at the time of execution. The *Penry* ruling was greeted with a great deal of criticism and ultimately rejected by many State legislatures. A trend has been set in motion by State legislatures to prohibit executing mentally retarded capital felons, in spite of the blessings of the Constitution. *See also* **Insanity; Insanity While Awaiting Execution; Penry v. Lynaugh**

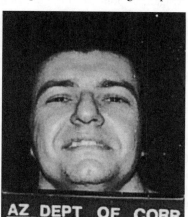

Claude Maturana is on death row in the State of Arizona. He has been diagnosed as mentally ill and unfit for execution, but with medication he would have the mental functioning level necessary to execute him under the laws of Arizona. However, medical officials refused to give him the medication that would allow the State to execute him. (Arizona Department of Corrections)

Mentally Retarded Mitigator

Three capital punishment jurisdictions, New York, South Carolina, and Virginia, have made mental retardation a statutory mitigating circumstance. If the penalty phase jury determines in those jurisdictions that a capital felon is mentally retarded, the death penalty may be rejected. *See also* **Extreme Mental or Emotional Disturbance; Mitigating Circumstances**

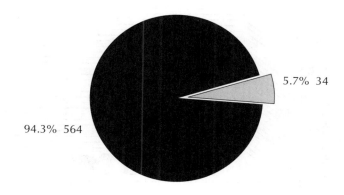

MENTALLY RETARDED CAPITAL FELONS EXECUTED 1976–1999

5.7% 34

94.3% 564

■ MENTALLY RETARDED EXECUTIONS
■ ALL OTHER EXECUTIONS

JURISDICTIONS PROHIBITING EXECUTION OF MENTALLY RETARDED CAPITAL FELONS

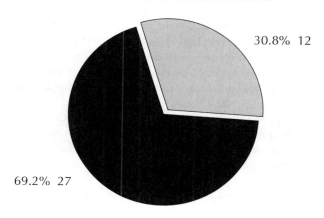

30.8% 12

69.2% 27

■ EXECUTION OF MENTALLY RETARDED PROHIBITED
■ EXECUTION OF MENTALLY RETARDED ALLOWED

Methods of Execution

The development of methods to execute capital felons has been shaped by a desire to bring about the most efficient and humane way of carrying out executions. While the common law permitted disemboweling, beheading, burning and quartering, Anglo-American jurisprudence resisted such methods of executions because of constitutional restraints on cruel and unusual punishments. The order in which execution methods developed in the United States was: hanging, firing squad, electrocution, lethal gas and lethal injection. *See also* **Electrocution; Firing Squad; Hanging; Lethal Gas; Lethal Injection**

Mexico

Mexico reserves capital punishment for extremely exceptional crimes. Its legal system is based on civil law.

METHODS OF EXECUTION USED 1976-1999

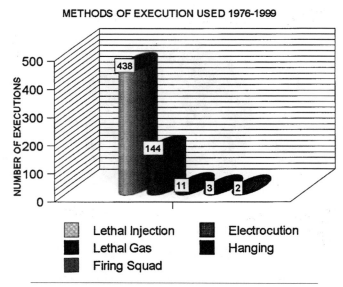

Lethal Injection   Electrocution
Lethal Gas   Hanging
Firing Squad

Mexico's constitution was adopted on February 5, 1917. Mexico is a federal republic composed of 31 states and a Federal District. The structure of the federal government consists of an executive branch, legislative branch, and judicial branch.

The federal court system consists of District Courts, Circuit Courts of Appeal, Courts of Appeal, and a Supreme Court. The trial system consists of a series of fact-gathering hearings before a single judge. Defendants have the right to attend the hearings and challenge the evidence presented. Court hearings are open to the public. Defendants have a constitutional right to an attorney at all stages of the criminal proceedings. *See also* **International Capital Punishment Nations**

Michigan   Since Michigan became a state in 1837, it has had no executions. The State abolished the punishment by statute in 1846. In 1964, the State inserted the ban in its constitution.

Micronesia   Capital punishment is not carried out in Micronesia. *See also* **International Capital Punishment Nations**

Military Death Penalty Law   From its inception, the United States Military has had the power to decree capital punishment during wartime. This authority, however, does not have a long history of being able to court martial and sentence members of the armed forces for capital offenses committed in the United States in peacetime. In the early history of the nation the powers of court martial were fixed in the Articles of War. Congress enacted the first Articles of War in 1789. The Articles of War adopted by Congress placed significant restrictions on court martial jurisdiction over capital offenses. While the death penalty was authorized for 14 military offenses, the Articles of War followed the English model of requiring the supremacy of civil court jurisdiction over ordinary capital crimes that were not special military offenses. In 1806, Congress debated and rejected a proposal to remove the death penalty from military jurisdiction.

Over the next two centuries, Congress expanded military jurisdiction. In 1863, Congress granted court martial jurisdiction to the military of common law capital crimes and the authority to impose the death penalty in wartime. In 1916, Congress granted to the military courts a general jurisdiction over common law felonies committed by service members, except for murder and rape committed within the United States during peacetime. Persons accused of murder or rape were to be turned over to the civilian authorities. In 1950, with the passage of the Uniform Code of Military Justice, Congress lifted the restriction on murder and rape.

It was not until 1983, that the military confronted a challenge to the constitutionality of the military capital punishment scheme in light of the United States Supreme Court's 1972, decision in *Furman v. Georgia*. In the case of *United States v. Matthews*, 16 M. J. 354 (1983), the military's highest court, the Court of Appeals for the Armed Forces (formerly the Court of Military Appeals) invalidated the military's capital punishment scheme. The court found that the military's death penalty procedures failed to specifically identify the aggravating factors for which the death penalty could be imposed. In making its ruling, the court indicated that either Congress or the President could remedy the defect and that the new procedures could be applied retroactively.

The President, Ronald Reagan, responded to the decision in *Matthews* on April 13, 1984. The President did so with an Executive Order promulgating the "Manual for Courts-Martial, United States, 1984." The Manual, as embodied in the Uniform Code of Military Justice and the Rules of Courts-Martial, reflects some of the concerns expressed by *Furman v. Georgia* in achieving a fair process for imposing capital punishment. (Although the opportunity has presented itself, the United States Supreme Court has never expressly ruled that *Furman v. Georgia* applied to military capital punishment.)

Under modern military capital punishment, crimes for which the death penalty may be imposed by the military include: desertion, assaulting or willfully disobeying a superior commissioned officer, mutiny, sedition, misbehavior before the enemy, subordinate compelling surrender, improper use of countersign, forcing a safeguard, aiding the enemy, spying, espionage, improper hazarding of a vessel, misbehavior of a sentinel or lookout, murder, felony murder, and rape. Most of the offenses punishable with death by the military are limited to wartime conduct.

A military capital prosecution is initiated by the convening authority, a high ranking commanding officer. The convening authority picks those service members who will serve as jurors. The jury must consist of no fewer than five members. The defendant is permitted to have at least one-third of the jury consisting of enlisted personnel. A defendant is not permitted to have a bench trial (judge only). Nor is a defendant permitted to plead guilty to a capital offense.

A defendant in a military capital trial cannot be convicted of a capital offense unless the jury unanimously finds him or her guilty beyond a reasonable doubt. If guilt is determined, the case proceeds to the penalty phase. At the penalty phase, the prosecution must prove the existence of at least one codified aggravating circumstance beyond a reasonable doubt. (One exception is a conviction for spying, which carries a mandatory death sentence.) The aggravating circumstances include:

1. That the offense was committed before or in the presence of the enemy, except that this circumstance shall not apply in the case of a violation of Article 118 or 120;
2. That in committing the offense the accused intended to:
   A. Cause substantial damage to the national security of the United States; or
   B. Cause substantial damage to a mission, system, or function of the United States, provided that this subsection shall apply only if substantial damage to the national security of the United States would have resulted had the intended damage been effected;
3. That the offense caused substantial damage to the national security of the United States, whether or not the accused intended such damage, except that this circumstance shall not apply in the case of a violation of Article 118 or 120;
4. That the offense was committed in such a way or under circumstances that the lives of persons other than the victim, if any, were unlawfully and substantially endangered, except that this circumstance shall not apply to a violation of Article 120;
5. That the accused committed the offense with the intent to avoid hazardous duty;
6. That, only in the case of a violation of Article 118 or 120, the offense was committed in time of war and in territory in which the United States or an ally of the United States was then an occupying power or in which the armed forces of the United States were then engaged in active hostilities;
7. That, only in the case of a violation of Article 118(1):
   A The accused was serving a sentence of confinement for 30 years or more or for life at the time of the murder;
   B. The murder was committed while the accused was engaged in the commission or attempted commission of any robbery, rape, aggravated arson, sodomy, burglary, kidnapping, mutiny, sedition, or piracy of an aircraft or vessel, or was engaged in flight or attempted flight after the commission or attempted commission of any such offense;
   C. The murder was committed for the purpose of receiving money or a thing of value;
   D. The accused procured another by means of compulsion, coercion, or a promise of an advantage, a service, or a thing of value to commit the murder;
   E. The murder was committed with the intent to avoid or to prevent lawful apprehension or effect an escape from custody or confinement;
   F. The victim was the President of the United States, the President-elect, the Vice President, or, if there was no Vice President, the officer next in the order of succession to the office of President of the United States, the Vice-President-elect, or any individual who is acting as President under the Constitution and laws of the United States, any Member of Congress or Member-of-Congress elect, or any judge of the United States;
   G. The accused then knew that the victim was any of the following persons in the execution of office: a commissioned, warrant, noncommissioned, or petty officer of the armed services of the United States; a member of any law enforcement or security activity or agency, military or civilian, including correctional custody personnel; or any firefighter;
   H. The murder was committed with intent to obstruct justice;
   I. The murder was preceded by the intentional infliction of substantial physical harm or prolonged, substantial mental or physical pain and suffering to the victim;
   J. The accused has been found guilty in the same case of another violation of Article 118;
8. That only in the case of a violation of Article 118(4), the accused was the actual perpetrator of the killing;
9. That, only in the case of a violation of Article 120:
   A. The victim was under the age of 12; or
   B. The accused maimed or attempted to kill the victim; or
10. That, only in the case of a violation of the law of war, death is authorized under the law of war for the offense.

The prosecution is required to give the defendant notice, prior to trial, of the aggravating circumstances that will be used at the penalty phase. Once the evidence in aggravation offered by the prosecution, and evidence in mitigation offered by the defendant, have been submitted to the jury, the jury is required to weigh all of the aggravating evidence in the case against evidence in mitigation. The death penalty may not be imposed unless the jury unanimously conclude that the aggravating circumstances substantially outweigh the mitigating circumstances. However, even if every juror agrees upon the existence of an aggravating circumstance and concludes that the evidence in aggravation outweighs the mitigating evidence, any juror is still free to choose a sentence less than death. Which means that the jury must unanimously conclude that death is an appropriate sentence. If death is not imposed the defendant must be sentenced to life without the possibility of parole.

When a death sentence is imposed, the record is initially reviewed by the convening authority, who has the power to reduce the sentence. If the convening authority approves the death sentence, the defendant will be moved to the military death row at the United States Disciplinary Barracks, Fort Leavenworth, Kansas.

Military Death Row Inmates 1999

Ronald Gray	Kenneth Parker
William Kreutzer	Jessie Quintanilla
Dwight J. Loving	Jose Simoy
James T. Murphy	Wade L. Walker

Once the convening authority reviews the death sentence, the record of trial then goes before one of the military justice system's four intermediate appellate courts: the Army, Navy-Marine Corps, Air Force, or Coast Guard Court of Criminal Appeals. The branch of service that the defendant is in dictates which intermediate appellate court reviews the sentence. If the intermediate appellate court affirms the death sentence, the case then goes before the military's highest court, the Court of Appeals for the Armed Forces. The Court of Appeals for the Armed Forces is a five-member court. Its judges are civilians appointed by the President with the advice and consent of the Senate to serve 15 year terms.

If the Court of Appeals for the Armed Forces affirms the sentence, the case may be reviewed by the United States Supreme Court. The Supreme Court's certiorari jurisdiction over military justice cases was authorized in 1983. If the Supreme Court affirms the death sentence or denies certiorari, the death sentence is then reviewed by the President. If the President approves the death sentence, the defendant may seek habeas corpus relief from the Federal courts. If habeas relief is ultimately denied, the defendant may then be executed by lethal injection. The President has the power to commute a death sentence.

From 1930 to 1999, the military executed 160 prisoners. The last death row inmate executed by the military in the 20th century was Army Private John Arthur Bennett. The execution of Bennett occurred on April 13, 1961. He was executed by hanging. He had been convicted of rape and attempted murder. *See also* **Burns v. Wilson; Coleman v. Tennessee; Dakota Executions; Ex Parte Milligan; Ex Parte Quirin; Houston Military Riot of 1917; Loving v. United States; Schick v. Reed; War Crimes**

Milke, Debra Jean *see* Child Killers

Miller, Samuel F.

Samuel F. Miller served as an associate justice of the United States Supreme Court from 1862 to 1890. While on the Supreme Court Miller was known as a moderate interpreter of the Constitution.

Miller was born in Richmond, Kentucky on April 5, 1816. He received a medical degree from Transylvania University in 1838. During a decade of medical practice Miller taught himself the law. In 1847 he was admitted to the bar in Kentucky. As a result of political activities as a lawyer in Iowa, Miller was appointed to the Supreme Court by President Abraham Lincoln in 1862.

Miller wrote a few capital punishment opinions while on the Supreme Court. The capital punishment opinion that Miller was best remembered for was *In Re Medley*. In that case Miller, writing for the Supreme Court, reversed a capital sentence as violating the Ex Post Facto Clause. In outlining the contours of ex post facto principles Miller wrote that "it may be said that any law which was passed after the commission of the offense for which the party is being tried is an ex post facto law when it inflicts a greater punishment than the law an-

nexed to the crime at the time it was committed or which alters the situation of the accused to his disadvantage; and that no one can be criminally punished in this country except according to a law prescribed for his government by the sovereign authority before the imputed offense was committed, or by some law passed afterwards, by which the punishment is not increased." Miller died on December 13, 1890.

Capital Punishment Opinions Written by Miller

Case Name	Opinion of the Court	Concurring Opinion	Dissenting Opinion
Ex Parte Gon-shay-ee	✓		
In Re Medley	✓		
Kring v. Missouri	✓		
Wiggins v. Utah	✓		

Miller v. Pate *Court:* United States Supreme Court; *Case Citation:* Miller v. Pate, 386 U.S. 1 (1967); *Argued:* January 11–12, 1967; *Decided:* February 13, 1967; *Opinion of the Court:* Justice Stewart; *Concurring Opinion:* None; *Dissenting Opinion:* None; *Appellate Defense Counsel:* Willard J. Lassers argued; Arthur G. Greenberg and Harry Golter on brief; *Appellate Prosecution Counsel:* Richard A. Michael argued; William G. Clark on brief; *Amicus Curiae Brief Supporting Prosecutor:* None; *Amicus Curiae Brief Supporting Defendant:* 1.

Issue Presented: Whether the defendant established that the prosecutor used false evidence to convict him?

Case Holding: The defendant established that the prosecutor used false evidence to convict him.

Factual and procedural background of case: The State of Illinois prosecuted the defendant, Lloyd Eldon Miller, for rape and murder of a child victim. A crucial element of the circumstantial evidence against the defendant was a pair of men's underwear, allegedly belonging to the defendant, which had stains that were identified by prosecution testimony as blood of the victim's blood type. The defendant was convicted and sentenced to death. The conviction and sentence were affirmed by the Illinois Supreme Court.

In a subsequent habeas corpus proceeding in a Federal District Court the defendant was allowed for the first time to have the underwear subjected to chemical analysis. The chemical testing revealed that the stains were not blood, but actually paint. The District Court, for another reason, ordered defendant's release or prompt retrial. A Federal Court of Appeals reversed. The United States Supreme Court granted certiorari to consider the issue.

Opinion of the Court by Justice Stewart: Justice Stewart observed that there were no eyewitnesses to the brutal crime which the defendant was charged with perpetrating. It was said that the only circumstantial link between the defendant and the crime during the trial was the purported blood stained underwear. The opinion noted that the underwear had been found by the police three days after the murder, and about a mile from the scene of the crime. The prosecutor's theory at trial was that the defendant had been wearing the shorts when he committed the murder, and that afterwards he removed and discarded them.

The opinion stated that during the presentation of the prosecutor's evidence, the victim's mother testified that her daughter had type "A" positive blood. The prosecutor also called a chemist for the State Bureau of Crime Identification. This witness testified that the stains on the underwear were blood and that the blood was type "A." Justice Stewart indicated that subsequent testing of the underwear conclusively proved that the alleged blood stains were nothing more than reddish paint. The opinion also stated that a memorandum was uncovered which showed that investigating officer informed the prosecutor that the underwear only contained paint stains. Justice Stewart concluded the opinion by stating: "More than 30 years ago this Court held that the Fourteenth Amendment cannot tolerate a state criminal conviction obtained by the knowing use of false evidence. There has been no deviation from that established principle. There can be no retreat from that principle here." The judgment of the Court of Appeals was reversed.

Mills v. Maryland

Court: United States Supreme Court; *Case Citation:* Mills v. Maryland, 486 U.S. 367 (1988); *Argued:* March 30, 1988; *Decided:* June 6, 1988; *Opinion of the Court:* Justice Blackmun; *Concurring Opinion:* Justice Brenna; *Concurring Opinion:* Justice White; *Dissenting Opinion:* Chief Justice Rehnquist, in which O'Connor, Scalia, and Kennedy, JJ., joined; *Appellate Defense Counsel:* George E. Burns, Jr. argued; Alan H. Murrell, Michael R. Braudes, and Julia Doyle Bernhardt on brief; *Appellate Prosecution Counsel:* Charles O. Monk II argued; J. Joseph Curran, Jr., Gary E. Bair and Richard B. Rosenblatt on brief; *Amicus Curiae Brief Supporting Prosecutor:* None; *Amicus Curiae Brief Supporting Defendant:* 1.

Issue Presented: Whether the Constitution is violated by an instruction to the penalty phase jury that it must unanimously agree on the existence of a mitigating circumstance?

Case Holding: An instruction given to the penalty phase jury that it must unanimously agree on the existence of a mitigating circumstance violates the Constitution.

Factual and procedural background of case: The defendant, Ralph Mills, was convicted of capital murder and sentenced to death by a Maryland court. On appeal the defendant challenged the sentence on the ground that Maryland's capital punishment statute, as applied to him, was unconstitutionally mandatory. He argued that the statute required imposition of the death sentence if the jury unanimously found an aggravating circumstance, but could not agree unanimously as to the existence of any particular mitigating circumstance. Thus, he asserted, even if some or all of the jurors were to believe that some mitigating circumstance or circumstances were present, unless they could unanimously agree on the existence of the same mitigating factor, the sentence necessarily would be death. The Maryland Court of Appeals rejected the argument and affirmed the conviction and sentence. The United States Supreme Court granted certiorari to consider how the sentencing jury was instructed.

Opinion of the Court by Justice Blackmun: Justice Blackmun indicated that in a capital prosecution, the penalty phase jury may not be precluded from considering, as a mitigating factor, any relevant circumstance. It was said that if the jury followed the instructions set out in the verdict form in the case, the jury would be precluded from considering mitigating evidence if only a single juror adhered to the view that such evidence should not be considered. Justice Blackmun found that while there was no extrinsic evidence of what the jury in the case actually thought, the portions of the record relating to the verdict form and the judge's instructions indicated that there was at least a substantial risk that the jury was misinformed. The opinion held: "We conclude that there is a substantial probability that reasonable jurors, upon receiving the judge's instructions in this case, and in attempting to complete the verdict form as instructed, well may have thought they were precluded from considering any mitigating evidence unless all 12 jurors agreed on the existence of a particular such circumstance. Under our cases, the sentencer must be permitted to consider all mitigating evidence. The possibility that a single juror could block such consideration, and consequently require the jury to impose the death penalty, is one we dare not risk." The judgment of the Maryland Court of Appeals was vacated insofar as the death sentence.

Concurring opinion by Justice Brennan: The concurring opinion of Justice Brennan stated succinctly: "I join the Court's opinion and agree fully with its analysis as to why, under our current death penalty jurisprudence, the death sentence in this case must be vacated. I write separately only because the judgment, which is without prejudice to further sentencing proceedings, does not expressly preclude the reimposition of the death penalty. Adhering to my view that the death penalty is in all circumstances cruel and unusual punishment prohibited by the Eighth and Fourteenth Amendments, I would direct that the resentencing proceedings be circumscribed such that the State may not reimpose the death sentence."

Concurring opinion by Justice White: Justice White stated in his concurring opinion the following: "The issue in this case is how reasonable jurors would have understood and applied their instructions. That is the issue the Court's opinion addresses, and I am persuaded that the Court reaches the correct solution. Hence, I join the Court's opinion."

Dissenting opinion by Chief Justice Rehnquist, in which O'Connor, Scalia, and Kennedy, JJ., joined: The Chief Justice dissented on the grounds that the Court departed from exiting law to find that the jury may have misinterpreted the trial court's instructions. The dissent stated: "[T]he relevant inquiry is not whether an impermissible interpretation of instructions to the jury, however improbable, is literally possible; it is instead 'what a reasonable juror could have understood the charge as meaning.' I think the instructions and charges to the jury in this case pass this test, and I would affirm [defendant's] sentence as well as his conviction." *See also* **Jury Unanimity; McKoy v. North Carolina**

Mills v. United States *Court:* United States Supreme Court; *Case Citation:* Mills v. United States, 164 U.S. 644 (1897); *Argued:* Not reported; *Decided:* January 4, 1897; *Opinion of the Court:* Justice Peckham; *Concurring Opinion:* None; *Dissenting Opinion:* None; *Appellate Defense Counsel:* Not represented; *Appellate Prosecution Counsel:* Dickinson argued and briefed; *Amicus Curiae Brief Supporting Prosecutor:* None; *Amicus Curiae Brief Supporting Defendant:* None.

Issue Presented: Whether the trial court properly instructed the jury on the crime of rape?

Case Holding: The trial court did not properly instruct the jury on the crime of rape, therefore the judgment against the defendant could not stand.

Factual and procedural background of case: The defendant, Mills, was convicted of rape and sentenced to death by the United States. The defendant was a citizen of the Cherokee Nation and the victim was not. The defendant appealed the judgment against him to the United States Supreme Court. In the appeal he contended that the trial court improperly instructed the jury on what was necessary to constitute the crime of rape. The United States Supreme Court granted certiorari to consider the issue.

Opinion of the Court by Justice Peckham: Justice Peckham held that the trial court did not properly inform the jury of what was necessary for the commission of rape. The opinion explained as follows:

> In [the jury instructions] we think the court did not explain fully enough so as to be understood by the jury what constitutes in law nonconsent on the part of the woman, and what is the force, necessary in all cases of nonconsent, to constitute this crime. He merely stated that if the woman did not give consent, the only force necessary to constitute the crime in that case was that which was incident to the commission of the act itself. That is true in a case where the woman's will or her resistance had been overcome by threats or fright, or she had become helpless or unconscious, so that, while not consenting, she still did not resist. But the charge in question covered much more extensive ground. It covered the case where no threats were made, where no active resistance was overcome, where the woman was not unconscious, but where there was simply nonconsent on her part, and no real resistance whatever. Such nonconsent as that is no more than a mere lack of acquiescence, and is not enough to constitute the crime of rape. Taking all the evidence in the case, the jury might have inferred just that amount of nonconsent in this case. Not that they were bound to do so, but the question was one for them to decide. The mere nonconsent of a female to intercourse, where she is in possession of her natural, mental, and physical powers, if not overcome by numbers, or terrified by threats, or in such place and position that resistance would be useless, does not constitute the crime of rape on the part of the man who has connection with her under such circumstances. More force is necessary when that is the character of nonconsent than was stated by the court to be necessary to make out that element of the crime. That kind of nonconsent is not enough, nor is the force spoken of then sufficient, which is only incidental to the act itself.

The judgment of the Federal trial court was reversed and the cause remanded for a new trial.

Case note: Under modern capital punishment jurisprudence the death penalty may not be imposed for the crime of rape, without an accompanying homicide. *See also* **Rape and Capital Punishment**

Minder v. Georgia *Court:* United States Supreme Court; *Case Citation:* Minder v. Georgia, 183 U.S. 559 (1902); *Argued:* December 3, 1901; *Decided:* January 6, 1902; *Opinion of the Court:* Chief Justice Fuller; *Concurring Opinion:* None; *Dissenting Opinion:* None; *Appellate Defense Counsel:* John Randolph Cooper argued; Herman Brosch, and Marion W. Harris on brief; *Appellate Prosecution Counsel:* J. M. Terrell argued and briefed; *Amicus Curiae Brief Supporting Prosecutor:* None; *Amicus Curiae Brief Supporting Defendant:* None.

Issue Presented: Whether the defendant was denied due process of law because the trial court would not grant him a continuance to depose witnesses?

Case Holding: The defendant was not denied due process of law because the trial court would not grant him a continuance to depose witnesses.

Factual and procedural background of case: The defendant, Isadore Minder, was convicted of capital murder and sentenced to death by the State of Georgia. The Supreme Court of Georgia affirmed the judgment. In doing so, the appellate court rejected the defendant's contention that he was denied due process of law because the trial court refused to postpone the trial and permit him to depose out-of-state witnesses. The United States Supreme Court granted certiorari to consider the issue.

Opinion of the Court by Chief Justice Fuller: The Chief Justice held that the defendant was not denied due process of law. The opinion reasoned as follows:

> The requirements of the 14th Amendment are satisfied if trial is had according to the settled course of judicial procedure obtaining in the particular state, and the laws operate on all persons alike and do not subject the individual to the arbitrary exercise of the powers of government. Because it is not within the power of the Georgia courts to compel the attendance of witnesses who are beyond the limits of the state, or because the taking or use of depositions of witnesses so situated in criminal cases on behalf of defendants is not provided for, and may not be recognized in Georgia, we cannot interfere with the administration of justice in that state on the ground of a violation of the 14th Amendment in these particulars.

The judgment of the Georgia Supreme Court was affirmed.

Minnesota Minnesota abolished capital punishment in 1911.

Minor Participation Mitigator Even though a defendant is convicted of capital murder, his or her role may have been minor when accomplices are involved. A majority of capital punishment jurisdictions have recognized this fact and made "minor participation" in a murder a statutory mitigating circumstance. The penalty phase jury may reject the death penalty in these jurisdictions, based upon this mitigator. *See also* **Mitigating Circumstances**

JURISDICTIONS USING MINOR PARTICIPATION MITIGATOR

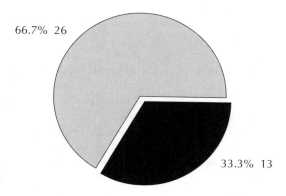

66.7% 26

33.3% 13

■ MINOR PARTICIPATION MITIGATOR JURISDICTIONS

■ ALL OTHER JURISDICTIONS

Minton, Sherman

Sherman Minton served as an associate justice of the United States Supreme Court from 1949 to 1956. While on the Supreme Court Minton was known as a conservative interpreter of the Constitution.

Minton was born in Georgetown, Indiana, on October 20, 1890. He was a 1915 graduate of Indiana University. Minton obtained a law degree from Yale in 1916. After law school Minton started a private law practice. In 1934 he was elected to the United States Senate. He was later nominated for a position as an appellate judge on the Seventh Circuit Court of Appeals. In 1949 President Harry S. Truman appointed Minton to the United States Supreme Court.

Minton was known to write only a few opinions in capital punishment cases. The staunch conservative philosophy espoused by Minton was best illustrated in his dissenting opinion in *Leyra v. Denno*. In *Leyra* the defendant argued that his initial involuntary confession tainted subsequent confessions, so as to preclude their use against him. The majority on the Court agreed with the defendant and reversed his capital sentence. Minton disagreed and wrote: "It seems to me the very essence of due process to submit to a jury the question of whether these later confessions were tainted by the prior coercion and promises which led to the [initial] confession. I am familiar with no case in which this Court has ever held that an invalid confession ipso facto invalidates all subsequent confessions as a matter of law. It does not seem to me a denial of due process for the State to allow the jury to say, under all the facts and circumstances in evidence and under proper instructions by the court, whether the subsequent confessions were tainted or were free and voluntary." Minton died on April 9, 1965.

Capital Punishment Opinions Written by Minton

Case Name	Opinion of the Court	Concurring Opinion	Dissenting Opinion
Burns v. Wilson		✓	
Leyra v. Denno			✓
Williams v. Georgia			✓

Miranda Warnings *see* Right to Remain Silent

Misdemeanor *see* Types of Crimes

Mississippi

The State of Mississippi is a capital punishment jurisdiction. The State reenacted its death penalty law after the United States Supreme Court decision in *Furman v. Georgia*, 408 U.S. 238 (1972), on April 23, 1974.

Mississippi has a three-tier legal system. The State's legal system is composed of a supreme court, court of appeals and courts of general jurisdiction. The Mississippi Supreme Court is presided over by a chief justice, two presiding justices and six associate justices. The Mississippi Court of Appeals is composed of a chief judge and nine judges. The courts of general jurisdiction in the State are called Circuit Courts. Capital offenses against the State of Mississippi are tried in the Circuit Courts.

Mississippi's capital punishment statute is triggered if a person commits a homicide under the following special circumstances:

a. Murder which is perpetrated by killing a peace officer, correction officer, or fireman while such officer or fireman is acting in his official capacity or by reason of an act performed in his official capacity, and with knowledge that the victim was a peace officer or fireman;

b. Murder which is perpetrated by a person who is under sentence of life imprisonment;

c. Murder which is perpetrated by use or detonation of a bomb or explosive device;

d. Murder which is perpetrated by any person who has been offered or has received anything of value for committing the murder, and all parties to such a murder, are guilty as principals;

e. When done with or without any design to effect death, by any person engaged in the commission of the crime of rape, burglary, kidnapping, arson, robbery, sexual battery, unnatural intercourse with any child under the age of twelve, or nonconsensual unnatural intercourse with mankind, or in any attempt to commit such felonies;

f. When done with or without any design to effect death, by any person engaged in the commission of the crime of felonious

Mike Moore is the Mississippi Attorney General. His office represents the State in capital punishment appellate proceedings. (Mississippi Attorney General Office)

abuse and/or battery of a child or in any attempt to commit such felony;

g. Murder which is perpetrated by the killing of any elected official of a county, municipal, state or federal government with knowledge that the victim was such public official.

Capital murder in Mississippi is punishable by death or life imprisonment with or without parole. A capital prosecution in Mississippi is bifurcated into a guilt phase and penalty phase. A jury is used at both phases of a capital trial. It is required that, at the penalty phase, the jury unanimously agree that a death sentence is appropriate before it can be imposed. If the penalty phase jury is unable to reach a verdict, the trial judge is required to impose a sentence of life imprisonment. The decision of a penalty phase jury is binding on the trial court under the laws of Mississippi.

In order to impose a death sentence upon a defendant under Mississippi law, it is required that the prosecutor establish the existence of at least one of the following statutory aggravating circumstances at the penalty phase:

a. The capital offense was committed by a person under sentence of imprisonment.
b. The defendant was previously convicted of another capital offense or of a felony involving the use or threat of violence to the person.
c. The defendant knowingly created a great risk of death to many persons.
d. The capital offense was committed while the defendant was engaged, or was an accomplice, in the commission of, or an attempt to commit, or flight after committing or attempting to commit, any robbery, rape, arson, burglary, kidnapping, aircraft piracy, sexual battery, unnatural intercourse with any child under the age of twelve, or nonconsensual unnatural intercourse with mankind, or felonious abuse and/or battery of a child, or the unlawful use or detonation of a bomb or explosive device.
e. The capital offense was committed for the purpose of avoiding or preventing a lawful arrest or effecting an escape from custody.
f. The capital offense was committed for pecuniary gain.
g. The capital offense was committed to disrupt or hinder the lawful exercise of any governmental function or the enforcement of laws.
h. The capital offense was especially heinous, atrocious or cruel.

Although the Federal Constitution will not permit jurisdictions to prevent capital felons from presenting all relevant mitigating evidence at the penalty phase, Mississippi has provided the following statutory mitigating circumstances that permit the jury to reject imposition of the death penalty:

a. The defendant has no significant history of prior criminal activity.
b. The offense was committed while the defendant was under the influence of extreme mental or emotional disturbance.

c. The victim was a participant in the defendant's conduct or consented to the act.
d. The defendant was an accomplice in the capital offense committed by another person and his participation was relatively minor.
e. The defendant acted under extreme duress or under the substantial domination of another person.
f. The capacity of the defendant to appreciate the criminality of his conduct or to conform his conduct to the requirements of law was substantially impaired.
g. The age of the defendant at the time of the crime.

Under Mississippi's capital punishment statute, a sentence of death is automatically reviewed by the Mississippi Supreme Court. Mississippi uses lethal injection to carry out death sentences (lethal gas was formerly used). The State's death row facility for men is located in Parchman, Mississippi; while the facility maintaining female death row inmates is located in Pearl, Mississippi.

Pursuant to the laws of Mississippi the Governor has exclusive authority to grant clemency in capital cases. The State's Parole Board investigates clemency requests.

From the start of modern capital punishment in 1976, through 1999, Mississippi executed four capital felons. During this period Mississippi did not execute any female capital felons, although one of its death row inmates during this period was female. A total of 65 capital felons were on death row in Mississippi in 1999. The 1999 death row population in the State was listed as: 37 black inmates and 28 white inmates. In 1999 the State had five juveniles on death row. The State permits capital punishment to be imposed on persons 16 years old or older. Mississippi does not prohibit the execution of mentally retarded capital felons.

Executions by Mississippi 1976–1999

Name	Race	Date of Execution	Method of Execution
Jimmy L. Gray	White	September 2, 1983	Lethal Gas
Edward E. Johnson	White	May 20, 1987	Lethal Gas
Connie R. Evans	Black	July 20, 1987	Lethal Gas
Leo Edwards	Black	June 21, 1989	Lethal Gas

MISSISSIPPI EXECUTIONS 1976–1999

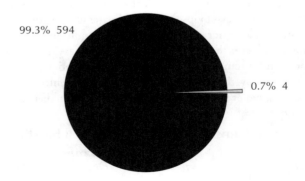

99.3% 594

0.7% 4

■ MISSISSIPPI EXECUTIONS
■ ALL OTHER EXECUTIONS

EXECUTIONS BY MISSISSIPPI 1930–1999

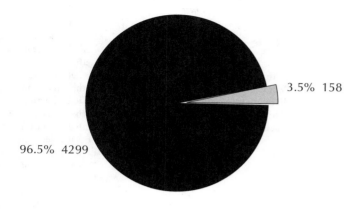

3.5% 158

96.5% 4299

■ MISSISSIPPI

■ ALL OTHER JURISDICTIONS

Missouri The State of Missouri is a capital punishment jurisdiction. The State reenacted its death penalty law after the United States Supreme Court decision in *Furman v. Georgia*, 408 U.S. 238 (1972), on September 28, 1975.

Missouri has a three-tier legal system. The State's legal system is composed of a supreme court, court of appeals and courts of general jurisdiction. The Missouri Supreme Court is presided over by a chief justice and six associate justices. The Missouri Court of Appeals is divided into three districts. Each district is composed of a chief judge and at least six judges. The courts of general jurisdiction in the State are called Circuit Courts. Capital offenses against the State of Missouri are tried in the Circuit Courts.

Missouri's capital punishment statute is triggered if a person commits a homicide under the following single special circumstance: The offender knowingly causes the death of another person after deliberation upon the matter.

Capital murder in Missouri is punishable by death or life imprisonment without parole. A capital prosecution in Missouri is bifurcated into a guilt phase and penalty phase. A jury is used at both phases of a capital trial. It is required that, at the penalty phase, the jury unanimously agree that a death sentence is appropriate before it can be imposed. If the penalty phase jury is unable to reach a verdict, the trial judge is required to impose a sentence of life imprisonment without parole. The decision of a penalty phase jury is binding on the trial court under the laws of Missouri.

In order to impose a death sentence upon a defendant under Missouri law, it is required that the prosecutor establish the existence of at least one of the following statutory aggravating circumstances at the penalty phase:

1. The offense was committed by a person with a prior record of conviction for murder in the first degree, or the offense was committed by a person who has one or more serious assaultive criminal convictions;

2. The murder in the first degree offense was committed while the offender was engaged in the commission or attempted commission of another unlawful homicide;

3. The offender by his act of murder in the first degree knowingly created a great risk of death to more than one person by means of a weapon or device which would normally be hazardous to the lives of more than one person;

4. The offender committed the offense of murder in the first degree for himself or another, for the purpose of receiving money or any other thing of monetary value from the victim of the murder or another;

5. The murder in the first degree was committed against a judicial officer, former judicial officer, prosecuting attorney or former prosecuting attorney, circuit attorney or former circuit attorney, assistant prosecuting attorney or former assistant prosecuting attorney, assistant circuit attorney or former assistant circuit attorney, peace officer or former peace officer, elected official or former elected official during or because of the exercise of his official duty;

6. The offender caused or directed another to commit murder in the first degree or committed murder in the first degree as an agent or employee of another person;

7. The murder in the first degree was outrageously or wantonly vile, horrible or inhuman in that it involved torture, or depravity of mind;

8. The murder in the first degree was committed against any peace officer, or fireman while engaged in the performance of his official duty;

9. The murder in the first degree was committed by a person in, or who has escaped from, the lawful custody of a peace officer or place of lawful confinement;

10. The murder in the first degree was committed for the purpose of avoiding, interfering with, or preventing a lawful arrest or custody in a place of lawful confinement, of himself or another;

11. The murder in the first degree was committed while the defendant was engaged in the perpetration or was aiding or encouraging another person to perpetrate or attempt to perpetrate a felony of any degree of rape, sodomy, burglary, robbery, kidnapping, or any felony offense;

12. The murdered individual was a witness or potential witness in any past or pending investigation or past or pending prosecution, and was killed as a result of his status as a witness or potential witness;

13. The murdered individual was an employee of an institution or facility of the department of corrections of this state or local correction agency and was killed in the course of performing his official duties, or the murdered individual was an inmate of such institution or facility;

14. The murdered individual was killed as a result of the hijacking of an airplane, train, ship, bus or other public conveyance;

15. The murder was committed for the purpose of concealing or attempting to conceal any felony offense;

16. The murder was committed for the purpose of causing or

attempting to cause a person to refrain from initiating or aiding in the prosecution of a felony offense;

17. The murder was committed during the commission of a crime which is part of a pattern of criminal street gang activity.

Although the Federal Constitution will not permit jurisdictions to prevent capital felons from presenting all relevant mitigating evidence at the penalty phase, Missouri has provided the following statutory mitigating circumstances that permit the jury to reject imposition of the death penalty:

1. The defendant has no significant history of prior criminal activity;
2. The murder in the first degree was committed while the defendant was under the influence of extreme mental or emotional disturbance;
3. The victim was a participant in the defendant's conduct or consented to the act;
4. The defendant was an accomplice in the murder in the first degree committed by another person and his participation was relatively minor;
5. The defendant acted under extreme duress or under the substantial domination of another person;
6. The capacity of the defendant to appreciate the criminality of his conduct or to conform his conduct to the requirements of law was substantially impaired;
7. The age of the defendant at the time of the crime.

Under Missouri's capital punishment statute, a sentence of death is automatically reviewed by the Missouri Supreme Court. Missouri provides for the election of lethal injection or lethal gas to carry out death sentences. The State's death row facility for men is located in Mineral Point, Missouri; while the facility maintaining female death row inmates is located in Chillicothe, Missouri.

Pursuant to the laws of Missouri the Governor has exclusive authority to grant clemency in capital cases. The Governor has the discretion to appoint a board of inquiry to investigate a request for clemency.

From the start of modern capital punishment in 1976, through 1999, Missouri executed 41 capital felons. During this period Missouri did not execute any female capital felons, although one of its death row inmates during this period was a female. A total of 84 capital felons were on death row in Missouri in 1999. The 1999 death row population in the State was listed as: 40 black inmates and 44 white inmates. In 1999 the State did not have any juveniles on death row. The State permits capital punishment to be imposed on persons 16 years old

Executions by Missouri 1976–1999

Name	Race	Date of Execution	Method of Execution
George Mercer	White	January 6, 1989	Lethal Injection
Gerald Smith	White	January 18, 1990	Lethal Injection
Wilford Stokes	Black	May 11, 1990	Lethal Injection
Leonard M. Laws	White	May 17, 1990	Lethal Injection
George C. Gilmore	White	August 31, 1990	Lethal Injection
Maurice Byrd	Black	August 23, 1991	Lethal Injection
Ricky L. Grubbs	White	October 21, 1992	Lethal Injection
Martsay Bolder	Black	January 27, 1993	Lethal Injection
Walter J. Blair	Black	July 21, 1993	Lethal Injection
Frederick Lashley	Black	July 28, 1993	Lethal Injection
Frank Guinan	White	October 6, 1993	Lethal Injection
Emmitt Foster	Black	May 3, 1995	Lethal Injection
Larry Griffin	Black	June 21, 1995	Lethal Injection
Anthony R. Murray	Black	July 26, 1995	Lethal Injection
Robert Sidebottom	White	November 15, 1995	Lethal Injection
Anthony J. LaRette	White	November 29, 1995	Lethal Injection
Robert O'Neal	White	December 6, 1995	Lethal Injection
Jeffery P. Sloan	White	February 21, 1996	Lethal Injection
Doyle Williams	White	April 10, 1996	Lethal Injection
Emmet Nave	N.A.	July 31, 1996	Lethal Injection
Thomas Battle	Black	August 7, 1996	Lethal Injection
Richard Oxford	White	August 21, 1996	Lethal Injection
Richard Zeitvogel	White	December 11, 1996	Lethal Injection
Eric Schneider	White	January 29, 1997	Lethal Injection
Ralph C. Feltrop	White	August 6, 1997	Lethal Injection
Donald E. Reese	White	August 13, 1997	Lethal Injection
Andrew Six	White	August 20, 1997	Lethal Injection
Samuel McDonald, Jr.	Black	September 24, 1997	Lethal Injection
Alan Bannister	White	October 22, 1997	Lethal Injection
Reginald Powell	Black	February 25, 1998	Lethal Injection
Milton Griffin-El	Black	March 25, 1998	Lethal Injection
Glennon Sweet	White	April 22, 1998	Lethal Injection
Kelvin Malone	Black	January 13, 1999	Lethal Injection
James Rodden	White	February 24, 1999	Lethal Injection
Roy M. Roberts	White	March 10, 1999	Lethal Injection
Roy Ramsey, Jr.	Black	April 14, 1999	Lethal Injection
Ralph E. Davis	Black	April 28, 1999	Lethal Injection
Jessie Wise	Black	May 26, 1999	Lethal Injection
Bruce Kilgore	Black	June 16, 1999	Lethal Injection
Robert Walls	White	June 30, 1999	Lethal Injection
David Leisure	White	September 1, 1999	Lethal Injection

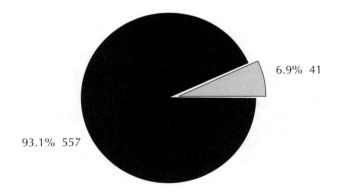

MISSOURI EXECUTIONS 1976–1999

6.9% 41

93.1% 557

■ MISSOURI EXECUTIONS
■ ALL OTHER EXECUTIONS

EXECUTIONS BY MISSOURI 1930–1999

97.7% 4354

2.3% 103

■ MISSOURI

■ ALL OTHER JURISDICTIONS

JURISDICTIONS THAT DO NOT HAVE STATUTORY MITIGATING CIRCUMSTANCES

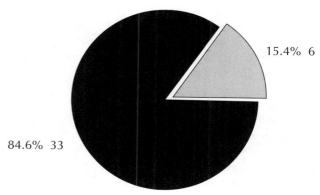

15.4% 6

84.6% 33

■ JURISDICTIONS WITHOUT STATUTORY MITIGATORS

■ ALL OTHER JURISDICTIONS

or older. Missouri does not prohibit the execution of mentally retarded capital felons.

Mistrial   A trial judge is vested with the authority to grant a mistrial over the defendant's objection, and discharge a jury whenever in his or her opinion there is a manifest necessity for the mistrial. A retrial after a mistrial properly granted is not prohibited by double jeopardy principles. However, an improperly granted mistrial to which the defendant objected, precludes a second prosecution for the same offense and acts as an acquittal. *See also* **Thompson v. United States**

Mitigating Circumstances   The phrase "mitigating circumstances" refers to some aspect of a defendant's character, record, or some extenuating aspect of a capital crime which, while it does not prevent the defendant from being found guilty of the crime, does make him or her less deserving of the penalty of death. Mitigating circumstances are factors that are introduced as evidence by a capital felon at the penalty phase, not guilt phase of a capital prosecution. There

Daniel Green (left) and Larry Demery (right) were found guilty of the 1993 capital murder of James Jordan, father of basketball legend Michael Jordan. The penalty phase juries in both cases found mitigating circumstances warranted rejection of the death penalty. Green and Demery were therefore sentenced to life imprisonment for their capital crime. (North Carolina Department of Corrections)

are two types of mitigating circumstances: statutory mitigating circumstances and non-statutory mitigating circumstances.

A majority of capital punishment jurisdictions have created a limited number of statutory mitigating circumstances. From a practical matter, the only difference between statutory and non-statutory mitigators is that the former

is embodied in statutes and the latter is not. This is so because it is constitutionally required that all relevant mitigating circumstances, whether statutory or non-statutory, be permitted at the penalty phase of a capital prosecution.

Submission to the penalty phase jury of an instruction on a relevant mitigating circumstance is not automatic. In order to establish that a capital felon is entitled to a requested penalty phase jury instruction on a proffered mitigating circumstance, the defendant must show that the circumstance is one which a jury could reasonably find had mitigating value, and that there is sufficient evidence of the existence of the circumstance to require it to be submitted to the jury. If the trial court determines the jury could not reasonably find the proffered mitigating circumstance exists in light of the evidence introduced, the jury will not be instructed to consider the mitigating circumstance.

There is no federal constitutional right to have the penalty phase factfinder treat proffered mitigating evidence as, in fact, mitigating. The law only requires that evidence considered mitigating by the capital defendant be presented in such a way as to allow the factfinder to determine if moral blameworthiness should be decreased.

M'Naghten Rule *see* **Insanity Defense**

Moldova   Moldova abolished capital punishment in 1995. *See also* **International Capital Punishment Nations**

Monaco   The death penalty was abolished officially by Monaco in 1962. *See also* **International Capital Punishment Nations**

Mongolia   Capital punishment is carried out in Mongolia. Mongolia uses the firing squad to carry out the death penalty. Its legal system is a mixture of Chinese, Russian and

Turkish systems of law. The nation's constitution was adopted on February 12, 1992.

The court system consists of local courts, provincial courts, a Supreme Court, and a Constitutional Court. Defendants are provided due process, legal defense, and a public trial. Defendants may question witnesses and appeal decisions. *See also* **International Capital Punishment Nations**

Montana The State of Montana is a capital punishment jurisdiction. The State reenacted its death penalty law after the United States Supreme Court decision in *Furman v. Georgia*, 408 U.S. 238 (1972), on March 11, 1974.

Montana has a two-tier legal system. The State's legal system is composed of a supreme court and courts of general jurisdiction. The Montana Supreme Court is presided over by a chief justice and six associate justices. The courts of general jurisdiction in the State are called District Courts. Capital offenses against the State of Montana are tried in the District Courts.

Montana's capital punishment statute is triggered if a person commits a homicide under the following special circumstances:

a. the person purposely or knowingly causes the death of another human being; or

b. the person attempts to commit, commits, or is legally accountable for the attempt or commission of robbery, sexual intercourse without consent, arson, burglary, kidnapping, aggravated kidnapping, felonious escape, felony assault, aggravated assault, or any other forcible felony and in the course of the forcible felony or flight thereafter, the person or any person legally accountable for the crime causes the death of another human being.

Capital murder in Montana is punishable by death, life imprisonment without parole, or imprisonment for a term of years. A capital prosecution in Montana is bifurcated into a guilt phase and penalty phase. A jury is used only at the guilt phase of a capital trial. The trial judge presides over the penalty phase of a capital prosecution and determines the sentence without a jury.

In order to impose a death sentence upon a defendant under Montana law, it is required that the prosecutor establish the existence of at least one of the following statutory aggravating circumstances at the penalty phase:

Joseph P. Mazurek is the Montana Attorney General. His office represents the State in capital punishment appellate proceedings. (Montana Attorney General Office)

1. The offense was deliberate homicide and was committed by a person serving a sentence of imprisonment in the state prison.

2. The offense was deliberate homicide and was committed by a defendant who had been previously convicted of another deliberate homicide.

3. The offense was deliberate homicide and was committed by means of torture.

4. The offense was deliberate homicide and was committed by a person lying in wait or ambush.

5. The offense was deliberate homicide and was committed as a part of a scheme or operation that, if completed, would result in the death of more than one person.

6. The offense was deliberate homicide and the victim was a peace officer killed while performing the officer's duty.

7. The offense was aggravated kidnapping that resulted in the death of the victim or the death by direct action of the defendant of a person who rescued or attempted to rescue the victim.

8. The offense was attempted deliberate homicide, aggravated assault, or aggravated kidnapping committed while incarcerated at the state prison by a person who has been previously:

    a. convicted of the offense of deliberate homicide; or

    b. found to be a persistent felony offender.

9. The offense was deliberate homicide and was committed by a person during the course of committing sexual assault, sexual intercourse without consent, deviate sexual conduct, or incest, and the victim was less than 18 years of age.

10. The offense was sexual intercourse without consent and the defendant has a previous conviction of sexual intercourse without consent in this state or of an offense under the laws of another state or of the United States that if committed in this state would be the offense of sexual intercourse without consent and the defendant inflicted serious bodily injury upon a person in the course of committing each offense.

Although the Federal Constitution will not permit jurisdictions to prevent capital felons from presenting all relevant mitigating evidence at the penalty phase, Montana has provided the following statutory mitigating circumstances that permit the judge to reject imposition of the death penalty:

a. The defendant has no significant history of prior criminal activity.

b. The offense was committed while the defendant was under the influence of extreme mental or emotional disturbance.

c. The defendant acted under extreme duress or under the substantial domination of another person.

d. The capacity of the defendant to appreciate the criminality of the defendant's conduct or to conform the defendant's conduct to the requirements of law was substantially impaired.

e. The victim was a participant in the defendant's conduct or consented to the act.

f. The defendant was an accomplice in an offense committed by another person, and the defendant's participation was relatively minor.

g. The defendant, at the time of the commission of the crime, was less than 18 years of age.

h. The court may consider any other fact that exists in mitigation of the penalty.

Under Montana's capital punishment statute, a sentence of death is automatically reviewed by the Montana Supreme Court. Montana uses lethal injection to carry out death sentences. The State's death row facility for men is located in Deer Lodge, Montana; while the facility maintaining female death row inmates is located in Warm Springs, Montana.

Pursuant to the laws of Montana the Governor has author-

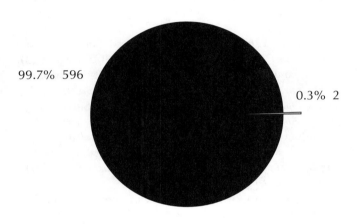

MONTANA EXECUTIONS 1976–1999

99.7% 596   0.3% 2

■ MONTANA EXECUTIONS
■ ALL OTHER EXECUTIONS

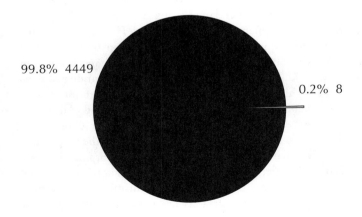

EXECUTIONS BY MONTANA 1930–1999

99.8% 4449   0.2% 8

■ MONTANA
■ ALL OTHER JURISDICTIONS

ity to grant clemency in capital cases. The Governor must obtain the approval of the State's Board of Pardons in order to grant clemency.

From the start of modern capital punishment in 1976, through 1999, Montana executed 2 capital felons. During this period Montana did not have any female capital felons. A total of 6 capital felons were on death row in Montana in 1999. The 1999 death row population in the State was listed as: 0 black inmates and 6 white inmates. In 1999 the State did not have any juveniles on death row. The State permits capital punishment to be imposed on persons 16 years old or older. Montana does not prohibit the execution of mentally retarded capital felons.

Executions by Montana 1976–1999

Name	Race	Date of Execution	Method of Execution
Duncan McKenzie	White	May 10, 1995	Lethal Injection
Terry A. Langford	White	February 24, 1998	Lethal Injection

Moody, William H.   William H. Moody served as an associate justice of the United States Supreme Court from 1906 to 1910. While on the Supreme Court Moody was known as a conservative interpreter of the Constitution.

Moody was born in Newbury, Massachusetts on December 23, 1853. He received an undergraduate degree from Harvard in 1876. Moody studied law as an apprentice and was admitted to the bar in Massachusetts in 1878. He garnered national attention as one of the prosecutors in the unsuccessful murder trial of Lizzie Borden. Moody went on to be elected to the United States House of Representatives in 1895, where he remained until he accepted an appointment in 1902 to be Secretary of the Navy. He was subsequently appointed United States Attorney General in 1904. President Theodore Roosevelt appointed Moody to the Supreme Court in 1906.

Moody was known to have authored only one capital punishment opinion. In *Keizo v. Henry* the Supreme Court was asked to decide whether the defendant was denied due process of law because eight members of the grand jury that indicted him may not have been citizens. Moody, writing for the Court, used a technical rule to avoid confronting the issue presented by the defendant. Moody wrote that the issue raised by the defendant may not be brought on a habeas petition to the Supreme Court, when the matter could have been properly brought in a direct appeal. He reasoned: "Where a court has jurisdiction, mere errors which have been committed in the course of the proceedings cannot be corrected upon a writ of habeas corpus, which may not, in this manner, usurp the functions of [an appeal]." Ill health caused Moody to resign from the Court in 1910. Moody died on July 2, 1917.

Moore, Blanche   In May of 1989, Blanche Moore's second husband, Reverend Dwight Moore was treated at a North Carolina hospital and diagnosed with arsenic poisoning. The police were informed of the diagnosis and launched an investigation. The investigation lead to a court order permitting the

Blanche Moore was sentenced to death for poisoning her boyfriend. The prosecutor had evidence that Moore also poisoned to death her father, her first husband and attempted to kill her second husband through poisoning. (North Carolina Department of Corrections)

exhumation of the bodies of Blanche's father P. D. Kiser, Sr., her first husband James N. Taylor, and a former boyfriend Raymond Reid. Autopsies of the three men all revealed that they died of arsenic poisoning. Blanche was subsequently indicted for the murder of all three men, and the attempted murder of her second husband.

Authorities ultimately only prosecuted Blanche for the murder of her former boyfriend Reid. During her trial, which was held in 1989, it was brought out that Blanche began dating Reid in 1979. Reid initially became ill in January of 1986. His illness began after spending New Year's Eve with Blanche and having eaten some of her homemade potato soup. Shortly after the meal Reid began experiencing severe symptoms of nausea, vomiting, and diarrhea. His condition became progressively worse, so that by May of 1986 he had to be admitted to a hospital. When he was admitted, Reid's symptoms including excessive nausea and vomiting, loose stools, skin rash, edema, dehydration, bone marrow damage, blood cell abnormalities, electrolyte abnormality, tachypnea (progressive shortness of breath), respiratory failure, tachycardia (fast heartbeat), low blood pressure, kidney malfunction and shutdown, and numbness and tingling in his hands and feet. Each of the symptoms was characteristic of arsenic poisoning, but hospital officials did not make such a diagnosis at the time.

During Reid's time in the hospital Blanche regularly visited him and brought him food. Reid's condition grew unexplainably worse during his hospitalization. His condition reached a life threatening stage and he had to be transferred to a larger hospital. His treating physician was never able to make a satisfactory diagnosis of the cause of Reid's multi-system failures.

Blanche visited Reid at the new hospital. She was observed regularly bringing him food items from home such as iced tea, frozen yogurt, milk shakes, and soups. Once Reid's condition reached the point where he could not speak or move his limbs, Blanche arranged to have his will drawn up leaving his entire estate to her. On October 7, 1986, Reid was pronounced dead from what hospital officials believed were complications attributable to Guillain-Barre syndrome. After Reid's death Blanche was reported as stating: "We cannot have an autopsy. He has been through too much. He wouldn't want to be cut on like this. We just — we cannot have one." No autopsy was performed at that time.

On June 13, 1989, Reid's body was exhumed. An autopsy revealed a concentration of arsenic in Reid's liver tissue 30 times higher than one might see in an average individual who was not having significant exposure to arsenic. The arsenic in Reid's brain tissue was approximately 67 times higher than that expected in a normal individual. As a result of these findings, the medical examiner concluded that Reid died as a result of the complications of arsenic poisoning. Trial testimony established that the arsenic levels in Reid's body had to be administered while he was in the hospital.

The prosecutor also presented the jury with extensive evidence concerning the deaths of Blanche's father, her first husband and the illness of her second husband — all victims of arsenic poisoning. Evidence was also introduced which established that Blanche forged a letter shifting the blame of Reid's death to someone else. The jury found Blanche guilty of capital murder and she was sentenced to death. Blanche is on death row in North Carolina.

Moore v. Dempsey

Court: United States Supreme Court; *Case Citation:* Moore v. Dempsey, 261 U.S. 86 (1923); *Argued:* January 9, 1923; *Decided:* February 19, 1923; *Opinion of the Court:* Justice Holmes; *Concurring Opinion:* None; *Dissenting Opinion:* Justice McReynolds, in which Sutherland J., joined; *Appellate Defense Counsel:* U. S. Bratton argued; Scipio A. Jones and Moorfield Storey on brief; *Appellate Prosecution Counsel:* Elbert Godwin argued and briefed; *Amicus Curiae Brief Supporting Prosecutor:* None; *Amicus Curiae Brief Supporting Defendant:* None.

Issue Presented: Whether the defendants presented sufficient allegations that their prosecution was dominated by mob violence so as to warrant a habeas corpus evidentiary hearing by the Federal District Court?

Case Holding: The defendants presented sufficient allegations that their prosecution was dominated by mob violence so as to warrant a habeas corpus evidentiary hearing by the Federal District Court.

Factual and procedural background of case: This case involved six black defendants, Frank Moore, Ed Hicks, J. E. Knox, Ed Coleman, Paul Hall and Frank Hicks, who were indicted for capital murder of a white victim by the State of Arkansas. The murder was highly publicized and resulted in random killing of blacks in the State. At the urging of concerned white citizens, the governor set the execution date of the defendants before they were fully prosecuted. All six defendants were eventually tried, convicted and sentenced to death. The Arkansas Supreme Court affirmed the judgments. The defendants filed a petition for habeas corpus relief in a Federal District Court, alleging that pretrial publicity denied them a fair trial. The District Court dismissed the petition without holding an evidentiary hearing to determine the merits of the petition. The United States Supreme Court granted certiorari to consider the issue.

Opinion of the Court by Justice Holmes: Justice Holmes ruled that the defendants presented sufficient allegations, that their prosecution was dominated by mob rule, so as to require an evidentiary hearing by the District Court. The opinion reasoned as follows:

> In *Frank v. Mangum*, it was recognized of course that if in fact a trial is dominated by a mob so that there is an actual interference with the course of justice, there is a departure from due process of law; and that "if the State, supplying no corrective process, carries into execution a judgment of death or imprisonment based upon a verdict thus produced by mob domination, the State deprives the accused of his life or liberty without due process of law." We assume in accordance with that case that the corrective process supplied by the State may be so adequate that interference by habeas corpus ought not to be allowed. It certainly is true that mere mistakes of law in the course of a trial are not to be corrected in that way. But if the case is that the whole proceeding is a mask—that counsel, jury and judge were swept to the fatal end by an irresistible wave of public passion, and that the State Courts failed to correct the wrong, neither perfection in the machinery for correction nor the possibility that the trial court and counsel saw no other way of avoiding an immediate outbreak of the mob can prevent this Court from securing to the [defendants] their constitutional rights.

The judgment of the District Court was reversed and the case remanded for an evidentiary hearing.

Dissenting opinion by Justice McReynolds, in which Sutherland J., joined: Justice McReynolds dissented from the Court's decision. He believed that the defendants failed to present adequate evidence to warrant an evidentiary hearing. Justice McReynolds wrote: "The matter is one of gravity. If every man convicted of crime in a state court may thereafter resort to the federal court and by swearing, as advised, that certain allegations of fact tending to impeach his trial are 'true to the best of his knowledge and belief,' and thereby obtain as of right further review, another way has been added to a list already unfortunately long to prevent prompt punishment. The delays incident to enforcement of our criminal laws have become a national scandal and give serious alarm to those who observe. Wrongly to decide the present cause probably will produce very unfortunate consequences." *See also* **Frank v. Mangum; Pretrial Publicity**

Moore v. Illinois

Court: United States Supreme Court; *Case Citation:* Moore v. Illinois, 408 U.S. 786 (1972); *Argued:* January 18, 1972; *Decided:* June 29, 1972; *Opinion of the Court:* Justice Blackmun; *Concurring and Dissenting Opinion:* Justice Marshall, in which Douglas, Stewart and Powell, JJ., joined; *Appellate Defense Counsel:* James J. Doherty argued; Gerald W. Getty on brief; *Appellate Prosecution Counsel:* Thomas J. Immel argued; William J. Scott, Joel M. Flaum, James B. Zagel and Jayne A. Carr on brief; *Amicus Curiae Brief Supporting Prosecutor:* None; *Amicus Curiae Brief Supporting Defendant:* 2.

Issue Presented: Whether the defendant's conviction and death sentence were valid when evidence was alleged to be suppressed and false evidence was alleged to be introduced against him?

Case Holding: The defendant's conviction was imposed validly, however, under the decision in *Furman v. Georgia* the sentence of death was invalid.

Factual and procedural background of case: The defendant, Lyman A. Moore, was convicted of capital murder and sentenced to death by the State of Illinois. The Illinois Supreme Court affirmed the conviction and sentence. In doing so, the appellate court rejected the defendant's argument that evidence had been suppressed and false evidence had been introduced against him. The United States Supreme Court granted certiorari to consider the issue.

Opinion of the Court by Justice Blackmun: Justice Blackmun rejected the defendant's allegations of suppressed and false evidence. However, the opinion held that in light of the Court's ruling in *Furman v. Georgia*, the defendant's death sentence could not stand, as it was imposed under procedures found unconstitutional in *Furman*. The judgment of the Illinois Supreme Court, insofar as it affirmed the death sentence, was reversed.

Concurring and dissenting opinion by Justice Marshall, in which Douglas, Stewart and Powell, JJ., joined: Justice Marshall concurred in the Court's decision to invalidate the death sentence. However, he dissented from the Court's decision to let the conviction stand. On the latter issue he wrote as follows: "My reading of the case leads me to conclude that the prosecutor knew that evidence existed that might help the defense, that the defense had asked to see it, and that it was never disclosed. It makes no difference whatever whether the evidence that was suppressed was found in the file of a police officer who directly aided the prosecution or in the file of the prosecutor himself. When the prosecutor consciously uses police officers as part of the prosecutorial team, those officers may not conceal evidence that the prosecutor himself would have a duty to disclose. It would be unconscionable to permit a prosecutor to adduce evidence demonstrating guilt without also requiring that he bear the responsibility of producing all known and relevant evidence tending to show innocence."

Case note: The case was one of three opinions issued by the Court, on the same day, invalidating death penalty statutes. *See also* **Furman v. Georgia; Stewart v. Massachusetts**

Moral Justification Mitigator

Capital murder committed by a defendant who believed the killing was morally justified, has been made a statutory mitigating circumstance in California, Colorado, Kentucky, Louisiana, New Mexico, and Tennessee. In these jurisdictions if the penalty phase jury finds evidence of the killing being morally justified the jury may refuse to recommend imposition of the death penalty. *See also* **Mitigating Circumstances**

Moratorium 2000

Moratorium 2000 is a nonprofit organization dedicated to obtaining a worldwide moratorium on the death penalty. Noted author and anti–death penalty advocate, Sister Helen Prejean is the honorary chairperson for the group.

The organization launched an ambitious campaign to gather one million signatures and letters from people opposed to the death penalty. This project was slated to culminate with delivery of the signatures and letters to the United States representative to the United Nations and to the Secretary General of the United Nations, on Human Rights Day, December 10, 2000.

Moratorium on Capital Punishment   In the late 1990s organizations throughout the nation began campaigns to bring about a halt to executions in the nation. Some groups seek to halt capital punishment for the purpose of implementing a method of imposing the punishment in a more fair and just manner. These organizations contend that the current methods for determining when the death penalty is imposed unfairly discriminates against minorities and the poor. Other groups are opposed to capital punishment per se, and therefore seek to abolish the punishment forever.

Some of the more prominent organizations that have called for a moratorium on capital punishment include: The American Bar Association, Amnesty International, United Nations Commission on Human Rights, and the American Civil Liberties Union.

In 1999, Nebraska legislators approved a bill calling for a moratorium and a study on the fairness of the death penalty's application. The State's governor vetoed the bill, but legislators voted unanimously to override the veto of the study portion of the bill. In January 2000, the governor of Illinois imposed a moratorium on the execution of inmates in the state.

International pressure has been placed on the United States from various European countries demanding that the nation ban capital punishment. The international opponents of capital punishment included a statement issued by Pope John Paul II asking the United States to abolish capital punishment.

Morgan v. Illinois   *Court:* United States Supreme Court; *Case Citation:* Morgan v. Illinois, 504 U.S. 719 (1992); *Argued:* January 21, 1992; *Decided:* June 15, 1992; *Opinion of the Court:* Justice White; *Concurring Opinion:* None; *Dissenting Opinion:* Justice Scalia, in which Rehnquist, C.J., and Thomas, J., joined; *Appellate Defense Counsel:* Allen H. Andrews III argued and briefed; *Appellate Prosecution Counsel:* Kenneth L. Gillis argued; Roland W. Burris, Terence M. Madsen, Jack O'Malley, Randall E. Roberts, Sally L. Dilgart, William D. Carroll, and Marie Quinlivan Czech on brief; *Amicus Curiae Brief Supporting Prosecutor:* None; *Amicus Curiae Brief Supporting Defendant:* 2.

Issue Presented: Whether, during voir dire of the jury for a capital offense, the Constitution permits a trial court to refuse inquiry into whether a potential juror would automatically impose the death penalty upon conviction of the defendant?

Case Holding: A trial court's refusal to inquire whether potential jurors would automatically impose the death penalty upon convicting a capital felon is inconsistent with and violates the Due Process Clause of the Fourteenth Amendment.

Factual and procedural background of case: The defendant, Derrick Morgan, was convicted in Cook County, Illinois, of first-degree murder and sentenced to death. During voir dire of the jury the trial court refused the defendant's request to ask if any jurors would automatically vote to impose the death penalty regardless of the facts in the case. On appeal to the Illinois Supreme Court the defendant argued that under the federal Constitution he had a right to voir dire the jury on the death-qualifying issue. The appellate court rejected the argument and affirmed the conviction and sentence. The United States Supreme Court granted certiorari to address the issue.

Opinion of the Court by Justice White: Justice White observed that due process demands that a jury provided to a capital defendant at the sentencing phase must be impartial and fair. Because of this impartiality requirement, the opinion held that a capital defendant may challenge for cause any prospective juror who would automatically vote for the death penalty. It was said that such a juror would fail to consider the evidence of aggravating and mitigating circumstances as instructed by the trial court.

The majority opinion ruled that on voir dire in a capital prosecution the trial court must, at a defendant's request, inquire into the prospective jurors' views on capital punishment. Justice White asserted that part of the guarantee of a defendant's right to an impartial jury is an adequate voir dire to identify unqualified jurors. It was held that the defendant could not exercise intelligently his challenge for cause against prospective jurors who would unwaveringly impose death after a finding of guilt, unless he was given the opportunity to identify such persons by questioning them at voir dire about their views on the death penalty. Justice White found that the trial court's voir dire was insufficient to satisfy the defendant's right to make inquiry.

The opinion concluded: "Because the 'inadequacy of voir dire' leads us to doubt that [the defendant] was sentenced to death by a jury empaneled in compliance with the Fourteenth Amendment, his sentence cannot stand. Accordingly, the judgment of the Illinois Supreme Court affirming [the defendant's] death sentence is reversed, and the case is remanded for further proceedings not inconsistent with this opinion."

Dissenting opinion by Justice Scalia, in which Rehnquist, C.J., and Thomas, J., joined: Justice Scalia argued in dissent that a juror should not be disqualified because he or she is pro–death penalty. He stated his position as follows: "The fact that a particular juror thinks the death penalty proper whenever capital murder is established does not disqualify him. To be sure, the law governing sentencing verdicts says that a jury may give less than the death penalty in such circumstances, just as ... the law governing guilt verdicts says that a jury may acquit despite proof of elements x, y, and z. But in neither case does the requirement that a more defense-favorable option be left available to the jury convert into a requirement that all jurors must, on the facts of the case, be amenable to entertaining that option." *See also* **Adams v. Texas; Boulden v. Holman; Darden v. Wainwright; Davis v. Georgia; Gray v. Mississippi; Jury Selection; Ross v. Oklahoma; Wainwright v. Witt; Witherspoon v. Illinois**

Morocco Capital punishment is allowed in Morocco. Morocco uses the firing squad to carry out the death penalty. Its legal system is a mixture of Islamic law and French and Spanish civil systems. The nation's constitution was adopted on March 10, 1972. The constitution of Morocco provides for a monarchy, with a parliament and an independent judiciary. Ultimate authority, however, rests with the King.

The judicial system consists of trials courts, Appeals Court, and a Supreme Court. Defendants have the right to bail and the right to retained or appointed counsel. *See also* **International Capital Punishment Nations**

Motive A defendant's motive or reason for committing an offense is not an element of a crime. Defendant's have contended, however, that failure to prove motive by the prosecution invalidates a conviction. This argument has never prevailed because motive, while helpful for the jury if shown, is not a prerequisite for a valid conviction. *See also* **Johnson v. United States**

Mozambique Mozambique abolished capital punishment in 1990. *See also* **International Capital Punishment Nations**

Mudgett, Herman Herman Mudgett, alias Dr. Henry H. Holmes, was born on May 16, 1860, in Gilmanton, New Hampshire. Mudgett was a bright youth. He graduated from high school at 16 and finished medical school at the University of Michigan when he was 24. Beneath the brilliance displayed by Mudgett was a side of him that would eventually lead him to murder hundreds of people.

Mudgett moved to Chicago in 1886, where he started a drugstore empire and built a hundred-room mansion. The mansion was secretly equipped with gas chambers, trap doors, acid vats, lime pits, fake walls and secret entrances. Authorities found evidence to prove that during the 1893 World's Fair, Mudgett rented rooms to visitors and, after killing them, tried to collect insurance. He lured countless women to his mansion with the promise of marriage, but would throw them down an elevator shaft and gas them to death, after they signed their life savings over to him. It was believed that he dismembered and skinned his victims and experimented with their corpses. When police grew suspicious about Mudgett he burned his mansion and fled Chicago. In the ruins of the mansion authorities found the remains of over 200 people.

When Mudgett left Chicago he ended up in Philadelphia. While in Philadelphia Mudgett convinced a friend, Benjamin F. Pitezel, to join him in an insurance scheme. The plan called for Pitezel to take out a $10,000 life insurance policy and fake his death. Mudgett betrayed Pitezel and killed him. He then took the money and ran off to Canada with Pitezel's wife and three children. It was not long before Mudgett killed the three children and abandoned their mother.

Philadelphia authorities were able to track down Mudgett and bring him back to stand trial for Pitezel's murder. His trial began on October 28, 1895. The jury convicted him on November 4 and he was sentenced to death. He was finally hanged on May 7, 1896. Before his execution Mudgett admitted to killing over 200 women in his Chicago mansion.

Multiple Homicide Aggravator A majority of capital punishment jurisdictions have made the killing of more than one victim in a single episode a statutory aggravating circumstance. In these jurisdictions the penalty phase jury may recommend a death sentence if the evidence reveals multiple homicides committed by the defendant in a single incident. *See also* **Aggravating Circumstances**

The State of California executed Keith William on May 3, 1996, after he was convicted of killing three victims in a single incident. (California Department of Corrections)

JURISDICTIONS USING MULTIPLE HOMICIDE AGGRAVATOR

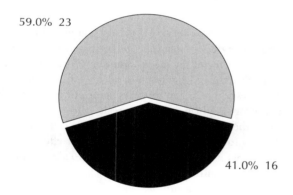

59.0% 23

41.0% 16

◼ MULTIPLE HOMICIDE AGGRAVATOR JURISDICTIONS
◼ ALL OTHER JURISDICTIONS

Source: Federal Bureau of Investigation, Supplementary Homicide Reports, 1976–97.

PERCENT OF HOMICIDES INVOLVING MULTIPLE VICTIMS 1986-1997

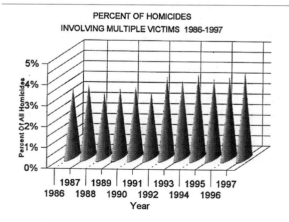

Mu'Min v. Virginia
Court: United States Supreme Court; Case Citation: Mu'Min v. Virginia, 500 U.S. 415 (1991); Argued: February 20, 1991; Decided: May 30, 1991; Opinion of the Court: Chief Justice Rehnquist; Concurring Opinion: Justice O'Connor; Dissenting Opinion: Justice Marshall, in which Blackmun and Stevens, JJ., joined; Dissenting Opinion: Justice Kennedy; Appellate Defense Counsel: John H. Blume argued; Mark E. Olive on brief; Appellate Prosecution Counsel: John H. McLees, Jr. argued; Mary Sue Terry, H. Lane Kneedler, Stephen D. Rosenthal, Jerry P. Slonaker and Thomas C. Daniel on brief; Amicus Curiae Brief Supporting Prosecutor: None; Amicus Curiae Brief Supporting Defendant: 1.

Issue Presented: Whether the trial judge's refusal to question prospective jurors about the specific contents of pretrial news reports of the crime to which they had been exposed violated the defendant's Sixth Amendment right to an impartial jury or his right to due process under the Fourteenth Amendment?

Case Holding: The trial judge's refusal to question prospective jurors about the specific contents of pretrial news reports of the crime to which they had been exposed did not violate the defendant's constitutional rights.

Factual and procedural background of case: The defendant, Dawud Majid Mu'Min, was charged with capital murder by the State of Virginia. The case received extensive pretrial publicity, partly out of community outrage over the fact that the defendant was serving a prison sentence for a previous murder conviction and was out of prison under a work program at the time of the second murder. During jury selection for the trial the judge refused to ask any of the defendant's proposed questions relating to the content of news items that potential jurors might have seen or read.

Initially, the judge questioned the prospective jurors as a group, asking four separate questions about the effect on them of pretrial publicity or information about the case obtained by other means. One juror who admitted to having formed a belief as to the defendant's guilt was excused for cause. Although 8 of the 12 jurors eventually chosen admitted that they had read or heard something about the case, none of them indicated that they had formed an opinion based on the outside information or would be biased in any way. The defendant was convicted and sentenced to death. The Virginia Supreme Court affirmed the conviction and sentence. In doing so, the appellate court ruled that, while a criminal defendant may ask on voir dire whether a juror has previously acquired any information about the case, the defendant does not have a constitutional right to explore the content of the acquired information, but is only entitled to know whether the juror can remain impartial in light of the previously obtained information. The United States Supreme Court granted certiorari to consider the issue.

Opinion of the Court by Chief Justice Rehnquist: The Chief Justice held that the trial judge's refusal to question prospective jurors about the specific contents of pretrial news reports to which they had been exposed, did not violate the defendant's constitutional rights. The opinion noted, as a general matter, that voir dire examination of potential jurors serves the dual purposes of enabling the trial court to select an impartial jury and assisting attorneys in exercising peremptory challenges. It was said that the Court's prior cases stressed the wide discretion granted to trial courts in conducting voir dire in the area of pretrial publicity and in other areas that might tend to show juror bias.

The opinion found that although precise inquiries about the contents of any news reports that a potential juror has read might reveal a sense of the juror's general outlook on life that would be of some use in exercising peremptory challenges, this benefit could not be a basis for making "content" questions about pretrial publicity a constitutional requirement, since peremptory challenges are not required by the Constitution. It was further said that while content questions might be helpful in assessing whether a juror is impartial, such questions are constitutionally compelled only if the trial court's failure to ask them renders the defendant's trial fundamentally unfair. Justice Rehnquist found the voir dire examination conducted by the trial court adequately covered the subject of possible bias by pretrial publicity. The judgment of the Virginia Supreme Court was affirmed.

Concurring opinion by Justice O'Connor: Justice O'Connor concurred in the Court's opinion. She wrote separately to express her views as to why the issue of voir dire "content" questions should not be elevated to a constitutional right. Justice O'Connor wrote:

> No one doubts that Dawud Majid Mu'Min's brutal murder of Gladys Nopwasky attracted extensive media coverage. For days on end, the case made headlines because it involved a macabre act of senseless violence and because it added fuel to an already heated political controversy about the wisdom of inmate work-release programs. But the question we decide today is not whether the jurors who ultimately convicted Mu'Min had previously read or heard anything about the case; everyone agrees that eight of them had. Nor is the question whether jurors who read that Mu'Min had confessed to the murder should have been disqualified as a matter of law.... The only question before us is whether the trial court erred by crediting the assurances of eight jurors that they could put aside what they had read or heard and render a fair verdict based on the evidence....
>
> The ... trial judge himself was familiar with the potentially prejudicial publicity to which the jurors might have been exposed. Hearing individual jurors repeat what the judge already knew might still have been helpful: a particular juror's tone of voice or demeanor might have suggested to the trial judge that the juror had formed an opinion about the case and should therefore be excused. I cannot conclude, however, that "content" questions are so indispensable that it violates the Sixth Amendment for a trial court to evaluate a juror's credibility instead by reference to the full range of potentially prejudicial information that has been reported. Accordingly, I join the Court's opinion.

Dissenting opinion by Justice Marshall, in which Blackmun and Stevens, JJ., joined: Justice Marshall believed that the majority opinion was wrong and therefore dissented. He stated his position on the issue as follows:

> Today's decision turns a critical constitutional guarantee — the Sixth Amendment's right to an impartial jury — into a hollow

formality. Dawud Majid Mu'Min's capital murder trial was preceded by exceptionally prejudicial publicity, and at jury selection 8 of the 12 jurors who ultimately convicted Mu'Min of murder and sentenced him to death admitted exposure to this publicity. Nonetheless, the majority concludes that the trial court was under no obligation to ask what these individuals knew about the case before seating them on the jury. Instead, the majority holds that the trial court discharged its obligation to ensure the jurors' impartiality by merely asking the jurors whether they thought they could be fair.

The majority's reasoning is unacceptable. When a prospective juror has been exposed to prejudicial pretrial publicity, a trial court cannot realistically assess the juror's impartiality without first establishing what the juror already has learned about the case. The procedures employed in this case were wholly insufficient to eliminate the risk that two-thirds of Mu'Min's jury entered the jury box predisposed against him. I dissent.

Dissenting opinion by Justice Kennedy: Justice Kennedy dissented from the Court's opinion. He believed that "content" questions were imperative for obtaining a fair trial in this case. Justice Kennedy articulated his concerns as follows:

> Our precedents mark the distinction between allegations that the individual jurors might have been biased from exposure to pretrial publicity, and the quite separate problem of a case tried in an atmosphere so corruptive of the trial process that we will presume a fair trial could not be held, nor an impartial jury assembled....
>
> ... Our inquiry, in my view, should be directed to the question of the actual impartiality of the seated jurors, and the related question whether the trial judge conducted an adequate examination of those eight jurors who acknowledged some exposure to press accounts of the trial....
>
> I fail to see how the trial court could evaluate the credibility of the individuals seated on this jury. The questions were asked of groups, and individual jurors attested to their own impartiality by saying nothing. I would hold, as a consequence, that, when a juror admits exposure to pretrial publicity about a case, the court must conduct a sufficient colloquy with the individual juror to make an assessment of the juror's ability to be impartial. The trial judge should have substantial discretion in conducting the voir dire, but, in my judgment, findings of impartiality must be based on something more than the mere silence of the individual in response to questions asked en masse.

Case note: Virginia executed Dawud Majid Mu'Min by lethal injection on November 13, 1997. *See also* **Stroble v. California; Pretrial Publicity; Jury Selection**

Murder

Murder is generally defined as the intentional or purposeful killing of another human being. Murder may be capital or noncapital. A defendant charged with capital murder is subject to receiving the death penalty. Whereas a defendant charged with noncapital murder is not subject to being punished with death. Capital murder and noncapital murder are distinguished by special circumstances. That is, murder punished as a capital offense has specific underlying statutorily created factors that permit imposition of the death penalty. For example, murder of a police officer or murder committed by firing a gun out of a moving car. Jurisdictions have created a variety of special circumstances which permit murder to be transformed into capital murder. *See also* **Death-Eligible Offenses**

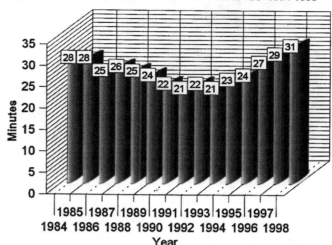

FREQUENCY OF MURDER IN THE U.S. IN MINUTES 1984-1998

Source: U.S. Department of Justice, Federal Bureau of Investigation, *Uniform Crime Reports* (1985–1999).

Murder, Inc.

Murder, Inc was the New York based arm of organized crime during the 1930s. The undisputed boss of Murder, Inc., was Louis "Lepke" Buchalter.

Before joining the national crime syndicate, Lepke was a small time Jewish labor racketeer operating in Manhattan's garment district. Lepke quickly caught the eyes of Meyer Lansky and Lucky Luciano when they formed the national crime syndicate. With Luciano's blessing, Lepke was placed in charge of the enforcement arm of the syndicate. Lepke did not disappoint his benefactors. With Lepke in charge, it has been estimated that over a thousand people were killed nationwide by Murder, Inc. It is believed that Lepke personally killed over a hundred people as the head of the most lethal crime group in American history.

For six years Lepke brought terror to those who opposed the syndicate. His downfall came after he carried out a hit on a Jewish candy store clerk named Joseph Rosen. The pressure placed on the syndicate because of the murder of Rosen sent Lepke into hiding. Lepke revealed himself to authorities only after Luciano assured him everything would come out okay. This was a mistake. Lepke and two of his associates, Emanuel Weiss and Louis Capone (no relation to Al), were indicted for Rosen's death. In what became one of the most publicized trials in the nation's history, Lepke, Weiss and Capone were convicted of Rosen's murder. The sentence handed down was death. Murder, Inc. was effectively put out of business.

Four years after the trial, Lepke, Weiss and Capone were electrocuted on March 4, 1944. Lepke's death marked the first time that an organized crime boss was executed by a government. *See also* **Buchalter v. New York**

Murder Mack

Lawrence Bittaker and Roy Norris met in 1978 while they were serving time together at the California Men's Colony at San Luis Obispo. The two men made a pack that when they got out of prison they would embark on a

Lawrence Bittaker is on California's death row. (California Department of Corrections)

killing spree that involved murdering girls between the ages of 13 to 19. Their plan included recording the events on videotape.

Bittaker was paroled on November 15, 1978. Upon his release, Bittaker obtained a van that he called "Murder Mack." Norris was released on June 15, 1979. The two men joined forces and began putting their murder spree plan into operation.

On June 24, 1979, 16-year-old Cindy Schaeffer disappeared following a church gathering and was never seen again. Eighteen-year-old Joy Hall disappeared from Redondo Beach on July 8. On September 2, Jacqueline Lamp, 13, and Jackie Gilliam, 15, disappeared while hitchhiking in the Redondo Beach area. Shirley Ledford, 16, was abducted on October 31. Ledford was fortunate in managing to escape and was found the day after her disappearance in a Tijunga residential district. Ledford had suffered near strangulation, mutilation of her breasts and face, and slashed arms.

Through a lucky break, authorities located and arrested Bittaker and Norris on November 20, in connection with an assault in Hermosa Beach in September. The victim of the assault in Hermosa Beach was unable to positively identify her attackers, however, the authorities held Bittaker and Norris for parole violations due to possession of drugs.

Within a short period of being detained, Norris became unglued and began telling authorities tales of murder. According to Norris, young girls had been approached at random, photographed by Bittaker, and offered rides in Murder Mack, drugs, and modeling jobs. Norris reported that the girls were abducted forcibly and driven to remote mountainous areas where they were raped, tortured, and murdered. The first corroborative evidence authorities had of Norris' confession was a tape recording of one of the victim's final moments alive and 500 photographs of smiling young girls that were found in the Murder Mack.

Norris eventually led authorities to shallow graves in San Dimas Canyon and the San Gabriel Mountains, where skeletal remains of two victims were found. Authorities charged Norris and Bittaker with five counts of murder. However, the police believed the two were linked to the disappearance of 30 or 40 other young victims.

On March 18, 1981 Norris pled guilty to five counts of murder. In return for his cooperation with authorities Norris was sentenced to 45 years to life, with the possibility of parole after 30 years. Bittaker had denied everything. During his trial

Bittaker testified that Norris informed him of the murders, but he had no personal knowledge or involvement in the killings. On February 17, a jury returned a guilty verdict against Bittaker. On March 24, in accordance with the penalty phase jury's recommendation, the judge sentenced Bittaker to death. Bittaker is on death row at San Quentin Prison. Norris is confined at Pelican Bay Prison.

Murder Victims Families for Reconciliation

Murder Victims Families for Reconciliation (MVFR) is a Massachusetts-based organization that was founded by Marie Deans, following the murder of her mother-in-law. Deans founded MVFR to provide a national forum for murder victims' family members, including family members of those executed. The executive director of MVFR is Renny Cushing. Under Cushing's leadership, MVFR promotes the idea that society honors the lives of murder victims not by supporting more killing, but by working to fashion a criminal justice system that holds murderers accountable without killing them. MVFR has

Renny Cushing is the executive director of Murder Victims Families for Reconciliation. (Renny Cushing)

worked to end the isolation of survivors of homicide victims and to reinforce and support the notion that it is okay to lose a loved one to murder and not want the government to kill the murderer. MVFR works actively in the areas of Public Education, Policy Reform and Victim Support. The organization's ongoing projects include speaking tours and a speakers' bureau, publication of *The Voice* newsletter, and a book, *Not in Our Name: Murder Victims Families Speak Out Against the Death Penalty*.

Murphy, Francis William

Francis William Murphy served as an associate justice of the United States Supreme Court from 1940 to 1949. While on the Supreme Court Murphy was known as a passionate liberal interpreter of the Constitution.

Murphy was born on April 13, 1890, in Harbor Beach, Michigan. Murphy was educated at the University of Michigan and was admitted to Michigan's bar in 1914. His career included practicing law, municipal judge, mayor of Detroit, governor of the Philippines and Michigan, and United States Attorney General. In 1940 President Franklin D. Roosevelt nominated Murphy to the Supreme Court.

While on the Supreme Court Murphy wrote a number of dissenting opinions in capital punishment cases. The dissenting opinion which best illustrated Murphy's reputation as a passionate liberal was written in *Williams v. New York*. In *Williams* the defendant argued that due process of law was violated by the trial court's use of information from a nondisclosed presentence probation report, in order to justify overriding the jury's recommendation of mercy and impose a death sentence. The majority on the Court found that due process was not violated. Murphy disagreed with the majority and wrote: "Due process of law includes at least the idea that a person accused of crime shall be accorded a fair hearing through all the stages of the proceedings against him. I agree with the Court as to the value and humaneness of liberal use of probation reports as developed by modern penologists, but, in a capital case, against the unanimous recommendation of a jury, where the report would concededly not have been admissible at the trial, and was not subject to examination by the defendant, I am forced to conclude that the high commands of due process were not obeyed." Murphy died on July 19, 1949.

Capital Punishment Opinions Written by Murphy

Case Name	Opinion of the Court	Dissenting Opinion	Concurring and Dissenting
Adamson v. California		✓	
Akins v. Texas		✓	
Fisher v. United States		✓	
Griffin v. United States		✓	
Malinski v. New York			✓
Taylor v. Alabama		✓	
Williams v. New York		✓	

Murray v. Giarratano *Court:* United States Supreme Court; *Case Citation:* Murray v. Giarratano, 492 U.S. 1 (1989); *Argued:* March 22, 1989; *Decided:* June 23, 1989; *Plurality Opinion:* Chief Justice Rehnquist announced the Court's judgment and delivered an opinion, in which White, O'Connor, and Scalia, JJ., joined; *Concurring Opinion:* Justice O'Connor; *Concurring Opinion:* Justice Kennedy, in which O'Connor, J., joined; *Dissenting Opinion:* Justice Stevens, in which Brennan, Marshall, and Blackmun, JJ., joined; *Appellate Defense Counsel:* Gerald T. Zerkin argued; Jonathan D. Sasser and Martha A. Geer on brief; *Appellate Prosecution Counsel:* Robert Q. Harris argued; Mary Sue Terry, H. Lane Kneedler, Stephen D. Rosenthal and Francis S. Ferguson on brief; *Amicus Curiae Brief Supporting Prosecutor:* 1; *Amicus Curiae Brief Supporting Defendants:* 2.

Issue Presented: Whether the Eighth Amendment or the Due Process Clause requires States to appoint counsel for indigent death row inmates seeking State post-conviction relief?

Case Holding: Neither the Eighth Amendment nor the Due Process Clause requires States to appoint counsel for indigent death row inmates seeking State post-conviction relief.

Factual and procedural background of case: This case was brought as a "class action" by indigent Virginia death row inmates who did not have counsel to pursue post-conviction proceedings. The class action was brought in a Federal District Court against various Virginia officials, alleging that the Federal Constitution required that they be provided with counsel at the State's expense for the purpose of pursuing collateral proceedings related to their convictions and sentences. The District Court concluded that Virginia provided constitutionally inadequate legal services to indigent death row inmates seeking post-conviction relief. The District Court therefore ordered Virginia to develop a program for the appointment of counsel, upon request, to indigent death row inmates wishing to pursue habeas corpus in State court, but not in Federal court. A Federal Court of Appeals affirmed. The United States Supreme Court granted certiorari to consider the issue.

Plurality opinion in which Chief Justice Rehnquist announced the Court's judgment and in which White, O'Connor and Scalia, JJ., joined: The Chief Justice ruled that neither the Eighth Amendment nor the Due Process Clause requires States to appoint counsel for indigent death row inmates seeking State post-conviction relief. It was said that State collateral proceedings are not constitutionally required as an adjunct to the state criminal proceeding, and serve a different and more limited purpose than either the trial or appeal. The Chief Justice reasoned that Eighth Amendment safeguards imposed at the trial stage—where the court and jury hear testimony, receive evidence, and decide the question of guilt and punishment—were sufficient to assure the reliability of the process by which the death penalty was imposed. The judgment of the Court of Appeals was reversed.

Concurring opinion by Justice O'Connor: Justice O'Connor wrote a concurring opinion in the case. In her concurrence she indicated the following: "I join in the Chief Justice's opinion. As his opinion demonstrates, there is nothing in the Constitution or the precedents of this Court that requires that a State provide counsel in postconviction proceedings. A postconviction proceeding is not part of the criminal process itself, but is instead a civil action designed to overturn a presumptively valid criminal judgment. Nothing in the Constitution requires the States to provide such proceedings, nor does it seem to me that the Constitution requires the States to follow any particular federal model in those proceedings."

Concurring opinion by Justice Kennedy, in which O'Connor, J., joined: Justice Kennedy concurred in the Court's judgment. He indicated that "[i]t cannot be denied that collateral relief proceedings are a central part of the review process for prisoners sentenced to death." He noted, however, that the requirement of meaningful access to courts can be achieved in various ways, without constitutionalizing the right to counsel at the post-conviction stage. Justice Kennedy argued that States should be free to develop and implement their own plans for meeting the legal needs of death row inmates seeking post-conviction relief. He concluded: "While Virginia has not adopted procedures for securing representation that are as far reaching and effective as those available in other States, no prisoner on death row in Virginia has been unable to obtain counsel to represent him in postconviction proceedings, and Virginia's prison system is staffed with institutional lawyers to assist in preparing petitions for post-conviction relief. I am not prepared to say that this scheme violates the Constitution."

Dissenting opinion by Justice Stevens, in which Brennan, Marshall, and Blackmun, JJ., joined: Justice Stevens dissented from the Court's decision. He believed that the efforts undertaken by Virginia to assist death row inmates seek post-conviction relief were constitutionally unacceptable. He stated his opinion thus:

> Two Terms ago this Court reaffirmed that the Fourteenth Amendment to the Federal Constitution obligates a State "to assure the indigent defendant an adequate opportunity to present his claims fairly in the context of the State's appellate process. The narrow question presented is whether that obligation includes appointment of counsel for indigent death row inmates who wish to pursue state postconviction relief. Viewing the facts in light of our precedents, we should answer that question in the affirmative....
>
> Ideally, "direct appeal is the primary avenue for review of a conviction or sentence, and death penalty cases are no exception. When the process of direct review ... comes to an end, a presumption of finality and legality attaches to the conviction and sentence." There is, however, significant evidence that in capital cases what is ordinarily considered direct review does not sufficiently safeguard against miscarriages of justice to warrant this presumption of finality. Federal habeas courts granted relief in only 0.25 percent to 7 percent of noncapital cases in recent years; in striking contrast, the success rate in capital cases ranged from 60 percent to 70 percent. Such a high incidence of uncorrected error demonstrates that the meaningful appellate review necessary in a capital case extends beyond the direct appellate process....
>
> The postconviction procedure in Virginia may present the first opportunity for an attorney detached from past proceedings to examine the defense and to raise claims that were barred on direct review by prior counsel's ineffective assistance. A fresh look may reveal, for example, that a prior conviction used to enhance the defendant's sentence was invalid; or that the defendant's mental illness, lack of a prior record, or abusive childhood should have been introduced as evidence in mitigation at his sentencing hearing. Defense counsel's failure to object to or assert such claims precludes direct appellate review of them. The postconviction proceeding gives inmates another chance to rectify defaults. In Virginia, therefore, postconviction proceedings are key to meaningful appellate review of capital cases....
>
> Of the 37 States authorizing capital punishment, at least 18 automatically provide their indigent death row inmates counsel to help them initiate state collateral proceedings. Thirteen of the 37 States have created governmentally funded resource centers to assist counsel in litigating capital cases. Virginia is among as few as five States that fall into neither group and have no system for appointing counsel for condemned prisoners before a postconviction petition is filed.
>
> The basic question in this case is whether Virginia's procedure for collateral review of capital convictions and sentences assures its indigent death row inmates an adequate opportunity to present their claims fairly. The District Court and Court of Appeals en banc found that it did not, and neither the State nor this Court's majority provides any reasoned basis for disagreeing with their conclusion. Simple fairness requires that this judgment be affirmed.

See also **Right to Counsel**

Murray v. Louisiana Court: United States Supreme Court; Case Citation: Murray v. Louisiana, 163 U.S. 101 (1896); Argued: Not reported; Decided: May 18, 1896; Opinion of the Court: Justice Shiras; Concurring Opinion: None; Dissenting Opinion: None; Appellate Defense Counsel: Thomas F. Maher argued and briefed; Appellate Prosecution Counsel: M. J. Cunningham argued; Alex Porter Morse on brief; Amicus Curiae Brief Supporting Prosecutor: None; Amicus Curiae Brief Supporting Defendant: None.

Issue Presented: Whether the exclusion of blacks from the grand jury that indicted the defendant required his case be removed to a Federal court for prosecution?

Case Holding: The exclusion of blacks from the grand jury that indicted the defendant did not require his case be removed to a Federal court for prosecution, because the Federal removal statute required racial discrimination emanate from a State's constitution or laws.

Factual and procedural background of case: The defendant, Jim Murray, was indicted for capital murder by the State of Louisiana. Prior to trial the defendant requested the indictment be dismissed, on the grounds that blacks were systematically excluded from the grand jury that indicted him. The trial court denied the request. The defendant then requested the case be removed to Federal court, on the grounds that blacks were excluded from the grand jury. The trial court also denied this request. The defendant was tried, convicted and sentenced to death. The Louisiana Supreme Court affirmed the judgment. In doing so, the appellate court rejected the defendant's contention that the case should have been removed to a Federal court. The United States Supreme Court granted certiorari to consider the issue.

Opinion of the Court by Justice Shiras: Justice Shiras held that the Federal removal statute did not authorize "a removal of the prosecution from the state court upon an allegation that jury commissioners or other subordinate officers had, without authority derived from the constitution and laws of the state, excluded [black] citizens from juries because of their race[.]" The opinion made clear that removal required racial discriminatory conduct that was based upon a State's constitution or laws. Justice Shiras found that the defendant's "petition for removal complained of the acts of the jury commissioners in illegally confining their summons to white citizens only, and in excluding from jury service citizens of the race and color of the [defendant], but did not aver that the jury commissioners so acted under or by virtue of the laws or constitution of the state; nor was there shown, during the course of the trial, that there was any statutory or constitutional enactment of the state of Louisiana which discriminated against persons on account of race, color, or previous condition of servitude, or which denied to them the equal protection of the laws." It was ruled that the defendant was not entitled to have his case removed to a Federal court because he did not allege racial discrimination under the constitution or laws of Louisiana. The judgment of the Louisiana Supreme Court was affirmed. *See also* **Discrimination in Grand or Petit Jury Selection**

N

Namibia Namibia abolished capital punishment in 1990. *See also* **International Capital Punishment Nations**

National Association for the Advancement of Colored People Legal Defense Fund

The National Association for the Advancement of Colored People Legal Defense Fund (LDF) was founded in 1940 under the leadership of the late Thurgood Marshall, who became the first African American United States Supreme Court Justice. For more than half a century, LDF has mounted legal attacks aimed at obtaining fairness in American society for blacks and other minorities. With a staff of 25 attorneys, assisted by lawyers throughout the country, LDF has participated in more cases before the United States Supreme Court than any institution other than the United States Solicitor General's office.

One of the areas in which LDF has concentrated its resources has been capital punishment. Attorneys for LDF were involved in such landmark decisions as *Furman v. Georgia,* 408 U.S. 238 (1972) (halting executions in the nation) and *Coker v. Georgia,* 433 U.S. 584 (1977) (prohibiting death penalty for rape). LDF has filed numerous amicus briefs throughout the country on behalf of capital felons.

The LDF is headquartered in New York City. In 1957, LDF became independent from its former parent organization, the National Association for the Advancement of Colored People.

National Center for Victims of Crime

The National Center for Victims of Crime (NCVC) is a Virginia based nonprofit organization founded in 1985. NCVC is a national resource and advocacy center for victims of crime. The purpose of NCVC is to bring about a national commitment to help victims of crime rebuild their lives. NCVC has advocated for laws and public policies that create resources and secure rights and protection for victims. Utilizing its national database, NCVC refers crime victims to services that include crisis intervention, research information, assistance with the criminal justice process, counseling and support groups.

National Coalition to Abolish the Death Penalty

The National Coalition to Abolish the Death Penalty (NCADP) is a Washington, D.C. based national coalition of organizations and individuals committed to the abolition of capital punishment. The organization was founded in 1976 and has nearly 140 national, state and local affiliates. The NCADP is considered by many to be the national leader of the capital punishment abolitionist movement.

The NCADP provides information, advocates for public policy and mobilizes and supports people and institutions that oppose capital punishment. Through consultations, providing materials, training, technical support, NCADP hopes to bring about total abolishment of capital punishment in the nation. The NCADP publishes and distributes several vital sources of information for abolitionists. *Lifelines,* the organization's newsletter, is produced bi-monthly and goes out to thousands of people across the globe. Articles included in this publication are written by NCADP affiliates, death row inmates, and abolitionists on the cutting edge of the anti–death penalty movement. The central purpose of *Lifelines* is to serve as a means of communication between abolitionists, death row inmates, and families that have been effected by capital crimes.

Native Americans and Capital Punishment

Federal law limits the circumstances under which Native Americans may be subject to capital punishment. Under Federal law, a capital offense that is committed solely on Native American land must be prosecuted by the governing tribal authority, unless such authority has consented to prosecution outside of its jurisdiction. Native Americans are subject to capital prosecution like anyone else for murder committed outside of Native American territory. *See also* **Dakota Executions**

Darrick Gerlaugh, a Native American, was executed by the State of Arizona on February 3, 1999. (Arizona Department of Corrections)

Native Americans Executed 1976–1999

Name	Date of Execution	Jurisdiction	Method of Execution
James "Red Dog" Allen	March 3, 1993	DE	Lethal Injection
Emmit Nave	July 31, 1996	MO	Lethal Injection
Scott Carpenter	May 8, 1997	OK	Lethal Injection
Robert West	July 29, 1997	TX	Lethal Injection
Daniel Remeta	March 31, 1998	FL	Electrocution
Darick Gerlaugh	February 3, 1999	AZ	Lethal Injection

Nauru Capital punishment has not been officially abolished in the nation of Nauru, but the punishment has not been imposed in recent memory. Nauru is a small Pacific island with about 10,500 inhabitants. The country gained independence in 1968. Its legal system is based on English common law. The nation adopted its constitution on January 29, 1968.

NATIVE AMERICANS EXECUTED 1976–1999

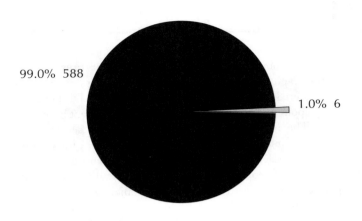

99.0% 588

1.0% 6

■ NATIVE AMERICANS
■ ALL OTHERS

NATIVE AMERICANS ON DEATH ROW
On April 1, 1999

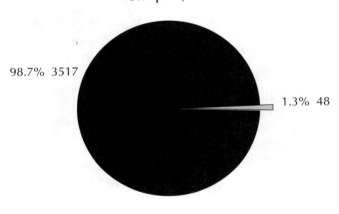

98.7% 3517

1.3% 48

■ NATIVE AMERICANS
■ ALL OTHERS

The judicial system consists of trial courts and an appellate court. Defendants have a right to a public trial and to legal counsel. *See also* **International Capital Punishment Nations**

Nazi Spies *see* **Espionage**

Neal v. Delaware
Court: United States Supreme Court; *Case Citation:* Neal v. Delaware, 103 U.S. 370 (1880); *Argued:* Not reported; *Decided:* October Term, 1880; *Opinion of the Court:* Justice Harlan; *Concurring Opinion:* None; *Dissenting Opinion:* Chief Justice Waite; *Dissenting Opinion:* Justice Field; *Appellate Defense Counsel:* Charles Devens argued; Anthony Higgins on brief; *Appellate Prosecution Counsel:* George Gray argued and briefed; *Amicus Curiae Brief Supporting Prosecutor:* None; *Amicus Curiae Brief Supporting Defendant:* None.

Issues Presented: (1) Whether the defendant satisfied the Fed-

eral statute requiring removal of a State criminal case when the laws of a State discriminate against a defendant because of race? (2) Whether the defendant established that in practice, Delaware officials have implemented the State's jury laws in such a manner as to systematically exclude blacks from all jury service?

Case Holdings: (1) The defendant did not satisfy the Federal statute requiring removal of a State criminal case when the laws of a State discriminate against a defendant because of race, insofar as the jury laws of Delaware were interpreted by the courts of the State in a race neutral manner. (2) The defendant established that in practice, Delaware officials have implemented the State's jury laws in such a manner as to systematically exclude blacks from all jury service, therefore his conviction and sentence could not stand.

Factual and procedural background of case: The defendant, William Neal, was indicted on a charge of rape by the State of Delaware. Prior to trial, the defendant filed a petition to have his case removed to a Federal District Court in Delaware, on the grounds that the State systematically excluded blacks from grand and petit juries. The relief sought was denied. The defendant was tried, convicted and sentenced to death. The Delaware Supreme Court affirmed the judgment. The United States Supreme Court granted certiorari to consider the issue of removal of the case to Federal Court.

Opinion of the Court by Justice Harlan: Justice Harlan stated that "[t]he essential question ... is whether, at the time the petition for removal was filed, citizens of the African race, otherwise qualified, were, by reason of the Constitution and laws of Delaware, excluded from service on juries because of their color." The opinion noted that "[t]he court below, all the judges concurring, held that no such exclusion was required or authorized by the Constitution or laws of the State, and, consequently, that the case was not embraced by the removal statute as construed by this court." Justice Harlan agreed with the conclusion of the lower courts that the laws of Delaware, as interpreted by the State's courts, did not discriminate against blacks in grand and petit jury selection. Consequently, the case was not appropriate for removal to a Federal court for prosecution.

The opinion pointed out that, while the State's laws may have been facially neutral and not subject to the Federal removal statute, the implementation of those laws was still subject to constitutional oversight. Justice Harlan wrote: "[The defendant] is not without remedy if the officers of the State charged with the duty of selecting jurors were guilty of the offence charged in his petition. A denial upon their part, of his right to a selection of grand and petit jurors without discrimination against his race, because of their race, would be a violation of the Constitution and laws of the United States, which the trial court was bound to redress." The opinion made clear "that while a [black] citizen, party to a trial involving his life, liberty, or property, cannot claim, as matter of right, that his race shall have a representation on the jury, and while a mixed jury, in a particular case, is not within the meaning of the Constitution, always or absolutely necessary to the equal protection of the laws, it is a right to which he is entitled, that in the selection of jurors to pass upon his life, liberty, or property, there shall be no exclusion of his race, and no discrimination against them, because of their color."

In turning to the evidence presented by the defendant, Justice Harlan found that the defendant had established that the jury laws of Delaware were implemented so as to systematically exclude blacks from grand and petit juries. He wrote:

> The showing thus made, including, as it did, the fact that no [black] citizen had ever been summoned as a juror in the courts of the State,—although its [black] population exceeded twenty thousand in 1870, and in 1880 exceeded twenty-six thousand, in a total population of less than one hundred and fifty thousand,—presented a prima facie case of denial, by the officers charged with the selection of grand and petit jurors, of that equality of protection which has been secured by the Constitution and laws of the United States. It was, we think, under all the circumstances, a violent presumption which the State court indulged, that such uniform exclusion of that race from juries, during a period of many years, was solely because, in the judgment of those officers, fairly exercised, the black race in Delaware were utterly disqualified, by want of intelligence, experience, or moral integrity, to sit on juries. The action of those officers in the premises is to be deemed the act of the State; and the refusal of the State court to redress the wrong by them committed was a denial of a right secured to the prisoner by the Constitution and laws of the United States.

The judgment of the Delaware Supreme Court was reversed.

Dissenting opinion by Chief Justice Waite: The Chief Justice dissented from the Court's decision. He argued that the evidence proffered by the defendant was not sufficient to sustain a finding of systematic discrimination. The Chief Justice also indicated that even if the discrimination was proven, the issue did not warrant reversal of the judgment.

Dissenting opinion by Justice Field: Justice Field dissented from the Court's decision. He argued "that the mere fact that no persons of the [black] race were selected as jurors is not evidence that such persons were excluded on account of their race or color." Justice Field stated that "the fact that [black] persons had never, since the act of Congress of May 1, 1875, been selected as jurors may be attributed to other causes than those of race and color."

Case note: Under modern capital punishment jurisprudence the death penalty may not be imposed for the crime of rape, without an accompanying homicide. *See also* **Discrimination in Grand or Petit Jury Selection; Rape and Capital Punishment**

Nebraska
The State of Nebraska is a capital punishment jurisdiction. The State reenacted its death penalty law after the United States Supreme Court decision in *Furman v. Georgia*, 408 U.S. 238 (1972), on April 20, 1973.

Nebraska has a three-tier legal system. The State's legal system is composed of a supreme court, court of appeals and courts of general jurisdiction. The Nebraska Supreme Court is presided over by a chief justice and six associate justices. The Nebraska Court of Appeals is composed of a chief judge and

five judges. The courts of general jurisdiction in the State are called District Courts. Capital offenses against the State of Nebraska are tried in the District Courts.

Nebraska's capital punishment statute is triggered if a person commits a homicide under the following special circumstances:

> The offender kills another person (1) purposely and with deliberate and premeditated malice, or (2) in the perpetration of or attempt to perpetrate any sexual assault in the first degree, arson, robbery, kidnapping, hijacking of any public or private means of transportation, or burglary, or (3) by administering poison or causing the same to be done; or if by willful and corrupt perjury or subornation of the same he purposely procures the conviction and execution of any innocent person.

Capital murder in Nebraska is punishable by death or life imprisonment without parole. A capital prosecution in Nebraska is bifurcated into a guilt phase and penalty phase. A jury is used only at the guilt phase of a capital trial. The trial judge presides over the penalty phase of a capital prosecution and determines the sentence without a jury. The trial judge is authorized to request two other judges to participate in the penalty phase. If a three judge panel is used, the judges must unanimously agree that death is the appropriate punishment.

In order to impose a death sentence upon a defendant under Nebraska law, it is required that the prosecutor establish the existence of at least one of the following statutory aggravating circumstances at the penalty phase:

a. The offender was previously convicted of another murder or a crime involving the use or threat of violence to the person, or has a substantial prior history of serious assaultive or terrorizing criminal activity;

b. The murder was committed in an effort to conceal the commission of a crime, or to conceal the identity of the perpetrator of such crime;

c. The murder was committed for hire, or for pecuniary gain, or the defendant hired another to commit the murder for the defendant;

d. The murder was especially heinous, atrocious, cruel, or manifested exceptional depravity by ordinary standards of morality and intelligence;

e. At the time the murder was committed, the offender also committed another murder;

f. The offender knowingly created a great risk of death to at least several persons;

g. The victim was a public servant having lawful custody of the offender or another in the lawful performance of his or her official duties and the offender knew or should have known that the victim was a public servant performing his or her official duties;

h. The murder was committed knowingly to disrupt or hinder the lawful exercise of any governmental function or the enforcement of the laws; or

i. The victim was a law enforcement officer engaged in the lawful performance of his or her official duties as a law enforcement officer and the offender knew or reasonably should have known that the victim was a law enforcement officer.

Although the Federal Constitution will not permit jurisdictions to prevent capital felons from presenting all relevant mitigating evidence at the penalty phase, Nebraska has provided the following statutory mitigating circumstances that permit the judge to reject imposition of the death penalty:

a. The offender has no significant history of prior criminal activity;

b. The offender acted under unusual pressures or influences or under the domination of another person;

c. The crime was committed while the offender was under the influence of extreme mental or emotional disturbance;

d. The age of the defendant at the time of the crime;

e. The offender was an accomplice in the crime committed by another person and his or her participation was relatively minor;

f. The victim was a participant in the defendant's conduct or consented to the act; or

---

NEBRASKA EXECUTIONS 1976–1999

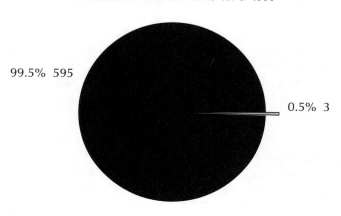

99.5% 595

0.5% 3

■ NEBRASKA EXECUTIONS

■ ALL OTHER EXECUTIONS

EXECUTIONS BY NEBRASKA 1930–1999

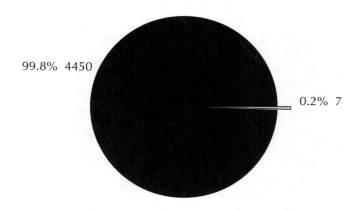

99.8% 4450

0.2% 7

■ NEBRASKA

■ ALL OTHER JURISDICTIONS

---

g. At the time of the crime, the capacity of the defendant to appreciate the wrongfulness of his or her conduct or to conform his or her conduct to the requirements of law was impaired as a result of mental illness, mental defect, or intoxication.

Under Nebraska's capital punishment statute, a sentence of death is automatically reviewed by the Nebraska Supreme Court. Nebraska uses the electric chair to carry out death sentences. The State's death row facility for men is located in Lincoln, Nebraska; while the facility maintaining female death row inmates is located in York, Nebraska.

Pursuant to the laws of Nebraska an Executive Panel, which includes the Governor, has authority to grant clemency in capital cases.

From the start of modern capital punishment in 1976, through 1999, Nebraska executed three capital felons. During this period Nebraska did not have any female capital felons on death row. A total of nine capital felons were on death row in Nebraska in 1999. The 1999 death row population in the State was listed as: one black inmate; seven white inmates; and one unidentified inmate. The State does not permit capital punishment to be imposed on persons 17 years old or younger. Nebraska prohibits the execution of mentally retarded capital felons.

Executions by Nebraska 1976–1999

Name	Race	Date of Execution	Method of Execution
Harold Otey	Black	September 2, 1994	Electrocution
John Joubert	White	July 17, 1996	Electrocution
Robert E. Williams	Black	December 2, 1997	Electrocution

Nebraskans Against the Death Penalty Nebraskans Against the Death Penalty (NADP) is the primary death penalty abolition organization in Nebraska. It was founded in 1981, after the State's governor vetoed a bill that would have repealed the death penalty in Nebraska. Work engaged in by NADP includes educating the public about the death penalty and charitable efforts toward death row inmates and those being prosecuted for capital crimes.

In 1999, NADP was instrumental in getting Nebraska's unicameral legislature to pass a bill that would have imposed a two-year moratorium on capital punishment and funded a study of the punishment. However, the State's governor vetoed the bill. The legislature was able to get enough votes to override that part of the bill which called for funding a two-year study of capital punishment. The study will cost between $120,000 and $160,000. It will analyze the nearly 1,300 homicides committed in Nebraska since 1973 based on race, gender, economic status and the crimes themselves. The study will be conducted by the Nebraska Crime Commission. The NADP is monitoring the process to promote a fair and honest study of the death penalty in Nebraska.

Neebe, Oscar W. *see* **Chicago Labor Riots of 1886**

Nepal Nepal abolished the death penalty for ordinary crimes in 1990, and abolished the punishment completely in 1997. *See also* International Capital Punishment Nations

Netherlands Capital punishment was abolished for ordinary crimes by the Netherlands in 1870, and was completely abolished as a punishment in 1982. *See also* **International Capital Punishment Nations**

Neubauer, Herman Otto *see* **Espionage**

Nevada The State of Nevada is a capital punishment jurisdiction. The State reenacted its death penalty law after the United States Supreme Court decision in *Furman v. Georgia*, 408 U.S. 238 (1972), on July 1, 1973.

Nevada has a two-tier legal system. The State's legal system is composed of a supreme court and courts of general jurisdiction. The Nevada Supreme Court is presided over by a chief justice and six associate justices. The courts of general jurisdiction in the State are called District Courts. Capital offenses against the State of Nevada are tried in the District Courts.

Nevada's capital punishment statute is triggered if a person commits a homicide under the following special circumstances:

a. Perpetrated by means of poison, lying in wait, torture or child abuse, or by any other kind of willful, deliberate and premeditated killing;

b. Committed in the perpetration or attempted perpetration of sexual assault, kidnaping, arson, robbery, burglary, invasion of the home, sexual abuse of a child or sexual molestation of a child under the age of 14 years; or

c. Committed to avoid or prevent the lawful arrest of any person by a peace officer or to effect the escape of any person from legal custody.

Capital murder in Nevada is punishable by death, life imprisonment without parole or imprisonment for a term of years. A capital prosecution in Nevada is bifurcated into a guilt phase and penalty phase. A jury is used at both phases of a capital trial. It is required that, at the penalty phase, the jury unanimously agree that a death sentence is appropriate before it can be imposed. If the penalty phase jury is unable to reach a verdict, the trial judge is required to declare a mistrial and convene another penalty phase proceeding that is composed of three judges, who must decide the punishment. The decision of a penalty phase jury is binding on the trial court under the laws of Nevada.

In order to impose a death sentence upon a defendant under Nevada law, it is required that the prosecutor establish the existence of at least one of the following statutory aggravating circumstances at the penalty phase:

1. The murder was committed by a person under sentence of imprisonment.

2. The murder was committed by a person who, at any time before a penalty hearing is conducted, is or has been con-

Members of the Nevada Supreme Court: (left to right sitting) *Justice Cliff Young, Justice Deborah A. Agosti, Justice Nancy A. Becker, and Chief Justice Robert E. Rose;* (left to right standing) *Justice A. William Maupin, Justice Myron E. Leavitt, and Justice Miriam Shearing.* (Nevada Supreme Court)

victed of another murder, or a felony involving the use or threat of violence to the person of another.

3. The murder was committed by a person who knowingly created a great risk of death to more than one person by means of a weapon, device or course of action which would normally be hazardous to the lives of more than one person.

4. The murder was committed while the person was engaged, alone or with others, in the commission of or an attempt to commit or flight after committing or attempting to commit, any robbery, arson in the first degree, burglary, invasion of the home or kidnaping in the first degree.

5. The murder was committed to avoid or prevent a lawful arrest or to effect an escape from custody.

6. The murder was committed by a person, for himself or another, to receive money or any other thing of monetary value.

7. The murder was committed upon a peace officer, correction officer or fireman who was killed while engaged in the performance of his official duty or because of an act performed in his official capacity, and the defendant knew or reasonably should have known that the victim was a peace officer, correction officer or fireman.

8. The murder involved torture or the mutilation of the victim.

9. The murder was committed upon one or more persons at random and without apparent motive.

10. The murder was committed upon a person less than 14 years of age.

11. The murder was committed upon a person because of the actual or perceived race, color, religion, national origin, physical or mental disability or sexual orientation of that person.

12. The defendant has, in the immediate proceeding, been convicted of more than one offense of murder in the first or second degree.

13. The person, alone or with others, subjected or attempted to subject the victim of the murder to nonconsensual sexual penetration immediately before, during or immediately after the commission of the murder.

Although the Federal Constitution will not permit jurisdictions to prevent capital felons from presenting all relevant mitigating evidence at the penalty phase, Nevada has provided the following statutory mitigating circumstances that permit the jury to reject imposition of the death penalty:

1. The defendant has no significant history of prior criminal activity.

2. The murder was committed while the defendant was under the influence of extreme mental or emotional disturbance.

3. The victim was a participant in the defendant's criminal conduct or consented to the act.

4. The defendant was an accomplice in a murder committed by another person and his participation in the murder was relatively minor.

5. The defendant acted under duress or under the domination of another person.

6. The youth of the defendant at the time of the crime.

7. Any other mitigating circumstance.

Under Nevada's capital punishment statute, a sentence of death is automatically reviewed by the Nevada Supreme Court. Nevada uses lethal injection to carry out death sentences (lethal gas was formerly used). The State's death row facility for men is located in Ely, Nevada; while the facility maintaining female death row inmates is located in Carson City, Nevada.

Pursuant to the laws of Nevada an Executive Panel, which includes the Governor, has authority to grant clemency in capital cases.

From the start of modern capital punishment in 1976, through 1999, Nevada executed 8 capital felons. During this period Nevada did not execute any female capital felons, although one of its death row inmates during this period was a female. A total of 86 capital felons were on death row in Nevada in 1999. The 1999 death row population in the State was listed as: 35 black inmates; 43 white inmates; and eight unidentified inmates. In 1999 the State had one juvenile on death row. The State permits capital punishment to be imposed on persons 16 years old or older. Nevada does not prohibit the execution of mentally retarded capital felons.

Executions by Nevada 1976–1999

Name	Race	Date of Execution	Method of Execution
Jesse Bishop	White	October 22, 1979	Lethal Gas
Carroll Cole	White	December 6, 1985	Lethal Injection
William P. Thompson	White	June 21, 1989	Lethal Injection
Sean P. Flannagan	White	June 23, 1989	Lethal Injection
Thomas Baal	White	June 3, 1990	Lethal Injection
Richard A. Moran	White	March 30, 1996	Lethal Injection
Roderick Abeyta	Hispanic	October 5, 1998	Lethal Injection
Alvaro Calambro	Asian	April 6, 1999	Lethal Injection

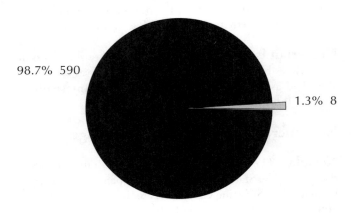

NEVADA EXECUTIONS 1976–1999

98.7% 590

1.3% 8

■ NEVADA EXECUTIONS
■ ALL OTHER EXECUTIONS

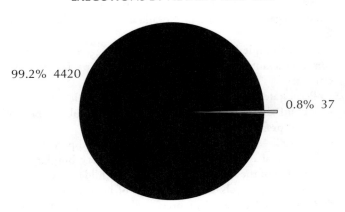

EXECUTIONS BY NEVADA 1930–1999

99.2% 4420

0.8% 37

■ NEVADA
■ ALL OTHER JURISDICTIONS

New Hampshire The State of New Hampshire is a capital punishment jurisdiction. The State reenacted its death penalty law after the United States Supreme Court decision in *Furman v. Georgia*, 408 U.S. 238 (1972), on January 1, 1991.

New Hampshire has a two-tier legal system. The State's legal system is composed of a supreme court and courts of general jurisdiction. The New Hampshire Supreme Court is presided over by a chief justice and four associate justices. The courts of general jurisdiction in the State are called Superior Courts. Capital offenses against the State of New Hampshire are tried in the Superior Courts.

New Hampshire's capital punishment statute is triggered if a person commits a homicide under the following special circumstances:

a. the murder of a law enforcement officer or a judicial officer acting in the line of duty or when the death is caused as a consequence of or in retaliation for such person's actions in the line of duty;

b. murder during the commission of, or while attempting to commit kidnaping;

c. by criminally soliciting a person to cause death or after having been criminally solicited by another for his personal pecuniary gain;

d. murder by the offender after being sentenced to life imprisonment without parole;

e. murder during the commission of, or while attempting to commit aggravated felonious sexual assault;

f. murder during the commission of, or while attempting to commit a drug offense.

Capital murder in New Hampshire is punishable by death or life imprisonment without parole. A capital prosecution in New Hampshire is bifurcated into a guilt phase and penalty phase. A jury is used at both phases of a capital trial. It is required that, at the penalty phase, the jury unanimously agree that a death sentence is appropriate before it can be imposed. If the penalty phase jury is unable to reach a verdict, the trial judge is required to impose a sentence of life imprisonment without parole. The decision of a penalty phase jury is binding on the trial court under the laws of New Hampshire.

In order to impose a death sentence upon a defendant under New Hampshire law, it is required that the prosecutor establish the existence of at least one of the following statutory aggravating circumstances at the penalty phase:

a. The defendant purposely killed the victim.

b. The defendant has been convicted of another state or federal offense resulting in the death of a person, for which a sentence of life imprisonment or a sentence of death was authorized by law.

c. The defendant has previously been convicted of two or more state or federal offenses punishable by a term of imprisonment of more than one year, committed on different occasions, involving the infliction of, or attempted infliction of, serious bodily injury upon another person.

d. The defendant has previously been convicted of two or more state or federal offenses punishable by a term of imprisonment of more than one year, committed on different occasions, involving the distribution of a controlled substance.

e. In the commission of the offense of capital murder, the defendant knowingly created a grave risk of death to one or more persons in addition to the victims of the offense.

f. The defendant committed the offense after substantial planning and premeditation.

g. The victim was particularly vulnerable due to old age, youth, or infirmity.

h. The defendant committed the offense in an especially heinous, cruel or depraved manner in that it involved torture or serious physical abuse to the victim.

i. The murder was committed for pecuniary gain.

j. The murder was committed for the purpose of avoiding or preventing a lawful arrest or effecting an escape from lawful custody.

Although the Federal Constitution will not permit jurisdictions to prevent capital felons from presenting all relevant mitigating evidence at the penalty phase, New Hampshire has provided the following statutory mitigating circumstances that permit the jury to reject imposition of the death penalty:

a. The defendant's capacity to appreciate the wrongfulness of his conduct or to conform his conduct to the requirements of law was significantly impaired, regardless of whether the capacity was so impaired as to constitute a defense to the charge.

b. The defendant was under unusual and substantial duress, regardless of whether the duress was of such a degree as to constitute a defense to the charge.

c. The defendant is punishable as an accomplice in the offense, which was committed by another, but the defendant's participation was relatively minor, regardless of whether the participation was so minor as to constitute a defense to the charge.

d. The defendant was youthful, although not under the age of 18.

e. The defendant did not have a significant prior criminal record.

f. The defendant committed the offense under severe mental or emotional disturbance.

g. Another defendant or defendants, equally culpable in the crime, will not be punished by death.

h. The victim consented to the criminal conduct that resulted in the victim's death.

i. Other factors in the defendant's background or character mitigate against imposition of the death sentence.

Under New Hampshire's capital punishment statute, a sentence of death is automatically reviewed by the New Hampshire Supreme Court. New Hampshire uses lethal injection to carry out death sentences. The State also provides for the use of hanging, if lethal injection was found unconstitutional. Pursuant to the laws of New Hampshire the Governor has exclusive authority to grant clemency in capital cases.

EXECUTIONS BY NEW HAMPSHIRE 1930–1999

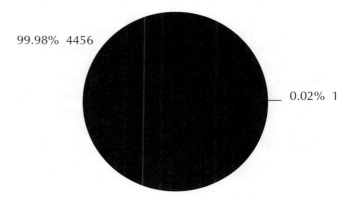

99.98% 4456

0.02% 1

■ NEW HAMPSHIRE

■ ALL OTHER JURISDICTIONS

From the start of modern capital punishment in 1976, through 1999, New Hampshire did not execute any prisoner. Nor did the State have anyone on death row during this period. The last execution by the State occurred in 1939.

The State permits capital punishment to be imposed on persons 17 years old or older. New Hampshire does not prohibit the execution of mentally retarded capital felons.

New Jersey The State of New Jersey is a capital punishment jurisdiction. The State reenacted its death penalty law after the United States Supreme Court decision in *Furman v. Georgia,* 408 U.S. 238 (1972), on August 6, 1982.

New Jersey has a two-tier legal system. The State's legal system is composed of a supreme court and courts of general jurisdiction. The New Jersey Supreme Court is presided over by a chief justice and six associate justices. The courts of general jurisdiction in the State are called Superior Courts (an appellate division exists as part of the Superior Courts). Capital offenses against the State of New Jersey are tried in the Superior Courts.

New Jersey's capital punishment statute is triggered if a person commits a homicide under the following special circumstances:

1. The offender purposely causes death or serious bodily injury resulting in death; or
2. The offender knowingly causes death or serious bodily injury resulting in death; or
3. The offender was an accomplice who procured the commission of the offense by payment or promise of payment of anything of pecuniary value; or who, as a leader of a narcotics trafficking network and in furtherance of a conspiracy, commanded or by threat or promise solicited the commission of the offense.

Capital murder in New Jersey is punishable by death or life imprisonment without parole. A capital prosecution in New Jersey is bifurcated into a guilt phase and penalty phase. A jury is used at both phases of a capital trial. It is required that, at the penalty phase, the jury unanimously agree that a death sentence is appropriate before it can be imposed. If the penalty phase jury is unable to reach a verdict, the trial judge is required to impose a sentence of life imprisonment without parole. The decision of a penalty phase jury is binding on the trial court under the laws of New Jersey.

In order to impose a death sentence upon a defendant under New Jersey law, it is required that the prosecutor establish the existence of at least one of the following statutory aggravating circumstances at the penalty phase:

a. The defendant has been convicted, at any time, of another murder;
b. In the commission of the murder, the defendant purposely or knowingly created a grave risk of death to another person in addition to the victim;
c. The murder was outrageously or wantonly vile, horrible or inhuman in that it involved torture, depravity of mind, or an aggravated assault to the victim;

d. The defendant committed the murder as consideration for the receipt, or in expectation of the receipt of anything of pecuniary value;
e. The defendant procured the commission of the offense by payment or promise of payment of anything of pecuniary value;
f. The murder was committed for the purpose of escaping detection, apprehension, trial, punishment or confinement for another offense committed by the defendant or another;
g. The offense was committed while the defendant was engaged in the commission of, or an attempt to commit, or flight after committing or attempting to commit murder, robbery, sexual assault, arson, burglary or kidnapping or the crime of contempt;
h. The defendant murdered a public servant, while the victim was engaged in the performance of his official duties, or because of the victim's status as a public servant;
i. The defendant: (i) as a leader of a narcotics trafficking network and in furtherance of a conspiracy committed, commanded or by threat or promise solicited the commission of the offense or (ii) committed the offense at the direction of a leader of a narcotics trafficking network in furtherance of a conspiracy;
j. The homicidal act that the defendant committed or procured through an explosion, flood, avalanche, collapse of a building, release or abandonment of poison gas, radioactive material or any other harmful or destructive substance;
k. The victim was less than 14 years old.

Although the Federal Constitution will not permit jurisdictions to prevent capital felons from presenting all relevant mitigating evidence at the penalty phase, New Jersey has provided the following statutory mitigating circumstances that permit the jury to reject imposition of the death penalty:

a. The defendant was under the influence of extreme mental or emotional disturbance insufficient to constitute a defense to prosecution;
b. The victim solicited, participated in or consented to the conduct which resulted in his death;
c. The age of the defendant at the time of the murder;
d. The defendant's capacity to appreciate the wrongfulness of his conduct or to conform his conduct to the requirements of the law was significantly impaired as the result of mental disease or defect or intoxication, but not to a degree sufficient to constitute a defense to prosecution;
e. The defendant was under unusual and substantial duress insufficient to constitute a defense to prosecution;
f. The defendant has no significant history of prior criminal activity;
g. The defendant rendered substantial assistance to the State in the prosecution of another person for the crime of murder; or
h. Any other factor which is relevant to the defendant's character or record or to the circumstances of the offense.

Under New Jersey's capital punishment statute, a sentence of death is automatically reviewed by the New Jersey Supreme Court. New Jersey uses lethal injection to carry out death sentences. Pursuant to the laws of New Jersey the Governor has exclusive authority to grant clemency in capital cases.

From the start of modern capital punishment in 1976, through 1999, New Jersey did not execute any capital felon. The last execution by New Jersey occurred in 1963. A total of 16 capital felons were on death row in New Jersey in 1999. The 1999 death row population in the State was listed as: seven black inmates and nine white inmates. The death row population included one female, but her sentence was overturned on appeal. The State does not permit capital punishment to be imposed on persons 17 years old or younger. New Jersey does not prohibit the execution of mentally retarded capital felons.

EXECUTIONS BY NEW JERSEY 1930–1999

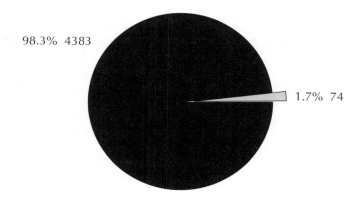

98.3% 4383

1.7% 74

- ■ (gray) NEW JERSEY
- ■ (black) ALL OTHER JURISDICTIONS

New Mexico   The State of New Mexico is a capital punishment jurisdiction. The State reenacted its death penalty law after the United States Supreme Court decision in *Furman v. Georgia*, 408 U.S. 238 (1972), on July 1, 1979.

New Mexico has a three-tier legal system. The State's legal system is composed of a supreme court, court of appeals and courts of general jurisdiction. The New Mexico Supreme Court is presided over by a chief justice and four associate justices. The New Mexico Court of Appeals is composed of a chief judge and nine judges. The courts of general jurisdiction in the State are called District Courts. Capital offenses against the State of New Mexico are tried in the District Courts.

New Mexico's capital punishment statute is triggered if a person commits a homicide under the following special circumstances:

1. by any kind of willful, deliberate and premeditated killing;
2. in the commission of or attempt to commit any felony; or
3. by any act greatly dangerous to the lives of others, indicating a depraved mind regardless of human life.

Members of the New Mexico Supreme Court: (left to right sitting) *Justice Joseph F. Baca, Chief Justice Pamela B. Minzner, and Justice Gene E. Franchini;* (left to right standing) *Justice Patricio M. Serna and Justice Petra J. Maes. (New Mexico Supreme Court)*

Capital murder in New Mexico is punishable by death or life imprisonment. A capital prosecution in New Mexico is bifurcated into a guilt phase and penalty phase. A jury is used at both phases of a capital trial. It is required that, at the penalty phase, the jury unanimously agree that a death sentence is appropriate before it can be imposed. If the penalty phase jury is unable to reach a verdict, the trial judge is required to impose a sentence of life imprisonment. The decision of a penalty phase jury is binding on the trial court under the laws of New Mexico.

In order to impose a death sentence upon a defendant under New Mexico law, it is required that the prosecutor establish the existence of at least one of the following statutory aggravating circumstances at the penalty phase:

A. the victim was a peace officer who was acting in the lawful discharge of an official duty when he was murdered;
B. the murder was committed with intent to kill in the commission of or attempt to commit kidnaping, criminal sexual contact of a minor or criminal sexual penetration;
C. the murder was committed with the intent to kill by the defendant while attempting to escape from a penal institution of New Mexico;
D. while incarcerated in a penal institution in New Mexico, the defendant, with the intent to kill, murdered a person who was at the time incarcerated in or lawfully on the premises of a penal institution in New Mexico;
E. while incarcerated in a penal institution in New Mexico, the defendant, with the intent to kill, murdered an employee of the corrections and criminal rehabilitation department;
F. the capital felony was committed for hire; and
G. the capital felony was murder of a witness to a crime or any person likely to become a witness to a crime, for the purpose of preventing report of the crime or testimony in any criminal proceeding, or for retaliation for the victim having testified in any criminal proceeding.

Although the Federal Constitution will not permit jurisdictions to prevent capital felons from presenting all relevant mitigating evidence at the penalty phase, New Mexico has provided the following statutory mitigating circumstances that permit the jury to reject imposition of the death penalty:

A. the defendant has no significant history of prior criminal activity;

B. the defendant acted under duress or under the domination of another person;

C. the defendant's capacity to appreciate the criminality of his conduct or to conform his conduct to the requirements of the law was impaired;

D. the defendant was under the influence of mental or emotional disturbance;

E. the victim was a willing participant in the defendant's conduct;

F. the defendant acted under circumstances which tended to justify, excuse or reduce the crime;

G. the defendant is likely to be rehabilitated;

H. the defendant cooperated with authorities; and

I. the defendant's age.

Under New Mexico's capital punishment statute, a sentence of death is automatically reviewed by the New Mexico Supreme Court. New Mexico uses lethal injection to carry out death sentences. The State's death row facility for men is located in Santa Fe, New Mexico. Pursuant to the laws of New Mexico the Governor has exclusive authority to grant clemency in capital cases.

From the start of modern capital punishment in 1976, through 1999, New Mexico did not execute any capital felon. The last execution by the State occurred in 1960. During the 1976–1999 period, New Mexico did not have any female capital felons. A total of four capital felons were on death row in New Mexico in 1999. The 1999 death row population in the State was listed as: zero black inmates; three white inmates; and one unidentified inmate. The State does not permit capital punishment to be imposed on persons 17 years old or younger. New Mexico prohibits the execution of mentally retarded capital felons.

EXECUTIONS BY NEW MEXICO 1930–1999

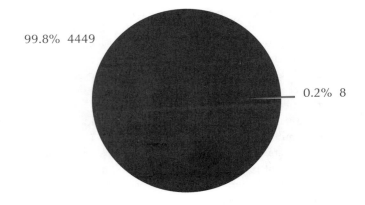

99.8% 4449

0.2% 8

■ NEW MEXICO

■ ALL OTHER JURISDICTIONS

New Mexico Coalition to Repeal the Death Penalty

The New Mexico Coalition to Repeal the Death Penalty is composed of organizations and individuals committed to repealing the death penalty in New Mexico. The organization has several committees including legislative, educational, faith, and media. Its legislative committee focuses on introducing bills to repeal the death penalty in the New Mexico legislature. The education committee provides resources and teaching materials for school groups, religious communities, and others interested in learning more about the death penalty. The faith committee works with individual faith communities and religious leaders to promote dialogue and action around the issue. The media committee focuses on publicizing the organization's message, as well as death penalty-related events in the community

Newton, Frances Elaine

On the evening of April 7, 1987, Houston police responded to a call of possible shooting at the home of Adrian Newton. When the police arrived they found 23-year-old Adrian dead from a bullet wound to his head. They also found Adrian's two children, seven-year-old Alton and 21-month-old Farrah, dead from gunshot wounds.

On April 21, 1987, 23-year-old Frances Elaine Newton, the wife of Adrian and mother of Alton and Farrah, filed a claim for a $50,000 life insurance policy she had taken out on her husband and children. The police arrested Frances the day after she filed the insurance claim and charged her with three counts of murder.

During the trial of Frances, which was held in 1988, the prosecutor was able to present strong circumstantial evidence that she murdered her husband and two children. The evidence revealed that Frances was having an affair with another man. A month before her husband and children were killed she took out a life insurance policy, effective immediately, on her family.

On the day of the murders, Frances asked her brother-in-law to leave the home because she wanted to discuss marital problems with her husband. The brother-in-law left. Within hours of his departure, the killings occurred. Frances claimed to have an alibi, in that around the time of the murders she visited the home of a relative named Sondra Nelms. However, Nelms' testimony provided the strongest evidence against Frances.

Nelms testified that when Frances arrived at her home she went to a nearby

Frances Elaine Newton is on death row in Texas after being convicted of killing her husband and two children for life insurance proceeds. (Texas Department of Criminal Justice)

abandoned house carrying a bag and that she left the bag in the house. Police later found the bag in the abandoned house. The bag contained the murder weapon.

Additional evidence during the trial revealed that the dress Frances wore on the day of the killings contained gunpowder residue. Frances was ultimately convicted of the murders by a jury and sentenced to death. She is on death row in Texas.

New York   The State of New York is a capital punishment jurisdiction. The State reenacted its death penalty law after the United States Supreme Court decision in *Furman v. Georgia*, 408 U.S. 238 (1972), on September 9, 1995.

New York has a three-tier legal system. The State's legal system is composed of a court of appeals, appellate division and courts of general jurisdiction. The New York Court of Appeals is presided over by a chief judge and six associate judges. The New York Supreme Court Appellate Division is divided into four departments. Each department is composed of a presiding chief justice and at least eight associate justices. The courts of general jurisdiction in the State are called Supreme Courts. Capital offenses against the State of New York are tried in the Supreme Courts.

New York's capital punishment statute is triggered if a person commits a homicide under the following special circumstances:

i. the intended victim was a police officer who was at the time of the killing engaged in the course of performing his official duties, and the defendant knew or reasonably should have known that the intended victim was a police officer; or

ii. the intended victim was a uniformed court officer, parole officer, probation officer, or employee of the division for youth, who was at the time of the killing engaged in the course of performing his official duties, and the defendant knew or reasonably should have known that the intended victim was such a uniformed court officer, parole officer, probation officer, or employee of the division for youth; or

iii. the intended victim was an employee of a state correctional institution or was an employee of a local correctional facility, who was at the time of the killing engaged in the course of performing his official duties, and the defendant knew or reasonably should have known that the intended victim was an employee of a state correctional institution or a local correctional facility; or

iv. at the time of the commission of the killing, the defendant was confined in a state correctional institution or was otherwise in custody upon a sentence for the term of his natural life, or upon a sentence commuted to one of natural life, or upon a sentence for an indeterminate term the minimum of which was at least fifteen years and the maximum of which was natural life, or at the time of the commission of the killing, the defendant had escaped from such confinement or custody while serving such a sentence and had not yet been returned to such confinement or custody; or

v. the intended victim was a witness to a crime committed on a prior occasion and the death was caused for the purpose of preventing the intended victim's testimony in any criminal action or proceeding whether or not such action or proceeding had been commenced, or the intended victim had previously testified in a criminal action or proceeding and the killing was committed for the purpose of exacting retribution for such prior testimony, or the intended victim was an immediate family member of a witness to a crime committed on a prior occasion and the killing was committed for the purpose of preventing or influencing the testimony of such witness, or the intended victim was an immediate family member of a witness who had previously testified in a criminal action or proceeding and the killing was committed for the purpose of exacting retribution upon such witness for such prior testimony; or

vi. the defendant committed the killing or procured commission of the killing pursuant to an agreement with a person other than the intended victim to commit the same for the receipt, or in expectation of the receipt, of anything of pecuniary value from a party to the agreement or from a person other than the intended victim acting at the direction of a party to such agreement; or

vii. the victim was killed while the defendant was in the course of committing or attempting to commit and in furtherance of robbery, burglary in the first degree or second degree, kidnaping in the first degree, arson in the first degree or second degree, rape in the first degree, sodomy in the first degree, sexual abuse in the first degree, aggravated sexual abuse in the first degree or escape in the first degree, or in the course of and furtherance of immediate flight after committing or attempting to commit any such crime or in the course of and furtherance of immediate flight after attempting to commit the crime of murder in the second degree; or

viii. as part of the same criminal transaction, the defendant, with intent to cause serious physical injury to or the death of an additional person or persons, causes the death of an additional person or persons; provided, however, the victim is not a participant in the criminal transaction; or

ix. prior to committing the killing, the defendant had been convicted of murder; or

x. the defendant acted in an especially cruel and wanton manner pursuant to a course of conduct intended to inflict and inflicting torture upon the victim prior to the victim's death; or

xi. the defendant intentionally caused the death of two or more additional persons within the state in separate criminal transactions within a period of twenty-four months when committed in a similar fashion or pursuant to a common scheme or plan; or

xii. the intended victim was a judge and the defendant killed such victim because such victim was, at the time of the killing, a judge.

Capital murder in New York is punishable by death or life imprisonment without parole. A capital prosecution in New York is bifurcated into a guilt phase and penalty phase. A jury is used at both phases of a capital trial. It is required that, at the penalty phase, the jury unanimously agree that a death sentence is appropriate before it can be imposed. If the penalty phase jury is unable to reach a verdict, the trial judge is required to impose a sentence of life imprisonment without parole. The decision of a penalty phase jury is binding on the trial court under the laws of New York.

Pursuant to the death penalty statute of New York, the prosecutor is not required to prove aggravating circumstances at the penalty phase of a capital trial. New York's law provides that whatever special circumstances were proven beyond a reasonable doubt at the guilt phase, are used as conclusive proof of the existence of aggravating circumstances, for the purposes of the penalty phase.

Although the Federal Constitution will not permit jurisdictions to prevent capital felons from presenting all relevant mitigating evidence at the penalty phase, New York has provided the following statutory mitigating circumstances that permit the jury to reject imposition of the death penalty:

a. The defendant has no significant history of prior criminal convictions involving the use of violence against another person;

b. The defendant was mentally retarded at the time of the crime, or the defendant's mental capacity was impaired or his ability to conform his conduct to the requirements of law was impaired but not so impaired in either case as to constitute a defense to prosecution;

c. The defendant was under duress or under the domination of another person, although not such duress or domination as to constitute a defense to prosecution;

d. The defendant was criminally liable for the present offense of murder committed by another, but his participation in the offense was relatively minor although not so minor as to constitute a defense to prosecution;

e. The murder was committed while the defendant was mentally or emotionally disturbed or under the influence of alcohol or any drug, although not to such an extent as to constitute a defense to prosecution; or

f. Any other circumstance concerning the crime, the defendant's state of mind or condition at the time of the crime, or the defendant's character, background or record that would be relevant to mitigation or punishment for the crime.

Under New York's capital punishment statute, a sentence of death is automatically reviewed by the New York Court of Appeals. New York uses lethal injection to carry out death sentences. The State's death row facility is located in Dannemora, New York. Pursuant to the laws of New York the Governor has exclusive authority to grant clemency in capital cases.

From the start of modern capital punishment in 1976, through 1999, New York did not execute any capital felon. The last execution in the State occurred in 1963. During the 1976–1999 period New York did not have any female capital felon on death row. A total of two capital felons were on death row in New York in 1999. The 1999 death row population in the State was listed as: one black inmate and one unidentified inmate. The State does not permit capital punishment to be imposed on persons 18 years old or younger. New York prohibits the execution of mentally retarded capital felons, except for capital murder by a person who was an inmate at the time of the crime.

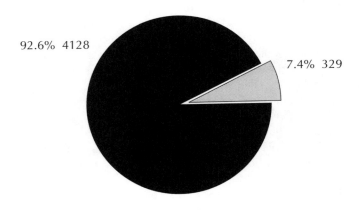

EXECUTIONS BY NEW YORK 1930–1999

92.6% 4128

7.4% 329

■ NEW YORK

■ ALL OTHER JURISDICTIONS

New Zealand   New Zealand abolished capital punishment for ordinary crimes in 1961, and completely abolished the punishment for all crimes in 1989. *See also* **International Capital Punishment Nations**

Next Friend Intervention *see* **Intervention by Next Friend**

Ng, Charles   Charles Ng, a former Marine and Hong Kong immigrant, was sentenced to death by the State of California on June 30, 1999. Ng was convicted of the murder of six men, three women and two baby boys. He spent 14 years fighting the charges, thus making his prosecution the longest in the history of California — and one of the costliest at $14

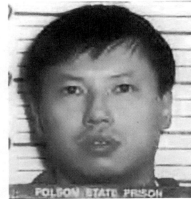

Charles Ng is on death row in the State of California after being convicted of killing 11 people. (California Department of Corrections)

million. Ng was arrested in Canada in 1985, and fought extradition for five years.

The evidence in Ng's trial revealed that he and an accomplice named Leonard Lake, who committed suicide while in police custody in 1985, lured the victims to a cabin in California's Gold Rush Country in 1984 and 1985. The cabin was equipped a bunker that was used as a prisoner's cell.

Video tapes revealed Ng and Lake tortured and raped their female victims before killing them. The police only recovered the bodies of two of the victims, but there was evidence of hundreds of pieces of charred bones around the cabin, leading authorities to conclude that the other victims were burned. Ng is on death row in California.

Nicaragua Capital punishment was abolished by Nicaragua in 1979. *See also* **International Capital Punishment Nations**

Niger Capital punishment has not been officially abolished by Niger, but the punishment has not been invoked in over a decade. Niger uses the firing squad to carry out the death penalty. Its legal system is based on French civil law and customary law. Niger revised its constitution on May 12, 1996.

The judicial system is composed of trial courts, a Court of Appeals, and a Supreme Court. Customary courts try cases involving divorce or inheritance. Defendants have the right to retained or appointed counsel, to confront witnesses, and enjoy a presumption of innocence. Defendants and prosecutors may appeal a judgment. *See also* **International Capital Punishment Nations**

Nigeria Capital punishment is on the law books of Nigeria. Nigeria uses hanging and the firing squad to carry out the death penalty. In 1998, Nigeria executed six prisoners. The nation's legal system is based on English common law and customary law. Nigeria has a partially defunct constitution (due to military rule) that was adopted in 1979.

The judicial system is composed of federal and state trial courts, appellate courts, and a federal Supreme Court. Trials in the court system are public. Defendants enjoy a presumption of innocence, have a right to legal counsel, and a right to confront witnesses. *See also* **International Capital Punishment Nations**

Night Stalker Between 1984–1985, the city of Los Angeles was gripped with fear, as the media proclaimed the city was being terrorized by an unidentified Night Stalker. During this period the infamous Night Stalker randomly stalked and murdered 13 people in their homes.

The police were at a loss for locating the Night Stalker until a break came through on September 1, 1985. On that day the police were able to obtain a picture of the Night Stalker and posted it throughout the city. On the day the picture was released, the Night Stalker was caught by residents of a neighborhood as he attempted to steal a car. The residents attacked

him and held him until the police arrived. That evening police arrested Richard Ramirez on suspicion of committing 19 murders.

Richard Ramirez received 13 death sentences by the State of California. (Los Angeles Police)

Ramirez was born February 29, 1960, to Mexican immigrant parents. He was reared in El Paso, Texas. He left home at age 18 and headed for Los Angeles. Ramirez was considered a dangerous youth by those who knew him. He was known to be a heavy drug user who listened religiously to satanic music. Eventually drugs and satanic music drove Ramirez to the point of rejecting his Catholic background, and embracing satanic worship.

Ramirez was not brought to trial until January 10, 1989. The trial ended in July. The jury deliberated until September 20, before they brought back guilty verdicts on each of the charges. On October 3, the penalty phase jury voted for the death penalty. The trial judge responded by sentencing Ramirez to death 13 times. The Night Stalker is on death row in California continuing to worship satan.

Nobles v. Georgia *Court:* United States Supreme Court; *Case Citation:* Nobles v. Georgia, 168 U.S. 398 (1897); *Argued:* Not reported; *Decided:* November 29, 1897; *Opinion of the Court:* Justice White; *Concurring Opinion:* None; *Dissenting Opinion:* None; *Appellate Defense Counsel:* Marion W. Harris argued; W. C. Glenn on brief; *Appellate Prosecution Counsel:* J. M. Terrell argued and briefed; *Amicus Curiae Brief Supporting Prosecutor:* None; *Amicus Curiae Brief Supporting Defendant:* None.

Issue Presented: Whether the defendant was entitled to a jury trial to determine her sanity before the trial court fixed a new date for her execution?

Case Holding: The defendant was not entitled to a jury trial to determine her sanity before the trial court fixed a new date for her execution, because such a requirement was not imposed under the common law.

Factual and procedural background of case: The defendant, Elizabeth Nobles, was convicted of capital murder and sentenced to death by the State of Georgia. The Georgia Supreme Court affirmed the judgment. When the case returned to the trial court it was necessary to fix a new execution date because the initial one had expired while the case was being appealed. The defendant objected to the new sentencing proceeding on the grounds that she had become insane, and requested a jury trial to determine whether she was insane. The trial court rejected the contention and set a new execution date. The defendant appealed the issue, but the State appellate court affirmed the judgment. The United States Supreme Court granted certiorari to consider the issue.

Opinion of the Court by Justice White: Justice White indicated that the defendant challenged the method of inquiry provided by the Georgia statutes for ascertaining whether a defendant who had been convicted of a crime was insane at the time of the inquiry. The defendant contended that the Georgia statutes afforded an opportunity to investigate the question of the insanity of a person convicted of crime only when the suggestion of insanity was made after conviction and sentence, but the statutes furnished no means of testing the question of insanity arising after conviction and before sentence. Justice White ultimately concluded that the defendant's argument was without merit, because she was not actually resentenced and therefore was not entitled to any presentencing protections in determining her sanity. The opinion reasoned as follows:

> Indeed, the question which arises on the record does not require a consideration of what would be due process of law under the fourteenth amendment, where insanity was suggested between verdict and sentence, or even at the time of sentence. This results from the fact that the suggestion of insanity relied on was made, not at the time of sentence, but long after the sentence had been imposed. As stated [in the record], the accused had been sentenced to death at the term of court where the verdict of guilty was found, and that when called into court again, ... it was for a resentence upon the verdict, because of the previous sentence having been regularly and legally superseded by the order of court. In the opinion of the supreme court of Georgia in this case, it finds this fact, and holds that under the Georgia statutes the [second] proceeding ..., although called a "resentence," was in legal effect but a fixing of a new date for the execution of the previous sentence; the date fixed in the prior sentence having expired. In other words, the supreme court of Georgia holds that the prior sentence remained in force, and that the subsequent action of the court was but a mere fixing of the date for its execution....
>
> From these considerations it follows that the only question which we are called upon to determine is whether, after a regular conviction and sentence, a suggestion of a then existing insanity is made, it is necessary, in order to constitute due process of law, that the question so presented should be tried by a jury in a judicial proceeding surrounded by all the safeguards and requirements of a common law jury trial, and even although by the state law full and adequate administrative and quasi judicial process is created for the purpose of investigating the suggestion. Without analysis of the contention, it might well suffice to demonstrate its obvious unsoundness by pointing to the absurd conclusion which would result from its establishment. If it were true that at common law a suggestion of insanity, after sentence, created on the part of a convict an absolute right to a trial of this issue by a judge and jury, then it would be wholly at the will of a convict to suffer any punishment whatever, for the necessity of his doing so would depend solely upon his fecundity in making suggestion after suggestion of insanity, to be followed by trial upon trial.....
>
> It being demonstrated by reason and authority that at common law a suggestion, made after verdict and sentence, of insanity, did not give rise to an absolute right on the part of a convict to have such issue tried before the court and to a jury, but addressed itself to the discretion of the judge, it follows that the

manner in which such question should be determined was purely a matter of legislative regulation. It was therefore a subject within the control of the state of Georgia.

The judgment of the Georgia Supreme Court was affirmed. *See also* **Insanity While Awaiting Execution**

Nofire v. United States

Court: United States Supreme Court; *Case Citation:* Nofire v. United States, 164 U.S. 657 (1897); *Argued:* Not reported; *Decided:* January 4, 1897; *Opinion of the Court:* Justice Brewer; *Concurring Opinion:* None; *Dissenting Opinion:* None; *Appellate Defense Counsel:* Not represented; *Appellate Prosecution Counsel:* Mr. Whitney argued and briefed; *Amicus Curiae Brief Supporting Prosecutor:* None; *Amicus Curiae Brief Supporting Defendant:* None.

Issue Presented: Whether the Federal court had jurisdiction over a murder committed by Cherokee citizens against an adopted Cherokee citizen?

Case Holding: The Federal court did not have jurisdiction over a murder committed by Cherokee citizens against an adopted Cherokee citizen.

Factual and procedural background of case: This case involved the prosecution of the defendant, Nofire, and several other unnamed defendants by the United States. The defendants were charged with the capital murder of a white person, Fred Rutherford, on the land of the Cherokee Nation. The defendants requested the Federal trial court dismiss the case because the victim, though white, was a citizen of the Cherokee Nation and therefore the court was without jurisdiction to prosecute the case. Under the laws of the Cherokee Nation any one marrying a member of the Cherokee Nation became a citizen thereof by adoption. The defendants established the victim had married a member of the Cherokee Nation. The trial court rejected the evidence of the victim's membership in the Cherokee Nation. The defendants were prosecuted, convicted and sentenced to death. The defendants appealed to the United States Supreme Court, alleging that the trial court did not have jurisdiction to prosecute them. The United States Supreme Court granted certiorari to consider the issue.

Opinion of the Court by Justice Brewer: Justice Brewer held that the Federal court did not have jurisdiction over the offense charged against the defendants. The opinion explained:

> ... [T]he courts of the Cherokee Nation have jurisdiction over offenses committed by one [of its citizens] upon the person of another, and this includes, by virtue of the statutes, both [Cherokees] by birth and [Cherokees] by adoption....
>
> ... [I]t is evident that Rutherford intended to change his nationality, and become a Cherokee citizen. He took the steps which the statute prescribed, and did, as he supposed, all that was requisite therefor. He was marrying a Cherokee woman, and thus to a certain extent allying himself with the Cherokee Nation. He sought and obtained the license which was declared legally prerequisite to such marriage if he intended to become an adopted citizen of that Nation. That he also obtained a marriage license from the United States authorities does not disprove this intention. It only shows that he did not intend that there should be any question anywhere, by any authority, as to the validity of his marriage. He asserted, and was permitted to exercise,

the right of suffrage as a Cherokee citizen. Suppose, during his lifetime, the Cherokee Nation had asserted jurisdiction over him as an adopted citizen; would he not have been estopped from denying such citizenship? Has death changed the significance of his actions? The Cherokee Nation ... has asserted its jurisdiction over the Cherokees who did the killing,—a jurisdiction which is conditioned upon the fact that the party killed was a Cherokee citizen. It appears, therefore, that Rutherford sought to become a citizen, took all the steps he supposed necessary therefor, considered himself a citizen, and that the Cherokee Nation in his lifetime recognized him as a citizen, and still asserts his citizenship. Under those circumstances, we think it must be adjudged that he was a citizen by adoption, and, consequently, the jurisdiction over the offense charged herein is, by the laws of the United States and treaties with the Cherokee Nation, vested in the courts of that Nation.

The judgment of the Federal trial court was reversed and the case remanded with instructions to surrender the defendants to the authorities of the Cherokee Nation. *See also* **Jurisdiction**

Nolo Contendere Plea

The phrase "nolo contendere" means no contest. In criminal prosecutions a nolo contendere plea has the effect of a guilty plea, insofar as the punishment for a crime may be imposed based upon the plea. However, a nolo contendere plea is technically not a plea of guilty, nor a plea of innocence. The nolo contendere plea was originally designed to permit a defendant to avoid civil consequences that might result from a plea of guilty. For example, a defendant who assaults a victim is subject to both criminal and civil prosecution. Thus, if a defendant entered a plea of guilty to the criminal charge of assault, the victim could merely take the record of the guilty plea into a civil court and use it as conclusive evidence in a civil case against the defendant for the same conduct. By entering a plea of nolo contendere, a defendant does not give the victim conclusive proof of his or her guilt for use in a civil case.

The nolo contendere plea is rare in capital prosecutions, but it has been used. *See also* **Wuornos, Aileen; Guilty Plea**

Non-Binding Jury Sentencing Determination *see* Binding/Nonbinding Jury Sentencing Determination

Non-Capital and Capital Sentencing

Very often the situation arises where a capital felon will be convicted of capital murder, in addition to non-capital crimes during the same trial. An issue that arises frequently in this situation is whether the capital felon has a right to serve the non-capital prison sentence before having to be executed on the capital offense conviction. The universal rule on this issue is that a capital felon receiving a sentence of imprisonment, in addition to a sentence of death, does not have a right to serve the term of imprisonment before being executed.

Non-Capital Punishment Jurisdictions *see* Capital Punishment Jurisdictions

Non-Discrimination Jury Instruction

A trend has begun wherein capital punishment statutes are expressly requiring trial judges to instruct penalty phase juries that they are not to consider the race, color, religious belief, national origin or sex of capital felons when deliberating on their fate. Courts have been quick to observe that statutory non-discrimination jury instructions are not intended to eliminate jury consideration of legitimate mitigating factors, such as inferences which can be drawn from a capital felon who had a culturally difficult and deprived background. *See also* **Jury Instructions; Race-Qualified Jury**

Non-Statutory Aggravating Circumstances *see* Aggravating Circumstances

Non-Statutory Mitigating Circumstances *see* Mitigating Circumstances

Non-Weighing Jurisdictions *see* Burden of Proof at the Penalty Phase

Norris, Roy *see* Murder Mack

Norris v. Alabama

Court: United States Supreme Court; *Case Citation:* Norris v. Alabama, 294 U.S. 587 (1935); *Argued:* February 15–18, 1935; *Decided:* April 1, 1935; *Opinion of the Court:* Chief Justice Hughes; *Concurring Opinion:* None; *Dissenting Opinion:* None; *Justice Taking No Part in Decision:* Justice McReynolds; *Appellate Defense Counsel:* Samuel S. Leibowitz argued; Walter H. Pollak, Osmond K. Fraenkel and Carl S. Stern on brief; *Appellate Prosecution Counsel:* Thomas E. Knight, Jr. argued and briefed; *Amicus Curiae Brief Supporting Prosecutor:* None; *Amicus Curiae Brief Supporting Defendant:* None.

Issue Presented: Whether the defendant established that blacks were systematically excluded from the grand jury that indicted him and the petit jury that convicted him?

Case Holding: The defendant established that blacks were systematically excluded from the grand jury that indicted him and the petit jury that convicted him, therefore his conviction and death sentence could not stand.

Factual and procedural background of case: The defendant, Clarence Norris, was one of seven defendants convicted of rape and sentenced to death by the State of Alabama. In *Powell v. Alabama*, the United States Supreme Court reversed the convictions of all seven defendants and ordered a new trial. After the remand, a motion for change of venue was granted and all the cases were transferred to another county. The defendant was tried separately, however, on remand. The jury convicted the defendant and he was again sentenced to death. On appeal, the Alabama Supreme Court affirmed the conviction and sentence. In doing so, the appellate court rejected the defendant's argument that his trial violated the Federal Constitution, on the grounds that blacks were systematically excluded from the grand jury that indicted him and the petit jury that convicted him. The United States Supreme Court granted certiorari to consider the issue.

Opinion of the Court by Chief Justice Hughes: The Chief Justice held that the defendant's trial violated the Constitution because blacks were excluded from the grand and petit juries involved with the prosecution. The opinion stated that: "Whenever by any action of a state, whether through its Legislature, through its courts, or through its executive or administrative officers, all persons of the African race are excluded, solely because of their race or color, from serving as grand jurors in the criminal prosecution of a person of the African race, the equal protection of the laws is denied to him, contrary to the Fourteenth Amendment of the Constitution of the United States.... The principle is equally applicable to a similar exclusion ... from service on petit juries. And although the state['s] statute defining the qualifications of jurors may be fair on its face, the constitutional provision affords protection against action of the state through its administrative officers in effecting the prohibited discrimination."

The Chief Justice found that the defendant adduced evidence to support the charge of unconstitutional discrimination in the actual administration of the state's grand and petit jury statute. It was said that blacks had not "served on any grand or petit jury in that county within the memory of witnesses who had lived there all their lives." The opinion indicated that county officials placed code words on forms that alerted them to which potential jurors on the master jury list were black. Through the use of such code words officials were able to systematically exclude blacks from all jury service. The Chief Justice found that such evidence "in itself made out a prima facie case of the denial of the equal protection which the Constitution guarantees." The judgment of the Alabama Supreme Court was reversed and the case remanded for a new trial.

Case note: Under modern capital punishment jurisprudence the death penalty may not be imposed for the crime of rape without an accompanying homicide. *See also* **Patterson v. Alabama; Powell v. Alabama; Rape and Capital Punishment**

North Carolina
The State of North Carolina is a capital punishment jurisdiction. The State reenacted its death penalty law after the United States Supreme Court decision in *Furman v. Georgia*, 408 U.S. 238 (1972), on June 1, 1977.

North Carolina has a three-tier legal system. The State's legal system is composed of a supreme court, court of appeals and courts of general jurisdiction. The North Carolina Supreme Court is presided over by a chief justice and six associate justices. The North Carolina Court of Appeals is composed of a chief judge and eleven associate judges. The courts of general jurisdiction in the State are called Superior Courts. Capital offenses against the State of North Carolina are tried in the Superior Courts.

North Carolina's capital punishment statute is triggered if a person commits a homicide under the following special circumstances:

> Murder perpetrated by means of poison, lying in wait, imprisonment, starving, torture, or by any other kind of willful, deliberate, and premeditated killing, or which shall be committed in the perpetration or attempted perpetration of any arson, rape or a sex offense, robbery, kidnapping, burglary, or other felony committed or attempted with the use of a deadly weapon.

Capital murder in North Carolina is punishable by death or life imprisonment without parole. A capital prosecution in North Carolina is bifurcated into a guilt phase and penalty phase. A jury is used at both phases of a capital trial. It is required that, at the penalty phase, the jury unanimously agree that a death sentence is appropriate before it can be imposed. If the penalty phase jury is unable to reach a verdict, the trial judge is required to impose a sentence of life imprisonment without parole. The decision of a penalty phase jury is binding on the trial court under the laws of North Carolina.

In order to impose a death sentence upon a defendant under North Carolina law, it is required that the prosecutor establish the existence of at least one of the following statutory aggravating circumstances at the penalty phase:

1. The capital felony was committed by a person lawfully incarcerated.
2. The defendant had been previously convicted of another capital felony or had been previously adjudicated delinquent in a juvenile proceeding for committing an offense that would be a capital felony if committed by an adult.
3. The defendant had been previously convicted of a felony involving the use or threat of violence to the person or had been previously adjudicated delinquent in a juvenile proceeding for committing an offense that would be a felony involving the use or threat of violence to the person if the offense had been committed by an adult.
4. The capital felony was committed for the purpose of avoiding or preventing a lawful arrest or effecting an escape from custody.
5. The capital felony was committed while the defendant was engaged, or was an aider or abettor, in the commission of, or an attempt to commit, or flight after committing or attempting to commit, any homicide, robbery, rape or a sex offense, arson, burglary, kidnapping, or aircraft piracy or the unlawful throwing, placing, or discharging of a destructive device or bomb.
6. The capital felony was committed for pecuniary gain.
7. The capital felony was committed to disrupt or hinder the lawful exercise of any governmental function or the enforcement of laws.
8. The capital felony was committed against a law-enforcement officer, employee of the Department of Correction, jailer, fireman, judge or justice, former judge or justice, prosecutor or former prosecutor, juror or former juror, or witness or former witness against the defendant, while engaged in the performance of his official duties or because of the exercise of his official duty.

9. The capital felony was especially heinous, atrocious, or cruel.

10. The defendant knowingly created a great risk of death to more than one person by means of a weapon or device which would normally be hazardous to the lives of more than one person.

11. The murder for which the defendant stands convicted was part of a course of conduct in which the defendant engaged and which included the commission by the defendant of other crimes of violence against another person or persons.

Although the Federal Constitution will not permit jurisdictions to prevent capital felons from presenting all relevant mitigating evidence at the penalty phase, North Carolina has provided the following statutory mitigating circumstances that permit the jury to reject imposition of the death penalty:

1. The defendant has no significant history of prior criminal activity.

2. The capital felony was committed while the defendant was under the influence of mental or emotional disturbance.

3. The victim was a voluntary participant in the defendant's homicidal conduct or consented to the homicidal act.

4. The defendant was an accomplice in or accessory to the capital felony committed by another person and his participation was relatively minor.

5. The defendant acted under duress or under the domination of another person.

6. The capacity of the defendant to appreciate the criminality of his conduct or to conform his conduct to the requirements of law was impaired.

7. The age of the defendant at the time of the crime.

8. The defendant aided in the apprehension of another capital felon or testified truthfully on behalf of the prosecution in another prosecution of a felony.

9. Any other circumstance arising from the evidence which the jury deems to have mitigating value.

Under North Carolina's capital punishment statute, a sentence of death is automatically reviewed by the North Carolina Supreme Court. North Carolina uses lethal injection to carry out death sentences (lethal gas was formerly used). The State's death row facility for men and women is located in Raleigh, North Carolina. Pursuant to the laws of North Carolina the Governor has exclusive authority to grant clemency in capital cases.

From the start of modern capital punishment in 1976, through 1999, North Carolina executed 15 capital felons. During this period North Carolina executed one female capital felon, although five of its death row inmates during this period were females. A total of 212 capital felons were on death row in North Carolina in 1999. The 1999 death row population in the State was listed as: 114 black inmates; 86 white inmates; and 12 unidentified inmates. In 1999 the State had two juveniles on death row. The State permits capital punishment to be imposed on persons 17 years old or older. North Car-

olina does not prohibit the execution of mentally retarded capital felons.

Executions by North Carolina 1976–1999

Name	Race	Date of Execution	Method of Execution
James Hutchins	White	March 16, 1984	Lethal Injection
Velma Barfield	White	November 2, 1984	Lethal Injection
John Rook	White	September 19, 1986	Lethal Injection
Michael McDougall	White	October 18, 1991	Lethal Injection
John S. Gardner, Jr.	White	October 23, 1992	Lethal Injection
David Lawson	White	June 15, 1994	Lethal Gas
Kermit Smith, Jr.	Black	January 24, 1995	Lethal Injection
Phillip L. Ingle	White	September 22, 1995	Lethal Injection
Ricky L. Sanderson	White	January 30, 1998	Lethal Gas
Zane B. Hill	White	August 14, 1998	Lethal Injection
John T. Noland	White	November 20, 1998	Lethal Injection
James Rich	White	March 26, 1999	Lethal Injection
Harvey L. Green	Black	September 24, 1999	Lethal Injection
Arthur Boyd	White	October 21, 1999	Lethal Injection
David J. Brown	Black	November 19, 1999	Lethal Injection

NORTH CAROLINA EXECUTIONS 1930–1999

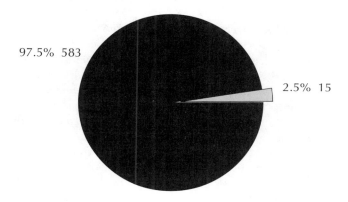

97.5% 583

2.5% 15

■ NORTH CAROLINA EXECUTIONS

■ ALL OTHER EXECUTIONS

EXECUTIONS BY NORTH CAROLINA 1930–1999

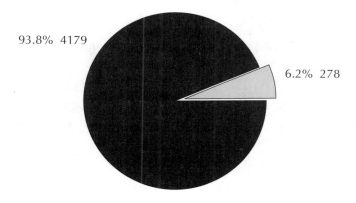

93.8% 4179

6.2% 278

■ NORTH CAROLINA

■ ALL OTHER JURISDICTIONS

North Carolina v. Alford *Court:* United States Supreme Court; *Case Citation:* North Carolina v. Alford, 400 U.S. 25 (1970); *Argued:* November 17, 196; *Reargued:* October 14, 1970; *Decided:* November 23, 1970; *Opinion of the Court:* Justice Whit; *Concurring Opinion:* None; *Concurring Statement:* Justice Black; *Dissenting Opinion:* Justice Brennan, in which Douglas and Marshall, JJ., joined; *Appellate Defense Counsel:* Doris R. Bray argued and briefed; *Appellate Prosecution Counsel:* Jacob L. Safron argued; Robert Morgan, and Andrew A. Vanore, Jr. on brief; *Amicus Curiae Brief Supporting Prosecutor:* None; *Amicus Curiae Brief Supporting Defendant:* 1.

Issue Presented: Whether a guilty plea that represents a voluntary and intelligent choice among the alternatives available to a defendant, especially one represented by competent counsel, is compelled within the meaning of the Fifth Amendment because it was entered to avoid the possibility of the death penalty?

Case Holding: A guilty plea that is voluntarily and intelligently made is not compelled within the meaning of the Fifth Amendment because it was entered to avoid the possibility of the death penalty.

Factual and procedural background of case: On December 2, 1963, the defendant, Alford, was indicted for the capital crime of first-degree murder by the State of North Carolina. At the time, the State's law provided for the penalty of life imprisonment when a plea of guilty was accepted to a first-degree murder charge. Defense counsel, in the face of strong evidence of guilt, recommended a guilty plea, but left the decision to the defendant. The prosecutor agreed to accept a plea of guilty to second-degree murder, which carried a penalty of from two to 30 years imprisonment.

Before the plea was finally accepted by the trial court, the court heard the sworn testimony of a police officer who summarized the State's case. Although there was no eyewitness to the crime, the testimony indicated that shortly before the killing the defendant took his gun from his house, stated his intention to kill the victim, and returned home with the declaration that he had carried out the killing. After the summary presentation of the State's case, the defendant took the stand and testified that he did not commit the murder, but that he was pleading guilty because he faced the threat of the death penalty if he did not do so. In response to the questions of his counsel, he acknowledged that his counsel had informed him of the difference between second and first-degree murder and of his rights in case he chose to go to trial. The trial court then asked the defendant if, in light of his denial of guilt, he still desired to plead guilty to second-degree murder and the defendant answered, "Yes, sir. I plead guilty on — from the circumstances that [my attorney] told me." The trial court accepted the guilty plea and sentenced the defendant to 30 years imprisonment.

The defendant filed a habeas corpus petition a Federal District Court, arguing his plea was unconstitutional because the threat of the death penalty coerced his decision to enter the plea of guilty. The District Court denied relief. However, a Court of Appeals granted relief after finding that the defendant's guilty plea was involuntary because it was motivated principally by fear of the death penalty. The United States Supreme Court granted certiorari to address the issue.

Opinion of the Court by Justice White: Justice White wrote that a guilty plea that represents a voluntary and intelligent choice among the alternatives available to a defendant, especially one represented by competent counsel, is not compelled within the meaning of the Fifth Amendment because it was entered to avoid the possibility of the death penalty. The opinion reasoned that an accused may voluntarily, knowingly, and understandingly consent to the imposition of a prison sentence, even though he or she is unwilling to admit participation in the crime, or even if his or her guilty plea contains a protestation of innocence. It was said that: "The standard was and remains whether the plea represents a voluntary and intelligent choice among the alternative courses of action open to the defendant. That he would not have pleaded except for the opportunity to limit the possible penalty does not necessarily demonstrate that the plea of guilty was not the product of a free and rational choice, especially where the defendant was represented by competent counsel whose advice was that the plea would be to the defendant's advantage."

Justice White concluded that it was error for the Court of Appeals to find the defendant's guilty plea was invalid. Therefore, the judgment of the Court of Appeals was reversed.

Concurring Statement by Justice Black: Justice Black issued a statement indicating he "concurs in the judgment and in substantially all of the opinion in this case."

Dissenting opinion by Justice Brennan, in which Douglas and Marshall, JJ., joined: Justice Brennan dissented on basis that the defendant had established that his guilty plea was not the product of free choice. The dissent reasoned and concluded, as follows: "I adhere to the view that, in any given case, the influence of such an unconstitutional threat 'must necessarily be given weight in determining the voluntariness of a plea.' And, without reaching the question whether due process permits the entry of judgment upon a plea of guilty accompanied by a contemporaneous denial of acts constituting the crime, I believe that at the very least such a denial of guilt is also a relevant factor in determining whether the plea was voluntarily and intelligently made. With these factors in mind, it is sufficient in my view to state that the facts set out in the majority opinion demonstrate that Alford was 'so gripped by fear of the death penalty' that his decision to plead guilty was not voluntary but was 'the product of duress as much so as choice reflecting physical constraint.' Accordingly, I would affirm the judgment of the Court of Appeals." See also **Guilty Plea**

North Dakota North Dakota abolished capital punishment in 1915.

Norway Norway abolished capital punishment for ordinary crimes in 1905, and abolished the punishment completely in 1979. *See also* **International Capital Punishment Nations**

Not Guilty by Reason of Insanity *see* Insanity Defense

Notice of Intent to Seek Death Penalty
In the case of *In re Oliver*, 333 U.S. 257 (1948) the United States Supreme Court held that the Constitution demanded that a defendant be given reasonable notice of a charge against him or her. The constitutional notice requirement is generally satisfied at the arraignment stage of a prosecution. At an arraignment a defendant is formally given a copy of the charging instrument and is informed by the trial court of the nature of the accusation against him or her.

In the context of a capital prosecution, a charging instrument will inform a defendant that he or she is accused of an offense that may be punished with death. As a general matter, the Constitution does not require death penalty notice beyond that which is provided in the charging instrument and explained by the trial judge during arraignment.

Statutory Notice Requirement: A minority of capital punishment jurisdictions statutorily require prosecutors provide defendants notice of the intent to seek the death penalty, prior to the trial and independent of the notice provided at the arraignment in the charging instrument. Several justifications have been proffered for the stringent statutory notice requirement: (1) it is an acknowledgment that the death penalty is unlike any other form of punishment in its finality, (2) it insures that the plea bargaining process is effectively and fairly carried out, and (3) it enables a defendant to timely make a more intelligent determination of what evidence to present at trial.

Notice in Multiple Murder Prosecution: In the case of *Grandison v. State*, 670 A.2d 398 (Md. 1995) the appellate court addressed the issue of notice to seek the death penalty in a multiple murder prosecution. The defendant in *Grandi-son* was prosecuted for committing two homicides. The prosecutor provided the defendant with statutory notice that the death penalty would be sought. However, the notice did not state that the death penalty would be sought for both homicides.

Subsequent to the defendant's convictions for multiple homicides, he appealed the convictions and argued that the statutory death penalty notice he received was inadequate. The defendant contended that he should have received notice that the death penalty would be sought for each murder. The *Grandison* court disagreed with the defendant in a cautious way. The court indicated that the record in the case revealed that the defendant was generally aware, before the trial started, that the death penalty would be sought for both murders. The court did not indicate what its decision on the issue would have been, if the record did not show that the defendant was aware before the trial that the death penalty was going to be sought for both murders.

The Lankford Notice Exception: The United States Supreme Court developed what has become known as the *Lankford* notice exception, in the case of *Lankford v. Idaho*, 500 U.S. 110 (1991). Under the *Lankford* notice exception, if subsequent to an arraignment a prosecutor explicitly indicates that the death penalty will not be sought in the case, such punishment may not be imposed, absent a timely notice that the punishment will in fact be sought. *See also* **Lankford v. Idaho; Prosecutor**

Notice of Statutory Aggravating Circumstances
In response to the critical role of statutory aggravating circumstances in death penalty cases, a large minority of capital punishment jurisdictions require by statute that prosecutors provide defendants with pretrial notice of the aggravating

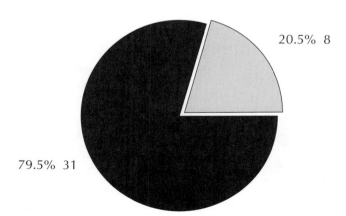

JURISDICTIONS STATUTORILY REQUIRING DEFENDANTS BE GIVEN PRETRIAL NOTICE OF INTENT TO SEEK THE DEATH PENALTY

20.5% 8

79.5% 31

■ NOTICE OF INTENT REQUIRED
■ NOTICE OF INTENT NOT REQUIRED

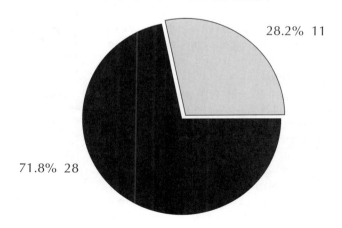

JURISDICTIONS REQUIRING BY STATUTE THAT PRETRIAL NOTICE OF AGGRAVATING CIRCUMSTANCES BE GIVEN

28.2% 11

71.8% 28

■ NOTICE OF AGGRAVATORS REQUIRED
■ NOTICE NOT REQUIRED

circumstances that will be used against them. In the case of *People v. Arias*, 913 P.2d 980 (Cal. 1996) it was held that pretrial notice of aggravating circumstances is adequate, if it gives a defendant a reasonable understanding of what to expect and prepare for at the penalty phase hearing.

Two primary concerns are addressed by the requirement of giving pretrial notice of aggravating circumstances. First, the requirement provides a defendant with sufficient time to prepare a penalty phase defense to the aggravating circumstances. Second, this requirement can facilitate the plea bargaining process by letting the defendant know the strength of the prosecutor's penalty phase evidence.

In four capital punishment jurisdictions, Delaware, Indiana, Nevada, and New Jersey, it is required by statute that prosecutors provide defendants with notice of aggravating circumstances, prior to the start of the penalty phase of a capital murder prosecution. This requirement means that the notice does not have to be given until after the trial. *See also* **Aggravating Circumstances**

O'Connor, Sandra Day

Sandra Day O'Connor was appointed an associate justice of the United States Supreme Court in 1981. While on the Supreme Court O'Connor has displayed a moderate to conservative philosophy in her interpretation of the Constitution.

O'Connor was born in El Paso, Texas on March 26, 1930. She graduated from Stanford University in 1950. O'Connor received her law degree from Stanford Law School in 1952. Her legal career included being a prosecutor, trial judge and appellate judge on the Arizona Court of Appeals. In 1981 President Ronald Reagan appointed O'Connor as the first female associate justice on the Supreme Court.

O'Connor has written a considerable number of opinions in capital punishment cases. One of her opinions which had the greatest influence across criminal law in general was the capital case of *Strickland v. Washington*. That case involved a defendant who alleged that he pled guilty to capital murder and was sentenced to death because his attorney was constitutionally ineffective. O'Connor, writing for the Court, established a constitutional test to determine whether an attorney's performance was deficient to the point of violating the constitutional right to have effective assistance of counsel. Under the *Strickland* test a defendant may prevail on an ineffective assistance of counsel claim only if he or she proves that the attorney's performance was deficient and that he or she suffered prejudice as a result of the

Capital Punishment Opinions Written by O'Connor

Case Name	Opinion of the Court	Concurring Opinion	Dissenting Opinion	Concurring and Dissenting
Arave v. Creech	✓			
Arizona v. Rumsey	✓			
Caldwell v. Mississippi		✓		
California v. Brown		✓		
California v. Ramos	✓			
Coleman v. Thompson	✓			
Eddings v. Oklahoma		✓		
Enmund v. Florida			✓	
Ford v. Wainwright				✓
Franklin v. Lynaugh		✓		
Harris v. Alabama	✓			
Heath v. Alabama	✓			
Herrera v. Collins		✓		
Johnson v. Texas			✓	
Lambrix v. Singletary			✓	
Lewis v. Jeffers	✓			
Lockhart v. Fretwell		✓		
McFarland v. Scott			✓	
Mu'Min v. Virginia		✓		
Murray v. Giarratano		✓		
Ohio A.P.A. v. Woodard		✓		
Parker v. Dugger	✓			
Payne v. Tennessee		✓		
Penry v. Lynaugh	✓			
Richmond v. Lewis	✓			
Riggins v. Nevada	✓			
Romano v. Oklahoma		✓		
Satterwhite v. Texas	✓			
Schiro v. Farley	✓			
Schlup v. Delo		✓		
Simmons v. South Carolina		✓		
Sochor v. Florida		✓		
South Carolina v. Gathers			✓	
Stanford v. Kentucky		✓		
Strickland v. Washington	✓			
Smith v. Murray	✓			
Thompson v. Oklahoma		✓		
Tison v. Arizona	✓			
Victor v. Nebraska	✓			

deficiency. O'Connor held that the defendant did not satisfy the test created by her. The test announced in *Strickland* is used across the board in determining allegations of ineffective assistance of counsel.

Ocuish, Hannah

Hannah Ocuish was the youngest known female to be executed in the nation. The State of Connecticut charged Hannah with strangling and stoning to death a 6-year-old child on July 21, 1786. The State convicted and sentenced her to death by hanging on October 12, 1786. On December 20, 1786, the death sentence was carried out. Hannah was 12 years old on the date of her execution. *See also* **Juveniles**

O'Dell v. Netherland

Court: United States Supreme Court; *Case Citation:* O'Dell v. Netherland, 521 U.S. 151 (1997); *Argued:* March 18, 1997; *Decided:* June 19, 1997; *Opinion of the Court:* Justice Thomas; *Concurring Opinion:* None; *Dissenting Opinion:* Justice Stevens, in which Souter, Ginsburg, and Breyer, JJ., joined; *Appellate Defense Counsel:* Not reported; *Appellate Prosecution Counsel:* Not reported; *Amicus Curiae Brief Supporting Prosecutor:* Not reported; *Amicus Curiae Brief Supporting Defendant:* Not reported.

Issue Presented: Whether the rule set out in *Simmons v. South Carolina*, that a capital defendant be permitted to inform the sentencing jury that he or she was parole ineligible, was a new rule and thereby inapplicable to the defendant's case?

Case Holding: The rule announced in *Simmons v. South Carolina* was a new rule and therefore inapplicable to the defendant's case.

Factual and procedural background of case: Virginia convicted the defendant, Joseph Roger O'Dell, of capital murder. During the sentencing phase the defendant requested the trial judge instruct the jury that he was ineligible for parole if sentenced to life in prison. The trial judge refused to give the instruction. The jury determined that the defendant presented a future danger and sentenced him to death. The Virginia Supreme Court affirmed the conviction and sentence.

The defendant filed a habeas corpus petition in a Federal District Court, arguing that under the United States Supreme Court's decision in *Simmons v. South Carolina* he had a constitutional right to have the jury instructed that he would not be eligible for parole if given a life sentence. The District Court agreed with the defendant, after concluding that *Simmons* did not announce a new rule and could therefore be relied upon by the defendant. The defendant's death sentence was vacated. A Federal Court of Appeals reversed the District Court's decision, after concluding *Simmons* announced a new rule after the defendant's conviction became final and could therefore not be relied upon by him. The United States Supreme Court granted certiorari to consider the issue.

Opinion of the Court by Justice Thomas: Justice Thomas ruled that the requirement under *Simmons*, that a penalty phase jury be instructed that a defendant is not eligible for parole if his future dangerousness is an issue in the case, was a new rule announced after the defendant's conviction became final and could therefore not be relied upon by him. It was said that the rule announced in *Simmons* was "new," because it was not dictated by precedent existing at the time the defendant's conviction became final.

The opinion pointed out that under the Court's precedents, a new constitutional rule cannot be applied to a conviction that had become final before the new rule was announced, unless the new rule fell within one of two narrow exceptions. Justice Thomas indicated that to circumvent the general bar to retroactive application of a new constitutional rule, the new rule must have (1) placed an entire category of primary conduct beyond the reach of criminal law or prohibited imposition of a certain type of punishment for a class of defendants because of their status or offense; or (2) was a watershed rule of criminal procedure implicating a criminal proceeding's fundamental fairness and accuracy.

The opinion found that the defendant's conviction became final in 1988, and *Simmons* was decided in 1994. Justice Thomas reasoned that at the time the defendant's conviction became final, no decision by the Court foreshadowed the rule announced in *Simmons*. The opinion rejected the defendant's argument that the Court's decisions in *Gardner v. Florida* and *Skipper v. South Carolina* foreshadowed or dictated the rule announced in *Simmons*. It was also determined that the rule in *Simmons* did not come within either of the two exceptions to the prohibition of retroactive application of a new constitutional rule. The judgment of the Court of Appeals was affirmed.

Dissenting opinion by Justice Stevens, in which Souter, Ginsburg, and Breyer, JJ., joined: Justice Stevens dissented from the Court's decision on the basis that *Simmons* did not announce a new rule. He stated his position as follows:

> ... This case is not about whether O'Dell was given a fair sentencing hearing; instead, the question presented is whether, despite the admittedly unfair hearing, he should be put to death because his trial was conducted before *Simmons* was decided. Because the Court regards the holding in *Simmons* as nothing more than a novel "court made rule," it rejects [the defendant's] plea. In my view, our decision in *Simmons* applied a fundamental principle that is as old as the adversary system itself, and that had been quite clearly articulated by this Court in two earlier opinions....
>
> ... [E]ven if the rule in *Simmons* could properly be viewed as a "new" rule, it is of such importance to the accuracy and fairness of a capital sentencing proceeding that it should be applied consistently to all prisoners whose death sentences were imposed in violation of the rule, whether they were sentenced before *Simmons* was decided or after. Moreover, to the extent that the fundamental principles underlying the rule needed explicit articulation by this Court, they clearly had been expressed well before O'Dell's 1988 sentencing proceeding.

Case note: Virginia executed Joseph Roger O'Dell by lethal injection on July 23, 1997. *See also* **Butler v. McKellar; Graham v. Collins; Gray v. Netherland; Lambrix v. Singletary; Retroactive Application of a New Constitutional Rule; Saffle v. Parks; Sawyer v. Smith**

Ohio The State of Ohio is a capital punishment jurisdiction. The State reenacted its death penalty law after the United States Supreme Court decision in *Furman v. Georgia*, 408 U.S. 238 (1972), on January 1, 1974.

Ohio has a three-tier legal system. The State's legal system is composed of a supreme court, court of appeals and courts of general jurisdiction. The Ohio Supreme Court is presided over by a chief justice and six associate justices. The Ohio Courts of Appeals are divided into twelve districts. Each district is composed of at least three judges. The courts of general jurisdiction in the State are called Courts of Common Pleas. Capital offenses against the State of Ohio are tried in the Courts of Common Pleas.

Ohio's capital punishment statute is triggered if a person commits a homicide under the following special circumstances:

A. The offender with prior calculation and design, caused the death of another or the unlawful termination of another's pregnancy.

B. The offender purposely caused the death of another or the unlawful termination of another's pregnancy while committing or attempting to commit, or while fleeing immediately after committing or attempting to commit, kidnaping, rape, aggravated arson or arson, aggravated robbery or robbery, aggravated burglary or burglary, or escape.

C. The offender purposely caused the death of another who is under thirteen years of age at the time of the commission of the offense.

D. The offender is under detention as a result of having been found guilty of or having pleaded guilty to a felony or who breaks that detention and caused the death of another.

E. The offender purposely caused the death of a law enforcement officer whom the offender knows or has reasonable cause to know is a law enforcement officer.

Members of the Ohio Supreme Court: (left to right sitting) *Justice Andrew Douglas, Chief Justice Thomas J. Moyer, and Justice Alice R. Resnick;* (left to right standing) *Justice Deborah L. Cook, Justice Francis E. Sweeney, Justice Paul E. Pfeifer, and Justice Evelyn L. Stratton.* (Ohio Supreme Court)

Capital murder in Ohio is punishable by death, life imprisonment without parole or imprisonment for a term of years. A capital prosecution in Ohio is bifurcated into a guilt phase and penalty phase. A jury is used at both phases of a capital trial. It is required that, at the penalty phase, the jury unanimously agree that a death sentence is appropriate before it can be imposed. If the penalty phase jury is unable to reach a verdict, the trial judge is required to impose a sentence of life imprisonment without parole or imprisonment for a term of years. The decision of a penalty phase jury is binding on the trial court under the laws of Ohio.

In order to impose a death sentence upon a defendant under Ohio law, it is required that the prosecutor establish the existence of at least one of the following statutory aggravating circumstances at the penalty phase:

1. The offense was the assassination of the president of the United States or a person in line of succession to the presidency, the governor or lieutenant governor of this state, the president-elect or vice president-elect of the United States, the governor-elect or lieutenant governor-elect of this state, or a candidate for any of the offices.

2. The offense was committed for hire.

3. The offense was committed for the purpose of escaping detection, apprehension, trial, or punishment for another offense committed by the offender.

4. The offense was committed while the offender was under detention or while the offender was at large after having broken detention.

5. Prior to the offense, the offender was convicted of an offense an essential element of which was the purposeful killing of or attempt to kill another, or the offense being prosecuted was part of a course of conduct involving the purposeful killing of or attempt to kill two or more persons by the offender.

6. The victim of the offense was a law enforcement officer.

7. The offense was committed while the offender was committing, attempting to commit, or fleeing immediately after committing or attempting to commit kidnapping, rape, aggravated arson, aggravated robbery, or aggravated burglary, and either the offender was the principal offender in the commission of the aggravated murder or, if not the principal offender, committed the aggravated murder with prior calculation and design.

8. The victim of the aggravated murder was a witness to an offense who was purposely killed to prevent the victim's testimony in any criminal proceeding and the aggravated murder was not committed during the commission, attempted commission, or flight immediately after the commission or attempted commission of the offense to which the victim was a witness, or the victim of the aggravated murder was a witness to an offense and was purposely killed in retaliation for the victim's testimony in any criminal proceeding.

9. The offender, in the commission of the offense, purposefully caused the death of another who was under thirteen

years of age at the time of the commission of the offense, and either the offender was the principal offender in the commission of the offense or, if not the principal offender, committed the offense with prior calculation and design.

Although the Federal Constitution will not permit jurisdictions to prevent capital felons from presenting all relevant mitigating evidence at the penalty phase, Ohio has provided the following statutory mitigating circumstances that permit the jury to reject imposition of the death penalty:

1. Whether the victim of the offense induced or facilitated it;
2. Whether it is unlikely that the offense would have been committed, but for the fact that the offender was under duress, coercion, or strong provocation;
3. Whether, at the time of committing the offense, the offender, because of a mental disease or defect, lacked substantial capacity to appreciate the criminality of the offender's conduct or to conform the offender's conduct to the requirements of the law;
4. The youth of the offender;
5. The offender's lack of a significant history of prior criminal convictions and delinquency adjudications;
6. If the offender was a participant in the offense but not the principal offender, the degree of the offender's participation in the offense and the degree of the offender's participation in the acts that led to the death of the victim;
7. Any other factors that are relevant to the issue of whether the offender should be sentenced to death.

Under Ohio's capital punishment statute, a sentence of death is automatically reviewed by the Ohio Supreme Court. Ohio provides a capital offender an option of choosing death by lethal injection or electrocution. The State's death row facility for men is located in Mansfield, Ohio; while the facility maintaining female death row inmates is located in Marysville, Ohio.

Pursuant to the laws of Ohio the Governor has authority to grant clemency in capital cases. Requests for clemency are investigated by the State's Adult Parole Authority, which can make a nonbinding recommendation.

From the start of modern capital punishment in 1976, through 1999, Ohio executed one capital felon. During this period Ohio did not have any female capital felons on death row. A total of 192 capital felons were on death row in Ohio in 1999. The 1999 death row population in the State was listed as: 95 black inmates; 90 white inmates; and seven unidentified inmates. The State does not permit capital punishment to be imposed on persons 17 years old or younger. Ohio does not prohibit the execution of mentally retarded capital felons.

Executions by Ohio 1976–1999

Name	Race	Date of Execution	Method of Execution
Wilford Berry	White	February 19, 1999	Lethal Injection

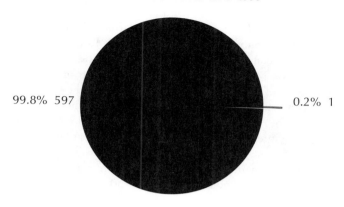

OHIO EXECUTIONS 1976–1999

99.8% 597   0.2% 1

▨ OHIO EXECUTIONS
■ ALL OTHER EXECUTIONS

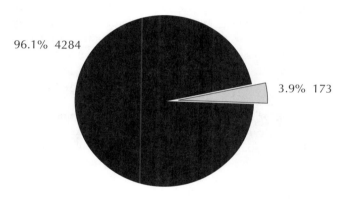

EXECUTIONS BY OHIO 1930–1999

96.1% 4284   3.9% 173

▨ OHIO
■ ALL OTHER JURISDICTIONS

Ohio Adult Parole Authority v. Woodard

Court: United States Supreme Court; *Case Citation:* Ohio Adult Parole Authority v. Woodard, 523 U.S. 272 (1998); *Argued:* December 10, 1997; *Decided:* March 25, 1998; *Opinion of the Court:* Chief Justice Rehnquist; *Concurring Opinion:* Justice O'Connor, in which Souter, Ginsburg and Breyer, JJ., joined; *Concurring and Dissenting Opinion:* Justice Stevens; *Appellate Defense Counsel:* Not reported; *Appellate Prosecution Counsel:* Not reported; *Amicus Curiae Brief Supporting Prosecutor:* Not reported; *Amicus Curiae Brief Supporting Defendant:* Not reported.

Issue Presented: Whether Ohio's clemency procedures for death row inmates violated the Due Process Clause or the Fifth Amendment privilege against self-incrimination?

Case Holding: Ohio's clemency procedures for death row inmates did not violate the Due Process Clause or the Fifth Amendment privilege against self-incrimination.

Factual and procedural background of case: The State of Ohio convicted the defendant, Eugene Woodard, of capital murder and sentenced him to death. He was sentenced to death for aggravated murder committed in the course of a car-jacking. The Ohio Supreme Court affirmed the conviction and sentence. Subsequently, the Ohio Adult Parole Authority (Authority) commenced its clemency investigation as required by State law. Pursuant to the death penalty statute of the State, in the case of an inmate under death sentence, the Authority must conduct a clemency hearing within 45 days of the scheduled date of execution. Prior to the hearing, the inmate may request an interview with one or more parole board members. Counsel for the inmate is not allowed at that interview. The Authority must ultimately make a recommendation to the Governor, even if the inmate subsequently obtains a stay of execution.

The Authority informed the defendant that he could have his voluntary interview with Authority members on a particular date, and that his clemency hearing would be held a week later. The defendant responded by filing a Federal civil rights law suit against the Authority, alleging that Ohio's clemency process violated his due process right and his right to remain silent. A Federal District Court granted judgment to the State. A Federal Court of Appeals reversed, after finding the defendant's constitutional due process rights and right to remain silent were infringed upon by Ohio's clemency procedures. The United States Supreme Court granted certiorari to consider the issues.

Opinion of the Court by Chief Justice Rehnquist: The Chief Justice ruled that giving a death row inmate the option of voluntarily participating in an interview as part of the clemency process does not violate his Fifth Amendment right to remain silent. It was said that the Fifth Amendment prohibited compelled self-incrimination. It was reasoned that any testimony by the defendant before the Authority would be voluntary, not compelled.

It was also held by the Chief Justice that the defendant did not establish a violation of the Due Process Clause in the nature of the clemency proceedings. It was said that traditional executive discretion existed in clemency proceedings and that such proceedings were rarely, if ever, appropriate subjects for judicial review.

The opinion concluded that neither the Due Process Clause nor the Fifth Amendment privilege against self-incrimination were violated by Ohio's clemency proceedings. The judgment of the Court of Appeals was reversed.

Concurring opinion by Justice O'Connor, in which Souter, Ginsburg and Breyer, JJ., joined: Justice O'Connor concurred in the Court's decision. She indicated that, while Ohio's clemency procedures satisfied due process, she believed that the Court was incorrect in finding that judicial intervention in clemency proceedings should rarely, if ever, occur. Justice O'Connor was of the opinion that clemency proceedings were subject to judicial scrutiny for fundamental fairness like any other criminal process.

Concurring and dissenting opinion by Justice Stevens: Justice Stevens concurred with the Court's resolution of the

Fifth Amendment claim. However, he dissented from the Court's resolution of the Due Process Clause issue. Justice Stevens believed that clemency proceedings were subject to judicial review for fundamental fairness. He also believed that the defendant's due process claim should have been remanded to the lower courts for a determination of whether Ohio's clemency procedures provided minimal due process safeguards. *See also* **Calderon v. Coleman; California v. Ramos; Clemency; Rose v. Hodges; Schick v. Reed**

Ohio Cult Murders In August of 1990, a Lake County, Ohio jury found cult leader Jeffrey Lundgren guilty of the kidnapping and murder of five of his followers. The trial court subsequently sentenced Lundgren to death.

Until 1987, Lundgren lived a modest life as a bible school teacher and temple guide for the Reorganized Church of Jesus Christ of Latter Day Saints, in Kirkland, Ohio. Lundgren had taken the position in 1984 when he and his wife and son moved from their home in Missouri. The church supported Lundgren and his family and provided them with housing.

Lundgren destroyed the church's trust in him when it was discovered that funds he was responsible for maintaining disappeared. In October of 1987 he was fired and evicted from church housing. Eventually Lundgren was excommunicated from the church.

By the time of Lundgren's expulsion from the church he had attracted a small following from those who listened during his bible school classes. Consequently, Lundgren decided to start his own religious cult. He was able to rent a farm in a rural area outside of Cleveland where he operated from. About 30 people lived with Lundgren. His followers called him "Dad" and gave him their paychecks for common group expenses.

Lundgren's cult teachings included the belief that Christ would return and build a temple in Kirkland. He also taught the inner circle of his cult that 10 followers had to be killed before Christ could establish Zion.

In January of 1989, Lundgren began telling his followers they had to go on a wilderness trip before Zion would be possible. At the beginning of April of that year the group began preparing for the wilderness trip. Those who worked left their jobs. Lundgren encouraged all of the followers to use up any of their available credit cards. On April 12, three of the followers secretly began digging a six-by-seven-foot pit in the dirt floor of Lundgren's barn.

One of the families that joined Lundgren's

Jeffrey Lundgren is on death row in Ohio after being convicted of killing five people. (Ohio Department of Corrections)

cult was Dennis and Cheryl Avery and their three daughters Trina, Rebecca, and Karen. The Avery family did not live on the farm, but they were faithful followers of Lundgren.

On April 17, the Averys were invited to dinner at Lundgren's farmhouse. After dinner, Lundgren went out to the barn with his son, Damon, and four followers. The Averys stayed in the house with Lundgren's wife Alice and other followers. At Lundgren's direction, each member of the Avery family was individually led out to the barn, where each was bound and gagged. After the men placed each Avery family member into the pit that was dug in the barn, Lundgren shot each person two or three times with a .45 caliber semiautomatic weapon. The men then filled the pit with dirt and stones. Afterwards, Lundgren and his followers went back to the farmhouse and held a prayer meeting.

The next day, April 18, Lundgren and his followers drove out to selected mountain campsites near Davis, West Virginia, where they lived in tents through October 1989. Some of the followers found jobs. While in West Virginia, Lundgren decided to take a second wife from among his followers. He chose follower Kathryn Johnson, who was already married to follower Larry Johnson. Dissension broke out over this decision. The group split up, with Lundgren and about ten of his followers moving to Missouri. In December, Larry Johnson contacted Federal authorities about the Avery murders.

On January 3, 1990, Kirtland police dug up the pit in the barn and found the Avery family. Lundgren had shot Dennis twice in the back and Cheryl three times in the torso. He shot Trina once in the head and twice in the body; Rebecca in the back and thigh; and Karen in the head and chest. Police discovered that a .45 caliber semiautomatic weapon, belonging to Lundgren, had fired all of the bullets they recovered. Lundgren bought the weapon in 1987 and sold it in West Virginia in 1989. On January 7, 1990, Federal authorities arrested Lundgren in California. He was extradited to Ohio.

The State of Ohio prosecuted Lundgren, his wife Alice and son Damon, as well as other members of the cult. Lundgren was the only member to receive the death penalty. He is now on Ohio's death row.

Ohioans to Stop Executions

Ohioans to Stop Executions (OTSE) was founded in 1987. Its purpose is to abolish the use of capital punishment in the State of Ohio. The OTSE has taken the position that capital punishment in Ohio is not implemented fairly, it fails to serve its legal purposes, and is overwhelmingly imposed on indigent, minority, underprivileged and disadvantaged members of society. The organization utilizes educational tools to make the public aware of the problems it associates with capital punishment.

Activities engaged in by OTSE include organizing vigils, lectures, training, and distributing a newsletter. The organization has made arrangements to be made aware of when an execution is pending in Ohio. When it obtains such information the organization will coordinate peaceful demonstrations, coordinate prayer vigils, services, and symbolic gestures such as bell ringing. OTSE also provides moral support to the inmate's family.

Oklahoma

The State of Oklahoma is a capital punishment jurisdiction. The State reenacted its death penalty law after the United States Supreme Court decision in *Furman v. Georgia*, 408 U.S. 238 (1972), on May 17, 1973.

Oklahoma has a three-tier legal system. The State's legal system is composed of a supreme court, court of appeals and courts of general jurisdiction. The Oklahoma Supreme Court is presided over by a chief justice, a vice chief justice and seven associate justices. The Oklahoma Court of Criminal Appeals is composed of a presiding judge, vice presiding judge and three judges. The highest court of criminal appeals in the State is the Court of Criminal Appeals. The courts of general jurisdiction in the State are called District Courts. Capital offenses against the State of Oklahoma are tried in the District Courts.

Oklahoma's capital punishment statute is triggered if a person commits a homicide under the following special circumstances:

A. The offender unlawfully and with malice aforethought causes the death of another human being.

B. The death of a human being results from the commission or attempted commission of murder of another person, shooting or discharge of a firearm or crossbow with intent to kill, intentional discharge of a firearm or other deadly weapon into any dwelling or building, forcible rape, robbery with a dangerous weapon, kidnaping, escape from lawful custody, first degree burglary, first degree arson, unlawful distributing or dispensing of controlled dangerous substances, or trafficking in illegal drugs.

C. The death of a child results from the willful or malicious injuring, torturing, maiming or using of unreasonable force by the offender or who shall willfully cause, procure or permit any of said acts to be done upon the child.

D. The offender unlawfully and with malice aforethought solicits another person or persons to cause the death of a human being in furtherance of unlawfully manufacturing, distributing or dispensing controlled dangerous substances.

W.A. Drew Edmondson is the Oklahoma Attorney General. His office represents the State in capital punishment appellate proceedings. (Oklahoma Attorney General Office)

Capital murder in Oklahoma is punishable by death, life imprisonment without parole, or imprisonment for a term of years. A capital prosecution in Oklahoma is bifurcated into a guilt phase and penalty phase. A jury is used at both phases of a capital trial. It is required that, at the penalty phase, The jury unanimously agree that a death sentence is appropriate before it can be imposed. If the penalty phase jury is unable to reach a verdict, the trial judge is required to impose imprisonment for life or term of years. The decision of a penalty phase jury is binding on the trial court under the laws of Oklahoma.

In order to impose a death sentence upon a defendant under Oklahoma law, it is required that the prosecutor establish the existence of at least one of the following statutory aggravating circumstances at the penalty phase:

1. The defendant was previously convicted of a felony involving the use or threat of violence to the person;
2. The defendant knowingly created a great risk of death to more than one person;
3. The person committed the murder for remuneration or the promise of remuneration or employed another to commit the murder for remuneration or the promise of remuneration;
4. The murder was especially heinous, atrocious, or cruel;
5. The murder was committed for the purpose of avoiding or preventing a lawful arrest or prosecution;
6. The murder was committed by a person while serving a sentence of imprisonment on conviction of a felony;
7. The existence of a probability that the defendant would commit criminal acts of violence that would constitute a continuing threat to society; or
8. The victim of the murder was a peace officer or guard of an institution under the control of the Department of Corrections, and such person was killed while in performance of official duty.

Oklahoma does not provide by statute any mitigating circumstances to the imposition of the death penalty. Even though the State does not provide statutory mitigating circumstances, the United States Supreme Court has ruled that all relevant mitigating evidence must be allowed at the penalty phase.

Under Oklahoma's capital punishment statute, a sentence of death is automatically reviewed by the Oklahoma Court of Criminal Appeals. Oklahoma uses lethal injection to carry out death sentences. The State provides for use of electrocution or firing squad, should lethal injection be found unconstitutional. The State's death row facility for men is located in McAlester, Oklahoma; while the facility maintaining female death row inmates is located in Oklahoma City, Oklahoma.

Pursuant to the laws of Oklahoma the Governor has authority to grant clemency in capital cases. The Governor requires the approval of the State's Pardon and Parole Board, in order to grant clemency.

From the start of modern capital punishment in 1976, through 1999, Oklahoma executed 19 capital felons. During this period Oklahoma did not execute any female capital felons, although three of its death row inmates during this period were females. A total of 151 capital felons were on death row in Oklahoma in 1999. The 1999 death row population in the State was listed as: 51 black inmates; 82 white inmates; and 18 unidentified inmates. In 1999 the State had three juveniles on death row. The State permits capital punishment to be imposed on persons 16 years old or older. Oklahoma does not prohibit the execution of mentally retarded capital felons.

Executions by Oklahoma 1976–1999

Name	Race	Date of Execution	Method of Execution
Charles Coleman	White	September 10, 1990	Lethal Injection
Robyn L. Parks	Black	March 10, 1992	Lethal Injection
Olan R. Robison	White	March 13, 1992	Lethal Injection
Thomas Grasso	White	March 20, 1995	Lethal Injection
Roger D. Stafford	White	July 1, 1995	Lethal Injection
Robert Brecheen	White	August 11, 1995	Lethal Injection
Benjamin Brewer	White	April 26, 1996	Lethal Injection
Stephan Hatch	White	August 9, 1996	Lethal Injection
Scott Carpenter	N.A.	May 8, 1997	Lethal Injection
Michael E. Long	White	February 20, 1998	Lethal Injection
Stephen Wood	White	August 5, 1998	Lethal Injection
Tuan Nguyen	Asian	December 10, 1998	Lethal Injection
John W. Duvall	White	December 17, 1998	Lethal Injection
John W. Castro	Hispanic	January 7, 1999	Lethal Injection
Sean Sellers	White	February 4, 1999	Lethal Injection
Scotty L. Moore	White	June 3, 1999	Lethal Injection
Norman L. Newsted	White	July 8, 1999	Lethal Injection
Cornel Cooks	Black	December 2, 1999	Lethal Injection
Bobby L. Ross	Black	December 9, 1999	Lethal Injection

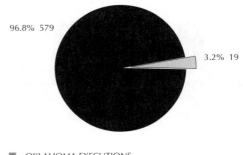

OKLAHOMA EXECUTIONS 1976–1999

96.8% 579

3.2% 19

■ OKLAHOMA EXECUTIONS
■ ALL OTHER EXECUTIONS

EXECUTIONS BY OKLAHOMA 1930–1999

98.2% 4378

1.8% 79

■ OKLAHOMA
■ ALL OTHER JURISDICTIONS

Oklahoma Bombing On April 19, 1995, Timothy James McVeigh etched his name in capital punishment history as the most lethal mass murderer in the history of the United States. On that date, in Oklahoma City, McVeigh intentionally triggered a bomb which killed 168 people. On August 14, 1997, McVeigh was sentenced to death by Federal authorities. An accomplice, Terry Lynn Nichols, was eventually sentenced to life imprisonment for his role in the mass murder.

At the guilt phase of McVeigh's trial, which began on April 24, 1997 and encompassed 23 days of testimony, the Federal government proved the following set of facts against him.

In the fall of 1994, McVeigh and Nichols sought, bought, and stole all the materials needed to construct a 3,000–6,000 pound bomb. In a letter to Michael and Lori Fortier written around September of 1994, McVeigh disclosed that he and Nichols had decided to take some type of positive offensive action against the federal government in response to the government's siege of the Branch Davidians in Waco, Texas in 1993. On a subsequent visit to their home, McVeigh told the Fortiers that he planned to blow up a Federal building. McVeigh later informed the Fortiers that he wanted to cause a general uprising in America and that the bombing would occur on the anniversary of the end of the Waco siege. McVeigh rationalized the inevitable loss of life by concluding that anyone who worked in the Federal building was guilty by association with those responsible for Waco.

McVeigh stated that he had figured out how to make a truck into a bomb using 55-gallon drums filled with ammonium nitrate combined with explosives. McVeigh demonstrated the shaped charge he intended to use for the bomb by arranging soup cans on the floor in the same triangle shape in which he was going to place 55-gallon barrels filled with ammonium nitrate combined with nitromethane in the truck. McVeigh also diagramed the truck, barrels, and fusing system on a piece of paper, and stated that he intended to use a Ryder truck. McVeigh told the Fortiers that he chose the Murrah Building in Oklahoma City, Oklahoma, as the target because he believed that (1) the orders for the attack at Waco emanated from the building, (2) the building housed people involved in the Waco raid, and (3) the building's U-shape and glass front made it an

Timothy James McVeigh was convicted and sentenced to death by the Federal government for killing 168 people. (Oklahoma State Police)

easy target. On a later trip through Oklahoma City, McVeigh showed Michael Fortier the Murrah Building, asking Fortier whether he thought a 20-foot rental truck would fit in front of the building.

On September 30, 1994, and October 18, 1994, McVeigh purchased a total of 4,000 pounds of ammonium nitrate from the McPherson branch of the Mid-Kansas Cooperative using the alias "Mike Havens." In October of 1994, McVeigh and Nichols stole seven cases of Tovex explosives and a box of Primadet nonelectric blasting caps from the Martin Marietta rock quarry near Marion, Kansas. On October 21, 1994, McVeigh purchased three drums of nitromethane at a race track outside of Dallas, Texas. Prior to the nitromethane purchase, McVeigh had sought bomb ingredients, including nitromethane, both in person and through the use of a prepaid telephone calling card under the name "Daryl Bridges." Using various aliases, McVeigh and Nichols rented a number of storage lockers in Kansas where they stored the bomb components. In order to fund their conspiracy, McVeigh and Nichols robbed a gun dealer in Arkansas in November of 1994.

Also, towards the end of 1994, McVeigh typed a number of letters discussing the justified use of violence against federal agents as retaliation for the events in Waco. McVeigh told his sister and one of his friends that he had moved from the propaganda stage to the action stage in his dispute with the Federal government. McVeigh then warned his sister that "something big" was going to happen in April, and asked her to extend her April 1995 Florida vacation. He also instructed her not to write to him any more lest she incriminate herself. The manner in which the bombing was carried out closely tracked several books bought by McVeigh, which he often encouraged his friends to read, describing how to make a powerful bomb mixing ammonium nitrate with nitromethane and romanticizing self-declared patriots who blow up Federal buildings. McVeigh was familiar with explosives and had detonated a pipe bomb prior to the attack on the Murrah Building.

From April 14 to 18, 1995, McVeigh stayed at the Dreamland Motel located in Junction City, Kansas. On April 14, 1995, McVeigh purchased a 1977 yellow Mercury Marquis from Junction City Firestone in Junction City, Kansas. While waiting to take possession of the car from the dealer, McVeigh made a phone call to Elliott's Body Shop in Junction City, Kansas, seeking a 20-foot Ryder truck for a one-way rental to Omaha. McVeigh eventually drove to Oklahoma City in the rented Ryder truck on the morning of April 19, 1995. McVeigh parked the bomb-filled truck in front of the Murrah Building and ran to the yellow Mercury that he and Nichols had stashed as a getaway car in a nearby alley a few days before the bombing. McVeigh hand-printed a sign inside the yellow Mercury, "Not Abandoned; Please do not tow; will move by April 23 (Needs Battery & Cable)." McVeigh deliberately parked the car so that a building would stand between the car and the blast, shielding McVeigh from the explosion.

At 9:02 on the morning of April 19, 1995, a massive explosion tore apart the Murrah Building in Oklahoma City,

Oklahoma, killing a total of 168 people and injuring hundreds more. The destruction of the Murrah Building killed 163 people in the building and five people outside. Fifteen children in the Murrah Building day care center, visible from the front of the building, and four children visiting the building were included among the victims. Eight Federal law enforcement officials also lost their lives. The explosion, felt and heard six miles away, tore a gaping hole into the front of the Murrah Building and covered the streets with glass, debris, rocks, and chunks of concrete.

Just 77 minutes after the blast, Oklahoma State Trooper Charles Hanger stopped the yellow Mercury driven by McVeigh because the car had no license tags. The stop occurred on Interstate 35, just before the exit for Billings, Oklahoma, precisely 77.9 miles north of the Murrah Building. Trooper Hanger arrested McVeigh upon discovering that he was carrying a concealed loaded gun. Trooper Hanger transported McVeigh to Noble County Jail in Perry, Oklahoma, where McVeigh was booked and incarcerated for unlawfully carrying a weapon and transporting a loaded firearm. Noble County authorities took custody of McVeigh's clothing and property, including earplugs, and issued him prison garb. Two days later, on April 21, 1995, the Federal government filed a Complaint against McVeigh for unlawful destruction by explosives. Oklahoma then transferred McVeigh to Federal custody on the Federal bombing charges. An FBI test performed later found that McVeigh's clothing and the earplugs contained explosives residue, including PETN, EGDN, and nitroglycerine — chemicals associated with the materials used in the construction of the bomb.

A subsequent inventory search of the yellow Mercury uncovered a sealed envelope containing documents arguing that the Federal government had commenced open warfare on the liberty of the American people and justifying the killing of government officials in the defense of liberty. Finally, three days after the arrest, Trooper Hanger found a Paulsen's Military Supply business card on the floor of his cruiser bearing McVeigh's fingerprints. McVeigh had written on the back of the card, "TNT @ $5/stick Need more" and "Call After 01, May, See if I can get some more."

On August 10, 1995, a Federal grand jury returned an 11-count indictment against McVeigh and Nichols charging: one count of conspiracy to use a weapon of mass destruction; one count of use of a weapon of mass destruction; one count of destruction by explosives; and eight counts of first-degree murder. On October 20, 1995, the government filed a Notice of Intent to Seek the Death Penalty. On February 19, 1996, the federal district court granted McVeigh's and Nichols' Motion for Change of Venue and transferred the case to Denver, Colorado. On October 25, 1996, the district court granted a Motion for Severance by McVeigh and Nichols and ordered that McVeigh's trial proceed first.

McVeigh's trial began with voir dire of prospective jurors on March 31, 1997. A jury of 12 with six alternates was sworn in by the district court on April 24, 1997, and opening state-

ments commenced that same day. On June 2, 1997, the jury returned guilty verdicts on all counts charged in the indictment. The penalty phase of trial commenced on June 4, 1997, and concluded with summations and jury instructions on June 12, 1997. The jury deliberated for two days before returning special findings recommending that McVeigh be sentenced to death. After denying McVeigh's motion for a new trial, the district court accepted the jury recommendation on August 14, 1997, sentencing McVeigh to death. *See also* **Mass Murder**

Oklahoma Coalition to Abolish the Death Penalty

The Oklahoma Coalition to Abolish the Death Penalty (OCADP) consists of organizations, individuals, human rights groups, churches and other faith-based organizations. The organization seeks to abolish the death penalty in Oklahoma. OCADP provides information regarding the death penalty, encourages activism among concerned citizens, offers support to the loved ones of murder victims, and offers support to death row inmates and their loved ones.

Oman

Capital punishment is allowed in Oman. In 1998, Oman executed six prisoners. Its legal system is based on English common law and Islamic law. Oman does not have a constitution. Oman is a monarchy which has been ruled by the Al Bu Sa'id family since the 18th century. It has no political parties or directly elected representative institutions.

The judicial system is composed of magistrate courts and a State Security Court. Defendants tried by the State Security Court are not permitted to have legal representation present. The laws of Oman do not specify the rights of defendants. There are no written rules of evidence or any legal provision for public trials. Criminal procedures have developed. Defendants are presumed innocent and have the right to present evidence and confront witnesses.

A defendant may hire an attorney, but there is no explicit right to be represented by counsel. A panel of three judges tries felonies and security offenses. *See also* **International Capital Punishment Nations**

Opening Statement *see* **Trial Structure**

Opposition to Capital Punishment

When the United States Supreme Court lifted the brief moratorium on capital punishment in 1976, it did so in the midst of strong opposition. During the ensuing decades, anti–death penalty advocates have grown larger in numbers and in their scope. There are literally thousands of national and international organizations that have formed for the express purpose of abolishing capital punishment in the United States and the world.

1. *Reasons for Opposing Capital Punishment:* Although the underlying motivation behind organizational and individual opposition to capital punishment varies, a few broad categories capture much of the impetus.

   A. *Religious grounds:* Although the Judeo-Christian scriptures expressly endorses capital punishment for such offenses as murder, adultery, blasphemy, sodomy, idolatry, and incest, many organizations and individuals use religion as the basis for opposing the death penalty. Death penalty opponents point to Cain, the first biblical murderer, being punished with banishment and not death. They also cling strongly to biblical teachings on redemption and forgiveness, and the biblical admonishment "Thou shalt not kill," as cornerstones that make capital punishment inconsistent with their understanding of religious thought.

B. *Philosophical grounds:* Many of the most influential philosophers, such as John Locke, Immanuel Kant, and Jean-Jacques Rousseau, did not oppose capital punishment, in spite of their development of and belief in the principle that human beings were born with a "natural right to life." Many opponents of the death penalty have taken the "natural right to life" principle as the basis for opposing capital punishment. It is argued that governmental taking of life as punishment, violates the condemned's "natural right to life." The fact that a condemned took the "natural right to life" of another, does not excuse or justify a government's actions in taking the life of the condemned.

One of the leading writers on capital punishment, Hugo Adam Bedau, has articulated the utilitarian philosophy against capital punishment. Bedau contends that punishment should be administered with the most efficient and socially benefiting sanction. He believes the death penalty is not the best means of punishment, because it is not the most efficient sanction and it does not benefit society — it in fact degrades society.

C. *Lack of deterrence:* One of the primary arguments made by proponents of capital punishment is that the punishment has a deterrent effect. Death penalty opponents contend that no supportable proof has ever been deduced which establishes that capital punishment has a meaningful deterrent effect. Death penalty opponents point to the historically consistent high level of homicides as irrefutable proof that capital punishment has no justifiable deterrent effect.

D. *Discrimination:* Death penalty opponents contend that capital punishment should be abolished because it is not meted out fairly in the nation. They point to statistics which show that capital punishment is disproportionately inflicted upon minorities and the poor.

E. *Risk of executing the innocent:* The justification for abolishing capital punishment that is embraced by most death penalty opponents is the risk of executing an innocent person. While no irrefutable evidence has ever been compiled to show that innocent persons were executed, a great deal of research has in fact given strong evidence that suggests many executed persons were in fact innocent. A study done in 1987 suggested that between 1900–1985 there were 23 prisoners executed in the United States who were actually innocent of the crimes charged.

Death penalty opponents argue that the risk of executing one innocent person is reason enough to abolish capital punishment.

2. *Nations That Have Abolished Capital Punishment Since 1976:* There have been about 59 countries that have abolished capital punishment since 1976. That figure includes nations that abolished the death penalty per se, and those nations which abolished the death penalty for ordinary crimes only.

3. *Constitutional Abolishment of Capital Punishment:* Most of the nations of the world that have abolished capital punishment have done so through legislative acts. However, a few countries have taken the step of abolishing capital punishment per se or limiting its application, through their constitutions. Nations that provide for the abolishment of capital punishment through their constitutions include: Austria, Belgium, Cape Verde, Colombia, Dominican Republic, Ecuador, Finland, Germany, Haiti, Holland, Honduras, Iceland, Italy, Luxemburg, Marshall Islands, Federated States of Micronesia, Monaco, Mozambique, Namibia, Netherlands, Nicaragua, Panama, Portugal, Sao Tomé and Príncipe, Spain, Sweden, Uruguay and Venezuela.

4. *International Agreements to Ban Capital Punishment:* The international arena has produced several documents that call for the outright abolishment of capital punishment or limitations on its application.

A. *Second Optional Protocol to the International Covenant on Civil and Political Rights:* This instrument was sponsored by the United Nations. It provides for the abolishment of the death penalty. However, it allows nations to retain the death penalty in wartime.

B. *Protocol to the American Convention on Human Rights to Abolish the Death Penalty:* The Organization of American States sponsored this instrument. Under this document capital punishment must be abolished by all nations, but may be retained in wartime.

C. *Protocol No. 6 to the Convention for the Protection of Human Rights and Fundamental Freedoms Concerning the Abolition of the Death Penalty:* The Council of Europe sponsored this covenant. It provides for the abolishment of the death penalty in peacetime.

D. *International Covenant on Civil and Political Rights:* The United Nations sponsored this agreement. It provides that capital punishment shall not be imposed for crimes committed by persons below 18 years of age and shall not be carried out on pregnant women.

E. *Convention on the Rights of the Child:* The United Nations sponsored this document. It provides that capital punishment shall not be imposed for offences committed by persons below 18 years of age.

F. *American Convention on Human Rights:* The Organization of American States sponsored this instrument. It provides that capital punishment shall not be imposed upon persons who were under 18 years of age or over 70 years of age, at the time the crime was committed. It also prohibits imposition of the death penalty on pregnant women.

5. *Public Opinion and the Death Penalty:* National studies have shown that 70 percent of Americans approve of the death penalty. However, when asked to choose between the death penalty and alternative harsh prison sentences, only 41 percent of Americans preferred the death penalty. In a 1997, poll it was reported that 53 percent of Americans believed that capital punishment did not deter criminal conduct.

See also **American Bar Association; American Civil Liberties Union; Amnesty International; California Coalition for Alternatives to the Death Penalty; Campaign to End the Death Penalty; Canadian Coalition Against the Death Penalty; Catholics Against Capital Punishment; Citizens Against Homicides; Citizens United for Alternatives to the Death Penalty; Coalition of Arizonans to Abolish the Death Penalty; Death Penalty Focus of California; Death Penalty Information Center; Death Penalty Institute of Oklahoma; Equal Justice USA; Friends Committee to Abolish the Death Penalty; Hands Off Cain; Homicide Survivors; Human Rights Watch; Kentucky Coalition to Abolish the Death Penalty; Lifespark; Louisiana Coalition to Abolish the Death Penalty; MacArthur Justice Center; Maryland Coalition Against State Executions; Moratorium 2000; Moratorium on Capital Punishment; Murder Victims Families for Reconciliation; National Association for the Advancement of Colored People Legal Defense Fund; National Coalition to Abolish the Death Penalty; Nebraskans Against the Death Penalty; New Mexico Coalition to Repeal the Death Penalty; Ohioans to Stop Executions; Oklahoma Coalition to Abolish the Death Penalty; Oregon Coalition to Abolish the Death Penalty; People of Faith Against the Death Penalty; Pope John Paul II; Protests Against Capital Punishment; Religious Organizing Against the Death Penalty Project; Security on Campus; Southern Center for Human Rights; Tennessee Coalition to Abolish State Killing; Texas Coalition to Abolish the Death Penalty; Unitarian Universalists Against the Death Penalty; United Nations Commission on Human Rights; United Students Against the Death Penalty; Virginians for Alternatives to the Death Penalty; Washington Coalition to Abolish the Death Penalty; Western Missouri Coalition to Abolish the Death Penalty**

Ordering Killing Aggravator

A minority of capital punishment jurisdictions provide that murder committed as a result of an order or command by another, is a statutory aggravating circumstance. In these jurisdictions the penalty phase jury may impose the death penalty if it finds that the murder was ordered by another. *See also* **Aggravating Circumstances**

Oregon

The State of Oregon is a capital punishment jurisdiction. The State reenacted its death penalty law after the

JURISDICTIONS USING ORDERING KILLING AGGRAVATOR

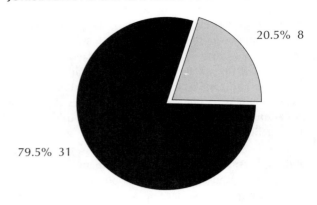

20.5% 8

79.5% 31

■ ORDERING KILLING AGGRAVATOR JURISDICTIONS
■ ALL OTHER JURISDICTIONS

United States Supreme Court decision in *Furman v. Georgia,* 408 U.S. 238 (1972), on December 7, 1978.

Oregon has a three-tier legal system. The State's legal system is composed of a supreme court, court of appeals and courts of general jurisdiction. The Oregon Supreme Court is presided over by a chief justice and six associate justices. The Oregon Court of Appeals is composed of a chief judge and nine judges. The courts of general jurisdiction in the State are called Circuit Courts. Capital offenses against the State of Oregon are tried in the Circuit Courts.

Oregon's capital punishment statute is triggered if a person commits a homicide under the following special circumstances:

1. a. The defendant committed the murder pursuant to an agreement that the defendant receive money or other thing of value for committing the murder.

   b. The defendant solicited another to commit the murder and paid or agreed to pay the person money or other thing of value for committing the murder.

   c. The defendant committed murder after having been convicted previously in any jurisdiction of any homicide.

   d. There was more than one murder victim in the same criminal episode.

   e. The homicide occurred in the course of or as a result of intentional maiming or torture of the victim.

   f. The victim of the intentional homicide was a person under the age of 14 years.

2. a. The victim was one of the following and the murder was related to the performance of the victim's official duties in the justice system: (A) a police officer; (B) a correctional, parole or probation officer or other person charged with the duty of custody, control or supervision of convicted persons; (C) a member of the Oregon State Police; (D) a judicial officer; (E) a juror or witness in a criminal proceeding; (F) an employee or officer of a court of justice; or (G) a member of the State Board of Parole and Post-Prison Supervision.

b. The defendant was confined in a state, county or municipal penal or correctional facility or was otherwise in custody when the murder occurred.

c. The defendant committed murder by means of an explosive.

d. The defendant personally and intentionally committed the homicide.

e. The murder was committed in an effort to conceal the commission of a crime, or to conceal the identity of the perpetrator of a crime.

f. The murder was committed after the defendant had escaped from a state, county or municipal penal or correctional facility and before the defendant had been returned to the custody of the facility.

Capital murder in Oregon is punishable by death, life imprisonment without parole, or imprisonment with parole. A capital prosecution in Oregon is bifurcated into a guilt phase and penalty phase. A jury is used at both phases of a capital trial. It is required that, at the penalty phase, the jury must unanimously agree that a death sentence is appropriate before it can be imposed. If the penalty phase jury is unable to reach a verdict, the trial judge is required to impose life imprisonment without parole, or imprisonment with parole. The decision of a penalty phase jury is binding on the trial court under the laws of Oregon.

In order to impose a death sentence upon a defendant under Oregon law, it is required that the penalty phase jury return an affirmative answer to each of the following questions:

Upon the conclusion of the presentation of the evidence, the court shall submit the following issues to the jury:

A. Whether the conduct of the defendant that caused the death of the deceased was committed deliberately and with the reasonable expectation that death of the deceased or another would result;

B. Whether there is a probability that the defendant would commit criminal acts of violence that would constitute a continuing threat to society;

C. If raised by the evidence, whether the conduct of the defendant in killing the deceased was unreasonable in response to the provocation, if any, by the deceased; and

D. Whether the defendant should receive a death sentence.

Although the Federal Constitution will not permit jurisdictions to prevent capital felons from presenting all relevant mitigating evidence at the penalty phase, Oregon has provided the following statutory mitigating circumstances that permit the jury to reject imposition of the death penalty:

The defendant's age, the extent and severity of the defendant's prior criminal conduct and the extent of the mental and emotional pressure under which the defendant was acting at the time the offense was committed.

Under Oregon's capital punishment statute, a sentence of death is automatically reviewed by the Oregon Supreme Court. Oregon uses lethal injection to carry out death sentences. The State's death row facility for men is located in Salem, Oregon. Pursuant to the laws of Oregon the Governor has exclusive authority to grant clemency in capital cases.

From the start of modern capital punishment in 1976, through 1999, Oregon executed two capital felons. During this period Oregon did not have any female capital felons on death row. A total of 26 capital felons were on death row in Oregon in 1999. The 1999 death row population in the State was listed as: one black inmate; 21 white inmates; and four unidentified inmates. The State does not permit capital punishment to be imposed on persons 17 years old or younger. Oregon does not prohibit the execution of mentally retarded capital felons.

Executions by Oregon 1976–1999

Name	Race	Date of Execution	Method of Execution
Douglas F. Wright	White	September 6, 1996	Lethal Injection
Harry C. Moore	White	May 16, 1997	Lethal Injection

OREGON EXECUTIONS 1976–1999

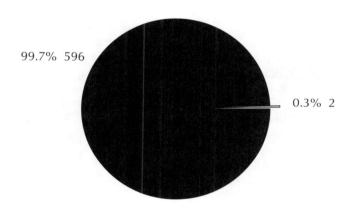

99.7% 596   0.3% 2

■ OREGON EXECUTIONS
■ ALL OTHER EXECUTIONS

EXECUTIONS BY OREGON 1930–1999

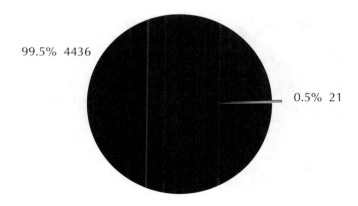

99.5% 4436   0.5% 21

■ OREGON
■ ALL OTHER JURISDICTIONS

Oregon Coalition to Abolish the Death Penalty

The Oregon Coalition to Abolish the Death Penalty (OCADP) is an organization formed for the purpose of abolishing the death penalty in Oregon. OCADP engages in efforts to educate the community, monitor death penalty cases, and advocate for humane and constitutional death row conditions of confinement. It also supports the needs and concerns of the families of victims, as well as the families of persons on death row.

Packer, Alfred

Alfred Packer was the first person prosecuted in the United States for cannibalism. Packer was born in Pennsylvania on November 21, 1842. He was a shoemaker by trade, but spent some time in the military before wandering out west. In 1873, while in Provo, Utah, he was hired as a guide for 20 men on a prospecting trip into the San Juan mountains of Colorado. In January of 1874 the group of prospectors stopped near Montrose, Colorado. While in the area they were warned not to try crossing the mountains until spring. Packer and five of prospectors decided to continue on into the mountains.

During early spring of 1874, Packer had alone appeared near the town of Gunnison. He told people that he was left behind by the prospectors due to a leg injury. A search along the trail taken by the prospectors revealed strips of human flesh. Authorities questioned Packer and he gave a confession to killing and eating all five men. Packer was jailed in Saguache, but escaped to Wyoming. For nine years Packer evaded capture. He was eventually captured in Cheyenne in 1883 and returned to Lake City to stand trial.

Packer was found guilty of murder and sentenced to be hanged in 1885. An appeal was taken and his conviction and sentence were reversed by the Colorado Supreme Court. Packer was retried and convicted of manslaughter and sentenced to 40 years imprisonment. Packer was released on parole in 1901. He would later die on April 23, 1907.

Alfred Packer was sentenced to death for the cannibal murders of five people, but his death sentence was reversed on appeal. (Colorado State Archives)

Paine, Lewis *see* Lincoln's Assassination

Pakistan

Capital punishment is allowed in Pakistan. Pakistan uses hanging and stoning to carry out the death penalty. In 1998, Pakistan executed four prisoners. Its legal system is based on English common law and Islamic law. The constitution of Pakistan was restored on December 30, 1985.

The judicial system is composed of magistrate courts, sessions court, High Court, and a Supreme Court. Defendants have a right to a public trial, enjoy a presumption of innocence, and have a right to retained counsel. Attorneys are appointed for indigents only in capital cases. There are no jury trials. Defendants may be admitted to bail and may appeal judgments. *See also* **International Capital Punishment Nations**

Palau

Capital punishment is not carried out in Palau. *See also* **International Capital Punishment Nations**

Palko v. Connecticut

Court: United States Supreme Court; *Case Citation:* Palko v. Connecticut, 302 U.S. 319 (1937); *Argued:* November 12, 1937; *Decided:* December 6, 1937; *Opinion of the Court:* Justice Cardozo; *Concurring Opinion:* None; *Dissenting Statement:* Justice Butler; *Appellate Defense Counsel:* David Goldstein argued; George A. Saden on brief; *Appellate Prosecution Counsel:* Wm. H. Comley argued and briefed; *Amicus Curiae Brief Supporting Prosecutor:* None; *Amicus Curiae Brief Supporting Defendant:* None.

Issue Presented: Whether the double jeopardy principles contained in the Fifth Amendment are applicable to States?

Case Holding: The double jeopardy principles contained in the Fifth Amendment are not applicable to States, therefore the judgment against the defendant could stand.

Factual and procedural background of case: The defendant, Palko, was prosecuted for capital murder by the State of Connecticut. The jury found the defendant guilty of murder in the second degree, and he was sentenced to confinement in the state prison for life. The prosecutor appealed the judgment to the Connecticut Supreme Court. The appellate court reversed the judgment and ordered a new trial.

At the second trial the defendant was convicted of capital murder and sentenced to death. The State appellate court affirmed the judgment. In doing so, the appellate court rejected the defendant's argument that double jeopardy principles of the Fifth Amendment prohibited a second prosecution of him. The United States Supreme Court granted certiorari to consider the issue.

Opinion of the Court by Justice Cardozo: Justice Cardozo ruled that the double jeopardy principles of the Fifth Amendment were applicable against the Federal government, but had no application to States. The opinion stated the matter as follows: "The argument for [the defendant] is that whatever is forbidden by the Fifth Amendment is forbidden by the Fourteenth also. The Fifth Amendment, which is not directed to the States, but solely to the federal government, creates immunity from double jeopardy. No person shall be 'subject for the same offense to be twice put in jeopardy of life or limb.' The Fourteenth Amendment ordains, 'nor shall any State deprive any person of life, liberty, or property, without due process of law.' To retry a defendant, though under one indictment and only one, subjects him, it is said, to double jeopardy in violation of the Fifth Amendment, if the prosecution is one on behalf of the United States. From this the consequence is said to follow that there is a denial of life or liberty without due process of law, if the prosecution is one on behalf of the people of a state." Justice Cardozo rejected the defendant's reasoning and affirmed the judgment of the Connecticut Supreme Court.

Dissenting statement by Justice Butler: Justice Butler issued a statement indicating he dissented from the Court's decision.

Case note: The rule laid down in this case would eventually be rejected by the Court in *Benton v. Maryland*, 395 U.S. 784 (1969), and the Fifth Amendment would be made applicable to States through the Fourteenth Amendment.

Panama   Capital Punishment is not carried out in Panama. *See also* **International Capital Punishment Nations**

Papua New Guinea   The death penalty has not been officially outlawed by Papua New Guinea, but it has not been invoked in recent memory. Papua New Guinea uses hanging as the method of execution. Its legal system is based on English common law. The nation's constitution was adopted on September 16, 1975.

The judicial system is composed of trial courts, National Court, and a Supreme Court. There are also village courts headed by lay persons, who adjudicate minor offenses under both customary and statutory law. Defendants have a right to public trials, to retained or appointed counsel, may confront witnesses, and appeal convictions. *See also* **International Capital Punishment Nations**

Paraguay   Paraguay abolished capital punishment in 1992. *See also* **International Capital Punishment Nations**

Pardon *see* **Clemency**

Parents of Murdered Children   Parents of Murdered Children (POMC) is an Ohio based group that was founded in 1978 by the Reverend and Mrs. Robert Hullinger, after their daughter was brutally murdered. POMC seeks to provide supportive services for the loved ones of homicide victims. Services provided by POMC include: participation in a self-help group; crisis intervention; assistance with problematic cases; advocacy; and information and referrals. Additionally, POMC sponsors conferences and in-depth therapeutic grief weekends.

Parker v. Dugger   *Court:* United States Supreme Court; *Case Citation:* Parker v. Dugger, 498 U.S. 308 (1991); *Argued:* November 7, 1990; *Decided:* January 22, 1991; *Opinion of the Court:* Justice O'Connor; *Concurring Opinion:* None; *Dissenting Opinion:* Justice White, in which Rehnquist, C.J., and Scalia and Kennedy, JJ., joined; *Appellate Defense Counsel:* Robert J. Link argued and briefed; *Appellate Prosecution Counsel:* Carolyn M. Snurkowski argued; Robert A. Butterworth and Mark C. Menser on brief; *Amicus Curiae Brief Supporting Prosecutor:* None; *Amicus Curiae Brief Supporting Defendant:* None.

Issue Presented: Whether the Florida Supreme Court erroneously affirmed the defendant's death sentence on the grounds that he proffered no mitigating evidence during the penalty phase?

Case Holding: The Florida Supreme Court erroneously affirmed the defendant's death sentence on the grounds that he proffered no mitigating evidence during the penalty phase.

Factual and procedural background of case: The defendant, Robert Parker, was convicted of two capital murder charges by the State of Florida. During the penalty phase an advisory jury found that sufficient aggravating circumstances existed to justify a death sentence as to both murders, but that sufficient mitigating circumstances existed to outweigh those aggravating factors, and therefore recommended that the defendant be sentenced to life imprisonment on both counts. The trial judge accepted the jury's recommendation as to one of the murders, but overrode the recommendation for the other and sentenced the defendant to death.

On appeal, the Florida Supreme Court found invalid two of the six statutory aggravating circumstances relied upon by the trial court to be impose the death sentence. The appellate court affirmed the death sentence after declaring that the trial court had found no mitigating circumstances to balance against the four properly applied aggravating factors. It was ruled by the appellate court that the facts suggesting the death sentence were "so clear and convincing that no reasonable person could differ."

The defendant filed a habeas corpus petition in a Federal District Court. The District Court found that the death sentence was unconstitutional because the Florida Supreme Court failed to consider non-statutory mitigating evidence submitted by the defendant. The District Court vacated the defendant's death sentence. A Federal Court of Appeals disagreed with the District Court and reversed its decision. The United States Supreme Court granted certiorari to consider the issue.

Opinion of the Court by Justice O'Connor: Justice O'Connor held that the Florida Supreme Court acted arbitrarily and capriciously by failing to treat adequately the defendant's non-statutory mitigating evidence. The opinion indicated that although the trial judge's order imposing the death sentence did not state explicitly what effect he gave the defendant's non-statutory mitigating evidence, the Court would conclude that the judge found and weighed such evidence before imposing the sentence. It was said that the record in the case contained substantial evidence, much of it uncontroverted, favoring mitigation.

The opinion reasoned that the State Supreme Court erred in concluding that the trial judge found no mitigating circumstances to balance against the aggravating factors, and consequently erred in its review of the defendant's death sentence. Justice O'Connor observed that the State Supreme Court did not conduct an independent reweighing of the evidence, since it explicitly relied on what it took to be the trial judge's findings of no mitigating circumstances. She noted that although a Federal court on habeas review must give deference to a State appellate court's resolution of an ambiguity in a state trial court's order, it need not do so where the State appellate court's conclusion is not fairly supported by the record in the case. Justice O'Connor concluded that the State Supreme Court's affirmance of the death sentence, based upon nonexistent findings, was invalid because it deprived the defendant of the individualized treatment to which he was entitled under the Constitution.

The judgment of the Court of Appeals was reversed and the case was remanded with instructions to return the case to the District Court to enter an order directing the State of Florida to initiate appropriate proceedings in state court so that the defendant's death sentence may be reconsidered in light of the entire record of his trial and sentencing hearing and the trial judge's findings. She expressed no opinion as to whether the Florida courts had to order a new sentencing hearing.

Dissenting opinion by Justice White, in which Rehnquist, C.J., and Scalia and Kennedy, JJ., joined: Justice White dissented from the Court's decision. He argued that the record in the case was not so clear as to reach the conclusion that the trial court in fact found the existence of non-statutory mitigating evidence. Because of the lack of precise record, Justice White believed the Court should have deferred to the Florida Supreme Court's determination that the trial court found no mitigating evidence. He concluded: "I cannot countenance the Court's ... imaginative reconstruction of the record in this case. Therefore, I dissent, and would affirm the judgment of the Court of Appeals" *See also* **Mitigating Circumstances**

Parole *see* **Life Imprisonment**

Parole Eligibility Jury Instruction   When a capital defendant's future dangerousness is at issue during the penalty phase, and the applicable law prohibits the defendant's release on parole, constitutional due process requires that the sentencing jury be instructed that the defendant would be ineligible for parole if given a life sentence. *See also* **Jury Instructions; Simmons v. South Carolina**

Parole/Probation Officer Aggravator   A minority of capital punishment jurisdictions have made the killing of a parole or probation officer a statutory aggravating circumstance. In such jurisdictions if the penalty phase jury finds that the victim was a parole or probation officer killed during the course of his or her work, the death penalty may be imposed. *See also* **Statutory Aggravating Circumstances**

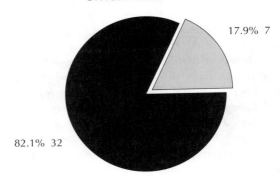

JURISDICITONS USING PAROLE/PROBATION
OFFICER AGGRAVATOR

17.9% 7

82.1% 32

■ PAROLE/PROBATION OFFICER AGGRAVATOR JURISDICTIONS
■ ALL OTHER JURISDICTIONS

Parole Watch   Parole Watch is a New York based nonprofit anti-crime advocacy group. The primary goal of Parole Watch is to inform the public when violent felons come up for parole, so that the public may have an opportunity to voice its opinion on the matter. Parole Watch has a goal of creating a nationwide database on parole information concerning violent inmates and to make that database available to the public on the Internet.

Parsons, Albert R. *see* **Chicago Labor Riots of 1886**

Passion, Prejudice or Arbitrariness *see* **Individualized Sentencing**

Patterson v. Alabama   *Court:* United States Supreme Court; *Case Citation:* Patterson v. Alabama, 294 U.S. 600 (1935); *Argued:* February 15–18, 1935; *Decided:* April 1, 1935; *Opinion of the Court:* Chief Justice Hughes; *Concurring Opinion:* None; *Dissenting Opinion:* None; *Justice Taking No Part in Decision:* Justice McReynolds; *Appellate Defense Counsel:* Walter H. Pollak argued; Osmond K. Fraenkel and Carl S. Stern on brief; *Appellate Prosecution Counsel:* Thomas E.

Knight, Jr. argued and briefed; *Amicus Curiae Brief Supporting Prosecutor:* None; *Amicus Curiae Brief Supporting Defendant:* None.

Issue Presented: Whether the defendant established that blacks were systematically excluded from the grand jury that indicted him and the petit jury that convicted him?

Case Holding: In light of the Court's determination of grand and petit jury racial discrimination in a companion case, *Norris v. Alabama*, the decision in this case would be remanded for the Alabama Supreme Court to address the issue.

Factual and procedural background of case: The defendant, Haywood Patterson, was one of seven defendants convicted of rape and sentenced to death by the State of Alabama. In *Powell v. Alabama*, the United States Supreme Court reversed the convictions of all seven defendants and ordered a new trial. After the remand, a motion for change of venue was granted and all the cases were transferred to another county. The defendant was tried separately, however, on remand. The jury found a verdict against him which the trial judge set aside as against the weight of evidence. He was then brought to trial for a third time and was again convicted and sentenced to death. On appeal, the Alabama Supreme Court affirmed the conviction and sentence. In doing so, the appellate court failed to address the defendant's argument that his trial violated the Federal Constitution, on the grounds that blacks were systematically excluded from the grand jury that indicted him and the petit jury that convicted him. The United States Supreme Court granted certiorari to consider the issue.

Opinion of the Court by Chief Justice Hughes: The Chief Justice ruled that because the Court found in a companion case, *Norris v. Alabama*, that blacks were systematically excluded from grand and petit juries in the county where the defendant was convicted, the defendant's case could not come out differently. However, because the Alabama Supreme Court had not addressed the issue, the Court determined the State appellate court should have an opportunity to address the matter. The opinion stated: "[The Court was] not convinced that the [State] court, in the presence of such a determination of constitutional right, confronting the anomalous and grave situation which would be created by a reversal of the judgment against Norris, and an affirmance of the judgment of death in the companion case of Patterson, who had asserted the same right, and having regard to the relation of the two cases and the other circumstances disclosed by the record, would have considered itself powerless to ... provide appropriate relief.... At least the state court should have an opportunity to examine its powers in the light of the situation which has now developed. We should not foreclose that opportunity." The judgment of the Alabama Supreme Court was vacated and the case remanded.

Case note: Under modern capital punishment jurisprudence the death penalty may not be imposed for the crime of rape without an accompanying homicide. *See also* **Norris v. Alabama; Powell v. Alabama; Rape and Capital Punishment**

Patton v. Mississippi *Court:* United States Supreme Court; *Case Citation:* Patton v. Mississippi , 332 U.S. 463 (1948); *Argued:* November 21–24, 1947; *Decided:* December 8, 1947; *Opinion of the Court:* Justice Black; *Concurring Opinion:* None; *Dissenting Opinion:* None; *Appellate Defense Counsel:* Thurgood Marshall argued and briefed; *Appellate Prosecution Counsel:* George H. Ethridge argued and briefed; *Amicus Curiae Brief Supporting Prosecutor:* None; *Amicus Curiae Brief Supporting Defendant:* None.

Issue Presented: Whether the defendant established that blacks were systematically excluded from the grand jury that indicted him and the petit jury that convicted him?

Case Holding: The defendant established that blacks were systematically excluded from the grand jury that indicted him and the petit jury that convicted him, therefore his conviction and sentence could not stand.

Factual and procedural background of case: The defendant, Patton, was convicted of capital murder and sentenced to death by the State of Mississippi. The Mississippi Supreme Court affirmed the judgment. In doing so, the appellate court rejected the defendant's contention that his conviction and sentence were invalid because blacks were systematically exclude from the grand jury that indicted him and the petit jury that convicted him. The United States Supreme Court granted certiorari to consider the issue.

Opinion of the Court by Justice Black: Justice Black noted that "[s]ixty-seven years ago this Court held that state exclusion of [blacks] from grand and petit juries solely because of their race denied [black] defendants in criminal cases the equal protection of the laws required by the Fourteenth Amendment." In turning to the defendant's case, Justice Black found that the defendant had been the victim of racial jury discrimination. The opinion ruled: "We hold that the State wholly failed to meet the very strong evidence of purposeful racial discrimination made out by the [defendant] upon the uncontradicted showing that for thirty years or more no [black] had served as a juror in the criminal courts of Lauderdale County. When a jury selection plan, whatever it is, operates in such way as always to result in the complete and long-continued exclusion of any representative at all from a large group of [blacks], or any other racial group, indictments and verdicts returned against them by juries thus selected cannot stand." The judgment of the Mississippi Supreme Court was reversed. *See also* **Discrimination in Grand or Petit Jury Selection**

Payne v. Arkansas *Court:* United States Supreme Court; *Case Citation:* Payne v. Arkansas, 356 U.S. 560 (1958); *Argued:* March 3, 1958; *Decided:* May 19, 1958; *Opinion of the Court:* Justice Whittaker; *Concurring Statement:* Justice Harlan; *Dissenting Opinion:* Justice Clark; *Dissenting Statement:* Justice Burton; *Appellate Defense Counsel:* Wiley A. Branton argued and briefed; *Appellate Prosecution Counsel:* Thorp Thomas argued; Bruce Bennett on brief; *Amicus Curiae Brief Supporting Prosecutor:* None; *Amicus Curiae Brief Supporting Defendant:* None.

Issue Presented: Whether the defendant's confession to capital murder was obtained in violation of due process of law?

Case Holding: The defendant's confession to capital murder was obtained in violation of due process of law and therefore his conviction cannot stand.

Factual and procedural background of case: The defendant, Payne, was convicted of capital murder and sentenced to death by the State of Arkansas. On appeal the Arkansas Supreme Court affirmed the conviction and sentence. In doing so, the appellate court rejected the defendant's contention that his confession was obtained in violation of the Federal Constitution. The United States Supreme Court granted certiorari to consider the issue.

Opinion of the Court by Justice Whittaker: Justice Whittaker held that the defendant's confession was obtained in violation of due process of law. The opinion laid out the facts supporting the Court's conclusion as follows:

> It is obvious from the totality of the course of conduct shown by undisputed evidence that the confession was coerced and did not constitute an "expression of free choice." That [the defendant] was not physically tortured affords no answer to the question whether the confession was coerced, for "[t]here is torture of mind as well as body; the will is as much affected by fear as by force…. A confession by which life becomes forfeit must be the expression of free choice."…
>
> The undisputed evidence in this case shows that [the defendant], a mentally dull 19-year-old youth, (1) was arrested without a warrant, (2) was denied a hearing before a magistrate at which he would have been advised of his right to remain silent and of his right to counsel, as required by Arkansas statutes, (3) was not advised of his right to remain silent or of his right to counsel, (4) was held incommunicado for three days, without counsel, advisor or friend, and though members of his family tried to see him they were turned away, and he was refused permission to make even one telephone call, (5) was denied food for long periods, and, finally, (6) was told by the chief of police "that there would be 30 or 40 people there in a few minutes that wanted to get him," which statement created such fear in [the defendant] as immediately produced the "confession." It seems obvious from the totality of this course of conduct and particularly the culminating threat of mob violence, that the confession was coerced and did not constitute an "expression of free choice," and that its use before the jury, over [the defendant's] objection, deprived him of "that fundamental fairness essential to the very concept of justice," and, hence, denied him due process of law, guaranteed by the Fourteenth Amendment.

The judgment of the Arkansas Supreme Court was reversed.

Concurring Statement by Justice Harlan: Justice Harlan issued a concurring statement indicating he joined the Court's reversal of the judgment.

Dissenting opinion by Justice Clark: Justice Clark dissented from the Court's decision. He believed that the confession was voluntary and was not obtained in violation of due process. Justice Clark also contended that the Court should not have disturbed the judgment because under Arkansas law the jury determined whether a confession was voluntary. He reasoned that under the Court's precedents it should have assumed that the jury found the confession was coerced and rejected it. Justice Clark concluded that "even if

the confession be deemed coerced, there is sufficient other evidence of guilt to sustain the conviction[.]"

Dissenting statement by Justice Burton: Justice Burton issued a dissenting statement indicating he believed the Court should "accept the conclusion of the state court and jury that [the defendant's] confession was voluntary." *See also* **Right to Remain Silent**

Payne v. Tennessee
Court: United States Supreme Court; *Case Citation:* Payne v. Tennessee, 501 U.S. 808 (1991); *Argued:* April 24, 1991; *Decided:* June 27, 1991; *Opinion of the Court:* Chief Justice Rehnquist; *Concurring Opinion:* Justice O'Connor, in which White and Kennedy, JJ., joined; *Concurring Opinion:* Justice Scalia, in which O'Connor and Kennedy, JJ., joined; *Concurring Opinion:* Justice Souter, in which Kennedy, J., joined; *Dissenting Opinion:* Justice Marshall, in which Blackmun, J., joined; *Dissenting Opinion:* Justice Stevens, in which Blackmun, J., joined; *Appellate Defense Counsel:* J. Brooke Lathram argued and briefed; *Appellate Prosecution Counsel:* Charles W. Burson argued; Kathy M. Principe on brief; *Amicus Curiae Brief Supporting Prosecutor:* 8; *Amicus Curiae Brief Supporting Defendant:* 1.

Issue Presented: Whether the Eighth Amendment bars the admission of victim impact evidence during the penalty phase of a capital trial?

Case Holding: The Eighth Amendment does not bar the admission of victim impact evidence during the penalty phase of a capital trial.

Factual and procedural background of case: The defendant, Pervis Tyrone Payne, was convicted of two capital murders by the State of Tennessee. During the penalty phase the prosecutor presented evidence of the impact of the deaths on the victims' family members. During the prosecutor's closing argument further statements were made as to the traumatic effect the deaths had on the victims' family. The defendant was sentenced to death for both murders. The Tennessee Supreme Court affirmed both convictions and sentences. In doing so, the appellate court rejected the defendant's contention that the admission of the victim impact evidence and the prosecutor's closing argument violated his Eighth Amendment rights under United States Supreme court decisions in *Booth v. Maryland* and *South Carolina v. Gathers*, which held that evidence and argument relating to the victim and the impact of the victim's death on the victim's family were per se inadmissible at a capital sentencing hearing. The United States Supreme Court granted certiorari to consider the issue.

Opinion of the Court by Chief Justice Rehnquist: The Chief Justice announced that it was time to overrule *Booth* and *Gathers*. He ruled that the Eighth Amendment erected no per se bar prohibiting a capital sentencing jury from considering victim impact evidence relating to the victim's personal characteristics and the emotional impact of the murder on the victim's family, or precluded a prosecutor from arguing such evidence at a capital sentencing hearing. The Chief Justice concluded that to the extent that the Court held to the contrary in *Booth* and *Gathers*, those cases were overruled. The judgment of the Tennessee Supreme Court was affirmed.

Concurring opinion by Justice O'Connor, in which White and Kennedy, JJ., joined: Justice O'Connor concurred in the Court's decision. In doing so, she outlined her understanding of the Court's ruling as follows:

> In my view, a State may legitimately determine that victim impact evidence is relevant to a capital sentencing proceeding. A State may decide that the jury, before determining whether a convicted murderer should receive the death penalty, should know the full extent of the harm caused by the crime, including its impact on the victim's family and community. A State may decide also that the jury should see "a quick glimpse of the life [the defendant] chose to extinguish," to remind the jury that the person whose life was taken was a unique human being.
>
> Given that victim impact evidence is potentially relevant, nothing in the Eighth Amendment commands that States treat it differently than other kinds of relevant evidence. "The Eighth Amendment stands as a shield against those practices and punishments which are either inherently cruel or which so offend the moral consensus of this society as to be deemed 'cruel and unusual.'" Certainly there is no strong societal consensus that a jury may not take into account the loss suffered by a victim's family or that a murder victim must remain a faceless stranger at the penalty phase of a capital trial. Just the opposite is true. Most States have enacted legislation enabling judges and juries to consider victim impact evidence. The possibility that this evidence may in some cases be unduly inflammatory does not justify a prophylactic, constitutionally based rule that this evidence may never be admitted. Trial courts routinely exclude evidence that is unduly inflammatory; where inflammatory evidence is improperly admitted, appellate courts carefully review the record to determine whether the error was prejudicial.
>
> We do not hold today that victim impact evidence must be admitted, or even that it should be admitted. We hold merely that if a State decides to permit consideration of this evidence, "the Eighth Amendment erects no per se bar." If, in a particular case, a witness' testimony or a prosecutor's remark so infects the sentencing proceeding as to render it fundamentally unfair, the defendant may seek appropriate relief under the Due Process Clause of the Fourteenth Amendment.

Concurring opinion by Justice Scalia, in which O'Connor and Kennedy, JJ., joined: Justice Scalia concurred in the Court's opinion. He wrote: "The Court correctly observes the injustice of requiring the exclusion of relevant aggravating evidence during capital sentencing, while requiring the admission of all relevant mitigating evidence. I have previously expressed my belief that the latter requirement is both wrong and, when combined with the remainder of our capital sentencing jurisprudence, unworkable. Even if it were abandoned, however, I would still affirm the judgment here. True enough, the Eighth Amendment permits parity between mitigating and aggravating factors. But more broadly and fundamentally still, it permits the People to decide (within the limits of other constitutional guarantees) what is a crime and what constitutes aggravation and mitigation of a crime."

Concurring opinion by Justice Souter, in which Kennedy, J., joined: Justice Souter wrote an opinion concurring in the Court's decision. He stated his views as follows:

> I join the Court's opinion addressing two categories of facts excluded from consideration at capital sentencing proceedings by *Booth v. Maryland* and *South Carolina v. Gathers*: information revealing the individuality of the victim and the impact of the crime on the victim's survivors. As to these two categories, I believe *Booth* and *Gathers* were wrongly decided.
>
> To my knowledge, our legal tradition has never included a general rule that evidence of a crime's effects on the victim and others is, standing alone, irrelevant to a sentencing determination of the defendant's culpability. Indeed, as the Court's opinion today, and dissents in *Booth* and *Gathers*, make clear, criminal conduct has traditionally been categorized and penalized differently according to consequences not specifically intended, but determined in part by conditions unknown to a defendant when he acted.

Dissenting opinion by Justice Marshall, in which Blackmun, J., joined: In his dissenting opinion, Justice Marshall expressed alarm over the Court's decision to overrule *Booth* and *Gathers*. He believed such a decision was a prelude to further erosion of rights he believed were fundamental to the Constitution. Justice Marshall wrote:

> Power, not reason, is the new currency of this Court's decisionmaking. Four Terms ago, a five-Justice majority of this Court held that "victim impact" evidence of the type at issue in this case could not constitutionally be introduced during the penalty phase of a capital trial. By another 5–4 vote, a majority of this Court rebuffed an attack upon this ruling just two Terms ago. Nevertheless, having expressly invited [Tennessee] to renew the attack, today's majority overrules *Booth* and *Gathers* and credits the dissenting views expressed in those cases. Neither the law nor the facts supporting *Booth* and *Gathers* underwent any change in the last four years. Only the personnel of this Court did.
>
> In dispatching *Booth* and *Gathers* to their graves, today's majority ominously suggests that an even more extensive upheaval of this Court's precedents may be in store. Renouncing this Court's historical commitment to a conception of "the judiciary as a source of impersonal and reasoned judgments," the majority declares itself free to discard any principle of constitutional liberty which was recognized or reaffirmed over the dissenting votes of four Justices and with which five or more Justices now disagree. The implications of this radical new exception to the doctrine of stare decisis are staggering. The majority today sends a clear signal that scores of established constitutional liberties are now ripe for reconsideration, thereby inviting the very type of open defiance of our precedents that the majority rewards in this case. Because I believe that this Court owes more to its constitutional precedents in general and to *Booth* and *Gathers* in particular, I dissent.

Dissenting opinion by Justice Stevens, in which Blackmun, J., joined: The dissenting opinion of Justice Stevens continued the theme of Justice Marshall's dissent. Justice Stevens believed the Court went too far in overruling precedents. He wrote:

> The novel rule that the Court announces today represents a dramatic departure from the principles that have governed our capital sentencing jurisprudence for decades. Justice Marshall is properly concerned about the majority's trivialization of the doctrine of stare decisis. But even if *Booth v. Maryland*, and *South Carolina v. Gathers*, had not been decided, today's decision would represent a sharp break with past decisions. Our cases provide no support whatsoever for the majority's conclusion that the prosecutor may introduce evidence that sheds no light on the defendant's guilt or moral culpability, and thus serves no purpose other than to encourage jurors to decide in

favor of death rather than life on the basis of their emotions rather than their reason.

Until today our capital punishment jurisprudence has required that any decision to impose the death penalty be based solely on evidence that tends to inform the jury about the character of the offense and the character of the defendant; evidence that serves no purpose other than to appeal to the sympathies or emotions of the jurors has never been considered admissible. Thus, if a defendant, who had murdered a convenience store clerk in cold blood in the course of an armed robbery, offered evidence unknown to him at the time of the crime about the immoral character of his victim, all would recognize immediately that the evidence was irrelevant and inadmissible. Evenhanded justice requires that the same constraint be imposed on the advocate of the death penalty....

Given the current popularity of capital punishment in a crime-ridden society, the political appeal of arguments that assume that increasing the severity of sentences is the best cure for the cancer of crime, and the political strength of the "victims' rights" movement, I recognize that today's decision will be greeted with enthusiasm by a large number of concerned and thoughtful citizens. The great tragedy of the decision, however, is the danger that the "hydraulic pressure" of public opinion that Justice Holmes once described — and that properly influences the deliberations of democratic legislatures — has played a role not only in the Court's decision to hear this case, and in its decision to reach the constitutional question without pausing to consider affirming on the basis of the Tennessee Supreme Court's rationale, but even in its resolution of the constitutional issue involved. Today is a sad day for a great institution.

Case note: The impact of the Court's decision on capital punishment was profound. The decision has enabled prosecutors to take full advantage of a weapon once thought to be too powerful to allow in capital prosecutions: empathy for the families of murder victims. In an effort to control the sweeping impact of the decision many courts scrutinize and limit the use of victim impact evidence. *See also* **Booth v. Maryland; California v. Brown; South Carolina v. Gathers; Victim Impact Evidence**

Peckham, Rufus W.   Rufus W. Peckham served as an associate justice of the United States Supreme Court from 1895 to 1909. While on the Supreme Court Peckham was known as a conservative interpreter of the Constitution.

Peckham was born on November 8, 1838 in Albany, New York. Peckham's education was obtained in private schools in the United States and abroad. He studied law as an apprentice in his father's law office and was admitted to the bar in New York in 1859. Peckham maintained a private practice for several years before taking a position as a prosecutor for Albany County. He eventually became a trial judge and was a member of New York's highest court. In 1895 President Grover Cleveland appointed Peckham to the Supreme Court.

Peckham wrote only a few capital punishment opinions while on the Supreme Court. The conservative interpretation of the Constitution that Peckham was known for was best illustrated in the case of *Valentina v. Mercer*. The defendant in the case pled guilty to capital murder and was sentenced to death by a New Jersey trial court. She asked the Supreme

Court to reverse the judgment on the grounds that New Jersey's procedure for accepting a guilty plea violated constitutional due process. Peckham, writing for the Court, rejected the argument. However, instead of addressing the constitutional challenge head-on, Peckham wrote that the Court did not have jurisdiction over the case because the issue presented was purely a state-law matter that did not involve a Federal constitutional question. Peckham died on October 24, 1909.

Capital Punishment Opinions Written by Peckham

Case Name	Opinion of the Court	Concurring Opinion	Dissenting Opinion
Elk v. United States	✓		
Mills v. United States	✓		
Stevenson v. United States	✓		
Tla-Koo-Yel-Lee v. United States	✓		
Valentina v. Mercer	✓		

Pecuniary Gain Aggravator   The phrase "pecuniary gain" encompasses more than just money, and can include anything that results in economic gain. The overwhelming majority of capital punishment jurisdictions have made pecuniary gain a statutory aggravating circumstance. In these jurisdictions the penalty phase jury may recommend the death penalty if it is determined that a capital felon committed murder for pecuniary gain. *See also* **Aggravating Circumstances**

JURISDICTIONS USING PECUNIARY GAIN AGGRAVATOR

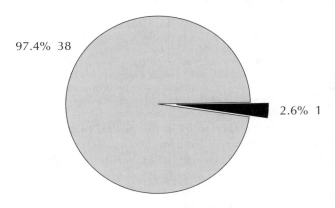

97.4% 38

2.6% 1

■ PECUNIARY GAIN AGGRAVATOR JURISDICTIONS

■ ALL OTHER JURISDICTIONS

Penalty Phase Discovery *see* **Discovery**

Penalty Phase Evidence   Capital felons have argued that the Federal Constitution requires that the standard for introducing evidence at the penalty phase be higher than that which is used at the guilt phase. Courts have rejected this contention. As a general rule, any relevant evidence may be introduced during the penalty phase. Wide latitude is granted to parties in introducing evidence in aggravation and mitigation during the capital penalty phase. The evidence, generally, need not satisfy the more restrictive rules of evidence that govern the guilt phase. Such evidence must have a direct bearing on the statutory prerequisites for imposition of the death penalty.

At the penalty phase the prosecutor and defense counsel may introduce and comment upon (1) any evidence raised at the guilt phase that is relevant to the special circumstances found in the indictment or information for which the capital felon was found guilty; (2) any other testimony or evidence relevant to the special circumstances found in the indictment or information; (3) evidence rebutting the existence of an aggravating or mitigating circumstance; (4) any presentence report that was produced; and (5) any mental examination report that was produced. *See also* **Hearsay; Hearsay Exception; Aggravating Circumstances; Mitigating Circumstances**

Penalty Phase Procedural Structure *see* **Trial Structure**

Penitentiary *see* **Death Row**

Pennsylvania
The State of Pennsylvania is a capital punishment jurisdiction. The State reenacted its death penalty law after the United States Supreme Court decision in *Furman v. Georgia*, 408 U.S. 238 (1972), on March 26, 1974.

Pennsylvania has a three-tier legal system. The State's legal system is composed of a supreme court, intermediate courts and courts of general jurisdiction. The Pennsylvania Supreme Court is presided over by a chief justice and six associate justices. The State has two intermediate appellate courts: The first intermediate court is called Superior Court and is composed of a president judge and 14 judges. The second intermediate court is called Commonwealth Court and is composed of a president judge and eight judges. The courts of general jurisdiction in the State are called Courts of Common Pleas. Capital offenses against the State of Pennsylvania are tried in the Courts of Common Pleas.

Members of the Pennsylvania Supreme Court: (left to right sitting) *Justice Stephen A. Zappala, Chief Justice John P. Flaherty, and Justice Ralph J. Cappy;* (left to right standing) *Justice Sandra Schultz Newman, Justice Ronald Castille, Justice Russell M. Nigro, and Justice Thomas G. Saylor.* (*Pennsylvania Supreme Court*)

Pennsylvania's capital punishment statute is triggered if a person commits a homicide under the following special circumstance: The offender commits an intentional killing.

Capital murder in Pennsylvania is punishable by death or life imprisonment. A capital prosecution in Pennsylvania is bifurcated into a guilt phase and penalty phase. A jury is used at both phases of a capital trial. It is required that, at the penalty phase, the jury unanimously agree that a death sentence is appropriate before it can be imposed. If the penalty phase jury is unable to reach a verdict, the trial judge is required to impose a sentence of life imprisonment. The decision of a penalty phase jury is binding on the trial court under the laws of Pennsylvania.

In order to impose a death sentence upon a defendant under Pennsylvania law, it is required that the prosecutor establish the existence of at least one of the following statutory aggravating circumstances at the penalty phase:

1. The victim was a firefighter, peace officer, public servant concerned in official detention, judge of any court in the unified judicial system, the Attorney General of Pennsylvania, a deputy attorney general, district attorney, assistant district attorney, member of the General Assembly, Governor, Lieutenant Governor, Auditor General, State Treasurer, State law enforcement official, local law enforcement official, Federal law enforcement official or person employed to assist or assisting any law enforcement official in the performance of his duties, who was killed in the performance of his duties or as a result of his official position.

2. The defendant paid or was paid by another person or had contracted to pay or be paid by another person or had conspired to pay or be paid by another person for the killing of the victim.

3. The victim was being held by the defendant for ransom or reward, or as a shield or hostage.

4. The death of the victim occurred while defendant was engaged in the hijacking of an aircraft.

5. The victim was a prosecution witness to a murder or other felony committed by the defendant and was killed for the purpose of preventing his testimony against the defendant in any grand jury or criminal proceeding involving such offenses.

6. The defendant committed a killing while in the perpetration of a felony.

7. In the commission of the offense the defendant knowingly created a grave risk of death to another person in addition to the victim of the offense.

8. The offense was committed by means of torture.

9. The defendant has a significant history of felony convictions involving the use or threat of violence to the person.

10. The defendant has been convicted of another Federal or State offense, committed either before or at the time of the offense at issue, for which a sentence of life imprisonment or death was imposable or the defendant was

undergoing a sentence of life imprisonment for any reason at the time of the commission of the offense.

11. The defendant has been convicted of another murder committed in any jurisdiction and committed either before or at the time of the offense at issue.

12. The defendant has been convicted of voluntary manslaughter, or a substantially equivalent crime in any other jurisdiction, committed either before or at the time of the offense at issue.

13. The defendant committed the killing or was an accomplice in the killing, while in the perpetration of a felony drug crime.

14. At the time of the killing, the victim was or had been involved, associated or in competition with the defendant in the sale, manufacture, distribution or delivery of any controlled substance or counterfeit controlled substance, and the defendant committed the killing or was an accomplice to the killing and the killing resulted from or was related to that association, involvement or competition to promote the defendant's activities in selling, manufacturing, distributing or delivering controlled substances or counterfeit controlled substances.

15. At the time of the killing, the victim was or had been a nongovernmental informant or had otherwise provided any investigative, law enforcement or police agency with information concerning criminal activity and the defendant committed the killing or was an accomplice to the killing and the killing was in retaliation for the victim's activities as a nongovernmental informant or in providing information concerning criminal activity to an investigative, law enforcement or police agency.

16. The victim was a child under 12 years of age.

17. At the time of the killing, the victim was in her third trimester of pregnancy or the defendant had knowledge of the victim's pregnancy.

18. At the time of the killing the defendant was subject to a court order restricting in any way the defendant's behavior toward the victim.

Although the Federal Constitution will not permit jurisdictions to prevent capital felons from presenting all relevant mitigating evidence at the penalty phase, Pennsylvania has provided the following statutory mitigating circumstances that permit the jury to reject imposition of the death penalty:

1. The defendant has no significant history of prior criminal convictions.

2. The defendant was under the influence of extreme mental or emotional disturbance.

3. The capacity of the defendant to appreciate the criminality of his conduct or to conform his conduct to the requirements of law was substantially impaired.

4. The age of the defendant at the time of the crime.

5. The defendant acted under extreme duress, although not such duress as to constitute a defense to prosecution or acted under the substantial domination of another person.

6. The victim was a participant in the defendant's homicidal conduct or consented to the homicidal acts.

7. The defendant's participation in the homicidal act was relatively minor.

8. Any other evidence of mitigation concerning the character and record of the defendant and the circumstances of his offense.

Under Pennsylvania's capital punishment statute, a sentence of death is automatically reviewed by the Pennsylvania Supreme Court. Pennsylvania uses lethal injection to carry out death sentences. The State has three sites for its death row facilities for men: Pittsburgh, Huntington and Graterford, Pennsylvania. The facility maintaining female death row inmates is located in Muncy, Pennsylvania.

Pursuant to the laws of Pennsylvania the Governor has authority to grant clemency in capital cases. The Governor is required to obtain the advice of the State's Board of Pardons.

From the start of modern capital punishment in 1976, through 1999, Pennsylvania executed three capital felons. During this period Pennsylvania did not execute any female capital felons, although four of its death row inmates during this period were females. A total of 225 capital felons were on death row in Pennsylvania in 1999. The 1999 death row population in the State was listed as: 139 black inmates; 70 white inmates; 14 Hispanic inmates; and two unidentified inmates. In 1999 the State had 2 juveniles on death row. The State permits capital punishment to be imposed on persons 16 years old or older. Pennsylvania does not prohibit the execution of mentally retarded capital felons.

Executions by Pennsylvania 1976–1999

Name	Race	Date of Execution	Method of Execution
Keith Zettlemoyer	White	May 2, 1995	Lethal Injection
Leon Moser	White	August 16, 1995	Lethal Injection
Gary Heidnick	White	July 6, 1999	Lethal Injection

PENNSYLVANIA EXECUTIONS 1976–1999

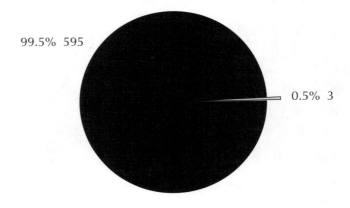

99.5% 595

0.5% 3

■ PENNSYLVANIA EXECUTIONS
■ ALL OTHER EXECUTIONS

EXECUTIONS BY PENNSYLVANIA 1930–1999

96.5% 4302

3.5% 155

■ PENNSYLVANIA

■ ALL OTHER JURISDICTIONS

Penry v. Lynaugh   *Court:* United States Supreme Court; *Case Citation:* Penry v. Lynaugh, 492 U.S. 302 (1989); *Argued:* January 11, 1989; *Decided:* June 26, 1989; *Opinion of the Court:* Justice O'Connor; *Concurring and Dissenting Opinion:* Justice Brennan, in which Marshall, J., joined; *Concurring and Dissenting Opinion:* Justice Stevens, in which Blackmun, J., joined; *Concurring and Dissenting Opinion:* Justice Scalia, in which Rehnquist, C. J., and White and Kennedy, JJ., joined; *Appellate Defense Counsel:* Curtis C. Mason argued and briefed; *Appellate Prosecution Counsel:* Charles A. Palmer argued; Jim Mattox, Mary F. Keller, Lou McCreary, Michael P. Hodge and William C. Zapalac on brief; *Amicus Curiae Brief Supporting Prosecutor:* None; *Amicus Curiae Brief Supporting Defendant:* 4.

Issues Presented: (1) Whether the Constitution is violated when a defendant proffers mitigating evidence that may be interpreted favorably or unfavorably and the trial court refuses to instruct the penalty phase jury on how it should consider and give effect to the defendant's mitigating evidence in imposing the sentence? (2) Whether the Constitution categorically prohibits executing a mentally retarded prisoner?

Case Holdings: (1) The Constitution is violated when a penalty phase jury is not instructed on how it may consider and give effect to the defendant's mitigating evidence in imposing its sentence. (2) The Constitution does not categorically prohibit executing a mentally retarded prisoner.

Factual and procedural background of case: The defendant, Johnny Paul Penry, was charged with capital murder by the State of Texas. He was found competent to stand trial, although a psychologist testified that he was mildly to moderately retarded and had the mental age of a 6½-year-old. At the guilt phase of the trial, the defendant raised an insanity defense. The jury rejected the defendant's insanity defense and found him guilty of capital murder. At the penalty phase of the trial, the defendant requested the trial court instruct the jury that it should interpret evidence of his mental retardation

and childhood abuse as mitigating circumstances and not as aggravating evidence. The trial court refused the request. The defendant was sentenced to death.

The Texas Court of Criminal Appeals affirmed the conviction and sentence. In doing so, the appellate court rejected the defendant's contention that his death sentence violated the Eighth Amendment because (1) the jury was not adequately instructed on how to consider all of his mitigating evidence and (2) because it was cruel and unusual punishment to execute a mentally retarded person. After the United States Supreme Court denied certiorari on direct review, the defendant filed a habeas corpus petition in a Federal District Court. The District Court denied relief. The defendant appealed, but the Court of Appeals denied relief. The United States Supreme Court granted certiorari under the habeas claim.

Opinion of the Court by Justice O'Connor: Justice O'Connor agreed with the defendant that the absence of instructions informing the jury that it could consider and give effect to his mitigating evidence of mental retardation and abused background, by declining to impose the death penalty, denied him the constitutional right to have his sentence imposed based upon a consideration of his disadvantaged background and mental problems. The opinion indicated that in order for the punishment imposed to be directly related to the personal culpability of the defendant, the sentencer must be allowed to consider and give effect to mitigating evidence relevant to a defendant's background, character, and crime. Justice O'Connor reasoned that full consideration of such mitigating evidence enhances the reliability of the jury's sentencing decision.

The opinion rejected the defendant's claim that the Constitution barred executing mentally retarded prisoners. Justice O'Connor went to great lengths to distinguish an "insane" prisoner from a prisoner who was merely mentally retarded. The opinion noted that under common law and the Court's own precedent, *Ford v. Wainwright*, an insane prisoner could not be executed. Justice O'Connor wrote that mentally retarded persons are individuals whose abilities and behavioral deficits can vary greatly depending on the degree of their retardation, their life experience, and the ameliorative effects of education and habilitation, therefore, as a generally matter the Constitution does not prohibit executing mentally retarded prisoners.

Accordingly, the opinion reversed the judgment because of the failure of the trial court to adequately instruct the jury, but affirmed that part of the judgment which found the defendant's mental retardation did not prevent him from being executed.

Concurring and dissenting opinion by Justice Brennan, in which Marshall, J., joined: Justice Brennan concurred and dissented on the following grounds: "I agree that the jury instructions given at sentencing in this case deprived [the defendant] of his constitutional right to have a jury consider all mitigating evidence that he presented before sentencing him to die. I would also hold, however, that the Eighth Amendment prohibits the execution of offenders who are mentally retarded and who thus lack the full degree of responsibility for their crimes that is a predicate for the constitutional imposition of the death penalty."

Concurring and dissenting opinion by Justice Stevens, in which Blackmun, J., joined: Justice Stevens concurred with the Courts reversal of the judgment on the issue of failure to instruct the jury properly. However, he believed the Constitution prohibited executing mentally retarded prisoners. He "would therefore reverse the judgment of the Court of Appeals in its entirety."

Concurring and dissenting opinion by Justice Scalia, in which Rehnquist, C. J., and White and Kennedy, JJ., joined: Justice Scalia concurred with the Court's finding that mentally retarded prisoners can be executed consistent with the Constitution. He dissented on the Court's decision that the jury was not adequately instructed. Justice Scalia argued that the Constitution was not offended by the trial court's refusal to provide specific instructions on how to interpret the defendant's mental retardation and childhood abuse. He wrote that "[t]he decision whether to impose the death penalty is a unitary one; unguided discretion not to impose is unguided discretion to impose as well. In holding that the jury had to be free to deem Penry's mental retardation and sad childhood relevant for whatever purpose it wished, the Court has come full circle, not only permitting but requiring what *Furman* once condemned ... [as] '[f]reakishly' and 'wantonly,' imposing the death penalty."

Case note: The decision in the case garnered a significant amount of negative commentary because of its determination that mentally retarded prisoners may be executed. Several states responded to the decision by enacting statutes that expressly prohibit the execution of mentally retarded prisoners. *See also* **Ford v. Wainwright; Insanity While Awaiting Execution; Mentally Retarded Capital Felon; Mitigating Circumstances**

People of Faith Against the Death Penalty

People of Faith Against the Death Penalty (PFADP) is a special project of the North Carolina Council of Churches. PFADP was created for the purpose of abolishing the death penalty through the mobilization and education of the religious community of North Carolina. The organization advocates supportive letter writing to death row inmates; lobbying lawmakers; and holding vigils at the prison gates when executions occur.

Per Curiam Opinion

A per curiam opinion is a written appellate opinion that does not assign the name of the appellate judge responsible for writing it. Per curiam opinions, as a general rule, do not create new principles of law. The United States Supreme Court has issued a number of per curiam capital punishment opinions. The most cited per curiam opinion by the Supreme Court was its ruling in *Furman v. Georgia*, 408 U.S. 238 (1972), which had the effect of striking down all capital punishment statutes in the nation. *See also* **Alcorta v. Texas; Arnold v. North Carolina; Cage v. Louisiana; Calderon v. Coleman; Coleman v. Alabama (II); Ciucci v. Illinois; Davis v. Georgia; Delo v. Lashley; Demosthenes v. Baal; Dobbs v. Zant; Espinosa v. Florida; Furman v. Georgia; Green v. Georgia; Hale v. Kentucky; Hildwin v. Florida; Maxwell v. Bishop; Powell v. Texas; Presnell v. Georgia; Roberts v. Louisiana (II); Rose v. Hodges; Shell v. Mississippi; Shepherd v. Florida; Sims v. Georgia (II); Stansbury v. California; Stephan v. United States; Stewart v. Massachusetts; Tuggle v. Netherland; Wainwright v. Goode; Zant v. Stephens (I)**

Peremptory Challenge *see* **Jury Selection**

Perovich v. United States

Court: United States Supreme Court; *Case Citation:* Perovich v. United States, 205 U.S. 86 (1907); *Argued:* January 21, 1907; *Decided:* March 11, 1907; *Opinion of the Court:* Justice Brewer; *Concurring Opinion:* None; *Dissenting Opinion:* None; *Appellate Defense Counsel:* Not represented; *Appellate Prosecution Counsel:* Mr. Cooley argued; Mr. Hoyt on brief; *Amicus Curiae Brief Supporting Prosecutor:* None; *Amicus Curiae Brief Supporting Defendant:* None.

Issue Presented: Whether the identity of the victim was sufficiently identified to sustain the judgment against the defendant?

Case Holding: The identity of the victim was sufficiently identified to sustain the judgment against the defendant, even though the victim's body was burned almost beyond recognition.

Factual and procedural background of case: The defendant, Vuko Perovich, was convicted of capital murder and sentenced to death by the United States. An appeal was filed on behalf of the defendant to the United States Supreme Court, alleging that the conviction was invalid because the prosecutor failed to prove the identity of the victim of the crime. The United States Supreme Court granted certiorari to consider the issue.

Opinion of the Court by Justice Brewer: Justice Brewer ruled that sufficient identification of the victim was established at the trial. The opinion addressed the issue as follows: "It is assigned for error that the court overruled a motion to instruct the jury to bring in a verdict of not guilty for the reason that the corpus delicti had not been proved.... While it is true there was no witness to the homicide and the identification of the body found in the cabin was not perfect, owing to its condition, caused by fire, yet, taking all the circumstances together, there was clearly enough to warrant the jury in finding that the partially burned body was that of [the named victim] and that he had been killed by the defendant." The judgment of the Federal trial court was affirmed. *See also* **Biddle v. Perovich; Corpus Delicti**

Persuasive Authority *see* **Binding Authority**

Peru Peru abolished capital punishment for ordinary crimes in 1979, but retains authority to impose the punishment for exceptional offenses. Its legal system is based on civil law. The nation adopted a constitution on December 31, 1993.

The judicial system consists of lower courts, superior courts, Supreme Court, and a Constitutional Tribunal. Defendants have the right to be present at their trial and have a right to retained or appointed counsel. *See also* **International Capital Punishment Nations**

Petit Jury *see* **Jury Selection**

Philippines Capital punishment is imposed by the Philippines. The Philippines carries out the death penalty by lethal injection. On February 9, 1999, the Philippines carried out its first execution since 1976. Its legal system is based on Spanish and Anglo-American law. The nation's constitution became effective on February 2, 1987.

The judicial system consists of local and regional trial courts, a National Court of Appeals, and a Supreme Court. The government has an anticorruption court, called Sandiganbayan, to hear criminal cases of misconduct brought against officials. Defendants have the right to counsel and be provided a speedy and public trial. Defendants are presumed innocent and have the right to confront witnesses against them and to appeal convictions. There is no jury system . All cases are heard by judges. *See also* **International Capital Punishment Nations**

Phyle v. Duffy *Court:* United States Supreme Court; *Case Citation:* Phyle v. Duffy, 334 U.S. 431 (1948); *Argued:* April 20–21, 1948; *Decided:* June 7, 1948; *Opinion of the Court:* Justice Black; *Concurring Opinion:* Justice Frankfurter, in which Douglas, Murphy and Rutledge, JJ., joined; *Dissenting Opinion:* None; *Appellate Defense Counsel:* Morris Lavine argued and briefed; *Appellate Prosecution Counsel:* Clarence Alinn argued and briefed; *Amicus Curiae Brief Supporting Prosecutor:* None; *Amicus Curiae Brief Supporting Defendant:* None.

Issue Presented: Whether the Due Process Clause required California provide the defendant with a judicial hearing to determine if he had returned to sanity as reported by a doctor in a non-judicial setting?

Case Holding: The constitutional issue presented would not be addressed in a habeas proceeding, because the defendant had another adequate remedy under State law.

Factual and procedural background of case: The defendant, Phyle, was convicted of capital murder and sentenced to death by the State of California. The California Supreme Court affirmed the conviction and sentence. After the defendant's trial ended he was found insane at a judicial hearing. Under the laws of California he could not be executed while insane. A subsequent determination was made that the defendant was sane and his execution was scheduled. The defendant filed a habeas corpus petition in the California Supreme Court challenging his scheduled execution, on the grounds that he was insane. In his habeas petition the defendant alleged that the doctor reached the determination of his return to sanity without notice, and without any opportunity on the defendant's part to obtain an original court hearing and adjudication of his sanity, or even to obtain a court review of the doctor's conclusion that he was sane. The defendant contended this procedure violated due process of law guaranteed to him by the Fourteenth Amendment of the Federal Constitution. The appellate court rejected the habeas petition. The United States Supreme Court granted certiorari to consider the issue.

Opinion of the Court by Justice Black: Justice Black ruled that the Court would not address the defendant's constitutional issue in a habeas proceeding, because under the laws of California the defendant had another remedy. The opinion indicated that under the laws of California, the method for challenging the determination that the defendant was sane, was through filing a writ of mandamus to "invoke judicial action to compel the warden to initiate judicial proceedings, and in which mandamus proceedings the court will hear and consider evidence to determine whether there is reason to believe that the [defendant] is insane." Justice Black reasoned that: "Applications for inquiries into sanity made by a defendant sentenced to death, unsupported by facts, and buttressed by no good reasons for believing that the defendant has lost his sanity, cannot, with any appropriate regard for society and for the judicial process, call for the delays in execution incident to full judicial inquiry. And a court can just as satisfactorily determine by mandamus as by direct application whether there are good reasons to have a full-fledged judicial inquiry into a defendant's sanity." The judgment of the California Supreme Court was affirmed.

Concurring opinion by Justice Frankfurter, in which Douglas, Murphy and Rutledge, JJ., joined: Justice Frankfurter concurred in the Court's decision. He wrote separately to express his view that the Court's ruling was contingent upon representations made by the State's counsel, that mandamus would be available for the defendant to use in challenging the decision that he had returned to sanity. *See also* **Insanity While Awaiting Execution; Solesbee v. Balkcom**

Pierre v. Louisiana *Court:* United States Supreme Court; *Case Citation:* Pierre v. Louisiana, 306 U.S. 354 (1939); *Argued:* February 3–6, 1939; *Decided:* February 27, 1939; *Opinion of the Court:* Justice Black; *Concurring Opinion:* None; *Dissenting Opinion:* None; *Appellate Defense Counsel:* Maurice R. Woulfe argued and briefed; *Appellate Prosecution Counsel:* John E. Fleury argued and briefed; *Amicus Curiae Brief Supporting Prosecutor:* None; *Amicus Curiae Brief Supporting Defendant:* None.

Issue Presented: Whether the defendant established that blacks were systematically excluded from the grand jury that indicted him and the petit jury that convicted him?

Case Holding: The defendant established that blacks were systematically excluded from the grand jury that indicted him and the petit jury that convicted him, therefore his conviction and death sentence could not stand.

Factual and procedural background of case: The defendant, Pierre, was convicted of capital murder and sentenced to death by the State of Louisiana. The Louisiana Supreme Court affirmed the judgment. In doing so, the appellate court rejected the defendant's argument that his conviction was void, because blacks were systematically excluded from the grand jury that indicted him and the petit jury that convicted him. The United States Supreme Court granted certiorari to consider the issue.

Opinion of the Court by Justice Black: Justice Black wrote that "[p]rinciples which forbid discrimination in the selection of Petit Juries also govern the selection of Grand Juries." It was said that in the prosecution of the defendant equal protection principles required "that, in the selection of jurors to pass upon his life …, there shall be no exclusion of his race, and no discrimination against them because of their color." The opinion found that the defendant produced sufficient evidence to establish that blacks were systematically excluded from the grand and petit juries involved in his prosecution. Justice Black noted that "[t]he fact that approximately one-half of the Parish's [or county's] population were [black] demonstrates that there could have been no lack of [black] residents over twenty-one years of age." The opinion "conclude[d] that the exclusion of [blacks] from jury service was not due to their failure to possess the statutory qualifications." The judgment of the Louisiana Supreme Court was reversed. *See also* **Discrimination in Grand or Petit Jury Selection**

Pitney, Mahlon

Mahlon Pitney served as an associate justice of the United States Supreme Court from 1912 to 1922. While on the Supreme Court Pitney was known for his conservative interpretation of the Constitution.

Pitney was born in Morristown, New Jersey on February 5, 1858. He attended Princeton University where he graduated in 1879. Pitney studied law as an apprentice in a law office and was admitted to the bar in New Jersey in 1882. His career included a private legal practice, member of the United States House of Representatives, member of the New Jersey senate and State supreme court judge. In 1912 President William Howard Taft appointed Pitney to the Supreme Court.

Pitney was known to have written only two capital punishment opinions. In *Lem Woon v. Oregon*, Pitney wrote the opinion of the Court. The issue presented in *Lem Woon* was whether the Constitution required Oregon to prosecute capital offenses by grand jury indictment. Pitney wrote the Federal Constitution did not require Oregon to prosecute capital offenses by grand jury indictment.

The opinion which gave Pitney the greatest legal notoriety was the decision in *Frank v. Mangum*. That case involved the prosecution of a Jewish American by the State of Georgia for the murder of a Christian woman. The case was emotionally turbulent, as local people sought swift justice against the defendant. The issue presented to the Supreme Court was whether the defendant's conviction and death sentence were obtained in violation of due process of law because of mob intimidation during his trial. Pitney, writing for the majority on the Court, found that there was no due process violation because of mob threats. (The defendant would eventually be lynched by a mob after his sentence was commuted by a Georgia governor.) Pitney died December 9, 1924.

Plain Error Rule

Under the plain error rule, an appellate court may address an assignment of error that was not properly preserved at the trial court level, if there was in fact (1) an error, (2) that is plain, and (3) affects substantial rights. There is no constitutional right to have plain error review in death penalty cases. *See also* **Jones v. United States (II)**

Plane Hijacking Aggravator

In a minority of capital punishment jurisdictions plane hijacking is a statutory aggravating circumstance. In these jurisdictions the death penalty may be imposed if it is found at the penalty phase that the victim was killed during a plane hijacking. *See also* **Aggravating Circumstances**

JURISDICTIONS USING PLANE HIJACKING AGGRAVATOR

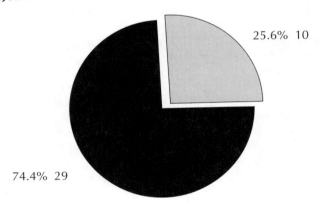

25.6% 10

74.4% 29

- ■ PLANE HIJACKING AGGRAVATOR JURISDICTIONS
- ■ ALL OTHER JURISDICTIONS

Plea Bargaining *see* **Guilty Plea; Nolo Contendere Plea**

Plurality Opinion

A plurality opinion is one where a majority of the members of an appellate court agree on the result reached in a case, but only a minority of its members agree with the reasoning used in the opinion that announces the appellate court's decision. The reasoning used in plurality opinion issued by an appellate court is considered persuasive authority, not binding authority on lower courts. The United States Supreme Court has issued a number of plurality capital punishment cases. *See also* **Barclay v. Florida; Burns v. Wilson; Coker v. Georgia; Franklin v. Lynaugh; Gardner v. Florida; Godfrey v. Georgia; Gregg v. Georgia; Harris v.**

South Carolina; Jurek v. Texas; Lilly v. Virginia; Lockett v. Ohio; Murray v. Giarratano; Proffitt v. Florida; Roberts v. Louisiana (I); Schad v. Arizona; Simmons v. South Carolina; Turner v. Pennsylvania; Watts v. Indiana; Woodson v. North Carolina

Pointer v. United States
Court: United States Supreme Court; *Case Citation:* Pointer v. United States, 151 U.S. 396 (1894); *Argued:* Not reported; *Decided:* January 22, 1894; *Opinion of the Court:* Justice Harlan; *Concurring Opinion:* None; *Dissenting Opinion:* None; *Appellate Defense Counsel:* S. B. Maxey argued; Jacob C. Hodges on brief; *Appellate Prosecution Counsel:* Mr. Whitney argued and briefed; *Amicus Curiae Brief Supporting Prosecutor:* None; *Amicus Curiae Brief Supporting Defendant:* None.

Issue Presented: Whether an indictment may set out two murder offenses?

Case Holding: An indictment may set out two murder offenses, in separate counts, which occurred close in time.

Factual and procedural background of case: The defendant, John Pointer, was indicted by the United States with committing two murders "at the Choctaw Nation, in [Native American] country[.]" The defendant was tried, convicted of both murders and sentenced to death. The defendant appealed to the United States Supreme Court, arguing that the indictment was defective because it improperly contained two murder offenses. The United States Supreme Court granted certiorari to consider the issue.

Opinion of the Court by Justice Harlan: Justice Harlan ruled that there was no merit to the defendant's contention that an indictment may not contain two murder offenses. The opinion reasoned as follows:

> While recognizing as fundamental the principle that the court must not permit the defendant to be embarrassed in his defense by a multiplicity of charges embraced in one indictment and to be tried by one jury, and while conceding that regularly or usually an indictment should not include more than one felony, the authorities concur in holding that a joinder in one indictment, in separate counts, of different felonies, at least of the same class or grade, and subject to the same punishment, is not necessarily fatal to the indictment ... and does not, in every case, by reason alone of such joinder, make it the duty of the court, upon motion of the accused, to compel the prosecutor to elect upon what one of the charges he will go to trial. The court is invested with such discretion as enables it to do justice between the government and the accused. If it be discovered at any time during a trial that the substantial rights of the accused may be prejudiced by a submission to the same jury of more than one distinct charge of felony among two or more of the same class, the court, according to the established principles of criminal law, can compel an election by the prosecutor....
>
> In the present case we cannot say, from anything on the fact of the indictment, that the court erred or abused its discretion in overruling the defendant's motion to quash the indictment or his motions for an election by the government between the two charges of murder. The indictment showed that the two murders were committed on the same day, in the same county and district, and with the same kind of instrument.... There was such close connection between the two killings in respect of

time, place, and occasion that it was difficult, if not impossible, to separate the proof of one charge from the proof of the other. It is, therefore, clear that the accused was not confounded in his defense by the union of the two offenses of murder in the same indictment, and that his substantial rights were not prejudiced by the refusal of the court to compel the prosecutor to elect upon which of the two charges he would proceed.

The judgment of the Federal trial court was affirmed. *See also* **Grand Jury**

Poland
Poland abolished capital punishment in 1997. *See also* **International Capital Punishment Nations**

Poland Brothers
Michael Kent Poland was born on June 11, 1940. His brother, Patrick Gene Poland, was born on March 8, 1950. On February 3, 1983, the Poland brothers were placed on death row by the State of Arizona. Michael was executed by lethal injection on June 16, 1999. Patrick is still on death row waiting to be executed.

The Poland brothers' journey to death row began on May 24, 1977. On that day a Purolator van containing $328,180 in cash, left Phoenix on a routine delivery to banks in various towns in northern Arizona. However, the van failed to make its deliveries. The police were notified and the abandoned van, with some $35,150 in cash, was discovered early the next day.

During the investigation into the apparent robbery, the police learned from witnesses that on the morning of May 24, the Purolator van was pulled over to the side of Highway I-17 by what appeared to be a police car. The witnesses identified the two uniformed police officers as Michael and Patrick. Neither of the Poland brothers was employed as a police officer.

The police further learned that on May 24 Michael and Patrick borrowed a pickup truck and tarpaulin from their father. The next day the brothers rented a boat at a marina on Lake Mead. A few days later, the brothers returned their father's truck with a new tarpaulin.

Michael Kent Poland, left, and his brother Patrick Gene Poland, right, received death sentences by the State of Arizona for killing two armored car security guards. Michael was executed on June 16, 1999. Patrick is still on death row. (Arizona Department of Corrections)

In the middle of June, the dead body of Cecil Newkirk, one of the guards of the Purolator van, surfaced on the Nevada side of Lake Mead. The body was partially covered by a canvas bag. A week later, authorities found the dead body of the other Purolator guard, Russell Dempsey, a short distance from where Cecil's body had been found. Autopsies indicated drowning as the cause of both deaths. Divers searching the area recovered a tarpaulin and a license plate bearing the insignia found on Arizona Department of Public Safety automobiles.

Authorities searched the homes of Michael and Patrick on July 27. They found a number of weapons, including a laser gun, large amounts of cash, and items of police-type paraphernalia. The police also discovered a scanner and scanner key which were capable of monitoring radio frequencies, a notebook listing local police frequencies. Both of the brothers had cars with siren-type burglar alarms which could be activated from inside or outside of the car. It was learned that the bothers purchased a "light bar" which could be placed on top of an automobile and would resemble a law enforcement light bar.

Finally, the police learned that, while neither Michael nor Patrick had regular employment, they made numerous large purchases during June and July of 1977. These purchases included appliances, furniture, motorcycles, and a business. The purchases were made in cash or by a cashier's check.

The Poland brothers were charged with the murder of the Purolator guards and robbery. The were tried together on October 23, 1979. They were both found guilty and on April 9, 1980, they were both sentenced to death. The conviction and sentences were reversed on appeal by the Arizona Supreme Court because of various reasons that included jury misconduct. A new trial was awarded. The brothers were again tried together on November 18, 1982. They were found guilty a second time. On February 3, 1983, they were again sentenced to death. The second judgments were affirmed on appeal. *See also* **Poland v. Arizona**

Poland v. Arizona
Court: United States Supreme Court; *Case Citation:* Poland v. Arizona, 476 U.S. 147 (1986); *Argued:* February 24, 1986; *Decided:* May 5, 1986; *Opinion of the Court:* Justice White; *Concurring Opinion:* None; *Dissenting Opinion:* Justice Marshall, in which Brennan and Blackmun, JJ., joined; *Appellate Defense Counsel:* H. K. Wilhelmsen argued; Marc E. Hammond on brief; *Appellate Prosecution Counsel:* Gerald R. Grant argued; Robert K. Corbin on brief; *Amicus Curiae Brief Supporting Prosecutor:* None; *Amicus Curiae Brief Supporting Defendant:* None.

Issue Presented: Whether the Double Jeopardy Clause bars a further capital sentencing proceeding when, on appeal from a sentence of death, the appellate court finds the evidence insufficient to support the only aggravating factor on which the sentencing court relied, but does not find the evidence insufficient to support the death penalty on other aggravating factors?

Case Holding: The Double Jeopardy Clause does not bar a further capital sentencing proceeding when, on appeal from a sentence of death, the appellate court finds the evidence insufficient to support the only aggravating factor on which the sentencing court relied, but does not find the evidence insufficient to support the death penalty on other aggravating factors.

Factual and procedural background of case: The defendants, Michael and Patrick Poland, were convicted and sentenced to death for capital murder during the course of a robbery by the State of Arizona. On appeal the Arizona Supreme Court reversed the convictions and death sentences. The appellate court found that the evidence was insufficient to support the trial judge's finding that the murder was "especially heinous, cruel, or depraved" (a statutory aggravating circumstance). It was determined by the appellate court that the trial judge erred in finding the "pecuniary gain" statutory aggravating circumstance did not apply to robbery of a bank. The appellate court remanded the case for a new trial.

At the second trial the defendants were again convicted of capital murder. At the second non-jury penalty phase proceeding the trial judge found the existence of both, the "pecuniary gain" and "especially heinous, cruel, or depraved" statutory aggravating circumstances. The sentence of death was again imposed on each defendant. The Arizona Supreme Court affirmed the convictions and death sentences. In doing so, the appellate court found that the evidence did not support finding the existence of the "especially heinous, cruel, or depraved" factor, but the evidence did sustain finding the existence of the "pecuniary gain" factor. The appellate court also rejected the defendants' argument that the Double Jeopardy Clause barred reimposition of the death penalty. The United States Supreme Court granted certiorari to consider the issue.

Opinion of the Court by Justice White: Justice White ruled that reimposing the death penalty on the defendants did not violate the Double Jeopardy Clause. The opinion acknowledged that in *Bullington v. Missouri* and *Arizona v. Rumsey*, the "Court held that a defendant sentenced to life imprisonment by a capital sentencing jury is protected by the Double Jeopardy Clause against imposition of the death penalty in the event that he obtains reversal of his conviction and is retried and reconvicted." Justice White stated that the decision in the case was not inconsistent with *Bullington* and *Rumsey*, because under those cases the relevant inquiry is whether there was a determination made that the prosecutor failed to prove its case for the death penalty and which meant that there was an acquittal on the sentence of death. The opinion addressed this issue as follows:

> At no point during [the defendants'] first capital sentencing hearing and appeal did either the sentencer or the reviewing court hold that the prosecution had "failed to prove its case" that [the defendants] deserved the death penalty. Plainly, the sentencing judge did not acquit, for he imposed the death penalty. While the Arizona Supreme Court held that the sentencing judge erred in relying on the "especially heinous, cruel, or depraved" aggravating circumstance, it did not hold that the prosecution had failed to prove its case for the death penalty. Indeed, the court clearly indicated that there had been no such failure

by remarking that "the trial court mistook the law when it did not find that the defendants 'committed the offense as consideration for the receipt, or in expectation of the receipt, of anything of pecuniary value,'" and that "[u]pon retrial, if the defendants are again convicted of first degree murder, the court may find the existence of this aggravating circumstance[.]"

The judgment of the Arizona Supreme Court was affirmed.

Dissenting opinion by Justice Marshall, in which Brennan and Blackmun, JJ., joined: Justice Marshall dissented from the majority decision. He believed that the Double Jeopardy Clause was violated by the imposition of the death sentences a second time. He wrote:

> In these cases, the trial judge found death to be the appropriate punishment because [the defendants'] offenses were "especially heinous, cruel, or depraved." On appeal, the Arizona Supreme Court held that the sole basis offered by the trial court to support its "conviction" of [the defendants] was insufficient as a matter of law....
>
> The majority believes that, since other aggravating circumstances might have been found to support the "convictions," it was permissible to remand the cases for further factfinding on those alternative factors. But this overlooks what our cases have said a conviction is in the sentencing context — a determination that death is the appropriate penalty, not separate trials on the existence of all statutory aggravating circumstances, conducted seriatim. In these cases, that determination was reversed because there was insufficient evidence to support the ground relied on by the trial judge in reaching it. Any remand for further factfinding on the question whether the death sentence should be imposed was thereafter prohibited. In no other circumstance would the Double Jeopardy Clause countenance the offer of a second chance to the State and the trial judge to find a better theory upon which to base a conviction. Nor should it do so here. I dissent.

See also **Arizona v. Rumsey; Bullington v. Missouri; Double Jeopardy Clause; Poland Brothers; Stroud v. United States**

Pope John Paul II

During the latter part of the 1990s, Pope John Paul II took an aggressive role in speaking out against the use of capital punishment in the United States. The Pope's strong anti–death penalty position bore fruit during his visit to the United States in January of 1999.

While speaking in St. Louis, Missouri the Pope criticized capital punishment as cruel and unnecessary. During a prayer service the Pope made a passionate plea for mercy and forgiveness. In attendance at the prayer service was Missouri Governor Mel Carnahan. On the day after the Pope's prayer service, Governor Carnahan commuted the death sentence of Darrell Mease to life imprisonment. Mease had been scheduled for execution during the Pope's visit to St. Louis. However, as a direct result of an unprecedented display of the Pope's influence, Mease was spared execution.

Portugal

Capital punishment was abolished by Portugal for ordinary crimes in 1867, and was completely abolished for all crimes in 1976. *See also* **International Capital Punishment Nations**

Post-Conviction Remedies *see* Habeas Corpus

Post-Furman Capital Punishment *see* Impact of the Furman Decision

Powell, Lewis F., Jr.

Lewis F. Powell, Jr., served as an associate justice of the United States Supreme Court from 1972 to 1987. While on the Supreme Court Powell was known as a moderate conservative interpreter of the Constitution.

Powell was born in Suffolk, Virginia on November 19, 1907. He was educated at Washington and Lee University where received a bachelor's degree in 1929 and a law degree in 1931. Powell also received a graduate degree from Harvard Law School in 1932. He led a relatively obscure and nonpolitical life as a practicing attorney until President Richard M. Nixon appointed him to the Supreme Court in 1972.

Powell wrote numerous capital punishment opinions while on the Supreme Court. The capital punishment opinion written by him which had the most impact was *McCleskey v. Kemp*. In *McCleskey* the defendant presented statistical evidence to establish that Georgia's capital punishment system was being implemented in a racially discriminatory manner. Powell, writing for the Court, acknowledged that the statistical evidence showed a racial disparity in capital prosecutions in Georgia. However, Powell concluded that such disparity did not sufficiently rise to the level of a constitutional violation. Powell died on August 25, 1998.

Capital Punishment Opinions Written by Powell

Case Name	Opinion of the Court	Plurality Opinion	Concurring Opinion	Dissenting Opinion	Concurring and Dissenting
Booth v. Maryland	✓				
Bullington v. Missouri				✓	
Burger v. Kemp				✓	
Coker v. Georgia					✓
Darden v. Wainwright	✓				
Eddings v. Oklahoma	✓				
Ford v. Wainwright			✓		
Furman v. Georgia				✓	
Gray v. Mississippi			✓		
McCleskey v. Kemp	✓				
Presnell v. Georgia				✓	
Proffitt v. Florida		✓			
Skipper v. South Carolina			✓		
Turner v. Murray				✓	
Zant v. Stephens (I)				✓	

Powell v. Alabama

Court: United States Supreme Court; *Case Citation:* Powell v. Alabama, 287 U.S. 45 (1932); *Argued:* October 10, 1932; *Decided:* November 7, 1932; *Opinion of the Court:* Justice Sutherland; *Concurring Opinion:* None; *Dissenting Opinion:* Justice Butler, in which McReynolds, J., joined; *Appellate Defense Counsel:* Walter H.

Pollak argued and briefed; *Appellate Prosecution Counsel:* Thomas E. Knight, Jr. argued and briefed; *Amicus Curiae Brief Supporting Prosecutor:* None; *Amicus Curiae Brief Supporting Defendant:* None.

Issue Presented: Whether the defendants had a Federal Constitutional right to appointment of counsel in their capital prosecutions by the State of Alabama?

Case Holding: The defendants had a Federal Constitutional right to appointment of counsel in their capital prosecutions by the State of Alabama.

Factual and procedural background of case: This case involved seven defendants, all black, convicted of rape and sentenced to death by the State of Alabama. The Alabama Supreme Court affirmed the convictions and sentences. In doing so, the appellate court rejected the defendants' argument that they were denied counsel. The United States Supreme Court granted certiorari to consider the issue.

Opinion of the Court by Justice Sutherland: Justice Sutherland ruled that the defendants were denied the right to counsel within the meaning of the Constitution. The issue was addressed by his opinion as follows:

> It is hardly necessary to say that the right to counsel being conceded, a defendant should be afforded a fair opportunity to secure counsel of his own choice. Not only was that not done here, but such designation of counsel as was attempted was either so indefinite or so close upon the trial as to amount to a denial of effective and substantial aid in that regard....
>
> April 6, six days after indictment, the trials began. When the first case was called, the court inquired whether the parties were ready for trial. The state's attorney replied that he was ready to proceed. No one answered for the defendants or appeared to represent or defend them. Mr. Roddy, a Tennessee lawyer not a member of the local bar, addressed the court, saying that he had not been employed, but that people who were interested had spoken to him about the case. He was asked by the court whether he intended to appear for the defendants, and answered that he would like to appear along with counsel that the court might appoint.... [The trial court also appointed a local lawyer named Mr. Moody.]
>
> It thus will be seen that until the very morning of the trial no lawyer had been named or definitely designated to represent the defendants. Prior to that time, the trial judge had appointed all the members of the bar for the limited purpose of arraigning the defendants. Whether they would represent the defendants thereafter, if no counsel appeared in their behalf, was a matter of speculation only, or, as the judge indicated, of mere anticipation on the part of the court....
>
> It is not enough to assume that counsel thus precipitated into the case thought there was no defense, and exercised their best judgment in proceeding to trial without preparation. Neither they nor the court could say what a prompt and thorough-going investigation might disclose as to the facts. No attempt was made to investigate. No opportunity to do so was given. Defendants were immediately hurried to trial.... Under the circumstances disclosed, we hold that defendants were not accorded the right of counsel in any substantial sense. To decide otherwise, would simply be to ignore actualities....
>
> ... [T]he necessity of counsel was so vital and imperative that the failure of the trial court to make an effective appointment of counsel was ... a denial of due process within the meaning of the Fourteenth Amendment. Whether this would be so in other criminal prosecutions, or under other circumstances, we

need not determine. All that it is necessary now to decide, as we do decide, is that in a capital case, where the defendant is unable to employ counsel, and is incapable adequately of making his own defense because of ignorance, feeble-mindedness, illiteracy, or the like, it is the duty of the court, whether requested or not, to assign counsel for him as a necessary requisite of due process of law; and that duty is not discharged by an assignment at such a time or under such circumstances as to preclude the giving of effective aid in the preparation and trial of the case.

The judgments of the Alabama Supreme Court were reversed and the case was remanded for a new trial.

Dissenting opinion by Justice Butler, in which McReynolds, J., joined: Justice Butler dissented from the Court's decision. He argued that the record did not support the claim of lack of counsel or ineffective assistance of counsel. Justice Butler wrote: "If there had been any lack of opportunity for preparation, trial counsel would have applied to the court for postponement. No such application was made. There was no suggestion, at the trial or in the motion for a new trial which they made, that Mr. Roddy or Mr. Moody was denied such opportunity or that they were not in fact fully prepared. The amended motion for new trial, by counsel who succeeded them, contains the first suggestion that defendants were denied counsel or opportunity to prepare for trial. But neither Mr. Roddy nor Mr. Moody has given any support to that claim. Their silence requires a finding that the claim is groundless for if it had any merit they would be bound to support it. And no one has come to suggest any lack of zeal or good faith on their part."

Case note: Under modern capital punishment jurisprudence the death penalty may not be imposed for the crime of rape without an accompanying homicide.

This case was significant because it marked the first time that the Court had enforced the Sixth Amendment right to counsel upon the States. The decision was limited, however, to appointment of counsel in capital cases. It would not be until 1963, that the Sixth Amendment right to counsel would be imposed upon States in non-capital cases. *See also* **Norris v. Alabama; Patterson v. Alabama; Rape and Capital Punishment; Right to Counsel**

Powell v. Texas *Court:* United States Supreme Court; *Case Citation:* Powell v. Texas, 492 U.S. 680 (1989); *Argued:* Not reported; *Decided:* July 3, 1989; *Opinion of the Court:* Per Curiam; *Concurring Opinion:* None; *Dissenting Opinion:* None; *Appellate Defense Counsel:* Not reported; *Appellate Prosecution Counsel:* Not reported; *Amicus Curiae Brief Supporting Prosecutor:* Not reported; *Amicus Curiae Brief Supporting Defendant:* Not reported.

Issue Presented: Whether it was error to permit psychiatrists to testify during the penalty phase that the defendant would be dangerous in the future?

Case Holding: It was error to permit psychiatrists to testify during the penalty phase that the defendant would be dangerous in the future, when the manner in which the psychiatrists obtained information about the defendant violated his constitutional rights.

Factual and procedural background of case: The defendant, Powell, was charged with capital murder by the State of Texas. Prior to his trial, the court ordered that a psychiatric examination be conducted to determine his competency to stand trial. The defendant and his counsel were not notified that the defendant would be examined on the issue of future dangerousness, and the defendant was not informed of his right to remain silent.

The guilt phase jury convicted the defendant of capital murder. During the penalty phase the psychiatrists who examined the defendant were permitted to testify that he would commit future acts of violence that would constitute a continuing threat to society. The penalty phase jury sentenced the defendant to death. On appeal the Texas Court of Criminal Appeals affirmed the conviction and sentence. In doing so, it rejected the defendant's claim that his constitutional rights were violated when the psychiatrists were allowed to testify on the issue of his future dangerousness. The United States Supreme Court granted certiorari to consider the issue.

Opinion of the Court was delivered Per Curiam: The opinion held that the testimony of the psychiatrists during the penalty phase violated the defendant's constitutional rights. It was said that under the Court's decisions in *Estelle v. Smith* and *Satterwhite v. Texas*, once a defendant is formally charged, the right to counsel precludes a psychiatric examination concerning future dangerousness without notice to counsel. Additionally, pursuant to *Estelle*, a capital defendant's constitutional right against compelled self-incrimination precludes subjecting a defendant to a psychiatric examination concerning future dangerousness without first informing the defendant of the right to remain silent, and that anything the defendant says can be used against him or her at a sentencing proceeding. The judgment of the Texas Court of Criminal Appeals was reversed. *See also* **Estelle v. Smith; Right to Counsel; Right to Remain Silent; Satterwhite v. Texas**

Precedent *see* **Binding Authority**

Pre-Furman Capital Punishment The decision of the United States Supreme Court in *Furman v. Georgia*, 408 U.S. 238 (1972), placed a moratorium on a form of punishment that had its origins in the American Colonies. The death penalty was commonly authorized for a wide variety of crimes in the American Colonies prior to the Revolution.

The American Colonies developed as an outgrowth of people migrating from England and other European nations. Virginia became the first colony when the first permanent English settlers arrived there in 1607. English settlers arrived to start the second colony in Massachusetts in 1620. By 1623 permanent settlements were made in New Hampshire. A year later New York was founded by Dutch families. The fifth colony, Maryland, was settled in 1634. Connecticut followed in 1635 and Rhode Island in 1636. Swedes settled Delaware in

1638. New Jersey was established in 1664. Pennsylvania was settled by Quakers in 1681. North Carolina was settled in 1653, and South Carolina was carved out of it in 1670. (The Carolinas actually formed a single colony until 1730.) Georgia, the last of the 13 colonies, was settled in 1733.

The colonists had from ten to 18 capital offenses. In 1636 the Massachusetts Bay Colony listed 13 crimes punishable by death. Most of the New England Colonies made 12 offenses capital. Rhode Island, with ten capital crimes, had the least number of all of the colonies. Offenses that were punishable by death typically included murder, treason, piracy, arson, rape, robbery, burglary, and sodomy. Execution of criminals was carried out by such methods as drowning, stoning, hanging, and beheading.

In 1682, Pennsylvania, under William Penn, limited capital punishment to murder. Following Penn's death in 1718, however, Pennsylvania greatly expanded the number of capital offenses.

After the Revolution the States uniformly followed the common law practice of making death the exclusive and mandatory sentence for certain specified offenses. Almost from the outset juries in the new nation reacted unfavorably to the harshness of mandatory death sentences. The States initially responded to public dissatisfaction with mandatory death statutes by limiting the classes of capital offenses. This mild effort at reform did not prevent juries from refusing to convict defendants rather than subject them to automatic death sentences.

In 1794, Pennsylvania addressed the problem by confining the mandatory death penalty to murder of the first degree. Other jurisdictions followed and within a generation the practice spread to most of the States. Ultimately, however, the division of murder into degrees was not a satisfactory means of identifying defendants appropriately punishable with death.

The next step taken, first by Tennessee in 1838, was to grant juries sentencing discretion in capital cases. Tennessee's decision

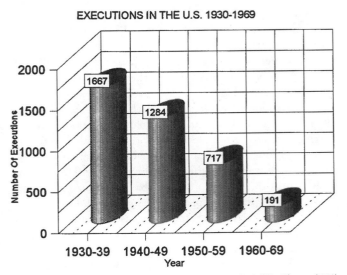

EXECUTIONS IN THE U.S. 1930-1969

Source: Bureau of Justice Statistics, Capital Punishment (1998)

to abandon mandatory death sentences was followed by Alabama in 1841 and Louisiana in 1846. By the turn of the century, the Federal government and 23 States had made death sentences discretionary for first-degree murder and other capital offenses. Fourteen additional States followed the trend by 1920. (In 1907 Kansas took the ultimate step and abolished capital punishment. Eight more states followed suit over the next ten years.) By 1963 all automatic death penalty statutes were replaced with discretionary jury sentencing.

Providing jury discretion in the imposition of capital punishment did not resolve dissatisfaction with capital punishment. In the early years of the 1960s, death penalty opponents litigated in courts throughout the nation in an effort to halt capital punishment. The activities of death penalty opponents during that period led to an unofficial moratorium on executions, after Luis Jose Monge was executed in the gas chamber at Colorado State Penitentiary, on June 2, 1967.

The focus of discontent with capital punishment was three-fold. Some people opposed the punishment because a disproportionate number of minorities were subjected to it. Other opponents found it unworkable because it was the poor in general who were subjected to the punishment. Finally, others were opposed to the punishment purely on the basis that it was a primitive and outmoded method of punishment.

The unofficial moratorium that was generated in 1967 became official on June 29, 1972, when the United States Supreme Court handed down its decision in *Furman*, which held that the procedures used to impose capital punishment violated the Cruel and Unusual Punishment Clause of the Eighth Amendment of the Federal Constitution. *See also* **Impact of the Furman Decision; Local Government Executions**

Pregnant Death Row Inmate *see* **Women and Capital Punishment**

Preliminary Hearing
The phrase "preliminary hearing" is typically used to describe any type of criminal hearing held before trial. However, the phrase has a technical meaning. In the strictest use of the phrase, preliminary hearing refers to a specific hearing held to determine whether sufficient evidence exists to submit a case to the grand jury for indictment consideration.

In all grand jury jurisdictions, a preliminary hearing is usually presided over by a court of limited jurisdiction, such as a magistrate court. At the preliminary hearing the magistrate must determine, without a jury, (1) whether there is probable cause to believe a felony crime was committed, and (2) whether there is probable cause to believe that the named defendant committed the felony. If probable cause is found for both issues presented to the magistrate, the case is bound over to a court of general jurisdiction for the purpose of having a grand jury consider the matter. If the magistrate finds that probable cause is lacking for one or both of the dispositive issues, the charge must be dismissed.

During a preliminary hearing a defendant has a right to be represented by counsel, to present evidence, and to cross examine witnesses. Generally trial court rules of evidence are relaxed at preliminary hearings.

Preparation for Execution
No single procedure is used by capital punishment jurisdictions in preparing a capital felon for execution, although similarities do exist for specific methods of execution. The protocol used by California, Arizona, and Oregon in preparing an inmate for death are set out below.

California Lethal Injection Protocol

When Execution Order Is Received: As soon as the execution order is received, the condemned inmate is moved into a special security area of the prison. Based on hourly checks, staff document his/her behavior and bring anything unusual to the warden's attention.

The inmate receives priority visiting privileges; no visitors are turned away without authorization of the warden. Every effort is made to accommodate visits by the inmate's attorney, including weekend or holiday visits if necessary.

Pre-Execution Reports: Two reports are prepared within three weeks of the established execution date. The first is 20 days before execution; the second is seven days before execution. Each report includes:

1. Psychiatric report — Results and interpretation of examinations, interviews and history of the inmate by three psychiatrists which will be used to determine the inmate's sanity.
2. Chaplain report — Comments on the inmate's spiritual and emotional well-being.
3. Summary of behavior — Observations noted by case worker and custody staff.
4. Cover letter from warden — Includes firsthand information from interviews, observations or communication with the inmate and his/her family or friends.

The seven day preexecution report discusses any changes that have occurred since the first report.

Sanity Review Requests: Within 30 to seven days before the execution, the inmate's attorney may submit current psychiatric information that may have a bearing on the sanity of the condemned inmate. This information will be provided to the panel of psychiatrists to consider in completion of the preexecution psychiatric reports.

Last 24 Hours: During the day before the execution, the warden will make special arrangements for visits by approved family members, spiritual advisors, and friends.

About 6 P.M. the day before the execution, the inmate will be moved to the death watch cell which is adjacent to the execution chamber. From then on, a three-member staff unit will provide a constant death watch.

Soon after he is rehoused, the inmate will be served his last dinner meal. The prison makes every effort to provide the meal requested by the inmate.

Between 7 and 10 P.M., the inmate may be visited by the assigned state chaplain and the warden. The inmate may read, watch television, or play the radio. He can request special food items and coffee or soft drinks.

The family, spiritual advisors and friends the inmate has selected as witnesses may arrive up to two hours before the scheduled execution.

About 30 minutes before the scheduled execution, the inmate is given a new pair of denim trousers and blue work shirt to wear. He is escorted into the execution chamber a few minutes before the appointed time and is strapped onto a table.

The inmate is connected to a cardiac monitor which is connected to a printer outside the execution chamber. An IV is started in two usable veins and a flow of normal saline solution is administered at a slow rate. (One line is held in reserve in case of a blockage or malfunction in the other.) The door is closed. The warden issues the execution order.

The Execution: In advance of the execution, syringes containing the following are prepared: 5.0 grams of sodium pentothal in 20–25 cc of diluent; 50 cc of pancuronium bromide; 50 cc of potassium chloride. Each chemical is lethal in the amounts administered.

At the warden's signal, sodium pentothal is administered, then the line is flushed with sterile normal saline solution. This is followed by pancuronium bromide, a saline flush, and finally, potassium chloride. As required by the California Penal Code, a physician is present to declare when death occurs.

After all witnesses have left, the body is removed with dignity and care. Typically, the family claims the body. If not, the State makes the arrangements.

Arizona Lethal Gas Protocol

Receipt of Execution Warrant: When an inmate receives a Warrant of Execution, a schedule is developed for submission of related forms and inmate movement. Inmates under a Warrant of Execution remain on death row until 48 to 24 hours prior to their scheduled execution. At that time, affected inmates are transferred to Death House.

Execution: One pound of sodium-cyanide is placed in a container underneath the gas chamber chair. The chair is made of perforated metal which allows the cyanide gas to pass through and fill the chamber. A bowl below the gas chamber contains sulfuric acid and distilled water. A lever is pulled and the sodium-cyanide falls into the solution, releasing the gas. It takes the prisoner several minutes to die. After the execution, the excess gas is released through an exhaust pipe which extends about 50 feet above Death House.

Oregon Lethal Injection Protocol

Receipt of Death Warrant:

1. Notifications:

    a. The Superintendent will personally notify the Director that the execution will commence at 12:01 A.M. or as soon thereafter as possible on the date specified in the warrant ordering execution. Such notification will be followed by a letter from the Superintendent to the Director confirming this information. The Director will subsequently notify the Governor of the date and time of the pending execution.

    b. The Superintendent, with the Assistant Superintendent of Security, will interview the inmate to be executed, provide the inmate with a copy of the death warrant, and document the interview.

    c. The Superintendent will send a letter to the medical examiner indicating the date and time of the scheduled execution, requesting that the medical examiner or his/her representative be present at the execution and be prepared to issue the certificate of death. The letter to the medical examiner will be sent by certified mail with a return receipt requested.

    d. The Superintendent or his/her designee will notify the Oregon State Police Superintendent's Office of the scheduled date and time of the execution, followed by a letter confirming the information.

2. Assembly of Supplies and Equipment:

    a. The Director shall prepare a written order to purchase the lethal substances as described by law and attach a certified copy of the judgment of the court imposing the punishment. The written order and copy of the judgment shall be submitted to the drug wholesaler at the time the lethal substances are purchased.

    b. The Superintendent or his/her designee will assemble the supplies and prepare the equipment necessary to effect the execution consistent with the law.

3. Selection of Executioner(s): The selection of the executioner(s) will be the responsibility of the Superintendent. The identity of the executioner(s) will remain confidential.

4. Arrangement will be made to ensure that the telephone company has installed two dedicated telephone lines, hereafter referred to as the emergency telephone lines, which will ring directly into the Intensive Management Unit execution room. The Director will advise the Governor and the Attorney General of the telephone process.

5. Special Security Team Preparations:

    a. The Assistant Superintendent of Security, or his/her designee subject to the Superintendent's approval, will select no less than six primary correctional personnel and no less than six alternate correctional personnel from a previously identified pool of correctional personnel to assist in conducting the execution procedure. These selected correctional personnel will be referred to as the special security team.

    b. The Assistant Superintendent of Security or his/her designee will conduct drills with the special security team simulating the movement of the inmate, restraints, and the lethal injection system. The Assistant Superintendent of Security or his/her designee will ensure that all members are fully aware of their roles during the procedure, and that the team is prepared to deal with any disruptive behavior which might be demonstrated by the inmate.

Witness Access Agreements:

1. Persons invited by the Superintendent of the Oregon State Penitentiary ("Penitentiary") who wish to attend and witness the execution of a Department inmate shall sign and strictly observe an access agreement drawn by the department that establishes the terms and conditions of access to the Penitentiary for the purpose of attending and witnessing the execution. The Superintendent will send to each invitee for the invitee's review and signature the original access agreement, together with the Superintendent's official invitation, via certified mail, return receipt requested. To accept the Superintendent's invitation, invitees must return the signed, original access agreement to the Superintendent no later than seven calendar days following receipt. Acceptance may also be made by faxing a copy of the signed agreement to the Superintendent no later than seven calendar days following receipt, provided that the Superintendent receives the signed original agreement by mail or hand-delivery no later than ten calendar days following invitee's receipt of the Superintendent's invitation. The Superintendent may, in his/her discretion, consistent with the policies expressed in these rules, extend the time for acceptance.

2. Terms and Conditions of Access: The witness access agreement shall specify, at a minimum, the following terms and conditions of access to the Penitentiary:

   a. Covenant to Strictly Adhere to Terms and Conditions of Access Agreement and Abide by Directions of Security Staff. In order to discharge its statutory responsibility to carry out death sentences imposed under Oregon law in a manner that is consistent with Oregon statutes and administrative rules, and with the safe, secure and orderly management and operation of the Oregon State Penitentiary, witnesses shall at all times strictly adhere to the terms and conditions of the access agreement, and abide by the directions of the Superintendent and security staff.

   b. Covenant of Nondisclosure. In order to protect the safety and security of Department staff and other persons involved in the conduct of the execution and the supervision of the condemned inmate, and the safety and security of their families, and to protect the personal privacy interests of such persons and insure their anonymity, witnesses shall not disclose either directly or indirectly in any manner whatsoever the physical appearance, attributes, characteristics or any other fact that would have a tendency to reveal the identity of any person, excluding only the Superintendent, that is directly involved in the conduct of the execution or supervision of the condemned inmate, specifically including: (1) the executioner(s); (2) medical professionals and medically trained persons; and (3) Department security staff and supervisors, including special security team members, and correctional officers supervising the condemned inmate in the execution room cell (M1). The covenant of nondisclosure will not apply to any information now or hereafter voluntarily disseminated by the Superintendent or Department to the public, or which otherwise becomes part of the public domain through lawful means.

   c. Remedies. Witnesses shall agree that in the event that they disclose information in violation of the access agreement, the Department is entitled to specific performance, including immediate issuance of a temporary restraining order or preliminary injunction enforcing the access agreement, and to judgment for damages caused by the witness' breach, and to any other remedies provided by law.

   d. Special Terms and Conditions of Access Applicable to Media Witnesses. Media witnesses, in addition to observing the general terms and conditions of access and covenant of nondisclosure applicable to all witnesses, shall return to the Oregon Department of Corrections Media Center at the Penitentiary immediately following the execution to brief those media representatives assembled regarding their observations of the execution and to answer the media representatives' questions. Media witnesses shall not file their own reports until after they have completed their responsibilities as pool reporters. Any media witness who fails to adhere to the terms and conditions of the access agreement may be barred from further access to the Penitentiary for purposes of attending, witnessing and reporting on executions. The Department may, in its discretion, also bar all other representatives of the media organization represented by the media witness.

   e. In addition to the covenant of nondisclosure and special terms and conditions for media witnesses, the access agreement may include such other terms and conditions governing access to the Penitentiary as the Department deems necessary or advisable in furtherance of the policies expressed in these and in other Department administrative rules.

Four Days Prior to Scheduled Execution Date:

1. Housing Assignment:

   a. No less than four days prior to the scheduled execution date, the condemned inmate will be moved to the Oregon State Penitentiary Intensive Management Unit (IMU) and celled in the execution room cell, M1.

   b. Security:

   A. Correctional officer(s) will be assigned by the Assistant Superintendent of Security or his/her designee to provide a 24-hour watch on the condemned inmate. The assigned correctional officer will maintain a log of all activities. The log entries must be written in ink, and cross-outs shall be legible and initialed. Copies of the logs will be hand-delivered to the Superintendent daily.

   B. Any unusual incident shall be prepared in accordance with the Department of Corrections procedure on Unusual Incident Reports.

2. Institutional Privileges:

    a. Mail: All incoming mail will be photocopied the last four days to ensure the inmate does not receive drug-infiltrated paper. The original letters will be maintained in the condemned inmate's property and a photocopy sent to the inmate.

    b. Visiting: At the discretion of the Superintendent, there may be daily visits with members of the inmate's family, approved religious representative(s), and such other persons as approved by the Superintendent or his/her designee, if they are on the approved visiting list and requested by the inmate. Visits must be arranged by appointment (i.e., dates, times and durations) through the Superintendent's Office. All visits will be restricted to basic visiting unless otherwise designated by the Superintendent.

    c. Telephone: Telephone privileges will be provided as approved by the Superintendent or his/her designee.

    d. Exercise: The condemned inmate will be permitted to exercise only in his/her cell.

    e. Clothing: New institutional clothing will be issued to the inmate and will be exchanged as needed. Clothing will be maintained in the secure confines of the Intensive Management Unit.

3. Personal Property Disposition: The Assistant Superintendent of Security or his/her designee will assure that a Personal Property Records form is signed by the inmate for disposition of personal property.

4. Food Preparations: The inmate will be served the same food as other inmates assigned to the Intensive Management Unit. At the discretion of the Superintendent, the inmate may be permitted a last meal of the inmate's choosing.

5. The Assistant Superintendent of Security or his/her designee will ensure the final preparations are made for the special security team.

6. The Assistant Director for Institutions or his/her designee and the Assistant Director for Programs or his/her designee will jointly work together to ensure that the equipment and supplies for the lethal injection are collected and deposited in secure storage located within the IMU.

7. The Oregon State Police will be notified by the Assistant Superintendent of Security so that adequate perimeter security will be established around the Penitentiary on the evening preceding the execution.

Forty-Eight Hours Prior to Execution:

1. The Superintendent or his/her designee will ensure that all arrangements as required by these rules have been accomplished.

2. The Assistant Superintendent of Security or his/her designee will conduct drills with the special security team to ensure that all team members are familiar with their duties and responsibilities.

3. The Assistant Superintendent of Security or his/her designee will have a process of identifying all witnesses and visitors who will be entering the facility on the evening of the execution.

4. The Superintendent or his/her designee will ensure that a sufficient number of staff have been scheduled to work the evening preceding the execution.

5. The Superintendent or his/her designee will ensure the necessary execution documents have been prepared/obtained to include:

    a. An appropriate certificate of death that reflects the cause of death as execution by lethal injection in the manner prescribed by law; and

    b. A form authorizing release of the body to be signed by the mortician.

Final Twenty-Four Hours to Execution:

1. An up-to-date log will be maintained on all execution related events which occur during the final 24 hours.

2. The Assistant Director for Programs or his/her designee will ensure that a medically trained individual will prepare and secure the necessary syringes with the lethal solutions. The necessary back-up syringes with the lethal solutions will be prepared and secured separately. This equipment and solutions will be provided to the Assistant Superintendent of Security or his/her designee for secure storage.

3. The Assistant Director for Programs or his/her designee will ensure that a medically trained individual will be available to insert an intravenous catheter(s) into an appropriate vein(s) of the condemned inmate.

4. The Superintendent will distribute written orders that all employees selected for special assignment duty will report to the Penitentiary at the appropriately designated time.

5. The Assistant Superintendent of Security will ensure that:

    a. All living units will be checked regularly;

    b. All towers will be posted;

    c. The reception desk staff will be provided with a list of the approved visitors and witnesses; and

    d. Escort officers will be identified for moving witnesses and visitors to the execution area.

6. The emergency telephone lines to the execution room will be checked at 6:00 P.M. and again at 9:00 P.M. Beginning at 9:30 P.M., they will be tested every half-hour until 11:30 P.M.

7. Approved Witnesses and Designated Media Representatives:

    a. Upon entering Penitentiary grounds, approved witnesses will remain in a designated staging area under staff supervision. Designated media representatives will remain in the Media Center until directed by staff to move their designated staging area.

    b. At the appropriate time, witnesses and media representatives will pass through the metal detector, be frisk searched, properly identified and have the back of their right hand stamped.

    c. Note pads, and pens or pencils issued by the Penitentiary to approved witnesses and media representatives will be the only items/equipment permitted inside the secure perimeter of the Penitentiary.

    d. The Department of Corrections Communications Manager will be stationed at the Media Center and will be the Department's contact person with the media.

8. The Assistant Superintendent of Programs or his/her designee will be assigned to the Administration Building and will be responsible for screening calls to the Penitentiary and ensuring that no unauthorized persons enter the Penitentiary.

9. The Assistant Superintendent of Programs or his/her designee will establish radio contact with the officer-in-charge of the IMU to ensure that messages can be conveyed in the event that the institutional telephone line or the emergency telephone lines become inoperable.

10. At 11:30 P.M., the Assistant Superintendent of Security or his/her designee will confirm accurate time for the clock used to conduct the execution.

Thirty Minutes Prior to Execution:

1. There will be no visits after the inmate has been moved to the execution room.

2. Movement of Inmates to Execution Room:

    a. The Special Security Team Leader will instruct the officer supervising cell M-1 to open the inmate's cell after restraints have been applied. The Special Security Team Leader will supervise the activities of the special security team members. The six special security team members will escort the inmate in security restraints from the cell and position and properly restrain the inmate on the table in the execution room.

    b. A medically trained person(s) will connect the heart monitor machine to the inmate.

    c. A medically trained person(s) will insert/connect intravenous catheters for lethal injection.

3. The Superintendent will accompany the executioner(s) to the execution room, and ensure that the confidentiality of the executioner(s) has not been compromised.

Twenty Minutes Prior to Execution:
The Assistant Superintendent of Administrative Services and/or other assigned personnel will escort the witnesses and all other approved visitors from the designated area to the IMU visiting processing station where they will enter the witness area. Two correctional captains will also be stationed in the witness area.

Execution Procedure:

1. The Assistant Superintendent of Security or his/her designee shall make a final inspection of all straps, and with the assistance of medically trained staff, make final inspection of the intravenous catheters, and the injection equipment. When it is determined all is in order, he/she shall so advise the Superintendent.

2. Upon receiving a signal from the Superintendent, the Assistant Superintendent of Security or his/her designee shall open the window coverings so that the witnesses can see the inmate in position on the table.

3. At 12:01 A.M. or as soon thereafter as possible, the Super-

intendent shall signal the executioner(s) to begin injection of lethal solutions by syringe(s) into the injection port of the intravenous catheters. As prescribed by law, the lethal solutions will include an ultra-short acting barbiturate in combination with a chemical paralytic agent and potassium chloride or other equally effective substances sufficient to cause death.

4. The executioner(s) shall signal the Superintendent when infusion of the lethal injection has been completed. Upon determining death of the inmate and time, the Superintendent will summon a medical professional to certify the inmate's death.

5. Once the inmate has been pronounced dead, the witnesses will be escorted from the witness area.

6. The Communications Manager will be notified of the time of the death and will inform the media assembled in the Oregon State Penitentiary Media Center. Media witnesses will be escorted to the Media Center where they will share information as prearranged.

7. The Assistant Superintendent, Security, or his/her designee will remain with the body in the execution room and supervise the removal of the body.

Stay of Execution: If, during any stage of the execution prior to infusion of the lethal injection, the Superintendent is notified that a stay of execution has been ordered, execution procedures shall be halted and the witnesses shall be removed.

Presentence Report
A presentence report represents a descriptive history of a defendant who has been convicted of a crime. Presentence reports are compiled by probation officers and submitted to trial judges for consideration prior to imposing sentence. The purpose of a presentence report is to give a trial judge an individualized assessment of a defendant, that includes a review of the defendant's family background and prior criminal history.

In the context of capital punishment, the United States Supreme Court has held that there is no Federal constitutional right to have a presentence report prepared in a capital prosecution. As a general rule, however, presentence reports are prepared prior to the start of a capital penalty phase proceeding. Courts permit penalty phase juries to consider relevant mitigating and aggravating aspects of a presentence report.

The United States Supreme Court had once held that a capital defendant did not have a constitutional right to see and contest information contained in a presentence report that was considered in imposing a death sentence. However, the Court eventually reversed its position and has held that information in a presentence report, to the extent it is relied upon to impose a sentence, must be seen by the defendant and an opportunity given to him or her to challenge information in the report. *See also* **Williams v. New York**

Presnell v. Georgia
Court: United States Supreme Court; *Case Citation:* Presnell v. Georgia, 439 U.S. 14 (1978); *Argued:* Not reported; *Decided:* November 6, 1978; *Opinion of*

the Court: Per Curiam; *Concurring Statement:* Justice Brennan; *Concurring Statement:* Justice Marshall; *Dissenting Opinion:* Justice Powell, in which Burger, C.J., and Rehnquist joined; *Appellate Defense Counsel:* Not reported; *Appellate Prosecution Counsel:* Not reported; *Amicus Curiae Brief Supporting Prosecutor:* Not reported; *Amicus Curiae Brief Supporting Defendant:* Not reported.

Issue Presented: Whether a sentence of death may be imposed under principles of felony murder, when the underlying non-capital offense conviction is invalid?

Case Holding: The Due Process Clause prohibits imposition of a death sentence under a felony murder theory, when the underlying non-capital offense conviction is invalid.

Factual and procedural background of case: The defendant, Presnell, was indicted by the State of Georgia on three counts of capital murder: (1) rape during the commission of murder; (2) kidnaping with bodily injury (aggravated sodomy) during the commission of murder; and (3) murder with malice aforethought. Only one victim was actually killed. During the guilt phase of the prosecution the jury returned a verdict of guilty of all three capital murder charges.

At the penalty phase of the defendant's trial, the jury was instructed by the trial judge that it could impose the death penalty (1) for rape if that offense was committed while the defendant was engaged in the commission of murder, (2) for kidnaping with bodily injury (aggravated sodomy) if that offense was committed while the defendant was engaged in the commission of rape, or (3) for murder if that offense was committed while the defendant was engaged in the commission of kidnaping with bodily harm (aggravated sodomy). The jury found that all three offenses were committed during the commission of the specified additional offenses, and it imposed three death sentences on the defendant.

On appeal, the Supreme Court of Georgia held that the first two death sentences imposed by the jury could not stand. Both sentences depended upon the defendant having committed forcible rape, and the appellate court determined that the jury had not properly convicted the defendant of that offense. The appellate court affirmed the death sentence for murder committed during the commission of kidnaping with bodily harm (aggravated sodomy). The Supreme Court of Georgia rejected the defendant's contention that the sentence affirmed was unconstitutional because the underlying rape charge was invalid. The United States Supreme Court granted certiorari to consider the issue.

Opinion of the Court was delivered Per Curiam: The per curiam opinion held that the death sentence affirmed by the Supreme Court of Georgia violated principles of due process. It was said that a fundamental principle of due process is that a sentence of death cannot rest on an invalid underlying conviction. The Court found that the underlying conviction for kidnaping with bodily injury was not proven, because the bodily injury (aggravated sodomy) element was not proven. Therefore the conviction and sentence of death were reversed.

Concurring Statement by Justice Brennan: Justice Brennan issued a statement concurring in the Court's judgment and indicating that he believed the death penalty violated the Constitution per se.

Concurring Statement by Justice Marshall: Justice Marshall issued a concurring statement indicating he joined the Court's judgment and pointed out that he believed that the death penalty in any proceeding was unconstitutional.

Dissenting opinion by Justice Powell, in which Burger, C.J., and Rehnquist joined: Justice Powell issued a dissenting opinion stating: "If, as the per curiam opinion for the Court states, the Supreme Court of Georgia had found [the defendant] guilty of kidnaping with bodily injury in spite of a failure of the jury to return a proper guilty verdict for that crime, I would join this decision. My review of the record and the opinion of the Georgia court, however, has convinced me that [the defendant's] conviction for that crime might well have been upheld on the basis of the jury's proper verdict. Because the opinion of the Supreme Court of Georgia is fundamentally ambiguous on this point, I would remand the case for clarification rather than vacating [the defendant's] sentence of death. Accordingly, I dissent." *See also* **Felony Murder**

Presumption of Innocence *see* **Burden of Proof at Guilt Phase**

Presumption of Innocence of Aggravators

Capital felons have argued that they have a Federal constitutional right to have trial courts instruct penalty phase juries that the law presumes a defendant is innocent of statutory aggravating circumstances and, consequently, the law presumes that the appropriate sentence for murder is punishment other than death. This contention has been uniformly rejected by courts considering the issue. Neither the Federal Constitution, nor any law, imposes a presumption of innocence of statutory aggravating circumstances. Conversely, there is no presumption of guilt of any statutory aggravating circumstance. *See also* **Aggravating Circumstances; Burden of Proof at Penalty Phase**

Presumption That Death Is the Proper Sentence

Capital felons have argued that death penalty statutes which provide that the trial court "shall impose" the death penalty if one or more aggravating circumstances are found and mitigating circumstances are held insufficient to call for leniency, creates an unconstitutional presumption that death is the proper sentence. This argument has been rejected as an improper reading of the phrase "shall impose." It has been said that the phrase merely directs trial courts as to what they must do, if the evidence finds that a death sentence is appropriate. The phrase does not require trial courts presume that death is appropriate. Such a presumption would be unconstitutional, if it was in fact required. *See also* **Walton v. Arizona**

Pretrial Publicity

The Due Process Clause of the Fourteenth Amendment guarantees to the criminally accused a fair trial by a panel of impartial jurors. Under Anglo-American jurisprudence there exists a presumption that a juror who has formed a pretrial opinion about the outcome of a case cannot be impartial.

The biggest obstacle to impaneling an impartial jury is pretrial publicity by the media. Unlike routine non-capital prosecutions, capital punishment prosecutions typically draw widespread pretrial media coverage. Such coverage oftentimes make it impossible for an impartial jury to be impaneled in the venue where the crime occurred. If it is determined before trial that media coverage of a crime was so extensive and prejudicial to the defendant, that selecting an impartial jury is unlikely, the defendant is constitutionally entitled to have the trial venue changed. *See also* **Buchalter v. New York; Darcy v. Handy; Due Process Clause; Irvin v. Dowd (II); Moore v. Dempsey; Mu'min v. Virginia; Rideau v. Louisiana; Stroble v. California; Venue**

Principal in the First Degree *see* Law of Parties

Principal in the Second Degree *see* Law of Parties

Prior Felony or Homicide Aggravator

A majority of capital punishment jurisdictions have made the existence of a prior felony or homicide a statutory aggravating circumstance. In these jurisdictions the death penalty may be imposed if it is found at the penalty phase that a defendant has a prior felony or homicide conviction.

Some courts have held that to be admissible during the penalty phase, a prior felony conviction judgment must have been entered against the capital defendant before the commission of the capital offense for which the death penalty is being sought. However, other courts have reasoned that contemporaneous convictions made prior to the capital sentencing phase may qualify as previous convictions in multiple victim prosecutions.

Courts restrict prosecutors to introducing only prior felony offenses during their penalty phase case-in-chief. Prosecutors may introduce evidence of prior non-felony convictions only as rebuttal evidence, if the capital felon opens the door to this by introducing evidence of good character or lack of a criminal history. Admissibility of evidence of prior convictions is limited to documents certifying the fact of a conviction, victim testimony or eyewitness testimony.

Evidence of unadjudicated conduct by the capital felon as an adult may be introduced in the prosecutor's penalty phase case-in-chief, only if the conduct involves violence against the victim. Unadjudicated conduct by a capital felon as a juvenile may only be introduced during the prosecutor's penalty phase case-in-chief, if the conduct involved a felonious crime of violence.

The factfinder at the penalty phase may not consider, as a statutory aggravator, a prior conviction that was unconstitutional and vacated. In order for a capital defendant to prevail on a claim that his or her death sentence was prejudicially based upon consideration of an unconstitutional prior conviction, he or she must show that the conviction was unconstitutional and that the punishment in the capital prosecution was enhanced in reliance upon the invalid conviction. *See also* **Johnson v. Mississippi; Aggravating Circumstances**

Prison Adjustment Mitigator

Capital felons have contended that evidence which indicates they can adjust well to prison life is relevant and mitigating and, therefore, they should be allowed to present such evidence during the penalty phase. Courts directly addressing this issue have agreed with capital felons and permit the introduction of prison adjustment evidence as non-statutory mitigating evidence. *See also* **Mitigating Circumstances**

Prison Chaplain

All capital punishment jurisdictions allow death row inmates to have access to spiritual advisors before execution. Although prison chaplains exist at all death penalty facilities, inmates may request that their own particular spiritual advisor speak with them before execution. *See also* **Spiritual Advisor**

Prisons *see* Death Row

Privilege Against Self-Incrimination *see* Right to Remain Silent

Pro Bono Legal Service

The Federal Constitution does not require jurisdictions provide legal counsel for indigents beyond the initial appeal. If the initial appeal process is unfavorable to a defendant, any subsequent collateral attack on the judgment does not require appointment of counsel. Consequently, the vast majority of collateral attacks on judgments are made pro se, i.e., by inmates without legal counsel.

Frequently in capital punishment cases attorneys will provide pro bono representation to death row inmates with legitimate grounds for collaterally attacking their judgment. Pro bono representation means that the attorney does not seek monetary compensation for his or her services.

JURISDICTIONS USING PRIOR FELONY OR HOMICIDE AGGRAVATOR

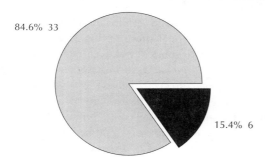

84.6% 33

15.4% 6

■ PRIOR FELONY OR HOMICIDE AGGRAVATOR JURISDICTIONS
■ ALL OTHER JURISDICTIONS

Probation Sentence A sentence to probation is not an option in capital punishment law. No death penalty statute authorizes a sentencing court to consider probation for a defendant convicted of capital murder.

Procedural Default of Constitutional Claims

Under the procedural default doctrine a defendant may forfeit any alleged error in a prosecution, by failing to present the issue to a court in the manner provided by general criminal procedural rules. It is said that the procedural default doctrine protects the integrity of the criminal justice system by imposing a forfeiture sanction for failure to follow applicable procedural rules, thereby deterring defendants from deviating from the jurisdiction's scheme.

The procedural default doctrine can be used to prevent a capital felon convicted in a State court from raising a federal constitutional claim in a federal court. That is, if a capital felon does not follow the procedures for presenting alleged constitutional errors to the attention of a State court, a federal court may employ the procedural default doctrine to preclude raising the issues in federal court.

Federal courts may not review Federal habeas corpus claims that were defaulted on by a defendant in a State habeas corpus proceeding, unless the defendant can demonstrate (1) cause for the default; (2) actual prejudice as a result of the alleged violation of federal law; or (3) that failure to consider the claims will result in a fundamental miscarriage of justice.

Although a tactical or intentional decision to forgo a procedural opportunity in State court normally cannot constitute cause to excuse a default on a claim, the failure of counsel to raise a constitutional issue reasonably unknown to him or her is a situation in which the "cause for the default" requirement is met. Establishing that the factual or legal basis for a claim was not reasonably available to counsel or that some interference by public officials made compliance impracticable, constitutes cause for the default. *See also* **Amadeo v. Zant; Coleman v. Thompson; Dugger v. Adams; In Re Jugiro; In Re Wood; Keizo v. Henry; Smith v. Murray**

Proffitt v. Florida *Court:* United States Supreme Court; *Case Citation:* Proffitt v. Florida, 428 U.S. 242 (1976); *Argued:* March 31, 1976; *Decided:* July 2, 1976; *Plurality Opinion:* Justice Powell announced the Court's judgment and delivered an opinion, in which Stewart and Stevens, JJ., joined; *Concurring Opinion:* Justice White, in which Burger, C. J., and Rehnquist, J., joined; *Concurring Statement:* Justice Blackmun; *Dissenting Statement:* Justice Brennan; *Dissenting Statement:* Justice Marshall; *Appellate Defense Counsel:* Clinton A. Curtis argued; Jack O. Johnson on brief; *Appellate Prosecution Counsel:* Robert L. Shevin argued; A. S. Johnston, George R. Georgieff, and Raymond L. Marky on brief; *Amicus Curiae Brief Supporting Prosecutor:* 2; *Amicus Curiae Brief Supporting Defendant:* 3.

Issue Presented: Whether the imposition of the sentence of death for the crime of murder under the law of Florida violates the Eighth and Fourteenth Amendments?

Case Holding: The imposition of the sentence of death for the crime of murder under the law of Florida does not violate Constitution.

Factual and procedural background of case: The defendant, Charles William Proffitt, was tried, found guilty, and sentenced to death for first-degree murder by the State of Florida. The conviction and sentence were under a new death penalty statute enacted by Florida, in response to the decision in *Furman v. Georgia*, which had the effect of invalidating all capital punishment statutes in the nation.

Under Florida's new death penalty statute, if a defendant was found guilty of a capital offense, a separate evidentiary penalty phase hearing was held before the trial judge and jury to determine the sentence. At the penalty phase the prosecution had to establish the existence of at least one statutory aggravating circumstance. The defense could present evidence in mitigation of the death penalty. The jury's verdict was determined by majority vote. However, it was only advisory. The actual sentence was determined by the trial judge. The new statute directed the trial judge to weigh the statutory aggravating and mitigating circumstances in determining the sentence to be imposed on a defendant. The new statute required that if the trial court imposed a sentence of death, it must set forth in writing its findings upon which the sentence of death was based as to the facts. The statute provided for automatic review by the Florida Supreme Court in all cases in which a death sentence had been imposed.

The defendant's conviction and death sentence were affirmed by the Florida Supreme Court. In doing so, the appellate court rejected the defendant's argument that Florida's new death penalty statute was unconstitutional. The United States Supreme Court granted certiorari to consider the constitutionality of Florida's new death penalty statute.

Plurality opinion in which Justice Powell announced the Court's judgment and in which Stewart and Stevens JJ., joined: Justice Powell made clear at the outset that imposition of the death penalty was not per se cruel and unusual punishment in violation of the Eighth and Fourteenth Amendments. The opinion then examined the procedures of Florida's new death penalty statute. Justice Powell wrote:

> On their face these procedures ... appear to meet the constitutional deficiencies identified in *Furman*. The sentencing authority in Florida, the trial judge, is directed to weigh ... aggravating factors against ... mitigating factors to determine whether the death penalty shall be imposed. This determination requires the trial judge to focus on the circumstances of the crime and the character of the individual defendant. He must, inter alia, consider whether the defendant has a prior criminal record, whether the defendant acted under duress or under the influence of extreme mental or emotional disturbance, whether the defendant's role in the crime was that of a minor accomplice, and whether the defendant's youth argues in favor of a more lenient sentence than might otherwise be imposed. The trial judge must also determine whether the crime was committed in the course of one of several enumerated felonies, whether it was committed for pecuniary gain, whether it was committed to assist in an escape from custody or to prevent a lawful arrest, and whether the crime was especially heinous, atrocious, or cruel. To

answer these questions ... the sentencing judge must focus on the individual circumstances of each homicide and each defendant.

In view of the procedures outlined in Florida's new death penalty statute, Justice Powell concluded: "Florida ... has responded to *Furman* by enacting legislation that passes constitutional muster. That legislation provides that after a person is convicted of first-degree murder, there shall be an informed, focused, guided, and objective inquiry into the question whether he should be sentenced to death. If a death sentence is imposed, the sentencing authority articulates in writing the statutory reasons that led to its decision. Those reasons, and the evidence supporting them, are conscientiously reviewed by a court which, because of its statewide jurisdiction, can assure consistency, fairness, and rationality in the evenhanded operation of the state law.... [T]his system serves to assure that sentences of death will not be 'wantonly' or 'freakishly' imposed." The opinion affirmed the judgment of the Florida Supreme Court.

Concurring opinion by Justice White, in which Burger, C. J., and Rehnquist, J., joined: Justice White wrote succinctly in his concurrence: "Under Florida law, the sentencing judge is required to impose the death penalty on all first-degree murderers as to whom the statutory aggravating factors outweigh the mitigating factors. There is good reason to anticipate, then, that as to certain categories of murderers, the penalty will not be imposed freakishly or rarely but will be imposed with regularity; and consequently it cannot be said that the death penalty in Florida as to those categories has ceased 'to be a credible deterrent or measurably to contribute to any other end of punishment in the criminal justice system.'"

Concurring Statement by Justice Blackmun: The concurring statement issued by Justice Blackmun read: "I concur in the judgment."

Dissenting statement by Justice Brennan: Justice Brennan issued a statement referencing to his dissent in *Gregg v. Georgia* as the basis for his dissent in this case.

Dissenting statement by Justice Marshall: Justice Marshall issued a statement referencing to his dissent in *Gregg v. Georgia* as the basis for his dissent in this case.

Case note: The decision in this case was significant because it was one of three decisions rendered by the Court in 1976, which had the effect of lifting the moratorium placed on capital punishment in the United States by the 1972 decision in *Furman v. Georgia. See also* **Gregg v. Georgia; Jurek v. Texas**

Prompt Presentment Rule *see* Arrest

Proportionality Review of Death Sentence *see* Appellate Review of Conviction and Death Sentence

Prosecution by Information An "information" is a criminal charging document that is drafted by a prosecutor and used to prosecute defendants. The use of an information came

about as an alternative to the grand jury indictment. The United States Supreme Court has held that use of an information by States to prosecute capital offenders does not violate the Federal Constitution. The Federal Constitution does, however, require Federal prosecutions of felony offenses be done by grand jury indictment. *See also* **Grand Jury; Hurtado v. California; Lem Woon v. Oregon**

Prosecutor The legal system in the United States may be divided into two broad categories: civil and criminal. In civil litigation individual citizens hire private attorneys to represent their interests. In criminal litigation a defendant has a constitutional right to be represented by private counsel (appointed or retained). However, the victim of a crime does not have a constitutional right to have a private attorney prosecute his or her case against a defendant. In criminal prosecutions government attorneys, called prosecutors, represent the interests of a crime victim.

Under modern capital punishment jurisprudence, the primary criticism facing prosecutors involves the broad discretion they have in prosecuting capital cases. A proper understanding of prosecutorial discretion in Anglo-American jurisprudence begins with its origin on the shores of England.

The Prosecutor Under Common Law: The English Crown made criminal prosecution an unregulated for-profit business. All crimes in England were punishable by fines and physical forms of punishment. Under the common law a fine included cash, as well as other personal and real property. Depending upon the nature of the offense, a convicted defendant's land could be confiscated by the Crown, as well as everything else he or she may have owned.

Although the English Parliament existed during the common law era, the Crown was the true sovereign authority. As the sovereign authority, it was the duty and responsibility of the Crown to maintain the peace and enforce the laws of the realm. This duty and responsibility meant apprehending and prosecuting law breakers. The Crown delegated, in large part, both its arrest and prosecution duties to the general public. In other words, both the Crown and common citizens carried out criminal prosecutorial duties.

Prosecution by the Crown. The English Crown employed numerous legal advisors. Some of the legal offices created by the Crown included: (1) King's advocate general, (2) King's attorney general, (3) King's solicitor general and (4) King's serjeants. Legal advisors employed by the Crown enjoyed the benefits of the inherent prerogative of the Crown, due to their association with the Crown. This meant that, in practice, legal advisors of the Crown were viewed literally as being above all other attorneys and treated with absolute deference in courts of law. It was said by one scholar that the Crown's attorney did not represent the Crown in court, because the Crown was theoretically always present. The attorney merely followed a case on behalf of the Crown. This framework of absolute deference to the Crown's attorneys, laid the seeds of prosecutorial discretion that is present in Anglo-American jurisprudence today.

In fulfilling its duty of prosecuting criminal offenders, the Crown relied primarily upon its attorney general, though King's serjeants were known to have played a minor role in this area of litigation as well. The Crown's attorney general did not prosecute all crimes, although it had the authority to do so. Instead, the attorney general limited its attention to major felony crimes like treason, murder, outlawry and robbery. The crime of murder and treason were of particular interest to the Crown, because the real property of defendants convicted of either offense escheated to the Crown. Enormous fines were appended to other major felony offenses.

The fact that the attorney general selected the cases it would prosecute (those bringing the greatest bounty to the Crown), was a prerogative act of discretion that could not be challenged by the courts or anyone, save the Crown itself. The attorney general represented the Crown and, as observed in *Skinner v. Dostert*, 278 S.E.2d 624 (W.Va. 1981), "[i]f the agent of the sovereign desired that a prosecution should [not occur], that was the end of the matter. The pubic subjects had no interest and could not be heard to complain."

Additionally, if the attorney general began a prosecution and decided it did not wish to proceed further, or if the prosecution was begun by a private citizen and the attorney general desired to terminate the action, it could do so by filing a *nolle prosequi*. It was noted by the court in *Skinner* that the nolle prosequi was "a statement by the [attorney general] that he would proceed no further in a criminal case…. The discretion to discontinue prosecution rested solely with the [attorney general] and it was unnecessary to obtain the permission of the court to give legal effect to this decision."

The underlying justification for permitting the attorney general to have absolute discretion in determining the fate of a prosecution, anchored itself to the fact that the Crown, as sovereign authority, was theoretically the only party interested in the prosecution.

Prosecution by citizens. Under the common law all citizens were permitted to prosecute criminal offenders in the name of the Crown. This privilege was monstrously abused because of the benefits that could be reaped by successful prosecutions. A citizen bringing a successful criminal prosecution could share in the proceeds of the invariably imposed fine.

Private prosecutors were also able to monetarily take advantage of the common law's rule that an acquittal could be appealed (rejected by Anglo-American jurisprudence). A defendant, acquitted of a crime, could be confined in jail pending an appeal of the acquittal. This situation usually resulted in the defendant entering a settlement agreement with the private prosecutor. The private prosecutor would agree to forgo an appeal in exchange for a monetary payment by the defendant.

Evolution of the Public Prosecutor in America:
The common law did not have a public prosecutor, as that term is understood today. Instead, the common law tolerated gross selective prosecution by the Crown's attorney general and wholesale prosecution by private citizens. Unfortunately this chaotic method of prosecuting criminals was transplanted to the American Colonies.

Fortunately, however, another method of prosecuting criminal defendants also took root in North America. This second method came not from England and the common law. When the Dutch founded the colony of New Netherland during the 17th century, they brought with them their system of prosecuting criminal defendants. A review of both methods of prosecution will follow.

Common law prosecution in the colonies. The Crown appointed an attorney general in all of the colonies. The first appointment was made in Virginia in 1643. The primary task of colonial attorneys general was to promote and protect the financial interests of the Crown. This meant that the bulk of the legal work performed by the colonial attorneys general was civil in nature.

Colonial attorneys general were also responsible for prosecuting criminal defendants. However, this duty was neglected. Rarely did colonial attorneys general prosecute criminal defendants. They intervened in this area only when a notorious major felony occurred. A routine murder was not considered notorious, unless it affected a colonial aristocrat.

The attitude of colonial attorneys general was the same as their brethren in England, *i.e.,* if the Crown did not obtain a substantial benefit from criminal prosecutions, there would be no prosecution by the sovereign authority whose duty it was to prosecute all crimes. Colonial judges did not challenge the discretion exercised by colonial attorneys general.

Two factors caused colonial judges to defer to the prosecutorial discretion of colonial attorneys general. First, the judges followed the legal principles of the common law. Under the common law it was held that the Crown's prosecutors had absolute discretion in deciding what course, if any, to take regarding a criminal offense. This common law principle was echoed in modern times in the case of *Newman v. United States*, 382 F.2d 479 (D.C. Cir. 1967) where it was said that "[f]ew subjects are less adapted to judicial review than the exercise by the [prosecutor] of his discretion in deciding when and whether to institute criminal proceedings, or what precise charge shall be made, or whether to dismiss a proceeding once brought."

The second factor which caused colonial judges to bow to the whim of colonial attorneys general, was the Crown. Colonial attorneys general were not ordinary attorneys. The Crown's prerogative was vested in colonial attorneys general when they carried out their legal duties. No colonial judge could muster the death-certain courage to tell the Crown when it should prosecute a criminal case.

The fact that colonial attorneys general rarely prosecuted criminal defendants, did not mean that vigorous criminal prosecutions were nonexistent in the colonies. Crime was routinely prosecuted. The citizens of the colonies prosecuted the vast majority of crimes.

The chaotic private prosecutorial method that existed in England was allowed to flourish in the colonies. The inducement used to encourage colonists to prosecute criminals was the same carrot used in England. Private prosecutors reaped monetary rewards for successfully prosecuting criminals. They also reaped rewards by intimidating defendants into settling criminal charges, prior to trial, by paying them monetary sums.

Criminal prosecution in New Netherland. The Dutch ventured to North America and settled a colony in the 17th century. They called their colony New Netherland (this colony comprised parts of Delaware, New Jersey, New York, Pennsylvania, and Connecticut). As would be expected, Dutch colonists brought with them the Dutch culture, social norms and system of government.

One aspect of the Dutch system of government that was brought with the colonists had a profound effect on Anglo-American jurisprudence. The legal system of the Dutch had an office called the *schout*. Although legal scholars rarely acknowledge the point, but it was the principles undergirding the office of schout which shaped the prosecutorial system that America would eventually adopt and utilize to this day.

The schout was a public prosecutor. Unlike the chaotic system of prosecution tolerated by the common law, Dutch law intrusted the task of prosecuting criminals in a single office — the office of schout. Dutch colonists did not haul their neighbors into criminal courts on real or monetarily imagined charges. If a criminal offense occurred, the office of schout prosecuted the crime.

When the English eventually took New Netherland from the Dutch, the term schout was buried. However, the idea of entrusting a public prosecutor with the responsibility for prosecuting all crimes took root and blossomed in America. The public prosecutor of today is a distant cousin of the common law and the first cousin of the schout.

Modern Day Public Prosecutor: The nation's prosecutorial system is a hybrid of the common law and the schout. When the American colonists threw off the yoke of the Crown, they also tossed out the common law's ad hoc approach to prosecuting criminal defendants. The nation unanimously moved in the direction of imposing the duty of prosecuting criminal defendants upon individual governments. Neither the nation nor its legal system was prepared to continue depending upon private citizens to prosecute criminals. Crime would be prosecuted, but it would be under the schout model.

Steven D. Stewart is the prosecutor for Clark County, Indiana. His office has prosecuted several capital cases during his tenure in office. (Clark County Prosecutor)

JURISDICTIONS THAT PROVIDE FOR POPULAR ELECTION OF CRIMINAL PROSECUTORS

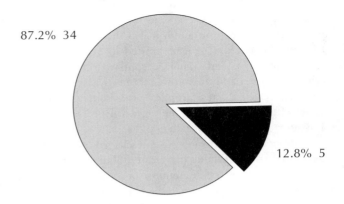

87.2% 34

12.8% 5

■ JURISDICTIONS THAT ELECT PROSECUTORS

■ ALL OTHER JURISDICTIONS

Today all jurisdictions have schouts, though they go by various names: district attorney, county prosecutor, state attorney, attorney general, or simply public prosecutor. A majority of capital punishment jurisdictions provide for the election of prosecutors on a local, usually county level.

Although Anglo-American jurisprudence rejected the common law's method of prosecuting crimes, the judiciary continues to adhere to the common law principle that a prosecutor has broad discretion regarding the disposition of criminal cases. Although the nation is not governed by a Crown, the judiciary continues to allow prosecutors to have almost unassailable prosecutorial power and authority.

The Powell propositions. In the case of *Wayte v. United States*, 470 U.S. 598 (1985), Justice Powell articulated the modern day justification for adhering to the common law's deference to prosecutors. Justice Powell reasoned as follows:

> This broad discretion rests largely on the recognition that the decision to prosecute is particularly ill-suited to judicial review. Such factors as the strength of the case, the prosecution's general deterrence value, the Government's enforcement priorities, and the case's relationship to the Government's overall enforcement plan are not readily susceptible to the kind of analysis the courts are competent to undertake. Judicial supervision in this area, moreover, entails systemic costs of particular concern. Examining the basis of a prosecution delays the criminal proceeding, threatens to chill law enforcement by subjecting the prosecutor's motives and decisionmaking to outside inquiry, and may undermine prosecutorial effectiveness by revealing the Government's enforcement policy. All these are substantial concerns that make the courts properly hesitant to examine the decision whether to prosecute.

Five propositions were offered by Justice Powell for the modern day deference to prosecutors: (1) inability to systematically analyze the prosecutor's decision making process; (2) oversight would be too costly; (3) wholesale review would clog up the system; (4) oversight would discourage prosecutions; and (5) oversight could make public, otherwise hidden agendas. The concerns expressed in the Powell propositions have merit. However, numerous commentators challenge the Powell propositions and the unbridled prosecutorial discretion they permit. At the core of arguments taken against deference to prosecutorial discretion stands one idea: prosecutors frequently abuse their discretion.

Death penalty charging discretion. The determination of whether to charge a person with a capital offense rests with the prosecutor. The power vested in the prosecutor is almost without limit.

Traditionally the determination of what penalty a convicted defendant will receive is made by the presiding judge, based upon the penalty range provided by statute. For example, if a prosecutor obtains a conviction for rape and the penalty for the offense is from five to 15 years imprisonment, the prosecutor cannot absolve the defendant from being subject to this penalty. At most, a prosecutor may recommend to the trial judge that the defendant receive probation or some other disposition. The court can accept or reject the recommendation. In other words, once a prosecutor charges a defendant with a crime the penalty automatically attaches and the prosecutor cannot, *sua sponte*, remove the defendant from exposure to the penalty (short of dismissing the charge).

Tradition is abandoned, however, in capital murder prosecutions. In this context the prosecutor can invade the traditionally exclusive domain of the trial judge. All capital punishment jurisdictions, except New Jersey, give prosecutors statutory discretion to waive the death penalty, sua sponte, for any death-eligible offense. It was said in *People ex rel. Carey v. Cousins*, 397 N.E.2d 809 (Ill. 1979), that the exercise of this discretion does not violate "the separation of powers provision of [federal or state constitutions], in that the prosecutor is given power to exercise a part of the sentencing process, which should properly be a judicial function."

The fact that a prosecutor waives or gives up the right to seek the death penalty in a case, does not mean that the case will not be prosecuted. The prosecution continues, but the maximum penalty a defendant would face upon conviction would be life imprisonment.

Capital felons consistently challenge death sentences on the grounds that the statutes under which they were convicted and sentenced gave unbridled discretion to prosecutors to seek or deny invoking death penalty provisions. This argument has never found a prevailing ear. In the case of *McCleskey v. Kemp*, 481 U.S. 279 (1987) the United States Supreme Court held the Federal Constitution does not mandate guidelines for prosecutors in administering the death penalty statutes.

Absent a showing of arbitrary and invidious discrimination, prosecutors have tremendous latitude when selecting those eligible cases in which the death penalty will actually be sought. That is, the decision to prosecute capitally cannot be intentionally based upon race, religion, gender, social status, or any other arbitrary classification. Prosecutors are also prohibited from basing the decision to capitally prosecute on a defendant's exercise of his or her statutory or constitutional rights.

Prosecutors are not required by the federal constitution to give reasons why they are seeking the death penalty. Political motivation is not per se a legal basis for challenging the propriety of a prosecutor's determination to seek the death penalty. Rather, the preeminent concern is whether a prosecutor has substantial evidence of statutory aggravating circumstances that would qualify a defendant for the death penalty. Courts have held that prosecutors may consider the wishes of a victim's family in deciding whether to seek the death penalty. *See also* **McCleskey v. Kemp; Notice of Intent to Seek the Death Penalty**

Prosecutor Aggravator A large minority of capital punishment jurisdictions provide that the killing of a prosecutor is a statutory aggravating circumstance. In such jurisdictions if it is shown at the penalty phase that the victim was a prosecutor killed because of his or her public work, the death penalty may be imposed. *See also* **Aggravating Circumstances**

JURISDICTIONS USING PROSECUTOR AGGRAVATOR

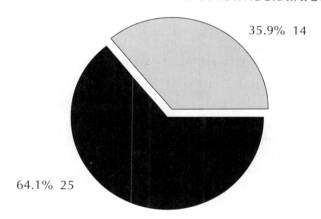

35.9% 14

64.1% 25

■ PROSECUTOR AGGRAVATOR JURISDICTIONS

■ ALL OTHER JURISDICTIONS

Protests Against Capital Punishment Thousands of national and international organizations have spoken out against capital punishment in the United States, and are actively seeking to abolish the punishment. Organized public opposition to the death penalty has been largely without incident. Peaceful demonstrations have been ongoing outside of prisons, state capitals, and the United States Supreme Court. Organized protests have involved candlelight vigils in front of prisons on the day of a scheduled execution. On rare occasions the police have been summoned to escort away a few overly aggressive demonstrators. Actual violence by organization members has not been reported.

One of the most intimidating death penalty protests occurred in February of 2000. This protest involved only two Texas death row inmates. The two inmates captured a female correctional officer and held her hostage. This incident was triggered by the inmates as a form of protest over the living conditions of death row. After less than 24 hours the two inmates released the correction officer unharmed without any concessions being made by authorities. *See also* **Opposition to Capital Punishment**

Public Trial   Under the Sixth Amendment of the Federal Constitution criminal defendants have a right to a "public trial." The constitutional right to a public trial seeks to prevent secretive prosecutions of citizens. Governments must prosecute criminal defendants in open court where the public may attend. Obviously qualifications exist to the right to a public trial. For example, courtrooms are limited in size so that only a fraction of a community may actually be able to attend a trial.

Although television cameras have the capacity to bring criminal trials into everyone's home, the right to a public trial does not extend to the right of the media to bring cameras into a courtroom. Trial courts have discretion to bar cameras from court proceedings. *See also* **Bill of Rights**

Public Viewing of Execution   All capital punishment jurisdictions impose restrictions on who may actually witness or view an execution. As outlined by the material under this heading, nonpublic executions were not always the norm in the nation.

Origin of Public Executions: The common law tolerated, for reasons that are forthcoming, having capital felons executed in full view of the public. Attending an execution was a routine part of life in England, under the common law. People gathered, much as they gather today at sporting events, with joy and enthusiasm to watch the condemned be put to death.

Anglo-American jurisprudence embraced England's practice of inviting the public to watch capital felons die. Public executions were an integral part of the early development of America. Prior to the 1830s all capital punishments in the United States were open to the public.

Neither England nor the United States permitted public executions for the sake of entertaining citizens. Two fundamental reasons guided the decision to allow the public to observe capital felons being put to death. One reason was aimed at the capital felon and the other was centered on the public.

The first justification for holding public executions involved the dehumanization of the capital felon. Capital crimes were offenses that society deemed unforgivable. Due to the perceived reprehensible nature of capital crimes, it was felt necessary to humiliate and degrade a capital offender by parading him or her in front of the public before, during and after execution. Whether or not a capital felon felt humiliated and degraded — as opposed to feeling scared to death — is an issue for psychologists to digest. Penologists believed capital felons felt dehumanized by being brought before the public for execution.

The second justification for holding public executions was grounded in the deterrent principle underpinning criminal punishment in general. It was thought that exposing the public to executions would deter others from committing, at minimum, capital crimes.

Movement Away from Public Executions: New York is historically credited with being the first jurisdiction to permit nonpublic executions. It did so by enacting a statute in 1835, which allowed the sheriff to hold executions out of public view (some revisionists have credited Pennsylvania with enacting a similar statute in 1834). Without realizing it, New York set in motion a penological reform movement that would eventually engulf the nation.

The New York statute was heralded as representing the evolving decency of society. Public executions were symbolic of a crude and unsophisticated society. Such a spectacle dehumanized not only the capital felon, it took away the humanity of those observing. In slow but steady fashion, the notion of evolving decency moved across the nation and jurisdictions began enacting statutes which took away the public's ability to view executions. The force of this movement touched down in England where, in 1868, that nation abolished the practice of holding public executions.

The theme of evolving decency came full circle in 1936. It was in 1936 that the last public execution occurred in the United States (some revisionists have suggested a later date). This execution took place in Owensboro, Kentucky. It was recorded that between ten and twenty thousand people came out to see the state of Kentucky hang 22-year-old Ramsey Bethea.

Judicial Challenges to Nonpublic Executions: Removal of executions from the public's eye has not gone unchallenged. Numerous attacks, cloaked in diverse motives, have been made to remove secrecy from executions. Some of the legal battles waged to reopen executions to the public are discussed below.

The right of the capital felon and the public. Penologists believed that public executions humiliated and degraded capital felons. This belief is difficult to digest when capital felons demand to have public executions. The first challenge to nonpublic executions came in 1890 and was made by a capital felon.

The United States Supreme Court picked up this challenge in the case of *Holden v. Minnesota*, 137 U.S. 483 (1890). The defendant in *Holden* had been sentenced to death for committing capital murder. At the time of his offense Minnesota permitted public executions (Minnesota currently does not allow capital punishment). However, shortly before his scheduled execution the state changed the law so that executions could no longer be held in public. The defendant argued that the change in law should not affect him, because at the time of his offense executions were public. It was contended by the defendant that the constitution's ban on ex post facto laws prohibited the new law from applying to him. The Supreme Court rejected the defendant's position and held that executions may be held out of public view. The decision in *Holden* has stood the test of time in championing the proposition that the general public does not have a right to attend an execution.

The media's right to film executions. The First Amendment is a powerful constitutional provision. In crystal clear words this amendment heralds the independence of the press (media), by proclaiming that governments cannot abridge the freedom of the press. Upon first impression it would seem that governments cannot bar the media from filming or photographing executions. This first impression has met a sad fate in judicial decisions.

In 1990 California was preparing to execute its first capital felon in 23 years. The recipient of this dubious distinction was named Robert Alton Harris. A local San Francisco television station, KQED, wanted to film the execution for posterity. The station approached California officials with a request to record the execution, but was turned down. Unperturbed, the station filed an equity proceeding, styled *KQED v. Vasquez*, No. C-90-1383 (N.D.Cal. August 6, 1991), in a federal district court seeking to force California to allow it to film Harris' execution. The district court rebuffed the station, and held that the state of California could constitutionally exclude cameras from its execution chamber.

In the case of *Halquist v. Dept. of Corrections*, 783 P.2d 1065 (Wash. 1989) a producer of radio and television documentaries asked officials in the state of Washington to allow him to videotape the execution of Charles Campbell. When the producer was turned down he filed an equity proceeding before the Washington Supreme Court. The producer contended that he had a right under the constitution of Washington to film the execution.

The state constitutional provision relied upon by the producer in *Halquist* provided that: "Every person may freely speak, write and publish on all subjects, being responsible for the abuse of that right." The producer argued that the latter state constitutional provision guaranteed him the right to film the execution. The court rebuffed this argument by noting that "the right to publish applies only to those who have previously and lawfully obtained information." The court also added that there was "a substantial difference between the right to publish already acquired information and the right to attend a proceeding for the purpose of news gathering." In placing the last nail in the producer's coffin, so to speak, the court observed that the United States Supreme Court took the position that "the First Amendment does not guarantee the press a constitutional right of special access to information not available to the public generally."

In *Garrett v. Estelle*, 556 F.2d 1274 (5th Cir. 1977) the State of Texas sought reversal of a Federal district court's decision ordering it to permit a television news cameraman to film executions. In reversing the decision of the Federal district court, the court of appeals held the following:

> Garrett asserts a first amendment right to gather news, which he contends can be limited only on account of a compelling state interest. He further argues that preventing him from using a motion picture camera to gather news denies him use of the tool of his trade and therefore denies him equal protection of the laws....
>
> News gathering is protected by the first amendment, for with-

out some protection for seeking out the news, freedom of the press could be eviscerated. This protection is not absolute, however. As the late Chief Justice Warren wrote for the Supreme Court, "The right to speak and publish does not carry with it the unrestrained right to gather information[.]"

> [T]he press has no greater right of access to information than does the public at large and ... the first amendment does not require government to make available to the press information not available to the public. This principle marks a limit to the first amendment protection of the press' right to gather news. Applying this principle to the present case, we hold that the first amendment does not invalidate nondiscriminatory prison access regulations.
>
> While we agree that the death penalty is a matter of wide public interest, we disagree that the protections of the first amendment depend upon the notoriety of an issue. The Supreme Court has held that the first amendment does not protect means of gathering news in prisons not available to the public generally, and this holding is not predicated upon the importance or degree of interest in the matter reported....
>
> Garrett next argues that to prevent his filming executions denies him equal protection of the law, since other members of the press are allowed free use of their usual reporting tools. This argument is also without merit. The Texas media regulation denies Garrett use of his camera, and it also denies the print reporter use of his camera, and the radio reporter use of his tape recorder. Garrett is free to make his report by means of anchor desk or stand-up delivery on the TV screen, or even by simulation. There is no denial of equal protection.

The right of a felon to videotape an execution. Capital felons have argued that the methods used to execute the death penalty are cruel and unusual. Several capital felons have sought to prove this argument by offering into evidence videotapes of capital felons being put to death. To obtain such evidence capital felons have to establish that they have a "right" to videotape executions.

In the case of *Campbell v. Blodgett*, 1993 U.S. App. LEXIS 1036 (9th Cir.), a capital felon, Charles Campbell, filed an action in a Federal district court seeking to force officials to allow him to videotape the hanging execution of Westley Allan Dodd. Campbell wanted to use the videotape in another proceeding where he had alleged that hanging was a cruel and unusual form of punishment. The Federal district court denied the request. Campbell appealed to a Federal court of appeals. The court of appeals stated that a videotape of Dodd's hanging would be insufficient proof that hanging was cruel and unusual, because it could not establish what degree of pain and suffering was endured. Therefore, the court of appeals affirmed the denial.

The case of *Fierro v. Gomez*, 1993 U.S. Dist. LEXIS 14445 (N.D.Cal.), presented a ray of hope for capital felons seeking to prove death penalty methods were cruel and unusual. Three capital felons brought this case into Federal court: David Fierro, Alejandro Gilbert Ruiz and Robert Alton Harris. In an effort to support their claim that California's use of lethal gas to execute felons was cruel and unusual punishment, the capital felons asked a Federal district court to issue an order permitting them to videotape the execution of Harris. The capital felons argued that the videotape would conclusively establish that death by lethal gas was cruel and unusual punishment.

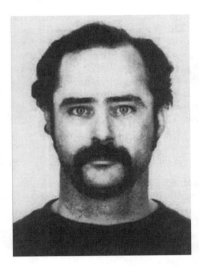

Robert Alton Harris' execution by the State of California was allowed to be video taped by a death row inmate, for the purpose of showing death by lethal gas violated the Cruel and Unusual Punishment Clause of the Federal Constitution. (California Department of Corrections)

The district court held that such a videotape would have some relevancy on the defendants' claim. Therefore, the district court issued an order allowing the capital felons to videotape the execution of Harris. The court explicitly required that only Harris be videotaped and not anyone else attending the execution.

In the case of *Petition of Thomas*, 155 F.R.D. 124 (D.Md. 1994), a capital felon challenged the state of Maryland's method of execution as being cruel and unusual punishment. In an effort to prove his claim, the defendant asked a federal district court to allow him to conduct discovery on the state. Part of the discovery that the defendant wanted to engage in was that of videotaping the execution of another capital felon. The court in that case ultimately ruled that the defendant could conduct discovery to support his challenge to the state's method of execution and, as part of that discovery, he could videotape the execution of a consenting death row inmate.

Statutory Limitations on Access to Executions: Methodically detailed rules and regulations have been promulgated by correctional agencies, which set out what the environment will consist of when an execution occurs. The overwhelming majority of capital punishment jurisdictions have provided, by statute, a few restrictions that help make up the rules and regulations for conducting an execution.

The material that follows reviews most of the statutory guidelines for carrying out the death penalty. It should be kept in mind that the bulk of the procedures for carrying out the death penalty are contained in administrative rules and regulations.

Attendance by family members of the victim. Only four capital punishment jurisdictions allow, by statute, family members of a victim to attend the execution. Two of the jurisdictions, Delaware and Louisiana, allow only one family member of the victim to attend the execution. Another jurisdiction, Ohio, sets the limit at three family members. The fourth jurisdiction, Washington, imposes no statutory limit on the number of family members that can attend the execution.

Family or friends of capital felon. Although the majority of capital punishment jurisdictions do not allow members of a victim's family to attend the execution, the situation is different for the capital felon. A majority of jurisdictions provide by statute that a capital felon's family or friends may attend the execution. Most of these statutes place restrictions on the number of family members and friends of the capital felon who may attend the execution.

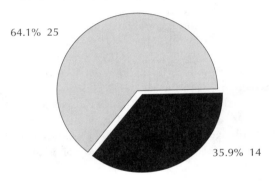

JURISDICTIONS THAT STATUTORILY PERMIT FAMILY OR FRIENDS OF CAPITAL FELON TO ATTEND THE EXECUTION

64.1% 25

35.9% 14

■ JURISDICTIONS ALLOWING FAMILY OR FRIENDS

■ ALL OTHER JURISDICTIONS

Media representation. Although no capital punishment jurisdiction currently allows executions to be televised, the unanimous bar is not found in statutes. Only four jurisdictions — Kentucky, Mississippi, South Carolina, and Tennessee — set out in statutes that audio-visual recorders are prohibited from being used at executions.

The majority of capital punishment jurisdictions do not provide by statute for media attendance at executions. The jurisdictions that do provide for media attendance by statute are divided into two types: (1) newspaper reporters only and (2) media generally (which includes newspaper, television and radio reporters).

1. Newspaper reporters only. Three capital punishment jurisdictions restrict, by statute, media presence at executions to that of newspaper reporters. Two of the jurisdictions, Alabama and Connecticut, do not set a numerical limitation on the number of newspaper reporters, while the third jurisdiction, Mississippi, limits the number at eight.

2. Media generally. The statutes in 11 capital punishment jurisdictions provide for general media representation at executions.

Execution witness room at North Carolina's Central Prison. (North Carolina Department of Corrections)

Jurisdictions Providing by Statute for General Media Representation at Executions

Jurisdiction	Total Media Representation
Kentucky	9
Utah	9
New Jersey	8
Tennessee	7
Pennsylvania	6
South Carolina	5
Ohio	3
South Dakota	1
Florida	no statutory limit
Oklahoma	no statutory limit
Washington	no statutory limit

Public representation. The majority of capital punishment jurisdictions provide by statute for limited "respectable citizen" representation at executions.[18] All of these jurisdictions, except for one, authorize correctional officials to select the public representation.

Public Representation at Executions

# of Jurisdictions	# of Public Representatives	# of Jurisdictions	# of Public Representatives
1	15	1	7
7	12	8	6
1	10	1	3
1	9	2	2
1	8	2	no statutory limit

Citizen representation at an execution is voluntary. Persons selected do not have to attend. It should also be noted that statutes use the phrase "respectable citizens," or "reputable citizens," to describe those who are selected as public representatives to attend executions, but fail to define the phrases.

Inmate representation. North Carolina is the only jurisdiction to provide by statute that a capital felon may invite inmate friends to view the execution. Four capital punishment jurisdictions — Alabama, Missouri, Ohio, and Texas — exclude by statute inmates from attending a capital felon's execution.

Spiritual advisor. Capital punishment jurisdictions permit prison chaplains or personal spiritual advisors to attend executions, at the request of condemned prisoners.

Physician representation. A majority of capital punishment jurisdictions provide by statute for the presence of physicians at executions. Some jurisdictions limit that representation to one. A few jurisdictions set the limit at two, while others allow three physicians to be in attendance. Finally, a few jurisdictions do not have a statutory limit.

Age restrictions. A minority of capital punishment jurisdictions provide statutory restrictions on the age of persons allowed to be in attendance at executions. Seven jurisdictions provide that no "minors" are to be in attendance, while two jurisdictions restrict attendance to persons 21 or over.

Other witnesses. All executions are attended by correctional commissioners or wardens (or their respective designated representatives), executioners, limited security personnel and, of course, the capital felon scheduled for execution. Statutes round out execution witnesses with a limited number of other individuals.

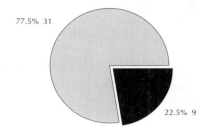

JURISDICTIONS THAT STATUTORILY ALLOWING PERSONAL SPIRITUAL ADVISORS TO ATTEND EXECUTIONS

77.5% 31

22.5% 9

■ JURISDICTIONS ALLOWING PERSONAL SPIRITUAL ADVISORS
■ ALL OTHER JURISDICTIONS

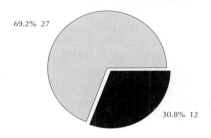

JURISDICTIONS THAT STATUTORILY PROVIDING FOR PHYSICIAN ATTENDANCE AT EXECUTIONS

69.2% 27

30.8% 12

■ JURISDICTIONS PROVIDING FOR PHYSICIAN ATTENDANCE
■ ALL OTHER JURISDICTIONS

1. Capital felon's counsel. A minority of capital punishment jurisdictions allow legal counsel for a capital felon to attend the execution.

2. Attorney general. The statutes in eight capital punishment jurisdictions allow the jurisdiction's attorney general to attend executions.

3. Prosecutor. Five capital punishment jurisdictions allow the prosecutor responsible for bringing about the capital felon's conviction and sentence to attend the execution.

4. Judge. It is provided in the statutes of four capital punishment jurisdictions that the judge who presided over the capital felon's case may attend the execution.

5. Court clerk. New Hampshire is the only jurisdiction that allows the clerk of the court, wherein the capital felon was convicted and sentenced, to attend the execution. *See also* **Holden v. Minnesota**

Pulley v. Harris   *Court:* United States Supreme Court; *Case Citation:* Pulley v. Harris, 465 U.S. 37 (1984); *Argued:* November 7, 1983; *Decided:* January 23, 1984; *Opinion of the Court:* Justice White; *Concurring Opinion:* Justice Stevens; *Dissenting Opinion:* Justice Brennan, in which Marshall, J., joined; *Appellate Defense Counsel:* Anthony G. Amsterdam argued; Quin Denvir, Charles M. Sevilla, Ezra Hendon and Michael J. McCabe on brief; *Appellate Prosecution Counsel:* Michael D. Wellington argued; John K. Van De Kamp, Daniel J. Kremer, Steven V. Adler and Harley D. Mayfield on brief; *Amicus Curiae Brief Supporting Prosecutor:* None; *Amicus Curiae Brief Supporting Defendant:* 1.

Issue Presented: Whether California's capital punishment statute was invalid under the Constitution because it failed to require the California Supreme Court to engage in proportionality review of death sentences?

Case Holding: The Constitution does not require proportionality review of death sentences by appellate courts.

Factual and procedural background of case: The defendant, Harris, was convicted of capital murder by the State of California and was sentenced to death. The California Supreme Court affirmed the conviction and sentence. In doing so, the appellate court rejected the defendant's claim that California's capital punishment statute was invalid under the federal Constitution because it failed to require the California Supreme Court to compare defendant's sentence with sentences imposed in similar capital cases and thereby to determine whether they were proportionate.

After habeas corpus relief was denied by State courts, the defendant sought habeas corpus relief in a Federal District Court. The District Court denied relief. However, a Federal Court of Appeals granted relief, after finding that comparative proportionality review was constitutionally required. The United States Supreme Court granted certiorari to consider the issue.

Opinion of the Court by Justice White: Justice White found that the Constitution did not demand appellate courts engage in proportionality review of death sentences. It was reasoned that the outcome of *Gregg v. Georgia* and its progeny did not hinge on proportionality review. Moreover, the opinion observed that merely becomes death penalty statutes in some jurisdictions require appellate courts engage in proportionality review, does not mean that such review is indispensable or constitutionally required.

Justice White concluded: "Any capital sentencing scheme may occasionally produce aberrational outcomes. Such inconsistencies are a far cry from the major systemic defects identified in *Furman*. As we have acknowledged in the past, 'there can be no perfect procedure for deciding in which cases governmental authority should be used to impose death.' As we are presently informed, we cannot say that the California procedures provided [the defendant] inadequate protection against the evil identified in *Furman*. The Court of Appeals therefore erred in ordering the writ of habeas corpus to issue. Its judgment is reversed, and the case is remanded for further proceedings consistent with this opinion."

Concurring opinion by Justice Stevens: Justice Stevens concurred with most of the Court's opinion. He was at odds with the majority's characterization of some of the Court's prior decisions. In summarizing his concurrence, Justice Stevens wrote: "[I]n each of the statutory schemes approved in our prior cases, as in the scheme we review today, meaningful appellate review is an indispensable component of the Court's determination that the State's capital sentencing procedure is valid. Like the Court, however, I am not persuaded that the particular form of review prescribed by statute in Georgia — comparative proportionality review — is the only method by which an appellate court can avoid the danger that the imposition of the death sentence in a particular case, or a particular class of cases, will be so extraordinary as to violate the Eighth Amendment."

Dissenting opinion by Justice Brennan, in which Marshall, J., joined: Justice Brennan argued long and forceful in dissenting from the majority's opinion. He believed that proportionality review was a constitutionally indispensable part of capital punishment. The dissent presented its position as follows:

> [I]n this case, the Court concludes that proportionality review of a death sentence is constitutionally unnecessary. Presumably this is so, even if a comparative review of death sentences imposed on similarly situated defendants might eliminate some, if only a small part, of the irrationality that currently surrounds the imposition of the death penalty. Because, in my view, the evidence available to the Court suggests that proportionality review does serve this limited purpose, I believe that the State of California, through a court of statewide jurisdiction, should be required to undertake proportionality review when examining any death sentence on appeal....

> The question directly presented by this case is whether the Federal Constitution requires a court of statewide jurisdiction to undertake comparative proportionality review before a death sentence may be carried out. The results obtained by many States that undertake such proportionality review, pursuant to either state statute or judicial decision, convince me that this form of appellate review serves to eliminate some, if only a small part, of the irrationality that infects the current imposition of death sentences throughout the various States. To this extent, I believe that comparative proportionality review is mandated by the Constitution....

> Disproportionality among sentences given different defendants can only be eliminated after sentencing disparities are identified. And the most logical way to identify such sentencing disparities is for a court of statewide jurisdiction to conduct comparisons between death sentences imposed by different judges or juries within the State. This is what the Court labels comparative proportionality review. Although clearly no panacea, such review often serves to identify the most extreme examples of disproportionality among similarly situated defendants. At least to this extent, this form of appellate review serves to eliminate some of the irrationality that currently surrounds imposition of a death sentence. If only to further this limited purpose, therefore, I believe that the Constitution's prohibition on the irrational imposition of the death penalty requires that this procedural safeguard be provided....

> Perhaps the best evidence of the value of proportionality review can be gathered by examining the actual results obtained in those States which now require such review. For example, since 1973, the statute controlling appellate review of death sentences in the State of Georgia has required that the Supreme Court of Georgia determine "[w]hether the sentence of death is excessive or disproportionate to the penalty imposed in similar cases, considering both the crime and the defendant." Pursuant to this statutory mandate, the Georgia Supreme Court has vacated at least seven death sentences because it was convinced that they were comparatively disproportionate.

> Similarly, other States that require comparative proportionality review also have vacated death sentences for defendants whose crime or personal history did not justify such an extreme penalty. (Citing numerous cases.)

> What these cases clearly demonstrate, in my view, is that comparative proportionality review serves to eliminate some, if only

a small part, of the irrationality that currently infects imposition of the death penalty by the various States. Before any execution is carried out, therefore, a State should be required under the Eighth and Fourteenth Amendments to conduct such appellate review. The Court's decision in *Furman*, and the Court's continuing emphasis on meaningful appellate review require no less.

The Court today concludes that our prior decisions do not mandate that a comparative proportionality review be conducted before any execution takes place.... At no point does the Court determine whether comparative proportionality review should be required in order to ensure that the irrational, arbitrary, and capricious imposition of the death penalty invalidated by *Furman* does not still exist. Even if I did not adhere to my view that the death penalty is in all circumstances cruel and unusual punishment, I could not join in such unstudied decisionmaking.

See also **Appellate Review of Conviction and Death Sentence**

Q

Qatar Capital punishment is carried out in Qatar. Qatar uses hanging and the firing squad to carry out the death penalty. Its legal system is a mixture of civil law and Islamic law. Qatar adopted a constitution on April 19, 1971.

Qatar is a monarchy without democratically elected institutions or political parties. It is governed by the ruling Al-Thani family through its head, the Amir. The Amir holds absolute power, that is influenced by religious law and consultation with leading citizens.

The criminal judicial system consists of the Shari'a (Islamic) Court and a rarely convened state security court. In the Shari'a Court, the same judge may preside over the trial case and the appeal. Trials in the Shari'a Court are not public. Defendants are not always permitted to be represented by counsel in the Shari'a court. There is no provision for bail in criminal cases. *See also* **International Capital Punishment Nations**

Queenan v. Oklahoma

Court: United States Supreme Court; *Case Citation:* Queenan v. Oklahoma, 190 U.S. 548 (1903); *Argued:* April 16, 17, 1903; *Decided:* June 1, 1903; *Opinion of the Court:* Justice Holmes; *Concurring Opinion:* None; *Dissenting Opinion:* None; *Appellate Defense Counsel:* Stillwell H. Russell argued; J. W. Johnson, C. B. Ames and H. H. Howard on brief; *Appellate Prosecution Counsel:* J. C. Robberts argued; C. H. Woods on brief; *Amicus Curiae Brief Supporting Prosecutor:* None; *Amicus Curiae Brief Supporting Defendant:* None.

Issue Presented: Whether the trial court committed error in refusing to permit the defendant's witness to render an opinion on the defendant's sanity at the time of the commission of the crime?

Case Holding: The trial court did not commit error in refusing to permit the defendant's witness to render an opinion on the defendant's sanity at the time of the commission of the crime, because the witness was not an expert.

Factual and procedural background of case: The defendant, Thomas P. Queenan, was indicted for capital murder by the State of Oklahoma. During his prosecution the defendant raised the defense of insanity. Defense counsel called as a witness, a lawyer who knew the defendant, and asked the lawyer if it was his opinion that the defendant was insane at the time of the commission of the crime. The prosecutor objected to the question, and the trial court refused to allow the lawyer to answer it. The defendant was convicted and sentenced to death. The Oklahoma Supreme Court affirmed the judgment. In doing so, the appellate court rejected the defendant's contention that he was denied due process of law because the trial court refused to permit his witness to render an opinion on his sanity. The United States Supreme Court granted certiorari to consider the issue.

Opinion of the Court by Justice Holmes: Justice Holmes held that the defendant was not denied due process of law because his witness was precluded from rendering an opinion on the issue of insanity. The opinion addressed the matter as follows:

A lawyer, called as a witness for the defendant, stated that he knew the prisoner quite well; that the prisoner was his barber for some years, and that he saw him on the day before the killing. He then described the appearance and conduct of the prisoner, and said that at the time he did not notice any difference from the prisoner's usual demeanor. He then was asked if, since the killing, he had formed an opinion as to the prisoner's mental condition at that time. This opinion he was not allowed to state.... Some states exclude such opinions, even when formed at the time.... [T]o let a witness who is not an expert state an opinion upon sanity which he has formed after the event, when a case has arisen and become a matter of public discussion, [may not] be justified.... It is unnecessary to lay down the rule that it never can be done, for instance, when the opinion clearly appears to sum up a series of impressions received at different times. It is enough to say that, at least, it should be done with caution and not without special reasons. In this case the only knowledge shown by the witness was the familiarity of a man with his barber. So far as the evidence went, his present opinion might have been the result of interested argument, and, leaving such suggestions on one side, no reason of necessity or propriety was shown for the statement that would not have applied to any other man who had had his hair cut in the prisoner's shop.

It does not appear that there was error in the ruling of the court.

The judgment of the Oklahoma Supreme Court was affirmed.

See also **Insanity Defense; Rules of Evidence**

Quirin, Richard *see* **Espionage**

Race and Capital Punishment   One of the historical criticisms of capital punishment in the United States is that the death penalty is disproportionately inflicted upon minority groups. The dominant factor behind the decision to invalidate capital punishment statutes in *Furman v. Georgia*, 408 U.S. 238 (1972), was statistical evidence which showed that minorities, particularly African Americans, were disproportionately represented in the execution chamber.

Post–*Furman* capital punishment is being challenged by anti–death penalty advocates on the grounds that the death penalty continues to be administered in a racially discriminatory manner. For example, between 1976–1999 minorities made up 44 percent of all executed prisoners. A snap shot of April 1, 1999, revealed that 53 percent of the prisoners on death row were minorities.

One capital punishment jurisdiction has taken the initiative to prevent racial discrimination in death sentencing. In 1998, the State of Kentucky passed legislation allowing death sentences to be challenged on racial grounds through the use of statistical evidence.

Kentucky Racial Justice Act of 1998:

1. No person shall be subject to or given a sentence of death that was sought on the basis of race.
2. A finding that race was the basis of the decision to seek a death sentence may be established if the court finds that race was a significant factor in decisions to seek the sentence of death in the Commonwealth at the time the death sentence was sought.
3. Evidence relevant to establish a finding that race was the basis of the decision to seek a death sentence may include statistical evidence or other evidence, or both, that death sentences were sought significantly more frequently:
    a. Upon persons of one race than upon persons of another race; or
    b. As punishment for capital offenses against persons of one race than as punishment for capital offenses against persons of another race.
4. The defendant shall state with particularity how the evidence supports a claim that racial considerations played a significant part in the decision to seek a death sentence in his or her case. The claim shall be raised by the defendant at the pre-trial conference. The court shall schedule a hearing on the claim and shall prescribe a time for the submission of evidence by both parties. If the court finds that race was the basis of the decision to seek the death sentence, the court shall order that a death sentence shall not be sought.
5. The defendant has the burden of proving by clear and convincing evidence that race was the basis of the decision to seek the death penalty. The Commonwealth may offer evidence in rebuttal of the claims or evidence of the defendant.

As the first of its kind in the nation, the Kentucky initiative must be placed in perspective. The legislation is concerned with the initiation of a capital prosecution. That is, it seeks to prevent prosecutors from using race as a basis for seeking the death penalty. In the final analysis, the Kentucky initiative falls short of providing the type of effective remedy sought by minorities and anti–death penalty advocates.

Studies have shown that two stages exist where improper motives, such as race, may play a role in capital punishment. The decision to seek the death penalty is one stage. The Kentucky initiative addresses that stage. The second stage is the determination by the jury of whether the death penalty should be imposed. The Kentucky initiative does not address this stage. It has been argued it is the second stage where the real problem of racial discrimination exists. In other words, even if prosecutors fairly and impartially chose cases for capital prosecution, juries may exhibit bias in making recommendations as to who actually should receive the punishment. *See also* **African Americans and Capital Punishment; Asians and Capital Punishment; Hispanics and Capital Punishment; Native Americans and Capital Punishment**

Race-Qualified Jury   It has been held that the constitutional guarantee of an impartial jury entitles a defendant, in a capital case involving interracial violence, to have prospective jurors questioned on the issue of racial bias. This right includes informing the prospective jurors of the race of the victim. This right is not automatic. To invoke the right of having a race-qualified jury, a defendant must specifically request the trial judge make an inquiry into racial opinions and beliefs. The requirements of this rule have not been extended outside of interracial violence criminal prosecutions. *See also* **Aldridge v. United States; Discrimination in Grand or Petit Jury Selection; Jury Selection; Non-Discrimination Jury Instruction; Turner v. Murray**

Raise or Waive Rule *see* Procedural Default of Constitutional Claims

Ramirez, Richard *see* Night Stalker

Rape *see* Sexual Assault

Rape and Capital Punishment

Under the common law all felonies were punishable by the infliction of death. The American Colonies incorporated the common law's position in their criminal statutes. The first codified capital punishment offenses in the American colonies were drawn up in 1636, by the Massachusetts Bay colony. The *Capital Laws of New England*, as they were called, provided the death penalty for the following crimes: rebellion, perjury, manstealing, rape, statutory rape, adultery, buggery, sodomy, murder, blasphemy, idolatry, witch craft, and assault in sudden anger.

All jurisdictions, at some point in the nation's development, provided the death penalty for offenses that did not involve the death of a human being. The constitutional issue of whether or not the death penalty could be inflicted for non-homicide offenses, was not addressed by the United States Supreme Court until it heard the case of *Coker v. Georgia*, 433 U.S. 584 (1977).

The narrow issue presented to the Supreme Court in *Coker*, was whether or not the Cruel and Unusual Punishment Clause prohibited imposition of the death penalty for the crime of rape of an adult woman. In addressing this issue the Court observed "that Georgia is the sole jurisdiction in the United States at the present time that authorizes a sentence of death when the rape victim is an adult woman, and only two other jurisdictions provide capital punishment when the victim is a child." With this observation in sight, the Supreme Court concluded:

> Rape is without doubt deserving of serious punishment; but in terms of moral depravity and of the injury to the person and to the public, it does not compare with murder, which does involve the unjustified taking of human life. Although it may be accompanied by another crime, rape by definition does not include the death of or even the serious injury to another person. The murderer kills; the rapist, if no more than that, does not. Life is over for the victim of the murderer; for the rape victim, life may not be nearly so happy as it was, but it is not over and normally is not beyond repair. We have the abiding conviction that the death penalty, which is unique in its severity and irrevocability, is an excessive penalty for the rapist who, as such, does not take human life.

The decision in *Coker* stands for the proposition that it is unconstitutional to impose capital punishment for the offense of rape of an adult, without more. Whether or not capital punishment may constitutionally be imposed for rape of a child was not directly addressed in *Coker*. The opinion gives

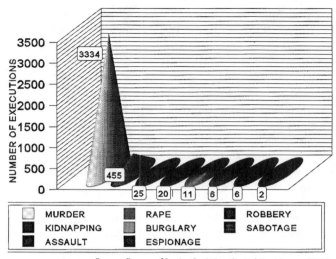

Source: Bureau of Justice Statistics, Capital Punishment (1977).

an indication that this, too, would be unconstitutional. However, in *Upshaw v. State*, 350 So.2d 1358 (Miss. 1977) and *Leatherwood v. State*, 548 So.2d 389 (Miss. 1989), the Mississippi Supreme Court indicated in dicta that *Coker* did not prohibit the death penalty for rape of a minor. But, in *Buford v. State*, 403 So.2d 943 (Fla. 1981) the Florida Supreme Court interpreted *Coker* as invalidating a statute in that jurisdiction which had imposed the death penalty for committing rape of a minor.

At this juncture in Anglo-American jurisprudence courts are almost unanimous in holding that *Coker* has prohibited imposition of the death penalty for any offense that does not involve the death of a victim. For example, in *Cook v. State*, 251 S.E.2d 230 (Ga. 1978), the Georgia Supreme Court interpreted *Coker* as invalidating statutes in that jurisdiction which had imposed the death penalty for armed robbery and kidnaping with bodily injury. Moreover, except for treason and espionage (Mississippi retains rape of a child as a capital crime), all offenses that have the death penalty as an authorized punishment require a homicide also occur. *See also* **Coker v. Georgia**

Rawlins v. Georgia

Court: United States Supreme Court; *Case Citation:* Rawlins v. Georgia, 201 U.S. 638 (1906); *Argued:* April 6, 1906; *Decided:* April 16, 1906; *Opinion of the Court:* Justice Holmes; *Concurring Opinion:* None; *Dissenting Opinion:* None; *Appellate Defense Counsel:* John Randolph Cooper and Oscar M. Smith argued and briefed; *Appellate Prosecution Counsel:* John C. Hart briefed; *Amicus Curiae Brief Supporting Prosecutor:* None; *Amicus Curiae Brief Supporting Defendant:* None.

Issue Presented: Whether the exclusion of professional persons from the grand jury that indicted the defendants denied them due process of law?

Case Holding: The exclusion of professional persons from the grand jury that indicted the defendants did not deny them due process of law.

Factual and procedural background of case: The defendants, J. G. Rawlins, Milton Rawlins, and Jesse Rawlins were convicted of capital murder and sentenced to death (a fourth defendant, Leonard Rawlins, was sentenced to life imprisonment) by the State of Georgia. The Georgia Supreme Court affirmed the judgments. In doing so, the appellate court rejected the defendants' contention that their convictions were invalid because "while there are in Lowndes county many lawyers, many preachers, ministers, many doctors, many engineers and firemen of railroad trains, and many dentists, as many as ten of each class named, or other large number of each of said class, all citizens and residents of said county, and being competent and qualified jurors, as to age and uprightness, experience and intelligence, and as to all the legal qualifications of a juror, yet each and every one of these classes of citizens, and each and every member thereof in the county, is expressly and purposely excluded from the grand jury service by the commissioners failing and refusing to put any of said names in the box, so that, not being in the box, they cannot be legally drawn for service." The United States Supreme Court granted certiorari to consider the issue.

Opinion of the Court by Justice Holmes: Justice Holmes held that the defendants were not denied due process of law because professional members of the community were excluded from grand jury service. The opinion explained as follows:

> When the question is narrowed to its proper form the answer does not need much discussion. The nature of the classes excluded was not such as was likely to affect the conduct of the members as jurymen, or to make them act otherwise than those who were drawn would act. The exclusion was not the result of race or class prejudice. It does not even appear that any of the defendants belonged to any of the excluded classes. The ground of omission, no doubt, was that pointed out by the state court,— that the business of the persons omitted was such that they either would have been entitled to claim exemption, or that probably they would have been excused. Even when persons liable to jury duty under the state law are excluded, it is no ground for challenge to the array, if a sufficient number of unexceptional persons are present. But if the state law itself should exclude certain classes on the bona fide ground that it was for the good of the community that their regular work should not be interrupted, there is nothing in the 14th Amendment to prevent it. The exemption of lawyers, ministers of the gospel, doctors, and engineers of railroad trains — in short, substantially the exemption complained of— is of old standing, and not uncommon in the United States. It could not be denied that the state properly could have excluded these classes had it seen fit, and that undeniable proposition ends the case.

The judgment of the Georgia Supreme Court was affirmed.

Recess *see* Time Between Guilt Phase and Penalty Phase

Reece v. Georgia
Court: United States Supreme Court; *Case Citation:* Reece v. Georgia, 350 U.S. 85 (1955); *Argued:* November 9, 1955; *Decided:* December 5, 1955; *Opinion of the Court:* Justice Clark; *Concurring Opinion:* None; *Dissenting*

Opinion: None; *Appellate Defense Counsel:* Daniel Duke argued and briefed; *Appellate Prosecution Counsel:* Eugene Cook argued; Robert H. Hall and E. Freeman Leverett on brief; *Amicus Curiae Brief Supporting Prosecutor:* None; *Amicus Curiae Brief Supporting Defendant:* None.

Issue Presented: Whether the defendant was denied due process of law by Georgia's requirement that a challenge to the composition of the grand jury must be made before an indictment was returned?

Case Holding: The defendant was denied due process of law by Georgia's requirement that a challenge to the composition of the grand jury must be made before an indictment was returned, when the defendant has shown that he was semi-literate and did not have counsel appointed until after the indictment was returned.

Factual and procedural background of case: The defendant, Amos Reece, was convicted of the rape and sentenced to death by the State of Georgia. The Georgia Supreme Court reversed the judgment and ordered a new trial. The defendant was convicted at the second trial and again sentenced to death. The Georgia Supreme Court affirmed the judgment. In doing so, the appellate court ruled that the defendant failed to timely raise, at the trial court level, his claim that blacks were systematically excluded from the grand jury that indicted him. The United States Supreme Court granted certiorari to consider the issue.

Opinion of the Court by Justice Clark: Justice Clark indicated that "[t]he indictment of a defendant by a grand jury from which members of his race have been systematically excluded is a denial of his right to equal protection of the laws." The opinion noted that Georgia law required that objections of a defendant to the composition of a grand jury be raised before the indictment was returned. The opinion found that Georgia's procedure did not afford the defendant an opportunity to object to the composition of the grand jury, because he was semi-literate and did not have counsel appointed until after the indictment was returned and he was arrested. Justice Clark stated that "it is utterly unrealistic to say that he had such opportunity when counsel was not provided for him until the day after he was indicted." It was reasoned in the opinion "that the assignment of counsel in a state prosecution at such time and under such circumstances as to preclude the giving of effective aid in the preparation and trial of a capital case is a denial of due process of law." Justice Clark found that the defendant's counsel could not effectively represent him on a key procedural issue, because under Georgia law the issue was lost before counsel was appointed.

The opinion found that the defendant had provided sufficient evidence to support his claim of racial discrimination in the composition of the grand jury. This evidence included documentation that no black person "had served on the grand jury in Cobb County for the previous 18 years." The opinion indicated that while the defendant made out a prima facie case of discrimination, the Court would not decide the issue. Instead, Justice Clark ruled that the Georgia Supreme

Court should first have an opportunity to address the merits of the claim. The judgment of the Georgia Supreme Court was vacated and the case remanded.

Case note: Under modern capital punishment jurisprudence the death penalty may not be imposed for the crime of rape without an accompanying homicide. *See also* **Discrimination in Grand or Petit Jury Selection; Rape and Capital Punishment**

Reed, Stanley Forman
Stanley Forman Reed served as an associate justice of the United States Supreme Court from 1938 to 1957. While on the Supreme Court Reed was known as a moderate in his interpretation of the Constitution.

Reed was born in Macon County, Kentucky on December 31, 1884. Reed was educated at Kentucky Wesleyan College where he received an undergraduate degree in 1902. Although Reed attended several law schools, he did not receive a law degree. He was admitted to the bar in Kentucky in 1910. Reed went on to hold several attorney positions with the Federal government, including appointment as United States Solicitor General in 1935. In 1938 President Franklin D. Roosevelt appointed Reed to the Supreme Court.

Reed issued a number of capital punishment opinions while on the Supreme Court. The capital punishment opinion which has kept Reed's name current in legal discussion, was his plurality opinion in *Francis v. Resweber*. The decision in *Francis* asked the question of whether the Constitution permitted a defendant to be executed more than once. The defendant in *Francis* was unsuccessfully executed by electrocution by the State of Louisiana. The defendant asked the Supreme Court to stop a second attempt at electrocuting him. The majority of the Court approved of a subsequent execution. Reed, announcing the decision of the Court and writing a plurality opinion, held: "For we see no difference from a constitutional point of view between a new trial for error of law at the instance of the state ... and an execution that follows a failure of equipment. When an accident, with no suggestion of malevolence, prevents the consummation of a sentence, the state's subsequent course in the administration of its criminal law is not affected on that account." In 1957 Reed retired from the Court. He died on April 2, 1980.

Capital Punishment Opinions Written by Reed

Case Name	Opinion of the Court	Plurality Opinion	Concurring Opinion	Dissenting Opinion
Adamson v. California	✓			
Akins v. Texas	✓			
Andres v. United States	✓			
Brown v. Allen	✓			
Cassell v. Texas			✓	
Fisher v. United States	✓			
Francis v. Resweber		✓		
Smith v. Baldi	✓			
United States v. Carignan	✓			

Rehnquist, William Hubbs
William Hubbs Rehnquist served as an associate justice of the United States Supreme Court from 1971 to 1986. In 1986 Rehnquist was appointed chief justice of the Supreme Court. While on the Supreme Court Rehnquist has been known as an ultra conservative in his interpretation of the Constitution.

Rehnquist was born on October 1, 1924, in Milwaukee, Wisconsin. In 1952 he graduated from Stanford University Law School. In 1953 Rehnquist began the private practice of law. In 1969 he took a position as an attorney with the Department of Justice. President Richard M. Nixon appointed him to the United States Supreme Court as an associate justice in 1971. President Ronald Reagan elevated Rehnquist to the position of chief justice of the Supreme Court in 1986.

Rehnquist has written a considerable number of capital punishment opinions. In all of his capital punishment opinions he has been consistent in taking a position that was ultra conservative and primarily pro-government. A case illustrating Rehnquist's ultra conservative constitutional views is *Dawson v. Delaware*. In that case the defendant was a member of a white racist prison gang. During the defendant's capital sentencing proceeding the prosecutor introduced evidence of the defendant's gang membership to show that he would be dangerous if spared the death penalty. The defendant argued to the Supreme Court that the prosecutor should not have been allowed to use his right-wing gang membership against him. Rehnquist, writing for the majority of the Court, agreed with the defendant that his membership in a prison hate group was not relevant for determining the proper sentence in the case. *See table on next page.*

Relevant Evidence
Relevant evidence is generally defined as any evidence having a tendency to make the existence of any fact that is of consequence more probable or less probable than it would be without such evidence. This definition is used to control admission of evidence at the guilt phase, as well as penalty phase of a capital prosecution. Any evidence that is relevant may be considered during the penalty phase of a capital prosecution. Evidence may be relevant at the guilt phase, but precluded from introduction on other evidentiary grounds. *See also* **Mitigating Circumstances**

Religion and Capital Punishment
In 1999, the National Jewish/Catholic Consultation issued a joint statement calling for the abolishment of capital punishment. The National Jewish/Catholic Consultation was co-sponsored by the National Council of Synagogues and the National Conference of Catholic Bishops' Committee for Ecumenical and Interreligious Affairs. The joint statement of condemnation of capital punishment by the National Jewish/Catholic Consultation was in keeping with a growing trend by religious institutions in the 1990s to publicly speak out against capital punishment in the nation. This trend was placed on the fast track by statements made by Pope John Paul II in the latter part of 1990s calling for a global end to capital

Capital Punishment Opinions Written by Rehnquist

Case Name	Opinion of the Court	Plurality Opinion	Concurring Opinion	Dissenting Opinion	Concurring and Dissenting
Adams v. Texas				✓	
Ake v. Oklahoma				✓	
Arizona v. Rumsey				✓	
Barclay v. Florida		✓			
Beck v. Alabama				✓	
Boyde v. California	✓				
Bracy v. Gramley	✓				
Buchanan v. Angelone	✓				
Butler v. McKellar	✓				
Calderon v. Ashmus	✓				
Caldwell v. Mississippi				✓	
California v. Brown	✓				
Dawson v. Delaware	✓				
Davis v. Georgia				✓	
Dobbert v. Florida	✓				
Estelle v. Smith			✓		
Felker v. Turpin	✓				
Ford v. Wainwright				✓	
Furman v. Georgia				✓	
Gardner v. Florida				✓	
Gray v. Netherland	✓				
Green v. Georgia				✓	
Heckler v. Chaney	✓				
Herrera v. Collins	✓				
Lilly v. Virginia			✓		
Lockett v. Ohio					✓
Lockhart v. Fretwell	✓				
Lonchar v. Thomas			✓		
Lowenfield v. Phelps	✓				
Mills v. Maryland					✓
Mu'Min v. Virginia	✓				
Murray v. Giarratano			✓		
Ohio A.P.A. v. Woodard	✓				
Payne v. Tennessee	✓				
Roberts v. Louisiana (II)				✓	
Romano v. Oklahoma	✓				
Ross v. Oklahoma	✓				
Sawyer v. Whitley	✓				
Schlup v. Delo				✓	
Sochor v. Florida					✓
Stewart v. Martinez-Villareal	✓				
Wainwright v. Witt	✓				
Whitmore v. Arkansas	✓				
Woodson v. North Carolina				✓	
Zant v. Stephens (II)			✓		

punishment. There was also a statement issued in 1999 by the Dalai Lama calling for a moratorium on capital punishment in the United States.

Religious Institutions That Issued Statements Calling for an End to Capital Punishment

American Baptist Churches in the U.S.A.
Benedictine Sisters of Cullman, Alabama
Christian Church (Disciples of Christ)
Christian Reformed Church
Church of the Brethren
Church Women United
Episcopal Church
Evangelical Lutheran Church
United Methodist Church

Fellowship of Reconciliation
Moravian Church In America
National Council of Churches of Christ
Orthodox Church in America
Presbyterian Church
Reorganized Church of Jesus Christ L.D.S.
Unitarian Universalist Association
United Church of Christ

Although many religious institutions in the nation have come out to oppose capital punishment, the religious community is not unanimous on this issue. There are religious based groups that support capital punishment. These groups point to the bible as justification for the death penalty. It has been noted that the bible imposes capital punishment for the following conduct: murder, rape, sodomy, incontinence, perjury, kidnapping, fornication, witchcraft, striking or cursing one's father or mother, theft, blasphemy, and sabbath desecration.

Religious Organizing Against the Death Penalty Project

The Philadelphia based Religious Organizing Against the Death Penalty Project (the Project) was created to bring together the religious community in the United States to work against capital punishment. The Project is coordinated by the criminal justice program of the American Friends Service Committee. The Project provides the religious communities with the tools and resources to become effective advocates for the abolition of the death penalty. Some of the practical work done by the Project includes: getting people to sign a pledge to express individual opposition to capital punishment; designing action plans for working for the abolition of the death penalty; addressing the spiritual needs of families of murder victims; working with family members of those on death row; organize anti–death penalty demonstrations and vigils; and testify and lobby against the death penalty.

Remand *see* **Appellate Review of Conviction and Death Sentence**

Reprieve *see* **Clemency**

Requesting Death The Federal Constitution does not prohibit a capital felon from waiving his or her right to put on mitigating evidence during the penalty phase and requesting to be sentenced to death. However, before a capital defendant is permitted to waive his or her right to put on mitigating evidence at the penalty phase and request a sentence of death, a trial court must evaluate the possible mitigating circumstances and inform the defendant of any potential merit they may have.

In addition to the right to request a death sentence at the penalty phase, a capital felon may request or volunteer to be executed once he or she is on death row. From 1976 to 1999, a request to be put to death was made by and granted to 75 death row inmates.

David Mason voluntarily dropped all appeals of his capital conviction and requested to be executed on August 24, 1993. The State of California honored Mason's request and executed him on August 24, 1993. (California Department of Corrections)

CAPITAL FELONS EXECUTED UPON REQUEST 1976–1999

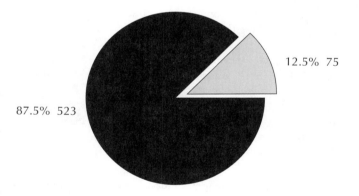

12.5% 75

87.5% 523

■ VOLUNTARY EXECUTIONS

■ ALL OTHER EXECUTIONS

Residual Doubt of Guilt Residual doubt of guilt refers to some inferential aspect of a valid conviction that suggests a defendant's innocence. Courts agree that a capital felon does not have a Federal constitutional right to present residual doubt of guilt evidence at the penalty phase. Some courts expressly preclude introduction of residual doubt of guilt evidence at the penalty phase for mitigation purposes. However, other courts hold that residual doubt of guilt is a valid nonstatutory mitigating circumstance for the penalty phase jury to consider. *See also* **Franklin v. Lynaugh; Mitigating Circumstances**

Respite *see* **Clemency**

Retrials and the Death Penalty Conviction of a capital crime does not mean that a sentence of death will be imposed. Life imprisonment is an option in capital prosecutions. Invariably a defendant convicted of a capital offense will seek to overturn the conviction, regardless of whether or not the death penalty was imposed. An issue that has twice been addressed by the United States Supreme Court involves seeking the death penalty at a retrial of a defendant, when the overturned sentence in the first trial was life imprisonment.

The Stroud Ruling. In the case of *Stroud v. United States*, 251 U.S. 15 (1919) the defendant was convicted of capital murder and was sentenced to life imprisonment. The defendant appealed his conviction. An appellate court overturned the conviction and granted the defendant a new trial. At the second trial the defendant was again convicted of murder, however, this time he was sentenced to death. The defendant appealed his second conviction to the United States Supreme Court.

The defendant's argument to the Supreme Court was that the Double Jeopardy Clause of the Fifth Amendment prohibited imposition of the death penalty at his second trial, because the first trial determined that the death penalty was inappropriate. This argument was rejected. The Supreme Court held that the death penalty may be constitutionally sought by a prosecutor at a retrial of a defendant, even though the punishment was not imposed at the first trial.

The Bullington Ruling. The ruling in *Stroud* remained unchallenged law until the United States Supreme Court heard the case of *Bullington v. Missouri*, 451 U.S. 430 (1981). The relevant facts of *Bullington* reveal that the defendant was indicted in 1977, for the capital murder of a woman during the commission of a kidnaping. After a lengthy trial the jury returned a verdict of guilty of capital murder. The prosecutor indicated he would seek the death penalty, therefore a sentencing hearing was held to determine the penalty. The sentencing jury returned a verdict of life imprisonment.

Shortly after the sentencing verdict was returned the defendant filed post-verdict motions. In the motions he asked the trial court to set aside the guilty verdict and acquit him or, in the alternative, set aside the guilty verdict and grant him a new trial. Due to a constitutional error at the trial, the presiding judge set aside the guilty verdict and granted the defendant a new trial.

Prior to the start of the second trial, the prosecutor filed a notice that he would again seek the death penalty. The defendant objected to this and filed a motion asking the trial court to quash the notice. The defendant argued that the Double Jeopardy Clause prevented the prosecutor from seeking the death penalty, after the jury rejected this in the first trial.

The trial court agreed with the defendant and prohibited the prosecutor from seeking the death penalty in the second trial. The prosecutor thereafter made an interlocutory appeal of the trial court's ruling to the Missouri Supreme Court. The

State high court agreed with the prosecutor that the Double Jeopardy Clause did not prevent him from seeking the death penalty in the second trial. The State high court then set aside the trial court's ruling.

Before the second trial began, the defendant made an interlocutory appeal of the State high court decision to the United States Supreme Court. The essence of the Supreme Court's response was that, when a penalty phase jury rejects the death penalty and life imprisonment is imposed, double jeopardy principles prohibit imposition of a death sentence after a subsequent retrial. However, if a defendant is given the death penalty in the first trial, which is subsequently reversed, he or she is still exposed to capital punishment at a retrial. *See also* **Bullington v. Missouri; Double Jeopardy Clause; Stroud v. United States**

Retribution Theory of Capital Punishment *see* Justifications for Capital Punishment

Retroactive Application of a New Constitutional Rule   Capital punishment decisions by the United States Supreme Court often proclaim new constitutional rules. A principle becomes a new rule if it breaks new ground, imposes a new obligation on the States or the Federal government, or was not dictated by precedent existing at the time the defendant's conviction became final.

A primary issue involving a new constitutional rule is whether it may be applied retroactively to capital cases decided prior to the announcement of the new rule. The general rule regarding retroactivity of a new constitutional rule is that, after a defendant's conviction has become final, he or she may not use a subsequently created constitutional rule to attack the conviction in a Federal habeas corpus proceeding. This prohibition has been applied to prevent the adoption of a new rule in cases actually being decided by the Supreme Court.

Two narrow exceptions have been carved out from the general prohibition against applying a new constitutional rule to convictions that have become final. A new rule may be applied retroactively if it: (1) placed an entire category of primary conduct beyond the reach of criminal law or prohibited imposition of a certain type of punishment for a class of defendants because of their status or offense; or (2) was a watershed rule of criminal procedure implicating a criminal proceeding's fundamental fairness and accuracy. *See also* **Butler v. McKellar; Graham v. Collins; Gray v. Netherland; Lambrix v. Singletary; O'Dell v. Netherland; Saffle v. Parks; Sawyer v. Smith**

Reverse *see* Appellate Review of Conviction and Death Sentence

Review of Death Sentence *see* Appellate Review of Conviction and Death Sentence

Rhode Island   Capital punishment is not carried out by the State of Rhode Island. In 1852, the State abolished capital punishment for most crimes, and later placed a ban on the punishment for all crimes.

Richetti, Adam *see* **Kansas City Massacre**

Richmond v. Lewis   *Court:* United States Supreme Court; *Case Citation:* Richmond v. Lewis, 506 U.S. 40 (1992); *Argued:* October 13, 1992; *Decided:* December 1, 1992; *Opinion of the Court:* Justice O'Connor; *Concurring Statement:* Justice Thomas; *Dissenting Opinion:* Justice Scalia; *Appellate Defense Counsel:* Timothy K. Ford argued; Judith H. Ramseyer and Carla Ryan on brief; *Appellate Prosecution Counsel:* Paul J. McMurdie argued; Grant Woods and Jack Roberts on brief; *Amicus Curiae Brief Supporting Prosecutor:* None; *Amicus Curiae Brief Supporting Defendant:* None.

Issue Presented: Whether the Arizona Supreme Court properly cured the constitutional error in the defendant's death sentence that was caused by the vague "especially heinous, cruel or depraved manner" statutory aggravating circumstance?

Case Holding: The State appellate court failed to cure the constitutional error in the defendant's death sentence that was caused by the "especially heinous, cruel or depraved manner" statutory aggravating circumstance; but the State appellate court would be given an opportunity to cure the defective death sentence.

Factual and procedural background of case: The defendant, Richmond, was convicted of capital murder by the State of Arizona. During the sentencing phase the trial court found three statutory aggravating circumstances were proven to exist. Included among the three aggravating factors found was the "especially heinous, cruel or depraved manner" aggravator. The trial court sentenced the defendant to death. The Arizona Supreme Court found that the "especially heinous, cruel or depraved manner" aggravator was vague, but that based upon a narrowing construction given to the aggravator it was constitutionally sound. The appellate court affirmed the conviction and sentence.

The defendant subsequently filed a habeas corpus petition in a Federal District Court, arguing that the "especially heinous, cruel or depraved manner" aggravator was constitutionally invalid. The District Court agreed with the defendant and granted relief. A Federal Court of Appeals affirmed. The United States Supreme Court granted certiorari to consider the issue.

Opinion of the Court by Justice O'Connor: Justice O'Connor ruled that the defendant's death sentence violated the Eighth Amendment, because the "especially heinous, cruel or depraved manner" aggravator was unconstitutionally vague at the time the sentencing judge gave it weight. It was held that the State appellate court did not cure the error, because that court did not actually reweigh the aggravating and mitigating circumstances in affirming the sentence.

The opinion concluded that the State appellate court must

be given an opportunity to correct the constitutional error by reweighing the aggravating and mitigating circumstances with the invalid "especially heinous, cruel or depraved manner" aggravator removed. The judgment of the Court of appeals was reversed and the case remanded with instructions that the State appellate court, within a reasonable period of time, either correct the constitutional error in the defendant's death sentence or vacate the sentence and impose a lesser sentence consistent with State law.

Concurring Statement by Justice Thomas: Justice Thomas issued a concurring statement indicating he agreed with the Court's judgment that the State appellate court failed to properly reweigh the aggravating and mitigating factors.

Dissenting opinion by Justice Scalia: Justice Scalia dissented from the Court's decision. He believed that any error caused by the failure of the State appellate court to properly reweigh the aggravating and mitigating factors was harmless error. *See also* **Heinous, Atrocious, Cruel or Depraved Aggravator; Lewis v. Jeffers; Maynard v. Cartwright; Shell v. Mississippi; Stringer v. Black; Walton v. Arizona**

Rideau v. Louisiana

Court: United States Supreme Court; *Case Citation:* Rideau v. Louisiana, 373 U.S. 723 (1963); *Argued:* April 29, 1963; *Decided:* June 3, 1963; *Opinion of the Court:* Justice Stewart; *Concurring Opinion:* None; *Dissenting Opinion:* Justice Clark, in which Harlan, J., joined; *Appellate Defense Counsel:* Fred H. Sievert, Jr. argued and briefed; *Appellate Prosecution Counsel:* Frank Salter argued; Jack P. F. Gremillion, Robert S. Link, Jr., John E. Jackson, Jr. and M. E. Culligan on brief; *Amicus Curiae Brief Supporting Prosecutor:* None; *Amicus Curiae Brief Supporting Defendant:* None.

Issue Presented: Whether due process of law required the location of the defendant's trial be changed because of the locally televised showing of the defendant confessing to the charge against him?

Case Holding: Due process of law required the location of the defendant's trial be changed because of the locally televised showing of the defendant confessing to the charge against him.

Factual and procedural background of case: The defendant, Wilbert Rideau, was arrested for capital murder by the State of Louisiana. While in jail awaiting prosecution, the defendant confessed to the crime. The confession was recorded on film and broadcast locally prior to the trial. Defense counsel requested the trial court change the venue of trial because of adverse pretrial publicity. The trial court denied the request. The defendant was convicted and sentenced to death. The Louisiana Supreme Court affirmed the conviction and sentence. In doing so, the appellate court rejected the defendant's contention that due process of law was violated by the trial court's denial of a change of venue. The United States Supreme Court granted certiorari to consider the issue.

Opinion of the Court by Justice Stewart: Justice Stewart ruled that it was a denial of due process of law to refuse the request for a change of venue after the local exposure to the defendant personally confessing in detail to the crime. He stated the Court's position as follows:

> The case now before us does not involve physical brutality. The kangaroo court proceedings in this case involved a more subtle but no less real deprivation of due process of law. Under our Constitution's guarantee of due process, a person accused of committing a crime is vouchsafed basic minimal rights. Among these are the right to counsel, the right to plead not guilty, and the right to be tried in a courtroom presided over by a judge. Yet in this case the people of [the] Parish saw and heard, not once but three times, a "trial" of Rideau in a jail, presided over by a sheriff, where there was no lawyer to advise Rideau of his right to stand mute....
>
> ... [W]e do not hesitate to hold, without pausing to examine a particularized transcript of the voir dire examination of the members of the jury, that due process of law in this case required a trial before a jury drawn from a community of people who had not seen and heard Rideau's televised "interview." "Due process of law, preserved for all by our Constitution, commands that no such practice as that disclosed by this record shall send any accused to his death."

The judgment of the Louisiana Supreme Court was reversed.

Dissenting opinion by Justice Clark, in which Harlan, J., joined: Justice Clark dissented from the Court's decision. He did not believe the record showed such adverse publicity as to warrant reversing the conviction. Justice Clark wrote that "[u]nless the adverse publicity is shown by the record to have fatally infected the trial, there is simply no basis for the Court's inference that the publicity, epitomized by the televised interview ... [made the defendant's] trial a meaningless formality." He added further that, "when the jurors testify that they can discount the influence of external factors and meet the standard imposed by the Fourteenth Amendment, that assurance is not lightly to be discarded." *See also* **Pretrial Publicity; Venue**

Riggins v. Nevada

Court: United States Supreme Court; *Case Citation:* Riggins v. Nevada, 504 U.S. 127 (1992); *Argued:* January 15, 1992; *Decided:* May 18, 1992; *Opinion of the Court:* Justice O'Connor; *Concurring Opinion:* Justice Kennedy; *Dissenting Opinion:* Justice Thomas, in which Scalia, J., joined; *Appellate Defense Counsel:* Mace J. Yampolsky argued; Jay Topkis, Neal H. Klausner and Steven C. Herzog on brief; *Appellate Prosecution Counsel:* James Tufteland argued; Rex Bell on brief; *Amicus Curiae Brief Supporting Prosecutor:* 4; *Amicus Curiae Brief Supporting Defendant:* 3.

Issue Presented: Whether forcing the defendant to use the antipsychotic drug Mellaril during his trial infringed upon the defendant's due process right to a fair trial?

Case Holding: Under the facts and circumstances of the case, forcing the defendant to use the antipsychotic drug Mellaril during his trial infringed upon his due process right to a fair trial.

Factual and procedural background of case: The State of Nevada charged the defendant, David Riggins, with capital murder. Prior to trial he complained of hearing voices and having sleep problems. The trial court ordered a psychiatric examination of the defendant's competency to stand trial. The defendant was found competent, but the examining psychiatrist prescribed the antipsychotic drug Mellaril for the defendant. Defense counsel made a motion to suspend the Mellaril's administration until after the defendant's trial, arguing that its use infringed upon his freedom, that its effect on his demeanor and mental state during trial would deny him due process, and that he had the right to show jurors his true mental state when he offered an insanity defense. The trial court denied the motion. The defendant was tried, convicted and sentenced to death. On appeal, the Nevada Supreme Court affirmed the conviction and sentence. In doing so, the appellate court rejected the defendant's contention that forced use of the Mellaril drug violated his constitutional rights. The United States Supreme Court granted certiorari to consider the issue.

Opinion of the Court by Justice O'Connor: Justice O'Connor ruled that the forced administration of antipsychotic medication during the defendant's trial violated his constitutional rights. It was said that a defendant has an interest in avoiding involuntary administration of antipsychotic drugs that is protected under the Due Process Clause. The opinion reasoned that once the defendant motioned the trial court to terminate his treatment, the State became obligated to establish both the need for Mellaril and its medical appropriateness. It was indicated that due process would have been satisfied had the State shown that the treatment was medically appropriate and, considering less intrusive alternatives, essential for the defendant's own safety or the safety of others. Additionally, the opinion noted that the State also might have been able to justify the treatment, if medically appropriate, by showing that an adjudication of guilt or innocence could not be obtained by using less intrusive means. However, Justice O'Connor found that the trial court allowed the drug's administration to continue without making any determination of the need for its continuation or any findings about reasonable alternatives, and it failed to acknowledge the defendant's liberty interest in freedom from antipsychotic drugs.

The opinion found that there was a strong possibility that the trial court's error impaired the defendant's constitutionally protected trial rights. While the precise consequences of forcing Mellaril upon the defendant could not be shown from the trial transcript, the testimony of doctors who examined the defendant established a strong possibility that his defense was impaired. It was said that Mellaril's side effects may have impacted not only the defendant's outward appearance, but also his trial testimony's content, his ability to follow the proceedings, or the substance of his communication with counsel. The judgment of the Nevada Supreme Court was reversed.

Concurring opinion by Justice Kennedy: Justice Kennedy concurred in the Court's decision. He wrote that medical evidence in the record indicated that involuntary medication with antipsychotic drugs posed a serious threat to the defendant's right to a fair trial. Justice Kennedy concluded that, "absent an extraordinary showing by the State, the Due Process Clause prohibits prosecuting officials from administering involuntary doses of antipsychotic medicines for purposes of rendering the accused competent for trial[.]"

Dissenting opinion by Justice Thomas, in which Scalia, J., joined: Justice Thomas dissented from the Court's decision. He believed that forced use of antipsychotic drugs did not deprive the defendant of a fair trial. Justice Thomas wrote: "I agree with the positions of the majority and concurring opinions in the Nevada Supreme Court: even if the State truly forced Riggins to take medication, and even if this medication deprived Riggins of a protected liberty interest in a manner actionable in a different legal proceeding, Riggins nonetheless had the fundamentally fair criminal trial required by the Constitution. I therefore would affirm his conviction." *See also* **Insanity**

Right to Counsel

Under the common law of England a defendant charged with treason or other felony was denied the aid of counsel. At the same time, however, parties in civil cases and defendants accused of misdemeanors were entitled to the full assistance of counsel. After 1688, the rule was abolished as to treason, but was otherwise adhered to until 1836, when by act of the English Parliament the full right was granted in respect of felonies generally.

The common law rule was rejected by the American Colonies. Before the adoption of the Federal Constitution, the Constitution of Maryland had declared: "That, in all criminal prosecutions, every man hath a right ... to be allowed counsel[.]" The right to counsel provided by Maryland was adopted by other Colonies as follows: the Constitution of Pennsylvania in 1776; the Constitution of New York in 1777; the Constitution of Massachusetts in 1780; and the Constitution of New Hampshire in 1784.

In the case of Pennsylvania, as early as 1701, the Penn Charter declared that "all Criminals shall have the same Privileges of Witnesses and Council as their Prosecutors." There was also a provision in the Pennsylvania statute of May 31, 1718, which provided that in capital cases counsel should be assigned to the prisoners. The original Constitution of New Jersey of 1776, contained a provision like that of the Penn Charter, to the effect that all criminals should be admitted to the same privileges of counsel as their prosecutors.

In Delaware's Constitution of 1776, it adopted the common law of England, but expressly excepted such parts as were repugnant to the rights and privileges contained in the Declaration of Rights. The Declaration of Rights, which was adopted on September 11, 1776, provided: "That in all Prosecutions for criminal Offences, every Man hath a Right ... to be allowed Counsel[.]"

North Carolina's Constitution of 1776, did not contain the guaranty to counsel, but a statute provided: "That every person accused of any crime or misdemeanor whatsoever, shall be entitled to council in all matters which may be necessary for his defense, as well to facts as to law[.] Similarly, in South Carolina the original Constitution of 1776, did not contain the provision as to counsel, but it was provided as early as 1731, by statute that every person charged with treason, murder, felony, or other capital offense, should be admitted to make full defense by counsel learned in the law. In Virginia there was no original constitutional provision on the subject of right to counsel, but as early as 1734, there was an act declaring that in all trials for capital offenses the prisoner, upon petition to the court, should be allowed counsel. In Connecticut's Constitution of 1818, it provided that "in all criminal prosecutions, the accused shall have a right to be heard by himself and by counsel." However, it appears that the English common law rule had been rejected by Connecticut in practice long prior to 1796. The 1777, Constitution of Georgia did not contain a guarantee with respect to counsel, but its Constitution of 1798, provided that "no person shall be debarred from advocating or defending his cause before any court or tribunal, either by himself or counsel, or both." The first Constitution adopted by Rhode Island in 1842, contained the guaranty with respect to the assistance of counsel in criminal prosecutions. However, as early as 1798, Rhode Island provided by statute that "in all criminal prosecutions, the accused shall enjoy the right ... to have the assistance of counsel for his defence[.]"

Sixth Amendment Right to Counsel: The Sixth Amendment to the Federal Constitution embodies the guarantee of the right to counsel. It is provided in the Sixth Amendment that: "In all criminal prosecutions, the accused shall ... have the Assistance of Counsel for his defence." The United States Supreme Court imposed the Sixth Amendment right to counsel upon States in the case of *Gideon v. Wainwright*, 372 U.S. 335 (1963). The decision in *Gideon* held that the Sixth Amendment required indigent criminal defendants be provided with legal counsel paid for by the government. The right to counsel extends to trial proceedings only. There is no Federal constitutional right to an attorney in post-conviction proceedings.

Right to Effective Assistance of Counsel: The Sixth Amendment right to counsel carries with it the right to have effective assistance of counsel. In *Strickland v. Washington*, 466 U.S. 668 (1984), the United States Supreme Court outlined the test for determining whether a defendant received effective assistance of counsel. *Strickland* held that a convicted defendant's claim that defense counsel's assistance was so defective as to require reversal of a capital conviction or setting aside of a death sentence, requires that the defendant show: (1) that defense counsel's performance was deficient and (2) that the deficient performance prejudiced the defense so as to deprive the defendant of a fair trial or sentencing. Failure to make the required showing of either deficient performance or sufficient prejudice defeats the ineffectiveness claim. Contemporary assessment of defense counsel's conduct is used when determining the deficient performance component of the test. The prejudice component is not dependent upon analysis under the law existing at the time of the deficient performance.

Right to Self-Representation: The constitutional right to counsel carries with it the right of self-representation. This right was first recognized by the United States Supreme Court in the case of *Faretta v. California*, 422 U.S. 806 (1975). The *Faretta* right, as it is called, may be exercised by a defendant charged with a capital offense. A capital defendant may waive his or her right to counsel and represent him/herself. The *Faretta* right is not absolute. The competency standard for waiving the right to counsel, is whether the defendant has sufficient present ability to consult with his or her lawyer with a reasonable degree of rational understanding, and a rational as well as factual understanding of the proceedings against him or her. Even when a trial court determines that a defendant is competent to waive the right to counsel and represent him/herself, the court may still appoint "stand-by" counsel for the defendant to consult with as needed. Courts unanimously agree that a defendant who represents him/herself cannot raise, on appeal, the issue of ineffective assistance of counsel. Some cases have permitted defendants who have utilized stand-by counsel to raise an ineffective assistance of counsel claim on issues that the stand-by counsel was consulted on.

Statutory Counsel in Capital Cases: The law presumes all attorneys are competent to handle any type of legal matter. This presumption is rebuttable. The statutes in some capital punishment jurisdictions rebut this presumption by requiring attorneys, appointed to capital cases for indigent defendants, have a specific number of years of experience as practicing attorneys generally, and in some instances such experience must be in criminal law. *See also* **Andersen v. Treat; Avery v. Alabama; Bill of Rights; Burger v. Kemp; Court Appointed Counsel; Darden v. Wainwright; Estelle v. Smith; Godinez v. Moran; Lockhart v. Fretwell; Murray v. Giarratano; Norris v. Alabama; Patterson v. Alabama; Powell v. Alabama; Powell v. Texas; Satterwhite v. Texas; Strickland v. Washington; Stroble v. California**

Right to Remain Silent

The Fifth Amendment guarantees the right against self-incrimination. This constitutional provision provides that: "No person ... shall be compelled in any criminal case to be a witness against himself."

In Court Silence: The right to remain silent is an expansive right. During a criminal trial the right to remain silent permits a defendant to sit mute during the trial. That is, a defendant cannot be compelled to testify against him/herself. Part of the protection of the constitutional right to remain silent, is that the failure of a defendant to testify in his or her own defense does not create any presumption against the defendant. If a defendant chooses not to testify at trial, no comment or argument about his or her failure to testify is permitted. If a prosecutor comments to the jury about a defendant's failure to testify, courts will generally grant a new trial.

A defendant's right not to be compelled to testify in a court proceeding is qualified. If a trial court grants a defendant immunity from prosecution, he or she may be compelled to testify or may be subject to being held in contempt of court.

Out of Court Silence: In addition to a defendants right to remain silent in court, he or she also has a right not to be

When I left my home on Tuesday, October 25, I was very emotionally distraught. I didn't want to live anymore. I felt like things could never get any worse. When I left home, I was going to ride around a little while and then go to my mom's. As I rode and rode and rode, I felt even more anxiety coming upon me about not wanting to live. I felt I couldn't be a good mom anymore but I didn't want my children to grow up without a mom. I felt I had to end our lives to protect us all from any grief or harm. ~~[crossed out]~~ I had never felt so lonely and so sad in my entire life. I was in love with someone very much, but he didn't love me and never would. I had a very difficult time accepting that. But I had hurt him very much and I could see why he could never love me. When I was @ John D. Long Lake, I had never felt so scared and unsure as I did then. I wanted to end my life so bad and was in my car ready to go down that ramp into the water and I did go part way, but I stopped. I went again and stopped. I then got out of the car and stood by the car frantic wreck. Why was everything so bad in my life? I had no answers to these questions. I dropped to the lowest when I allowed my children to go down that ramp into the water without me. I took off running and screaming "Oh God! Oh God, NO!" What have I done? Why did you let this happen? I wanted to turn around and go back, but I knew it was too late. I was an absolute mental case! I couldn't believe what I had done. I love my children with all my ♥. That will never change. I have prayed to them for forgiveness and hope that they will find it in their ♥ to forgive me. I never

meant to hurt them!! I am sorry for what has happened and I know that I need some help. I don't think I will ever be able to forgive myself for what I have done. My children, Michael and Alex, are with our Heavenly Father now and I know that they will never be hurt again. As a mom, that means more than words could ever say.

I knew from day one, the truth would prevail, but I was so scared I didn't know what to do. It was very tough emotionally to sit and watch my family hurt like they did. It was time to bring a piece of mind to everyone, including myself. My children deserve to have the best and now they will. I broke down on Thursday, November 3 and told Sheriff Howard Wells the truth. It wasn't easy, but after the truth was out, I felt like the world was lifted off my shoulders. I know now that it is going to be a tough and long road ahead of me. At the very moment, I don't feel I will be able to handle what's coming, but I have prayed to God that he give me the strength to survive each day and to face those times and situations in my life that will be extremely painful. I have put my total faith in God and He will take care of me.

Susan V. Smith
11/3/94
5:05 p.m.

Witness
Chief D. Alfrion, 781, Cruceinville, S.C.
Danny Regan, SLED, Cty SC

The voluntary handwritten confession of Susan Smith to the 1994, murder of her two children. A South Carolina jury spared Smith the death penalty, and she was sentenced to prison for life.

forced or tricked into making incriminating statements by government officials outside of a courtroom. In the case of *Miranda v. Arizona*, 384 U.S. 436 (1966), the United States Supreme Court held that a suspect who has been formally arrested, must be warned prior to any questioning (1) that he or she has the right to remain silent, (2) that anything he or she says can be used against him or her in a court of law, (3) that he or she has the right to the presence of an attorney, and (4) that if he or she cannot afford an attorney one will be appointed for him or her prior to any questioning if he or she so desires. After *Miranda* warnings have been given, a suspect may knowingly and intelligently waive these rights and agree to answer questions or make a statement. However, unless and until such warnings and waiver are demonstrated by the prosecution at trial, no evidence obtained as a result of interrogation can be used against a suspect. The voluntariness of a confession or incriminating statements must be determined by the trial judge and may not be submitted to the jury for determination.

In determining whether an individual was in custody, for Fifth Amendment purposes, a court must examine all of the circumstances surrounding the interrogation, but the ultimate inquiry is simply whether there was a formal arrest or restraint on freedom of movement of the degree associated with a formal arrest. The initial determination of custody depends on the objective circumstances of the interrogation, not on the subjective views harbored by either the interrogating officers or the person being questioned. A police officer's subjective view that the individual under questioning is a suspect, if undisclosed, does not bear upon the question of whether the individual is in custody for purposes of *Miranda*.

An officer's knowledge or beliefs may bear upon the custody issue if they are conveyed, by word or deed, to the individual being questioned. Those beliefs are relevant only to the extent they would affect how a reasonable person in the position of the individual being questioned would gauge the breadth of his or her freedom of action. Even a clear statement from an officer that the person under interrogation is a prime suspect is not, in itself, dispositive of the custody issue. The weight and pertinence of any communications regarding the officer's degree of suspicion will depend upon the facts and circumstances of the particular case. In sum, an officer's views concerning the nature of an interrogation, or beliefs concerning the potential culpability of the individual being questioned, may be one among many factors that bear upon the assessment of whether that individual was in custody, but only if the officer's views or beliefs were somehow manifested to the individual under interrogation and would have affected how a reasonable person in that position would perceive his or her freedom to leave.

The prophylactic safeguards of *Miranda* have been extended to pretrial court ordered psychiatric examinations of defendants charged with capital offenses. It has been held that a defendant's constitutional right against compelled self-incrimination precludes subjecting him or her to a psychiatric examination without first informing the defendant of the right to remain silent, and that anything the defendant says can be used against him or her at a capital sentencing proceeding.

Courts have ruled that the inherent unreliability of an involuntary confession requires its exclusion from the penalty phase of a capital prosecution as a proffered non-statutory aggravating circumstance. The exclusion of such evidence is not diminished by the mere fact that a capital felon pled guilty to the crimes related to the confessions. *See also* **Bill of Rights; Bram v. United States; Estelle v. Smith; Fikes v. Alabama; Hardy v. United States; Harris v. South Carolina; Jackson v. Denno; Leyra v. Denno; Lisenba v. California Malinski v. New York; Payne v. Arkansas; Powell v. Texas; Rogers v. Richmond; Sims v. Georgia (I); Spano v. New York; Stansbury v. California; Stewart v. United States; Stroble v. California; Thomas v. Arizona; Townsend v. Sain; Turner v. Pennsylvania; Watts v. Indiana; Wilson v. United States; Ziang v. United States**

Right to Trial by Jury *see* Jury Trial

Ripper Crew Cult Murders The Ripper Crew was a satanic cult composed of Robin Gecht, Edward Spreitzer and brothers Andrew and Thomas Kokoraleis. Authorities believed that during 1981–1982 the cult members abducted and murdered 18 women, many of whom were prostitutes, from the streets of Chicago.

The Ripper Crew murdered their victims in ritualistic fashion. They would cut off the left breast of a victim and eat it as Gecht read passages from the bible.

On October 6, 1992, authorities got a break in their investigation of the numerous unsolved disappearances of women from the Chicago streets. On that day, one of the Ripper

Top, left to right: *Thomas Kokoraleis and Robin Gecht received long prison sentences for their roles in the Ripper Crew murders. (Chicago Police)* Bottom, left to right: *Andrew Kokoraleis and Edward Spreitzer received death setences for their roles in the Ripper Crew murders. Kokoraleis was executed on March 16, 1999. Spreitzer is on death row. (Chicago Police)*

guilty and sentenced to 120 years in prison. Authorities were never able to obtain sufficient evidence to prosecute him for the murder of any of the victims. Thomas Kokoraleis was convicted of the death of one victim and sentenced to life imprisonment, but obtained a reversal of the conviction on appeal. Subsequently he entered a plea bargain and was sentenced to 70 years in prison.

On April 2, 1984, Spreitzer pled guilty to four counts of murder and was sentenced to life imprisonment for each murder. Spreitzer was prosecuted in 1986 for the murder of another victim and was sentenced to death on March 20 of that year. He is now on death row.

Andrew Kokoraleis was prosecuted for the murder of one victim and was sentenced to life imprisonment. He was subsequently prosecuted for the death of another victim. He was found guilty and on March 18, 1985, was sentenced to death. On March 16, 1999, the State of Illinois executed Andrew Kokoraleis by lethal injection.

Robbery   The crime of robbery is a felony offense that is generally defined as the unlawful taking of property of another, from his or her person or in his or her presence, through the use or threat of force or violence. Robbery, without more, cannot be used to inflict the death penalty. The Eighth Amendment of the United States Constitution prohibits this as cruel and unusual punishment. However, the crime of robbery can play a role in a capital prosecution. If robbery occurs during the commission of a homicide it may form the basis of a death-eligible offense, and therefore trigger a capital prose-

Crew's victims was found alive beside a Chicago railroad track. Her left breast had been severed.

The victim was able to identify Gecht, as one of her attackers.

Gecht was arrested on October 20, and shortly thereafter all the members of the Ripper Crew were arrested. It did not take long before the Ripper Crew began pointing fingers at each other and telling authorities about some of their victims.

Gecht was prosecuted in September of 1983 on attempted murder charges involving the surviving victim. He was found guilty and sentenced to 120 years in prison.

cution. *See also* **Felony Murder Rule; Rape and Capital Punishment; Robbery Aggravator**

Robbery Aggravator   The crime of robbery committed during the course of a homicide is a statutory aggravating circumstance in a majority of capital punishment jurisdictions. As a statutory aggravating circumstance, evidence of robbery is used at the penalty phase of a capital prosecution for the factfinder to consider in determining whether to impose the death penalty. *See also* **Aggravating Circumstances; Felony Murder Rule; Robbery**

JURISDICTIONS USING ROBBERY AGGRAVATOR

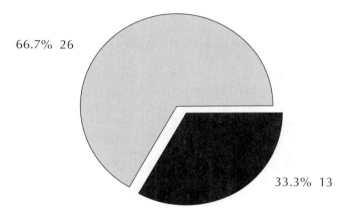

66.7% 26

33.3% 13

█ ROBBERY AGGRAVATOR JURISDICTIONS

█ ALL OTHER JURISDICTIONS

Roberts, Owen J.   Owens J. Roberts served as an associate justice of the United States Supreme Court from 1930 to 1945. While on the Supreme Court Roberts was known as a justice whose judicial philosophy was not "black or white." Roberts took constitutional positions that swung from conservative, to moderate, to liberal.

Roberts was born in Germantown, Pennsylvania on May 2, 1875. He was educated at the University of Pennsylvania where he received an undergraduate degree in 1895 and a law degree in 1898. His career included being a prosecutor and law professor at the University of Pennsylvania. In 1930 President Herbert Hoover appointed Roberts to the Supreme Court.

Roberts was known to have written only three capital punishment opinions while on the Supreme Court. The capital punishment opinion which has kept Robert's name relevant in this area of the law was his opinion for the Supreme Court in *Buchalter v. New York*. The decision in *Buchalter* involved death sentences that were returned against three members of New York's infamous Murder, Inc., crime organization. In *Buchalter* Roberts affirmed the judgments against the defendants, although clear evidence indicated the defendants' trial was marred by extensive pretrial publicity. Roberts took a conservative approach to the issue of pretrial publicity and deferred to the ruling by New York courts that due process of law was not infringed upon because of pretrial publicity. Roberts retired from the Court in 1945 in order to return to academia. He died on May 17, 1955.

Capital Punishment Opinions Written by Roberts

Case Name	Opinion of the Court	Concurring Opinion	Dissenting Opinion
Buchalter v. New York	✓		
Lisenba v. California	✓		
Snyder v. Massachusetts			✓

Roberts v. Louisiana (I)

Court: United States Supreme Court; *Case Citation:* Roberts v. Louisiana, 428 U.S. 325 (1976); *Argued:* March 30–31, 1976; *Decided:* July 2, 1976; *Plurality Opinion:* Justice Stevens announced the Court's judgment and delivered an opinion, in which Stewart and Powell, JJ., joined; *Concurring Statement:* Justice Brenna; *Concurring Statement:* Justice Marshall; *Dissenting Opinion:* Justice White, in which Burger, C. J., and Blackmun and Rehnquist, JJ., joined; *Dissenting Statement:* Chief Justice Burge; *Dissenting Statement:* Justice Blackmun; *Appellate Defense Counsel:* Anthony G. Amsterdam argued; Jack Greenberg, James M. Nabrit III, Peggy C. Davis, James E. Williams, and Richard P. Ieyoub on brief; *Appellate Prosecution Counsel:* James L. Babin argued; William J. Guste, Jr., Walter L. Smith, L. J. Hymel, Jr., and Frank T. Salter, Jr. on brief; *Amicus Curiae Brief Supporting Prosecutor:* 2; *Amicus Curiae Brief Supporting Defendant:* 1.

Issue Presented: Whether the mandatory imposition of the sentence of death for the crime of first-degree murder under the law of Louisiana violates the Eighth and Fourteenth Amendments?

Case Holding: The mandatory imposition of the sentence of death for the crime of first-degree murder under the law of Louisiana violates the Constitution.

Factual and procedural background of case: On August 18, 1973, the defendant, Stanislaus Roberts, and three accomplices murdered a gas station attendant in Louisiana. The defendant was charged with first-degree murder under Louisiana's new death penalty statute, which was enacted in response to the invalidation of all death penalty statutes by the decision in *Furman v. Georgia*. The State's post–*Furman* death penalty statute mandated imposition of the death penalty for five categories of homicide. If a verdict of guilty of first-degree murder was returned, death was mandated regardless of any mercy recommendation.

The defendant was found guilty of first-degree murder and sentenced to death. The Louisiana Supreme Court affirmed, after rejecting the defendant's claim that the new mandatory death penalty statute was unconstitutional. The United States Supreme Court granted certiorari to address the issue.

Plurality opinion in which Justice Stevens announced the Court's judgment and in which Stewart and Powell JJ., joined: Justice Stevens asserted at the outset that the imposition of the death penalty was not per se cruel and unusual punishment violative of the Eighth and Fourteenth Amendments.

However, it was concluded that Louisiana's mandatory death penalty statute violated the Eighth and Fourteenth Amendments. The plurality opinion gave the following reasons for the judgment of the Court:

The history of mandatory death penalty statutes indicates a firm society view that limiting the scope of capital murder is an inadequate response to the harshness and inflexibility of a mandatory death sentence statute. A large group of jurisdiction[s] first responded to the unacceptable severity of the common-law rule of automatic death sentences for all murder convictions by narrowing the definition of capital homicide. Each of these jurisdictions found that approach insufficient and subsequently substituted discretionary sentencing for mandatory death sentences.

The futility of attempting to solve the problems of mandatory death penalty statutes by narrowing the scope of the capital offense stems from our society's rejection of the belief that every offense in alike legal category calls for an identical punishment without regard to the past life and habits of a particular offender....

The constitutional vice of mandatory death sentence statute — lack of focus on the circumstances of the particular offense and the character and propensities of the offender — is not resolved by Louisiana's limitation of first-degree murder to various categories of killings. The diversity of circumstances presented in cases falling within the single category of killings during the commission of a specified felony, as well as the variety of possible offenders involved in such crimes, underscores the rigidity of Louisiana's enactment.... Even the other more narrowly drawn categories of first-degree murderer in the Louisiana law afford no meaningful opportunity for consideration of mitigating factors presented by the circumstances of the particular crime or by the attributes of the individual offender.

Louisiana's mandatory death sentence statute also fails to comply with *Furman's* requirements that standardless jury discretion be replaced by procedures that safeguard against the arbitrary and capricious imposition of death sentences. The State claims that it has adopted satisfactory procedures by taking all sentencing authority from juries in capital murder cases. This was accomplished, according to the State, by deleting the jury's pre–*Furman* authority to return a verdict of guilty without capital punishment in any murder case.

Under the current Louisiana system, however, every jury in a first-degree murder case is instructed on the crimes of second-degree murder and manslaughter and permitted to consider those verdicts even if there is not a scintilla of evidence to support the lesser verdicts. And, if a lesser verdict is returned, it is treated as an acquittal of all greater charges. This responsive verdict procedure not only lacks standards to guide the jury in selecting among first-degree murders, but it plainly invites the jurors to disregard their oaths and choose a verdict for a lesser offense whenever they feel the death penalty is inappropriate. There is an element of capriciousness in making the jurors' power to avoid the death penalty dependent on their willingness to accept this invitation to disregard the trial judge's instructions. The Louisiana procedure neither provides standards to channel jury judgments nor permits review to check the arbitrary exercise of the capital jury's de facto sentencing discretion.

The judgment of the Louisiana Supreme Court was reversed insofar as it upheld the death sentence imposed upon the defendant.

Concurring Statement by Justice Brennan: Justice Brennan wrote that he concurred in the judgment for the reasons stated in his dissenting opinion in *Gregg v. Georgia*.

Concurring Statement by Justice Marshall: Justice Marshall wrote that he concurred in the judgment for the reasons stated in his dissenting opinion in *Gregg v. Georgia.*

Dissenting opinion by Justice White, in which Burger, C. J., and Blackmun and Rehnquist, JJ., joined: Justice White believed that Louisiana's new death penalty statute did not violate the Constitution. He wrote, "[a]s I see it, we are ... in no position to rule that the State's present law, having eliminated the overt discretionary power of juries, suffers from the same constitutional infirmities which led this Court to invalidate the Georgia death penalty statute in *Furman v. Georgia.*" It was reasoned by the dissent that: "Louisiana [has] returned to the mandatory capital punishment system for certain crimes. [Its] legislature[] ha[s] not deemed mandatory punishment, once the crime is proved, to be unacceptable; nor have ... juries rejected it, for the death penalty has been imposed with some regularity. Perhaps we would prefer that the[] State[] had adopted a different system, but the issue is not our individual preferences but the constitutionality of the mandatory system[] chosen by the[] ... State[]. I see no warrant under the Eighth Amendment for refusing to uphold the[] statute[]."

Dissenting statement by Chief Justice Burger: The Chief Justice issued a statement indicating he dissented for the reasons set forth in his dissent in *Furman v. Georgia.*

Dissenting statement by Justice Blackmun: Justice Blackmun issued a statement indicating he dissented for the reasons set forth in his dissent in *Furman v. Georgia.*

Case note: This case was one of numerous cases decided by the Court in 1976, which invalidated death sentences that were imposed under mandatory death sentence statutes. Subsequent to the decision in this case, Louisiana amended its death penalty statute so as to comply with the Constitution. *See also* **Mandatory Death Penalty Statutes; Roberts v. Louisiana (II); Sumner v. Shuman; Woodson v. North Carolina**

Roberts v. Louisiana (II)
Court: United States Supreme Court; *Case Citation:* Roberts v. Louisiana, 431 U.S. 633 (1977); *Argued:* March 28, 1977; *Decided:* June 6, 1977; *Opinion of the Court:* Per Curiam; *Concurring Opinion:* None; *Dissenting Opinion:* Justice Blackmun, in which White and Rehnquist, JJ., joined; *Dissenting Opinion:* Justice Rehnquist, in which White, J., joined; *Dissenting Statement:* Chief Justice Burger; *Appellate Defense Counsel:* Garland R. Rolling argued and briefed; *Appellate Prosecution Counsel:* Louise Korns argued; William J. Guste, Jr. and Harry F. Connick on brief; *Amicus Curiae Brief Supporting Prosecutor:* 3; *Amicus Curiae Brief Supporting Defendant:* None.

Issue Presented: Whether Louisiana's mandatory death penalty requirement for killing a law enforcement officer in the line of duty violated the Eighth and Fourteenth Amendments?

Case Holding: A mandatory death sentence imposed for killing a law enforcement officer in the line of duty violates the Constitution.

Factual and procedural background of case: The defendant, Harry Roberts, was convicted of capital murder by the State of Louisiana. The victim of the offense was a police officer who, at the time of his death, was engaged in the performance of his lawful duties. As required by Louisiana's death penalty statute, punishment for the offense was a mandatory death sentence. The defendant was, accordingly, sentenced to death. The Louisiana Supreme Court affirmed the conviction and sentence. The United States Supreme Court granted certiorari to consider the constitutional validity of the mandatory death sentence.

Opinion of the Court was delivered Per Curiam: The per curiam opinion noted that shortly before the defendant filed his petition with the Court, it decided the case of *Roberts v. Louisiana (I)*, wherein it was held that Louisiana could not enforce its mandatory death penalty statute for a conviction of first-degree murder where the victim was not a police officer. Therefore, the outcome of the case was dictated by *Roberts v. Louisiana (I)*. The Court pointed out that "it is essential that the capital-sentencing decision allow for consideration of whatever mitigating circumstances may be relevant to either the particular offender or the particular offense."

The opinion went on to reason as follows: "To be sure, the fact that the murder victim was a peace officer performing his regular duties may be regarded as an aggravating circumstance. There is a special interest in affording protection to these public servants who regularly must risk their lives in order to guard the safety of other persons and property. But it is incorrect to suppose that no mitigating circumstances can exist when the victim is a police officer. Circumstances such as the youth of the offender, the absence of any prior conviction, the influence of drugs, alcohol, or extreme emotional disturbance, and even the existence of circumstances which the offender reasonably believed provided a moral justification for his conduct are all examples of mitigating facts which might attend the killing of a peace officer and which are considered relevant in other jurisdictions."

The Court found that imposition of a mandatory sentence of death for killing a police officer violated the Constitution. Therefore, the judgment of the Louisiana Supreme Court was reversed and the case remanded.

Dissenting opinion by Justice Blackmun, in which White and Rehnquist, JJ., joined: Justice Blackmun argued that the Constitution did not prohibit Louisiana from enforcing a mandatory death penalty for killing a police officer. He wrote that he " would uphold the State's power to impose such a punishment ... and I would reject any statements or intimations to the contrary in the Court's prior cases."

Dissenting opinion by Justice Rehnquist, in which White, J., joined: Justice Rehnquist articulated strong disagreement with the majority's decision. He believed that Louisiana had a constitutional right to enforce its mandatory death sentence statute. The dissent wrote: "The Court today holds that the State of Louisiana is not entitled to vindicate its substantial interests in protecting the foot soldiers of an ordered society by mandatorily sentencing their murderers to death. This is so even though the State has demonstrated to a jury in a fair trial, beyond a reasonable doubt, that a particular defendant was the murderer, and that he committed the act while possessing 'a specific intent to kill, or to inflict great bodily harm upon, ... a peace officer who was engaged in the performance of his lawful duties....' That holding would have shocked those who drafted the Bill of Rights on which it purports to rest, and would commend itself only to the most imaginative observer as being required by today's 'evolving standards of decency.'"

Dissenting statement by Chief Justice Burger: The Chief Justice issued a statement which read: "I would sustain the Louisiana statute and I therefore dissent on the basis of my dissenting statement in *Roberts v. Louisiana (I)*, and that of Mr. Justice White in *Woodson v. North Carolina*.

Case note: The decision in this case was issued as a per curiam opinion, rather than a memorandum order, because it involved a different provision of Louisiana's death penalty statute than did the plurality opinion in *Roberts v. Louisiana (I)*. See *also* **Mandatory Death Penalty Statutes; Roberts v. Louisiana (I); Sumner v. Shuman; Woodson v. North Carolina**

Robinson v. United States
Court: United States Supreme Court; *Case Citation:* Robinson v. United States, 324 U.S. 282 (1945); *Argued:* February 8, 1945; *Decided:* March 5, 1945; *Opinion of the Court:* Justice Black; *Concurring Opinion:* None; *Dissenting Opinion:* Justice Rutledge, in which Murphy, J., joined; *Appellate Defense Counsel:* Robert E. Hogan argued and briefed; *Appellate Prosecution Counsel:* Edward J. Ennis argued and briefed; *Amicus Curiae Brief Supporting Prosecutor:* None; *Amicus Curiae Brief Supporting Defendant:* None.

Issue Presented: Whether under the Federal Kidnapping Act a sentence of death may only be imposed if the victim's injuries were permanent or the injuries were in existence at the time of the defendant's sentencing?

Case Holding: Under the Federal Kidnapping Act a sentence of death may be imposed even though the victim's injuries were not permanent or the injuries were not in existence at the time of the defendant's sentencing.

Factual and procedural background of case: The defendant, Robinson, was indicted by the United States for violating the Federal Kidnapping Act (Act). The Act authorized the death sentence when the kidnapped victim was harmed. The evidence presented to the jury was to the effect that the kidnapping victim yielded to capture only after the defendant had twice violently struck her on the head with an iron bar; that while held in custody the victim's lips were abraised and made swollen by repeated applications of tape on her mouth; and that wounds resulting from those assaults were not healed when she was liberated after six days of captivity. There was no evidence introduced that the injuries inflicted were permanent, or that the victim still suffered from them when the defendant was tried. The trial court instructed the jury that in determining whether the victim had been liberated unharmed they were limited to a consideration of her condition

at the time she was liberated, and that they were not authorized to recommend the death penalty if at the time of her liberation she had recovered from her injuries. The jury convicted the defendant and sentenced him to death.

The defendant appealed the judgment to a Federal Court of Appeals, arguing that under the Act a sentence of death could only be imposed if the victim's injuries were permanent or the injuries had to be in existence at the time of sentencing. The Court of Appeals rejected the argument and affirmed the conviction and sentence. The United States Supreme Court granted certiorari to consider the issue.

Opinion of the Court by Justice Black: Justice Black rejected the defendant's argument that the Act required the victim's injuries be permanent. The opinion found that the term "permanent injury" was not used in the Act. Justice Black stated the Court's position as follows: "The quality of the injury to which Congress referred is not defined. It may be possible that some types of injury would be of such trifling nature as to be excluded from the category of injuries which Congress had in mind. We need indulge in no speculation in regard to such a category. The injuries inflicted upon his victim were of such degree that they cannot be read out of the Act's scope without contracting it to the point where almost all injuries would be excluded. We find no justification whatever for grafting the word permanent onto the language which Congress adopted." The opinion stated further: "One thing about this Act is not uncertain, and that is the clear purpose of Congress to authorize juries to recommend and judges to inflict the death penalty, under certain circumstances, for kidnappers who harmed their victims. And we cannot doubt that a kidnaper who violently struck the head of his victim with an iron bar, as evidence showed that this [defendant] did, comes within the group Congress had in mind. This purpose to authorize a death penalty is clear even though Congress did not unmistakably mark some boundary between a pin prick and a permanently mutilated body. It is for Congress and not for us to decide whether it is wise public policy to inflict the death penalty at all. We do not know what provision of law, constitutional or statutory, gives us power wholly to nullify the clearly expressed purpose of Congress to authorize the death penalty because of a doubt as to the precise congressional purpose in regard to hypothetical cases that may never arise."

The opinion also rejected the defendant's contention that the victim's injuries had to be in existence at the time of his sentencing. Justice Black wrote: "Nor can we construe the proviso as precluding the death sentence where the kidnapped person's injuries have been healed at the time sentence is imposed. It is not to be assumed that Congress intended a matter of such grave consequence to defendants and the public to turn on the fortuitous circumstance of the length of time that a case is pending in the courts. Far too many contingencies are involved, for example, the time it takes to apprehend a criminal, the condition of the trial docket, and the uncertainties of appeals. We would long hesitate before interpreting the Act so as to make the severity of sentence turn upon the date sentence is ultimately imposed, even if the language of the Act more readily lent itself to such a construction than this one does. At the very least, the proviso's language must mean that the kidnapped person shall not be suffering from injuries when liberated; the kidnapped person here was still suffering from her injuries when liberated." The judgment of the Court of Appeals was affirmed.

Dissenting opinion by Justice Rutledge, in which Murphy, J., joined: Justice Rutledge dissented from the Court's decision. He believed the Act should not have been interpreted so as to impose the death penalty on the defendant under the facts of the case. Justice Rutledge argued as follows:

> This case involves the law's extreme penalty. That penalty should not rest on doubtful command or vague and uncertain conditions. The words used here, for its imposition, are too general and unprecise, the purposes Congress had in using them too obscure and contradictory, the consequences of applying them are too capricious, whether for the victim or for the kidnapper, to permit their giving foundation for exercise of the power of life and death over the citizen, though he be [a] convicted criminal. Other penalties might be rectified with time, if wrong. This one cannot be.

> ... I think the statute turns the power to impose the death penalty upon facts so vaguely defined that only judicial legislation can remedy the defect. This is not the kind of thing courts should be left to work out case by case through the gradual process of inclusion and exclusion. This business rather belongs to Congress, not to the courts. As the Court's opinion states, though I think in contradiction of its judgment, "It is for Congress and not for us to decide whether it is wise public policy to inflict the death penalty at all." Congress' mandate in such matters must be clear; otherwise we, not Congress, decide. In this one it is beyond understanding.

Case note: Under modern capital punishment law, the death penalty may not be imposed for crimes that do not involve death. *See also* **Rape and Capital Punishment**

Rogers v. Alabama

Court: United States Supreme Court; *Case Citation:* Rogers v. Alabama, 192 U.S. 226 (1904); *Argued:* January 4, 1904; *Decided:* January 18, 1904; *Opinion of the Court:* Justice Holmes; *Concurring Opinion:* None; *Dissenting Opinion:* None; *Appellate Defense Counsel:* Wilford H. Smith argued and briefed; *Appellate Prosecution Counsel:* Massey Wilson argued and briefed; *Amicus Curiae Brief Supporting Prosecutor:* None; *Amicus Curiae Brief Supporting Defendant:* None.

Issue Presented: Whether the defendant established that blacks were systematically excluded from the grand jury that indicted him?

Case Holding: The defendant established that blacks were systematically excluded from the grand jury that indicted him, therefore the judgment against him could not stand.

Factual and procedural background of case: The defendant, Dan Rogers, was convicted of capital murder and sentenced to death by the State of Alabama. The Alabama Supreme Court affirmed the judgment. In doing so, the appellate court rejected the defendant's contention that the judgment against him was invalid because blacks were systemati-

cally excluded from the grand jury that indicted him. The United States Supreme Court granted certiorari to consider the issue.

Opinion of the Court by Justice Holmes: Justice Holmes held that the defendant presented sufficient evidence to find that blacks were systematically excluded from the grand jury. It was said that under new provisions of the State's constitution blacks were disqualified from serving on grand juries. The opinion concluded as follows: "We are of opinion that the Federal question is raised by the record, and is properly before us. That question is disposed of by *Carter v. Texas*, and it was error not to apply that decision. The result of that and the earlier cases may be summed up in the following words of the judgment delivered by Mr. Justice Gray: 'Whenever, by any action of a state, whether through its legislature, through its courts, or through its executive or administrative officers, all persons of the African race are excluded, solely because of their race or color, from serving as grand jurors in the criminal prosecution of a person of the African race, the equal protection of the laws is denied to him, contrary to the 14th Amendment of the Constitution of the United States.'" The judgment of the Alabama Supreme Court was reversed. *See also* **Carter v. Texas; Discrimination in Grand or Petit Jury Selection**

Rogers v. Peck

Court: United States Supreme Court; *Case Citation:* Rogers v. Peck, 199 U.S. 425 (1905); *Argued:* November 6, 1905; *Decided:* November 27, 1905; *Opinion of the Court:* Justice Day; *Concurring Opinion:* None; *Dissenting Opinion:* None; *Appellate Defense Counsel:* Tracy L. Jeffords argued; T. W. Moloney and F. M. Butler on brief; *Appellate Prosecution Counsel:* Clarke C. Fitts argued and briefed; *Amicus Curiae Brief Supporting Prosecutor:* None; *Amicus Curiae Brief Supporting Defendant:* None.

Issue Presented: Whether detaining the defendant in solitary confinement until her execution was in violation of due process of law?

Case Holding: Detaining the defendant in solitary confinement until her execution was not in violation of due process of law, as such confinement was provided for by State law.

Factual and procedural background of case: The defendant, Mary Mabel Rogers, was convicted of capital murder by the State of Vermont. Pursuant to statutory authority, the trial court sentenced the defendant to three months hard labor, to be followed by three months of solitary confinement, which would be followed by execution by hanging. The Vermont Supreme Court affirmed the judgment. Subsequently, the defendant filed a habeas corpus petition in a Federal District Court, alleging she was being held in solitary confinement in violation of due process of law. The District Court dismissed the petition. The United States Supreme Court granted certiorari to consider the issue.

Opinion of the Court by Justice Day: Justice Day held that confinement of the defendant in solitary confinement was authorized by the State's death penalty laws. The opinion ruled that due process of law was not violated in the manner in which the defendant was sentenced. Justice Day disposed of the case as follows:

> The court, in sentencing the [defendant] to be hanged …, imposed a sentence of three months at hard labor until within three months of the time fixed for the execution, and three months of solitary confinement next before the day of execution....
>
> … In the present case no sentence or law is being violated, and, assuming the [defendant] to be held in solitary confinement, there is nothing to prevent her having relief at the hands of the state authorities, and nothing to show that the [defendant] is being deprived of her liberty in violation of any right secured to her by the Federal Constitution.
>
> The extent of the right of the Federal courts to interfere by the writ of habeas corpus with the proceedings of courts and other authorities of a state is carefully defined by statute. When a prisoner is in jail he may be released upon habeas corpus when held in violation of his constitutional rights. In the case before us, assuming for this purpose that the [defendant] has been properly convicted and sentenced of one of the gravest offenses known to the law, she is properly restrained of her liberty while in custody, for the purpose of making the sentence effectual. If her custodian is improperly restricting her freedom more than is necessary or legal under state law, there is no reason to suppose that the state authorities will not afford the necessary relief. And certainly there is nothing in this branch of the case to justify Federal interference with the local authority intrusted with the keeping of the prisoner.
>
> The reluctance with which this court will sanction Federal interference with a state in the administration of its domestic law for the prosecution of crime has been frequently stated in the deliverances of the court upon the subject. It is only where fundamental rights, specially secured by the Federal Constitution, are invaded, that such interference is warranted.
>
> We are unable to find that the [defendant] has sustained any violation of rights secured by the Federal Constitution by the proceedings of the executive or judicial departments of the state of Vermont.

The judgment of the District Court was affirmed.

Rogers v. Richmond

Court: United States Supreme Court; *Case Citation:* Rogers v. Richmond, 365 U.S. 534 (1961); *Argued:* November 8–9, 1960; *Decided:* March 20, 1961; *Opinion of the Court:* Justice Frankfurter; *Concurring Opinion:* None; *Dissenting Opinion:* Justice Stewart, in which Clark, J., joined; *Appellate Defense Counsel:* Louis H. Pollak and Jacob D. Zeldes argued and briefed; *Appellate Prosecution Counsel:* Abraham S. Ullman and Robert C. Zampano argued; Arthur T. Gorman on brief; *Amicus Curiae Brief Supporting Prosecutor:* None; *Amicus Curiae Brief Supporting Defendant:* None.

Issue Presented: Whether it was error for the courts of Connecticut to focus upon the truth or falsity of the defendant's confessions, in permitting their use at trial?

Case Holding: It was error for the courts of Connecticut to focus upon the truth or falsity of the defendant's confessions, in permitting their use at trial, when the relevant constitutional inquiry was whether the confessions were coerced.

Factual and procedural background of case:

The defendant, Rogers, was found guilty of capital murder and sentenced to death by the State of Connecticut. On appeal, Connecticut Supreme Court of Errors affirmed the judgment. In doing so, the appellate court rejected the defendant's con-

tention that his confessions were involuntary. The defendant filed a habeas corpus petition in a Federal District Court, arguing that his conviction violated the Due Process Clause because it was based upon his involuntary confessions. The District Court denied relief. A Federal Court of Appeals affirmed. The United States Supreme Court granted certiorari to consider the issue.

Opinion of the Court by Justice Frankfurter:

Justice Frankfurter held that the defendant's conviction could not stand because the State courts used the wrong test in determining the voluntariness of the confessions. It was said that the State courts focused upon whether the confessions were "probably" true, instead of ascertaining whether the confessions were coerced. Justice Frankfurter addressed the issues as follows:

> Our decisions under that Amendment have made clear that convictions following the admission into evidence of confessions which are involuntary, i.e., the product of coercion, either physical or psychological, cannot stand. This is so not because such confessions are unlikely to be true but because the methods used to extract them offend an underlying principle in the enforcement of our criminal law: that ours is an accusatorial and not an inquisitorial system — a system in which the State must establish guilt by evidence independently and freely secured and may not by coercion prove its charge against an accused out of his own mouth....
>
> From a fair reading of [the record], we cannot but conclude that the question whether Rogers' confessions were admissible into evidence was answered by reference to a legal standard which took into account the circumstance of probable truth or falsity. And this is not a permissible standard under the Due Process Clause of the Fourteenth Amendment. The attention of the trial judge should have been focused, for purposes of the Federal Constitution, on the question whether the behavior of the State's law enforcement officials was such as to overbear [the defendant's] will to resist and bring about confessions not freely self-determined — a question to be answered with complete disregard of whether or not [the defendant] in fact spoke the truth. The employment instead, by the trial judge and the Supreme Court of Errors, of a standard infected by the inclusion of references to probable reliability resulted in a constitutionally invalid conviction, pursuant to which Rogers is now detained "in violation of the Constitution." A defendant has the right to be tried according to the substantive and procedural due process requirements of the Fourteenth Amendment. This means that a vital confession, such as is involved in this case, may go to the jury only if it is subjected to screening in accordance with correct constitutional standards. To the extent that in the trial of Rogers evidence was allowed to go to the jury on the basis of standards that departed from constitutional requirements, to that extent he was unconstitutionally tried and the conviction was vitiated by error of constitutional dimension.

The judgment of the Court of appeals was reversed and the case remanded for a new trial.

Dissenting opinion by Justice: Stewart, in which Clark, J., joined:

Justice Stewart dissented from the Court's decision. He argued that the Court should have remanded the case for a hearing to determine whether the confessions were involuntary. Justice Stewart believed that "[w]here, as here, the state trial court's determination of admissibility was at least partly affected by the impermissible factor of probable reliability, ... there can be no question of the federal court's duty to hold such a hearing." *See also* **Right to Remain Silent**

Rolling, Danny *see* Gainsville Ripper Murders

Romania   Romania abolished capital punishment in 1989. *See also* **International Capital Punishment Nations**

Romano v. Oklahoma

Court: United States Supreme Court; *Case Citation:* Romano v. Oklahoma, 512 U.S. 1 (1994); *Argued:* March 22, 1994; *Decided:* June 13, 1994 *Opinion of the Court:* Chief Justice Rehnquist; *Concurring Opinion:* Justice O'Connor; *Dissenting Opinion:* Justice Blackmun; *Dissenting Opinion:* Justice Ginsburg, in which Blackmun, Stevens, and Souter, JJ., joined; *Appellate Defense Counsel:* Not reported; *Appellate Prosecution Counsel:* Not reported; *Amicus Curiae Brief Supporting Prosecutor:* Not reported; *Amicus Curiae Brief Supporting Defendant:* Not reported.

Issue Presented: Whether admission of evidence of an unrelated prior death sentence at the defendant's penalty phase proceeding violated the Constitution?

Case Holding: Admission of evidence of an unrelated prior death sentence at the defendant's penalty phase proceeding did not violate the Constitution.

Factual and procedural background of case: John Joseph Romano was convicted of capital murder by the State of Oklahoma. During the penalty phase of his trial the prosecutor introduced a copy of the judgment and death sentence the defendant had received for another, unrelated murder. The jury sentenced the defendant to a second sentence of death. In affirming the conviction and sentence, the Oklahoma Court of Criminal Appeals acknowledged that the evidence of the defendant's prior death sentence was irrelevant to determining the appropriateness of the second death sentence, but found that admission of the evidence did not violate the United States Supreme Court's decision in *Caldwell v. Mississippi,* or so infect the sentencing determination with unfairness as to amount to a denial of due process. The United States Supreme Court granted certiorari to consider the issue.

Opinion of the Court by Chief Justice Rehnquist: The Chief Justice held that admission of evidence regarding the defendant's prior death sentence did not amount to constitutional error. It was said that under *Caldwell* prosecutors are prohibited from introducing evidence that misleads the jury as to its role in the sentencing process. The opinion found that admission of the evidence did not contravene the principle established in *Caldwell,* because the evidence did not affirmatively mislead the jury regarding its role in the sentencing process so as to diminish its sense of responsibility for the capital sentencing decision. The Chief Justice pointed out that the evidence was not false at the time it was admitted, and did not even pertain to the jury's sentencing role.

The opinion acknowledged that the evidence may have been irrelevant, but that the jury's consideration of it did not render the sentencing proceeding so unreliable that it violated

the Constitution. The Chief Justice found that the fact that the evidence may have been irrelevant as a matter of State law did not render its admission a Federal constitutional error.

It was also said that introduction of the evidence did not so infect the trial with unfairness as to render the jury's imposition of the death penalty a denial of due process. The Chief Justice wrote that presuming the trial court's instructions were followed, the instruction did not offer the jurors any means by which to give effect to the irrelevant evidence of the defendant's prior death sentence. The opinion concluded: "Even assuming that the jury disregarded the trial court's instructions and allowed the evidence of [the defendant's] prior death sentence to influence its decision, it is impossible to know how this evidence might have affected the jury. It seems equally plausible that the evidence could have made the jurors more inclined to impose a death sentence, or it could have made them less inclined to do so. Either conclusion necessarily rests upon one's intuition. To hold on the basis of this record that the admission of evidence relating to [the defendant's] sentence in the [other] case rendered [his] sentencing proceeding for [this] murder fundamentally unfair would thus be an exercise in speculation, rather than reasoned judgment."

Concurring opinion by Justice O'Connor: Justice O'-Connor concurred in the Court's decision on the basis that the evidence introduced was truthful. She wrote as follows:

> ... I believe that [defendant's] *Caldwell* claim fails because the evidence here was accurate, at the time it was admitted. [The defendant's] sentencing jury was told that he had been sentenced to death — and indeed he had been. Introducing that evidence is no different than providing the jury with an accurate description of a State's appellate review process. Both may (though we can never know for sure) lessen the jury's sense of responsibility, but neither is unconstitutional. Though evidence like that involved in this case can rise to the level of a *Caldwell* violation, to do so the evidence must be both inaccurate and tend to undermine the jury's sense of responsibility.
>
> It may well have been better practice for the State to agree to accept [the defendant's] stipulation offer, or to excise the sentencing information before submitting the Judgment and Sentence form to the jury. But under our precedents, because this evidence was accurate, I do not believe its introduction violated the Constitution.

Dissenting opinion by Justice Blackmun: Justice Blackmun dissented from the Court's decision. He argued that the Constitution precluded introduction of evidence of the defendant's prior death sentence because it "created an unacceptable risk of leading the jurors to minimize the importance of their roles." Justice Blackmun concluded that "[e]ven if this particular constitutional error were not present in this case, I would vacate Romano's death sentence and remand for resentencing in adherence to my view that the death penalty cannot be imposed fairly within the constraints of our Constitution."

Dissenting opinion by Justice Ginsburg, in which Blackmun, Stevens, and Souter, JJ., joined: Justice Ginsburg argued in her dissent that the principle established by *Caldwell* controlled the facts of the case and the sentence should therefore be vacated. She wrote: "In my view, this principle, reiterated throughout the Court's *Caldwell* opinion covers the present case: the jury's consideration of evidence at the capital sentencing phase of … Romano's trial, that a prior jury had already sentenced Romano to death, infected the jury's life-or-death deliberations as did the prosecutorial comments condemned in *Caldwell*. Accordingly, I would vacate the death sentence imposed upon Romano and remand for a new sentencing hearing." *See also* **Prior Felony or Homicide Aggravator**

Rooney v. North Dakota

Court: United States Supreme Court; *Case Citation:* Rooney v. North Dakota, 196 U.S. 319 (1905); *Argued:* January 12, 1905; *Decided:* January 23, 1905; *Opinion of the Court:* Justice Harlan; *Concurring Opinion:* None; *Dissenting Opinion:* None; *Appellate Defense Counsel:* B. F. Spalding argued; Seth Newman on brief; *Appellate Prosecution Counsel:* Emerson Hall Smith argued; W. H. Barnett on brief; *Amicus Curiae Brief Supporting Prosecutor:* None; *Amicus Curiae Brief Supporting Defendant:* None.

Issue Presented: Whether application of a new death penalty statute to the defendant violated ex post facto principles?

Case Holding: Application of a new death penalty statute to the defendant did not violate ex post facto principles, because the new law only made minor procedural changes that did not adversely impact the defendant.

Factual and procedural background of case: The defendant, John Rooney, was convicted of capital murder and sentenced to death by the State of North Dakota. The North Dakota Supreme Court affirmed the judgment. In doing so, the appellate court rejected the defendant's contention that the application of new death penalty procedures to him violated ex post facto principles. The United States Supreme Court granted certiorari to consider the issue.

Opinion of the Court by Justice Harlan: Justice Harlan ruled that the changes in the State's death penalty law involved procedural matters that did not implicate the Ex Post Facto Clause. It was said that the new law merely (1) extended the time before execution, (2) required convicted capital felons be maintained in the State penitentiary prior to execution, and (3) required the execution take place within the State penitentiary. Under prior law county jails were used to hold capital felons and execution of a death sentence was done in the yard of a county jail. Justice Harlan disposed of the case as follows:

> We are of opinion that [the new statute] is not repugnant to the constitutional provision declaring that no state shall pass an ex post facto law. It did not create a new offense, nor aggravate or increase the enormity of the crime for the commission of which the accused was convicted, nor require the infliction upon the accused of any greater or more severe punishment than was prescribed by law at the time of the commission of the offense. The changes, looked at in the light of reason and common sense and applied to the present case, are to be taken as favorable, rather than as unfavorable, to him. It may be sometimes difficult to say whether particular changes in the law are or are not in mitigation of the punishment for crimes previously committed. But it must be taken that there is such mitigation when, by the later law, there is an enlargement of the period of confinement prior to the actual execution of the criminal by hanging. The giving, by the later statute, of three months additional time to live, after the rendition of judgment, was clearly to his advantage, for the court must assume that every rational person desires to live as long as he may. If the shortening of the time of confinement, whether in the county jail or in the penitentiary, before execution, would have increased, as undoubtedly it would have increased, the punishment to the disadvantage of a criminal sentenced to be hung, the enlargement of such time must be deemed a change for his benefit. So that a statute which mitigates the rigor of the law in force at the time a crime was committed cannot be regarded as ex post facto with reference to that crime. Besides, the extension of the time to live, given by the later law, increased the opportunity of the accused to obtain a pardon or commutation from the governor of the state before his execution.
>
> Nor was the punishment, in any substantial sense, increased or made more severe by substituting close confinement in the penitentiary prior to execution for confinement in the county jail.…
>
> The objection that the later law required the execution of the sentence of death to take place within the limits of the penitentiary rather than in the county jail, as provided in the previous statute, is without merit. However material the place of confinement may be in case of some crimes not involving life, the place of execution, when the punishment is death, within the limits of the state, is of no practical consequence to the criminal. On such a matter he is not entitled to be heard.…
>
> We are of opinion that the [new] law … did not alter the situation to the material disadvantage of the criminal, and, therefore, was not ex post facto when applied to his case in the particulars mentioned.

The judgment of the North Dakota Supreme Court was affirmed. *See also* **Ex Post Facto Clause**

Rose v. Hodges

Court: United States Supreme Court; *Case Citation:* Rose v. Hodges, 423 U.S. 19 (1975); *Argued:* Not reported; *Decided:* November 11, 1975; *Opinion of the Court:* Per Curiam; *Concurring Opinion:* Non; *Dissenting Opinion:* Justice Brennan, in which Marshall, J., joined; *Dissenting Statement:* Justice Douglas; *Appellate Defense Counsel:* Not reported; *Appellate Prosecution Counsel:* Not reported; *Amicus Curiae Brief Supporting Prosecutor:* Not reported; *Amicus Curiae Brief Supporting Defendant:* Not reported.

Issue Presented: Whether the Constitution requires that, following commutation of a death sentence by a State's Governor, a defendant is entitled to have his or her sentence determined anew by a jury?

Case Holding: The Constitution does not require that, following commutation of a death sentence by a State's Governor, a defendant is entitled to have his or her sentence determined anew by a jury.

Factual and procedural background of case: The defendants, Hodges and Lewis, were convicted and sentenced to death for capital murder by the State of Tennessee. On July 31, 1972, the Tennessee Court of Criminal Appeals affirmed the judgments of conviction, but reversed and remanded the case to the trial court on the issue of punishment, based upon the decision by the United States Supreme Court in *Furman v. Georgia*.

On August 7, 1972, the Governor of Tennessee commuted the defendants' death sentences to 99 years imprisonment. On August 8, 1972, the State filed a timely petition for rehearing in the State Court of Criminal Appeals. The Court of Criminal Appeals then found the commutations by the Governor to be valid and a proper exercise of executive authority, and held its previous remand to be naught, thus affirming the convictions and commuted sentences. The Tennessee Supreme Court denied certiorari.

The defendants then filed a habeas corpus petitioned with a Federal District Court asserting, that their Fourteenth Amendment rights were violated by the illegal commutation of their sentences. The District Court dismissed the petition for failure to exhaust State remedies.

The defendants appealed to a Federal Court of Appeals. The Court of Appeals held that since the death sentences had been vacated at the time of the Governor's commutation order, there were no viable death sentences to commute, therefore the commutations were invalid. The United States Supreme Court granted certiorari to consider the issue.

Opinion of the Court was delivered Per Curiam: The per curiam opinion found that the federal courts lacked jurisdiction to address the issue presented by the defendants. The opinion ruled: "Whether or not the sentences imposed upon [the defendants] were subject to commutation by the Governor, and the extent of his authority under the circumstances of this case, are questions of Tennessee law which were resolved in favor of sustaining the action of the Governor by the Tennessee Court of Criminal Appeals.... It was not the province of a federal habeas court to re-examine these questions."

The opinion rejected the defendants' contention that their Constitutional right to jury trial was infringed by the Tennessee proceedings. It was held that: "A jury had already determined their guilt and sentenced them to death. The Governor commuted these sentences to a term of 99 years after this Court's decision in *Furman v. Georgia*. Neither *Furman* nor any other holding of this Court requires that following such a commutation the defendant shall be entitled to have his sentence determined anew by a jury. If Tennessee chooses to allow the Governor to reduce a death penalty to a term of years without resort to further judicial proceedings, the United States Constitution affords no impediment to that choice." The judgment of the Court of Appeals was reversed.

Dissenting opinion by Justice Brennan, in which Marshall, J., joined: Justice Brennan dissented from the Court's disposition of the case. He wrote: "I dissent on two grounds: first, because the Court errs in reading the record to include a final holding of the Court of Appeals declaring the commutations to be invalid; and, second, because if there were such a final holding, summary disposition of the question of the validity of the commutations — certainly one of first impression in this Court — is particularly inappropriate." Ultimately, Justice Brennan urged strongly that the Court should have allowed the case to be fully briefed and argued, before resolving the critical issue presented.

Dissenting statement by Justice Douglas: Justice Douglas issued a statement indicating that he "would deny certiorari." *See also* **Calderon v. Coleman; California v. Ramos; Clemency; Ohio Adult Parole Authority v. Woodard; Schick v. Reed**

Rosenberg, Julius and Ethel

One of the most famous capital punishment cases in the history of the United States was the Federal prosecution of Julius and Ethel Rosenberg. The Rosenbergs ultimately became the first husband and wife to be executed by the United States.

Julius was born on May 12, 1918. Ethel was born on September 28, 1915. The couple wedded in 1930. The Rosenbergs lived a modest and obscure life until August 17, 1950, when they were indicted for conspiring to commit espionage in wartime, in violation of the Federal Espionage Act of 1917.

The prosecution of the Rosenbergs came at a time when the nation was gripped in the witchhunt for communist sympathizers. The Rosenbergs were members of the American Communist Party. Their involvement with the American Communist Party played a significant role in giving credence to charges that they aided the Soviet Union in stealing the secrets to the atomic bomb from the United States.

The Rosenbergs' trial began on March 6, 1951, at the Federal District Court in New York City. After a lengthy jury trial they were found guilty, and on April 5, 1951, they were sentenced to death by Judge Irving R. Kaufman. The Rosenbergs maintained their innocence up to and including the moment of their executions at Sing Sing Prison on June 19, 1953. *See also* **Rosenberg v. United States**

Julius and Ethel Rosenberg during happier times. (New York State Library)

Rosenberg v. United States

Court: United States Supreme Court; *Case Citation:* Rosenberg v. United States, 346 U.S. 273 (1953); *Argued:* June 18, 1953; *Decided:* June 19, 1953; *Opinion of the Court:* Chief Justice Vinson; *Concurring Opinion:* Justice Jackson, in which Vinson, C.J., and Reed, Burton, and Minton, JJ., joined; *Concurring Opinion:* Justice Clark, in which Vinson, C.J., and Reed, Jackson, Burton and Minton, JJ., joined; *Dissenting Opinion:* Justice Black; *Dissenting Opinion:* Justice Frankfurter; *Dissenting Opinion:* Justice Douglas; *Appellate Defense Counsel:* Daniel G. Marshall argued; Emanuel H. Bloch, John F. Finerty and Fyke Farmer on brief; *Appellate Prosecution Counsel:* Acting Solicitor General Stern argued; Attorney General Brownell on brief; *Amicus Curiae Brief Supporting Prosecutor:* None; *Amicus Curiae Brief*

Supporting Defendants: Denied amicus brief of Dr. W. E. B. DuBois.

Issue Presented: Whether the Atomic Energy Act of 1946 rendered the Federal District Court powerless to impose the death penalty upon the defendants under the Espionage Act of 1917?

Case Holding: The Atomic Energy Act of 1946 did not render the Federal District Court powerless to impose the death penalty upon the defendants under the Espionage Act of 1917.

Factual and procedural background of case: The defendants, Julius Rosenberg and Ethel Rosenberg, were convicted and sentenced to death by the United States for conspiring to violate the Espionage Act of 1917, by communicating to a foreign government, in wartime, secret atomic and other military information. A Federal Court of Appeals affirmed the convictions and sentences. The United States Supreme Court denied certiorari review. Thereafter, several unsuccessful collateral attacks on the sentences were made.

An attorney who had not been retained by the defendants, but who purported to represent them as a "next friend," applied to Justice Douglas for a stay of execution and a writ of habeas corpus, contending that the Atomic Energy Act of 1946 rendered the Federal District Court powerless to impose the death penalty under the Espionage Act of 1917. On June 17, 1953, Justice Douglas denied a writ of habeas corpus but granted a stay of execution, effective until the applicability of the Atomic Energy Act could be determined in the lower courts. The Attorney General of the United States thereafter petitioned the Supreme Court (which was in recess) to convene in Special Term and to vacate the stay. The Supreme Court was convened in Special Term on June 18 and the case was argued on that day. On June 19, the Supreme Court announced its decision in a per curiam opinion, which vacated the stay. The per curiam opinion read:

> The question which has been and now is urged as being substantial is whether the provisions of the Atomic Energy Act of 1946, rendered the District Court powerless to impose the death sentence under the Espionage Act of 1917, under which statute the indictment was laid.
>
> Although this question was raised and presented for the first time to Mr. Justice Douglas by counsel who have never been employed by the Rosenbergs, and who heretofore have not participated in this case, the full Court has considered it on its merits.
>
> We think the question is not substantial. We think further proceedings to litigate it are unwarranted. A conspiracy was charged and proved to violate the Espionage Act in wartime. The Atomic Energy Act did not repeal or limit the provisions of the Espionage Act. Accordingly, we vacate the stay entered by Mr. Justice Douglas on June 17, 1953.
>
> We are entering this order in advance of the preparation of full opinions which will be filed with the Clerk.

The Special Term was adjourned. Thereafter the defendants were executed on June 19. Subsequent to the issuance of the per curiam opinion, the Supreme Court issued signed opinions.

Opinion of the Court by Chief Justice Vinson: The Chief Justice held that Justice Douglas had power to issue the stay, just as all members of the Court have such authority. It was said that the full Court had made no practice of vacating stays issued by single Justices, but that in unusual circumstances the Court would exercise its discretion to vacate a stay of a single Justice. The opinion indicated that a stay should issue only if there is a substantial question to be preserved for further proceedings in the courts. The Chief Justice found that the question of whether the Atomic Energy Act rendered the District Court powerless in the case to impose the death penalty under the Espionage Act was not substantial, and further proceedings to litigate it were unwarranted.

The opinion ruled the Atomic Energy Act did not repeal or limit the penalty provisions of the Espionage Act. It was said that the partial overlap of the two statutes could not repeal the earlier act, unless the intention of the legislature to repeal the earlier statute was clear and manifest. The Chief Justice stated that instead of repealing the penalty provisions of the Espionage Act, the Atomic Energy Act expressly preserved them in undiminished force. It was determined that since the crux of the charges against the defendants alleged overt acts committed before the Atomic Energy Act was enacted, that Atomic Energy Act could not cover the offenses charged.

The Chief Justice concluded that "[i]n the circumstances of this case, in which the Rosenbergs were represented at their trial and in all subsequent proceedings by able and zealous counsel of their own choice, intervention by a stranger as 'next friend,' without authorization by the Rosenbergs and through counsel who had never been retained by them, is to be discountenanced."

Concurring opinion by Justice Jackson, in which Vinson, C.J., and Reed, Burton, and Minton, JJ., joined: Justice Jackson concurred in the Court's opinion. He believed that the Atomic Energy Act did not, by text or intention, supersede the earlier Espionage Act. In addressing the issue of the "next friend" petitioner in the case, Justice Jackson wrote:

> ... The stay was granted solely on the petition of one Edelman, who sought to appear as "next friend" of the Rosenbergs. Of course, there is power to allow such an appearance, under circumstances such as incapacity of the prisoner or isolation from counsel, which make it appropriate to enable the Court to hear a prisoner's case. But in these circumstances the order which grants Edelman standing further to litigate this case in the lower courts cannot be justified.
>
> Edelman is a stranger to the Rosenbergs and to their case. His intervention was unauthorized by them and originally opposed by their counsel. What may be Edelman's purpose in getting himself into this litigation is not explained, although inquiry was made at the bar....
>
> Vacating this stay is not to be construed as indorsing the wisdom or appropriateness to this case of a death sentence. That sentence, however, is permitted by law and, as was previously pointed out, is therefore not within this Court's power of revision.

Concurring opinion by Justice Clark, in which Vinson, C.J., and Reed, Jackson, Burton and Minton, JJ., joined: Justice Clark concurred in the opinion of the Court. He agreed that Justice Douglas had authority to issue the stay under the circumstances presented to him. Justice Clark indicated that in his judgment the Atomic Energy Act did not invalidate the death sentences. He wrote: "In any event, the Government could not have invoked the Atomic Energy Act against these defendants. The crux of the charge alleged overt acts committed in 1944 and 1945, years before that Act went into effect. While some overt acts did in fact take place as late as 1950, they related principally to defendants' efforts to avoid detection and prosecution of earlier deeds. Grave doubts of unconstitutional ex post facto criminality would have attended any prosecution under that statute for transmitting atomic secrets before 1946. Since the Atomic Energy Act thus cannot cover the offenses charged, the alleged inconsistency of its penalty provisions with those of the Espionage Act cannot be sustained."

Dissenting opinion by Justice Black: Justice Black dissented from the Court's opinion. He argued that he did "not believe that Government counsel or th[e] Court has had time or an adequate opportunity to investigate and decide the very serious question raised in asking this Court to vacate the stay granted by Mr. Justice Douglas." Justice Black saw the resolution of the case as a rush to judgment without adequate information. He wrote that "the time ha[d] been too short for [him] to give this question the study it deserves."

The dissenting opinion disagreed with the Court's position that it could set aside the stay entered by Justice Douglas. Justice Black stated that he "found no statute or rule of court which permits the full Court to set aside a mere temporary stay entered by a Justice in obedience to his statutory obligations." He concluded that:

> I am aware also of the argument that Mr. Justice Douglas should not have considered and that we should not now consider the point here involved because the Rosenbergs' lawyers had not originally raised it on appeal. I cannot believe, however, that if the sentence of a citizen to death is plainly illegal, this Court would allow that citizen to be executed on the grounds that his lawyers had "waived" plain error. An illegal execution is no less illegal because a technical ground of "waiver" is assigned to justify it.
>
> ... It is my view based on the limited arguments we have heard that after passage of the Atomic Energy Act of 1946 it was unlawful for a judge to impose the death penalty for unlawful transmittal of atomic secrets unless such a penalty was recommended by the jury trying the case. I think this question should be decided only after time has been afforded counsel for the Government and for the defendants to make more informed arguments than we have yet heard and after this Court has had an opportunity to give more deliberation than it has given up to this date. This I think would be more nearly in harmony with the best judicial traditions.

Dissenting opinion by Justice Frankfurter: Justice Frankfurter dissented from the majority opinion. He argued that the imposition of the death penalty under the Espionage Act was foreclosed by the procedures of the Atomic Energy Act. Justice Frankfurter wrote:

> It is suggested that the overt acts laid in the indictment all occurred before the effective date of the Atomic Energy Act and that hence the indictment did not charge any offense committed after that effective date. But, again, the offense charged in the indictment was a conspiracy, not one or more overt acts. As

the judge told the jury, they had to find a conspiracy in order to convict, a conspiracy aimed principally at obtaining atomic secrets and characterized as such by the overt acts alleged, but a conspiracy, I cannot too often repeat, alleged to have been continuous to a date certain in 1950. The Government having tried the Rosenbergs for a conspiracy, continuing from 1944 to 1950, to reveal atomic secrets among other things, it flies in the face of the charge made, the evidence adduced and the basis on which the conviction was secured now to contend that the terminal date of the Rosenberg conspiracy preceded the effective date of the Atomic Energy Act....

> It thus appears — although, of course, I would feel more secure in my conviction had I had the opportunity to make a thorough study of the lengthy record in this case — that the conspiracy with which the Rosenbergs were charged is one falling in part within the terms of the Atomic Energy Act, passed by Congress in 1946 and specifically dealing with classified information pertaining to the recent developments in atomic energy. There remains the question whether the sentence for such a conspiracy could be imposed under the Espionage Act.

> Congress was not content with the penal provisions of the Espionage Act of 1917 to prevent disclosure of atomic energy information. The relevant provisions of the Atomic Energy Act of 1946 differ in several respects from those of the Espionage Act. For one thing the 1946 Act makes possible the death penalty for disclosures in time of peace as well as in war. Some disclosures which fell generally within the Espionage Act now specifically fall under 10 of the Atomic Energy Act. The decisive thing in this case is that under the Espionage Act the power to impose a sentence of death was left exclusively to the discretion of the court, while under the Atomic Energy Act a sentence of death can be imposed only upon recommendation of the jury.

> Surely it needs only statement that with such a drastic difference in the authority to take life between the Espionage Act and the Atomic Energy Act, it cannot be left within the discretion of a prosecutor whether the judge may impose the death sentence wholly on his own authority or whether he may do so only upon recommendation of the jury. Nothing can rest on the prosecutor's caprice in placing on the indictment the label of the 1917 Act or of the 1946 Act. To seek demonstration of such an absurdity, in defiance of our whole conception of impersonality in the criminal law, would be an exercise in self-stultification. The indorsement of an indictment, the theory under which the prosecutor is operating, his belief or error as to the statute which supports an indictment or under which sentences may be imposed, are all wholly immaterial.

Dissenting opinion by Justice Douglas: Justice Douglas dissented from the Court's opinion. In doing so, he defended his decision to grant the stay of execution. Justice Douglas wrote:

> When the motion for a stay was before me, I was deeply troubled by the legal question tendered. After twelve hours of research and study I concluded, as my opinion indicated, that the question was a substantial one, never presented to this Court and never decided by any court. So I issued the stay order.

> Now I have had the benefit of an additional argument and additional study and reflection. Now I know that I am right on the law.

> The Solicitor General says in oral argument that the Government would have been laughed out of court if the indictment in this case had been laid under the Atomic Energy Act of 1946. I agree. For a part of the crime alleged and proved antedated that Act. And obviously no criminal statute can have retroactive application. But the Solicitor General misses the legal point on which my stay order was based. It is this — whether or not the

death penalty can be imposed without the recommendation of the jury for a crime involving the disclosure of atomic secrets where a part of that crime takes place after the effective date of the Atomic Energy Act.

The crime of the Rosenbergs was a conspiracy that started prior to the Atomic Energy Act and continued almost four years after the effective date of that Act. The overt acts alleged were acts which took place prior to the effective date of the new Act. But that is irrelevant for two reasons. First, acts in pursuance of the conspiracy were proved which took place after the new Act became the law. Second, ... no overt acts were necessary; the crime was complete when the conspiracy was proved. And that conspiracy, as defined in the indictment itself, endured almost four years after the Atomic Energy Act became effective.

The crime therefore took place in substantial part after the new Act became effective, after Congress had written new penalties for conspiracies to disclose atomic secrets. One of the new requirements is that the death penalty for that kind of espionage can be imposed only if the jury recommends it. And here there was no such recommendation. To be sure, this espionage included more than atomic secrets. But there can be no doubt that the death penalty was imposed because of the Rosenbergs' disclosure of atomic secrets. The trial judge, in sentencing the Rosenbergs to death, emphasized that the heinous character of their crime was trafficking in atomic secrets....

But the Congress in 1946 adopted new criminal sanctions for such crimes. Whether Congress was wise or unwise in doing so is no question for us. The cold truth is that the death sentence may not be imposed for what the Rosenbergs did unless the jury so recommends.

Some say, however, that since a part of the Rosenbergs' crime was committed under the old law, the penalties of the old law apply. But it is law too elemental for citation of authority that where two penal statutes may apply — one carrying death, the other imprisonment — the court has no choice but to impose the less harsh sentence.

A suggestion is made that the question comes too late, that since the Rosenbergs did not raise this question on appeal, they are barred from raising it now. But the question of an unlawful sentence is never barred. No man or woman should go to death under an unlawful sentence merely because his lawyer failed to raise the point. It is that function among others that the Great Writ serves....

Here the trial court was without jurisdiction to impose the death penalty, since the jury had not recommended it.

See also **Demosthenes v. Baal; Espionage; Intervention by Next Friend; Rosenberg, Julius and Ethel; Treason; Whitmore v. Arkansas**

Ross v. Aguirre

Court: United States Supreme Court; *Case Citation:* Ross v. Aguirre, 191 U.S. 60 (1903); *Argued:* October 14, 1903; *Decided:* November 2, 1903; *Opinion of the Court:* Justice McKenna; *Concurring Opinion:* None; *Dissenting Opinion:* None; *Appellate Defense Counsel:* W. C. Van Fleet argued; W. B. Treadwell on brief; *Appellate Prosecution Counsel:* U. S. Webb argued; E. B. Power and C. N. Post on brief; *Amicus Curiae Brief Supporting Prosecutor:* None; *Amicus Curiae Brief Supporting Defendant:* None.

Issue Presented: Whether an amendment to California's grand jury statute was valid?

Case Holding: The amendment to California's grand jury statute was valid.

Factual and procedural background of case: The defendant, Burt Ross, was convicted of capital murder and sentenced to death by the State of California. The California Supreme Court affirmed the judgment and the United States Supreme Court denied review. The defendant thereafter filed a habeas corpus petition in a Federal District Court, alleging that the grand jury which indicted him was selected under an invalid law, therefore the judgment against him was obtained in violation of due process of law. The District Court denied relief. The United States Supreme Court granted certiorari to consider the issue.

Opinion of the Court by Justice McKenna: Justice McKenna held that the law under which the grand jury was selected was valid. The opinion indicated that the defendant's argument involved the title given to a statutory amendment to the procedure for selecting grand juries. The defendant contended that the amendment was invalid because the title of the new law was not descriptive of its content, as required by the State's constitution. Justice McKenna rejected the argument and held that the amendment "has but one purpose and contains but one subject. It amends particular sections; it does not revise a whole code." The judgment of the District Court was affirmed.

Ross v. Oklahoma

Court: United States Supreme Court; *Case Citation:* Ross v. Oklahoma, 487 U.S. 81 (1988); *Argued:* January 19, 1988; *reargued* April 18, 1988; *Decided:* June 22, 1988; *Opinion of the Court:* Chief Justice Rehnquist; *Concurring Opinion:* None; *Dissenting Opinion:* Justice Marshall, in which Brennan, Blackmun and Stevens, JJ., joined; *Appellate Defense Counsel:* Gary Peterson argued; Thomas G. Smith, Jr. on brief; *Appellate Prosecution Counsel:* Robert A. Nance argued; Robert H. Henry on brief; *Amicus Curiae Brief Supporting Prosecutor:* None; *Amicus Curiae Brief Supporting Defendant:* 1.

Issue Presented: Whether the defendant's right to a fair trial was violated because the trial court refused to strike a juror for cause?

Case Holding: The defendant's right to a fair trial was not violated because the trial court refused to strike a juror for cause.

Factual and procedural background of case: The defendant, Bobby Lynn Ross, was charged with capital murder by the State of Oklahoma. During jury selection the trial court refused to strike a prospective juror for cause, who had declared that he would vote to impose death automatically if the jury found the defendant guilty. The defendant exercised one of its peremptory challenges to remove the prospective juror. The jury found the defendant guilty and sentenced him to death. The Oklahoma Court of Criminal Appeals affirmed the conviction and sentence. In doing so, the appellate court rejected the defendant's argument that the trial court's refusal to strike the prospective juror for cause violated his Federal constitutional rights. The United States Supreme Court granted certiorari to consider the issue.

Opinion of the Court by Chief Justice Rehnquist: The Chief Justice ruled that the defendant's constitutional right to an impartial jury and fair trial were not violated by the trial judge's refusal to strike the prospective juror for cause. It was said in the opinion that "[a]lthough the trial court erred in failing to dismiss prospective juror ... for cause, the error did not deprive [the defendant] of an impartial jury or of any interest provided by the State." The Chief Justice commented that "[t]he Constitution entitles a criminal defendant to a fair trial, not a perfect one."

The opinion further held that: "Any claim that the jury was not impartial ... must focus ... on the jurors who ultimately sat. None of those 12 jurors ... was challenged for cause by [the defendant], and he has never suggested that any of the 12 was not impartial. '[T]he Constitution presupposes that a jury selected from a fair cross section of the community is impartial, regardless of the mix of individual viewpoints actually represented on the jury, so long as the jurors can conscientiously and properly carry out their sworn duty to apply the law to the facts of the particular case.'"

The Chief Justice indicated that the fact that the defendant had to use a peremptory challenge to cure the trial court's error did not mean that the Constitution was violated, because peremptory challenges are not of constitutional dimension but are merely a means to achieve the end of an impartial jury. The judgment of the Oklahoma Court of Criminal Appeals was affirmed.

Dissenting opinion by Justice Marshall, in which Brennan, Blackmun, and Stevens, JJ., joined: Justice Marshall dissented from the Court's decision. He argued that the Constitution protected the defendant from having to use a peremptory challenge to strike a juror that should have been removed for cause. The dissent reasoned as follows:

> Neither the State nor this Court disputes that the trial court "erred" when it refused to strike [the] juror ... for cause from the jury.... [The juror] twice stated during voir dire that if he were to find Ross guilty of murder, he would automatically vote to impose the death penalty; there is no question that [the juror] was not the fair and impartial juror guaranteed to [the defendant] by the Sixth Amendment. The Court concludes, however, that the trial court's error does not require resentencing because it was "cure[d]" by the defense's use of one of a limited number of peremptory challenges to remove the biased juror. I believe that this conclusion is irreconcilable with this Court's holding just last Term that a similar Sixth Amendment error in capital jury selection requires resentencing if "the composition of the jury panel as a whole could possibly have been affected by the trial court's error."...
>
> I would reverse the judgment of the Oklahoma Court of Criminal Appeals to the extent that it left undisturbed the sentence of death.

See also **Adams v. Texas; Boulden v. Holman; Darden v. Wainwright; Davis v. Georgia; Gray v. Mississippi; Jury Selection; Morgan v. Illinois; Wainwright v. Witt; Witherspoon v. Illinois**

Routier, Darlie Lynn

On the night of June 6, 1996, Texas authorities received a report that Devon Routier and his brother Damon Routier were stabbed to death in their home in Rowlett, Texas. Authorities also received a report that the mother of the children, Darlie Lynn Routier, had her throat slashed at the time the children were killed. The initial report indicated that Darlie and her two sons were attacked by an intruder in their home. During the alleged attack, Darlie's husband and their third infant son were asleep in another part of the home.

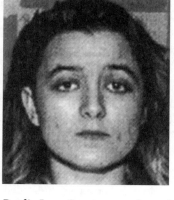

Darlie Lynn Routier was charged with killing two of her sons in 1996. She was prosecuted for the death of one of the children and was convicted. Darlie is on death row in Texas. (Texas Department of Criminal Justice)

The death of Darlie's two sons and her own injury attracted the attention of the media and the tragedy was subsequently broadcast throughout the nation. Sympathy poured into the suburban town of Rowlett from all over the country. Before the nation's prayers and condolences found full expression — they turned to horror and anger. Twelve days after the alleged attack, Darlie was arrested by authorities and charged with the murder of her two sons.

Authorities believed Darlie's neck wound was self-inflicted for the purpose of covering up her role in killing her two children. The motive alleged by authorities was money. It was said that the family's middle-class income was not sufficient to support Darlie in the lifestyle she wanted, therefore she removed the expenses brought on by her two sons by killing them.

Although Darlie maintained her innocence, on February 1, 1997 a jury convicted her of the murder of Damon. On February 4, Darlie was sentenced to death. Authorities decided not to prosecute her for the murder of her second child. Darlie is on death row in Texas.

Rules of Evidence

The admission of evidence at the guilt phase of a capital prosecution is controlled by rules of evidence. However, as a general matter, the rules of evidence are not applied during the penalty phase of a capital prosecution. The rationale for not imposing evidentiary rules at the penalty phase is that, in determining the appropriate sentence, the jury must possess the fullest information possible concerning the capital felon's life, character, criminal record, and the circumstances of the particular offense. Stringently applied evidentiary rules would limit the flow of relevant evidence at the penalty phase. *See also* **Hearsay; Hearsay Exceptions; Queenan v. Oklahoma; Thompson v. Missouri**

Russia

Capital punishment is imposed by Russia. Russia uses the firing squad to carry out the death penalty. In 1996, former Russian President Boris Yeltsin imposed a moratorium on the death penalty. In 1999, President Yeltsin commuted the death sentence of all prisoners condemned to death. The commutation affected 716 death row inmates. The actions taken President Yeltsin did not outlaw capital punishment in Russia. Only the Russian legislature has authority to abolish capital punishment in the nation. Its legal system is based on civil law. The nation adopted a constitution on December 12, 1993.

Under the 1993, constitution of Russia the government is composed of an executive branch, legislative branch, and judicial branch. The executive branch consists of an elected President and a government headed by a Prime Minister. There is a bicameral legislature consisting of the State Duma and the Federation Council.

The judicial system consists of regional courts and a Supreme Court. Defendants have the right to retained or appointed counsel and enjoy a presumption of innocence. Because Russia has not fully made a transition to democratic institutions, different criminal procedure rules exist. It was reported that 80 regions of the country did not use adversarial jury trials. In these regions the trial judge or panel of judges conduct the trial. In other regions adversarial jury trials are optional for defendants charged with crimes carrying a penalty of 15 years or more. *See also* **International Capital Punishment Nations**

Rutledge, Wiley B.

Wiley B. Rutledge served as an associate justice of the United States Supreme Court from 1943 to 1949. While on the Supreme Court Rutledge was known as a liberal interpreter of the Constitution.

Rutledge was born on July 20, 1894 in Cloverport, Kentucky. He received an undergraduate degree from the University of Wisconsin in 1914. Rutledge received a law degree in 1922 after graduating from a law school in Colorado. He went on to become dean of Washington University College of Law and Iowa College of Law. In 1939 Rutledge was appointed by President Franklin D. Roosevelt as an appellate judge on the Court of Appeals for the District of Columbia. President Roosevelt appointed Rutledge to the Supreme Court in 1943.

Rutledge wrote only three known capital punishment opinions. The capital punishment case of *Fisher v. United States* illustrated Rutledge's liberal philosophy. In *Fisher* the defendant argued that he was denied due process of law because of the trial court's refusal to instruct the jury on the defendant's mental deficiency, so as to allow for a sentence less than death. The majority on the Court rejected the argument. Rutledge dissented. He argued that fundamental fairness required such an instruction. The position argued by Rutledge would eventually become constitutional law under modern capital punishment. Rutledge died on September 10, 1949.

Capital Punishment Opinions Written by Rutledge

Case Name	Opinion of the Court	Dissenting Opinion	Concurring and Dissenting
Fisher v. United States		✓	
Malinski v. New York			✓
Robinson v. United States		✓	

Rwanda

Capital punishment is permitted in Rwanda. Rwanda uses the firing squad to carry out the death penalty. In 1998, Rwanda executed 24 prisoners. Its legal system is based on German and Belgian civil law. Rwanda adopted a new constitution on May 5, 1995.

The judicial system consists of trial courts, Court of Appeal, and a Supreme Court. The law provides for public trials and a right to retained legal counsel. *See also* **International Capital Punishment Nations**

Sacco and Vanzetti

In August of 1927, the State of Massachusetts executed Nicola Sacco and Bartolomeo Vanzetti by electrocution. In August of 1977, Governor Michael Dukakis of Massachusetts signed a proclamation that cleared the names of Sacco and Vanzetti for the crimes which sent them to their deaths.

Sacco and Vanzetti were Italian immigrants who had arrived in the United States in 1908. Sacco was a shoe worker by trade and Vanzetti was a fish peddler. Both men were charged with the murders of a paymaster and a security guard, and the theft of more than $15,000 from a shoe factory in South Braintree, Massachusetts, on April 15, 1920.

The trial of Sacco and Vanzetti took place between May 31 and July 14, 1921. The evidence against them boiled down to two circumstantial facts. First, Sacco possessed a pistol of the type used in the murders. Second, they were arrested at a garage as they attempted to claim an automobile that was seen during the South Braintree crimes. This evidence proved sufficient for the jury to return guilty verdicts against both men.

The guilty verdicts against Sacco and Vanzetti caused an international crisis. Support from around the world poured into Massachusetts imploring the State not to execute the two men. The international community viewed the convictions as based upon deep seated prejudice against immigrants.

Left to right: *Nicola Sacco and Bartolomeo Vanzetti were executed on August 23, 1927, for a crime many believe they did not commit. (Massachusetts State Police)*

During the six years that followed their convictions every effort was made to obtain a new trial for Sacco and Vanzetti. All efforts proved futile, even after the 1925 confession of another condemned man named Celestine Madeiros. Celestine claimed that he was a member of a gang that committed the South Braintree crimes. On August 23, 1927, Sacco and Vanzetti were electrocuted.

Saffle v. Parks *Court:* United States Supreme Court; *Case Citation:* Saffle v. Parks, 494 U.S. 484 (1990); *Argued:* November 1, 1989; *Decided:* March 5, 1990; *Opinion of the Court:* Justice Kennedy; *Concurring Opinion:* None; *Dissenting Opinion:* Justice Brennan, in which Marshall, Blackmun and Stevens, JJ., joined; *Appellate Defense Counsel:* Vivian Berger argued and briefed; *Appellate Prosecution Counsel:* Robert A. Nance argued; Robert H. Henry on brief; *Amicus Curiae Brief Supporting Prosecutor:* 1; *Amicus Curiae Brief Supporting Defendant:* None.

Issue Presented: Whether the defendant may obtain Federal habeas relief, when to do so requires the creation of a new constitutional rule after the defendant's capital conviction became final?

Case Holding: The defendant cannot obtain Federal habeas relief, when to do so required the creation of a new constitutional rule after the defendant's capital conviction became final.

Factual and procedural background of case: The defendant, Robyn Parks, was convicted and sentenced for capital murder by the State of Oklahoma. The Oklahoma Court of Criminal Appeals affirmed the conviction and sentence. Subsequent to the defendant's conviction becoming final, he filed a habeas corpus petition in a Federal District Court arguing that his sentence was invalid because the trial court instructed the penalty phase jury not to have sympathy for him during its deliberations. The defendant couched this argument in terms of precluding the jury from considering mitigating evidence submitted by him. The District Court denied relief and dismissed the petition. A Federal Court of Appeals reversed after finding that the instruction was unconstitutional because it in effect told the jury to disregard the mitigating evidence that the defendant had presented. The United States Supreme Court granted certiorari to consider the issue.

Opinion of the Court by Justice Kennedy: Justice Kennedy concluded that the defendant was not entitled to Federal habeas relief. The opinion said that the principle advanced by the defendant required creation of a new rule of Federal con-

stitutional law. The Court's precedents dictated that a new rule of constitutional law could neither be announced nor applied in a case on collateral review, unless it came within one of two exceptions. It was held that the principal advocated by the defendant did not come within the two exceptions to the prohibition against retroactive application of a new rule after a defendant's capital conviction became final.

The opinion pointed out that a principle becomes a new rule if it "breaks new ground," "imposes a new obligation on the States or the Federal Government," or was not "dictated by precedent existing at the time the defendant's conviction became final." Justice Kennedy found that for the Court to hold that the Constitution prohibited trial courts from giving antisympathy instructions at the penalty phase would constitute a new rule, because the Court's precedents did not foreshadow such a rule.

Having decided that the relief the defendant sought would necessitate the creation of a new rule, the opinion turned to the issue of whether the new rule came within either of the two exceptions to the general principle that new rules will not be applied on collateral review. The first exception permits the retroactive application of a new rule if the rule placed an entire category of primary conduct beyond the reach of criminal law or prohibited imposition of a certain type of punishment for a class of defendants because of their status or offense. Justice Kennedy found that the defendant could not invoke this exception. The rule sought by the defendant would neither decriminalize a class of conduct nor prohibit the imposition of capital punishment on a particular class of persons.

The second exception allowed retroactive application of a new rule that was a watershed rule of criminal procedure implicating a criminal proceeding's fundamental fairness and accuracy. This exception was found to be inapplicable, because the new rule was not a rule of criminal procedure implicating the fundamental fairness and accuracy the proceeding. The judgment of the Court of Appeals was reversed.

Dissenting opinion by Justice Brennan, in which Marshall, Blackmun and Stevens, JJ., joined: Justice Brennan dissented from the majority's decision. He believed the Court distorted the issue presented by the defendant, and that the relief sought by the defendant did not require creation of a new rule; it required enforcement of existing law. Justice Brennan stated his position as follows:

> Today, the Court holds that [the defendant] is not entitled to relief because his claim would require the application of a "new rule" that may not be applied retroactively on collateral review. The Court displays undue eagerness to apply the new standard for retroactivity announced in *Butler v. McKellar*, at the expense of thoughtful legal analysis. I cannot countenance such carelessness when a life is at stake. I dissent....
>
> [The defendant] does not ... raise a claim challenging how the jury considered mitigating evidence.... [H]e argues that his jury could have believed it could not consider his mitigating evidence's bearing on moral culpability at all. Thus, his claim clearly falls within the holdings of *Lockett v. Ohio* and *Eddings v. Oklahoma* even under the majority's reading of those cases. The real question in this case is whether the rule of *Lockett* and

Eddings was violated. Resolution of [the defendant's] claim involves only the otherwise familiar inquiry into the sufficiency of the jury instructions, not the recognition of a new principle of law....

For the same reasons that *Lockett* and *Eddings* compel the conclusion that [the defendant] does not seek a "new rule" ... these cases also compel the conclusion that [the defendant] was denied an individualized sentencing determination as required by the Eighth Amendment....

The instructions at the sentencing phase of [the defendant's] trial may well have misled the jury about its duty to consider the mitigating evidence [the defendant's] presented. Until today, the Court consistently has vacated a death sentence and remanded for resentencing when there was any ambiguity about whether the sentencer actually considered mitigating evidence. The Court's failure to adhere to this fundamental Eighth Amendment principle is inexcusable. Distorting [the defendant's] claim and our precedents in order to hide behind the smokescreen of a new standard of retroactivity is even more so.

Case note: Oklahoma executed Robyn Parks by lethal injection on March 10, 1992. *See also* **Butler v. Mckellar; Graham v. Collins; Gray v. Netherland; Lambrix v. Singletary; O'Dell v. Netherland; Retroactive Application of a New Constitutional Rule; Sawyer v. Smith**

St. Clair v. United States

Court: United States Supreme Court; *Case Citation:* St. Clair v. United States, 154 U.S. 134 (1894); *Argued:* Not reported; *Decided:* May 26, 1894; *Opinion of the Court:* Justice Harlan; *Concurring Opinion:* None; *Dissenting Opinion:* None; *Appellate Defense Counsel:* F. J. Kierce argued and briefed; *Appellate Prosecution Counsel:* Mr. Conrad argued and briefed; *Amicus Curiae Brief Supporting Prosecutor:* None; *Amicus Curiae Brief Supporting Defendant:* None.

Issues Presented: (1) Whether the indictment against the defendant was invalid due to its failure to state where the offense occurred? (2) Whether a verdict stating "guilty" was invalid to sustain a conviction for capital murder?

Case Holdings: (1) The indictment against the defendant was not invalid due to its failure to state where the offense occurred, because allegations of crimes committed on the high seas do not need the specificity required of crimes committed on land. (2) A verdict stating "guilty" was not invalid to sustain a conviction for capital murder, where it is possible to infer from the record that no other conviction was intended.

Factual and procedural background of case: The defendant, Thomas St. Clair, was indicted for capital murder by the United States. Also named in the indictment were Herman Sparf and Hans Hansen. The murder took place on the high seas. The case was prosecuted in a Federal District Court in California. The defendant, who was tried separately, was convicted and sentenced to death. The defendant appealed to the United States Supreme Court alleging that the Federal court did not have jurisdiction over the case because the indictment failed to state where the victim was actually killed; and that the verdict against him was invalid because it merely stated "guilty." The United States Supreme Court granted certiorari to consider the issues.

Opinion of the Court by Justice Harlan: Justice Harlan ruled that the defendant's jurisdiction issue was without merit and that the Federal District Court had jurisdiction to prosecute the case. The opinion reasoned as follows:

The objection ... that the indictment did not sufficiently show on what part of the high seas the offense charged was committed, is met by the averment that the offense was committed on board of an American vessel, on the high seas, within the jurisdiction of the court, and within the admiralty and maritime jurisdiction of the United States, and not within the jurisdiction of any particular state of the Union. Nothing more was required to show the locality of the offense. The doctrine of venue in indictments at the common law is inapplicable to cases of this kind.... The reason of the common law for laying the venue so particularly in offenses on land does not in any manner apply to the offense on the high seas, for no jury ever did or could come from the visne or vicinage on the high seas to try the cause, and no summons could issue for such a purpose.

The opinion next turned to the defendant's contention that the verdict was invalid because it only stated "guilty." Justice Harlan, in rejecting the argument, reasoned as follows:

This contention cannot be sustained. We said in [a previous case] that, while the record of a criminal case must state what will affirmatively show the offense, the steps without which the sentence cannot be good, and the sentence itself, all parts of the record must be interpreted together; giving effect to every part if possible, and supplying a deficiency in one part by what appears elsewhere in the record. The indictment contained but one charge, that of murder. The accused was arraigned, and pleaded not guilty of that charge. And while the jury had the physical power to find him guilty of some lesser crime necessarily included in the one charged, or of an attempt to commit the offense so charged, if such attempt was a separate offense, the law will support the verdict with every fair intendment, and therefore will, by construction, supply the words as charged in the indictment. The verdict of "Guilty" in this case will be interpreted as referring to the single offense specified in the indictment.

The judgment of the Federal District Court was affirmed. *See also* **Jurisdiction; Sparf v. United States**

Saint Kitts and Nevis

Capital punishment may be imposed in the island nation of Saint Kitts and Nevis. Saint Kitts and Nevis use hanging as the method of carrying out the death penalty. Its legal system is based on English common law. Saint Kitts and Nevis adopted a constitution on September 19, 1983.

The court system is composed of magistrate courts and a High Court. Appeals may be taken to the Eastern Caribbean Court of Appeal. Final appeal may be made to the Judicial Committee of the Privy Council in England. Defendants have a right to public trials and the right to retained legal counsel. Indigent defendants in capital cases have a right to appointed counsel. *See also* **International Capital Punishment Nations**

Saint Lucia

Saint Lucia permits capital punishment. Saint Lucia uses hanging as the method of carrying out the death penalty. Its legal system is based on English common law. A constitution was adopted by the nation on February 22, 1979.

The court system is composed of magistrate courts and a

High Court. Appeals may be taken to the Eastern Caribbean Court of Appeal. Final appeal may be made to the Judicial Committee of the Privy Council in England. Defendants have a right to a public trial and enjoy a presumption of innocence. In cases involving capital punishment, indigent defendants have a right to appointed legal counsel. In cases not involving capital punishment, defendants must obtain their own legal counsel. Defendants have the right to appeal. *See also* **International Capital Punishment Nations**

Saint Vincent and the Grenadines

Capital punishment is permitted in Saint Vincent and the Grenadines. Saint Vincent and the Grenadines uses hanging as the method of carrying out the death penalty. Its legal system is based on English common law. A constitution was adopted by Saint Vincent and the Grenadines on October 27, 1979.

The court system is composed of magistrate courts and a High Court. Appeals may be taken to the Eastern Caribbean Court of Appeal. Final appeal may be made to the Judicial Committee of the Privy Council in England. Defendants have a right to a public trial and enjoy a presumption of innocence. Defendants also have a right to retained legal counsel. In cases involving capital punishment, indigent defendants have a right to appointed legal counsel. Defendants have the right to appeal. *See also* **International Capital Punishment Nations**

Salem Village Witch Hangings

In 1692, a mass hysteria engulfed Salem Village, Massachusetts. The hysteria centered around wild accusations of witchcraft being practiced by people in the town. The accusations caused the arrest of dozens of people. Trials were held and many were found guilty and sentenced to death. During the period June through September of 1692, a total of 19 men and women who had been convicted of witchcraft, were taken to a place called Gallows Hill and hanged. One of the condemned, an elderly man, was actually executed by having heavy stones pressed against his body for several days.

The Salem Village witch hangings have been traced to 1689, with the arrival of Samuel Parris and his family. Parris was invited to Salem Village to preach in the town's church. In February of 1692, Parris' nine-year-old daughter, Betty, became strangely ill. Her symptoms were manifested by cries of pain that caused her to throw herself on the floor wildly. Shortly after Betty's illness began, several of her playmates began to display similar behavior. One of the town's doctors suggested the children were victims of supernatural powers. This nonmedical diagnosis inflamed gossip of witchcraft being practiced in the town.

When additional children began mimicking the behavior of Betty and her playmates, several women decided to conjure up a potion that would counter the evil spirits afflicting the children. This was a mistake. The women were arrested for practicing witchcraft on February 29. In March a trial was held and one of the women confessed to being a witch. This confession launched hysteria that swept through the town and re-sulted in a relentless quest to find and prosecute all suspected witches.

A special court was set up to prosecute suspected witches. The court was presided over by five judges and a jury. The defendants did not have legal counsel and could not call witnesses to testify under oath on their behalf. The judges forced the defendants to have their bodies examined for marks that would indicate sorcery. Suspect after suspect was brought into court for trial during the months of June through September. Guilty verdicts were constantly handed down and executions swiftly carried out. At some point near the end of the prosecutions, sanity returned to the town and not guilty verdicts began to replace the automatic guilty verdicts. Unfortunately sanity returned only after 19 innocent people were hung and one man was pressed to death by stones.

Samoa

Capital punishment may be imposed in Samoa, but the punishment has not been invoked in over a decade. Its legal system is based on English common law and customary law. A constitution was adopted by Samoa on January 1, 1962. *See also* **International Capital Punishment Nations**

San Marino

Capital punishment was abolished in San Marino for ordinary crimes in 1848, and for all crimes in 1865. *See also* **International Capital Punishment Nations**

São Tomé and Príncipe

São Tomé and Príncipe abolished capital punishment in 1990. *See also* **International Capital Punishment Nations**

Satterwhite v. Texas

Court: United States Supreme Court; *Case Citation:* Satterwhite v. Texas, 486 U.S. 249 (1988); *Argued:* December 8, 1987; *Decided:* May 31, 1988; *Opinion of the Court:* Justice O'Connor; *Concurring Opinion:* Justice Marshall, in which Brennan and Blackmun, JJ., joined; *Concurring Statement:* Justice Blackmun; *Dissenting Opinion:* None; *Justice Taking No Part In Decision:* Justice Kennedy; *Appellate Defense Counsel:* Richard D. Woods argued; Stephen Takas on brief; *Appellate Prosecution Counsel:* Charles A. Palmer argued; Jim Mattox, F. Scott McCown, Paula C. Offenhauser and Mary F. Keller on brief; *Amicus Curiae Brief Supporting Prosecutor:* None; *Amicus Curiae Brief Supporting Defendant:* 1.

Issue Presented: Whether it was harmless error to introduce psychiatric testimony, that was obtained in violation of *Estelle v. Smith*, at the defendant's capital penalty phase hearing?

Case Holding: It was not harmless error to introduce psychiatric testimony, that was obtained in violation of *Estelle v. Smith*, at the defendant's capital penalty phase hearing.

Factual and procedural background of case: The defendant, John T. Satterwhite, was charged with capital murder by the State of Texas. Prior to trial the defendant underwent two court ordered psychiatric evaluations to determine his competency to stand trial and future dangerousness. Both examinations were taken without the knowledge of the defendant's counsel.

The defendant was convicted of capital murder by a jury. During the penalty phase, the prosecutor introduced testimony from the psychiatrist who examined the defendant, indicating that the defendant had "a severe antisocial personality disorder and is extremely dangerous and will commit future acts of violence." The jury returned a verdict recommending the death penalty, which the trial court imposed.

On appeal to the Texas Court of Criminal Appeals, the defendant argued that the testimony by the psychiatrist during the penalty phase violated his constitutional rights, because his attorney was never informed of the psychiatric evaluations that formed the basis of the testimony. The appellate court held that the admission of the psychiatrist's testimony violated the defendant's Sixth Amendment right, as recognized by the United States Supreme Court in *Estelle v. Smith*, but that the constitutional violation was subject to harmless error analysis, and that the error was harmless. The appellate court affirmed the defendant's conviction and sentence. The United States Supreme Court granted certiorari to consider the issue.

Opinion of the Court by Justice O'Connor: Justice O'Connor held that the use of the psychiatrist's testimony at the capital sentencing proceeding, on the issue of future dangerousness, violated the Sixth Amendment. The opinion held that under *Estelle*, defense counsel must be given advance notice of a psychiatric examination and the content of the information sought.

The opinion next discussed the harmless error rule. Under this rule, if the prosecutor can prove beyond a reasonable doubt that a constitutional error did not contribute to the verdict, the error is harmless and the verdict may stand. Justice O'Connor announced that the harmless error rule applied to the admission of psychiatric testimony in violation of the Sixth Amendment. It was acknowledged that the evaluation of the consequences of an error in the penalty phase of a capital case may be difficult because of the discretion that is given to the sentencer. However, it was reasoned that a reviewing court can make an intelligent judgment about whether the erroneous admission of psychiatric testimony might have affected a capital sentencing jury.

Justice O'Connor ruled that the Texas Court of Criminal Appeals improperly held that the erroneous admission of psychiatric testimony was harmless beyond a reasonable doubt. The judgment of the Texas Court of Criminal Appeals was reversed.

Concurring opinion by Justice Marshall, in which Brennan and Blackmun, JJ., joined: Justice Marshall concurred in the Court's decision. He believed, however, that the Court was wrong in extending harmless error analysis to an *Estelle* violation. He addressed this issue as follows:

> I agree with the Court that the psychiatric examination on which [the psychiatrist] testified at the capital sentencing proceeding was in bald violation of *Estelle v. Smith*, and that [the defendant's] death sentence should be vacated. I write separately because I believe the Court errs in applying harmless-error analysis to this Sixth Amendment violation. It is my view that the unique nature of a capital sentencing determination should

cause this Court to be especially hesitant ever to sanction harmless-error review of constitutional errors that taint capital sentencing proceedings, and even if certain constitutional errors might properly be subject to such harmless-error analysis, a violation of *Estelle v. Smith* is not such an error.

> Until today's ruling, this Court never had applied harmless-error analysis to constitutional violations that taint the sentencing phase of a capital trial. In deciding to apply harmless-error analysis to the Sixth Amendment violation in this case, I believe the Court fails to adequately consider the unique nature of a capital sentencing proceeding and a sentencer's decision whether a defendant should live or die. The Court's analysis is also flawed in that it fails to accord any noticeable weight to the qualitative difference of death from all other punishments....

> Because of the moral character of a capital sentencing determination and the substantial discretion placed in the hands of the sentencer, predicting the reaction of a sentencer to a proceeding untainted by constitutional error on the basis of a cold record is a dangerously speculative enterprise.... The threat of an erroneous harmless-error determination thus looms much larger in the capital sentencing context than elsewhere.

Concurring Statement by Justice Blackmun: Justice Blackmun issued a concurring statement indicating he joined Justice Marshall's concurrence "because I agree that harmless-error analysis is inappropriate where the error is a Sixth Amendment violation under *Estelle v. Smith*, which results in the erroneous admission of psychiatric testimony in a capital-sentencing proceeding." *See also* **Estelle v. Smith; Harmless Error Rule; Powell v. Texas; Right to Counsel**

Saudi Arabia Saudia Arabia permits capital punishment. Saudi Arabia carries out the death penalty using stoning and beheading. In 1998, Saudi Arabia executed 29 prisoners. Its legal system is based on Shari'a (Islamic) law. Saudia Arabia does not have a constitution. Saudi Arabia is a monarchy without democratically elected representative institutions or political parties. The nation is ruled by King Fahd Bin Abd Al-Aziz Al Saud. The Government has declared the Islamic holy book the Koran, and the Sunna of the Prophet Muhammad, to be the nation's constitution.

Shari'a courts exercise jurisdiction over criminal cases. Shari'a courts include summary courts, courts of common pleas, and courts of appeal. Defendants may choose any person to represent them by a power of attorney filed with the court. Defendants usually appear without an attorney before a judge, who determines guilt or innocence. Most trials are not open to the public.

The King reviews cases involving capital punishment. The King has the authority to commute death sentences and grant pardons, except for capital crimes committed against individuals. In such cases, he may request the victim's next of kin to pardon the defendant. *See also* **International Capital Punishment Nations**

Sawyer v. Smith *Court:* United States Supreme Court; *Case Citation:* Sawyer v. Smith, 497 U.S. 227 (1990); *Argued:* April 25, 1990; *Decided:* June 21, 1990; *Opinion of the Court:* Justice Kennedy; *Concurring Opinion:* Justice None; *Dissenting*

Opinion: Justice Marshall, in which Brennan, Blackmun and Stevens, JJ., joined; *Appellate Defense Counsel:* Catherine Hancock argued; Elizabeth W. Cole on brief; *Appellate Prosecution Counsel:* Dorothy A. Pendergast argued; John M. Mamoulides and Terry M. Boudreaux on brief; *Amicus Curiae Brief Supporting Prosecutor:* 1; *Amicus Curiae Brief Supporting Defendant:* 3.

Issue Presented: Whether the defendant could challenge his death sentence under a new constitutional rule announced after his conviction became final?

Case Holding: The defendant could not challenge his death sentence under a new constitutional rule announced after his conviction became final.

Factual and procedural background of case: The defendant, Robert Wayne Sawyer, was convicted and sentenced to death for capital murder by the State of Louisiana. The Louisiana Supreme Court affirmed the conviction and sentence. Subsequent to the defendant's conviction and death sentence becoming final in 1984, the defendant filed a habeas corpus petition in a Federal District Court arguing that the prosecutor's closing argument during the penalty phase of his trial diminished the jury's sense of responsibility for the capital sentencing decision, in violation of a new rule announced in 1985, by the United States Supreme Court in *Caldwell v. Mississippi.* The District Court dismissed the petition.

While the defendant's appeal of the denial of his habeas corpus petition was pending in a Federal Court of Appeals, the United States Supreme Court issued an opinion in the noncapital punishment case of *Teague v. Lane,* 489 U.S. 288 (1989), wherein it was held that defendants whose convictions had become final are generally prohibited from utilizing any new rule announced by the Court in subsequent habeas corpus proceedings. Consequently, the Court of Appeals affirmed the District Court's denial of relief, after finding that *Caldwell* announced a new rule within the meaning of *Teague.* The United States Supreme Court granted certiorari to consider the issue.

Opinion of the Court by Justice Kennedy: Justice Kennedy ruled that the defendant was not entitled to Federal habeas relief, because *Caldwell* announced a new rule, as defined by *Teague,* that did not come within either of the *Teague* exceptions. It was noted that under the decision in *Teague* a new rule of constitutional law established after a defendant's conviction had become final may not be used to attack the conviction in a Federal habeas corpus proceeding unless the new rule (1) placed an entire category of primary conduct beyond the reach of criminal law or prohibited imposition of a certain type of punishment for a class of defendants because of their status or offense; or (2) was a watershed rule of criminal procedure implicating a criminal proceeding's fundamental fairness and accuracy. Justice Kennedy found that *Caldwell's* new constitutional rule did not come within either of the *Teague* exceptions.

The opinion noted that the new rule announced in *Caldwell,* prohibiting prosecutors during the closing argument of a capital penalty phase proceeding from making statements that diminished the jury's sense of responsibility for the capital sentencing decision, was not dictated by any precedent existing at the time the defendant's conviction became final. It was said that no case prior to *Caldwell* invalidated a prosecutorial argument as impermissible under the Eighth Amendment.

Because the defendant sought the benefit of a new rule that did not come within either of the *Teague* exceptions, his claim for habeas corpus relief was found to be without merit. The judgment of the Court of Appeals was affirmed.

Dissenting opinion by Justice Marshall, in which Brennan, Blackmun and Stevens, JJ., joined: Justice Marshall dissented from the majority's decision. He believed that the rule announced in *Caldwell* was not precluded from use by the defendant in attacking his death sentence. Justice Marshall argued as follows:

> The Court refuses to address Sawyer's *Caldwell* claim on the merits. Instead, it holds that *Caldwell* created a "new" rule within the meaning of *Teague v. Lane,* and that *Caldwell's* protection against misleading prosecutorial argument is not ... essential to the fundamental fairness of a capital proceeding. To reach this result, the majority misrepresents the source and function of *Caldwell's* prohibitions, thereby applying its newly-crafted retroactivity bar to a case in which the State has no legitimate interest in the finality of the death sentence it obtained through intentional misconduct....
>
> In *Teague,* the plurality declared that a case announces a new rule "if the result was not dictated by precedent existing at the time the defendant's conviction became final." This Term, the Court held that the "'new rule' principle ... validates reasonable, good-faith interpretations of existing precedents made by state courts even though they are shown to be contrary to later decisions." I continue to regard the Court's effort to curtail the scope of federal habeas as inconsistent with Congress's intent to provide state prisoners with an opportunity to redress "unlawful state deprivations of their liberty interests through a fresh and full review of their claims by an Article III court."

Case note: Louisiana executed Robert Wayne Sawyer by lethal injection on March 5, 1993. *See also* **Butler v. McKellar; Graham v. Collins; Gray v. Netherland; Lambrix v. Singletary; O'Dell v. Netherland; Retroactive Application of a New Constitutional Rule; Saffle v. Parks; Sawyer v. Whitley**

Sawyer v. Whitley

Court: United States Supreme Court; *Case Citation:* Sawyer v. Whitley, 505 U.S. 333 (1992); *Argued:* February 25, 1992; *Decided:* June 22, 1992; *Opinion of the Court:* Chief Justice Rehnquist; *Concurring Opinion:* Justice Blackmun; *Concurring Opinion:* Justice Stevens, in which Blackmun and O'Connor, JJ., joined; *Dissenting Opinion:* None; *Appellate Defense Counsel:* R. Neal Walker argued; Nicholas J. Trenticosta and Sarah L. Ottinger on brief; *Appellate Prosecution Counsel:* Dorothy A. Pendergast argued; John M. Mamoulides on brief; *Amicus Curiae Brief Supporting Prosecutor:* 2; *Amicus Curiae Brief Supporting Defendant:* 1.

Issue Presented: Determining the proper standard to use when a defendant brings a successive, abusive, or defaulted Federal habeas claim alleging "actual innocence" of the death penalty?

Case Holding: A defendant filing a successive, abusive, or defaulted Federal habeas claim alleging "actual innocence" of the death penalty, must show by clear and convincing evidence that, but for a constitutional error, no reasonable juror would have found him or her eligible for the death penalty under the applicable State law.

Factual and procedural background of case: The State of Louisiana convicted the defendant, Robert Wayne Sawyer, of capital murder and sentenced him to death. After the defendant exhausted his State and Federal post-conviction remedies, he filed a second habeas corpus petition in a Federal District Court. The defendant's conviction and sentence were previously affirmed by the United States Supreme Court in *Sawyer v. Smith.*

In the second habeas petition the defendant alleged that the prosecutor failed to produce exculpatory evidence and that his trial counsel's failure to introduce mental health records as mitigating evidence during the penalty phase of his prosecution constituted ineffective assistance of counsel. The District Court barred the petition and claims as abusive or successive use of the habeas procedure. A Federal Court of Appeals affirmed, holding that the defendant had not shown cause for failure to raise his claims in his earlier petition, and that it could not otherwise reach the claims' merits because he had not shown that he was "actually innocent" of the death penalty under Louisiana law. The United States Supreme Court granted certiorari to consider the issue.

Opinion of the Court by Chief Justice Rehnquist: The Chief Justice noted that a defendant seeking a second or subsequent habeas corpus remedy must show cause and prejudice before a court will reach the merits of a successive, abusive, or defaulted claim. It was said that even if a defendant cannot meet the standard, a court may hear the merits of such claims if failure to hear them would result in a miscarriage of justice. The miscarriage of justice exception applies where a defendant is "actually innocent" of the crime of which he or she was convicted or the penalty which was imposed. The Chief Justice held that, in the context of a claim of "actual innocence" of the death penalty, in order to establish "actual innocence" a defendant must show by clear and convincing evidence that, but for a constitutional error, no reasonable juror would have found him or her eligible for the death penalty under the applicable State law.

The opinion found that the defendant failed to show that he was actually innocent of the death penalty to which he had been sentenced. The judgment of the Court of Appeals was affirmed.

Concurring opinion by Justice Blackmun: Justice Blackmun concurred in the Court's judgment in the case. He indicated that he did not agree, however, a Federal court was absolutely barred from reviewing a capital defendant's abusive, successive, or procedurally defaulted claim unless the defendant can meet the "clear and convincing evidence" standard announced in the case. Justice Blackmun believed that a lesser standard of proof was more appropriate.

Concurring opinion by Justice Stevens, in which Blackmun and O'Connor, JJ., joined: Justice Stevens concurred in the judgment of the Court. He believed, however, the Court was wrong in erecting a "clear and convincing evidence" standard in order for a capital defendant to have an abusive, defaulted, or successive claim reviewed by a Federal court. Justice Stevens wrote as follows: "... I see no reason to depart from settled law, which clearly requires a defendant pressing a defaulted, successive, or abusive claim to show that a failure to hear his claim will 'probably result' in a fundamental miscarriage of justice. In my opinion, a corresponding standard governs a defaulted, successive, or abusive challenge to a capital sentence: The defendant must show that he is probably — that is, more likely than not —'innocent of the death sentence.'"

Case note: Louisiana executed Robert Wayne Sawyer by lethal injection on March 5, 1993. *See also* **Actual Innocence Claim; Herrera v. Collins; Sawyer v. Smith; Schlup v. Delo**

Scalia, Antonin

Scalia, Antonin Antonin Scalia was appointed to serve as an associate justice of the United States Supreme Court in 1986. While on the Supreme Court Scalia has displayed an ultra conservative interpretation of the Constitution.

Scalia was born in Trenton, New Jersey on March 11, 1936. He attended Georgetown University and received a law degree from Harvard Law School in 1960. Scalia taught administrative law at the University of Chicago before being appointed as an appellate judge on the Court of Appeals for the District of Columbia. In 1986 President Ronald Reagan appointed Scalia to the Supreme Court.

While on the Supreme Court Scalia has written a number of capital punishment opinions. His opinions in this area have displayed his ultra conservative judicial ideology. For example, in *Lankford v. Idaho* the defendant was sentenced to death after being mislead that the death penalty would not be sought. The majority of the Supreme Court believed due process of law prohibited imposition of the death sentence under the facts of the case. However, Scalia dissented. Scalia believed that the mere fact that the defendant was found guilty of the crime of capital murder was sufficient notice that the death penalty would be sought.

Capital Punishment Opinions Written by Scalia

Case Name	Opinion of the Court	Concurring Opinion	Dissenting Opinion	Concurring and Dissenting
Booth v. Maryland			✓	
Buchanan v. Angelone		✓		
Dobbs v. Zant		✓		
Gray v. Mississippi				✓
Herrera v. Collins		✓		
Hitchcock v. Dugger	✓			
Johnson v. Texas		✓		

Case Name	Opinion of the Court	Concurring Opinion	Dissenting Opinion	Concurring and Dissenting
Kyles v. Whitley			✓	
Lambrix v. Singletary	✓			
Lankford v. Idaho			✓	
Lilly v. Virginia		✓		
Loving v. United States		✓		
McKoy v. North Carolina			✓	
Morgan v. Illinois			✓	
Payne v. Tennessee		✓		
Penry v. Lynaugh				✓
Richmond v. Lewis			✓	
Schad v. Arizona		✓		
Schlup v. Delo			✓	
Simmons v. South Carolina			✓	
Sochor v. Florida				✓
South Carolina v. Gathers			✓	
Stanford v. Kentucky	✓			
Stewart v. Martinez-Villareal			✓	
Thompson v. Oklahoma			✓	
Tuggle v. Netherland		✓		
Tuilaepa v. California		✓		
Walton v. Arizona		✓		

Schad v. Arizona

Court: United States Supreme Court; *Case Citation:* Schad v. Arizona, 501 U.S. 624 (1991); *Argued:* February 27, 1991; *Decided:* June 21, 1991; *Plurality Opinion:* Justice Souter announced the Court's judgment and delivered an opinion, in which Rehnquist, C.J., and O'Connor and Kennedy JJ., joined; *Concurring Opinion:* Justice Scalia; *Dissenting Opinion:* Justice White, J., filed a dissenting opinion, in which Marshall, Blackmun, and Stevens, JJ., joined; *Appellate Defense Counsel:* Denise I. Young argued; John M. Bailey on brief; *Appellate Prosecution Counsel:* R. Wayne Ford argued; Robert K. Corbin and Ronald L. Crimson on brief; *Amicus Curiae Brief Supporting Prosecutor:* 24; *Amicus Curiae Brief Supporting Defendant:* None.

Issues Presented: (1) Whether the defendant was entitled to a jury instruction on the lesser included offense of robbery, when the jury was instructed on the lesser included offense of second-degree murder? (2) Whether the defendant's first-degree murder conviction under jury instructions that did not require agreement on whether the defendant was guilty of premeditated murder or felony murder was unconstitutional?

Case Holdings: (1) The defendant was not entitled to a jury instruction on the lesser included offense of robbery, when the jury was instructed on the lesser included offense of second-degree murder. (2) The defendant's first-degree murder conviction under jury instructions that did not require agreement on whether the defendant was guilty of premeditated murder or felony murder was constitutional.

Factual and procedural background of case: The defendant, Edward Harold Schad, was charged with capital murder during the commission of robbery by the State of Arizona. During the guilt phase of the prosecution the defendant requested the trial court instruct the jury on the lesser included offense of robbery, but the trial court refused. However, the trial court agreed to instruct the jury on the lesser included offense of second-degree murder. Additionally, the prosecutor sought and obtained an instruction on both premeditated murder and felony murder. The trial court did not instruct the jury that it had to agree on a single murder theory. The jury convicted the defendant of first-degree murder, and he was sentenced to death. The Arizona Supreme Court affirmed the conviction and sentence. In doing so, the appellate court rejected the defendant's contention that the trial court erred in refusing to give an instruction on the lesser included offense of robbery, and in not requiring the jury to agree on a single theory of murder. The United States Supreme Court granted certiorari to consider the issues.

Plurality opinion in which Justice Souter announced the Court's judgment and in which Rehnquist, C.J., and O'Connor and Kennedy, JJ., joined: Justice Souter ruled that the defendant did not have a constitutional right to have the guilt phase jury instructed on the lesser included offense of robbery. The opinion recognized that in *Beck v. Alabama* the Court held unconstitutional a statute which prohibited lesser included offense instructions in capital cases. Justice Souter noted that *Beck* was based on the concern that a jury convinced that the defendant had committed some violent crime, but not convinced that he or she was guilty of a capital offense, might nonetheless vote for a capital conviction if the only alternative was to set him or her free with no punishment at all. It was ruled that this concern simply was not implicated in the defendant's case, since the jury was given the option of finding him guilty of the lesser included offense of second-degree murder. Justice Souter stated that it would be irrational to assume that the jury chose a capital murder conviction, rather than second-degree murder, as its means of keeping a "robber" off the streets.

Next, Justice Souter ruled that Arizona's characterization of first-degree murder as a single crime that did not require the jury to agree on one of its alternative forms, premeditated murder or felony murder, was not unconstitutional. It was said that the real issue presented by the defendant's argument was whether it was constitutionally acceptable to permit the jury to reach one verdict based on any combination of the alternative findings. Justice Souter found that the Due Process Clause did place limits on a State's capacity to define different states of mind as merely alternative means of committing a single offense. He indicated that it was impossible to lay down any single test for determining when two means are so disparate as to exemplify two inherently separate offenses. Instead, the concept of due process must serve as the measurement of the level of definitional and verdict specificity permitted by the Constitution.

Justice Souter reasoned that in translating the due process demands for fairness and rationality into concrete judgments about the adequacy of legislative determinations, courts should look both to history and widely shared State practices as guides to fundamental values. In using this process, he found it significant that Arizona's equation of the mental states of premeditated and felony murder as a species of the blameworthy state of mind required to prove a single offense of first-degree murder, was supported by substantial historical and contemporary data. In view of those observations, the opinion concluded that the jury's options in the case did not fall beyond the constitutional bounds of fundamental fairness and rationality. The judgment of the Arizona Supreme Court was affirmed.

Concurring opinion by Justice Scalia: Justice Scalia concurred in the Court's decision. He believed that the defendant's argument that the jury should have been instructed to agree on a single theory, did not require due process analysis. He wrote that it had long been the general rule that, when a single crime can be committed in various ways, jurors need not agree upon the method of commission. Justice Scalia indicated that first-degree murder was a traditional crime and that juries traditionally have not been required to agree on the method of its commission.

Dissenting opinion by Justice White, J., filed a dissenting opinion, in which Marshall, Blackmun, and Stevens, JJ., joined: Justice White dissented from the majority decision. He believed that both of the defendant's arguments were decided incorrectly by the Court. Justice White stated his position as follows:

> Because I disagree with the result reached on each of the two separate issues before the Court, and because what I deem to be the proper result on either issue alone warrants reversal of [the defendant's] conviction, I respectfully dissent.
>
> It is true that we generally give great deference to the States in defining the elements of crimes. I fail to see, however, how that truism advances the plurality's case. There is no failure to defer in recognizing the obvious: that premeditated murder and felony murder are alternative courses of conduct by which the crime of first-degree murder may be established....
>
> ... [A] verdict that simply pronounces a defendant "guilty of first-degree murder" provides no clues as to whether the jury agrees that the three elements of premeditated murder or the two elements of felony murder have been proven beyond a reasonable doubt. Instead, it is entirely possible that half of the jury believed the defendant was guilty of premeditated murder and not guilty of felony murder/robbery, while half believed exactly the reverse. To put the matter another way, the plurality affirms this conviction without knowing that even a single element of either of the ways for proving first-degree murder, except the fact of a killing, has been found by a majority of the jury, let alone found unanimously by the jury, as required by Arizona law. A defendant charged with first-degree murder is at least entitled to a verdict — something [the defendant] did not get in this case as long as the possibility exists that no more than six jurors voted for any one element of first-degree murder, except the fact of a killing....
>
> When the State chooses to proceed on various theories, each of which has lesser included offenses, the relevant lesser included instructions and verdict forms on each theory must be given in order to satisfy *Beck*. Anything less renders *Beck*, and the due process it guarantees, meaningless.

See also **Beck v. Alabama; Hopkins v. Reeves; Hopper v. Evans; Lesser Included Offense Instruction**

Schick v. Reed *Court:* United States Supreme Court; *Case Citation:* Schick v. Reed, 419 U.S. 256 (1974); *Argued:* October 23, 1974; *Decided:* December 23, 1974; *Opinion of the Court:* Chief Justice Burger; *Concurring Opinion:* None; *Dissenting Opinion:* Justice Marshall, in which Douglas and Brennan, JJ., joined; *Appellate Defense Counsel:* Homer E. Moyer, Jr. argued; Robert N. Sayler on brief; *Appellate Prosecution Counsel:* Louis F. Claiborne argued; Harry R. Sachse on brief; *Amicus Curiae Brief Supporting Prosecutor:* None; *Amicus Curiae Brief Supporting Defendant:* None.

Issue Presented: Whether the President of the United States may commute a death sentence to life imprisonment, with a condition that the defendant not be eligible for parole?

Case Holding: The President of the United States may commute a death sentence to life imprisonment, with a condition that the defendant not be eligible for parole.

Factual and procedural background of case: The defendant, Maurice L. Schick, was sentenced to death by a military court in 1954. On March 25, 1960, President Eisenhower, acting under the authority of the Constitution, commuted the defendant's death sentence as follows:

> [P]ursuant to the authority vested in me as President of the United States by Article II, Section 2, Clause 1, of the Constitution, the sentence to be put to death is hereby commuted to dishonorable discharge, forfeiture of all pay and allowances becoming due on and after the date of this action, and confinement at hard labor for the term of his [defendant's] natural life. This commutation of sentence is expressly made on the condition that the said Maurice L. Schick shall never have any rights, privileges, claims, or benefits arising under the parole and suspension or remission of sentence laws of the United States and the regulations promulgated thereunder governing Federal prisoners confined in any civilian or military penal institution or any acts amendatory or supplementary thereof.

The action of the President substituted a life sentence for the death sentence imposed in 1954, subject to the conditions described in the commutation. Had the defendant originally received a sentence of life imprisonment, he would have been eligible for parole consideration in March 1969. The condition in the President's order of commutation barred parole at any time.

As a result of the decision of the United States Supreme Court in *Furman v. Georgia*, the defendant challenged the President's authority to condition commutation of his sentence. The defendant filed a habeas corpus petition in a Federal District Court contending that based upon *Furman* he was entitled to be resentenced to a life term with the possibility of parole, and that the President was without authority to condition a commuted death sentence. The District Court dismissed the petition without granting relief. A Court of Appeals affirmed. The United States Supreme Court granted certiorari to consider the matter.

Opinion of the Court by Chief Justice Burger: Chief Justice Burger indicated that it was not necessary, for the disposition of the case, to decide whether *Furman* applied to death sentences imposed by the military. The opinion confined itself to a resolution of the power of the President to condition a commuted death sentence.

The Chief Justice noted "that Presidents throughout our history as a Nation have exercised the power to pardon or commute sentences upon conditions that are not specifically authorized by statute. Such conditions have generally gone unchallenged and ... attacks have been firmly rejected by the courts." The opinion went on to uphold the authority of the President to condition the defendant's commuted death sentence as follows:

> A fair reading of the history of the English pardoning power, from which our [Article II, Section 2, Clause 1] derives, of the language of that clause itself, and of the unbroken practice since 1790 compels the conclusion that the power flows from the Constitution alone, not from any legislative enactments, and that it cannot be modified, abridged, or diminished by the Congress. Additionally, considerations of public policy and humanitarian impulses support an interpretation of that power so as to permit the attachment of any condition which does not otherwise offend the Constitution. The plain purpose of the broad power conferred by [the Constitution], was to allow plenary authority in the President to "forgive" the convicted person in part or entirely, to reduce a penalty in terms of a specified number of years, or to alter it with conditions which are in themselves constitutionally unobjectionable. If we were to accept [defendant's] contentions, a commutation of his death sentence to 25 or 30 years would be subject to the same challenge as is now made, i. e., that parole must be available to [him] because it is to others. That such an interpretation of [the Constitution] would in all probability tend to inhibit the exercise of the pardoning power and reduce the frequency of commutations is hardly open to doubt. We therefore hold that the pardoning power is an enumerated power of the Constitution and that its limitations, if any, must be found in the Constitution itself. It would be a curious logic to allow a convicted person who petitions for mercy to retain the full benefit of a lesser punishment with conditions, yet escape burdens readily assumed in accepting the commutation which he sought.

> Petitioner's claim must therefore fail. The no-parole condition attached to the commutation of his death sentence is similar to sanctions imposed by legislatures such as mandatory minimum sentences or statutes otherwise precluding parole; it does not offend the Constitution. Similarly, the President's action derived solely from his [constitutional] powers; it did not depend upon ... any ... statute fixing a death penalty for murder.... Of course, the President may not aggravate punishment; the sentence imposed by statute is therefore relevant to a limited extent. But, as shown, the President has constitutional power to attach conditions to his commutation of any sentence. Thus, even if *Furman v. Georgia* applies to the military, a matter which we need not and do not decide, it could not affect a conditional commutation which was granted 12 years earlier.

The opinion went on to affirm the judgment of the Court of Appeals.

Dissenting opinion by Justice Marshall, in which Douglas and Brennan, JJ., joined: Justice Marshall dissented from the Court's opinion. He believed that a fair resolution of the case could only be achieved by addressing the application of *Furman.* He wrote:

> The Court today denies [the defendant] relief from the no-parole condition of his commuted death sentence, paying only lip service to our intervening decision in *Furman v. Georgia.* Because I believe the retrospective application of *Furman* requires us to vacate [the defendant's] sentence and substitute the only lawful alternative — life with the opportunity for parole, I respectfully dissent....

> [T]he no-parole condition is constitutionally defective in the face of the retrospective application of Furman and the extra-legal nature of the Executive action. I would nullify the condition, and direct the lower court to remand the case for resentencing to the only alternative available — life with the opportunity for parole — and its attendant benefits.

See also **Calderon v. Coleman; California v. Ramos; Clemency; Military Death Penalty Law; Ohio Adult Parole Authority v. Woodard; Rose v. Hodges**

Schiro v. Farley

Court: United States Supreme Court; *Case Citation:* Schiro v. Farley, 510 U.S. 222 (1994); *Argued:* November 1, 1993; *Decided:* January 19, 1994; *Opinion of the Court:* Justice O'Connor; *Concurring Opinion:* None; *Dissenting Opinion:* Justice Blackmun; *Dissenting Opinion:* Justice Stevens, in which Blackmun, J., joined; *Appellate Defense Counsel:* Not reported; *Appellate Prosecution Counsel:* Not reported; *Amicus Curiae Brief Supporting Prosecutor:* Not reported; *Amicus Curiae Brief Supporting Defendant:* Not reported.

Issue Presented: Whether the Double Jeopardy Clause required reversal of the defendant's sentence of death?

Case Holding: The Double Jeopardy Clause did not require reversal of the defendant's sentence of death.

Factual and procedural background of case: The State of Indiana charged the defendant, Thomas Schiro, with one count of committing capital murder "intentionally," and a second count of committing capital murder during the course of a rape. A guilt phase jury convicted the defendant of the second count of committing capital murder during a rape, but did not return a verdict on the first count. At the penalty phase the jury recommended life imprisonment. However, the trial court imposed a death sentence, after finding the prosecutor proved the statutory aggravating circumstance that the defendant committed the murder by "intentionally" killing the victim while committing rape. The Indiana Supreme Court affirmed the conviction and sentence on direct appeal and on a habeas appeal.

The defendant subsequently filed a habeas corpus petition in a Federal District Court, contending that the guilt phase jury's failure to convict him on the first count of capital murder operated as an acquittal of intentional murder, and that the Double Jeopardy Clause prohibited the use of the intentional murder aggravating circumstance at the penalty phase. The District Court rejected the argument and dismissed the petition. A Federal Court of Appeals affirmed the dismissal. The United States Supreme Court granted certiorari to consider the issue.

Opinion of the Court by Justice O'Connor: Justice O'-Connor ruled that the Double Jeopardy Clause did not require reversal of the defendant's death sentence. It was said that the defendant's argument that his sentencing proceeding amounted to a successive prosecution for intentional murder in violation of the Double Jeopardy Clause was inconsistent with the Court's prior decisions. Justice O'Connor indicated that because a second sentencing proceeding following retrial ordinarily is constitutional, an initial sentencing proceeding following trial on the issue of guilt does not violate the Double Jeopardy Clause Constitution. The opinion found that, as applied to successive prosecutions, the Double Jeopardy Clause is written in terms of risk of trial and conviction, not punishment. The judgment of the Court of Appeals was affirmed.

Dissenting opinion by Justice Blackmun: Justice Blackmun argued in his dissent that the Double Jeopardy Clause was applicable to a capital sentencing proceeding. He wrote as follows:

> The "trial-like" nature of [the defendant's] capital sentencing proceeding, and the trauma he necessarily underwent in defending against the sentence of death, are directly analogous to guilt-phase proceedings, and thus bring the Double Jeopardy Clause into play.
>
> ... [T]he jury's failure to convict [him] of intentional murder impliedly acquitted him under the Double Jeopardy Clause.... [T]here is no question that [he] could not have been reprosecuted for intentional murder. Nor is there any question that the aggravator required the prosecution to prove again at sentencing, beyond a reasonable doubt, the identical elements of that murder charge. Thus, "the jury ha[d] already acquitted the defendant of whatever was necessary to impose the death sentence...." This sentence cannot be tolerated under the Double Jeopardy Clause.

Dissenting opinion by Justice Stevens, in which Blackmun, J., joined: Justice Stevens argued in his dissent that the Double Jeopardy Clause barred imposition of the death penalty. He wrote: "The jury found Thomas Schiro guilty of felony murder, but not intentional murder. Thereafter, in a separate sentencing hearing, the same jury unanimously concluded that Schiro did not deserve the death penalty, presumably because he had not intended to kill. Nevertheless, ... the trial judge overrode the jury's recommendation and sentenced Schiro to death.... [T]he judge found that Schiro had intentionally killed his victim. That finding, like the majority's holding today, violated the central purpose of the Double Jeopardy Clause. After the issue of intent had been raised at trial and twice resolved by the jury, ... it was constitutionally impermissible for the trial judge to reexamine the issue. Because the death sentence rests entirely on that unauthorized finding, the law requires that it be set aside." *See also* **Double Jeopardy Clause**

Schlup v. Delo
Court: United States Supreme Court; *Case Citation:* Schlup v. Delo, 513 U.S. 298 (1995); *Argued:* October 3, 1994; *Decided:* January 23, 1995; *Opinion of the Court:* Justice Stevens; *Concurring Opinion:* Justice O'Connor; *Dissenting Opinion:* Chief Justice Rehnquist, in which Kennedy and Thomas, JJ., joined; *Dissenting Opinion:* Justice Scalia, in which Thomas, J., joined; *Appellate Defense Counsel:* Not reported; *Appellate Prosecution Counsel:* Not reported; *Amicus Curiae Brief Supporting Prosecutor:* Not reported. *Amicus Curiae Brief Supporting Defendant:* Not reported

Issue Presented: Whether the burden of proof on an actual innocence claim requires the defendant demonstrate by clear and convincing evidence that but for a constitutional error, no reasonable juror would have found him guilty.

Case Holding: The burden of proof on an actual innocence claim does not require the defendant demonstrate by clear and convincing evidence that but for a constitutional error, no reasonable juror would have found him guilty; instead, the defendant must show that, in light of the new evidence, it is more likely than not that no reasonable juror would have found him guilty beyond a reasonable doubt.

Factual and procedural background of case: The defendant, Lloyd E. Schlup, was convicted and sentenced to death for capital murder by the State of Missouri. On direct appeal, the Missouri Supreme Court affirmed the conviction and sentence. The defendant subsequently filed State and Federal habeas corpus petitions, but was denied relief.

The defendant filed a second Federal habeas petition in a District Court alleging that constitutional error at his trial deprived the jury of critical evidence that would have established his innocence. The District Court dismissed the petition without addressing its merits after concluding that the defendant could not satisfy the threshold showing of "actual innocence." The District Court ruled that the burden of proof on an actual innocence claim required the defendant demonstrate by clear and convincing evidence that but for a constitutional error, no reasonable juror would have found him guilty. A Federal Court of Appeals affirmed. The United States Supreme Court granted certiorari to consider whether the "clear and convincing evidence" standard used was the correct standard for the defendant's actual innocence claim.

Opinion of the Court by Justice Stevens: Justice Stevens ruled that the lower Federal courts applied the wrong standard of proof to the defendant's actual innocence claim. The opinion pointed out that under the Court's holding in *Sawyer v. Whitley*, in order for a defendant who had exhausted his or her right to file a habeas corpus petition in Federal court, the defendant had to bring an actual innocence claim and demonstrate by clear and convincing evidence that, but for the alleged constitutional error, no reasonable juror would have imposed the death penalty on him or her. Justice Stevens believed the burden imposed by *Sawyer* for showing actual innocence of punishment, was too high for showing actual innocence of the crime for which a defendant was convicted.

The opinion ruled that better standard of proof for an actual innocence claim premised on guilt of the crime, was the standard of announced by the Court in the non-capital case of *Murray v. Carrier*, 477 U.S. 478 (1986). It was said that under *Murray*, when a defendant raises a claim of actual innocence to avoid a procedural bar to the consideration of the merits of his or her constitutional claims, the defendant must show that, in light of the new evidence, it is "more likely than not" that no reasonable juror would have found him guilty beyond a reasonable doubt. It was said that the focus on actual innocence means that a court is not bound by the admissibility rules that would govern at trial, but may consider the probative force of relevant evidence that was either wrongly excluded or unavailable at trial. The reviewing court must make a probabilistic determination about what reasonable, properly instructed jurors would do. The opinion added that it is presumed that a reasonable juror would consider fairly all of the evidence presented and would conscientiously obey the trial court's instructions requiring proof beyond a reasonable doubt.

The judgment of the Court of Appeals was reversed and the case was remanded with instructions that the defendant's petition be evaluated under *Murray's* actual innocence standard.

Concurring opinion by Justice O'Connor: Justice O'Connor wrote in her concurring opinion that she agreed with the Court's reasoning and adoption of *Murray's* actual innocence standard to capital cases. She pointed out that she believed "[t]he Court today does not sow confusion in the law. Rather, it properly balances the dictates of justice with the need to ensure that the actual innocence exception remains only a 'safety valve' for the 'extraordinary case.'"

Dissenting opinion by Chief Justice Rehnquist, in which Kennedy and Thomas, JJ., joined: The Chief Justice dissented from the Court's opinion on the grounds that confusion would result from having two different actual innocent standards in capital cases. The dissent wrote: "The Court decides that the threshold standard for a showing of 'actual innocence' in a successive or abusive habeas petition is that set forth in *Murray v. Carrier*, rather than that set forth in *Sawyer v. Whitley*.... I believe the *Sawyer* standard should be applied to claims of guilt or innocence as well as to challenges to a petitioner's sentence. But, more importantly, I believe the Court's exegesis of the *Carrier* standard both waters down the standard suggested in that case, and will inevitably create confusion in the lower courts."

Dissenting opinion by Justice Scalia, in which Thomas, J., joined: Justice Scalia wrote in his dissenting opinion that he believed the Court should not disturb lower court rulings involving successive or abusive habeas corpus petitions, when there has been no abuse of discretion. He argued that no evidence was shown to demonstrate that the Court of Appeals or District Court abused their discretion in denying the defendant's successive petition. *See also* **Actual Innocence Claim; Herrera v. Collins; Sawyer v. Whitley**

Schwab, Michael *see* **Chicago Labor Riots of 1886; Schwab v. Berggren**

Schwab v. Berggren
Court: United States Supreme Court; *Case Citation:* Schwab v. Berggren, 143 U.S. 442 (1892); *Argued:* Not reported; *Decided:* February 29, 1892; *Opinion of the Court:* Justice Harlan; *Concurring Opinion:*

None; *Dissenting Opinion:* None; *Appellate Defense Counsel:* Benjamin F. Butler argued; Moses Salomon on brief; *Appellate Prosecution Counsel:* George Hunt argued; E. S. Smith on brief; *Amicus Curiae Brief Supporting Prosecutor:* None; *Amicus Curiae Brief Supporting Defendant:* None.

Issue Presented: Whether the defendant had a constitutional right to be present in person when the State appellate court affirmed his death sentence?

Case Holding: The defendant did not have a constitutional right to be present in person when the State appellate court affirmed his death sentence, because such right was only according at the trial court level when the original sentence was pronounced.

Factual and procedural background of case: The defendant, Michael Schwab, was prosecuted, along with seven other defendants, for the capital murder of a police officer by the State of Illinois. The other defendants were August Spies, Samuel Fielden, Albert R. Parsons, Adolph Fischer, George Engel, Louis Lingg, and Oscar W. Neebe. All of the defendants were found guilty by a jury. Schwab and six of the other defendants were sentenced to death. One defendant, Neebe, was sentenced to 15 years imprisonment. The Illinois Supreme Court affirmed all of the judgments. In *Ex Parte Spies*, the United States Supreme Court affirmed all of the judgments.

The defendant, Schwab, had his sentence commuted to life imprisonment by the governor of Illinois (Fielden's sentence was also commuted to life imprisonment). Subsequently, the defendant filed a habeas corpus petition in a Federal District Court, alleging his constitutional rights were violated because he was not present when the State appellate court affirmed the original death sentence, therefore his detention under the commutation was unlawful. The petition was dismissed. The United States Supreme Court granted certiorari to consider the issue.

Opinion of the Court by Justice Harlan: Justice Harlan ruled that the Constitution was not violated because the defendant was not present when the original death sentence was affirmed by the State appellate court. The opinion stated the following:

> At common law, it was deemed essential in capital cases that inquiry be made of the defendant, before judgment was passed, whether he had anything to say why the sentence of death should not be pronounced upon him; thus giving him an opportunity to allege any ... objection to further proceedings against him. This privilege was deemed of such substantial value to the accused that the judgment would be reversed if the record did not show that it was accorded to him.
>
> But this rule of the common law, as the authorities clearly show, applied to the court of original jurisdiction which pronounced the sentence, and not to an appellate court[.]
>
> ... [N]either reason nor public policy require that he shall be personally present pending proceedings in an appellate court whose only function is to determine whether ... there appear any error of law to the prejudice of the accused.... We do not mean to say that the appellate court may not, under some circumstances, require his personal presence, but only that his presence is not essential to its jurisdiction to proceed with the case.

The judgment of the District Court was affirmed. *See also*

Allocution; Chicago Labor Riots of 1886; Ex Parte Spies; Fielden v. Illinois

Scott, Roger *see* Child Killers

Scottsboro Boys

The obscure town of Scottsboro, Alabama became the focus of national and international attention after two girls, Victoria Price and Ruby Bates, reported to authorities that they were raped on March 24, 1931, by nine African Americans while onboard a freight train. The nine Scottsboro boys, as they became known, were: Roy Wright (13), Eugene Williams (13), Andy Wright (17), Haywood Patterson (17), Olen Montgomery (17), Willie Roberson (17), Ozzie Powell (16), Charles Weems (21) and Clarence Norris (21).

On April 19, 1931, the Scottsboro boys were prosecuted without counsel and, except for Roy Wright (mistrial), were found guilty and sentenced to death. The death sentences were overturned by the United States Supreme Court. Eventually charges were dropped against four of the Scottsboro boys: Roy Wright, Eugene Williams, Olen Montgomery, and Willie Roberson.

Haywood Patterson was convicted again on the rape charge in January of 1936 and sentenced to 75 years imprisonment. In 1948, Patterson escaped from prison and fled to Michigan. The governor of Michigan refused to extradite Patterson back to Alabama.

In 1937, Andy Wright, Charlie Weems, and Ozzie Powell were again convicted, but sentenced to prison terms. Clarence Norris was also convicted again in 1937, but he was sentenced to death. The death sentence was commuted to life imprisonment by Alabama's governor in 1938. In October of 1976, Alabama governor George Wallace granted a pardon to Norris. *See also* **Norris v. Alabama; Patterson v. Alabama; Powell v. Alabama**

Search and Seizure Clause *see* Bill of Rights

Security on Campus

Security on Campus (SOC) is a nonprofit organization founded in 1987, by Howard and Connie Clery after their daughter was brutally raped and murdered on a college campus. The primary work of SOC is that of advocating the prevention of college and university campus crime. SOC also works to assist campus crime victims in the enforcement of their legal rights.

Self-Defense

When properly invoked, self-defense will excuse a homicide. Self-defense is an affirmative defense that a defendant must prove. In order to establish self-defense a defendant must show that, in committing a homicide he or she was acting under a reasonable belief that he or she was in imminent danger of death or great bodily harm, and that his or her conduct in causing death was necessary in order to avoid death or great bodily harm. *See also* **Affirmative Defenses; Allison v. United States; Andersen v. United States; Hick-**ory v. United States; Starr v. United States; Thompson v. United States; Wallace v. United States

Self-Incrimination *see* Right to Remain Silent

Self-Representation *see* Right to Counsel

Senegal

Capital punishment has not been abolished by Senegal, but it has been more than a decade since the punishment has been imposed. Senegal uses the firing squad to carry out the death penalty. Its legal system is based on French civil law. Senegal adopted its constitution on March 3, 1963.

The judicial system is composed of trial courts, Court of Appeal, and a Constitutional Council. Defendants enjoy a presumption of innocence, have the right to confront witnesses, the right to a public trial, and the right to have an attorney. *See also* **International Capital Punishment Nations**

Sentence for Non-Capital Crime

It is often the situation that a capital defendant will be convicted of non-capital crimes during the trial of a capital offense. Occasionally trial courts do not sentence capital felons on the non-capital convictions until after a penalty phase capital verdict is returned. Capital defendants sentenced to death under such circumstances have argued that their Federal constitutional due process rights are violated by not being sentenced on the non-capital crimes before the capital penalty phase proceeding begins.

This argument is raised by capital felons convicted in the few jurisdictions that allow a sentence of life imprisonment with the possibility of parole, as an option to a sentence of death for capital murder. Capital felons in such jurisdictions seek to have trial judges impose punishment for the non-capital convictions, prior to the start of the capital penalty phase, so that they can argue to the penalty phase jury that, in view of the sentence for the non-capital crimes, they will not be released on parole if the jury recommended a sentence of life imprisonment. Courts have rejected this due process argument as a basis for invalidating death sentences.

Sentencing Proceeding *see* Trial Structure

Sequestration of Jury

The purpose of sequestering the jury is to insulate jurors from extraneous influences. Courts have not hesitated to reverse capital convictions or death sentences when sufficient evidence has been proffered to show improper communication was made with a juror or jurors. There are reported cases where death sentences have been vacated because court personnel and law enforcement agents made improper remarks to penalty phase jurors regarding the need for capital felons to be put to death. *See also* **Mattox v. United States**

Serial Killer

A serial killer is defined as a person who kills three or more victims over a period of time. It has been esti-

that 85 percent of the world's serial killers are in the United States. Serial killers tend to be white males, between the ages 25–35, and educated. Most victims of serial killers are chosen randomly. Some serial killers randomly target a specific group, such as college women, prostitutes, gays, or young children. Serial killers tend to sexually attack their victims before killing them. There has also been a pattern of showing pleasure from mutilating the bodies of victims. *See also* **Bundy, Theodore; Cleveland State University Racial Murders; Coleman and Brown; Freeway Killer; Gacy, John Wayne; Mass Murder; Mudgett, Herman; Night Stalker; Wuornos, Aileen**

Sexual Assault

The crime of sexual assault may be a felony or misdemeanor, depending upon the nature of the unlawful contact, e.g., mere fondling or copulation. Sexual assault, without more, cannot be used to inflict the death penalty. The Eighth Amendment of the United States Constitution prohibits this as cruel and unusual punishment. However, the crime of sexual assault can play a role in a capital prosecution. If sexual assault occurs during the commission of a homicide it may form the basis of a death-eligible offense, and therefore trigger a capital prosecution. *See also* **Death-Eligible Offenses; Felony Murder Rule; Rape and Capital Punishment; Sexual Assault Aggravator**

Sexual Assault Aggravator

A majority of capital punishment jurisdictions have made sexual assault a statutory aggravating circumstance. As such, the death penalty may be imposed if it is found at the penalty phase that the murder was committed during the course of sexual assault. *See also* **Aggravating Circumstances; Felony Murder Rule; Sexual Assault**

JURISDICTIONS USING SEXUAL ASSAULT AGGRAVATOR

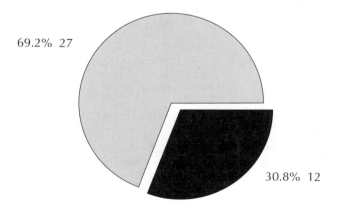

69.2% 27

30.8% 12

■ SEXUAL ASSAULT AGGRAVATOR JURISDICTIONS

■ ALL OTHER JURISDICTIONS

Seychelles

Capital punishment has not been imposed in Seychelles since it gained its independence from England on June 29, 1976.

The judicial system of Seychelles includes a Supreme Court (trial court), Constitutional Court, and a Court of Appeal. A jury is used in cases involving murder or treason. Trials are public, and defendants enjoy a presumption of innocence. Defendants have the right to counsel, to confront witnesses, and to appeal. *See also* **International Capital Punishment Nations**

Shell v. Mississippi

Court: United States Supreme Court; *Case Citation:* Shell v. Mississippi, 498 U.S. 1 (1990); *Argued:* Not reported; *Decided:* October 29, 1990; *Opinion of the Court:* Per Curiam; *Concurring Opinion:* Justice Marshall; *Dissenting Opinion:* None; *Appellate Defense Counsel:* Not reported; *Appellate Prosecution Counsel:* Not reported; *Amicus Curiae Brief Supporting Prosecutor:* Not reported; *Amicus Curiae Brief Supporting Defendant:* Not reported.

Issue Presented: Whether the statutory aggravating circumstance "especially heinous, atrocious or cruel" was properly defined so as to sustain the defendant's death sentence?

Case Holding: The statutory aggravating circumstance "especially heinous, atrocious or cruel" was not properly defined so as to sustain the defendant's death sentence.

Factual and procedural background of case: The defendant, Shell, was convicted and sentenced to death for capital murder by the State of Mississippi. The defendant's death sentence was imposed based upon evidence at the penalty phase which established that the murder was especially heinous, atrocious or cruel. On appeal to the Mississippi Supreme Court, the defendant argued that the trial court did not define the terms "especially heinous, atrocious or cruel," in a constitutionally acceptable manner. The State appellate court rejected the argument and affirmed the conviction and sentence. The United States Supreme Court granted certiorari to consider the issue.

Opinion of the Court was delivered Per Curiam: The per curiam opinion ruled that "[a]lthough the trial court in this case used a limiting instruction to define the 'especially heinous, atrocious, or cruel' factor, that instruction is not constitutionally sufficient." The opinion held that the statutory aggravating circumstance was too vague even with the definition supplied by the trial court. The judgment of the Mississippi Supreme Court was reversed, insofar as it left standing the sentence of death.

Concurring opinion by Justice Marshall: Justice Marshall indicated that he was writing a concurring opinion only for the purpose of providing legal analysis that was not contained in the brief per curiam opinion. In carrying out his purpose, he wrote the following:

> Obviously, a limiting instruction can be used to give content to a statutory factor that "is itself too vague to provide any guidance to the sentencer" only if the limiting instruction's own "definitions are constitutionally sufficient," that is, only if the limiting instruction itself "provide[s] some guidance to the sentencer." The trial court's definitions of "heinous" and "atrocious" in this case clearly fail this test; like "heinous" and "atrocious" themselves, the phrases [used by the trial court]

"extremely wicked or shockingly evil" and "outrageously wicked and vile" could be used by "[a] person of ordinary sensibility [to] fairly characterize almost every murder." Indeed, there is no meaningful distinction between these latter formulations and the "outrageously or wantonly vile, horrible and inhuman" instruction expressly invalidated in *Godfrey v. Georgia.*

Nor is it of any consequence that the trial court defined "cruel" in an arguably more concrete fashion than "heinous" or "atrocious." It has long been settled that when a case is submitted to the jury on alternative theories the unconstitutionality of any of the theories requires that the conviction [or verdict] be set aside. Even assuming that the trial court permissibly defined "cruel," the instruction in this case left the jury with two constitutionally infirm, alternative bases on which to find that [the defendant] committed the charged murder in an "especially heinous, atrocious or cruel" fashion.

See also **Heinous, Atrocious, Cruel or Depraved Aggravator; Maynard v. Cartwright; Lewis v. Jeffers; Richmond v. Lewis; Stringer v. Black; Walton v. Arizona**

Shepherd v. Florida
Court: United States Supreme Court; *Case Citation:* Shepherd v. Florida, 341 U.S. 50 (1951); *Argued:* March 9, 1951; *Decided:* April 9, 1951; *Opinion of the Court:* Per Curiam; *Concurring Opinion:* Justice Jackson, in which Frankfurter, J., joined; *Dissenting Opinion:* None; *Appellate Defense Counsel:* Franklin H. Williams and Robert L. Carter argued; Alex Akerman, Jr. and Thurgood Marshall on brief; *Appellate Prosecution Counsel:* Reeves Bowen argued; Richard W. Ervin and Howard S. Bailey on brief; *Amicus Curiae Brief Supporting Prosecutor:* Not reported; *Amicus Curiae Brief Supporting Defendant:* Not reported.

Issue Presented: Whether the defendants established that their convictions and sentences were invalid because blacks were systematically excluded from the grand jury that indicted them?

Case Holding: The defendants established that their convictions and sentences were invalid because blacks were systematically excluded from the grand jury that indicted them.

Factual and procedural background of case: Two defendants in this case, Shepard and another unnamed defendant, were convicted of rape and sentenced to death by the State of Florida. The Florida Supreme Court affirmed judgments. In doing so, the appellate court rejected the defendants' argument that their convictions were invalid because blacks were systematically excluded from the grand jury that indicted them. The United States Supreme Court granted certiorari to consider the issue.

Opinion of the Court was delivered Per Curiam: The per curiam opinion ruled that the disposition of the case was controlled by its decision in *Cassell v. Texas.* In *Cassell* it was held that jury discrimination may be proved in other ways than by evidence of long-continued unexplained absence of blacks from jury duty, such as by admissions from jury commissioners that they chose only whom they knew, and that they knew no blacks. The judgments of the Florida Supreme Court were reversed.

Concurring opinion by Justice Jackson, in which Frankfurter, J., joined: Justice Jackson concurred in the Court's decision. He wrote separately to set out facts that the per curiam opinion failed to mention, and to stress his belief that the case required reversal for reasons more significant than that chosen by the Court. Justice Jackson gave the following account of the case:

Newspapers published as a fact, and attributed the information to the sheriff, that these defendants had confessed. No one, including the sheriff, repudiated the story. Witnesses and persons called as jurors said they had read or heard of this statement. However, no confession was offered at the trial. The only rational explanations for its nonproduction in court are that the story was false or that the confession was obtained under circumstances which made it inadmissible or its use inexpedient....

But that is not all. Of course, such a crime stirred deep feeling and was exploited to the limit by the press [because the victim was white]. These defendants were first taken to the county jail of Lake County. A mob gathered and demanded that defendants be turned over to it. By order of court, they were quickly transferred for safekeeping to the state prison, where they remained until about two weeks before the trial. Meanwhile, a mob burned the home of defendant Shepherd's father and mother and two other ... houses. [Blacks] were removed from the community to prevent their being lynched. The National Guard was called out on July 17 and 18 and, on July 19, the 116th Field Artillery was summoned from Tampa. The [blacks] of the community abandoned their homes and fled.

Every detail of these passion-arousing events was reported by the press.... These and many other articles were highly prejudicial, including a cartoon published at the time of the grand jury, picturing ... electric chairs and headed, "No Compromise — Supreme Penalty"....

... Under these circumstances, for the Court to reverse these convictions upon the sole ground that the method of jury selection discriminated against the [black] race, is to stress the trivial and ignore the important. While this record discloses discrimination which under normal circumstances might be prejudicial, this trial took place under conditions and was accompanied by events which would deny defendants a fair trial before any kind of jury. I do not see, as a practical matter, how any [black] on the jury would have dared to cause a disagreement or acquittal. The only chance these [defendants] had of acquittal would have been in the courage and decency of some sturdy and forthright white person of sufficient standing to face and live down the odium among his white neighbors that such a vote, if required, would have brought. To me, the technical question of discrimination in the jury selection has only theoretical importance. The case presents one of the best examples of one of the worst menaces to American justice. It is on that ground that I would reverse.

Case note: Under modern capital punishment jurisprudence the death penalty may not be imposed for the crime of rape, without an accompanying death. *See also* **Discrimination in Grand or Petit Jury Selection; Rape and Capital Punishment**

Shiras, George, Jr.
George Shiras, Jr., served as an associate justice of the United States Supreme Court from 1892 to 1903. While on the Supreme Court Shiras displayed a judicial philosophy that straddled between moderate and conservative.

Shiras was born on January 26, 1832, in Pittsburgh, Pennsylvania. Shiras' educational training included studying law at

Yale Law School. During his years of private practice in Allegheny County Shiras became an extremely successful litigator. His clients included railroad companies and other large corporations. In 1892 President Benjamin Harrison appointed Shiras to the Supreme Court.

While on the Supreme Court Shiras wrote several capital punishment decisions. Shiras' capital punishment opinions reflected a moderate constitutional philosophy. This was best illustrated in the case of *Murray v. Louisiana*. In that case the defendant was convicted of murder and sentenced to death by the State of Louisiana. The defendant argued to the Supreme Court that his prosecution should have been removed to a Federal court because blacks were excluded from the grand jury that indicted him. Shiras, writing for the Supreme Court, acknowledged the existence of a Federal statute which required removal of a State criminal case to Federal court, if the statutes or constitution of the State discriminated against blacks in jury service. However, Shiras found that, while the defendant presented some evidence of racial discrimination in grand juror selection, he could not point to any statute or constitutional provision of the State of Louisiana that permitted such discrimination. Consequently, Shiras found that the defendant did not have a right to be tried in a Federal court. Shiras retired from the Court in 1903. He died on August 2, 1924.

Capital Punishment Opinions Written by Shiras

Case Name	Opinion of the Court	Concurring Opinion	Dissenting Opinion
Bird v. United States (I)	✓		
Hallinger v. Davis	✓		
Lewis v. United States	✓		
Murray v. Louisiana	✓		
Thompson v. United States	✓		

Siblings *see* Apelt Brothers; Gutierrez Brothers; LaGrand Brothers; Poland Brothers

Sierra Leone Capital punishment is allowed in Sierra Leone. Sierra Leone uses the firing squad and hanging to carry out the death penalty. In 1998, the nation executed 24 prisoners. Its legal system is base on English law and customary law. Sierra Leone adopted a constitution on October 1, 1991. The judicial system includes trial courts and appellate courts. *See also* **International Capital Punishment Nations**

Simmons v. South Carolina *Court:* United States Supreme Court; *Case Citation:* Simmons v. South Carolina, 512 U.S. 154 (1994); *Argued:* January 18, 1994; *Decided:* June 17, 1994; *Plurality Opinion:* Justice Blackmun announced the Court's judgment and delivered an opinion, in which Stevens, Souter, and Ginsburg, JJ., joined; *Concurring Opinion:* Justice Souter, in which Stevens, J., joined; *Concurring Opinion:* Justice Ginsburg; *Concurring Opinion:* Justice O'Connor, in which Rehnquist, C.J., and Kennedy, J., joined; *Dissenting Opinion:* Justice Scalia, in which Thomas, J., joined; *Appellate Defense Counsel:* Not reported; *Appellate Prosecution Counsel:* Not reported; *Amicus Curiae Brief Supporting Prosecutor:* Not reported; *Amicus Curiae Brief Supporting Defendant:* Not reported.

Issue Presented: Whether the Due Process Clause of the Fourteenth Amendment was violated by the refusal of the trial court to instruct the penalty phase jury that, under State law, the defendant was ineligible for parole?

Case Holding: Where a defendant's future dangerousness is at issue during that penalty phase, and State law prohibits the defendant's release on parole, due process requires that the sentencing jury be informed that the defendant is parole ineligible.

Factual and procedural background of case: Jonathan Dale Simmons was convicted of capital murder by the State of South Carolina. During the penalty phase of the defendant's trial, the prosecutor argued that his future dangerousness was a factor for the jury to consider when deciding whether to sentence him to death or life imprisonment. As a consequence of the prosecutor's argument on future dangerousness, the defendant asked the trial judge to instruct the penalty phase jury that under South Carolina death penalty law, he was ineligible for parole if given a life imprisonment sentence. The judge refused to give the instruction. Prior to returning its verdict on punishment, the jury asked the trial court whether life imprisonment carried with it the possibility of parole. The trial court instructed the jury not to consider parole in reaching its verdict, and that the terms life imprisonment and death sentence were to be understood to have their plain and ordinary meaning. The jury returned a death sentence.

On appeal, the South Carolina Supreme Court affirmed the defendant's conviction and sentence. In doing so, the appellate court rejected the defendant's contention that the Federal Constitution required the jury be instructed that he was not eligible for parole. The United States Supreme Court granted certiorari to consider the issue.

Plurality opinion in which Justice Blackmun announced the Court's judgment and in which Stevens, Souter and Ginsburg, JJ., joined: Justice Blackmun ruled that the defendant was entitled to have the jury instructed that he was not eligible for parole. The opinion found that where a defendant's future dangerousness is at issue during the penalty phase of a capital prosecution, and the applicable law prohibits his or her release on parole, due process requires that the sentencing jury be informed that the defendant is parole ineligible. It was said that a capital felon cannot be executed on the basis of information which he or she had no opportunity to deny or explain. Justice Blackman indicated that the defendant's jury reasonably may have believed that he could be released on parole if he were not executed. He reasoned that to the extent that this misunderstanding pervaded the jury's deliberations, it had the effect of creating a false choice between sentencing the defendant to death and sentencing him to a limited period of incarceration. The opinion concluded that the trial court's refusal to apprise the jury of information so crucial to its determination, particularly when the prosecutor alluded to the defendant's future dangerousness, could not be reconciled with the Court's well established precedents interpreting the Due Process Clause. The judgment of the South Carolina Supreme Court was reversed.

Concurring opinion by Justice Souter, in which Stevens, J., joined: Justice Souter wrote that he concurred with the plurality's opinion "that, at least when future dangerousness is an issue in a capital sentencing determination, the defendant has a due process right to require that his sentencing jury be informed of his ineligibility for parole."

Concurring opinion by Justice Ginsburg: Justice Ginsburg indicated the following in her concurring opinion: "When the prosecution urges a defendant's future dangerousness as cause for the death sentence, the defendant's right to be heard means that he must be afforded an opportunity to rebut the argument. To be full and fair, that opportunity must include the right to inform the jury, if it is indeed the case, that the defendant is ineligible for parole."

Concurring opinion by Justice O'Connor, in which Rehnquist, C.J., and Kennedy, J., joined: Justice O'Connor wrote in her concurring opinion that where the prosecution puts a defendant's future dangerousness in issue, and the only available alternative sentence to death is life imprisonment without possibility of parole, due process entitles the defendant to inform the sentencing jury, either by argument or instruction, that he or she is parole ineligible. It was said by Justice O'Connor that if the prosecution does not argue future dangerousness, parole may not be a proper issue for the jury's consideration even if the only alternative sentence to death, is life imprisonment without the possibility of parole.

Dissenting opinion by Justice Scalia, in which Thomas, J., joined: Justice Scalia dissented from the Court's judgment on the basis that he did not believe the Due Process Clause incorporated the issue decided. He argued that there was no precedent to extend due process to a State law determination of whether a jury should be apprised of parole ineligibility. Justice Scalia believed that extending constitutional due process to this State law issue was unnecessary and that "[t]here is really no basis for such a pronouncement, neither in any near uniform practice of our people nor in the jurisprudence of this Court." *See also* **Parole Eligibility Jury Instruction**

Sims v. Georgia (I)   *Court:* United States Supreme Court; *Case Citation:* Sims v. Georgia, 385 U.S. 538 (1967); *Argued:* December 6–7, 1966; *Decided:* January 23, 1967; *Opinion of the Court:* Justice Clark; *Concurring Opinion:* None; *Dissenting Statement:* Justice Black; *Appellate Defense Counsel:* Jack Greenberg argued; James M. Nabrit III, Anthony G. Amsterdam and Howard Moore, Jr. on brief; *Appellate Prosecution Counsel:* Dewey Hayes and E. Freeman Leverett argued; Arthur K. Bolton on brief; *Amicus Curiae Brief Supporting Prosecutor:* None; *Amicus Curiae Brief Supporting Defendant:* None.

Issue Presented: Whether it was constitutional error for the trial court to fail to determine the voluntariness of the defen-

dant's confession, before allowing the jury to consider the confession?

Case Holding: The record is silent as to whether the trial court made a determination of the voluntariness of the defendant's confession, therefore the case would be reversed and remanded for a hearing on the issue.

Factual and procedural background of case: The defendant, Sims, was convicted of rape and sentenced to death by the State of Georgia. The Supreme Court of Georgia affirmed the conviction and sentence. In doing so, the appellate court rejected the defendant's claim that his right to a fair trial was violated by the trial judge's failure to determine the voluntariness of his confession, prior to its admission into evidence before the jury, as required by the United States Supreme Court's ruling in *Jackson v. Denno*. The defendant also argued unsuccessfully that the selection of the grand jury that indicted him and the petit jury that convicted him were done in violation of the Federal Constitution. The United States Supreme Court granted certiorari to consider both issues, but only addressed the *Jackson* claim.

Opinion of the Court by Justice Clark: Justice Clark indicated that in *Jackson* the Court laid down a constitutional rule that a jury was not to hear a confession, unless and until the trial judge had determined that it was freely and voluntarily given. It was said that under *Jackson* a jury, if it so chooses, may give absolutely no weight to a confession in determining the guilt or innocence of the defendant, but it is not for the jury to make the primary determination of voluntariness. Justice Clark held further that under *Jackson* a trial judge need not make formal findings of fact or write an opinion, but the judge's conclusion that the confession was voluntary must appear from the record with unmistakable clarity.

In turning to the defendant's case, Justice Clark ruled that there was no actual ruling or finding in the record showing that the trial judge determined the voluntariness of the defendant's confession before allowing it to be introduced into evidence. Consequently, the opinion reversed the judgment of the Georgia Supreme Court and remanded the case for a hearing to determine whether the defendant's confession was voluntary.

Dissenting statement by Justice Black: Justice Black issued a statement indicating he dissented for the reasons set out in his concurring and dissenting opinion in *Jackson v. Denno*.

Case note: Under modern capital punishment jurisprudence the death penalty may not be imposed for the crime of rape without an accompanying homicide. *See also* **Jackson v. Denno; Rape and Capital Punishment; Right to Remain Silent; Sims v. Georgia (II)**

Sims v. Georgia (II)   *Court:* United States Supreme Court; *Case Citation:* Sims v. Georgia, 389 U.S. 404 (1967); *Argued:* Not reported; *Decided:* December 18, 1967; *Opinion of the Court:* Per Curiam; *Concurring Opinion:* None; *Dissenting Opinion:* None; *Appellate Defense Counsel:* Jack Greenberg, James M. Nabrit III, Anthony G. Amsterdam and Howard Moore, Jr. on brief; *Appellate Prosecution Counsel:*

Not represented; *Amicus Curiae Brief Supporting Prosecutor:* Not reported; *Amicus Curiae Brief Supporting Defendant:* Not reported.

Issues Presented: (1) Whether the prosecutor rebutted the defendant's claim that his confession was involuntary? (2) Whether the grand jury which indicted the defendant and the petit jury which convicted him, were selected in a racially discriminatory manner?

Case Holdings: (1) The prosecutor failed to rebut the defendant's claim that his confession was involuntary. (2) The grand jury which indicted the defendant and the petit jury which convicted him, were selected in a racially discriminatory manner.

Factual and procedural background of case: The defendant, Sims, was convicted of rape and sentenced to death by the State of Georgia. The Supreme Court of Georgia affirmed the conviction and sentence. However, the United States Supreme Court reversed the judgment, in *Sims v. Georgia (I)*, and remanded the case for the Georgia courts to determine whether the defendant's confession was voluntary. On remand the case was submitted to the trial judge who had presided at the defendant's original trial. The trial judge merely reviewed the transcript of the trial and determined that the defendant's confession had been voluntary and denied a new trial. The Georgia Supreme Court affirmed. The United States Supreme Court granted certiorari to consider the adequacy of the trial court's determination, as well as address the defendant's previously deferred claim that the selection of the grand jury that indicted him and the petit jury that convicted him were done in violation of the Federal Constitution.

Opinion of the Court was delivered Per Curiam: The per curiam opinion found that the trial court failed to adequately review the defendant's claim that his confession was involuntary. It was said that the State failed to rebut the defendant's allegation that he had been subjected to physical violence prior to his confession. The opinion held that a confession produced by violence or threats of violence is involuntary and cannot constitutionally be used against the person giving it. In view of the State's failure to provide evidence to contradict the defendant's allegations, the opinion found that the confession was involuntary and should not have been used at his trial.

The Court also took the time in the per curiam opinion to resolve the defendant's claim that the grand jury which indicted him, and the petit jury that convicted him were selected in a racially discriminatory manner, in that all blacks were systematically excluded from both. The opinion found that the evidence revealed that the grand and petit jury lists were drawn from the county tax digests which separately listed taxpayers by race in conformity with then existing Georgia law. Blacks constituted 24.4 percent of the individual taxpayers in the county where the defendant was prosecuted. However, they amounted to only 4.7 percent of the names on the grand jury list and 9.8 percent of the names on the master jury list from which the defendant's grand and petit juries were selected.

The opinion concluded that the facts adduced were virtually indistinguishable from a jury selection process condemned by the Court in *Whitus v. Georgia*. Accordingly, it was said that the juries by which the defendant was indicted and tried were selected in a manner that did not comport with constitutional requirements. The judgment of the Georgia Supreme Court was reversed. *See also* **Coleman v. Alabama (I)**; **Coleman v. Alabama (II)**; **Discrimination in Grand or Petit Jury Selection**; **Sims v. Georgia (I)**; **Whitus v. Georgia**

Singapore Singapore permits capital punishment. Singapore uses hanging as the method of execution. In 1998, Singapore executed 28 prisoners. Its legal system is based on English common law. A constitution was adopted by the nation on June 3, 1959.

The judicial system consists of District Courts, High Court, and a Court of Appeal. Defendants enjoy a presumption of innocence and the right of appeal. They have the right to be represented by an attorney and confront witnesses against them. Trials are public and are presided over by judges. There are no jury trials. *See also* **International Capital Punishment Nations**

Sioux Mass Executions *see* **Dakota Executions**

Sixth Amendment *see* **Bill of Rights**

Skipper v. South Carolina *Court:* United States Supreme Court; *Case Citation:* Skipper v. South Carolina, 476 U.S. 1 (1986); *Argued:* February 24, 1986; *Decided:* April 29, 1986; *Opinion of the Court:* Justice White; *Concurring Opinion:* Justice Powell, in which Burger, C. J., and Rehnquist, J., joined; *Dissenting Opinion:* None; *Appellate Defense Counsel:* David I. Bruck argued and briefed; *Appellate Prosecution Counsel:* Harold M. Coombs, Jr. argued; T. Travis Medlock on brief; *Amicus Curiae Brief Supporting Prosecutor:* 1; *Amicus Curiae Brief Supporting Defendant:* None.

Issue Presented: Whether exclusion at the penalty phase of witnesses who would have testified that the defendant was well-behaved in jail, violated the defendant's constitutional right to introduce all relevant mitigating evidence?

Case Holding: Exclusion at the penalty phase of witnesses who would have testified that the defendant was well-behaved in jail, violated the defendant's constitutional right to introduce all relevant mitigating evidence.

Factual and procedural background of case: The defendant, Ronald Skipper, was convicted of capital murder by the State of South Carolina. During the penalty phase the defendant sought to introduce testimony from two jailers and a "regular visitor" who would testify that he had made a good adjustment during the 7 months he had spent in jail between his arrest and trial. The trial judge ruled such evidence irrelevant and inadmissible. The defendant was sentenced to death. The South Carolina Supreme Court affirmed the death sentence, after rejecting the defendant's contention that the trial court had committed constitutional error in excluding the testimony of the jailers and regular visitor. The United States Supreme Court granted certiorari to consider the issue.

Opinion of the Court by Justice White: Justice White held that the trial court's exclusion from the sentencing hearing of the testimony of the jailers and the regular visitor denied the defendant his right to place before the sentencing jury all relevant evidence in mitigation of punishment. The opinion reasoned: "The exclusion by the state trial court of relevant mitigating evidence impeded the sentencing jury's ability to carry out its task of considering all relevant facets of the character and record of the individual offender. The resulting death sentence cannot stand, although the State is of course not precluded from again seeking to impose the death sentence, provided that it does so through a new sentencing hearing at which [the defendant] is permitted to present any and all relevant mitigating evidence that is available."

The judgment of the Supreme Court of South Carolina was reversed insofar as it affirmed the death sentence.

Concurring opinion by Justice Powell, in which Burger, C. J., and Rehnquist, J., joined: Justice Powell concurred in the Court's judgment, but for reasons different than those asserted in the majority opinion. He argued that the evidence should not have been excluded because it was actually rebuttal testimony to evidence by the prosecutor that the defendant would be dangerous in prison. Justice Powell believed that it was not necessary to assert that the evidence was constitutionally required because it was mitigating per se. *See also* **Bell v. Ohio; Delo v. Lashley; Eddings v. Oklahoma; Hitchcock v. Dugger; Lockett v. Ohio; Mitigating Circumstances**

Slovakia Slovakia abolished capital punishment in 1990. *See also* **International Capital Punishment Nations**

Slovenia Slovenia abolished capital punishment in 1989. *See also* **International Capital Punishment Nations**

Smith v. Baldi *Court:* United States Supreme Court; *Case Citation:* Smith v. Baldi, 344 U.S. 561 (1953); *Argued:* April 29–30, 1952; reargued October 13–14, 1952; *Decided:* February 9, 1953; *Opinion of the Court:* Justice Reed; *Concurring Opinion:* None; *Dissenting Opinion:* Justice Frankfurter, in which Black and Douglas, JJ., joined; *Appellate Defense Counsel:* Thomas D. McBride argued; Herbert S. Levin on brief; *Appellate Prosecution Counsel:* Randolph C. Ryder argued; Robert E. Woodside and Frank P. Lawley, Jr. on brief; *Amicus Curiae Brief Supporting Prosecutor:* None; *Amicus Curiae Brief Supporting Defendant:* 1.

Issues Presented: (1) Whether due process permitted the State to allow the defendant to plead guilty before a determination of his sanity was made? (2) Whether due process required the State to appoint a psychiatrist to assist the defendant with his insanity defense?

Case Holdings: (1) Due process permitted the State to allow the defendant to plead guilty before a determination of his san-

ity was made, because a procedure was in place to allow the defendant to plead not guilty by reason of insanity. (2) Due process did not require the State to appoint a psychiatrist to assist the defendant with his insanity defense.

Factual and procedural background of case: The defendant, Smith, was charged with capital murder by the State of Pennsylvania. The defendant agreed to enter a plea of guilty to the charge. Part of the agreement called for the defendant to have a hearing to determine if he was insane at the time of the murder. If insanity was established his plea would turn into not guilty by reason of insanity. At the conclusion of the sanity hearing, the trial court found the defendant was sane at the time of the offense and sentenced him to death.

The Pennsylvania Supreme Court affirmed the conviction and sentence. The defendant then filed a petition for habeas corpus relief in State court, which was denied. An appeal from the denial of habeas relief was filed with the United States Supreme Court, but certiorari was denied on the grounds that the appeal was not timely filed. The defendant then filed a habeas corpus petition in a Federal District Court, alleging that he was denied due process in not having his sanity determined before he entered a plea of guilty; in not having a State appointed psychiatrist to help prepare his insanity defense; and that he could not be executed because he was insane. The District Court denied habeas relief. A Federal Court of Appeals affirmed. The United States Supreme Court granted certiorari to consider the issues.

Opinion of the Court by Justice Reed: Justice Reed indicated, as a preliminary matter, that a denial of certiorari by the Court to review a decision of a State supreme court affirming a conviction in a criminal prosecution should be given no weight in subsequent habeas corpus proceedings in a federal court. It was said that the Court's denial of the defendant's first appeal carried no weight in the determination of the issues presented.

The opinion held that due process was not violated by a procedure which allowed the defendant to plead guilty before a determination of his sanity was made, because the procedure allowed him to withdraw the guilty plea if found insane and enter a plea of not guilty by reason of insanity. Justice Reed also held that it was not the constitutional duty of the State, even upon request, to appoint a psychiatrist to make a pretrial examination into the defendant's sanity. The opinion rejected the defendant's claim that, as an insane person he could not be executed, because the evidence established that he was sane. The judgment of the Court of Appeals was affirmed.

Dissenting opinion by Justice Frankfurter, in which Black and Douglas, JJ., joined: Justice Frankfurter dissented from the Court's opinion and judgment based on two primary grounds. First, he argued that the defendant "was deprived of a fair opportunity to establish his insanity." Justice Frankfurter believed that the insanity procedure utilized by the State was a trap void of due process and unconstitutional.

The second reason given for dissenting, was that the psychiatrist relied upon by the State "had himself been committed [to a mental institution] because of an incurable mental disease which had deprived him of 'any judgment or insight.'" Justice Frankfurter indicated that it was not until the case was presented to the Court that the defendant learned that the State's psychiatrist was himself insane. He concluded that "to allow the victim of this testimony, which, in any event, has been brought into doubt, to go to his death without an opportunity for reassessment, by either State or federal court, of the basis for the rejection of his plea of insanity would constitute a denial of due process no less gross than if the sentence had been imposed without any hearing at all on the issue of sanity."

Case note: The case's rejection of the defendant's right to have court appointed assistance of counsel to help with his insanity defense, no longer holds as valid law. In subsequent capital and non-capital cases, the Court has ruled that an indigent defendant is constitutionally entitled to appointment of psychiatric assistance where the issue of insanity is in question. *See also* **Brown v. Allen; Insanity; Insanity Defense**

Smith v. Mississippi
Court: United States Supreme Court; *Case Citation:* Smith v. Mississippi, 162 U.S. 592 (1896); *Argued:* Not reported; *Decided:* April 13, 1896; *Opinion of the Court:* Justice Harlan; *Concurring Opinion:* None; *Dissenting Opinion:* None; *Appellate Defense Counsel:* Cornelius J. Jones argued and briefed; *Appellate Prosecution Counsel:* Frank J. Johnston argued and briefed; *Amicus Curiae Brief Supporting Prosecutor:* None; *Amicus Curiae Brief Supporting Defendant:* None.

Issues Presented: (1) Whether the exclusion of blacks from the grand jury that indicted the defendant required his case be removed to a Federal court for prosecution? (2) Whether the defendant established that blacks were systematically excluded from the grand jury that indicted him?

Case Holdings: (1) The exclusion of blacks from the grand jury that indicted the defendant did not require his case be removed to a Federal court for prosecution, because the Federal removal statute required racial discrimination emanate from a State's constitution or laws. (2) The defendant did not establish that blacks were systematically excluded from the grand jury that indicted him, because the defendant failed to present any evidence of such discrimination.

Factual and procedural background of case: The defendant, Charley Smith, was indicted for capital murder by the State of Mississippi. Prior to trial the defendant requested the indictment be dismissed on the grounds that blacks were systematically excluded from the grand jury that indicted him. The trial court denied the request. The defendant next requested the case be removed to a Federal court because of the exclusion of blacks from the grand jury. This request was also denied by the trial court. The defendant was tried, convicted and sentenced to death. The Mississippi Supreme Court affirmed the judgment. In doing so, the appellate court found that the defendant did not establish a right to have the case removed to a Federal court. The United States Supreme Court granted certiorari to consider the issue.

Opinion of the Court by Justice Harlan: Justice Harlan held that the defendant failed to show that he satisfied the requirement of the Federal removal statute in order to have his case prosecuted in a Federal court. It was said that the removal statute required racial discrimination be based on a State's constitution or laws. The opinion found that "[n]either the constitution nor the laws of Mississippi, by their language, reasonably interpreted, or as interpreted by the highest court of the state, show that the accused was denied ... any right secured to him by any law providing for the equal civil rights of citizens of the United States, or of all persons within the United States."

The opinion also found that the defendant's claim of racial discrimination was not supported by any evidence. Justice Harlan wrote: "The facts stated in the written motion to quash, although that motion was verified by the affidavit of the accused, could not be used as evidence to establish those facts, except with the consent of the state prosecutor, or by order of the trial court. No such consent was given. No such order was made. The grounds assigned for quashing the indictment should have been sustained by distinct evidence introduced, or offered to be introduced, by the accused. He could not, of right, insist that the facts stated in the motion to quash should be taken as true simply because his motion was verified by his affidavit. The motion to quash was therefore unsupported by any competent evidence. Consequently, it cannot be held to have been erroneously denied." The judgment of the Mississippi Supreme Court was affirmed. *See also* **Discrimination in Grand or Petit Jury Selection**

Smith v. Murray
Court: United States Supreme Court; *Case Citation:* Smith v. Murray, 477 U.S. 527 (1986); *Argued:* March 4, 1986; *Decided:* June 26, 1986; *Opinion of the Court:* Justice O'Connor; *Concurring Opinion:* None; *Dissenting Opinion:* Justice Stevens, in which Marshall, Brennan and Blackmun, JJ., joined; *Dissenting Statement:* Justice Brennan, in which Marshall, J., joined; *Appellate Defense Counsel:* J. Lloyd Snook III argued; Richard J. Bonnie on brief; *Appellate Prosecution Counsel:* James E. Kulp argued; William G. Broaddus and Frank S. Ferguson on brief; *Amicus Curiae Brief Supporting Prosecutor:* None; *Amicus Curiae Brief Supporting Defendant:* 3.

Issue Presented: Whether the defendant defaulted his underlying constitutional claim by failing to present it before the Virginia Supreme Court on direct appeal?

Case Holding: The defendant defaulted his underlying constitutional claim by failing to present it before the Virginia Supreme Court on direct appeal.

Factual and procedural background of case: The defendant, Michael Smith, was charged with capital murder by the State of Virginia. Prior to trial the defendant was examined by a psychiatrist who was appointed by the trial court at the request of defense counsel. During the psychiatric examination, the defendant disclosed facts about the murder and prior incidents of deviant sexual conduct, including an incident where he tore the clothes off a girl on a school bus before deciding not to rape her. Following a jury trial, the defendant was convicted of capital murder. At the penalty phase, the prosecutor called the psychiatrist to the stand, and, over the defense counsel's objection, the psychiatrist described the defendant's aborted rape incident on the school bus. The defendant was sentenced to death.

On appeal to the Virginia Supreme Court, the defendant raised a number of claims but did not assign any error concerning the admission of the psychiatrist's testimony at the penalty phase. The appellate court affirmed the conviction and sentence, with out addressing any issue concerning the prosecutor's use of the psychiatric testimony. After exhausting state remedies, the defendant filed a habeas corpus petition in a Federal District Court. One of the issues raised in the habeas petition was that the trial court committed constitutional error in allowing the psychiatrist to testify about the aborted school bus rape incident. The District Court dismissed the petition, finding the defendant defaulted his right to argue the claim involving the psychiatrist's testimony because the issue was never raised on direct appeal to the Virginia Supreme Court. A Federal Court of Appeals affirmed. The United States Supreme Court granted certiorari to consider the issue.

Opinion of the Court by Justice O'Connor: Justice O'Connor ruled that the defendant defaulted his constitutional claim as to the admission of the psychiatrist's testimony by failing to present it before the Virginia Supreme Court on direct appeal. It was said that the defendant did not carry his burden of showing good cause for his noncompliance with Virginia's rules of procedure. The opinion found that defense counsel made a deliberate, tactical decision not to pursue the claim in State court. It was said that defense counsel's decision not to press the claim in State court was not an error of such magnitude that it rendered his performance constitutionally deficient. Justice O'Connor said that even assuming the psychiatrist's testimony should not have been presented to the jury, its admission did not pervert the jury's deliberations concerning the ultimate question of whether the death penalty should be imposed. The judgment of the Court of Appeals was affirmed.

Dissenting opinion by Justice Stevens, in which Marshall, Brennan and Blackmun, JJ., joined: Justice Stevens dissented from the Court's ruling. He believed that the significance of the error alleged by the defendant warranted addressing the issue on its merits. The dissenting opinion stated:

The record in this case unquestionably demonstrates that [the defendant's] constitutional claim is meritorious, and that there is a significant risk that he will be put to death because his constitutional rights were violated.

The Court does not take issue with this conclusion. It is willing to assume that (1) [the defendant's] Fifth Amendment right against compelled self-incrimination was violated; (2) his Eighth Amendment right to a fair, constitutionally sound sentencing proceeding was violated by the introduction of the evidence from that Fifth Amendment violation; and (3) those constitutional violations made the difference between life and death in the jury's consideration of his fate. Although the constitutional

violations and issues were sufficiently serious that this Court decided to grant certiorari, ... this Court concludes that [the defendant's] presumably meritorious constitutional claim is procedurally barred and that [the defendant] must therefore be executed.

In my opinion, the Court should reach the merits of [the defendant's] argument. To the extent that there has been a procedural "default," it is exceedingly minor — perhaps a kind of "harmless" error....

I fear that the Court has lost its way in a procedural maze of its own creation and that it has grossly misevaluated the requirements of "law and justice" that are the federal court's statutory mission under the federal habeas corpus statute.

Dissenting statement by Justice Brennan, in which Marshall, J., joined: Justice Brennan issued a statement indicating that his dissent in a non-capital case, *Murray v. Carrier*, 477 U.S. 478 (1986), was to be incorporated by reference in this case as his dissenting opinion. In *Murray v. Carrier* the Court also decided not to reach the merits of a case because of procedural default in failing to bring the issue before a State court. Justice Brennan explained in *Murray v. Carrier* the basis of his belief that procedural default should not be used to defeat constitutional claims as follows:

The competing interests implicated by a prisoner's petition to a federal court to review the merits of a procedurally defaulted constitutional claim are easily identified. On the one hand, "there is Congress' expressed interest in providing a federal forum for the vindication of the constitutional rights of state prisoners." In enacting [the habeas statute], "Congress sought to interpose the federal courts between the States and the people, as guardians of the people's federal rights — to protect the people from unconstitutional action." This interest is at its strongest where the state court has declined to consider the merits of a constitutional claim, for without habeas review no court will ever consider whether the [defendant's] constitutional rights were violated.

These interests must be weighed against the State's interest in maintaining the integrity of its rules and proceedings, an interest that would be undermined if the federal courts were too free to ignore procedural forfeitures in state court. The criminal justice system in each State is structured both to determine the guilt or innocence of defendants and to resolve all questions incident to that determination, including the constitutionality of the procedures leading to the verdict. Each State's complement of procedural rules facilitates this process by "channeling, to the extent possible, the resolution of various types of questions to the stage of the judicial process at which they can be resolved most fairly and efficiently." Procedural default rules protect the integrity of this process by imposing a forfeiture sanction for failure to follow applicable state procedural rules, thereby deterring litigants from deviating from the State's scheme. Generally, the threat of losing the right to raise a claim in state proceedings will be sufficient to ensure compliance with the State's procedural rules: a defendant loses nothing by raising all of his claims at trial since the state-court judgment will have no res judicata effect in later habeas proceedings, while he retains the possibility of obtaining relief in the state courts. Nonetheless, to the extent that federal habeas review of a procedurally defaulted claim is available, the broad deterrent effect of these procedural default rules is somewhat diminished....

The particular question we must decide in this case is whether counsel's inadvertent failure to raise a substantive claim of error can constitute "cause" for the procedural default.... [T]o say that the petitioner should be bound to his lawyer's tactical decisions is one thing; to say that he must also bear the burden of his lawyer's inadvertent mistakes is quite another. Where counsel is unaware of a claim or of the duty to raise it at a particular time, the procedural default rule cannot operate as a specific deterrent to noncompliance with the State's procedural rules. Consequently, the State's interest in ensuring that the federal court help prevent circumvention of the State's procedural rules by imposing the same forfeiture sanction is much less compelling. To be sure, applying procedural default rules even to inadvertent defaults furthers the State's deterrent interests in a general sense by encouraging lawyers to be more conscientious on the whole. However, as the Court has pointed out in another context, such general deterrent interests are weak where the failure to follow a rule is accidental rather than intentional.

I believe that this incremental state interest simply is not sufficient to overcome the heavy presumption against a federal court's refusing to exercise jurisdiction clearly granted by Congress.

Case note: A few weeks after the Court's opinion was filed, Virginia executed Michael Smith by electrocution on July 31, 1986. *See also* **Amadeo v. Zant; Coleman v. Thompson; Dugger v. Adams; Procedural Default of Constitutional Claims**

Snyder v. Massachusetts

Court: United States Supreme Court; *Case Citation:* Snyder v. Massachusetts, 291 U.S. 97 (1934); *Argued:* November 7, 1933; *Decided:* January 8, 1934; *Opinion of the Court:* Justice Cardozo; *Concurring Opinion:* None; *Dissenting Opinion:* Justice Roberts, in which Brandeis, Sutherland and Butler, JJ., joined; *Appellate Defense Counsel:* A. C. Webber argued; Henry P. Fielding on brief; *Appellate Prosecution Counsel:* Joseph E. Warner argued and briefed; *Amicus Curiae Brief Supporting Prosecutor:* None; *Amicus Curiae Brief Supporting Defendant:* None.

Issue Presented: Whether the Federal Constitution requires a defendant be permitted to accompany a jury to view the crime scene?

Case Holding: The Federal Constitution does not require a defendant be permitted to accompany a jury to view the crime scene, because such observations do not constitute evidence.

Factual and procedural background of case: The defendant, Snyder, was convicted of capital murder and sentenced to death by the State of Massachusetts. The Massachusetts Supreme Court affirmed the judgment. In doing so, the appellate court rejected the defendant's contention that his Federal constitutional rights were violated when the trial court refused to allow him to accompany the jury on their visit to the crime scene. The United States Supreme Court granted certiorari to consider the issue.

Opinion of the Court by Justice Cardozo: Justice Cardozo held that the defendant was not denied any right guaranteed by the Constitution because he was not permitted to accompany the jury to the crime scene. Justice Cardozo expressed the Court's position as follows:

The commonwealth of Massachusetts is free to regulate the procedure of its courts in accordance with its own conception of policy and fairness, unless in so doing it offends some principle of justice so rooted in the traditions and conscience of our people as to be ranked as fundamental. Its procedure does not run foul of the Fourteenth Amendment because another method may seem to our thinking to be fairer or wiser or to give a surer promise of protection to the prisoner at the bar....

We assume in aid of the [defendant] that in a prosecution for a felony the defendant has the privilege under the Fourteenth Amendment to be present in his own person whenever his presence has a relation, reasonably substantial, to the fullness of his opportunity to defend against the charge. Thus, the privilege to confront one's accusers and cross-examine them face to face is assured to a defendant by the Sixth Amendment in prosecutions in the federal courts, and in prosecutions in the state courts is assured very often by the Constitutions of the states. For present purposes we assume that the privilege is reinforced by the Fourteenth Amendment, though this has not been squarely held....

... Nowhere in the decisions of this court is there a dictum, and still less a ruling, that the Fourteenth Amendment assures the privilege of presence when presence would be useless.... Many motions before trial are heard in the defendant's absence, and many motions after trial or in the prosecution of appeals. Confusion of thought will result if we fail to mark the distinction between requirements in respect of presence that have their source in the common law, and requirements that have their source, either expressly or by implication, in the Federal Constitution. Confusion will result again if the privilege of presence be identified with the privilege of confrontation, which is limited to the stages of the trial when there are witnesses to be questioned.... So far as the Fourteenth Amendment is concerned, the presence of a defendant is a condition of due process to the extent that a fair and just hearing would be thwarted by his absence, and to that extent only.

... We consider a bare inspection and nothing more, a view where nothing is said by any one to direct the attention of the jury to one feature or another. The Fourteenth Amendment does not assure to a defendant the privilege to be present at such a time. There is nothing he could do if he were there, and almost nothing he could gain. The only shred of advantage would be to make certain that the jury had been brought to the right place and had viewed the right scene. If he felt any doubt about this, he could examine the bailiffs at the trial and learn what they had looked at. The risk that they would lie is no greater than the risk that attaches to testimony about anything. Constitutional law, like other mortal contrivances, has to take some chances. Here the chance is so remote that it dwindles to the vanishing point. If the bailiffs were to bear false witness as to the place they had shown, the lie would be known to the jury. There is no immutable principle of justice that secures protection to a defendant against so shadowy a risk. The argument is made that conceivably the place might have been changed and in a way that would be material. In that event the fact could be brought out by appropriate inquiry. There could be inquiry of witnesses in court and of counsel out of court. Description would disclose the conditions at the view, and the defendant or his witnesses could prove what the conditions were before. He could do nothing more though he had been there with the jury. Indeed, the record makes it clear that upon request he would have been allowed to go there afterwards in company with his counsel. Opportunity was ample to learn whatever there was need to know.

If the risk of injustice to the prisoner is shadowy at its greatest, it ceases to be even a shadow when he admits that the jurors were brought to the right place and shown what it was right to see. That, in substance is what happened here.

The judgment of the Massachusetts Supreme Court was affirmed.

Dissenting opinion by Justice Roberts, in which Brandeis, Sutherland and Butler, JJ., joined: Justice Roberts dissented from the Court's decision. He believed the Constitution required the defendant's presence at the jury view, particularly because the trial court instructed the jury to consider their observations as evidence in rendering their decision in the case. Justice Roberts wrote as follows:

> In the light of the universal acceptance of this fundamental rule of fairness that the prisoner may be present throughout his trial, it is not a matter of assumption but a certainty that the Fourteenth Amendment guarantees the observance of the rule....
>
> If ... a view of the premises where crime is alleged to have been committed is a part of the process of submission of data to the triers of fact, upon which judgment is to be founded; if the knowledge thereby gained is to play its part with oral testimony and written evidence in striking the balance between the state and the prisoner, it is a part of the trial. If this is true, the Constitution secures the accused's presence. In this conclusion all the courts, save those of Massachusetts, agree. Such difference of view as the authorities exhibit as to the prisoner's right to be present at a view arises out of a disagreement on the question whether the view is a part of the trial, whether it is, in effect the taking of evidence. The great weight of authority is that it forms a part of the trial, and for that reason a defendant who so desires is entitled to be present.... It is true there is disagreement as to the nature and function of a view. On the one hand, the assertion is that its purpose is merely to acquaint the jury with the scene and thus enable them better to understand the testimony, and hence it forms no part of the trial and is not the taking of evidence. On the other, the suggestion is that the jury are bound to carry in mind what they see and form their judgment from the knowledge so obtained, and so the view amounts to the taking of evidence. The distinction seems too fine for practical purposes; but, however that may be, discussion of this abstract question is unimportant in a case like the present where the view was held to be evidence, and the jury were expressly so instructed.

See also **Jury View**

Sochor v. Florida

Court: United States Supreme Court; *Case Citation:* Sochor v. Florida, 504 U.S. 527 (1992); *Argued:* March 2, 1992; *Decided:* June 8, 1992; *Opinion of the Court:* Justice Souter; *Concurring Opinion:* Justice O'Connor; *Concurring and Dissenting Opinion:* Chief Justice Rehnquist, in which White and Thomas, JJ., joined; *Concurring and Dissenting Opinion:* Justice Stevens, in which Blackmun, J., joined; *Concurring and Dissenting Opinion:* Justice Scalia; *Appellate Defense Counsel:* Gary Caldwell argued; Richard L. Jorandby and Eric Cumfer on brief; *Appellate Prosecution Counsel:* Carolyn M. Snurkowski argued; Robert A. Butterworth and Celia A. Terenzio on brief; *Amicus Curiae Brief Supporting Prosecutor:* 1; *Amicus Curiae Brief Supporting Defendant:* 1.

Issue Presented: Whether the Florida Supreme Court cured the trial court's constitutional error in weighing an invalid statutory aggravating circumstance, in imposing the death penalty on the defendant?

Case Holding: The Florida Supreme Court did not cure the trial court's error in considering an invalid aggravating circumstance, because it neither reweighed the evidence nor applied harmless error analysis to the evidence.

Factual and procedural background of case: The defendant, Dennis Sochor, was convicted of capital murder by the State of Florida. During the penalty phase an advisory jury and the trial court found four statutory aggravating circumstances existed. Two of the aggravating circumstances found were called "heinousness" and "coldness" aggravators. The jury recommended the death penalty and the trial court adopted the recommendation. The Florida Supreme Court affirmed the conviction and sentence. In doing so, the appellate court found that the defendant's contention that the jury instruction on the heinousness factor was unconstitutionally vague had been waived for failure to object. The appellate court also held that the evidence failed to support the trial judge's finding of the coldness factor, but nevertheless affirmed the death sentence. The United States Supreme Court granted certiorari to consider the issue.

Opinion of the Court by Justice Souter: Justice Souter found that the application of the heinousness factor did not result in reversible error. It was said that the Court lacked jurisdiction to address the claim that the jury instruction on the heinousness factor was unconstitutionally vague, because the State appellate court indicated that its rejection of the claim was based on an alternative state ground.

The opinion found that the application of the coldness factor constituted an Eighth Amendment error that went uncorrected by the State appellate court. It was said that the constitutional error occurred when the trial judge weighed the coldness factor. Justice Souter indicated that the State appellate court did not cure the error. The opinion found that the State appellate court did not reweigh the evidence independently or perform harmless error analysis in order to cure the error. The judgment of the Florida Supreme Court was reversed as to the punishment.

Concurring opinion by Justice O'Connor: Justice O'Connor concurred in the Court's opinion. She wrote separately to state that her understanding of the Court's opinion was "that an appellate court can[not] fulfill its obligations of meaningful review by simply reciting the formula for harmless error." It was further said in her concurrence that "[a]n appellate court's bald assertion that an error of constitutional dimensions was 'harmless' cannot substitute for a principled explanation of how the court reached that conclusion."

Concurring and dissenting opinion by Chief Justice Rehnquist, in which White and Thomas, JJ., joined: The Chief Justice filed an opinion concurring in part and dissenting in part with the Court's decision. The Chief Justice indicated that he agreed with the Court's rejection of the defendant's claim on the "heinousness" factor. He also agreed with the Court that the trial court committed constitutional error in weighing the invalid "coldness" factor. The Chief Justice dissented, however, with the Court's conclusion that the State appellate court did not cure the error. It was said by the Chief Justice that the Florida Supreme Court applied harmless error analysis to the error in order to cure it.

Concurring and dissenting opinion by Justice Stevens, in

which Blackmun, J., joined: Justice Stevens wrote an opinion concurring in part and dissenting in part with the Court's decision. He agreed with the Court's disposition of the defendant's claim on the "coldness" factor. Justice Stevens disagreed with the Court's rejection of the defendant's claim on the "heinousness" factor. Justice Stevens stated his dissenting position as follows:

> [The defendant's] failure to object to the instruction at trial did not deprive the Florida Supreme Court or this Court of the power to correct the obvious constitutional error. First, [the defendant] did object to the vagueness of this aggravating circumstance in a [m]otion ... at the start of trial, however, that motion was denied. Second, the Florida Supreme Court, though noting that [the defendant] had failed to make a contemporaneous objection to the instruction at the time of trial, nevertheless went on to reach the merits of [the defendant's] claim. Thus, the Florida Supreme Court, far from providing us with a plain statement that [the defendant's] claim was procedurally barred, has merely said that the claim was "not preserved for appeal," and has given even further indication that [the defendant's] claim was not procedurally barred by proceeding to the merits, albeit in the alternative. Third, and most important, the state court may review a fundamental error despite a party's failure to make a contemporaneous objection in the trial court and it unquestionably has the power to review this error even though the error may not have been properly preserved for appeal.... Under these circumstances, the State has waived any possible procedural objection to our consideration of the erroneous jury instruction and this Court, contrary to its protestation, is not "without authority" to address [the defendant's] claim.

Concurring and dissenting opinion by Justice Scalia: Justice Scalia wrote an opinion concurring in part and dissenting in part with the Court's decision. He agreed with the Court's rejection of the defendant's claim on the "heinousness" factor. Justice Scalia dissented from the Court's "holding that the death sentence in this case is unconstitutional because the Florida Supreme Court failed to find 'harmless error' after having invalidated the trial judge's 'coldness' finding." He believed the issue was a State law matter that did not raise a Federal question. *See also* **Heinous, Atrocious, Cruel or Depraved Aggravator; Invalid Aggravator**

Solesbee v. Balkcom

Court: United States Supreme Court; *Case Citation:* Solesbee v. Balkcom, 339 U.S. 9 (1950); *Argued:* November 15, 1949; *Decided:* February 20, 1950; *Opinion of the Court:* Justice Black; *Concurring Opinion:* None; *Dissenting Opinion:* Justice Frankfurter; *Justice Taking No Part in Decision:* Justice Douglas; *Appellate Defense Counsel:* Benjamin E. Pierce argued and briefed; *Appellate Prosecution Counsel:* Eugene Cook argued; Claude Shaw and J. R. Parham on brief; *Amicus Curiae Brief Supporting Prosecutor:* None; *Amicus Curiae Brief Supporting Defendant:* None.

Issue Presented: Whether due process requires a judicial tribunal, rather than the office of a Governor, determine if a defendant is insane prior to execution?

Case Holding: Due process does not require a judicial tribunal, rather than the office of a Governor, determine if a defendant is insane prior to execution.

Factual and procedural background of case: The defendant, Solesbee, was convicted of capital murder and sentenced to death by the State of Georgia. The conviction and sentence were affirmed by the Georgia Supreme Court. Prior to the defendant's execution he asked the Governor to postpone execution on the ground that after conviction and sentence he had become insane. Acting under authority granted by statute, the Governor appointed three physicians who examined the defendant and declared him sane.

The defendant then filed a habeas corpus petition in a State trial court, alleging that the Federal Due Process Clause required that his claim of insanity after sentence be originally determined by a judicial tribunal after notice and hearings in which he could be represented by counsel, cross examine witnesses and offer evidence. The trial court rejected the claim and dismissed the petition. The Georgia Supreme Court affirmed. The United States Supreme Court granted certiorari to consider the issue.

Opinion of the Court by Justice Black: Justice Black made clear at the outset of the opinion that the Court was not addressing the issue of the constitutionality of executing an insane person. The opinion indicated that the defendant's only challenge was the non-judicial procedure used by Georgia for determining whether a death row inmate was insane prior to execution. In rejecting the defendant's claim that due process required a judicial tribunal determine his sanity to be executed, Justice Black wrote the following:

> Where a state policy is against execution of a condemned convict who has become insane after conviction and sentence, it is not a denial of due process under the Fourteenth Amendment to vest discretionary authority in the Governor (aided by physicians) to determine whether a condemned convict has become insane after sentence and, if so, whether he should be committed to an insane asylum — even though the Governor's decision is not subject to judicial review and the statute makes no provision for an adversary hearing at which the convict may appear in person or by counsel or through friends and cross-examine witnesses and offer evidence.
>
> We are unable to say that it offends due process for a state to deem its Governor an "apt and special tribunal" to pass upon a question so closely related to powers that from the beginning have been entrusted to governors. And here the governor had the aid of physicians specially trained in appraising the elusive and often deceptive symptoms of insanity. It is true that governors and physicians might make errors of judgment. But the search for truth in this field is always beset by difficulties that may beget error. Even judicial determination of sanity might be wrong....
>
> [The Court's precedents] stand for the universal common-law principle that upon a suggestion of insanity after sentence, the tribunal charged with responsibility must be vested with broad discretion in deciding whether evidence shall be heard. This discretion has usually been held nonreviewable by appellate courts. The heart of the common-law doctrine has been that a suggestion of insanity after sentence is an appeal to the conscience and sound wisdom of the particular tribunal which is asked to postpone sentence. We cannot say that the trust thus reposed in judges should be denied governors, traditionally charged with saying the last word that spells life or death. There is no indication that either the Governor or the physicians who acted on [the defendant's] application violated the humanitarian policy of Georgia against execution of the insane. We hold

that the Georgia statute as applied is not a denial of due process of law.

The judgment of the Georgia Supreme Court was affirmed.

Dissenting opinion by Justice Frankfurter: Justice Frankfurter dissented from the Court's decision. He believed that under a scheme which allowed a Governor to determine a defendant's sanity prior to execution, due process required the defendant be allowed to present evidence on the issue and challenge contrary evidence with the assistance of counsel. Justice Frankfurter wrote: "It is a groundless fear to assume that it would obstruct the rigorous administration of criminal justice to allow the case to be put for a claim of insanity, however informal and expeditious the procedure for dealing with the claim. The time needed for such a fair procedure could not unreasonably delay the execution of the sentence unless in all fairness and with due respect for a basic principle in our law the execution should be delayed. The risk of an undue delay is hardly comparable to the grim risk of the barbarous execution of an insane man because of a hurried, one-sided, untested determination of the question of insanity[.]" *See also* **Insanity While Awaiting Execution; Phyle v. Duffy**

Solomon Islands

Solomon Islands Capital punishment was abolished on the Solomon Islands in 1966. *See also* **International Capital Punishment Nations**

Somalia

Somalia Somalia permits capital punishment. Somalia uses the firing squad to carry out the death penalty. Its legal system is a mixture of English and Italian law and customary law. Somalia's constitution became effective on September 23, 1979.

Somalia has been without a central government since 1991. In a conference in Cairo, Egypt, in December 1997, fighting factions in the nation signed the "Cairo Declaration." The Declaration provided for a 13-person council of Presidents, a Prime Minister, and a National Assembly.

There is no national judicial system. Some regions of the country have established local courts. The judiciary in most regions rely on some combination of traditional or customary law, Shari'a (Islamic) law, and the penal code of the pre–1991 overthrow of the government. The right to legal counsel and the right to appeal do not exist in those areas that apply customary or Shari'a law. *See also* **International Capital Punishment Nations**

Souter, David H.

Souter, David H. David H. Souter was appointed as an associate justice of the United States Supreme Court in 1990. While on the Supreme Court Souter has displayed a moderate judicial philosophy in his interpretation of the Constitution.

Souter was born in Melrose, Massachusetts on September 17, 1939. Souter graduated from Harvard University in 1961. His educational training included studying law at Harvard Law School and Oxford University. In addition to serving on the supreme court of New Hampshire, Souter was appointed in 1990 as an appellate judge for the First Circuit Court of Appeals. A few months after his Federal appellate appointment, President George Bush appointed Souter to the Supreme Court.

Souter has authored a few capital punishment opinions since his elevation to the Supreme Court. The moderate philosophy Souter brought to the Court was best illustrated in the case of *Sochor v. Florida*. In that case the defendant was sentenced to death under an invalid aggravating circumstance. Souter, writing for the Court, found that the supreme court of Florida failed to perform the necessary analysis that could have cured the problem caused by the use of an invalid factor and, therefore, reversed the death sentence.

Capital Punishment Opinions Written by Souter

Case Name	Opinion of the Court	Plurality Opinion	Concurring Opinion	Dissenting Opinion	Concurring and Dissenting
Calderon v. Thompson				✓	
Felker v. Turpin			✓		
Graham v. Collins				✓	
Kyles v. Whitley	✓				
Payne v. Tennessee			✓		
Schad v. Arizona		✓			
Simmons v. South Carolina			✓		
Sochor v. Florida	✓				
Strickler v. Greene					✓
Stringer v. Black				✓	
Tuilaepa v. California			✓		

South Africa

South Africa South Africa abolished capital punishment for ordinary crimes in 1995, and for all crimes in 1997. *See also* **International Capital Punishment Nations**

South Carolina

South Carolina The State of South Carolina is a capital punishment jurisdiction. The State reenacted its death penalty law after the United States Supreme Court decision in *Furman v. Georgia*, 408 U.S. 238 (1972), on July 2, 1974.

South Carolina has a three-tier legal system. The State's legal system is composed of a supreme court, court of appeals and courts of general jurisdiction. The South Carolina Supreme Court is presided over by a chief justice and four associate justices. The South Carolina Court of Appeals is composed of a chief judge and eight associate judges. The courts of general jurisdiction in the State are called Circuit Courts. Capital offenses against the State of South Carolina are tried in the Circuit Courts.

South Carolina's capital punishment statute is triggered if a person commits a homicide under the following special circumstance: Murder committed with malice aforethought.

Capital murder in South Carolina is punishable by death, life imprisonment without parole or imprisonment for a term of years. A capital prosecution in South Carolina is bifurcated into a guilt phase and penalty phase. A jury is used at both phases of a capital trial. It is required that, at the penalty phase, the jury unanimously agree that a death sentence is appropriate before it can be imposed. If the penalty phase jury is unable to reach a verdict, the trial judge is required to impose a sentence of imprisonment for a term of years. The decision of a penalty phase jury is binding on the trial court under the laws of South Carolina.

In order to impose a death sentence upon a defendant under South Carolina law, it is required that the prosecutor establish the existence of at least one of the following statutory aggravating circumstances at the penalty phase:

1. The murder was committed during the commission of: (a) criminal sexual conduct; (b) kidnaping; (c) burglary; (d) robbery; (e) larceny; (f) killing by poison; (g) drug trafficking; (h) physical torture; or (i) dismemberment of a person.
2. The offender had a prior conviction for murder.
3. The offender knowingly created a great risk of death to more than one person.
4. The offender committed the murder for money or a thing of monetary value.
5. The murder of a judicial officer, solicitor, or other officer of the court.
6. The offender directed another to commit murder or committed murder as an agent of another person.
7. The murder of a law enforcement officer, corrections employee or fireman.
8. The murder of a family member of an official listed in (5) and (7) above with the intent to impede or retaliate against the official.
9. Two or more persons were murdered by the defendant by one act or pursuant to one scheme.
10. The murder of a child 11 years of age or under.
11. The murder of a witness or potential witness committed at any time during the criminal process for the purpose of impeding prosecution of any crime.

Although the Federal Constitution will not permit jurisdictions to prevent capital felons from presenting all relevant mitigating evidence at the penalty phase, South Carolina has provided the following statutory mitigating circumstances that permit the jury to reject imposition of the death penalty:

1. The defendant has no significant history of prior criminal conviction.
2. The murder was committed while the defendant was under the influence of mental or emotional disturbance.
3. The victim was a participant in the defendant's conduct or consented to the act.

4. The defendant was an accomplice in the murder committed by another person and his participation was relatively minor.
5. The defendant acted under duress or under the domination of another person.
6. The capacity of the defendant to appreciate the criminality of his conduct or to conform his conduct to the requirements of law was substantially impaired.
7. The age or mentality of the defendant at the time of the crime.
8. The defendant was provoked by the victim into committing the murder.
9. The defendant was below the age of 18 at the time of the crime.
10. The defendant had mental retardation at the time of the crime.

Under South Carolina's capital punishment statute, a sentence of death is automatically reviewed by the South Carolina Supreme Court. South Carolina provides for lethal injection or electrocution to carry out death sentences. The State's death row facility for men is located in Ridgeville, South Carolina; while the facility maintaining female death row inmates is located in Columbia, South Carolina. Pursuant to the laws of South Carolina the Governor has exclusive authority to grant clemency in capital cases.

From the start of modern capital punishment in 1976, through 1999, South Carolina executed 24 capital felons. During this period South Carolina did not have any female capital felons on death row. A total of 69 capital felons were on death row in South Carolina in 1999. The 1999 death row population in the State was listed as: 37 black inmates and 94

Executions by South Carolina 1976–1999

Name	Race	Date of Execution	Method of Execution
Joseph C. Shaw	White	January 11, 1985	Electrocution
James T. Roach	White	January 10, 1986	Electrocution
Ronald Woomer	White	April 27, 1990	Electrocution
Donald Gaskins	White	September 6, 1991	Electrocution
Sylvester Adams	Black	August 18, 1995	Lethal Injection
Robert South	White	May 31, 1996	Lethal Injection
Fred Kornahrens	White	July 19, 1996	Lethal Injection
Michael Torrence	White	September 6, 1996	Lethal Injection
Larry G. Bell	White	October 4, 1996	Electrocution
Doyle C. Lucas	White	November 15, 1996	Lethal Injection
Frank Middleton, Jr.	Black	November 22, 1996	Lethal Injection
Michael E. Elkins	White	June 13, 1997	Lethal Injection
Earl Matthews	Black	November 7, 1997	Lethal Injection
John Arnold	White	March 6, 1998	Lethal Injection
John Plath	White	July 10, 1998	Lethal Injection
Sammy Roberts	White	September 25, 1998	Lethal Injection
Larry Gilbert	Black	December 4, 1998	Lethal Injection
J. D. Gleaton	Black	December 4, 1998	Lethal Injection
Louis Truesdale	Black	December 11, 1998	Lethal Injection
Andy Smith	Black	December 18, 1998	Lethal Injection
Ronnie Howard	Black	January 8, 1999	Lethal Injection
Joseph E. Atkins	White	January 25, 1999	Lethal Injection
Leroy J. Drayton	Black	November 12, 1999	Lethal Injection
David Rocheville	White	December 3, 1999	Lethal Injection

white inmates. In 1999 the State had 5 juveniles on death row. The State permits capital punishment to be imposed on persons 16 years old or older. South Carolina does not prohibit the execution of mentally retarded capital felons.

SOUTH CAROLINA EXECUTIONS 1976–1999

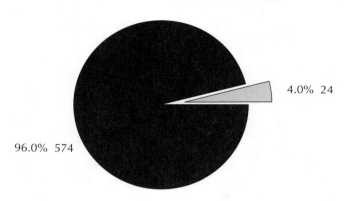

4.0% 24

96.0% 574

■ SOUTH CAROLINA EXECUTIONS
■ ALL OTHER EXECUTIONS

EXECUTIONS BY SOUTH CAROLINA 1930–1999

95.8% 4271

4.2% 186

■ SOUTH CAROLINA
■ ALL OTHER JURISDICTIONS

South Carolina v. Gathers *Court:* United States Supreme Court; *Case Citation:* South Carolina v. Gathers, 490 U.S. 805 (1989); *Argued:* March 28, 1989; *Decided:* June 12, 1989; *Opinion of the Court:* Justice Brennan; *Concurring Statement:* Justice White; *Dissenting Opinion:* Justice O'Connor, in which Rehnquist, C. J., and Kennedy, J., joined; *Dissenting Opinion:* Justice Scalia; *Appellate Defense Counsel:* William Isaac Diggs argued; Joseph L. Savitz III on brief; *Appellate Prosecution Counsel:* Donald J. Zelenka argued; T. Travis Medlock and Charles M. Condon on brief; *Amicus Curiae Brief Supporting Prosecutor:* 6; *Amicus Curiae Brief Supporting Defendant:* 2.

Issue Presented: Whether it was constitutionally improper during the penalty phase for the prosecutor to provide remarks about personal characteristics of the defendant?

Case Holding: It was constitutionally improper during the

penalty phase for the prosecutor to provide remarks about personal characteristics of the defendant, because such information inhibits reasoned deliberation by the jury in assessing the penalty to give the defendant.

Factual and procedural background of case: The defendant, Demetrius Gathers, was convicted of capital murder and sentenced to death by the State of South Carolina. On appeal, the South Carolina Supreme Court reversed the death sentence on the grounds that during the penalty phase the prosecutor improperly interjected remarks about the victim being a religious person. The United States Supreme Court granted certiorari to consider the issue.

Opinion of the Court by Justice Brennan: Justice Brennan held that the prosecutor's remarks about the religious background of the victim interjected impermissible information to the jury during the penalty phase. It was said that the victim's religious life and other personal characteristics had no bearing on whether the defendant warranted receiving a sentence of death. The opinion reasoned that the Constitution required the jury make a reasoned decision on whether to impose a sentence of death. Justice Brennan found that emotional appeal to the jury through presentation of personal characteristics of the victim inhibited rational decisionmaking by the jury. The judgment of the South Carolina Supreme Court was affirmed.

Concurring Statement by Justice White: Justice White issued a statement indicating he concurred in the Court's decision.

Dissenting opinion by Justice O'Connor, in which Rehnquist, C. J., and Kennedy, J., joined: Justice O'Connor dissented from the Court's decision. She believed that the Constitution permitted personal characteristics of the victim to be brought out during the penalty phase. Justice O'Connor wrote as follows: "Because the Eighth Amendment itself requires "that the penalty imposed in a capital case be proportional to the harm caused and the defendant's blameworthiness," I would reject a rigid Eighth Amendment rule which prohibits a sentencing jury from hearing argument or considering evidence concerning the personal characteristics of the victim. I would thus reverse the judgment of the South Carolina Supreme Court in this case."

Dissenting opinion by Justice Scalia: Justice Scalia dissented from the Court's decision. He argued that a jury had a right to hear of admirable qualities of the victim. Justice Scalia believed there was no justification for isolating the victim from the penalty phase, when the reason for the defendant's sentence was the death of the victim. *See also* **Booth v. Maryland; California v. Brown; Payne v. Tennessee; Victim Impact Evidence**

South Dakota The State of South Dakota is a capital punishment jurisdiction. The State reenacted its death penalty law after the United States Supreme Court decision in *Furman v. Georgia*, 408 U.S. 238 (1972), on January 1, 1979.

South Dakota has a two-tier legal system. The State's legal

system is composed of a supreme court and courts of general jurisdiction. The South Dakota Supreme Court is presided over by a chief justice and four associate justices. The courts of general jurisdiction in the State are called Circuit Courts. Capital offenses against the State of South Dakota are tried in the Circuit Courts.

South Dakota's capital punishment statute is triggered if a person commits a homicide under the following special circumstances:

> A premeditated design to effect the death of the person killed or of any other human being, or a homicide when committed by a person engaged in the perpetration of, or attempt to perpetrate, any arson, rape, robbery, burglary, kidnapping, or unlawful throwing, placing, or discharging of a destructive device or explosive. Homicide is also a capital offense if committed by a person who perpetrated, or who attempted to perpetrate, any arson, rape, robbery, burglary, kidnapping or unlawful throwing, placing or discharging of a destructive device or explosive and who subsequently effects the death of any victim of such crime to prevent detection or prosecution of the crime.

Capital murder in South Dakota is punishable by death or life imprisonment. A capital prosecution in South Dakota is bifurcated into a guilt phase and penalty phase. A jury is used at both phases of a capital trial. It is required that, at the penalty phase, the jury unanimously agree that a death sentence is appropriate before it can be imposed. If the penalty phase jury is unable to reach a verdict, the trial judge is required to impose a sentence of life imprisonment. The decision of a penalty phase jury is binding on the trial court under the laws of South Dakota.

In order to impose a death sentence upon a defendant under South Dakota law, it is required that the prosecutor establish the existence of at least one of the following statutory aggravating circumstances at the penalty phase:

1. The offense was committed by a person with a prior record of felony conviction;
2. The defendant by the defendant's act knowingly created a great risk of death to more than one person in a public place by means of a weapon or device which would normally be hazardous to the lives of more than one person;
3. The defendant committed the offense for the benefit of the defendant or another, for the purpose of receiving money or any other thing of monetary value;
4. The defendant committed the offense on a judicial officer, former judicial officer, prosecutor, or former prosecutor while such prosecutor, former prosecutor, judicial officer, or former judicial officer was engaged in the performance of such person's official duties or where a major part of the motivation for the offense came from the official actions of such judicial officer, former judicial officer, prosecutor, or former prosecutor;
5. The defendant caused or directed another to commit murder or committed murder as an agent or employee of another person;
6. The offense was outrageously or wantonly vile, horrible, or inhuman in that it involved torture, depravity of mind, or an aggravated battery to the victim. Any murder is

wantonly vile, horrible, and inhuman if the victim is less than 13 years of age;
7. The offense was committed against a law enforcement officer, employee of a corrections institution, or fire fighter while engaged in the performance of such person's official duties;
8. The offense was committed by a person in, or who has escaped from, the lawful custody of a law enforcement officer or place of lawful confinement;
9. The offense was committed for the purpose of avoiding, interfering with, or preventing a lawful arrest or custody in a place of lawful confinement, of the defendant or another; or
10. The offense was committed in the course of manufacturing, distributing, or dispensing narcotics.

South Dakota does not provide by statute any mitigating circumstances to the imposition of the death penalty. Even though the State does not provide statutory mitigating circumstances, the United States Supreme Court has ruled that all relevant mitigating evidence must be allowed at the penalty phase.

Under South Dakota's capital punishment statute, a sentence of death is automatically reviewed by the South Dakota Supreme Court. South Dakota uses lethal injection to carry out death sentences. Pursuant to the laws of South Dakota the Governor has exclusive authority to grant clemency in capital cases.

From the start of modern capital punishment in 1976, through 1999, South Dakota did not execute any capital felon. A total of 2 capital felons were on death row in South Dakota in 1999. The 1999 death row population in the State was listed as: 0 black inmates and 2 white inmates. Both death row inmates were male. In 1999 the State did not have any juvenile on death row. The State permits capital punishment to be imposed on persons 16 years old or older. South Dakota does not prohibit the execution of mentally retarded capital felons.

EXECUTIONS BY SOUTH DAKOTA 1930–1999

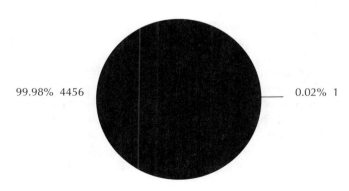

99.98% 4456   0.02% 1

■ SOUTH DAKOTA
■ ALL OTHER JURISDICTIONS

Southern Center for Human Rights

Southern Center for Human Rights   The Southern Center for Human Rights (the Center) is a nonprofit, public interest legal project. It was founded in 1976, to enforce the constitutional protection against cruel and unusual punishment. The Center challenges discrimination against minorities, the poor and the disadvantaged in the criminal justice system of the South.

The Center carries out its objectives in a variety of ways. It provides direct legal representation to the condemned and the imprisoned, recruiting attorneys from throughout the nation to take on such work; supporting the efforts of local attorneys, community groups and individuals; involving students and other volunteers in human rights work; and disseminating information to the press and public about human rights abuses and denials of due process.

Members of the Center's staff have written articles that have appeared in books, newspapers, law reviews and other publications; have taught courses on capital punishment and prisoners' rights at the law schools at Harvard, Yale, Georgetown, Emory, Georgia State and other universities; have responded to invitations to testify before the committees of the United States Senate, the United States House of Representatives, and several state legislatures; and have appeared in the media and public forums in order to educate the press and public about criminal justice and corrections issues.

The Center carries out this work with a staff of nine attorneys. Attorney Stephen B. Bright has been the director of the Center since 1982. He has taught courses on criminal law, capital punishment, prisoners' rights and international human rights at Yale, Harvard, Georgetown, Emory, Northeastern, Florida State and St. Mary's law schools.

The Center has a death penalty project which challenges racial discrimination in the imposition of the death penalty. The death penalty project uses a strategy which combines litigation, community involvement and public education. The project provides direct legal representation to those facing the death penalty at trials, on appeal, and in post-conviction proceedings; engages in efforts to bring about greater participation by people who have been excluded from the criminal justice system; challenges the imposition of the death penalty upon people with mental illnesses, children, and other disenfranchised groups and educates lawyers about how best to defend those groups in capital cases; recruits lawyers to provide representation to those facing the death penalty, publishes materials and provides advice to lawyers defending those facing death; provides materials to and collaborates with other organizations, community groups and individuals in efforts to educate communities about the injustices in the use of the death penalty and involve them in seeking solutions; and draws national and international attention to and increases public involvement in these issues through workshops, public hearings, and the media.

The Center has been instrumental in establishing other organizations. It helped establish and provided staff for organizations in Alabama, Texas and Louisiana which provide representation to persons facing the death penalty in those states.

Sovereignty Doctrine *see* Dual Sovereignty

Spain   Spain abolished capital punishment for ordinary crimes in 1978, and for all crimes in 1995. *See also* **International Capital Punishment Nations**

Spano v. New York   *Court:* United States Supreme Court; *Case Citation:* Spano v. New York, 360 U.S. 315 (1959); *Argued:* April 27, 1959; *Decided:* June 22, 1959; *Opinion of the Court:* Chief Justice Warren; *Concurring Opinion:* Justice Douglas, in which Black and Brennan, JJ. Joined; *Concurring Opinion:* Justice Stewart, in which Douglas and Brennan, JJ., joined; *Dissenting Opinion:* None; *Appellate Defense Counsel:* Herbert S. Siegal argued; Rita D. Schechter on brief; *Appellate Prosecution Counsel:* Irving Anolik argued; Daniel V. Sullivan and Walter E. Dillon on brief; *Amicus Curiae Brief Supporting Prosecutor:* None; *Amicus Curiae Brief Supporting Defendant:* None.

Issue Presented: Whether the defendant's confession to capital murder was involuntary and therefore inadmissible at his trial?

Case Holding: The defendant's confession to capital murder was involuntary and therefore inadmissible at his trial.

Factual and procedural background of case: The defendant, Vincent Joseph Spano, was arrested for capital murder by the State of New York. While being detained the defendant was interrogated for eight hours by the police, in spite of requests to see his attorney. The defendant eventually confessed to the murder. A jury convicted the defendant of capital murder and he was sentenced to death. The New York Court of Appeals affirmed the conviction and sentence. In doing so, the appellate court rejected the defendant's argument that his confession was taken in violation of the Federal Constitution. The United States Supreme Court granted certiorari to consider the issue.

Opinion of the Court by Chief Justice Warren: The Chief Justice held that the defendant's confession was not voluntary and its use at trial violated the Due Process Clause of the Fourteenth Amendment. The opinion pointed out that the constitutional abhorrence to the use of involuntary confessions did not turn alone on their inherent untrustworthiness. It was said that the prohibition also turned on the deep-rooted feeling that the police must obey the law while enforcing the law. The Chief Justice wrote "that in the end life and liberty can be as much endangered from illegal methods used to convict those thought to be criminals as from the actual criminals themselves." The opinion went onto to set out the interrogation tactics used against the defendant as follows:

> [The defendant] was a foreign-born young man of 25 with no past history of law violation or of subjection to official interrogation, at least insofar as the record shows. He had progressed only one-half year into high school and the record indicates that he had a history of emotional instability. He did not make a narrative statement, but was subject to the leading questions of a skillful prosecutor in a question and answer confession. He was subjected to questioning not by a few men, but by

many. They included Assistant District Attorney Goldsmith, one Hyland of the District Attorney's Office, Deputy Inspector Halks, Lieutenant Gannon, Detective Ciccone, Detective Motta, Detective Lehrer, Detective Marshal, Detective Farrell, Detective Leira, Detective Murphy, Detective Murtha, Sergeant Clarke, Patrolman Bruno and Stenographer Baldwin. All played some part, and the effect of such massive official interrogation must have been felt. [The defendant] was questioned for virtually eight straight hours before he confessed, with his only respite being a transfer to an arena presumably considered more appropriate by the police for the task at hand. Nor was the questioning conducted during normal business hours, but began in early evening, continued into the night, and did not bear fruition until the not-too-early morning. The drama was not played out, with the final admissions obtained, until almost sunrise. In such circumstances slowly mounting fatigue does, and is calculated to, play its part. The questioners persisted in the face of his repeated refusals to answer on the advice of his attorney, and they ignored his reasonable requests to contact the local attorney whom he had already retained and who had personally delivered him into the custody of these officers in obedience to the bench warrant.

We conclude that [the defendant's] will was overborne by official pressure, fatigue and sympathy falsely aroused, after considering all the facts in their post-indictment setting. Here a grand jury had already found sufficient cause to require [the defendant] to face trial on a charge of first-degree murder, and the police had an eyewitness to the shooting. The police were not therefore merely trying to solve a crime, or even to absolve a suspect. They were rather concerned primarily with securing a statement from [the] defendant on which they could convict him. The undeviating intent of the officers to extract a confession from [the defendant] is therefore patent. When such an intent is shown, this Court has held that the confession obtained must be examined with the most careful scrutiny, and has reversed a conviction on facts less compelling than these.

The judgment of the New York Court of Appeals was reversed.

Concurring opinion by Justice Douglas, in which Black and Brennan, JJ. joined: Justice Douglas concurred in the Court's decision. He wrote separately to express his opinion that the defendant's constitutional right to counsel was violated by the interrogation. Justice Douglas wrote: "We do not have here mere suspects who are being secretly interrogated by the police ... nor witnesses who are being questioned in secret administrative or judicial proceedings[.] This is a case of an accused, who is scheduled to be tried by a judge and jury, being tried in a preliminary way by the police. This is a kangaroo court procedure whereby the police produce the vital evidence in the form of a confession which is useful or necessary to obtain a conviction. They in effect deny him effective representation by counsel. This seems to me to be a flagrant violation of the principle ... that the right of counsel extends to the preparation for trial, as well as to the trial itself.... When he is deprived of that right after indictment and before trial, he may indeed be denied effective representation by counsel at the only stage when legal aid and advice would help him. This secret inquisition by the police when defendant asked for and was denied counsel was [a] serious ... invasion of his constitutional rights[.]"

Concurring opinion by Justice Stewart, in which Douglas and Brennan, JJ., joined: Justice Stewart concurred in the Court's decision. He believed, like Justice Douglas, that the right to counsel was the triggering constitutional violation in the case. Justice Stewart wrote:

> While I concur in the opinion of the Court, it is my view that the absence of counsel when this confession was elicited was alone enough to render it inadmissible under the Fourteenth Amendment.
>
> Our Constitution guarantees the assistance of counsel to a man on trial for his life in an orderly courtroom, presided over by a judge, open to the public, and protected by all the procedural safeguards of the law. Surely a Constitution which promises that much can vouchsafe no less to the same man under midnight inquisition in the squad room of a police station.

See also **Harris v. South Carolina; Right to Remain Silent; Turner v. Pennsylvania; Watts v. Indiana**

Sparf v. United States
Court: United States Supreme Court; *Case Citation:* Sparf v. United States, 156 U.S. 51 (1895); *Argued:* Not reported; *Decided:* January 21, 1895; *Opinion of the Court:* Justice Harlan; *Concurring and Dissenting Opinion:* Justice Brewer, in which Brown, J., joined; *Concurring and Dissenting Opinion:* Justice Gray, in which Shiras, J., joined; *Appellate Defense Counsel:* F. J. Kierce argued and briefed; *Appellate Prosecution Counsel:* Mr. Conrad argued and briefed; *Amicus Curiae Brief Supporting Prosecutor:* None; *Amicus Curiae Brief Supporting Defendant:* None.

Issues Presented: (1) Whether Sparf's conviction was invalid due to the introduction of Hansen's confession? (2) Whether the trial court committed error in failing to instruct the jury on lesser included offenses to capital murder?

Case Holdings: (1) Sparf's conviction was invalid due to the introduction of Hansen's confession, because there was no evidence of a conspiracy between the defendants to kill the victim. (2) The trial court did not commit error in failing to instruct the jury on lesser included offenses to capital murder, because no evidence was introduced on lesser included offenses.

Factual and procedural background of case: The defendants, Herman Sparf and Hans Hansen, were indicted for capital murder by the United States. Also named in the indictment was Thomas St. Clair. The murder took place on the high seas. The case was prosecuted in a Federal District Court in California. The defendants, who were tried together, were convicted and sentenced to death. In the defendants appeal to the United States Supreme Court, Sparf contended that his conviction was invalid because the trial court allowed Hansen's confession to be used against him; and both defendants argued that their convictions were invalid because the trial court refused to instruct the jury that they could return a verdict of guilty of a lesser included offense. The United States Supreme Court granted certiorari to consider the issues.

Opinion of the Court by Justice Harlan: Justice Harlan first examined the contention by Sparf that Hansen's confession could not be used against him. The opinion found that "the confession and declarations of Hansen ... were incompetent as evidence against Sparf." Justice Harlan reasoned as follows: "If the evidence made a case of conspiracy to kill and murder, the rule is settled that after the conspiracy has come to an end, and whether by success or by failure, the admissions of one conspirator by way of narrative of past facts are not admissible in evidence against the others. The same rule is applicable where the evidence does not show that the killing was pursuant to a conspiracy, but yet was by the joint act of the defendants."

His opinion next turned to the issue of whether the trial court should have instructed the jury on lesser included offenses. Justice Harlan ruled that no evidence was presented which would have justified an instruction on lesser included offenses. He wrote as follows:

> ... A verdict of guilty of an offense less than the one charged would have been in flagrant disregard of all the proof, and in violation by the jury of their obligation to render a true verdict. There was an entire absence of evidence upon which to rest a verdict of guilty of manslaughter or of simple assault. A verdict of that kind would have been the exercise by the jury of the power to commute the punishment for an offense actually committed, and thus impose a punishment different from that prescribed by law....
>
> We are of opinion that the court below did not err in saying to the jury that they could not, consistently with the law arising from the evidence, find the defendants guilty of manslaughter, or of any offense less than the one charged; that if the defendants were not guilty of the offense charged, the duty of the jury was to return a verdict of not guilty. No instruction was given that questioned the right of the jury to determine whether the witnesses were to be believed or not, nor whether the defendant was guilty or not guilty of the offense charged. On the contrary, the court was careful to say that the jury were the exclusive judges of the facts, and that they were to determine — applying to the facts the principles of law announced by the court — whether the evidence established the guilt or innocence of the defendants of the charge set out in the indictment.

The judgment of the District Court was affirmed as to Hansen, but is reversed as to Sparf, with directions for a new trial as to him.

Concurring and dissenting opinion by Justice Brewer, in which Brown, J., joined: Justice Brewer concurred in the Court's affirmance of the judgment against Hansen. He dissented from the Court's reversal of Sparf's judgment, on the grounds that Sparf did not make a proper objection during the trial. Justice Brewer wrote:

> But it is conceded that this confession was material, relevant, and competent, was properly admitted in evidence on the single trial then pending, and properly heard by the jury. The real burden of complaint is that, when the court admitted the testimony, it ought to have instructed the jury that it was evidence only against Hansen, and not against Sparf.... I do not question the proposition that a confession made by one of two defendants in the absence of the other is to be considered by the jury only as against the one making it, and I admit that, if a separate objection had been made by Sparf, the court would have been called upon to formally sustain such objection, and instruct the jury that such testimony was to be considered by them only as against Hansen. If an instruction had been asked, as is the proper way, the attention of the court would have been directed to the matter, and an adverse ruling would have rightly presented the error which is now relied upon.

Concurring and dissenting opinion by Justice Gray, in which Shiras, J., joined: Justice Gray concurred in the Court's reversal of Sparf's judgment. He dissented from the Court's affirmance of Hansen's judgment. Justice Gray wrote:

> The defendants requested the judge to instruct the jury that "under the indictment in this case the defendants may be convicted of murder or manslaughter or of an attempt to commit murder or manslaughter; and if, after a full and careful consideration of all the evidence before you, you believe beyond a reasonable doubt that the defendants are guilty either of manslaughter, or of an assault with intent to commit murder or manslaughter, you should so find your verdict." The judge refused to give this instruction, and the defendants excepted to the refusal....
>
> The judge, by instructing the jury that they were bound to accept the law as given to them by the court, denied their right to decide the law. And by instructing them that, if a felonious homicide by the defendants was proved, there was nothing in the case to reduce it below the grade of murder, and they could not properly find it to be manslaughter, and by declining to submit to them the question whether the defendants were guilty of manslaughter only, he denied their right to decide the fact....
>
> For the twofold reason that the defendants, by the instructions given by the court to the jury, have been deprived both of their right to have the jury decide the law involved in the general issue, and also of their right to have the jury decide every matter of fact involved in that issue[.]

See also **Lesser Included Offense Instruction; St. Clair v. United States**

Spaziano v. Florida

Court: United States Supreme Court; *Case Citation:* Spaziano v. Florida, 468 U.S. 447 (1984); *Argued:* April 17, 1984; *Decided:* July 2, 1984; *Opinion of the Court:* Justice Blackmun; *Concurring Statement:* Justice White, in which Rehnquist, J., joined; *Concurring and Dissenting Opinion:* Justice Stevens, in which Brennan and Marshall, JJ., joined; *Appellate Defense Counsel:* Craig S. Barnard argued; Richard L. Jorandby, Richard H. Burr III, and Richard B. Greene on brief; *Appellate Prosecution Counsel:* Mark C. Menser argued; Jim Smith on brief; *Amicus Curiae Brief Supporting Prosecutor:* 1; *Amicus Curiae Brief Supporting Defendant:* None.

Issue Presented: Whether the Constitution requires a capital sentencing jury's recommendation of life imprisonment be final?

Case Holding: There is no constitutional requirement that a capital jury's recommendation of life imprisonment be final.

Factual and procedural background of case: The defendant, Joseph Robert Spaziano, was indicted and tried for first-degree murder by the State of Florida. After the jury returned a verdict of guilty of first-degree murder, a sentencing hearing was conducted before the same jury, which returned an advisory verdict recommending life imprisonment. The trial judge rejected the recommendation and, after weighing the aggravating and mitigating circumstances, imposed a death sentence.

On appeal, the Florida Supreme Court affirmed the conviction, but reversed the death sentence because of the trial judge's consideration of a confidential portion of a presentence investigation report, without letting either party review a copy of the confidential portion. On remand, the trial court again imposed the death penalty. The Florida Supreme Court affirmed the sentence. In doing so, the appellate court rejected the defendant's contention the federal Constitution prohibited the trial court from overriding the jury's recommendation of life imprisonment. The United States Supreme Court granted certiorari to address the issue.

Opinion of the Court by Justice Blackmun: Justice Blackmun rejected the defendant's argument that the Constitution prohibits a trial court from overriding a capital jury's recommendation of life imprisonment. It was said that the fundamental issue in a capital sentencing proceeding is the determination of the appropriate punishment to be imposed on an individual, and in making such determination the Constitution does not guarantee a right to a binding jury verdict. The opinion reasoned that nothing in the safeguards against arbitrary and discriminatory application of the death penalty necessitated by the qualitative difference of the penalty requires that the sentence be imposed by a jury. Justice Blackmun made clear that the fact that the majority of jurisdictions with capital sentencing statutes give the life-or-death decision to the jury, does not establish that contemporary standards of fairness and decency are offended by the jury override.

The opinion held further: "We see nothing that suggests that the application of the jury-override procedure has resulted in arbitrary or discriminatory application of the death penalty, either in general or in this particular case. Regardless of the jury's recommendation, the trial judge is required to conduct an independent review of the evidence and to make his own findings regarding aggravating and mitigating circumstances. If the judge imposes a sentence of death, he must set forth in writing the findings on which the sentence is based." The Court went on to affirm the judgment of the Florida Supreme Court.

Concurring Statement by Justice White, in which Rehnquist, J., joined: Justice White issued a statement indicating he joined the Court's opinion and judgment except for its dictum on a nondispositive issue not discussed here.

Concurring and dissenting opinion by Justice Stevens, in which Brennan and Marshall, JJ., joined: Justice Stevens concurred with the Court's resolution of a nondispositive issue involving the statute of limitations (not discussed here). However, he dissented from the Court's determination that the Constitution did not provide the defendant with a right to have the jury determine his sentence. The dissent pointed out that in 82 cases arising under the capital punishment statute enacted by Florida in 1972, trial judges sentenced defendants to death after a jury had recommended a sentence of life imprisonment. Justice Stevens wrote that "[t]he question presented is whether the Constitution of the United States permits [the defendant's] execution when the prosecution has been unable to persuade a jury of his peers that the death penalty is the appropriate punishment for his crime." The dissent went on to state its position and reasoning as follows:

The judgment of the people's representatives firmly supports the conclusion that the jury ought to make the life-or-death decision necessary in capital cases....

The same consideration that supports a constitutional entitlement to a trial by a jury rather than a judge at the guilt or innocence stage — the right to have an authentic representative of the community apply its lay perspective to the determination that must precede a deprivation of liberty — applies with special force to the determination that must precede a deprivation of life. In many respects capital sentencing resembles a trial on the question of guilt, involving as it does a prescribed burden of proof of given elements through the adversarial process. But more important than its procedural aspects, the life-or-death decision in capital cases depends upon its link to community values for its moral and constitutional legitimacy....

That the jury provides a better link to community values than does a single judge is supported not only by our cases, but also by common sense. Juries — comprised as they are of a fair cross section of the community are more representative institutions than is the judiciary; they reflect more accurately the composition and experiences of the community as a whole, and inevitably make decisions based on community values more reliably, than can that segment of the community that is selected for service on the bench. Indeed, as the preceding discussion demonstrates, the belief that juries more accurately reflect the conscience of the community than can a single judge is the central reason that the jury right has been recognized at the guilt stage in our jurisprudence. This same belief firmly supports the use of juries in capital sentencing, in order to address the Eighth Amendment's concern that capital punishment be administered consistently with community values. In fact, the available empirical evidence indicates that judges and juries do make sentencing decisions in capital cases in significantly different ways, thus supporting the conclusion that entrusting the capital decision to a single judge creates an unacceptable risk that the decision will not be consistent with community values.

Thus, the legitimacy of capital punishment in light of the Eighth Amendment's mandate concerning the proportionality of punishment critically depends upon whether its imposition in a particular case is consistent with the community's sense of values. Juries have historically been, and continue to be, a much better indicator as to whether the death penalty is a disproportionate punishment for a given offense in light of community values than is a single judge. If the prosecutor cannot convince a jury that the defendant deserves to die, there is an unjustifiable risk that the imposition of that punishment will not reflect the community's sense of the defendant's "moral guilt." The Florida statute is thus inconsistent with "the need for reliability in the determination that death is the appropriate punishment in a specific case."

See also **Harris v. Alabama; Jury Override**

Speck, Richard

Richard Speck was born on December 6, 1941, in Kirkwood, Illinois. His family left Illinois and moved to Dallas, Texas when he was a child. Speck had a troubled childhood that included arrests, drugs and alcohol. He was married for a short period in the mid 1960s. His wife filed for divorce, on the grounds of cruelty, in January of 1966. After the divorce was filed Speck left Dallas and went to Chicago to live with one of his sisters.

Chicago proved to be too much for Speck. Drugs and alcohol were his only means of coping with the city's fast pace life. Although he was able to find work at a shipyard, the pay did not support his addictions. Speck resorted to stealing.

Richard Speck escaped death sentences imposed for eight murders in 1966, because of the moratorium imposed on capital punishment by the United States Supreme Court in 1972. (Dallas County Sheriff)

On July 13, 1966, Speck decided to burglarize a residence near South Chicago Community Hospital. The home Speck selected was occupied by nine student nurses. Speck approached the home by knocking on the door. He was armed with a gun and knife. When his knock at the door was answered, Speck forced his way into the home. Six of the girls who lived in the home were present. He told the girls he needed money and that he would not harm them. He made the girls lie on the floor and tied them up. As Speck rumbled through the home three other girls arrived. Speck quickly subdued them and tied them up.

Once Speck had retrieved all the valuables he could carry he decided to kill all of the girls. He led the girls, one at a time, into a room where he stabbed and strangled them to death. Only one victim was raped. Because of the number of girls in the home, Speck did not realize that one of them had rolled under a bed and was hiding. Speck left the home believing he had killed all nine of the girls.

Once Speck left, the lone survivor contacted the police and gave a description of the attacker. The police were able to lift Speck's fingerprints from the crime scene and make a positive identification of him. A massive manhunt followed.

Several days after the murders Speck's photograph was circulated throughout city, along with description of a tattoo he had on his arm reading "Born to Raise Hell." At the time Speck was living at a shelter for derelicts. Once he realized his identity was known, Speck went back to the shelter and slit his wrist in a suicide attempt. Shelter officials called an ambulance and Speck was taken to a hospital — the same hospital where his victims had been taken. When Speck arrived at the hospital he was recognized by the treating physician, as a result of the tattoo on his arm reading "Born to Raise Hell." Hospital officials contacted the police.

Speck was placed under arrest while in the hospital. He was eventually charged with eight counts of murder. On April 3, 1967, his trial began. On April 15, the jury found Speck guilty of eight counts of murder. The trial judge sentenced him to death on the same day.

Speck avoided the death penalty as a result of the United States Supreme Court decision in *Furman v. Georgia*, 408 U.S. 238 (1972), which placed a moratorium on capital punishment. He was resentenced to eight consecutive terms of 50 to 150 years each. Speck died in prison on December 5, 1991, from a massive heart attack.

Speedy Trial Clause *see* Bill of Rights

Spencer v. Texas

Court: United States Supreme Court; *Case Citation:* Spencer v. Texas, 385 U.S. 554 (1967); *Argued:* October 17–18, 1966; *Decided:* January 23, 1967; *Opinion of the Court:* Justice Harlan; *Concurring Opinion:* Justice Stewart; *Dissenting Opinion:* Chief Justice Warren, in which Fortas, J., joined; *Dissenting Statement:* Justice Brennan and Douglas, J.; *Appellate Defense Counsel:* Michael D. Matheny argued; Joe B. Goodwin on brief; *Appellate Prosecution Counsel:* Leon Douglas argued; Waggoner Carr and Hawthorne Phillips on brief; *Amicus Curiae Brief Supporting Prosecutor:* None; *Amicus Curiae Brief Supporting Defendant:* None.

Issue Presented: Whether a Texas rule that permitted the jury to be informed of the defendant's prior murder conviction offended the Due Process Clause?

Case Holding: The Texas rule that permitted the jury to be informed of the defendant's prior murder conviction did not offend the Due Process Clause.

Factual and procedural background of case: The defendant, Spencer, was charged with capital murder by the State of Texas. At the time of the prosecution, Texas had a recidivist statute which permitted the jury to be told of any prior conviction that a defendant had, for the purpose of enhancing punishment upon conviction. During the defendant's prosecution the trial judge permitted the prosecutor to inform the jury that the defendant had previously been convicted of murder. The trial judge instructed the jury that they could only consider the prior conviction for sentencing purposes, if they found the defendant guilty. The defendant was found guilty and sentenced to death. The Texas Court of Criminal Appeals affirmed the conviction and sentence. In doing so, the appellate court rejected the defendant's argument that the recidivist procedure violated the Due Process Clause of the Federal Constitution. The United States Supreme Court granted certiorari to consider the issue.

Opinion of the Court by Justice Harlan: Justice Harlan ruled that Texas' recidivist statute was not unconstitutional. He wrote that States had wide leeway in dividing responsibility between judge and jury in criminal cases, and that it was not unconstitutional for the jury to assess the punishment in a criminal case, or to make findings regarding prior convictions. It was pointed out that the possibility of prejudice from such evidence was outweighed by the validity of the State's purpose in permitting introduction of the evidence. Justice Harlan ruled that the defendant's interests were protected by the trial court's limiting instructions. It was concluded that States had power to promulgate their own rules of evidence to try their crimes as long as those rules are not prohibited by the

Federal Constitution. The judgment of the Texas Court of Criminal Appeals was affirmed.

Concurring opinion by Justice Stewart: Justice Stewart concurred in the Court's decision. He indicated that, while he may not personally favor Texas' recidivist rule, the rule was not offensive to the Constitution. The concurrence stated: "[T]he question for decision is not whether we applaud or even whether we personally approve the procedures followed in these recidivist cases. The question is whether those procedures fall below the minimum level the Fourteenth Amendment will tolerate. Upon that question I am constrained to join the opinion and judgment of the Court."

Dissenting opinion by Chief Justice Warren, in which Fortas, J., joined: The Chief Justice dissented from the Court's decision. He stated his position as follows: "It seems to me that the use of prior-convictions evidence in th[is] case[] is fundamentally at odds with traditional notions of due process, not because this procedure is not the nicest resolution of conflicting but legitimate interests of the State and the accused, but because it needlessly prejudices the accused without advancing any legitimate interest of the State. If I am wrong in thinking that the introduction of prior-convictions evidence serves no valid purpose I am not alone, for the Court never states what interest of the State is advanced by this procedure. And this failure, in my view, undermines the logic of the Court's opinion."

Dissenting statement by Justice Brennan and Douglas, J.: Justices Brennan and Douglas issued a statement indicating they dissented from the Court's opinion.

Case note: Under modern capital punishment law, use of prior convictions are generally confined to the separate penalty phase of a capital prosecution as aggravating circumstances. Additionally, modern rules of evidence greatly restrict the circumstances under which prior convictions may be introduced to the jury during the guilt phase of a capital prosecution. *See also* **Prior Felony or Homicide Aggravator; Rules of Evidence**

Spies, August *see* **Chicago Labor Riots of 1886**

Spiritual Advisor
Hollywood popularized the notion of a capital felon going to the execution chamber with a priest close at hand. The classic depiction of this scenario involved Pat O'Brien playing a priest who attended James Cagney, as he was ushered to the death chamber. Reality is not far behind Hollywood's fictional accounts of executions. A majority of capital punishment jurisdictions allow by statute for spiritual advisors to be present at executions. Two types of spiritual advisors are provided for in statutes: (1) prison chaplains and (2) personal spiritual advisors.
1. Prison chaplain. Five capital punishment jurisdictions permit by statute for prison chaplains to attend executions. Three of those jurisdictions, Indiana, Kentucky, and Wyoming, limit prison chaplain representation to one chaplain. The remaining two jurisdictions, Alabama and

Texas, do not limit the number of prison chaplains that may attend an execution.
2. Personal spiritual advisor. A majority of capital punishment jurisdictions statutorily allow capital felons to invite their own personal spiritual advisors to be present at executions. These jurisdictions vary on the number of personal spiritual advisors that may be in attendance.

In addition to access to spiritual advisors during the executions, capital felons have access to religious services while on death row.

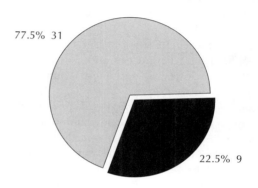

JURISDICTIONS STATUTORILY ALLOWING PERSONAL
SPIRITUAL ADVISORS TO ATTEND EXECUTIONS

77.5% 31

22.5% 9

■ JURISDICTIONS ALLOWING PERSONAL SPIRITUAL ADVISORS
■ ALL OTHER JURISDICTIONS

Spisak, Frank G., Jr. *see* **Cleveland State University Racial Murders**

Spreitzer, Edward *see* **Ripper Crew Cult Murders**

Sri Lanka
Sri Lanka permits capital punishment but the punishment has not been imposed in over a decade. Sri Lanka uses hanging to carry out the death penalty. Its legal system is a complex mixture of English common law, Roman-Dutch law, Islamic law, Sinhalese law and customary law. Sri Lanka adopted a constitution on August 16, 1978.

The judicial system is composed of High Courts, Courts of Appeal, and a Supreme Court.

Defendants are tried in public by juries. They may be represented by the counsel of their choice, and have the right to appeal. Indigent defendants have the right to appointed counsel. *See also* **International Capital Punishment Nations**

Standing of Capital Felon's Relative to Stop Execution *see* **Intervention by Next Friend**

Stanford v. Kentucky
Court: United States Supreme Court; *Case Citation:* Stanford v. Kentucky, 492 U.S. 361 (1989); *Argued:* March 27, 1989; *Decided:* June 26, 1989; *Opinion of the Court:* Justice Scalia; *Concurring Opinion:* Justice

O'Connor; *Dissenting Opinion:* Justice Brennan, in which Marshall, Blackmun, and Stevens, JJ., joined; *Appellate Defense Counsel in Case No. 87-5765:* Frank W. Heft, Jr. argued; J. David Niehaus and Daniel T. Goyette on brief; *Appellate Defense Counsel in Case No. 87-6026:* Nancy A. McKerrow argued and briefed; *Appellate Prosecution Counsel in Case No. 87-5765:* Frederic J. Cowan argued; Elizabeth Ann Myerscough and David A. Smith on brief; *Appellate Prosecution Counsel in Case No. 87-6026:* John M. Morris III argued; William L. Webster on brief; *Amicus Curiae Brief Supporting Prosecutor:* 1; *Amicus Curiae Brief Supporting Defendant:* 10.

Issue Presented: Whether the imposition of capital punishment on an individual for a capital crime committed at 16 or 17 years of age constitutes cruel and unusual punishment under the Eighth Amendment?

Case Holding: The imposition of capital punishment on an individual for a capital crime committed at 16 or 17 years of age does not constitute cruel and unusual punishment under the Eighth Amendment.

Factual and procedural background of case: The decision in this case involved two separate prosecutions that were consolidated for disposition. The first case, No. 87-5765, concerned Kevin Stanford. This defendant was approximately 17 years and 4 months old at the time he committed murder in Kentucky. A Kentucky juvenile court, after conducting hearings, transferred him for trial as an adult to be prosecuted for capital murder. The defendant was convicted and sentenced to death. The Kentucky Supreme Court affirmed the conviction and death sentence, after rejecting the defendant's contention that the death sentence violated the Eighth Amendment because of his age at the time of the crime.

The second case, No. 87-6026, involved Heath Wilkins. This defendant was approximately 16 years and 6 months old when he committed murder in Missouri. He was certified for trial as an adult to be prosecuted for capital murder. This defendant pleaded guilty and was sentenced to death. The Missouri Supreme Court affirmed the conviction and sentence, after rejecting the defendant's argument that his death sentence violated the Eighth Amendment because of his age at the time of the crime.

The United States Supreme Court granted certiorari for both cases and consolidated them for disposition.

Opinion of the Court by Justice Scalia: Justice Scalia rejected the defendants' contention that the Constitution prohibited imposition of the death penalty against them, because of their ages at the time of the commission of their offenses. It was pointed out that under the common law a rebuttable presumption existed that a person 14 years old or younger was incapable of committing a felony. The opinion noted that in accordance with this common law tradition, at least 281 offenders under 18, and 126 under 17, have been executed in the United States.

The opinion ruled that in determining whether a punishment violated evolving standards of decency, the Court looks not to its own subjective conceptions, but, rather, to the conceptions of modern American society as reflected by objective evidence. Justice Scalia held that the primary and most reliable evidence of national consensus, the pattern of federal and state laws, failed to show a settled consensus against the execution of 16-and 17-year-old offenders. It was said that of the States that permit capital punishment, 15 decline to impose it on 16-year-olds and 12 on 17-year-olds. Justice Scalia reasoned that this did not establish the degree of national agreement the Court has previously thought sufficient to label a punishment cruel and unusual.

It was concluded in the opinion that: "We discern neither a historical nor a modern societal consensus forbidding the imposition of capital punishment on any person who murders at 16 or 17 years of age. Accordingly, we conclude that such punishment does not offend the Eighth Amendment's prohibition against cruel and unusual punishment." The judgments of the Kentucky Supreme Court the Missouri Supreme Court were therefore affirmed.

Concurring opinion by Justice O'Connor: Justice O'Connor concurred in the Court's judgment. She cautioned, however, that "[t]he day may come when there is such general legislative rejection of the execution of 16-or 17-year-old capital murderers that a clear national consensus can be said to have developed."

Dissenting opinion by Justice Brennan, in which Marshall, Blackmun, and Stevens, JJ., joined: Justice Brennan dissented from the majority opinion. In doing so, he made clear that he "believe[d] that to take the life of a person as punishment for a crime committed when below the age of 18 is cruel and unusual and hence is prohibited by the Eighth Amendment."

The dissent articulated the basis of its rejection of the majority opinion as follows: "There are strong indications that the execution of juvenile offenders violates contemporary standards of decency: a majority of States decline to permit juveniles to be sentenced to death; imposition of the sentence upon minors is very unusual even in those States that permit it; and respected organizations with expertise in relevant areas regard the execution of juveniles as unacceptable, as does international opinion. These indicators serve to confirm in my view my conclusion that the Eighth Amendment prohibits the execution of persons for offenses they committed while below the age of 18, because the death penalty is disproportionate when applied to such young offenders and fails measurably to serve the goals of capital punishment."

Case note: The majority decision in the case garnered a significant degree of national legal commentary, which both praised and rebuked the Court's ruling. A few states reacted to the opinion by statutorily prohibiting imposition of the death penalty upon persons who were under 18 years of age at the time of the commission of a capital offense. *See also* **Juveniles; Thompson v. Oklahoma**

Stansbury v. California

Court: United States Supreme Court; *Case Citation:* Stansbury v. California, 511 U.S. 318 (1994); *Argued:* Not reported; *Decided:* April 26, 1994; *Opinion of the Court:* Per Curiam; *Concurring Statement:* Justice Blackmun; *Dissenting Opinion:* None; *Appellate Defense Counsel:* Not reported; *Appellate Prosecution Counsel:* Not reported; *Amicus Curiae Brief Supporting Prosecutor:* Not reported; *Amicus Curiae Brief Supporting Defendant:* Not reported.

Issue Presented: Whether the initial determination of custody, for *Miranda* purposes, depends on the objective circumstances of a police interrogation or on the subjective views harbored by either the interrogating officers or the person being questioned?

Case Holding: The initial determination of custody, for *Miranda* purposes, depends on the objective circumstances of a police interrogation, not on the subjective views harbored by either the interrogating officers or the person being questioned.

Factual and procedural background of case: The defendant, Robert Edward Stansbury, was charged with capital murder by the State of California. Prior to trial the defendant motioned the trial court to exclude from evidence incriminating statements he made to the police before his arrest. The defendant argued that the police did not give him the warnings required by the United States Supreme Court's decision in the non-capital case of *Miranda v. Arizona*, 384 U.S. 436 (1966). The trial court denied the motion on the grounds that the defendant was not in custody when he made the statements and thus was not entitled to *Miranda* warnings. The defendant was found guilty of capital murder and sentenced to death. The California Supreme Court affirmed the conviction and sentence. In doing so, the appellate court rejected the defendant's contention that his *Miranda* rights were violated.

The United States Supreme Court granted certiorari to consider the issue.

Opinion of the Court was delivered Per Curiam: The per curiam opinion found that the defendant's *Miranda* rights were violated when the police obtained incriminating statements from him during questioning at police headquarters. The opinion held that under *Miranda* when a person is questioned by law enforcement officers after being taken into custody or otherwise deprived of his or her freedom of action in any significant way, he or she must first be warned of the right to remain silent, that any statement made may be used as evidence against him or her, and that he or she has a right to the presence of an attorney, either retained or appointed. It was said that statements elicited in noncompliance with *Miranda* may not be admitted for certain purposes in a criminal trial.

The opinion noted that an officer's obligation to administer *Miranda* warnings attaches only where there has been such a restriction on a person's freedom as to render him or her in custody. It was ruled that in determining whether an individual was in custody, a court must examine all of the circumstances surrounding the interrogation, but the ultimate inquiry is simply whether there was a formal arrest or restraint on freedom of movement of the degree associated with a formal arrest. The initial determination of custody depends on the objective circumstances of the interrogation, not on the subjective views harbored by either the interrogating officers

or the person being questioned. It was further held that a police officer's subjective view that the individual under questioning is a suspect, if undisclosed, does not bear upon the question whether the individual is in custody for purposes of *Miranda*.

In looking at the record in the case, the opinion found that the California Supreme Court's analysis of whether the defendant was in custody was not consistent in all respects with the Court's precedents. It was said that the State appellate court's conclusion that the defendant's *Miranda* rights were not triggered until he had become the focus of the police's suspicions, was incorrect because the officers' subjective and undisclosed suspicions did not bear upon the question whether the defendant was in custody for purposes of *Miranda*. The judgment of the California Supreme Court was reversed.

Concurring Statement by Justice Blackmun: Justice Blackmun issued a concurring statement indicating that he joined the Court's per curiam opinion and that "even if [he] were not persuaded that the judgment must be reversed for the reasons stated in that opinion, [he] would adhere to [his] view that the death penalty cannot be imposed fairly within the constraints of our Constitution. [He] therefore would vacate the death sentence on that ground, too." *See also* **Right to Remain Silent**

Starr v. United States
Court: United States Supreme Court; *Case Citation:* Starr v. United States, 153 U.S. 614 (1894); *Argued:* Not reported; *Decided:* May 14, 1894; *Opinion of the Court:* Chief Justice Fuller; *Concurring Opinion:* None; *Dissenting Opinion:* None; *Appellate Defense Counsel:* A. H. Garland argued and briefed; *Appellate Prosecution Counsel:* Mr. Conrad argued and briefed; *Amicus Curiae Brief Supporting Prosecutor:* None; *Amicus Curiae Brief Supporting Defendant:* None.

Issue Presented: Whether the trial court correctly instructed the jury on the defense of self-defense?

Case Holding: The trial court incorrectly instructed the jury on the defense of self-defense, because its instruction required the jury to disregard the defense if it was shown that the defendant prevented the victim from identifying himself as a Federal deputy marshal.

Factual and procedural background of case: The defendant, Henry Starr, was indicted for capital murder by the United States. The victim of the crime was a Federal deputy marshal who was attempting to arrest the defendant. During the trial the defendant contended that he did not know the victim was an officer of the law and that the killing occurred in self-defense. The jury convicted the defendant and he was sentenced to death. The defendant appealed to the United States Supreme Court, alleging that the trial court erroneously instructed the jury on self-defense. The United States Supreme Court granted certiorari to consider the issue.

Opinion of the Court by Chief Justice Fuller: The Chief Justice held that the trial court did not correctly instruct the jury on self-defense. It was said that under the trial court's instruction the jury was informed that self-defense was invalid if the defendant prevented the victim from identifying himself as a Federal marshal. The opinion reasoned that "if [the] defendant had no knowledge, was not informed, and was not chargeable with notice of [the victim's] mission or official character, the fact, if there was evidence tending to show it, that defendant prevented the giving of notice had no such relation to defendant's claim of exemption from liability founded on his ignorance, and the appearance of the facts to him[.]" The Chief Justice explained the fundamental principles of self-defense as follows:

> First. A man, who, in the lawful pursuit of his business, is attacked by another under circumstances which denote an intention to take away his life, or do him some enormous bodily harm, may lawfully kill the assailant, provided he uses all the means in his power, otherwise, to save his own life, or prevent the intended harm, such as retreating as far as he can, or disabling his adversary without killing him, if it be in his power. Secondly. When the attack upon him is so sudden, fierce, and violent that a retreat would not diminish, but increase, his danger, he may instantly kill his adversary, without retreating at all. Thirdly. When, from the nature of the attack, there is reasonable ground to believe that there is a design to destroy his life, or commit any felony upon his person, the killing of the assailant will be excusable homicide, although it should afterwards appear that no felony was intended.

The judgment of the Federal trial court was reversed and the cause remanded for a new trial. *See also* **Self-Defense**

Statutory Aggravating Circumstances *see* **Aggravating Circumstances**

Statutory Mitigating Circumstances *see* **Mitigating Circumstances**

Stay of Execution   As a general rule, trial courts are required to set an execution date in the order sentencing a defendant to death. However, under modern capital punishment jurisprudence, a capital felon may not be executed prior to exhausting direct appellate review of the judgment. Therefore, any initial execution date is automatically stayed until after direct appellate review has been exhausted. Once direct appellate review is exhausted and collateral or habeas corpus relief is subsequently sought by a capital felon, he or she must file an application with the appropriate court seeking to stay enforcement of the scheduled execution.

1. *Seeking a Stay from the United States Supreme Court:* A stay of execution is not automatic, pending the filing and consideration of a petition for a writ of certiorari from the United States Supreme Court. The conditions that must be met include: (1) there must be a reasonable probability that four members of the Court would consider the underlying issue sufficiently meritorious for the grant of certiorari or the notation of probable jurisdiction; (2) there must be a significant possibility of reversal of the lower court's decision; and (3) there must be a likelihood that irreparable harm will result if that decision is not stayed. A stay of execution should first be sought from a Federal Court of Appeals. The Supreme Court generally places considerable weight on the decision reached by a Federal Court of Appeals.

2. *Eleventh Hour Stay.* The fact that a capital felon has unsuccessfully exhausted all avenues of appeal, does not automatically mean that he or she will be executed on the appointed day and time for execution. Eleventh hour stays (last minute) are not uncommon. Various reasons may trigger an eleventh hour stay. For example, Alabama death row inmate Robert Lee Tarver had eaten his last meal and was about two hours away from execution in January 2000, when the United States Supreme Court issued a stay of his execution to consider Tarver's challenge to the state's use of the electric chair. (The Supreme Court, on a 5–4 vote, later decided not to review the matter.)

   Once the eleventh hour approaches, the most crucial factor in the execution process is the operation of the phone lines. It is imperative that split second communication is possible between the officials in the execution chamber and any potential judge or executive officer that has the authority to halt the execution. The execution protocol that follows is used at the Oregon State Penitentiary for the final twenty-fours in a capital felon's life.

3. *Oregon State Penitentiary Countdown to Execution.*

   A. One Day. Twenty-four hours prior to execution a medically trained individual prepares and secures the necessary syringes with the lethal solutions, and separately prepares and secures back-up syringes. Secure storage is the responsibility of the assistant superintendent of security.

   Penitentiary staff work in concert with the Oregon State Police, the Salem Police and the Marion County Sheriff's office for perimeter security including crowd control, traffic control and penitentiary access. Inmate visiting may be limited or suspended the day before and after an execution.

   A media center is set up on penitentiary grounds to accommodate the needs of the media. Only media who have arranged for credentials prior to the execution are admitted to the media center.

   The inmate's last meal is personally prepared and served about 6 P.M. by a staff member assigned by the food services manager.

   An emergency command center is established in the superintendent's office to manage institutional affairs during the hours preceding and immediately following an execution. The assistant superintendent of Program Services is assigned to manage the command center.

   The emergency telephone lines in the Execution Room are checked at 6 P.M. and again at 9 P.M. At 9:30 P.M. they are tested every half-hour until 11:30 P.M. The command center will establish radio contact with the officer-in-charge of the Intensive Management Unit (IMU) to ensure that messages can be conveyed in the event that institutional or emergency telephone lines become inoperable.

All witnesses and designated media representatives gather in pre-arranged locations at approximately 10 P.M. They remain under staff supervision while on penitentiary grounds. Prior to being escorted to the IMU they are briefed by staff about procedures and what to expect; they are also visited by a counselor who offers information on the psychological effects of witnessing an execution. Security procedures require witnesses to pass through one or more metal detectors. Witnesses may not carry recording devices once they assemble on penitentiary grounds. The only hand-carried items allowed within the penitentiary are note pads and pens or pencils issued by the department.

B. The Final Minutes. At 11:30 P.M. the assistant superintendent, Security, confirms that the clock used to determine the time to carry out the execution is accurate. The superintendent accompanies the executioner(s) to the execution room and ensures that the confidentiality of the executioner is not compromised.

Once restraints have been applied to the inmate, the Special Security Team leader instructs the officer supervising the execution room cell to open the cell door. The leader supervises the activities of the Special Security Team members, who escort the inmate in security restraints from the cell and position and properly restrain the inmate on the table. There are no visits once the inmate has been moved to the execution room.

Medically trained individuals connect a heart monitor to the inmate which helps determine when death has occurred. They also insert two intravenous catheters — one primary and one back-up — in the most appropriate locations on the inmate's body, usually the arms and/or hands.

Following insertion of the intravenous catheters the witnesses are escorted to the witness area. Two correctional captains are stationed in the witness area to assist witnesses and maintain decorum. If at any point in the execution process a stay of execution is ordered, the superintendent shall halt all execution procedures and the witnesses shall be removed.

C. The Execution. Immediately prior to execution, the assistant superintendent, Security, inspects all straps, and with the assistance of medically trained staff, makes a final inspection of the intravenous catheters and the injection equipment. Upon authorization from the superintendent the window coverings are lifted so the witnesses can see the inmate in position on the table. The table is designed to slightly elevate the inmate's head so witnesses have full view of the actual execution.

If no stay of execution has been received via the open phone lines to the governor and the attorney general, as soon after midnight as possible, the superintendent signals the executioner to begin injection of lethal solutions into the injection port of the intravenous catheters. As prescribed by law, the lethal solutions include an ultra-short acting barbiturate in combination with a chemical paralytic agent and potassium chloride or other equally effective substances sufficient to cause death.

The executioner signals the superintendent when infusion of the lethal substances has been completed. Once death occurs, the time is noted. The superintendent summons a medical professional to officially certify the inmate's death. The superintendent announces the time of death to the witnesses. The time of death is conveyed via telephone to the communications manager who announces it to the media assembled in the media center.

After the witnesses leave the execution area, they are joined by the superintendent who conveys the inmates last words. Media witnesses are escorted to the media center to share their experiences and impressions with their colleagues as prearranged. Other witnesses are escorted off of penitentiary grounds.

The assistant superintendent, Security, will remain to supervise the removal of the body. The body is released to a funeral home after the body is properly identified using identification photographs for comparison. The State Police are notified when the execution is complete and the body is ready for removal.

The inmate's predesignated contact person will be notified to contact the funeral home to which the inmate's body was taken. This contact person will also receive the inmate's personal property and any amount of money in the inmate's trust account, after deducting any expenses incurred by the department and related to the death of the inmate.

See also **Barefoot v. Estelle; Lonchar v. Thomas**

Stein v. New York *Court:* United States Supreme Court; *Case Citation:* Stein v. New York, 346 U.S. 156 (1953); *Argued:* December 18, 1952; *Decided:* June 15, 1953; *Opinion of the Court:* Justice Jackson; *Concurring Opinion:* None; *Dissenting Opinion:* Justice Black; *Dissenting Opinion:* Justice Frankfurter; *Dissenting Opinion:* Justice Douglas, in which Black, J., joined; *Appellate Defense Counsel Case No. 391:* John J. Duff argued; Philip J. O'Brien on brief; *Appellate Defense Counsel Case No. 392:* J. Bertram Wegman argued; I. Maurice Wormser and Richard J. Burke on brief; *Appellate Defense Counsel Case No. 393:* Peter L. F. Sabbatino argued; Thomas J. Todarelli on brief; *Appellate Prosecution Counsel:* John J. O'Brien and John C. Marbach argued; Burton C. Meighan on brief; *Amicus Curiae Brief Supporting Prosecutor:* None; *Amicus Curiae Brief Supporting Defendant:* None.

Issue Presented: Whether the Constitution permits the jury to determine whether a confession was voluntary?

Case Holding: The Constitution permits the jury to determine whether a confession was voluntary, as this issue is one that States are free to determine.

Factual and procedural background of case: This case

involved the prosecution of three defendants, Stein, Wissner and Calman, for capital murder by the State of New York. Two of the defendants gave confessions, which, over the objections of the defendants, were introduced to the jury. Under the procedure used by New York the jury determined whether a confession was voluntary. The jury returned verdicts of guilty and the defendants were sentenced to death. The New York Court of Appeals affirmed. The United States Supreme Court granted certiorari to consider whether it was constitutionally permissible for the jury to determine whether a confession was voluntary.

Opinion of the Court by Justice Jackson: Justice Jackson ruled that the Constitution did not require the trial court, rather than the jury, determine whether a confession was voluntary. The opinion addressed the matter as follows:

> An attack on the fairness of New York procedure is that [the defendants] could not take the witness stand to support, with their own oaths, the charges their counsel made against the state police without becoming subject to general cross-examination....
>
> It is not impossible that cross-examination could be employed so as to work a denial of due process. But no basis is laid for such a contention here. Appellate courts leave an exceptional discretion to trial courts to prevent abuse and injustice. But here the defendants took no step which would call for or permit an exercise of such discretion. They made no request for a ruling by the trial court and made no offer or suggestion of readiness to testify, however restricted the cross-examination might be. We do not know whether, or how far, the court would have permitted any line of cross-examination, nor what specific limitation defendants would have claimed. We will not adjudge a trial court guilty of constructive abuse by imputing to it a ruling that never was made on a proposition that never was put to it....
>
> ... In trial of a coercion issue, as of every other issue, when the prosecution has made a case to go to the jury, an accused must choose between the disadvantage from silence and that from testifying. The Constitution safeguards the right of a defendant to remain silent; it does not assure him that he may remain silent and still enjoy the advantages that might have resulted from testifying. We cannot say that [the defendants] have been denied a fair hearing of the coercion charge....
>
> The Fourteenth Amendment does not forbid jury trial of the issue. The states are free to allocate functions as between judge and jury as they see fit.

The judgment of the New York Court of Appeals was affirmed.

Dissenting opinion by Justice Black: Justice Black dissented from the Court's decision. He argued that the Court's decision had narrowed the protection afforded by the constitutional right not to be a witness against oneself. Justice Black believed the procedure utilized by New York posed an unacceptable choice to defendants: testify on involuntariness of a confession and be subject to cross examination, or refrain from testifying and thereby leave the prosecutor's evidence on voluntariness of the confession unchallenged. This choice, contended Justice Black, was unconstitutional.

Dissenting opinion by Justice Frankfurter: Justice Frankfurter dissented from the Court's decision. He was concerned that the confessions were in fact involuntary, though the jury found them voluntary. He wrote that "the Court now holds that a criminal conviction sustained by the highest court of a State, and more especially one involving a sentence of death, is not to be reversed for a new trial, even though there entered into the conviction a coerced confession which in and of itself disregards the prohibition of the Due Process Clause of the Fourteenth Amendment."

Dissenting opinion by Justice Douglas, in which Black, J., joined: Justice Douglas dissented from the Court's decision. He believed that permitting the jury to determine the voluntariness of a confession compelled defendants to testify against themselves. Justice Douglas argued that the procedure should be struck down as violating due process of law.

Case note: The decision in the case was not long lived, as the Court eventually ruled that the Constitution did not permit the jury to determine whether a confession was voluntary. *See also* **Jackson v. Denno**

Stephan v. United States
Court: United States Supreme Court; *Case Citation:* Stephan v. United States, 319 U.S. 423 (1943); *Argued:* Not reported; *Decided:* June 1, 1943; *Opinion of the Court:* Per Curiam; *Concurring Opinion:* None; *Dissenting Opinion:* None; *Appellate Defense Counsel:* Nicholas Salowich argued; James E. McCabe on brief; *Appellate Prosecution Counsel:* Charles Fahy argued and briefed; *Amicus Curiae Brief Supporting Prosecutor:* Not reported; *Amicus Curiae Brief Supporting Defendant:* Not reported.

Issue Presented: Whether the defendant could appeal from a Federal District Court directly to the United States Supreme Court?

Case Holding: The defendant could not appeal from a Federal District Court directly to the United States Supreme Court, because Congress established Federal Courts of Appeals for the purpose of hearing direct appeals from District Courts..

Factual and procedural background of case: The defendant, Stephan, was convicted of treason and sentenced to death by the United States. The judgment was affirmed by a Federal Court of Appeals. The United States Supreme Court denied appellate review. The defendant thereafter filed a direct appeal with the United States Supreme Court, contending that an 1889 Federal statute permitted a direct appeal.

Opinion of the Court was delivered Per Curiam: The per curiam opinion held that the defendant could not appeal directly from a Federal District Court to the Supreme Court. It was said that the 1889 statute relied upon by the defendant no longer reflected the procedure for bringing an appeal to the Court. The opinion indicated that "[t]he fact that the words of [the 1889 statute] have lingered on in the successive editions of the United States Code is immaterial." The opinion noted that the statute referenced to was enforce before Congress created Federal Courts of Appeal. The defendant's application for appeal was denied.

Stevens, John Paul
John Paul Stevens was appointed as an associate justice of the United States Supreme Court in 1975. While on the Supreme Court Stevens has displayed a judicial philosophy that straddles between moderate and liberal.

Stevens was born in Chicago, Illinois on April 20, 1920. He was a 1941 graduate of Chicago University. In 1947 Stevens received a law degree from Northwestern University School of Law. Stevens developed a successful law practice before being nominated in 1970 as an appellate judge on the Seventh Circuit Court of appeals. In 1975 President Gerald Ford appointed Stevens to the Supreme Court.

While on the Supreme Court Stevens has authored a considerable number of capital punishment opinions. In general, Stevens' capital punishment opinions have reflected an honest effort to assure that the merits of an issue dictate the constitutional outcome of his opinions, either for the Court or otherwise. Unlike many of his contemporaries on the bench, Stevens has shown tremendous discipline in separating personal beliefs and public opinion from the individual fairness that must be brought to every case. Commentators have praised his rare ability to consistently interpret the Constitution on the merits of the issues and not on other immaterial and extraneous factors.

The capital punishment opinion which best illustrates Stevens' quintessential constitutional philosophy is *Lankford v. Idaho*. In that case the defendant was sentenced to death by the trial court, even though the prosecutor had led the defendant to believe that the death penalty would not be sought. The defendant argued to the Supreme Court that he had a constitutional right to notice that the death penalty would be sought. Stevens, writing for the Court, indicated that no special notice of intent to seek the death penalty was required by the Constitution. He wrote that so long as a defendant is made aware of the possibility of the death penalty during arraignment, the Constitution is satisfied. However, Stevens held that the Constitution would not accept circumstances that mislead a defendant into believing that the death penalty would not be sought, only to have such a punishment imposed. In reversing the defendant's death sentence, Stevens wrote: "If notice

Capital Punishment Opinions Written by Stevens

Case Name	Opinion of the Court	Plurality Opinion	Concurring Opinion	Dissenting Opinion	Concurring and Dissenting
Baldwin v. Alabama				✓	
Barclay v. Florida			✓		
Barefoot v. Estelle			✓		
Beck v. Alabama	✓				
Burger v. Kemp	✓				
Cabana v. Bullock				✓	
Calderon v. Coleman				✓	
California v. Ramos				✓	
Cooper v. Oklahoma	✓				
Delo v. Lashley				✓	
Dobbert v. Florida				✓	
Felker v. Turpin			✓	✓	
Franklin v. Lynaugh				✓	
Gardner v. Florida		✓			
Graham v. Collins				✓	
Gray v. Netherland				✓	
Harris v. Alabama				✓	
Hopkins v. Reeves				✓	
Johnson v. Mississippi	✓				
Jurek v. Texas		✓			
Kyles v. Whitley			✓		
Lambrix v. Singletary				✓	
Lankford v. Idaho	✓				
Lilly v. Virginia		✓			
Lockhart v. Fretwell				✓	
Loving v. United States			✓		
McCleskey v. Kemp				✓	
Murray v. Giarratano				✓	
O'Dell v. Netherland				✓	
Ohio A.P.A. v. Woodard					✓
Payne v. Tennessee				✓	
Penry v. Lynaugh					✓
Pulley v. Harris			✓		
Roberts v. Louisiana (I)		✓			
Sawyer v. Whitley			✓		
Schiro v. Farley				✓	
Schlup v. Delo	✓				
Smith v. Murray				✓	
Sochor v. Florida					✓
Spaziano v. Florida					✓
Strickler v. Greene	✓				
Thompson v. Oklahoma		✓			
Tuilaepa v. California			✓		
Wainwright v. Witt			✓		
Walton v. Arizona				✓	
Yates v. Aiken	✓				
Zant v. Stephens (II)	✓				

is not given, and the adversary process is not permitted to function properly, there is an increased chance of error, and with that, the possibility of an incorrect result…. [The defendant's] lack of adequate notice that the judge was contemplating the imposition of the death sentence created an impermissible risk that the adversary process may have malfunctioned in this case."

Stevenson v. United States
Court: United States Supreme Court; *Case Citation:* Stevenson v. United States, 162 U.S. 313 (1896); *Argued:* Not reported; *Decided:* April 13, 1896; *Opinion of the Court:* Justice Peckham; *Concurring Opinion:*

None; *Dissenting Opinion:* None; *Appellate Defense Counsel:* Fred Beall argued and briefed; *Appellate Prosecution Counsel:* Mr. Dickinson argued and briefed; *Amicus Curiae Brief Supporting Prosecutor:* None; *Amicus Curiae Brief Supporting Defendant:* None.

Issue Presented: Whether the trial court committed error in refusing to instruct the jury that it could return a verdict of guilty of manslaughter?

Case Holding: The trial court committed error in refusing to instruct the jury that it could return a verdict of guilty of manslaughter, because evidence was introduced to make manslaughter a possible sentence.

Factual and procedural background of case: The defendant, Stevenson, was convicted of capital murder and sentenced to death by the United States. The defendant appealed to the United States Supreme Court, alleging that he was denied due process of law because the trial court refused to instruct the jury that it could return a verdict of guilty of manslaughter. The United States Supreme Court granted certiorari to consider the issue.

Opinion of the Court by Justice Peckham: Justice Peckham ruled that the trial court improperly refused to instruct the jury that a verdict of manslaughter could be returned if supported by the evidence. The opinion explained the issue as follows:

> ... The evidence as to manslaughter need not be uncontradicted or in any way conclusive upon the question. So long as there is some evidence upon the subject, the proper weight to be given it is for the jury to determine. If there were any evidence which tended to show such a state of facts as might bring the crime within the grade of manslaughter, it then became a proper question for the jury to say whether the evidence were true, and whether it showed that the crime was manslaughter instead of murder. It is difficult to think of a case of killing by shooting, where both men were armed, and both in readiness to shoot, and where both did shoot, in which the question would not arise, for the jury to answer, whether the killing was murder, or manslaughter, or a pure act of self-defense. The evidence might appear to the court to be simply overwhelming to show that the killing was in fact murder, and not manslaughter, or an act performed in self-defense, and yet, so long as there was some evidence relevant to the issue of manslaughter, the credibility and force of such evidence must be for the jury, and cannot be a matter of law for the decision of the court....
>
> The ruling of the learned judge was to the effect that, in this case, the killing was either murder, or else it was done in the course of self-defense, and that under no view which could possibly be taken of the evidence would the jury be at liberty to find the defendant guilty of manslaughter. The court passed upon the strength, credibility, and tendency of the evidence, and decided, as a matter of law, what, it seems to us, would generally be regarded as a question of fact, viz. whether, under all the circumstances which the jury might, from the evidence, find existed in the case, the defendant was guilty of murder, or whether he killed the deceased, not in self-defense, but unlawfully and unjustly, although without malice. The presence or absence of malice would be the material consider-
> ation in the case, provided the jury should reject the theory of self-defense; and yet this question of fact is, under the evidence in the case, determined by the trial court as one of law, and against the defendant....
>
> A judge may be entirely satisfied, from the whole evidence in the case, that the person doing the killing was actuated by malice; that he was not in any such passion as to lower the grade of the crime from murder to manslaughter by reason of any absence of malice; and yet, if there be any evidence fairly tending to bear upon the issue of manslaughter, it is the province of the jury to determine from all the evidence what the condition of mind was, and to say whether the crime was murder or manslaughter.

The judgment of the Federal trial court was reversed and the cause remanded for a new trial.

Stewart, Potter

Potter Stewart served as an associate justice of the United States Supreme Court from 1958 to 1981. While on the Supreme Court Stewart was known as a moderate interpreter of the Constitution.

Stewart was born on January 23, 1915 in Jackson, Michigan. He received educational training at University School, Yale and Cambridge. Stewart obtained a law degree from Yale Law School in 1941. In 1954 he was appointed as an appellate judge to the Sixth Circuit Court of Appeals. President Dwight Eisenhower appointed Stewart to the Supreme Court in 1958.

Stewart wrote a number of capital punishment opinions while on the Supreme Court. Stewart's capital punishment decisions reflected the moderate philosophy he brought to the Constitution. For example, he voted with the majority to place a moratorium on capital punishment in *Furman v. Georgia*. However, Stewart pointed out in his concurring opinion in *Furman* that he did not believe the Constitution barred capital punishment per se. Stewart argued that the Constitution prohibited imposition of capital punishment in an arbitrary and capricious manner. In *Woodson v. North Carolina*, writing for the Court, Stewart found North Carolina's mandatory death penalty law offensive to the Constitution. He wrote that "[t]he belief no longer prevails that every offense in a like legal category calls for an identical punishment without regard

Capital Punishment Opinions Written by Stewart

Case Name	Opinion of the Court	Plurality Opinion	Concurring Opinion	Dissenting Opinion
Boulden v. Holman	✓			
Estelle v. Smith			✓	
Furman v. Georgia			✓	
Godfrey v. Georgia		✓		
Gregg v. Georgia		✓		
Lane v. Brown	✓			
Miller v. Pate	✓			
Rideau v. Louisiana	✓			
Rogers v. Richmond				✓
Spano v. New York			✓	
Spencer v. Texas			✓	✓
Townsend v. Sain				✓
United States v. Jackson	✓			
Witherspoon v. Illinois	✓			
Woodson v. North Carolina		✓		

to the past life and habits of a particular offender." In *Witherspoon v. Illinois,* again writing for the Court, Stewart struck down a statute which authorized the prosecutor to exclude from the jury, for cause, any venireperson who said that he or she was opposed to capital punishment and who indicated that he or she had conscientious scruples against inflicting the death penalty. Stewart reasoned in *Witherspoon:* "Whatever else might be said of capital punishment, it is at least clear that its imposition by a hanging jury cannot be squared with the Constitution. The State of Illinois has stacked the deck against the [defendant]. To execute this death sentence would deprive him of his life without due process of law." Stewart died on December 7, 1985.

Stewart v. Martinez-Villareal   *Court:* United States Supreme Court; *Case Citation:* Stewart v. Martinez-Villareal, 523 U.S. 637 (1998); *Argued:* February 25, 1998; *Decided:* May 18, 1998; *Opinion of the Court:* Chief Justice Rehnquist; *Concurring Opinion:* None; *Dissenting Opinion:* Justice Scalia , in which Thomas, J., joined; *Dissenting Opinion:* Justice Thomas, in which Scalia, J., joined; *Appellate Defense Counsel:* Not reported; *Appellate Prosecution Counsel:* Not reported; *Amicus Curiae Brief Supporting Prosecutor:* Not reported; *Amicus Curiae Brief Supporting Defendant:* Not reported.

Issue Presented: Whether the defendant's incompetency claim under *Ford v. Wainwright* was brought as a second or successive habeas application under the Antiterrorism and Effective Death Penalty Act, when the District Court failed to address the merits of the issue during its resolution of the defendant's initial habeas petition?

Case Holding: The defendant's incompetency claim under *Ford v. Wainwright* was not a second or successive habeas application under the Antiterrorism and Effective Death Penalty Act, because the District Court failed to address the merits of the issue during its resolution of the defendant's initial habeas petition.

Factual and procedural background of case: The defendant, Ramon Martinez-Villareal, was convicted and sentenced to death for capital murder by the State of Arizona. The Arizona Supreme Court affirmed the conviction and sentence on direct appeal. The defendant's habeas corpus petition in State court was unsuccessful. He filed three Federal habeas petitions that were denied on the ground that he did not exhaust his state remedies. The defendant filed a fourth Federal habeas petition alleging that he was insane and could not be executed under the United States Supreme Court decision in *Ford v. Wainwright.* The Federal District Court rejected the claim as premature because an execution date had not been given in the case. However, the District Court reached the merits of another issue raised in the petition and vacated the death sentence. A Federal Court of Appeals reversed the ruling by the District Court and reinstated the death sentence.

On remand to the District Court the defendant sought to reopen his *Ford* claim. While the District Court was considering whether to allow the defendant to reopen the *Ford* claim,

Arizona issued a death warrant setting the date of his execution. The District Court ultimately ruled that under Congress' recently enacted Antiterrorism and Effective Death Penalty Act of 1996 (AEDP Act), it lacked jurisdiction to reopen the *Ford* claim because it was a "successive" habeas application. Under the AEDP Act, Federal District Courts were barred from entertaining successive habeas applications unless a defendant obtained permission from a Federal Court of Appeals. The defendant asked a Court of Appeals for permission to have the District Court review the merits of the *Ford* claim. The Court of Appeals ruled that the *Ford* claim did not constitute a successive application for habeas relief, therefore the defendant did not need its permission to have the issue addressed by the District Court. The United States Supreme Court granted certiorari to consider the issue.

Opinion of the Court by Chief Justice Rehnquist: The Chief Justice held that the defendant's *Ford* claim was not a second or successive petition under the AEDP Act. It was said that the fact that this was the second time that the defendant asked the District Court to provide relief on his *Ford* claim did not mean that there were two separate applications for habeas relief. The Chief Justice indicated that there was only one application for habeas relief, and the District Court should have ruled on the merits of each claim presented in the application when it became ripe. The opinion found that since the defendant was entitled to an adjudication of all of the claims presented in his earlier petition, the Court of Appeals correctly held that he was not required to get authorization to have the *Ford* claim heard. The Chief Justice also wrote that the initial three habeas corpus petitions filed by the defendant were inconsequential, because they were dismissed on procedural grounds that did not involve the merits of the claims alleged. The judgment of the Court of Appeals was affirmed and the case remanded for a hearing on the merits of the defendant's *Ford* claim in the District Court.

Dissenting opinion by Justice Scalia , in which Thomas, J., joined: Justice Scalia dissented from the Court's decision. He argued that, because Arizona thoroughly examined the defendant and concluded he was competent to be executed, he should not be permitted to challenge that determination in Federal court.

Dissenting opinion by Justice Thomas, in which Scalia, J., joined: Justice Thomas dissented from the Court's decision on the grounds that the defendant's *Ford* claim was a second or successive claim under the AEDP Act. He reasoned that the District Court's failure to address the *Ford* claim initially was through no fault of the District Court; the claim was simply premature insofar as no execution date had been set. Justice Thomas believed that once the execution date was established, a new, second or successive, habeas proceeding was instituted and controlled by the AEDP Act. He wrote that "[b]ecause this filing was a 'second or successive habeas corpus application,' [the defendant's] *Ford* claim should have been dismissed." *See also* **Felker v. Turpin; Habeas Corpus**

Stewart v. Massachusetts   *Court:* United States Supreme Court; *Case Citation:* Stewart v. Massachusetts, 408 U.S. 845 (1972); *Argued:* Not reported; *Decided:* June 29, 1972; *Opinion of the Court:* Per Curiam; *Concurring Opinion:* None; *Dissenting Opinion:* None; *Appellate Defense Counsel:* Not reported; *Appellate Prosecution Counsel:* Not reported; *Amicus Curiae Brief Supporting Prosecutor:* Not reported; *Amicus Curiae Brief Supporting Defendant:* Not reported.

Issue Presented: Whether imposition of the death penalty under the procedures used by Massachusetts violated the Constitution?

Case Holding: Imposition of the death penalty under the procedures used by Massachusetts violated the Constitution.

Factual and procedural background of case: The defendant, Stewart, was convicted of a capital offense by the State of Massachusetts and sentenced to death. The conviction and sentence were upheld by the Massachusetts Supreme Court. The United States Supreme Court granted certiorari to consider whether imposition of capital punishment under the State's laws violated the Constitution.

Opinion of the Court was delivered Per Curiam: The per curiam opinion was one paragraph which held that, in light of *Furman v. Georgia*, the defendant's death sentence violated the Constitution.

Case note: Subsequent to the decision in the case, Massachusetts enacted a new death penalty statute. However, in 1984, the Massachusetts Supreme Court found the new death penalty statute was unconstitutional. As a result of the State appellate court's decision, Massachusetts does not impose capital punishment.

Additionally, the case was one of three opinions issued by the Court, on the same day, invalidating death penalty statutes. *See also* **Moore v. Illinois; Furman v. Georgia**

Stewart v. United States   *Court:* United States Supreme Court; *Case Citation:* Stewart v. United States, 366 U.S. 1 (1961); *Argued:* February 21, 1961; *Decided:* April 24, 1961; *Opinion of the Court:* Justice Black; *Concurring Opinion:* None; *Dissenting Opinion:* Justice Frankfurter, in which Harlan and Whittaker, JJ., joined; *Dissenting Opinion:* Justice Clark, in which Whittaker, J., joined; *Appellate Defense Counsel:* Edward L. Carey argued; Robert L. Ackerly and Walter E. Gillcrist on brief; *Appellate Prosecution Counsel:* Carl W. Belcher argued; Wayne G. Barnett, Beatrice Rosenberg and Jerome M. Feit on brief; *Amicus Curiae Brief Supporting Prosecutor:* None; *Amicus Curiae Brief Supporting Defendant:* None.

Issue Presented: Whether it was constitutional error for the trial court to deny the defendant's request for a mistrial after the prosecutor informed the jury the defendant did not testify at his first two trials?

Case Holding: It was constitutional error for the trial court to deny the defendant's request for a mistrial after the prosecutor informed the jury the defendant did not testify at his first two trials.

Factual and procedural background of case: The defendant, Willie Stewart, was prosecuted three times for the same capital murder by the District of Columbia. The defendant was sentenced to death on each of the first two convictions, but the convictions were reversed because of trial errors. During the first two trials the defendant's defense was insanity and he did not testify. The defendant decided to testify at his third trial, though he still relied on the defense of insanity. During the third trial, on cross examination, the prosecutor alluded to the two earlier trials by asking the defendant, "This is the first time you have gone on the stand, isn't it, Willie?" Defense counsel immediately requested a mistrial on the ground that it was prejudicial to inform the jury of the defendant's failure to take the stand in his previous trials. The trial judge denied the request. The defendant was convicted and sentenced to death. The District of Columbia Court of Appeals affirmed the conviction and sentence. In doing so, the appellate court rejected the defendant's contention that the prosecutor's question violated his Fifth Amendment right not to be a witness against himself. The United States Supreme Court granted certiorari to consider the issue.

Opinion of the Court by Justice Black: Justice Black held that the prosecutor's question was prejudicial and the trial court should have granted a mistrial. It was said that the Fifth Amendment provides in unequivocal terms that no person may "be compelled in any criminal case to be a witness against himself." Justice Black indicated that part of the protection of the Fifth Amendment is that the failure of a defendant to testify in his or her own defense does not create any presumption against the defendant. If a defendant chooses not to testify, no comment or argument about his or her failure to testify is permitted.

The opinion reasoned that the jury's awareness of the defendant's failure to testify at his first two trials could have affected its deliberations. Justice Black stated that "the jury might well have thought it likely that [the defendant] elected to feign this 'testimony' out of desperation brought on by his failure to gain acquittal without it in the two previous trials." The opinion concluded: "[W]e agree with the point made by the Government in its brief—that it is regrettable when the concurrent findings of 36 jurors are not sufficient finally to terminate a case. But under our system, a man is entitled to the findings of 12 jurors on evidence fairly and properly presented to them. Petitioner may not be deprived of his life until that right is accorded him. That right was denied here by the prosecutor's improper questions." The judgment of the Court of Appeals was reversed.

Dissenting opinion by Justice Frankfurter, in which Harlan and Whittaker, JJ., joined: Justice Frankfurter dissented from the Court's decision. He believed the error caused by the prosecutor's question did not have any meaningful impact on the outcome of the trial. Justice Frankfurter wrote: "Stewart never intelligibly answered the questions. The jury was not told and did not know as a fact that he had not previously taken the stand. The Court now finds that the jury may nevertheless have inferred the information from the leading form of the prosecutor's questions. But this conclusion should not be reached merely on the basis of the broad generalization that 'such an inference will in all likelihood be drawn from leading questions of this kind.' Such an abstraction does not get us to the heart of the question before us. That question, in one aspect, is whether it is likely that this jury in the circumstances of this case drew the inference from this leading question. It is not only not likely, but overwhelmingly unlikely."

Dissenting opinion by Justice Clark, in which Whittaker, J., joined: Justice Clark dissented from the Court's decision. He argued that the prosecutor's question was a nonexistent factor for the jury. Justice Clark stated his position as follows: "[A]s I read the Government's brief, it conceded only that the question asked Willie 'was of but negligible importance to the government's case.' The sole issue, it said, was whether the question was prejudicial.... [The Government's] position was that one could not assume, as the Court does, that 'the jury noted and focused attention on a question given so little emphasis that it was overlooked by the trial judge.' I add that in the light of the long trial, the uncontradicted evidence as to Willie's malingering and the fact that the question was never mentioned again during the remaining three days of the trial, the jury did not need, nor as a matter of relevancy was it able, to go through the mental gymnastics the Court supposes." *See also* **Right to Remain Silent**

Stigma of Death Sentence on Family

Capital felons have sought to introduce, as penalty phase non-statutory mitigating evidence, testimony from family members on how a sentence of death would have an adverse social impact on them in the community. Courts have refused to allow such evidence on the grounds that it is not mitigating nor relevant to individualized sentencing of capital felons. *See also* **Individualized Sentencing; Mitigating Circumstances**

Stone, Harlan F.

Harlan F. Stone served as an associate justice of the United States Supreme Court from 1925 to 1941; and served as chief justice of the Supreme Court from 1941 to 1946. While on the Supreme Court Stone's judicial philosophy floated between moderate and liberal in his interpretation of the Constitution.

Stone was born in Chesterfield, New Hampshire on October 11, 1872. He received an undergraduate degree from Amherst College in 1894 and a law degree from Columbia Law School in 1898. In addition to being a successful attorney, Stone served as dean of Columbia Law School and as United States Attorney General. In 1925 President Calvin Coolidge nominated Stone to the Supreme Court. In 1941 President Franklin D. Roosevelt nominated Stone as chief justice.

While on the Supreme Court Stone wrote only a few capital punishment opinions. The most important capital punishment opinion authored by Stone was handed down in *Ex Parte Quirin*. That case involved the prosecution of eight German soldiers for spying in the United States. The issue pre-

sented to the Court was whether the detention and prosecution of the defendants as spies by a military commission, appointed by Order of the President, was in conformity with the laws and Constitution of the United States. Stone upheld the prosecution of the defendants by a military commission. He wrote: "The spy who secretly and without uniform passes the military lines of a belligerent in time of war, seeking to gather military information and communicate it to the enemy, or an enemy combatant who without uniform comes secretly through the lines for the purpose of waging war by destruction of life or property, are familiar examples of belligerents who are generally deemed not to be entitled to the status of prisoners of war, but to be offenders against the law of war subject to trial and punishment by military tribunals." Stone died on April 22, 1946.

Capital Punishment Opinions Written by Stone

Case Name	Opinion of the Court	Concurring and Dissenting
Ex Parte Quirin	✓	
Hill v. Texas	✓	
Malinski v. New York		✓

Storti v. Massachusetts

Court: United States Supreme Court; *Case Citation:* Storti v. Massachusetts, 183 U.S. 138 (1901); *Argued:* November 19–20, 1901; *Decided:* December 2, 1901; *Opinion of the Court:* Justice Brewer; *Concurring Opinion:* None; *Dissenting Opinion:* None; *Appellate Defense Counsel:* G. Philip Wardner argued; W. M. Stockbridge on brief; *Appellate Prosecution Counsel:* H. M. Knowlton argued; Arthur W. DeGoosh on brief; *Amicus Curiae Brief Supporting Prosecutor:* None; *Amicus Curiae Brief Supporting Defendant:* None.

Issue Presented: Whether prosecution of the defendant for capital murder violated a treaty between the United States and Italy?

Case Holding: Prosecution of the defendant for capital murder did not violate a treaty between the United States and Italy, insofar as the treaty required equality of treatment of Italian citizens living in the United States.

Factual and procedural background of case: The defendant, Luigi Storti, was convicted of capital murder and sentenced to death by the State of Massachusetts. The Massachusetts Supreme Court affirmed the judgment. The defendant thereafter filed a habeas corpus petition in a Federal District Court. In the petition the defendant alleged that he was a citizen of Italy and a subject of its King. The defendant further alleged that his detention was contrary to a treaty between the United States and the King of Italy. The District Court dismissed the petition and denied relief. The United States Supreme Court granted certiorari to consider the issue.

Opinion of the Court by Justice Brewer: Justice Brewer held that the judgment against the defendant was not in violation of the treaty between the United States and Italy. In disposing of the issue, Justice Brewer wrote: "It is averred that the proceedings in the Massachusetts courts are in conflict with the rights secured by the treaty between Italy and the

United States, but the articles of the treaty referred to only require equality of treatment and that the same rights and privileges be accorded to a citizen of Italy that are given to a citizen of the United States under like circumstances, and there is nothing in the petition tending to show a lack of such equality of treatment. The petition, therefore, is plainly without merit." The judgment of the District Court was affirmed.

Story, Joseph

Joseph Story served as an associate justice of the United States Supreme Court from 1811 to 1845. While on the Supreme Court Story was known as a moderate interpreter of the Constitution.

Story was born in Marblehead, Massachusetts on September 18, 1779. He was a graduate of Harvard University in 1789. Story studied the law privately and established a law practice in 1801. His career included authoring an influential treatises on the law, bank president, member of Congress and member of the Massachusetts legislature. President James Madison appointed Story to the Supreme Court in 1811.

Story was known to have authored only one capital punishment opinion while on the Supreme Court (some early decisions by the Court did not disclose the actual sentence defendants received). In *United States v. Smith* the Court was asked to decide whether the defendant could be punished with death for plundering a ship. Story, writing for the majority, interpreted the Federal Piracy Act as providing for capital punishment for plundering a ship. He reached the decision even though the language of the Piracy Act was vague in its definition. Story grafted principles from the law of nations onto the Piracy Act in order to sustain the judgment against the defendant. Story died September 10, 1845.

Strauder v. West Virginia

Court: United States Supreme Court; *Case Citation:* Strauder v. West Virginia, 100 U.S. 303 (1879); *Argued:* Not reported; *Decided:* October Term, 1879; *Opinion of the Court:* Justice Strong; *Concurring Opinion:* None; *Dissenting Statement:* Justice Field, in which Clifford, J., joined; *Appellate Defense Counsel:* Charles Devens argued; George O. Davenport on brief; *Appellate Prosecution Counsel:* Robert White argued; James W. Green on brief; *Amicus Curiae Brief Supporting Prosecutor:* None; *Amicus Curiae Brief Supporting Defendant:* None.

Issue Presented: Whether the defendant's capital prosecution under the laws of West Virginia should have been removed to a Federal court?

Case Holding: The defendant's capital prosecution under the laws of West Virginia should have been removed to a Federal court, because the defendant established that the State's jury statute systematically excluded blacks from serving on grand and petit juries.

Factual and procedural background of case: The defendant, Strauder, was convicted of capital murder and sentenced to death by the State of West Virginia. The West Virginia Supreme Court affirmed the judgment. In doing so, the appellate rejected the defendant's argument that his case should

have been removed for prosecution in a Federal court because blacks were systematically excluded from serving on grand and petit juries in the State. The United States Supreme Court granted certiorari to consider the issue.

Opinion of the Court by Justice Strong: Justice Strong held that the defendant's trial should have been removed to a Federal court. The opinion pointed out that "[t]he right to a trial by jury is guaranteed to every citizen of West Virginia by the Constitution of that State[.]" However, Justice Strong found that the jury statute of the State discriminated against blacks and barred their participation in grand and petit juries. In addressing the Federal removal statute, the opinion stated:

> But there is express authority to protect the rights and immunities referred to in the Fourteenth Amendment, and to enforce observance of them by appropriate congressional legislation. And one very efficient and appropriate mode of extending such protection and securing to a party the enjoyment of the right or immunity, is a law providing for the removal of his case from a State court, in which the right is denied by the State law, into a Federal court, where it will be upheld.
>
> We have heretofore considered and affirmed the constitutional power of Congress to authorize the removal from State courts into the circuit courts of the United States, before trial, of criminal prosecutions for alleged offenses against the laws of the State, when the defense presents a Federal question, or when a right under the Federal Constitution or laws is involved.

Justice Strong concluded that the defendant "made a case for removal into the Federal Circuit Court[.]" The judgment of the West Virginia Supreme Court was reversed.

Dissenting statement by Justice Field, in which Clifford, J., joined: Justice Field issued a statement indicating he dissented from the Court's decision. *See also* **Discrimination in Grand or Petit Jury Selection**

Strickland v. Washington

Court: United States Supreme Court; *Case Citation:* Strickland v. Washington, 466 U.S. 668 (1984); *Argued:* January 10, 1984; *Decided:* May 14, 1984; *Opinion of the Court:* Justice O'Connor; *Concurring and Dissenting Opinion:* Justice Brennan; *Dissenting Opinion:* Justice Marshall; *Appellate Defense Counsel:* Richard E. Shapiro argued; Joseph H. Rodriguez on brief; *Appellate Prosecution Counsel:* Carolyn M. Snurkowski argued; Jim Smith and Calvin L. Fox on brief; *Amicus Curiae Brief Supporting Prosecutor:* 2; *Amicus Curiae Brief Supporting Defendant:* 1.

Issue Presented: Determining the proper standards for judging a criminal defendant's contention that the Constitution requires a capital conviction or death sentence to be set aside because defense counsel's assistance at the trial or sentencing was ineffective?

Case Holding: A convicted defendant's claim that defense counsel's assistance was so defective as to require reversal of a capital conviction or setting aside of a death sentence, requires that the defendant show: (1) that defense counsel's performance was deficient and (2) that the deficient performance prejudiced the defense so as to deprive the defendant of a fair trial or sentencing. Failure to make the required showing of either deficient performance or sufficient prejudice defeats the ineffectiveness claim.

Factual and procedural background of case: The defendant, Washington, pleaded guilty in a Florida trial court to an indictment that included three capital murder charges. In preparing for the penalty phase hearing, defense counsel spoke with the defendant about his background, but did not seek out character witnesses or request a psychiatric examination. Defense counsel's decision not to present evidence concerning the defendant's character and emotional state was a strategic decision aimed at preventing the prosecutor from cross-examining the defendant and from presenting psychiatric evidence of its own. Defense counsel did not request a presentence report because it would have included the criminal history and thereby would have undermined a claim of no significant prior criminal record. At the conclusion of the penalty phase proceeding the trial judge sentenced the defendant to death on each of the murder counts. The Florida Supreme Court affirmed.

The defendant then sought collateral relief in state court on the ground that defense counsel had rendered ineffective assistance at the sentencing proceeding. The trial court denied relief, and the Florida Supreme Court affirmed.

Next, the defendant filed a habeas corpus petition in a Federal District Court alleging ineffective assistance of counsel. After an evidentiary hearing, the District Court denied relief. The District Court concluded that although defense counsel made errors in judgment in failing to investigate mitigating evidence further than he did, no prejudice to the defendant's sentence resulted from any such error in judgment. A Federal Court of Appeals ultimately reversed, stating that the Sixth Amendment accorded criminal defendants a right to counsel rendering reasonably effective assistance. The Court of Appeals outlined standards for judging whether a defense counsel fulfilled the duty to investigate mitigating circumstances and whether counsel's errors were sufficiently prejudicial to justify reversal. The Court of Appeals remanded the case for application of the standards by the District Court. The United States Supreme Court granted certiorari to consider the issue.

Opinion of the Court by Justice O'Connor: Justice O'Connor wrote that the Sixth Amendment right to counsel, embodies the right to effective assistance of counsel. It was said that the benchmark for judging any claim of ineffectiveness must be whether defense counsel's conduct so undermined the proper functioning of the adversarial process that the trial cannot be relied on as having produced a just result. Justice O'Connor indicated that this principle applied to a capital sentencing proceeding.

The opinion held that a convicted defendant's claim that defense counsel's assistance was so defective as to require reversal of a capital conviction or setting aside of a death sentence, requires that the defendant show: (1) that defense counsel's performance was deficient and (2) that the deficient performance prejudiced the defense so as to deprive the defendant of a fair trial or sentencing. Failure to make the required show-

ing of either deficient performance or sufficient prejudice defeats the ineffectiveness claim.

Justice O'Connor explained the components of the test for ineffective assistance of counsel. It was said that the proper standard for judging attorney performance is that of reasonably effective assistance, considering all the circumstances. When a convicted defendant complains of the ineffectiveness of defense counsel's assistance, the defendant must show that defense counsel's representation fell below an objective standard of reasonableness. The opinion indicated that judicial scrutiny of defense counsel's performance must be highly deferential, and a fair assessment of attorney performance requires that every effort be made to eliminate the distorting effects of hindsight, to reconstruct the circumstances of defense counsel's challenged conduct, and to evaluate the conduct from defense counsel's perspective at the time. A court must indulge a strong presumption that defense counsel's conduct falls within the wide range of reasonable professional assistance.

With regard to the required showing of prejudice, Justice O'Connor wrote that the proper standard requires the defendant to show that there is a reasonable probability that, but for defense counsel's unprofessional errors, the result of the proceeding would have been different. It was said that a reasonable probability was a probability that was sufficient to undercut confidence in the outcome of the proceeding.

Applying the test to the case, Justice O'Connor ruled that the facts of the case made it clear that defense counsel's conduct at and before the defendant's sentencing proceeding could not be found unreasonable. The opinion added that, even assuming defense counsel's conduct was unreasonable, the defendant suffered insufficient prejudice to warrant setting aside his death sentence. The judgment of the Court of Appeals was reversed.

Concurring and dissenting opinion by Justice Brennan: Justice Brennan dissented from the Court's judgment by stating: "Adhering to my view that the death penalty is in all circumstances cruel and unusual punishment forbidden by the Eighth and Fourteenth Amendments, I would vacate [the defendant's] death sentence and remand the case for further proceedings[.]" However, he concurred with the Court's opinion. He indicated his reasons for concurring in the Court's opinion as follows:

> I join the Court's opinion because I believe that the standards it sets out today will both provide helpful guidance to courts considering claims of actual ineffectiveness of counsel and also permit those courts to continue their efforts to achieve progressive development of this area of the law. Like all federal courts and most state courts that have previously addressed the matter, the Court concludes that "the proper standard for attorney performance is that of reasonably effective assistance." And, rejecting the strict "outcome-determinative" test employed by some courts, the Court adopts as the appropriate standard for prejudice a requirement that the defendant "show that there is a reasonable probability that, but for counsel's unprofessional errors, the result of the proceeding would have been different," defining a "reasonable probability" as "a probability sufficient to

undermine confidence in the outcome." I believe these standards are sufficiently precise to permit meaningful distinctions between those attorney derelictions that deprive defendants of their constitutional rights and those that do not; at the same time, the standards are sufficiently flexible to accommodate the wide variety of situations giving rise to claims of this kind.

With respect to the performance standard, I agree with the Court's conclusion that a "particular set of detailed rules for counsel's conduct" would be inappropriate. Precisely because the standard of "reasonably effective assistance" adopted today requires that counsel's performance be measured in light of the particular circumstances of the case, I do not believe our decision "will stunt the development of constitutional doctrine in this area." Indeed, the Court's suggestion that today's decision is largely consistent with the approach taken by the lower courts, simply indicates that those courts may continue to develop governing principles on a case-by-case basis in the common-law tradition, as they have in the past. Similarly, the prejudice standard announced today does not erect an insurmountable obstacle to meritorious claims, but rather simply requires courts carefully to examine trial records in light of both the nature and seriousness of counsel's errors and their effect in the particular circumstances of the case.

Dissenting opinion by Justice Marshall: Justice Marshall dissented from the Court's judgment and opinion. He believed that the test created by the Court would cause more problems than it would resolve. On this issue he wrote: "The state and lower federal courts have developed standards for distinguishing effective from inadequate assistance. Today, for the first time, this Court attempts to synthesize and clarify those standards. For the most part, the majority's efforts are unhelpful. Neither of its two principal holdings seems to me likely to improve the adjudication of Sixth Amendment claims.... Most importantly, the majority fails to take adequate account of the fact that the focus of this case is a capital sentencing proceeding."

In his dissent Justice Marshall contended that the defendant had established ineffective assistance of counsel. He wrote: "If counsel had investigated the availability of mitigating evidence, he might well have decided to present some such material at the hearing. If he had done so, there is a significant chance that [the defendant] would have been given a life sentence. In my view, those possibilities, conjoined with the unreasonableness of counsel's failure to investigate, are more than sufficient to establish a violation of the Sixth Amendment and to entitle [the defendant] to a new sentencing proceeding."

Case note: The decision in the case was extremely important because it constitutionalized the standard courts use to determine the performance of defense counsel in criminal litigation generally. The test developed in the opinion has been criticized to some degree, on the grounds that it incorrectly placed the burden on defendants to establish actual prejudice, once they have established deficient performance by counsel. Critics contend that once deficient performance is established, relief should be granted or, alternatively, the prosecutor should have the burden of showing no prejudice resulted from the deficient performance. *See also* **Burger v. Kemp; Right to Counsel**

Strickler v. Greene

Court: United States Supreme Court; *Case Citation:* Strickler v. Greene, 119 S.Ct. 1936 (1999); *Argued:* March 3, 1999; *Decided:* June 17, 1999; *Opinion of the Court:* Justice Stevens; *Concurring and Dissenting Opinion:* Justice Souter, in which Kennedy, J., joined; *Appellate Defense Counsel:* Not reported; *Appellate Prosecution Counsel:* Not reported; *Amicus Curiae Brief Supporting Prosecutor:* Not reported; *Amicus Curiae Brief Supporting Defendant:* Not reported.

Issue Presented: Whether the defendant was prejudiced by the prosecutor's failure to reveal evidence that the defendant could have used to impeach the prosecutor's star witness against him?

Case Holding: The defendant was not prejudiced by the prosecutor's failure to reveal evidence that the defendant could have used to impeach the prosecutor's star witness against him.

Factual and procedural background of case: The defendant, Thomas Strickler, was convicted and sentenced to death for capital murder by the State of Virginia. The Virginia Supreme Court affirmed the conviction and sentence. Subsequent to the appellate court's decision the defendant learned that the prosecutor withheld evidence that would have impeached much of the testimony of the prosecutor's primary witness. The defendant unsuccessfully sought State habeas corpus relief on the grounds that his constitutional rights, articulated by the United States Supreme Court in *Brady v. Maryland*, were violated because the prosecutor failed to disclose exculpatory and critical impeachment evidence.

The defendant then filed a habeas corpus petition in a Federal District Court. The District Court granted relief after finding the prosecutor violated *Brady* by withholding the evidence. A Court of Appeals reversed the District Court for two reasons: the defendant waived the right to raise the issue because it was not brought out at his trial; and any error was harmless. The United States Supreme Court granted certiorari to consider the issue.

Opinion of the Court by Justice Stevens: Justice Stevens held that the although the defendant demonstrated good cause for failing to raise his *Brady* claim timely, the State of Virginia did not violate *Brady* by failing to disclose the exculpatory evidence.

The opinion observed that there are three essential components of a *Brady* violation: (1) the evidence at issue must be favorable to the accused, either because it is exculpatory, or because it is impeaching; (2) the evidence must have been suppressed by the prosecutor, either willfully or inadvertently; and (3) prejudice must have ensued. Justice Stevens found that the record in the case established the first two components of a *Brady* claim. It was said that the third component, establishing prejudice, was not shown by the record. Justice Stevens wrote that in order to obtain relief, the defendant had to convince the Court that there was a reasonable probability that his conviction or sentence would have been different had the suppressed evidence been disclosed to him. It was pointed out that the issue was not whether the defendant would more likely than not have received a different verdict with the suppressed evidence, but whether in its absence he received a fair trial, understood as a trial resulting in a verdict worthy of confidence. The opinion found that other evidence in the record provided strong support for the conclusion that the defendant would have been convicted of capital murder and sentenced to death, even if the prosecutor's key witness had been severely impeached or the witness' testimony was excluded entirely. The judgment of the Court of Appeals was affirmed.

Concurring and dissenting opinion by Justice Souter, in which Kennedy, J., joined: Justice Souter filed an opinion concurring in part and dissenting in part. He stated his position as follows: "I look at this case much as the Court does, … that Strickler has shown cause to excuse the procedural default of his *Brady* claim. Like the Court, I think it clear that the materials withheld were exculpatory as devastating ammunition for impeaching [the prosecutor's star witness]. Even on the question of prejudice or materiality, over which I ultimately part company with the majority, I am persuaded that Strickler has failed to establish a reasonable probability that, had the materials withheld been disclosed, he would not have been found guilty of capital murder. As the Court says, however, the prejudice enquiry does not stop at the conviction but goes to each step of the sentencing process: the jury's consideration of aggravating, death-qualifying facts, the jury's discretionary recommendation of a death sentence if it finds the requisite aggravating factors, and the judge's discretionary decision to follow the jury's recommendation. It is with respect to the penultimate step in determining the sentence that I think Strickler has carried his burden. I believe there is a reasonable probability (which I take to mean a significant possibility) that disclosure of the [suppressed] materials would have led the jury to recommend life, not death, and I respectfully dissent."

Case note: Four days after the Court's decision was decided, Virginia executed Thomas Strickler by lethal injection on July 21, 1999. *See also* **Brady v. Maryland; Exculpatory Evidence; Kyles v. Whitley**

Stringer v. Black

Court: United States Supreme Court; *Case Citation:* Stringer v. Black, 503 U.S. 222 (1992); *Argued:* December 9, 1991; *Decided:* March 9, 1992; *Opinion of the Court:* Justice Kennedy; *Concurring Opinion:* None; *Dissenting Opinion:* Justice Souter, in which Scalia and Thomas, JJ., joined; *Appellate Defense Counsel:* Kenneth J. Rose argued; James W. Craig and Louis D. Bilionis on brief; *Appellate Prosecution Counsel:* Marvin L. White, Jr. argued; Mike Moore on brief; *Amicus Curiae Brief Supporting Prosecutor:* 14; *Amicus Curiae Brief Supporting Defendant:* None.

Issue Presented: Whether the defendant was precluded from relying on the decision in *Maynard v. Cartwright* because the decision announced a new rule after the defendant's conviction became final?

Case Holding: The defendant was not precluded from relying on the decision in *Maynard v. Cartwright* because the decision did not announce a new rule.

Factual and procedural background of case: The defendant, James R. Stringer, was convicted of capital murder by a Mississippi jury. During the penalty phase the jury found that there were three statutory aggravating factors. These included the "especially heinous, atrocious or cruel" aggravator. The defendant was sentenced to death. The Mississippi Supreme Court, on direct review, affirmed the conviction and sentence.

After the defendant exhausted State post-conviction relief without success, he filed a habeas corpus petition in a Federal District Court, alleging that the "especially heinous, atrocious or cruel" aggravator was so vague as to render his death sentence arbitrary, and in violation of the United States Supreme Court decision in *Maynard v. Cartwright*. The District Court denied relief. A Federal Court of Appeals ultimately affirmed, after holding that the defendant was not entitled to rely on *Maynard* in his habeas corpus proceeding because that decision was issued after his sentence became final and announced a new rule. The United States Supreme Court granted certiorari to consider the issue.

Opinion of the Court by Justice Kennedy: Justice Kennedy held that in a Federal habeas corpus proceeding, a defendant whose death sentence became final before *Maynard* was decided was not foreclosed from relying on that case. The opinion indicated that when a defendant seeks Federal habeas relief based on a principle announced after his or her conviction became final, a Federal court must determine whether the decision in question announced a new rule, i.e., was not dictated by precedent existing when the judgment became final. If the answer is yes and neither of two exceptions apply, the decision is not available to the defendant.

It was ruled by the Court that *Maynard* did not announce a new rule. Justice Kennedy stated that *Maynard's* invalidation of Oklahoma's "especially heinous, atrocious, or cruel" aggravating circumstance was based upon another decision by the Court which had invalidated Georgia's statutory aggravating circumstance of "outrageously or wantonly vile, horrible and inhuman" as vague and imprecise. Consequently, the opinion found that the defendant was not foreclosed from relying on *Maynard* to attack the validity of Mississippi's "especially heinous, atrocious, or cruel" aggravator. Th judgment of the Court of Appeals was reversed.

Dissenting opinion by Justice Souter, in which Scalia and Thomas, JJ., joined: Justice Souter dissented from the majority's decision. He argued that *Maynard* did announce a new rule when it invalidated Oklahoma's "especially heinous, atrocious, or cruel" aggravator as vague. Justice Souter contended that because *Maynard* announced a new rule after the defendant's conviction became final, he was not entitled to rely upon it to challenge his death sentence. *See also* **Heinous, Atrocious, Cruel or Depraved Aggravator; Lewis v. Jeffers; Maynard v. Cartwright; Richmond v. Lewis; Shell v. Mississippi; Walton v. Arizona**

Stroble v. California

Court: United States Supreme Court; *Case Citation:* Stroble v. California, 343 U.S. 181

(1952); *Argued:* March 6, 1952; *Decided:* April 7, 1952; *Opinion of the Court:* Justice Clark; *Concurring Opinion:* None; *Dissenting Opinion:* Justice Frankfurter; *Dissenting Opinion:* Justice Douglas, in which Black, J., joined; *Appellate Defense Counsel:* John D. Gray and A. L. Wirin argued; Fred Okrand, Clore Warne and Loren Miller on brief; *Appellate Prosecution Counsel:* Adolph Alexander argued; Edmund G. Brown, William V. O'Connor, and Frank W. Richards on brief; *Amicus Curiae Brief Supporting Prosecutor:* None; *Amicus Curiae Brief Supporting Defendant:* None.

Issue Presented: Whether the defendant was denied due process as a result of his confession, interrogation without counsel, pretrial publicity, and waiver of jury determination on the issue of his sanity?

Case Holding: The defendant was not denied due process as a result of his confession, interrogation without counsel, pretrial publicity, and waiver of jury determination on the issue of his sanity.

Factual and procedural background of case: The defendant, Stroble, was convicted of capital murder and sentenced to death by the State of California. On appeal to the California Supreme Court, the defendant argued that his conviction violated the Due Process Clause of the Federal Constitution because of the following: (1) that his confession was coerced; (2) that he did not have counsel present during interrogation by the prosecutor; (3) that a fair trial was impossible because of inflammatory newspaper reports inspired by the prosecutor; and (4) that he was deprived of counsel in the course of his sanity hearing. The State appellate court rejected the contentions and affirmed the conviction and sentence. The United States Supreme Court granted certiorari to consider the issue.

Opinion of the Court by Justice Clark: Justice Clark ruled that the burden of showing essential unfairness in a State court trial is upon the defendant. It was said that a defendant's burden was not established through speculation, but must be shown "as a demonstrable reality." In addressing the defendant's involuntary confession allegation, Justice Clark held that if the confession which the defendant made shortly after his arrest was in fact involuntary, the conviction could not stand, even though the evidence apart from that confession might have been sufficient to sustain the jury's verdict. It was said that when the question on review of a State court conviction is whether there has been a violation of the Due Process Clause by the introduction of an involuntary confession, the Court must make an independent determination on the undisputed facts. It was then concluded that in the light of all the circumstances of the case, the Court could not say that the defendant's confession was the result of coercion, either physical or psychological. The Court rejected the defendant's contention that the delay in taking him to a magistrate, after his warrantless arrest, showed that his confession was coerced.

The opinion next addressed the defendant's claim of denial of counsel during interrogation by the prosecutor. Justice Clark held that based upon the record in the case, there was no showing of prejudice resulting from the refusal of the pros-ecutor to allow defense counsel to speak with the defendant during the interrogation. It was said that defense counsel came to the prosecutor's office at the request of the defendant's son-in-law merely to inquire of the defendant as to his guilt. Justice Clark indicated that at no point did the defendant himself ask for counsel. The opinion reasoned that in light of these facts, the prosecutor's refusal to interrupt the interrogation of the defendant so that defense counsel could make inquiry for the defendant's son-in-law, did not constitute a deprivation of due process. Justice Clark noted that while prosecutors should always honor a request of defense counsel for an interview with a client, upon the record in the case there was no showing of prejudice.

Justice Clark rejected the defendant's claim that pretrial publicity engendered by the prosecutor deprived him of a fair trial. It was reasoned that newspaper accounts of his arrest and confession were not so inflammatory as to make a fair trial impossible, even though a period of only six weeks intervened between the day of his arrest and confession and the beginning of his trial. The opinion also rejected the defendant's claim of denial of counsel during his sanity hearing. Justice Clark found that the defendant had counsel when he knowingly waived the right to trial by jury on the issue of insanity. The judgment of the California Supreme Court was affirmed.

Dissenting opinion by Justice Frankfurter: Justice Frankfurter dissented from the Court's decision. He believed that the defendant was denied a fair trial as a result of pretrial publicity. Justice Frankfurter addressed this issue as follows:

> One of the [defendant's] grounds for attacking his conviction is that the trial lacked fundamental fairness because the district attorney himself initiated the intrusion of the press into the process of the trial. Such misconduct, the [defendant] contends, subverted the adjudicatory process by which guilt is determined in Anglo-Saxon countries, so as to offend what the Due Process Clause of the Fourteenth Amendment protects. The issue was raised after verdict, and the Supreme Court of California might have disposed of the claim by ruling that it had not been made at the stage of the proceeding required by State law. That court, however, chose not to do so. It permitted the [defendant] to invoke the Due Process Clause and thereby tendered a federal constitutional issue, as this Court recognizes, for our disposition....
>
> ... [The] California court's own reading of the record [showed] circumstances tending to establish guilt and adduced outside the courtroom before the trial had even begun were avidly exploited by press and other media, actively promoted by the prosecutor. The State court sanctioned this as not only permissible but as an inevitable ingredient of American criminal justice. That sanction contradicts all our professions as to the establishment of guilt on the basis of what takes place in the courtroom, subject to judicial restrictions in producing proof and in the general conduct of the proceedings. Jurors are of course human beings and even with the best of intentions in the world they are ... "extremely likely to be impregnated by the environing atmosphere...."
>
> And so I cannot agree to uphold a conviction which affirmatively treats newspaper participation instigated by the prosecutor as part of "the traditional concept of the 'American way of the conduct of a trial.'" Such passion as the newspapers stirred in this case can be explained (apart from mere commercial

exploitation of revolting crime) only as want of confidence in the orderly course of justice. To allow such use of the press by the prosecution as the California court here left undisciplined, implies either that the ascertainment of guilt cannot be left to the established processes of law or impatience with those calmer aspects of the judicial process which may not satisfy the natural, primitive, popular revulsion against horrible crime but do vindicate the sober second thoughts of a community. If guilt here is clear, the dignity of the law would be best enhanced by establishing that guilt wholly through the processes of law unaided by the infusion of extraneous passion. The moral health of the community is strengthened by according even the most miserable and pathetic criminal those rights which the Constitution has designed for all.

Dissenting opinion by Justice Douglas, in which Black, J., joined: Justice Douglas dissented from the Court's decision based upon the confession given by the defendant. He believed that confession was involuntary. Justice Douglas wrote:

> ... The practice of obtaining confessions prior to arraignment breeds the third-degree and the inquisition. As long as it remains lawful for the police to hold persons incommunicado, coerced confessions will infect criminal trials in violation of the commands of due process of law.
>
> The facts of this case illustrate the evils of this police practice. While the defendant was being held by the police prior to his arraignment, a lawyer tried to see him. The police refused the lawyer's repeated requests. It was only after a confession was obtained that the lawyer was allowed to talk with the prisoner. This was lawless conduct, condemned by the Supreme Court of California. It was not only lawless conduct; it was conduct that produced a confession.
>
> This confession as well as subsequently obtained confessions were used at the trial. The fact that the later confessions may have been lawfully obtained or used is immaterial. For once an illegal confession infects the trial, the verdict of guilty must be set aside no matter how free of taint the other evidence may be.
>
> Moreover, the fact that the accused started talking shortly after he was arrested and prior to the time he was taken before the District Attorney does not save the case. That talk was accompanied or preceded by blows and kicks of the police; and the Supreme Court of California assumed that it was part and parcel of the first confession obtained through "physical abuse or psychological torture or a combination of the two."

Case note: The Court's resolution of the confession and right to counsel claim would come out differently under modern capital and non-capital punishment law. Constitutional safeguards were subsequently developed by the Court to prohibit obtaining and using involuntary confessions; in addition to stringent constitutional requirements concerning interrogation when counsel is requested. *See also* **Mu'Min v. Virginia; Pretrial Publicity; Right to Counsel; Right to Remain Silent**

Strong, William

William Strong served as an associate justice of the United States Supreme Court from 1870 to 1880. While on the Supreme Court Strong was known as a moderate in his interpretation of the Constitution.

Strong was born in Somers, Connecticut on May 6, 1808. He was educated at Yale University where he received an undergraduate degree and law degree. Strong was admitted to the bar in Pennsylvania in 1832. Strong's career included being elected to the United States House of Representatives and serving on the supreme court of Pennsylvania. In 1870 President Ulysses S. Grant appointed Strong to the Supreme Court.

While on the Supreme Court Strong is known to have written only one capital punishment opinion (during the early history of the Court justices oftentimes failed to state what sentence a defendant received). In *Strauder v. West Virginia* the defendant was convicted of murder and sentenced to death. The defendant argued before the Supreme Court that his conviction was invalid because under the laws of West Virginia blacks were prohibited from serving on juries. Strong, writing for the Court, agreed with the defendant. Strong wrote that equal protection guarantees embodied in the Constitution prohibited West Virginia from excluding blacks from serving on juries because of their race. Strong retired from the Court in 1880. He died on August 19, 1895.

Stroud v. United States

Court: United States Supreme Court; *Case Citation:* Stroud v. United States, 251 U.S. 15 (1919); *Argued:* October 22, 1919; *Decided:* November 24, 1919; *Opinion of the Court:* Justice Day; *Concurring Opinion:* None; *Dissenting Opinion:* None; *Appellate Defense Counsel:* Martin J. O'Donnell argued; Isaac B. Kimbrell on brief; *Appellate Prosecution Counsel:* United States Assistant Attorney General Stewart argued and briefed; *Amicus Curiae Brief Supporting Prosecutor:* None; *Amicus Curiae Brief Supporting Defendant:* None.

Issue Presented: Whether the Double Jeopardy Clause prohibits successive prosecutions of a capital defendant for the same capital offense?

Case Holding: When a capital defendant is granted a new trial because of trial errors, the Constitution does not prohibit a subsequent prosecution for the same capital offense.

Factual and procedural background of case: The defendant, Robert F. Stroud, was indicted by the United States for killing a prison guard while confined in a federal prison at Leavenworth, Kansas. The defendant was convicted in May, 1916, and sentenced to be hanged. A federal Court of Appeals reversed this judgment. The defendant was tried again in 1917. At the second trial the jury found the defendant guilty, but did not impose the death penalty. The United States Supreme Court reversed the second judgment. A third trial was held and the defendant was convicted and sentenced to death. The United States Supreme Court granted certiorari to address whether the Constitution prohibited prosecuting the defendant after the first judgment was reversed.

Opinion of the Court by Justice Day: Justice Day acknowledged that "[t]he protection afforded by the Constitution is against a second trial for the same offense." The opinion ruled that principles of double jeopardy are not absolute, but are qualified. One such qualification involved setting aside a judgment because of trial errors. The opinion addressed the matter as follows: "[T]he conviction and sentence upon the former trials were reversed upon writs of error sued out by the [defendant]. The only thing the appellate court could do was to award a new trial on finding error in the proceeding, thus the [defendant] himself invoked the action of the court which resulted in a further trial. In such cases he is not placed in second jeopardy within the meaning of the Constitution." The conviction and sentence of death were affirmed. *See also* **Arizona v. Rumsey; Bullington v. Missouri; Double Jeopardy Clause; Poland v. Arizona; Retrials and the Death Penalty**

Structure of Capital Trial *see* Trial Structure

Styers, James *see* Child Killers

Subpoena *see* Compulsory Process Clause

Substantial Capacity Test *see* Insanity Defense

Successive Prosecutions In murder prosecutions involving more than one victim, the Federal Constitution does not prohibit separate trials of a defendant for each murder. Defendants have contended that due process should prevent separate prosecutions when this is done merely in an attempt to assure that the death penalty will be obtained. This argument has been rejected. *See also* **Ciucci v. Illinois**

Sudan Capital punishment is allowed in Sudan. Sudan uses hanging, stoning, crucifixion, and the firing squad to carry out the death penalty. Its legal system is based on English common law and Islamic law. The most recent constitution adopted by Sudan was done so on October 10, 1985.

The judicial system includes trial courts, special security courts, and a Constitutional Court. Defendants have the right to counsel, and the courts are required to provide free legal counsel for indigent defendants accused of crimes punishable by death or life imprisonment. *See also* **International Capital Punishment Nations**

Sumner v. Shuman *Court:* United States Supreme Court; *Case Citation:* Sumner v. Shuman, 483 U.S. 66 (1987); *Argued:* April 20, 1987; *Decided:* June 22, 1987; *Opinion of the Court:* Justice Blackmun; *Concurring Opinion:* None; *Dissenting Opinion:* Justice White, in which Rehnquist, C. J., and Scalia, J., joined; *Appellate Defense Counsel:* Daniel Markoff argued; N. Patrick Flanagan III on brief; *Appellate Prosecution Counsel:* Brain McKay argued; Brooke A. Nielsen on brief; *Amicus Curiae Brief Supporting Prosecutor:* None; *Amicus Curiae Brief Supporting Defendant:* 2.

Issue Presented: Whether a statute that mandates the death penalty for a prison inmate who is convicted of murder while serving a life sentence without possibility of parole violates the Eighth and Fourteenth Amendments?

Case Holding: A statute that mandates the death penalty for a prison inmate who is convicted of murder while serving a life sentence without possibility of parole violates the Constitution.

Factual and procedural background of case: The defen-

dant, Raymond Wallace Shuman, was serving a life sentence without possibility of parole, when he was convicted and sentenced to death for the capital murder of a fellow prisoner by the State of Nevada. The defendant's death sentence was rendered under a provision of the State's statute mandating the death penalty under those circumstances. The Nevada Supreme Court affirmed conviction and death sentence. However, in a habeas corpus proceeding in a Federal District Court, the defendant's death sentence was vacated on the grounds that the mandatory capital punishment statute violated the Eighth and Fourteenth Amendments. A Federal Court of Appeals affirmed. The United States Supreme Court granted certiorari to consider the issue.

Opinion of the Court by Justice Blackmun: Justice Blackmun held that a statute that mandates the death penalty for a prison inmate who is convicted of murder while serving a life sentence without possibility of parole violated the Eighth and Fourteenth Amendments. The opinion in the case reasoned as follows:

> The Nevada mandatory capital-sentencing statute under which Shuman was sentenced to death precluded a determination whether any relevant mitigating circumstances justified imposing on him a sentence less than death. Redefining the offense as capital murder and specifying that it is a murder committed by a life-term inmate revealed only two facts about [the defendant]—(1) that he had been convicted of murder while in prison, and (2) that he had been convicted of an earlier criminal offense which, at the time committed, yielded a sentence of life imprisonment without possibility of parole. These two elements had to be established at Shuman's trial to support a verdict of guilty of capital murder. After the jury rendered that verdict of guilty, all that remained for the trial judge to do was to enter a judgment of conviction and impose the death sentence. The death sentence was a foregone conclusion.
>
> These two elements of capital murder do not provide an adequate basis on which to determine whether the death sentence is the appropriate sanction in any particular case. The fact that a life-term inmate is convicted of murder does not reflect whether any circumstance existed at the time of the murder that may have lessened his responsibility for his acts even though it could not stand as a legal defense to the murder charge. This Court has recognized time and again that the level of criminal responsibility of a person convicted of murder may vary according to the extent of that individual's participation in the crime. Just as the level of an offender's involvement in a routine crime varies, so too can the level of involvement of an inmate in a violent prison incident. An inmate's participation may be sufficient to support a murder conviction, but in some cases it may not be sufficient to render death an appropriate sentence, even though it is a life-term inmate or an inmate serving a particular number of years who is involved....
>
> ... In Shuman's case, a sentencing authority may likely find relevant his behavior during his 15 years of incarceration, including whether the inmate murder was an isolated incident of violent behavior or merely the most recent in a long line of such incidents. There is no reason to believe that several of the mitigating circumstances listed in Nevada's current guided-discretion statute could not be equally applicable to a murder committed by a life-term inmate. Hence, the mandatory capital-sentencing procedure pursuant to which Shuman's death sentence was imposed "create[d] the risk that the death penalty

w[ould] be imposed in spite of factors which may call for a less severe penalty."

The judgment of the Court of Appeals was affirmed.

Dissenting opinion by Justice White, in which Rehnquist, C. J., and Scalia, J., joined: Justice White dissented from the majority decision. In doing so, he wrote: "Today the Court holds that the Eighth Amendment prohibits a State from imposing a mandatory death sentence on a prisoner who, while serving a life term for a first-degree murder conviction, murders a fellow inmate. The Court reasons that the Constitution requires that such an inmate be afforded the opportunity to present mitigating evidence to the sentencer, and, in so reasoning, quite obviously assumes that cases will arise under the type of statute at issue here in which an inmate will be able, through the presentation of such mitigating evidence, to persuade a sentencer not to impose a death sentence. In my view, the Constitution does not bar a state legislature from determining, in this limited class of cases, that, as a matter of law, no amount of mitigating evidence could ever be sufficient to outweigh the aggravating factors that characterize a first-degree murder committed by one who is already incarcerated for committing a previous murder and serving a life sentence. Accordingly, I dissent." *See also* **Mandatory Death Penalty Statutes; Roberts v. Louisiana (I); Roberts v. Louisiana (II); Woodson v. North Carolina**

Suriname Suriname has not abolished capital punishment, but the punishment has not been imposed in over a decade. Suriname uses the firing squad to carry out the death penalty. Its legal system is based on Dutch law and French law. The constitution of Suriname was ratified on September 30, 1987.

The judicial system consists of trial courts and an appellate court. Defendants have the right to a public trial and to retained or appointed legal counsel. Trials are before a single judge, with the right of appeal. *See also* **International Capital Punishment Nations**

Surratt, Mary *see* **Lincoln's Assassination**

Sutherland, George George Sutherland served as an associate justice of the United States Supreme Court from 1922 to 1938. While on the Supreme Court Sutherland was known as a conservative interpreter of the Constitution.

Sutherland was born in Buckinghamshire, England on March 25, 1862. Sutherland's family immigrated to the United States during his adolescent years and settled in Utah. He was a graduate of Brigham Young University in 1881, and thereafter studied law at the University of Michigan Law School. His career included serving in the Utah legislature, the United States House of Representatives and the United States Senate. In 1922 President Warren G. Harding appointed Sutherland to the Supreme Court.

While on the Supreme Court Sutherland was known to issue only one capital punishment opinion. The case of *Powell v. Alabama* involved death sentences handed down against seven black defendants for the crime of rape. The primary issue presented to the Supreme Court was that the defendants, all indigent, did not have legal representation. Sutherland, writing for the Court, stepped out of his conservative judicial reputation to establish a precedent that paved the way to the constitutional requirement that a defendant has a right to counsel for all criminal offenses carrying imprisonment as a penalty. In *Powell*, Sutherland reversed the judgments against the defendants and wrote that in capital punishment cases, an indigent defendant has a constitutional right to counsel if requested. Sutherland retired from the Court in 1938. He died on July 18, 1942.

Swain v. Alabama *Court:* United States Supreme Court; *Case Citation:* Swain v. Alabama, 380 U.S. 202 (1965); *Argued:* December 8, 1964; *Decided:* March 8, 1965; *Opinion of the Court:* Justice White; *Concurring Statement:* Justice Harlan; *Concurring Statement:* Justice Black; *Dissenting Opinion:* Justice Goldberg, in which Warren, C.J., and Douglas, J., joined; *Appellate Defense Counsel:* Constance Baker Motley argued; Jack Greenberg, James M. Nabrit III, Orzell Billingsley, Jr., Peter A. Hall and Michael Meltsner on brief; *Appellate Prosecution Counsel:* Leslie Hall argued; Richmond M. Flowers on brief; *Amicus Curiae Brief Supporting Prosecutor:* None; *Amicus Curiae Brief Supporting Defendant:* None.

Issue Presented: Whether the defendant established a prima facie case of racial discrimination in the selection of the grand jury that indicted him and the petit jury that convicted him?

Case Holding: The defendant did not establish a prima facie case of racial discrimination in the selection of the grand jury that indicted him and the petit jury that convicted him, because blacks were in the jury pool although none where selected to serve on either jury.

Factual and procedural background of case: The defendant, Robert Swain, was convicted of rape and sentenced to death by the State of Alabama. The Alabama Supreme Court affirmed the judgment. In doing so, the appellate court rejected the defendant's contention that the judgment against him was void on the grounds that blacks were systematically excluded from the grand jury that indicted him and the petit jury that convicted him. The United States Supreme Court granted certiorari to consider the issue.

Opinion of the Court by Justice White: Justice White ruled that blacks were not systematically excluded from the grand and petit juries. It was said that blacks were included in the grand and petit jury pool, although none actually served on either jury. Justice White indicated that a defendant in a criminal case was not constitutionally entitled to a proportionate number of his or her race on the grand or petit juries.

The opinion found that the prosecutor's use of peremptory strikes to remove blacks from the jury panel did not constitute denial of equal protection of the laws. It was further said that peremptory strikes based on race in a particular case did not raise a prima facie case of discrimination under the Constitution to establish systematic striking. Justice White concluded that "[t]otal exclusion of [blacks] from venires by state officials creates an inference of discrimination, but this rule of proof cannot be applied where it is not shown that the State is responsible for the exclusion of [blacks] through peremptory challenges." The judgment of the Alabama Supreme Court was affirmed.

Concurring Statement by Justice Harlan: Justice Harlan issued a statement indicating he concurred in the Court's decision.

Concurring Statement by Justice Black: Justice Black issued a statement indicating he concurred in the Court's decision.

Dissenting opinion by Justice Goldberg, in which Warren, C.J., and Douglas, J., joined: Justice Goldberg dissented from the decision by the Court. He argued that the defendant presented sufficient evidence to establish racial discrimination in jury selection. Justice Goldberg wrote as follows:

> [The defendant], a 19-year-old [black], was indicted in Talladega County for the rape of a 17-year-old white girl, found guilty, and sentenced to death by an all-white jury. The [defendant] established by competent evidence and without contradiction that not only was there no [black] on the jury that convicted and sentenced him, but also that no [black] within the memory of persons now living has ever served on any petit jury in any civil or criminal case tried in Talladega County, Alabama. Yet, of the group designated by Alabama as generally eligible for jury service in that county, 74 percent (12,125) were white and 26 percent (4,281) were [black].
>
> Under well-established principles this evidence clearly makes out a prima facie case of the denial of the equal protection which the Constitution guarantees....
>
> It is clear that, unless the State here can "justify such an exclusion as having been brought about for some reason other than racial discrimination," this conviction cannot stand. Long continued omission of [blacks] from jury service establishes a prima facie case of systematic discrimination. The burden of proof is then upon the State to refute it....
>
> I deplore the Court's departure from its [precedents]. By affirming [the defendant's] conviction on this clear record of jury exclusion because of race, the Court condones the highly discriminatory procedures used in Talladega County under which [blacks] never have served on any petit jury in that county. By adding to the present heavy burden of proof required of defendants in these cases, the Court creates additional barriers to the elimination of practices which have operated in many communities throughout the Nation to nullify the command of the Equal Protection Clause in this important area in the administration of justice.

Case note: Under modern capital punishment jurisprudence the death penalty may not be imposed for the crime of rape, without an accompanying homicide. *See also* **Discrimination in Grand or Petit Jury Selection; Jury Selection; Rape and Capital Punishment**

Swaziland Capital punishment is permitted in Swaziland. Swaziland uses hanging as the method of carrying out the death penalty. Its legal system is based on Roman-Dutch law. The last constitution promulgated by the nation was on October 13, 1978.

The judicial system is composed of magistrate courts, a High Court, and a Court of Appeals. Defendants have the right to legal counsel. Court appointed counsel is provided in capital cases. *See also* **International Capital Punishment Nations**

Sweden Sweden abolished capital punishment for ordinary crimes in 1921, and completely abolished the punishment in 1972. *See also* **International Capital Punishment Nations**

Switzerland Switzerland abolished capital punishment for ordinary crimes in 1942, and completely abolished the punishment in 1992. *See also* International Capital Punishment Nations

Sympathy for Victim *see* Victim Impact Evidence

Syria Capital punishment is allowed in Syria. Syria uses hanging and the firing squad to carry out the death penalty. Its legal system is based on civil law and Islamic law. A constitution was adopted by the nation on March 13, 1973.

The judicial system is composed of trial courts, security courts, Court of Cassation, and a Supreme Constitutional Court. Defendants are entitled to retained or appointed legal counsel. Defendants are presumed innocent and may confront their accusers. Trials are public. There are no juries. Defendants may appeal. *See also* **International Capital Punishment Nations**

T

Taft, William Howard William Howard Taft served as chief justice of the United States Supreme Court from 1921 to 1930. While on the Supreme Court Taft was known as a moderate interpreter of the Constitution.

Taft was born in Cincinnati, Ohio on September 15, 1857. He was educated at Yale University and received a law degree from Cincinnati Law School in 1880. Taft's career included being a trial court judge in Ohio, an appellate court judge for the Sixth Circuit Court of Appeals, United States Solicitor General and President of the United States. As Solicitor General Taft argued two capital punishment cases before the Supreme Court: *Alexander v. United States* and *Ball v. United States (I)*. In 1921 President Warren G. Harding nominated Taft as chief justice for the Supreme Court.

While on the Supreme Court Taft was known to write only one capital punishment opinion (early criminal cases by the Supreme Court frequently failed to state what sentence a defendant received). In *Kelley v. Oregon* the Supreme Court was asked to decide whether the defendant had a constitutional right to serve out a prior imprisonment sentence before he could be executed for another crime. Taft, writing for the Court, held that the defendant did not have a constitutional right to serve out a prior imprisonment sentence before he could be executed for another crime. Taft wrote: "The penitentiary is no sanctuary, and life in it does not confer immunity from capital punishment provided by law. He has no vested constitutional right to serve out his unexpired sentence." Taft died on March 8, 1930.

Taiwan Capital punishment is permitted in Taiwan. Taiwan uses the firing squad and lethal injection to carry out the death penalty. In 1998, Taiwan executed 32 prisoners. Its legal system is based on civil law. The nation adopted a constitution on January 1, 1947.

The judicial system of Taiwan is composed of district courts, high courts, and a Supreme Court. Defendants have a right to public trials and to legal counsel. Judges, rather than juries, decide trials. Parties and witnesses are interrogated by a single judge, not directly by a defense attorney or prosecutor. Defendants may not be compelled testify. The Supreme Court automatically reviews life imprisonment and death sentences. Prosecutors have the right to appeal verdicts of not guilty. *See also* **International Capital Punishment Nations**

Tajikistan Tajikistan permits capital punishment. Tajikistan uses the firing squad to carry out the death penalty. Its legal system is based on civil law. A constitution was adopted by the nation on November 6, 1994.

The judicial system is composed of district courts, regional courts, national courts, and a Constitutional Court. Trials are public and defendants have the right to retained or appointed counsel. *See also* **International Capital Punishment Nations**

Talton v. Mayes *Court:* United States Supreme Court; *Case Citation:* Talton v. Mayes, 163 U.S. 376 (1896); *Argued:* Not reported; *Decided:* May 18, 1896; *Opinion of the Court:* Justice White; *Concurring Opinion:* None; *Dissenting Statement:* Justice Harlan; *Appellate Defense Counsel:* L. D. Yarrell argued and briefed; *Appellate Prosecution Counsel:* R. C. Garland argued and briefed; *Amicus Curiae Brief Supporting Prosecutor:* None; *Amicus Curiae Brief Supporting Defendant:* None.

Issue Presented: Whether the indictment returned against the defendant by the Cherokee Nation was invalid due to the grand jury being composed of only five people?

Case Holding: The indictment returned against the defendant by the Cherokee Nation was not invalid due to the grand jury being composed of only five people, because the composition of the grand jury was a matter exclusively within the control of the Cherokee Nation.

Factual and procedural background of case: The defendant, Bob Talton, was convicted of capital murder and sentenced to death by the Cherokee Nation. Both the defendant and the victim were members of the Cherokee Nation. The defendant filed a habeas corpus petition in a Federal District Court, alleging the judgment against him was invalid because he was indicted by a grand jury consisting of only five people. The District Court denied relief and dismissed the petition. The United States Supreme Court granted certiorari to consider the issue.

Opinion of the Court by Justice White: Justice White held that the indictment returned against the defendant was valid, even though the grand jury was composed of only five people. The opinion noted that when the grand jury returned the indictment against the defendant, the laws of the Cherokee Nation required the grand jury be composed of only five people. It was said that during the pendency of the defendant's prosecution, the Cherokee Nation changed the law and required the grand jury be composed of 13 people. Justice White found the subsequent change in the law did not invalidate the former requirement. The opinion went on to express the legal basis for the deference the Court had to accord the laws of the Cherokee Nation:

> By treaties and statutes of the United States the right of the Cherokee Nation to exist as an autonomous body, subject always to the paramount authority of the United States, has been recognized. And from this fact there has consequently been conceded to exist in that Nation power to make laws defining offenses and providing for the trial and punishment of those who violate them when the offenses are committed by one member of the tribe against another one of its members within the territory of the Nation....
>
> The crime of murder committed by one Cherokee ... upon the person of another within the jurisdiction of the Cherokee Nation is, therefore, clearly not an offense against the United States, but an offense against the local laws of the Cherokee Nation. Necessarily, the statutes of the United States which provide for an indictment by a grand jury, and the number of persons who shall constitute such a body, have no application, for such statutes relate only, if not otherwise specially provided, to grand juries impaneled for the courts of and under the laws of the United States....
>
> True it is that in many adjudications of this court the fact has been fully recognized that, although possessed of these attributes of local self-government when exercising their tribal functions, all such rights are subject to the supreme legislative authority of the United States.... But the existence of the right in congress to regulate the manner in which the local powers of the Cherokee Nation shall be exercised does not render such local powers federal powers arising from and created by the constitution of the United States.... The question whether a statute of the Cherokee Nation which was not repugnant to the constitution of the United States or in conflict with any treaty or

law of the United States had been repealed by another statute of that Nation, and the determination of what was the existing law of the Cherokee Nation as to the constitution of the grand jury, was solely a matter within the jurisdiction of the courts of that Nation, and the decision of such a question in itself necessarily involves no infraction of the constitution of the United States. Such has been the decision of this court with reference to similar contentions arising upon an indictment and conviction in a state court.

The judgment of the Federal District Court was affirmed.

Dissenting statement by Justice Harlan: Justice Harlan issued a statement indicting he dissented from the Court's decision. *See also* **Grand Jury**

Taney, Roger B.

Roger B. Taney served as chief justice of the United States Supreme Court from 1836 to 1864. While on the Supreme Court Taney was known as a conservative interpreter of the Constitution.

Taney was born in Calvert County, Maryland on March 17, 1777. He was a graduate of Dickinson College in 1795. Taney studied law on his own and was admitted to the bar in Maryland in 1799. Taney's career included being elected to the Maryland legislature and being appointed United States Attorney General. In 1836 President Andrew Jackson nominated Taney as chief justice of the Supreme Court.

While on the Supreme Court Taney was known to have written only one capital punishment opinion (early decisions by the Court frequently failed to state the type of sentence a criminal defendant received). In *Ex Parte Gordon* the defendant asked the Supreme Court to issue an order halting his execution, while it reviewed his petition for appeal. Taney, writing for the Court, denied the relief on the grounds that the Court did not have authority to issue an order halting an execution. Taney died on October 12, 1864.

Tanzania

Tanzania allows capital punishment. Tanzania uses hanging to carry out the death penalty. Its legal system is based on English common law. A constitution was adopted by the nation on April 25, 1977.

The legal system is composed of trial courts, High Court, and Court of Appeal.

Criminal trials are open to the public. Defendants have the right to counsel and the right to appeal. *See also* **International Capital Punishment Nations**

Taylor v. Alabama

Court: United States Supreme Court; *Case Citation:* Taylor v. Alabama, 335 U.S. 252 (1948); *Argued:* April 30, May 3, 1948; *Decided:* June 21, 1948; *Opinion of the Court:* Justice Burton; *Concurring Opinion:* Justice Frankfurter; *Dissenting Opinion:* Justice Murphy, in which Douglas and Rutledge, JJ., joined; *Justice Taking No Part in Decision:* Justice Black; *Appellate Defense Counsel:* Nesbitt Elmore argued; Thurgood Marshall on brief; *Appellate Prosecution Counsel:* Bernard F. Sykes argued and briefed; *Amicus Curiae Brief Supporting Prosecutor:* None; *Amicus Curiae Brief Supporting Defendant:* None.

Issue Presented: Whether the defendant was deprived of due process when the Alabama Supreme Court denied him permission to file a petition for a writ of coram nobis in the trial court?

Case Holding: The defendant was not deprived of due process when the Alabama Supreme Court denied him permission to file a petition for a writ of coram nobis in the trial court.

Factual and procedural background of case: The defendant, Samuel Taylor, was convicted of rape and sentenced to death by the State of Alabama. The Alabama Supreme Court affirmed the conviction and sentence. Shortly before his scheduled execution, the defendant filed a petition in the Alabama Supreme Court seeking an order granting him permission to file a petition for a writ of coram nobis in the trial court. As grounds for the request, the defendant argued that his confession to committing the crime was involuntary. The appellate court denied the request and dismissed the petition. The United States Supreme Court granted certiorari to consider the issue.

Opinion of the Court by Justice Burton: Justice Burton held that the Due Process Clause was not violated when the defendant was denied permission to file a petition for writ of coram nobis with the trial court. In finding that due process was not violated in the case, Justice Burton indicated that there was no allegation by the defendant that false testimony was presented at the trial. Nor did the defendant deny his guilt. The opinion reasoned that the purported evidence of a forced confession, if true, was known to the defendant at the time of trial, but he did not raise the issue then. Under the circumstances of the case, the opinion found that the Alabama Supreme Court's denial of permission to file a petition for a writ of coram nobis was not arbitrary. The judgment of the Alabama Supreme Court was affirmed.

Concurring opinion by Justice Frankfurter: Justice Frankfurter concurred in the Court's decision. He wrote that Alabama provided procedures to ensure that a defendant received a fair trial, and provided procedures for review of convictions and sentences. Justice Frankfurter believed that Alabama's procedures satisfied due process and that the defendant was not denied due process in the case.

Dissenting opinion by Justice Murphy, in which Douglas and Rutledge, JJ., joined: Justice Murphy dissented from the Court's decision. He believed that the Due Process Clause was violated in the case. Justice Murphy wrote as follows:

> One of the fixed principles of due process, as guaranteed by the Fourteenth Amendment, is that no conviction in a state court is valid which is based in whole or in part upon an involuntary confession. Wherever a confession is shown to be the product of mental or physical coercion rather than reasoned and voluntary choice, the conviction is void. And it is void even though the confession is in fact true and even though there is adequate evidence otherwise to sustain the conviction.
>
> The problem in this case is whether the [defendant], having been found guilty of rape and sentenced to death, is now entitled to a hearing on his allegation that the confession introduced at the trial was obtained by coercive methods. The Supreme

Court of Alabama refused to allow a hearing on the theory that the allegation was unreasonable. In affirming that refusal, however, this Court relies upon considerations which are either irrelevant, inconclusive or contrary to the constitutional principle just discussed.

Fortunately, this Court has not yet made a final and conclusive answer to [the defendant's] All that has been decided here is that the Supreme Court of Alabama did not err in declining to permit him to file a petition for writ of coram nobis in the Alabama courts. Nothing has been held which prejudices petitioner's right to proceed by way of habeas corpus in a federal district court, now that he has exhausted his state remedies. He may yet obtain the hearing which Alabama has denied him.

Case note: Under modern capital punishment law, the death penalty may not be imposed for the crime of rape, without an accompanying homicide. *See also* **Coram Nobis; Rape and Capital Punishment**

Tennessee

Tennessee The State of Tennessee is a capital punishment jurisdiction. The State reenacted its death penalty law after the United States Supreme Court decision in *Furman v. Georgia,* 408 U.S. 238 (1972), on February 27, 1974.

Tennessee has a three-tier legal system. The State's legal system is composed of a supreme court, court of appeals and courts of general jurisdiction. The Tennessee Supreme Court is presided over by a chief justice and four associate justices. The Tennessee Court of Criminal Appeals is divided into three divisions. Each division has four judges. The courts of general jurisdiction in the State are called Criminal Courts. Capital offenses against the State of Tennessee are tried in the Criminal Courts.

Members of the Tennessee Supreme Court: (left to right standing) *Justice Frank F. Drowota, III, Justice Adolpho A. Birch, Jr., Justice William M. Barker, and Justice Janice M. Holder;* (seated) *Chief Justice E. Riley Anderson. (Tennessee Supreme Court)*

Tennessee's capital punishment statute is triggered if a person commits a homicide under the following special circumstances:

1. Premeditated and intentional killing of another;
2. A killing of another committed in the perpetration of or attempt to perpetrate any first degree murder, arson, rape, robbery, burglary, theft, kidnaping, aggravated child abuse, aggravated child neglect or aircraft piracy; or
3. A killing of another committed as the result of the unlawful throwing, placing or discharging of a destructive device or bomb.

Capital murder in Tennessee is punishable by death or life imprisonment with or without parole. A capital prosecution in Tennessee is bifurcated into a guilt phase and penalty phase. A jury is used at both phases of a capital trial. It is required that, at the penalty phase, the jury unanimously agree that a death sentence is appropriate before it can be imposed. If the penalty phase jury is unable to reach a verdict, the trial judge is required to impose a sentence of life imprisonment. The decision of a penalty phase jury is binding on the trial court under the laws of Tennessee.

In order to impose a death sentence upon a defendant under Tennessee law, it is required that the prosecutor establish the existence of at least one of the following statutory aggravating circumstances at the penalty phase:

1. The murder was committed against a person less than 12 years of age and the defendant was 18 years of age, or older;
2. The defendant was previously convicted of one or more felonies, other than the present charge, whose statutory elements involve the use of violence to the person;
3. The defendant knowingly created a great risk of death to two or more persons, other than the victim murdered, during the act of murder;
4. The defendant committed the murder for remuneration or the promise of remuneration or employed another to commit the murder for remuneration or the promise of remuneration;
5. The murder was especially heinous, atrocious, or cruel in that it involved torture or serious physical abuse beyond that necessary to produce death;
6. The murder was committed for the purpose of avoiding, interfering with, or preventing a lawful arrest or prosecution of the defendant or another;
7. The murder was knowingly committed, solicited, directed, or aided by the defendant, while the defendant had a substantial role in committing or attempting to commit, or was fleeing after having a substantial role in committing or attempting to commit, any first degree murder, arson, rape, robbery, burglary, theft, kidnapping, aircraft piracy, or unlawful throwing, placing or discharging of a destructive device or bomb;
8. The murder was committed by the defendant while the defendant was in lawful custody or in a place of lawful confinement or during the defendant's escape from lawful custody or from a place of lawful confinement;
9. The murder was committed against any law enforcement officer, corrections official, corrections employee, emergency medical or rescue worker, emergency medical technician, paramedic or firefighter, who was engaged in the performance of official duties;
10. The murder was committed against any present or former judge, district attorney general or state attorney general, assistant district attorney general or assistant state attorney general due to or because of the exercise of the victim's official duty or status and the defendant knew that the victim occupied such office;
11. The murder was committed against a national, state, or local popularly elected official, due to or because of the official's lawful duties or status, and the defendant knew that the victim was such an official;

12. The defendant committed mass murder, which is defined as the murder of three or more persons whether committed during a single criminal episode or at different times within a 48-month period;

13. The defendant knowingly mutilated the body of the victim after death; or

14. The victim of the murder was 70 years of age or older; or the victim of the murder was particularly vulnerable due to a significant handicap or significant disability, whether mental or physical.

Although the Federal Constitution will not permit jurisdictions to prevent capital felons from presenting all relevant mitigating evidence at the penalty phase, Tennessee has provided the following statutory mitigating circumstances that permit the jury to reject imposition of the death penalty:

1. The defendant has no significant history of prior criminal activity;

2. The murder was committed while the defendant was under the influence of extreme mental or emotional disturbance;

3. The victim was a participant in the defendant's conduct or consented to the act;

4. The murder was committed under circumstances which the defendant reasonably believed to provide a moral justification for the defendant's conduct;

5. The defendant was an accomplice in the murder committed by another person and the defendant's participation was relatively minor;

6. The defendant acted under extreme duress or under the substantial domination of another person;

7. The youth or advanced age of the defendant at the time of the crime;

8. The capacity of the defendant to appreciate the wrongfulness of the defendant's conduct or to conform the defendant's conduct to the requirements of the law was substantially impaired as a result of mental disease or defect or intoxication which was insufficient to establish a defense to the crime but which substantially affected the defendant's judgment; and

9. Any other mitigating factor which is raised by the evidence produced by either the prosecution or defense at either the guilt or sentencing hearing.

Under Tennessee's capital punishment statute, a sentence of death is automatically reviewed by the Tennessee Supreme Court. Tennessee uses lethal injection to carry out death sentences. Inmates on death row as of December 31, 1998 may choose between lethal injection and electrocution. The State's death row facilities for men and women are located in Nashville, Tennessee.

Pursuant to the laws of Tennessee the Governor has authority to grant clemency in capital cases. The Governor may commute a capital felon's death sentence to life imprisonment if the Tennessee Supreme Court determines the sentence warrants commutation.

From the start of modern capital punishment in 1976,

through 1999, Tennessee did not execute any capital felon. A total of 104 capital felons were on death row in Tennessee in 1999. The 1999 death row population in the State was listed as: 34 black inmates; 63 white inmates; and 7 unidentified inmates. Two death row inmates were female. The State does not permit capital punishment to be imposed on persons 17 years old or younger. Tennessee prohibits the execution of mentally retarded capital felons.

EXECUTIONS BY TENNESSEE 1930–1999

97.9% 4364   2.1% 93

▪ TENNESSEE
■ ALL OTHER JURISDICTIONS

Tennessee Coalition to Abolish State Killing The Tennessee Coalition to Abolish State Killing was formed for the purpose of working to abolish capital punishment in Tennessee and the United States. The organization is active in working to educate the public about capital punishment.

Texas The State of Texas is a capital punishment jurisdiction. The State reenacted its death penalty law after the United States Supreme Court decision in *Furman v. Georgia*, 408 U.S. 238 (1972), on January 1, 1974.

Texas has a three-tier legal system. The State's legal system is composed of a supreme court, court of appeals and courts of general jurisdiction. The Texas Supreme Court is presided over by a chief justice and eight associate justices. The Texas Court of Criminal Appeals is composed of a presiding judge and eight judges. The Court of Criminal Appeals has the final appellate jurisdiction over all criminal cases. The courts of general jurisdiction in the State are called District Courts. Capital

John Cornyn is the Texas Attorney General. His office represents the State in capital punishment appellate proceedings. (Texas Attorney General Office)

offenses against the State of Texas are tried in the District Courts.

Texas' capital punishment statute is triggered if a person commits a homicide under the following special circumstances:

1. the offender murders a peace officer or fireman who is acting in the lawful discharge of an official duty;
2. the offender intentionally commits the murder in the course of committing or attempting to commit kidnaping, burglary, robbery, aggravated sexual assault, arson, or obstruction or retaliation;
3. the offender commits the murder for remuneration or the promise of remuneration or employs another to commit the murder for remuneration or the promise of remuneration;
4. the offender commits the murder while escaping or attempting to escape from a penal institution;
5. the offender, while incarcerated in a penal institution, murders another who is employed in the operation of the penal institution;
6. the offender while incarcerated murders another;
7. the offender murders more than one person:
8. the offender murders an individual under six years of age.

Capital murder in Texas is punishable by death or life imprisonment. A capital prosecution in Texas is bifurcated into a guilt phase and penalty phase. A jury is used at both phases of a capital trial. It is required that, at the penalty phase, the jury unanimously agree that a death sentence is appropriate before it can be imposed. If the penalty phase jury is unable to reach a verdict, the trial judge is required to impose a sentence of life imprisonment. The decision of a penalty phase jury is binding on the trial court under the laws of Texas.

In order to impose a death sentence upon a defendant under Texas law, it is required that the jury answer the first two following special issues affirmatively and the third special issue negatively:

1. whether there is a probability that the defendant would commit criminal acts of violence that would constitute a continuing threat to society; and
2. in cases in which the jury charge at the guilt phase permitted the jury to find the defendant guilty as an accomplice, whether the defendant actually caused the death of the deceased or did not actually cause the death of the deceased but intended to kill the deceased or another or anticipated that a human life would be taken.
3. Whether, taking into consideration all of the evidence, including the circumstances of the offense, the defendant's character and background, and the personal moral culpability of the defendant, there is a sufficient mitigating circumstance or circumstances to warrant that a sentence of life imprisonment rather than a death sentence be imposed.

Texas does not provide by statute any mitigating circumstances to the imposition of the death penalty. Even though the State does not provide statutory mitigating circumstances, the United States Supreme Court has ruled that all relevant mitigating evidence must be allowed at the penalty phase.

Under Texas' capital punishment statute, a sentence of death is automatically reviewed by the Texas Court of Criminal Appeals. Texas uses lethal injection to carry out death sentences. The State's death row facility for men is located in Huntsville, Texas; while the facility maintaining female death row inmates is located in Gatesville, Texas.

Pursuant to the laws of Texas the Governor has authority to grant clemency in capital cases. The Governor must obtain the consent of the State's Board of Pardons and Paroles in order to grant clemency.

From the start of modern capital punishment in 1976, through 1999, Texas executed 199 capital felons. During this

Executions by Texas 1976–1989

Name	Race	Date of Execution	Method of Execution
Charlie Brooks	Black	December 7, 1982	Lethal Injection
James Autry	White	March 14, 1984	Lethal Injection
Ronald O'Bryan	White	March 31, 1984	Lethal Injection
Thomas Barefoot	White	October 30, 1984	Lethal Injection
Dovle Skillern	White	January 16, 1985	Lethal Injection
Stephen P. Morin	White	March 13, 1985	Lethal Injection
Jesse Rosa	Hispanic	May 15 1985	Lethal Injection
Charles Milton	Black	June 25, 1985	Lethal Injection
Henry M. Porter	Hispanic	July 9, 1985	Lethal Injection
Charles Rumbaugh	White	September 11, 1985	Lethal Injection
Charles W. Bass	White	March 12, 1986	Lethal Injection
Jeffrey A. Barney	White	April 16, 1986	Lethal Injection
Jay Pinkerton	White	May 15, 1986	Lethal Injection
Rudy Esquivel	Hispanic	June 9, 1986	Lethal Injection
Kenneth Brock	White	June 18, 1986	Lethal Injection
Randy Woolls	White	August 20, 1986	Lethal Injection
Larry Smith	Black	August 22, 1986	Lethal Injection
Charles Wicker	White	August 26, 1986	Lethal Injection
Michael W. Evans	Black	December 4, 1986	Lethal Injection
Richard Andrade	Hispanic	December 18, 1986	Lethal Injection
Ramon Hernandez	Hispanic	January 30, 1987	Lethal Injection
Elisio Moreno	Hispanic	March 4, 1987	Lethal Injection
Anthony Williams	Black	May 28, 1987	Lethal Injection
Elliott Johnson	Black	June 24, 1987	Lethal Injection
John R. Thompson	White	July 8, 1987	Lethal Injection
Joseph Starvaggi	White	September 10, 1987	Lethal Injection
Robert Streetman	White	January 7, 1988	Lethal Injection
Donald G. Franklin	Black	November 3, 1988	Lethal Injection
Raymond Landry	Black	December 13, 1988	Lethal Injection
Leon R. King	Black	March 22, 1989	Lethal Injection
Stephen McCoy	White	May 24, 1989	Lethal Injection
James Paster	White	September 20, 1989	Lethal Injection
Carlos Luna	Hispanic	December 7, 1989	Lethal Injection

period Texas executed one female capital felon. The State had 8 females on death row during this period. A total of 437 capital felons were on death row in Texas in 1999. The 1999 death row population in the State was listed as: 181 black inmates; 162 white inmates; 87 Hispanic inmates; and 7 unidentified inmates. In 1999 the State had 24 juveniles on death row. The State permits capital punishment to be imposed on persons 17 years old or older. Texas does not prohibit the execution of mentally retarded capital felons.

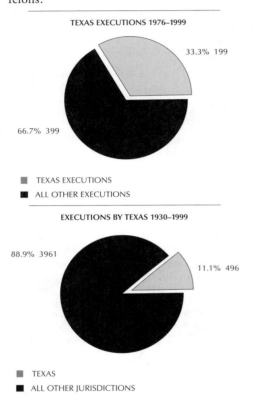

TEXAS EXECUTIONS 1976–1999

33.3% 199

66.7% 399

■ TEXAS EXECUTIONS
■ ALL OTHER EXECUTIONS

EXECUTIONS BY TEXAS 1930–1999

88.9% 3961

11.1% 496

■ TEXAS
■ ALL OTHER JURISDICTIONS

Texas Coalition to Abolish the Death Penalty
The Texas Coalition to Abolish the Death Penalty (TCADP) is a group of organizations and individuals who work for the abolition of the death penalty. The organization believes that capital punishment is not a deterrent to crime, but in fact perpetuates violence. TCADP holds vigils at prison gates and county courthouses whenever executions are scheduled.

Thailand
Thailand permits capital punishment. Thailand uses the firing squad to carry out the death penalty. Its legal system is based on civil law. The nation adopted a new constitution on October 11, 1997.

Executions by Texas 1990–1994

Name	Race	Date of Execution	Method of Execution
Jerome Butler	Black	April 21, 1990	Lethal Injection
Johnny R. Anderson	White	May 17, 1990	Lethal Injection
James Smith	Black	June 26, 1990	Lethal Injection
Mikel Derrick	White	July 18, 1990	Lethal Injection
Lawrence L. Buxton	Black	February 26, 1991	Lethal Injection
Ignacio Cuevas	Hispanic	May 23, 1991	Lethal Injection
James Bird	White	June 17, 1991	Lethal Injection
James Russell	Black	September 19, 1991	Lethal Injection
G. W. Green	White	November 12, 1991	Lethal Injection
Joe A. Cordova	Hispanic	January 22, 1991	Lethal Injection
Johnny F. Garrett	White	February 11, 1992	Lethal Injection
David M. Clark	White	February 28, 1992	Lethal Injection
Edward Ellis	White	March 3, 1992	Lethal Injection
William W. White	Black	April 23, 1992	Lethal Injection
Justin L. May	White	May 7, 1992	Lethal Injection
Jesus Romero	Hispanic	May 20, 1992	Lethal Injection
Robert Black	White	May 22, 1992	Lethal Injection
Curtis L. Johnson	Black	August 11, 1992	Lethal Injection
James Demouchette	Black	September 22, 1992	Lethal Injection
Jeffrey Griffin	Black	November 19, 1992	Lethal Injection
Kevin Lincecum	Black	December 10, 1992	Lethal Injection
Carlos Santana	Hispanic	March 23, 1993	Lethal Injection
Ramon Montoya	Hispanic	March 25, 1993	Lethal Injection
Darryl Stewart	Black	May 5, 1993	Lethal Injection
Leonel Herrera	Hispanic	May 12, 1993	Lethal Injection
James Sawyers	White	May 18, 1993	Lethal Injection
Markham D. Smith	White	June 29, 1993	Lethal Injection
Curtis Harris	Black	July 1, 1993	Lethal Injection
Danny Harris	Black	July 30, 1993	Lethal Injection
Joseph Jernigan	White	August 5, 1993	Lethal Injection
David L. Holland	White	August 12, 1993	Lethal Injection
Carl Kelly	Black	August 20, 1993	Lethal Injection
Ruben Cantu	Hispanic	August 24, 1993	Lethal Injection
Richard Wilkerson	Black	August 31, 1993	Lethal Injection
Johnny James	White	September 3, 1993	Lethal Injection
Antonio Bonham	Black	September 27, 1993	Lethal Injection
Anthony Cook	White	November 10, 1993	Lethal Injection
Clifford Phillips	Black	December 15, 1993	Lethal Injection
Harold Barnard	White	February 2, 1994	Lethal Injection
Freddie L. Webb	Black	March 31, 1994	Lethal Injection
Richard L. Beavers	White	April 4, 1994	Lethal Injection
Larry Anderson	White	April 26, 1994	Lethal Injection
Paul Rougeau	Black	May 3, 1994	Lethal Injection
Stephen Nethery	White	May 26, 1994	Lethal Injection
Denton Crank	White	June 14, 1994	Lethal Injection
Robert Drew	White	August 2, 1994	Lethal Injection
Jessie Guttierrez	Hispanic	September 16, 1994	Lethal Injection
George Lott	White	September 20, 1994	Lethal Injection
Walter Williams	Black	October 5, 1994	Lethal Injection
Warren Bridge	White	November 22, 1994	Lethal Injection
Herman Clark	Black	December 6, 1994	Lethal Injection
Raymond Kinnamon	White	December 11, 1994	Lethal Injection

Executions by Texas 1995–1997

Name	Race	Date of Execution	Method of Execution
Jesse D. Jacobs	White	January 4, 1995	Lethal Injection
Mario S. Marquez	Hispanic	January 17, 1995	Lethal Injection
Clifton Russell	White	January 31, 1995	Lethal Injection
Willie R. Williams	Black	January 31, 1995	Lethal Injection
Jeffrey D. Motley	White	February 7, 1995	Lethal Injection
Billy C. Gardner	White	February 16, 1995	Lethal Injection

Name	Race	Date of Execution	Method of Execution
Samuel Hawkins	Black	February 21, 1995	Lethal Injection
Noble D. Mays	White	April 6, 1995	Lethal Injection
Fletcher T. Mann	White	June 1, 1995	Lethal Injection
Ronald K. Allridge	Black	June 8, 1995	Lethal Injection
John Fearance, Jr.	Black	June 20, 1995	Lethal Injection
Karl Hammond	Black	June 21, 1995	Lethal Injection
Vernon Sattiewhite	Black	August 15, 1995	Lethal Injection
Carl Johnson	Black	September 19, 1995	Lethal Injection
Harold J. Lane	White	October 4, 1995	Lethal Injection
Bernard Amos	Black	December 6, 1995	Lethal Injection
Hai H. Yuong	Asian	December 7, 1995	Lethal Injection
Esequel Banda	Hispanic	December 11, 1995	Lethal Injection
James M. Briddle	White	December 12, 1995	Lethal Injection
Leo Jenkins	White	February 9, 1996	Lethal Injection
Kenneth Granviel	Black	February 27, 1996	Lethal Injection
Joe Gonzales	Hispanic	September 18, 1996	Lethal Injection
Richard Brimage, Jr.	White	February 10, 1997	Lethal Injection
John K. Barefield	Black	March 12, 1997	Lethal Injection
David L. Herman	White	April 2, 1997	Lethal Injection
David Spence	White	April 3, 1997	Lethal Injection
Billy L. Woods	White	April 14, 1997	Lethal Injection
Kenneth Gentry	White	April 16, 1997	Lethal Injection
Benjamin Boyle	White	April 21, 1997	Lethal Injection
Ernest O. Baldree	White	April 29, 1997	Lethal Injection
Terry Washington	Black	May 6, 1997	Lethal Injection
Anthony R. Westley	Black	May 13, 1997	Lethal Injection
Clifton Belyeu	White	May 16, 1997	Lethal Injection
Richard Drinkard	White	May 19, 1997	Lethal Injection
Clarence Lackey	White	May 20, 1997	Lethal Injection
Bruce Callins	Black	May 21, 1997	Lethal Injection
Larry W. White	White	May 22, 1997	Lethal Injection
Robert Madden	White	May 28, 1997	Lethal Injection
Patrick Rogers	White	June 2, 1997	Lethal Injection
Kenneth Harris	White	June 3, 1997	Lethal Injection
Dorsey J. Bey	Black	June 4, 1997	Lethal Injection
Davis Losada	Hispanic	June 4, 1997	Lethal Injection
Earl Behringer	White	June 11, 1997	Lethal Injection
David Stoker	White	June 16, 1997	Lethal Injection
Eddie J. Johnson	Black	June 17, 1997	Lethal Injection
Irineo Montoya	Hispanic	June 18, 1997	Lethal Injection
Robert West	N.A.	July 29, 1997	Lethal Injection
James C. L. Davis	Black	September 9, 1997	Lethal Injection
Jessel Turner	Black	September 22, 1997	Lethal Injection
Benjamin Stone	White	September 25, 1997	Lethal Injection
Johnny Cockrum	White	September 30, 1997	Lethal Injection
Dwight D. Adanandus	Black	October 1, 1997	Lethal Injection
Ricky L. Green	White	October 8, 1997	Lethal Injection
Kenneth R. Ransom	Black	October 28, 1997	Lethal Injection
Aua Lauti	Asian	November 4, 1997	Lethal Injection
Aaron L. Fuller	White	November 6, 1997	Lethal Injection
Michael E. Sharp	White	November 19, 1997	Lethal Injection
Charlie Livingston	Black	November 21, 1997	Lethal Injection
Michael Lockhart	White	December 9, 1997	Lethal Injection

Executions by Texas 1998–1999

Name	Race	Date of Execution	Method of Execution
Karla F. Tucker	White	February 3, 1998	Lethal Injection
Steven Renfro	White	February 3, 1998	Lethal Injection
Jerry L. Hogue	White	March 11, 1998	Lethal Injection
Joseph Cannon	White	April 24, 1998	Lethal Injection
Lesley L. Gosch	White	April 24, 1998	Lethal Injection
Frank B. McFarland	White	April 29, 1998	Lethal Injection
Robert A. Carter	Black	May 18, 1998	Lethal Injection

The judicial system consists of trial courts, courts of appeal, a Supreme Court and a Constitution Court. Defendants enjoy a presumption of innocence. They have the right to retained or appointed legal counsel. There is no trial by jury. Felony crimes are tried by two or more judges. Trials are public. *See also* **International Capital Punishment Nations**

Theory of Accountability

The theory of accountability is nothing more than a restatement of the liability theories of principal in the second degree and accessory before the fact, without a distinction being made as to presence or absence at the crime scene. To sustain a murder charge under the theory of accountability, the prosecutor must show (1) the defendant solicited, aided, abetted, agreed or attempted to aid another person in planning or committing murder, (2) the defendant's act or conduct occurred before or during the commission of murder, and (3) the defendant acted with concurrent specific intent to promote or facilitate the murder.

Under the theory of accountability it is not necessary that the defendant be shown to have had the specific intent to kill or that he or she took part in a preconceived plan to commit murder. Additionally, where individuals conspire to commit a crime wherein they contemplate violence may be necessary to carry out the plan, all such persons are liable for acts done in furtherance of the plan, so that if death occurs all are liable for murder whether present or not during the commission of the crime.

To sustain a prosecution for murder premised on the theory of accountability it is not necessary to have a disposition against the principal killer. The fact that the actual killer of the victim is acquitted will not preclude prosecution of a defendant under the theory of accountability, when it is shown the defendant cooperated in planning the felony which resulted in the victim's death and was an active participant in the felony.

Thiede v. Utah

Court: United States Supreme Court; *Case Citation:* Thiede v. Utah, 159 U.S. 510 (1895); *Argued:* Not reported; *Decided:* November 11, 1895; *Opinion of the Court:* Justice Brewer; *Concurring Opinion:* None; *Dissenting Opinion:* None; *Appellate Defense Counsel:* Not represented;

Name	Race	Date of Execution	Method of Execution
Pedro C. Muniz	Hispanic	May 19, 1998	Lethal Injection
Clifford H. Boggess	White	June 11, 1998	Lethal Injection
Johnny Pyles	White	June 15, 1998	Lethal Injection
Leopoldo Narvaiz	Hispanic	June 26, 1998	Lethal Injection
Genaro R. Camacho	Hispanic	August 26, 1998	Lethal Injection
Delbert Teague	White	September 9, 1998	Lethal Injection
David Castillo	Hispanic	September 23, 1998	Lethal Injection
Javier Cruz	Hispanic	October 1, 1998	Lethal Injection
Jonathan Nobles	White	October 7, 1998	Lethal Injection
Kenneth McDuff	White	November 17, 1998	Lethal Injection
Daniel L. Corwin	White	December 7, 1998	Lethal Injection
Jeff Emery	White	December 8, 1998	Lethal Injection
James R. Meanes	Black	December 15, 1998	Lethal Injection
John G. Moody	White	January 5, 1999	Lethal Injection
Troy Farris	White	January 13, 1999	Lethal Injection
Martin Vega	Hispanic	January 27, 1999	Lethal Injection
George Cordova	Hispanic	February 10, 1999	Lethal Injection
Danny L. Barber	White	February 11, 1999	Lethal Injection
Andrew Cantu	Hispanic	February 16, 1999	Lethal Injection
Norman Green	Black	February 24, 1999	Lethal Injection
Charles Rector	Black	March 25, 1999	Lethal Injection
Robert E. White	White	March 30, 1999	Lethal Injection
Aaron Foust	White	April 28, 1999	Lethal Injection
Jose Cruz	Hispanic	May 4, 1999	Lethal Injection
Clydell Coleman	Black	May 5, 1999	Lethal Injection
William H. Little	White	June 1, 1999	Lethal Injection
Joseph S. Faulder	White	June 17, 1999	Lethal Injection
Charles Tuttle	White	July 1, 1999	Lethal Injection
Tyrone Fuller	Black	July 7, 1999	Lethal Injection
Ricky Blackmon	White	August 4, 1999	Lethal Injection
Charles Boyd	Black	August 5, 1999	Lethal Injection
Kenneth D. Dunn	Black	August 10, 1999	Lethal Injection
James O. Earhart	White	August 11, 1999	Lethal Injection
Joseph Trevino	Hispanic	August 18, 1999	Lethal Injection
Raymond Jones	White	September 1, 1999	Lethal Injection
Willis Barnes	Black	September 10, 1999	Lethal Injection
William Davis	Black	September 14, 1999	Lethal Injection
Richard W. Smith	White	September 21, 1999	Lethal Injection
Alvin Crane	White	October 12, 1999	Lethal Injection
Jerry McFadden	White	October 14, 1999	Lethal Injection
Domingo Cantu	Hispanic	October 28, 1999	Lethal Injection
Desmond Jennings	Black	November 16, 1999	Lethal Injection
John M. Lamb	White	November 17, 1999	Lethal Injection
Jose Gutierrez	Hispanic	November 18, 1999	Lethal Injection
David M. Long	White	December 8, 1999	Lethal Injection
James Beathard	White	December 9, 1999	Lethal Injection
Robert Atworth	White	December 14, 1999	Lethal Injection
Sammie Felder	Black	December 15, 1999	Lethal Injection

Appellate *Prosecution Counsel:* Mr. Dickinson argued and briefed; *Amicus Curiae Brief Supporting Prosecutor:* None; *Amicus Curiae Brief Supporting Defendant:* None.

Issue Presented: Whether the defendant was denied due process of law when a juror was called upon to act as an interpreter for a witness?

Case Holding: The defendant was not denied due process of law when a juror was called upon to act as an interpreter for a witness, because the defendant consented to this arrangement.

Factual and procedural background of case: The defendant, Charles Thiede, was convicted of capital murder and sentenced to death by the State of Utah. The Utah Supreme Court affirmed the judgment. In doing so, the appellate court rejected the defendant's contention that he was denied due process of law because one of the jurors acted as an interpreter for a witness. The United States Supreme Court granted certiorari to consider the issue.

Opinion of the Court by Justice Brewer: Justice Brewer held that the defendant was not denied due process of law because a juror was called upon to act as an interpreter for one of the witnesses. The opinion explained the Court's reasoning as follows: "The record discloses that when [the witness] was called ... [a juror] was sworn as interpreter.... This juror was asked if he fully understood the peculiar dialect of the German language which the witness spoke, and replied that he did, whereupon, with the consent of defendant, he was sworn to act as an interpreter.... We cannot see that in this any substantial right of the defendant was prejudiced. The juror certainly heard all that the witness stated, and was therefore fully prepared to act with the other jurors in considering his testimony, and, as his interpretation of the witness' testimony was with the consent of the defendant, the latter cannot now question its propriety." The judgment of the Utah Supreme Court was affirmed.

Thiel, Werner *see* Espionage

Thomas, Clarence
Clarence Thomas was appointed as an associate justice of the United States Supreme Court in 1991. While on the Supreme Court Thomas has revealed an ultra conservative philosophy in his interpretation of the Constitution.

Thomas was born in Pin Point, Georgia on June 23, 1948. He was a graduate of Holy Cross College in 1971. Thomas received a law degree from Yale University Law School in 1974. He rose quickly in his legal career and was appointed an appellate judge for the Court of Appeals of the District of Columbia in 1990. In 1991 President George Bush nominated Thomas to the Supreme Court.

While on the Supreme Court Thomas has written a number of capital punishment opinions. His capital punishment opinions have been consistent in revealing the ultra conservative philosophy he has brought to other areas of the law. A decision which best illustrates Thomas' ultra conservative philosophy is *O'Dell v. Netherland.* In that case the defendant asked the Supreme Court to find that it was constitutional error for the trial court to refuse to instruct the penalty phase jury that he was parole ineligible, for the purpose of obtaining a life imprisonment sentence. Thomas, writing for the Court, acknowledged that a recent decision by the Court required such an instruction be given if requested. However, Thomas wrote that its previous decision on this issue created a new rule of law that would not be applied retroactive, so as to benefit the defendant. Thomas affirmed the death sentence in the case.

Capital Punishment Opinions Written by Thomas

Case Name	Opinion of the Court	Concurring Opinion	Dissenting Opinion
Dawson v. Delaware			✓
Godinez v. Moran	✓		
Graham v. Collins		✓	
Hopkins v. Reeves	✓		
Johnson v. Texas		✓	
Jones v. United States (II)	✓		
Lilly v. Virginia		✓	
Lockhart v. Fretwell		✓	
Loving v. United States		✓	
McFarland v. Scott			✓
O'Dell v. Netherland	✓		
Riggins v. Nevada			✓
Stewart v. Martinez-Villareal	✓		

Thomas v. Arizona

Court: United States Supreme Court; *Case Citation:* Thomas v. Arizona, 356 U.S. 390 (1958); *Argued:* March 4–5, 1958; *Decided:* May 19, 1958; *Opinion of the Court:* Justice Clark; *Concurring Opinion:* None; *Dissenting Statement:* Chief Justice Warren, and Black, Douglas and Brennan, JJ.; *Appellate Defense Counsel:* W. Edward Morgan argued and briefed; Appellate *Prosecution Counsel:* Wesley E. Polley and John G. Pidgeon argued; Robert Morrison and James H. Green, Jr. on brief; *Amicus Curiae Brief Supporting Prosecutor:* None; *Amicus Curiae Brief Supporting Defendant:* None.

Issue Presented: Whether the defendant's confession, given before a judicial officer, was voluntary?

Case Holding: The defendant's confession, given before a judicial officer, was voluntary.

Factual and procedural background of case: The defendant, Thomas, was convicted of capital murder and sentenced to death. The Arizona Supreme Court affirmed the conviction and sentence. In doing so, the appellate court rejected the defendant's contention that his confession was involuntary. The defendant filed a habeas corpus petition in a Federal District Court. The petition was dismissed. A Federal Court of Appeals affirmed. The United States Supreme Court granted certiorari to consider the issue.

Opinion of the Court by Justice Clark: Justice Clark ruled that the defendant's confession, given before a judicial officer, was not involuntary. The opinion stated: "On all the undisputed facts here, [the defendant's] confession before the Justice of the Peace is not shown to be the product of fear, duress or coercion.... [The defendant's] reliance on certain disputed facts is misplaced, for this Court's inquiry is limited to the undisputed portions of the record when either the trial judge or the jury, with superior opportunity to gauge the truthfulness of witnesses' testimony, has found the confession to be voluntary." The judgment of the Court of Appeals was affirmed.

Dissenting statement by Chief Justice Warren, and Black, Douglas and Brennan, JJ.: The Chief Justice and Justices Black, Douglas and Brennan issued a joint statement indicating they dissented from the Court's decision. *See also* **Right to Remain Silent**

Thomas v. Texas

Court: United States Supreme Court; *Case Citation:* Thomas v. Texas, 212 U.S. 278 (1909); *Argued:* November 3, 1908; *Decided:* February 23, 1909; *Opinion of the Court:* Chief Justice Fuller; *Concurring Opinion:* None; *Dissenting Opinion:* None; *Appellate Defense Counsel:* Noah Allen argued; Frederick S. Tyler on brief; Appellate *Prosecution Counsel:* Robert Vance Davidson argued; James DuBose Walthall on brief; *Amicus Curiae Brief Supporting Prosecutor:* None; *Amicus Curiae Brief Supporting Defendant:* None.

Issue Presented: Whether the defendant established that blacks were systematically excluded from the grand jury that indicted him and the petit jury that convicted him?

Case Holding: The defendant failed to establish that blacks were systematically excluded from the grand jury that indicted him and the petit jury that convicted him.

Factual and procedural background of case: The defendant, Marcellus Thomas, was convicted of capital murder and sentenced to death by the State of Texas. The Texas Court of Criminal Appeals affirmed the judgment. In doing so, the appellate court rejected the defendant's contention that blacks were systematically excluded from the grand jury that indicted him and the petit jury that convicted him. The United States Supreme Court granted certiorari to consider the issue.

Opinion of the Court by Chief Justice Fuller: The Chief Justice held that "whether such discrimination was practiced in this case was a question of fact, and the determination of that question adversely to [the defendant] by the trial court and by the court of criminal appeals was decisive, so far as this court is concerned, unless it could be held that these decisions constitute such abuse as amounted to an infraction of the Federal Constitution, which cannot be presumed, and which there is no reason to hold on the record before us." The opinion added that "the careful opinion of the court of criminal appeals, setting forth the evidence, justifies the conclusion of that court that [blacks were] not intentionally or otherwise discriminated against in the selection of the grand and petit jurors." The Chief Justice noted that one black was on the grand jury that indicted the defendant, and several blacks were in the petit jury pool, "although it happened that none of them were drawn out of the jury box." The judgment of the Texas Court of Criminal Appeals was affirmed. *See also* **Discrimination in Grand or Petit Jury Selection**

Thompson v. Missouri

Court: United States Supreme Court; *Case Citation:* Thompson v. Missouri, 171 U.S. 380

(1898); *Argued:* Not reported; *Decided:* May 31, 1898; *Opinion of the Court:* Justice Harlan; *Concurring Opinion:* None; *Dissenting Opinion:* None; *Appellate Defense Counsel:* Charles F. Joy argued; M. C. Early on brief; *Appellate Prosecution Counsel:* E. C. Crow argued and briefed; *Amicus Curiae Brief Supporting Prosecutor:* None; *Amicus Curiae Brief Supporting Defendant:* None.

Issue Presented: Whether application to the defendant of a new rule of evidence that was not the law at the time of his offense violated ex post facto principles?

Case Holding: Application to the defendant of a new rule of evidence that was not the law at the time of his offense did not violate ex post facto principles.

Factual and procedural background of case: The defendant, Thompson, was indicted for capital murder by the State of Missouri. The victim of the crime was killed through the use of strychnine. During the trial the prosecutor sought to establish that a prescription for strychnine was written by the defendant, as well as a threatening letter written to the victim before his death. To connect the defendant to the writings the prosecutor introduced, for handwriting comparison purposes, letters written by the defendant to his wife. The jury ultimately convicted the defendant and he was sentenced to death. On appeal, the Missouri Supreme Court reversed the judgment and awarded a new trial, on the grounds that under the rules of evidence the letters written by the defendant to his wife could not be introduced.

Prior to the defendant's second trial, the Missouri legislature amended the rules of evidence so as to permit handwriting samples to be introduced into evidence for comparison purposes. During the defendant's second trial the letters written to his wife were again introduced into evidence. The defendant was convicted a second time and sentenced to death. The State appellate court affirmed the judgment. In doing so, the appellate court rejected the defendant's contention that ex post facto principles precluded application of the new evidence rule to his case. The United States Supreme Court granted certiorari to consider the issue.

Opinion of the Court by Justice Harlan: Justice Harlan held that the statute of Missouri relating to the comparison of writings was not ex post facto when applied to prosecutions for crimes committed prior to its passage. It was said that the Court could not "perceive any ground upon which to hold a statute to be ex post facto which does nothing more than admit evidence of a particular kind in a criminal case upon an issue of fact which was not admissible under the rules of evidence as enforced by judicial decisions at the time the offense was committed." Justice Harlan presented the Court's reasoning as follows:

> ... The Missouri statute, when applied to this case, did not enlarge the punishment to which the accused was liable when his crime was committed, nor make any act involved in his offense criminal that was not criminal at the time he committed the murder of which he was found guilty. It did not change the quality or degree of his offense. Nor can the new rule ... be characterized as unreasonable; certainly not so unreasonable as

materially to affect the substantial rights of one put on trial for crime. The statute did not require less proof, in amount or degree, than was required at the time of the commission of the crime charged upon him. It left unimpaired the right of the jury to determine the sufficiency or effect of the evidence declared to be admissible, and did not disturb the fundamental rule that the state, as a condition of its right to take the life of an accused, must overcome the presumption of his innocence, and establish his guilt beyond a reasonable doubt. Whether he wrote the prescription for strychnine, or the threatening letter to the [victim], was left for the jury; and the duty of the jury, in that particular, was the same after as before the passage of the statute. The statute did nothing more than remove an obstacle arising out of a rule of evidence that withdrew from the consideration of the jury testimony which, in the opinion of the legislature, tended to elucidate the ultimate, essential fact to be established, namely, the guilt of the accused. Nor did it give the prosecution any right that was denied to the accused. It placed the state and the accused upon an equality, for the rule established by it gave to each side the right to have disputed writings compared with writings proved to the satisfaction of the judge to be genuine. Each side was entitled to go to the jury upon the question of the genuineness of the writing upon which the prosecution relied to establish the guilt of the accused....

> Of course, we are not to be understood as holding that there may not be such a statutory alteration of the fundamental rules in criminal trials as might bring the statute in conflict with the ex post facto clause of the constitution. If, for instance, the statute had taken from the jury the right to determine the sufficiency or effect of the evidence which it made admissible, a different question would have been presented. We mean now only to adjudge that the statute is to be regarded as one merely regulating procedure, and may be applied to crimes committed prior to its passage without impairing the substantial guaranties of life and liberty that are secured to an accused by the supreme law of the land.

The judgment of the Missouri Supreme Court was affirmed.
See also **Ex Post Facto Clause; Rules of Evidence**

Thompson v. Oklahoma *Court:* United States Supreme Court; *Case Citation:* Thompson v. Oklahoma, 487 U.S. 815 (1988); *Argued:* November 9, 1987; *Decided:* June 29, 1988; *Plurality Opinion:* Justice Stevens announced the Court's judgment and delivered an opinion, in which Brennan, Marshall, and Blackmun, JJ., joined; *Concurring Opinion:* Justice O'Connor; *Dissenting Opinion:* Justice Scalia, in which Rehnquist, C.J., and White, J., joined; *Justice Taking No Part in Decision:* Justice Kennedy; *Appellate Defense Counsel:* Harry F. Tepker, Jr., argued; Victor L. Streib on brief; Appellate *Prosecution Counsel:* David W. Lee argued; Robert H. Henry, William H. Luker, Susan Stewart Dickerson, Sandra D. Howard, and M. Caroline Emerson on brief; *Amicus Curiae Brief Supporting Prosecutor:* 20; *Amicus Curiae Brief Supporting Defendant:* 8.

Issue Presented: Whether the Cruel and Unusual Punishment Clause bars executing a convicted capital felon who was 15 years old at the time of the commission of the crime?

Case Holding: The Cruel and Unusual Punishment Clause prohibits the execution of a person who was under 16 years of age at the time of the commission of his or her capital offense.

Factual and procedural background of case: The defendant,

William Wayne Thompson, was charged with capital murder by the State of Oklahoma. At the time of the commission of the offense the defendant was 15 years old. The defendant was tried as an adult, found guilty and sentenced to death. The Oklahoma Court of Criminal Appeals affirmed the conviction and sentence. In doing so, the appellate court rejected the defendant's argument that the federal Constitution prohibited executing him because of his age at the time of the commission of the offense. The United States Supreme Court granted certiorari to consider the issue.

Plurality opinion in which Justice Stevens announced the Court's judgment and in which Brennan, Marshall, and Blackman, JJ., joined: Justice Stevens noted that in determining whether the Eighth Amendment's prohibition against cruel and unusual punishment applied to the defendant's claim, the Court must be guided by the evolving standards of decency that mark the progress of a maturing society. In so doing, the Court had to review relevant legislative enactments and jury determinations and consider the reasons why a civilized society may accept or reject the death penalty for a person less than 16 years old at the time of the crime.

The opinion observed that almost a majority of capital punishment jurisdictions require by statute that a defendant must have attained at least the age of 16 at the time of a capital offense, in order to be sentenced to death. Justice Stevens contended that such a near majority consensus supported the conclusion that it would offend civilized standards of decency to execute a person who was less than 16 years old at the time of his or her offense. It was also said that this conclusion was consistent with the views expressed by respected professional organizations, by other nations that share the Anglo-American heritage, and by the leading members of the Western European community.

Justice Stevens found that the behavior of juries, as evidenced by statistics demonstrating that, although between 18 and 20 persons under the age of 16 were executed during the first half of the 20th century, no such execution has taken place since 1948 despite the fact that thousands of murder cases were tried during that period. Further, only 5 of the 1,393 persons sentenced to death for capital murder during the years 1982 through 1986 were less than 16 at the time of the offense. He concluded that such evidence leads to the unambiguous conclusion that the imposition of the death penalty on a 15-year-old offender is now generally abhorrent to the conscience of the community.

It was also said in the opinion that a juvenile's reduced culpability, and the fact that the application of the death penalty to this class of offenders does not measurably contribute to the essential purposes underlying the penalty, also support the conclusion that the imposition of the penalty on persons under the age of 16 constitutes unconstitutional punishment. Justice Stevens reasoned that given a juvenile's reduced culpability, as well as his or her capacity for growth and society's fiduciary obligations to its children, the retributive purpose underlying the death penalty was simply inapplicable to the execution of a 15-year-old offender.

Moreover, he argued that the deterrence rationale for the penalty is equally unacceptable with respect to such offenders. The likelihood that the teenage offender has made the kind of cold-blooded, cost-benefit analysis that attaches any weight to the possibility of execution is virtually nonexistent. Further, the opinion noted that statistics demonstrate that the vast majority of persons arrested for capital murder are over 16 at the time of the offense. Therefore, it was "fanciful" to believe that a 15-year-old would be deterred by the knowledge that a small number of persons his or her age have been executed during the 20th century. The opinion went on to vacate the judgment of the Oklahoma Court of Criminal Appeals.

Concurring opinion by Justice O'Connor: Justice O'Connor concurred in the Court's judgment. She wrote that although a national consensus forbidding the execution of any person for a crime committed before the age of 16 probably exists, this conclusion should not unnecessarily be adopted as a matter of constitutional law without better evidence than was before the Court.

Dissenting opinion by Justice Scalia, in which Rehnquist, C.J., and White, J., joined: Justice Scalia rejected the Court's judgment that the Constitution barred executing a defendant who was under 16 years of age at the time of the capital offense. He presented his position on the issue as follows:

> … William Wayne Thompson is not a juvenile caught up in a legislative scheme that unthinkingly lumped him together with adults for purposes of determining that death was an appropriate penalty for him and for his crime. To the contrary, Oklahoma first gave careful consideration to whether, in light of his young age, he should be subjected to the normal criminal system at all. That question having been answered affirmatively, a jury then considered whether, despite his young age, his maturity and moral responsibility were sufficiently developed to justify the sentence of death. In upsetting this particularized judgment on the basis of a constitutional absolute, the plurality pronounces it to be a fundamental principle of our society that no one who is as little as one day short of his 16th birthday can have sufficient maturity and moral responsibility to be subjected to capital punishment for any crime. As a sociological and moral conclusion that is implausible; and it is doubly implausible as an interpretation of the United States Constitution.
>
> The text of the Eighth Amendment, made applicable to the States by the Fourteenth, prohibits the imposition of "cruel and unusual punishments." The plurality does not attempt to maintain that this was originally understood to prohibit capital punishment for crimes committed by persons under the age of 16; the evidence is unusually clear and unequivocal that it was not. The age at which juveniles could be subjected to capital punishment was explicitly addressed in Blackstone's Commentaries on the Laws of England, published in 1769 and widely accepted at the time the Eighth Amendment was adopted as an accurate description of the common law. According to Blackstone, not only was 15 above the age at which capital punishment could theoretically be imposed; it was even above the age (14) up to which there was a rebuttable presumption of incapacity to commit a capital (or any other) felony…. The historical practice in this country conformed with the common-law understanding that 15-year-olds were not categorically immune from commission of capital crimes. One scholar has documented 22 executions, between 1642 and 1899, for crimes committed under the age of 16….

When the Federal Government, and ... a majority of the States that include capital punishment as a permissible sanction, allow for the imposition of the death penalty on any juvenile who has been tried as an adult, which category can include juveniles under 16 at the time of the offense, it is obviously impossible for the plurality to rely upon any evolved societal consensus discernible in legislation — or at least discernible in the legislation of this society, which is assuredly all that is relevant. Thus, the plurality falls back upon what it promises will be an examination of "the behavior of juries." It turns out not to be that, perhaps because of the inconvenient fact that no fewer than five murderers who committed their crimes under the age of 16 were sentenced to death, in five different States, between the years 1984 and 1986. Instead, the plurality examines the statistics on capital executions, which are of course substantially lower than those for capital sentences because of various factors, most notably the exercise of executive clemency. Those statistics show, unsurprisingly, that capital punishment for persons who committed crimes under the age of 16 is rare. We are not discussing whether the Constitution requires such procedures as will continue to cause it to be rare, but whether the Constitution prohibits it entirely.

See also **Juveniles; Stanford v. Kentucky**

Thompson v. United States   *Court:* United States Supreme Court; *Case Citation:* Thompson v. United States, 155 U.S. 271 (1894); *Argued:* Not reported; *Decided:* December 3, 1894; *Opinion of the Court:* Justice Shiras; *Concurring Opinion:* None; *Dissenting Opinion:* None; *Appellate Defense Counsel:* A. H. Garland argued and briefed; *Appellate Prosecution Counsel:* Mr. Whitney argued and briefed; *Amicus Curiae Brief Supporting Prosecutor:* None; *Amicus Curiae Brief Supporting Defendant:* None.

Issues Presented: (1) Whether principles of double jeopardy prevented the retrial of the defendant after the trial court granted a mistrial of the first prosecution? (2) Whether the jury was properly instructed to consider evidence of the victim's previous threats to the defendant as evidence against the defendant?

Case Holdings: (1) Principles of double jeopardy did not prevent the retrial of the defendant after the trial court granted a mistrial of the first prosecution, because manifest necessity for the mistrial was shown. (2) The jury was improperly instructed to consider evidence of the victim's previous threats to the defendant as evidence against the defendant, because such evidence should have received as tending to establish self-defense.

Factual and procedural background of case: The defendant, Thomas Thompson, was convicted of capital murder and sentenced to death by the United States. At the trial it was determined that both the defendant and the victim were Native Americans. The defendant appealed the judgment against him to the United States Supreme Court. In the appeal the defendant alleged that the trial court improperly declared a mistrial and that his subsequent retrial violated the Double Jeopardy Clause. It was also contended that the trial court improperly instructed the jury on previous threats made by the victim, so as to preclude the jury from considering such threats

as evidence tending to establish self-defense. The United States Supreme Court granted certiorari to consider the issues.

Opinion of the Court by Justice Shiras: Justice Shiras indicated that the trial court granted a mistrial, over the defendant's objection, after it was learned that one of the petit jurors was also a member of the grand jury that indicted the defendant. The opinion held that it was not error for the trial court to grant a mistrial under the circumstances presented. In rejecting the double jeopardy argument, Justice Shiras wrote: "As to the question raised by the plea of former jeopardy ... courts of justice are invested with the authority to discharge a jury from giving any verdict whenever, in their opinion, taking all the circumstances into consideration, there is a manifest necessity for the act, or the ends of public justice would otherwise be defeated, and to order a trial by another jury; and that the defendant is not thereby twice put in jeopardy, within the meaning of the fifth amendment to the constitution of the United States."

In turning to the defendant's second assignment of error, Justice Shiras ruled that the trial court improperly instructed the jury to consider previous threats by the victim as evidence against the defendant. The opinion addressed the matter as follows:

> ... The learned judge seems to have regarded such evidence not merely as not extenuating or excusing the act of the defendant, but as evidence from which the jury might infer special spite, special ill will, on the part of the defendant....
>
> While it is no doubt true that previous threats will not, in all circumstances, justify, or perhaps even extenuate, the act of the party threatened in killing the person who uttered the threats, yet it by no means follows that such threats, signifying ill will and hostility on the part of the deceased, can be used by the jury as indicating a similar state of feeling on the part of the defendant. Such an instruction was not only misleading in itself, but it was erroneous in the present case, for the further reason that it omitted all reference to the alleged conduct of the deceased at the time of the killing, which went to show an intention then and there to carry out the previous threats.

The judgment of the Federal trial court was reversed and the case remanded for a new trial. *See also* **Double Jeopardy Clause; Mistrial; Self-Defense**

Three-Judge Panel *see* **Jury Trial**

Tison v. Arizona   *Court:* United States Supreme Court; *Case Citation:* Tison v. Arizona, 481 U.S. 137 (1987); *Argued:* November 3, 1986; *Decided:* April 21, 1987; *Opinion of the Court:* Justice O'Connor; *Concurring Opinion:* None; *Dissenting Opinion:* Justice Brennan, in which Marshall, Blackmun and Stevens, JJ., joined; *Appellate Defense Counsel:* Alan M. Dershowitz argued; Stephen H. Oleskey, Cynthia O. Hamilton, Susan Estrich, and Nathan Dershowitz on brief; *Appellate Prosecution Counsel:* William J. Schafer III argued; Robert K. Corbin on brief; *Amicus Curiae Brief Supporting Prosecutor:* None; *Amicus Curiae Brief Supporting Defendant:* None.

Issue Presented: Whether the Eighth Amendment prohibits the death penalty in the intermediate case of the defendant whose participation is major and whose mental state is one of reckless indifference to the value of human life?

Case Holding: The Constitution permits the death penalty in the intermediate case of the defendant whose participation is major and whose mental state is one of reckless indifference to the value of human life.

Factual and procedural background of case: The defendants, brothers Raymond and Ricky Tison, were prosecuted for capital murder by the State of Arizona. The defendants, along with other accomplices, helped a relative escape from prison. During the prison escape and afterwards, several people were killed. Both defendants were convicted and sentenced to death. After the Arizona Supreme Court affirmed the defendants' convictions for capital murder under that State's felony murder statute, the defendants collaterally attacked their death sentences in state post-conviction proceedings. The defendants alleged that under the United States Supreme Court decision in *Enmund v. Florida*, they could not be sentenced to death because they did not intend to kill. The State appellate court determined that *Enmund* did not preclude executing them because they played an active part in planning and executing the prison escape and in the events that lead to the murders, and that they did nothing to interfere with the killings nor to disassociate themselves from the killers afterward. The United States Supreme Court granted certiorari to consider the issue.

Opinion of the Court by Justice O'Connor: Justice O'Connor recognized that under *Enmund* the death penalty could not be imposed upon a defendant who neither took life, attempted to take life, nor intended to take life. The opinion distinguished the facts contemplated by *Enmund* from the conduct of the defendants. Justice O'Connor wrote that the defendants' conduct fell "outside the category of felony murderers for whom *Enmund* explicitly held the death penalty disproportional: their degree of participation in the crimes was major rather than minor, and the record would support a finding of the culpable mental state of reckless indifference to human life."

It was said that although the defendants neither intended to kill the victims nor inflicted the fatal wounds, the record might support a finding that they had the culpable mental state of reckless indifference to human life. The opinion ruled that the Constitution did not prohibit the death penalty as disproportionate in the case of a defendant whose participation in a felony that results in murder is major and whose mental state is one of reckless indifference.

Because the Arizona Supreme Court did not analyze the case under the standard adopted by the opinion, the judgments were vacated and the case remanded for further consideration.

Dissenting opinion by Justice Brennan, in which Marshall, Blackmun and Stevens, JJ., joined: Justice Brennan argued in dissent that the felony murder doctrine could not be used to impose a death sentence on a person who neither killed nor intended to kill. In ridiculing the felony murder doctrine he said that it "is a living fossil from a legal era in which all felonies were punishable by death; in those circumstances, the state of mind of the felon with respect to the murder was understandably superfluous, because he or she could be executed simply for intentionally committing the felony. Today, in most American jurisdictions and in virtually all European and Commonwealth countries, a felon cannot be executed for a murder that he or she did not commit or specifically intend or attempt to commit."

The dissent criticized the Court for creating a new doctrine of liability out of the felony murder rule. Justice Brennan wrote concisely: "The Court has chosen ... to announce a new substantive standard for capital liability: a defendant's 'major participation in the felony committed, combined with reckless indifference to human life'.... I join no part of this."

Finally, Justice Brennan contended that even under the new culpability standard announced by the Court, its analysis should not have ended on that point. The dissent reasoned: "Creation of a new category of culpability is not enough to distinguish this case from *Enmund*. The Court must also establish that death is a proportionate punishment for individuals in this category. In other words, the Court must demonstrate that major participation in a felony with a state of mind of reckless indifference to human life deserves the same punishment as intending to commit a murder or actually committing a murder. The Court does not attempt to conduct a proportionality review of the kind performed in past cases raising a proportionality question[.]"

Case note: The majority opinion in the case received some legal criticism because of its distortion of the common law felony murder rule. *See also* **Enmund v. Florida; Felony Murder Rule; Mens Rea**

Tla-Koo-Yel-Lee v. United States

Court: United States Supreme Court; *Case Citation:* Tla-Koo-Yel-Lee v. United States, 167 U.S. 274 (1897); *Argued:* Not reported; *Decided:* May 24, 1897; *Opinion of the Court:* Justice Peckham; *Concurring Opinion:* None; *Dissenting Opinion:* None; *Appellate Defense Counsel:* Not represented; Appellate *Prosecution Counsel:* Mr. Conrad argued and briefed; *Amicus Curiae Brief Supporting Prosecutor:* None; *Amicus Curiae Brief Supporting Defendant:* None.

Issue Presented: Whether the trial court committed error in limiting the defendant's ability to show that a key witness was biased and had a motive to testify falsely?

Case Holding: The trial court committed error in limiting the defendant's ability to show that a key witness was biased and had a motive to testify falsely.

Factual and procedural background of case: The defendant, Tla-Koo-Yel-Lee, and Tak-Ke (both Native Americans) were indicted for capital murder by the United States. Separate trials occurred. During the defendant's trial two alleged eyewitnesses to the crime testified. One of the witnesses,

Tlak-Sha, was the wife of Tak-Ke (she would eventually testify against her husband). The defendant attempted to show bias and motive to testify falsely on the part Tlak-Sha, by establishing that she was having a relationship with the other eyewitness to the crime. The defense's theory was that Tlak-Sha wanted to get rid of her husband, therefore she was motivated to testify falsely against the defendant in order to bolster her testimony against her husband when his trial took place. The trial court would not allow the defendant to question Tlak-Sha about her relationship with the other witness. The jury convicted the defendant and he was sentenced to death. The defendant appealed to the United States Supreme Court, alleging it was error for the trial court to limit his questioning of Tlak-Sha. The United States Supreme Court granted certiorari to consider the issue.

Opinion of the Court by Justice Peckham: Justice Peckham held that it was critical for the defendant to be able to question Tlak-Sha about her relationship with the other alleged eyewitness. It was said that the defendant had a right "to show to the jury, if possible, the bias, if any, of the witness against the defendant, or to show that her credibility was not to be depended upon by the jury." Justice Peckham found that the questions the defendant sought to ask Tlak-Sha "were directed to the purpose of showing material facts bearing upon the character and credibility of the witness[.]" The judgment of the Federal trial court was reversed and the case remanded for a new trial.

Togo Capital punishment may be imposed in Togo, but the punishment has not been used in over a decade. Togo uses the firing squad to carry out the death penalty. Its legal system is based on French law. Togo adopted a constitution on September 27, 1992.

The judicial system consists of trial courts, appellate courts and a Supreme Court. Trials are open to the public. Defendants have the right to retained or appointed legal counsel and to appeal. They may confront witnesses and enjoy a presumption of innocence. *See also* **International Capital Punishment Nations**

Tonga Capital punishment may be used in Tonga, but the punishment has not been carried out in over a decade. Its legal system is based on English law. Tonga comprises 169 small islands in the South Pacific. Most of the approximately 105,000 inhabitants are Polynesian. Tonga is a constitutional monarchy governed by a King. Tonga adopted a constitution on November 4, 1875.

The judicial system consists of a Supreme Court (trial court) and Court of Appeals. The law provides for the right to a public trial. Defendants are prosecuted by indictment. Defendants are entitled to counsel. The King has the right to commute a death sentence in cases of murder or treason. *See also* **International Capital Punishment Nations**

Torture Aggravator Torture refers to the infliction of great pain and suffering. A large minority of capital punish-

ment jurisdictions have made torture a statutory aggravating circumstance. In such jurisdictions the death penalty may be imposed if it is found at the penalty phase that the victim was tortured before being killed. *See also* **Aggravating Circumstances**

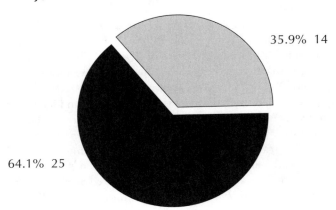

JURISDICTIONS USING TORTURE AGGRAVATOR

35.9% 14

64.1% 25

■ TORTURE AGGRAVATOR JURISDICTIONS

■ ALL OTHER JURISDICTIONS

Townsend v. Sain *Court:* United States Supreme Court; *Case Citation:* Townsend v. Sain, 372 U.S. 293 (1963); *Argued:* February 19, 1962; reargued October 8–9, 1962; *Decided:* March 18, 1963; *Opinion of the Court:* Chief Justice Warren; *Concurring Opinion:* Justice Goldberg; *Dissenting Opinion:* Justice Stewart, in which Clark, Harlan and White, JJ., joined; *Appellate Defense Counsel:* George N. Leighton argued and briefed; Appellate *Prosecution Counsel:* Edward J. Hladis argued; Daniel P. Ward on brief; *Amicus Curiae Brief Supporting Prosecutor:* None; *Amicus Curiae Brief Supporting Defendant:* None.

Issue Presented: Whether the Federal District Court was required to hold an evidentiary hearing on the defendant's habeas corpus petition alleging his confession was involuntary?

Case Holding: The Federal District Court was required to hold an evidentiary hearing on the defendant's habeas corpus petition alleging his confession was involuntary, where the State court record was underdeveloped.

Factual and procedural background of case: The defendant, Charles Townsend, was convicted of capital murder and sentenced to death by the State of Illinois. The Illinois Supreme Court affirmed the conviction and sentence. In doing so, the appellate court rejected the defendant's contention that his confession was involuntarily obtained. The defendant filed a habeas corpus petition in a Federal District Court alleging that his conviction violated the Federal Constitution because of the admission in evidence of a confession obtained while he was under the influence of drugs, including a truth serum, administered by a police physician. The District Court dismissed the petition without an evidentiary hearing. A Federal Court of Appeals affirmed. The United States Supreme Court granted certiorari to consider the issue.

Opinion of the Court by Chief Justice Warren: The Chief Justice set out the underlying facts of the defendant's confession. It was said that the defendant was arrested by Chicago police shortly before or after 2 a. m. on New Year's Day 1954. The defendant was 19 years old at the time and a heroin addict. He was under the influence of heroin before his arrest. During the initial interrogation he denied committing any crime. It was said that the defendant began complaining that he had pains in his stomach, that he was suffering from withdrawal symptoms, that he wanted a doctor, and that he was in need of a dose of narcotics. A police physician was summoned. The doctor gave the defendant a combined dosage by injection of ⅛-grain of phenobarbital and ½₃₀-grain of hyoscine. The opinion noted that it was the hyoscine that was alleged to have the properties of a truth serum. The doctor also left the defendant four or five ¼-grain tablets of phenobarbital. The medication alleviated the discomfort of the withdrawal symptoms, and the defendant promptly responded to questioning by confessing to the murder charge.

The Chief Justice wrote that "[i]t is difficult to imagine a situation in which a confession would be less the product of a free intellect, less voluntary, than when brought about by a drug having the effect of a 'truth serum.'" It was said that "[a]ny questioning by police officers which in fact produces a confession which is not the product of a free intellect renders that confession inadmissible." The opinion held that the defendant satisfactorily alleged a deprivation of constitutional rights that entitled him to an evidentiary hearing before the District Court. As a guide for District Court's in making the determination of whether to hold an evidentiary hearing on a habeas corpus petition, the Chief Justice set out the following:

> Where the facts are in dispute, the Federal District Court must grant an evidentiary hearing if (1) the merits of the factual dispute were not resolved in the state hearing, either at the time of the trial or in a collateral proceeding; (2) the state factual determination is not fairly supported by the record as a whole; (3) the fact-finding procedure employed by the State Court was not adequate to afford a full and fair hearing; (4) there is a substantial allegation of newly discovered evidence; (5) the material facts were not adequately developed at the state-court hearing; or (6) for any reason it appears that the state trier of fact did not afford the applicant a full and fair fact hearing. When the state trier of fact has made no express findings, the District Court must hold an evidentiary hearing if the State Court did not decide the issues of fact tendered to it, if the State Court applied an incorrect standard of constitutional law, or if, for any other reason, the District Court is unable to reconstruct the relevant findings of the state trier of fact. The Federal District Court must carefully scrutinize the state-court record in order to determine whether the factual determinations of the State Court are fairly supported by the record. Even if all the relevant facts were presented in the state-court hearing, it is the Federal Judge's duty to disregard the state findings and take evidence anew, if the procedure employed by the State Court appears to be seriously inadequate for the ascertainment of the truth.

Where newly discovered evidence which could not reasonably have been presented to the State Court is alleged, the Federal Court must grant an evidentiary hearing, unless the allegation of newly discovered evidence is irrelevant, frivolous or incredible. If, for any reason not attributable to the inexcusable neglect of the applicant, evidence crucial to the adequate consideration of his constitutional claim was not developed at the state hearing, the Federal Court must grant an evidentiary hearing. The duty to try the facts anew exists in every case in which the State Court has not, after a full hearing, reliably found the relevant facts.

The judgment of the Court of Appeals was reversed and the case remanded.

Concurring opinion by Justice Goldberg: Justice Goldberg concurred with the Court's decision. He wrote separately to express his disagreements with the arguments made in the dissenting opinion of Justice Stewart. Justice Goldberg indicated that he disagreed with Justice Stewart's conclusion that the voluntariness of the confession was properly resolved at the trial. He also wrote that he disagreed with Justice Stewart's position that the guidelines for District Courts was inappropriate. Justice Goldberg argued that "[t]he setting of certain standards is essential to disposition of this case and a definition of their scope and application is an appropriate exercise of this Court's adjudicatory obligations."

Dissenting opinion by Justice Stewart, in which Clark, Harlan and White, JJ., joined: Justice Stewart dissented from the Court's decision. He believed that the jury properly resolved the issue of the voluntariness of the confession. He also argued that evidence independent of the confession established the defendant's guilt beyond a reasonable doubt. Justice also thought it was unnecessary for the Court to set out standards for holding habeas corpus evidentiary hearings. He wrote: "The Court has done little more today than to supply new phrases — imprecise in scope and uncertain in meaning — for the habeas corpus vocabulary of District Court judges. And because they purport to establish mandatory requirements rather than guidelines, the tests elaborated in the Court's opinion run the serious risk of becoming talismanic phrases, the mechanistic invocation of which will alone determine whether or not a hearing is to be had." *See also* **Habeas Corpus; Right to Remain Silent**

Trailside Killer During the period 1979–1981, David Carpenter placed Northern California in terror because of the numerous dead bodies that were turning up alongside hiking and biking trails. Carpenter's path to becoming the "Trailside Killer" began in 1961 when, at the age of 33, he brutally attacked a woman with a hammer. He was prosecuted for the crime and sentenced to prison for 14 years. In 1970, Carpenter was released from prison. Within months of his release he was arrested for kidnapping and robbery. He was sentenced to seven years for the crimes. He was released in 1977.

Carpenter's life appeared to change on the surface when he was released from prison in 1977. He found steady work in San Francisco in a photo print shop. Two years after Carpenter's release dead bodies began to surface along trailsides.

David Carpenter was sentenced to death for committing seven murders between the period 1979–1981. (California Department of Corrections)

August 20, 1979, the naked body of Edda Kane was discovered on a hiking trail in Mt. Tamalpais State Park, near San Francisco. She had been shot in the head. On March 8, 1980, the body of Barbara Swartz was found in a park along an unpaved trail. She had been stabbed to death. On June 4, 1980, the body of Anna Menjivas was discovered dead in Mt. Tamalpais State Park. She had been shot to death. On October 15, 1980, the body of Anne Alderson was found near a park jogging trail. She had been shot in the head three times.

On November 29, 1980, the bodies of Shauna May and Diana O'Connell were found in a shallow grave near Point Reyes Park. Both women had been shot in the head. Also on November 29, in another section of Point Reyes Park, authorities found the bodies of Richard Stowers and Cynthia Moreland. They had also been shot to death.

On March 29, 1981, Stephen Haertle and Ellen Hansen were ambushed while hiking in Henry Cowle State Park, near Santa Cruz. Hansen was shot to death. Haertle was shot but survived the attack. He was able to give authorities a description of the attacker. On May 24, 1981, the decomposing body of Heather Scaggs was along a trail in Big Basin Redwood State Park, north of San Francisco. She had been shot to death.

Before authorities found Scaggs' body, her reported disappearance had led authorities to Carpenter. Scaggs worked with Carpenter at the print shop. On May 1, Carpenter arranged to meet Scaggs alone for the purpose of selling his car to her. When Scaggs did not return home the police were notified by her boyfriend and informed of her plans to purchase a car from Carpenter.

When the police located Carpenter on May 14, they immediately recognized him from the composite sketch given by Haertle. Carpenter was taken into custody (ten days later the remains of Scaggs were found).

The real evidence connecting Carpenter to the murders came after authorities were able to locate the gun used in several of the murders. Carpenter had sold the gun to a suspect who was being prosecuted for robbery. The barrel markings of the gun matched the bullets that killed Hansen and Scaggs.

Carpenter was prosecuted for the murder of Scaggs and Hansen in 1984. A jury convicted him of the killings and on July 6, 1984, he was sentenced to death. On May 10, 1988, a jury convicted Carpenter of the murder of Moreland, Stowers, O'Connell, May, and Alderson. He was sentenced to death for those murders. Carpenter is on death row in California.

Transcript of Proceeding   All trial level, in-court, proceedings in a capital prosecution are recorded. This includes trial level post-conviction collateral proceedings, such as habeas corpus and coram nobis proceedings. The purpose of recording all trial court level proceedings is for appellate courts to review the record when defendants prosecute appeals. An issue that once plagued defendants, who were indigent, was that of obtaining transcripts free of charge for direct appeals and appeals from collateral attacks on their judgments. It was not until the non-capital case of *Griffin v. Illinois*, 351 U.S. 12 (1956), was decided that the United States Supreme Court ruled that the Constitution required an indigent defendant be provided with a free transcript for an initial direct appeal of his or her conviction. The decision in *Griffin* was extended to appeals from post-conviction collateral proceedings in the capital case of *Lane v. Brown*, 372 U.S. 477 (1963). *See also* **Chessman v. Teets; Lane v. Brown**

Treason   Article III, Section 3, of the Federal Constitution provides for treason as follows: "Treason against the United States shall consist only in levying war against them, or in adhering to their enemies, giving them aid and comfort. No person shall be convicted of treason unless on the testimony of two witnesses to the same overt act, or on confession in open court." The crime of treason has been made punishable by death under Federal law.

The United States Supreme Court has held that under modern capital punishment jurisprudence the death penalty may not generally be imposed for a crime that does not involve a homicide. However, it is doubtful that the Supreme Court would extend this ruling to the crime of treason against the nation. *See also* **Espionage; Kawakita v. United States; Rape and Capital Punishment; Rosenberg v. United States**

Trial Structure   The determination of whether a defendant is guilty of committing a capital offense, and if so, whether he or she should be sentenced to death, are the two issues that make up a single capital trial. All capital punishment jurisdictions decide the issues of guilt and punishment for a capital offense through two separate phases: guilt phase and penalty phase. The separation of a capital trial into two phases serves the federal constitutional purpose of attempting to secure fair and rational imposition of the death penalty as punishment

Capital felons have raised various Federal constitutional arguments for having a separate jury preside over the guilt phase and penalty phase of a capital prosecution. Courts have unanimously ruled that there is no constitutional right to have a different jury hear the guilt phase evidence and penalty phase evidence. A primary consideration in rejecting this argument is that there is no Federal constitutional right to have a jury preside over the penalty phase. When the same jury is seated in both the guilt and penalty phases of a capital prosecution, evidence that is admitted at the guilt phase may be considered by the jury at the penalty phase.

The format for conducting a guilt phase and penalty phase proceeding are generally the same: opening statements, case-in-chief, rebuttal, closing arguments, and charge to the jury.

Opening Statements. The prosecutor and defense counsel are afforded an opportunity to make opening statements to the factfinder at the guilt phase and penalty phase. The opening statement is a nonargumentative summary presentation of the type of evidence each party intends to present to the factfinder. The prosecutor's opening statement generally is given first. In a few capital punishment jurisdictions, a defendant may give his or her penalty phase opening statement first.

Case-in-Chief. Once opening statements have been given, the actual evidence of both parties will be presented. This stage is called case-in-chief. During the guilt phase the prosecutor will always present its case-in-chief first, because the prosecutor has the burden of proving a defendant's guilt. During the penalty phase prosecutors generally give their case-in-chief first, but some jurisdictions permit the defendant to give his or her penalty phase case-in-chief first.

The prosecutor's guilt phase case-in-chief will consist of testimonial and physical evidence that proves each element of the charged offense. The prosecutor's penalty phase case-in-chief will consist of testimonial and physical evidence only on the issue of proving aggravating circumstances.

The prosecutor's examination of witnesses that it calls will be through direct examination. What this means is that the questioning must generally be open-ended and not leading. The capital felon will be afforded an opportunity to cross examine all witnesses called by the prosecutor. Leading questions are permitted on cross examination.

At the conclusion of the prosecutor's guilt phase case-in-chief, the capital felon may, but does not have to, present his or her case-in-chief. A capital felon does not have to put on a guilt phase case-in-chief, because of the presumption of innocence afforded a defendant by Anglo-American jurisprudence. The defendant must put on a penalty phase case-in-chief because there is no presumption of innocence at the penalty phase. The evidence presented by the capital felon during his or her guilt phase case-in-chief will consist of testimonial and physical evidence showing his or her innocence of the crime. The evidence presented by the capital felon during his or her penalty phase case-in-chief will consist of testimonial and physical evidence on the issue of mitigating circumstances.

The capital felon's questioning of witnesses called by him or her will be through direct examination. The prosecutor will be given an opportunity to cross examine witnesses called by the capital felon.

Rebuttal. In the event that an issue was brought out during either of the capital felon's case-in-chiefs, that was not addressed during either of the prosecutor's case-in-chiefs, the trial court has the discretion to allow the prosecutor to pre-

sent rebuttal evidence. Rebuttal evidence refers to evidence that is proffered to explain, repel, counteract, or disprove facts given in evidence by the opposing party. Likewise, if during a prosecutor's rebuttal matters are brought out that were not addressed in a capital felon's case-in-chief, the defendant may present rebuttal evidence.

Closing Arguments. At the conclusion of the presentation of all evidence during the guilt phase and penalty phase, both sides are given an opportunity to give closing arguments at the guilt phase and penalty phase. The purpose of the closing argument is to allow both parties to argue reasons why the factfinder should reject the evidence of the other party. The general rule is that the prosecutor gives its closing argument last. However, a few jurisdictions require the capital felon give his or her penalty phase closing argument last.

Charge to the Jury. If a jury presided over the guilt phase and penalty phase, the trial judge will read jury instructions to the jury at both phases, before the jury retires to deliberate. The charge to the jury informs it of the law that must be applied to the facts presented during the guilt phase and penalty phase. *See also* **Trifurcated Trial**

Trial Transcript *see* Transcript of Proceeding

Tried in Absentia

The Federal Constitution guarantees every defendant the right to be present at criminal proceedings against him or her. This right, however, does not prevent the prosecution of a defendant for capital murder or any crime, in absentia, so long as his or her absence was voluntary and for the purpose of evading prosecution.

Trifurcated Trial

The legal concept of a trifurcated trial has its origin in civil litigation. In the context of civil litigation a trifurcated trial involves holding a trial on liability, a separate trial on general damages and a separate trial on the issue of punitive damages. This civil law trial scheme has found its way into criminal law in a few jurisdictions.

In the context of capital punishment, a trifurcated trial occurs when a capital felon raises the defense of insanity. The trial involving the defense of insanity would take place as follows. First, a trial on the issue of the capital felon's guilt would take place. Next, if the factfinder rendered a verdict of guilty of a capital offense, another proceeding would be held on the issue of the capital felon's defense of insanity. Finally, if the factfinder determined the capital felon was sane at the time of the offense, a penalty phase proceeding would be held to determine whether the capital felon should be sentenced to death. Currently only the capital punishment jurisdictions of California and Colorado employ a trifurcated trial when a capital felon raises the defense of insanity.

In opinions issued by a few courts, the term trifurcated trial is used to describe a capital prosecution that involves an advisory penalty phase jury. In this situation, a defendant's guilt is determined at the guilt phase proceeding. Next, a penalty phase proceeding is held wherein an advisory jury is used.

After the advisory jury renders its recommendation to the trial judge, the trial judge then makes specific findings of fact and conclusions of law as to the penalty to be imposed. It is the separate roles of the advisory jury and the trial court, in conjunction with the guilt phase, that has caused some courts to describe the process as a trifurcated trial. *See also* **Insanity Defense; Trial Structure**

Trinidad and Tobago

Trinidad and Tobago Capital punishment may be carried out in Trinidad and Tobago. Trinidad and Tobago uses hanging as the method of execution. Its legal system is based on English common law. The nation adopted a constitution on August 1, 1976.

The court system consists of a High Court and Court of Appeal. Trials are heard before a judge and jury. Appeals can be filed with the Judicial Committee of the Privy Council in England. Defendants have the right to bail and to an attorney. The law requires a person accused of murder to have an attorney. *See also* **International Capital Punishment Nations**

Tucker, Karla Faye

Tucker, Karla Faye On February 3, 1998, Karla Faye Tucker was executed by the State of Texas. The method of execution was lethal injection. At the time of Tucker's execution she was only the second woman to be executed since the reinstatement of the death penalty in 1976.

The execution of Tucker brought a wave of condemnation from around the world. During Tucker's time on death row she attracted national and international attention and support. She was widely recognized because of her religious conversion and willingness to accept responsibility for the crimes she committed. Her religious supporters included Pope John Paul II and Pat Robertson, founder of the Christian Coalition, and Sister Helen Prejean.

> *Press Release Statement by Mary Robinson United Nations High Commissioner for Human Rights, February 4, 1998*
> I was saddened to learn of the death by lethal injection last night of Karla Faye Tucker who was put to death for murders she committed 15 years ago.
> This was the first execution of a woman in the state of Texas since 1863 and the first in the United States since 1984.
> The increasing use of the death penalty in the United States

and in a number of other states is a matter of serious concern and runs counter to the international community's expressed desire for the abolition of the death penalty.

> As far back as 1971 the United Nations General Assembly called on states to progressively restrict use of the death penalty with a view to its abolition.
> Last year, the Commission on Human Rights called on states which have not yet abolished the death penalty to consider suspending executions with a view to abolishing the death penalty completely.
> The International Covenant on Civil and Political Rights as well as the American and European Conventions on Human Rights have additional protocols providing for the abolition of capital punishment.
> The international trend against the death penalty was evident in the Security Council Resolutions establishing the tribunals for crimes committed in the former Yugoslavia and Rwanda. The Council decided that there would be no application of the death penalty even for crimes against humanity and participation in genocide.
> My own views on the death penalty are reflected in the opening declaration of the Second Protocol to the International Covenant: "abolition of the death penalty contributes to enhancement of human dignity and progressive development of human rights." I have full sympathy for the families of the victims of murder and other crimes but I do not accept that one death justifies another.

The events that led Tucker to the death chamber began in June of 1983. During that time period she and her boyfriend, Daniel Ryan Garrett, murdered Jerry Lynn Dean and Deborah Thornton. Tucker confessed to killing both Dean and Thornton with a pickaxe. Tucker left the pickaxe embedded in Thornton's chest. Garrett died of natural causes in June of 1993. *See also* **Women and Capital Punishment**

Tuggle v. Netherland

Tuggle v. Netherland *Court:* United States Supreme Court; *Case Citation:* Tuggle v. Netherland, 516 U.S. 10 (1995); *Argued:* Not reported; *Decided:* October 30, 1995; *Opinion of the Court:* Per Curiam; *Concurring Opinion:* Justice Scalia; *Dissenting Opinion:* None; *Appellate Defense Counsel:* Not reported; *Appellate Prosecution Counsel:* Not reported; *Amicus Curiae Brief Supporting Prosecutor:* Not reported; *Amicus Curiae Brief Supporting Defendant:* Not reported.

Issue Presented: Whether a death sentence based on multiple statutory aggravating circumstances may automatically be sustained when one aggravating factor is invalid, but the remaining factors are valid?

Case Holding: A death sentence based on multiple statutory aggravating circumstances may not automatically be sustained when one aggravating factor is invalid, but the remaining factors are valid.

Factual and procedural background of case: The defendant, Lem Davis Tuggle, was convicted of capital murder by a Virginia jury. During the penalty phase the prosecutor presented unrebutted psychiatric testimony that the defendant had a high probability of future dangerousness. The defendant was unable to rebut the evidence because he was indigent and could not afford to hire a psychiatric expert to testify on his behalf. The trial court would not appoint a psychiatric expert

Karla Faye Tucker was executed by the State of Texas on February 3, 1998. As a result of Tucker becoming a "born again Christian," and admitting her guilt in killing two people, she attracted national and international support to try and prevent her execution. (Texas Department of Criminal Justice)

for the defendant. The penalty phase jury found that the prosecutor established two statutory aggravating circumstances, future dangerousness and vileness, and accordingly sentenced the defendant to death. The Virginia Supreme Court affirmed the conviction and sentence.

Shortly after the Virginia Supreme Court affirmed the defendant's conviction and sentence, the United States Supreme Court rendered a decision in *Ake v. Oklahoma*, which held that when the prosecutor presents psychiatric evidence of an indigent defendant's future dangerousness in a capital sentencing proceeding, due process requires that the State provide the defendant with the assistance of an independent psychiatrist. At the time of *Ake*, the defendant's case was pending before the United States Supreme Court. In a memorandum opinion the Supreme Court vacated the defendant's death sentence and remanded the case to the Virginia Supreme Court with instructions reconsider the case in light of *Ake*.

On remand, the Virginia Supreme Court invalidated the future dangerousness aggravating circumstance because of the *Ake* error. The appellate court nevertheless reaffirmed the defendant's death sentence on the grounds that the vileness aggravating factor permitted the sentence to survive.

The defendant next filed a habeas corpus petition in a Federal District Court, contending that the Virginia Supreme Court applied the wrong analysis in affirming his sentence based on the vileness aggravating factor. The District Court denied relief. A Federal Court of Appeals affirmed. The United States Supreme Court granted certiorari to consider the issue.

Opinion of the Court was delivered Per Curiam: The per curiam opinion held that under the Court's decision in *Zant v. Stephens (II)*, a death sentence supported by multiple statutory aggravating circumstances need not always be set aside if one aggravator is found to be invalid. The opinion ruled that both the Virginia Supreme Court and the Court of Appeals misinterpreted *Zant* as permitting a death sentence to be upheld on the basis of one valid aggravating circumstance, regardless of the reasons for which another aggravating factor may have been found to be invalid. It was said that *Zant* did not sanction automatic affirmance of a death sentence, where an aggravating circumstance is found invalid, but other valid aggravating factors remain. Under *Zant* courts are required to analyze the possible prejudicial effect on the sentencing decision by the evidence used to establish the invalid aggravating factor.

It was said in the per curiam opinion that the *Ake* error prevented the defendant from developing his own psychiatric evidence to rebut the prosecutor's evidence and to enhance his defense in mitigation. As a result, the prosecutor's psychiatric evidence went unchallenged and may have unfairly increased its persuasiveness in the eyes of the jury. It was reasoned that the absence of such evidence may well have affected the jury's ultimate decision, based on all of the evidence before it, to sentence the defendant to death rather than life imprisonment. The judgment of the Court of Appeals was reversed and the case was remanded for harmless error analysis of the *Ake* violation.

Concurring opinion by Justice Scalia: Justice Scalia concurred with the Court's judgment. He indicated in his concurring opinion that this was "a simple case and should be simply resolved." Justice Scalia believed that the case had become unnecessarily complicated, when it was quite clear what the law required under the facts of the case.

Case note: After the case was remanded to the Court of Appeals it was determined that the *Ake* violation was in fact harmless error. Virginia subsequently executed Lem Davis Tuggle by lethal injection on December 12, 1996. *See also* **Ake v. Oklahoma; Invalid Aggravator; Zant v. Stephens(II)**

Tuilaepa v. California   *Court:* United States Supreme Court; *Case Citation:* Tuilaepa v. California, 114 S.Ct. 2630 (1994); *Argued:* March 22, 1994; *Decided:* June 30, 1994; *Opinion of the Court:* Justice Kennedy; *Concurring Opinion:* Justice Scalia; *Concurring Opinion:* Justice Souter; *Concurring Opinion:* Justice Stevens, in which Ginsburg, J., joined; *Dissenting Opinion:* Justice Blackmun; *Appellate Defense Counsel:* Not reported; *Appellate Prosecution Counsel:* Not reported; *Amicus Curiae Brief Supporting Prosecutor:* Not reported; *Amicus Curiae Brief Supporting Defendant:* Not reported.

Issue Presented: Whether three of California's capital penalty phase statutory sentencing factors are unconstitutionally vague?

Case Holding: The challenged capital penalty phase statutory sentencing factors are not unconstitutionally vague.

Factual and procedural background of case: The defendants, Paul Palalaua Tuilaepa and William Arnold Proctor, were convicted and sentenced to death for capital murder in separate cases by the State of California. Both defendants' convictions and sentences were affirmed by the California Supreme Court. Both defendants had argued unsuccessfully to the State appellate court that the following penalty phase statutory factor was vague and therefore violated the federal Constitution: (1) a requirement that the sentencer consider the circumstances of the crime of which the defendant was convicted and the existence of any special circumstances found to be true.

Additionally, Tuilaepa unsuccessfully contended before the State appellate court that the following two penalty phase statutory factors were vague and therefore violated the federal Constitution: (2) a requirement that the sentencer consider the presence or absence of criminal activity involving the use or attempted use of force or violence, or the express or implied threat to use force or violence; and (3) a requirement that the sentencer consider the defendant's age at the time of the crime. The United States Supreme Court granted certiorari for both cases and consolidated them to address the constitutionality of the three factors.

Opinion of the Court by Justice Kennedy: Justice Kennedy observed that the Court's constitutional vagueness review was deferential, and relied on the basic principle that a factor is not unconstitutional if it has some common sense core of meaning that criminal juries should be capable of understanding.

He stated further: "We have held, under certain sentencing schemes, that a vague propositional factor used in the sentencing decision creates an unacceptable risk of randomness, the mark of the arbitrary and capricious sentencing process prohibited by *Furman v. Georgia.* Those concerns are mitigated when a factor does not require a yes or a no answer to a specific question, but instead only points the sentencer to a subject matter."

The opinion found that the defendants' challenge to the requirement that the sentencer consider the circumstances of the crime of which the defendant was convicted and the existence of any special circumstances found to be true, was at some odds with settled principles, because the circumstances of the crime are a traditional subject for consideration by the sentencer. The Court found this factor instructed the jury in understandable terms. It was said that the requirement that the sentencer consider the presence or absence of criminal activity involving the use or attempted use of force or violence, or the express or implied threat to use force or violence, was framed in conventional and understandable terms as well. Asking a jury to consider matters of historical fact was a permissible part of the sentencing process. Finally, the opinion found that the requirement that the sentencer consider the defendant's age at the time of the crime, might pose a dilemma for the jury in determining the bearing age ought to have in fixing the penalty, but that difficulty in application was not the equivalent of vagueness. Justice Kennedy concluded "that none of the three factors is defined in terms that violate the Constitution." The judgments of the California Supreme Court were affirmed.

Concurring opinion by Justice Scalia: Justice Scalia's concurring opinion stated succinctly: "It is my view that, once a State has adopted a methodology to narrow the eligibility for the death penalty, thereby ensuring that its imposition is not 'freakish,' the distinctive procedural requirements of the Eighth Amendment have been exhausted. Today's decision adheres to our cases which acknowledge additional requirements, but, since it restricts their further expansion, it moves in the right direction. For that reason, and without abandoning my prior views, I join the opinion of the Court."

Concurring opinion by Justice Souter: In his concurrence, Justice Souter stated: "I join the Court's opinion because it correctly recognizes that factors adequate to perform the function of genuine narrowing, as well as factors that otherwise guide the jury in selecting which defendants receive the death penalty, are not susceptible to mathematical precision; they must depend for their requisite clarity on embodying a 'common sense core of meaning[.]'"

Concurring opinion by Justice Stevens, in which Ginsburg, J., joined: Justice Stevens concurred in the Courts judgment. He indicated that prior precedent decided these issue in this case. The concurring opinion stated:

> The question is whether, in addition to adequately narrowing the class of death-eligible defendants, the State must channel the jury's sentencing discretion when it is deciding whether to impose the death sentence on an eligible defendant by requiring the trial judge to characterize relevant sentencing factors as aggravating or mitigating. In *Zant v. Stephens,* we held that the incorrect characterization of a relevant factor as an aggravating factor did not prejudice the defendant; it follows, I believe, that the failure to characterize factors such as the age of the defendant or the circumstances of the crime as either aggravating or mitigating is also unobjectionable. Indeed, I am persuaded that references to such potentially ambiguous, but clearly relevant, factors actually reduces the risk of arbitrary capital sentencing....
> ... Matters such as the age of the defendant at the time of the crime, the circumstances of the crime, and the presence or absence of force or violence are, in my opinion, relevant to an informed, individualized sentencing decision.... If, as we held in *Zant,* it is not constitutional error for the trial judge to place an incorrect label on the prosecutor's evidence, it necessarily follows that refusing to characterize ambiguous evidence as mitigating or aggravating is also constitutionally permissible. Indeed, as I have indicated, I think the identification of additional factors that are relevant to the sentencing decision reduces the danger that a juror may vote in favor of the death penalty because he or she harbors a prejudice against a class of which the defendant is a member.
> ...I conclude that the sentencing factors at issue in these cases are consistent with the defendant's constitutional entitlement to an individualized "determination that death is the appropriate punishment in a specific case."

Dissenting opinion by Justice Blackmun: In dissenting from the majority decision, Justice Blackmun wrote: "Adhering to my view that the death penalty cannot be imposed fairly within the constraints of our Constitution, I would vacate [the defendants'] death sentences. Even if I did not hold this view, I would find that the three challenged factors do not withstand a meaningful vagueness analysis because 'as a practical matter [they] fail to guide the sentencer's discretion.'" *See also* **Void for Vagueness Doctrine**

Tunisia

Tunisia permits capital punishment. Tunisia uses hanging and the firing squad to carry out the death penalty. Its legal system is based on French civil law and Islamic law. Tunisia adopted a constitution on June 1, 1959.

The court system is composed of trial courts, courts of appeal, and a Court of Cassation. Defendants have a right to be represented by counsel, question witnesses, and appeal verdicts. Both the defendant and the prosecutor may appeal. Trials are open to the public. *See also* **International Capital Punishment Nations**

Turkey

Capital punishment may be used in Turkey, but the punishment has not been used in over a decade. Turkey uses hanging to carry out the death penalty. Its legal system is a mixture of various European legal systems. The nation adopted a constitution on November 7, 1982.

The judicial system is composed of trial courts, State Security Courts, High Court of Appeals, and a Constitutional Court. Defendants have the right to a public trial and retained or appointed counsel. There is no jury system. All cases are decided by a judge or a panel of judges. *See also* **International Capital Punishment Nations**

Turkmenistan Turkmenistan abolished the death penalty on December 27, 1999. *See also* **International Capital Punishment Nations**

Turner v. Murray *Court:* United States Supreme Court; *Case Citation:* Turner v. Murray, 476 U.S. 28 (1986); *Argued:* December 12, 1985; *Decided:* April 30, 1986; *Opinion of the Court:* Justice White; *Concurring Statement:* Chief Justice Burger; *Concurring and Dissenting Opinion:* Justice Brennan; *Concurring and Dissenting Opinion:* Justice Marshall, in which Brennan, J., joined; *Dissenting Opinion:* Justice Powell, in which Rehnquist, J., joined; *Appellate Defense Counsel:* J. Lloyd Snook III argued and briefed; Appellate *Prosecution Counsel:* James E. Kulp argued; William G. Broaddus and Robert H. Anderson III on brief; *Amicus Curiae Brief Supporting Prosecutor:* None; *Amicus Curiae Brief Supporting Defendant:* None.

Issue Presented: Whether the trial judge committed constitutional error during jury selection by refusing the defendant's request to question prospective jurors on racial prejudice?

Case Holding: The trial judge committed constitutional error during jury selection by refusing the defendant's request to question prospective jurors on racial prejudice.

Factual and procedural background of case: The defendant, Willie Lloyd Turner, was indicted by the State of Virginia for capital murder. During jury selection the trial judge refused the defendant's request to question the prospective jurors on racial prejudice. The request was made because the victim was white and the defendant was black. The jury convicted the defendant and he was sentenced to death. The Virginia Supreme Court upheld the conviction and sentence. In doing so, the appellate court rejected the defendant's argument that the trial judge deprived him of a fair trial by refusing to question the prospective jurors on racial prejudice. The defendant raised the issue again in a habeas corpus petition he filed a Federal District Court. The District Court dismissed the petition. A Court of Appeals affirmed the dismissal. The United States Supreme Court granted certiorari to consider the issue.

Opinion of the Court by Justice White: Justice White determined that the defendant's rights under the Constitution were violated by the trial judge's refusal to voir dire the jury panel for racial bias. The opinion held: "We hold that a capital defendant accused of an interracial crime is entitled to have prospective jurors informed of the race of the victim and questioned on the issue of racial bias. The rule we propose is minimally intrusive; as in other cases involving 'special circumstances,' the trial judge retains discretion as to the form and number of questions on the subject, including the decision whether to question the venire individually or collectively. Also, a defendant cannot complain of a judge's failure to question the venire on racial prejudice unless the defendant has specifically requested such an inquiry."

The judgment of the Court of Appeals was reversed, insofar as the sentence imposed.

Concurring Statement by Chief Justice Burger: The Chief Justice issued a statement indicating he concurred in the Court's judgment.

Concurring and dissenting opinion by Justice Brennan: Justice Brennan issued an opinion concurring in part and dissenting in part with the Court's decision in the case. He agreed with the Court's reversal of the defendant's sentence, but disagreed with the Court's determination not to reverse the conviction. Justice Brennan stated his position as follows:

The Court's judgment vacates [the defendant's] sentence of death while refusing to disturb his conviction. Adhering to my view that the death penalty is in all circumstances cruel and unusual punishment prohibited by the Eighth and Fourteenth Amendments, I agree that the death sentence in this case must be vacated. But even if I did not hold that view, I would still find that the sentence was unconstitutionally imposed in this case. In my view, the constitutional right of a defendant to have a trial judge ask the members of the venire questions concerning possible racial bias is triggered whenever a violent interracial crime has been committed. The reality of race relations in this country is such that we simply may not presume impartiality, and the risk of bias runs especially high when members of a community serving on a jury are to be confronted with disturbing evidence of criminal conduct that is often terrifying and abhorrent. In analyzing the question of when the Constitution requires trial judges to accommodate defendants' requests for inquiries into racial prejudice, I, like the Court, am influenced by what the Court correctly describes as the "ease" with which the risk may be minimized.

In any event, I cannot fully join either the Court's judgment or opinion. For in my view, the decision in this case, although clearly half right, is even more clearly half wrong. After recognizing that the constitutional guarantee of an impartial jury entitles a defendant in a capital case involving interracial violence to have prospective jurors questioned on the issue of racial bias—a holding which requires that this case be reversed and remanded for new sentencing—the Court disavows the logic of its own reasoning in denying …. Turner a new trial on the issue of his guilt. It accomplishes this by postulating a jury role at the sentencing phase of a capital trial fundamentally different from the jury function at the guilt phase and by concluding that the former gives rise to a significantly greater risk of a verdict tainted by racism. Because I believe that the Court's analysis improperly intertwines the significance of the risk of bias with the consequences of bias, and because in my view the distinction between the jury's role at a guilt trial and its role at a sentencing hearing is a distinction without substance in so far as juror bias is concerned, I join only that portion of the Court's judgment granting [the defendant] a new sentencing proceeding, but dissent from that portion of the judgment refusing to vacate the conviction.

Concurring and dissenting opinion Justice Marshall, in which Brennan, J., joined: Justice Marshall issued an opinion concurring in the Court's reversal of the defendant's death sentence, but dissenting from the Court's decision not to reverse the conviction. Justice Marshall outlined his concerns as follows:

… I believe that a criminal defendant is entitled to inquire on voir dire about the potential racial bias of jurors whenever the case involves a violent interracial crime. As the Court concedes, "it is plain that there is some risk of racial prejudice influencing a jury whenever there is a crime involving interracial violence." To my mind that risk plainly outweighs the slight cost of allowing the defendant to choose whether to make an inquiry concerning such possible prejudice….

Even if I agreed with the Court that a per se rule permitting inquiry into racial bias is appropriate only in capital cases, I could not accept the Court's failure to remedy the denial of such inquiry in this capital case by reversing [the defendant's] conviction. Henceforth any capital defendant accused of an interracial crime may inquire into racial prejudice on voir dire. When, as here, the same jury sits at the guilt phase and the penalty phase, these defendants will be assured an impartial jury at both phases. Yet [the defendant] is forced to accept a conviction by what may have been a biased jury. This is an incongruous and fundamentally unfair result. I therefore concur only in the Court's judgment vacating [the defendant's] sentence, and dissent from the Court's refusal to reverse the conviction as well.

Dissenting opinion by Justice Powell, in which Rehnquist, J., joined: Justice Powell dissented from the Court's judgment in the case. He believed the Court was wrong in making race-qualified juries a per se requirement in capital prosecutions. Justice Powell articulated his position as follows:

> The Court today adopts a per se rule applicable in capital cases, under which "a capital defendant accused of an interracial crime is entitled to have prospective jurors informed of the race of the victim and questioned on the issue of racial bias." This rule is certain to add to the already heavy burden of habeas petitions filed by prisoners under sentence of death....
>
> In effect, the Court recognizes a presumption that jurors who have sworn to decide the case impartially nevertheless are racially biased. Such a presumption is flatly contrary to our [precedents]. The facts of this case demonstrate why it is unnecessary and unwise for this Court to rule, as a matter of constitutional law, that a trial judge always must inquire into racial bias in a capital case involving an interracial murder, rather than leaving that decision to be made on a case-by-case basis. Before today the facts that a defendant is black and his victim was white were insufficient to raise "a constitutionally significant likelihood that, absent questioning about racial prejudice," an impartial jury would not be seated....
>
> The per se rule announced today may appear innocuous. But the rule is based on what amounts to a constitutional presumption that jurors in capital cases are racially biased. Such presumption unjustifiably suggests that criminal justice in our courts of law is meted out on racial grounds. It is not easy to reconcile the Court's holding today with the principles announced and applied in [other cases]. The manner in which [the defendant] was tried and sentenced, and particularly the jurors who fulfilled their civic duty to sit in his case, reflected not a trace of the racial prejudice that the Court's new rule now presumes. *See also* **Race-Qualified Jury**

Turner v. Pennsylvania
Court: United States Supreme Court; *Case Citation:* Turner v. Pennsylvania, 338 U.S. 62 (1949); *Argued:* November 16–17, 1948; *Decided:* June 27, 1949; *Plurality Opinion:* Justice Frankfurter announced the Court's judgment and delivered an opinion, in which Murphy and Rutledge, JJ., joined; *Concurring Opinion:* Justice Douglas; *Concurring Statement:* Justice Black; *Dissenting Opinion:* Justice Jackson; *Dissenting Statement:* Chief Justice Vinson, and Reed and Burton, JJ.; *Appellate Defense Counsel:* Edwin P. Rome argued and briefed; *Appellate Prosecution Counsel:* Colbert C. McClain argued and briefed; *Amicus Curiae Brief Supporting Prosecutor:* None; *Amicus Curiae Brief Supporting Defendant:* None.

Issue Presented: Whether the defendant's confession was obtained in violation of due process of law, and thereby invalidated his conviction and death sentence?

Case Holding: The defendant's confession was obtained in violation of due process of law, therefore his conviction and death sentence were invalid.

Factual and procedural background of case: The defendant, Turner, was detained as a suspect in a capital murder by the State of Pennsylvania. After his arrest the defendant was interrogated by police officers for five days before he gave a confession to committing the crime. The record report of the interrogation revealed the following: "The [defendant] was not permitted to see friends or relatives during the entire period of custody; he was not informed of his right to remain silent until after he had been under the pressure of a long process of interrogation and had actually yielded to it. With commendable candor the district attorney admitted that a hearing was withheld until interrogation had produced [a] confession. The delay of five days thus accounted for was in violation of a Pennsylvania statute which requires that arrested persons be given a prompt preliminary hearing."

The jury returned a verdict of guilty and the death penalty was imposed. The Pennsylvania Supreme Court affirmed the conviction and sentence. In doing so, the appellate court rejected the defendant's contention that his confession was taken in violation of due process of law. The United States Supreme Court granted certiorari to consider the issue.

Plurality opinion in which Justice Frankfurter announced the Court's judgment and in which Murphy and Rutledge, JJ., joined: Justice Frankfurter held that the case was controlled by the Court's decision in *Watts v. Indiana.* The opinion held as follows: "Putting this case beside the considerations set forth in our opinion in *Watts v. Indiana,* leaves open no other possible conclusion than that [the defendant's] confession was obtained under circumstances which made its use at the trial a denial of due process. We must, accordingly, reverse the judgment and remand the case."

Concurring opinion by Justice Douglas: Justice Douglas concurred in the Court's decision. He described the defendant's interrogation as follows:

> During this confinement [the defendant] was subject to continual interrogations by a number of police officers, who questioned him individually and in small groups. The day of his arrest he was questioned about three hours in the afternoon and again in the evening. The next two days he was questioned three to four hours in the afternoon. The next day the questioning was intensified and he was again subjected to both day and evening sessions. On the 7th of June, the day he finally confessed, the interrogations were intensive, once again being held afternoon and evening. [The defendant] denied his guilt, even after being informed that other suspects had issued statements incriminating him. About eleven o'clock in the evening, after three hours of interrogation, [the defendant] finally indicated that he wished to make a statement. This confession was set down on paper the next day, and [the defendant] signed it after he had been committed by a magistrate.
>
> These interrogations had been conducted by at least seven different officers. They were conducted in [the defendant's] cell

in a small office, and in a room which had a stand-up screen where suspects were put for identification. It was admitted that the reason [the defendant] was not brought before a magistrate was because he had not given the answers which the police wanted and which they believed he could give.

The case is but another vivid illustration of the use of illegal detentions to exact confessions. It is governed by *Watts v. Indiana.*

Concurring opinion by Justice Black: Justice Black issued a statement indicating he concurred in the Court's judgment.

Dissenting opinion by Justice Jackson: Justice Jackson dissented from the Court's decision in the case. He referenced to his concurring and dissenting opinion written in a companion case, *Watts v. Indiana*, as the basis for his dissent. In *Watts*, Justice Jackson wrote that he believed involuntary confessions were not invalid under the Constitution. He believed such confessions assured the accuracy of convictions. Justice Jackson reasoned as follows in the dissenting part of his *Watts* opinion: "If the right of interrogation be admitted, then it seems to me that we must leave it to trial judges and juries and state appellate courts to decide individual cases, unless they show some want of proper standards of decision. I find nothing to indicate that any of the courts below in these cases did not have a correct understanding of the Fourteenth Amendment, unless this Court thinks it means absolute prohibition of interrogation while in custody before arraignment."

Dissenting statement by Chief Justice Vinson and Reed and Burton, JJ.: Chief Justice Vinson and Justices Reed and Burton issued a joint statement indicating they dissented from the Court's decision and believed the judgment should be affirmed.

Case note: This case was one of three cases decided by the Court, on the same day, involving involuntary confessions. In each of the cases the Court applied due process principals to invalidate the capital convictions. In subsequent decades the Court would apply the Fifth Amendment right to remain silent to review claims from State prisoners that their confessions were involuntary. *See also* **Harris v. South Carolina; Right to Remain Silent; Watts v. Indiana**

Tuvalu Capital punishment is not carried out in Tuvalu. *See also* International Capital Punishment Nations

Twitchell v. Pennsylvania
Court: United States Supreme Court; *Case Citation:* Twitchell v. Pennsylvania, 74 U.S. 321 (1868); *Argued:* Not reported; *Decided:* December Term, 1868; *Opinion of the Court:* Chief Justice Chase; *Concurring Opinion:* None; *Dissenting Opinion:* None; *Appellate Defense Counsel:* Mr. Hubbell argued and briefed; Appellate Prosecution Counsel: B. H. Brewster on brief; *Amicus Curiae Brief Supporting Prosecutor:* None; *Amicus Curiae Brief Supporting Defendant:* None.

Issue Presented: Whether the adequate charging notice requirement of the Sixth Amendment could be used to challenge the sufficiency of a State indictment?

Case Holding: The adequate charging notice requirement of the Sixth Amendment could not be used to challenge the sufficiency of a State indictment, because the Sixth Amendment was not applicable to States.

Factual and procedural background of case: The defendant, Twitchell, was convicted of capital murder and sentenced to death by the State of Pennsylvania. The Pennsylvania Supreme Court affirmed the judgment. In doing so, the appellate court rejected the defendant's contention that the indictment against him failed to adequately inform him of the nature of the charge against him, in violation of the Federal Constitution. The United States Supreme Court granted certiorari to consider the issue.

Opinion of the Court by Chief Justice Chase: The Chief Justice acknowledged that the Sixth Amendment requires a defendant "be informed of the nature and cause of the accusation." However, it was said that the rights under the Sixth Amendment were only applicable against the Federal government. The Chief Justice indicated that prior decisions of the Court made clear that the "amendments contain no expression indicating an intention to apply them to State governments." The judgment of the Pennsylvania Supreme Court was affirmed.

Case note: The Court would eventually rule in *Duncan v. Louisiana,* 391 U.S. 145 (1968), that the Sixth Amendment was applicable to States through the Fourteenth Amendment.

Two-Witness Conviction Requirement The death penalty statute of Connecticut has a unique provision which holds that no person may be convicted of any crime punishable by death without testimony of at least two eyewitnesses. The Supreme Court of Connecticut has qualified the two-witness requirement in two respects. First, the court has recognized that the Federal Constitution does not impose such an evidentiary requirement on the State. Second, it has been held that the requirement is satisfied when the prosecutor presents more than one witness to provide circumstantial evidence from which a jury may infer a defendant's guilt. The two-witness requirement is applicable to the guilt phase only and has no application to the penalty phase of a capital prosecution.

The crime of treason, as provided for in the Federal Constitution, requires that offense be proven by two witnesses. *See also* **Treason**

Types of Crimes Criminal offenses are generally categorized as misdemeanor or felony. The death penalty may not be based upon commission of a misdemeanor offense. The United States Supreme Court has restricted infliction of the death penalty to felony offenses that involve homicides. *See also* **Rape and Capital Punishment**

U

Uganda Uganda allows capital punishment. Uganda uses the firing squad and hanging to carry out the death penalty. Its legal system is based on English common law and customary law. Uganda adopted a constitution on October 8, 1995.

The judicial system is composed of a High Court, Court of Appeal, Constitutional Court, and a Supreme Court. Defendants have the right to retain counsel and in capital cases indigent defendants have the right to appointed counsel. Defendants also have the right to bail and the right to appeal. *See also* **International Capital Punishment Nations**

Ukraine Ukraine recognizes capital punishment. Ukraine uses the firing squad to carry out the death penalty. Its legal system is based on civil law. The nation adopted a constitution on June 8, 1996.

The judicial system consists of district courts, regional courts, a Supreme Court, and a Constitutional Court. Under Ukraine's current court system, cases are decided by judges and two lay assessors. Trials are public. Defendants have a right to counsel and the right against self-incrimination. Defendants enjoy a presumption of innocence. *See also* **International Capital Punishment Nations**

Unitarian Universalists Against the Death Penalty Unitarian Universalists Against the Death Penalty (UUADP) was organized in California in November of 1996. The UUADP is an independent affiliate of the Unitarian Universalist Association (UUA). Its purpose is to implement the mandate of UUA resolutions opposing the death penalty by providing education, encouraging participation in state and national abolition groups, and providing resources to help individuals and congregations to become more effective voices against the death penalty. Work engaged in by UUADP includes taking part in anti–death penalty vigils and rallies, writing letters to political leaders, and coordinating workshops and programs.

United Arab Emirates The death penalty is allowed in the United Arab Emirates. The United Arab Emirates uses the firing squad, stoning, and beheading to carry out the death penalty. Its legal system is based on Islamic law. The nation promulgated a constitution on December 2, 1971.

The judicial system is composed of emirate and federal trial courts, and a federal Supreme Court. Defendants have a right to legal counsel and in capital cases the right to appointed counsel. Defendants are presumed innocent. There are no jury trials. All trials are public, except national security cases. Death sentences may be appealed to the ruler of the emirate where the offense was committed or to the President of the United Arab Emirates. *See also* **International Capital Punishment Nations**

United Nation's Commission on Human Rights On April 3, 1998, the United Nations Commission on Human Rights issued a resolution calling for a moratorium and eventual abolishment of executions in the United States. The resolution was prompted by a report generated by the United Nations Special Rapporteur on Extrajudicial, Summary or Arbitrary Executions. The Special Rapporteur, Bacre Waly Ndiaye (Senegal), visited the United States from September 21 to October 8, 1997, for the purpose of investigating reports which suggested that compliance with international agreements relating to fair trials and specific restrictions on the death penalty were not being fully observed in the United States.

In his report, the Special Rapporteur found that the defendants who received the death penalty in the United States were not necessarily those who committed the most heinous crimes. The report indicated that factors other than the crime itself appeared to influence the imposition of a death sentence. The Special Rapporteur concluded that race and economic status, both of the victims and the defendants, were key factors in determining whether the death penalty was imposed.

The report of the Special Rapporteur was also critical of alleged political influences upon the use of the death penalty. The report cited the election of judges as a compromise of the impartiality of the judicial system, which directly impacted on capital prosecutions. There was also criticism of the discretionary powers of the prosecutor as to whether or not to seek the death penalty. The report found prosecutors often abused their discretion for political reasons when making the decision of whether to seek the death penalty in a given case.

The jury system also came under attack in the Special Rapporteur's report. It was said that people with reservations regarding the death penalty were less likely to sit as jurors. Further, that jurors were most likely to be people predisposed to imposing capital punishment.

The report of the Special Rapporteur noted that the practice of imposing capital punishment on juveniles by many jurisdictions was a direct violation international law. The Special Rapporteur also condemned the practice of executing mentally retarded persons.

United States Attorney General Capital offenses that violate Federal law are prosecuted by the office of the United States Attorney General. Each State is assigned a number of assistant attorney generals, which number depends upon the volume of litigation carried on in the State. The assistant attorney generals are required to obtain the approval of the

Attorney General before seeking the death penalty against a defendant.

If a defendant's conduct violates both Federal law and the law of a State, prosecution by a Federal assistant attorney general takes precedent over the State's right to prosecute the defendant. A State does not lose its right to prosecute a defendant while waiting for a Federal prosecution to conclude. As a practical matter, in most instances both jurisdictions will not prosecute a defendant.

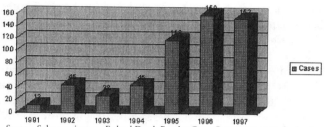

Federal Death Penalty Cases By Year of Indictment

Source: Subcommittee on Federal Death Penalty Cases Committee on Defender Services Judicial Conference of the United States, "Federal Death Penalty Cases: Recommendations Concerning the Cost and Quality of Defense Representation" May 1998.

United States Courts of Appeal *see* **Federal Government**

United States District Courts *see* **Federal Government**

United States Government *see* **Federal Government**

United States Supreme Court *see* **Federal Government**

United States v. Bevans *Court:* United States Supreme Court; *Case Citation:* United States v. Bevins, 16 U.S. 336 (1818); *Argued:* February 14, 1818; *Decided:* February 21, 1818; *Opinion of the Court:* Chief Justice Marshall; *Concurring Opinion:* None; *Dissenting Opinion:* None; *Appellate Defense Counsel:* Mr. Webster argued and briefed; Appellate *Prosecution Counsel:* Mr. Wheaton argued and briefed; *Amicus Curiae Brief Supporting Prosecutor:* None; *Amicus Curiae Brief Supporting Defendant:* None.

Issue Presented: Whether a Federal court in Massachusetts had jurisdiction to prosecute the defendant for a murder committed on a military ship anchored in the Boston harbor?

Case Holding: The Federal court in Massachusetts did not have jurisdiction to prosecute the defendant for a murder committed on a military ship anchored in the Boston harbor, because such an offense had to be committed on waters outside the territory of any State.

Factual and procedural background of case: The defendant, William Bevins, was charged with capital murder by the United States. At the time of the crime the defendant was enlisted in the United States military. The victim was also in the

military. The crime occurred on board a war ship anchored in a harbor in Boston, Massachusetts. The defendant was prosecuted in a Federal court in Massachusetts. A jury convicted the defendant of capital murder. Prior to imposing the death penalty the trial court certified the following question to the United States Supreme Court: Did the trial court have jurisdiction to prosecute the offense?

Opinion of the Court by Chief Justice Marshall: The Chief Justice ruled that the trial court did not have jurisdiction to hear the case. It was said that to bring the case within the jurisdiction of Federal courts, the crime had to occur on water that was out of the jurisdiction of any State. The Chief justice found that the site of the murder described in the indictment was "unquestionably within the original jurisdiction of Massachusetts[.]" The opinion concluded "that a murder committed on board a ship of war, lying within the harbor of Boston, is not cognizable in the [Federal] court for the district of Massachusetts[.]" *See also* **Certified Question; Jurisdiction**

United States v. Carignan *Court:* United States Supreme Court; *Case Citation:* United States v. Carignan, 342 U.S. 36 (1951); *Argued:* October 8, 1951; *Decided:* November 13, 1951; *Opinion of the Court:* Justice Reed; *Concurring Opinion:* Justice Douglas, in which Black and Frankfurter, JJ., joined; *Dissenting Opinion:* None; *Justice Taking No Part in Decision:* Minton; *Appellate Defense Counsel:* Harold J. Butcher argued and briefed; Appellate *Prosecution Counsel:* Philip Elman argued; Robert S. Erdahl and Beatrice Rosenberg on brief; *Amicus Curiae Brief Supporting Prosecutor:* None; *Amicus Curiae Brief Supporting Defendant:* None.

Issue Presented: Whether the defendant's confession was obtained in violation of his right to prompt arraignment before a magistrate as required by Rule 5 of the Federal Rules of Criminal Procedure?

Case Holding: Rule 5 of the Federal Rules of Criminal Procedure was inapplicable to the case, but the defendant was entitled to a new trial on different grounds.

Factual and procedural background of case: The defendant, Carignan, was convicted of capital murder and sentenced to death by the United States. Federal jurisdiction was premised upon the murder occurring in the Territory of Alaska. A Federal Court of Appeals reversed the conviction and sentence, after finding the defendant's confession was obtained in violation of his right to be promptly arraigned before a neutral magistrate as required by Rule 5 of the Federal Rules of Criminal Procedure. The United States Supreme Court granted certiorari to consider the issue.

Opinion of the Court by Justice Reed: Justice Reed held that Rule 5 was inapplicable as a basis for reversing the judgment, because at the time of the defendant's confession he was properly being held in jail for another offense. It was said that the police could not present the defendant for arraignment on a murder charge when they did not have a basis to charge him for murder, until he confessed.

The opinion found that the defendant was entitled to a new trial on an issue that was not passed upon by the Court of Appeals. Justice Reed indicated that when the admissibility of the defendant's confession was in issue in the trial court, the judge committed reversible error in refusing to permit the defendant to testify out of the presence of the jury to facts the defendant believed indicated the involuntary character of the confession. Justice Reed wrote: "We think it clear that this defendant was entitled to such an opportunity to testify. An involuntary confession is inadmissible. Such evidence would be pertinent to the inquiry on admissibility and might be material and determinative." The judgment of the Court of Appeals was affirmed on different grounds.

Concurring opinion by Justice Douglas, in which Black and Frankfurter, JJ., joined: Justice Douglas concurred in the Court's decision. He believed the conviction should have been set aside because the police used the initial arrest as a screen to interrogate the defendant about the crime they really wanted to arrest him for. Justice Douglas stated: "[A] time-honored police method for obtaining confessions is to arrest a man on one charge (often a minor one) and use his detention for investigating a wholly different crime. This is an easy short cut for the police. How convenient it is to make detention the vehicle of investigation! Then the police can have access to the prisoner day and night. Arraignment for one crime gives some protection. But when it is a pretense or used as the device for breaking the will of the prisoner on long, relentless, or repeated questionings, it is abhorrent. We should free the federal system of that disreputable practice which has honeycombed the municipal police system in this country. We should make illegal such a perversion of a 'legal' detention."

See also **Arraignment**

United States v. Jackson
Court: United States Supreme Court; *Case Citation:* United States v. Jackson, 390 U.S. 570 (1968); *Argued:* December 7, 1967; *Decided:* April 8, 1968; *Opinion of the Court:* Justice Stewart; *Concurring Opinion:* None; *Dissenting Opinion:* Justice White, in which Black , J., joined; *Justice Not Taking Part in Decision:* Justice Marshall; *Appellate Defense Counsel:* Steven B. Duke argued; Stephen I. Traub and Ira B. Grudberg on brief; Appellate *Prosecution Counsel:* Ralph S. Spritzer argued; Richard A. Posner, Beatrice Rosenberg and Marshall Tamor Golding on brief; *Amicus Curiae Brief Supporting Prosecutor:* None; *Amicus Curiae Brief Supporting Defendant:* None.

Issue Presented: Whether the death penalty provision of the Federal Kidnaping Act impermissibly infringed upon the defendants' constitutional rights by encouraging non-jury trials and guilty pleas?

Case Holding: The death penalty provision of the Federal Kidnaping Act impermissibly infringed upon the defendants' constitutional rights by encouraging non-jury trials and guilty pleas.

Factual and procedural background of case: A Federal grand jury in Connecticut returned an indictment charging the defendants, Charles Jackson, Glenn Motte, and John Albert Walsh, Jr., with violating the Federal Kidnaping Act (FKA). The FKA provided that interstate kidnapers "shall be punished (1) by death if the kidnaped person has not been liberated unharmed, and if the verdict of the jury shall so recommend, or (2) by imprisonment for any term of years or for life, if the death penalty is not imposed." The Federal District Court dismissed the count of the indictment charging the defendants with violating the FKA, because it made "the risk of death" the price for asserting the right to trial by jury and therefore impaired the free exercise of that constitutional right. The Federal Government appealed directly to the United States Supreme Court.

Opinion of the Court by Justice Stewart: Justice Stewart held that the FKA created an offense punishable by death "if the verdict of the jury shall so recommend." The latter passage was interpreted as requiring a lesser sentence than death if a defendant waived the right to jury trial or pleaded guilty. Justice Stewart found that the death penalty provision of the FKA imposed an impermissible burden upon the exercise of constitutional rights, insofar as it encouraged guilty pleas and non-jury trials by defendants in order to avoid the death penalty provision of the statute. It was said that this "encouragement" to give up constitutional rights made the death penalty provision unconstitutional. Justice Stewart reasoned in the opinion as follows:

> ... Whatever might be said of Congress' objectives, they cannot be pursued by means that needlessly chill the exercise of basic constitutional rights. The question is not whether the chilling effect is "incidental" rather than intentional; the question is whether that effect is unnecessary and therefore excessive. In this case the answer to that question is clear.... Whatever the power of Congress to impose a death penalty for violation of the Federal Kidnaping Act, Congress cannot impose such a penalty in a manner that needlessly penalizes the assertion of a constitutional right.
>
> It is no answer to urge, as does the Government, that federal trial judges may be relied upon to reject coerced pleas of guilty and involuntary waivers of jury trial. For the evil in the federal statute is not that it necessarily coerces guilty pleas and jury waivers but simply that it needlessly encourages them. A procedure need not be inherently coercive in order that it be held to impose an impermissible burden upon the assertion of a constitutional right. Thus the fact that the Federal Kidnaping Act tends to discourage defendants from insisting upon their innocence and demanding trial by jury hardly implies that every defendant who enters a guilty plea to a charge under the Act does so involuntarily. The power to reject coerced guilty pleas and involuntary jury waivers might alleviate, but it cannot totally eliminate, the constitutional infirmity in the capital punishment provision of the Federal Kidnaping Act.

The opinion ruled that the death penalty provision was severable from the remainder of the statute, therefore the District Court committed error in dismissing the kidnaping count of the indictment. The judgment of the District Court was reversed.

Dissenting opinion by Justice White, in which Black , J., joined: Justice White dissented from the Court's decision. He argued that the FKA could be interpreted in such a way so as to avoid infringing upon constitutional rights of defendants. Justice White stated his position as follows:

> The Court strikes down a provision of the Federal Kidnaping Act which authorizes only the jury to impose the death penalty. No question is raised about the death penalty itself or about the propriety of jury participation in its imposition, but confining the power to impose the death penalty to the jury alone is held to burden impermissibly the right to a jury trial because it may either coerce or encourage persons to plead guilty or to waive a jury and be tried by the judge. In my view, however, if the vice of the provision is that it may interfere with the free choice of the defendant to have his guilt or innocence determined by a jury, the Court needlessly invalidates a major portion of an Act of Congress. The Court itself says that not every plea of guilty or waiver of jury trial would be influenced by the power of the jury to impose the death penalty. If this is so, I would not hold the provision unconstitutional but would reverse the judgment, making it clear that pleas of guilty and waivers of jury trial should be carefully examined before they are accepted, in order to make sure that they have been neither coerced nor encouraged by the death penalty power in the jury.
>
> Because this statute may be properly interpreted so as to avoid constitutional questions, I would not take the first step toward invalidation of statutes on their face because they arguably burden the right to jury trial.

Case note: Under modern capital punishment jurisprudence the death penalty may not be imposed for the crime of kidnaping, without an accompanying homicide. *See also* **Rape and Capital Punishment**

United States v. Klintock

Court: United States Supreme Court; *Case Citation:* United States v. Klintock, 18 U.S. 144 (1820); *Argued:* February 14, 1820; *Decided:* February 25, 1820; *Opinion of the Court:* Chief Justice Marshall; *Concurring Opinion:* None; *Dissenting Opinion:* None; *Appellate Defense Counsel:* Mr. Winder argued and briefed; Appellate *Prosecution Counsel:* United States Attorney General argued and briefed; *Amicus Curiae Brief Supporting Prosecutor:* None; *Amicus Curiae Brief Supporting Defendant:* None.

Issues Presented: (1) Whether the defendant could be prosecuted for piracy when he was under the commission of another country? (2) Whether fraudulent conduct used to acquire a ship constitutes piracy?

Case Holdings: (1) The defendant could be prosecuted for piracy when he was under the commission of another country, because the purported country was nonexistent. (2) Fraudulent conduct used to acquire a ship does not in and of itself constitute piracy, but it may form part of the offense.

Factual and procedural background of case: The defendant, Ralph Klintock, was charged by the United States with piracy, a capital offense. The defendant was accused of fraudulently taking a Danish ship, the Norberg, from the Caribbean Sea. The trial occurred in a Federal District Court in Georgia. The defendant was convicted of piracy. The District Court, before imposing the death sentence, certified the following questions to the United States Supreme Court: (1) Could the defendant be punished under the Piracy Act when he was under commission from another country? (2) Could fraudulent conduct constitute piracy?

Opinion of the Court by Chief Justice Marshall: The Chief Justice ruled that the commission under which the defendant allegedly sailed was issued by "a republic of whose existence we know nothing[.]" It was said that the mere fact that the defendant was operating under a commission from a nonexistent country was not a justification for excusing the crime.

The opinion also found that "[a]lthough the fraud practiced on the [Danish ship] may not of itself constitute piracy, yet it is an ingredient in the transaction which has no tendency to mitigate the character of the offense." The Chief Justice concluded that "general piracy ... by persons on board of a vessel not at the time belonging to the subjects of any foreign power, but in possession of a crew acting in defiance of all law, and acknowledging obedience to no government whatever, is within the true meaning of [the Piracy Act], and is punishable in the Courts of the United States." *See also* **Certified Question; United States v. Pirates; United States v. Smith**

United States v. Palmer

Court: United States Supreme Court; *Case Citation:* United States v. Palmer, 16 U.S. 610 (1818); *Argued:* March 13, 1818; *Decided:* March 14, 1818; *Opinion of the Court:* Chief Justice Marshall; *Concurring Opinion:* None; *Dissenting Opinion:* None; *Appellate Defense Counsel:* Not represented; Appellate *Prosecution Counsel:* Mr. Blake argued and briefed; *Amicus Curiae Brief Supporting Prosecutor:* None; *Amicus Curiae Brief Supporting Defendant:* None.

Issue Presented: Whether piratical robbery may be punished with death, when robbery on land was not punishable with death by the United States?

Case Holding: Piratical robbery may be punished with death, although robbery on land was not punishable with death by the United States.

Factual and procedural background of case: The defendants in the case, John Palmer, Thomas Wilson and Barney Calloghan, were charged by the United States with piratical robbery, a capital offense. Prior to trial the Federal court certified the following question to the United States Supreme Court: Could the crime of robbery be punished with death as required under the Piracy Act, when robbery on land was not punished with death.

Opinion of the Court by Chief Justice Marshall: The Chief Justice ruled that, "[h]ad the intention of congress been to render the crime piracy dependent on the punishment affixed to the same offense, if committed on land, this intention must have been expressed in very different terms from those which have been selected [in the statute]." After finding no statutory language limiting imposition of the death penalty for piratical robbery, the Chief Justice held "that a robbery committed on the high seas, although such robbery, if committed on land, would not, by the laws of the United States, be punishable with death, is piracy [and punishable with death]." *See also* **Certified Question**

United States v. Pirates

Court: United States Supreme Court; *Case Citation:* United States v. Pirates, 18 U.S. 184

(1820); *Argued:* February 21, 1820; *Decided:* March 1, 1820; *Opinion of the Court:* Justice Johnson; *Concurring Opinion:* None; *Dissenting Opinion:* None; *Appellate Defense Counsel:* Mr. Webster and Mr. Winder argued and briefed; *Appellate Prosecution Counsel:* United States Attorney General argued and briefed; *Amicus Curiae Brief Supporting Prosecutor:* None; *Amicus Curiae Brief Supporting Defendant:* None.

Issues Presented: (1) Whether a foreign defendant who murders another foreigner aboard an American ship may be prosecuted under the Piracy Act? (2) Whether a commission from a belligerent nation immunizes a defendant from being prosecuted for piracy under the Piracy Act? (3) Whether piracy may occur when a ship is anchored near the shore?

Case Holdings: (1) A foreign defendant who murders another foreigner aboard an American ship may be prosecuted under the Piracy Act, because national character is lost when piracy is entered into. (2) A commission from a belligerent nation does not immunize a defendant from being prosecuted for piracy under the Piracy Act, because national character is lost when piracy is entered into. (3) Piracy may occur when a ship is anchored near the shore.

Factual and procedural background of case: This case was a consolidation of three separate prosecutions for capital piracy by the United States. In one case the defendant, John Furlong, was charged with two counts of piratical murder, one count of piratical seizure of a vessel and one count of piratical robber. In the second case the defendants, Benjamin Brailsford and James Griffen, were charged with general piracy. In the third case the defendants, David Bowers and Henry Mathews, were charged with two counts of piratical robbery. All of the defendants were tried and found guilty of each charge against them. The District Courts, before imposing death sentences, certified the following questions to the United States Supreme Court: (1) Could a foreigner who killed another foreigner aboard an American ship be prosecuted under the Piracy Act? (2) Does a commission from a belligerent protect a person from being prosecuted for piracy under the Piracy Act? (3) May piracy occur when a vessel is anchored within a marine league of the shore?

Opinion of the Court by Justice Johnson: Justice Johnson ruled the United States had jurisdiction of a piratical murder committed by a foreigner against another foreigner, on board an American vessel. The opinion stated that when a ship is taken "and proceed[s] on a piratical cruise, the crew [loses] all claim to national character, and whether citizens or foreigners, bec[o]me equally punishable under the act[.]"

It was said in the opinion that a commission from a belligerent nation would not immunize piratical conduct from the Piracy Act. Justice Johnson reasoned that, because national character is lost when piracy is undertaken, the fact of obtaining a commission from a belligerent nation is irrelevant.

Finally, the opinion stated that anchorage of a ship does not defeat an act of piracy. Justice Johnson wrote: "It is historically known, that in prosecuting trade with many places, vessels lie at anchor in open situations, under the lay of the land. Such vessels are neither in a river, haven, basin or bay, and are no where, unless it be on the seas. Being at anchor is immaterial, for this might happen in a thousand places in the open ocean[.]" *See also* **Certified Question; United States v. Klintock; United States v. Smith**

United States v. Smith

Court: United States Supreme Court; *Case Citation:* United States v. Smith, 18 U.S. 153 (1820); *Argued:* February 21, 1820; *Decided:* February 25, 1820; *Opinion of the Court:* Justice Story; *Concurring Opinion:* None; *Dissenting Opinion:* Justice Livingston; *Appellate Defense Counsel:* Mr. Webster argued and briefed; *Appellate Prosecution Counsel:* United States Attorney General argued and briefed; *Amicus Curiae Brief Supporting Prosecutor:* None; *Amicus Curiae Brief Supporting Defendant:* None.

Issue Presented: Whether the defendant could be punished with death for plundering a ship?

Case Holding: The defendant could be punished with death for plundering a ship.

Factual and procedural background of case: The defendant, Thomas Smith, was charged by the United States with piracy, a capital offense. The defendant was accused of taking and plundering a ship in the Caribbean Sea. The trial occurred in a Federal District Court in Virginia. The defendant was convicted of piracy. The District Court, before imposing a sentence of death, certified the following question to the United States Supreme Court: (1) Could the defendant be punished under the Piracy Act for plundering a ship?

Opinion of the Court by Justice Story: Justice Story noted that the provision under the Piracy Act which the defendant was prosecuted provided "that if any person or persons whatsoever, shall, upon the high seas, commit the crime of piracy, as defined by the law of nations, and such offender or offenders shall be brought into, or found in the United States, every such offender or offenders shall, upon conviction thereof, be punished with death." The opinion found that the latter imprecise definition of piracy did not offend the Constitution. It was said that the conduct attributed to the defendant constituted piracy under the law of nations. Justice Story concluded: "The special verdict finds that the prisoner is guilty of the plunder and robbery charged in the indictment; and finds certain additional facts from which it is most manifest that he and his associates were, at the time of committing the offense, freebooters upon the sea, not under the acknowledged authority, or deriving protection from the flag or commission of any government. If, under such circumstances, the offense be not piracy, it is difficult to conceive any which would more completely fit the definition."

Dissenting opinion by Justice Livingston: Justice Livingston dissented from the Court's opinion. He argued that the provision under the Piracy Act that the defendant was convicted violated the Constitution. Justice Livingston contended that Congress had no authority to define piracy in terms of whatever could be found in law books pertaining to the law of nations. *See also* **Certified Question; United States v. Klintock; United States v. Pirates**

United Students Against the Death Penalty
The United Students Against the Death Penalty is an organization formed for the purpose of abolishing the use of the death penalty in Connecticut. The group consists of college students, and concerned citizens, from around the State of Connecticut.

Unlawfully Obtaining Custody of Defendant
Under the common law a criminal defendant could be unlawfully abducted and brought within the jurisdiction of a court for prosecution. In such a situation, a defendant may be able to prosecute a civil lawsuit against his or her abductor, but the defendant could not obtain release from the criminal jurisdiction of the court merely because of improper means in obtaining custody of him or her. The United States Supreme Court has indicated that, even in the context of a capital offense, the Constitution does not prohibit the prosecution of a defendant who has been illegally brought within the jurisdiction of the prosecuting court, so long as the court has jurisdiction over the offense. *See also* **Ex Parte Johnson**

Uruguay
Uruguay abolished capital punishment in 1907. *See also* International Capital Punishment Nations

Utah
The State of Utah is a capital punishment jurisdiction. The State reenacted its death penalty law after the United States Supreme Court decision in *Furman v. Georgia*, 408 U.S. 238 (1972), on July 1, 1973.

Utah has a three-tier legal system. The State's legal system is composed of a supreme court, court of appeals and courts of general jurisdiction. The Utah Supreme Court is presided over by a chief justice and four associate justices. The Utah Court of Appeals is composed of a presiding judge and six judges. The courts of general jurisdiction in the State are called District Courts. Capital offenses against the State of Utah are tried in the District Courts.

Members of the Utah Supreme Court: (left to right) Justice Michael D. Zimmerman, Chief Justice Richard C. Howe, Associate Chief Justice Christine M. Durham, Justice I. Daniel Stewart, and Justice Leonard H. Russon. (Utah Supreme Court)

Utah's capital punishment statute is triggered if a person commits a homicide under the following special circumstances:

a. the homicide was committed by a person who is confined in a jail or other correctional institution;

b. the homicide was committed incident to one act, scheme, course of conduct, or criminal episode during which two or more persons were killed, or during which the offender attempted to kill one or more persons in addition to the victim who was killed;

c. the offender knowingly created a great risk of death to a person other than the victim and the actor;

d. the homicide was committed while the offender was engaged in the commission of, or an attempt to commit, or flight after committing or attempting to commit, aggravated robbery, robbery, rape, rape of a child, object rape, object rape of a child, forcible sodomy, sodomy upon a child, forcible sexual abuse, sexual abuse of a child, aggravated sexual abuse of a child, child abuse of a child under the age of 14 years, or aggravated sexual assault, aggravated arson, arson, aggravated burglary, burglary, aggravated kidnaping, kidnaping, or child kidnaping;

e. the homicide was committed for the purpose of avoiding or preventing an arrest of the defendant or another by a peace officer acting under color of legal authority or for the purpose of effecting the defendant's or another's escape from lawful custody;

f. the homicide was committed for pecuniary or other personal gain;

g. the defendant committed, or engaged or employed another person to commit the homicide pursuant to an agreement or contract for remuneration or the promise of remuneration for commission of the homicide;

h. the offender was previously convicted of aggravated murder, murder, or of a felony involving the use or threat of violence to a person;

i. the homicide was committed for the purpose of:
  A. preventing a witness from testifying;
  B. preventing a person from providing evidence or participating in any legal proceedings or official investigation;
  C. retaliating against a person for testifying, providing evidence, or participating in any legal proceedings or official investigation; or
  D. disrupting or hindering any lawful governmental function or enforcement of laws;

j. the victim is or has been a local, state, or federal public official, or a candidate for public office, and the homicide is based on, is caused by, or is related to that official position, act, capacity, or candidacy;

k. the victim is or has been a peace officer, law enforcement officer, executive officer, prosecuting officer, jailer, prison official, firefighter, judge or other court official, juror, probation officer, or parole officer, and the victim is either on duty or the homicide is based on, is caused by, or is related to that official position, and the actor knew, or reasonably should have known, that the victim holds or has held that official position;

l. the homicide was committed by means of a destructive device, bomb, explosive, incendiary device, or similar device which was planted, hidden, or concealed in any place, area, dwelling, building, or structure, or was mailed or delivered;

m. the homicide was committed during the act of unlawfully assuming control of any aircraft, train, or other public conveyance by use of threats or force with intent to obtain any valuable consideration for the release of the public conveyance or any passenger, crew member, or any other person aboard, or to direct the route or movement of the public conveyance or otherwise exert control over the public conveyance;

n. the homicide was committed by means of the administration of a poison or of any lethal substance or of any substance administered in a lethal amount, dosage, or quantity;

o. the victim was a person held or otherwise detained as a shield, hostage, or for ransom;

p. the offender was under a sentence of life imprisonment or a sentence of death at the time of the commission of the homicide; or

q. the homicide was committed in an especially heinous, atrocious, cruel, or exceptionally depraved manner, any of which must be demonstrated by physical torture, serious physical abuse, or serious bodily injury of the victim before death.

Capital murder in Utah is punishable by death or life imprisonment with or without parole. A capital prosecution in Utah is bifurcated into a guilt phase and penalty phase. A jury is used at both phases of a capital trial. It is required that, at the penalty phase, the jury unanimously agree that a death sentence is appropriate before it can be imposed. If the penalty phase jury is unable to reach a verdict, the trial judge is required to impose a sentence of life imprisonment. The decision of a penalty phase jury is binding on the trial court under the laws of Utah.

Utah does not provide statutory aggravating circumstances for the penalty phase jury to consider. The State imposes a death sentence based upon a conviction for one of the guilt phase special circumstances. The penalty phase jury is permitted to reject the death penalty based upon evidence of the following statutory mitigating circumstances (or any nonstatutory mitigators):

a. the defendant has no significant history of prior criminal activity;

b. the homicide was committed while the defendant was under the influence of mental or emotional disturbance;

c. the defendant acted under duress or under the domination of another person;

d. at the time of the homicide, the capacity of the defendant to appreciate the wrongfulness of his conduct or to conform his conduct to the requirement of law was impaired as a result of mental disease, intoxication, or influence of drugs;

e. the youth of the defendant at the time of the crime;

f. the defendant was an accomplice in the homicide committed by another person and the defendant's participation was relatively minor; and

g. any other fact in mitigation of the penalty.

Under Utah's capital punishment statute, a sentence of death is not automatically reviewed by the Utah Supreme Court. A capital felon must initiate an appeal of a death sentence. Utah permits capital felons to choose between death by firing squad or lethal injection. The State's death row facility for men is located in Draper, Utah. Pursuant to the laws of Utah, an Executive Panel that includes the Governor has authority to grant clemency in capital cases.

From the start of modern capital punishment in 1976, through 1999, Utah executed 6 capital felons. During this period it did not have any female capital felons on death row. A total of 11 capital felons were on death row in Utah in 1999. The 1999 death row population in the State was listed as: 2 black inmates; 7 white inmates; and 2 unidentified inmates. In 1999 the State did not have juveniles on death row. The State permits capital punishment to be imposed on persons 16 years old or older. Utah does not prohibit the execution of mentally retarded capital felons.

Executions by Utah 1976–1999

Name	Race	Date of Execution	Method of Execution
Gary Gilmore	White	January 17, 1977	Firing Squad
Dale P. Selby	Black	August 28, 1987	Lethal Injection
Arthur Bishop	White	June 10, 1988	Lethal Injection
William Andres	Black	July 30, 1992	Lethal Injection
John A. Taylor	White	January 26, 1996	Firing Squad
Joseph Parsons	White	October 15, 1999	Lethal Injection

Utter Disregard for Human Life Aggravator

Idaho is the only capital punishment jurisdiction using the utter disregard for human life aggravator. If this aggravator is found to exist at the penalty phase the death penalty may be imposed. The utter disregard for human life statutory aggravator has been found unconstitutionally vague where no definition has been crafted to provide reasonable understanding of the type of conduct it seeks to capture. However, the utter disregard for human life aggravator has been found to pass constitutional muster when appropriate definitional language is included. The meaning attached to this aggravator is that a capital felon acted in cold-blood, without feeling, sympathy or lack of emotion. *See also* **Arave v. Creech; Aggravating Circumstances**

Uzbekistan

Capital punishment is allowed in Uzbekistan. Uzbekistan uses the firing squad to carry out the death penalty. The crimes punishable by death include murder, espionage, and treason. Its legal system is based on Russian civil law. The nation adopted a new constitution on December 8, 1992. The judicial system is composed of district courts, regional courts, and a Supreme Court. Trials are open to the public. The is no jury system. Trials are presided over by a judge and two lay assessors. Defendants have the right to retained or appointed legal counsel, and the right to confront witnesses. *See also* **International Capital Punishment Nations**

Valdez v. United States   *Court:* United States Supreme Court; *Case Citation:* Valdez v. United States, 244 U.S. 432 (1917); *Argued:* April 23–24, 1917; *Decided:* June 11, 1917; *Opinion of the Court:* Justice McKenna; *Concurring Opinion:* None; *Dissenting Opinion:* Justice Clarke, in which White, C.J., joined; *Appellate Defense Counsel:* Timothy T. Ansberry argued; Challen B. Ellis on brief; Appellate *Prosecution Counsel:* Mr. Davis argued; Mr. Warren on brief; *Amicus Curiae Brief Supporting Prosecutor:* None; *Amicus Curiae Brief Supporting Defendant:* None.

Issue Presented: Whether the absence of the defendant during the trial judge's visit to the crime scene denied him due process of law?

Case Holding: The absence of the defendant during the trial judge's visit to the crime scene did not deny him due process of law.

Factual and procedural background of case: The defendant, Emilio Valdez, was convicted of capital murder and sentenced to death under the United States' territorial jurisdiction of the Philippine Islands. The Philippine Islands Supreme Court affirmed the judgment. In doing so, the appellate court rejected the defendant's contention that he had a right to be present when the trial court viewed the site of the crime. The United States Supreme Court granted certiorari to consider the issue.

Opinion of the Court by Justice McKenna: Justice McKenna held that the defendant did not have a right to be present when the trial judge visited the site of the crime. It was noted that counsel for the defendant was present during the visit. Justice McKenna reasoned that the Court "must assume that the judge, in his inspection of the scene of the homicide, was not improperly addressed by anyone, and, in the presence of counsel, did no more than visualize the testimony of the witnesses,— giving it a certain picturesqueness, it may be, but not adding to or changing it." It was also said that to require the presence of the defendant during such visit would lead to the absurd conclusion "that an accused is entitled to be with the judge in his meditations, and that he could entertain no conception nor form any judgment without such personal presence." The judgment of the Philippine Islands Supreme Court was affirmed.

Dissenting opinion by Justice Clarke, in which White, C.J., joined: Justice Clarke dissented from the Court's decision. He argued that the defendant had a right to be personally present when the trial court visited the crime scene. Justice Clarke wrote: "It has long been familiar, textbook, law, that a viewing of the premises where the crime is alleged to have been committed is part of the trial.... It is very clear to my mind ... that the viewing of the scene of the murder by the judge without the presence of the accused requires that it be reversed and a new trial granted." *See also* **Jury View**

Valentina v. Mercer   *Court:* United States Supreme Court; *Case Citation:* Valentina v. Mercer, 201 U.S. 131 (1906); *Argued:* February 27, 1906; *Decided:* March 12, 1906; *Opinion of the Court:* Justice Peckham; *Concurring Opinion:* None; *Dissenting Opinion:* None; *Appellate Defense Counsel:* James M. Trimble argued and briefed; Appellate *Prosecution Counsel:* Robert H. McCarter argued and briefed; *Amicus Curiae Brief Supporting Prosecutor:* None; *Amicus Curiae Brief Supporting Defendant:* None.

Issue Presented: Whether the procedure used by New Jersey for a defendant desiring to plead guilty to a crime comports with the Federal Constitution?

Case Holding: The procedure used by New Jersey for a defendant desiring to plead guilty to a crime does not raise a Federal constitutional issue, but is a matter of State law only.

Factual and procedural background of case: The defendant, Anna Valentina, was indicted by the State of New Jersey for capital murder. The defendant desired to plead guilty. Under the laws of the State, a defendant desiring to plead guilty was entitled to have a trial solely to determine the degree of guilt. In the case of the defendant the degree of guilt was first degree murder or second degree murder. A trial on the degree of the defendant's guilt was held. The defendant was convicted of committing murder in the first degree and was thereafter sentenced to death. The New Jersey Supreme Court affirmed the judgment. The defendant thereafter filed a petition for habeas corpus relief in a Federal District Court, alleging she was denied a trial to determine her guilt or innocence. The petition was dismissed. The United States Supreme Court granted certiorari to consider the issue.

Opinion of the Court by Justice Peckham: Justice Peckham held that the Court did not have jurisdiction to review the merits of the defendant's claim, because it did not involve a question of Federal law. The opinion set out the Court's reasoning as follows:

> The contention of the counsel for the [defendant] is that the proceedings upon the trial, which resulted in [the defendant's] sentence to death, did not amount to a trial at common law, or a proceeding authorized by any statute. That it was a mere inquiry to determine the degree of murder of which defendant was guilty, and hence she has never had a trial by due process of law, and the action of the state court was without jurisdiction. A perusal of the charge of the court to the jury shows that the whole case was presented to the jury upon the evidence that was produced in court. Upon all the evidence given the court stated to the jury that there was no evidence to show that the defendant killed the deceased in her necessary self-defense, and the court instructed the jury that it would not be justified in acquitting the defendant on the ground of self-defense. The court further said that there was no question of manslaughter in the case, and that, not only as a necessary conclusion from the evidence, but upon the admitted facts in the case, the defendant was guilty of the crime of murder, and the only question left for the

consideration of the jury was whether it was murder in the first degree or second degree. The court gave an extended explanation as to what constituted murder in the first degree and what constituted murder in the second degree....

The charge of the court was the subject of review by the court of last resort of the state of New Jersey, and it was held by that court to be without error. Upon the record in this case there can, in our judgment, be no possible doubt that the [defendant] has had a valid trial by a court having jurisdiction of the subject matter and of the person of the accused, and that there was no loss of jurisdiction over either at any time during the trial. What effect was to be given by the court to the admission of counsel (above set forth) was a question of law for the court to decide, and the charge of the court did not oust it of jurisdiction to proceed in the trial of the case. This is to us so plain a proposition that it is unnecessary to enlarge upon it.

Having no power to review on this writ any other question than that of the jurisdiction of the court in the trial and sentence pronounced upon the verdict of guilty, and concluding that there was the necessary jurisdiction the order of the [federal court] refusing the writ of habeas corpus is affirmed.

See also **Guilty Plea**

Vampire Clan Murders

On November 29, 1996, four Kentucky teenagers drove to Eustice, Florida to help 15-year-old Heather Wendorf run away from home. The four teenagers were: Rodrick Ferrell (16), Dana Cooper (19), Howard Anderson (16), and Charity Keesee (16). The Kentucky teenagers were members of a cult called the Vampire Clan. Authorities believe about 30 teenagers were members of the Vampire Clan. The Vampire Clan's connection with Heather was through Rodrick. He met and became friends with her during a two year period that he lived in Eustice.

Rodrick was the leader of the Vampire Clan. He told members of Vampire Clan he could open the Gates of Hell once he killed a large number of people and drank their blood. Part of the ritual of the cult was that of cutting each other's arms and sucking the blood. They would also kill small animals and drink the blood.

When the Vampire Clan arrived in Eustice they found Heather. The cult then drove to a cemetery where Rodrick and Heather performed a blood drinking ritual that made her a fellow vampire. Shortly afterwards, Rodrick and Howard went to the home of Heather's parents, Richard and Naoma Wen-

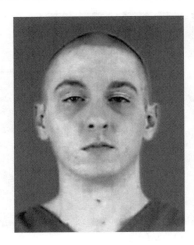

Rodrick Ferrell was sentenced to death for the murder of Richard and Naoma Wendorf. (Florida Department of Corrections)

dorf. While inside the home Rodrick used a crowbar to beat the couple to death, as Howard looked on. Rodrick burned a "V" sign surrounded by circular marks into Richard Wendorf's body. After the murders the Vampire Clan and Heather left Florida driving the Wendorf's utility vehicle.

When authorities discovered the bodies of Richard and Naomi, they initially believed Heather was a kidnap victim. After further investigation she became a suspect in the murders. It did not take authorities long to locate the cult. With the help of the mother of one of the cult members, authorities captured the cult in Louisiana.

A grand jury returned murder indictments against Rodrick and Howard. Dana and Charity were indicted as accessories before the fact. No indictment was returned against Heather, as it appeared she did not know that her parents would be killed.

The Vampire Clan members were tried separately and each was found guilty. On February 27, 1998, Rodrick was sentenced to death. On April 1, 1998, Howard was given two life sentences. On July 15, 1998, Dana was given two sentences of 15 years. On August 13, 1998, Charity was given two sentences of 10 years.

Vanuatu

Capital punishment is not carried out in Vanuatu. *See also* **International Capital Punishment Nations**

Vatican City State

Capital punishment was abolished by the Vatican City State in 1969. *See also* **International Capital Punishment Nations**

Venezuela

Venezuela abolished capital punishment in 1863. *See also* **International Capital Punishment Nations**

Venue

Venue refers to the place in which a crime occurred. Geographically criminal venue is generally a county. A defendant is entitled to be tried in the venue where the crime was committed. A defendant may seek to change trial venue when pretrial negative publicity makes it unlikely that an impartial jury can be selected from the area. *See also* **Irvin v. Dowd (II); Pretrial Publicity; Rideau v. Louisiana**

Verdict *see* Jury Unanimity

(Left to right): *Dana Cooper, Howard Anderson, and Charity Keesee. Cooper and Keesee received stiff prison sentences for their role in the murder of Richard and Naoma Wendorf. Anderson received two sentences of life imprisonment. (Florida Department of Corrections)*

Vermont The death penalty is not carried out by the State of Vermont. It was abolished for most crimes in 1965, and subsequently for all crimes.

Victim Impact Evidence Victim impact evidence involves personal characteristics of the victim and the emotional, economic and social impact of the crime on the victim's immediate family. This type of evidence was once found to violate the Federal Constitution as being too prejudicial for use at the penalty phase of a capital prosecution. However, it is now recognized that victim impact evidence does not offend the Federal Constitution and may be admissible at a capital penalty phase proceeding for the penalty phase jury to consider as non-statutory aggravating evidence.

As a result of the emotional appeal and prejudice of victim impact evidence, courts are generally strict in the type of victim evidence they will permit the jury to consider. Highly inflammatory or irrelevant victim impact evidence is usually barred from introduction at the penalty phase. Victim impact evidence is admitted at the penalty phase proceeding only after there is present in the record evidence of one or more statutory aggravating circumstances.

Victim impact evidence is to be distinguished from sympathy for the victim. The death penalty may not be imposed based upon sympathy for the victim. Imposition of a sentence of death must be grounded upon the interplay of mitigating and aggravating circumstances. *See also* **Booth v. Maryland; California v. Brown; Payne v. Tennessee; South Carolina v. Gathers**

Victim's Family's Right to Attend Execution The family members of a murder victim do not have a Federal constitutional right to be present at the execution of a capital felon. Jurisdictions have absolute authority to admit or deny public access to an execution. Only a few jurisdictions provide by statute for the attendance of family members of the victim at an execution. *See also* **Public Viewing of Execution**

Victim's Opinion About the Death Penalty In a few capital prosecutions, victims of capital murder have left behind documented opinions about their views on the death penalty. Such views have been for and against the death penalty. Courts have prohibited capital defendant's from introducing victim opinions that opposed capital punishment. And, too, courts have barred prosecutors from introducing as victim impact evidence, documented statements by capital murder victims approving of the death penalty. Courts have precluded such evidence on both sides, because it goes to the issue of the appropriate sentence to be imposed. The determination of the appropriate sentence must be made purely upon factors that aggravated a murder, as well as factors surrounding the character of the capital defendant and the circumstances of the crime that mitigate the punishment. *See also* **Individualized Sentencing**

Victor v. Nebraska *Court:* United States Supreme Court; *Case Citation:* Victor v. Nebraska, 511 U.S. 1 (1994); *Argued:* January 18, 1994; *Decided:* March 22, 1994; *Opinion of the Court:* Justice O'Connor; *Concurring Opinion:* Justice Kennedy; *Concurring Opinion:* Justice Ginsburg; *Concurring and Dissenting Opinion:* Justice Blackmun, in which Souter, J., joined; *Appellate Defense Counsel:* Not reported; *Appellate Prosecution Counsel:* Not reported; *Amicus Curiae Brief Supporting Prosecutor:* Not reported; *Amicus Curiae Brief Supporting Defendant:* Not reported.

Issue Presented: Whether the guilt phase juries in the defendants' capital trials were properly instructed on the meaning of the "beyond a reasonable doubt" standard of proof?

Case Holding: The guilt phase juries in the defendants' capital trials were properly instructed on the meaning of the "beyond a reasonable doubt" standard of proof.

Factual and procedural background of case: This case involved two consolidated cases that presented the same issue. In the first case the defendant, Clarence Victor, was convicted and sentenced to death by the State of Nebraska. In the second case the defendant, Alfred Arthur Sandoval, was convicted and sentenced to death by the State of California. Both defendants unsuccessfully challenged their convictions, in their respective State Supreme Courts, on the grounds that the trial judges erroneously instructed the guilt phase juries on the meaning of "beyond a reasonable doubt." Both defendants contended that the erroneous instructions violated the Due Process Clause of the Federal Constitution. The United States Supreme Court granted certiorari for both cases to consider the issue.

Opinion of the Court by Justice O'Connor: Justice O'Connor noted that prosecutors must prove beyond a reasonable doubt every element of a charged offense. She wrote that taken as a whole, the instructions in both cases correctly conveyed the concept of reasonable doubt. The opinion ruled that there was no reasonable likelihood that the jurors understood the instructions to allow convictions based on proof less than that of beyond a reasonable doubt.

It was also said that the Constitution does not dictate that any particular form of words be used in advising the jury of the government's burden of proof at the guilt phase, so long as, taken as a whole, the instructions correctly convey the concept of reasonable doubt. The opinion stated that the proper inquiry is not whether an instruction "could have" been applied unconstitutionally, but whether there is a reasonable likelihood that the jury did so apply it unconstitutionally. The judgments of the Nebraska Supreme Court and California Supreme Court were affirmed.

Concurring opinion by Justice Kennedy: Justice Kennedy concurred in the Court's decision. He indicated that the California instruction contained a term that was problematic, but it was not fatal to the instruction as a whole.

Concurring opinion by Justice Ginsburg: Justice Ginsburg concurred in the Court's opinion. She was concerned that both instructions contained terms that were obscure, but that "the instructions adequately conveyed to the jurors that they should focus exclusively upon the evidence, and that they should convict only if they had an 'abiding conviction' of the defendants' guilt."

Concurring and dissenting opinion by Justice Blackmun, in which Souter, J., joined: Justice Blackmun concurred in the Court's opinion of the validity of the instruction in Sandoval's case, but dissented from the Court's judgment. He indicated that he dissented from the opinion and judgment of the Court Victor's case. It was said by Justice Blackmun that the instruction in Victor's case had the same flaws that the Court disapproved of in *Cage v. Louisiana*. Justice Blackmun wrote: "The majority today purports to uphold and follow *Cage*, but plainly falters in its application of that case. There is no meaningful difference between the jury instruction delivered at Victor's trial and the jury instruction issued in *Cage*, save the fact that the jury instruction in Victor's case did not contain the two words 'grave uncertainty.' But the mere absence of these two words can be of no help to the State, since there is other language in the instruction that is equally offensive to due process." The basis of Justice Blackmun's dissent in the judgment of Sandoval's case was his "view that the death penalty cannot be imposed fairly within the constraints of our Constitution." *See also* **Burden of Proof at Guilt Phase; Cage v. Louisiana**

Vietnam Capital punishment is allowed in Vietnam. Vietnam uses the firing squad to carry out the death penalty. In 1998, the nation executed 18 prisoners. Its legal system is based on French civil law. The nation adopted a constitution on April 15, 1992. The judicial system consists of the district courts, provincial courts and a Supreme People's Court. Trials generally are open to the public. Defendants have the right to be present at their trial and to have a lawyer. Those convicted have the right to appeal. *See also* **International Capital Punishment Nations**

Viewing Execution *see* Public Viewing of Execution

Vigilance Committee of San Francisco During the 1850s lawlessness was at its height in San Francisco, California. The gold rush fever broke down the organs of government and crime went largely unpunished. In an effort to bring crime under control a few leading citizens of the city helped form the famous Vigilance Committee in 1851. The Committee took on the task of prosecuting lawbreakers as an unofficial organ of government. The Committee prosecuted criminals from 1851–1852, before yielding to the official law enforcement organs of government.

One of the leading supporters of the Committee was James King, a former banker. On October 8, 1855, King launched the publication of newspaper called the Evening Bul-

letin. King used the newspaper as a voice to rally citizens to help fight rampant crime and corruption, even though the Committee had disbanded.

Shortly after King started his newspaper, a notorious gambler named Charles Cora, shot and killed a local United States marshal named William H. Richardson. Cora was arrested by the local sheriff. King believed the sheriff would accept a bribe and allow Cora to escape. Consequently, King announced in his newspaper that if Cora escaped, the sheriff must hang in his place.

King received widespread public support for his attack on the sheriff. In response to that support, King launched attacks on other local government officials. One of the politicians taken on by King was James P. Casey, a city supervisor. King informed the public that Casey was an ex-convict who was imprisoned in New York's Sing Sing Prison. King's attack on Casey was the last effort on his part to fight crime and corruption in the city. On May 14, 1856, Casey shot King as he was leaving his newspaper headquarters. King died in his home on May 20. Casey was arrested for the shooting.

During the few days that King was at home clinging to life, over 10,000 people crowded around his home daily to hear the latest on his condition. At the same time, his supporters began to reorganize the Vigilance Committee in the event that he died. When King in fact died, almost 4,000 people had joined the Committee, which was spearheaded by William T. Coleman, a prominent member of the old Committee of 1851.

On the day of King's death, the members of the Committee marched to the jail where Casey was being held and removed him. Casey was taken to a lodge where the Committee had hastily set up headquarters. Shortly after taking Casey, the Committee returned to the jail and took Cora.

On May 21, both Casey and Cora were prosecuted by the Committee for murder. The trial was presided over by a jury and both men had "lawyers." The jury found Casey guilty of murdering King, and found Cora guilty of murdering marshal Richardson. They were both sentenced to death.

On May 22, King and Casey were taken atop a city building and prepared for execution. Thousands of people lined the streets below. At precisely 20 minutes after one o'clock, the bodies of both men were tossed from the building as ropes snapped their necks.

Vinson, Fred M. Fred M. Vinson served as chief justice of the United States Supreme Court from 1946 to 1953. While on the Supreme Court Vinson was known as a conservative interpreter of the Constitution.

Vinson was born in Louisa, Kentucky on January 22, 1890. He received his law degree from Center College in 1911. Vinson

Capital Punishment Opinions Written by Vinson

Case Name	Opinion of the Court	Plurality Opinion	Concurring Opinion	Dissenting Opinion
Burns v. Wilson		✓		
Kawakita v. United States				✓
Rosenberg v. United States	✓			

had a modest and obscure legal practice in Kentucky. He developed national contacts after his election to the United States House of Representatives, beginning in 1923. He was appointed as an appellate judge on the Court of Appeals for the District of Columbia in 1937. In 1946 President Harry S. Truman appointed Vinson chief justice of the Supreme Court.

During Vinson's relatively short tenure on the Supreme Court he wrote only a few capital punishment opinions. The opinion which has endeared his name to capital punishment jurisprudence was written for the Court in *Rosenberg v. United States*. In that case Vinson rejected an appeal by a "next of friend" seeking to stop the execution of Julius and Ethel Rosenberg. The opinion in the case was actually issued after the Rosenbergs were executed. Vinson died on September 8, 1953.

Virginia The State of Virginia is a capital punishment jurisdiction. The State reenacted its death penalty law after the United States Supreme Court decision in *Furman v. Georgia*, 408 U.S. 238 (1972), on October 1, 1975.

Virginia has a three-tier legal system. The State's legal system is composed of a supreme court, court of appeals and courts of general jurisdiction. The Virginia Supreme Court is presided over by a chief justice and six associate justices. The Virginia Court of Appeals is composed of a chief judge and nine judges. The courts of general jurisdiction in the State are called Circuit Courts. Capital offenses against the State of Virginia are tried in the Circuit Courts.

Virginia's capital punishment statute is triggered if a person commits a homicide under the following special circumstances:
1. The willful, deliberate, and premeditated killing of any person in the commission of abduction, when such abduction was committed with the intent to extort money or a pecuniary benefit or with the intent to defile the victim of such abduction;
2. The willful, deliberate, and premeditated killing of any person by another for hire;
3. The willful, deliberate, and premeditated killing of any person by a prisoner confined in a state or local correctional facility, or while in the custody of an employee thereof;
4. The willful, deliberate, and premeditated killing of any person in the commission of robbery or attempted robbery;
5. The willful, deliberate, and premeditated

Members of the Virginia Supreme Court: (left to right) *Justice Lawrence L. Koontz, Jr., Justice Leroy R. Hassell, Sr., Justice A. Christian Compton, Chief Justice Harry L. Carrico, Justice Elizabeth B. Lacy, Justice Barbara M. Keenan, and Justice Cynthia D. Kinser. (Virginia Supreme Court)*

Executions by Virginia 1976–1996

Name	Race	Date of Execution	Method of Execution
Frank Coppola	White	August 10, 1982	Electrocution
Linwood Briley	Black	October 12, 1984	Electrocution
James Briley	Black	April 18, 1985	Electrocution
Morris Mason	Black	June 25, 1985	Electrocution
Michael Smith	Black	July 31, 1986	Electrocution
Richard Whitley	White	July 6, 1987	Electrocution
Earl Clanton	Black	April 14, 1988	Electrocution
Alton Waye	Black	August 30, 1989	Electrocution
Richard T. Boggs	White	July 19, 1990	Electrocution
Wilbert L. Evans	Black	October 17, 1990	Electrocution
Buddy E. Justus	White	December 13, 1990	Electrocution
Albert Clozza	White	July 24, 1991	Electrocution
Derick L. Peterson	Black	August 22, 1991	Electrocution
Roger K. Coleman	White	May 20, 1992	Electrocution
Edward Fitzgerald	White	July 23, 1992	Electrocution
Willie L. Jones	Black	September 15, 1992	Electrocution
Timothy Bunch	White	December 10, 1992	Electrocution
Charles Stampfer	Black	January 19, 1993	Electrocution
Syvasky Poyner	Black	March 18, 1993	Electrocution
Andrew Chabrol	White	June 17, 1993	Electrocution
Joseph Wise	Black	September 14, 1993	Electrocution
David Pruett	White	December 16, 1993	Electrocution
Johnny Watkins, Jr.	Black	March 3, 1994	Electrocution
Timothy Spencer	Black	April 27, 1994	Electrocution
Dana R. Edmonds	Black	January 24, 1995	Lethal Injection
Willie L. Turner	Black	May 25, 1995	Lethal Injection
Dennis W. Stockton	White	September 27, 1995	Lethal Injection
Mickey W. Davidson	White	October 19, 1995	Lethal Injection
Herman C. Barnes	Black	November 13, 1995	Lethal Injection
Walter Correll	White	January 4, 1996	Lethal Injection
Richard Townes, Jr.	Black	January 23, 1996	Lethal Injection
Joseph Savino	White	July 17, 1996	Lethal Injection
Ronald Bennett	Black	November 21, 1996	Lethal Injection
Gregory W. Beaver	White	December 3, 1996	Lethal Injection
Larry A. Stout	Black	December 10, 1996	Lethal Injection
Lem Tuggle	White	December 12, 1996	Lethal Injection
Ronald L. Hoke	White	December 16, 1996	Lethal Injection

Executions by Virginia 1997–1999

Name	Race	Date of Execution	Method of Execution
Michael C. George	White	February 6, 1997	Lethal Injection
Coleman Gray	Black	February 26, 1997	Lethal Injection
Roy B. Smith	White	July 17, 1997	Lethal Injection

Name	Race	Date of Execution	Method of Execution
Joseph R. O'Dell	White	July 23, 1997	Lethal Injection
Carlton J. Pope	Black	August 19, 1997	Lethal Injection
Mario B. Murphy	Hispanic	September 17, 1997	Lethal Injection
Dawud M. Mu'Min	Black	November 13, 1997	Lethal Injection
Michael C. Satcher	Black	December 9, 1997	Lethal Injection
Thomas Beaver	White	December 11, 1997	Lethal Injection
Tony A. Mackall	Black	February 10, 1998	Lethal Injection
Douglas Buchanan	White	March 18, 1998	Lethal Injection
Ronald Watkins	Black	March 25, 1998	Lethal Injection
Angel F. Breard	Hispanic	April 14, 1998	Lethal Injection
Dennis W. Eaton	White	June 18, 1998	Lethal Injection
Danny L. King	White	July 23, 1998	Lethal Injection
Lance Chandler	Black	August 20, 1998	Lethal Injection
Johnile DuBois	Black	August 31, 1998	Lethal Injection
Kenneth Stewart	White	September 23, 1998	Electrocution
Dwayne A. Wright	Black	October 14, 1998	Lethal Injection
Ronald L. Fitzgerald	Black	October 21, 1998	Lethal Injection
Kenneth Wilson	Black	November 17, 1998	Lethal Injection
Kevin W. Cardwell	Black	December 3, 1998	Lethal Injection
Mark A. Sheppard	Black	January 20, 1998	Lethal Injection
Tony L. Fry	White	February 4, 1999	Lethal Injection
George A. Quesinberry	White	March 9, 1999	Lethal Injection
David L. Fisher	White	March 25, 1999	Lethal Injection
Carl H. Chichester	Black	April 13, 1999	Lethal Injection
Arthur R. Jenkins	White	April 20, 1999	Lethal Injection
Eric C. Payne	White	April 28, 1999	Lethal Injection
Ronald D. Yeatts	White	April 29, 1999	Lethal Injection
Thomas Strickler	White	July 21, 1999	Lethal Injection
Marlon Williams	Black	August 17, 1999	Lethal Injection
Everett L. Mueller	White	September 16, 1999	Lethal Injection
Jason Joseph	Black	October 19, 1999	Lethal Injection
Thomas L. Royal, Jr.	Black	November 9, 1999	Lethal Injection
Andre Graham	Black	December 9, 1999	Lethal Injection

killing of any person in the commission of, or subsequent to, rape or attempted rape, forcible sodomy or attempted forcible sodomy or object sexual penetration;

6. The willful, deliberate, and premeditated killing of a law-enforcement officer;

7. The willful, deliberate, and premeditated killing of more than one person as a part of the same act or transaction;

8. The willful, deliberate, and premeditated killing of more than one person within a three-year period;

9. The willful, deliberate, and premeditated killing of any person in the commission of or attempted commission of a drug offense;

10. The willful, deliberate, and premeditated killing of any person by another pursuant to the direction or order of one who is engaged in a continuing criminal enterprise;

11. The willful, deliberate and premeditated killing of a pregnant woman by one who knows that the woman is pregnant and has the intent to cause the involuntary termination of the woman's pregnancy without a live birth; and

12. The willful, deliberate and premeditated killing of a person under the age of 14 by a person age 21 or older.

Capital murder in Virginia is punishable by death or life imprisonment. A capital prosecution in Virginia is bifurcated into a guilt phase and penalty phase. A jury is used at both phases of a capital trial. It is required that, at the penalty phase, the jury unanimously agree that a death sentence is appropriate before it can be imposed. If the penalty phase jury is unable to reach a verdict, the trial judge is required to impose a sentence of life imprisonment. The decision of a penalty phase jury is binding on the trial court under the laws of Virginia.

In order to impose a death sentence upon a defendant under Virginia law, it is required that the prosecutor prove the following statutory aggravating circumstance at the penalty phase:

> There is a probability based upon evidence of the prior history of the defendant or of the circumstances surrounding the commission of the offense of which he is accused that he would commit criminal acts of violence that would constitute a continuing serious threat to society, or that his conduct in committing the offense was outrageously or wantonly vile, horrible or inhuman, in that it involved torture, depravity of mind or aggravated battery to the victim.

Although the Federal Constitution will not permit jurisdictions to prevent capital felons from presenting all relevant mitigating evidence at the penalty phase, Virginia has provided the following statutory mitigating circumstances that permit the jury to reject imposition of the death penalty:

(i) The defendant has no significant history of prior criminal activity, (ii) the capital felony was committed while the defendant was under the influence of extreme mental or emotional disturbance, (iii) the victim was a participant in the defendant's conduct or consented to the act, (iv) at the time of the commission of the capital felony, the capacity of the defendant to appreciate the criminality of his conduct or to conform his conduct to the requirements of law was significantly impaired, (v) the age of the defendant at the time of the commission of the capital offense or (vi) mental retardation of the defendant.

Under Virginia's capital punishment statute, a sentence of death is automatically reviewed by the Virginia Supreme Court. Virginia permits a capital felon to choose between death by lethal injection or electrocution. The State's death row facility for men is located in Waverly, Virginia. Pursuant to the laws of Virginia the Governor has exclusive authority to grant clemency in capital cases.

From the start of modern capital punishment in 1976, through 1999, Virginia executed 73 capital felons. During this period Virginia did not have any female capital felon on death row. A total of 37 capital felons were on death row in Virginia in 1999. The 1999 death row population in the State was listed as: 15 black inmates; 19 white inmates; and 3 unidentified inmates. In 1999 the State had 3 juveniles on death row. The State permits capital punishment to be imposed on persons 16 years old or older. Virginia does not prohibit the execution of mentally retarded capital felons.

VIRGINIA EXECUTIONS 1976–1999

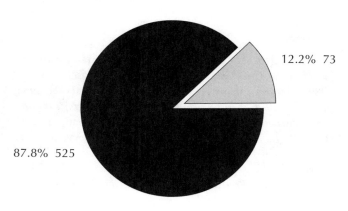

12.2% 73

87.8% 525

◼ VIRGINIA EXECUTIONS
◼ ALL OTHER EXECUTIONS

EXECUTIONS BY VIRGINIA 1930–1999

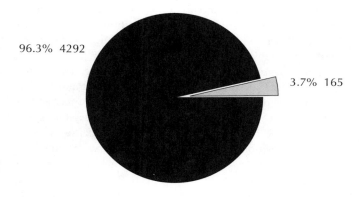

96.3% 4292

 3.7% 165

◼ VIRGINIA
◼ ALL OTHER JURISDICTIONS

Virginians for Alternatives to the Death Penalty

Virginians for Alternatives to the Death Penalty (VADP) was founded in 1991, in Charlottesville, Virginia. VADP was formed for the purpose of educating Virginians about alternative punishments to the death penalty. Under the leadership of its executive director, Henry Heller, VADP sponsors statewide public forums that highlight what it believes are the injustices of the death penalty. The organization circulates a newsletter that provides State and national death penalty information. VADP also has a program designed to work closely with the families of murder victims.

Void for Vagueness Doctrine   The void for vagueness doctrine is a legal tool used to invalidate laws that are obscure or misleading in their meaning or application. This doctrine forces lawmakers to strive for simplicity and clarity in drafting laws. *See also* **Godfrey v. Georgia; Tuilaepa v. California**

Voir Dire *see* **Jury Selection**

Volunteer to Be Executed *see* **Requesting Death**

W

Wainwright v. Goode   *Court:* United States Supreme Court; *Case Citation:* Wainwright v. Goode, 464 U.S. 78 (1983); *Argued:* Not reported; *Decided:* November 28, 1983; *Opinion of the Court:* Per Curiam; *Concurring Opinion:* None; *Dissenting Opinion:* Justice Brennan, in which Marshall, J., joined; *Appellate Defense Counsel:* Not reported; *Appellate Prosecution Counsel:* Not reported; *Amicus Curiae Brief Supporting Prosecutor:* Not reported; *Amicus Curiae Brief Supporting Defendant:* Not reported.

Issue Presented: Whether consideration by a trial court of an impermissible aggravating circumstance during the penalty phase of a capital prosecution required reversal of the defendant's sentence of death?

Case Holding: Where the record indicates the State's highest court reweighed aggravating and mitigating circumstances, excluding the impermissible aggravator, and thereafter affirms the death sentence, any error in a trial court's consideration of an impermissible aggravator is harmless error.

Factual and procedural background of case: The defendant, Arthur Goode, was convicted and sentenced to death for capital murder by the State of Florida. The Florida Supreme Court affirmed the conviction and sentence. After exhausting State post-conviction remedies, the defendant filed a habeas corpus petition in a Federal District Court, alleging that the sentencing judge considered a non-statutory aggravating circumstance, future dangerousness, that was impermissible under Florida law. The District Court denied relief. However, a Federal Court of Appeals reversed after concluding that from the record the State appellate court's finding that the sentencing judge did not rely on the future dangerousness aggravator was not fairly supported by the record as a whole, and that the execution of the defendant would be in violation of the Eighth Amendment. The United States Supreme Court granted certiorari to consider the issue.

Opinion of the Court was delivered Per Curiam: The per curiam opinion ruled that assuming that the issue of whether the sentencing judge had relied on a non-statutory aggravating circumstance was a question of law, it was an issue of State law that was resolved by the Florida Supreme Court. It was said that the Florida Supreme Court's resolution should have been accepted by the Court of Appeals, since the views of a State's highest court with respect to State law are binding on the federal courts.

As an alternative disposition of the issue, the per curiam opinion held: "Even if the Court of Appeals were correct in concluding that the sentencing judge had relied on a factor unavailable to him under state law, it erred in reversing the District Court's dismissal of [the defendant's] habeas corpus petition. It does not appear that if the sentencing judge did consider such a factor, the balancing process of comparing aggravating and mitigating circumstances, as prescribed by the Florida statute, was so infected as to render the death sentence constitutionally impermissible. Whatever may have been true of the sentencing judge, there is no claim that in conducting its independent reweighing of the aggravating and mitigating circumstances the Florida Supreme Court considered [the defendant's] future dangerousness. Thus, there is no basis for concluding that the procedures followed by the State produced an arbitrary or freakish sentence forbidden by the Eighth Amendment." The judgment of the Court of Appeals was reversed.

Dissenting opinion by Justice Brennan, in which Marshall, J., joined: Justice Brennan expressed his disapproval of the Court's summary disposition of the case, as well as the judgment of the Court. He stated his concerns as follows:

> Even if I were to accept the prevailing view that the death penalty is constitutionally permissible under certain circumstances, I would nonetheless object to the Court's summary reversal of the decision of the Court of Appeals. By taking this step, the Court adds to a growing and disturbing trend toward summary disposition of cases involving capital punishment.
>
> When an intervening decision of this Court may affect a lower court's decision, our practice has generally been to grant the petition for certiorari, vacate the lower court judgment, and remand for further consideration in light of the intervening decision.... That the Court today chooses to reverse summarily instead of remanding ..., not only contradicts our general prac-

tice, but also demonstrates once again the Court's disquieting readiness to dispose of cases involving the death penalty on the merits without benefit of full briefing or oral argument.

Wainwright v. Witt   *Court:* United States Supreme Court; *Case Citation:* Wainwright v. Witt, 469 U.S. 412 (1985); *Argued:* October 2, 1984; *Decided:* January 21, 1985; *Opinion of the Court:* Justice Rehnquist; *Concurring Opinion:* Justice Stevens; *Dissenting Opinion:* Justice Brennan, in which Marshall, J., joined; *Appellate Defense Counsel:* William C. McLain argued and briefed; *Appellate Prosecution Counsel:* Robert J. Landry argued; Jim Smith on brief; *Amicus Curiae Brief Supporting Prosecutor:* 1; *Amicus Curiae Brief Supporting Defendant:* None.

Issue Presented: Determining the proper standard for evaluating when a prospective juror may be excluded for cause because of his or her views on capital punishment?

Case Holding: The proper standard for determining when a prospective juror may be excluded for cause because of his or her views on capital punishment, is whether the juror's views would prevent or substantially impair the performance of his or her duties as a juror in accordance with his or her instructions and oath. This standard does not require that a juror's bias be proved with unmistakable clarity.

Factual and procedural background of case: The defendant, Johnny Paul Witt, was convicted of capital murder and sentenced to death by the State of Florida. On direct appeal to the Florida Supreme Court, he argued that several prospective jurors had been improperly excluded for "cause" because of their opposition to capital punishment, in violation of the decision by the United States Supreme Court in *Witherspoon v. Illinois*. The appellate court rejected the argument and affirmed the conviction and sentence.

After unsuccessfully seeking post-conviction review in the State courts, the defendant filed a federal petition for a writ of habeas corpus. The federal District Court denied relief. However, a federal Court of Appeals reversed and granted the writ, holding that, on the basis of the voir dire questioning by the prosecutor, one of the prospective jurors was improperly excused for cause under *Witherspoon*. The United States Supreme Court granted certiorari to consider whether the federal Court of Appeals applied the correct standard in reviewing the case.

Opinion of the Court by Justice Rehnquist: Justice Rehnquist determined that the Court of Appeals applied the wrong standard in evaluating the defendant's claim. The opinion held that the proper standard for determining when a prospective juror may be excluded for cause because of his or her views on capital punishment, is whether the juror's views would prevent or substantially impair the performance of his or her duties as a juror in accordance with his or her instructions and oath. It was further ruled that this standard does not require that a juror's bias be proved with unmistakable clarity.

The opinion found that the Court of Appeals committed error by focusing unduly on the lack of clarity of the questioning of the prospective juror, and in focusing on whether the juror's answers indicated that she would automatically vote against the death penalty.

Justice Rehnquist ruled that under the facts of this case, the prospective juror in question was properly excused for cause. The opinion found that there were adequate written indicia of the trial judge's factual finding to satisfy its decision to grant a challenge for cause. The transcript of voir dire showed that the prospective juror was questioned in the presence of both counsels and the trial judge, that at the end of the colloquy between the prosecutor and the juror the prosecutor challenged for cause, and that the challenge was sustained. The opinion held that nothing more was required. The trial court was not required to write a specific finding or announce for the record its conclusion that, or its reasons why, the prospective juror was biased. The trial court's finding was therefore presumed correct, absent a contrary showing. The opinion concluded that there was ample support for the trial court's finding that the prospective juror's views would have prevented or substantially impaired the performance of her duties as a juror. The judgment of the Court of Appeals was reversed.

Concurring opinion by Justice Stevens: Justice Stevens concurred in the Court's judgment, but did not join the Court's opinion "[b]ecause the Court's opinion contains so much discussion that is unnecessary to the resolution of this case[.]"

Dissenting opinion by Justice Brennan: Justice Brennan dissented from the majority opinion because of his fundamental belief that the Constitution prohibited imposition of the death penalty. As a second basis for dissenting, Justice Brennan argued that the Court was abandoning principles laid down in *Witherspoon* on death-qualified juries. The dissent contended as follows:

> In *Witherspoon v. Illinois*, the Court recognized that the voir dire practice of "death qualification"—the exclusion for cause, in capital cases, of jurors opposed to capital punishment-can dangerously erode this "inestimable safeguard" by creating unrepresentative juries "uncommonly willing to condemn a man to die." To protect against this risk, *Witherspoon* and its progeny have required the State to make an exceptionally strong showing that a prospective juror's views about the death penalty will result in actual bias toward the defendant before permitting exclusion of the juror for cause.
>
> The Court of Appeals below correctly applied the stringent *Witherspoon* standards to the voir dire colloquy between the prosecutor and prospective juror[.] Reversing this decision, the Court today abandons *Witherspoon's* strict limits on death-qualification and holds instead that death-qualification exclusions be evaluated under the same standards as exclusions for any other cause. Championing the right of the State to a jury purged of all possibility of partiality toward a capital defendant, the Court today has shown itself willing to ignore what the Court in *Witherspoon* and its progeny thought crucial: the inevitable result of the quest for such purity in the jury room in a capital case is not a neutral jury drawn from a fair cross section of the community but a jury biased against the defendant, at least with respect to penalty, and a jury from which an identifiable segment of the community has been excluded. Until today it had been constitutionally impermissible for the State to require a defen-

dant to place his life in the hands of such a jury; our fundamental notions of criminal justice were thought to demand that the State, not the defendant, bear the risk of a less than wholly neutral jury when perfect neutrality cannot, as in this situation it most assuredly cannot, be achieved. Today the State's right to ensure exclusion of any juror who might fail to vote the death penalty when the State's capital punishment scheme permits such a verdict vanquishes the defendant's right to a jury that assuredly will not impose the death penalty when that penalty would be inappropriate.

See also **Adams v. Texas; Boulden v. Holman; Darden v. Wainwright; Davis v. Georgia; Gray v. Mississippi; Jury Selection; Morgan v. Illinois; Ross v. Oklahoma; Witherspoon v. Illinois**

Waite, Morrison R.

Morrison R. Waite served as chief justice of the United States Supreme Court from 1874 to 1888. While on the Supreme Court Waite was known as a conservative interpreter of the Constitution.

Waite was born in Lyme, Connecticut on November 19, 1816. He was educated at Yale University and graduated in 1837. Waite studied law with his father, who was a lawyer and judge. In 1839 Waite was admitted to the Ohio bar. Waite was a successful lawyer who gained national prominence after his representation of the United States in arbitration proceedings against England for post–Civil War claims. Waite succeeded in obtaining a settlement from England in the amount of $15 million. In 1874 President Ulysses S. Grant nominated Waite as chief justice of the Supreme Court.

Waite was known to only issue a few capital punishment opinions while on the Supreme Court (frequently the Court issued criminal law opinions which did not indicate what punishment the defendant received). In the case of *Ex Parte Spies* eight defendants (seven received death sentences) sought to have the judgments against them reversed because an Illinois statute did not disqualify jurors who had prior knowledge of a case. (The defendants' prosecution gained national attention because they were anarchists.) Waite, writing for the Court, rejected the defendants' argument that the statute violated due process of law. He wrote that the statute was valid because it required jurors give an oath that they could fairly and impartially decide the issues in the case. Waite died on March 23, 1888.

Capital Punishment Opinions Written by Waite

Case Name	Opinion of the Court	Concurring Opinion	Dissenting Opinion
Bush v. Kentucky			✓
Ex Parte Spies	✓		
Neal v. Delaware			✓

Waiver

In spite of the many constitutional and statutory protections afforded a capital felon, he or she may waive the vast majority of such protections. For example, capital felons generally may waive the right to appeal a capital "conviction." In all waiver situations, a record must be made which shows that a defendant voluntarily and knowingly gave up a right guaranteed to him or her. *See also* **Requesting Death**

Waiver of Right to Counsel *see* Right to Counsel

Wallace v. United States

Court: United States Supreme Court; *Case Citation:* Wallace v. United States, 162 U.S. 466 (1896); *Argued:* Not reported; *Decided:* April 20, 1896; *Opinion of the Court:* Chief Justice Fuller; *Concurring Opinion:* None; *Dissenting Opinion:* None; *Appellate Defense Counsel:* J. D. Hill argued; J. H. Pratt on brief; Appellate *Prosecution Counsel:* Mr. Conrad argued and briefed; *Amicus Curiae Brief Supporting Prosecutor:* None; *Amicus Curiae Brief Supporting Defendant:* None.

Issue Presented: Whether the trial court committed error in preventing the defendant from proffering evidence that the victim previously threatened him?

Case Holding: The trial court committed error in preventing the defendant from proffering evidence that the victim previously threatened him, because the defendant's defense was self-defense.

Factual and procedural background of case: The defendant, Jerry Wallace, was convicted of capital murder and sentenced to death by the United States. The defendant appealed to the United States Supreme Court, alleging that the trial court committed error in not allowing him to put on evidence that the victim had previously threatened him. The United States Supreme Court granted certiorari to consider the issue.

Opinion of the Court by Chief Justice Fuller: The Chief Justice held that, because the defendant's defense was self-defense, he had a right to put on evidence showing the victim previously threatened him. The opinion addressed the matter as follows:

> If Jerry Wallace believed, and had reasonable ground for the belief, that he was in imminent danger of death or great bodily harm from [the victim], at the moment he fired, and would not have fired but for such belief, and if that belief, founded on reasonable ground, might, in any view the jury could properly take of the circumstances surrounding the killing, have excused his act, or reduced the crime from murder to manslaughter, then the evidence in respect of [the victim's] threats was relevant, and it was error to exclude it....
>
> Where a difficulty is intentionally brought on for the purpose of killing the deceased, the fact of imminent danger to the accused constitutes no defense; but where the accused embarks in a quarrel with no felonious intent or malice, or premeditated purpose of doing bodily harm or killing, and, under reasonable belief of imminent danger he inflicts a fatal wound, it is not murder.

The judgment of the Federal trial court was reversed and the cause remanded for a new trial. *See also* **Self-Defense**

Walton v. Arizona

Court: United States Supreme Court; *Case Citation:* Walton v. Arizona, 497 U.S. 639 (1990); *Argued:* January 17, 1990; *Decided:* June 27, 1990; *Opinion of the Court:* Justice White; *Concurring Opinion:* Justice Scalia; *Dissenting Opinion:* Justice Brennan, in which Marshall, J., joined; *Dissenting Opinion:* Justice Blackmun, in which Brennan, Marshall, and Stevens, JJ., joined; *Dissenting Opinion:* Justice Stevens; *Appellate Defense Counsel:* Timothy K. Ford argued; Denise I. Young on brief; *Appellate Prosecution Counsel:* Paul J. McMurdie argued; Robert K. Corbin and Jessica Gifford Funkhouser on brief; *Amicus Curiae Brief Supporting Prosecutor:* 1; *Amicus Curiae Brief Supporting Defendant:* 1.

Issues Presented: (1) Whether every finding of fact underlying the capital sentencing decision must be made by a jury, not by a judge? (2) Whether Arizona's death penalty statute violated the Eighth and Fourteenth Amendments because it imposed on defendants the burden of establishing, by a preponderance of the evidence, the existence of mitigating circumstances sufficiently substantial to call for leniency? (3) Whether the requirement under Arizona's death penalty statute that the trial court "shall impose" the death penalty if one or more aggravating circumstances are found and mitigating circumstances are held insufficient to call for leniency, created an unconstitutional presumption that death is the proper sentence? (4) Whether the statutory aggravating circumstance "especially heinous, cruel or depraved" was unconstitutionally vague?

Case Holdings: (1) Every finding of fact underlying the capital sentencing decision does not have to be made by a jury, and can be made by a judge. (2) Arizona's death penalty statute did not violate the Constitution by imposing on defendants the burden of establishing, by a preponderance of the evidence, the existence of mitigating circumstances sufficiently substantial to call for leniency. (3) The requirement under Arizona's death penalty statute that the trial court "shall impose" the death penalty if one or more aggravating circumstances are found and mitigating circumstances are held insufficient to call for leniency, did not create an unconstitutional presumption that death is the proper sentence. (4) The statutory aggravating circumstance "especially heinous, cruel or depraved," as construed by the Arizona Supreme Court, was not unconstitutionally vague.

Factual and procedural background of case: The defendant, Jeffrey Walton, was convicted and sentenced to death for capital murder by the State of Arizona. The conviction and sentence were upheld by the Arizona Supreme Court. In doing so, the appellate court rejected the defendant's argument (1) that the Constitution required a jury return the death sentence verdict; (2) that the federal Constitution prohibited the State's requirement that he prove penalty phase mitigating circumstances by a preponderance of the evidence; (3) that the statutory requirement which provided that the court "shall impose" the death penalty if one or more aggravating circumstances are found and mitigating circumstances are held insufficient to call for leniency, created an unconstitutional presumption that death is the proper sentence; and (4) that the statutory aggravating circumstance of "especially heinous, cruel or depraved" was constitutionally vague. The United States Supreme Court granted certiorari to consider the issues.

Opinion of the Court by Justice White: Justice White ruled that, under prior precedent by the Court, Arizona's requirement that the judge make the determination of punishment did not violate the Constitution. It was said that the Constitution did not require that every finding of fact underlying a sentencing decision be made by a jury rather than by a judge.

Justice White rejected the defendant's contention that the Constitution prohibited the State from requiring him to prove mitigating circumstances by a preponderance of the evidence. It was said that the defendant's constitutional rights were not violated by placing on him the burden of proving by a preponderance of the evidence the existence of mitigating circumstances sufficiently substantial to call for leniency, since Arizona's method of allocating the burdens of proof did not lessen the State's burden to prove the existence of aggravating circumstances.

The opinion also rejected the defendant's argument that the State's death penalty statute created an unconstitutional presumption that death is the proper sentence by requiring that the court "shall impose" the death penalty under the specified circumstances. It was said that the statute neither precluded the trial court from considering any type of mitigating evidence nor automatically imposed a death sentence for certain types of murder. The opinion ruled that states were free to structure and shape consideration of mitigating evidence in an attempt to achieve a more rational and equitable administration of the death penalty.

The Court found that the "especially heinous, cruel or depraved" statutory aggravating circumstance, as construed by the Arizona Supreme Court, furnished sufficient guidance to the sentencer to satisfy the Constitution. It was said that although juries must be instructed in more than bare terms about an aggravating circumstance that is unconstitutionally vague on its face, trial judges are presumed to know the law and to apply narrower definitions in their decisions. The judgment of the Arizona Supreme Court was affirmed.

Concurring opinion by Justice Scalia: Justice Scalia concurred in the Court's judgment but indicated he did not agree with some of the Court's reasoning.

Dissenting opinion by Justice Brennan: Justice Brennan wrote very critical of the majority's resolution of the issues presented. He wrote in dissent: "In the past, 'this Court has gone to extraordinary measures to ensure that the prisoner sentenced to be executed is afforded process that will guarantee, as much as is humanly possible, that the sentence was not imposed out of whim, passion, prejudice, or mistake;' but today's decisions reflect, if anything, the opposing concern that States ought to be able to execute prisoners with as lit-

tle interference as possible from our established Eighth Amendment doctrine."

Dissenting opinion by Justice Blackmun: Justice Blackmun believed that the majority incorrectly resolved the issues presented. He wrote in his dissent: "In my view, two Arizona statutory provisions, pertinent here, run afoul of the established Eighth Amendment principle that a capital defendant is entitled to an individualized sentencing determination which involves the consideration of all relevant mitigating evidence. The first is the requirement that the sentencer may consider only those mitigating circumstances proved by a preponderance of the evidence. The second is the provision that the defendant bears the burden of establishing mitigating circumstances 'sufficiently substantial to call for leniency.' I also conclude that Arizona's 'heinous, cruel or depraved' aggravating circumstance, as construed by the Arizona Supreme Court, provides no meaningful guidance to the sentencing authority and, as a consequence, is unconstitutional."

Dissenting opinion by Justice Stevens: Justice Stevens believed that the Constitution required a jury make the capital sentencing determination. The dissent issued by Justice Stevens stated: "The Court holds in ... its opinion that a person is not entitled to a jury determination of facts that must be established before the death penalty may be imposed. I am convinced that the Sixth Amendment requires the opposite conclusion." *See also* **Burden of Proof at Penalty Phase; Heinous, Atrocious, Cruel or Depraved Aggravator; Jury Trial; Lewis v. Jeffers; Maynard v. Cartwright; Richmond v. Lewis; Shell v. Mississippi; Stringer v. Black**

War Crimes On February 24, 1864, Andersonville Prison was opened near Americus, Georgia. The prison was used by the Confederate Army for holding Union prisoners of war

The execution of Captain Henry Wirz, the only Confederate soldier executed for war crimes during the Civil War. (National Archives)

during the Civil War. By August of 1864, the prison held 45,613 Union prisoners. During the first 14 months of the prison's operation it was estimated that 12,912, Union prisoners died. It was found that the vast majority of the deaths were due to deliberate starvation imposed by prison officials and the barbaric conditions maintained at the prison.

During the period that most of the deaths occurred at Andersonville, Confederate Captain Henry Wirz was in charge. Wirz was born in Zurich, Switzerland in 1822. He was educated at the University of Zurich, and later obtained a medical degree while studying in Paris and Berlin. In 1849, Wirz immigrated to the United States. He set up a medical practice in Kentucky.

When the Civil War broke out Wirz enlisted in the Confederate Army. He was wounded in 1863 and rendered unfit for the battlefield. In April of 1864, Wirz was placed in command of the Andersonville Prison.

After the war ended Wirz returned to civilian life. Shortly after returning to his medical practice Wirz was arrested and charged with war crimes, as a result of the large number of deaths at the Andersonville Prison. On May 10, 1865, Wirz was transported to Washington, D.C. to stand trial. A military court prosecuted Wirz and found him guilty of war crimes. He was sentenced to death. On November 10, 1865, Wirz was led to the gallows in the Old Capital Prison yard. As hundreds of spectators looked on, Wirz's body swung from the gallows and he entered history as the only Confederate soldier executed for war crimes.

Warren, Earl

Earl Warren served as chief justice of the United States Supreme Court from 1953 to 1969. While on the Supreme Court Warren was known as an ultra liberal interpreter of the Constitution.

Warren was born in Los Angeles, California on March 19, 1891. He was educated at the University of California at Berkeley, where he received an undergraduate degree and law degree. Warren was admitted to the California bar in 1914. His career included being elected attorney general and Governor of California. In 1953 President Dwight D. Eisenhower nominated Warren chief justice of the Supreme Court.

While on the Supreme Court Warren issued only a few capital punishment opinions (frequently the Court issued criminal law opinions which did not indicate what punishment the defendant received). The case of *Spano v. New York* illustrates the ultra liberal philosophy espoused by Warren. In *Spano* the defendant confessed to murder. He appealed alleging that his confession was involuntary. Warren, writing for the Court, agreed with the defendant. The opinion issued by Warren detailed the methods of questioning employed against the defendant. However, no physical force or intimidation was used against him. Warren held that the mere fact of repeated interrogation made the confession involuntary. Warren died July 9, 1974.

Capital Punishment Opinions Written by Warren

Case Name	Opinion of the Court	Concurring Opinion	Dissenting Opinion
Fikes v. Alabama	✓		
Spano v. New York	✓		
Spencer v. Texas			✓
Townsend v. Sain	✓		

Washington

The State of Washington is a capital punishment jurisdiction. The State reenacted its death penalty law after the United States Supreme Court decision in *Furman v. Georgia*, 408 U.S. 238 (1972), on November 4, 1975.

Washington has a three-tier legal system. The State's legal system is composed of a supreme court, court of appeals and courts of general jurisdiction. The Washington Supreme Court is presided over by a chief justice and eight associate justices. The Washington Court of Appeals is divided into three divisions. Each division has at least five judges. The courts of general jurisdiction in the State are called Superior Courts. Capital offenses against the State of Washington are tried in the Superior Courts.

Washington's capital punishment statute is triggered if a person commits a homicide under the following special circumstances:

1. The victim was a law enforcement officer, corrections officer, or fire fighter;
2. At the time of the act resulting in the death, the person was serving a term of imprisonment, had escaped, or was on authorized or unauthorized leave from a state facility or program;
3. At the time of the act resulting in death, the person was in custody in a county or county-city jail as a consequence of having been adjudicated guilty of a felony;
4. The person committed the murder pursuant to an agreement that he or she would receive money or any other thing of value for committing the murder;
5. The person solicited another person to commit the murder and had paid or had agreed to pay money or any other thing of value for committing the murder;
6. The person committed the murder to obtain or maintain his or her membership or to advance his or her position in the hierarchy of an organization, association, or identifiable group;
7. The murder was committed during the course of or as a result of a shooting where the discharge of the firearm, is either from a motor vehicle or from the immediate area of a motor vehicle that was used to transport the shooter or the firearm, or both, to the scene of the discharge;
8. The victim was a judge; juror or former juror; prospective, current, or former witness in an adjudicative proceeding; prosecuting attorney; deputy prosecuting attorney; defense attorney; a member of the indeterminate sentence review board; or a probation or parole officer;
9. The person committed the murder to conceal the commission of a crime or to protect or conceal the identity

of any person committing a crime, including, but specifically not limited to, any attempt to avoid prosecution as a persistent offender;

10. There was more than one victim and the murders were part of a common scheme or plan or the result of a single act of the person;

11. The murder was committed in the course of, in furtherance of, or in immediate flight from a robbery, rape, burglary, kidnaping, or arson;

12. The victim was regularly employed or self-employed as a newsreporter and the murder was committed to obstruct or hinder the investigative, research, or reporting activities of the victim;

13. At the time the person committed the murder, there existed a court order, issued in this or any other state, which prohibited the person from either contacting the victim, molesting the victim, or disturbing the peace of the victim, and the person had knowledge of the existence of that order;

14. At the time the person committed the murder, the person and the victim were family or household members and the person had previously engaged in a pattern or practice of three or more of the following crimes committed upon the victim within a five-year period, regardless of whether a conviction resulted: (a) harassment or (b) any criminal assault.

Capital murder in Washington is punishable by death or life imprisonment without parole. A capital prosecution in Washington is bifurcated into a guilt phase and penalty phase. A jury is used at both phases of a capital trial. It is required that, at the penalty phase, the jury unanimously agree that a death sentence is appropriate before it can be imposed. If the penalty phase jury is unable to reach a verdict, the trial judge is required to impose a sentence of life imprisonment without parole. The decision of a penalty phase jury is binding on the trial court under the laws of Washington.

Washington does not set out any penalty phase statutory aggravating circumstances. In order to impose a death sentence upon a defendant under Washington law, it is required that the jury answer the following question affirmatively: Having in mind the crime of which the defendant has been found guilty, are you convinced beyond a reasonable doubt that there are not sufficient mitigating circumstances to merit leniency?

Although the Federal Constitution will not permit jurisdictions to prevent capital felons from presenting all relevant mitigating evidence at the penalty phase, Washington has provided the following statutory mitigating circumstances that permit the jury to reject imposition of the death penalty:

1. Whether the defendant has or does not have a significant history, either as a juvenile or an adult, of prior criminal activity;

2. Whether the murder was committed while the defendant was under the influence of extreme mental disturbance;

3. Whether the victim consented to the act of murder;

4. Whether the defendant was an accomplice to a murder committed by another person where the defendant's participation in the murder was relatively minor;

5. Whether the defendant acted under duress or domination of another person;

6. Whether, at the time of the murder, the capacity of the defendant to appreciate the wrongfulness of his or her conduct or to conform his or her conduct to the requirements of law was substantially impaired as a result of mental disease or defect;

7. Whether the age of the defendant at the time of the crime calls for leniency; and

8. Whether there is a likelihood that the defendant will pose a danger to others in the future.

Under Washington's capital punishment statute, a sentence of death is automatically reviewed by the Washington Supreme Court. Washington permits a capital felon to choose between lethal injection and hanging as the method of execution. The State's death row facility for men is located in Walla Walla, Washington. Pursuant to the laws of Washington the Governor has exclusive authority to grant clemency in capital cases.

From the start of modern capital punishment in 1976, through 1999, Washington executed 3 capital felons. During this period it did not have any female capital felons on death row. A total of 17 capital felons were on death row in Washington in 1999. The 1999 death row population in the State was listed as: 3 black inmates; 13 white inmates; and 1 unidentified inmate. The State does not permit capital punishment to be imposed on persons 17 years old or younger. Washington prohibits the execution of mentally retarded capital felons.

Executions by Washington 1976–1999

Name	Race	Date of Execution	Method of Execution
Westley A. Dodd	White	January 5, 1993	Hanging
Charles Campbell	White	May 27, 1994	Hanging
Jeremy Sagastegui	White	October 13, 1998	Lethal Injection

WASHINGTON EXECUTIONS 1976–1999

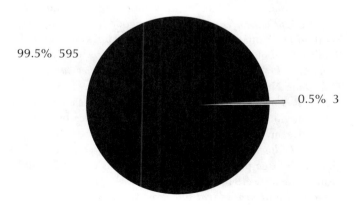

99.5% 595

0.5% 3

■ WASHINGTON EXECUTIONS
■ ALL OTHER EXECUTIONS

EXECUTIONS BY WASHINGTON 1930–1999

98.9% 4407

1.1% 50

■ WASHINGTON

■ ALL OTHER JURISDICTIONS

Washington Coalition to Abolish the Death Penalty

The Washington Coalition to Abolish the Death Penalty (WCADP) was created in 1984. The organization is composed of 21 community, religious, and legal organizations. Through public education and activism, WCADP works to increase opposition to the death penalty in the general public and among the State of Washington's leaders. WCADP publishes a quarterly newsletter, offers written resources and speakers about the death penalty, coordinates activities around the state, works with the media and the legislature, and offers support to death row inmates in Washington.

Watts v. Indiana

Court: United States Supreme Court; *Case Citation:* Watts v. Indiana, 338 U.S. 49 (1949); *Argued:* November 16–17, 1948; *Decided:* June 27, 1949; *Plurality Opinion:* Justice Frankfurter announced the Court's judgment and delivered an opinion, in which Murphy and Rutledge, JJ., joined; *Concurring Opinion:* Justice Douglas; *Concurring Statement:* Justice Black; *Concurring Statement:* Justice Jackson; *Dissenting Statement:* Chief Justice Vinson, and Reed and Burton, JJ.; *Appellate Defense Counsel:* Thurgood Marshall argued; Franklin H. Williams on brief; *Appellate Prosecution Counsel:* Frank E. Coughlin argued and briefed; *Amicus Curiae Brief Supporting Prosecutor:* None; *Amicus Curiae Brief Supporting Defendant:* None.

Issue Presented: Whether the defendant's confession was obtained in violation of due process of law, and thereby invalidated his conviction and death sentence?

Case Holding: The defendant's confession was obtained in violation of due process of law, therefore his conviction and death sentence were invalid.

Factual and procedural background of case: The defendant, Watts, was arrested on suspicion of capital murder by the State of Indiana. The circumstances occurring after his arrest were reported as follows:

> ... They took him ... to State Police Headquarters, where he was questioned by officers in relays from about 11:30 that night

until sometime between 2:30 and 3 o'clock the following morning. The same procedure of persistent interrogation from about 5:30 in the afternoon until about 3 o'clock the following morning, by a relay of six to eight officers, was pursued on Thursday the 13th, Friday the 14th, Saturday the 15th, Monday the 17th. Sunday was a day of rest from interrogation. About 3 o'clock on Tuesday morning, November 18, the [defendant] made an incriminating statement after continuous questioning since 6 o'clock of the preceding evening. The statement did not satisfy the prosecutor who had been called in and he then took [the defendant] in hand. [The defendant], questioned by an interrogator of 20 years' experience as lawyer, judge and prosecutor, yielded a more incriminating document.

Until his inculpatory statements were secured, the [defendant] was a prisoner in the exclusive control of the prosecuting authorities. He was kept for the first two days in solitary confinement in a cell aptly enough called 'the hole' in view of its physical conditions.... Apart from the five night sessions, the police intermittently interrogated Watts during the day and on three days drove him around town, hours at a time, with a view to eliciting identifications and other disclosures. Although the law of Indiana required that [the defendant] be given a prompt preliminary hearing before a magistrate, with all the protection a hearing was intended to give him, the [defendant] was not only given no hearing during the entire period of interrogation but was without friendly or professional aid and without advice as to his constitutional rights. Disregard of rudimentary needs of life — opportunities for sleep and a decent allowance of food — are also relevant, not as aggravating elements of [the defendant's] treatment, but as part of the total situation out of which his confessions came and which stamped their character.

Armed with a confession by the defendant, the prosecutor was able to get the jury to return a guilty verdict and death sentence. The Indiana Supreme Court affirmed the conviction and sentence. In do so, the appellate court rejected the defendant's contention that his confession was obtained in violation of due process of law. The United States Supreme Court granted certiorari to consider the issue.

Plurality opinion in which Justice Frankfurter announced the Court's judgment and in which Murphy and Rutledge, JJ., joined: Justice Frankfurter held that it was the judgment of the Court that the confession given by the defendant was obtained in violation of the Due Process Clause. Justice Frankfurter expressed his opinion as to the requirements of due process as follows:

> A confession by which life becomes forfeit must be the expression of free choice. A statement to be voluntary of course need not be volunteered. But if it is the product of sustained pressure by the police it does not issue from a free choice. When a suspect speaks because he is overborne, it is immaterial whether he has been subjected to a physical or a mental ordeal.... We would have to shut our minds to the plain significance of what here transpired to deny that this was a calculated endeavor to secure a confession through the pressure of unrelenting interrogation. The very relentlessness of such interrogation implies that it is better for the prisoner to answer than to persist in the refusal of disclosure which is his constitutional right. To turn the detention of an accused into a process of wrenching from him evidence which could not be extorted in open court with all its safeguards, is so grave an abuse of the power of arrest as to offend the procedural standards of due process....

In holding that the Due Process Clause bars police procedure which violates the basic notions of our accusatorial mode of prosecuting crime and vitiates a conviction based on the fruits of such procedure, we apply the Due Process Clause to its historic function of assuring appropriate procedure before liberty is curtailed or life is taken. We are deeply mindful of the anguishing problems which the incidence of crime presents to the States. But the history of the criminal law proves overwhelmingly that brutal methods of law enforcement are essentially self-defeating, whatever may be their effect in a particular case.

The judgment of the Indiana Supreme Court was reversed.

Concurring opinion by Justice Douglas: Justice Douglas concurred in the Court's judgment. He addressed the issue of custodial interrogation as follows: "It would be naive to think that this protective custody was less than the inquisition. The man was held until he broke. Then and only then was he arraigned and given the protection which the law provides all accused. Detention without arraignment is a time-honored method for keeping an accused under the exclusive control of the police. They can then operate at their leisure. The accused is wholly at their mercy. He is without the aid of counsel or friends; and he is denied the protection of the magistrate. We should unequivocally condemn the procedure and stand ready to outlaw, any confession obtained during the period of the unlawful detention. The procedure breeds coerced confessions. It is the root of the evil. It is the procedure without which the inquisition could not flourish in the country."

Concurring Statement by Justice Black: Justice Black issued a statement indicating he concurred in the Court's judgment.

Concurring Statement by Justice Jackson: Justice Jackson issued a dissenting opinion in the case which actually stated his position in two companion cases decided by the Court. Although he placed his dissent in this case, Justice Jackson actually concurred in the judgment of this case. He did not provide any reasons for his concurrence in the judgment.

Dissenting statement by Chief Justice Vinson, and Reed and Burton, JJ.: Chief Justice Vinson and Justices Reed and Burton issued a joint statement indicating they dissented from the Court's decision and believed the judgment should be affirmed.

Case note: This case was one of three cases decided by the Court, on the same day, involving involuntary confessions. In each of the cases the Court applied due process principals to invalidate the capital convictions. In subsequent decades the Court would apply the Fifth Amendment right to remain silent to review claims from State prisoners that their confessions were involuntary. *See also* **Harris v. South Carolina; Right to Remain Silent; Turner v. Pennsylvania**

Wayne, James M.

James M. Wayne served as an associate justice of the United States Supreme Court from 1835 to 1867. While on the Supreme Court Wayne was known as a moderate interpreter of the Constitution.

Wayne was born in 1790 in Savannah, Georgia. He was educated at Princeton University where he graduated in 1808. Wayne studied the law and was admitted to practice in Geor-

gia. His career included serving as a trial judge, mayor of Savannah, State legislator and a member of Congress. In 1835 President Andrew Jackson nominated Wayne to the Supreme Court.

While on the Supreme Court Wayne was known to have written only one capital punishment case (frequently the Court issued opinions in criminal cases that did not indicate what punishment a defendant received). In *Ex Parte Wells* the Supreme Court was asked to decide whether the President had authority to pardon the defendant's death sentence upon the condition that the defendant remain in prison for life. Wayne, writing for the Court, ruled that the President had authority to pardon the defendant's death sentence upon the condition that the defendant remain in prison for life, because pardons may be absolute as well as conditional. Wayne died on July 7, 1867.

Weighing Jurisdictions *see* Burden of Proof at the Penalty Phase

Weinberger Kidnapping

On July 4, 1956, one-month-old Peter Weinberger was kidnapped from his home in Westbury, New York. The child was abducted while unattended and sleeping on a patio. The kidnapper left a ransom note demanding $2,000 for the child's safe return. Although the ransom note indicated the child would be killed if the police were notified, the child's parents, Morris and Betty Weinberger, contacted the local police.

Several days after the kidnapping, the police arranged a phony ransom package and dropped it off at a site designated by the kidnapper. However, the kidnapper did not show up. On July 10, the kidnapper called the Weinberger home and left instructions where to deliver the money a second time. The phony ransom package was again dropped off. The kidnapper did not show up however. Instead, the police found a note telling the Weinbergers where they could find the baby if everything went correctly.

The Federal Bureau of Investigation (FBI) was called into to help with the case. The FBI immediately had the handwriting on the two ransom notes analyzed. On August 22, the FBI found a possible match to the handwriting. A similarity was found between the handwriting on the ransom notes and that of Angelo LaMarca. LaMarca had a Federal criminal arrest record for bootlegging.

Angelo LaMarca was executed on August 7, 1958. (U.S. Department of Justice/FBI)

On August 23, LaMarca was arrested at his home in Plainview, New York by FBI agents. LaMarca initially denied involvement in the kidnapping, but later gave a confession. He informed authorities that he was in debt and that the kidnapping occurred on impulse, as he was driving around Westbury trying to figure out how to get the money he needed. LaMarca told the FBI that he had abandoned the baby alive in some heavy brush just off a highway exit right after the kidnapping. A search of the area described by LaMarca was made. The child was found — dead.

LaMarca was prosecuted by the State of New York for murder. He was convicted and on December 14, 1956, he was sentenced to death. On August 7, 1958, LaMarca was executed by electrocution at Sing Sing Prison.

West Memphis Cult Murders　On May 5, 1993, the dead bodies of three boys were discovered in a shallow stream in West Memphis, Arkansas. The boys, all eight years old, were beaten to death. One of them had been sexually mutilated. For weeks authorities were baffled by the crimes and had no lead on who was responsible for what appeared to be ritual-like murders.

A break in the investigation occurred when police interviewed a teenager named Jesse Misskelley. Initially Misskelley denied any knowledge of the murders. However, after failing a lie detector test Misskelley brokedown and confessed.

Misskelley told authorities that he was a member of a satanic cult whose leader was 19-year-old Damien Wayne Echols. The other member of the cult was a youth named Jason Baldwin. According to Misskelley, the trio engaged in the ritualistic killing and eating of dogs. Under Echols' leadership, the trio decided to make a sacrifice of three children. They randomly targeted the victims. Echols was said to have sexually mutilated one of the victims as part of a ritual.

Authorities arrested the trio and prosecuted them for three murders. Misskelley's trial was held first. On February 4, 1994, he was found guilty and sentenced to prison for life. The trial of Echols and Baldwin was held together in March. The jury convicted them of all three murders on March 18. The following day Baldwin was sentenced to life imprisonment and Echols was sentenced to death. Echols is now on death row.

West Virginia　The death penalty was finally abolished by the State of West Virginia in 1965.

Western Missouri Coalition to Abolish the Death Penalty　The Western Missouri Coalition to Abolish the Death Penalty was founded for the purpose of working to abolish the death penalty in the nation. The organization promotes letter writing to death row inmates and engages in educational efforts to reconcile communities with inmates. It also works in a supportive way to assist the families of murder victims.

Westmoreland v. United States　*Court:* United States Supreme Court; *Case Citation:* Westmoreland v. United States, 155 U.S. 545 (1895); *Argued:* Not reported; *Decided:* January 7, 1895; *Opinion of the Court:* Justice Brewer; *Concurring Opinion:* None; *Dissenting Opinion:* None; *Appellate Defense Counsel:* C. L. Herbert argued; Robert H. West on brief; Appellate *Prosecution Counsel:* Whitney argued and briefed; *Amicus Curiae Brief Supporting Prosecutor:* None; *Amicus Curiae Brief Supporting Defendant:* None.

Issue Presented: Whether the indictment against the defendant was defective in failing to allege he knew that he was giving the victim poison and that the poison was ingested in the victim's stomach?

Case Holding: The indictment against the defendant was not defective in failing to allege he knew that he was giving the victim poison and that the poison was ingested in the victim's stomach, because the absence of such allegations did not prevent the defendant from preparing a defense to the charge against him.

Factual and procedural background of case: The defendant, Thomas Westmoreland, was convicted of capital murder and sentenced to death by the United States. The defendant appealed to the United States Supreme Court, alleging that the indictment against him was defective because it failed to allege that he knew the substance which he administered to the deceased was a deadly poison, and that the poison was taken into the stomach of the deceased. The United States Supreme Court granted certiorari to consider the issue.

Opinion of the Court by Justice Brewer: Justice Brewer held that the defendant's assignment of error was without merit and that the indictment was sufficient in giving him notice of the charge against him. The opinion explained as follows:

> … It is charged that he administered the strychnine and other poisons with the unlawful and felonious intent to take the life of the deceased, and that, so administered, they did have the effect of causing death. It matters not whether he knew the exact character of the strychnine or other poisons. It was murder if he unlawfully and feloniously administered any poison with the design of taking life, and that which he so administered did produce death. At the common law, though it was necessary to allege the kind of poison administered, nevertheless proof of the use of a different kind of poison was regarded as an immaterial variance…. So, also, it is unnecessary to aver that the poison was taken into the stomach of the deceased. The crime would be complete if the poison was by hypodermic injection, or otherwise, introduced into the body of the deceased, and, affecting the heart or other organ, caused the death. The indictment need not specify in detail the mode in which the poison affected the body, or the particular organ upon which its operation was had. It is enough to charge that poison was administered, and that such poison, so administered, caused the death.

The judgment of the Federal trial court was affirmed.

Wheeler v. United States　*Court:* United States Supreme Court; *Case Citation:* Wheeler v. United States, 159 U.S. 523 (1895); *Argued:* Not reported; *Decided:* November 11, 1895; *Opinion of the Court:* Justice Brewer; *Concurring Opinion:*

None; *Dissenting Opinion:* None; *Appellate Defense Counsel:* Not represented; Appellate *Prosecution Counsel:* Mr. Whitney argued and briefed; *Amicus Curiae Brief Supporting Prosecutor:* None; *Amicus Curiae Brief Supporting Defendant:* None.

Issue Presented: Whether the trial court committed error in allowing the victim's five year old son to testify?

Case Holding: The trial court did not commit error in allowing the victim's five year old son testify, because the record discloses the child understood the difference between truth and falsehood.

Factual and procedural background of case: The defendant, George L. Wheeler, was convicted of capital murder and sentenced to death by the United States. The defendant appealed to the United States Supreme Court, alleging that it was error for the trial court to allow the victim's five-year-old son to testify. The United States Supreme Court granted certiorari to consider the issue.

Opinion of the Court by Justice Brewer: Justice Brewer held that it was not error to allow the child to testify. The opinion reasoned as follows:

> … The boy, in reply to questions put to him on his voir dire, said, among other things, that he knew the difference between the truth and a lie; that if he told a lie, the bad man would get him, and that he was going to tell the truth. When further asked what they would do with him in court if he told a lie, he replied that they would put him in jail. He also said that his mother had told him that morning to "tell no lie," and, in response to a question as to what the clerk said to him when he held up his hand, he answered, "Don't you tell no story." Other questions were asked as to his residence, his relationship to the deceased, and as to whether he had ever been to school, to which latter inquiry he responded in the negative….
>
> That the boy was not by reason of his youth, as a matter of law, absolutely disqualified as a witness is clear. While no one should think of calling as a witness an infant only two or three years old, there is no precise age which determines the question of competency. This depends on the capacity and intelligence of the child, his appreciation of the difference between truth and falsehood, as well as of his duty to tell the former. The decision of this question rests primarily with the trial judge, who sees the proposed witness, notices his manner, his apparent possession or lack of intelligence, and may resort to any examination which will tend to disclose his capacity and intelligence, as well as his understanding of the obligations of an oath. As many of these matters cannot be photographed into the record, the decision of the trial judge will not be disturbed on review, unless from that which is preserved it is clear that it was erroneous.

The judgment of the Federal trial court was affirmed.

White, Bryon R.

Byron R. White served as an associate justice of the United States Supreme Court from 1962 to 1993. While on the Supreme Court White was known for a judicial philosophy that swayed between conservative and moderate.

White was born in Fort Collins, Colorado on June 8, 1917. He graduated from the University of Colorado in 1938. White played professional football while studying law at Yale University Law School, where he received a law degree in 1946.

Capital Punishment Opinions Written by White

Case Name	Opinion of the Court	Plurality Opinion	Concurring Opinion	Dissenting Opinion	Concurring and Dissenting
Adams v. Texas	✓				
Barefoot v. Estelle	✓				
Booth v. Maryland				✓	
Brady v. Maryland			✓		
Cabana v. Bullock	✓				
Clemons v. Mississippi	✓				
Coker v. Georgia		✓			
Coleman v. Thompson			✓		
Dugger v. Adams	✓				
Enmund v. Florida	✓				
Franklin v. Lynaugh		✓			
Furman v. Georgia			✓		
Gardner v. Florida			✓		
Godfrey v. Georgia				✓	
Graham v. Collins	✓				
Gregg v. Georgia			✓		
Herrera v. Collins			✓		
Jackson v. Denno	✓				
Johnson v. Mississippi			✓		
Jurek v. Texas			✓		
Lockett v. Ohio					✓
Maynard v. Cartwright	✓				
McKoy v. North Carolina			✓		
Mills v. Maryland			✓		
Morgan v. Illinois	✓				
North Carolina v. Alford	✓				
Parker v. Dugger				✓	
Poland v. Arizona	✓				
Proffitt v. Florida			✓		
Pulley v. Harris	✓				
Roberts v. Louisiana (I)				✓	
Schad v. Arizona				✓	
Skipper v. South Carolina	✓				
Sumner v. Shuman				✓	
Swain v. Alabama	✓				
Turner v. Murray	✓				
United States v. Jackson				✓	
Walton v. Arizona	✓				
Witherspoon v. Illinois				✓	
Woodson v. North Carolina				✓	
Zant v. Stephens (II)			✓		

In 1962 President John F. Kennedy, a lifelong friend of White, appointed him to the Supreme Court.

While on the Supreme Court White wrote a considerable number of capital punishment opinions. White's capital punishment opinions were more conservative than moderate. For example, in *Clemons v. Mississippi* White wrote for the Court in holding that the Constitution did not prevent a State appellate court from upholding a death sentence that was based in part on an invalid or improperly defined aggravating circumstance, either by reweighing of the aggravating and mitigating evidence or by harmless error review. In *Enmund v. Florida* White held the Constitution prohibited imposition of the death penalty upon a co-defendant who neither took life, attempted to take life, nor intended to take life. In *North Carolina v. Alford* White ruled that a guilty plea that is voluntarily and intelligently made is not compelled within the meaning of the Fifth Amendment merely because it was made to avoid the possibility of the death penalty. White retired from the Supreme Court in 1993.

White, Edward D.

Edward D. White served as an associate justice of the United States Supreme Court from 1894 to 1910, and as chief justice from 1910 to 1921. While on the Supreme Court White was known as a conservative interpreter of the Constitution.

White was born in Lafourche Parish, Louisiana on November 3, 1845. He attended Georgetown College. White studied law privately and was admitted to the Louisiana bar in 1868. White's career included service on the Louisiana supreme court and an appointment to fill a vacancy in the United States Senate. In 1894 President Grover Cleveland appointed White as an associate justice to the Supreme Court. President William Howard Taft appointed White chief justice in 1910.

While on the Supreme Court White wrote only a few capital punishment opinions (frequently the Court issued criminal opinions that did not indicate the punishment a defendant received). The decision in *Bram v. United States* represented an important capital punishment opinion rendered by White, because the decision had application to criminal law in general. In *Bram* the defendant confessed to capital murder. On appeal the defendant argued that the confession was involuntary even though force was not used to extract the confession. White, writing for the Court, held that the defendant's confession was not voluntarily given, even though physical force was not used against him, as it was enough that he was in a situation that precluded him from exercising free will. White died on May 19, 1921.

Capital Punishment Opinions Written by White

Case Name	Opinion of the Court	Concurring Opinion	Dissenting Opinion
Bram v. United States	✓		
Hickory v. United States	✓		
Itow v. United States	✓		
Nobles v. Georgia	✓		
Talton v. Mayes	✓		

White v. Texas *Court:* United States Supreme Court; *Case Citation:* White v. Texas, 310 U.S. 530 (1940); *Argued:* May 20, 1940; *Decided:* May 27, 1940; *Opinion of the Court:* Justice Black; *Concurring Opinion:* None; *Dissenting Opinion:* None; *Appellate Defense Counsel:* F. S. K. Whittaker argued; Carter Wesley on brief; Appellate *Prosecution Counsel:* Lloyd W. Davidson argued; William J. Fanning on brief; *Amicus Curiae Brief Supporting Prosecutor:* None; *Amicus Curiae Brief Supporting Defendant:* None.

Issue Presented: Whether the State of Texas presented sufficient grounds to obtain a rehearing of the United States Supreme Court's memorandum opinion reversing the defendant's conviction and death sentence because his confession was illegally obtained?

Case Holding: The State of Texas failed to present sufficient grounds to obtain a rehearing of the United States Supreme Court's memorandum opinion reversing the defendant's conviction and death sentence, because his confession was illegally obtained.

Factual and procedural background of case: The defendant, White, was convicted of rape and sentenced to death by the State of Texas. The Texas Court of Criminal Appeals affirmed the judgment. The defendant appealed to the United Sates Supreme Court. The Supreme Court, by memorandum opinion, reversed the judgment on the grounds that the conviction was obtained as a result of an illegally obtained confession, in violation of its decision in *Chambers v. Florida*. The State requested a rehearing of the Supreme Court's memorandum decision.

Opinion of the Court by Justice Black: Justice Black ruled that the State did not present grounds to permit a rehearing. The opinion pointed out that the State contended that the defendant had denied ever having signed the confession, therefore he should not be allowed to contend that the State's use of the confession violated his constitutional right to due process. Justice Black reasoned that "[s]ince ... the confession was presented by the State to the jury as that of [the defendant], we must determine whether the record shows that, if signed at all, the confession was obtained and used in such manner that [the defendant's] trial fell short of that procedural due process guaranteed by the Constitution." The opinion then set out the following facts regarding the defendant's confession:

> [The defendant] is an illiterate farmhand who was engaged, at the time of his arrest, upon a plantation about ten miles from Livingston, Texas. On the day following the crime with which he has been charged, he was called from the field in which he was picking cotton and was taken to the house of the brother-in-law of the ... victim of the crime, where 15 or 16 [blacks] of the vicinity were at the time in custody without warrants or the filing of charges. Taken to the county court house, and thence to the Polk County jail, [the defendant] was kept there six or seven days. According to his testimony, armed Texas Rangers on several successive nights took him handcuffed from the jail "up in the woods somewhere," whipped him, asked him each time about a confession and warned him not to speak to any one about the nightly trips to the woods. During the period of his

arrest up to and including the signing of the alleged confession, [the defendant] had no lawyer, no charges were filed against him and he was out of touch with friends or relatives.…

Before carrying [the defendant] to Beaumont, where the alleged confession was taken, the Sheriff talked about an hour and a half with him. The Rangers who had been taking [the defendant] to the woods at night knew the county attorney was going to Beaumont to get a statement; they, too, went there and were in and out of the eighth floor room of the jail in Beaumont, with the elevator locked, where [the defendant] was interrogated from approximately 11:00 P.M. to 3:00 or 3:30 A.M. The alleged confession was reduced to writing after 2 A.M. Immediately before it was taken down, the prisoner was repeatedly asked by the private prosecutor whether he was ready to confess. [The defendant] then began to cry, and the typing of the confession, upon which the State's case substantially rested, was completed by the county attorney about daylight. Two citizens of Beaumont signed it as witnesses.

Justice Black concluded that "[d]ue process of law, preserved for all by our Constitution, commands that no such practice as that disclosed by this record shall send any accused to his death." The State's request for rehearing was denied.

Case note: Under modern capital punishment jurisprudence the death penalty may not be imposed for the crime of rape, without an accompanying homicide. *See also* **Chambers v. Florida; Crimes Not Involving Homicide; Right to Remain Silent**

Whitmore v. Arkansas

Court: United States Supreme Court; *Case Citation:* Whitmore v. Arkansas, 495 U.S. 149 (1990); *Argued:* January 10, 1990; *Decided:* April 24, 1990; *Opinion of the Court:* Chief Justice Rehnquist; *Concurring Opinion:* None; *Dissenting Opinion:* Justice Marshall, in which Brennan, J., joined; *Appellate Defense Counsel:* Arthur L. Allen argued; John Harris on brief; Appellate *Prosecution Counsel:* J. Steven Clark argued; Clint Miller on brief; *Amicus Curiae Brief Supporting Prosecutor:* 2; *Amicus Curiae Brief Supporting Defendant:* None.

Issue Presented: Whether a third party has standing to challenge the validity of a death sentence imposed on a capital defendant who has knowingly, intelligently, and voluntarily elected to forgo the right of appeal to the State Supreme Court?

Case Holding: A third party does not have standing to challenge the validity of a death sentence imposed on a capital defendant who has knowingly, intelligently, and voluntarily elected to forgo the right of appeal to the State Supreme Court.

Factual and procedural background of case: The defendant, Ronald Simmons, was convicted and sentenced to death by the State of Arkansas. After his sentence was imposed the defendant waived his right to automatic appeal of his conviction and sentence. Under Arkansas law a convicted and sentenced capital felon can forgo direct appeal only if he or she has been judicially determined to have the capacity to understand the choice between life and death, and to knowingly and intelligently waive any and all rights to appeal his or her sentence. The trial court conducted a hearing and determined that the defendant was competent to waive further proceedings. The Arkansas Supreme Court reviewed the competency

determination and affirmed the trial court's decision that the defendant had knowingly and intelligently waived the right to appeal.

While the State appellate court was reviewing the record on the defendant's waiver of appeal, a death row inmate, Jonas Whitmore, petitioned the court to intervene in the proceeding as a "next friend," of the defendant. The appellate court determined that Whitmore did not have standing to intervene and denied his petition. Subsequently the United States Supreme Court granted Whitmore's petition for certiorari.

Opinion of the Court by Chief Justice Rehnquist: The Chief Justice held that Whitmore lacked standing to proceed with his claim in the Court. The opinion pointed out that before a Federal court can consider the merits of a legal claim, the person seeking to invoke the court's jurisdiction must establish the requisite standing to litigate. To do so, the person must prove the existence of a case or controversy by clearly demonstrating that he or she has suffered an injury in fact, which is concrete in both a qualitative and temporal sense. He or she must show that the injury fairly can be traced to the challenged action, and is likely to be redressed by a favorable decision. The Chief Justice found that Whitmore did not satisfy the standing requirement.

In directly addressing Whitmore's claim that he had standing as the defendant's "next friend," the opinion ruled that the scope of the Federal "next friend" standing doctrine was no broader than the "next friend" standing permitted under the Federal habeas corpus statute. It was said that a necessary condition for "next friend" standing was a showing by the proposed "next friend" that the real party in interest is unable to litigate his or her own cause due to mental incapacity, lack of access to court, or other similar disability. The Chief Justice held that the prerequisite was not satisfied in the case, because the record established that an evidentiary hearing was held and that it was determined that the defendant knowingly, intelligently, and voluntarily waived of his right to appeal. The judgment of the Arkansas Supreme Court was affirmed.

Dissenting opinion by Justice Marshall, in which Brennan, J., joined: Justice Marshall dissented from the majority decision. He believed that Whitmore had standing, and that the Constitution prohibited Arkansas from failing to review the defendant's death sentence. Justice Marshall expressed his opinion thus:

The Court today allows a State to execute a man even though no appellate court has reviewed the validity of his conviction or sentence. In reaching this result, the Court does not address the constitutional claim presented by petitioner: whether a State must provide appellate review in a capital case despite the defendant's desire to waive such review. Rather, it decides that petitioner does not have standing to raise that issue before this Court. The Court rejects petitioner's argument that he should be allowed to proceed as Ronald Gene Simmons "next friend," relying on the federal common-law doctrine that a competent defendant's waiver of his right to appeal precludes another person from appealing on his behalf. If petitioner's constitutional claim is meritorious, however, Simmons' execution violates the Eighth Amendment. The Court would thus permit an unconstitutional execution on the basis of a common-law doctrine that the Court has the power to amend.

Given the extraordinary circumstances of this case, then, consideration of whether federal common law precludes Jonas Whitmore's standing as Ronald Simmons' next friend should be informed by a consideration of the merits of Whitmore's claim. For the reasons discussed herein, the Constitution requires that States provide appellate review of capital cases notwithstanding a defendant's desire to waive such review. To prevent Simmons' unconstitutional execution, the Court should relax the common-law restriction on next-friend standing and permit Whitmore to present the merits question on Simmons' behalf. By refusing to address that question, the Court needlessly abdicates its grave responsibility to ensure that no person is wrongly executed....

Our cases and state courts' experience with capital cases compel the conclusion that the Eighth and Fourteenth Amendments require appellate review of at least death sentences to prevent unjust executions. I believe the Constitution also mandates review of the underlying convictions. The core concern of all our death penalty decisions is that States take steps to ensure to the greatest extent possible that no person is wrongfully executed. A person is just as wrongfully executed when he is innocent of the crime or was improperly convicted as when he was erroneously sentenced to death. States therefore must provide review of both the convictions and sentences in death cases....

A defendant's voluntary submission to a barbaric punishment does not ameliorate the harm that imposing such a punishment causes to our basic societal values and to the integrity of our system of justice. Certainly a defendant's consent to being drawn and quartered or burned at the stake would not license the State to exact such punishments. Nor could the State knowingly execute an innocent man merely because he refused to present a defense at trial and waived his right to appeal. Similarly, the State may not conduct an execution rendered unconstitutional by the lack of an appeal merely because the defendant agrees to that punishment.

This case thus does not involve a capital defendant's so-called "right to die." When a capital defendant seeks to circumvent procedures necessary to ensure the propriety of his conviction and sentence, he does not ask the State to permit him to take his own life. Rather, he invites the State to violate two of the most basic norms of a civilized society -that the State's penal authority be invoked only where necessary to serve the ends of justice, not the ends of a particular individual, and that punishment be imposed only where the State has adequate assurance that the punishment is justified. The Constitution forbids the State to accept that invitation.

Case note: The State of Arkansas executed Ronald Simmons by lethal injection on June 25, 1990. Arkansas executed Jonas Whitmore by lethal injection on May 11, 1994. *See also* **Demosthenes v. Baal; Intervention by Next Friend; Rosenberg v. United States**

Whittaker, Charles E.

Charles E. Whittaker served as an associate justice of the United States Supreme Court from 1957 to 1962. While on the Supreme Court Whittaker was known as a conservative interpreter of the Constitution.

Whittaker was born in Troy, Kansas on February 22, 1901. He received a law degree from the University of Kansas City Law School in 1923. Whittaker maintained a successful law practice before being appointed a Federal trial judge in 1954. President Dwight D. Eisenhower appointed Whittaker to the Supreme Court in 1957.

During Whittaker's brief tenure on the Supreme Court he was known to write only two capital punishment opinions. In *Williams v. Oklahoma*, Whittaker, writing for the Court, held that imposition of the death penalty for the crime of kidnaping was not disproportionate to that offense. Writing for the Court in *Payne v. Arkansas*, Whittaker reversed a death sentence after finding the defendant's confession was extracted involuntarily. In 1962 Whittaker retired from the Court. He died on November 26, 1973.

Whitus v. Georgia

Court: United States Supreme Court; *Case Citation:* Whitus v. Georgia, 385 U.S. 545 (1967); *Argued:* December 7, 1966; *Decided:* January 23, 1967; *Opinion of the Court:* Justice Clark; *Concurring Opinion:* None; *Dissenting Opinion:* None; *Appellate Defense Counsel:* Charles Morgan, Jr. and P. Walter Jones argued and briefed; *Appellate Prosecution Counsel:* Fred B. Hand, Jr. and E. Freeman Leverett argued; Arthur K. Bolton on brief; *Amicus Curiae Brief Supporting Prosecutor:* None; *Amicus Curiae Brief Supporting Defendant:* None.

Issue Presented: Whether the defendants established that blacks were systematically excluded from the grand jury which indicted them and the petit jury which convicted them of capital murder?

Case Holding: The defendants established that blacks were systematically excluded from the grand jury which indicted them and the petit jury which convicted them of capital murder, therefore their convictions cannot stand.

Factual and procedural background of case: The defendants, Whitus and Davis, were convicted of capital murder and sentenced to death by the State of Georgia. The Georgia Supreme Court affirmed the convictions and sentences. The defendants filed a habeas corpus petition in a Federal District Court, alleging that blacks were systematically excluded from the grand jury that indicted them and the petit jury that convicted them. The District Court dismissed the petition and a Federal Court of Appeals affirmed. The United States Supreme Court summarily vacated that Court of Appeals' judgment and remanded the case to the District Court for a hearing on the claim of discrimination. On remand the District Court dismissed the petition on the ground that the claim had been waived. However, but the Court of Appeals reversed, holding that blacks had been systematically excluded from both grand and petit juries. The United States Supreme Court granted certiorari to consider the issue.

Opinion of the Court by Justice Clark: Justice Clark ruled that the defendants had established that blacks were systematically excluded from the grand jury that indicted them and the petit jury that convicted them. The opinion stated: "The proof offered by [the defendants], including the use by the State of a system of jury selection which had been previously condemned, constituted a prima facie case of purposeful discrimination, which shifted the burden of proof to the State. The State, which submitted no explanation for the continued use of the condemned system ... failed to meet the burden of rebutting the prima facie case." Justice Clark noted that "[f]or over fourscore years it has been federal statutory law, and the law of this Court as applied to the States through the Equal Protection Clause of the Fourteenth Amendment, that a conviction cannot stand if it is based on an indictment of a grand jury or the verdict of a petit jury ... which ... exclude[s] [blacks] by reason of their race." The judgment of the Court of Appeals was affirmed. *See also* **Coleman v. Alabama (I); Coleman v. Alabama (II); Discrimination in Grand or Petit Jury Selection; Sims v. Georgia (II)**

Wiggins v. Utah

Court: United States Supreme Court; *Case Citation:* Wiggins v. Utah, 93 U.S. 30 (1876); *Argued:* Not reported; *Decided:* October Term, 1876; *Opinion of the Court:* Justice Miller; *Concurring Opinion:* None; *Dissenting Opinion:* Justice Clifford; *Appellate Defense Counsel:* George H. Williams argued and briefed; Appellate *Prosecution Counsel:* Solicitor General Phillips argued and briefed; *Amicus Curiae Brief Supporting Prosecutor:* None; *Amicus Curiae Brief Supporting Defendant:* None.

Issue Presented: Whether it was reversible error to exclude testimony by a defense witness that the murder victim had previously made threats against the defendant?

Case Holding: It was reversible error to exclude testimony by a defense witness that the murder victim had previously made threats against the defendant, even though the threats were not communicated to the defendant.

Factual and procedural background of case: The defendant, Jack Wiggins, was convicted of capital murder and sentenced to death by the Territory of Utah. The Utah Supreme Court affirmed the judgment. In doing so, the appellate court rejected the defendant's contention that he was denied due process of law by the trial court's refusal to allow his witness to testify that the victim had previously made threats against the defendant. The United States Supreme Court granted certiorari to consider the issue.

Opinion of the Court by Justice Miller: Justice Miller ruled that it was reversible error to exclude testimony by a defense witness that would have shown that the victim had communicated threats against the defendant. The opinion reasoned as follows: "Although there is some conflict as to the admission of threats of the deceased against the prisoner in a case of homicide, where the threats had not been communicated to him, there is a modification of the doctrine in more recent times.... Where the question is as to what was deceased's attitude at the time of the fatal encounter, recent threats may become relevant to show that this attitude was one hostile to defendant, even though such threats were not communicated to defendant. The evidence ... may be relevant to show that, at the time of the meeting, the deceased was seeking defendant's life." Justice Miller believed that the relaxed standard on such evidence was pertinent to the case, because there was evidence that before the defendant fired the fatal shots that killed the victim, a gun the victim was carrying had previously discharged. The judgment of the Utah Supreme Court was reversed and a new trial awarded.

Dissenting opinion by Justice Clifford: Justice Clifford dissented from the Court's decision. He argued that the exception which would have allowed the evidence to be admitted was appropriate only in cases where a defendant has raised the defense of self-defense. Justice Clifford noted that the defendant did not raise the defense of self-defense. He also believed that the issue was one that was grounded in State law and was therefore not appropriate for the Court to address.

Wilkerson v. Utah

Court: United States Supreme Court; *Case Citation:* Wilkerson v. Utah, 99 U.S. 130 (1878); *Argued:* October Term, 1878; *Decided:* October Term, 1878; *Opinion of the Court:* Justice Clifford; *Concurring Opinion:* None; *Dissenting Opinion:* None; *Appellate Defense Counsel:* E. D. Hoge argued; P. L. Williams on brief; Appellate *Prosecution Counsel:* Solicitor General argued and briefed; *Amicus Curiae Brief Supporting Prosecutor:* None; *Amicus Curiae Brief Supporting Defendant:* None.

Issue Presented: Whether a sentence death by firing squad, upon conviction of a capital offense, violates the Constitution as cruel and unusual punishment?

Case Holding: Death by firing squad, upon conviction of a capital offense, does not violate the Constitution as cruel and unusual punishment.

Factual and procedural background of case: The defendant, Wilkerson, was convicted and sentenced to death for capital murder by the Territory of Utah. The trial court ordered that the defendant be put to death by firing squad. The defendant appealed to "the Supreme Court of the Territory, where the judgment of the subordinate court was affirmed." The appellate court rejected the defendant's contention that death by firing squad was unconstitutional. The United States Supreme Court granted certiorari to consider the issue.

Opinion of the Court by Justice Clifford: Justice Clifford observed that Utah's criminal code did not set out a method for carrying out a death sentence. The code merely provided "that every person guilty of murder in the first degree shall suffer death[.]" The opinion ruled that: "Had the statute prescribed the mode of executing the sentence, it would have been the duty of the court to follow it, unless the punishment to be inflicted was cruel and unusual, within the meaning of the eighth amendment to the Constitution.... Statutory directions being given that the prisoner when duly convicted shall suffer death, without any statutory regulation specifically pointing out the mode of executing the command of the law, it must be that the duty is devolved upon the court authorized to pass the sentence to determine the mode of execution and to impose the sentence prescribed."

The decision noted that under Utah's prior code, 1852–1876, the method of execution of the death penalty was set out. Prior law "provided that 'when any person shall be convicted of any crime the punishment of which is death, ... he shall suffer death by being shot, hung, or beheaded, as the court may direct,' or as the convicted person may choose."

Justice Clifford traced the history of carrying out the death penalty by firing squad to the military. The opinion found "[m]ilitary laws ... do not say how a criminal offending against such laws shall be put to death, but leave it entirely to the custom of war; and ... shooting or hanging is the method determined by such custom[.]" Further, "[f]or mutiny, desertion, or other military crime it is commonly by shooting; for murder not combined with mutiny, for treason, and piracy accompanied with wounding or attempt to murder, by hanging[.]"

It was concluded by Justice Clifford that "[c]ruel and unusual punishments are forbidden by the Constitution, but ... the punishment of shooting as a mode of executing the death penalty for the crime of murder in the first degree is not included in that category, within the meaning of the eighth amendment." The judgment of the Supreme Court of the Territory of Utah was affirmed.

Case note: The decision in the case, finding death by firing squad did not violate the Constitution, has gone undisturbed for over 100 years. The case has also been cited over the decades as authority for the constitutionality of death by hanging. *See also* **Firing Squad**

Williams v. Georgia

Court: United States Supreme Court; *Case Citation:* Williams v. Georgia, 349 U.S. 375 (1955); *Argued:* April 18, 1955; *Decided:* June 6, 1955; *Opinion of the Court:* Justice Frankfurter; *Concurring Opinion:* None; *Dissenting Opinion:* Justice Clark, in which Reed and Minton, JJ., joined; *Dissenting Opinion:* Justice Minton, in which Reed and Clark, JJ., joined; *Appellate Defense Counsel:* Eugene Gressman argued; Carter Goode on brief; *Appellate Prosecution Counsel:* E. Freeman Leverett and Robert H. Hall argued; Eugene Cook on brief; *Amicus Curiae Brief Supporting Prosecutor:* None; *Amicus Curiae Brief Supporting Defendant:* 1.

Issue Presented: Whether blacks were systematically excluded as jurors in the defendant's case?

Case Holding: The State's confession of error made it unnecessary for the Court to decide the issue and the case would be remanded.

Factual and procedural background of case: The defendant, Williams, was convicted of capital murder and sentenced to death by the State of Georgia. The Georgia Supreme Court affirmed the conviction and sentence. The defendant then filed a habeas corpus petition with the trial court alleging for the first time that blacks were systematically excluded from the jury that presided at his trial. The trial court dismissed the petition. The State appellate court affirmed the dismissal, after concluding that the defendant waived the issue by not raising it before trial as required by Georgia law. The United States Supreme Court granted certiorari to consider the issue.

Opinion of the Court by Justice Frankfurter: Justice Frankfurter held that the case would be remanded for reconsideration by the State appellate court, in light of the State's confession of error during oral argument of the case. The opinion found that the evidence revealed that the trial court used white tickets to place the name of potential white jurors and yellow tickets for potential black jurors, for the purpose of systematically controlling the types of cases blacks would participate in. Justice Frankfurter wrote that "[t]he facts of this case are extraordinary, particularly in view of the use of yellow and white tickets by a judge of the Fulton County Superior Court almost a year after the State's own Supreme Court had condemned the practice[.]" The opinion concluded: "Fair regard for the principles which the Georgia courts have enforced in numerous cases and for the constitutional commands binding on all courts compels us to reject the assumption that the courts of Georgia would allow this man to go to his death as the result of a conviction secured from a jury which the State admits was unconstitutionally impaneled." The judgment of the Georgia Supreme Court was reversed and the case remanded.

Dissenting opinion by Justice Clark, in which Reed and Minton, JJ., joined: Justice Clark dissented from the Court's decision. He believed it was wrong for the Court to reverse the case because under Georgia law the defendant waived the error by not timely raising the issue. Justice Clark reasoned: "And orderly administration of the laws often imposes hardships upon those who have not properly preserved their rights. In any event, the resolution of these conflicting interests should be a matter wholly for the Georgia courts."

Dissenting opinion by Justice Minton, in which Reed and Clark, JJ., joined: Justice Minton dissented from the Court's decision. Like Justice Clark, Justice Minton believed that the Court should not have interfered with the State appellate court's determination that the defendant failed to timely race the issue of jury discrimination. Justice Minton wrote:

> Georgia has a rule of law that the jury panel must be challenged at the threshold, that is, as Georgia expresses it, before the panel is "put upon the defendant." If the panel is not thus challenged, the issue cannot later be raised and is considered as waived "once and for all."
>
> This is a reasonable rule. It gives the State an opportunity to meet the challenge and to justify the [jury panel], or, if it is improperly constituted, an opportunity to correct it.

See also **Confession of Error; Discrimination in Grand or Petit Jury Selection**

Williams v. Mississippi

Court: United States Supreme Court; *Case Citation:* Williams v. Mississippi, 170 U.S. 213 (1898); *Argued:* Not reported; *Decided:* April 25, 1898; *Opinion of the Court:* Justice McKenna; *Concurring Opinion:* None; *Dissenting Opinion:* None; *Appellate Defense Counsel:* Cornelius J. Jones argued and briefed; *Appellate Prosecution Counsel:* C. B. Mitchell argued and briefed; *Amicus Curiae Brief Supporting Prosecutor:* None; *Amicus Curiae Brief Supporting Defendant:* None.

Issue Presented: Whether the defendant's capital prosecution should have been removed from the Mississippi trial court into a Federal trial court, due to alleged racial discrimination in the selection of grand and petit juries?

Case Holding: The defendant's capital prosecution could

not be removed from the Mississippi trial court into a Federal trial court, due to alleged racial discrimination in the selection of grand and petit juries, because such alleged discrimination was not based upon the State's constitution or statutes.

Factual and procedural background of case: The defendant, Henry Williams, was convicted of capital murder and sentenced to death by the State of Mississippi. The Mississippi Supreme Court affirmed the judgment. In doing so, the appellate court rejected the defendant's contention that the trial court should have permitted removal of his case to a Federal trial court, because of systematic exclusion of blacks from the grand and petit juries involved with his case. The United States Supreme Court granted certiorari to consider the issue.

Opinion of the Court by Justice McKenna: Justice McKenna rejected the defendant's argument that his case should have been removed to a Federal trial court. The opinion indicated that the Federal removal statute established a narrow basis for removing State prosecutions into Federal court. Justice McKenna addressed the scope of the removal statute as follows:

> ... [I]t has been uniformly held that the constitution of the United States, as amended, forbids, so far as civil and political rights are concerned, discriminations by the general government or by the states against any citizen because of his race; but it has also been held, in a very recent case, to justify a removal from a state court to a federal court of a cause in which such rights are alleged to be denied, that such denial must be the result of the constitution or laws of the state, not of the administration of them....
>
> It is not asserted by [the defendant] that either the constitution of the state or its laws discriminate in terms against [blacks], either as to the elective franchise or the privilege or duty of sitting on juries. These results, if we understand [the plaintiff], are alleged to be effected by the powers vested in certain administrative officers.
>
> It cannot be said, therefore, that the denial of the equal protection of the laws arises primarily from the constitution and laws of Mississippi; nor is there any sufficient allegation of an evil and discriminating administration of them. The only allegation is ... [that] by granting discretion to [administrative] officers, as mentioned in the several sections of the constitution of the state, and the statute of the state adopted under the said constitution, the use of which discretion can be and has been used by said officers ... [to deny blacks] the right to be selected as jurors...; and that this denial to them of the right to equal protection and benefits of the laws of the state of Mississippi on account of their color and race, resulting from the exercise of the discretion partial to the white citizens, is in accordance with the purpose and intent of the framers of the present constitution of said state....
>
> It will be observed that there is nothing direct and definite in this allegation either as to means or time as affecting the proceedings against the accused. There is no charge against the officers to whom is submitted the selection of grand or petit jurors, or those who procure the lists of the jurors.... We gather from the [defendant's allegations] that certain officers are invested with discretion in making up lists of electors, and that this discretion can be and has been exercised against [blacks], and from these lists jurors are selected. The supreme court of Mississippi, however, decided, in a case presenting the same questions as the one at bar, "that jurors are not selected from or with reference to any lists furnished by such election officers."

This comment is not applicable to the constitution of Mississippi and its statutes. They do not on their face discriminate between the races, and it has not been shown that their actual administration was evil; only that evil was possible under them.

The judgment of the Mississippi Supreme Court was affirmed.

See also **Discrimination in Grand or Petit Jury Selection**

Williams v. New York

Court: United States Supreme Court; *Case Citation:* Williams v. New York , 337 U.S. 241 (1949); *Argued:* April 21, 1949; *Decided:* June 6, 1949; *Opinion of the Court:* Justice Black; *Concurring Opinion:* None; *Dissenting Opinion:* Justice Murphy; *Dissenting Statement:* Justice Rutledge; *Appellate Defense Counsel:* John F. Finerty argued and briefed; Appellate *Prosecution Counsel:* Solomon Klein argued and briefed; *Amicus Curiae Brief Supporting Prosecutor:* None; *Amicus Curiae Brief Supporting Defendant:* None.

Issue Presented: Whether the Due Process Clause prohibits a trial judge from considering extraneous information when imposing a death sentence, without first giving the defendant an opportunity to contest the information?

Case Holding: The Due Process Clause does not prohibit a trial judge from considering extraneous information when imposing a death sentence, without first giving the defendant an opportunity to contest the information.

Factual and procedural background of case: The defendant, Williams, was convicted of capital murder by a jury in New York. The jury recommended life imprisonment, but the trial judge imposed a sentence of death. In giving reasons for imposing the death sentence, the trial judge stated in open court that the evidence upon which the jury had convicted the defendant was considered in the light of additional information obtained through the court's probation department, and through other sources. Under a statute in the State a trial judge was given authority to consider such evidence when imposing a sentence. The Court of Appeals of New York affirmed the conviction and sentence, over the defendant's contention that consideration of information by the trial court for which he was not privy, violated the Due Process Clause of the Federal Constitution. The United States Supreme Court granted certiorari to consider the issue.

Opinion of the Court by Justice Black: Justice Black rejected the defendant's argument that the Constitution prohibited the trial court from considering extraneous evidence during sentencing, without affording him an opportunity to challenge the evidence. Justice Black reasoned as follows:

> The due process clause should not be treated as a device for freezing the evidential procedure of sentencing in the mold of trial procedure. So to treat the due process clause would hinder if not preclude all courts — state and federal — from making progressive efforts to improve the administration of criminal justice....
>
> ... Leaving a sentencing judge free to avail himself of out-of-court information in making such a fateful choice of sentences does secure to him a broad discretionary power, one susceptible of abuse. But in considering whether a rigid constitutional barrier should be created, it must be remembered that there is possibility of abuse wherever a judge must choose between life

imprisonment and death. And it is conceded that no federal constitutional objection would have been possible if the judge here had sentenced [the defendant] to death because [the defendant's] trial manner impressed the judge that [the defendant] was a bad risk for society, or if the judge had sentenced him to death giving no reason at all. We cannot say that the due process clause renders a sentence void merely because a judge gets additional out-of-court information to assist him in the exercise of this awesome power of imposing the death sentence.

[The defendant] was found guilty after a fairly conducted trial. His sentence followed a hearing conducted by the judge. Upon the judge's inquiry as to why sentence should not be imposed, the defendant made statements. His counsel made extended arguments. The case went to the highest court in the state, and that court had power to reverse for abuse of discretion or legal error in the imposition of the sentence. That court affirmed. We hold that [the defendant] was not denied due process of law.

The judgment of the Court of Appeals of New York was affirmed.

Dissenting opinion by Justice Murphy: Justice Murphy dissented from the Court's decision. He argued that due process required the defendant be afforded an opportunity to confront the information relied upon by the trial judge in imposing the death penalty. Justice Murphy argued as follows:

[The defendant] was convicted of murder by a jury, and sentenced to death by the judge. The jury which heard the trial unanimously recommended life imprisonment as a suitable punishment for the defendant. They had observed him throughout the trial, had heard all the evidence adduced against him, and in spite of the shocking character of the crime of which they found him guilty, were unwilling to decree that his life should be taken. In our criminal courts the jury sits as the representative of the community; its voice is that of the society against which the crime was committed. A judge even though vested with statutory authority to do so, should hesitate indeed to increase the severity of such a community expression.

He should be willing to increase it, moreover, only with the most scrupulous regard for the rights of the defendant. The record before us indicates that the judge exercised his discretion to deprive a man of his life, in reliance on material made available to him in a probation report, consisting almost entirely of evidence that would have been inadmissible at the trial. Some, such as allegations of prior crimes, was irrelevant. Much was incompetent as hearsay. All was damaging, and none was subject to scrutiny by the defendant.

Due process of law includes at least the idea that a person accused of crime shall be accorded a fair hearing through all the stages of the proceedings against him. I agree with the Court as to the value and humaneness of liberal use of probation reports as developed by modern penologists, but, in a capital case, against the unanimous recommendation of a jury, where the report would concededly not have been admissible at the trial, and was not subject to examination by the defendant, I am forced to conclude that the high commands of due process were not obeyed.

Dissenting statement by Justice Rutledge: Justice Rutledge issued a statement dissenting from the Court's decision.

Case note: The position taken by Justice Murphy would eventually be adopted by the Court under modern capital punishment law. *See also* **Presentence Report**

Williams v. Oklahoma *Court:* United States Supreme Court; *Case Citation:* Williams v. Oklahoma, 358 U.S. 576

(1959); *Argued:* January 21, 1959; *Decided:* February 24, 1959; *Opinion of the Court:* Justice Whittaker; *Concurring Opinion:* None; *Dissenting Statement:* Justice Douglas; *Appellate Defense Counsel:* John A. Ladner, Jr. argued and briefed; *Appellate Prosecution Counsel:* Mac Q. Williamson argued; Sam H. Lattimore on brief; *Amicus Curiae Brief Supporting Prosecutor:* None; *Amicus Curiae Brief Supporting Defendant:* None.

Issues Presented: (1) Whether the Double Jeopardy Clause prohibited Oklahoma from prosecuting the defendant for kidnaping, after prosecuting him for murder of the victim who was kidnaped? (2) Whether imposition of the death penalty for the crime of kidnaping was disproportionate to that offense?

Case Holdings: (1) The Double Jeopardy Clause did not prohibit Oklahoma from prosecuting the defendant for kidnaping, after prosecuting him for murder of the victim who was kidnaped. (2) Imposition of the death penalty for the crime of kidnaping was not disproportionate to that offense.

Factual and procedural background of case: The defendant, Williams, entered a plea of guilty to capital murder and was sentenced to life imprisonment by the State of Oklahoma. Thereafter, he was charged in another Oklahoma court with the crime of kidnaping involving the same victim of the murder prosecution. While represented by counsel and after being warned by the trial court that conviction might result in a death sentence, the defendant plead guilty to the kidnaping charge. The trial court sentenced the defendant to death. Under Oklahoma law, kidnaping and murder were separate and distinct offenses, and the defendant made no claim prior to his conviction that he was being put twice in jeopardy for the same offense. The Oklahoma Criminal Court of Appeals affirmed the conviction and sentence. In doing so, the appellate court rejected the defendant's contention that double jeopardy principles prohibited his prosecution for kidnaping, and that imposition of the death penalty for kidnaping was disproportionate to the offense. The United States Supreme Court granted certiorari to consider the issues.

Opinion of the Court by Justice Whittaker: Justice Whittaker ruled that double jeopardy principles were not violated by the defendant's conviction and sentence for murder and kidnapping of the same victim. He also rejected the defendant's contention that the sentence of death was disproportionate for the crime of kidnaping. Justice Whittaker reasoned as follows:

Since kidnaping and murder are separate and distinct crimes under Oklahoma law, the court's consideration of the murder as a circumstance involved in the kidnaping cannot be said to have resulted in punishing [the defendant] a second time for the same offense nor to have denied him due process of law in violation of the Fourteenth Amendment....

This Court cannot say that the death sentence for kidnaping, which was within the range of punishments authorized for that crime by Oklahoma law, denied to [the defendant] due process of law or any other constitutional right. [The defendant's] further claim that the sentence to death for kidnaping was "disproportionate" to that crime and to the life sentence that had earlier been imposed upon him for the "ultimate" crime of murder proceeds on the basis that the sentence for kidnaping was excessive, that the murder was the greater offense, and that the sentence for the lesser crime of kidnaping ought not, in conscience and with due regard for fundamental fairness, exceed the life sentence that was imposed in another jurisdiction for the murder. But the Due Process Clause of the Fourteenth Amendment does not, nor does anything in the Constitution, require a State to fix or impose any particular penalty for any crime it may define or to impose the same or "proportionate" sentences for separate and independent crimes. Therefore we cannot say that the sentence to death for the kidnaping, which was within the range of punishments authorized for that crime by the law of the State, denied to [the defendant] due process of law or any other constitutional right." The judgment of the Oklahoma Criminal Court of Appeals was affirmed.

Dissenting statement by Justice Douglas: Justice Douglas issued a dissenting statement indicating he believed the defendant "was in substance tried for murder twice in violation of the guarantee against double jeopardy[.]"

Case note: Under modern capital punishment jurisprudence the death penalty may not be imposed for kidnaping, without an accompanying death. *See also* **Double Jeopardy Clause; Rape and Capital Punishment**

Wilson v. United States *Court:* United States Supreme Court; *Case Citation:* Wilson v. United States, 162 U.S. 613 (1896); *Argued:* Not reported; *Decided:* April 27, 1896; *Opinion of the Court:* Chief Justice Fuller; *Concurring Opinion:* None; *Dissenting Opinion:* None; *Appellate Defense Counsel:* Not represented; *Appellate Prosecution Counsel:* United States Assistant Attorney General Dickinson on brief; *Amicus Curiae Brief Supporting Prosecutor:* None; *Amicus Curiae Brief Supporting Defendant:* None.

Issue Presented: Whether the defendant's confession was made voluntarily?

Case Holding: The defendant's confession was made voluntarily where there was no evidence of improper inducements, threats or promises.

Factual and procedural background of case: The defendant, Wilson, was convicted of capital murder and sentenced to death by the United States. Federal jurisdiction was premised on the victim being killed "at the Creek Nation in the [Native American] country[.]" The United States Supreme Court granted certiorari to consider the question of whether the defendant's confession was voluntary.

Opinion of the Court by Chief Justice Fuller: The Chief Justice ruled that the defendant's confession was voluntary. It was said that "[a] confession, if freely and voluntarily made, is evidence of the most satisfactory character." The Chief Justice noted that "from the very nature of such evidence, it must be subjected to careful scrutiny, and received with great caution, a deliberate, voluntary confession of guilt is among the most effectual proofs in the law, and constitutes the strongest evidence against the party making it that can be given of the facts stated in such confession." The opinion held that a confession is involuntary when "made either in consequence of inducements of a temporal nature, held out by one in authority touching the charge preferred, or because of a threat or promise, by or in the presence of such person, which, operating upon the fears or hopes of the accused in reference to the charge, deprives him of that freedom of will or self-control essential to make his confession voluntary within the meaning of the law." The Chief Justice concluded that "[t]ested by these conditions, there seems to have been no reason to exclude the confession of the accused; for the existence of any such inducements, threats, or promises seems to have been negatived by the statement of the circumstances under which it was made." The judgment of conviction and sentence of death were affirmed. *See also* **Right to Remain Silent**

Winston v. United States *Court:* United States Supreme Court; *Case Citation:* Winston v. United States, 172 U.S. 303 (1899); *Argued:* Not reported; *Decided:* January 3, 1899; *Opinion of the Court:* Justice Gray; *Concurring Opinion:* None; *Dissenting Statement:* Justice Brewer and McKenna, J.; *Appellate Defense Counsel in Case No. 431:* George Kearney argued and briefed; *Appellate Defense Counsel in Case No. 432:* Samuel D. Truitt argued and briefed; *Appellate Defense Counsel in Case No. 433:* F. S. Key Smith argued and briefed; *Appellate Prosecution Counsel:* Henry E. Davis argued and briefed; *Amicus Curiae Brief Supporting Prosecutor:* None; *Amicus Curiae Brief Supporting Defendant:* None.

Issue Presented: Whether Congress required the defendants present mitigating evidence before their respective juries could return qualified noncapital verdicts against them?

Case Holding: Congress did not require the defendants present mitigating evidence before their respective juries could return qualified noncapital verdicts against them, therefore imposition of such a requirement by the trial courts necessitated new trials for each defendant.

Factual and procedural background of case: This matter involved three separate capital prosecutions by the District of Columbia. The defendants, Winston, Strather and Smith, were each convicted of capital murder. Under a new law passed by Congress, juries were empowered to return a qualified verdict of "without capital punishment," which meant a defendant could only be sentenced to life imprisonment. The jury in each of the defendants' cases were instructed that they could only qualify their verdicts if mitigating evidence was presented by the defendants. Subsequently, each defendant received an unqualified verdict of guilty and each was sentenced to death. The District of Columbia Court of Appeals affirmed the judgments. Each defendant then filed an appeal with the United States Supreme Court, alleging that the Federal statute did not require the jury find mitigating evidence before it could return a qualified verdict. The United States Supreme Court granted certiorari to consider the issue and consolidated the cases for disposition.

Opinion of the Court by Justice Gray: Justice Gray agreed with the defendants that Congress did not require juries find mitigating evidence before extending mercy by rendering a qualified verdict of "without capital punishment." In discussing the merits of the case, the opinion outlined legislative efforts to ameliorate the hardship of mandatory death penalty statutes:

> The hardship of punishing with death every crime coming within the definition of murder at common law, and the reluctance of jurors to concur in a capital conviction, have induced American legislatures, in modern times, to allow some cases of murder to be punished by imprisonment, instead of by death. That end has been generally attained in one of two ways:
>
> In some states and territories, statutes have been passed establishing degrees of the crime of murder, requiring the degree of murder to be found by the jury, and providing that the courts shall pass sentence of death in those cases only in which the jury return a verdict of guilty of murder in the first degree, and sentence of imprisonment when the verdict is guilty of murder in the lesser degree.
>
> The difficulty of laying down exact and satisfactory definitions of degrees in the crime of murder, applicable to all possible circumstances, has led other legislatures to prefer the more simple and flexible rule of conferring upon the jury, in every case of murder, the right of deciding whether it shall be punished by death or by imprisonment. This method has been followed by congress in the act of 1897....
>
> The right to qualify a verdict of guilty by adding the words "without capital punishment" is thus conferred upon the jury in all cases of murder. The act does not itself prescribe, nor authorize the court to prescribe, any rule defining or circumscribing the exercise of this right, but commits the whole matter of its exercise to the judgment and the consciences of the jury. The authority of the jury to decide that the accused shall not be punished capitally is not limited to cases in which the court or the jury is of opinion that there are palliating or mitigating circumstances. But it extends to every case in which, upon a view of the whole evidence, the jury is of opinion that it would not be just or wise to impose capital punishment. How far considerations of age, sex, ignorance, illness, or intoxication, of human passion or weakness, of sympathy or clemency, or the irrevocableness of an executed sentence of death, or an apprehension that explanatory facts may exist which have not been brought to light, or any other consideration whatever, should be allowed weight in deciding the question whether the accused should or should not be capitally punished, is committed by the act of congress to the sound discretion of the jury, and of the jury alone....
>
> The instructions of the judge to the jury in each of the three cases now before this court clearly gave the jury to understand that the act of congress did not intend or authorize the jury to qualify their verdict by the addition of the words "without capital punishment," unless mitigating or palliating circumstances were proved.
>
> This court is of opinion that these instructions were erroneous in matter of law, as undertaking to control the discretionary power vested by congress in the jury, and as attributing to congress an intention unwarranted either by the express words or by the apparent purpose of the statute....

The judgments of the Court of Appeals were reversed and the cases remanded for new trials.

Dissenting statement by Justice Brewer and McKenna, J.: Justices Brewer and McKenna issued a statement indicating they dissented from the Court's decision.

Wirz, Henry *see* War Crimes

Wisconsin
The death penalty was formally abolished by the State of Wisconsin in 1853.

Witherspoon v. Illinois
Court: United States Supreme Court; *Case Citation:* Witherspoon v. Illinois, 391 U.S. 510 (1968); *Argued:* April 24, 1968; *Decided:* June 3, 1968; *Opinion of the Court:* Justice Stewart; *Concurring Opinion:* Justice Douglas; *Dissenting Opinion:* Justice Black, in which Harlan and White, JJ., joined; *Dissenting Opinion:* Justice White; *Appellate Defense Counsel:* Albert E. Jenner, Jr. argued; Thomas P. Sullivan, Jerold S. Solovy, and John C. Tucker on brief; Appellate *Prosecution Counsel:* Donald J. Veverka and James B. Zagel argued; William G. Clark, John J. O'Toole, John J. Stamos, Elmer C. Kissane, and Joel Flaum on brief; *Amicus Curiae Brief Supporting Prosecutor:* 1; *Amicus Curiae Brief Supporting Defendant:* 6.

Issue Presented: Whether the State of Illinois may provide by statute that the prosecutor may exclude from the jury, for cause, any venireperson who said that he or she was opposed to capital punishment and who indicated that he or she had conscientious scruples against inflicting the death penalty?

Case Holding: The Constitution prohibits enforcement of a statute which authorizes the prosecutor to exclude from the jury, for cause, any venireperson who said that he or she was opposed to capital punishment and who indicated that he or she had conscientious scruples against inflicting the death penalty.

Factual and procedural background of case: The defendant, Witherspoon, was adjudged guilty of capital murder and sentenced to death by an Illinois jury. At the time of the prosecution Illinois had a statute which allowed the prosecutor to challenge for "cause" in murder trials "any juror who shall, on being examined, state that he has conscientious scruples against capital punishment, or that he is opposed to the same." At the defendant's trial the prosecutor, under that statute, eliminated nearly half the venire of prospective jurors by challenging all who expressed qualms about the death penalty. Most of the venirepersons thus challenged for cause were excluded, with no effort to find out whether their scruples would invariably compel them to vote against capital punishment. On appeal, the defendant challenged the constitutionality of the statute, but the Illinois Supreme Court affirmed the conviction and sentence. The United States Supreme Court granted certiorari to consider the issue.

Opinion of the Court by Justice Stewart: Justice Stewart observed that neither on the basis of the record in the case, nor as a matter of judicial notice, could it be concluded that the exclusion of jurors opposed to capital punishment resulted in an unrepresentative jury on the issue of guilt or that such exclusion substantially increased the risk of conviction. The opinion ruled, however, that while it was not shown that the jury was biased with respect to guilt, it was self-evident that, in its distinct role as arbiter of the punishment to be imposed, the jury fell woefully short of the impartiality to which a defendant is entitled under the Constitution.

The opinion reasoned that a person who opposed the death penalty, no less than one who favors it, can make the discretionary choice of punishment entrusted to him or her by the State and can thus obey the oath taken as a juror. However, the opinion continued, in a nation where so many have come to oppose capital punishment, a jury from which all such people have been excluded cannot perform the task demanded of it — that of expressing the conscience of the community on the ultimate question of life or death.

Justice Stewart wrote that just as a State may not entrust the determination of whether a defendant is innocent or guilty to a tribunal organized to convict, so it may not entrust the determination of whether a defendant should live or die to a tribunal organized to return a verdict of death. No sentence of death can be carried out, regardless of when it was imposed, if the voir dire testimony indicated that the jury that imposed or recommended that sentence was chosen by excluding venirepersons for "cause" simply because they voiced general objections to capital punishment or expressed conscientious or religious scruples against its infliction.

The opinion concluded: "Whatever else might be said of capital punishment, it is at least clear that its imposition by a hanging jury cannot be squared with the Constitution. The State of Illinois has stacked the deck against the [defendant]. To execute this death sentence would deprive him of his life without due process of law." The judgment of the Illinois Supreme Court was reversed, insofar as the sentence of death.

Concurring opinion by Justice Douglas: Justice Douglas concurred in the judgment, but argued that the conviction and sentence should have been reversed. The concurrence stated its position as follows: "Although the Court reverses as to penalty, it declines to reverse the verdict of guilt rendered by the same jury. It does so on the ground that petitioner has not demonstrated on this record that the jury which convicted him was 'less than neutral with respect to guilt,' because of the exclusion of all those opposed in some degree to capital punishment. The Court fails to find on this record 'an unrepresentative jury on the issue of guilt.' But we do not require a showing of specific prejudice when a defendant has been deprived of his right to a jury representing a cross-section of the community. We can as easily assume that the absence of those opposed to capital punishment would rob the jury of certain peculiar qualities of human nature as would the exclusion of women from juries. I would not require a specific showing of a likelihood of prejudice, for I feel that we must proceed on the assumption that in many, if not most, cases of class exclusion on the basis of beliefs or attitudes some prejudice does result and many times will not be subject to precise measurement. Indeed, that prejudice 'is so subtle, so intangible, that it escapes the ordinary methods of proof.' In my view, that is the essence of the requirement that a jury be drawn from a cross-section of the community."

Dissenting opinion by Justice Black, in which Harlan and White, JJ., joined: Justice Black dissented from the majority opinion. In doing so, he gave the following reasons:

As I see the issue in this case, it is a question of plain bias. A person who has conscientious or religious scruples against capital punishment will seldom if ever vote to impose the death penalty. This is just human nature, and no amount of semantic camouflage can cover it up. In the same manner, I would not dream of foisting on a criminal defendant a juror who admitted that he had conscientious or religious scruples against not inflicting the death sentence on any person convicted of murder (a juror who claims, for example, that he adheres literally to the Biblical admonition of "an eye for an eye"). Yet the logical result of the majority's holding is that such persons must be allowed so that the "conscience of the community" will be fully represented when it decides "the ultimate question of life or death." While I have always advocated that the jury be as fully representative of the community as possible, I would never carry this so far as to require that those biased against one of the critical issues in a trial should be represented on a jury....

The majority opinion attempts to equate those who have conscientious or religious scruples against the death penalty with those who do not in such a way as to balance the allegedly conflicting viewpoints in order that a truly representative jury can be established to exercise the community's discretion in deciding on punishment. But for this purpose I do not believe that those who have conscientious or religious scruples against the death penalty and those who have no feelings either way are in any sense comparable. Scruples against the death penalty are commonly the result of a deep religious conviction or a profound philosophical commitment developed after much soul-searching. The holders of such scruples must necessarily recoil from the prospect of making possible what they regard as immoral. On the other hand, I cannot accept the proposition that persons who do not have conscientious scruples against the death penalty are "prosecution prone."

Dissenting opinion by Justice White: Justice White dissented from the decision of the majority. He believed Illinois had a right to provide for jurors to be excluded for cause if they indicated reservations about the propriety of the death penalty. In his dissent he argued as follows:

The Court does not hold that imposition of the death penalty offends the Eighth Amendment. Nor does it hold that a State Legislature may not specify only death as the punishment for certain crimes, so that the penalty is imposed automatically upon a finding of guilt, with no discretion in judge or jury. Either of these holdings might furnish a satisfactory predicate for reversing this judgment. Without them, the analytic basis of the result reached by the Court is infirm; the conclusion is reached because the Court says so, not because of reasons set forth in the opinion.

The Court merely asserts that this legislative attempt to impose the death penalty on some persons convicted of murder, but not on everyone so convicted, is constitutionally unsatisfactory....

The Court does not deny that the legislature can impose a particular penalty, including death, on all persons convicted of certain crimes. Why, then, should it be disabled from delegating the penalty decision to a group who will impose the death penalty more often than would a group differently chosen?

See also **Adams v. Texas; Boulden v. Holman; Darden v. Wainwright; Davis v. Georgia; Gray v. Mississippi; Jury Selection; Morgan v. Illinois; Ross v. Oklahoma; Wainwright v. Witt**

Witnessing an Execution *see* Public Viewing of Execution

Witness Aggravator   A large minority of capital punishment jurisdictions have made the killing of a witness a statutory aggravating circumstance. If it is found at the penalty phase that the victim was a witness who was killed because of his or her role as a witness in a prosecution, the death penalty may be imposed. *See also* **Aggravating Circumstances**

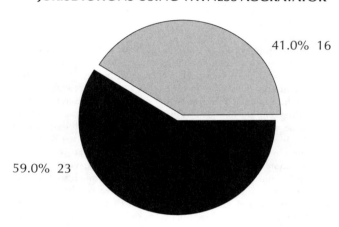

JURISDICTIONS USING WITNESS AGGRAVATOR

41.0% 16

59.0% 23

■ WITNESS AGGRAVATOR JURISDICTIONS

■ ALL OTHER JURISDICTIONS

Women and Capital Punishment   Women have historically made up only a small percentage of persons committing homicides. This fact explains why women have always been a minute percentage of persons executed in the nation. For example, of the 598 capital felons executed between the period 1976–1999, only three were women. The three women executed during this period were, in order of execution: Velma Margie Barfield, Karla Faye Tucker, and Judias Buenoano. From the American Colonial period to 1999, female executions constituted 3 percent of all executions in America. Betty Lou Beets became the first women executed in the 21st century when Texas executed her on February 24, 2000. Prior to the resumption of capital punishment in 1976, the last female executed was Elizabeth Ann Duncan. She was executed by California on August 8, 1962.

Gender Discrimination. Death penalty advocates have long argued that more women would be represented in the ranks of death row, if changes were made that would alter the gender biasness exhibited in capital prosecutions. That is, it has been postured that society has been conditioned to give less punishment to women for the same crimes committed by men. Most reputable studies have supported the argument that the judicial system punishes women less severely than men. However, in the area of capital punishment no viable so-

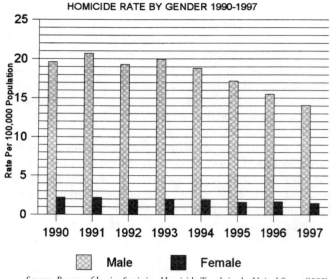

HOMICIDE RATE BY GENDER 1990-1997

■ Male   ■ Female

Source: Bureau of Justice Statistics, Homicide Trends in the United States (1998)

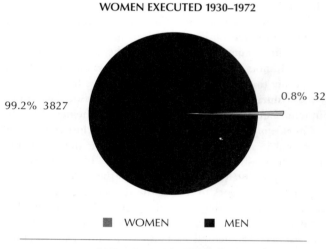

WOMEN EXECUTED 1930–1972

99.2% 3827

0.8% 32

■ WOMEN   ■ MEN

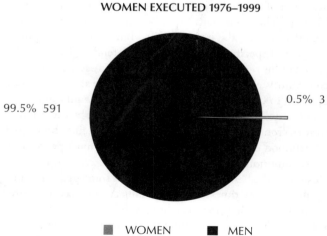

WOMEN EXECUTED 1976–1999

99.5% 591

0.5% 3

■ WOMEN   ■ MEN

lution to the acknowledged biased underrepresentation of women on death row has been put forward.

Female Death Sentences 1976–1996

Year	Total Death Sentences	Female Death Sentences
1976	234	3
1977	138	1
1978	186	4
1979	152	4
1980	175	2
1981	230	3
1982	269	5
1983	253	4
1984	284	8
1985	270	5
1986	304	3
1987	287	5
1989	261	11
1990	251	7
1991	269	6
1992	289	10
1993	291	6
1994	317	5
1995	325	7
1996	317	1

Source: U.S. Department of Justice, Capital Punishment 1997.

While there has been a general historical hesitancy to subject women to capital punishment in the United States, isolated incidents have been documented where women were indiscriminately subjected to capital punishment. For example in 1692, mass hysteria raged in Salem Village, Massachusetts over rumors of witchcraft being practiced. Numerous women were hung during this period after being tried and convicted of witchcraft.

WOMEN ON DEATH ROW
APRIL 1999

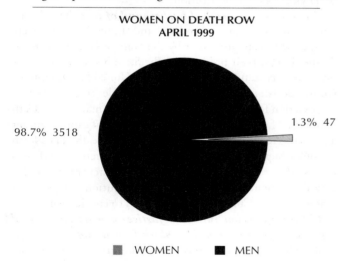

98.7% 3518   1.3% 47

■ WOMEN   ■ MEN

Pregnant Capital Felon. The United States Supreme Court has not been given an opportunity to rule upon the following question: May a female capital felon be executed while pregnant? Regardless of how the Supreme Court would address the question, a majority of capital punishment jurisdictions have answered it by enacting statutes that prohibit executing female capital felons while they are pregnant.

Statutes vary in how they address the issue of a female capital felon who alleges she is pregnant. The following two statutes illustrate this point.

JURISDICTIONS THAT HAVE STATUTES PROHIBITING THE EXECUTION OF A PREGNANT CAPITAL FELON

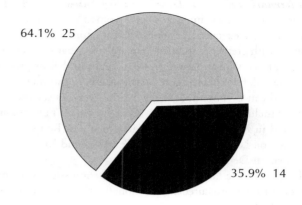

64.1% 25

35.9% 14

■ JURISDICTIONS HAVING PREGNANCY STATUTES

■ ALL OTHER JURISDICTIONS

Alabama Code § 15-18-86: (a) If there is reason to believe that a female convict is pregnant, the sheriff must, with the concurrence of a judge of the circuit court, summon a jury of six disinterested persons, as many of whom must be physicians as practicable. The sheriff must also give notice to the district attorney or, in his absence, to any attorney who may be appointed by a circuit judge to represent the state and who has authority to issue subpoenas for witnesses. (b) The jury, under the direction of the sheriff or officer acting in his place, must proceed to ascertain the fact of pregnancy and must state their conclusion in writing, signed by them and the sheriff. If such jury is of opinion, and so find, that the convict is with child, the sheriff or officer acting in his place must suspend the execution of the sentence and transmit the finding of the jury to the Governor. (c) Whenever the Governor is satisfied that such convict is no longer with child, he must issue his warrant to the sheriff appointing a day for her to be executed according to her sentence, and the sheriff or other officer must execute the sentence of the law on the day so appointed.

Wyoming Statutes Annotated §§ 7-13-912 and 913: (a) If there is good reason to believe that a female sentenced to death is pregnant, the director of the department of corrections shall immediately give written notice to the court in which the judgment of death was rendered and to the district attorney. The execution of the death sentence shall be suspended pending further order of the court. (b) Upon receiving notice as provided in subsection (a) of this section, the court shall appoint a jury of three (3) physicians to inquire into the supposed pregnancy and to make a written report of their findings to the court.

* * *

(a) If the court determines the female is not pregnant, the director of the department of corrections shall execute the death sentence. (b) If the court determines the female is pregnant, the court shall order the execution of the sentence suspended until it is determined that the female is no longer pregnant at which time the court shall issue a warrant appointing a new date for the execution of the sentence.

Pregnancy is not a permanent barrier to the imposition of the death penalty. Once a pregnancy has ended, the death penalty may be carried out. None of the capital punishment jurisdictions that have statutes addressing the issue of a pregnant capital felon, indicate what happens to the child that is born to a pregnant capital felon.

International Use of Death Penalty Aainst Women. All reports indicate that internationally women make up a small percentage of executed prisoners. China appears to execute women with greater frequency than any other nation. Because China protects information on the actual number of prisoners executed, no reliable figure on the number of women it has executed can be obtained. A few of the known execution of women include: Chen Yanfang, Wang Liwen, and Du Youyu, executed in May of 1996; Shao Miaomiao and Rong Fenbo, executed on November 24, 1995; Wen Yana and Xie Xiuyun, executed on December 15, 1995.

In spite of the fact that women represent a small percentage of prisoners executed internationally, they are victims of wholesale discrimination in courtrooms around the world. A major instrument that has been put in place to end discrimination against women in courtrooms and all aspects of life, is the Women's Human Rights Treaty or the Convention to End All Forms of Discrimination Against Women. This treaty establishes a minimum set of standards for ending discrimination against women. It has been ratified by over 165 countries. The United States is not a party to the treaty. Article 2 of the treaty, shown below, addresses discrimination in courtrooms.

Article 2 of the Convention to End All Forms of Discrimination Against Women: States Parties condemn discrimination against women in all its forms, agree to pursue by all appropriate means and without delay a policy of eliminating discrimination against women and, to this end, undertake:

a. To embody the principle of the equality of men and women in their national constitutions or other appropriate legislation if not yet incorporated therein and to ensure, through law and other appropriate means, the practical realization of this principle;

b. To adopt appropriate legislative and other measures, including sanctions where appropriate, prohibiting all discrimination against women;

c. To establish legal protection of the rights of women on an equal basis with men and to ensure through competent national tribunals and other public institutions the effective protection of women against any act of discrimination;

d. To refrain from engaging in any act or practice of discrimination against women and to ensure that public authorities and institutions shall act in conformity with this obligation;

e. To take all appropriate measures to eliminate discrimination against women by any person, organization or enterprise;

f. To take all appropriate measures, including legislation, to modify or abolish existing laws, regulations, customs and practices which constitute discrimination against women;

g. To repeal all national penal provisions which constitute discrimination against women.

See also **Barfield, Velma Margie; Beets, Betty Lou; Buenoano, Judias V.; Dugan, Eva; Salem Village Witch Hangings; Tucker, Karla Faye**

Woodson v. North Carolina

Court: United States Supreme Court; *Case Citation:* Woodson v. North Carolina, 428 U.S. 280 (1976); *Argued:* March 31, 1976; *Decided:* July 2, 1976; *Plurality Opinion:* Justice Stewart announced the Court's judgment and delivered an opinion, in which Powell and Stevens JJ., joined; *Concurring Statement:* Justice Brennan; *Concurring Statement:* Justice Marshall; *Dissenting Opinion:* Justice White, in which Burger, C. J., and Rehnquist, J., joined; *Dissenting Opinion:* Justice Rehnquist; *Dissenting Statement:* Justice Blackmun; *Appellate Defense Counsel:* Anthony G. Amsterdam argued; Jack Greenberg, James M. Nabrit III, Peggy C. Davis, Adam Stein, Charles L. Becton, Edward H. McCormick, and W. A. Johnson on brief; *Appellate Prosecution Counsel:* Sidney S. Eagles, Jr. argued; Rufus L. Edmisten, James E. Magner, Jr., Jean A. Benoy, Noel L. Allen and David S. Crump on brief; *Amicus Curiae Brief Supporting Prosecutor:* 2; *Amicus Curiae Brief Supporting Defendant:* 1.

Issue Presented: Whether mandatory imposition of a death sentence for the crime of first-degree murder under the law of North Carolina violates the Eighth and Fourteenth Amendments?

Case Holding: Mandatory imposition of a death sentence for the crime of first-degree murder under the law of North Carolina violates the Constitution.

Factual and procedural background of case: The defendants, James Tyrone Woodson and Luby Waxton, were charged with capital murder by the State of North Carolina. At the time of their prosecution the State had enacted a new death penalty statute in response to the United States Supreme Court's decision in *Furman v. Georgia.* Under the new statute, a conviction for capital murder resulted in a mandatory death sentence. The defendants were found guilty of capital murder and, as was required by statute, sentenced to death. The North Carolina Supreme Court affirmed the convictions and sentences, after rejecting the defendants' argument that mandatory death sentences violated the constitution. The United States Supreme Court granted certiorari to consider the issue.

Plurality opinion in which Justice Stewart announced the Court's judgment and in which Powell and Stevens JJ., joined: Justice Stewart wrote in his plurality opinion that although at the time the Eighth Amendment was adopted, all the States provided mandatory death sentences for specified offenses, the reaction of jurors and legislators to the harshness of those provisions led to the replacement of automatic death penalty statutes with discretionary jury sentencing. He observed that the two crucial indicators of evolving standards of decency respecting the imposition of punishment in society, jury determinations and legislative enactments, conclusively point to the repudiation of automatic death sentences. The opinion indicated that "[t]he belief no longer prevails that every offense in a like legal category calls for an identical punishment without regard to the past life and habits of a particular offender." It was held that North Carolina's mandatory death penalty statute was a constitutionally impermissible departure from contemporary standards respecting imposition of the unique and irretrievable punishment of death.

The opinion reasoned that North Carolina's statute failed to provide a constitutionally tolerable response to *Furman's* rejection of unbridled jury discretion in the imposition of capital sentences. It was said that central to the limited holding in that case was the conviction that vesting a jury with standardless sentencing power violated the Eighth and Fourteenth Amendments, yet that constitutional deficiency is not eliminated by the mere formal removal of all sentencing power from juries in capital cases. Justice Stewart wrote that in view of the historic record, it may reasonably be assumed that many juries under mandatory statutes will continue to consider the grave consequences of a conviction in reaching a verdict. However, the North Carolina statute provided no standards to guide the jury in determining which murderers shall live and which shall die. The North Carolina statute impermissibly treated all persons convicted of a designated offense not as uniquely individual human beings, but as members of a faceless, undifferentiated mass to be subjected to the blind infliction of the death penalty. Accordingly, the judgment of the North Carolina Supreme Court was reversed, insofar as it upheld the death sentences imposed upon the defendants.

Concurring Statement by Justice Brennan: In concurring in the Court's judgment, Justice Brennan issued a statement indicating that "[f]or the reasons stated in my dissenting opinion in *Gregg v. Georgia*, I concur in the judgment that sets aside the death sentence imposed under the North Carolina death sentence statute as violative of the Eighth and Fourteenth Amendments."

Concurring Statement by Justice Marshall: Justice Marshall issued a concurring statement that read: "For the reasons stated in my dissenting opinion in *Gregg v. Georgia*, I am of the view that the death penalty is a cruel and unusual punishment forbidden by the Eighth and Fourteenth Amendments. I therefore concur in the Court's judgment."

Dissenting opinion by Justice White, in which Burger, C. J., and Rehnquist, J., joined: Justice White dissented from the Court's judgment. In doing so, he wrote: "The issues in the case are very similar, if not identical, to those in *Roberts v. Louisiana*. For the reasons stated in my dissenting opinion in that case, I reject [the defendants'] arguments that the death penalty in any circumstances is a violation of the Eighth Amendment and that the North Carolina statute, although making the imposition of the death penalty mandatory upon proof of guilt and a verdict of first-degree murder, will nevertheless result in the death penalty being imposed so seldom and arbitrarily that it is void under *Furman v. Georgia*. As is also apparent from my dissenting opinion in *Roberts v. Louisiana*, I also disagree with the two additional grounds which the plurality sua sponte offers for invalidating the North

Carolina statute. I would affirm the judgment of the North Carolina Supreme Court."

Dissenting opinion by Justice Rehnquist: Justice Rehnquist opposed the judgment of the Court. In concise terms his dissenting opinion articulated his concerns with the judgment of the Court and the reasoning of the plurality opinion:

> Contrary to the plurality's assertions, they would import into the Cruel and Unusual Punishments Clause procedural requirements which find no support in our cases. Their application will result in the invalidation of a death sentence imposed upon a defendant convicted of first-degree murder under the North Carolina system, and the upholding of the same sentence imposed on an identical defendant convicted on identical evidence of first-degree murder under the Florida, Georgia, or Texas systems -a result surely as "freakish" as that condemned in the separate opinions in *Furman*....
>
> One of the principal reasons why death is different is because it is irreversible; an executed defendant cannot be brought back to life. This aspect of the difference between death and other penalties would undoubtedly support statutory provisions for especially careful review of the fairness of the trial, the accuracy of the factfinding process, and the fairness of the sentencing procedure where the death penalty is imposed. But none of those aspects of the death sentence is at issue here. [The defendants] were found guilty of the crime of first-degree murder in a trial the constitutional validity of which is unquestioned here. And since the punishment of death is conceded by the plurality not to be a cruel and unusual punishment for such a crime, the irreversible aspect of the death penalty has no connection whatever with any requirement for individualized consideration of the sentence.
>
> The second aspect of the death penalty which makes it "different" from other penalties is the fact that it is indeed an ultimate penalty, which ends a human life rather than simply requiring that a living human being be confined for a given period of time in a penal institution. This aspect of the difference may enter into the decision of whether or not it is a "cruel and unusual" penalty for a given offense. But since in this case the offense was first-degree murder, that particular inquiry need proceed no further.
>
> The plurality's insistence on individualized consideration of the sentencing, therefore, does not depend upon any traditional application of the prohibition against cruel and unusual punishment contained in the Eighth Amendment. The punishment here is concededly not cruel and unusual, and that determination has traditionally ended judicial inquiry in our cases construing the Cruel and Unusual Punishments Clause. What the plurality opinion has actually done is to import into the Due Process Clause of the Fourteenth Amendment what it conceives to be desirable procedural guarantees where the punishment of death, concededly not cruel and unusual for the crime of which the defendant was convicted, is to be imposed. This is squarely contrary to ... any other decision of this Court.

Dissenting statement by Justice Blackmun: Justice Blackmun issued a dissenting statement indicating that "I dissent for the reasons set forth in my dissent in *Furman v. Georgia*."

Case note: This case was one of numerous cases decided by the Court in 1976, which invalidated death sentences that were imposed under mandatory death sentence statutes. Subsequent to the decision in this case, North Carolina amended its death penalty statute so as to comply with the Constitution. *See also* **Mandatory Death Penalty Statutes; Roberts v. Louisiana (I); Roberts v. Louisiana (II); Sumner v. Shuman**

Wrongly Convicted *see* Actual Innocence Claim

Wuornos, Aileen   On January 16, 1991, Aileen Wuornos confessed to Florida officials that she killed six of the seven men they suspected her of killing. When the media learned of Aileen's capture and confession, they called her the nation's first female serial killer (she was in fact not the first female serial killer).

Aileen was born with the name Aileen Pittman on February 29, 1956, in Rochester, Michigan. Her parents were divorced when she was born, and her biological father hanged himself in prison, where he was serving time for rape and kidnapping. Her mother abandoned her and a sibling. Aileen was then adopted by her grandparents, the Wuornos. At about age 14, Aileen was raped by a family friend and became pregnant. Her grandfather forced her to give up the child for adoption.

Aileen left home at age 16 and began a life of prostitution. At about age 20, she settled in Florida, and began working as a highway prostitute at least four days of the week. Beginning in 1989, Aileen's life as a prostitute turned into that of being a serial killer.

On December 1, 1989, a deputy sheriff in Volusia County, Florida discovered an abandoned vehicle belonging to Richard Mallory. Mallory's body was found December 13, several miles away in a wooded area. Mallory had been shot several times.

On June 1, 1990, police officers discovered the nude body of David Spears in a remote area in Southwest Citrus County, Florida. He had died of six bullet wounds to the torso.

On June 6, 1990, police officers discovered the body of Charles Carskaddon in Pasco County, Florida. The medical examiner found nine small caliber bullets in his lower chest and upper abdomen.

In June of 1990, Peter Siems left his Florida home headed for New Jersey. The police later found his car in Orange Springs, Florida on July 4, 1990. A palm print on the interior door handle of the car matched that of Aileen. Siems' body has never been found.

On August 4, 1990, law enforcement officers found the body of Troy Burress in a wooded area along State Road 19 in Marion County, Florida. His body was substantially decomposed, but evidence showed it had been shot twice.

On September 12, 1990, police officers in

Aileen Wuornos worked as a highway prostitute in Florida. She confessed to killin six men over a period of time, but claimed that the killings were justified because the men would have seriously injured or killed her. (Florida Department of Corrections)

Marion County found the body of Charles Richard Humphreys. The body was fully clothed, and had been shot six times in the head and torso.

On November 19, 1990, the body of Walter Jeno Antonio was found near a remote logging road in Dixie County, Florida. His body was nearly nude, and had been shot four times in the back and head.

Florida police investigating the seven murders had circumstantial evidence implicating Aileen in each of the murders. She was eventually arrested. After her arrest Aileen gave a voluntary confession to killing Mallory, Spears, Carskaddon, Burress, Humphreys, and Antonio. She denied killing Siems. Aileen maintained that she killed in self-defense, resisting violent assaults by men whom she solicited while working as a prostitute.

Aileen's first trial was for the murder of Mallory. The trial began on January 13, 1992. The jury convicted her on January 27. The jury recommended death two days later on January 29. The trial judge imposed a sentence of death. Aileen later entered a plea of no contest to the murder of Humphrey, Burress, and Spears. She was sentenced to death for their murders. In separate proceedings Aileen enter a plea of guilty to killing Carskaddon and Antonio. She was sentenced to death for those murders. Aileen is now on death row in Florida. *See also* **Women and Capital Punishment**

Wynne v. United States   *Court:* United States Supreme Court; *Case Citation:* Wynne v. United States, 217 U.S. 234 (1910); *Argued:* February 28; March 1, 1910; *Decided:* April 4, 1910; *Opinion of the Court:* Justice Lurton; *Concurring Opinion:* None; *Dissenting Opinion:* None; *Appellate Defense Counsel:* Henry E. Davis argued; Frank E. Thompson and Charles F. Clemons on brief; *Appellate Prosecution Counsel:* Mr. Fowler argued and briefed; *Amicus Curiae Brief Supporting Prosecutor:* None; *Amicus Curiae Brief Supporting Defendant:* None.

Issue Presented: Whether the United States had jurisdiction to prosecute the defendant for murder committed in a harbor of the territory of Hawaii?

Case Holding: The United States had jurisdiction to prosecute the defendant for murder committed in a harbor of the territory of Hawaii, because Hawaii was not a State and Congress provided for such prosecution by statute.

Factual and procedural background of case: The defendant, John Wynne, was convicted of murder and sentenced to death by the United States. The crime occurred on board the steamer Rosecrans, an American vessel, while lying in the harbor of Honolulu, in the territory of Hawaii. On appeal to the United States Supreme Court, the defendant argued that Hawaii, not the United States, had jurisdiction to prosecute him. The United States Supreme Court granted certiorari to consider the issue.

Opinion of the Court by Justice Lurton: Justice Lurton held that the United States had jurisdiction to prosecute the defendant. The opinion outlined the Court's reasoning as follows:

That there existed an organized political community in the Hawaiian Islands, exercising political, civil, and penal jurisdiction throughout what now constitutes the territory of Hawaii, including jurisdiction over the bay or haven in question, when that territory was acquired under the joint resolution of Congress ... did not prevent the operation of [federal law]. [Hawaii] did not constitute one of the states of the United States[.]

Unless, therefore, there was something in the legislation of Congress ... providing a government for the territory of Hawaii, which excluded the operation of [federal law], the jurisdiction of the courts of the United States over the bay here in question, in respect of the murder there charged to have been committed, was beyond question....

It was within the power of Congress to confer upon its courts exclusive jurisdiction over all offenses committed within the territory, whether on land or water. This it did not elect to exercise. It provided for the establishment of a district court of the United States, with all of the powers and jurisdiction of a district court and of a circuit court of the United States. It provided also for the organization of local courts with the jurisdiction conferred by the existing laws of Hawaii upon its local courts except as such laws were in conflict with the act itself or the Constitution and laws of the United States. If it be true, as claimed, that the territorial courts exercise jurisdiction over homicides in the harbor of Honolulu, under and by virtue of the laws of Hawaii thus continued in force, it only establishes that there may be concurrent jurisdiction in respect of certain crimes when committed in certain places, and is far from establishing that the courts of the Union have been deprived of a jurisdiction which they have at all times claimed and exercised over certain offenses when committed upon the high seas, or in any arm of the sea, or in any river, basin, haven, creek, or bay within the admiralty and maritime jurisdiction of the United States, and out of the jurisdiction of any particular state.

The judgment of the Federal District Court was affirmed. *See also* **Jurisdiction**

Wyoming

The State of Wyoming is a capital punishment jurisdiction. The State reenacted its death penalty law after the United States Supreme Court decision in *Furman v. Georgia*, 408 U.S. 238 (1972), on February 28, 1977.

Wyoming has a two-tier legal system. The State's legal system is composed of a supreme court and courts of general jurisdiction. The Wyoming Supreme Court is presided over by a chief justice and four associate justices. The courts of general jurisdiction in the State are called District Courts. Capital offenses against the State of Wyoming are tried in the District Courts.

Wyoming's capital punishment statute is triggered if a person commits a homicide under the following special circumstances:

Homicide committed with premeditated malice, or in the perpetration of, or attempt to perpetrate, any sexual assault, arson, robbery, burglary, escape, resisting arrest, kidnaping or abuse of a child under the age of sixteen years.

Capital murder in Wyoming is punishable by death or life imprisonment. A capital prosecution in Wyoming is bifurcated into a guilt phase and penalty phase. A jury is used at both phases of a capital trial. It is required that, at the penalty phase, the jury unanimously agree that a death sentence is appropriate before it can be imposed. If the penalty phase jury is unable to reach a verdict, the trial judge is required to impose a sentence of life imprisonment. The decision of a penalty phase jury is binding on the trial court under the laws of Wyoming.

In order to impose a death sentence upon a defendant under Wyoming law, it is required that the prosecutor establish the existence of at least one of the following statutory aggravating circumstances at the penalty phase:

i. The murder was committed by a person:
   A. Confined in a jail or correctional facility;
   B. On parole or on probation for a felony;
   C. After escaping detention or incarceration; or
   D. Released on bail pending appeal of his conviction.
ii. The defendant was previously convicted of another murder in the first degree or a felony involving the use or threat of violence to the person;
iii. The defendant knowingly created a great risk of death to two or more persons;
iv. The murder was committed while the defendant was engaged, or was an accomplice, in the commission of, or an attempt to commit, or flight after committing or attempting to commit, any aircraft piracy or the unlawful throwing, placing or discharging of a destructive device or bomb;
v. The murder was committed for the purpose of avoiding or preventing a lawful arrest or effecting an escape from custody;
vi. The murder was committed for compensation, the collection of insurance benefits or other similar pecuniary gain;
vii. The murder was especially atrocious or cruel, being unnecessarily torturous to the victim;
viii. The murder of a judicial officer, former judicial officer, district attorney, former district attorney, defending attorney, peace officer, juror or witness, during or because of the exercise of his official duty;
ix. The defendant knew or reasonably should have known the victim was less than 17 years of age or older than 65 years of age;
x. The defendant knew or reasonably should have known the victim was especially vulnerable due to significant mental or physical disability;
xi. The defendant poses a substantial and continuing threat of future dangerousness or is likely to commit continued acts of criminal violence;
xii. The defendant killed another human being purposely and with premeditated malice and while engaged in, or as an accomplice in the commission of, or an attempt to commit, or flight after committing or attempting to commit, any robbery, sexual assault, arson, burglary, kidnaping or abuse of a child under the age of sixteen years.

Although the Federal Constitution will not permit jurisdictions to prevent capital felons from presenting all relevant mitigating evidence at the penalty phase, Wyoming has provided the following statutory mitigating circumstances that permit the jury to reject imposition of the death penalty:

i. The defendant has no significant history of prior criminal activity;

ii. The murder was committed while the defendant was under the influence of extreme mental or emotional disturbance;

iii. The victim was a participant in the defendant's conduct or consented to the act;

iv. The defendant was an accomplice in a murder committed by another person and his participation in the homicidal act was relatively minor;

v. The defendant acted under extreme duress or under the substantial domination of another person;

vi. The capacity of the defendant to appreciate the criminality of his conduct or to conform his conduct to the requirements of law was substantially impaired;

vii. The age of the defendant at the time of the crime;

viii. Any other fact or circumstance of the defendant's character or prior record or matter surrounding his offense which serves to mitigate his culpability.

Under Wyoming's capital punishment statute, a sentence of death is automatically reviewed by the Wyoming Supreme Court. Wyoming uses lethal injection to carry out death sentences (with lethal gas available if lethal injection found constitutionally invalid). The State's death row facility for men is located in Rawlings, Wyoming; while the facility maintaining female death row inmates is located in Lusk, Wyoming. Pursuant to the laws of Wyoming the Governor has authority to grant clemency in capital cases.

From the start of modern capital punishment in 1976, through 1999, Wyoming executed 1 capital felon. During this period Wyoming did not have any female capital felons on death row. A total of 2 capital felons were on death row in Wyoming in 1999. The 1999 death row population in the State was listed as: 0 black inmates and 2 white inmates. In 1999 the State had no juveniles on death row. The State permits capital punishment to be imposed on persons 16 years old or older. Wyoming does not prohibit the execution of mentally retarded capital felons.

Executions by Wyoming 1976–1999

Name	Race	Date of Execution	Method of Execution
Mark Hopkinson	White	January 22, 1992	Lethal Injection

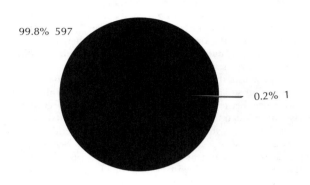

EXECUTIONS BY WYOMING 1976–1999

99.8% 597   0.2% 1

■ WYOMING EXECUTIONS
■ ALL OTHER EXECUTIONS

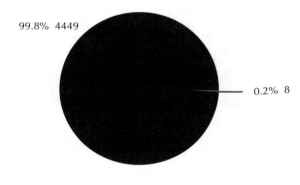

EXECUTIONS BY WYOMING 1930–1999

99.8% 4449   0.2% 8

■ WYOMING
■ ALL OTHER JURISDICTIONS

Yates v. Aiken *Court:* United States Supreme Court; *Case Citation:* Yates v. Aiken, 484 U.S. 211 (1988); *Argued:* December 2, 1987; *Decided:* January 12, 1988; *Opinion of the Court:* Justice Stevens; *Concurring Opinion:* None; *Dissenting Opinion:* None; *Appellate Defense Counsel:* David I. Bruck argued and briefed; Appellate *Prosecution Counsel:* Donald J. Zelenka argued; T. Travis Medlock on brief; *Amicus Curiae Brief Supporting Prosecutor:* None; *Amicus Curiae Brief Supporting Defendant:* None.

Issue Presented: Whether States may use presumptions that shift the burden of persuasion, on an element of an offense, to the defendant?

Case Holding: The Constitution prohibits States from using presumptions that shift the burden of persuasion, on an element of an offense, to the defendant.

Factual and procedural background of case: The defendant, Yates, was prosecuted for capital murder during the course of armed robbery by the State of South Carolina. The defendant testified during the guilt phase that his accomplice did the shooting and that he did not intend for anyone to be killed. The trial court instructed the guilt phase jury "that malice is implied or presumed from the use of a deadly weapon." The jury convicted the defendant and he was sentenced to death.

On direct review, the South Carolina Supreme Court affirmed the conviction and death sentence. Subsequently the defendant brought a habeas corpus proceeding in the State appellate court, arguing that the burden shifting instruction given at trial was unconstitutional in light of recent decisions by the United States Supreme Court. The State appellate court disagreed and dismissed the petition. The defendant appealed to the United States Supreme Court. In a memorandum order, the nation's highest Court vacated the State appellate court's denial of habeas relief and remanded the case for further consideration in light of recent decisions by the Court. On remand, the State appellate court again denied relief. The United States Supreme Court granted certiorari to fully consider the issue.

Opinion of the Court by Justice Stevens: Justice Stevens, writing for a unanimous Court, held that the defendant's conviction could not stand in light of recent non-capital decisions involving burden shifting jury instructions. It was said that the Due Process Clause prohibits jury instructions that have the effect of relieving the State of its burden of proof on the critical question of intent in a criminal prosecution. The opinion reasoned: "The Due Process Clause of the Fourteenth Amendment 'protects the accused against conviction except upon proof beyond a reasonable doubt of every fact necessary to constitute the crime with which he is charged.' This 'bedrock, axiomatic and elementary [constitutional] principle,' prohibits the State from using evidentiary presumptions in a jury charge that have the effect of relieving the State of its burden of persuasion beyond a reasonable doubt of every essential element of a crime. The prohibition protects the 'fundamental value determination of our society,' ... that 'it is far worse to convict an innocent man than to let a guilty man go free.'"

The judgment of the South Carolina Supreme Court was reversed.

Yemen Capital punishment is allowed in Yemen. Yemen uses the firing squad to carry out the death penalty. In 1998, the nation executed 17 prisoners. Its legal system is a mixture of English common law, Turkish law, Islamic law and customary law. The nation adopted a constitution on May 16, 1991.

The judicial system is composed of trial courts and appellate courts. There is no jury system. Defendants have the right to retained or appointed counsel. *See also* **International Capital Punishment Nations**

Youth and Capital Punishment *see* Juveniles

Yugoslavia (Serbia) Capital punishment is recognized by Yugoslavia. Yugoslavia uses the firing squad to carry out the death penalty. Its legal system is based on civil law. The constitution of the nation was adopted on April 27, 1992. *See also* **International Capital Punishment Nations**

Z

Zambia Capital punishment is recognized in Zambia. Zambia uses hanging to carry out the death penalty. Its legal system is based on English common law and customary law. The nation adopted a constitution on August 2, 1991.

The judicial system is composed of trial courts and a Supreme Court. Customary or traditional, courts handle most petty criminal cases in rural areas. Trials in regular courts are open to the public. Defendants have the right to legal counsel and the right to confront witnesses. *See also* **International Capital Punishment Nations**

Zant v. Stephens (I) *Court:* United States Supreme Court; *Case Citation:* Zant v. Stephens, 456 U.S. 410 (1982); *Argued:* February 24, 1982; *Decided:* May 3, 1982; *Opinion of the Court:* Per Curiam; *Concurring Opinion:* None; *Dissenting Opinion:* Justice Marshall, in which Brennan, J., joined; *Dis-*

senting Opinion: Justice Powell; *Appellate Defense Counsel:* John Charles Boger argued; James C. Bonner, Jr., Jack Greenberg, James M. Nabrit III, Joel Berger, Deborah Fins, and Anthony G. Amsterdam on brief; *Appellate Prosecution Counsel:* Daryl A. Robinson argued; Michael J. Bowers, Robert S. Stubbs II, Marion O. Gordon and John C. Walden on brief; *Amicus Curiae Brief Supporting Prosecutor:* 1; *Amicus Curiae Brief Supporting Defendant:* 1.

Issue Presented: Whether the Georgia Supreme Court constitutionally may sustain a death sentence, when an invalid statutory aggravating circumstance is used, so long as at least one of several statutory aggravating circumstances found by the jury is valid and supports the sentence?

Case Holding: Insufficient information exists to determine the rationale for the curative rule used by the Georgia Supreme Court, therefore a decision on the issue presented is held in abeyance pending an answer by the Georgia Supreme Court to the following certified question: What are the premises of state law that support the conclusion that the death sentence in this case is not impaired by the invalidity of one of the statutory aggravating circumstances found by the jury?

Factual and procedural background of case: The defendant, Stephens, was convicted of capital murder in a Georgia trial court. The penalty phase jury found the existence of three statutory aggravating circumstances specified in the Georgia death penalty statute and imposed the death penalty. On appeal, the Georgia Supreme Court set aside as invalid one of the statutory aggravating circumstances found by the jury. However, the appellate court upheld the death sentence, concluding that the evidence supported the jury's findings of the remaining statutory aggravating circumstances and that therefore the sentence was not impaired.

After exhausting state post-conviction remedies, the defendant filed habeas corpus petition in a federal District Court, which denied relief. However, a federal Court of Appeals reversed the death sentence after finding the sentence could not be cured by removing the invalid statutory aggravating circumstance. The United States Supreme Court granted certiorari to consider the issue.

Opinion of the Court was delivered Per Curiam: It was said in the per curiam opinion that despite the clarity of Georgia's rule removing an invalid statutory aggravating circumstance and independently determining whether a death sentence may be sustained with the remaining aggravating factors, "there is considerable uncertainty about the state-law premises of that rule." It was said that the Georgia Supreme Court had never explained the rationale for its rule. Moreover, "[i]t may be that implicit in the rule is a determination that multiple findings of statutory aggravating circumstances are superfluous, or a determination that the reviewing court may assume the role of the jury when the sentencing jury recommended the death penalty under legally erroneous instructions."

The Court was hesitant about resolving the issue presented, without a thorough understanding of Georgia's curative rule. The opinion held that: "In view of the foregoing uncertainty, it would be premature to decide whether such determinations, or any of the others we might conceive as a basis for the Georgia Supreme Court's position, might undermine the confidence we expressed in *Gregg v. Georgia*, that the Georgia capital-sentencing system, as we understood it then, would avoid the arbitrary and capricious imposition of the death penalty and would otherwise pass constitutional muster. Suffice it to say that the state-law premises of the Georgia Supreme Court's conclusion of state law are relevant to the constitutional issue at hand."

The Court went on to rule as follows: "The Georgia Supreme Court under certain circumstances will decide questions of state law upon certification from this Court. We invoke that statute to certify the following question: What are the premises of state law that support the conclusion that the

death sentence in this case is not impaired by the invalidity of one of the statutory aggravating circumstances found by the jury?" The certified question was sent to the Georgia Supreme Court and the decision of the case was held in abeyance pending a response.

Dissenting opinion by Justice Marshall, in which Brennan, J., joined: Justice Marshall dissented from the Court's opinion in the case. He did not believe a death sentence could be cured when an invalid aggravator was used. The dissenting opinion reasoned as follows: "In today's decision, a majority of this Court intimates that a post hoc construction of a death penalty statute by the State's highest court may remedy the fact that a jury was improperly instructed with respect to the very factors that save the Georgia statute from unconstitutionality. Because I cannot see how the Georgia Supreme Court's response to this Court's certification could constitutionally justify the imposition of the death penalty in this case, I must dissent.... [W]hether or not the Georgia Supreme Court's construction of the statute in response to this Court's certification might avoid the constitutional infirmity inherent in [the defendant's] sentence in some future case, it can do nothing to alter the fact that [the defendant's] death sentence may have been based in part on consideration of an unconstitutional aggravating circumstance."

Dissenting opinion by Justice Powell: Justice Powell dissented from the Court's disposition of the case. In his dissent he indicated "I am in essential agreement with the views expressed by Justice Marshall in ... his dissenting opinion.... I would not hold, however, that the case must be remanded for resentencing by a jury." Justice Powell stated that he would have certified a question to the Georgia Supreme Court to ascertain whether the appellate court had statutory "authority to find that the instruction was harmless error beyond a reasonable doubt." *See also* **Certified Question; Invalid Aggravator; Tuggle v. Netherland; Zant v. Stephens (II)**

Zant v. Stephens (II)

Zant v. Stephens (II) *Court:* United States Supreme Court; *Case Citation:* Zant v. Stephens, 462 U.S. 862 (1983); *Argued:* February 24, 1982; *Decided:* June 22, 1983; *Opinion of the Court:* Justice Stevens; *Concurring Opinion:* Justice White; *Concurring Opinion:* Justice Rehnquist; *Dissenting Opinion:* Justice Marshall, in which Brennan, J., joined; *Appellate Defense Counsel:* James C. Bonner, Jr., Jack Greenberg, James M. Nabrit III, Joel Berger, John Charles Boger, Deborah Fins, and Anthony G. Amsterdam on supplemental brief; *Appellate Prosecution Counsel:* Michael J. Bowers, Attorney General of Georgia, William B. Hill, Jr., Senior Assistant Attorney General, Robert S. Stubbs II, Executive Assistant Attorney General, and Marion O. Gordon on supplemental brief; *Amicus Curiae Supplemental Brief Supporting Prosecutor:* None; *Amicus Curiae Supplemental Brief Supporting Defendant:* None.

Issue Presented: Whether the Georgia Supreme Court constitutionally may sustain a death sentence, when an invalid statutory aggravating circumstance is used, so long as at least one of several statutory aggravating circumstances found by the jury is valid and supports the sentence?

Case Holding: The Constitution permits appellate courts to sustain a death sentence, when an invalid statutory aggravating circumstance is used, so long as at least one of several statutory aggravating circumstances found by the jury is valid and supports the sentence.

Factual and procedural background of case: The opinion in this case resulted from the certified question sent to the Georgia Supreme Court by the United States Supreme Court in *Zant v. Stephens (I)*. The certified question required the State appellate court to explain the rationale used by it in finding that an invalid statutory aggravating circumstance used in the defendant's case, did not affect the validity of his death sentence.

In response to the certified question, the Georgia Supreme Court explained that under Georgia law the finding of a statutory aggravating circumstance serves a limited purpose. That purpose is to merely identify those members of the class of persons convicted of murder who are eligible for the death penalty, without furnishing any further guidance to the jury in the exercise of its discretion in determining whether the death penalty should be imposed.

Opinion of the Court by Justice Stevens: Justice Stevens wrote that the limited function served by the jury's finding of a statutory aggravating circumstance does not render Georgia's death penalty scheme invalid under the holding in *Furman v. Georgia*. It was said that under Georgia's scheme, the jury is required to find and identify in writing at least one valid statutory aggravating circumstance in order to impose the death penalty, and the State appellate court must review the record of every death penalty proceeding to determine whether the sentence was arbitrary or disproportionate.

The opinion held that the narrowing function of statutory aggravating circumstances was properly achieved in this case by the two valid aggravating circumstances upheld by the Georgia Supreme Court, because those two factors adequately differentiate this case in an objective, evenhanded, and substantively rational way from the many Georgia murder cases in which the death penalty may not be imposed. Moreover, the Georgia Supreme Court reviewed the defendant's death sentence to determine whether it was arbitrary, excessive, or disproportionate.

The opinion rejected the argument by the defendant that his death sentence was impaired on the grounds that the jury instruction with regard to the invalid statutory aggravating circumstance may have unduly affected the jury's deliberations. The Court reasoned that the evidence used to establish the invalid statutory aggravating circumstance was readily admissible for other purposes and would have been heard by the jury regardless. The opinion went on to reverse the judgment of the federal Court of Appeals.

Concurring opinion by Justice White: Justice White concurred in the Court's opinion. He wrote that he agreed "with the Court that there [was] no ... problem since the evidence

supporting the invalid aggravating circumstances was properly before the jury."

Concurring opinion by Justice Rehnquist: Justice Rehnquist concurred in the Court's judgment. He drew particular attention to the lack of impact the invalid aggravator had on the decision to impose the death penalty. The concurrence stated:

> While agreeing with the Court's judgment, I write separately to make clear my understanding of the application of the Eighth and Fourteenth Amendments to the capital sentencing procedures and used in this case. I agree with the Court's treatment of the factual and procedural background of the case, and with its characterization of the question presented for review. In brief, we must decide ... whether the erroneous presentation to a jury of an invalid aggravating circumstance requires vacating the death sentence imposed by that jury....
>
> In the present case ... the erroneous submission to the jury of an invalid aggravating circumstance simply cannot satisfy whatever standard may plausibly be based on [prior cases]. As the Court points out, the only real impact resulting from the error was the evidence properly before the jury was capable of being fit within a category that the judge's instructions labeled "aggravating." The evidence in question -respondent's prior convictions -plainly was an aggravating factor, which, as we held in *Gregg*, the jury was free to consider. The fact that the instruction gave added weight to this no doubt played some role in the deliberations of some jurors. Yet, the Georgia Supreme Court was plainly right in saying that the "mere fact that some of the aggravating circumstances presented were improperly designated statutory;" had "an inconsequential impact on the jury's decision regarding the death penalty."... Whatever a defendant must show to set aside a death sentence, the present case involved only a remote possibility that the error had any effect on the jury's judgment; the Eighth Amendment did not therefore require that the defendant's sentence be vacated.

Dissenting opinion by Justice Marshall, in which Brennan, J., joined: Justice Marshall dissented from the Court's decision in the case. He stated his position as follows:

> Even if I accepted the prevailing view that the death penalty may constitutionally be imposed under certain circumstances, I could scarcely join in upholding a death sentence based in part upon a statutory aggravating circumstance so vague that its application turns solely on the "whim" of the jury.
>
> The submission of the unconstitutional statutory aggravating circumstance to the jury cannot be deemed harmless error on the theory that "in Georgia, the finding of an aggravating circumstance does not play any role in guiding the sentencing body in the exercise of its discretion, apart from its function of narrowing the class of persons convicted of murder who are eligible for the death penalty." If the trial judge's instructions had apprised the jury of this theory, it might have been proper to assume that the unconstitutional statutory factor did not affect the jury's verdict. But such instructions would have suffered from an even more fundamental constitutional defect -a failure to provide any standards whatsoever to guide the jury's actual sentencing decision. If this Court's decisions concerning the death penalty establish anything, it is that a capital sentencing scheme based on "standardless jury discretion" violates the Eighth and Fourteenth Amendments.
>
> In any event, the jury that sentenced [the defendant] to death was never informed of this "threshold" theory, which was invented for the first time by the Georgia Supreme Court more than seven years later. Under the instruction actually given, a juror might reasonably have concluded, as has this Court in

construing essentially identical instructions, that any aggravating circumstances, including statutory aggravating circumstances, should be balanced against any mitigating circumstances in the determination of the defendant's sentence. There is no way of knowing whether the jury would have sentenced [the defendant] to death if its attention had not been drawn to the unconstitutional statutory factor.

See also **Certified Question; Invalid Aggravator; Tuggle v. Netherland; Zant v. Stephens (I)**

Ziang v. United States
Court: United States Supreme Court; *Case Citation:* Ziang v. United States, 266 U.S. 1 (1924); *Argued:* April 7–8, 1924; *Decided:* Oct. 13, 1924; *Opinion of the Court:* Justice Brandeis; *Concurring Opinion:* None; *Dissenting Opinion:* None; *Appellate Defense Counsel:* Wm. C. Dennis argued; Frederic D. McKenney, James A. O'Shea, Charles Fahy, and John W. Davis on brief; *Appellate Prosecution Counsel:* Peyton Gordon argued and briefed; *Amicus Curiae Brief Supporting Prosecutor:* None; *Amicus Curiae Brief Supporting Defendant:* None.

Issue Presented: Whether the defendant's confession and incriminating statements were voluntarily given to the police?

Case Holding: The defendant's confession and incriminating statements were not voluntarily given to the police, therefore his conviction and sentence could not stand.

Factual and procedural background of case: The defendant, Sung Wan Ziang, was convicted of capital murder and sentenced to death by the District of Columbia. On appeal, the District of Columbia Court of Appeals affirmed the judgment. In doing so, the appellate court rejected the defendant's argument that his confession and incriminating statements were obtained illegally. The United States Supreme Court granted certiorari to consider the issue.

Opinion of the Court by Justice Brandeis: Justice Brandeis held that the defendant's confession and incriminating statements were not voluntarily given and should have been excluded from the trial. The opinion set out the facts and law of the case as follows:

> ... [T]he detectives took [the defendant] to Hotel Dewey; and, without entering his name in the hotel registry, placed him in a bedroom on an upper floor. In that room he was detained continuously one week. Throughout the period, he was sick and, most of the time, in bed. A physician was repeatedly called. It was a police surgeon who came. In vain [the defendant] asked to see his brother, with whom he lived in New York, who had nursed him in his illness, who had come to Washington at his request in January, who had returned with him to New York, and whom, as he later learned, the detectives had also brought to Washington, were detaining in another room of the hotel, and were subjecting to like interrogation.
>
> [The defendant] was held in the hotel room without formal arrest, incommunicado. But he was not left alone. Every moment of the day, and of the night, at least one member of the police force was on guard inside his room. Three ordinary policemen were assigned to this duty. Each served eight hours; the shifts beginning at midnight, at 8 in the morning, and at 4 in the afternoon. Morning, afternoon, and evening (and at least on one occasion after midnight) the prisoner was visited by the superintendent of police and/or one or more of the detectives.

> The sole purpose of these visits was to interrogate him. Regardless of [the defendant's] wishes and protest, his condition of health, or the hour, they engaged him in conversation. He was subjected to persistent, lengthy, and repeated cross-examination. Sometimes it was subtle, sometimes severe. Always the examination was conducted with a view to entrapping [the defendant] into a confession of his own guilt and/or that of his brother. Whenever these visitors entered the room, the guard was stationed outside the closed door.
>
> On the eighth day, the accusatory questioning took a more excruciating form. A detective was in attendance throughout the day. In the evening, [the defendant] was taken from Hotel Dewey to [the crime scene]. There, continuously for ten hours, this sick man was led from floor to floor minutely to examine and re-examine the scene....
>
> On the ninth day, at 20 minutes past 5 in the morning, [the defendant] was taken ... to the station house and placed formally under arrest. There the interrogation was promptly resumed. Again the detectives were in attendance, day and evening, plying their questions, pointing out alleged contradictions, arguing with the prisoner, and urging him to confess, lest his brother be deemed guilty of the crime. Still the statements secured failed to satisfy the detectives' craving for evidence. On the tenth day, [the defendant] was bundled up, was again taken to the [crime scene], was again questioned there for hours.... On the eleventh day, a formal interrogation of [the defendant] was conducted at the station house by the detectives in the presence of a stenographer. On the twelfth day, the verbatim typewritten report of the interrogation (which occupies 12 pages of the printed record) was read to [the defendant], in his cell at the jail. There he signed the report and initialed each page. On the thirteenth day, for the first time, [the defendant] was visited by the chief medical officer of the jail, in the performance of his duties.
>
> ... In the federal courts, the requisite of voluntariness is not satisfied by establishing merely that the confession was not induced by a promise or a threat. A confession is voluntary in law if, and only if, it was, in fact, voluntarily made. A confession may have been given voluntary, although it was made to police officers, while in custody, and in answer to an examination conducted by them. But a confession obtained by compulsion must be excluded whatever may have been the character of the compulsion, and whether the compulsion was applied in a judicial proceeding or otherwise.... The undisputed facts showed that compulsion was applied. As to that matter there was no issue upon which the jury could properly have been required or permitted to pass. The alleged oral statements and the written confession should have been excluded.

The judgment of the Court of Appeals was reversed and a new trial awarded. *See also* **Right to Remain Silent**

Zimbabwe
Capital punishment is permitted in Zimbabwe. Zimbabwe uses hanging to carry out the death penalty. Its legal system is based on English common law and Roman-Dutch law. The nation adopted a constitution on December 21, 1979.

The judicial system consists of magistrate courts, a High Court, and a Supreme Court. Defendants have the right to legal counsel. In capital cases the government provides an attorney for all defendants unable to afford one. The right to appeal exists in all cases and is automatic in cases in which the death penalty is imposed. Trials are open to the public except in certain security cases. Defendants enjoy a presumption of innocence and the right to question witnesses. *See also* **International Capital Punishment Nations**

Bibliography

Abbott, Geoffrey, *The Book of Execution: An Encyclopedia of Methods of Judicial Execution*, Hodder Headline, 1995.

Aguirre, Adalberto and David V. Baker, *Race, Racism, and the Death Penalty in the United States*, Vande Vere, 1991.

Arriens, Jan, *Welcome to Hell: Letters and Writings from Death Row*, Northeastern University Press, 1997.

Baldus, David C., Charles A. Pulaski, and George Woodworth, *Equal Justice and the Death Penalty: A Legal and Empirical Analysis*, Northeastern University Press, 1990.

Bedau, Hugo A., *The Death Penalty in America: Current Controversies*, Oxford University Press, 1998.

Berns, Walter, *For Capital Punishment: Crime and the Morality of the Death Penalty*, University Press of America, 1991.

Bessler, John D., *Death in the Dark: Midnight Executions in America*, Northeastern University Press, 1998.

Block, Eugene B., *When Men Play God: The Fallacy of Capital Punishment*, Cragmont, 1983.

Bohm, Robert M., *Deathquest: An Introduction to the Theory and Practice of Capital Punishment in the United States*, Anderson, 1999.

Bovee, Marvin H., *Christ and the Gallows: Or, Reasons for the Abolition of Capital Punishment*, AMS Press, 1983.

Brandon, Craig, *The Electric Chair: An Unnatural American History*, McFarland, 1999.

Cabana, Donald A., *Death at Midnight: The Confession of an Executioner*, Northeastern University Press, 1998.

Costanzo, Mark, *Just Revenge: Costs and Consequences of the Death Penalty*, St. Martin's, 1997.

Coyne, Randall, and Lyn Entzeroth, *Capital Punishment and the Judicial Process*, Carolina Academic Press, 1994.

Dicks, Shirley, *Young Blood: Juvenile Justice and the Death Penalty*, Prometheus Books, 1995.

Gatrell, V. A., *The Hanging Tree: Execution and the English People, 1770–1868*, Oxford University Press, 1996.

Gillespie, Kay, *The Unforgiven: Utah's Executed Men*, Signature Books, 1997.

Gottfried, Ted, *Capital Punishment: The Death Penalty Debate*, Enslow, 1997.

Grabowski, John F., *The Death Penalty*, Lucent Books, 1998.

Gross, Bob, *Death Penalty: A Guide for Christians*, Books on Demand, 1991.

Haas, Kenneth C., and James A. Inciardi, *Challenging Capital Punishment: Legal and Social Science Approaches*, Books on Demand, 1988.

Haines, Herbert H., *Against Capital Punishment: The Anti-Death Penalty Movement in America, 1972–1994*, Oxford University Press, 1999.

Hanks, Gardner C., *Against the Death Penalty*, Herald Press, 1997.

Hearn, Daniel Allen, *Legal Executions in New England: A Comprehensive Reference, 1623–1960*. McFarland, 1999.

_____, *Legal Executions in New York State: A Comprehensive Reference, 1639–1963*. McFarland, 1997.

Herda, D. J., *Furman v. Georgia: The Death Penalty Case*, Enslow, 1994.

Jackson, Bruce, and Diane Christian, *Death Row*, Transaction, 1980.

King, William M., *Going to Meet a Man: Denver's Last Legal Public Execution, 27 July 1886*, University Press of Colorado, 1990.

Koosed, Margery B., *Capital Punishment: The Philosophical, Moral, and Penological Debate over Capital Punishment*, Garland, 1996.

Latzer, Barry, *Death Penalty Cases: Leading US Supreme Court Cases on Capital Punishment*, Butterworth-Heinemann, 1997.

Marquart, James W., Sheldon Olson and Jonathan R. Sorenson, *The Rope, the Chair, and the Needle: Capital Punishment in Texas, 1923–1990*, University of Texas Press, 1998.

Martin, Robert P., *The Death Penalty: God's Will or Man's Folly*, Simpson, 1992.

Megivern, James J., *The Death Penalty: An Historical and Theological Survey*, Paulist Press, 1997.

Mello, Michael A., *Dead Wrong: A Death Row Lawyer Speaks Out Against Capital Punishment*, University of Wisconsin Press, 1999.

Miller, Arthur S. and Jeffrey H. Bowman, *Death by Installments: The Ordeal of Willie Francis*, Greenwood, 1988.

Nakell, Barry, and Kenneth A. Hardy, *The Arbitrariness of the Death Penalty*, Temple University Press, 1987.

O'Shea, Kathleen A., *Women and the Death Penalty in the United States, 1900–1998*, Greenwood, 1999.

O'Sullivan, Carol, *Death Penalty: Identifying Propaganda Techniques*, Greenhaven, 1990.

Palmer, Louis J., Jr., *The Death Penalty: An American Citizen's Guide to Understanding Federal and State Laws*, McFarland, 1998.

_____, *Organ Transplants from Executed Prisoners: An Argument for the Creation of Death Sentence Organ Removal Statutes*, McFarland, 1999.

Pojman, Louis P., and Jeffrey Reiman, *The Death Penalty: For and Against*, Rowman & Littlefield, 1997.

Prejean, Helen, *Dead Man Walking: An Eyewitness Account of the Death Penalty in the United States*, Random House, 1994.

Radelet, Michael L., *Facing the Death Penalty*, Temple University Press, 1990.

Randa, Laura E., *Society's Final Solution: A History and Discussion of the Death Penalty*, University Press of America, 1997.

Reed, Emily F., *The Penry Penalty: Capital Punishment and Offenders with Mental Retardation*, University Press of America, 1993.

Russell, Gregory D., *The Death Penalty and Racial Bias: Overturning Supreme Court Assumptions*, Greenwood, 1993.

Sarat, Austin, *The Killing State: Capital Punishment in Law, Politics, and Culture*, Oxford University Press, 1998.

Schabas, William S., *The Abolition of the Death Penalty in International Law*, Cambridge University Press, 1997.

Schonebaum, Steve, *Does Capital Punishment Deter Crime?*, Greenhaven Press, 1998.

Schwed, Roger E., *Abolition and Capital Punishment: The United States' Judicial, Political, and Moral Barometer*, AMS Press, 1983.

Sheleff, Leon S., *Ultimate Penalties: Capital Punishment, Life Imprisonment, Physical Torture*, Ohio State University Press, 1987.

Steffen, Lloyd H., *Executing Justice: The Moral Meaning of the Death Penalty*, Pilgrim Press/The United Church Press, 1998.

Streib, Victor L., *A Capital Punishment Anthology*, Anderson, 1997.

Vila, Bryan, and Cynthia Morris, *Capital Punishment in the United States: A Documentary History*, Greenwood, 1997.

Weinglass, Leonard, *Race for Justice: Mumia Abu-Jamal's Fight Against the Death Penalty*, Common Courage Press, 1995.

White, Welsh S., *The Death Penalty in the Nineties: An Examination of the Modern System of Capital Punishment*, University of Michigan Press, 1994.

Williams, Bill, *Tit for Tat: The Conspiracy to Abolish the Death Penalty*, BADM Books, 1997.

Winters, Paul A., *The Death Penalty: Opposing Viewpoints*, Greenhaven, 1997.

Zimring, Franklin E., and Gordon J. Hawkins, *Capital Punishment and the American Agenda*, Cambridge University Press, 1990.

Index